JOHN

JOHN

ZONDERVAN
Exegetical
Commentary
ON THE
New Testament

EDWARD W. KLINK III

CLINTON E. ARNOLD
General Editor

ZONDERVAN
ACADEMIC

For my mom, Kimberly Grace Klink

ZONDERVAN ACADEMIC

John
Copyright © 2016 by Edward W. Klink III

Requests for information should be addressed to:
Zondervan, 3900 *Sparks Drive SE, Grand Rapids, Michigan 49546*

Library of Congress Cataloging-in-Publication Data
Names: Klink, Edward W., III, 1975- author.
Title: John / by Edward W. Klink, III.
Other titles: Zondervan exegetical commentary on the New Testament.
Description: Grand Rapids, Michigan: Zondervan, [2016] | Series: Zondervan exegetical
      commentary on the New Testament | Includes bibliographical references and index.
Identifiers: LCCN 2016023256 | ISBN 9780310243601 (hardcover)
Subjects: LCSH: Bible. John—Commentaries.
Classification: LCC BS2615.53 K58 2016 | DDC 226.5/07—dc23
LC record available at https://lccn.loc.gov/2016023256

Cover design: *Tammy Johnson*
Interior design: *Beth Shagene*

Printed in the United States of America

22 23 24 25 26 27 28 29 30 31 32 /TRM/ 22 21 20 19 18 17 16 15 14 13 12 11 10 9 8 7 6 5

Contents

Series Introduction 7

Author's Preface 11

Abbreviations 15

Introduction 21

Select Bibliography 75

Commentary on John 81

Theology of John 927

Scripture Index 941

Other Ancient Literature Index 960

Subject Index 962

Author Index 966

Series Introduction

This generation has been blessed with an abundance of excellent commentaries. Some are technical and do a good job of addressing issues that the critics have raised; other commentaries are long and provide extensive information about word usage and catalogue nearly every opinion expressed on the various interpretive issues; still other commentaries focus on providing cultural and historical background information; and then there are those commentaries that endeavor to draw out many applicational insights.

The key question to ask is: What are you looking for in a commentary? This commentary series might be for you if

- you have taken Greek and would like a commentary that helps you apply what you have learned without assuming you are a well-trained scholar.
- you would find it useful to see a concise, one- or two-sentence statement of what the commentator thinks the main point of each passage is.
- you would like help interpreting the words of Scripture without getting bogged down in scholarly issues that seem irrelevant to the life of the church.
- you would like to see a visual representation (a graphical display) of the flow of thought in each passage.
- you would like expert guidance from solid evangelical scholars who set out to explain the meaning of the original text in the clearest way possible and to help you navigate through the main interpretive issues.
- you want to benefit from the results of the latest and best scholarly studies and historical information that help to illuminate the meaning of the text.
- you would find it useful to see a brief summary of the key theological insights that can be gleaned from each passage and some discussion of the relevance of these for Christians today.

These are just some of the features that characterize the new Zondervan Exegetical Commentary on the New Testament series. The idea for this series was refined over time by an editorial board who listened to pastors and teachers express what they wanted to see in a commentary series based on the Greek text. That board consisted of myself, George H. Guthrie, William D. Mounce, Thomas R. Schreiner, and Mark L. Strauss along with Zondervan senior editor at large Verlyn Verbrugge, and former Zondervan senior acquisitions editor Jack Kuhatschek. We also enlisted a board of consulting editors who are active pastors, ministry leaders, and seminary professors to help in the process of designing a commentary series that will be useful to the church. Zondervan senior acquisitions editor Katya Covrett has now been shepherding the process to completion, and Constantine R. Campbell is now serving on the board.

We arrived at a design that includes seven components for the treatment of each biblical passage. What follows is a brief orientation to these primary components of the commentary.

Literary Context

In this section, you will find a concise discussion of how the passage functions in the broader literary context of the book. The commentator highlights connections with the preceding and following material in the book and makes observations on the key literary features of this text.

Main Idea

Many readers will find this to be an enormously helpful feature of this series. For each passage, the commentator carefully crafts a one- or two-sentence statement of the big idea or central thrust of the passage.

Translation and Graphical Layout

Another unique feature of this series is the presentation of each commentator's translation of the Greek text in a graphical layout. The purpose of this diagram is to help the reader visualize, and thus better understand, the flow of thought within the text. The translation itself reflects the interpretive decisions made by each commentator in the "Explanation" section of the commentary. Here are a few insights that will help you to understand the way these are put together:

1. On the far left side next to the verse numbers is a series of interpretive labels that indicate the function of each clause or phrase of the biblical text. The corresponding portion of the text is on the same line to the right of the label. We have not used technical linguistic jargon for these, so they should be easily understood.

2. In general, we place every clause (a group of words containing a subject and a predicate) on a separate line and identify how it is supporting the principal assertion of the text (namely, is it saying when the action occurred, how it took

place, or why it took place?). We sometimes place longer phrases or a series of items on separate lines as well.

3. Subordinate (or dependent) clauses and phrases are indented and placed directly under the words that they modify. This helps the reader to more easily see the nature of the relationship of clauses and phrases in the flow of the text.

4. Every main clause has been placed in bold print and pushed to the left margin for clear identification.

5. Sometimes when the level of subordination moves too far to the right — as often happens with some of Paul's long, involved sentences! — we reposition the flow to the left of the diagram, but use an arrow to indicate that this has happened.

6. The overall process we have followed has been deeply informed by principles of discourse analysis and narrative criticism (for the Gospels and Acts).

Structure

Immediately following the translation, the commentator describes the flow of thought in the passage and explains how certain interpretive decisions regarding the relationship of the clauses were made in the passage.

Exegetical Outline

The overall structure of the passage is described in a detailed exegetical outline. This will be particularly helpful for those who are looking for a way to concisely explain the flow of thought in the passage in a teaching or preaching setting.

Explanation of the Text

As an exegetical commentary, this work makes use of the Greek language to interpret the meaning of the text. If your Greek is rather rusty (or even somewhat limited), don't be too concerned. All of the Greek words are cited in parentheses following an English translation. We have made every effort to make this commentary as readable and useful as possible even for the nonspecialist.

Those who will benefit the most from this commentary will have had the equivalent of two years of Greek in college or seminary. This would include a semester or two of working through an intermediate grammar (such as Wallace, Porter, Brooks and Winbery, or Dana and Mantey). The authors use the grammatical language that is found in these kinds of grammars. The details of the grammar of the passage, however, are discussed only when it has a bearing on the interpretation of the text.

The emphasis in this section of the text is to convey the meaning. Commentators examine words and images, grammatical details, relevant OT and Jewish background to a particular concept, historical and cultural context, important text-critical issues, and various interpretational issues that surface.

Theology in Application

This, too, is a unique feature for an exegetical commentary series. We felt it was important for each author not only to describe what the text means in its various details, but also to take a moment and reflect on the theological contribution that it makes. In this section, the theological message of the passage is summarized. The authors discuss the theology of the text in terms of its place within the book and in a broader biblical-theological context. Finally, each commentator provides some suggestions on what the message of the passage is for the church today. At the conclusion of each volume in this series is a summary of the whole range of theological themes touched on by this book of the Bible.

Our sincere hope and prayer is that you find this series helpful not only for your own understanding of the text of the New Testament, but as you are actively engaged in teaching and preaching God's Word to people who are hungry to be fed on its truth.

CLINTON E. ARNOLD, general editor

Author's Preface

I was honored to be invited to contribute the volume on the Gospel of John for the Zondervan Exegetical Commentary on the New Testament series, but I accepted with fear and trembling. My concern was not related to the common assumption that more than enough commentaries have been written in the modern era, especially on the Fourth Gospel. I am convinced that every generation must exegete Scripture in and for the church. I also saw more than enough space for my approach to the exegetical and theological issues in the Fourth Gospel to contribute to the academic discussion and to help the church understand the message of the Gospel. No, my fear was much more personal. In short, I felt unworthy. Who am I to offer a public exegesis of this significant book in the sacred Word of God? My agreement to write the commentary does not mean I am now more convinced of my own worthiness — not at all! Rather, I received this task as part of my faithfulness and obedience to God and his calling for my life and ministry. I wrote every page of this book for the church, specifically the local churches and pastors that will be assisted by the exegesis of this Gospel and the explication of its message — the gospel.

In the nearly six years it took me to write this commentary, my own ministerial assignment was shifted from the academy to the church. After nearly a decade as a professor at Talbot School of Theology, Biola University in southern California, I exchanged the podium for the pulpit, serving now as the senior pastor at Hope Evangelical Free Church in northern Illinois. I have training and gifting for the academy, yet I sensed an unmistakable call to serve in the local church. I do not believe that my PhD in New Testament and research/writing gifts are any less significant or functional by serving as a pastor, for I believe that the pastorate allows them to be placed in the context in which they are the most natural — in spite of the anti-intellectualism prevalent in so much of American evangelicalism. While I am thankful to be serving as an adjunct professor in the New Testament Department at Trinity Evangelical Divinity School, I cherish the thought that at least one contributor to the ZECNT series shares a post with the majority of its readers: the local pastor.

There are numerous people and institutions that deserve thanks. I am still surprised that the editors of ZECNT, especially the general editor, Clint Arnold, entrusted this task to me. The numerous insights along the way, not only from Clint but all the members of the editorial committee, as well as the editorial team at

Zondervan, especially Christopher Beetham, were more than helpful. The deficiencies in this commentary are entirely my own. The entire design of this commentary series is very well conceived and considerably more useful for the church than many commentaries currently in print.

The commentary was almost entirely written while I was still teaching at Talbot/Biola, and I cannot thank that institution and its leaders enough for the assistance and support given to me. I received not only grants from Biola University but also received a significant sabbatical from Talbot School of Theology. I would like to thank the deans who served during my years of service for all the resources they provided me: Dennis Dirks, Mike Wilkins, Clint Arnold, and Scott Rae. I would also like to thank my New Testament colleagues for their constant encouragement and prayer: Darian Lockett, Jon Lunde, Ken Berding, Matt Williams, Joanne Jung, Michelle Lee-Barnwall, and Doug Huffman. I could mention so many other Talbot colleagues who supported me along the way. During my years at Talbot/Biola I experienced a unique community of support and grace that was a blessing not only to my career but also to my family. This commentary, the majority of which was written in office 218 of the Talbot East building, is very much the result of the blessed environment in which I worked.

There were numerous students who read through some or all of the commentary and provided helpful feedback. Thanks are especially due to the graduate students in my Exegesis of John classes and the undergraduate students in my Gospel of John classes for their careful reading of various versions of the manuscript. Their insights into the text and interest in exegetical method motivated me and reminded me of the importance of this task. But no one provided more assistance than Jason Smith, my former teaching assistant, who not only read over large portions of the commentary but also spent countless hours working on the diagrams. I am so very thankful for the assistance Jason gave to me and to this commentary.

I would also like to thank my church family at Hope Evangelical Free Church in Roscoe, Illinois for recently welcoming my family and me as their senior pastor and for supporting me as I finished this commentary even while beginning my ministry with them. I want to thank the elders for having the vision and courage to invite a pastor-theologian to shepherd the flock they oversee. I would especially like to thank my ministerial team for their support and partnership in the gospel: Brad Schreiner, Jim Oakley, Kevin Dick, Fana Timoti, Vera Juhlin, Pat Noble, Carolyn Scherrer, and Dana Butts.

No person felt the burden of the production of this commentary more than my wife, Laura. For six years she constantly and graciously provided me with the time and blessing I needed to work on this massive project in the midst of regular work and life, including the birth of our third child! I could not have done this without her full support and encouragement. Not one word could have been typed had she not participated with me in this task. Laura shares in every way the fruit of this labor. I would also like to thank my children, Jacob, Benjamin, and Ruth, for their patience as their dad finished this book. I love each of them and hope that the message of the Gospel of John will be written into their hearts and lives as they believe in Jesus Christ and learn to have life in his name (20:31).

Finally, I am dedicating this commentary to my mom, Kimberly Grace Klink. It was not easy for her to raise a son as a single mom, but she did it. She sacrificed in innumerable ways for me, giving me the love and support of two parents! I have never met a more giving person, and I hope she can receive this commentary as my gift to her.

Abbreviations

1 En.	1 Enoch
1 Macc	1 Maccabees
2 En.	2 Enoch
2 Macc	2 Maccabees
AB	Anchor Bible
ABR	*Australian Biblical Review*
ABRL	Anchor Bible Reference Library
AD	*anno Domini*
AGJU	Arbeiten zur Geschichte des antiken Judentums und des Urchristentums
AJPS	*Asian Journal of Pentecostal Studies*
AnBib	Analecta Biblica
ANF	*Ante-Nicene Fathers*
Ann.	*Annales* (Tacitus)
ANTC	Abingdon New Testament Commentaries
Ant.	*Jewish Antiquities* (Josephus)
AsTJ	*Asbury Theological Journal*
AThR	*Anglican Theological Review*
2 Bar.	2 Baruch
b. Shabbat	Babylonian Talmud: Shabbat
b. Sukkah	Babylonian Talmud: Sukkah
Barn.	Barnabas
BAR	*Biblical Archaeology Review*
BBB	Bonner biblische Beiträge
BBC	Blackwell Bible Commentaries
BBR	*Bulletin for Biblical Research*
BC	before Christ
BCOT	Baker Commentary on the Old Testament
BDAG	Bauer, W., F. W. Danker, W. F. Arndt, and F. W. Gingrich. *Greek-English Lexicon of the New Testament and Other Early Christian Literature.* 3d ed. Chicago: University of Chicago Press, 2000
BDF	Blass, F., A. Debrunner, and R. W. Funk. *A Greek Grammar of the New Testament and Other Early Christian Literature.* Chicago: University of Chicago Press, 1961

BECNT	Baker Exegetical Commentary on the New Testament
BeO	*Bibbia e oriente*
BETL	Bibliotheca Ephemeridum Theologicarum Lovaniensium
BGBE	Beiträge zur Geschichte der biblischen Exegese
Bib	*Biblica*
BibTS	Biblical Tools and Studies
BibInt	Biblical Interpretation Series
B.J.	*Bellum judaicum* (Josephus)
BLG	Biblical Language: Greek
BNTC	Black's New Testament Commentaries
BR	*Biblical Research*
BSac	*Bibliotheca Sacra*
BSNA	Biblical Scholarship in North America
BSR	*Biblioteca di Scienze Religiose*
BT	*The Bible Translator*
BTB	*Biblical Theology Bulletin*
BTL	Biblical Theology for Life
BTNT	Biblical Theology of the New Testament
BZ	*Biblische Zeitschrift*
BZNW	Beihefte zur Zeitschrift für die neutestamentliche Wissenschaft
BZNWKAK	Beihefte zur Zeitschrift für die neutestamentliche Wissenschaft und die Kunde der älteren Kirche
CBQ	*Catholic Biblical Quarterly*
CBQMS	Catholic Biblical Quarterly Monograph Series
CD	Karl Barth. *Church Dogmatics*. Edinburgh: T&T Clark, 1956–75
CIT	Current Issues in Theology
CNTC	Calvin's New Testament Commentaries
Colloq	*Colloquium*
ConBNT	Coniectanea Neotestamentica
CTJ	*Calvin Theological Journal*
CTM	*Concordia Theological Monthly*
CTR	*Criswell Theological Review*
CurBR	*Currents in Biblical Research*
DDSR	*Duke Divinity School Review*
Did	*Didaskalia*
Did.	Didache
DRev	*Downside Review*
ECC	Eerdmans Critical Commentary
ECS	Early Christian Studies
EcumRev	*Ecumenical Review*
EJL	*Early Judaism and Its Literature*
Enc	*Encounter*
ENT	Erläuterungen Neuen Testament

2 Esd	2 Esdras
ESV	English Standard Version
ETL	*Ephemerides Theologicae Lovanienses*
EUS	European University Studies
EvQ	*Evangelical Quarterly*
ExAud	*Ex Auditu*
ExpTim	*Expository Times*
FC	Fathers of the Church
FCNTECW	Feminist Companion to the New Testament and Early Christian Writings
FPCC	Faith and Practice of the Christian Community
GNB	Good News Bible
GOTR	*Greek Orthodox Theological Review*
GTJ	*Grace Theological Journal*
HACL	History, Archaeology, and Culture of the Levant
Haer.	*Adversus haereses* (Irenaeus)
HBT	*Horizons in Biblical Theology*
HCSB	Holman Christian Standard Bible
Hist. eccl.	*Historia ecclesiastica* (Eusebius)
HM	Hallische Monographien
Hor	*Horizons*
HTCNT	Herder's Theological Commentary on the New Testament
HTR	*Harvard Theological Review*
ICC	International Critical Commentary
Ign. *Magn.*	Ignatius, *To the Magnesians*
IEJ	*Israel Exploration Journal*
IJST	*International Journal of Systematic Theology*
Int	*Interpretation*
IRM	*International Review of Mission*
IVPNTC	InterVarsity Press New Testament Commentary
JAMA	*Journal of the American Medical Association*
JB	Jerusalem Bible
JBL	*Journal of Biblical Literature*
JECH	*Journal of Early Christian History*
JES	*Journal of Ecumenical Studies*
JETS	*Journal of the Evangelical Theological Society*
JPaleolimnol	*Journal of Paleolimnology*
JQR	*Jewish Quarterly Review*
JR	*Journal of Religion*
JSNT	*Journal for the Study of the New Testament*
JSNTSup	Journal for the Study of the New Testament Supplement Series
JSOTSup	Journal for the Study of the Old Testament Supplement Series
JTI	*Journal of Theological Interpretation*

JTS	*Journal of Theological Studies*
JTSA	*Journal of Theology for Southern Africa*
Jub.	Jubilees
J.W.	*Jewish War* (Josephus)
KJV	King James Version
KNT	Kommentar zum Neuen Testament
LCC	Library of Christian Classics
LFHCC	A Library of Fathers of the Holy Catholic Church
LitTh	*Literature and Theology*
LNTS	The Library of New Testament Studies
LQ	*Lutheran Quarterly*
LSJ	Liddell, H. G., R. Scott, H. S. Jones. *A Greek-English Lexicon*. 9th ed. with revised supplement. Oxford: Clarendon, 1996
LTJ	*Lutheran Theological Journal*
LW	*Luther's Works*, American Edition. J. Pelikan and H. T. Lehmann. 55 vols. St. Louis: Concordia/Philadelphia: Fortress, 1955 – 86
LXX	Septuagint (the Greek Old Testament)
MarStud	*Marian Studies*
m. 'Abot	Mishnah: 'Abot
m. Kelim	Mishnah: Kelim
m. Nid.	Mishnah: Niddah
m. Shabbat	Mishnah: Shabbat
m. Sukkah	Mishnah: Sukkah
ModTheol	*Modern Theology*
MTZ	*Münchener theologische Zeitschrift*
NA^{28}	*Novum Testamentum Graece*, Nestle-Aland, 28th ed.
NAC	New American Commentary
NASB	New American Standard Bible
NBC	A New Biblical Commentary
NCB	New Century Bible
NCBC	New Cambridge Bible Commentary
NEB	New English Bible
Neot	*Neotestamentica*
NICNT	New International Commentary on the New Testament
NICOT	New International Commentary on the Old Testament
NIGTC	New International Greek Testament Commentary
NIV	New International Version
NJB	New Jerusalem Bible
NovT	*Novum Testamentum*
NovTSup	Supplements to Novum Testamentum
NPNF	*Nicene and Post-Nicene Fathers*
NRSV	New Revised Standard Version
NSBT	New Studies in Biblical Theology

NT	New Testament
NTAbh	Neutestamentliche Abhandlungen
NTL	New Testament Library
NTOA	Novum Testamentum et Orbis Antiquus
NTS	*New Testament Studies*
NTTS	New Testament Tools and Studies
NTTSD	New Testament Tools, Studies, and Documents
Odes Sol.	Odes of Solomon
OT	Old Testament
𝔓	Papyrus (manuscript)
PBM	Paternoster Biblical Monographs
PCNT	Paideia: Commentaries on the New Testament
PL	Patrologia Latina [= *Patrologiae Cursus Completus*: Series Latina]. Edited by J.-P. Migne. 217 vols. Paris, 1844–1864
PNTC	Pillar New Testament Commentary
Posterity	*On the Posterity of Cain* (Philo)
Presb	*Presbyterion*
ProcGLM	*Proceedings: Eastern Great Lakes and Midwest Biblical Societies*
ProEccl	*Pro Ecclesia*
PRSt	*Perspectives in Religious Studies*
PSB	*Princeton Seminary Bulletin*
Pss. Sol.	Psalms of Solomon
RefR	*Reformed Review*
ResQ	*Restoration Quarterly*
RevExp	*Review and Expositor*
RSR	*Recherches de science religieuse*
RSV	Revised Standard Version
RThom	*Revue thomiste*
RTR	*Reformed Theological Review*
RV	Revised Version
SBB	Stuttgarter biblische Beiträge
SBET	*Scottish Bulletin of Evangelical Theology*
SBFLA	*Studii Biblici Franciscani Liber Annus*
SBG	Studies in Biblical Greek
SBLDS	Society of Biblical Literature Dissertation Series
SBLMS	Society of Biblical Literature Monograph Series
SBLStBL	Society of Biblical Literature Studies in Biblical Literature
SBT	Studies in Biblical Theology
ScEs	*Science et esprit*
SCJ	*Stone-Campbell Journal*
Scorp.	*Scorpiace* (Tertullian)
SemeiaSt	Semeia Studies
SGBCNT	Story of God Bible Commentary: New Testament

Sir	Sirach
SMR	*St. Mark's Review*
SNTSMS	Society for New Testament Studies Monograph Series
SP	Sacra Pagina
Spec.	*De specialibus legibus* (Philo)
SSEJC	Studies in Scripture in Early Judaism and Christianity
ST	*Studia Theologica*
StBibLit	Studies in Biblical Literature (Lang)
Stim	*Stimulus*
SVTQ	*St. Vladimir's Theological Quarterly*
SWR	Studies in Woman and Religion
SymS	Symposium Series
TBei	*Theologische Beiträge*
TDNT	*Theological Dictionary of the New Testament.* Edited by G. Kittel and G. Friedrich. Translated by G. W. Bromiley. 10 vols. Grand Rapids: Eerdmans, 1964–1976
TENTS	Texts and Editions for New Testament Study
ThTo	*Theology Today*
T. Levi	Testament of Levi
Tob	Tobit
TJ	*Trinity Journal*
ThSt	Theologische Studiën
TS	Texts and Studies
TS	*Theological Studies*
TTCSST	T&T Clark Studies in Systematic Theology
TTE	*The Theological Educator*
TynBul	*Tyndale Bulletin*
TZ	*Theologische Zeitschrift*
Vita	*Vita* (Josephus)
WBC	Word Biblical Commentary
WCF	Westminster Confession of Faith
WesTJ	*Wesleyan Theological Journal*
Wis	Wisdom of Solomon
Wor	*Worship*
WSC	Westminster Shorter Catechism
WTJ	*Westminster Theological Journal*
WUNT	Wissenschaftliche Untersuchungen zum Neuen Testament
ZNW	*Zeitschrift für die neutestamentliche Wissenschaft und die Kunde der älteren Kirche*
ZSNT	Zacchaeus Studies: New Testament
ZTK	*Zeitschrift für Theologie und Kirche*

Introduction to John

The Gospel of John might be described as needing no introduction at all. This particular Gospel and book of the Christian Bible has been one of the most frequented and theologically significant in the entire canon, maybe in all the literature of the world. Yet possibly for that very reason it has also been one of the most abused and distorted and at the center of a host of interpretive and theological debates. And while this Gospel is itself intended to provide an introduction to *the gospel* of Jesus Christ, it still requires its own introduction, if only because of its sacred purpose and the importance of its subject matter.

Prolegomena

The modern commentary is expected to provide a certain amount of space to giving an introduction to the text to be commented upon, almost always in relation to its historical context. The author, origin (date, provenance, and audience), and purpose of the document are usually explored and defended with the methodological assumption that such data is significant for the interpretation to follow. It is unquestionable that this historical information about the text to be commented upon is vital to correctly understand its meaning and application. Yet it is rare for commentators to defend or even explain this implicit methodological foundation. This is unfortunate for two primary reasons.

First, it minimizes the hermeneutical issues involved in any kind of interpretation. Presumably, modern commentaries take for granted that the commentary genre is an overtly historical task and therefore feel no need to explain their method and its philosophical and theological underpinnings to the reader. But this is hardly the case. Not only does the text carry its own interpretive commands innate to its origin and nature, but the act of interpretation forces the interpreter to make a plethora of methodological assumptions regarding the text in view.

The second reason is even more important: it minimizes that the text in view is in fact the biblical text, that is, part of Christian Scripture. The very reason why there is so much interest in this particular text is treated as methodologically unimportant to the task at hand. By definition, then, this text raises the interpretive stakes.

For its author is not merely historical but also divine; and its audience is not merely confined to the ancient world but still exists and receives this text in the modern world. Without denying that this text has an origin and purpose in a time long past, as Scripture it must also be understood to have a divine origin and eternal purpose that demands its reception in every generation — even those still to come.

The dual origin of this text is the constant issue facing the interpreter. And after two millennia, with even greater cultural and historical distance between this (now ancient) text and the (contemporary) reader, the interpretive gap is even more of an issue. It would be an understatement to say that this gap has been the subject of much disagreement and debate over the last few centuries; there is no way a commentary on a biblical Gospel can avoid this issue. In fact, a biblical Gospel, maybe specifically the Gospel of John, is where these interpretive tensions or "gaps" (i.e., "Lessing's Ditch") are the most apparent. For certainly a book that begins, "In the beginning … with God" (1:1) is not easily given a date or provenance that is functional for the modern historical-critical method.

In light of the above discussion and the last few centuries of hermeneutical debate we can summarize two basic approaches to the biblical texts that confront the interpreter and this commentary: *critical* and *confessional*. It is often assumed that the critical approach takes its directives from the ancient context and historical identity of the text, and the confessional approach takes its directives from the contemporary ecclesial context and divine identity of the text, but as we will see below neither of these are entirely accurate. It is only partly correct to pit the approaches against one another in a manner that pits history against theology. While the critical approach is almost required to deny any divine authority to the interpretive task, the confessional approach not only embraces unhesitatingly the ancient context and historical identity of the text as part of the means of revelation but does so specifically for theological reasons. That is, while the critical approach cannot find warrant to move from the authoritative foundation of the natural (historical) to the supernatural, the confessional approach cannot find warrant to stop the move from the supernatural to the natural, since creation is a subset and necessary corollary of the Creator.

The critical approach finds its roots in what has for about two centuries been called "historical criticism." While the church has always practiced a historical reading of Scripture, the Enlightenment's rationalistic demands developing in the seventeenth and eighteenth centuries within and outside the church pressured a more "scientific" interpretive method to provide warrant for belief or disbelief in the doctrines derived from the Bible, with sophisticated historiographical methods dictating the terms of interpretation by the nineteenth century.[1] Early versions of historical criticism function "in godlike fashion," making a new kind of dogmatic claim that

---

1. Richard E. Burnett, "Historical Criticism," in *Dictionary for Theological Interpretation of the Bible*, ed. Kevin J. Van- hoozer et al. (Grand Rapids: Baker Academic, 2005), 290 – 93 (291).

silenced the dogma of the church.[2] More contemporary versions, however, are more admissive of their perspectival nature and simply argue (along with the confessional approach) that their perspective is the most faithful to the object of study, that is, verifiable by their own standards of ethics and warrant.[3]

In a recent and more sophisticated work on the critical approach, Barton argues that the plain sense of a text should not be equated with its original sense or what it "meant." Rather, "biblical critics are concerned with what texts mean, now equally as much as then."[4] Barton argues that the difference between critical and confessional approaches is not historical but literary, "the *kind* of text" being studied.[5] Barton's analysis establishes a common point of difference between the critical and confessional approaches: *the nature and function of the biblical text itself*. This means that history and its application is not the difference, as is commonly assumed. A confessional approach is just as concerned with the historical context and identity of the text as the critical approach, just for different reasons and with different warrant. Both approaches believe that the ancient context of the Bible is a determiner of its meaning. And both approaches feel the need to disregard certain historical judgments made to the text by the other approach. Just as the confessional approach will challenge historical value judgments of the critical approach to the biblical events (e.g., Jesus's resurrection from the dead or walking on water), so also the critical approach will challenge historical value judgments of the confessional approach to the biblical text (e.g., inerrancy). In this sense, then, both approaches rely on history and theology (or ideology), but do so from very different foundations, neither of which are value neutral.

What are the foundations upon which each approach establishes its authority? Is there a verifiable foundation upon which objective truth judgments can be established for determining meaning? Even by the standards of the critical approach, not without faith! Barton claims as much when he argues that the critical approach honors the text "as part of the givenness of a world we did not make."[6] But what exactly is this "givenness" and from whom has this been given? With what is almost a version of the cosmological or teleological argument, Barton's use of "givenness" is an ideological starting point that logically grounds the meaning of the text in the historical "world" to which it naturally relates. The confessional approach is no less theological (ideological) when it honors the text as part of the givenness of the God who claimed to write it. But this "givenness" is also a theological starting point that logically grounds the meaning of the text in the God to whom it naturally relates.[7]

---

2. Burnett, "Historical Criticism," 291.

3. See Van A. Harvey, *The Historian and the Believer: The Morality of Historical Knowledge and Christian Belief*, rev. ed. (Urbana: University of Illinois Press, 1996).

4. John Barton, *The Nature of Biblical Criticism* (Louisville: Westminster John Knox, 2007), 7.

5. Ibid., 23.

6. Ibid., 182.

7. Cf. Scott R. Swain, *Trinity, Revelation, and Reading: A Theological Introduction to the Bible and Its Interpretation* (London: T&T Clark, 2011), 7.

Both can be said to rely on the self-attestation of the text itself, but only the confessional approach ultimately trusts itself to the witness of the biblical text.[8] The ultimate difference, then, is what each approach believes to be the foundational "given": the world or God — an ironic choice in light of the Gospel of John. In this commentary we chose the Creator over *his* creation.[9]

In short, *the exploration of what this Gospel means cannot begin until we have explained what this Gospel is, for interpretation is guided by the nature of its object.* And these two approaches have differently defined objects in view, even when both are interpreting the Gospel of John, and the difference in object yields different warrants, guidance, and insights into its meaning. The issue was never history against theology or ancient versus ecclesial context, but which "givenness" is the most appropriate foundation for grounding the meaning of the text. It is the argument of this commentary that only the confessional approach can handle not only the God of the biblical text but also its full historicity, denouncing any dichotomy between history and theology by claiming that God both uses and is made known by the historical reality to which the text points and through which the text communicates. Using the Gospel's own terms, when "the Word became flesh" (1:14), it was "*the Word*" and not "the flesh" that was the primary agent of the encounter and therefore the primary ground of meaning.[10] Similarly, the paradox of Scripture is most suitably handled by the confessional approach.[11]

The above discussion has tried to situate the introductory topics regarding this particular kind of text in its divine identity as Christian Scripture. If one does not begin with this definition of the text — the Gospel of John, then they are not only reading in an entirely different manner but also in a deficient and inappropriate manner. The fact that commentators rarely define or defend their methodological foundation gives further warrant for such prolegomena here. For this reason we must include in the introduction to this commentary a section on methodology befitting Christian Scripture, and it is that section with which we must begin.

The Doctrine of Scripture and Methodology

The prolegomena which we covered above has magnified the importance of defining rightly the object of our study, the ontology of the Gospel of John. Before we can explain what the Gospel *does* we must first explain what the Gospel *is*. And since the Gospel of John is part of Christian Scripture, it must be dealt with accordingly. To do this, however, we must first apply the doctrine of Scripture specifically to this Gospel.

---

8. Cf. Harvey, *Historian and the Believer*, 42.

9. For a theological critique of Barton, see R. W. L. Moberly, "Biblical Criticism and Religious Belief," *JTI* 2 (2008): 71 – 100.

10. The "flesh" is a subset of "the Word" from which (whom) it was created. Cf. R. Michael Allen, *The Christ's Faith: A Dog-*

matic Account, TTCSST 2 (London: T&T Clark, 2009), 119.

11. Helpful here is Vern S. Poythress, "Dispensing with Merely Human Meaning: Gains and Losses from Focusing on the Human Author, Illustrated by Zephaniah 1:2 – 3," *JETS* 57 (2014): 481 – 99.

Doctrine of Scripture

To define the Gospel as part of Christian Scripture is to place it in a much larger communicative context than simply the first-century context in which it took on its literary "flesh." By categorizing the Gospel as Scripture, we are depicting it in light of its "origin, function, and end in divine self-communication"; yet we are also depicting the manner in which it must be read and the kinds of responses appropriate to its nature: "'Scripture' is a shorthand term for the nature and function of the biblical writings in a set of communicative acts which stretch from God's merciful self-manifestation to the obedient hearing of the community of faith."[12] While such language might not be common vernacular in an introduction to an exegetical commentary, it should be, for the object of interpretation demands to be treated according to its true and sacred nature. Not to treat this Gospel as Scripture is itself a form of eisegesis, and it is a disobedient hearing of the (canonical) text's own claim and of the God by whom it was authored.

The doctrine of Scripture is necessary for the exegetical task in two ways. First, it gives *insight* to the interpretive rules demanded by the object of interpretation. In a sense, Scripture becomes its own kind of genre: "If genre is a function of communal reception and usage as well as of inherent characteristics, then the genre of the biblical texts is that of 'holy Scripture.'"[13] Functionally, then, the doctrine of Scripture explains the (theological) genre of the Bible and the generic conventions to be followed by the faithful reader.

Second, the doctrine of Scripture gives *oversight* to its constituent parts and unifies their functions. Three are immediately apparent: (1) since the Gospel speaks in time-and-space history, a doctrinal framework is needed to make sure history remains subservient to the God of creation; (2) since the Gospel speaks in literary form, a doctrinal framework is needed to make sure words stay subservient to the Word; and (3) since the Gospel speaks about the things of God, a doctrinal framework is needed to make sure theology is defined by the person and work of God himself, the true subject matter of the things of God. In short, *the doctrine of Scripture gives oversight to the historical, literary, and theological components of the revelation of God, which we will refer to as creation, canon, and creed in order to match their doctrinal nature.* A brief explanation of each is in order.

Creation

The doctrine of Scripture provides the necessary requirements for understanding the historical content and context of the Gospel. To make interpretive judgments

---

12. John Webster, *Holy Scripture: A Dogmatic Sketch*, CIT 1 (Cambridge: Cambridge University Press, 2003), 5.

13. Francis Watson, *Text, Church and World: Biblical Interpretation in Theological Perspective* (Edinburgh: T&T Clark, 1994), 227.

regarding the meaning of the Gospel by comparing it to the historical (and social-cultural) setting in which it originated and occurred without the oversight or mediation of the doctrine of Scripture is to conflate the meaning of the text to its historical context. The Bible is not to be read as any other book. The view that supposes texts are wholly limited and confined by their immediate circumstances of origin, and that as soon as they stray from their appointed time and place they will be misread and misunderstood, embraces a historical perception of this body of writings that is theologically foreign to them.[14] This is not to say that Scripture is unhistorical or less historical — not at all! It is to say, rather, that it is more; it speaks from a more comprehensive position.

A doctrine of Scripture allows the biblical narrative, with all its historical necessity and detail, not to bow the knee to the claims of historical naturalism. "For a Christian theological account of Scripture … the problem … is not the affirmation that the biblical texts have a 'natural history,' but the denial that texts with a 'natural history' may function within the communicative divine economy, and that such a function is ontologically definitive of the text. It is this denial — rather than any purely methodological questions — which has to form the focus of dogmatic critique."[15] Helpful here is Billings, who explains that every interpreter implicitly answers two questions when they interpret the Bible: (1) Is revelation grounded in inherent, universal human capacities or in the particularity of God's action with Israel and in Jesus Christ?; and (2), Is Scripture received from within a deistic hermeneutic or with a Trinitarian hermeneutic?[16] In both cases the latter option is necessitated by a doctrinally defined reading of Scripture, for an interpretation that is naturalistic and/or deistic is poorly matched to the divine character of Scripture. For this reason the interpreter is given dogmatic reasons to believe that God was involved in the entire messy process, from the historical event to the textual expression of the text of Scripture (composition, transmission, and reception). This requires a highly theological account of "history," not only as a tool of interpretation but also as a philosophical construct.

A sophisticated account of a theology of history has been provided by Rae, who argues that in relation to biblical interpretation "the very idea of history requires both the biblical doctrine of creation, and a teleology, an account, that is, of the directedness of history towards some goal."[17] Similar to our discussion of historical criticism above, Rae argues that theology had been excluded from the consideration of biblical texts, which ironically is itself a dogmatic presupposition.[18] The key for

---

14. Edward W. Klink III and Darian R. Lockett, *Understanding Biblical Theology: A Comparison of Theory and Practice* (Grand Rapids: Zondervan, 2012), 160.

15. Webster, *Holy Scripture*, 19.

16. J. Todd Billings, *The Word of God for the People of God: An Entryway to the Theological Interpretation of Scripture* (Grand Rapids: Eerdmans, 2010), 71–104.

17. Murray A. Rae, *History and Hermeneutics* (London: T&T Clark, 2005), 2.

18. Rae, *History and Hermeneutics*, 19–20.

Rae (and others)[19] is the logical priority of Scripture: "We simply cannot proceed to investigate the Bible's witness to revelation by assuming that we know apart from revelation what history is. The order of knowing must be reversed."[20] Since all history doctrinally finds its purpose (*telos*) in the person and work of God, history only has meaning in the purposes of God. This is why the doctrine of creation is so important (and must be related) to the doctrine of Scripture. Creation implies that the world is invested with a *telos*. "There is a reason for its being, and history, in consequence, is to be understood as the space and time opened up for the world to become what it is intended to be."[21] History becomes God's own confession, under his creative, providential, and redemptive purposes, to extend himself to the world. The referentiality and meaning of Scripture, therefore, is given definition not only by its placement in the originating (historical) context but also in the fuller context of God's communicative grace.

The history in this Gospel, therefore, cannot be understood by rational inquiry without recourse to revelation. Nor can its purpose and meaning be reduced to a set of laws or by comparison to apparent analogous entities — to do so would be naturalistic and deistic. Rather, history, once understood to be framed by the Alpha and Omega (Rev 22:13), becomes a subset of creation — and therefore the Creator — and is embedded with promise and purpose that is revealed in the person and work of Jesus Christ, who is both its ground and goal.[22] The incarnation, as the Gospel records it, is not something entirely new but is the magnified, replacement grace (1:14) of a God who had been active and present in his creation since "the beginning" (1:1).

Canon

The doctrine of Scripture not only gives definition to the material nature behind the text but also to the literary nature of the text itself. Since such a doctrine provides a "conceptual framework, suggested by the narrative itself, for interpreting that narrative," it becomes essential for the exegetical task.[23] Vanhoozer suggests that by referring to Scripture as a divine "speech act," the classical doctrines of revelation, inspiration, and infallibility can be integrated and interpreted.[24] As a speech act, Scripture can speak not merely in *word* (what God says) but also in *action* (what God does).[25] "The notion of a divine speech act addresses both the problem of the nature of God's activity and the problem of the nature of biblical language. Scripture

---

19. See Karl Barth, *Church Dogmatics*, ed. T. F. Torrance and G. W. Bromiley (Edinburgh: T&T Clark, 1956 – 75), I/2:58 (hereafter *CD*).

20. Rae, *History and Hermeneutics*, 29. See also Webster, *Holy Scripture*, 6.

21. Rae, *History and Hermeneutics*, 51.

22. Cf. Augustine, *Teaching Christianity*, ed. John E. Rotelle, trans. Edmund Hill (Hyde Park: New City, 1996), 2.44.152.

23. Kevin J. Vanhoozer, *First Theology: God, Scripture, and Hermeneutics* (Downers Grove: InterVarsity Press, 2002), 129.

24. On speech act theory, see Jeannine K. Brown, *Scripture as Communication: Introducing Biblical Hermeneutics* (Grand Rapids: Baker Academic, 2007), 32 – 35, 111 – 14, 270. Cf. Billings, *The Word of God for the People of God*, 206 – 10.

25. Vanhoozer, *First Theology*, 130.

is neither simply the recital of the acts of God nor merely a book of inert propositions. Scripture is rather composed of divine-human speech acts that, through what
they say, accomplish several authoritative cognitive, spiritual and social functions."[26]

In this way, then, Scripture, including this Gospel, speaks by word and action in
a multitude of modes and manners, that is, illocutionary acts, which simultaneously
form a unitary act. A right reading of the Gospel will interpret the illocutionary infer-
ences, or communicative intentionality, provided by the text itself through primary
(explicit) and secondary (implicit) data. In this Gospel the inference is made explicit
(20:30 – 31): that the reader would come to believe in Jesus Christ and have life in
his name. This intentional communication, as a subset of the doctrine of Scripture,
makes it more than a communicative act — it is a missional act: "the self-presentation
of the triune God, the free work of sovereign mercy in which God wills, establishes
and perfects saving fellowship with himself in which humankind comes to know,
love and fear him above all things."[27] Scripture as a whole, and the Gospel of John in
particular, is the communicative grace of God.

By *canon*, then, we refer to more than the collection of biblical books;[28] we are
referring here primarily to Scripture's function and identity, both of which have
implications for interpreting the Gospel of John. First, according to its *function as
canon*, this Gospel cannot be treated as if it were a single unit. Without denying that
the Gospel took on literary "flesh" in the context of a particular historical author and
audience, as the Word of God it was always intended (doctrinally) to be read as part
of a collection. Though an argument could be made that the Gospel was originally
created (historically) with this intention from its inception,[29] our argument is more
dogmatic than historical. Since this Gospel makes up one of many parts of God's
intentional communicative Word, then this Gospel must be viewed as functioning
cooperatively. This in no way denies that the Gospel had value and meaning for its
particular historical context, only that its meaning is so tied to its larger canonical
context that the latter extends and even explains the former. Again, while the critical
approach demands that only the historical context be determinative for meaning, the
confessional approach understands that in the providence of God this Gospel's historical and canonical contexts function symphonically to communicate the intended
fullness of the Word of God.

Second, according to its *identity as canon*, this Gospel cannot be treated as if it
were (another) source to the Word of God but must be treated as the very source of
the Word of God. That is, the Bible is not a window to that which is inspired but is
itself the inspiration. When we speak of Scripture, we are speaking about the source

---

26. Vanhoozer, *First Theology*, 131.

27. Webster, *Holy Scripture*, 13.

28. See John Webster, *Word and Church: Essays in Christian
Dogmatics* (Edinburgh: T&T Clark, 2011), 11 – 17.

29. See D. Moody Smith, "When Did the Gospels Become
Scripture?" *JBL* 119 (2000): 3 – 20; Cf. Edward W. Klink III,
*The Sheep of the Fold: The Audience and Origin of the Gospel of
John*, SNTSMS 141 (Cambridge: Cambridge University Press,
2010), 252 – 54.

of revelation and claiming (dogmatically) that Scripture is the locus of revelation, not merely a mediator of revelation. This issue is easily confusing and needs to be attended to carefully (for further definition, see "Text versus Event" below). This is not to deny in any way that the text is referring to real historical people, places, and events but to claim that the revelation, inclusive of real events, is located in the inscripturated account; God is giving divine commentary on his own actions in history. Again, while the critical approach is tempted to find meaning behind the text (in the event), the confessional approach realizes that this text, as a divinely inspired communicative act, is God's revelation *per se* (in or by itself).

The Gospel of John cannot be read as just any other book. Its form, function, and canonical identity are not ancillary to its interpretation and meaning; they are determinative. Even the reality to which it points cannot be defined without recourse to revelation, nor can its meaning be determined outside of its canonical context. Rather, the Gospel, once understood to be framed by the rest of Scripture, becomes a subset of the biblical canon and embedded with the full significance of the Word of God. Canon is not ultimately a historical account of the biblical collection but "a trinitarian and soteriological account of revelation … in which God establishes saving fellowship with humanity and so makes himself known to us."[30] In this way, then, the Bible is addressing not merely the past but the present and not merely an ancient audience but the contemporary church. Stated more straightforwardly, this Gospel mediates *the* gospel.

Creed

The doctrine of Scripture not only gives definition to what lies behind the text (creation) and to the text itself (canon) but also guides the reader to the goal of the text or its true subject matter. In light of God's use of creation in Scripture and the canon of Scripture, the biblical speech act can be described as "Jesus Christ's own self-utterance."[31] And if this Gospel fits the generic form of a biography (see below), then it is more accurately an autobiography, for this word about God is also the Word of God. Since Scripture is God's communicative act, then its message and subject matter are about him — his person and his work. It is in this way that this Gospel proclaims *the* gospel.

To read this Gospel in a manner unbefitting of Scripture, as a mere historical account of the religious reflections or traditions of some first-century Christian group, is to read anthropocentrically in a manner that puts humanity and not God as the source and subject matter. Quite simply, if this Gospel were only written by and to a Christian group in the first century, then the reader would have every reason to use the resources of the first century to reconstruct the group(s) and its intended communication. However, if this Gospel was written also by God, then the same

---

30. Webster, *Word and Church*, 27.   31. Ibid., 35.

is true: the reader should make every effort to interpret the Gospel according to its author and his intended communication.

One of the consequences of the critical approach, however, is the loss of connection between the doctrines of the church and the text of Scripture. This is primarily because Scripture is expected, according to scholarly rules of interpretation, to be grounded historically in the first century, thereby excluding by methodological necessity eternal theological truths. The text becomes historically grounded in a manner that a faithful reading of the text's "literal sense" is in reference to subjects driven by and derived from the context of the Gospel's origin, not "figuration or typology [which] was a natural extension of literal interpretation" in earlier eras of biblical interpretation.[32] The doctrines of the creeds, according to this approach, are entirely imposed upon the text of Scripture. Helpful here is Yeago, who explains that Scripture speaks not merely with concepts, the use of explicit words or terms, but also judgments, which can use a variety of concepts but in a manner that speaks beyond them, making a further implicit referential claim.[33] A text *uses* concepts but *makes* judgments. "The only way to uncover the judgments made in a text is to pay close attention to what is said and implied, to the specific, contingent ways in which its conceptual resources are deployed."[34] In this way, then, the text may make judgments beyond its use of concepts, with the Trinity being a classical example, so that it may (and does!) speak to subject matters not contained by any one concept.

Since context is so determinative of how and to what the interpreters "pay close attention," the critical and confessional approaches will "uncover" different judgments in the text. For example, what looks like historical discrepancies or even unimportant detail to the critical approach will have a much different and contingent significance for the confessional approach. The critical approach interprets the conceptual resources by the text as referring to historical issues — the belief of the "Johannine commmunity" standing behind the Gospel or even simply the historical event itself. But the confessional approach interprets those same conceptual resources in a manner that can (and does!) also refer to the divine context and content of the text (Scripture). The confessional approach, for example, interprets the Gospel's depiction of the relation between the Father and the Son as reflective of the Trinitarian identity of God, even if the concept (the Trinity) is not used. If God is Trinitarian in nature, then depictions of him, even if partial, are also reflective of the Trinity. In a sense, *without denying the logical priority and authority of Scripture, the subject matter of Scripture functions in a circular manner, not only as the result of a reading of Scripture but also as a guide for further readings.*[35]

---

32. Hans W. Frei, *The Eclipse of Biblical Narrative: A Study in Eighteenth and Nineteenth Century Hermeneutics* (New Haven: Yale University Press, 1980), 2.

33. David S. Yeago, "The New Testament and the Nicene Dogma: A Contribution to the Recovery of Theological Exegesis," *ProEccl* 3 (1994): 152–64.

34. Ibid., 162.

35. Helpful here is Carl R. Trueman, *The Creedal Imperative* (Wheaton: Crossway, 2012).

The subject matter of Scripture has been deemed by the church to be clear, which it summarized by the doctrine called the perspicuity of Scripture. Its clarity is not, however, because the meaning of the text and its subject matter are obvious. Rather, it is because of the (doctrinal) conviction "that Scripture has the capacity to address and transform the human being, and to offer a reliable guide to human action."[36] Webster defines it well: "Scripture's clarity is neither an intrinsic element of the text as text nor simply a fruit of exegetical labour; it is that which the text becomes as it functions in the Spirit-governed encounter between the self-presenting saviour and the faithful reader. To read is to be caught up by the truth-bestowing Spirit of God."[37] The doctrine of Scripture guides the reader to look rightly at the text, that is, to look for the self-presentation of God through the work and person of Jesus Christ by the empowering Holy Spirit. The Gospel of John may not say all that Scripture in its entirety is saying, but it is speaking about the same thing, just as there can be four Gospels that all speak to the same unitary subject matter. To use a metaphor, reading Scripture is like listening to a symphony, so that even when we listen to only one instrument (a biblical book), we are always aware of the part it plays in the symphony (the whole of Scripture) and thus read it in light of its symphonic cooperation. We read the Gospel of John, therefore, as part of and in light of the gospel of Jesus Christ.

Methodology

Our discussion of the doctrine of Scripture above is directly related to methodology, for we cannot begin to draw out ("exegesis") its meaning until we have defined its nature. Although there are presuppositions and stances that one must adopt from the start, a robust doctrine of Scripture is expressed methodologically not by a rigidly defined procedure but by a posture that is sensitive to the narrative's own movements, pressures, and expectations (explicit and implicit) demanded from an obedient, believing reader. It is an art as much as a science, yet some basic principles or postured practices can be explained.

Historical-Critical/Grammatical and Theological Exegesis

Since this Gospel is a historical narrative, it is essential that its historical nature be properly treated. Yet its historical nature cannot render mute its nature as Christian Scripture, which commonly occurs, even if only partially, in light of the dominance of the critical approach and its concerns. Over the last few decades it has been common for confessional interpreters to distance themselves from many of the tenets of the historical-critical method and yet try to maintain their "historical" methodology by removing "critical" and referring to their method as historical-grammatical, with the

---

36. John Yocum, "Scripture, Clarity of," in Vanhoozer, *Dictionary for Theological Interpretation of the Bible*, 727–30 (727).

37. Webster, *Holy Scripture*, 95.

"grammatical" suggesting that they attend more confessionally to the literal sense of the text.[38] The strength of the historical-grammatical method for interpreting a historical narrative is obvious, but there is also a potential weakness: history — as in the historical context in which the Gospel was written — must serve as the foundation for all other methods. Blomberg states it plainly: "This does not mean that I reject theological and literary analyses; indeed, I find them crucial. However, they can be engaged in legitimately only when built on the appropriate historical foundations."[39]

The demand for a historical foundation raises a potential weakness of the method: Does a historical foundation make doctrine secondary? Our discussion above would push against such a hierarchy, not only because there can be no conception of history (i.e., creation) without God but also because the nature of Scripture requires the foundation of doctrine in order to rightly interpret this unique text. To make historical analyses the foundation limits from the start what the interpreter sees in and does with the text. And as we discussed above, as necessary as history is for reading a historical text, the tenets (dogmas) of history are unable to grasp or express the nature of Scripture. The concern, therefore, is that history as an interpretive science is unqualified to grasp the fullness of the biblical text and its subject matter.[40] A method is in grave danger if it grounds a reading of Scripture on a historical foundation in such a manner that doctrine or theology seem to be an imposition that must be guarded against.[41]

A recent response to the historical-grammatical method by others within the confessional approach has been an overtly theological method often called "theological interpretation of Scripture."[42] This approach has been variously defined, rarely applied to the biblical text — more theoretical than exegetical in form, and the object of much confusion and criticism.[43] While this "theological interpretation" movement, if it may be called that, has brought to light several important issues regarding the confessional approach, it may have only tipped the imbalance to the other side. Even more, neither side — the historical-grammatical or theological interpretation of Scripture, if they may be referred to as "sides" — actually admit imbalance. The proponents of the historical-grammatical method believe they are doing theology —

38. See Craig L. Blomberg, "The Historical-Critical/Grammatical View," in *Biblical Hermeneutics: Five Views*, ed. Stanley E. Porter and Beth M. Stovell (Downers Grove: InterVarsity Press, 2012), 27 – 47.

39. Blomberg, "Historical-Critical/Grammatical View," 28.

40. See Karl Barth, *The Epistle to the Romans*, trans. Edwyn C. Hoskyns, 6th ed. (Oxford: Oxford University Press, 1933), 6 – 7.

41. For example, see Blomberg, "The Historical-Critical/Grammatical View," 28: "I am convinced that all of the other approaches must build on the historical-critical/grammatical approach in order to function legitimately."

42. See Daniel J. Treier, *Introducing Theological Interpreta-*tion of Scripture: Recovering a Christian Practice* (Grand Rapids: Baker Academic, 2008). Cf. Stephen Fowl, *Theological Interpretation of Scripture* (Eugene, OR: Cascade, 2009).

43. For a critique, see D. A. Carson, "Theological Interpretation of Scripture: Yes, but …," in *Theological Commentary: Evangelical Perspectives*, ed. R. Michael Allen (London: T&T Clark, 2012), 187 – 207. For a defense, see Kevin J. Vanhoozer, "Theological Commentary and 'The Voice from Heaven': Exegesis, Ontology, and the Travail of Biblical Interpretation," in *On the Writing of New Testament Commentaries: Festschrift for Grant R. Osborne on the Occasion of His 70th Birthday*, ed. Stanley E. Porter and Eckhard J. Schnabel; TENTS 8 (Leiden: Brill, 2013), 269 – 98.

and they are, even if they do place it on a primary, historical foundation; and the proponents of theological interpretation of Scripture believe they are concerned with the text's original, historical location — and they are, even if they subsume it under a theological starting point within which it is easy to misplace.

What, then, is the methodological approach of this commentary in response to a historical narrative like the Gospel of John? The answer of this commentary is balance according to the nature (ontology) of Scripture: *to qualify the interpretation/ exegesis of Scripture as either historical or theological is to make a false dichotomy from the start.* Exegesis of Scripture can only be properly both, meeting the demands of a historical narrative that also bears the identity of Scripture. To choose between historical and theological emphases, therefore, is to pit the text against itself, as our discussion above has tried to explain, for creation and Creator cannot be divided. What does this look like? In general the approach of this commentary will begin with certain presuppositions that hold tightly to the necessity and meaning-deriving use of history while at the same time limiting the tenets of historical science by the doctrine of Scripture. But this does not provide a step-by-step procedure, for it is directed equally by both the text's historical concepts and context and the text's judgments and (theological) subject matter. In fact, the art of this kind of interpretation is the ability to allow both of these aspects of the text and its direction for meaning to be cooperatively active and interrelated in the exegetical process. As much as it is an art, it is only because it is a creative balance of two sciences. If there is a foundation, it is God since by definition Scripture is his spoken word; yet this does not distance history but embraces it, since God is the Creator of his creation. And because there is a God, there is a goal (*telos*); the communicative intention of God — in historical event and written expression — becomes the goal of interpretation.

In short, our method is the application to the text of what Webster calls "biblical reasoning," where the text is read and applied by both exegetical and dogmatic reasoning.[44] In this approach the words of the historical authors "are not wholly identical with the divine Word, but they are the subject of a special mission, they are 'sent from God,'" an embassy of God in which "Scripture is the textual settlement," extending the prophetic and apostolic speech into the church's present.[45] Exegesis, therefore, at least as this commentary will attempt to perform it, is an intellectual engagement with the living and gracious communication and self-presentation of God. It is no less than participation in the depths of the life of God by means of his Word to the world. A commentary, then, may be the most fitting genre for interpretation, since it remains closest to the text's own literal sense, functioning more as "contemplative paraphrase rather than as repository of textual-historical information."[46] For the purpose of a commentary, an exegete is not to speak but to listen so that the only word heard and understood is the Word of God.

---

44. John Webster, "Biblical Reasoning," *AThR* 90 (2008): 733–51.

45. Ibid., 740.

46. Ibid., 749.

Text versus Event

One distinction not always recognized in the interpretation of a historical narrative in light of the doctrine of Scripture is the manner in which *history* is defined and its meaning textually mediated. To state the issue briefly, what is the object to be interpreted: the event behind the text or the textual account?[47] The difference is stark and involves two very different interpretive acts. Although our approach will involve the latter, text-based focus, we will explain the interpretive results of both.

The event focus treats the historical narrative (the Gospel) as a window through which the interpretive act is mediated. *The meaning is derived from the event about which the text speaks.* While such an interpretation would claim to be text based, it is functionally making the text one source (even if primary) among many texts that are useful, since all textual information is important and functionally authoritative — with no distinction between inspired and uninspired texts (i.e., there *is not* a functional necessity for a doctrine of Scripture). In this way many judgments are made regarding the textually mediated event that find no warrant in the text itself, since focus on the event allows for numerous impositions to the reality (or subject matter) about which the text is speaking.[48] In short, the locus of revelation (i.e., where the revelation is located) is not the text but the event behind the text, the "revelation in history."[49]

The text focus, in sharp contrast, does not treat the text as a mediating source between the interpreter and the object of interpretation; rather, the text *is* the object of interpretation. *The meaning is derived from the text which speaks about an event.* While such an interpretation still claims to be based on real history (an event), it is functionally making the account provided by the text the only authoritative source, since it combines both the account of the event *and* its interpretation. In fact, to bring event reconstructions from other sources is prohibited without warrant from the text (the Gospel) itself, because there is a dramatic distinction between inspired and uninspired texts (i.e., there *is* a functional necessity for a doctrine of Scripture). In this way all judgments made regarding the event are directed by the (inspired) text alone, since the focus on the text demands that nothing be added to the account and especially to its meaning (subject matter) except that which the text allows. In short, the locus of revelation is not the event behind the text but the text as Scripture, so that revelation is located in the text in a manner that includes not only the recorded account but also the interpretation (whether explicit or implicit) of the account.[50]

---

47. See John H. Sailhamer, *The Pentateuch as Narrative: A Biblical-Theological Commentary* (Grand Rapids: Zondervan, 1995), 16 – 22.

48. See Mark Alan Bowald, "Rendering Mute the Word: Overcoming the Deistic Tendencies in Modern Hermeneutics; Kevin Vanhoozer as a Test Case," *WTJ* 69 (2007): 367 – 81.

49. Bowald, "Rendering Mute the Word," 17: "In such an approach the events lying behind the text of Scripture are read as a salvation history within which God makes known his will to humanity."

50. Cf. Benjamin B. Warfield, *Revelation and Inspiration* (Oxford: Oxford University Press, 1927), 48.

It was Frei's landmark monograph, *The Eclipse of Biblical Narrative*, that declared a major (false) turn had taken place in biblical hermeneutics in which the "ostensive" or apparent reference (i.e., the event behind the text) had become the locus of meaning, making the text itself, ironically, less applicable to the interpretive task.[51] "It so happens that reversal coincides with the Enlightenment project of describing the world without reference to God," which suggests that the biblical text had lost its doctrinal status as Scripture.[52] But while Frei rightly diagnosed this developing hermeneutical error, he wrongly suggested that the response was not to develop a more robust doctrine of Scripture but rather to redefine *history*. In sum, Frei collapsed the history into narrative.[53] While he was correct when he argued against the separation of text and reality, he was mistaken when he argued that there should be no distinction between the witness of the text and the reality of which it speaks. Not to separate the witness from its subject matter is to make a categorical mistake.[54]

Frei and several after him came to adopt a "narrative theology," in which the general hermeneutical category of narrativity was imported into theology as a foundational explanatory category — a new kind of "natural theology" that he so strongly opposed in regard to making history a foundational explanatory category. Contra Frei, God became "flesh" (John 1:14), not narrative! Yet contra event focus, the biblical narrative is neither expendable nor merely one of many sources through which God communicates. It is neither "narrative" nor "history" that can function as the foundational explanatory category; only the category of Scripture defined above can keep the necessary distinction and yet hold in their proper relations the narrative witness and its true subject matter, the (historical) person and (theological) work of Jesus Christ.

The text-focus approach guides the interpreter in a plethora of ways, two of which can be briefly summarized. First, because Scripture is both the authorized account of the event and its interpretation, the details of the narrative are paramount for interpretation. What is included is important, and what is not included is also important in its exclusion. To try to reconstruct what is not revealed in Scripture, unless the text gives implicit warrant, potentially creates a different story than the narrative. Even more, interpreting an event is entirely different than interpreting a text, primarily at the level of perspective. Events remain open to multiple perspectives. The meaning or sense of an event lies in the ability of the onlooker to gather the appropriate data and evaluate it from a certain (limited) vantage point. Narrative texts, however, provide readers with a privileged perspective on an event; they have the advantage of the author's guidance and perspective on the event.[55] Thus, the world of

51. Frei, *The Eclipse of Biblical Narrative*, especially 1–16.
52. Rae, *History and Hermeneutics*, 40.
53. See Hans W. Frei, *The Identity of Jesus Christ: The Hermeneutical Basis of Dogmatic Theology* (Philadelphia: Fortress, 1975), for his constructive proposal.

54. Paul C. McGlasson, *Invitation to Dogmatic Theology: A Canonical Approach* (Grand Rapids: Brazos, 2006), 119–23: "Frei wrongly identified all distinction between sign and signified with natural theology; he simply failed to observe that such a distinction is in fact essential to classical theology" (121).
55. Sailhamer, *The Pentateuch as Narrative*, 22.

the event "reaches us through the mediation of the words, selected and combined to form their own logic," offering the reader "a pre-interpreted image of reality" instead of the raw material given from the event itself.[56] Quite simply, the reader enters the world of the narrative — and it alone — not as a narrative theologian (Frei) but as a faithful listener to the Word of God. There is no better place from which to access what is real and true than from the words of Scripture. In fact, the reader is actually in a preferred position, beyond even those who were present at the historical event.

Second, in light of the hermeneutical turn to the event behind the text, the Gospels are rarely read without recourse to reconstructive comparison. This raises numerous issues, both historical and theological, most of which bump into the guiding paradox that God ordained four Gospels and yet there is one gospel of Jesus Christ. Only a few comments can be made here. Any attempt to reconstruct a singular event between the Gospel accounts not only places the locus of meaning in the event itself (and not the Scriptural witness) but at best creates a fifth Gospel of sorts; or worse, it is functionally combining the four Gospels into one historical Gospel, which has already been rejected by the church (i.e., Tatian's *Diatessaron*, which means "through four").[57] The church believes that the singular gospel is not a singular witness, a Gospel narrative, but a singular subject matter, a gospel message. The unitary nature of the Gospels can only be at the level of their message, with all four playing their own parts in a united and symphonic form.

Furthermore, if a unitary reconstruction of the Gospels is to occur, it is not in regard to the historical witnesses (the narrative Gospels) but in regard to their theological subject matter. As strongly as the church must maintain the need for the separation of the four Gospels, it must also pursue their unification into one gospel. This means that each Gospel must be interpreted for the individual Gospel's role or contribution to the one gospel, not in a manner that combines their events but in a manner that prepares to hear in unison their individual roles in the symphony of the gospel. For this reason our commentary on John will not engage in historical reconstruction with the other three Gospels but will focus on the witnessing role of the Fourth Gospel, as an exegetical commentary should, providing the material from which the subject matter can later be derived. This in no way denies a unified historical account of events, but places the pursuit of reconstructing the event under the category of apologetics, not interpretation or theology. We will at times in this commentary address interpretive issues driven by reconstruction of events and between the Gospels, such as the temple cleansing or the date of the crucifixion, not because it is methodologically required or even preferable but because it is pastorally relevant to the reader.

56. Meir Sternberg, *The Poetics of Biblical Narrative: Ideological Literature and the Drama of Reading* (Bloomington: Indiana University Press, 1987), 162.

57. Cf. Francis Watson, "Are There Still Four Gospels: A Study in Theological Hermeneutics," in *Reading Scripture With the Church: Toward a Hermeneutic for Theological Interpretation*, ed. A. K. M. Adam, Stephen E. Fowl, Kevin J. Vanhoozer, and Francis Watson (Grand Rapids: Baker Academic, 2006), 95 – 116 (98).

Canonical Connections and "Impressions"

Another distinction not always recognized in the interpretation of a historical narrative in light of the doctrine of Scripture is the manner in which its literary context is defined and its meaning textually connected. To state the issue briefly, how does the doctrine of Scripture give definition to the nature and function of the canonical context of this Gospel? There are two important ways in which the doctrine of Scripture gives literary definition to our interpretation of the Gospel.

First, the doctrine of Scripture demands that this Gospel be viewed as one part of a larger whole. This does not mean the Gospel has no definable literary boundary within which the narrative should be read and interpreted, for certainly the Gospel is its own literary unit with a functional structure, bearing meaning as an individual and intentional form of communication. Yet by its placement in the biblical canon, the doctrinal logic also explains that this book is incomplete on its own and was never intended to be read in isolation. In a sense, just as there are four Gospels and yet one gospel, so also there are sixty-six biblical books and yet one Bible. For this reason the message of this Gospel is not only grounded in its historical connections but also in its literary-canonical connections. Thus, our interpretation of the Gospel should assume that its divinely intended communication will make canonical connections in both directions — not merely to that which precedes it in space-time history (the OT) but also to that which it precedes (the rest of the NT).[58] That is, the connection between this Gospel and the rest of Scripture is canonical before it is chronological.[59] This assumption, however, is based upon a doctrinal presupposition about the unified and interconnected nature of Scripture and its author, God himself. Any interpretation of the Gospel that makes connections to historical parallels and backgrounds but not also to canonical connections and therefore to the full subject matter of the Bible is not rightly conceiving of the Gospel as Scripture.

Second, befitting the literary connections demanded by the canon of Scripture, a necessary corollary is that Scripture, as the real Word of God, is connected to the Gospel of John not only as a unified witness and text (canon) but also as a unified subject matter and message (content). Again, however, the logic for this is doctrinal, demanded by the fact that the intentional self-communication of God incorporates the whole of Scripture and works in a unified manner, without denying a distinction in roles and comprehensiveness assigned (by God) to the individual books within

---

58. Poythress, "Dispensing with Merely Human Meaning," 493–94, describes what impressions, or what he calls "resonances," might look like between Zephaniah 1 and other parts of Scripture.

59. Contra Peter J. Gentry and Stephen J. Wellum, *Kingdom through Covenant: A Biblical-Theological Understanding of the Covenants* (Wheaton: Crossway, 2012), 94–95, who argue for a reading that is more chronological than canonical. For Gen-try and Wellum, the canon is eclipsed by redemptive history into which the texts are embedded. That is, redemptive history is the larger and visible sequential development of God's plan (e.g., "typology") which serves as the frame of reference and interpretation for the text of Scripture. This is, unfortunately, to reverse the proper hermeneutical order regarding the text of Scripture and the history with which it relates.

Scripture. This means, in one sense, that the subject matter of Scripture must ultimately be derived from the full divine self-communication, and this Gospel is a necessary part of that communication. This also means, however, that the full divine self-communication is needed to understand each of the parts; the whole canon is expected to cooperate in the interpretation of its parts, and the Gospel of John is one of those parts. Thus, the connection is not merely to concepts but judgments, and the full canon is needed to interpret this Gospel in light of the revealed intentions of God.

This literary function of both concepts and judgments is important when interpreting the Gospel of John. For example, from its very first words (1:1) this Gospel is intentionally connecting itself (its story and theology) to the Old Testament, with interpretive language like quotations, allusions, and echoes only partly depicting the cooperative intentions. In light of our discussion above, especially in regard to the unified nature and function of the whole of Scripture, we are doctrinally committed to assuming that the books of the Bible are interconnected in their very being (ontology) and therefore their subject matter, and not merely when they use the same words and phrases. Not even typology is sufficiently warranted to be the category of connection across Scripture, for it is utilizing and therefore limited by historical categories dependent upon reading extratextual (or behind-the-text) realities like persons, events, and institutions through which the subject matter is attempted to be derived.[60] While wanting to affirm the text's ability to describe God's economy in the fullness of its historical account (function — what God does) or what theologians describe as the economic Trinity, we must also affirm the text's ability to describe God in the fullness of his own unique nature (ontology — who God is) or what theologians refer to as the immanent Trinity (see comments on 20:21 – 22). While redemptive history is well suited to grasp God's economy (function), it is unable on its own to account for or describe God's immanence (ontology).[61]

This might sound strange on the ears of the contemporary exegete, for the division of labor between biblical studies and (systematic) theology has resulted in the former focusing on the economic Trinity (history) and the latter focusing on the immanent Trinity (doctrine) — even though both are addressing the same subject matter! While we would not be warranted to assume such interconnection with any other set of books, Christian Scripture demands that we do so. In this way, then, our

60. Gentry and Wellum, *Kingdom through Covenant*, 87 – 108. While Gentry and Wellum argue that typology uses both "historical and textual realities" (103), as we discussed above, the textual realities are really functioning only as a window to access the historical realities behind the text. Again, historical tenets and not a doctrine of Scripture have become the primary determiners of meaning, with the category of "redemptive history" replacing the role and control that had previously been provided by "canon" — so much so that typology in redemptive history is described as "God-given patterns" (94) and therefore assumed "textual."

61. See C. Kavin Rowe, "The Doctrine of God Is a Hermeneutic: The Biblical Theology of Brevard S. Childs," in *The Bible as Christian Scripture: The Work of Brevard S. Childs*, ed. Christopher R. Seitz and Kent Harold Richards, BSNA 25 (Atlanta: Society of Biblical Literature, 2013), 155 – 69 (162).

reading of this Gospel is sensitive to links by means of both concepts (explicit) and judgments (implicit), with the latter being interpreted by the text's own carefully designed details and intentions. Thus, a particular pericope is read in light of the full canonical context and guided by the textually mediated clues so that "judgments" (not only economic but also immanent) are not read into the text in a foreign manner but naturally arise from the narrative pressures themselves.

This kind of narrative sensitivity to the contextual judgments applied by the use of a term or word was hardly foreign to the ancient world. In fact, the modern tendency to squabble over the precise meaning of a word would have been foreign to an ancient audience. Downing has helpfully shown that the widespread contemporary expectation of and insistence on clarity in the use of words is not justified in texts from the ancient Greco-Roman world.[62] "To read ancient authors as though they 'must' have shared the concern evinced by some among us for connotative precision risks making a category mistake, a mistake in the genre of verbal articulation deployed."[63] In contrast to strict construals of the meaning of words, words functioned more like names; they were "expected to evoke in hearer's minds shared impressions of people and events and things, and shared ideas, generalities, abstract concepts."[64] Words were assumed in the ancient world to make similar "mental impressions" upon the reader, with the implication that those impressions had a creative and flexible freedom within the bounds of appropriate meaning.[65] And the bounds of appropriate meaning are derived from the narrative itself. Some words make impressions that speak of two things simultaneously — e.g., the "exaltation" or "lifting up" of Jesus (see comments on 3:14), whereas other words are intended to bear significant theological freight, often repeatedly throughout the Gospel (see comments on 1:17). Throughout the commentary we will refer to "impressions" derived from our interpretation of the narrative's details or intentions in regard to the use of a word/term or even in some instances a paragraph or scene. Again, it is important to note that by "impression" we refer not only to the historical and literary connotations suggested by the use of a word but also to the theological (doctrinal) connotations by means of its relation to the rest of the canon.[66]

The Biblical Reader

If our method is rooted in God as the primary communicator and the text as the primary mediator, which includes not only the historical author and context but

---

62. F. Gerald Downing, "Ambiguity, Ancient Semantics, and Faith," *NTS* 56 (2009): 139–62. For example, the prevalent use of dictionaries today finds its genesis not in the ancient world but in Europe in the eighteenth century.

63. Downing, "Ambiguity," 146.

64. Ibid., 146.

65. Downing adds that this is all the more likely in narrative and gives the Fourth Gospel as an example of intentional and admissible ambiguity.

66. Cf. Peter J. Leithart, *Deep Exegesis: The Mystery of Reading Scripture* (Waco, TX: Baylor University Press, 2009), 75–108.

also the canonical context, then there is also the need of a primary reader. While it is common to assume that the primary reader is not the contemporary church but the ancient or original reader, such an assumption would conflict with the nature and role of this Gospel as Christian Scripture. This is not to deny or remove the original reader as a coparticipating reader but to claim for doctrinal reasons that the truly "biblical" reader is the church (past, present, and future).[67]

When we speak of the biblical reader, we are addressing one very important aspect of Christian discipleship. "A Christian theological depiction of the hermeneutical situation will involve the development of a Christian theological anthropology of reading ... which makes extensive appeal to the language and belief structure of Christian faith."[68] Two aspects can be briefly summarized. First, *the biblical reader is an active participant in the Word of God.* The reader is to be envisaged as located within the interpretive context we have outlined above, involving the self-communicating of God and the functional doctrine of Scripture (involving creation, canon, and creed). "The reader is an actor within the larger web of events and activities, supreme among which is God's act in which God speaks God's Word through the text of the Bible to the people of God.... As a participant in this historical process, the reader is spoken to in the text."[69] The biblical reader is expected to respond faithfully to God's communication through Scripture.

Second, *the biblical reader is a passive recipient of the Word of God.* Since Scripture is God's self-communicative act, a gracious encounter between the holy God and his fallen world, a truly Christian reading is not within the range of human competence, primarily because the reader's capacities are distorted by sin — "by choice of wrong ends to which to put the text; by desire to fashion that which the text says into something which pleases, rather than *something which disturbs or judges or commands or calls to repentance.*"[70] A truly biblical reading of Scripture requires that we love its author (God); if this is daunting, we are to be reminded (from Scripture) that our love is grounded in the fact that God initiated love: "We love because he first loved us" (1 John 4:19). In short, a biblical reading requires that the reader become a certain kind of person, one who through the Spirit is liberated from self-concern and the pursuit of self-interest, and one willing to love and pursue the ends for which God designed human life.[71] This kind of reading is the source and symptom of Christian discipleship. The biblical reader, therefore, is expected to relinquish himself to God's

---

67. See Kevin J. Vanhoozer, *Is There a Meaning in This Text?: The Bible, the Reader, and the Morality of Literary Knowledge* (Grand Rapids: Zondervan, 1998). We are not suggesting here that the church, as the reading and interpreting community, is the source and determiner of Scripture's meaning. Quite the opposite: a biblical reader is submissive to Scripture as the Word of God that comes from the outside.

68. Webster, *Word and Church*, 76.

69. Ibid., 77.

70. Ibid., 79 (emphasis added).

71. Ibid., 83. Cf. Kevin J. Vanhoozer, "The Spirit of Understanding: Special Revelation and General Hermeneutics," in *Disciplining Hermeneutics: Interpretation in Christian Perspective*, ed. Roger Lundin (Grand Rapids: Eerdmans, 1997), 131–65.

communication through Scripture. The most competent reader of Scripture will be the one who stands under (not over) it.[72]

The Gospel of John and Interpretation

We have worked hard to locate the Gospel of John in its divine context as Christian Scripture; now we must locate this Gospel in its historical context — the first-century Jewish and Greco-Roman world. For as much as God spoke out of his timelessness, he also spoke into a time-bound situation involving people, places, and processes. While the interpretation of this Gospel in light of the doctrine of Scripture might be uncommon, the Gospel has a long history of being examined and defined in relation to its originating historical context.[73] For this reason our introduction must also address the necessary elements of the historical context into which God spoke through this Gospel.

The historical circumstances in which the Gospel of John came to life are not easily defined or explained. The origin of the Gospel, in fact, is often referred to quite pessimistically as "the Johannine Problem." In the words of one commentator, "Everything we want to know about this book is uncertain, and everything about it that is apparently knowable is a matter of dispute."[74] As much as there is truth in this statement, it is more accurately a summary of the scholarly discussions over the last two centuries regarding the Gospel, which has spent as much time looking "behind the text" as it has spent reading it. The full truth is not quite so pessimistic. The Gospel of John is clearly concerned to root itself in its necessary historical and theological foundations and to guide the reader to see and understand how it serves as a witness to the life, death, and resurrection of Jesus Christ, as well as to his church, beginning with the twelve disciples. The Gospel is well aware of the historical context into and through which it speaks, and its message embraces the historical context in great detail — for Jesus the Word "became flesh" (1:14), was crucified under Pilate (18:28 – 19:27), and was resurrected (20:1 – 10) in real history. Without getting sidetracked by the countless explorations into the Gospel's context by those assuming the

72. It is important to note that a Christian reading of Scripture is not a wax nose that is subject to any definition and a limitless range of meaning. Rather, it is based upon the subject matter and direction of Scripture itself, which was confirmed and established by the creeds of the historical Christian church. Some traditions within the Christian faith may adopt a narrower and more contextually defined confessional statement (e.g., the Westminster Confession of Faith), but a Christian reading of Scripture cannot deny the properly basic tenets of Christianity. Thus, a so-called Christian reading that denies the Trinity is not properly Christian since the doctrine of the Trinity is central to the subject matter of Scripture and the historic faith of the church. This standard does not assume an objective definition outside of Scripture itself, but it does assume by the providence of God and the guidance of the Spirit that the historic, universal Christian church and its creedal judgments serve as authorized fences inside which Christian readings must dwell.

73. See Thomas L. Brodie, *The Gospel according to John: A Literary and Theological Commentary* (New York: Oxford University Press, 1993), 3 – 10.

74. George R. Beasley-Murray, *John*, 2nd ed., WBC 36 (Nashville: Thomas Nelson, 1999), xxxii.

critical approach to the Gospel, our discussion below will offer an introduction to the exegetically important topics related to the historical and social-cultural context of the Gospel necessary for a thorough interpretation of its contents and subject matter.

Authorship

The Gospel is formally anonymous, which means that its author's name does not appear in the text of the work itself. This does not mean, however, that the text is intentionally anonymous, shielding its author's identity from the readers. From its beginning the Gospel speaks in a first person manner identical to other ancient books that were also formally anonymous but not intentionally anonymous (e.g., Lucian's *Life of Demonax*). For this reason, then, the Gospel was not intended to be formally anonymous, which almost certainly explains the title added to the Gospel sometime after its completion (see below). Quite simply, book "publishing" in the ancient world was entirely different from today. Authors commonly spoke in the first person in a formally anonymous document because their works would have been circulated in the first instance among friends or acquaintances of the author, who would know the author personally from the oral context in which the work was first read. Knowledge of authorship would be passed on when copies were made for other (less familiar) readers, and the name would be noted with a brief title on the outside of the scroll or on a label affixed to the scroll.[75] This is not to claim that the Gospel was only intended for the immediate context of readers (on audience, see below) but to explain the manner in which texts were "published" in the ancient world.

"The Gospel According to John"

The title added to the Gospel when passed to those less (personally) familiar with the author was "The Gospel according to John" (ΕΥΑΓΓΕΛΙΟΝ ΚΑΤΑ ΙΩΑΝΝΗΝ). The title and comparative titles in related literature are important to our understanding of the author and his relation to the text.[76] Several questions need to be answered. First, how is the title to be interpreted? The title departs from the almost-standard title of books in antiquity, which lists the author first (in the genitive case) followed by the title of the content. Thus, one would have expected the title to read, "John's Biography of Jesus," like other biographies around the first century (on genre, see below). But it is significant that the name of the author is last and that the text is not called a biography of Jesus but "the Gospel." Since all four Gospels have the same title prefacing four different authors, the title is making a striking claim: there is *one* gos-

75. Richard Bauckham, *Jesus and the Eyewitnesses: The Gospels as Eyewitness Testimony* (Grand Rapids: Eerdmans, 2008), 300.

76. The following is relying heavily on Martin Hengel, "The Titles of the Gospels and the Gospel of Mark," in his *Studies in the Gospel of Mark*, trans. John Bowden (London: SCM, 1985), 64–84.

pel written or expressed in *four* different accounts — "according to" Matthew, Mark, Luke, and John. Thus, there is one gospel and four Gospels, with each Gospel offering a necessary perspective, witness, and interpretation of the one and only gospel. The title, then, is making both a historical and theological statement.

Second, when was the title attached to the Gospel of John? From the beginning of the manuscript tradition (ca. AD 200 onward), the only title for all four canonical Gospels is in this form.[77] No other title was ever used for any of the Gospels in known literature, a remarkable fact which demands that the titles be viewed as early and even original.[78] In short, "the universality of these ascriptions of authorship and the fact that they seem never to have been disputed indicate they became established usage as soon as the Gospels were circulating."[79] The titles became such a standard that even the apocryphal Gospels, the majority of which came into being as early as the first half of the second century but clearly later than the canonical Gospels, borrowed the form of the canonical title: "The Gospel according to" Thomas, Peter, Philip, Matthias, Mary, and so on. Even the Gospels of particular groups were given titles matching the canonical Gospel form. The early origin and application of the title suggests, therefore, that it offered significant instruction regarding the authorial connection to each particular account and situated each Gospel to the gospel. While the title of the Gospel might not be defined as inspired, its intimate connection to the origin of the inspired Gospel text provides it with a certain amount of authority in its own right. For this reason, in spite of the plethora of names suggested for the author of the Fourth Gospel, especially in the last two centuries, to suggest a name other than "John" is to disregard the author-designating title affixed to the Gospel from its earliest stage of origin. That is, the burden of proof is on those who want to argue against Johannine authorship.

Third, what are the practical roles of the title? One of the clear roles is to define the four Gospels as *the gospel*, a term which speaks beyond its genre (see below) to its message, its subject matter, and even its purpose — to "evangelize" or "announce good news," according to its etymology and secular use in the ancient world. The term *gospel* throughout the NT is the oral proclamation about Jesus Christ — who he was, what he accomplished through his life, death, and resurrection, and the promise of his future return — involving a call to repentance and faith. The apostle Paul refers to the gospel as "the gospel of God," from and about God, which "he [God] promised beforehand through his [OT] prophets in the Holy Scriptures" (Rom 1:1 – 2).[80] Thus, as much as this Gospel is a record of the life of Jesus, it is also God's announcement of eternal life for the world.

---

77. With the exception of a short form in manuscripts Vaticanus and Sinaiticus, which merely have "According to...."

78. Cf. Graham N. Stanton, *Jesus of Nazareth in New Testament Preaching*, SNTSMS 27 (Cambridge: Cambridge University Press, 1974), 78 – 80.

79. Bauckham, *Jesus and the Eyewitnesses*, 304.

80. See Jonathan T. Pennington, *Reading the Gospels Wisely: A Narrative and Theological Introduction* (Grand Rapids: Baker, 2012), 3 – 17.

There is another important role communicated by the title. By affixing the title to this Gospel the text is grounded in the eyewitness testimony of its author. Richard Bauckham has written a paradigm-shifting monograph that has convincingly argued for the nature and function of the Gospels as eyewitness testimonies. While a complete survey of Bauckham's contribution is beyond the scope of this commentary, one of the primary implications is how the category of eyewitness testimony is essential to grasp correctly the history and theology contained within and projected by the Gospel. According to Bauckham, "Testimony offers us ... both a reputable historiographic category for reading the Gospels as history, and also a theological model for understanding the Gospels as the entirely appropriate means of access to the historical reality of Jesus."[81] It is the theological aspect of testimony that offers a significant advancement to the traditional (historical) understanding, for it adds the historically grounded assumption that the author is not a dispassionate objective observer but a participant, one who was personally connected "to the events and whose direct experience enabled him to understand and interpret the significance of what he had seen."[82] In the ancient world eyewitnesses were not just data gatherers but data interpreters; they did not conceal the meaning, as if they were blocking the view, but served as the required connection to the object, the spectacles necessary for corrective vision. As Byrskog explains, "Involvement was not an obstacle to a correct understanding of what they perceived as historical truth. It was rather the essential means to a correct understanding of what really happened."[83] There was no dichotomy between fact and meaning or between empirical report and engaged interpretation. You could not have one without the other, for they are, quite simply, the two sides of the same coin. The reader of the Gospel is not going to an event behind the text (see "Text versus Event"), as if the text and the author are mere tools for (historical) reconstruction and are expendable; the reader is reading through the eyes and ears (the testimony) of the authorial witness.

The affixed title, therefore, not only situates the Gospel to a particular author but also situates the author as a particular kind of witness. And while the Gospel proper does not name the author, it clearly gives definition to the nature and function of his witness. The formal (but not intentional) anonymity of this Gospel allows the author to function both inside and outside the Gospel. In this way the title of the Gospel becomes an essential component of the Gospel, a judgment drawn from the Gospel proper that can appropriately be reapplied to it. With this title the Fourth Gospel is rightly declared to be both a *textual participant* in the fourfold Gospel account and propagator of the gospel, and also a *personal participant* in the living subject matter of the Gospel/gospel: Jesus Christ. For this reason the identity of the author is as

---

81. Bauckham, *Jesus and the Eyewitnesses*, 5.
82. Ibid., 9.

83. Samuel Byrskog, *Story as History — History as Story: The Gospel Tradition in the Context of Ancient Oral History*, WUNT 123 (Tübingen: Mohr Siebeck, 2000), 154.

much a hermeneutical (theological) issue as a historical one. To treat the authorship of the Fourth Gospel as an isolated debate is to compartmentalize inappropriately the message from its messenger. It is an act that subjects a testimony (and its author) to interpretive violence and is rooted in "the temptation to reduce the voice of the Other to our own."[84] For this Gospel, the identity of the author cannot merely be a historical plaything about which there are several unconfirmed suggestions. The author of this Gospel is its eyewitness and therefore is personally and authoritatively connected to the very message of the text. For a fuller explanation of these issues, see comments on 21:24.

The Identity of "John"

The author of the Gospel only explicitly reveals his identity as the "Beloved Disciple" (see 21:23 – 24; on the Beloved Disciple, see comments on 13:23), befitting the formally anonymous nature of the Gospel. There are several reasons why this literary technique is utilized by the author, so that the formal anonymity is serving a greater hermeneutical purpose than mere identification (see comments on 21:24). Yet the historical identity of the Beloved Disciple is also significant. Recent scholarship has offered several diverse suggestions concerning his identity. Although not a comprehensive list, several of the most prominent or interesting suggestions include the following: the apostle Thomas, Mary Magdalene, Lazarus, and even the Samaritan woman.[85] None of these suggestions finds any internal or external support; that is, not only do none of these options (or well over a dozen others) find any warrant from the Gospel itself, even if they have traits that overlap with the Beloved Disciple, but none of them were ever recognized as the Gospel's author by the (orthodox) church.

It is unavoidable and necessary to claim with the affixed title of the Gospel that the author of the Gospel was named John. From as early as the second century the author of the Gospel was identified as the apostle John, the son of Zebedee (see Irenaeus, *Haer.* 3.1.2), and from at least that point (if not earlier) the church has unanimously attributed the authorship of the Gospel to the apostle John. The apostolic authorship of John stood firmly until the middle of the eighteenth century, shielded by dogmatic considerations that guarded against any so-called scientific progress.[86]

---

84. Kevin J. Vanhoozer, "The Hermeneutics of I-Witness Testimony: John 21:20 – 24 and the 'Death' of the 'Author,'" in *Understanding Poets and Prophets: Essays in Honor of George Wishart Anderson*, ed. A. Graeme Auld, JSOTSup 152 (Sheffield: Sheffield Academic Press, 1993), 366 – 87 (368).

85. *Thomas*: James H. Charlesworth, *The Beloved Disciple: Whose Witness Validates the Gospel of John?* (Valley Forge, PA: Trinity Press International, 1995), 414 – 21. Charlesworth also lists and evaluates twenty-two other identification proposals (127 – 224). *Mary Magdalene*: Joseph A. Grassi, *The Secret Identity of the Beloved Disciple* (Mahwah, NJ: Paulist Press, 1992); Esther A. de Boer, *The Gospel of Mary: Beyond a Gnostic and a Biblical Mary Magdalene* (New York: Continuum, 2005). *Lazarus*: Ben Witherington III, *What Have They Done with Jesus?* (San Francisco: Harper, 2006), 141 – 56. *The Samaritan Woman*: James P. Carse, *The Gospel of the Beloved Disciple* (San Francisco: Harper, 1997).

86. Cf. Stephen C. Neill and Tom Wright, *The Interpretation of the New Testament 1861 – 1986*, 2nd ed. (Oxford: Oxford University Press, 1988), 359.

Only when issues arose that were less concerned with credibility and biblical authority were other authors able to be suggested.[87] If the church is not an authority on the identification of the author on its own right, at least this fact suggests that the evidence is so convincing regarding the identification of the apostle John that there was no definable dissent for nearly two millennia. This matches the title affixed to the Gospel, "according to John." Thus, both statements commenting upon the author of the Gospel and the manuscript tradition of the Gospel itself declare forthrightly that the author is John. To argue that someone with another name wrote the Gospel is to argue with no evidential support from either the manuscript tradition or the history of the church.

There is another "John" mentioned briefly in some of the postapostolic tradition, however, that some believe strongly suggests it is not John the apostle but one called John the elder who should be rightly identified as the author of the Gospel. The recent works of Hengel and Bauckham have gone a long way to make this "other John" a reasonable candidate.[88] Hengel and Bauckham explore the traditional external evidence, especially the famous fragment from the prologue of Papias (Eusebius, *Hist. eccl.* 3.39.4), in order to argue that "John the elder" is the author of the Gospel. This John, not the apostle, is the Beloved Disciple; he is not one of the Twelve but is a Jerusalem disciple of Jesus. The proposal of John the elder not only accounts for the formal anonymity and the fact that there is no evidence that the Gospel was ever regarded as anonymous (unlike Hebrews) but also explains the *eventual* attribution to John the apostle. According to Bauckham, the lesser-known John the elder was replaced by the fame of the better-known and more prestigious John the apostle.[89] Confusion over the formal anonymity allowed oral tradition to eclipse John the elder for John the apostle, which was solidified by Irenaeus when he applied the title "apostle" to the author of the Gospel (*Haer.* 1.9.2 – 3; 2.22.5; 3.3.4), not in a technical manner but in order to indicate the author was a reliable authority and authorized by Christ. The looseness of the title "apostle" as an application to the reliable witnesses of Christ soon became connected to the Gospel, and once he was considered an apostle, John the elder became indistinguishable from the son of Zebedee. Thus, while there are eighteen centuries of voices claiming John the apostle wrote the Gospel, Bauckham suggests that they are all repeating the mistaken interpretation of Irenaeus and ignoring the earliest tradition (from Asia) regarding the origin of the Gospel.

---

87. See Andreas J. Köstenberger, "Early Doubts of the Apostolic Authorship of the Fourth Gospel in the History of Modern Biblical Criticism," in his *Studies on John and Gender: A Decade of Scholarship*, StBibLit 38 (New York: Peter Lang, 2001), 17 – 47.

88. Hengel's proposal is found in his *The Johannine Question* (London: SCM, 1989); Bauckham's proposal is most comprehensively located in his *Jesus and the Eyewitnesses*.

89. Richard Bauckham, "Papias and Polycrates on the Origin of the Gospel of John," in *The Testimony of the Beloved Disciple: Narrative, History, and Theology in the Gospel of John* (Grand Rapids: Baker, 2007), 33 – 72 (35). According to Bauckham, the external evidence — the tradition in Asia from Papias early in the second century to Polycrates at its end — claiming the author was John the Elder was unchallenged in Asia before the third century, but had transitioned to the son of Zebedee in Egyptian works around the middle of the second century (69 – 70).

As much as the external evidence from the postapostolic period does suggest that there are two distinct "Johns" in earliest Christianity, not only is the exact identity of the one called John the elder vague and difficult to define with precision but there is even less warrant for attributing the authorship of the Gospel to him and not John the apostle. The brilliance of Bauckham's interpretation of the postapostolic evidence is still unable to offer a reading that is demanded by the tradition. Quite simply, Bauckham offers a revised reconstruction of the origin of the Gospel by reinterpreting the bulk of the tradition that clearly attributes authorship to the apostle John through the lens of a few statements in the tradition that could be read differently in regard to an individual named John the elder. While not impossible, neither the external evidence itself nor the internal evidence allow such a conclusion.[90] Just as the author waits until the epilogue to declare his identity as the Beloved Disciple (see 21:23 – 24), he also waits until the epilogue to connect the Beloved Disciple to one of the sons of Zebedee (see 21:2), thereby making clear that John the son of Zebedee, the apostle John, is the author of the Fourth Gospel.

The apostolic authorship of the Gospel adds an important dimension to the nature of its authority. Related to what we discussed above, just as the formal (but not intentional) anonymity of the author makes him a *textual participant* in its narrative account, and just as the authorial eyewitness makes him a *personal participant* in its living subject matter, so also does the identity of the author as John the apostle make him an *apostolic participant* in its message and therefore uniquely qualified in every way to serve as a herald of the gospel of Jesus Christ. Again, the identity of the author is as much a hermeneutical (theological) issue as a historical one; the message and the messenger unite to become part of "the foundation of the apostles and prophets, with Christ Jesus himself as the chief cornerstone" (Eph 2:20).

Genre and Literary Forms

As important as it is to define this Gospel as Scripture, which we described above as its own kind of genre, we must also understand what it is and does according to the cultural conventions of its literary genre and other literary forms. As we discussed above, this commentary is engaged in the interpretation of a text; without denying there was an author, audience, and a particular social-historical context out of which this text was created, the object of our interpretation is the textual form and identity of the Gospel itself.[91] For this reason we must define carefully not only its dogmatic form and function according to a doctrine of Scripture but also its literary

---

90. See Andreas J. Köstenberger and Stephen O. Stout, "'The Disciple Jesus Loved': Witness, Author, Apostle — A Response to Richard Bauckham's *Jesus and the Eyewitnesses*," *BBR* 18 (2008): 209 – 31; see also Charles E. Hill, "What Papias Said about John (and Luke): A 'New' Papian Fragment," *JTS* 49 (1998): 582 – 629.

91. See D. Moody Smith, *Johannine Christianity: Essays on Its Setting, Sources, and Theology* (Edinburgh: T&T Clark, 1984).

form and function according to the conventions of a text or narrative. After defining the genre of the Fourth Gospel, we will also give definition to three other common literary forms (subgenres) utilized by the Gospel.[92] Our goal is to gain an overview of the conventions of the Gospel's genre and literary forms in order to more competently handle the narrative's communicative act.

The Gospel in Narrative Form

Genre, or a text's type of literature, is extremely important for the interpretive task.[93] The term *genre* is used to understand a text, both descriptively and prescriptively, according to a generally recognizable type of writing with a certain style, purpose, and identifiable features. A text's genre has particular conventions that both designate the nature of the text and the manner in which it "works." Genre is important because it guides the reader to handle the text with a more precise literary competence, so that the text is handled according to its own nature and cultural conventions. While genre is just that — generic and not specific, it plays an important role in understanding and utilizing the intended act of communication between author, text, and reader.

The Gospels have long been discussed in regard to their genre or literary type. At least since the work of Burridge, it has become standard to recognize and interpret the Gospels as Greco-Roman biographies.[94] Burridge convincingly explained how the Gospels share a family resemblance with the wide-ranging form of Greco-Roman biographies from the Hellenistic period both before and after the life and ministry of Jesus. The Gospels, therefore, are not a newly invented genre but have been adapted to a recognizable literary form that is both biographical and historical.[95] But others have rightly pushed beyond Burridge's definition to see the Gospels as stemming just as equally from the Old Testament Scriptures. Loveday Alexander, for example, considers the Gospels to be unique biographies in light of their kerygmatic nature. According to Alexander, "It is to the biblical tradition, surely, that we should look for the origins of the 'religious intensity' of the Gospel narratives and their rich ideological intertextuality with the biblical themes of covenant, kingdom, prophecy, and promise — all features hard to parallel in Greek biography."[96] Something similar was argued by Adela Yarbro Collins, who not only wants to see an equal connection to both Greco-Roman biographical and the Old Testament (Jewish) Scriptures but also

---

92. We will only overview here literary forms that occur frequently in the Gospel. A literary form that only occurs once in the Gospel, like the testamentary "farewell speech" in the farewell discourse (see comments before 13:1), will be defined for the purpose of interpretation when it occurs.

93. See Gerald L. Borchert, *John 1–11*, NAC 25A (Nashville: Broadman & Holman, 1996), 27–30.

94. See Richard A. Burridge, *What Are the Gospels? A Com-*

parison with Graeco-Roman Biography, SNTSMS 70 (Cambridge: Cambridge University Press, 1992; repr., 2nd ed.; Grand Rapids: Eerdmans, 2004).

95. See Craig S. Keener, *The Gospel of John: A Commentary*, 2 vols. (Peabody, MA: Hendrickson, 2003), 1:3–34.

96. Loveday Alexander, "What Is a Gospel?," in *The Cambridge Companion to the Gospels*, ed. Stephen Barton (Cambridge: Cambridge University Press, 2006), 13–33 (27–28).

a shared emphasis between the historical and didactic. That is, while the goal of a more historical genre serves to give "an account of an important series of events," a more didactic genre has as its goal the instruction of the reader "not only about the life of a particular individual but also about the way of life that he founded."[97]

This is not to deny that the Gospels are Greco-Roman biographies; it is simply to add that the generic conventions of the Gospels also borrow from the Old Testament Scriptures and their similar but more didactic historical-biographical narratives. Collins, in reference to the Gospel of Mark, for example, refers to its genre as an "eschatological historical narrative."[98] However we title or even define the generic conventions of the Gospels, it is clear that they include three aspects: biographical (on Jesus), historical (on real events), and theological-didactic (on a subject matter pertinent for the reader). That is, in collaboration with the doctrine of Scripture we discussed above, the generic conventions of this Gospel are rooted in both its theological identity (as Scripture) and its literary-historical identity (as historical biography). The prescriptive role of genre demands that the reader engage with its subject matter according to and through all of its innate conventions. The reader, then, must work hard to grasp the manner in which this Gospel is using all of its generic conventions and forms to guide the reading and interpreting process, a process which includes a personal engagement with and through the text itself — God's Word.

What are some of the generic conventions that are important for a proper reading of the Gospel of John, rooted in its dual identity as both (ancient) historical biography and Christian Scripture? Several can be briefly stated.[99] First, the Gospel genre demands the reader take seriously the history about which it speaks. It is important to note, however, the radical difference between ancient and modern biographies. Ancient biographies often mix chronological and topical elements in a flexible manner, treat words of characters in a more paraphrastic and selective manner, and have little to no concern for sensory details of the story and the inner person — the latter of which is a major difference from modern biographies. If this Gospel had been written in this century, we would probably have read about "the waves lapping at the shore of the Sea of Galilee" and heard a description of "coarse dry sand trod underfoot in the Judean desert."[100] While ancient biographies postured themselves differently to the "life" they are presenting, they were not in any way divorced from or unconcerned with the real historical reality about which they write. In fact, the four Gospels reflect vested interest in the historical details, serving as eyewitnesses of the actual person and events, as we discussed above.

Second, the Gospel genre presents the character and life of the subject of the biography to the reader as one to be emulated. The reader is invited not merely to

---

97. Adela Yarbro Collins, *Mark*, Hermeneia (Minneapolis: Fortress, 2007), 31.

98. Collins, *Mark*, 42.

99. The following is adapted from Pennington, *Reading the Gospels Wisely*, 31 – 35.

100. Mark Allan Powell, *What Is Narrative Criticism?* (Minneapolis: Fortress, 1990), 71.

appreciate the "life" displayed in the biography but to share in its admirable qualities, even share in its riches and resources. This is all the more significant in the Gospels and with the life of Jesus, whose life was lived for the purpose of gathering life-sharing participants. The reader of the Gospel of John is even invited to believe in the life lived by Jesus and to enjoin their life to his, thereby receiving "life in his name" (see 20:31).

Third, related to the previous point, the dual identity of the Gospels directs the reader to engage with the Gospels as a communicative act directed at them. The Gospels are not dissociated from the reader, mere tools about and for another, but written intentionally — both by the historical author and God himself — to the reader as proclamation. Said another way, "We should come to the Gospel narratives as we do to a sermon; they are to be treated not as mere conveyors of (historical or doctrinal) information but as instruments of transformation."[101] The Gospels announce and define *the* gospel, and they have been and should continue to be the church's primary mediums for declaring the salvation of the world. To read them without this ultimate goal is to deny their literary intention and goal.

Basic Story Form

Beyond the generic conventions of the Gospel, the reader must be able to relate to it as narrative, that is, as a story. What stories are and how they work has been discussed since Aristotle's famous work, *Poetics*, which provided a basic analysis of the primary parts of a story.[102] In short, Aristotle explained that the foundation of a story is its plot, which must have a beginning, middle, and end. Modern literary criticism has developed further Aristotle's premise, showing how a story can be seen to have a more developed emplotment trajectory. For example, Gustav Freytag argued that the basic plot structure has five components or acts: introduction, rising action, a climax or turning point, falling action, and resolution.[103] This "story arc" is what develops the plot and therefore allows the story to work. "In large part the meaning of a narrative comes through paying attention to its form."[104] The reader of any narrative must be sensitive to the form the story takes and how it functions.[105] For the form of the story becomes the structural guide to its interpretation and meaning.

This sensitivity to form can happen at the macro- and microlevel of the Gospel. At the macrolevel, along with what we discussed above regarding genre, the Gospel as a whole functions as a complete and unified story, which this commentary will continue to develop and explicate as it moves through the narrative. The plot of the entire Gospel centers upon the life and mission of Jesus. But this is no common life,

---

101. Pennington, *Reading the Gospels Wisely*, 34.

102. The standard edition is the translation of Stephen Halliwell in the Loeb Classical Library (Cambridge, MA: Harvard University Press, 1995).

103. Gustav Freytag, *Die Technik des Dramas* (Leipzig: S. Hirzel, 1863).

104. Pennington, *Reading the Gospels Wisely*, 173.

105. Although we are dealing primarily with structure here, we could also have covered some of the literary tools common to narrative, especially literary tools utilized by the Fourth Gospel: irony, misunderstanding, and symbolism. For a good overview, see Borchert, *John 1–11*, 55–59.

for the life of Jesus is one that fulfills the purpose of the Father and finds its ultimate expression in the coming of the Spirit. In this sense, the plot of this Gospel involves the life of the Trinitarian God. The prologue introduces the basic plot of the Gospel, guiding the reader to understand the key characters and issues in the coming narrative. The entire Gospel, therefore, tells a single story that could be analyzed according to the emplotment form discussed above.

Yet the Gospel must also be analyzed at the microlevel, since it is clearly broken into smaller units that are also designed with a functioning emplotment. As much as this Gospel is one story, it is also comprised of a plethora of smaller stories which each bear a definable plot, even if less complex or technical. Since the early church all four Gospels have been seen as being an organized collection of different episodes (e.g., Eusebius) that unite to form a full narrative Gospel. In the modern period a smaller unit or episode is called a "pericope" (pl.: pericopae), a term from the Greek which can mean "a piece cut out," hence a section or a smaller unit. While there are clear boundary markers between pericopae, because the pericopae participate fittingly in the larger narrative interpreters do not always agree which boundary markers are determinative for determining a pericope.

The boundaries of a pericope, however, are only part of its interpretation, for just as the entire Gospel is emplotted, so also is each pericope. While not every pericope is a smaller unit of the narrative, for there are other pericopae (with definitive boundaries) in the Gospel that bear the conventions of other subgenres that would not follow the same emplotment structure (e.g., dialogues), each pericope that is narrative in genre will bear the basic story form. As helpful as Freytag's five-part emplotment structure is for reading narratives, a simpler form can be defined as having four acts, or what we will call in this commentary a four-scene structure:

SCENE 1: Introduction and Setting
SCENE 2: Conflict
SCENE 3: Resolution
SCENE 4: Conclusion and Interpretation

These four scenes are like handles, allowing the interpreter to grasp at the narrative's precise, intentional, and developing movements. They also allow us to be directed by the narrative itself. That is, we are not interpreting an event but the interpretive telling of an event, with an emplotment that bears its own interpretive prejudice and authority. By being directed by the emplotment, we interpret the text according to its own rules and expectation — an especially important procedure when dealing with Christian Scripture. It is important to note these narrative handles are not intended to hinder the story but to provide the lenses that allow the fullness of the story — both its precision and beauty — to be seen and experienced.[106] In order

---

106. By "experience," we mean that stories are intended to engage the imagination. See Leland Ryken, *Words of Life: A Literary Introduction to the New Testament* (Grand Rapids: Baker, 1987), 17, 23.

to be faithful to the basic story form, a brief summary of each of the four scenes is in order.

Scene 1 provides the *introduction and setting*, explaining the characters, setting or context, and issues important for interpretation. By interpreting the text and not the event (see above), things included by the narrative are to be given foremost importance, whereas things not stated should only be allowed interpretive weight when the context or pericope itself implies its functional participation.

Scene 2 introduces the plot's *conflict*. The conflict of the pericope could be more complexly divided into "rising tension" and "climax," and at times a more complex conflict is needed for the interpretation of a pericope that demands a rising or developing conflict, but the majority of pericopae can be rightly interpreted by the functional category of conflict. The conflict of the pericope is the problem or issue to be resolved; it is the engine that moves the story from its source to its solution and will help establish the issue being addressed regarding the meaning of the pericope.

Scene 3 explains how the conflict comes to a suitable *resolution*. Again, the resolution might be given an unexpected solution that is more complex in nature, yet the resolution should (and will) match or be equal to the nature of the conflict. The nature of the resolution will guide the reader to understand the subject matter being addressed by the narrative's emplotment.

Scene 4 provides the *conclusion and interpretation* to the pericope, even if the interpretation is only given by implication. At times the force of the macrolevel narrative and its macrolevel plot makes a detailed conclusion or interpretation unnecessary, but the narrative pericopae will not leave the reader stranded. Each pericope will conclude similar to how it began: it will guide the reader to see the issue(s) at hand and their solutions and will explicitly or implicitly instruct the reader to appropriately engage with its story and subject matter.

The basic story form is not only important for interpretation but also for preaching and teaching. A pericope, whether a basic story form or some other subgenre, is a fully containable unit with the larger Gospel narrative. Although they must work cumulatively within the full Gospel, they can also stand on their own as units for interpretation and instruction. This commentary will argue that this Gospel can be divided into forty-eight pericopae (see Structure and Outline below). Not all pericopae are equivalent in length, since the boundary markers and four-scene structure for emplotment are the primary determinations of a pericope. And since some pericopae are more complex in nature, a preacher/teacher may want to divide a pericope into even smaller teaching units. The goal, however, is to understand how this Gospel's parts all work together as a unified and developing story.

Dialogue

One of the unique features of this Gospel is the occurrence of lengthy dialogues, conversational exchanges between Jesus and either an individual or a group regarding religious and theological matters. The Johannine dialogues have long been noted but only briefly defined, and usually in relation to dialogue-like forms in the Synoptics, which are quite different in form and function from those found in John. Unfortunately, interpreters have minimized the functional importance of the dialogues of Jesus in the narrative of the Gospel and have, therefore, misjudged their important role in directing and establishing the theology of the Gospel. While interpreters might admit in principle that the form of a particular scene is a dialogue, in practice the dialogue is given little interpretive force or explanation. What becomes the focus instead are the *words* of Jesus, as if the purpose of the dialogue is simply to serve as a frame around the Jesus sayings. But the Gospel's dialogues are not the Johannine version of the Synoptics' pronouncement story, a narrative setting intended to serve a dramatic saying. Rather than serving as mere contexts or frames for Jesus's statement, dialogues function as unified wholes that work *with* the words of Jesus. Not only do the dialogues make much less sense as independent entities but they are also essential to the movement of the narrative and the strategy of its plot.

In the twentieth century C. H. Dodd provided the most focused analysis of dialogues in the Gospel, and most scholars since Dodd normally rely on his now sixty-year-old conclusions. Dodd analysed the Johannine dialogues under the category, "The Sayings," a title that immediately (and unfortunately) subordinates the dialogues to pronouncement-like stories. The elaborate nature of John's dialogues forces Dodd to conclude that John has left the example of the Synoptics, which he suggests borrowed forms of Jewish origin, and borrowed instead from the Hellenistic world where "there was a long tradition of the use of dialogue as a vehicle for philosophical or religious teaching."[107] Dodd's primary concern was not the function of the John's dialogues but the relation between John's dialogues and "the primitive Christian tradition."[108]

In this century the conclusions of Dodd have indirectly received a renewed interest. Dodd's suggestions regarding the Hellenistic world have been heeded, driven now by the more integrative approaches, especially by further comparisons with Greco-Roman "dramatic" literature and the application of narrative criticism. Recent work in narrative theory, for example, has made clear that narrative may be spoken of as dramatic in the sense that it does as much "showing" as it does "telling"; a dramatic narrative is a mediated presentation that uses a variety of linguistic and nonlinguistic strategies as a specific act of communication. More recently, scholars like Parsenios and Brant have provided extensive analyses of John's dramatic modes of narration. Parsenios argues that John, employing devices from ancient dramas, actually "thinks in dramatic categories" in a context in which dramatic thinking was common to literature.[109] Parsenios argues with P. E. Easterling that the prevalence and influence

---

107. C. H. Dodd, *Historical Tradition in the Fourth Gospel* (Cambridge: Cambridge University Press, 1963), 319.

108. Ibid., 321.

109. George L. Parsenios, *Departure and Consolation: The Johannine Farewell Discourses in Light of Greco-Roman Literature*, NovTSup 117 (Leiden: Brill, 2005), 18.

of dramatic thinking was so extensive that one can speak of the "the theatricalization of ancient culture."[110] Brant also employs a full range of the dramatic conventions of the Greco-Roman world and applies them to John.[111] Though she goes too far at times, she does offer helpful analytic tools that "provide heuristic devices for differentiating and identifying the various services rendered by Johannine dialogue in the construction of its dramatic world and action."[112] This is not to say that John is a drama instead of a biography; it is simply to suggest that an awareness of these dramatic modes and their performative natures are helpful in assessing the function of dialogues and dramatic conventions in the Gospel.[113]

The Function and Form of the Dialogues

There are two significant functions of the dialogues in the Gospel of John. *First, the dialogues serve an important role in the developing story of the Gospel.* The function of a dialogue is not merely the meaning of the language in the interaction but also what the language *does*. As much as dialogues do contain meaning, they also move and develop the plot. Thus, they are intimately connected to what has come before and where the plot of the Gospel is moving. The dialogue brings meaning to Jesus's person and work so that the characters — and therefore the readers — are exhorted to take a particular action, thereby moving the plot along toward its ultimate goal: "that you may believe" (20:31). The dialogues cannot be divorced from the narrative movement and emplotment of the Gospel as a whole. The dialogues are not tangents for John; they are necessary elements in the developing story of Jesus, which ultimately involves the (dialogical) conflict between God and humanity.

Second, the dialogues serve to give meaning and direction to the pericope/scene in which they occur. The interactive movement and patterns of the individual dialogue also provide the controls needed to interpret and understand the message of the passage. The conventions of the dialogue give meaning to the verbal exchanges, helping observe and interpret tactical maneuvers between dialogue participants (interlocutors), for a dialogue is not guided by the pattern of conflict and resolution like a basic story form but by the interactive movement and patterns of ancient dialogue. Such insights into the function of a dialogue provide lenses with which to understand the passage's details (e.g., playful words and phrases) and developing movement. Only by understanding the dialogical structure of the scene can the reader make sense of not only its details but also the rhetorical meaning of the interaction.

By means of these particular dialogue functions, three different forms (or kinds)

---

110. P. E. Easterling, "From Repertoire to Canon," in *The Cambridge Companion to Greek Tragedy*, ed. P. E. Easterling (Cambridge: Cambridge University Press, 1997), 226.

111. See Jo-Ann A. Brant, *Dialogue and Drama: Elements of Greek Tragedy in the Fourth Gospel* (Peabody, MA: Hendrickson, 2004).

112. Ibid., 75–76.

113. See Harold W. Attridge, "Genre Bending in the Fourth Gospel," *JBL* 121 (2002): 3–21; cf. Parsenios, *Departure and Consolation*, 1–11.

of dialogues occur in the Gospel of John: social challenge, legal challenge, and rhetorical challenge dialogues.[114] We shall discuss them each in turn. The first kind of Johannine dialogue can be called a *social challenge dialogue*, which takes the form of an informal debate. The purpose of the social challenge is not to debate formally a principle, idea, or point of law but to challenge the honor and authority of one's interlocutor. It was common for challenge dialogues to involve both irony and the playful use of words, in which the poetic battle involved the creation of competitive possibilities and realities.

The second kind of dialogue can be called a *legal challenge dialogue*, which takes the form of a formal debate. As a formal debate the purpose is not merely to challenge the honor or authority of one's interlocutor but to debate formally a principle, idea, or point of law.[115] The structure of the legal challenge is different than the informal dialogues (social and rhetorical), which are less concerned with technical content. It was common for legal dialogues to contain forensic elements similar to a trial: accusations of legal infractions, testimonies, scrutiny of witnesses, and rendering of judgment.[116] This basic structure provides handles to grasp the movement of legal dialogues and the subject matter being addressed by both interlocutors.[117]

The third kind of Johannine dialogue can be called a *rhetorical challenge dialogue*, which takes the form of a creative discussion of antitheses rather than a social or legal exchange of ideas.[118] A rhetorical dialogue is not void of a social challenge, but unlike social or legal dialogues where the logic of the argument and carefully timed presentation is central to the debate, in a rhetorical dialogue interlocutors are allowed "to lay out the conflicting propositions and commitments that give rise to their plight or provoke antagonism."[119] The grounds for challenge are more immediately established, as each interlocutor sets the deeds or position in diametric opposition with that of the other. A rhetorical dialogue is not intending to advance an argument but to intensify conflict between two parties that have already agreed to disagree. The goal of a rhetorical dialogue was not toward invitation but toward exclusion. It is possible that people of differing social statuses would engage in a rhetorical dialogue rather than a social or a legal dialogue. There was no need to mediate between or determine the victorious position, only to reestablish the antithetical positions.

---

114. The following are adapted from Brant, *Dialogue and Drama.*

115. Cf. Jerome Neyrey, "The Trials (Forensic) and Tribulations (Honor Challenges) of Jesus: John 7 in Social-Science Perspective," *BTB* 26 (1996): 107–24. While there is a legitimate distinction between social and legal dialogues, Brant helpfully explains that there is also a necessary overlap between them, since they are not different genres but different "patterns that fit into or weave into each other to form the conflict" (*Dialogue and Drama*, 142).

116. Brant, *Dialogue and Drama*, 140. See also Jerome H. Neyrey, *The Gospel of John*, NCBC (Cambridge: Cambridge University Press, 2007), 153, who suggests that this exchange "resembles a fencing match; thrust and parry, lunge and retreat."

117. As Brant explains regarding the use of forensic motifs and features in the crafting of this scene, "The Gospel writer seems to have borrowed from the contents of the [formal debate] without making use of its entire form and blended it into the design of the larger contest" (*Dialogue and Drama*, 142). Cf. Stephen Motyer, *Your Father the Devil? A New Approach to John and "the Jews"* (Carlisle: Paternoster, 1997), 144–45.

118. See Brant, *Dialogue and Drama*, 115–23.

119. Ibid., 116.

Seven Formal Dialogues

Our above analysis has introduced the generic function and form of dialogues as used by the Gospel. We have not yet classified each dialogue by their form and function. While there are several dialogical scenes in the Gospel where a particular interaction borrows a conventional aspect of a dialogue, what we might call partial or informal dialogues, there are only a limited number of formal dialogues in the Gospel that manifest the recognizable conventions and categories of the dialogue genre proper. The formal dialogues in the Gospel, then, are substantial enough in size to utilize observable conventions of technically defined social, legal, or rhetorical dialogues. It is important to note that the three kinds of dialogues are not mutually exclusive; dialogues often utilize and combine conventions from more than one kind of dialogue. This is especially common between the social and legal dialogues, since both are "insider" dialogues. Thus, while there is a legitimate distinction between the three types of dialogues in John, there is also a necessary overlap between them, since they are not different genres but different "patterns that fit into and weave into each other to form the conflict."[120]

We would like to suggest that there are seven formal dialogues in the Gospel between Jesus and the following character(s):

1. Nicodemus (3:1 – 21) — *social*
2. Samaritan Woman (4:1 – 42) — *rhetorical*
3. Jewish Crowd (6:22 – 71) — *social*
4. Jewish Authorities and the Jewish Crowd (7:14 – 52) — *social*
5. Jewish Authorities (8:12 – 59) — *legal*
6. Jewish Authorities (9:1 – 41) — *legal*
7. Jewish Crowd (10:22 – 42) — *social*

The number seven has a rhetorical significance frequently utilized by the Gospel and may be intentional. With the first and last dialogue falling under the pattern of a social dialogue, the entire public ministry of Jesus is framed by the conflict between the Word and the world. All seven substantial dialogues occur in the first half of the Gospel, that is, during the public ministry of Jesus (chs. 3, 4, 6, 7, 8, 9, 10). The dialogues include what is probably an intentional variety of interlocutors: two involve individuals (one Jewish man and one Samaritan woman), two and a half involve the Jewish authorities, and two and a half involve the crowd. The dialogues also utilize all three kinds of dialogues: four social dialogues, two legal dialogues, and one rhetorical dialogue.

There is nothing magical about the occurrence of seven dialogues in John; the concern of this commentary is merely to provide some guidelines for interpreting the dialogues. The occurrence of seven dialogues, however, does match well the Gospel's

---

120. Ibid., 142.

own proclivity for seven. It suggests that the dialogues are not merely literary conventions utilized by the author in the telling of the story of Jesus but, like the seven "signs," facilitate the Gospel's plot by depicting in graphic detail the conflict between God and humanity over honor, law, and identity in a manner that allows for robust theological interaction. In contrast to serving as the context for Jesus's one-liners, dialogues in the Gospel of John play a significant role in the narrative. Using the conventions and patterns of ancient dialogue, the Gospel's dialogues offer a dramatic theological presentation that engages the reader at numerous levels, drawing them more fully into the depth of the Gospel story that began in the conflict between darkness and the light (1:5) and ends at the cross.

Monologue

The Gospel is also unique in its use of extended discourses or monologues of Jesus. The Synoptic Gospels have few monologues that are substantial in length in comparison to the Fourth Gospel, which according to Dodd "worked on a radically different principle of composition."[121] As he did with dialogues, Dodd bases the monologues in this Gospel upon a comparison with potentially related "sayings" in the Synoptics. Similar to his concern with the dialogue, Dodd's primary concern was not the function of John's monologues but the relation between John's dialogues and "the primitive stage of tradition."[122] Dodd's goal was to uncover the origin of the monologues in the various "branches of oral tradition" and "the variations belong[ing] to its pre-literary history."[123] Dodd's primary concern, therefore, was not the function of John's monologues in the narrative but the relation between John's monologues and "the common deposit of tradition," which he suggests was shared by all four Gospels though applied by the Fourth Gospel in a radically different "pattern" and by a "different channel."[124]

Similar to our discussion above regarding dialogues, our concern with the monologues of John is in regard to their narrative function.[125] A monologue is similar to a dialogue in that it is set in the context of an engagement and conflict, but rather than engaging point for point it allows for a lengthy argument. Like the three types of dialogue, a monologue can contain elements of rhetoric, challenge, and conflict, but it does so in a sustained presentation. The function of a monologue is similar to a dialogue in another way: its significance is not merely the meaning of the language and the propositions of the argument but also what the language *does*. As much as monologues do contain meaning, they also move and develop the plot. Thus, they are intimately connected to what has come before and where the plot of John is

---

121. Dodd, *Historical Tradition*, 315.
122. Ibid., 337.
123. Ibid., 343.
124. Ibid., 365, 388, 404. Cf. Rudolf Bultmann, *The Gospel of John: A Commentary*, ed. R. W. N. Hoare and J. K. Riches, trans. G. R. Beasley-Murray (Philadelphia: Westminster, 1971), 6–7.
125. Cf. Keener, *John*, 1:68–76.

moving. At times a monologue may even contain within it a brief dialogue between speaker and audience, reflective of the implicit dialogical nature of a monologue. The monologue brings meaning to Jesus's person and work so that the listeners — and therefore the readers — are exhorted to take a particular action. For this reason each pericope containing a monologue is controlled by the linear movement and patterns of the monologue and not by scenes centered upon conflict and resolution. This is not a tangent for John; it is a necessary element in the developing story of Jesus.

Unlike Dodd, our concern is not with the "sayings" of Jesus as traditionally defined in Gospels scholarship but with substantial monologues that performed generic functions in the Gospel narrative. While there are several partial or informal monologues, there are only a limited number of substantial monologues in the Gospel that manifest the recognizable conventions and categories of the monologue genre proper. This commentary would like to suggest that there are four substantial monologues in the Gospel:

1. The Identity of (the Son of) God (5:19 – 47)
2. The Shepherd and the Sheep (10:1 – 21)
3. "The Hour has Come" (12:20 – 50)
4. The Farewell Discourse (13:31 – 16:33)

All four substantial monologues occur during the public ministry of Jesus, which includes Jesus's final but private address to his disciples. As a whole, the monologues provide robust insight into the identity of Jesus and the work given to him from the Father. The monologues also serve the narrative by facilitating the Gospel's plot, depicting in great detail God's own argument and explication of his person and work in the world.

Origin: Date, Provenance, and Audience

The author of this Gospel is well aware of the historical conditions and context out of which his message was communicated. Like the formal anonymity of the author, however, the origin of the Gospel could also be described as formally anonymous. The dominance of the critical approach over the last few centuries has made the issues surrounding the Gospel's origin the interpretive key to the Gospel. The confessional approach — the approach of this commentary — is also concerned with the historical situation in which the Gospel was created, but for different reasons and with different warrant (see above). For this reason our analysis below will not address these issues of origin as if they are the building foundation for the interpretation to follow. They are not for both methodological reasons as well as an important textual reason: the Gospel is formally anonymous in regard to its origin. At best the origin of the Gospel can only be implied (or reconstructed) from the narrative account.

Since the Gospel is only implicit in its account of its origin, we too should only be concerned with its historical and social-cultural context in a general manner; anything too specific goes beyond what the Gospel itself warrants. We would even argue that much of the discussion of this Gospel's origin is more appropriately applied to apologetics, the defense of the faith and its Scripture, than interpretation, the explication of Scripture and its meaning. This is not to minimize apologetics in any way but to admit that it is not the concern of this commentary. Nor is our concern the history of discussion regarding the Fourth Gospel and its interpretation, as if the Gospel can be analyzed in a manner that distances the text from its communicative intention and subject matter.[126] Rather, our goal is to interpret the Gospel as it demands to be received. For this reason it is necessary to locate the Gospel in its context of origin in order to allow for a conversation between the original record and the (contemporary) reader to occur in relationship to the subject matter. Most of the historical and social-cultural issues will be addressed in the commentary proper as needed, but a summary of some of the traditional origin issues in regard to this Gospel is in order.

Date

The Gospel gives the reader no explicit date of origin. In fact, its record is concerned with an earlier era, the life and ministry of Jesus, and not the life and ministry of its author. Ironically, most of modern discussion regarding date concerns the time period about which the Gospel does not speak. That is, the date is often in reference to the historical time and place of the author and not the subject about which he spoke, Jesus Christ. Much of this is driven by the methodological dogmas of the critical approach we discussed above.

The majority of scholars reconstruct the date of origin for the Gospel to be somewhere between AD 70 and 135; the former date because of the narrator's mention of Peter's death (21:19), which occurred around AD 65 or 66, and the latter date because a NT manuscript ($\mathfrak{P}^{52}$) containing part of the Gospel (18:31–32) was found that can be dated to around AD 135.[127] Certainly the latter date is far too late. Based upon the use of terms and phrases in the Gospel, such as the designation "Sea of Tiberias" in explaining the "Sea of Galilee," the best range of dates for the Gospel would be AD 70–95.[128] But even then this is just an educated guess. It is also pressing the evidence beyond what is needed for interpretation, for not only is little precision gained by such a detail — a general first-century context is clearly sufficient — but the interpretive dates the Gospel itself is concerned with is in the first third of the first century,

---

126. See Charles E. Hill, *The Johannine Corpus in the Early Church* (Oxford: Oxford University Press, 2004), who takes on what he calls "the myth of orthodox Johannophobia." Cf. Ernst Haenchen, *A Commentary on the Gospel of John*, 2 vols., ed. Robert W. Funk and Ulrich Busse, trans. Robert W. Funk, Hermeneia (Philadelphia: Fortress, 1984), 1:2–39; Rudolf Schnackenburg, *The Gospel According to St. John*, 3 vols., trans. Kevin Smyth, HTCNT (New York: Herder and Herder, 1968, 1980, 1982), 1:192–217.

127. Cf. D. Moody Smith, *John*, ANTC (Nashville: Abingdon, 1999), 42.

128. See Andreas J. Köstenberger, *A Theology of John's Gospel and Letters: The Word, the Christ, the Son of God*, BTNT (Grand Rapids: Zondervan, 2009), 82–83.

the context of Jesus's ministry. That is, the context directly related to the content and subject matter of the text. This is not to deny that the Gospel author is writing after the events of record and with an interpretive perspective. It is simply to claim that the author is neither making his later date obvious or significant for interpretation nor overly assuming his matured perspective from the start. As we discussed above, since the Gospel is the record of an eyewitness, the Gospel narrative serves to merge the date of event and the date of the text's origin into a united and singular witness that cannot be separated without doing damage to both.

Provenance

The Gospel also gives the reader no explicit place of origin. Its record is concerned with the location in which Jesus lived and ministered and not the location of its author, though most of modern discussion of provenance concerns the location of the author and not the locations about which the Gospel itself speaks. Evidence in the early church suggests that the Fourth Gospel had its origin in Ephesus. According to Eusebius, the apostle John went to serve in Asia (*Hist. eccl.* 3.1.1); according to Irenaeus, "John, the disciple of the Lord ... published the Gospel while living in Ephesus in Asia" (*Haer.* 3.1.2). Modern scholars have challenged an Ephesian origin by preferring comparison drawn from internal evidence (e.g., affinities between John and Philo for a supposed origin in Alexandria) over and against the external evidence drawn from the early church.

While it is entirely probable that the Gospel had its origin in Ephesus just as Eusebius and Irenaeus report, there is nothing significant about this place or the tradition promoting it.[129] Again, the Gospel is formally anonymous in regard to the place of its origin, and it would certainly be a mistake to place interpretive controls on the reconstructed social-cultural location of this proposal regarding the Gospel's origin. Hoskyns is probably closer to the point: "The Gospel was assuredly written down at a particular time and in a particular place ... and this cannot be irrelevant for our understanding of his book.... But the author has done his best, apparently with intention, to cover up his tracks. For his theme is not his own workshop but the workshop of God, and to this we have no direct access!"[130] This is not to minimize a real place or origin but to claim that the subject matter of this Gospel can only be

---

129. Sjef van Tilborg, *Reading John in Ephesus*, NovTSup 83 (Leiden: Brill, 1996), has recently given support to the tradition regarding Ephesus by showing how the Gospel can be illuminated against the context of life in first-century Ephesus based upon inscriptions and other sources. Yet even he admits that this tradition is not without criticism, and that he is "not going to try and prove that the Johannine Gospel belongs in Ephesus" (3). Rather, Tilborg uses Ephesian texts and data from the first century and compares/contrasts them to John as "interference,"

which he explains as "the mutual influence which two systems exercise on each other if they come together" (4). In this way Tilborg provides a concrete embedding of the text of John in the textually mediated history and life of the first-century city of Ephesus. While this cannot prove the Ephesian tradition, it offers a helpful reconstruction that is highly feasible.

130. Edwyn Clement Hoskyns, *The Fourth Gospel*, ed. Francis Noel Davey, 2nd ed. (London: Faber and Faber, 1947), 18–19.

defined when God is viewed as a participating (if not primary) source of origin. The provenance of importance for the interpretation of the Gospel is the locations described and articulated by the narrative itself. And as we will see, at times the thematic importance of a location is what matters most to the narrative (e.g., the use of "garden" in chs. 18 – 20; see comments on 19:41).

Audience

The early church had several traditions regarding the origins of the Gospels, including the audience for whom they were written. Over the last century, however, those traditions have been developed so as to take on a life of their own. Gospels research has now considered it axiomatic that the four evangelists wrote for and in response to their own particular Christian communities. In the last few decades elaborate reconstructions of the four Gospel communities have been proposed, using technical reading techniques that attempt to get "behind the text" of each Gospel. The quest for the historical Jesus that occupied much of the nineteenth century largely gave way to the quest for the early church in the twentieth century. The basic assumption is that by discovering the identity of the audience and its social and historical location, the Gospel can be rightly interpreted according to its original occasion and intended purpose.

The Johannine Community

While all four Gospels have been interpreted through the lens of their reconstructed audience, the uniqueness of the Gospel of John has almost required that it receive the most robust and detailed reconstruction of its audience, what is now commonly called the "Johannine community."[131] It is impossible to separate the reconstructions of the Gospel's audience from its authorship, source, and origin issues or in fact from the rest of the Johannine literature. Once the majority of critical scholarship held that John the apostle may not be the author, as was traditionally believed, then a wave of varying theories were presented in its place, leading to the current reconstructions of the audience. Initially it was believed that if it were not the apostle, at least one of his close companions completed the work from his memoirs. This thesis was held and adapted so that it was assumed that the apostle was not the author, but someone after him, a disciple of his most probably. Although it was C. Hermann Weisse (1838) who was the first to suggest that a group of followers or disciples of the apostle wrote the Gospel, using notes which the apostle left when he died, it was probably Ludwig Baumgarten-Crusius (1843) who first used the idea of a Johannine community or "circle" in defense of John's authenticity. Later

---

131. The following is adapted from Klink, *The Sheep of the Fold*, 24 – 35.

both Michel Nicholas (1864) and Carl H. von Weizsäcker (1901) argued that the Fourth Gospel was written by a pupil of John or a member of the Ephesian church, the location where it was assumed John originated. Thus, from as early as 1860, the disputed origin of the Gospel made the ground ripe for the establishment of a group of Johannine disciples out of which the Gospel found its origin.

The next century brought forth a growing consensus that the Gospel was in some way a creation of a Johannine community, that is, the work and ideas of the disciples of the apostle. In discussing the relation between the Gospel of John and the Johannine letters, James Moffatt's 1918 New Testament introduction summarizes the current understanding of Johannine literature by stating the general position many scholars had come to agree upon: "Their relationship on the disjunctive hypothesis is accounted for by the common language of a group or school in Asia Minor...."[132] Thus, through the first six decades of the twentieth century, the discussion in NT scholarship focused on the enigma of the Gospel and its relationship to the other Johannine writings. The more "orthodox" defended the authorship of the apostle, the less "orthodox" assumed some type of Johannine group as the responsible party for some or, more probably, all of the Johannine writings. The Johannine oddities and the various proposals concerning the background of the Gospel presented by these causes, not unlike current Johannine scholarship, were certainly present. In the 1920s, the influence of form criticism and its picture of the origin of the Gospels also played a role. The uncertainty of the origin, authorship, and sources of the Gospel of John and its relation to the other Johannine writings made the audience reconstructions of the Gospel appear to many scholars to be a most plausible explanation.

Martyn, Meeks, and Methodological Precision

It was in the 1960s, in the high point of redactional activity in all four of the Gospels, that the face of Johannine community reconstructions was drastically affected. In 1968, J. Louis Martyn published the first edition of *History and Theology in the Fourth Gospel*.[133] Martyn's thesis became "a paradigm" in Johannine studies by combining two growing conclusions into this one work: the Jewish nature of the Gospel as its background and origin and the reality that John was a book of many compositional levels.[134] Martyn himself states his purpose in his introduction:

> Our first task ... is to say something as specific as possible about the actual circumstances in which John wrote his Gospel. How are we to picture daily life in John's

---

132. James Moffatt, *An Introduction to the Literature of the New Testament* (New York: Charles Scribner's Sons, 1918), 389.

133. J. Louis Martyn, *History and Theology in the Fourth Gospel*, 3rd ed., NTL (Louisville: Westminster John Knox, 2003).

134. D. Moody Smith, "The Contribution of J. Louis Martyn to the Understanding of the Gospel of John," in *The Conversation Continues: Studies in Paul and John*, ed. R. T. Fortna and B. R. Gaventa (Nashville: Abingdon, 1990), 275–94 (293). See also John Ashton, *Understanding the Fourth Gospel* (Oxford: Clarendon, 1991), 107.

church? Have elements of its peculiar daily experiences left their stamp on the Gospel penned by one of its members? May one sense even in its exalted cadences the voice of a Christian theologian who writes *in response to contemporary events and issues* which concern, or should concern, all members of the Christian community in which he lives?[135]

According to Martyn, the text of John needs to be read on two levels: one that reflected the tradition of the church and the other that was involved in the contemporary issues of the particular community.[136] For Martyn, each writer in the NT handled these two issues and their relationship in different ways. This is in part because although each drew from a similar pool of tradition, each had unique social and religious circumstances which they faced. In this way Martyn can say, "Consequently, when we read the Fourth Gospel, we are listening both to tradition and to a new and unique interpretation of that tradition."[137] Methodologically, then, according to Martyn one could compare how different writers of the NT adapted the common tradition to their specific circumstances; thus, the different application denotes something of the historical circumstance in which each "community" lived and ministered. The Gospel text "presents its witness on two levels: (1) It is a witness to an *einmalig* ["back then"] event during Jesus's earthly lifetime.... (2) The text is also a witness to Jesus's powerful presence in actual events experienced by the Johannine church."[138] In this way, Martyn has not only assumed a Johannine "community" but has even provided a method by which interpreters may take a "glimpse" through a once-clouded window into the actual historical circumstances that were faced by the audience that authored, for itself and by itself, the text of the Gospel of John. The influence from Martyn's first edition in 1968 to the current day is massive. Since then it has been the common assumption that the Fourth Gospel was written in and for a specific "community."

Following in Martyn's trail, there have been many and various proposals given to delineate the exact nature, circumstances, and historical development of the "community" in which the text of the Fourth Gospel was written. Two primary methodological approaches to the reconstruction of the audience of the Gospel can be briefly defined. The first approach is rooted in the traditional, historical introductory questions applied to the Gospels. Although Martyn had the earliest impact on "community" interpretation in John, he was not actually the first example of the more recent audience reconstructions. Two years before Martyn, Raymond Brown, in the first volume of his commentary on John, sketched as a "working hypothesis" his now famous five stages in the production of the document. He only hinted at different events or conditions in the community for whom the Gospel was intended.[139] This

135. Martyn, *History and Theology*, 29 (emphasis original).
136. Ibid., 30–31.
137. Ibid., 30.
138. Ibid., 40.
139. See Raymond E. Brown, *The Gospel According to John*, 2 vols., AB 29 and 29A (New York: Doubleday, 1966, 1970), 1:xxxiv–xl, xcviii–cii.

initial publication of Brown's view of the audience was to become much more explicit in his *The Community of the Beloved Disciple* (1979).[140] This work is by far the most comprehensive and thorough explanation of the individual stages of the community and the many groups, for and against the authoring Johannine group, that were related in some way to the Johannine community. Yet like Martyn, Brown is performing a traditional historical-critical excavation of the Gospel text and its tradition, an approach wrapped up in the other introductory issues of the Gospel, growing from a desire to explicate the peculiarities of the Gospel in its historical situation.

The second approach to the reconstruction of the audience of the Gospel began shortly after Martyn. This methodological approach was initiated by Wayne Meeks's article "The Man from Heaven in Johannine Sectarianism" (1972).[141] Using the methods of the sociology of knowledge, Meeks examines the descent/ascent motif in the Fourth Gospel and argues that it comprises a myth by which the Johannine Christians understood and strengthened their status as a sectarian counterculture "group." Once the audience behind John was assumed to be a recognizable "group," various approaches were then used to define its functional makeup. Meeks's provocative article did much to fashion a view of the audience of John that dominated scholarship for years to come. While debate raged over the use of the term "sect" or "sectarian" to describe the "community,"[142] the view of the Johannine Christians as a minority group in their culture and their emphasis on the in-group/out-group distinction became a basic assumption of later scholarship. Meeks's proposal was a spark that ignited a plethora of social-scientific investigations in regard to the reconstruction of the Johannine community.

The Audience of the Gospel of John: An Evaluation

At the very end of the twentieth century, the methodological assumptions regarding the audience of the Gospels that had been growing in precision over the past generation were given a major challenge by the 1998 book, *The Gospels for All Christians: Rethinking the Gospel Audience*, edited by Richard Bauckham and contributed to by several other British scholars.[143] This critique of what had been a general consensus has led to a methodological debate over the audience of the Gospels and an evaluation of the appropriate methods for interpreting the Gospels.[144] Since the publication of that volume, each of the Gospels has received a level of evaluation regarding the

140. Raymond E. Brown, *The Community of the Beloved Disciple: The Life, Loves, and Hates of an Individual Church in New Testament Times* (New York: Paulist, 1979).

141. Wayne A. Meeks, "The Man from Heaven in Johannine Sectarianism," *JBL* 91 (1972): 44–72.

142. See Brown, *The Community of the Beloved Disciple*, 14–17, 88–91.

143. Richard Bauckham, ed., *The Gospels for All Christians:*

Rethinking the Gospel Audiences (Grand Rapids: Eerdmans, 1998).

144. For an overview of the contemporary-audience debate, see Edward W. Klink III, "Gospel Audience and Origin: The Current Debate," in *The Audience of the Gospels: Further Conversation about the Origin and Function of the Gospels in Early Christianity*, ed. Edward W. Klink III, LNTS 353 (London: T&T Clark, 2010), 1–26.

warrant of reconstructing a particular audience, including the Gospel of John.[145] As much as the old consensus (community reconstruction) has been given a sharp rebuke in regard to method and presupposition, it has hardly been outrightly rejected. If anything, the audience debate has simply brought a bit more balance to the use of the theories and approaches applied to the interpretation of the Gospels.[146]

The Gospels demand to be read in light of their original social-historical context and in a manner that facilitates the communicative intention of the Gospel according to its nature as both ancient text and contemporary Scripture. The assumption of this commentary is that the Johannine-community construct is methodologically a flawed category for interpreting the Gospel. Three reasons for this can be briefly summarized.[147] First, the Gospel audience must be defined "relationally" and not territorially. The Gospel envisages a wide range of readers, not those confined to a particular space and time. Second, the Gospel audience cannot be reconstructed from a "mirror reading" of the Gospel, for this abuses the genre of the Gospel and assumes an overly narrow audience entirely foreign to this kind of genre. Third, the Gospel itself does not yield itself to be read by or intended for a narrow, specific audience. In contrast, the Gospel is written in such a way that its audience — its intended reader — is still unknown. It is better to assume that the Gospel was intended for a broad readership and was intended to cooperate with the general witness of early Christianity. This assumption matches well the confessional approach discussed above, which intends to take seriously the "humanness" of the Gospel and yet maintain that the Gospel, as part of Scripture, is also a "divine" communication.[148]

Structure and Outline

Scholarship on the Gospel of John has widely agreed that the Gospel should be divided into four main sections: Prologue (1:1 – 18), Book of Signs (1:19 – 12:50), Book of Glory (13:1 – 20:31), and Epilogue (21:1 – 25). One scholar even makes the remarkable claim, "The divisions are unquestionable," though he is uncomfortable with the titles.[149] While scholars are right to see a major section break between chapter 12 and chapter 13, the place at which the narrative transitions out of the public ministry of Jesus, there is no warrant for dividing the Gospel into only two major sections or "acts." This two-part division of the Gospel is rooted more in source-critical theories (e.g., chs. 1 – 12 are part of the "Signs Source") than in the synchronic

---

145. A full evaluation and critique of the methods and assumptions of the reconstruction of a Johannine community was provided by Klink, *The Sheep of the Fold*. For a recent survey of the Johannine-audience debate, see Wally V. Cirafesi, "The Johannine Community Hypothesis (1968 – Present): Past and Present Approaches and a New Way Forward," *CBR* 12 (2014): 173 – 93.

146. For a more recent discussion of the issues from several perspectives regarding the audience debate, see the essays in Klink, *The Audience of the Gospels*.

147. The following is the thrust of the argument in Klink, *The Sheep of the Fold*.

148. Helpful here is Webster, *Holy Scripture*, 28 – 29.

149. Köstenberger, *Theology of John*, 167.

presentation of the narrative itself. It was apparently Bultmann who was the first to suggest the hypothetical "Signs Source,"[150] but Dodd seems to have been the most influential proponent of this two-part structure of the Gospel, without any substantial warrant besides the source-critical assumption of the conjoining of two sources ("signs" and "glory") which were supposedly the original foundation for the Gospel narrative.[151] Determining the literary structure of the Gospel is difficult and must be held loosely, but this division should be rejected by the narrative itself. For example, since the Gospel author describes the entire narrative as something like "a book of signs" (see comments on 20:31), certainly it is inaccurate to label only the first half of the Gospel with such a title.

One of the primary reasons why it is difficult to establishing *the* structure of the Gospel of John is because the narrative is crafted with several key themes that are repeatedly handled and developed throughout the progression of the narrative, which makes it possible to suggest all kinds of parallels, connections, and even chiasms. Without claiming that our proposed structure has correctly grasped this narrative, the analysis of this commentary has attempted to weigh the development of the Gospel as a narrative against the more formal considerations of literary structure. Our outline attempts to follow the movements and subject matter of the narrative, though it must be admitted that this structure is no more authoritative than the chapter and verse divisions, now common in all Bibles, which formed no part of the original text.[152] According to our interpretation, the Gospel is best divided into ten major sections:

I. Prologue (1:1 – 18)

II. The First Week: An Introduction to the Narrative Proper (1:19 – 51)

III. The Beginning of Jesus's Public Ministry (2:1 – 4:54)

IV. The Confession of the Son of God (5:1 – 8:11)

V. The Controversy over the Son of God (8:12 – 10:42)

VI. The Conclusion of Jesus's Public Ministry (11:1 – 12:50)

VII. The Farewell Discourse (13:1 – 17:26)

VIII. The Crucifixion (18:1 – 19:42)

IX. The Resurrection (20:1 – 31)

X. Epilogue (21:1 – 25)

The narrative is framed by the significant functions of the prologue and epilogue, and the narrative proper is divided into distinct but developing sections which serve to form one unitary story. The titles are simply derived from the subject matter of those sections, befitting their place in the development of the narrative.

---

150. Bultmann, *John*, 6 – 7. It was more fully developed by Robert T. Fortna, *The Gospel of Signs: A Reconstruction of the Narrative Source Underlying the Fourth Gospel* (Cambridge: Cambridge University Press, 1970), 87 – 98, 108.

151. C. H. Dodd, *The Interpretation of the Fourth Gospel* (Cambridge: Cambridge University Press, 1953), 289 – 91.

152. Cf. D. A. Carson, *The Gospel according to John*, PNTC (Grand Rapids: Eerdmans, 1991), 104.

The ten major sections can be divided into forty-eight distinct pericopae, smaller units or episodes which make up the larger sections. These divisions are equally as subjective as the larger divisions, but are based on the narrative's own boundary markers and change in subject matter. The commentary itself is divided into chapters based upon these forty-eight pericopae. While it is suggested that each pericope is a complete unit and therefore suitable for preaching, it must be admitted that some pericopae in this Gospel are complex enough or bear such a significant subject matter that a single pericope might be too much to exposit in one sermon or teaching session. For this reason we are providing a fuller outline of the Gospel that will show what our exegesis yielded to be even smaller episodes or units. The complete outline of the Gospel proposed by this commentary is the following:

I. Prologue (1:1 – 18)
   A. Introduction to the Word (1:1 – 5)
   B. Witness to the Word (1:6 – 8)
   C. Manifestation of the Word (1:9 – 14)
   D. Uniqueness of the Word (1:15 – 18)
II. The First Week: An Introduction to the Narrative Proper (1:19 – 51)
   A. The Witness of John (1:19 – 34)
      1. John, the Voice in the Wilderness (1:19 – 28)
         a. "Not Me": Jewish Authorities Question John (vv. 19 – 22)
         b. "But Him": John's Declaration of the Christ (vv. 23 – 28)
      2. Jesus, the Lamb and Son of God (1:29 – 34)
         a. John's Witness to the Lamb of God (vv. 29 – 31)
         b. The Spirit's Witness to the Son of God (vv. 32 – 34)
   B. The First Disciples (1:35 – 51)
      1. Andrew, the Anonymous Disciple, and Peter (1:35 – 42)
         a. "Come and See": Jesus's Invitation to the Disciples (vv. 35 – 39)
         b. The Naming of Peter (vv. 40 – 42)
      2. Philip and Nathanael (1:43 – 51)
         a. The "Good" that Comes from Nazareth (vv. 43 – 49)
         b. The Revelation of the Son of Man (vv. 50 – 51)
III. The Beginning of Jesus's Public Ministry (2:1 – 4:54)
   A. The First Sign: The Wedding at Cana (2:1 – 11)
      1. Invitation to a Wedding in Cana (vv. 1 – 3)
      2. Jesus, his Mother, and a Shortage of Wine (v. 4)
      3. From Purification Water to Celebratory Wine (vv. 5 – 8)
      4. The First Sign of Jesus's Glory (vv. 9 – 11)
   B. The Cleansing of the Temple: The Promise of the Seventh Sign (2:12 – 25)
      1. The House of God and a House of Business (vv. 12 – 17)
      2. A Challenge of Temple Authority (vv. 18 – 20)

3. The True Temple, the Body of Jesus (vv. 21 – 22)

4. Jesus's Witness to the Nature of Humanity (vv. 23 – 25)

C. Nicodemus, New Birth, and the Unique Son (3:1 – 21)

    1. Nicodemus's Provocative Introduction (vv. 1 – 2)

    2. First Verbal Exchange: "Born New" (vv. 3 – 4)

    3. Second Verbal Exchange: "Born from Water and Spirit" (vv. 5 – 10)

    4. Jesus's Victory Announcement: The Cross (vv. 11 – 15)

    5. Narrator's Commentary (vv. 16 – 21)

D. The Baptist, the True Bridegroom, and the Friend of the Bridegroom (3:22 – 36)

    1. Introduction to the Baptism of Jesus (vv. 22 – 24)

    2. Baptism Controversy (vv. 25 – 26)

    3. The Bridegroom and the Friend of the Bridegroom (vv. 27 – 30)

    4. Narrator's Commentary (vv. 31 – 36)

E. The Samaritan Woman, Living Water, and True Worshippers (4:1 – 42)

    1. Jesus's Return to Galilee through Samaria (vv. 1 – 6)

    2. First Verbal Exchange: Jesus's Provocative Request for Water (vv. 7 – 9)

    3. Second Verbal Exchange: "Living Water" (vv. 10 – 12)

    4. Third Verbal Exchange: Well of Eternal Life (vv. 13 – 15)

    5. Fourth Verbal Exchange: The Woman and Her Husbands (vv. 16 – 18)

    6. Fifth Verbal Exchange: True Worship and Worshippers (vv. 19 – 24)

    7. Sixth Verbal Exchange: The Confession of Christ (vv. 25 – 26)

    8. Interlude: Jesus's Disciples, True Food, and the Harvest (vv. 27 – 38)

    9. "The Savior of the World" (vv. 39 – 42)

F. The Second Sign: The Healing of the Royal Official's Son (4:43 – 54)

    1. The Honorless Prophet Returns to Galilee (vv. 43 – 46)

    2. Royal Official's Dying Son (v. 47)

    3. "Your Son Lives" (vv. 48 – 50)

    4. The "Sign" of Life (vv. 51 – 54)

IV. The Confession of the Son of God (5:1 – 8:11)

A. The Third Sign: The Healing of the Lame Man on the Sabbath (5:1 – 18)

    1. A Man Lame for Thirty-Eight Years (vv. 1 – 5)

    2. Get Up — Even on the Sabbath! (vv. 6 – 10)

    3. Sin No Longer (vv. 11 – 15)

    4. The Work of God, Father and Son (vv. 16 – 18)

B. The Identity of (the Son of) God: Jesus Responds to the Opposition (5:19 – 47)

    1. Like Father, like Son (vv. 19 – 24)

    2. Life and Judgment of the Son (vv. 25 – 29)

    3. Witnesses to the Son (vv. 30 – 47)

        a. The Insufficiency of Jesus's Witness (vv. 30 – 32)

        b. The Witness of John the Baptist (vv. 33 – 35)

        c. The Witness of the Works of Jesus (v. 36)

d. The Witness of the Father (vv. 37 – 38)

e. The Witness of Scripture (vv. 39 – 40)

f. The Insufficiency of Human Recognition (vv. 41 – 47)

C. The Fourth Sign: The Feeding of a Large Crowd (6:1 – 15)

1. Jesus on a Mountain at Passover (vv. 1 – 4)

2. From Where Shall We Buy Bread? (vv. 5 – 9)

3. The Hospitality of Jesus (vv. 10 – 13)

4. He is the Prophet, Make Him a King! (vv. 14 – 15)

D. "I AM" Walks across the Sea (6:16 – 21)

1. The Disciples Depart without Jesus (vv. 16 – 17)

2. Jesus Walks on the Stirring Sea (vv. 18 – 19)

3. The Encounter with (the Son of) God (v. 20)

4. The Disciples Receive Jesus (v. 21)

E. The Bread of Life (6:22 – 71)

1. The Crowd Pursues Jesus (vv. 22 – 24)

2. First Verbal Exchange: "When Did You Come Here?" (vv. 25 – 27)

3. Second Verbal Exchange: The Work of God (vv. 28 – 29)

4. Third Verbal Exchange: God Gave You Bread, Not Moses (vv. 30 – 33)

5. Fourth Verbal Exchange: Jesus Is the Bread, Not Manna (vv. 34 – 40)

6. Fifth Verbal Exchange: "I Am the Living Bread" (vv. 41 – 51)

7. Sixth Verbal Exchange: Life in the Flesh and Blood of Jesus (vv. 52 – 59)

8. The Crowd Deserts Jesus (vv. 60 – 71)

a. The Offense of Some "Disciples" (vv. 60 – 66)

b. The Confession of the "Twelve" (vv. 67 – 71)

F. Private Display of Suspicion (7:1 – 13)

1. The Feast of the Jews (vv. 1 – 2)

2. The Ridicule of Jesus by His Brothers (vv. 3 – 5)

3. The Response of Jesus to His Brothers (vv. 6 – 9)

4. The Reluctance toward Jesus because of the Jews (vv. 10 – 13)

G. Public Display of Rejection (7:14 – 52)

1. The Authority of Jesus (7:14 – 24)

a. Scene Introduction: Temple, Tabernacles, and Timing (v. 14)

b. First Verbal Exchange: The Source of Jesus's Teaching (vv. 15 – 19)

c. Second Verbal Exchange: The Source of Jesus's Miracles (vv. 20 – 24)

2. The Identity of Jesus (7:25 – 36)

a. Third Verbal Exchange: The Nature of Jesus's Origin (vv. 25 – 29)

b. Narrator's Interlude: Control in Confusion and Confrontation (vv. 30 – 32)

c. Fourth Verbal Exchange: The Nature of Jesus's Mission (vv. 33 – 36)

3. The Spirit of Jesus (7:37 – 44)

a. Final Exhortation of Jesus: The Promise of the Spirit (vv. 37 – 38)

b. Narrator's Interlude: The Interpretation of Jesus's Statement (v. 39)

c. Final Reaction of the Crowd (vv. 40 – 44)

4. The Internal Divisions of Unbelief (7:45 – 52)

   a. First Verbal Exchange: Jewish Authorities Challenge the Temple Police (vv. 45 – 46)

   b. Second Verbal Exchange: Jewish Authorities Challenge the Crowd (vv. 47 – 49)

   c. Third Verbal Exchange: Nicodemus Challenges the Jewish Authorities (vv. 50 – 52)

H. The Trial of Jesus regarding a Woman Accused of Adultery (7:53 – 8:11)

   1. Teaching in the Temple (7:53 – 8:2)

   2. The Law of Moses and Adultery (vv. 3 – 6a)

   3. The Finger of God (vv. 6b – 8)

   4. The Law of Christ (vv. 9 – 11)

V. The Controversy over the Son of God (8:12 – 10:42)

A. "The Light of the World": The Accusations of Jesus the Judge (8:12 – 59)

   1. First Accusation: The Charge against Inappropriate Belief (vv. 12 – 30)

      a. First Verbal Exchange: The Authority and Judgment of the Son (vv. 12 – 20)

         (1) Charge: "I Am the Light of the World" (v. 12)

         (2) Responses: The Witness of the Father and Son (vv. 13 – 18)

         (3) Verdict: "You Know neither Me nor My Father" (vv. 19 – 20)

      b. Second Verbal Exchange: The Origin of the Son (vv. 21 – 30)

         (1) Charge: "You Will Die in Your Sin" (v. 21)

         (2) Responses: "You Are from the World; I Am Not from This World" (vv. 22 – 27)

         (3) Verdict: "You Will Know That I Am" (vv. 28 – 30)

   2. Second Accusation: The Charge against Illegitimate Origin (vv. 31 – 59)

      a. First Verbal Exchange: The Identity of the People of God (vv. 31 – 47)

         (1) Charge: True Disciples Abide in My Word (vv. 31 – 32)

         (2) Responses: Abraham and the Father (vv. 33 – 43)

         (3) Verdict: "You Belong to Your Father, the Devil" (vv. 44 – 47)

      b. Second Verbal Exchange: The Counterclaim by the Jews: Heresy! (vv. 48 – 59)

         (1) Charge: "You Are a Samaritan and Have a Demon" (v. 48)

         (2) Responses: "Before Abraham Was [Born], I Am" (vv. 49 – 58)

         (3) Verdict: The Attempted Stoning of Jesus (v. 59)

B. The Fifth Sign: The Testimony of the Blind Man (9:1 – 41)

   1. The Healing of the Man Blind from Birth (vv. 1 – 7)

      a. Blindness and Sin: "Rabbi, Who Sinned?" (vv. 1 – 2)

      b. Blindness and "the Works of God" (vv. 3 – 5)

      c. Jesus Heals the Blind Man (vv. 6 – 7)

   2. The Judgment of Jesus *In Absentia*: Preliminary Hearing in the Sabbath Healing Case (vv. 8 – 34)

      a. First Verbal Exchange: The Blind Man and the Neighbors (vv. 8 – 12)

      b. Second Verbal Exchange: The Blind Man and the Jewish Authorities, Part 1 (vv. 13 – 17)

      c. Third Verbal Exchange: The Blind Man's Parents and the Jewish Authorities (vv. 18 – 23)

      d. Fourth Verbal Exchange: The Blind Man and the Jewish Authorities, Part 2 (vv. 24 – 34)

   3. The Confession of the Blind Man (vv. 35 – 41)

a. First Verbal Exchange: Jesus Encounters the Blind Man (vv. 35 – 38)

b. Second Verbal Exchange: Jesus Judges the Pharisees (vv. 39 – 41)

C. The Shepherd and the Sheep (10:1 – 21)

1. An "Illustration": The Door, the Shepherd, and the Sheep (vv. 1 – 5)

2. Narrator's Commentary (v. 6)

3. The Interpretation of the "Illustration" (vv. 7 – 18)

a. "I Am the Door of the Sheep" (vv. 7 – 10)

b. "I Am the Good Shepherd" (vv. 11 – 18)

4. Narrator's Commentary (vv. 19 – 21)

D. The Son of the Father (10:22 – 42)

1. Narrator's Introduction (vv. 22 – 23)

2. First Verbal Exchange: "I and the Father Are One" (vv. 24 – 30)

3. Second Verbal Exchange: Blasphemy or Belief? (vv. 31 – 39)

4. Narrator's Conclusion (vv. 40 – 42)

VI. The Conclusion of Jesus's Public Ministry (11:1 – 12:50)

A. The Sixth Sign: The Death and Resurrection of Lazarus (11:1 – 57)

1. The Death of Lazarus, Belief, and the Glory of God (vv. 1 – 16)

2. "I Am the Resurrection and the Life": The Dialogue between Mary and Martha and Jesus (vv. 17 – 37)

3. The Resurrection of Lazarus, Belief, and the Glory of God (vv. 38 – 44)

4. The (Prophetic) Response of the Jews to the Sign of Jesus (vv. 45 – 57)

B. The Anointing of Jesus (12:1 – 11)

1. Gift for a King (vv. 1 – 3)

2. But What about the Poor? (vv. 4 – 6)

3. Preparation for a Corpse (vv. 7 – 8)

4. The Public Response toward Jesus (vv. 9 – 11)

C. The Royal Entrance of Jesus into Jerusalem (12:12 – 19)

1. Preparations for a King (vv. 12 – 13)

2. The Royal Entrance of the King (vv. 14 – 15)

3. The True Nature of Jesus's Kingship (v. 16)

4. "The Whole World Has Gone after Him": Public Responses to Jesus (vv. 17 – 19)

D. "The Hour has Come": The Final Public Statement of Jesus (12:20 – 50)

1. Narrator's Introduction (vv. 20 – 22)

2. The Glorification of the Son (vv. 23 – 26)

3. The Mission of the Son (vv. 27 – 36)

4. Narrator's Commentary: The Unbelief of the People (vv. 37 – 43)

5. The Witness of the Son (vv. 44 – 50)

VII. The Farewell Discourse (13:1 – 17:26)

A. Introduction: The Love of Jesus (13:1 – 30)

1. Jesus and the Washing of His Disciples' Feet (13:1 – 20)

a. Jesus Washes His Disciples' Feet (vv. 1 – 5)

          b. Jesus's Dialogue with Peter (vv. 6 – 11)

          c. Jesus Explains His Foot Washing (vv. 12 – 20)

      2. Jesus Announces His Betrayal (13:21 – 30)

          a. The Prophecy of a Betrayer (vv. 21 – 22)

          b. Jesus's Dialogue with the Beloved Disciple (vv. 23 – 26)

          c. The Entrance of Satan and Departure of Judas (vv. 27 – 30)

   B. The Farewell Discourse (13:31 – 16:33)

      1. Prologue: Glory, Departure, and Love (13:31 – 38)

          a. The Glory and Departure of the Son of Man (vv. 31 – 33)

          b. A New Commandment: Love One Another (vv. 34 – 35)

          c. The Prophecy of Peter's Betrayal (vv. 36 – 38)

      2. I Am the Way and the Truth and the Life (14:1 – 14)

          a. "I Go and Prepare a Place for You" (vv. 1 – 4)

          b. Not Just a Place but a Person — The "I Am" (vv. 5 – 7)

          c. The Father, the Son, and "the Works" in the Name of the Son (vv. 8 – 14)

      3. I Will Give You the Paraclete (14:15 – 31)

          a. An Introduction to "Another Paraclete" (vv. 15 – 21)

          b. Participation with the Father and the Son in the Spirit (vv. 22 – 24)

          c. The Peace of Christ in the Spirit (vv. 25 – 31)

      4. I Am the True Vine (15:1 – 17)

          a. An Illustration of the Vine, the Farmer and the Branches (vv. 1 – 8)

          b. Remain in the Love of God (vv. 9 – 11)

          c. The Love Commandment (vv. 12 – 17)

      5. I Have Also Experienced the Hate of the World (15:18 – 27)

          a. The Source of the World's Hatred (vv. 18 – 21)

          b. The Judgment against the World (vv. 22 – 25)

          c. The Witness of the Paraclete (vv. 26 – 27)

      6. I Will Empower You by the Paraclete (16:1 – 15)

          a. "An Hour is Coming" (vv. 1 – 4a)

          b. The True Object of Faith (vv. 4b – 6)

          c. The Ministry of the Paraclete (vv. 7 – 15)

          d. The Paraclete's Conviction of the World (vv. 7 – 11)

          e. The Paraclete's Guidance of the Church (vv. 12 – 15)

      7. I Will Turn Your Grief into Joy (16:16 – 24)

          a. Confusion regarding Seeing God (vv. 16 – 18)

          b. The Coming Transition from Grief to Joy (vv. 19 – 24)

      8. Epilogue: Speaking Plainly, Departure, and Peace (16:25 – 33)

          a. The Christian Faith and the Coming "Hour" (vv. 25 – 28)

          b. The Misbelief of the Disciples (vv. 29 – 30)

          c. A Final Exhortation: "I Have Overcome the World" (vv. 31 – 33)

   C. Conclusion: The Prayer of Jesus (17:1 – 26)

      1. Prayer for the Glory of the Father and the Son (vv. 1 – 8)

      2. Prayer for the Present Disciples (vv. 9 – 19)

      3. Prayer for the Future Disciples (vv. 20 – 26)

VIII. The Crucifixion (18:1 – 19:42)

    A. The Arrest of Jesus (18:1 – 12)

      1. Betrayal in the Garden (vv. 1 – 3)

      2. "Whom Do You Seek?" (vv. 4 – 9)

      3. The Cup from the Father (vv. 10 – 11)

      4. Jesus, Arrested and Bound (v. 12)

    B. The Jewish Trial and Its Witnesses (18:13 – 27)

      1. Jesus Delivered to the Jewish Authorities (vv. 13 – 14)

      2. The First Denial of Peter (vv. 15 – 18)

      3. The Witness of Christ and His Disciples (vv. 19 – 24)

      4. The Second and Third Denials of Peter (vv. 25 – 27)

    C. The Roman Trial before Pilate (18:28 – 40)

      1. Jesus Delivered to the Roman Authorities (v. 28)

      2. Pilate and the Jews: "What Accusation Do You Bring?" (vv. 29 – 32)

      3. Pilate and Jesus: "What is Truth?" (vv. 33 – 38a)

      4. The Negotiation of Jesus (vv. 38b – 40)

    D. The Verdict: "Crucify Him!" (19:1 – 16)

      1. Treatment for a King (vv. 1 – 3)

      2. "Behold, the Man!" (vv. 4 – 7)

      3. Authority "from Above" (vv. 8 – 11)

      4. The Judgment Seat (vv. 12 – 16)

    E. The Crucifixion of Jesus (19:17 – 27)

      1. "Place of the Skull" (vv. 17 – 18)

      2. The Title of the King (vv. 19 – 22)

      3. The Tunic of the Priest (vv. 23 – 24)

      4. The Family of the Son (vv. 25 – 27)

    F. The Death and Burial of Jesus (19:28 – 42)

      1. "It Is Completed" (vv. 28 – 30)

      2. Testimony to the Perfect Sacrifice (vv. 31 – 37)

      3. Buried in a Garden and a New Tomb (vv. 38 – 42)

IX. The Resurrection (20:1 – 31)

    A. The Empty Tomb (20:1 – 10)

      1. The Location of Jesus (vv. 1 – 2)

      2. Run to the Tomb (vv. 3 – 7)

      3. Belief in the Resurrection (vv. 8 – 9)

      4. The Location of the Disciples (v. 10)

    B. The Appearance to Mary Magdalene (20:11 – 18)

      1. The Throne of Grace (vv. 11 – 12)

2. "Why Are You Weeping?" (vv. 13 – 15)

3. The Ascension (vv. 16 – 17)

4. "I Have Seen the Lord" (v. 18)

C. The Appearance to the Disciples (20:19 – 23)

1. The Peace of God (vv. 19 – 20)

2. The Mission of God (v. 21)

3. The Spirit of God (v. 22)

4. The Ministerial Authority of God (v. 23)

D. The Appearance to Thomas and the Purpose of the Gospel (20:24 – 31)

1. The "Absent Thomas" (v. 24)

2. The Witness of the Disciples (v. 25)

3. Not Unbelieving but Believing (vv. 26 – 27)

4. Belief in Testimony (vv. 28 – 29)

5. The Purpose of the Gospel (vv. 30 – 31)

X. Epilogue (21:1 – 25)

A. The Mission of the Church: Jesus and the Fishermen (21:1 – 14)

1. Fishermen without Fish (vv. 1 – 3)

2. Disciples without Jesus (vv. 4 – 6)

3. "It Is the Lord!" (vv. 7 – 8)

4. Jesus's Third Appearance to the Disciples (vv. 9 – 14)

B. The Ministers of the Church: Peter's Reinstatement and the Beloved Disciple's Testimony (21:15 – 25)

1. The Love and Sheep of Jesus (vv. 15 – 19)

2. "You Follow Me!" (vv. 20 – 23)

3. The Origin of the Gospel (vv. 24 – 25)

Select Bibliography

Ansberry, Christopher B., Casey A. Strine, Edward W. Klink III, and David Lincicum. "Pseudepigraphy and the Canon." Pages 125 – 57 in *Evangelical Faith and the Challenge of Historical Criticism*. Edited by Christopher M. Hays and Christopher B. Ansberry. London: SPCK, 2013.

Aquinas, Thomas. *Commentary on the Gospel of John*. 3 vols. Translated by Fabian Larcher and James A. Weisheipl. Washington, DC: The Catholic University of America Press, 2010.

Arterbury, Andrew E. "Breaking the Betrothal Bonds: Hospitality in John 4." *CBQ* 72 (2010): 63 – 83.

Ashton, John. *Understanding the Fourth Gospel*. Oxford: Clarendon, 1991.

Attridge, Harold W. "Genre Bending in the Fourth Gospel." *JBL* 121 (2002): 3 – 21.

Augustine. *On the Gospel of St. John*. In vol. 7 of *The Nicene and Post-Nicene Fathers*, Series 1. Edited by Philip Schaff. 1886 – 1889. 14 vols. Repr., Peabody, MA: Hendrickson, 1994.

Barrett, C. K. *The Gospel according to John: An Introduction with Commentary and Notes on the Greek Text*. 2nd ed. Philadelphia: Westminster, 1978.

Barth, Karl. *Witness to the Word: A Commentary on John 1*. Edited by Walter Fürst. Translated by Geoffrey W. Bromiley. Grand Rapids: Eerdmans, 1986. Repr., Eugene, OR: Wipf & Stock, 2003.

Bauckham, Richard. *God Crucified: Monotheism and Christology in the New Testament*. Grand Rapids: Eerdmans, 1998.

———. *Jesus and the Eyewitnesses: The Gospels as Eyewitness Testimony*. Grand Rapids: Eerdmans, 2006.

———. *The Testimony of the Beloved Disciple: Narrative, History, and Theology in the Gospel of John*. Grand Rapids: Baker, 2007.

Bauer, W., W. F. Arndt, F. W. Gingrich, and F. W. Danker. *A Greek-English Lexicon of the New Testament and Other Early Christian Literature*. 3rd ed. Chicago: University of Chicago Press, 2000.

Beasley-Murray, George R. *John*. WBC 36. 2nd ed. Nashville: Thomas Nelson, 1999.

Bernard, J. H. *A Critical and Exegetical Commentary on the Gospel according to St. John*. 2 vols. ICC. New York: Charles Scribner's Sons, 1929.

Blass, F., A. Debrunner, and R. W. Funk. *A Greek Grammar of the New Testament and Other Early Christian Literature*. Chicago: University of Chicago Press, 1961.

Boisemard, M.-E., and A. Lamouille. *L'Évangile de Jean*. Paris: Cerf, 1977.

Borchert, Gerald L. *John 1 – 11*. NAC 25A. Nashville: Broadman & Holman, 1996.

———. *John 12 – 21*. NAC 25B. Nashville: Broadman & Holman, 2002.

Bultmann, Rudolf. *The Gospel of John: A Commentary*. Edited by R. W. N. Hoare and J. K. Riches.

Translated by G. R. Beasley-Murray. Philadelphia: Westminster, 1971.

Brant, Jo-Ann A. *Dialogue and Drama: Elements of Greek Tragedy in the Fourth Gospel*. Peabody, MA: Hendrickson, 2004.

———. *John*. PCNT. Grand Rapids: Baker Academic, 2011.

Brodie, Thomas L. *The Gospel according to John: A Literary and Theological Commentary*. New York: Oxford University Press, 1993.

Brooke, G. J., and J.-D. Kaestli, eds. *Narrativity in Biblical and Related Texts*. Leuven: Leuven University Press, 2000.

Brown, Raymond E. *The Death of the Messiah: From Gethsemane to the Grave. A Commentary on the Passion Narratives of the Four Gospels*. 2 vols. New York: Doubleday, 1994.

———. *The Gospel according to John*. 2 vols. AB 29 and 29A. New York: Doubleday, 1966, 1970.

Bruce, F. F. *The Gospel of John: Introduction, Exposition, and Notes*. Grand Rapids: Eerdmans, 1983.

Bruner, Frederick Dale. *The Gospel of John: A Commentary*. Grand Rapids: Eerdmans, 2012.

Calvin, John. *The Gospel according to St. John 1 – 10*. Edited by David W. Torrance and Thomas F. Torrance. Translated by T. H. L. Parker. CNTC 4. Grand Rapids: Eerdmans, 1995.

———. *The Gospel according to St. John 11 – 21 & the First Epistle of John*. Edited by David W. Torrance and Thomas F. Torrance. Translated by T. H. L. Parker. CNTC 5. Grand Rapids: Eerdmans, 1994.

Capes, David B., April D. DeConick, Helen K. Bond, and Troy A. Miller, eds. *Israel's God and Rebecca's Children: Christology and Community in Early Judaism and Christianity*. Waco, TX: Baylor University Press, 2007.

Carson, D. A. *The Gospel according to John*. PNTC. Grand Rapids: Eerdmans, 1991.

Charlesworth, James H. *The Beloved Disciple: Whose Witness Validates the Gospel of John?* Valley Forge, PA: Trinity Press International, 1995.

Chrysostom, John. *Homilies on the Gospel of John and the Epistles to the Hebrews*. In vol. 14 of *The Nicene and Post-Nicene Fathers*, Series 1. Edited by Philip Schaff. 1886 – 1889. 14 vols. Repr., Peabody, MA: Hendrickson, 1994.

Culpepper, R. Alan. *Anatomy of the Fourth Gospel: A Study in Literary Design*. Philadelphia: Fortress, 1983.

Cyril of Alexandria. *Commentary on the Gospel according to Saint John*. 2 vols. Edited by Henry Parry Lidden. Translated by Philip Edward Pusey and Thomas Randall. LFHCC 43 and 48. London: Rivingtons, 1874 – 1885.

Dodd, C. H. *Historical Tradition in the Fourth Gospel*. Cambridge: Cambridge University Press, 1963.

———. *The Interpretation of the Fourth Gospel*. Cambridge: Cambridge University Press, 1953.

Downing, F. Gerald. "Ambiguity, Ancient Semantics, and Faith." *NTS* 56 (2009): 139 – 62.

Duke, Paul D. *Irony in the Fourth Gospel*. Atlanta: John Knox, 1985.

Edwards, Mark. *John*. BBC. Malden, MA: Blackwell, 2004.

Fortna, Robert T. *The Gospel of Signs: A Reconstruction of the Narrative Source Underlying the Fourth Gospel*. Cambridge: Cambridge University Press, 1970.

Frei, Hans W. *The Eclipse of Biblical Narrative: A Study in Eighteenth and Nineteenth Century Hermeneutics*. New Haven: Yale University Press, 1974.

Godet, Frederic L. *Commentary on John's Gospel*. 3rd ed. Translated by Timothy Dwight. New York: Funk and Wagnalls, 1886. Repr., Grand Rapids: Kregel, 1978.

Gundry, Robert H. *Jesus the Word according to John the Sectarian: A Paleofundamentalist Manifesto for Contemporary Evangelicalism, Especially Its Elites, in North America*. Grand Rapids: Eerdmans, 2002.

Haenchen, Ernst. *A Commentary on the Gospel of John*. 2 vols. Edited by Robert W. Funk and Ulrich Busse. Translated by Robert W. Funk. Hermeneia. Philadelphia: Fortress, 1984.

Heil, John Paul. *Blood and Water: The Death and Resurrection of Jesus in John 18–21*. CBQMS 27. Washington, DC: Catholic Biblical Association of America, 1995.

Hengel, Martin. *The Johannine Question*. Translated by John Bowden. London: SCM/Philadelphia: Trinity Press International, 1989.

Hoskyns, Edwyn Clement. *The Fourth Gospel*. 2nd ed. Edited by Francis Noel Davey. London: Faber and Faber, 1947.

Hunt, Steven A., D. Francois Tolmie, and Ruben Zimmermann, eds. *Character Studies in the Fourth Gospel: Literary Approaches to Sixty Figures in John*. WUNT 314. Tübingen: Mohr Siebeck, 2013.

Keener, Craig S. *The Gospel of John: A Commentary*. 2 vols. Peabody, MA: Hendrickson, 2003.

Kittel, G., and G. Friedrich, eds. *Theological Dictionary of the New Testament*. 10 vols. Translated by G. W. Bromiley. Grand Rapids: Eerdmans, 1964–1976.

Klink III, Edward W., ed. *The Audience of the Gospels: The Origin and Function of the Gospels in Early Christianity*. LNTS 353. London: T&T Clark, 2010.

———. "Light of the World: Cosmology and the Johannine Literature." Pages 74–89 in *Cosmology and New Testament Theology*. Edited by Jonathan T. Pennington and Sean M. McDonough. LNTS 355. London: T&T Clark, 2009.

———. *The Sheep of the Fold: The Audience and Origin of the Gospel of John*. SNTSMS 141. Cambridge: Cambridge University Press, 2007.

———. "What Concern is That to You and to Me? John 2:1–11 and the Elisha Narratives." *Neot* 39 (2005): 273–87.

Klink III, Edward W., and Darian R. Lockett. *Understanding Biblical Theology: A Comparison of Theory and Practice*. Grand Rapids: Zondervan, 2012.

Koester, Craig R., and Reimund Bieringer, eds. *The Resurrection of Jesus in the Gospel of John*. WUNT 222. Tübingen: Mohr Siebeck, 2008.

Köstenberger, Andreas J. *John*. BECNT. Grand Rapids: Baker, 2004.

———. *A Theology of John's Gospel and Letters: The Word, the Christ, the Son of God*. BTNT. Grand Rapids: Zondervan, 2009.

La Potterie, Ignace de. *La Vérité dans Saint Jean*. 2 vols. Rome: Pontifical Biblical Institute, 1977.

Leithart, Peter J. *Deep Exegesis: The Mystery of Reading Scripture*. Waco: Baylor University Press, 2009.

Lightfoot, R. H. *St. John's Gospel*. Oxford: Oxford University Press, 1956.

Lincoln, Andrew T. *The Gospel according to Saint John*. BNTC 4. London: Continuum, 2005.

———. *Truth on Trial: The Lawsuit Motif in the Fourth Gospel*. Peabody, MA: Hendrickson, 2000.

Lindars, Barnabas. *The Gospel of John*. NCB. Grand Rapids: Eerdmans, 1972.

Luther, Martin. *Sermons on the Gospel of St. John*. LW 22–24, 69. St. Louis: Concordia, 1957–2009.

Malina, Bruce J., and Richard L. Rohrbaugh. *Social-Science Commentary on the Gospel of John*. Minneapolis: Fortress, 1998.

Martyn, J. Louis. *History and Theology in the Fourth Gospel*. 3rd ed. NTL. Louisville: Westminster John Knox, 2003.

McHugh, John F. *A Critical and Exegetical Commentary on John 1–4.* ICC. London: T&T Clark, 2009.

Meeks, Wayne A. "The Man from Heaven in Johannine Sectarianism." *JBL* 91 (1972): 44–72.

Metzger, Bruce M. *A Textual Commentary on the Greek New Testament.* 2nd ed. Stuttgart: Deutsche Bibelgesellschaft, 1994.

Michaels, J. Ramsey. *The Gospel of John.* NICNT. Grand Rapids: Eerdmans, 2010.

Moloney, Francis J. *The Gospel of John.* SP 4. Collegeville, MN: Liturgical Press, 1998.

Morris, Leon. *The Gospel according to John.* Rev. ed. NICNT. Grand Rapids: Eerdmans, 1995.

Motyer, Stephen. *Your Father the Devil? A New Approach to John and "the Jews."* Carlisle: Paternoster, 1997.

Moule, C. F. D. *An Idiom Book of New Testament Greek.* 2nd ed. Cambridge: Cambridge University Press, 1959.

Moulton, J. H., W. F. Howard, and N. Turner. *A Grammar of New Testament Greek.* 4 vols. Edinburgh: T&T Clark, 1908–76.

Moulton, J. H., and G. Milligan. *Vocabulary of the Greek Testament.* London: Hodder & Stoughton, 1930. Repr., Peabody, MA: Hendrickson, 1997.

Newbigin, Lesslie. *The Light Has Come: An Exposition of the Fourth Gospel.* Grand Rapids: Eerdmans, 1982.

Neyrey, Jerome H. *The Gospel of John.* NCBC. Cambridge: Cambridge University Press, 2007.

———. *An Ideology of Revolt: John's Christology in Social-Science Perspective.* Philadelphia: Fortress, 1988.

Okure, Teresa. *The Johannine Approach to Mission: A Contextual Study of John 4:1–42.* WUNT 2.31. Tübingen: Mohr Siebeck, 1988.

Origen. *Commentary on John.* ANF 9. Peabody, MA: Hendrickson, 1994.

———. *Commentary on the Gospel of John: Books 13–32.* Translated by Ronald E. Heine. FC 80. Washington, DC: Catholic University of America Press, 1993.

Parsenios, George L. *Departure and Consolation: The Johannine Farewell Discourses in Light of Greco-Roman Literature.* NovTSup 117. Leiden: Brill, 2005.

———. *Rhetoric and Drama in the Johannine Lawsuit Motif.* WUNT 258. Tübingen: Mohr Siebeck, 2010.

Pink, Arthur W. *Exposition of the Gospel of John.* 3 vols. Cleveland: Cleveland Bible Truth Depot, 1929. Repr., Grand Rapids: Zondervan, 1975.

Porter, Stanley E. *Idioms of the Greek New Testament.* 2nd ed. BLG 2. Sheffield: Sheffield Academic Press, 1994.

———. *Verbal Aspect in the Greek of the New Testament, with Reference to Tense and Mood.* SBG 1. New York: Peter Lang, 1989.

Reinhartz, Adele. *The Word in the World: The Cosmological Tale in the Fourth Gospel.* SBLMS 45. Atlanta: Scholars Press, 1992.

Richardson, Alan. *The Gospel according to St. John.* London: SPCK, 1959.

Ridderbos, Herman N. *The Gospel of John: A Theological Commentary.* Translated by John Vriend. Grand Rapids: Eerdmans, 1997.

Robertson, A. T. *A Grammar of the Greek New Testament in the Light of Historical Research.* Nashville: Broadman, 1934.

Ryle, John Charles. *Expository Thoughts on the Gospels, St. John.* 3 vols. London: James Clarke, 1957.

Sanders, E. P. *Judaism: Practice and Belief: 63 BCE–66 CE.* Philadelphia: Fortress, 1992.

Schlatter, Adolf. *Der Evangelist Johannes: Wie er spricht, denkt und glaubt: Ein Kommentar zum Vierten Evangelium.* 4th ed. Stuttgart: Calwer, 1975.

———. *Das Evangelium nach Johannes: Ausgelegt für Bibelleser.* Erläuterungen zum Neuen Testament 3. Stuttgart: Calwer, 1962.

Schnackenburg, Rudolf. *The Gospel according to St. John.* 3 vols. Translated by Kevin Smyth. HTCNT. New York: Herder and Herder, 1968, 1980, 1982.

Smith, D. Moody. *John.* ANTC. Nashville: Abingdon, 1999.

Stevick, Daniel B. *Jesus and His Own: A Commentary on John 13–17.* Grand Rapids: Eerdmans, 2011.

Stibbe, Mark W. G. *John.* Readings: A New Biblical Commentary. Sheffield: JSOT Press, 1993.

Temple, William. *Readings in St. John's Gospel.* London: Macmillan, 1947.

Thompson, Marianne Meye. *The God of the Gospel of John.* Grand Rapids: Eerdmans, 2001.

Van Belle, G., J. G. Ven Der Watt, and P. Maritz, eds. *Theology and Christology in the Fourth Gospel: Essays by Members of the SNTS Johannine Writings Seminar.* BETL 184. Leuven: Leuven University Press, 2005.

Vanhoozer, Kevin J., gen. ed. *Dictionary for Theological Interpretation of the Bible.* London: SPCK/Grand Rapids: Baker, 2005.

———. "The Hermeneutics of I-Witness Testimony: John 21:20–24 and the 'Death' of the 'Author.'" Pages 366–87 in *Understanding Poets and Prophets: Essays in Honor of George Wishart Anderson.* Edited by A. Graeme Auld. JSOTSup 152. Sheffield: Sheffield Academic Press, 1993.

———. *Is There a Meaning in This Text? The Bible, the Reader, and the Morality of Literary Knowledge.* Grand Rapids: Zondervan, 1998.

Wahlde, Urban C. von. *The Gospel and Letters of John.* 3 vols. ECC 3. Grand Rapids: Eerdmans, 2010.

Wallace, Daniel B. *Greek Grammar beyond the Basics: An Exegetical Syntax of the New Testament.* Grand Rapids: Zondervan, 1996.

Westcott, B. F. *The Gospel according to St. John: The Authorized Version with Introduction and Notes.* London: John Murray, 1903.

Whitacre, Rodney A. *John.* IVPNTC 4. Downers Grove, IL: InterVarsity Press, 1999.

Witherington III, Ben. *John's Wisdom: A Commentary on the Fourth Gospel.* Louisville: Westminster John Knox, 1995.

Wright, N. T. *Jesus and the Victory of God.* Christian Origins and the Question of God 2. Minneapolis: Fortress, 1996.

———. *The New Testament and the People of God.* Christian Origins and the Question of God 1. Minneapolis: Fortress, 1992.

———. *The Resurrection of the Son of God.* Christian Origins and the Question of God 3. Minneapolis: Fortress, 2003.

Zahn, Theodor. *Das Evangelium des Johannes.* 6th ed. KNT 4. Leipzig: Deichert, 1921.

John 1:1 – 18

CHAPTER 1

Literary Context

John begins his Gospel with a prologue, a common feature in ancient writings, which serves not only as an introduction to the main character of the biography but also makes the reader aware of the issues and forces at work — both seen and unseen — surrounding the subject's life. Even more, the prologue of John provides the reader with an appropriate vision and presuppositions for the remainder of the narrative. Although it is technically a prologue, it is also a narrative, the narrative of the Word, Jesus Christ, the subject of the biography. This narrative introduction tells the reader *who* Jesus is and *what* Jesus has done; the rest of the Gospel will explain *how* Jesus acts on behalf of God in the human story.

➡ **I. Prologue (1:1 – 18)**
II. The First Week: An Introduction to the Narrative Proper (1:19 – 51)
   A. The Witness of John (1:19 – 34)
   B. The First Disciples (1:35 – 51)

Main Idea

The Gospel begins with a prologue that introduces the narrative. The introduction includes the plight of the world and the arrival of the unique Son, the revelation (Word) of God, through whom the readers are invited to become children of the Father. It is an introduction not merely to the Gospel but also *the* gospel: the Son that God sent dwells among us, the fallen world that God loves.

Translation

John 1:1–18

1a	Introduction to the Word (1–5)	**In the beginning was the Word,**
b	Association	and **the** **Word was with God,**
c	Identification	and **the** **Word was God.**
2a	Inference of 1a–c	**This** **Word was in the beginning with God.**
3a	Agency (+)	Through the Word
b	Event	**everything came into existence,**
c		and
d	Agency (–)	without the Word
e	Emphatic Contrast to 3a	**not one thing came into existence**
f		that has been made.
4a	Assertion	**In the Word was life,**
b	Description	and **the** life was the **light of humanity;**
5a	Action	and **the** **light shined in the darkness,**
b	Reaction	and **the** **darkness did not ☽ recognize it.**
	Witness to the Word (6–8)	
6a	Character Entrance	**There came a man**
b	Description	who was sent from God,
7a	Identification	**his name was John.**
b	Assertion	**This one came as a witness,**
c	Purpose	in order to witness concerning the light,
	Desired Result	so that all might believe through him.
8a	Clarification	**This one was not the light,** but
b	Contrasting Purpose	he came only to witness concerning the light.
9a	Identification of the Word (9–14)	**It was the true light,**
b	Description	the one that gives light to every person,
c	Description	that was coming into the world.
10a	Assertion	**He was in the world,**
b	Interchange: Action	and **the world came into existence through him,** A
c	Interchange: Reaction	and **the world did not know him.** B
11a	Interchange: Action	**He came to what belongs to him,** A
b	Interchange: Reaction	and **his own people did not receive him.** B
12a		But
b	Contrasting Action to 11b	to all who received him,
c	Result	**he gave to them the right to become children of God,**
d	Description of 12b	to those who believe in his name,
13a	Sphere of Origen as Basis:	who were born
b	(–)	not from blood,
c	(–)	nor from the desire of the flesh,
d	(–)	nor from the will of a husband, but
e	(+)	from God.

14a	Event	And **the Word became flesh**
b	Action	and **made his dwelling among us,**
c	Reaction	and **we saw his glory,**
d	Description	glory as the unique Son from the Father,
e	Description	full of grace and truth.
	Uniqueness of the Word (15–18)	
15a	Action	**John witnessed concerning him and has cried out, saying:**
b	Reference	*"This was he of whom I said:*
c	Assertion	*'He who follows me has surpassed me,*
d	Basis	*because he was prior to me.'"*
	Explanation (16–18)	
16a	Basis	Because out of his fullness
b	Result	**we all have received grace in place of grace;**
17a	Explanation	for the law was given through Moses;
b	Contrast	grace and truth came through Jesus Christ.
18a	Main Problem of John's Gospel	**No one has ever seen God;**
b	Main Resolution of John's Gospel	**the unique Son, . . .**
c	Identification	God,
d	Relationship (Description of 1b)	who is in the bosom of the Father,
e	Action	**. . . he revealed him.**

Structure and Literary Form

Numerous scholars have argued that the prologue of John was not part of the original Gospel. But the lack of a formal introduction at 1:19, as well as a similar style and content between the prologue and the rest of the Gospel, makes such a position unlikely. In fact, in the early twentieth century there was an "almost unanimous" consensus in Johannine scholarship favoring the unity of prologue with Gospel, a consensus that was only fortified by contemporary literary criticism.[1] Some have argued against viewing these verses as a formal prologue,[2] and others have proposed a different breakdown of the prologue.[3] But it is difficult to deny an intentional literary purpose to these opening verses, as if the Gospel could have functioned without them. There is no textual evidence that the prologue ever existed apart from the Gospel. There is also internal evidence that enforces the prologue's relation to the rest of the Gospel, not only by subject matter but also in linguistic agreement.[4]

1. Keener, *John*, 1:334.

2. See P. J. Williams, "Not the Prologue of John," *JSNT* 33 (2011): 375 – 86.

3. See J. Ramsey Michaels, *The Gospel of John*, NICNT (Grand Rapids: Eerdmans, 2010), 45 – 46.

4. See Vern S. Poythress, "Testing for Johannine Authorship by Examining the Use of Conjunctions," *WTJ* 46 (1984): 350 – 69.

Exegetical Outline

→ **I. Prologue (1:1 – 18)**
  A. Introduction to the Word (1:1 – 5)
  B. Witness to the Word (1:6 – 8)
  C. Manifestation of the Word (1:9 – 14)
  D. Uniqueness of the Word (1:15 – 18)

Explanation of the Text

The prologue of John is the cornerstone for the entire Gospel, the lens through which the Gospel must be read. It is of great importance that the magnificent language and imagery of the prologue not detract the reader from grasping its functional significance for explaining and directing the rest of the Gospel.

IN DEPTH: The Prologue

Beginnings of ancient books were important. In recent years scholars have become increasingly aware of the significance of beginnings and endings for their understanding of the Gospels "because each provides important clues about the meaning of the material that lies in between."[5] The beginning of narratives, often in the form of a preface or prologue, provides information regarding purpose, method, and contents: key information needed to understand the rest of the narrative.

While all types of narrative beginnings are important, prologues had a uniquely dramatic force in ancient writings. Reminiscent of the openings of classic dramas, prologues were often used to introduce the important characters in the narrative, situate them within the story, and give some understanding of their importance. John clearly does this with the character of his biography. But there is a further function of prologues that is important: prologues would project the plot by explaining both seen and unseen forces within the action. Hooker explains this function: "It was customary for the Greek dramatist to introduce the theme of his play in a 'prologue,' which provided members of his audience with the vital information that would enable them to comprehend the plot, and to understand the unseen forces — the desires and plans of the gods — which were at work in the story."[6] While John does not reveal the desires and plans of the gods, he does, in dramatist fashion, explain the desires and plans of *the* God. The prologue, in this sense, prescribes the reader's compre-

---

5. Morna D. Hooker, "Beginnings and Endings," in *The Written Gospel*, ed. Markus Bockmuehl and Donald A. Hagner (Cambridge: Cambridge University Press, 2005), 184.
6. Ibid., 186.

hension of the plot and explains the behind-the-scene activities of God. This is no mere background issue, for it is rooted in the narrative's own emplotment; yet it is also not merely theological abstraction, for it is connected to real events described by the narrative. What is explained are the "unseen forces" that are at work in and around the real events described by the narrative. Thus, the prologue is guiding the reader to see the invisible (God) in the visible (historical persons and events).

Interestingly, it was common in classic prologues that the deliverer of the prologue, often a character in the play, or in our case the narrator, "would continue to comment on the action of subsequent scenes."[7] Our examination of the prologue, therefore, must be careful to delineate exactly the plot and the unseen forces; moreover, we should expect to be guided in our reading of both of them throughout the Gospel. As we will see, this is exactly what the Gospel of John provides. The prologue is for the reader of John a guide — its own interpreter — to the meaning of the entire Gospel.

Since the prologue's conceptualization of the plot and explanation of unseen forces in the Gospel is central to the rest of the Gospel, a synopsis of the plot told by the prologue is necessary. An examination of the emplotment of the Gospel of John reveals two narrative strands developing throughout the narrative.[8] This two-strand plot is related to each of the forces discussed above: the visible (historical persons and events) and the invisible (God). Neither strand of the plot is complete on its own; in fact, each strand is supported by the other. This is vital information that the prologue reveals to the reader. This is what the prologue is prescribing for the reader and is what must be understood if the remainder of the Gospel's message is to be grasped.

The first of the two strands within the plot is the historical story. This is read plainly from the narrative. The vast majority of the narrative is set in the early first-century CE in Palestine. Thus, this story is historical in that it deals with the Jesus of history. Without taking away the nature of emplotment, the historical story is clearly meant to be read as true accounts of what really happened (cf. 21:24). Reinhartz argues that the historical story is "accessible to all readers of the Fourth Gospel and might be described as the primary 'signified' or content towards which the Gospel as signifier is generally thought to point."[9]

The second of the two strands within the plot is the cosmological story. According to Reinhartz, "specific hints in the Gospel intimate that its story goes well beyond the temporal and geographical boundaries."[10] One need look no

---

7. Ibid.

8. The following is adapted from Adele Reinhartz, *The Word in the World: The Cosmological Tale in the Fourth Gospel,* SBLMS 45 (Atlanta: Scholars Press, 1992).

9. Reinhartz, *Word in the World*, 2.

10. Ibid.

further in the narrative than 1:1. From the very beginning the story told by the Fourth Evangelist is the story of the Word who was with God and was God. The setting of this second story is not Palestine in the first century but the cosmos in eternity itself. Interestingly, the cosmological story is the very first thing introduced to the reader. Since the prologue is intended to guide the reader "to comprehend the plot" and "to understand the unseen forces," it is clear that the cosmological story is central to the cumulative story told by the Fourth Gospel. The cosmological story is not in conflict with the historical story but functions as the metastory, the narrative framework in which the events of the historical story take place. Even more, the events of the historical story are defined and explained by the cosmological story; without the cosmological story the historical story would be incomplete. In this way the story of John is not merely about Jesus of history but must also include Jesus the Word. The two are interconnected in the narrative itself. While the cosmological story narrates the arrival of the Son, the historical story narrates the events of his arrival into the world. Both stories reach their climax in the crucifixion and resurrection of Jesus, where the events of history (Jesus the man; disciples; the world) meet the cosmos (Jesus the one sent from above; God; the coming Paraclete) in a unified way. In this way, John is able to speak simultaneously and integratively of both real history and divine activity.

1:1a In the beginning (Ἐν ἀρχῇ). The opening statement echoes the style, vocabulary, syntax, and general sense of the opening statement of Genesis, "In the beginning God created the heavens and the earth" (Gen 1:1). This is not merely an echo but serves conceptually to embrace John within its biblical-theological framework, a framework in which an explicit connection — a continuation, even development — with the Old Testament is being presented, including both the God of and the story told by the Old Testament. In Genesis "in the beginning" introduces the story of the "old" creation; in John it introduces the story of the "new creation."[11] The opening prepositional phrase is directing the action from the past into the present, focusing its attention on its subject matter about whom this biography speaks.

The term "beginning" (ἀρχή) can also be understood to mean "origin" in the sense of a basic cause. In this sense, the term combines two meanings: "in the beginning of history" and "at the root of the universe."[12] Since this strategy of double meaning is common for John, it is likely being intentionally considered here. The term, therefore, is not referring to the first point in a temporal sequence but to that which lies beyond time.[13] The phrase does more than echo the OT and connect the two testaments; it also frames the rest of the historical narra-

11. F. F. Bruce, *The Gospel of John: Introduction, Exposition, and Notes* (Grand Rapids: Eerdmans, 1983), 29.

12. Leon Morris, *The Gospel according to John*, rev. ed., NICNT (Grand Rapids: Eerdmans, 1995), 65. Cf. Michaels, *John*, 49 – 50.

13. C. K. Barrett, *The Gospel according to John: An Introduction with Commentary and Notes on the Greek Text*, 2nd ed. (Philadelphia: Westminster, 1978), 152.

tive. Our discussion above should make clear that the prologue is here explaining the cosmological strand of the plot of John. Whatever activity occurs in the historical strand of the plot does not remove its being influenced and understood by means of the cosmological strand of the plot. This frame functions to explain what happens in the historical strand — the unseen forces. Even before Jesus is introduced as a son, a brother, or a Jew, he is introduced as being located in the domain of God. The context in which the Fourth Gospel begins is not Palestinian but primordial.

1:1b was the Word (ἦν ὁ λόγος). The imperfect verb "was" (ἦν) provides a controlling force on the connection between "the Word" and "in the beginning." The action of the verb "is conceived of by the language user as being in process ... its internal structure is seen as unfolding."[14] The continuous tense of the verb intentionally denies discernable temporal sequence "in time," for the Word "was" existing before time, or as we shall see in the next clause, "with God." This continuous tense is to be contrasted with the aorist tense form of "was" (ἐγένετο), which becomes an important term in the prologue. Even more, although the meanings of the Greek verbs behind "was" (ἦν, from εἰμί) and "were made" (ἐγένετο, from γίνομαι; e.g., v. 3) often overlap, John repeatedly uses the two verbs in con-

cert to establish something of a contrast (e.g., see 8:58). Thus, when John uses the two verbs in the same context, "was" (ἦν) frequently indicates "existence," whereas "was" (ἐγένετο) indicates "coming into being" or "coming into use." [15] In this way, the verb "was" (ἦν) here implies that the Word be understood as already in existence. "The Word" has no origin, for its (his) existence is beyond time and history.[16]

While the connection to Genesis may have been obvious for the original readers, the subject change from "in the beginning God ..." to "in the beginning was the Word" may have been surprising. The subject about whom the narrative speaks is described by a Greek term that we will simply translate as "Word" (λόγος). Some assume that John's use of this theological term without explanation implies that it was not unfamiliar to his readers.[17] Certainly the term might be recognizable, but its direct connection to Jesus assumes that Jesus, not merely his religious-philosophical context, determines its meaning. Since the term is not common in the NT as a designation of Christ, and even its two occurrences outside of the prologue have genitive modifiers ("Word of life" in 1 John 1:1; "Word of God" in Rev 19:13), it is likely that John will provide an explanation of the term in the Gospel as a whole.

IN DEPTH: "Word"

Much of the discussion surrounding the meaning of "Word" (λόγος) has centered upon its background. Although the background of the term is elusive, in light of its being the first descriptive title given to the subject of John's biography a

14. Stanley E. Porter, *Idioms of the Greek New Testament,* 2nd ed., BLG 2 (Sheffield: Sheffield Academic Press, 1994), 21.
15. Carson, *John,* 114.
16. Hoskyns, *Fourth Gospel,* 137.

17. B. F. Westcott, *The Gospel according to St. John: The Authorized Version with Introduction and Notes* (London: John Murray, 1903), 2; Barrett, *John,* 152.

discussion is in order. Four basic meanings are possible:[18] (1) In the Platonist sense, the term denotes a self-subsistent Form or Idea. (2) In the Stoic sense, the term denotes either the internal concept or external expression of the same. (3) For Plotinus and the Neoplatonists, the term denotes the first, ontologically necessary (noncontingent) emanation from the absolute primary principle of all things and is more commonly spoken of not as Word but as "Mind" (νοῦς). (4) In the OT/Jewish sense, the term denotes the Word of God as Creator of all things, revelatory of God's will and sovereignly effective of his decrees concerning human history. The fourth option, the OT/Jewish background, is the more likely conceptual pool from which John is drawing, reflected in the direct interrelationship between the prologue and OT words, themes, and issues.[19]

While the term "Word" (λόγος) is best understood to have an OT background, we can assume it would have resonated with both Jew and Gentile: "The Jew will remember that 'by the Word of the Lord were the heavens made'; the Greek will think of the rational principle of which all natural laws are particular expressions. Both will agree that this Logos is the starting-point of all things."[20] But John has a much fuller understanding than any of his predecessors, for he provides a "Christian" understanding rooted in the church's understanding of Jesus Christ. That is, while the numerous semantic and conceptual links to "Word" (λόγος) provide some explanatory support for its Johannine meaning, for John certainly had to use known and suitable categories in order to express his meaning, at best they simply reveal the plethora of antecedent associations, and at worst they are unable to fully express the true meaning of the term.[21] Although we find most satisfactory an OT background for the "Word," we are even more persuaded that John is not relying primarily on a background but on a foreground. For it is Jesus who embodies the "Word" (λόγος) in his flesh. It is likely for this reason that after 1:14 the term is never used again.

This first descriptive title of the subject of the Gospel conveys a meaning rooted in an OT background and a christological foreground that entails the following descriptions. "Word" reflects the truth that it is the very nature of God to reveal himself. God is not to be thought of as removed and indifferent, for he reveals himself.[22] In light of Jesus, the Word of God is intentionally personal. Rooted in the OT's use of the term, the Word is God's self-expression in creation,

18. The following is adapted from John F. McHugh, *A Critical and Exegetical Commentary on John 1 – 4*, ICC (London: T&T Clark, 2009), 7 – 9.

19. See Ben Witherington III, *John's Wisdom: A Commentary on the Fourth Gospel* (Louisville: Westminster John Knox, 1995), 19.

20. William Temple, *Readings in St. John's Gospel* (London: Macmillan, 1947), 4.

21. Cf. Carson, *John*, 116; Barrett, *John*, 154.

22. Morris, *John*, 66.

revelation, and salvation.[23] The personification of Word makes it a perfect categorical description for God's ultimate self-disclosure, his Son. For this reason the "Word" encapsulates Jesus's entire ministry in a way that demands that all his works and words be understood within this framework. Even still, the term is only a place holder, the provisional designation of something — or someone — that will be filled in later.[24] The entire Gospel is needed to explain this term.

1:1c and the Word was with God, and the Word was God (καὶ ὁ λόγος ἦν πρὸς τὸν θεόν, καὶ θεὸς ἦν ὁ λόγος). As important as it was for John to provide a simple statement of the Word's existence, he could not for long withhold his relation to God. The Word "was with God" (ἦν πρὸς τὸν θεόν). Several grammatical details need explaining. In this clause "was" (ἦν) carries a different sense than the previous use: while "was the Word" denotes existence, "was with" denotes presence.[25] The prepositional phrase "with God" (πρὸς τὸν θεόν) has an ambiguity that can suggest both presence ("with") and relationship ("toward").[26] Although the preposition with the accusative classically implies motion ("toward"), it can also be used in the sense of accompaniment, primarily due to the general weakening in Hellenistic Greek of the distinction between prepositions of motion and location (e.g., between the prepositions "into" [εἰς] and "in" [ἐν]; cf. 1:18).[27] The preposition πρός ("with") was being used in the place of the preposition παρά ("beside/near/with") to communicate presence (cf. 17:5).[28] The preposition's meaning, however, is not merely controlled by our understanding of its use in Hellensitic Greek, for the verb to which the preposition relates can also override a preposition's traditional force.[29] Thus, while πρός with the accusative is normally transitive ("toward"), the stative verb ἦν ("was") overrides the transitive force of the preposition, yielding the translation "with" and reflecting the idea of presence.

IN DEPTH: God

While often taken for granted, the meaning of God (θεός) is not quite so obvious. It was a term that the early Christians, especially the NT writers, spent a lot of energy wrestling with. "The word *theos* for Greek-speakers (and its equivalents in other languages spoken in the first century) was not univocal, and the early Christians made out a fairly thorough case for understanding it in a particular

23. Carson, *John*, 116.
24. Barth, *Witness to the Word*, 19–27.
25. Cf. Brown, *John*, 1:4.
26. Brodie, *John*, 137.
27. Brown, *John*, 1:4. Barrett, *John*, 155, describes this meaning as "unquestionable in New Testament Greek."
28. BDF § 239.1.
29. Daniel B. Wallace, *Greek Grammar beyond the Basics: An Exegetical Syntax of the New Testament* (Grand Rapids: Zondervan, 1996), 358–59.

sense."[30] Usually, especially in John 1:1c, the meaning of God is assumed and the meaning of "Word" (i.e., Jesus) is what needs to be defined. But if in the statement "the Word was God" the word "God" predicates something about the Word, the nature of the predication needs to be determined.

Several things can be stated regarding the meaning of *God* (θεός). First, *God* "is not a proper name, but a term that makes a predication about the person or reality named."[31] Because in Hebrew, Greek, and English *God* is used as a name or designation of a specific figure and as a label for a class of being, it often functions like a name, like *Dad* or *Mom* function for children as the name of their parent, even though neither label is the parent's name.

Second, as a predicating label, *God* in the first century would carry several different meanings: deity in general, a particular heathen god or goddess, pagan deities at large, angels, human rulers or judges, persons of valor or rank, god-like persons, as well as the one true God of Israel.[32] But since the determinative context for John is the OT, the meaning of the label *God* must be derived from its OT meaning. In the OT there is only one God, defined with qualifying phrases such as "God of gods" or "Most High God" in order to make clear to whom or to what *God* refers (e.g., Deut 10:17; Dan 3:26). Thus, it is best to view the entire OT as providing the qualifying meaning of the God being referred to in 1:1.

Third, since *God* could function as a qualifying predication, the specific and descriptive characterization of a figure (e.g., "Word") would be attained through the delineation of certain functions or activities rather than through the mere use of the term *God*. That is, the meaning of *God* is rooted not in "what God is" but in "who God is"; not in the "nature of God" (i.e., Greek philosophy) but in the "identity of God" (i.e., the God of Israel).[33] In this sense, *God* is defined not by ontological categories but by relational or personal categories.[34] Thus, even when speaking of attributes of divinity, such as eternal existence, the power to create, and omniscience, we must say that such attributes belong to God, not to "divinity." "If 'divinity' or 'divine status' is predicated of a figure, it will necessarily imply a relationship to the one God."[35]

Who is, therefore, God according to John? While a full description will be established throughout this commentary, a brief summary is in order. In almost every case the term *God* is applied in John to the God of Israel. However, the

30. N. T. Wright, *The New Testament and the People of God*, Christian Origins and the Question of God 1 (Minneapolis: Fortress, 1992), xiv.

31. Marianne Meye Thompson, *The God of the Gospel of John* (Grand Rapids: Eerdmans, 2001), 22.

32. Murray J. Harris, *Jesus as God: The New Testament Use*

of Theos *in Reference to Jesus* (Grand Rapids: Baker, 1992), 29.

33. Richard Bauckham, *God Crucified: Monotheism and Christology in the New Testament* (Grand Rapids: Eerdmans, 1998), 8.

34. Ibid., 8–9.

35. Thompson, *God of the Gospel of John*, 47–48.

most frequent characterization of God, derived from Jesus's own words, is Father, for Jesus calls God "my Father" and refers to him regularly as "the Father" or "the Father who sent me." The word "Father" is the most common term in John, occuring about 120 times.[36] Except in 1:1 and 1:18, every other use of "God" (eighty-three times) in John is either explicitly referring to the Father (e.g., 5:18; 6:27; 8:41 – 42) or implicitly referring to the Father, based upon (1) a contextual connection with sonship (e.g., 1:12 – 13, 34, 49; 3:16 – 18, 36; 5:25; 10:36; 11:4, 27, 52); (2) an accompanying mention of the Father (e.g., 4:23 – 24; 5:42 – 44; 6:27 – 29, 32 – 33, 45 – 46; 8:42, 54; 10:35 – 36; 11:40 – 41; 13:3; 14:1 – 2; 16:2 – 3, 27; 17:3 – 5; 20:17); or (3) the qualifying adjective "alone" (μόνος; e.g., 5:44; 17:3).[37] The overwhelming evidence is that God in John is the Father. Even the prologue implies such a qualifier, though from the perspective of the "children of God" (τέκνα θεοῦ; 1:12 – 13). The fact that 1:1 and 1:18 are the only two occurrences for which there might not be a direct allusion is almost certainly for rhetorical purposes. By leaving God implicitly undefined, the focus is placed solely on the Word. Since "God" is known by his attributes, the Word will make the Father known (1:18), with 1:1 functioning as the opening statement about the Word, the subject of the biography.

By understanding the meaning of "God" to be a predication of identity, the second clause of 1:1 is now made clearer. The statement "and the Word was with God" (καὶ ὁ λόγος ἦν πρὸς τὸν θεόν) must be explained further than mere presence. In this context "with" denotes personal intercourse rather than simply spatial juxtaposition or personal accompaniment. That is, the preposition "with" (πρός), when used with divine persons, must point to eternal intercommunion.[38] But the prepositional phrase is intending to delineate the Word — which may explain why this verse does not make explicit reference to the Father. The Word was first described "in the beginning" and now "with God." The former speaks of location, whereas the latter speaks of belonging. The

Word belongs to God.[39] This must first be grasped before the relation can be defined.

The final clause of 1:1 unequivocally posits how the Word belongs to God: "and the Word was God" (καὶ θεὸς ἦν ὁ λόγος). Two issues need to be addressed regarding this third clause: the anarthrous "God" (θεός) and the nature of the predication. The anarthrous "God" has led some to imply the Word is less than God, a "god." But several reasons can be given to show that "God" in this third clause is the Most High God, the Father. First, though an argument from silence, if John wanted to define Jesus as less than God — as a god — he certainly chose a poor term to do it. There is a perfect word for "divine" (θεῖος) that would have given Jesus a

36. Ibid., 228.
37. Harris, *Jesus as God*, 53 – 55. 20:28 is an exception.
38. Ibid., 57.

39. Karl Barth, *Witness to the Word: A Commentary on John 1*, ed. Walter Fürst, trans. Geoffrey W. Bromiley (Grand Rapids: Eerdmans, 1986; repr., Eugene, OR: Wipf & Stock, 2003), 20 – 21.

lesser-than-God "god" status, clearly distinguishing God from god, or "the Word" from "God." Second, and this is not an argument from silence, such a designation in 1:1c of the Word (i.e., Jesus) being a lesser god would stand in direct contradiction to the titles, roles, and relationship explicated by the remainder of the Gospel.

But there is a third reason that is directly related to the grammatical construction of the clause. This clause, "the Word was God" (θεὸς ἦν ὁ λόγος), contains a predicate nominative: the subject (the known entity) is "the Word" (ὁ λόγος), the predicate is "God" (θεός), and the copula is "was" (ἦν). Normally a predicate nominative is anarthrous and follows the verb. In this case the anarthrous predicate is before the verb. An established rule defines what this structure communicates: an anarthrous preverbal predicate nominative "is normally qualitative, sometimes definite, and only rarely indefinite."[40] Not only is an indefinite meaning for "God" (θεός) rare (i.e., "a god") but it would also need to be reflected by the context — which it is clearly not!

What, then, is the distinction between qualitative and definite uses, and how is it recognized? Beginning with the latter, the predicate can be recognized as qualitative or definite only by the context. Not only does 1:1b demand a distinction (qualitative) between God and Word, but the vast majority of definite anarthrous preverbal predicate nominatives are monadic (i.e., one-of-a-kind terms, such as titles), in genitive constructions, or are proper names, thus minimizing the likelihood that this predicate nominative is definite. The most grammatically probable and theologically accurate candidate for "God" (θεός) is qualitative. A qualitative use means that "the Word" contains all the attributes and qualities that "God" (1:1b) contains yet remains distinct. That is, while being God, the Word is not so equated with God that the Word alone encapsulates God (this would be a definite use). This is not to deny the affirmation that the Word *was* God; it is, rather, to affirm the denial that the Word is God *in total*. The Word is fully God, but God is not fully the Word. This is the qualitative nature of the predicate nominative in 1:1c. Theologians have expressed this qualitative nature of the Word as God: the Word shares the *essence* of the Father, though the Word is not the *person* of the Father. The Word is God but is not the Father. The remainder of the Gospel is needed to qualify the nature of the relation.

John 1:1 is clearly triadic, with each of the three clauses having the same subject, "the Word" (ὁ λόγος), and the same verb, "was" (ἦν). The three statements taken together are the foundation upon which the message of the Gospel rests. Ever since Chrysostom, commentators have discussed the three affirmations each clause makes. We have argued that the Word is described in three related ways: the *preexistence* of the Word (1:1a), the *presence* of the Word (1:1b), and the *person* of the Word (1:1c). The three clauses move progressively to define the Word in relation to God, with the third clause providing a climactic and qualified statement of the Word's participation in/as God. "God must be understood from the outset as the 'one who speaks,' the God who reveals himself."[41] In a real way, then, the Gospel of John begins: "Thus saith the Lord...." Every word from God, starting from the "beginning" (Gen 1:1), has culminated in this definitive word (Heb 1:1 – 2), the Word of God.

1:2 This Word was in the beginning with God (οὗτος ἦν ἐν ἀρχῇ πρὸς τὸν θεόν). The demonstrative pronoun "this" (οὗτος) is commonly used at the beginning of a narrative to refer to a person who has just been mentioned.[42] While it might

---

40. Wallace, *Greek Grammar*, 262.
41. Bultmann, *John*, 35.
42. BDAG 740.

also be translated "this one," thus showing the emphasis assumed by the pronoun in the context of this discourse, it is often translated with personal overtones as "this man" or more comfortably translated as a simple pronoun, "he." However, what the translation "he" gains in its ability to describe Jesus as a person (which v. 14 will make explicit), it loses with regard to its antecedent, the Word.

Since it is more than likely that John is beginning his Gospel in an exegetically coalescing way with Genesis 1:1 – 5, almost in commentary form, it is best to allow pronouns which have "the Word" as the antecedent to remain reflective of the Word and not to impose too early the personal overtone. Moving too quickly to v. 14 removes vv. 1 – 5 from their exegetical heritage. In this way, the full explanation of what God was doing in Genesis by his word will be allowed to be manifest in the Word without any loss to the incarnation of the Word in v. 14. In order to maintain a remnant of the antecedent, we shall translate all such pronouns as "the Word."[43]

After refocusing on "the Word," the remainder of the verse is a repetition of the statements made in the first two clauses of v. 1. While the language is similar to v. 1, the subject has necessarily shifted contexts. From the viewpoint of the Gospel, that which was from "the beginning" is related directly to that which continued in the coming and work of Jesus Christ in time — and still continues. In this sense, v. 2 serves to declare that "though the 'score' of the prologue may be that of Genesis 1, the content is that of the Gospel."[44] Verse 2 resituates "this Word" into the context already described in a new way and makes certain that v. 1 is never to be read merely as an allusion to Genesis 1 but as preceding Genesis 1, as the Word will claim for himself (cf. 8:58).[45]

1:3 Through the Word everything came into existence, and without the Word not one thing came into existence that has been made (πάντα δι᾽ αὐτοῦ ἐγένετο, καὶ χωρὶς αὐτοῦ ἐγένετο οὐδὲ ἕν. ὃ γέγονεν). Just as the Word is in relation to God, so also is the Word to be seen in relation to the entire world. This relation is not from afar but intimate, for in two parallel clauses, the first positive and the second negative, the Word is described as the one through whom existence came. The Word did not come toward creation; creation has come through the Word. The entire verse is centered around the threefold use of a verb twice translated as "came into existence" (ἐγένετο) and once as "has been made" (γέγονεν), the difference merely being a reflection of the change in aspectual force. The aorists look back to the moment when creation took place, whereas the perfect looks forward to the significance of the event in the present.[46] The verbal pressure of "existence" (ἐγένετο) reflects the "pure expression of the idea of creation; it excludes both the idea of emanation, and the conception of an original duality of light and darkness, according to which the world was formed by a tragic collision of both of these powers."[47] The creation through the Word is not the arrangement of chaotic stuff but creation *ex nihilo*.[48]

It is important to note that the verb "made" (ἐγένετο) is consistently used to describe creation in the LXX of Genesis 1, where it serves as

---

43. It is interesting to note that while modern translations prefer to use "he," older translations more commonly used "it" (e.g., the Geneva Bible).

44. Herman N. Ridderbos, *The Gospel of John: A Theological Commentary*, trans. John Vriend (Grand Rapids: Eerdmans, 1997), 25.

45. Adolf Schlatter, *Der Evangelist Johannes: Wie er spricht, denkt und glaubt: Ein Kommentar zum Vierten Evangelium*, 4th ed. (Stuttgart: Calwer, 1975), 2 – 3.

46. Francis J. Moloney, *The Gospel of John*, SP 4 (Collegeville, MN: Liturgical Press, 1998), 35 – 36.

47. Bultmann, *John*, 37 – 38.

48. Note the repetition of "and there was" (καὶ ἐγένετο) in Gen 1:3, 5, 8, 9, 11, 13, 15, 19, 20, 23, 24, 30.

a foundational term that expresses the creation power and activity of God. The use of this term in the prologue is employing a significant intentionality. It is also clear that the eleven occurrences of the verb (or a related term) in the prologue (see vv. 3, 6, 10, 12, 14, 15, 17, 18) in its variously translated forms, "made/came/became" (γίνομαι), is intentionally deploying the same functional meaning initiated by the use of the term in its twenty-three occurrences in Genesis 1 (see Gen 1:3, 5, 6, 8, 9, 11, 13, 14, 15, 19, 20, 23, 24, 30, 31).[49] This term's grounding in Genesis will be carefully established in the prologue and utilized throughout the Gospel to take on a "creation" emphasis in order to declare the transformative power and work of Jesus Christ (see comments on v. 17). The term's "numerous nuances relating to being and manner of being" are utilized by the Gospel to help describe in historical terms the cosmological actions of the Son of God.[50]

The first clause describes the coming into existence of all things through the Word. It begins with a substantival adjective "everything" (πάντα) that, since it is anarthrous, almost certainly emphasizes things in their individual form — the existence of every single thing. Before John states in v. 10 that "the world" as a whole "came into existence through him" (ὁ κόσμος δι' αὐτοῦ ἐγένετο), he first describes the act of creation in all of its detail. The prepositional phrase "through him" (δι' αὐτοῦ) stands firmly between "everything" and "existence," which establishes a "boundary within which everything that is in the world finds itself."[51] Not only did the Word create "everything" but also "everything" has a necessarily mediated relation-

ship to everything else for it depends upon the Word of God. This mediation must also include God the Father.

The second clause describes the inability of anything to come into existence without the Word. This clause is emphatic with its immediate repetition of the first clause in the negative. The negation is not mere emphasis but brings to completion the idea of the totality of the Word's position (e.g., "with God" and "was God") and power (i.e., as mediator). Life itself, as v. 4 will explain further, belongs neither to nature nor to humanity independently. Their existence is because of their relation to the Word of God.[52]

The exact relation between v. 3 and v. 4 is unclear, most notably concerning the last phrase: "that has been made" (ὃ γέγονεν). There are two possible ways of punctuating vv. 3 – 4: (1) a full stop is placed at the end of v. 3, after "that has been made"(ὃ γέγονεν); or (2) a full stop is placed after "not one thing" (οὐδὲ ἕν), and takes the words "that [which has] has been made" (ὃ γέγονεν) as the initial words of the sentence in v. 4. Option 1 is to be preferred for making much better contextual sense. For example, and most importantly, option 2 would require "that has been made" (ὃ γέγονεν) to be referring to the incarnation not creation. Such a transition is overwhelmingly unlikely. Furthermore, option 2 is loaded with grammatical difficulties, reflected by the many manuscript adjustments, that are nearly insurmountable.[53]

1:4 In the Word was life, and the life was the light of humanity (ἐν αὐτῷ ζωὴ ἦν, καὶ ἡ ζωὴ ἦν τὸ φῶς τῶν ἀνθρώπων). The role of the Word in creation

---

49. Cf. Jan A. du Rand, "The Creation Motif in the Fourth Gospel: Perspectives on Its Narratological Function within a Judaistic Background," in *Theology and Christology in the Fourth Gospel: Essays by Members of the SNTS Johannine Writings Seminar*, ed. G. van Belle, J. G. Van der Watt, and P. Maritz, BETL 184 (Leuven: Leuven University Press, 2005), 21 – 46 (38 – 40).

50. BDAG 196.

51. Barth, *Witness to the Word*, 34; cf. Cyril of Alexandria, *John* 1.5; Chrysostom, *John* 5.2.22.

52. Hoskyns, *Fourth Gospel*, 142.

53. See Bruce M. Metzger, *A Textual Commentary on the Greek New Testament*, 2nd ed. (Stuttgart: Deutsche Bibelgesellschaft, 1994), 168.

(existence) found in v. 3 is further manifested in v. 4. If the Word mediates existence, he also qualitatively defines life. Life was found "in him/it/the Word" (ἐν αὐτῷ). Such a statement transitions from creation in total to the creation of life, the pinnacle of creation. The past tense "was" (ἦν) is continually used by John (six times in vv. 1 – 4), but this is not describing a past-tense reality. In contrast, "the tense is to be understood from the perspective of one who looks at the present in light of its origin, which is antecedent to all human experience."[54] The "life" that was in the Word is still in the Word. Life is not mediated "through" the Word (δι' αὐτοῦ) but is "in" the Word (ἐν αὐτῷ). Jesus embodies life. "Life" (ζωή) is an important term for John. It occurs thirty-six times in John, whereas no other NT writing uses it more than seventeen times (Revelation). Thus, over twenty-five percent of all the uses of the term in the NT are found in John.

John's prologue is made especially difficult with the use of such loaded terms, from which interpreters can find many interesting parallels.[55] In light of vv. 1 – 3 it is quite logical to assume that "life" is in connection to creation and thus refers to physical life. Yet in the remainder of the Gospel the term is related specifically to salvation. "Life" is either resurrection life or spiritual life that is its foretaste.[56] While interpreters feel forced to decide between these two options for the use of the term here, to separate the connection between the Word (Jesus) and life in the context of the prologue is to create a false dichotomy between physical and spiritual realities — something that is foreign to the Gospel. In fact, as we will see, it is quite routine for John to use a word in one way and to be simultaneously intending a further, secondary meaning (on "impressions," see Introduction). As the prologue's terse

introduction of Jesus as "life," it must be referring to life in the fullest of all its possible senses. Only in this way is an understanding given to passages which speak of the life Jesus brings (e.g., 10:10), a life rooted from the beginning and ultimately in God himself.

John transitions in v. 4b from the nature of the Word to the nature of the life: "the life was the light of humanity" (ἡ ζωὴ ἦν τὸ φῶς τῶν ἀνθρώπων). The added article before "life" is best understood as an anaphoric use of the article, which denotes a previous reference.[57] The meaning of life has not changed but is being carried forward. Also, the genitive modifying "light," "of humanity" (τῶν ἀνθρώπων), is best understood as an objective genitive: the light "for" humanity. Calling forth "light" was God's first act in creation (Gen 1:3), and it is by embodying the "light" that Jesus acts on behalf of creation. The ambiguity of the phrase makes the connection to Genesis 1:1 – 5 of crucial importance, especially because this is the first mention of humanity. "Everything is still totally qualitative: life in its absolute meaning, light as the gift that makes human life possible, and humans as such in their dependence on the light without reference to place and time."[58] The text is not describing a specific relation to the light nor particular recipients of the light. Rather, what Genesis 1:1 – 5 makes implicit reference to in v. 4 is the light that people require to live, whether they are aware of it or not.[59]

1:5 and the light shined in the darkness, and the darkness did not recognize it (καὶ τὸ φῶς ἐν τῇ σκοτίᾳ φαίνει, καὶ ἡ σκοτία αὐτὸ οὐ κατέλαβεν). The discussion shows a progression from general (qualitative) in v. 4 to specific in v. 5. Even more, the verse shows with intentional ambiguity the

54. Ridderbos, *John*, 38.
55. See Keener, *John*, 1:381 – 87.
56. Carson, *John*, 119.
57. Wallace, *Greek Grammar*, 217 – 20.
58. Ridderbos, *John*, 38.
59. Cf. Martin Luther, *Sermons on the Gospel of St. John*, LW 22 – 24, 69 (St. Louis: Concordia, 1957 – 2009), 22:10.

movement from a context of physical creation to a context of spiritual salvation. The intentional play between creation and salvation in the verses above is important here, with the Genesis 1 connection by the prologue depicting something like a new creation. At the first creation, God "spoke" into a darkness that "covered the face of the deep" (Gen 1:2) and said: "Let there be light" (Gen 1:3a). "And there was light" (Gen. 1:3b). At the second creation the light — the Life, the Word — "shined in the darkness." While Genesis reflects the lack of light's presence, John reflects the manifestation of light's power. The present tense "shined" (φαίνει), translated as a historical present, reveals the continuation of light from the Light.

But the relationship of the light to the darkness is not merely one of physical conflict. The verb in the second clause can be translated as either "overcome" or "recognize" (κατέλαβεν). The former emphasizes the physical confrontation between light and darkness and explains that the darkness could not "overcome" or "overpower" the light. This is certainly a viable meaning based upon the nature of the verb and was assumed to be the meaning by most Greek commentators since Origen. Yet the latter rightly emphasizes the developing narrative context, even in the prologue,[60] and the misunderstandings that will become so prevalent throughout the Gospel between Jesus and his opponents. The latter translation, "recognize," more comprehensively grasps the implicit narrative context without denying the fact that such an encounter is a conflict to "overcome." This understanding of "recognize" (κατέλαβεν) so reflects the narrative context that Morris claims the verb almost assumes the reader will "think of darkness as equivalent to certain people, or perhaps the human race at large."[61] The

implicit narrative is what the Gospel will reveal in its remainder: Christ's appearance as the "Light of the World" is met with direct and robust confrontation by the darkness (cf. 3:19–20; 8:12; 9:5; 12:35). While the idea of "overcoming" the light is necessarily present (see comments on 12:31), it is not merely a physical confrontation that is being referenced. The greater confrontation, the one more deeply rooted, is the spiritual encounter. John has probably deliberately chosen, as he often does, a term that is speaking simultaneously on multiple levels (on "impressions," see Introduction). In this way the opening section of the prologue concludes.

1:6 There came a man who was sent from God, his name was John (Ἐγένετο ἄνθρωπος ἀπεσταλμένος παρὰ θεοῦ, ὄνομα αὐτῷ Ἰωάννης). A new section begins in v. 6. A new introducion is needed. This new section continues the introduction a prologue performs. As we stated above, the prologue is guiding the reader to see the invisible (God) in the visible (historical persons and events). The invisible Word was introduced. Now something visible is being introduced: "a man" (ἄνθρωπος). And it is this man who serves as a witness to the Word. In vv. 6–7 the witness, John, is introduced; in v. 8 the nature of John's witness is explained.

The word translated "came" (ἐγένετο) echoes back to v. 3 where it is used three times. We argued above that v. 3 was centered upon this term, where it expressed the creative force of God *ex nihilo*. While there is undoubtedly an intended contrast between the Word and John regarding the use of this term, the very visible presence of the term in v. 6 suggests that a related force is also at work here.[62] The related force is the work of God "creating" a witness to the Word. John could have

---

60. Edward W. Klink III, "Light of the World: Cosmology and the Johannine Literature," in *Cosmology and New Testament Theology*, ed. Jonathan T. Pennington and Sean M. McDonough, LNTS 355 (London: T&T Clark, 2009), 81–82.

61. Morris, *John*, 76.
62. The remainder of the prologue will confirm the importance of this verb.

used the imperfect "was" (ἦν), which would have described John from the inside. But John chose the aorist which "signals that the story is moving into historical time...."[63]

The end of the clause brings explanatory force to what the aorist implies: John was sent from God. The periphrastic construction, "who was sent from God" (ἀπεσταλμένος παρὰ θεοῦ), not only coordinates effectively with the creative force of "came" (ἐγένετο), but the perfect passive participle also places stress on the abiding quality of the one sent rather than on the once-for-all fact of the mission. Even the verb for "sent" (ἀπεσταλμένος) was traditionally used to entrust, charge, or commission someone with a message or task.[64] In the majority of the term's uses in secular Greek and the LXX, all the emphasis is on the authority of the sender, and the sender is almost universally divine. It has been described as "a technical term for divine authorization."[65] Even the preposition "from" (παρά) instead of "by" (ὑπό) gives emphasis to the envoy's origin rather than to his commissioner. Fitting with the prologue's intention to explain unseen forces, John finds a point of connection with the historical world but carefully portrays how even this history is subsumed under the creative (cosmological) working of God (see comments on v. 17).

The importance of this transition from vv. 1 – 5 to v. 6 cannot be missed. The prologue "plunges us" into the inside of history that has until now been seen only from the outside and only through and under the Word.[66] The transition is not a mere entrance into history but a focus upon a person who is only introduced by the following: "His name was John" (ὄνομα αὐτῷ Ἰωάννης). The name "John" without any qualification is used eighteen times in the Gospel and on every occasion refers to John the Baptist.[67] The lack of detail might imply two things. First, it might imply that the audience was aware of John the Baptist. Second, it might imply that the focus was as much on the task of the person as it was his identity (see comments on 19:35). Both of these are probably intended here and for a related reason. In a manner similar to the Synoptics and early Christian preaching (Acts 1:21 – 22; 10:37; 13:24 – 25), when the evangelist approaches the public ministry of Jesus, he begins with the witness of John the Baptist. The context in mind here is not first-century history but salvation history, in which others commissioned or "sent" from God served as forerunners of God and for God: Moses (Exod 3:10 – 15), the prophets (e.g., Isa 6:8; Jer 1:4 – 7), and even, in the Gospel of John, Jesus himself (3:17). Why is there a need for a witness to the Word? "This witness was ordained, not for Christ's sake but for ours," for John the Baptist is for us "the herald of divine grace."[68]

1:7 This one came as a witness, in order to witness concerning the light, so that all might believe through him (οὗτος ἦλθεν εἰς μαρτυρίαν, ἵνα μαρτυρήσῃ περὶ τοῦ φωτός, ἵνα πάντες πιστεύσωσιν δι᾽ αὐτοῦ). The use of "this one" (οὗτος) for John is identical to its use in v. 2 for the Word. Since it is often used at the beginning of a narrative, its use here gives warrant for seeing the beginning of a new section at v. 6 (cf. v. 2). The force of "came" (ἦλθεν) is certainly enforced by the divine commissioning in v. 6; the fact that he "came" is a result of

---

63. McHugh, *John*, 21.

64. Thomas Aquinas, *Commentary on the Gospel of John*, 3 vols., trans. Fabian Larcher and James A. Weisheipl (Washington, DC: The Catholic University of America Press, 2010), 1:47, suggests the term is connected to the office (not nature) of an angel, a messenger of God.

65. Karl H. Rengstorf, "ἀποστέλλω," *TDNT* 1:399.

66. Barth, *Witness to the Word*, 48.

67. This does not include the four occurrences of "Simon, son of John" (1:42; 21:15, 16, 17).

68. John Calvin, *The Gospel according to St. John 1 – 10*, ed. David W. Torrance and Thomas F. Torrance, trans. T. H. L. Parker, CNTC 4 (Grand Rapids: Eerdmans, 1995), 13 – 14.

his being "sent from God." The task for which John was commissioned is clearly stated: he came as a witness. Although the preposition "as a" (εἰς) can denote purpose, it is best left for the second clause. In the first clause the vocational use of the preposition suggests it be translated "as a witness" (εἰς μαρτυρίαν).[69] This translation coincides well with the commissioning in v. 6.

The term "witness" (μαρτυρία) is important to the Fourth Gospel, and several studies have examined it at length.[70] The term is best understood to carry its primary, legal meaning of testifying or bearing witness to the true state of affairs by one who has fuller knowledge or superior position.[71] The theme of witness will be continually developed throughout the Gospel. While the term "witness" certainly bears much theological weight, it never does so in isolation from the circumstancial accuracy to which it points.[72] In fact, to separate the two is to misunderstand the nature of "witness" (see comments on 21:24).[73] At the least, v. 7 is introducing the position and task of the witness to the Word, a man named John. The position of John, not his person, is the most important thing.

If the first clause defines the commission of John — as a witness, the second clause states the object to which John witnesses — the light. The second clause contains the first of two "in order to/ so that" (ἵνα) clauses that function epexegetically with "as a witness" (εἰς μαρτυρίαν). The indefinite expression "concerning the light" (περὶ τοῦ φωτός) gives minimal content of the testimony itself, but in light of vv. 4 – 5 makes clear that the focus of the testimony is the Word. Since the meaning of "light"

in vv. 6 – 8 can only be understood in reference to what came before (vv. 4 – 5) and what follows (v. 9) in the prologue, the apparent abruptness of v. 6 or the argument that vv. 6 – 8 were added later must be given less credence.

Finally, the third clause states the purpose of the witness. This second "in order to/so that" (ἵνα) clause is dependent on the first and demands that the witness not be viewed as an end in itself. The term "believe" (πιστεύσωσιν) could be translated as an ingressive aorist ("might come to believe"), though the theological weight of John's definitive witness makes the constative aorist preferable even if more vague in English. In light of the prologue's intention, the clause seems to be referring to the all-inclusive witness of John, not merely his local witness. The local witness of John will follow in vv. 35 – 42. Here the cooperative tension between the historical and cosmological strands of the plot is helpful. While John the Baptist clearly has a real and necessary historical impact, he is also part of the larger act of God in salvation history — a theme picked up by the other Gospels. While it is possible grammatically for "through him" (δι᾽ αὐτοῦ) to be referring to the Word, it is almost certainly referring instead to John. In the Gospel of John people do not believe *through* Jesus but *in* him. As Westcott explains, John is described here in the office of prophet, or more specifically, as "the completed type of the prophet."[74]

1:8 This one was not the light, but he came only to witness concerning the light (οὐκ ἦν ἐκεῖνος τὸ φῶς, ἀλλ᾽ ἵνα μαρτυρήσῃ περὶ τοῦ φωτός). As much as there is a relation beween John and the object to

---

69. BDAG 290.

70. See, for example, Andrew T. Lincoln, *Truth on Trial: The Lawsuit Motif in the Fourth Gospel* (Peabody, MA: Hendrickson, 2000).

71. Cf. Bultmann, *John*, 50 – 51; McHugh, *John*, 24 – 25.

72. Contra Andrew T. Lincoln, "The Beloved Disciple as Eyewitness and the Fourth Gospel as Witness," *JSNT* 85 (2002): 3 – 26.

73. Morris, *John*, 80, summaries well the seven witnesses to Jesus in the Gospel: each of the three persons of the Trinity, the works of Jesus, Scripture, John the Baptist, and a collection of human witnesses.

74. Westcott, *John*, 5.

which he witnesses, there is also a contrast. After stating what John is not — he is not the light — the restatement of clause two from v. 7 gives additional emphasis to the object to which he is a witness. Our translation is marked by the contextual nuance of this restatement. As important as the witness is, he is still only a witness. This negation and restatement not only make emphatic the contrast between the witness and the object but may also have been a statement into a historical context that had John the Baptist in an exalted position. However, if there were historical circumstances demanding a response to the Baptist's ministry, the narrative of John does not directly refer to them. His greatness can "only" be seen as derivative, entirely defined by the object to which he witnesses.

1:9 It was the true light, the one that gives light to every person, that was coming into the world (Ἦν τὸ φῶς τὸ ἀληθινόν, ὃ φωτίζει πάντα ἄνθρωπον, ἐρχόμενον εἰς τὸν κόσμον). The Word was introduced, rooted firmly in the cosmological strand of the plot of the Gospel. The witness to the Word was made manifest, being distinguished from the Word but centralized as directing the movement of the historical strand of the plot of the Gospel. Having plunged the Word into the history of the world, the prologue is now able to make manifest the Word, leading to the coalescence of the cosmological and historical strands of the plot — the incarnation (v. 14). The focus has now shifted so that the work of the Word is now a work in the world. This shift in focus gives warrant to considering vv. 9–14 as a distinct section within the prologue. As part of the prologue, this section is guiding the reader to see the invisible in the visible with the climax being the incarnation — the visible manifestation of the Word.

The coalescence of the cosmological and his-

torical strands of the plot forces John to speak of them both in a sentence that becomes somewhat awkward. The first clause implicitly transitions to the Word with the phrase, "It was the true light" (Ἦν τὸ φῶς τὸ ἀληθινόν). The implied pronoun of the verb is the subject of the predicate nominative, and the antecedent of the pronoun can be no other than the Word. As we discussed in vv. 1–5, the Word has not been personalized yet into Jesus (not until v. 17); we have been sensitive in our translation to allow the prologue to continue to develop the Word until the Word becomes flesh; hence our translation of the implied pronoun as a neuter "it." After making a sharp distinction between the light and the witness in v. 8, it is certain that the "it" in v. 9 is no other than the Word. Further evidence for this is provided by the lack of a personal introduction of the Word and, more obviously, by the fact that the man named John cannot be described as "coming into the world." The light is the "true" light, made emphatic by the double, postpositive article (τὸ φῶς τὸ ἀληθινόν). The emphasis is to make clear that this light is the light *par excellence*, and its qualifier, "true," implies that it is real, authentic, and genuine even if it is not recognized as such (vv. 10–11).[75]

The second clause begins with a relative pronoun clause that stands in apposition to the first clause. The neuter relative pronoun and verb are clearly modifying "light" and is best translated as "the one that gives light to" (ὃ φωτίζει). The verb was traditionally used of physical light: "to shine" and "to illuminate."[76] While "to illuminate" or "to enlighten" was common to the LXX and thereafter in Greek religious literature, the conceptual understanding in the prologue is so heavily rooted in the Word that it is best to avoid using an idea of enlightenment that might be understood in distinction from the Word. Thus, our translation

---

75. McHugh, *John*, 28–32.   76. Ibid., 32.

remains more generic, allowing the Word to define the nature of the illumination. This is especially important since the phrase immediately following, "every person" (πάντα ἄνθρωπον), has been taken by some to refer to a prenatal enlightenment, an idea suggested in some Jewish texts (cf. 2 Esd 7:21), and to others to refer to an unavoidable universal enlightenment. While we have avoided the former with our translation of the clause, we cannot avoid the latter except by understanding its meaning in light of the entire Gospel. It is important to note that the light given to "every person" is for John's Gospel not systematic theology's concept of general revelation but — fitting with the cosmological strand of John's plot — revelation in general, which is divisive and confrontational.[77]

The translation for the first and second clauses is ultimately based upon the grammatically ambiguous third clause. A majority of commentators regard the participle "was coming" (ἐρχόμενον) to be working periphrastically with the main verb. The translation, then, which has also been adopted by the NIV, would place emphasis on the durative nature of the verb — that the light was "continually coming" to the world, first implicitly through the prophets and saints and finally in its fullest sense by means of the incarnation. Unfortunately, it is impossible to regard the participle as periphrastic. By definition, "no elements may intervene between the auxiliary verb and the participle except for those

which completely or directly modify the participle (not the verb)...."[78] It makes more sense to interpret it as an attributive participle. In this way it functions as an afterthought, qualifying "light" (φῶς) in a way similar to a relative clause: "(a light) that came into the world."[79] The emphasis is also different, for it is not to be viewed as durative but as a second introduction. The Word has already been introduced; now the coming of the Word is introduced. The manifestation of the Word is an introduction to a "coming," made fully manifest in the incarnation (v. 14).

1:10 He was in the world, and the world came into existence through him, and the world did not know him (ἐν τῷ κόσμῳ ἦν, καὶ ὁ κόσμος δι᾽ αὐτοῦ ἐγένετο, καὶ ὁ κόσμος αὐτὸν οὐκ ἔγνω). Verse 10 moves quickly from "coming into the world" to "was in the world." Although "world" is first mentioned in v. 9, it is in v. 10 where it begins to receive important definition, which becomes foundational to the use of this central term in the Gospel.[80] Verse 10 begins with an important transition from v. 9: the "coming" has become an arrival. What was "coming into the world" is now simply "in the world" (ἐν τῷ κόσμῳ). The two prepositional phrases are back-to-back in John's placement: "coming into the world. In the world ..." (ἐρχόμενον εἰς τὸν κόσμον. ἐν τῷ κόσμῳ). The transition is quick but meaningful.

IN DEPTH: "World"

The term "world" (κόσμος) appears seventy-eight times in the Gospel of John, over five times more frequently than in the Synoptics (fourteen times). The term "world" (κόσμος) could refer to the physical universe, a sense John clearly rec-

77. Cf. Carson, *John*, 123 – 24.
78. Porter, *Idioms*, 45. See also BDF § 412.4; McHugh, *John*, 34. Contra Carson, *John*, 121 – 22.
79. Schnackenburg, *John*, 1:255.
80. For a fuller discussion, see Klink, "Light of the World," 74 – 76.

ognized (cf. 17:5; 21:25). However, the term can also refer to the universe as a personal entity, as is common in Jewish literature, or more directly to humanity as a group. This understanding of "world" is relational in nature and is most clearly reflected in v. 10. In this verse an excellent contrast is presented in the Johannine usage of "world," allowing the term to function both as the physical, created universe as well as the living, relational world, its anthropomorphic self. In this way, what we call mankind or humanity may also be called "the world."

The relational sense of "world" (κόσμος) in the Johannine literature generates significant scholarly confusion. Older descriptions of John's dualism[81] combined with more recent sociological assumptions of a sectarian-like Johannine community have led to the reconstruction of an introspective group which views itself in isolation from "this world" (see Introduction).[82] More recent research has advocated the more complex relational nature of the term. The "world" is the place or realm where God is at work, the place that is the main focus of God's attention.[83] It is a "dimension of encounter" between God and man.[84] Or more fully, "The world is thus the arena of the light's salvific invasion of darkness … 'the lost' that Jesus came to seek and to save."[85] The language of evil that pervades the Gospel's depiction of the "world" does not classify it in a completely negative sense. Although those who remain in the darkness remain evil, out of this same "dark world" come those whom Jesus came to save.[86] This more recent understanding of the Johannine "world" views the term as more relationally complex than previous descriptions of Johannine dualism. It appears that the personification of the "world" in John is the portrait of a class of people. This understanding of the term is necessary in order to grasp the "dimension of encounter" that in v. 10 is portrayed in an intentionally relational manner.

Verse 10 is carefully and, arguably, intentionally matching v. 1 with its tripartite structure. "With the same urgency with which v. 1 taught the deity of the Word, v. 10 now teaches its turning to the world."[87] The verse holds in wonderful tension the transcendence of the Word and the immanence of "him" who has arrived. Interestingly, the second clause reuses a familiar term in the prologue, "came" (ἐγένετο), echoing back to vv. 3 – 5 where creation itself is supported by the Word (see comments on v. 17). The one who has arrived in the world is the source of the world. The Creator of the world is present in the world. As in v. 2 where v. 1 is restated but with a new context in mind, v. 10 echoes back

81. Due in no small part to the influence of Rudolf Bultmann, *Theology of the New Testament*, trans. Kendrick Grobel, 2 vols. (London: SCM Press, 1951, 1955), 2:21.

82. Cf. Ashton, *Understanding the Fourth Gospel*, 206 – 8.

83. Margaret Davies, *Rhetoric and Reference in the Fourth Gospel*, JSNTSup 69 (Sheffield: JSOT Press, 1992), 155.

84. David Rensberger, *Johannine Faith and Liberating Community* (Philadelphia: Westminster, 1988), 137.

85. Keener, *John*, 1:329.

86. See Stanley B. Marrow, "Κόσμος in John," *CBQ* 64 (2002): 90 – 102.

87. Barth, *Witness to the Word*, 63.

to the very creation of the world; here, however, the new information is that the one through whom the world came into existence is not described with a title but with a personal pronoun.[88] Thus, even the first two clauses of v. 10 must now be made personal: "He was in the world" (ἐν τῷ κόσμῳ ἦν), and the world "came into existence through him" (δι᾽ αὐτοῦ ἐγένετο).

While the first two clauses of v. 10 allow "world" (κόσμος) to function as the physical, created universe, the term is shown in its living, relational sense in the third clause. The world, quite simply, "did not know him" (αὐτὸν οὐκ ἔγνω). This statement cannot be seen as promoting some form of ontological dualism, for the second clause makes clear that the "world" that did not know him is the same "world" that he made. McHugh argues that the threefold use of "world" (κόσμος) in v. 10 almost serves to provide a definition of the sense in which John is going to use the term in the remainder of the Gospel. Rooted in the Old Testament, "In the Fourth Gospel ['the world'] ὁ κόσμος denotes the divinely created world which has, as Genesis teaches, rejected God, but which is at the same time not beyond salvation, rather the opposite: it is certain to be saved."[89] Here again the cosmological and historical strands of John's plot coalesce, presenting a dramatic tension that moves the narrative along.

In light of the parallel thought in v. 11b, the verb "know" (ἔγνω) is almost certainly to be taken in an Old Testament sense and means a knowing and responding with moral commitment.[90] The sense of the verb could equally imply that the world did not "recognize" (cf. v. 5) or "respond" to him. Carrying forward the sense of "knowing" from the Old Testament, the depiction is more comprehensive than mere intellectual knowledge; it was not that the world failed to perceive of his existence but that the world failed to relate with humble obedience and trust (e.g., Jer 31:34).[91] The rest of John will explicate the nature of this failure to "know." Our translation prefers to keep the broader term "know," which carries the comprehensive understanding of the knowledge of God so central to the Old Testament, as well as the story of the God of the Old Testament now being told according to John.

1:11 He came to what belongs to him, and his own people did not receive him (εἰς τὰ ἴδια ἦλθεν, καὶ οἱ ἴδιοι αὐτὸν οὐ παρέλαβον). The prologue now makes a significant claim with a playful use of one word in two different genders: "what belongs"/"his own people" (ἴδια/ ἴδιοι). The first clause is almost speaking about the world as the "property" or "possession" (τὰ ἴδια) of the Word,[92] not as the Word's "home"[93] but as his creation that properly "belongs to him."[94] Here one might prefer the term "property," yet the relation between the Word and the world is more intimate than "possession" can express. Thus, the development of v. 11 from v. 10 begins cosmologically, as the first clause locates not merely the creation of the world by the Word but the innate ownership and belonging that exists between them.

In the second clause, the same term has been changed from a neuter, "what belongs" (τὰ ἴδια), to a masculine, "his own people" (οἱ ἴδιοι). Since

---

88. Although the implied subject of the first clause could be logically neuter ("it was in the world"), the direct object of the third clause, though antecedentally referring to "it," must grammatically be translated as a masculine pronoun, "him" (αὐτὸν). It seems as if John is allowing what should be referring back to be pointing forward (to v. 14). The incarnational context is being described by John, not here with large theological concepts but with a mere personal pronoun.

89. McHugh, *John*, 41.
90. Ibid., 40.
91. Barrett, *John*, 162.
92. BDAG 467.
93. Contra John W. Pryor, "Jesus and Israel in the Fourth Gospel: John 1:11," *NovT* 32 (1990): 201–18.
94. See Schnackenburg, *John*, 1:258–61.

we have seen the careful use of different genders already in the prologue, we should expect no less here. The flow of v. 11 would seem, therefore, to be as follows: while the first clause shows the intimacy between the Creator and his world, the second clause shows the intimacy between the man and his race. With this explicit movement, the referent can be none other than Israel/the Jewish people, of which Jesus was a member. This is also not foreign to the Old Testament, where Israel is frequently depicted as God's special people (Exod 19:5; 23:22; Deut 7:6; 14:2; 26:18; Isa 43:21; Ezek 13:18 – 23; Mal 3:17). In this sense, John is making "his own people" (οἱ ἴδιοι) a theological category by an association with the covenantal language so frequent in the OT.[95]

It is important to note, however, that there is an intentionally subtle relationship between "what belongs" (τὰ ἴδια) and "his own people" (οἱ ἴδιοι). First, the movement from the neuter to the masculine reflects the progressing intimacy that God will extend throughout the remainder of the Gospel. As much as God loves the "world" (3:16), it is the world in all its specifics that God extends himself toward. Second, the masculine is not intended to be entirely distinguishable from the neuter; just as the "coming" man is still the Word, so also Jewish people are still of the world. In fact, John provides theological description of the worldliness of God's covenant people. Excluding the prologue, there are thirty-eight occurrences of "world" (κόσμος) that carry negative connotations. In many of these references it is Israel who is representative of the world. For example, the hatred of the world in 7:7 is specifically the hatred of the Jews mentioned in 7:1 (cf. 8:23; 9:39). In the farewell discourse this hatred is carried over and applied to the disciples (15:18 – 19), yet it is the Jews who are doing the hating (15:20, 25; 16:1 – 3).

This subtle relationship between "what belongs" (τὰ ἴδια) and "his own people" (οἱ ἴδιοι) of v. 11, and even between "world" (κόσμος) in v. 10, becomes central to the story the Gospel tells. The Gospel as a whole sees Israel as interconnected with the world; "his own people" who should have received him — the Jewish nation — is no different than the world they thought they were opposing. At the deepest level, therefore, what we might call the primary historical referent of v. 11b, Israel, is also representative of a much larger referent, the world, or what we have been calling the primary cosmological referent. John's depiction of the manifestation of the Word in the world is made more detailed and graphic in v. 11: creation rejects its Creator; the loved reject their Lover. When Jesus was not received by the people to whom he belonged, God himself was not received by the world that belonged to him.

1:12 But to all who received him, he gave to them the right to become children of God, to those who believe in his name (ὅσοι δὲ ἔλαβον αὐτόν, ἔδωκεν αὐτοῖς ἐξουσίαν τέκνα θεοῦ γενέσθαι, τοῖς πιστεύουσιν εἰς τὸ ὄνομα αὐτοῦ). Verse 11 made clear that all creation, even the people with whom God had made covenant, rejected the one to whom they owe existence and allegiance. In essence, vv. 10 – 11 describe how the manifestation of the Word-man has been met with rejection. If the result is the rejection of God, the cause is a crisis of identity. The world has become distinct from its Creator. But there is a new creation! For as v. 12 will reveal, the Creator is not done creating. Even without relying on his chiastic interpretation, Neyrey may be correct when he describes this verse as "the functional center of the prologue."[96] In this verse the prologue shifts from tragedy to triumph.

Verse 12 begins with a pendent nominative, which we translated as "but to all" (ὅσοι δὲ), which

---

95. Pryor, "Jesus and Israel in the Fourth Gospel," 214.

96. Neyrey, *John*, 44.

functions as an emotional and strong contrast to the rejectors of the last two verses, putting emphasis on them as the beneficiaries of the one who has come.[97] At the same time, it leaves open the exact identity of the beneficiaries — an identity to be shortly described. John simply begins v. 12 by telling that some "received him" (ἔλαβον αὐτόν), in sharp contrast to those described in vv. 10 – 11. The term "received" (ἔλαβον) can have a more general meaning related to reception ("receive what is offered") or a more specific meaning related to authority ("accept or recognize someone's authority"). Interestingly, the term is found to have the latter meaning in 5:43 and 13:20, and in both cases it is equated with "to believe" (cf. 5:44 and 13:19), matching the context of v. 12.[98]

The second clause contains two significant parts that are loaded with significant terminology. Combined, the two parts become a narrative movement that introduces the source and nature of the benefits to be received. First, "He gave to them the right" (ἔδωκεν αὐτοῖς ἐξουσίαν). The source of the benefits is the Word-man. The grammatical subject is still the Word, or the "he." The one who receives the Word will be benefited by him. What looked like a tragic story has been triumphantly reversed. The noun we translated as "right" (ἐξουσίαν) is difficult to define with precision. In this context, the term denotes the right to do something or the power to do something.[99] But which one: "right" or "power"? In the context it can only be the former since John does not speak of power (an inherent ability) but of status (an authorization, an imparted title to a new status).[100]

Second, "to become children of God" (τέκνα θεοῦ γενέσθαι). The nature of the benefits is becoming children of God. In the Gospel of John, the term "children" (τέκνα) refers to Christians, whereas "son" (υἱός) is always reserved for Christ.[101] The latter term can be used in the NT to refer to Christians, most clearly in the two classic Pauline passages (Rom 8 and Gal 3 – 4) dealing with adoptive sonship. While it is difficult to define the difference in meaning between the two terms, one can speak generally of a nuance between the terms' usages. The term "children" describes the offspring from the viewpoint of the relationship to their progenitors and is therefore normally used of small children with an accompanying awareness of their weakness, their utter dependence on their parents, and their total trust. In contrast, generally speaking, "sons" is more adaptable and more comfortably used for maturing or adult offspring.[102] Thus, "children of God" (τέκνα θεοῦ) functions innately as a more intimate and affectionate term. The plural use of the term may reflect the communal nature of the conferred status, an issue addressed later in the Gospel, but the emphasis is primarily on the derived status, not its corporately independent function. Ultimately, one must "become" a child of God. It is almost certain that we are to understand "become" (γενέσθαι) in a similar manner to "came into existence" (ἐγένετο) in v. 3 and v. 6 where it expressed, as we argued above, the creative force of God *ex nihilo* (see comments on v. 17). Such children are a new creation; they are those not of this world (17:6, 16), who have received the spiritual rebirth from above (3:1 – 11).[103] To say that they have "become" children of God places the emphasis on the Word that provided the possibility. The "children" are only what they have been given.[104]

97. Wallace, *Greek Grammar*, 51 – 52.
98. McHugh, *John*, 44.
99. See BDAG 352.
100. Morris, *John*, 87; Cf. Dodd, *Interpretation*, 270.
101. Barrett, *John*, 163.

102. McHugh, *John*, 46.
103. Hoskyns, *Fourth Gospel*, 146.
104. Theodor Zahn, *Das Evangelium des Johannes*, 6th ed., KNT 4 (Leipzig: Deichert, 1921), 73.

The third clause of v. 12 makes explicit to whom this right is given: "to those who believe in his name" (τοῖς πιστεύουσιν εἰς τὸ ὄνομα αὐτοῦ). The potent central clause of v. 12 is bookended by two parallel phrases: those that "receive him" are those "who believe in his name." These phrases are parallel ways to describe the same spiritual change: when one ceases to rely on one's own merits and achievements and comes to trust in the Word (Christ).[105] Two things in this final clause are worthy of comment. First, "believe" is a central term for John, used a total of ninety-eight times, which towers above the use of the term by other NT authors (even more than Paul — fifty-four times). Such belief yields allegiance to the Word and complete trust in the Word, as appropriate for (small) children.

Second, this belief is specifically directed "in his name." The concept of a "name" in the ancient world was not merely a label but comprised the character of a person. When, for example, the psalmist spoke of the name of God (Ps 20:1), he did not have in mind simply the uttering of the name; he was speaking of all that "God" means.[106] However, to what name is John referring? While "life" and "light" were in the Word (vv. 3 – 4), the Word has not yet been given any additional name, much less a personal name; he has only otherwise been referred to with a pronoun. Since the almost exact phrase occurs at the end of the Gospel just before the epilogue (20:31), where the name of Jesus is stated, by implication the rest of the Gospel is needed to make manifest the name, that is, the character of the person in whom the children of God are to believe.

1:13 Who were born not from blood, nor from the desire of the flesh, nor from the will of a hus-band, but from God (οἳ οὐκ ἐξ αἱμάτων οὐδὲ ἐκ θελήματος σαρκὸς οὐδὲ ἐκ θελήματος ἀνδρὸς ἀλλ’ ἐκ θεοῦ ἐγεννήθησαν). The possibility described in v. 12 is given a description in v. 13. In one sense the concept of "birth" conceptually agrees with the notion of becoming "children" of God. But more must be implied since all of v. 13 centers around the concept of birth, and birth is important for John as a whole (cf. ch. 3). "Birth" is an important Johannine metaphor, referring to something both natural and supernatural. It is undeniable that this birth is from the outside and requires an intermediary. Some have been concerned to see those "who were born" as referring to "children of God" and not to "those who believe" in order to deny that faith would proceed from regeneration.[107] But the explicit instrumentality of v. 13, ending with the emphatic statement of finality, "but from God" (ἀλλ’ ἐκ θεοῦ), makes any other agency appear absurd. John has made certain that the birth he describes can be nothing but "procreation by God."[108]

This "procreation by God" is commented upon by an emphatic fourfold string of the preposition "from" (ἐξ, ἐκ), three negative and one positive. The three negatives provide three important denials regarding birth "from God." First, birth "from God" is not "from blood" (οὐκ ἐξ αἱμάτων). In ancient thought, blood was often considered the means of procreation; it is the matter from which life is generated (Josephus, *Ant.* 4.310). Thus, the first negation is to explain that God's "children" are not created by natural means.

Second, birth "from God" is not "from the desire of the flesh" (οὐδὲ ἐκ θελήματος σαρκὸς). The term translated "desire" (θελήματος) could also be translated as "will," but the use here is reminiscent of sexual desire, "the desire that arises out of the human bodily constitution."[109] While the genitive

105. Morris, *John*, 88.
106. Ibid.
107. See Bultmann, *John*, 59.
108. Ridderbos, *John*, 47.
109. Morris, *John*, 89.

modifier "of the flesh" (σαρκὸς) makes more certain the sexual connotation, it is important not to import the use of the term "flesh" with the negative or evil sense so commonly intended by the apostle Paul. For John the flesh is merely the body with all its needs and wants. The natural urges of the body are intended to be in sharp contrast to the source of the children of God, which is supernatural and entirely from the outside of a person.

Third, birth "from God" is not "from the will of a husband" (οὐδὲ ἐκ θελήματος ἀνδρός). The term translated "will" (θελήματος) is the same term from the second clause. But the context gives it a slightly different meaning. While its use here might have a similar sense, sexual desire, it is more likely referring to human volition in general. This is especially the case if the three denials are to be seen as having some form of development: the science of birth, the sexuality of birth, and the selection of birth, with each clause reflecting upon and moving beyond the previous. But the "birth" of which John speaks cannot be understood by human science nor rooted in human sexuality nor controlled by human selection. It is not something a person decides for it ultimately resides in the will of God (cf. 6:44). While the genitive modifier "husband" (ἀνδρός) could also have the more general meaning "man," our translation is to be preferred because without losing the sense of volition, it also locates the volition in the patriarchial authority of the ancient world. Thus, rather than reflecting a general conflict of wills (humanity in general against God), it reflects the conflict between two viable authorities (the patriarch of the human family against the Patriarch of the children of God).

Contrasting the threefold denial is the positive statement, "but from God" (ἀλλ᾽ ἐκ θεοῦ). Even though the entire verse has already been deny-

ing all other options, the strong adversative "but" is a fitting finale. Verses 12–13 make explicit the source and nature of this "new creation." Beyond the process of nature, beyond every Jewish or other genealogy, beyond every action of the body, and beyond every will of human authority, there are children who have been brought into existence by the creative power and will of God.[110] What the Word "gave" (ἔδωκεν) to the children of God "sweeps all other foundations from under our feet and sets us on this one alone."[111]

1:14a And the Word became flesh and made his dwelling among us (Καὶ ὁ λόγος σὰρξ ἐγένετο καὶ ἐσκήνωσεν ἐν ἡμῖν). The clause being emphatically introduced concerns "the Word" (ὁ λόγος).[112] This is the first appearance of "the Word" since v. 1, and the last time it will appear in the Gospel. Its appearance recollects the Word's identity as God from v. 1, yet it also serves as an *inclusio* which holds together all the activities of the Word that have been building progressively throughout the prologue. The background mystery of the "Word" has now faded, and its (or his) foreground is now clearly in view. Whatever theory one began with when first hearing the term no longer predominates. For the reader of John, the Word has become God coming and acting in the world. As a term for God's ultimate self-disclosure, it has now become disclosed in the flesh.

The Word "became flesh" (σὰρξ ἐγένετο). The Word-God is also the Word-man; God is found in the Word to be a "him" (v. 10). And this is not wordplay. The term translated "flesh" (σάρξ) is probably the harshest term for the body and therefore is a potent term to describe the Word as a real human being. While the term "man/human" (ἄνθρωπος) might be more common, "flesh" is no less comprehensive, for it refers not merely to the

---

110. Hoskyns, *Fourth Gospel*, 147.
111. Barth, *Witness to the Word*, 84; Cf. Luther, *John*, 22:101.

112. See John D. Denniston, *The Greek Particles* (Oxford: Oxford University Press, 1934), 317; Cf. BDAG 495.

flesh but also to the bones, blood, and soul — the whole human being.[113] It is the basic meaning of "flesh" (σάρξ) that is significant for John. For the reality to which it points, more than anything else in material creation, is diametrically opposed to the "Word" (λόγος). "Flesh is the most vulnerable, the most corruptible, the most easily destructible, part of the human body — in a word the most impermanent. The Logos is Eternal.... They are literally poles apart...."[114] Yet, and here is the paradox, in becoming "flesh" the Word does not cease to be God. The Word is the God-man.

The synthesis of these two poles is empahsized by the term "became" (ἐγένετο), the seventh use of this significant term! — which harkens back to its emphatic use earlier in the prologue, in which it spoke of creation *ex nihilo* (see comments on v. 17). If this meaning is carried forward to v. 14, Barth is correct when he claims, "The well-known paradox of the verse lies already in the *egeneto*."[115] The paradox of the statement is not that he came into the world, for that was already declared in v. 9; rather, the paradox is that he came in this way — in the "flesh."[116] The translation "became" is important because it refers to the actual nature of the Word. The Word has not changed, but the Word does now exist in the flesh.[117] Interestingly, v. 14 echoes v. 1 not merely with a restatement of the Word but with a predication of the Word, for it too begins with a qualitative predicate nominative construction. Verses 1 and 14 form a grammatical *inclusio*. Just as v. 1 predicated that the Word "was God," v. 14 predicates that the Word "became flesh." Just as v. 1 did not speak merely about "God" but about the one who "was God," so also the importance of v. 14 is not merely regarding the term "flesh" but about the one who "became" flesh. Three things can be stated regarding the meaning of "the Word became flesh" in the context of the prologue.

First, the notion of "became" does not allow for the implication that the Word transitioned from "God" to "human." The grammatical meaning is quite unequivocal, especially in light of the *inclusio* with v. 1. Just as the Word is God, so also the Word "became flesh." What is predicated is equally demanded in both statements by the very nature of the *inclusio*, with each functionally supporting the other. Thus, the Word-God became flesh without ceasing to be the Word-God. In this person ("flesh") was the Word, with the Word merely being first in the chronological ordering. As Schlatter explains it, "What emerged out of the Word was flesh."[118] "No change takes place, no transubstantiation, no replacing the Word's mode of being by another, no dissolution of the *logos* in *sarx*, and also no development of a mixture of both, but a full union in which nothing is taken away from the divine ... and nothing is added to the creaturely...."[119] This is the paradox that John describes in his prologue.

Second, while the meaning of "flesh" is not less than the fact that the Word became "human," it also expresses much more. In the context of John and beginning with the prologue, the meaning of "became flesh" entails much more than embracing human nature; it means embracing a human nature that is in hostile opposition to God. By becoming "flesh" the Word embraced humanity in its fullness, the very *nature* and *state* of Adam. He took a "servant form which is proper to human nature under the sign of the fall and in the sphere of darkness, of the fallen and corrupted human nature which needs to be sanctified and redeemed."[120]

---

113. McHugh, *John*, 51 – 52.

114. Ibid., 53.

115. Barth, *Witness to the Word*, 86.

116. Willem Nicol, *The Sēmeia in the Fourth Gospel: Tradition and Redaction*, NovTSup 32 (Leiden: Brill, 1972), 87.

117. See Ridderbos, *John*, 50.

118. Schlatter, *Der Evangelist Johannes*, 22.

119. Barth, *Witness to the Word*, 91.

120. Ibid., 88.

This becoming "was his humility, not his glory."[121] This does not imply that the Word embraced the spiritual condition of the flesh; it merely describes the spiritual context the Word took upon himself. The Word lived in darkness as the Light.

Third, the full meaning of the statement "and the Word became flesh" (Καὶ ὁ λόγος σὰρξ ἐγένετο) is not found in metaphysics but in the message of the Gospel.[122] As John will make clear, the person of Christ is not removed from the work of Christ. This may be the reason why John chose the term "flesh" instead of "man/human," for the former is intimately bound up with the notion of sacrifice, a use the Gospel will make explicit in 6:51 – 56. The imagery of sacrifice, which involves the graphic elements of flesh and blood, is redefined in light of the Gospel, where the sacrifice — the flesh — is nothing less than the Word-was-God.

Verse 14 continues to say that the Word not only "became flesh" but also "made his dwelling among us" (ἐσκήνωσεν ἐν ἡμῖν). The term "made his dwelling" (ἐσκήνωσεν) could be translated as "pitched his tent" (from σκηνόω; the noun σκηνή means "tent"), but in this context is best translated as "made his dwelling." The verb could be an ingressive aorist, which stresses the beginning of a state, or it could be a constative aorist, which views the action as a whole. It is probably best to understand "became" as an ingressive, with its stress on the new nature of the Word, and "made his dwelling" as a constative, providing a summary of the location of the Word. While a constative aorist can denote a temporary visit, the context of the prologue and the conven-

tional use of the term referring to settling down permanently in a place argues strongly against a brief dwelling (cf. Rev 12:12). Yet the term almost certainly was intended to arouse other associations.

The unusual verb "made his dwelling" (ἐσκήνωσεν), only occurring elsewhere in Revelation — an important connection to note — is certainly intending to recall many older traditions of God's presence dwelling with Israel.[123] One tradition stands out as primary and formative (as well as logically prior): the Sinai/Mosaic covenant and wilderness traditions of the ark and tent.[124] With the biblical echo of God "dwelling" with his people and the postbiblical echo of the glory of God making its "residence" (*shekinah*) in the tabernacle and temple, it is quite easy to see the evangelist declaring that the Word-became-flesh is the very dwelling (residence) of God. While God did dwell with his people and reveal his glory to them in the Old Testament, never has he dwelled and revealed in this manner. By alluding to such themes and traditions, John is declaring that the dwelling of God among his people has now occurred *par excellence*. The incarnation is both a fulfillment and a replacement: John proclaims Jesus as the fulfillment of patterns, prophecies, and traditions associated with the tabernacle and temple (both old and new).[125] Yet the incarnation is an unprecedented newness.[126]

1:14b and we saw his glory, glory as the unique Son from the Father, full of grace and truth (καὶ ἐθεασάμεθα τὴν δόξαν αὐτοῦ, δόξαν ὡς μονογενοῦς παρὰ πατρός, πλήρης χάριτος καὶ ἀληθείας). With the third "and" (καὶ) the climactic witness comes

121. Augustine, *John* 2.16.18.

122. Contra Frederic L. Godet, *Commentary on John's Gospel*, 3rd ed., trans.Timothy Dwight (New York: Funk and Wagnalls, 1886; repr., Grand Rapids: Kregel, 1978), 268 – 71 and 291 – 98.

123. Craig R. Koester, *Dwelling of God: The Tabernacle in the Old Testament, Intertestamental Jewish Literature, and the New Testament*, CBQMS 22 (Washington, DC: Catholic Bibli-

cal Association of America, 1989), 6.

124. See Mary L. Coloe, *God Dwells with Us: Temple Symbolism in the Fourth Gospel* (Collegeville, MN: Liturgical Press, 2001), 31 – 63 (61).

125. Cf. Hoskyns, *Fourth Gospel*, 148.

126. See Paul M. Hoskins, *Jesus as the Fulfillment of the Temple in the Gospel of John*, PBM (Milton Keynes: Paternoster, 2006), 124.

to its potent conclusion. The verb "we saw" (ἐθεασάμεθα) is one of two common NT verbs for seeing with the physical eye (the other is ὁράω). Because the object being seen is "glory," many interpreters have tried to define the term as seeing with the eyes of faith or as reflecting a "pervading postresurrectional perspective,"[127] but such supernatural emphasis might eclipse what v. 14 is trying to show, namely, that a real, physical man was the object seen. It is not a verb used to describe the seeing of visions; it is language used to describe what can be seen and "touched" (cf. 1 John 1:1). Had the object been something unavoidably physical, every translator would have allowed the verb to maintain its basic meaning of physical sight. The occurrence of "glory" should not neglect the immediate context in which John chose two physical words: "flesh" and now "see." Thus, even though McHugh calls translations like ours "unduly feeble renderings" since it lacks a sense of wonder, we prefer to communicate that the "glory" that was seen was real "flesh."[128]

Several questions have been raised regarding the implied first person plural of "we saw" (ἐθεασάμεθα). To whom is the "we" referring? Several options have been raised, including the following five options (general to specific): (1) universal "we": the world in general; (2) ecclesial "we": the universal church; (3) apostolic "we": the witness of apostolic authority; (4) historical "we": those physically present with Jesus; (5) sectarian "we": the Johannine community. While not all of these options are mutually exclusive, in light of the context of John, option (4), the historical "we," is in closest agreement with the emphasis on a real, physical presence ("flesh") and a real, physical seeing. Helpful here is Bauckham, who describes a common function of "we" in ancient Greek which

is intended "to give added force and authority to the self-reference." Without denying that the "we" represents real eyewitnesses, this "we of authoritative testimony" in v. 14 serves as an *inclusio* with the authoritative "we" of 21:24.[129] The "we" of "we saw his glory," therefore, is intended to imply that a real man was witnessed, and that this witness is an authoritative account, as the remainder of the Gospel will reveal.

What was physically seen was "his glory" (τὴν δόξαν αὐτοῦ). The "glory" of God in the Old Testament, a meaning certainly present in the mind of John, is God's majestic splendor and power revealed in the miracles in Egypt which were signs of his greatness (Num 14:22), at the giving of the law (Exod 24:16 – 17; Deut 5:24), and at great moments when God appeared to chosen servants, such as Moses (Exod 33:18, 22) and Ezekiel (Ezek 10:4, 18 – 19). In light of its OT context, "glory" is "the manifestation of God's being, nature and presence, in a manner accessible to human experience."[130] Of course, the manner was nothing less than the "flesh" of a man — the incarnation of the Word. Hence, it was not "a glory" but "his glory," the glory of a person. Interestingly, the manifestation of the "glory of God" in the OT was still incomplete. The hope of the OT was that the glory of God would be exalted above all the earth so that all nations would see his glory (Isa 66:18). While John is not promoting an entirely realized eschatology as some have tried to emphasize, he is clearly showing that the hopes of the OT are being realized in the person of Jesus, the one who will be "exalted/lifted up" (see 3:14; 8:28; 12:32, 34).

Verse 14 closes with two clauses that provide a description of this glory. The first clause claims that this glory was "glory as the unique Son from the Father" (δόξαν ὡς μονογενοῦς παρὰ πατρός).

127. Cf. Borchert, *John*, 1:120.
128. McHugh, *John*, 57.
129. Bauckham, *Jesus and the Eyewitnesses*, 370 – 83 (73).
130. Dodd, *Interpretation*, 206.

This statement does not denote an improper comparison but a proof of identity.[131] That is, it is not a focus on comparison ("glory similar to that of") but a focus on quality ("glory which truly is that of").[132]

This glory that was seen was nothing other than the "unique Son" (μονογενοῦς). The difficulty of defining this ambiguous term makes its significance here and in v. 18 all the more complex. A large amount of ink has been spilled regarding the two possible meanings of this word: "only begotten (son)" or "only/unique." In compound adjectives like "unique Son" (μονογενής) the -γενής suggests deriviation in general rather than birth. Nouns as the first part of the compound give the source, whereas adverbs describe the nature of the deriviation. Thus, the μονο- implies something about the nature of the derivation, namely, that it is unparalleled.[133] Etymologically, therefore, the term (μονογενής) "is not associated with begetting (γεννᾶσθαι) but with existence (γίγνεσθαι)."[134] The nature of the existence being described can have two senses: (1) manner: a more particular, derivative sense meaning "of sole descent," and (2) class: a more general, nonderivative meaning of "only" or "unique, unparalleled, incomparable." While related, the difference is a matter of emphasis. Sense (1) emphasizes the manner of derivation (i.e., "only son," since the child in v. 14 is male), whereas sense (2) emphasizes the class of derivation ("only" or "unique"). The translation that is best suited to the context of the prologue and the Gospel as a whole combines both senses by translating μονογενής as "unique Son."

This title needs to be viewed in relation to this section of the prologue, vv. 9 – 14, in which John has already introduced the concept of "children of God" and the nature of their derivation. Verse 14 is not emphasizing that the "unique Son" is similar to these "children"; in sharp contrast, it is claiming for him an ultimate uniqueness.[135] Thus, while the concept of the Word's sonship is certainly implied by the use of "unique Son" (μονογενής), what is made emphatic is that it is unparalleled, incomparable, and wholly other. Both the "children" and the "Son" relate to the Father and are derived, in some sense, "from" him but in manners and classes that are entirely dissimilar.[136]

There is also good evidence to understand John's use of "unique Son" (μονογενής) as part of his rhetorical technique. It is almost certainly significant that the term's root, -γενής (from the verb γίγνεσθαι in classical Greek) had transitioned to γίνομαι by the time of the NT.[137] The centrality of γίνομαι (often in the form of ἐγένετο) as the creative action of God that has run throughout the prologue reaches its climax here. John has shown a precise development in the prologue so as to make clear that the "unique Son" (μονογενής) is the ultimate and final creative act of God. Without denying that the term implies "sonship," by using a form of this verbal root John has made certain that we not miss the "uniqueness." This climactic term, supported by the developing threads of its verbal root throughout the prologue, serves to introduce an important category for understanding the person and mission of the Word (see comments on v. 17).

The uniqueness of the Son is made certain by the prepositional phrase that immediately follows: "from the Father" (παρὰ πατρός). The use of "Father" convinces many that the idea of "sonship" is the primary meaning conveyed by the term.[138]

131. Calvin, *John 1 – 10*, 21.

132. BDAG 1104; Cf. McHugh, *John*, 58.

133. F. Büchsel, "μονογενής," *TDNT* 4:737 – 41.

134. Harris, *Jesus as God*, 86.

135. This is made evident by the fact that in the Gospel of John, "son" (υἱός) is used solely for Jesus.

136. See Schlatter, *Der Evangelist Johannes*, 26.

137. LSJ 349.

138. Cf. Barnabas Lindars, *The Gospel of John*, NCB (Grand Rapids: Eerdmans, 1972), 96.

However, the context demands that this "Son" be seen as without parallel; the Son is different from other "children of God" (v. 12) in kind and not merely degree (the "only *genus*"). Hence, the impression given to the reader is not merely that the Son is related to the Father but that he is incomparable to all other children. While the force of the preposition can be source, in this context it also implies agency. That "from the Father" (παρὰ πατρός) implies a sending can be seen from the fact that in v. 6 John was also sent "from God" (παρὰ θεοῦ). The "unique Son," therefore, is the agent of God. "Unique Son" conveys both the sonship and mission of Jesus.[139] And this mission is on behalf of the other children he so eminently surpasses.

Until now the prologue had only spoken of the Word in relation to "God"; this is the first use of the title "Father." Since we have already seen that v. 14 forms in *inclusio* with v. 1, it appears that the title "Father" is working in relation to the meaning of "God" and providing insight into God's identity. God is the Word-made-flesh *and* the Father. With what is certainly a carefully selected impression given by "unique Son" (μονογενής), John provides us with our first introduction to the Father and the Son. The beginning of the *inclusio* pronounces the Word's relation to God; the end of the *inclusio* pronounces God's relation to the Word as Father and Son. In this way the mission of God is announced: the sending of the Son from the Father into the world.

What makes the Word-become-flesh unique is that he is "full of grace and truth" (πλήρης χάριτος καὶ ἀληθείας). The phrase is almost certainly an allusion to Exodus 34:6. Interestingly, in Exodus 33:18 Moses begs God, "Now show me your glory." The Lord replies by agreeing to "cause all my goodness to pass in front of you" (33:19). The Lord's goodness, therefore, is the glory of God. And "grace and truth" become terms in the Old Testament that define the goodness which is God's glory.[140] The use of "glory" and "grace and truth" in v. 14, therefore, implies that God's original expression of covenantal faithfulness to his people, Israel, has been transcended. The sending of the "unique Son" from the Father is the ultimate expression and source of God's covenantal faithfulness.[141] The unique Word-become-flesh is God's glory and covenantal faithfulness. He is explicit evidence that God is a Father to his children.

1:15 John witnessed concerning him and has cried out, saying: "This was he of whom I said: 'He who follows me has surpassed me, because he was prior to me'" (Ἰωάννης μαρτυρεῖ περὶ αὐτοῦ καὶ κέκραγεν λέγων, Οὗτος ἦν ὃν εἶπον, Ὁ ὀπίσω μου ἐρχόμενος ἔμπροσθέν μου γέγονεν, ὅτι πρῶτός μου ἦν). The Word was introduced in vv. 1 – 5, given a witness in vv. 6 – 8, and made manifest in vv. 9 – 14; the prologue now shifts to its fourth and final section where the uniqueness of the Word is explained (vv. 15 – 18). Several commentators, as well as the NA[27], suggest that the final section of the prologue begins at v. 14. But the matching grammatical structure between vv. 9 – 14 and 1 – 5, the narrative development of v. 14 as the climax of vv. 9 – 14, and the textual evidence strongly suggests that v. 14 be viewed as the conclusion of the third section of the prologue. Thus, vv. 15 – 18 fulfill the role of an ancient prologue by providing the final stage of the lens through which the Gospel must be read, giving a concluding introduction to the character(s) and unseen forces at work in the story.

The final section of the prologue begins by

---

139. Westcott, *John*, 12.
140. Carson, *John*, 129.

141. Andreas J. Köstenberger, "John," in *Commentary on the New Testament Use of the Old Testament*, ed. G. K. Beale and D. A. Carson (Grand Rapids: Baker Academic, 2007), 422.

reminding the reader of the superiority of the "unique Son." The opening statement, "John witnessed concerning him and has cried out" (Ἰωάννης μαρτυρεῖ περὶ αὐτοῦ καὶ κέκραγεν), combines verb tenses (present; perfect) in a manner that makes the past witness have a continuing effect. Our translation attempts to keep the tension that the verb tenses create while conveying their sense: the historical person of John gives a permanent witness. The Baptist is said to have "cried out" (κέκραγεν), which is not used for emotional or irrational cries but with a special sense for inspired speech, as for the speech of Jesus (7:28; 12:44), the cries of the Spirit (Luke 1:41 – 42), or the cries of a prophet (Rom 9:27).[142] The function of the term "saying" (λέγων) is used to transition the reader from the prophetic introduction to the actual words of the prophet.[143]

The emphasis on the permanent witness of the Baptist makes sense of the next phrase, "This was he of whom I said" (οὗτος ἦν ὃν εἶπον). The verbal difference from 1:30 should not be pressed too closely; the difference is merely a change in perspective. In v. 6 the Baptist was spoken of in the third person, but for the first time in the Gospel and for the only time in the prologue a person is introduced as a speaker. In this sense the "was" (ἦν) hints at a backward look. The nuance signals that a shift has taken place; the only perspective to be had is on this side of the incarnation. The Old Testament has crossed over into the New. The connection to the creative acts in Genesis (vv. 1 – 5) has given way to the creative acts of the Word (vv. 9 – 14). God has become "the Father." The voice of an Old Testament prophet, therefore, has become the voice of an apostle; the Baptist no longer looks *for* the Coming One, but *at* him.[144]

According to the witness of John, "He who follows me has surpassed me, because he was prior

to me" (ὁ ὀπίσω μου ἐρχόμενος ἔμπροσθέν μου γέγονεν, ὅτι πρῶτός μου ἦν). This statement playfully moves from the historical chronology (and implied rank) that Jesus first "follows" John to the surpassing greatness of Jesus rooted in his cosmological chronology (and implied rank) that Jesus was actually "prior" to John. That is, the Baptist is stating unequivocally that the successor is greater than the forerunner because the successor is the true forerunner. The Baptist moves the comparison beyond his own historical ministry and harkens back to the Word who was "in the beginning." It is interesting to note that the phrase translated as "(He) has surpassed me" (ἔμπροσθέν μου γέγονεν) uses the now technical verb (γέγονεν, from γίνομαι) which has become for the prologue a central term (see comments on v. 17). The appearance of the Son is not merely before the time of the Baptist but before the creation of the world. The cosmological and historical strands of the prologue have so coalesced that the reader is to see them as providing a constant paradox regarding Jesus. He is at one and the same time after *and* before John. Jesus "followed" John and yet was always "before" him. The reader is learning from the prologue to grasp the deep significance attached to words that describe the person of Jesus, who is dwelling not only "among us" but also "in the beginning with God." Although the Baptist has not yet pointed to a specific individual (cf. v. 33), he is able to announce in general terms the advent of the long-awaited Coming One.[145]

1:16 Because out of his fullness we all have received grace in place of grace (ὅτι ἐκ τοῦ πληρώματος αὐτοῦ ἡμεῖς πάντες ἐλάβομεν, καὶ χάριν ἀντὶ χάριτος). Following the witness of the Baptist, the narrator adds his own explanation. The transition from the Baptist to the evangelist is not

---

142. Bultmann, *John*, 75.
143. Schlatter, *Der Evangelist Johannes*, 28 – 29.

144. Barth, *Witness to the Word*, 111 – 12.
145. Carson, *John*, 130 – 31.

intending for v. 15 to be viewed as an awkward insertion or parenthesis[146] but as what the narrator (who describes the "unseen") sees as a "representative position" directly from the "apostolic and prophetic witness."[147] The Baptist stands on the continental divide between the cosmological and historical strands of John's plot, and his witness is foundational to the Gospel's own witness. Thus, the content of vv. 16–18 serves as an exposition of the basic statement of v. 15, all of which is part of the presentation of the prologue, which in this final section serves to exhibit the uniqueness of the Word.

The evangelist declares that "out of his fullness we all have received grace in place of grace." (ἐκ τοῦ πληρώματος αὐτοῦ ἡμεῖς πάντες ἐλάβομεν καὶ χάριν ἀντὶ χάριτος). The term "fullness" (πληρώματος) only occurs this once in John. The term looks back to the fullness of the Word, who is described in v. 14 as "full of grace and truth." The recipient of the fullness is the "we all"; an expression that has come to stand not only for the "we" of v. 14 but for all true Christians. The language here implies that Christians become participants in the fullness of Christ. Such a union looks toward the coming of the Spirit (14:15–18). But the fullness that "we all have received" should not diminish that what is received is from "his fullness." The "his" (αὐτοῦ) ties this "fullness" to a "him," the one whom the entire prologue has been introducing. The prologue has carefully articulated the coming of the Word from "with God" to "among us," moving from creation through the Old Testament to the "unique Son." Recognizing this development is important as we turn to the description of what is received.

That which is received is described as "grace in place of grace" (καὶ χάριν ἀντὶ χάριτος), a phrase which is an interpretive crux. The difficulty is rooted in the force of the preposition we translated "in place of" (ἀντί), but the complexity is multiplied because not only is the term a *hapax legomenon* in the Gospel but the four occurrences of "grace" in the Gospel are all in the prologue. While there are a plethora of interpretive options, some of which include suboptions, there are two that are most likely: (1) accumulation, which takes ἀντί as meaning "upon" or "in addition to"; and (2) replacement, which takes ἀντί as meaning "instead of" or "in place of." Option (1) refers to the inexhaustible bounty of God's grace, resulting in a constant flow of graces; option (2) refers to an exchange of sorts, from one kind of grace to another. It is important to say that both options have material power, theological truth, and possible compatibility with the context. Yet while (1) is clearly the translation favored by modern translations, (2) is deemed more satisfactory. A brief explanation is needed.[148]

The most common use of the prepositon (ἀντί) is "instead of, in place of." It is by far the most common meaning in the LXX (e.g., Gen 22:13) and in the Hellenistic papyri. In fact, there is no parallel use of option (1) in all of Greek literature. Rather, when "in addition to" is being described, it is not ἀντί that is used but "upon" (ἐπί), for example as in Sirach 26:15: "grace upon grace" (χάρις ἐπὶ χάριτι). The lack of evidence demands that either John is coining a unique usage of the preposition (ἀντί) or that he is intending option (2). Commentators in favor of option (1) will frequently suggest that a parallel can be found in Philo (*Posterity* 145), but Philo speaks not of "grace" but of "graces," which do not accumulate but replace one another. Even Philo is using ἀντί in the sense of option (2), its

146. As suggested by Brown, *John*, 1:15.
147. Barth, *Witness to the Word*, 113.

148. The following relies on Ruth B. Edwards, "XAPIN ANTI XAPITOΣ (John 1:16): Grace and the Law in the Johannine Prologue," *JSNT* 32 (1988): 3–15.

common meaning. Thus, since there is no lexical evidence for option (1), we must assume that John is using option (2). What is the sense, then, of "grace in place of grace?" To determine this we must include an analysis of v. 17.

1:17 for the law was given through Moses; grace and truth came through Jesus Christ (ὅτι ὁ νόμος διὰ Μωϋσέως ἐδόθη, ἡ χάρις καὶ ἡ ἀλήθεια διὰ Ἰησοῦ Χριστοῦ ἐγένετο). In light of v. 16 we have determined that the preposition ἀντί has a common meaning of "in place of." Thus, the "we all" have received out of the fullness of Christ "grace in place of grace." "Grace in place of grace" is referring in some manner to the contrast between Moses and Jesus, law and grace. But this contrast must be defined with theological precision.

So what is the relationship between "law/Moses" and "grace and truth/Jesus" in v. 17 and therefore "grace in place of grace" in v. 16? Although the two clauses are not in antithetic parallelism, they are in the form of a parallelism. For this reason some form of contrast is certainly in view. Yet while we would want to assume that there is a difference between law and grace and between Moses and Jesus and hence a level of tension, we would also want to assume that materially, because of the united subject matter of Scripture, we have something similar in both instances, something of the same substance (on the doctrine of Scripture, see Introduction). Although the context of the prologue has given us some clues, the difference is made clearer by the choice of verbs used to describe each side of the parallels: "was given" (ἐδόθη) and "came" (ἐγένετο). With the Old Testament as a context for so much of the prologue, it is undeniable that God was the giver of things to his people in the old covenant. But something new has been given in the new covenant, and John chose a word, "came" (ἐγένετο), that has become for him a central term.

IN DEPTH: "Came/Made/Became" (ἐγένετο/γίνομαι)

The magnificent language and imagery of the prologue as well as its seemingly disjointed nature often detract the reader from grasping the prologue's collective significance. What holds the prologue together and directs its message is the carefully crafted use of one variously translated Greek verb (γίνομαι). The verb is quite flexible in meaning, which is why it appears in so many different forms in translation, making it undetectable to the English reader: "made," "came," "become/became," the "unique" Son. Since its meaning contains "numerous nuances relating to being and manner of being,"[149] it serves as an excellent medium to express the coming and arrival of the incarnate Word of God. This single Greek verb occurs in every section of the prologue, forming what is like a highway upon which the message and meaning of the prologue travels.

The significance of the verb, however, is not merely its repeated occurrence but its progressive development throughout the prologue. Beginning in v. 3, the verb is used emphatically three times to describe Jesus as the one through whom all things "came" (ἐγένετο) into being, with different verbal tenses ex-

---

149. BDAG 196.

pressing both the completed act of creation (aorist) and its continuing effects (perfect). The idea of "creation" behind the use of the verb in v. 3 depicts Jesus as central to all the creativity of God.

In v. 6 the verb is used again, though this time to describe the arrival of John (the Baptist), who "came" (ἐγένετο) beneath the sending mission of God. While there is an intended contrast between John (witness) and Jesus (the one witnessed to), the explicit use of the word in v. 6 implies that a related force is also at work here. John would not have used the same verb four times in six verses without allowing them to work in a coordinated manner. The related force influencing v. 6 is that behind the witness of John is the God of creation (v. 3), who is working in creation. John could have used the imperfect "was" (ἦν), which would have described John from the inside. Instead John signals to the reader that even the ministry of the Baptist is subsumed under the creative working of God.

After being used again in v. 10 in a manner similar to v. 3, helping to carry forward the developing force of the verb, the term is used for a sixth time in v. 12 to describe the "creative" force of God when those who believe "become" (γενέσθαι) children of God. This transformation can only be described (with Paul) as a new creation, connecting this use of the verb with its emphatic use in v. 3 regarding the creation of the world.

The seventh (a significant number) occurrence of the verb occurs in v. 14 when John describes how the Word "became" (ἐγένετο) flesh. This is the ultimate manifestation of God's "creative" activity. The God who had been working from the outside was now on the inside; the Creator is now with his creation. In v. 14 Jesus is also described with a new title that is taken from the word's root: "the unique Son" (μονογενής; repeated in v. 18). By means of this eighth use Jesus has become the pinnacle of creation, the center of human history and all created things. The ninth use of the verb in v. 15 reinforces Jesus's place in history and the plan of God, making clear that Jesus "existed" not only before the time of the Baptist but before the creation of the world.

Finally, the verb is used for a tenth (another significant number) time in v. 17 to describe how the gospel of Jesus Christ is the ultimate "creative" act of God: the law was given through Moses, but grace and truth "came" (ἐγένετο) through Jesus Christ. The same power that God used to create the world (see v. 3) is also at work in the person and ministerial work of Jesus Christ. The children of God were born out of the same power that was used to create the world. With one verb the prologue of John describes with progressive precision the important characters, overall plot, and unseen forces at work in the story; something entirely missed in the English translation.

The above discussion not only gives evidence of a unified prologue (1:1 – 18) but also gives warrant for using the cosmological vision cast by the prologue to interpret and understand the historical events described by the remainder of the Gospel. Even more, the verb makes several other meaning-significant appearances through the Gospel. Direct examples include 4:14; 5:6, 9; 6:19; and 8:58. Indirect examples include 3:9; 6:25; 9:27, 39; and 19:36. While we will not explore each of those examples in depth, the same "creative" and transformative vision of the work of God through Jesus Christ crafted by the prologue should, based upon the context, be equally applied to those occurrences.

The larger context of the prologue makes certain that v. 17 ought not to be classified as synonymous or antithetical parallelism but as "synthetic" or "progressive" parallelism.[150] The old covenant is as much grace as the new, but it is in the new covenant that grace is given its ultimate and final expression. *The progression of the prologue has moved from a God who has "given" to his people to a God who has "come" to his people.* Such statements can only be grounded in a larger biblical theology. The Old Testament would be poorly interpreted if the old covenant was not inclusive of God's grace (see 5:45 – 47; cf. Rom 7:12 – 16). The law was never given *by* Moses but *through* him (cf. Acts 7:53). The argument that our interpretation demands that "the grace of God [be] available in two grades" is to pit Scripture against itself.[151]

If "the law" provides "light for the path" (Ps 119:105), "grace and truth" describe the nature of the true Light. The context behind v. 17 is the giving of the law in Exodus 34. Not only does v. 17 explicitly refer to the giving of the law but "grace and truth" explicate the phrases in Exodus 34:6. With the context of Exodus 33 – 34 almost certainly echoing in the background, v. 17 is presenting a rich image. In the giving of the law, God revealed himself to Moses when "Yahweh passed before him" as the God of grace and truth, steadfast love, and faithfulness (Exod 34:6). But even though he prayed to see God (Exod 33:18), Moses was not able to see God's glory. Only after he had passed by would God remove from Moses his hand that covered him (Exod 33:18 – 22). Thus, it was not merely the law that Moses mediated but the reflection of the glory of God. But what Moses was unable to see, Jesus Christ is! Who was greater than Moses? The one to whom Moses directed his worship (Exod 34:8): the Word-who-is-God. For "what Moses saw of the revelation of Yahweh's glory was nothing other than the revelation of God in Jesus Christ (cf. Jn. 12:41)."[152] Grace and truth are embodied in a person so that "this former manifestation of God's gracious love and favor has been replaced by a new, personal, and unique manifestation through his Son."[153]

This is the last occurrence of "grace" (χάρις) in the Gospel. From this point on, "grace" has no meaning outside of "Jesus Christ" — the name introduced here for the first time in the Gospel. Now the Word, Life, Light, and "unique Son" are known as Jesus Christ. Although the proper name is used again in 17:3, it is likely that the formal occurrence

---

150. Cf. J. Jeremias, "Μωϋσῆς," *TDNT* 4:873.
151. Barrett, *John*, 168.
152. Ridderbos, *John*, 58.
153. Edwards, "ΧΑΡΙΝ ΑΝΤΙ ΧΑΡΙΤΟΣ," 9.

in 20:31 ("that you may believe that Jesus is the Christ") is to be understood to form an *inclusio* with 1:17, embracing the whole Gospel, so that the reader is invited to believe in Jesus as the Christ, the Son of God, through whom the grace and truth promised in the old covenant were brought into "being" (ἐγένετο).[154]

1:18 No one has ever seen God; the unique Son, God, who is in the bosom of the Father, he revealed him (Θεὸν οὐδεὶς ἑώρακεν πώποτε· μονογενὴς θεὸς ὁ ὢν εἰς τὸν κόλπον τοῦ πατρὸς ἐκεῖνος ἐξηγήσατο). The prologue ends with the final declaration of the uniqueness of the Word. What makes the Word, who is Jesus Christ, ultimately unique is his position beside the Father. The statement begins by asserting a universal principle, "No one has ever seen God" (Θεὸν οὐδεὶς ἑώρακεν πώποτε). "In this sentence the whole historical relationship of men to God is set forth."[155] With the echo of Exodus 33 – 34 still in the background, such a statement is potent. The desire to see God resides deep within the human soul, even if the true weight of such a sight is itself unknowable — death (Exod 33:20). Yet the OT strongly assumes that God is invisible (e.g., Deut 4:12; Ps 97:2), and the idea is developed even further in later Judaism.[156] Even passages that speak of men "seeing" God, the theophanies of the OT (e.g., Exod 24:9 – 11), in no way imply that God's essential being had been seen. Until now God has only been seen in shadows and figures, not in his person. That the final statement of the prologue begins with such a negation "emphasizes that the fundamental theme of the Gospel is the revelation of God."[157]

The meaning of the opening clause is quite clear: no person can see God. The exception is Jesus Christ, described here as "the unique Son, God" (μονογενὴς θεὸς). Although some reliable manuscripts exchange "son" (υἱός) for "God," the superior manuscripts do not, and matters related to scribal habits make it likely that it is not the more primitive text.[158] Unfortunately, the text-critical issue is not the only problem regarding this phrase, for both "unique Son" (μονογενής) and "God" (θεός) may be understood adjectively or substantively. That "unique Son" (μονογενής) is anarthrous suggests that it is not functioning adjectively, since other Johannine occurrences have both "unique Son" (μονογενής) and the noun it qualifies as articular (cf. 3:16, 18; 1 John 4:9). It is best, then, to understand the term as a substantive, carrying the meaning determined for it in v. 14, "unique Son." This probably explains why the term "son" was often exchanged for "God" in some textual traditions.[159] In four of its eight uses in the NT (Luke 7:12; John 3:16, 18; 1 John 4:9), "unique Son" (μονογενής) functions as an attributive adjective modifying "Son" (υἱός). In the other three occasions, the term stands alone, but the context makes clear that it implies sonship (John 1:14; Heb 11:17; Luke 9:38). The only occasion in the NT where "unique Son" (μονογενής) is not used of a "son" is in Luke 8:42, where it qualifies an "only daughter" (θυγάτηρ μονογενής). Such an analysis confirms our analysis in v. 14.

Since "unique Son" (μονογενής) is not functioning adjectively with "God" (θεός), the corollary is that "God" stands in epexegetical apposition to "unique Son": "The unique Son, God." As Wallace explains, an appositive functions very much like a predicate nominative. The difference, however, is that while a predicate nominative makes an

---

154. McHugh, *John*, 69.
155. Hoskyns, *Fourth Gospel*, 152.
156. See Keener, *John*, 1:423 – 24.
157. Barrett, *John*, 169.

158. See Harris, *Jesus as God*, 74 – 83.
159. Cf. Benjamin J. Burkholder, "Considering the Possibility of a Theological Corruption in Joh 1,18 in Light of Its Early Reception," *ZNW* 103 (2012): 64 – 83.

assertion about the subject, the appositive makes an *assumption*, not an assertion.[160] Hence we will translate the term as "God" instead of "who is God," even though the latter is possible. In the context of the prologue what can now be assumed is that the "unique Son" is God; it need not be asserted, even though the assumption needs to be made explicit for the clause that follows. The anarthrous "God" (θεός) is not indefinite, made certain by the use of "he" (ἐκεῖνος). It is significant that both terms are anarthrous substantives, for it draws attention to the uniqueness of the familial status of Jesus Christ as the one and only Son of God (in the case of the "unique Son" [μονογενής]) and to his possession of the attributes of deity (in the case of "God" [θεός]).[161] The awkward grammar merely serves to emphasize this significant theological reality. With an intentional allusion to v. 1, an *inclusio* is formed that declares that the Word-God is Jesus the Son.

The position of the unique Son is described by another appositional, though this time adjectival, phrase: "who is in the bosom of the Father" (ὁ ὢν εἰς τὸν κόλπον τοῦ πατρός). The phrase, "the bosom of the Father" (τὸν κόλπον τοῦ πατρός), can be loosely translated as "the side of the Father," but is best understood as "the bosom" (τὸν κόλπον). The metaphor most frequently denotes the most intimate human relationships; for example, marriage (Deut 13:6), mother and child (1 Kgs 3:20), and God's care for Israel (Num 11:12). Almost certainly it continues the *inclusio* between vv. 1 and 18 by expressing "with God" (πρὸς τὸν θεόν) of v. 1 in another way. Thus, in combination with the present participle and the preposition "in" (εἰς),[162] the metaphor expresses the continuing and intimate union of the Son and the Father. Once understood to refer to the entirety of the Son in his person,

such a union with the Father reflects upon the very ministry of Jesus himself. When the Word became flesh, he did not cease to perform his cosmic activities as if the incarnation demanded an episodic interruption of his true being. At the same time, by taking on flesh, God himself fully shares in humanity, creating an intimacy between the Father and his "children" (cf. 13:23).

The prologue ends by explaining that the intimate position of the Son becomes the source of the revelation of the Father: "he revealed him" (ἐκεῖνος ἐξηγήσατο). The choice of the verb is a significant conclusion to the prologue. In the NT (only in Luke – Acts) the term can mean "to recount, relate, report, describe, or explain," though in classical Greek it can also mean "to impart" and "to interpret."[163] We must be careful not to demand the determination of a precise meaning but must allow the term to have real meaning without denying its multifacted "impressions" (see Introduction).[164] In the context of the verse what is unique about Jesus is that he provides for some to "see" God. Translating the verb as "has revealed him" allows us to focus on the revelatory act of the Son without losing the multifacted nature of his revelation. For it is important to remember that the final word of the prologue is not about revelation *per se* but about the revealer, the "exegete," a word ultimately derived from the verb "to reveal, report, explain, interpret" (ἐξηγεῖσθαι). The focus is on "the Word," who is himself the original, primary, and authentic revelation. In this way the prologue ends where it began (v. 1), strategically concluding with v. 18, which looks back over the prologue from its peak and presses forward into the Gospel narrative with the full recollection that the revelation of God has arrived.

160. Wallace, *Greek Grammar*, 48.
161. Harris, *Jesus as God*, 92.
162. Wallace, *Greek Grammar*, 360. Cf. McHugh, *John*, 70.
163. See McHugh, *John*, 73 – 77.
164. Cf. R. Roberts, "La Double Intention du Mot Final du Prologue Johannique," *RThom* 87 (1987): 435 – 41.

IN DEPTH: The Eternal Generation of the Son

Many theologians in the history of the church have supported the doctrine called the eternal generation of the Son. Likely deriving from Origen, the phrase denotes the inter-Trinitarian relationship between the Father and the Son. "Generation" suggests that there is a divine sonship prior to the incarnation, and that there is a clear distinction of persons within the one Godhead (see comments on 5:26). The doctrine is affirmed in confessions like the Niceno-Constantinopolitan Creed (AD 381) and post-Reformation statements like the Westminster Confession of Faith (WCF 2.3). The doctrine is strongly supported by 1:18, especially the use of the term long but wrongly translated as "only begotten" (μονογενής). Since the term is more accurately translated as "unique Son," support for the doctrine in recent years has decreased. Some have even claimed the doctrine lacks biblical support.

Although our interpretation of the term "unique Son" (μονογενής) goes against the idea of "only begotten," and therefore distances that term from the concept of "generation" (see comments on 1:14), there is no reason to deny the doctrine of the eternal generation of the Son. The eternal generation of the Son is not best drawn from a few dubious proof texts but is rooted in a rigorous and comprehensive Trinitarian hermeneutic.[165] Scripture's subject matter depicts the Trinitarian relationship between the Father and the Son in a manner that is nicely summarized by the doctrine of eternal generation.[166] The idea of eternal generation corresponds fittingly to what God has shown of himself in his own eternal being (the imminent Trinity). For "God has given form and order to the history of salvation because he intends not only to save us through it but also to reveal himself through it. The economy is shaped by God's intention to communicate his identity and character."[167] And when the Son and Holy Spirit are depicted in human history, they behave as they truly are: "Their eternal personalities, we might say, are exhibited here in time."[168] Thus, the doctrine of the eternal generation of the Son can rightly be drawn from the subject matter of Scripture, with 1:18 giving a glimpse into the very nature of God and the intimate union between God the Father and God the Son.

165. Helpful here is Keith E. Johnson, "Augustine, Eternal Generation, and Evangelical Trinitarianism," *TrinJ* 32 (2011): 141 – 63.

166. See John V. Dahms, "The Generation of the Son," *JETS* 32 (1989): 493 – 501.

167. Fred Sanders, *The Deep Things of God: How the Trinity Changes Everything* (Wheaton: Crossway, 2010), 133.

168. Ibid., 151.

Theology in Application

The Gospel begins with a prologue that describes the ultimate goal of God the Father: to create "children of God" by means of his "unique Son," Jesus Christ, who is the very expression (Word) of God. The prologue introduces not merely theological themes but a vision of God for his people and his world, finding fullest expression in the person and work of Jesus Christ. The prologue, introducing Christ for the rest of the Gospel narrative, is also introducing Christ for the rest of the world. The prologue simultaneously introduces the Gospel and pronounces the gospel.

Jesus the Word

The God who spoke creation into existence offered his climactic statement in the person of the Word. The Word reflects the truth that it is the very nature of God to reveal himself. In Jesus, God is intentionally personal. The Word is God's self-expression in creation, revelation, and salvation. The Word is the message and person of God, making manifest his love for the world and shining his light in the darkness. It is not the voice of a stranger but of a shepherd, which the sheep recognize and follow (cf. 10:3 – 5). It is Jesus the Word who speaks on behalf of God. Jesus is the very voice of God; his statements and actions are entirely God's. Everything God has ever said, is saying, and will say is made manifest in Jesus the Word.

It is one of the primary tasks of the church to listen to God. The Word of God is the voice of God. The voice to which the church must become fixated is the Word of God made fully manifest in Jesus Christ. Jesus the Word is not a word in the past but is fully present, for Jesus is the same yesterday, today, and forever (Heb 13:8). The Gospel of John, then, does not merely tell us what Jesus (of Nazareth) once said; it tells us what Jesus (the Word of God) is saying. John proclaims in Jesus the Word of God for the people of God.

Jesus the Unique Son of God

Jesus Christ is God incarnate. Jesus existed before time itself and is the one through whom creation came into existence. He is the one in whom life is found and is the light of humanity. He is in intimate communion with the Father and is, when received, the one through whom the right to become "children of God" is possible. All of this is because Jesus, God himself, came to us, the world. Jesus is God dwelling with us. God walked out of the stone temple, the holy of holies, and has put on "flesh." He is us ("flesh") before God the Father and he is God "among us." Yet his presence "among us" is not merely as our God but also as our brother. Jesus, as the unique Son, finds kinship with the children of God. The uniqueness of being the children of God is eclipsed by the unique Son, yet both find relation to God and to one another. It is one thing to understand that God has extended himself to his creation by sending the Word-made-flesh, but it is another to grasp that Jesus does not merely share our flesh but is an intimate brother, providing intimacy with the Father to his siblings. Jesus is unique not only in his relation to the Father but also in his relation to his "brothers and sisters."

The Plight of the World

The subtle shift from the created life of humanity in v. 4 to the spiritual life of humanity in v. 5 is summative of the entire redemptive storyline. Jesus did not just come to the world he created; he came to the *fallen* world. The life that the Word has in himself (cf. 5:26) is not just the life that begins at creation but is also the life of the new creation that begins with the sending of the Son by the Father. The Son was sent to shine "in the darkness." Yet the world was so darkened by sin that it did not recognize (v. 5), know (v. 10), or receive (v. 11) the light, the Light of humanity, the very one that created the world. It is for this reason that the Light came, the bearer of life, that he might reclaim the world that he created and the people that he loves, to whom he gives the right to become his children. The testimony of the church now incorporates Jesus, his story, and the life resurrected in his person. The prologue emphasizes that life — all creation — belongs to God. But physical life is only an aspect of the life that God provides through Jesus. The life of the church, then, is founded and strengthened by the Life, the Light of humanity, and only through his life, which is now finally entering the church's own testimony.

The Witness of John

John the Baptist reflects a God who initiates, intercedes, and introduces himself to the world. The choice of verbs in v. 6 suggests that God acted on behalf of himself to create a witness to the Word, the one in whom it is necessary to believe (v. 7). Even those used by God to witness to God are to be subsumed under the creative working of God. The Baptist introduces the public ministry of Jesus, that is, the public ministry of God.

The ministry of the Baptist should provide a model for all Christian ministry in that it constantly serves as a witness to Jesus Christ and is intentional about maintaining its role as the witness and *not* the light (v. 8). In that sense, the ministry of the church is, like the Baptist's, prophetic. Like a prophet, contemporary Christian witness speaks into the circumstances of which he or she is a part, bringing a message that is external to the prophet, the gospel, calling people to belief in Jesus.

The Children of God

The plight of the world was a misplaced identity. Creation had rejected its Creator, the loved had rejected the Lover. When Jesus was not received by the people to whom he belonged, God himself was not received by the world that belonged to him. If the result is the rejection of God, the cause is a crisis of identity. The world has become distinct from its Creator. But God in his love was not done creating. There is a new creation — a new status. The plight has turned to promise because of the authority of a person who welcomes children to the Father. As hard as it is to believe, faith is the only requirement. God does the rest. No one does this for him or herself; no one does this from within himself — we may not even desire this gift. "But God," a statement that evokes worship and adoration, does this. There is no other foundation "but God," and the work he does through his "unique Son," Jesus Christ.

The church only knows itself in relation to God. This new identity defines the individual against his or her past, but also defines the community over and against all its "natural" diversity. Just as Genesis depicts the creation of humanity on the sixth day as the pinnacle of creation, so the children of God, the new creation, become the pinnacle of God's creative activity in and through Jesus Christ. Amidst all ethnic, cultural, and natural diversity, the church becomes an embassy in which a true people find true unity and familial relationship through the unique Son, Jesus Christ.

God with Us

In Jesus Christ the world meets God. In Jesus, God personally embraced humanity, taking upon himself its spiritual plight, and dwelled among us. While God did dwell with his people and reveal his glory in the Old Testament, never had he dwelled and revealed in this manner before. Jesus Christ is the dwelling of God *par excellence*, fulfilling and replacing patterns, prophecies, and traditions associated with the tabernacle and temple. No longer does God command his people to make for him a dwelling (Exod 25:9), for he has made one for himself *ex nihilo* in Jesus Christ. The presence of God in Jesus makes the relation between Jesus and the church all the more significant. Since God is present with his people, the church then becomes the temple of God (1 Cor 3:16). The unique presence of God through the Son in the children of God transforms the church into the dwelling place of God. The church becomes the very body of Christ, with every individual a member of it (1 Cor 12:27). Just as Jesus manifests God in the world, so the church manifests Christ in the world. Through word and deed, the church is an ambassador of God through Christ. This is more than a calling; it is part of the church's identity.

The Revelation of God

Jesus Christ is the unique Son of God, sent from the Father, to become the ultimate expression of the grace of God. He completes and fulfills all previously received grace from God. The Gospel of John invites the reader to believe in Jesus as the Christ, the Son of God, through whom the grace and truth promised in the old covenant were brought into being. In a world that is unable to see God, Jesus brings sight to the blind — light in the darkness, presenting the Father in word and deed. The church also bears witness to God through Christ as it embraces Christ and reflects his life and coparticipates as the "light" of the world (Matt 5:14).

CHAPTER 2

John 1:19 – 34

Literary Context

Since this pericope immediately follows the prologue, it serves as the beginning of the narrative proper. It forms a secondary, though clearly subsidiary, introduction to the Gospel as it describes the appearance of Jesus the Word into the world, the historical context of first-century Israel near Jerusalem. The voice of the narrative is no longer the narrator's alone but now also includes the characters with whom Jesus engages and ministers. The prologue's introduction to the Baptist as a prophetic-apostolic witness to Jesus is made manifest in human history as John the "voice crying in the wilderness" is made public. The scene is first-century Israel just outside Jerusalem in Bethany on the other side of the Jordan, where John is drawing attention from the Jewish authorities because of his ministry and message, which includes a water baptism (v. 25). The ministry of John is primarily as witness to Christ; he has been "sent" by God for this very task.

I. Prologue (1:1 – 18)

➡ **II. The First Week: An Introduction to the Narrative Proper (1:19 – 51)**

A. The Witness of John (1:19 – 34)

B. The First Disciples (1:35 – 51)

Main Idea

Jesus is introduced to Israel (and the world) at his entrance into world history with titles that manifest his ministry to redeem the world from sin. Jesus is both the sacrificial Lamb and the offered son of Abraham. The Baptist's message is a reflection of a person who has seen who God is and what God has done: "Not me, but him!"

Translation

John 1:19–34

19a	Scene 1	Now **this is the witness of John,**
b	Setting	when the Jews from Jerusalem sent [to him] priests and Levites
c	Purpose	in order to ask him,
d	Question	*"Who are you?"*
20a	Response	And **he confessed and did not deny, and he confessed:**
b	Emphatic Denial	*"I am not the Christ."*
21a		And **they asked him,**
b	Question	*"Who are you, then? Are you Elijah?"*
c	Response	And **he said,**
d	Denial	*"I am not."*
e	Question	*"Are you the Prophet?"*
f	Response	And **he answered,**
g	Denial	*"No."*
22a		Finally **they said to him,**
b	Question	*"Who are you?*
c	Purpose	*In order that we may give an answer to those who sent us:*
d	Restatement	*What do you say about yourself?"*
23a	Response	**He said,**
b	Prophecy/OT Quotation	*"I am a voice crying out in the wilderness,*
c		'Make straight the way of the Lord,' (Isa 40:3)
d		*just as Isaiah the prophet said."*
24a	Aside: Clarification of 19b	And **some who were sent belonged to the Pharisees.**
25a		And **they asked him and said to him,**
b	Question	*"Why, then, do you baptize if you are not the Messiah, nor Elijah, nor the Prophet?"*
26a	Response	And **John answered them saying,**
b	Assertion	*"I baptize with water, but there is one among you whom you do not know.*
27a	Emphatic Contrast	*He is the one who comes after me; I am not worthy to untie the strap of his sandal."*
28a	Conclusion/Place	**These things occurred**
b	Description #1	in Bethany,
c	Description #2	on the other side of the Jordan,
d	Description #3	where John was baptizing.
29a	Scene 2/Setting	**On the next day he saw Jesus coming toward him and said,**
b	Confession/Allusion: OT & NT	*"Behold, the Lamb of God,*
c	Description	*the one who takes away the sin of the world.*
30a		*This is the one about whom I said,*
b	Assertion (Cf. 1:15)	*'A man who follows me has surpassed me,*
c	Basis	*because he was prior to me.'*
31a	Assertion	*And I myself did not know him,*
b	John's Purpose	*but the reason I came baptizing with water was in order that he might be ☜*
		revealed to Israel."
32a	Climax	And **John witnessed, saying,**
b	Prophecy/Allusion: Isa 11:2	*"I saw the Spirit descend like a dove from heaven,*
c		*and he remained upon him.*

33a	Restatement of 31a	*And I myself did not know him,*
b	Contrast	*but the one who sent me to baptize with water told me,*
c	Recollection	*'The man upon whom you see the Spirit descend and remain,*
d		*he is the one who baptizes with the Holy Spirit.'*
34a	Conclusion/Fulfillment	*And I have seen and I have born witness that he is the Son of God."*

Structure and Literary Form

The "witness" (μαρτυρία) of John serves as a framing motif that forms an *inclusio* in 1:19 – 34. The structure of this pericope is different than the basic story form, with its conflict-resolution structure (see Introduction). Rather, the pericope is given direction by the designation of "days," which guide the reader through the first "week" of Jesus's ministry. The first "week" of the ministry of Jesus serves as the structure for the remainder of chapter 1 (see comments before 2:1), with two pericopae (vv. 19 – 34 and vv. 35 – 51) that function as an introduction to the narrative proper. In the first pericope, the events take place on the first two days of Jesus's first week: day one: vv. 19 – 28, and day two: vv. 29 – 34.

Exegetical Outline

→ **A. The Witness of John (1:19 – 34)**
    1. John, the Voice in the Wilderness (1:19 – 28)
        a. "Not Me": Jewish Authorities Question John (vv. 19 – 22)
        b. "But Him": John's Declaration of the Christ (vv. 23 – 28)
    2. Jesus, the Lamb and Son of God (1:29 – 34)
        a. John's Witness to the Lamb of God (vv. 29 – 31)
        b. The Spirit's Witness to the Son of God (vv. 32 – 34)

Explanation of the Text

The beginning of the narrative proper is crafted in such a manner that it forms a secondary and clearly subsidiary introduction to the Gospel. This secondary introduction locates the Word, Jesus Christ, in the historical context of the first century. Like the Synoptics, the Fourth Gospel begins with John the Baptist, though the nature of the Baptist's role is unique in John. The prologue has already described the role of the Baptist as prophetic-apostolic witness to Jesus. Here the witness of the Baptist is given its public voice. That "witness" (μαρτυρία) of John becomes an *inclusio* that frames 1:19 – 34.

1:19 Now this is the witness of John, when the Jews from Jerusalem sent [to him] priests and

Levites in order to ask him, "Who are you?" (Καὶ αὕτη ἐστὶν ἡ μαρτυρία τοῦ Ἰωάννου, ὅτε ἀπέστειλαν [πρὸς αὐτὸν] οἱ Ἰουδαῖοι ἐξ Ἱεροσολύμων ἱερεῖς καὶ Λευίτας ἵνα ἐρωτήσωσιν αὐτόν, Σὺ τίς εἶ;). The opening of the narrative proper begins with the established witness of John the Baptist. The nature of the witness is intended to be carried over from the prologue, for this opening statement is not primarily a historical note but is intending to "bring out the official character" of the Baptist's witness.[1] The verb "is" (ἐστὶν) functions as a perfective present, or as Wallace suggests, a *testimonium* present.[2] The *testimonium* of the Baptist who came "in order to witness" (1:7) is now given his first occasion.

The "witness" is given its first juridical testing when some ambassadors are sent to cross-examine the witness. The scene is full of lawsuit imagery and forensic overtones.[3] The witness of the Baptist is of such a character that it drew an official delegation from Jerusalem. We cannot know with certainty what attracted the delegation to John. That they were "sent" (ἀπέστειλαν) — the same word used for the sending of the Baptist (1:6) — renders their visit to the Baptist as official business. The members of the delegation, "priests and Levites" (ἱερεῖς καὶ Λευίτας), also imply that it was an official visit and may even reflect the nature of the delegation.

This is the only place where priests and Levites are mentioned in John, so there is no other use from which we may derive John's assumption regarding these groups. In general, both priests and Levites belonged to the lower ranks of the clergy. Priests were rarely high in social status. The Levites were even lower; forbidden to take part in the offering of sacrifice, they usually provided service as musicians, doormen, and the police force of the temple.[4] It has been argued that the lower rank of the priests and Levites might imply that the authorities in Jerusalem were initially content to send a low-ranking delegation to gather intel regarding the Baptist's pretensions and activities.[5] While this is certainly possible, it might be implying too much. Priests and Levites were "the employees of the nation for the purposes of maintaining the worship of God in the temple, and teaching and judging the people."[6]

Even beyond their roles and titles, the purpose for which they were sent reveals the official nature of the delegation. They were sent "in order to ask" (ἵνα ἐρωτήσωσιν) a specific question of Baptist: Who are you? (σὺ τίς εἶ;). This question regarding his identity bears the weight of questions regarding his origins, intentions, and message. With the language of an official sending, and the sending of an official delegation, such a question makes clear that it was not an informal visit or a visit out of curiosity, as if they were merely interested in John's baptism as a purification ritual.[7] This was an official visit with religious and political implications. In a world that was without prophets, John was a prophetic voice. And his sudden and unexpected appearance had created quite a stir. The people had been listening to John, so an official delegation was sent to provide a report. The religious-political tensions are highlighted by the sending party, "the Jews," who in the Fourth Gospel serve as the primary interlocutor of Jesus.

1. Bultmann, *John*, 86.
2. Wallace, *Greek Grammar*, 532.
3. Lincoln, *Truth on Trial*, 58 – 65.
4. McHugh, *John*, 115.
5. Ibid.
6. E. P. Sanders, *Judaism: Practice and Belief: 63 BCE – 66 CE* (Philadelphia: Fortress, 1992), 182.
7. As suggested by Carson, *John*, 142, and Brown, *John*, 1:43.

IN DEPTH: "The Jews"

"The Jews" (οἱ Ἰουδαῖοι) are collectively an important character in the Fourth Gospel, and their introduction in the first verse of the narrative proper is significant. "The Jews" are mentioned in the Gospel seventy-one times; in the Synoptics they are only mentioned seventeen times. Over half of the occurrences are in conflict scenes where they are opposed to Jesus and his ministry. At the same time, the Jews are not always portrayed negatively; some Jews appear to be believers (cf. 8:31; 11:45; 12:11), and even Jesus is called a "Jew" by the Samaritan woman (4:9). The term has been viewed as problematic in the contemporary, postholocaust world.[8] The complexity of the term and its frequent occurrence will demand a developing analysis throughout the narrative, but a few things can be stated as an introductory summary.

First, at the most basic level "the Jews" (οἱ Ἰουδαῖοι) must be understood in their historical context. In the context of the first century the term is best understood by drawing its meaning from the post-Old Testament period when both "Jew" and "Israelite" were used to indicate that a person belonged to the ancestry of Israel and the religious community of Judaism.[9] In the context of the Gospel the term is regularly applied by John to Judaism and its official leaders, the center of which is at Jerusalem. "The Jews" are not always described negatively, as noted above, but they are clearly recognizable to the reader of John as a frequent opponent of Jesus. They defend the letter of the law (5:16), refuse to accept the authority of Jesus and his messianic status (9:22), and, after denying his kingship, ultimately deny their own status as the people of God (19:14–16).[10] Thus, as much as the Gospel is written with Jewish ink, the Gospel's use of "the Jews" demands, at least in part, some level of separation from the evangelist.

Second, our translation, "the Jews" (οἱ Ἰουδαῖοι), though not without debate, best allows for the narrative development of the term and a particularly Johannine duality of meaning. The search for the term's meaning solely in its literary or social-historical context often undermines the use of the term in John. In a very real sense Jesus (and the Gospel) is in conflict with "the Jews." But it could be no other way for the Word is in conflict with his entire creation. To exclude the Jews would be to exclude a part of creation from its Creator. Reinhartz makes an interesting claim: "The Fourth Gospel's polemic against the Jews undermines its declaration of God's boundless love for the world."[11] But

---

8. See, for example, Reimund Bieringer, Didier Pollefeyt, and Frederique Vandecasteele-Vanneuville, eds., *Anti-Judaism and the Fourth Gospel* (Louisville: Westminster John Knox, 2001). One contributor, a Jewish scholar, Adele Reinhartz, "'Jews' and Jews in the Fourth Gospel," 213, explains regard-

ing her initial encounters with the Gospel that "each Johannine usage of the term *Jew* felt like a slap in the face."

9. Ridderbos, *John*, 62.

10. Barrett, *John*, 172.

11. Reinhartz, "'Jews' and Jews in the Fourth Gospel," 227.

the reverse is in fact the case; it is not love that is the problem but sin. The Word is the Light shining in the darkness. And as the Baptist will shortly declare, this light is the "Lamb of God," a particularly significant term for "the Jews." But this Lamb is not simply intended for Jews but for the sin of the "world" (1:29). This is God's love.

1:20 And he confessed and did not deny, and he confessed: "I am not the Christ" (καὶ ὡμολόγησεν καὶ οὐκ ἠρνήσατο, καὶ ὡμολόγησεν ὅτι Ἐγὼ οὐκ εἰμὶ ὁ Χριστός). The repetitive style of the verse sets the Baptist's response in a framework of solemnity. It is not uncommon for the two verbs, "confess" (ὁμολογέω) and "deny" (ἀρνέομαι), to be used in the same context and by way of contrast (cf. Josephus, *Ant.* 6.151). The former often carries a judicial connotation and is best translated as "confess," making certain that the statement by the Baptist be taken as having a forensic meaning as part of the legal examination. Yet while the positive-negative combination is common enough, this is the only occurrence of a triple combination (positive-negative-positive) in the Gospel. This tautological introduction to the Baptist's confession is not to be understood as an editorial enhancement,[12] or as a message directed at the Baptist's disciples who claimed him as Messiah,[13] but as a necessary use of repetition "to express the form of the confession."[14] The fullness of the introduction is a necessary correlate to the fullness of the denial.

The confession of John is stated emphatically: "I am not the Christ" (ἐγὼ οὐκ εἰμὶ ὁ χριστός). The emphatic "I" (ἐγώ) simultaneously declares that he is not and another is. The declaration about himself is entirely in the negative. The Baptist's role as the prophet-apostle, which was established in the

prologue, is now in full effect. John has become "the normative image of the Christian preacher, apostle, and missionary, the perfect prototype of the true evangelist, whose one goal is self-effacement before Christ."[15]

The Baptist denies in full that he is "the Christ" (ὁ Χριστός). In this context "Christ" is used in an undefined sense, almost certainly denoting "the Messiah" and "the anointed one" but without determining precisely how that title was to be understood.[16] For the Jew it clearly had messianic connotations; for the gentile it was often understood as a personal name. While it is undeniable that John assumes the former in this context, the fact that the latter use was applied in 1:17 implies that the undefined "Christ" is not entirely a mystery. But the Baptist's indefinite use of the title is intended to separate himself from the "Christ"; only after he has separated himself will the Baptist be able to define "the Christ."

Although we are not given the exact question(s) from the interlocutors, the Baptist's response implies that the topic was in reference to messianic hopes and expectations, which were undoubtedly high in the time of Jesus. The expectations were almost certainly varied in two ways. First, claims about the messiah could generally be defined along three messianic identities: (1) Davidic messiah, (2) priestly messiah, and (3) "the Prophet" (Deut

---

12. Cf. Brown, *John*, 1:43.
13. Cf. Schnackenburg, *John*, 1:288.
14. Calvin, *John 1 – 10*, 27.

15. Walter Wink, *John the Baptist in the Gospel Tradition*, SNTSMS 7 (Cambridge: Cambridge University Press, 1968), 105.
16. McHugh, *John*, 116.

18:15–19). While we can assume that "Davidic" and "priestly" were the most prominent, none of the identities were mutually exclusive. It is more than likely that a conglomerate messianic identity was basic to the common first-century Jew. Second, there is evidence that the nonappearance of the messiah shifted the expectations from a physical sense, a warrior-king of God who would lead a national independence movement, to a spiritual sense, a chosen one of God who would be filled with the Spirit.[17] The diversity of expectations explains why Jesus expressly refused to accept the title of "Messiah," especially when it was attached to warrior-king expectations (cf. 18:11, 36).

1:21 And they asked him, "Who are you, then? Are you Elijah?" And he said, "I am not." "Are you the Prophet?" And he answered, "No" (καὶ ἠρώτησαν αὐτόν, Τί οὖν σύ; Ἡλίας εἶ; καὶ λέγει, Οὐκ εἰμί. Ὁ προφήτης εἶ σύ; καὶ ἀπεκρίθη, Οὔ). In v. 20 the questions asked by the interlocutors were not even given; it was the Baptist's answer that was the focus. In v. 21 the opposite is the case without in any way minimizing the continuing force of the strong negative of v. 20. Whether it was out of curiosity or a further exploration of the nature and source of the Baptist's activity, the investigators from Jerusalem continue with an onslaught of questions. The question of his identity is equally a question of mission and purpose, which in a heated religious-political context might explain the continued questioning.

The interlocutors ask him two further questions; the first asks, "Are you Elijah?" (Ἡλίας εἶ;). The question is rooted in the promise made by the prophet Malachi. Malachi 3:1–4 claims that God (Yahweh) was to send a "messenger" to purify the temple and its priesthood in order to prepare the way for his own coming. In Malachi 4:5–6 (= 3:23–24 MT) God declares, "I will send you the

prophet Elijah," in order to turn people's hearts so that God might not "come and strike the land with a curse." This "messenger" was often considered a forerunner not of the divine judge but of the messiah and, in light of the later passage, was often identified as Elijah. This is the background that the Synoptics presuppose as they describe the Baptist. Matthew 3:4 and Mark 1:6 both record that John wore a camel-hair tunic and leather belt, the same apparel worn by Elijah the prophet (2 Kgs 1:8). Luke 1:17 is even more direct: Zechariah's son will go before the Lord "in the spirit and power of Elijah" to turn people's hearts, quoting directly from the two passages in Malachi. Even more, in the Synoptics Jesus himself identifies John the Baptist as the promised Elijah (Matt 11:14; 17:12; Mark 9:13; cf. Luke 1:17, where it is an angel speaking). Yet the Baptist denies being Elijah: "And he said, 'I am not'" (καὶ λέγει· οὐκ εἰμί).

The second question asks, "Are you the Prophet?" (ὁ προφήτης εἶ σύ). The question is rooted in the promise of the "prophet like Moses" in Deuteronomy 18:15–19, to whom reference is also made in John 6:14; 7:40 (cf. Acts 3:22; 7:37). The Jewish tradition conceived of all sorts of "prophets" who would appear before the coming messiah (cf. Matt 16:14; Mark 6:15; Luke 9:19; 1 Macc 4:46; 14:41; 4 Ezra 2:18), but the traditions were inconsistent and did not provide a clear picture overall. However, there was more specific belief and hope that "the Prophet," a new prophet, would be sent to the assistance of Israel, though it too was still inconsistent and unclear. The "Prophet" was given greater emphasis in Samaritan and Qumran literature.[18] Clearly, therefore, the question by the interlocutors is reflecting currents within Judaism regarding an eschatological prophet, similar to the currents regarding Elijah. Yet the Baptist denies being the Prophet: "And he answered, 'no'" (καὶ ἀπεκρίθη,

---

17. Ibid., 154–56.   18. See Keener, *John*, 1:436–37.

οὔ.). The negative answer to the second question is narrated as stronger in force.

1:22 Finally they said to him, "Who are you? In order that we may give an answer to those who sent us: What do you say about yourself?" (εἶπαν οὖν αὐτῷ, Τίς εἶ; ἵνα ἀπόκρισιν δῶμεν τοῖς πέμψασιν ἡμᾶς· τί λέγεις περὶ σεαυτοῦ;). The conjunction (οὖν) in the narrative context is used to reflect the finality of the questioning; hence our translation "finally." After receiving negative answers to all their questions, the interrogators finally resort to asking him a generic question regarding his identity. Instead of giving their own suggestion, they ask him what he thinks "about himself" (περὶ σεαυτοῦ). They needed a positive statement to report to their superiors, who had sent them. This is a clear sign that the delegation was official.

1:23 He said, "I am a voice crying out in the wilderness, 'Make straight the way of the Lord,' just as Isaiah the prophet said" (ἔφη, Ἐγὼ φωνὴ βοῶντος ἐν τῇ ἐρήμῳ, Εὐθύνατε τὴν ὁδὸν κυρίου, καθὼς εἶπεν Ἡσαΐας ὁ προφήτης). The witness of the Baptist can only be the voice of the prophet. "He is no more than a voice."[19] John replies to the delegates from Jerusalem with a citation from Isaiah 40:3, a text also used at the beginning of his ministry in all three Synoptics. It is significant that the Baptist applies the words of Isaiah directly to himself; it is probably best to understand the final statement, "Just as Isaiah the prophet said" (καθὼς εἶπεν Ἡσαΐας ὁ προφήτης), as also belonging to the Baptist.

The use of the quotation is significant for two reasons. First, it locates the Baptist's role within the broad and expected work of God. The Baptist's declaration resonates through Isaiah 40:3 by connecting the Baptist with the great prophecy of the coming kingdom of God. The cry of the Baptist is one of penitence and conversion, without which the coming one cannot be received. Even more, the "crying voice" is "in the wilderness," which harkens back to the exile and stirs afresh the image of the return of the covenant people from exile.

Second, the point of the quotation is that it gives no prominence to the person about whom it speaks. He is not an important person; he is no more than a voice—a "voice" who announces the "Word" and his activities. The statement, "Make straight the way of the Lord" (εὐθύνατε τὴν ὁδὸν κυρίου), emphasizes that the Baptist's real function is not to teach but to introduce. It is the "Word" that is central to the Baptist and to the eschatological promise of God rooted in Isaiah.

Interestingly, after the closing words of v. 23 in which Isaiah the prophet is named, the only other occasion when the Gospel quotes from Isaiah is in 12:38–41, where the prophet is named three times. The verses in John 12 are openly presented as the reflections of the evangelist perceiving in the public ministry of Jesus the fulfillment of prophecies in the book of Isaiah, forming a thematic *inclusio* that locates the public ministry of Jesus within the eschatological promises of the prophet Isaiah.

1:24 And some who were sent belonged to the Pharisees (Καὶ ἀπεσταλμένοι ἦσαν ἐκ τῶν Φαρισαίων). Some suppose that the delegation first mentioned in v. 19 is given a further introduction here (e.g., "Now they had been sent by the Pharisees," RSV). The more likely meaning is that "some who were sent belonged to the Pharisees," implying that some of the delegates were from the party of the Pharisees. The preposition "belong to" (ἐκ) functions as a partitive genitive.[20] Thus, it speaks of a group within the group. This fits best with the interconnected questioning that clearly continues from v. 19, but is also historically plausible since it is very likely that some of the priests and Levites

---

19. Barrett, *John*, 173.

20. Cf. BDF § 164.

would belong to the party of the Pharisees even if they were not the majority.

The Pharisees are mentioned by the time of Jonathan of the Maccabeans, like the other two parties (cf. Josephus, *Ant.* 13.171). Having their origin in the "piety" movements that had joined forces against Antiochus IV Epiphanes (175–163 BC), who attempted to turn the Jewish faith into a Greek religion, the Pharisees were "experts in the laws of their country" who "enjoyed the highest esteem of the whole nation" (Josephus, *J.W.* 1.648). But at best the Pharisees had popular support and indirect authority, for they were neither politically connected nor aristocratic. The Pharisees were strict and precise in regards to the law (Josephus, *J.W.* 2.162). One of the distinguishing marks of the Pharisees was commitment to "the traditions of the elders" as supplementing or amending biblical law (cf. Josephus, *Ant.* 13.297; Mark 7:1–13). Their popular support and concern for the law meant they generally controlled the teaching of many synagogues, though it would be historically inaccurate to give to the Pharisees sole concern for the law for it was properly basic to Judaism to be devoted to the law. In the Gospel of John the Pharisees are the ever-watchful and suspicious adversaries of Jesus. They keep the people under surveillance and influence them with their propaganda (cf. 4:1; 7:32, 47–52; 11:46; 12:19, 42), and are experts in religious matters (cf. 3:1–2, 10; 7:47–49; 8:13; 9:16, 28–29, 40–41).[21]

1:25 And they asked him and said to him, "Why, then, do you baptize if you are not the Messiah, nor Elijah, nor the Prophet?" (καὶ ἠρώτησαν αὐτὸν καὶ εἶπαν αὐτῷ, Τί οὖν βαπτίζεις εἰ σὺ οὐκ εἶ ὁ Χριστὸς οὐδὲ Ἠλίας οὐδὲ ὁ προφήτης;). The priests and Levites who belonged to the party of the Pharisees pose a further question to the Baptist.

It is important to remember that the Gospel has not yet mentioned the baptism of John. The narrative takes it for granted that the readers are familiar with the tradition of John the Baptist. The question by the Pharisees might presuppose broader knowledge of a messianic baptism.[22] There are, however, no extant Jewish traditions which indicate that the messiah, Elijah, or the Prophet would baptize; only the Baptist describes such a baptism (1:33). With such a lack of evidence regarding a messianic baptism, the question may be referring not to the baptism but to the official status of the one who does such baptisms: "Why do you perform what appears to be an official act if you have no official status?"[23]

1:26 And John answered them saying, "I baptize with water, but there is one among you whom you do not know (ἀπεκρίθη αὐτοῖς ὁ Ἰωάννης λέγων, Ἐγὼ βαπτίζω ἐν ὕδατι· μέσος ὑμῶν ἕστηκεν ὃν ὑμεῖς οὐκ οἴδατε). John's response answers both the nature of his baptism and his official status. Regarding the baptism, John states nothing surprising, for water was almost assumed for baptism as well as for other symbolic reasons. The reader familiar with the Synoptics would expect John's opening statement to be contrasted with a greater kind of baptism, the baptism in the Holy Spirit that all three Synoptic Gospels refer to in a corresponding manner (Matt 3:11; Mark 1:7–8; Luke 3:16; cf. John 1:33). But John's comparison is not between water and spirit but between "I" and "him." In light of the greatness of Jesus, the topic of baptism fades away, for the subject matter of baptism "is among you" (μέσος ὑμῶν ἕστηκεν). The intention is not to minimize the role of baptism but to make clear that baptism is not an end in itself. As in the prologue, John is a witness to Jesus and nothing else. Whatever the secondary purpose of his baptism might be, the primary purpose is to bear witness to the

21. This paragraph relies heavily on Sanders, *Judaism*, 380–451.

22. Helpful here is Keener, *John*, 1:440–48.
23. Barrett, *John*, 174.

hidden messiah. His baptism is intended to prepare the people for him.[24] But there is more. The baptism no longer needs to look forward, for the one about whom John bears witness, the one about whom baptism refers, was there among them. The presence of the Word minimizes not only the role of the baptism but also the person of the Baptist. Yet in this moment the Baptist and his baptism serve as a rebuking witness to his interlocutors, who do not know who stands among them ("whom you do not know" [ὃν ὑμεῖς οὐκ οἴδατε]).

1:27 He is the one who comes after me; I am not worthy to untie the strap of his sandal (ὁ ὀπίσω μου ἐρχόμενος, οὗ οὐκ εἰμὶ [ἐγὼ] ἄξιος ἵνα λύσω αὐτοῦ τὸν ἱμάντα τοῦ ὑποδήματος). Jesus is incomparably greater than John, and John, as a good witness, makes it known. John's role is logically prior, though only on the plane of historical temporality (for the Word was in the beginning), and he is a prepatory witness to prepare the way for Jesus (vv. 22–23). John explains this emphatically by defining himself as not "worthy" (ἄξιος) enough to perform probably the most demeaning task assigned to household servants: caring for the feet of one's master. Some ancient sources even considered the task too demeaning for servants to have to perform for their masters, for to do such work was to be a slave.[25] Thus, although ancient teachers in Judaism usually expected disciples to function as servants, later rabbis allowed for one caveat: unlike slaves, they did not tend to the teacher's sandals.[26] The Baptist's argument reversed the normal social norm in order to magnify the greatness of Christ. "The sum of it is that he wants to abase himself as much as he can lest any degree of honor wrongly given to him should obscure the superiority of

Christ."[27] His relation is to the ministry of Christ; he is "a" prophet who prepares the way for "the" prophet. Any relation to his person can only be described in terms of a slave.

1:28 These things occurred in Bethany, on the other side of the Jordan, where John was baptizing (ταῦτα ἐν Βηθανίᾳ ἐγένετο πέραν τοῦ Ἰορδάνου, ὅπου ἦν ὁ Ἰωάννης βαπτίζων). The topographic reference, at the level of the narrative, serves to close this section of the pericope (as elsewhere; cf. 6:59; 8:20; 11:54) by marking a division in the text. The reference also underscores the historical importance of John's conduct and the trustworthiness of the narrative as referring to what really happened in a real place.[28] The Bethany most commonly mentioned in the Gospels is southeast of Jerusalem and is best known for being the home of Mary, Martha, and Lazarus (11:1). The Bethany referred to here, however, is located "across the Jordan," from the vantage point of the western side.

1:29 On the next day he saw Jesus coming toward him and said, "Behold, the Lamb of God, the one who takes away the sin of the world" (Τῇ ἐπαύριον βλέπει τὸν Ἰησοῦν ἐρχόμενον πρὸς αὐτὸν καὶ λέγει, Ἴδε ὁ ἀμνὸς τοῦ θεοῦ ὁ αἴρων τὴν ἁμαρτίαν τοῦ κόσμου). The first occurrence of "on the next day" (τῇ ἐπαύριον) signifies that this is the second day of Jesus's ministry and continues the creative theological image that we will develop below (see comments before 2:1). It also signifies a scene change: John's witness before the Jewish leadership has broadened to a witness before all Israel (v. 31). The narrator explains that the Baptist "saw" (βλέπει) Jesus coming. Just as the Jews came "toward him" (πρὸς αὐτὸν), that is, the Baptist in v. 19, so also now the unique Son comes toward him in

---

24. Carson, *John*, 146.
25. Cf. Diogenes Laertius, *Lives of Eminent Philosophers* 6.2.44.
26. See Keener, *John*, 1:448.

27. Calvin, *John 1–10*, 30–31.
28. Ridderbos, *John*, 68. Cf. Dodd, *Historical Tradition*, 233–47.

v. 29. The one about whom the Baptist had borne witness was now before him in the flesh.

Yet the voice of the prophet did not cease to be needed. The Word-in-flesh still needed a witness. John addresses those present before Jesus in a significant manner. Several aspects of the testimony need explanation. First, John begins the witness with the particle of exclamation, "Behold" (ἴδε). The conventionalized particle is used in Greek to draw attention to what follows. When used before a verb, it serves as a "prompter of attention," but when used before a noun, as in this case, it serves as a "marker of strong emphasis."[29] The Fourth Gospel uses it in the latter sense when there is a challenge to perceive with the mind a truth not outwardly evident to human eyes. For example, it is used as a marker of strong emphasis in 19:14 when Pilate says to the Jews, "Behold, your king" (ἴδε ὁ βασιλεὺς ὑμῶν).[30] Thus, the particle sets the tone regarding the importance of the person being emphatically introduced.

Second, Jesus is introduced as "the Lamb of God" (ὁ ἀμνὸς τοῦ θεοῦ). With the Old Testament no doubt providing the background, and in light of the reference to the removal of "sin," the pronouncement in v. 29 can only be understood as pointing to Jesus as the "Lamb of God" who reconciles the world to God. This is a fitting development to the prologue's description of the coming of the Word to the world. The exact meaning of the sacrificial title, however, is difficult to determine. There are several options worth exploring:[31] 1) *The Passover lamb*; however, the Passover victim was not always a lamb; 2) *The "lamb" of Isaiah 53:7*; however, the context makes no direct allusion to this text; 3) *The "lamb" of daily sacrifices*; however, the context again makes no direct allusion; 4) *The*

triumphant Lamb of Revelation (5:6; 14:1 – 4; 17:14; 22:1, 3); though the ruling lamb is slain, the context in the Gospel focuses more directly on removing sin, not conquering enemies; 5) *The lamb provided by God* (Gen 22:8); though clearly focusing on God's initiative and connecting to a central allusion in Jewish thought, the context makes no direct allusion to this narrative; 6) *A guilt offering* (e.g., Lev 14, especially v. 25); however, neither a guilt offering nor a sin offering was characteristically a lamb. Each of these options is possible, yet none of them secure direct allusions in the text. Before a conclusion can be drawn, the third aspect of the Baptist's testimony regarding Jesus requires explanation.

Third, the Lamb of God is described as "the one who takes away the sin of the world" (ὁ αἴρων τὴν ἁμαρτίαν τοῦ κόσμου). The questions surrounding the nature of the "lamb" receive some insight from this participial qualifier and subsequent clause. The term here translated "to take away" (αἴρω), used frequently by the evangelist, can mean "take away," "remove" (2:16; 11:39; 19:38; 20:2, 13, 15) and "destroy" (10:18; 11:48; 15:2; 19:15, 31). Its use with cognate words for "sin" finds strong support in the LXX (Exod 28:38; 34:7; Lev 10:17; 1 Sam 15:25; 25:28; Mic 7:18), and it is synonymous with other "removal" terms (cf. Isa 53:11 – 12). Though only implicit in our translation, the term here is best understood as a future present: *the one who is to take away* the sin of the world.[32] Although more clarity as to what prefigures "the Lamb of God" is not provided, the message of the Baptist's testimony is made certain. Jesus — the Word, the Light, the Life — is *the* Lamb of God and the Lamb *of* God, so that his person, ministry, and ultimately his death acts for the reconciliation of the world to God. It is the "chief office of Christ."[33] The emphasis is not

---

29. BDAG 468.

30. McHugh, *John*, 125 – 26.

31. For a fuller list of options and more detailed discussion, see Morris, *John*, 127 – 30; McHugh, *John*, 126 – 34; Keener, *John*, 1:452 – 54. Cf. Origen, *John*, 6.30 – 38.

32. BDF § 323.

33. According to Calvin, *John 1 – 10*, 32.

merely on him but on those for whom he serves. The sacrificial act has narrowed from many lambs to one Lamb, and yet its benefits have broadened from one nation to the whole world.

Our discussion regarding method in the Introduction allows our exegetical decision here not to be forced to choose between the purview of the Baptist or the evangelist, and even allows the full biblical canon to speak into the meaning and scope of the referent. In an important way, the historical witness of John the Baptist coalesces with the narrative witness of the evangelist, both of which are placed within the canonical witness of all Scripture. Even though "Lamb of God" is spoken by the Baptist and is therefore controlled in part by his context and level of understanding (in contrast to the narrator's creativity), the term cannot be ultimately contained by the Baptist's purview. Out of the Baptist's limited concept of messianic service and sacrifice protruded a full statement of the person and work of Jesus Christ for which the rest of the biblical canon is needed to explain. All the biblical allusions above, therefore, become part of the (canonical) context of the Gospel. The Lamb of God is Jesus, the crucified one. No NT passage concerning the sacrifice of Christ (e.g., in Paul) is excluded from the interpretive purview, for the allusion to the OT and NT images is not only welcome but necessary. Ultimately, the title ascribed to Jesus here at his first appearance in the Gospel narrative is coterminous with his last moments of life: Jesus is a Passover sacrifice (18:28; 19:36).

1:30 "This is the one about whom I said, 'A man who follows me has surpassed me, because he was prior to me'" (οὗτός ἐστιν ὑπὲρ οὗ ἐγὼ εἶπον, Ὀπίσω μου ἔρχεται ἀνὴρ ὃς ἔμπροσθέν μου γέγονεν, ὅτι πρῶτός μου ἦν). This statement from the Baptist echoes his previous statement as recorded in

the prologue (see comments on 1:15). The verbal differences are merely a change in perspective. That perspectival change, however, allows v. 30 to highlight the humanity of Jesus. The eternal Word became "a man." With these words the Baptist calls our attention to the fulfillment of his own prophecy. The prophetic witness of the Baptist has moved Jesus from the background to the immediate foreground, allowing for himself to be removed from the foreground and placed in the background.

1:31 "And I myself did not know him, but the reason I came baptizing with water was in order that he might be revealed to Israel" (κἀγὼ οὐκ ᾔδειν αὐτόν, ἀλλ' ἵνα φανερωθῇ τῷ Ἰσραὴλ διὰ τοῦτο ἦλθον ἐγὼ ἐν ὕδατι βαπτίζων). The inclusion of the implied subject allows John to emphasize that he did not know Jesus. The use of the pluperfect "know" (ᾔδειν, from οἶδα), which carries here the meaning of an imperfect tense, suggests that it need not be inferred that John did not know Jesus at all, but only that he did not know he was "the unique Son."[34] Yet, that is the reason for which John came. John came to make known one he did not know. Not only is the one to whom John witnesses beyond him but even his mission is beyond him. The relation of the Baptist to Jesus is defined in full by the relation of Jesus to Israel (and the world).

What is this "revelation" to Israel, and how does the baptism of John facilitate it? "Israel" (Ἰσραήλ), used only four times in the Gospel (cf. 1:49; 3:10; 12:13), carries no negative connotations, unlike "the Jews" (see comments on 1:19). Thus, what was hidden from "the Jews" is revealed to Israel, even if the exact public disclosure of that revelation is not clearly designated by the Gospel.[35] The subject matter of John's revelatory witness to Israel is a "he."[36] This revelation, however, was set in the

---

34. McHugh, *John*, 134 – 35. Cf. Barrett, *John*, 177.
35. Michaels, *John*, 113.

36. Schlatter, *Der Evangelist Johannes*, 50.

context of an assignment: baptism with water. Even before this element of baptism is contrasted with a greater baptismal element (v. 33), the reader is already aware that John's water baptism reflects the inferiority and provisionality of his mission (cf. v. 27). It was not a cleansing baptism like the one to come but served its purpose as a sign of the one to come. Just as the lamb of Moses was a sign of the Lamb of God, so also the baptism of John was a sign of the baptism of Christ. The "sin[ners] of the world" (v. 29) are to receive John's baptism as a call to penitence. The cleansing revelation "to Israel" was ultimately a preparatory cleansing designed to introduce "the one who takes away the sin of the *world.*"

1:32 And John witnessed saying, "I saw the Spirit descend like a dove from heaven, and he remained upon him" (Καὶ ἐμαρτύρησεν Ἰωάννης λέγων ὅτι Τεθέαμαι τὸ πνεῦμα καταβαῖνον ὡς περιστερὰν ἐξ οὐρανοῦ, καὶ ἔμεινεν ἐπ' αὐτόν). The centrality of "witness" in the Gospel has already been explained (see 1:7). The subject matter of the witness gives further insight into John's perception of Jesus. The verb John uses to describe what he "saw" (θεάομαι) is used in the NT to denote seeing with the physical eye, though it can carry along with physical sight a sense of perception that is "above and beyond what is merely seen with the eye."[37] The last time it was used was in 1:14, where the dual emphasis of real sight (i.e., not a vision; "we saw …") was tied to real perception (i.e., a deeper perception; " … his glory").

Both elements are contained in the use of the verb in this context.

John testified to seeing "the Spirit" (τὸ πνεῦμα). The dualistic view of the universe common to Western European philosophy might initiate an unhelpful mental impression regarding this term, especially in light of the Old Testament where its meaning necessarily consisted of a physical reality (e.g., wind).[38] Thus John describes the physicality of what he saw: the Spirit "descend like a dove" (καταβαῖνον ὡς περιστερὰν). Such a depiction provides explanation of the physical nature of the Spirit, even if the specifications of "like a dove" cannot be fully explained.[39] With Calvin, we rest comfortably saying that the Spirit appeared "under the form of a dove," that is, "a sure and infallible sign of the presence of the Spirit."[40] That the Spirit was connected to God is made clear by the description of the Spirit descending "from heaven" (ἐξ οὐρανοῦ).[41]

The Spirit did not merely descend toward Jesus but also "remained upon him" (ἔμεινεν ἐπ' αὐτόν). The verb, "remained" (ἔμεινεν), is best understood as a consummative (or perfective) aorist, which implies the result is permanent.[42] The combination of "the Spirit descending like a dove" and "remaining upon him" are best understood as reflecting Isaiah 11:2 ("The Spirit of the LORD will rest upon him"). The link between Isaiah 11 and v. 32 is duly noted in early Christian writings.[43] Full and permanent possession of the Spirit was taken to be the distinctive characteristic of the messiah. The stress of the scene is that the Spirit descended and

---

37. BDAG 445.

38. See McHugh, *John*, 136–38, for a helpful overview of the OT/Jewish context of this term.

39. For a survey of options, see Keener, *John*, 1:457–61.

40. Calvin, *John 1–10*, 43.

41. Contra McHugh, *John*, 138, reading the narrative's depiction of "the Spirit" here apart from Trinitarian doctrine forces an even greater imposition upon the text (on method, see Introduction).

42. Wallace, *Greek Grammar*, 559. Cf. J. H. Moulton, W. F. Howard, and N. Turner, *A Grammar of New Testament Greek*, 4 vols. (Edinburgh: T&T Clark, 1908–76), 3:72.

43. See Gary M. Burge, *The Anointed Community: The Holy Spirit in the Johannine Tradition* (Grand Rapids: Eerdmans, 1987), 54–59.

remained *upon him*. The importance of the sign is not to be missed. The early church preached that "God anointed Jesus of Nazareth with the Holy Spirit and power" (Acts 10:38). This is what John the Baptist saw. The Baptist serves as a prophetic-apostolic witness who was able to see truly "the visible occurrence and the invisible truth … set side by side."[44] The Baptist is not Elijah or the Prophet, and is certainly not the Christ; rather, he is the one who sees and points, the one who understands in order to testify to what he has seen. He is nothing more, for nothing more is needed. Once the Spirit descends "upon him," all attention has moved appropriately from the witness to his subject matter.

1:33 "And I myself did not know him, but the one who sent me to baptize with water told me, 'The man upon whom you see the Spirit descend and remain, he is the one who baptizes with the Holy Spirit'" (κἀγὼ οὐκ ᾔδειν αὐτόν, ἀλλ᾿ ὁ πέμψας με βαπτίζειν ἐν ὕδατι ἐκεῖνός μοι εἶπεν, Ἐφ᾿ ὃν ἂν ἴδῃς τὸ πνεῦμα καταβαῖνον καὶ μένον ἐπ᾿ αὐτόν, οὗτός ἐστιν ὁ βαπτίζων ἐν πνεύματι ἁγίῳ). After repeating his statement that until the time of the descent of the Spirit he did not know him, the Baptist gives an account for his ability to recognize the "Coming One" by means of the Spirit. Like a prophet who receives a "word from the Lord," the Baptist explains that his commission from God[45] also included a clue to the identity of the one to whom he would witness: the descending Spirit. No mention of the dove is made in this explanation. The purpose of the explanation serves primarily to give warrant to the Baptist's recognition of the "Coming One," but it also serves to implicate God as the primary actor.

It had always been God who had been working behind the ministry of the Baptist (see comments on 1:6). From this point onward even the ministry of Jesus is defined not merely by his own historical person or even by his own divine attributes, but by the activities of the Father and the Spirit.

Not only does the Spirit's witness eclipse the witness of the Baptist but Jesus's baptism eclipses the baptism of the Baptist. John explains regarding the one upon whom the Spirit descends and remains: "He is the one who baptizes" (οὗτός ἐστιν ὁ βαπτίζων). The Baptist is not just inferior to the person of Jesus; his baptism is inferior to the baptism of Jesus. The substantival participle, "the one who baptizes" (ὁ βαπτίζων), describes Jesus the way John "the Baptist" is traditionally described.[46] It is highly significant that John, unlike the Synoptics, never calls John "the Baptist," even though we have used that qualifier. For the Gospel of John, only Jesus is the Baptist. And true baptism can only be performed with the Holy Spirit. Jesus is the one who baptizes, and he will do so "with the Holy Spirit" (ἐν πνεύματι ἁγίῳ). The preposition is best translated as "with" or "by means of," for the Spirit is not merely a gift Jesus bestows (cf. 20:22) but the nexus of his messianic ministry.[47]

The unification of Jesus and the Spirit connects the promises of God in the Old Testament to the person and ministry of Jesus and the Spirit. Jesus is "the coming Davidic king" upon whom the Lord promised to pour out his Spirit (Isa 11:1–9); he is the servant/elect one upon whom God will put his Spirit (Isa 42:1); he is the prophet who announces, "The Spirit of the Sovereign LORD is on me, because the LORD has anointed me to proclaim good

---

44. Hoskyns, *Fourth Gospel*, 177.

45. This pericope has been centered upon two different missions: the Jews who were sent from the authority in Jerusalem and the Baptist who was sent from the authority in heaven.

46. Similar to the participle in 1:29, "the one who takes away" (ὁ αἴρων), it is likely that this is a future present. Cf. BDF § 323.

47. See Cornelis Bennema, "Spirit-Baptism in the Fourth Gospel: A Messianic Reading of 1,33," *Biblica* 84 (2003): 35–60: "In fact, 'to baptize with the Holy Spirit' is Jesus's ministry; it is shorthand for Jesus's salvific programme of revelation and cleansing by means of the Spirit" (59).

news to the poor" (Isa 61:1). The Spirit is the sign of the promised age, a time when God's people would have the Spirit poured out on them (Ezek 36:25 – 26), resulting in a cleansing with water. The descent of the Spirit upon Jesus was simultaneously an attestation of who Jesus is and an announcement that the promised age of the Spirit had dawned.[48] This is what the Baptist (now in a qualified sense) was sent to reveal to Israel.

1:34 "And I have seen and I have borne witness that he is the Son of God" (κἀγὼ ἑώρακα, καὶ μεμαρτύρηκα ὅτι οὗτός ἐστιν ὁ υἱὸς τοῦ θεοῦ). The pericope concludes with the Baptist's declaration, made emphatic with two perfect-tense verbs, that he has physically seen and judicially and prophetically given testimony regarding the one to whom he was to serve as a forerunner. And this is what the Lord said through the Baptist, "He is the Son of God" (οὗτός ἐστιν ὁ υἱὸς τοῦ θεοῦ). The use of "he" (οὗτός), now common to the reader, continues to emphasize the one to whom he points. The an-

nouncement is that Jesus is the Son of God (on this title, see comments on 1:49).

A textual variant plagues this announcement. Although the external evidence strongly supports "the Son" (ὁ υἱὸς), the internal evidence is often taken to argue in favor of "the elect/chosen one" (ὁ ἐκλεκτός).[49] As suggestive as the internal evidence favoring the reading of "the elect one" is, it is difficult to deny the age and diversity of witnesses that favor the reading of "the Son."[50] But even more, "the Son" also finds internal agreement with the theological terminology of the Gospel. The designation "the Son of God" not only fits the immediate context but is formative in John from start to finish, beginning with the careful description of the "unique Son" (1:14) and ending with the purpose of the Gospel (20:31). For this reason it is also appropriate that John, the first eyewitness of Jesus recorded in the Gospel, should also be the first to identify Jesus as "the Son of God," the same title the author wants all readers to recognize and confess.

Theology in Application

After the prologue, the Fourth Gospel introduces the arrival of the Word, Jesus Christ, into the historical context of the first century. All four Gospels begin with the ministry of John the Baptist, who is described as a forerunner who announces the person and ministry of Jesus. But the Baptist is displayed differently in John's Gospel, giving a more emphatic prophetic-apostolic witness to Jesus. The Baptist introduces Jesus not merely to Israel but to the world — even to the reader of the Gospel. It is through the self-effacement of the one who offered "renewal cleansings" that our attention is drawn to the one who can truly cleanse and renew.

The Nature of Human Religion

Jesus was introduced by the Baptist in a religious context that was confused, self-righteous, and self-determined. The grace of God given to the Jews (to us!) had been diluted and demeaned in such a way that they had become the self-declared

---

48. Cf. Carson, *John*, 152.
49. See McHugh, *John*, 142.
50. Metzger, *Textual Commentary*, 172.

and self-righteous judges of religious identity and activity. The Baptist's prophetic message speaks past their religious traditions and man-made authority structures by denying emphatically the concepts and structures they impose on his message. The reason for this is clear: it was not the Baptist's message but the message of God; it was the "word of the Lord." This word, however, was his definitive "Word," the last and culminating message from a gracious God. Would the Jewish leaders, Israel, and the world listen to this witness?

The church is so founded in the work and person of Christ and is so aware of its corporate testimony of sin and darkness that it is intentionally self-critical regarding its practices and postures. The origin of the church is, by definition, found in freedom from self-righteousness and is now founded solely upon the righteousness of Christ. The church is, however, not different by nature from the Jewish leaders, Israel, or the world; the church is only different in Christ, in the grace received, and in the righteousness it is empowered only now to express.

God Is the Primary Actor

It was not just the prologue that displayed the creative "coming" of God to the world; the beginning of the narrative proper displays a similar activity as the Son of God enters the historical scene. The entire ministry of the Baptist begins (cf. 1:6 "came," ἐγένετο) and ends (v. 33) with God, who is working behind the scenes to make himself known. He is the primary actor and stage director, with a plot that is driven forward by his actions and his identity. Made emphatic is God's self-disclosure, which he reveals to the Baptist (v. 33) so that the Baptist might reveal him to Israel and the world. We, like the Baptist, would not know him if it were not for "the one who sent me ... told me" (v. 33). This is not human religion; it is a God who acts without being asked and without being wanted, receiving nothing in return but what is already owed him. This is the gospel of Jesus Christ.

The church narrates God to the world. The ease with which a person puts himself or herself at the center, or his or her experiences as the plumb line, is the archenemy of the church. God and God alone is the primary actor in the world and the primary subject matter of the church's message. The church lives its life in and for God through Jesus Christ and serves as an ambassador to the world for God, announcing his message of grace and proclaiming his coming judgment. The church knows and proclaims that Jesus Christ is the Alpha and Omega, the beginning and the end. All things are defined in, by, and through Christ.

The Nature of Christian Witness

The message of the Baptist is a message of humble recognition of God. The Baptist, like Isaiah the prophet, is only able to cry out in self-disgust (cf. Isa 6:5). The message of the Baptist is a message of self-effacement. The Baptist is neither the true witness nor the one who can truly offer baptism, for God himself creates the witness and provides the true baptism (v. 33). It is for this reason the Fourth Gospel never called John "the Baptist," for he was merely the first Christian witness to the true Baptist.

The witness of the church is, therefore, like the Baptist, entirely and necessarily expendable. Unlike human religion, a Christian witness is a self-effacer who has seen God and can only muster, "Woe is me!" A true Christian witness is less than a servant; he or she is a self-proclaimed slave to Christ (v. 27). Like the Baptist we can only speak an emphatic "No!" regarding ourselves (vv. 20–21), but can declare an emphatic "Yes!" regarding the "revelation" we have been told (v. 31): Jesus is the Lamb, the Son of God.

The Trinitarian God

From the very beginning of the arrival of the Son of God, the Father and Spirit were present and active. The Gospel of John is Trinitarian from the start. The very first verse of the Gospel centers upon the persons of God, Father and Son (1:1). Even more, it is the Son that makes the Father known (1:18), and the Son is accompanied by the empowering Spirit (v. 32). The Gospel story moves beyond Abraham and his son to God the Father and his Son. This Greco-Roman biography is ultimately about the "life" (βίος) of the Trinitarian God.

The church is emphatically Trinitarian. When the church prays, it prays to the Father, through the Son, and by the power of the Spirit. When the church serves, it serves in the power of the Spirit, through the Son, and to the glory of the Father. Just as John and the rest of the Gospels focus on Christ, so also Christ in all four Gospels focuses on God. To be Christocentric, therefore, is to be theocentric, that is, Trinitarian. The church is Trinitarian from start to finish.

Jesus the Lamb of God and Son of God

The moment Jesus arrives on the scene he is immediately introduced by the Baptist with a title of redemption: "The Lamb of God" (v. 29). Although the exact nature of the metaphor is complex and undefined, its deep roots in the Old Testament (Passover lamb, the "lamb" of Isa 53, daily sacrifices, and the lamb God provided to Abraham in Gen 22:8) and in the New Testament (the triumphant lamb of Revelation) make certain that this Lamb removes sin. The Baptist announces as much when he describes the Lamb as "the one who takes away the sin of the world." This is a unique Lamb. The reason is clear: he is also the "unique Son" of God. The collective imagery of the Lamb of God and the Son of God, along with the accompanying Spirit, gives the overt impression that Jesus's person and actions are priestly in nature and function. God offered the Son that he did not demand from Abraham (Gen 22), and he offered the Lamb that no shepherd could offer.

The message of the church is Christ crucified, foolishness and a stumbling block to the world (1 Cor 1:23), but grace and truth to the children of God. The church is only the church because of a crucified God, and it finds honor in what the world considers shame. The church then finds in Jesus not merely a brother but also a high priest, through whom God is accessed and sin atoned for. The church lives in the grace of God through Christ, and worships the only one who is worthy, a slain Lamb (Rev 5).

John 1:35 – 51

Literary Context

After the prologue introduced the historical and cosmological plot of the Gospel, and the first pericope of the narrative proper described the introduction of Jesus by John to Israel, this pericope begins the ministry of Jesus, providing further introduction to his identity and his first disciples. This pericope together with the former (1:19 – 34) is best understood as the introduction to the narrative proper. Thus, all of chapter 1 serves as an introduction: the prologue (1:1 – 18) casts the vision by providing vital information regarding the subject of the biography, the plot, and the unseen forces at work in the story; the introduction to the narrative proper (1:19 – 51) sets the stage by moving the main character on the scene and locating him in the surrounding context. Thus, by the end of this pericope the first "week" (cf. comments on 2:1) is past and the ministry of Jesus is officially underway.

I. Prologue (1:1 – 18)

II. The First Week: An Introduction to the Narrative Proper (1:19 – 51)

   A. The Witness of John (1:19 – 34)

➡   **B. The First Disciples (1:35 – 51)**

Main Idea

Jesus is finally on center stage, and the identity of Jesus as the revelation of God is given emphatic explanation. The disciples of Jesus are learning who Jesus is and what it means to be his disciples, and are invited to "come and see."

Translation

(See pages 142–43.)

John 1:35–51

35a	Scene 1/Setting	**On the next day John was present again,**
b	Character Entrance	along with two of his disciples.
36a		And **looking directly at Jesus as he was walking by, he said,**
b	Confession: Allusion to OT & NT	*"Behold, the Lamb of God."*
37a	Reaction	And **his two disciples heard him and**
b		**followed Jesus.**
38a	Response	But **Jesus turned and saw them following and said to them,**
b	Question	*"What do you seek?"*
c	Response	And **they said to him,**
d	Honorific Address	*"Rabbi*
e	Aside	*(which is translated teacher),*
f	Question	*where are you staying?"*
39a	Climatic Response	**He said to them,**
b	Invitation	*"Come and you see."*
c	Response	Then **they came and saw where he was staying,**
d	Conclusion of Scene 1	and **they remained beside him that day;**
e	Time	**it was about the tenth hour.**
40a	Identification	**Andrew ...**
b	Relationship	**the brother of Simon Peter**
c	Description	**... was one of the two who heard from John and followed him.**
41a	Andrew's Reaction #1	**The first thing he did was find his brother,**
b	Character Entrance	**Simon,**
c		and **said to him:**
d	Exclamation	*"We have found the Messiah!"*
e	Aside	(which is translated Christ).
42a	Andrew's Reaction #2	**He led him to Jesus.**
b	Intensifying Description	Looking directly at him
c	Reaction to 42a	**Jesus said to him:**
d	Identification	*"You are Simon,*
e	Relationship	*son of John,*
f	Reidentification	*you will be called Cephas"*
g	Aside	(which is translated Peter).
43a	Scene 2/Setting	**On the next day Jesus desired to leave for Galilee,**
b	Character Entrance	and **he found Philip.**
c		And **Jesus said to him,**
d	Invitation/Command	*"Follow me."*
44a	Place	Now **Philip was from Bethsaida,**
b	Association	**from the city of Andrew and Peter.**
45a	Character Entrance	**Philip found Nathanael**
b	Response to 43c	and **said to him,**
c	Fulfillment of OT	*"We have found the one about whom Moses wrote in the Law and the Prophets,*
d	Identification/Relationship	*Jesus, the son of Joseph,*
e	Place	*from Nazareth."*

46a	Response	And **Nathanael said to him,**
b	Skeptical Question	*"What good thing is able to come from Nazareth?"*
c	Response	**Philip said to him,**
d	Invitation	*"Come and see."*
47a	Pronouncement	**Jesus saw Nathanael coming to him and he said concerning him,**
b	Allusion: Ps 32:2	*"Behold, a true Israelite, in whom there is no deceit."*
48a	Response	**Nathanael said to him,**
b	Question of Means	*"How do you know me?"*
c	Answer	**Jesus answered and said to him,**
d		*"I saw you while you were still under the fig tree before Philip called you."*
49a	Pronouncement	**Nathanael answered him:**
b	Honorific Address	*"Rabbi,*
c	Allusion: Exod 4:22–23	*you are the Son of God,*
d	Allusion: Zeph 3:15; Isa 44:6	*you are King of Israel."*
50a	Response	**Jesus answered and said to him,**
b	Rhetorical Question	*"Because I told you that I saw you under the fig tree you believe.*
c	Promise	*You shall see greater things than these."*
51a	Conclusion/Promise	And **he said,**
b	Amen Formula	*"Truly, truly I say to you,*
c	Promise/Allusion: Gen 28:12	*you will see heaven open and the angels of God ascending and*
d		*descending*
e	Allusion: Dan 7:13–14	*upon the Son of Man."*

Structure and Literary Form

This is the second of two pericopae that serve as an introduction to the narrative proper. In 1:1 – 18 Jesus was introduced from above as the Word who is coming to the world. In 1:19 – 51 Jesus is introduced from below as Jesus who is ministering in the world. In 1:19 – 34, the focus was on the Baptist's witness to Jesus, but in this pericope the focus is on Jesus's self-witness and his growing band of disciples. The structure of this pericope is different than the basic story form, with its conflict-resolution structure (see Introduction). The structure continues to be given direction by the designation of "days," which guide the reader through the first "week" of Jesus's ministry. The events take place on the second two days of Jesus's first week: day three: vv. 35 – 42, and day four: vv. 43 – 51.

Exegetical Outline

➡ **B. The First Disciples (1:35 – 51)**
    1. Andrew, the Anonymous Disciple, and Peter (1:35 – 42)
        a. "Come and See": Jesus's Invitation to the Disciples (vv. 35 – 39)
        b. The Naming of Peter (vv. 40 – 42)
    2. Philip and Nathanael (1:43 – 51)
        a. The "Good" that Comes from Nazareth (vv. 43 – 49)
        b. The Revelation of the Son of Man (vv. 50 – 51)

Explanation of the Text

The Gospel transitions from the public ministry of the Baptist to the public ministry of Jesus. The Fourth Gospel emphasizes the Baptist's witness to Jesus, through which the first disciples attach themselves to Jesus. It is the witness of John that directs the disciples to Jesus. The Synoptics, however, depict Jesus less as the recipient and more as the initiator, calling the disciples to himself (cf. Matt 4:18 – 22; 9:9; Mark 1:16 – 20; 2:13 – 14; Luke 5:1 – 11, 27 – 28). Harmonizations that attempt to reconstruct a first and second "call" of the disciples receive no support from the Fourth Gospel. Yet they need not be viewed as antithetical. In both cases God is extending himself to his people, witnessing to the person of the Son. Even more, John is intentionally linking Jesus's person and ministry to the person and ministry of the Baptist, connecting the Christian movement to the movement of God that culminated with the Baptist but began at the beginning of the story told by the OT. It is almost certainly for this reason that the apostolic tradition concerning Jesus always began with the public ministry and baptizing activity of John the Baptist (cf. Acts 1:21 – 22; 10:37, 39; 13:24, 26).

1:35 On the next day John was present again, along with two of his disciples (Τῇ ἐπαύριον πάλιν εἱστήκει ὁ Ἰωάννης καὶ ἐκ τῶν μαθητῶν αὐτοῦ δύο). The second occurrence of "on the next day" (τῇ ἐπαύριον) signifies that this is the third day of Jesus's ministry and continues the creative theological image that we will develop below (see comments before 2:1). It also signifies a scene change. The natural flow of the text implies that the location is the same as the preceding day. The two disciples with John, though unnamed, will reflect the ministerial goal of the Baptist: not only to provide a transition from water to Spirit baptism but to transition from having disciples to being a disciple.

1:36 And looking directly at Jesus as he was walking by, he said, "Behold, the Lamb of God" (καὶ ἐμβλέψας τῷ Ἰησοῦ περιπατοῦντι λέγει, Ἴδε ὁ ἀμνὸς τοῦ θεοῦ). At the surface level this appears to be a dramatic restatement of 1:29. There are, however, two mild differences. First, in v. 29 the Baptist's announcement was before the public of Israel, but here the announcement is before John's own disciples. The ministry of the Baptist finds its fulfillment in the ministry of Jesus. Second, in v. 29 the Baptist saw Jesus "coming toward him" (ἐρχόμενον πρὸς αὐτόν), but here the Baptist saw Jesus "as he was walking by" (περιπατοῦντι). The verb of motion instructs us regarding the transition that has taken place.[1] Jesus was now acting on his own; he had begun his ministry. Prophecy and promise now wore flesh. The verb chosen to depict John's visual focus on Jesus, "look directly at" (ἐμβλέπω), emphasizes the intensity of the stare. John now knew who to look for, finally matching what he had long known about him. John's witness is complete; he is not mentioned again in this scene. The last words he utters are the most significant. His ministry of cleansing is necessarily and wonderfully replaced.

1:37 And his two disciples heard him speaking and followed Jesus (καὶ ἤκουσαν οἱ δύο μαθηταὶ αὐτοῦ λαλοῦντος καὶ ἠκολούθησαν τῷ Ἰησοῦ). The disciples listen to their teacher and respond accordingly. The Baptist is no longer named or described, for his ultimate value is found in his witness, which continues its force in the present context. This verse describes the fruit of the Baptist's witness.[2]

---

1. Cf. Michaels, *John*, 118.

2. Cf. Barth, *Witness to the Word*, 147.

The disciples may not have yet understood the fullness of the object of the witness (cf. v. 38), but they trust the witness and respond in obedience. The fruit of the Baptist's witness was that they "followed Jesus" (ἠκολούθησαν τῷ Ἰησοῦ). In this Gospel "follow" is often used in reference to discipleship (e.g., 1:43; 8:12; 12:26; 21:19, 20, 22). Even the first steps of discipleship are not best viewed as superficial but representative of the nature of true discipleship and the true disciple.[3]

1:38 But Jesus turned and saw them following and said to them, "What do you seek?" And they said to him, "Rabbi (which is translated teacher), where are you staying?" (στραφεὶς δὲ ὁ Ἰησοῦς καὶ θεασάμενος αὐτοὺς ἀκολουθοῦντας λέγει αὐτοῖς, Τί ζητεῖτε; οἱ δὲ εἶπαν αὐτῷ, Ῥαββί [ὃ λέγεται μεθερμηνευόμενον Διδάσκαλε], ποῦ μένεις;). This is the first recorded action of the Word in the world. The particular focus on the fact that Jesus "turned" (στραφεὶς) strongly suggests more than that Jesus merely turned around physically.[4] Its use elsewhere in the Gospels (cf. Matt 9:22; 16:23; Luke 7:9, 44; 10:23; 14:25; 22:61) is always connected to Jesus and always denotes a sudden or remarkable change of attitude on his part, and is nearly always followed by a wholly unexpected saying. But more might be suggested. The Hebrew verb underlying "to turn" (στρέφω) would evoke instinctively the insistent prayers for the "return of God" to his people: "Turn, O Lord! How long?" (Ps 90:13 NRSV; cf. Pss 80:4 [80:5 MT], 8[9], 19[20]; 85:6[7]). It was the normal word for the return of God to Israel, and for the return of Israel to God. With this verb Zechariah opens his program for rebuilding the community after the exile: "'Return to me,' declares the Lord Almighty, 'and I will return to you'" (Zech 1:3), and Malachi, the last postexilic prophet, speaks in nearly identical words (Mal 3:7). The implication, then, is that the moment the two

Israelites turned from the Baptist toward Jesus he turned toward them, toward his people, answering the long-standing prayers echoed throughout the Psalms and redeeming the promises made in Zechariah and Malachi at the end of the Old Testament.

The first words of the Word are a question: "What do you seek?" (τί ζητεῖτε;). Jesus will ask the same question on two different occasions, both at crucial points in the narrative (18:4, 7; 20:15). In all three instances the question leads to a self-disclosure of some kind. The two followers respond with their own question: "Where are you staying?" (ποῦ μένεις;). They are not avoiding his question but telling him exactly what they are looking for: they are looking for someone to follow. They want to go where he is "staying" because he is now their leader, their teacher. In effect they are asking him: "To where will you be leading us?" Even the title used to address Jesus, "rabbi" (ῥαββί), which the narrator explains is to be understood as meaning "teacher," confirms the intention of the two followers. In the historical context, the interpretation of the Law had long passed from the priests to the scholars or scribes, who were increasingly viewed as the spiritual authorities of the people. The title "rabbi" was an honorific title that accorded the individual with the highest status as a teacher. The translation provided by the narrator, something not uncommon in John (cf. 1:41, 42; 4:25; 9:7; 11:16; 19:17; 20:16, 24; 21:2), gives direction to the narrative meaning, which in this case places the question of the followers in context.

1:39 He said to them, "Come and see." Then they came and saw where he was staying, and they remained beside him that day; it was about the tenth hour (λέγει αὐτοῖς, Ἔρχεσθε καὶ ὄψεσθε. ἦλθαν οὖν καὶ εἶδαν ποῦ μένει, καὶ παρ' αὐτῷ ἔμειναν τὴν ἡμέραν ἐκείνην· ὥρα ἦν ὡς δεκάτη). Jesus responds to the counterquestion with an

---

3. Hoskyns, *Fourth Gospel*, 179.

4. McHugh, *John 1–4*, 149–50. Cf. Aquinas, *John*, 1:116.

invitation: "Come and see" (ἔρχεσθε καὶ ὄψεσθε).[5] The followers respond positively based upon their actions. While the question they posed to Jesus, "Where are you staying?" (ποῦ μένεις;), would initially seem to be less concrete as a more general reference to sitting under Jesus's teaching, here the followers actually "came and saw where he was staying" (ἦλθαν οὖν καὶ εἶδαν ποῦ μένει). Without denying that a much longer "stay" was intended and that a teaching element was included, the narrative highlights the presence of Jesus, the Word. In connection with the repeated and therefore emphatic "come and see," the three occurrences of "staying" (μένω; once in v. 38; twice in v. 39) acquire an importance that is strongly reminiscent of an essential element in the prologue (1:14): the Word "made his dwelling among us" (ἐσκήνωσεν ἐν ἡμῖν). This event was recorded "down to the hour."[6] The Word-become-flesh was dwelling with humanity, dwelling with those for whom he came. God had made his dwelling among men, and had invited men to join him, and "they remained beside him" (παρ᾽ αὐτῷ ἔμειναν).

This climactic moment in redemptive history, crafted to emphasize the initial encounter between humanity and God in the person of Jesus Christ, is loaded with a kind of cryptic irony. First, it is striking that nothing regarding Jesus's self-revelation or their confession of him as the Christ is stated. In later interactions this is usually made emphatic. Even more, the fact that the two followers were shortly thereafter able to declare, "We have found the Messiah!" (v. 41), makes certain that such interaction took place. Second, in spite of the sparse information given regarding the interaction, a very specific time reference is given as an aside by the evangelist: "It was about the tenth hour" (ὥρα ἦν ὡς δεκάτη), that is, about 4:00 p.m.[7] It seems more exegetically sound to let the time reference serve as an emphatic announcement of this first encounter between the Incarnate One and his first disciples (i.e., between God and humanity). Several fanciful allegories for the symbolic meaning of the "tenth hour" have been offered, but none find a root in the narrative details. Ultimately, this "toneless" note of time pushes the mystery upon the reader.[8]

1:40 Andrew the brother of Simon Peter was one of the two who heard from John and followed him (Ἦν Ἀνδρέας ὁ ἀδελφὸς Σίμωνος Πέτρου εἷς ἐκ τῶν δύο τῶν ἀκουσάντων παρὰ Ἰωάννου καὶ ἀκολουθησάντων αὐτῷ). Only after the first encounter is already described does the narrator provide any names of the two followers/disciples, and even then only one of the two disciples is named. The named disciple is called Andrew, a Greek name; yet Andrew is found in the Talmud and cannot be used to prove any Greek connections on the part of his family.[9] Andrew is identified only by means of his relation to his brother, Simon Peter, even though he has yet to appear on the scene. It is simply taken for granted that the readers would know Simon Peter. Simon is his Jewish name, whereas Peter is not assigned until v. 42. As is common in ancient literature, the more obscure is described in terms of his relationship to the more famous. By defining Andrew by means of his famous brother, the Gospel shows itself to be connected to the historical circumstances of early Christianity, since Peter's name was widely

---

5. The two Greek verbs have been translated with the English idiom "come and see," in which the sense of the future indicative "see" (ὄψεσθε) is only implied but understood.

6. Ridderbos, *John*, 82.

7. The evidence almost unanimously supports understanding the time system to be Jewish and not Roman. While certain official days began at midnight, when reckoning the legal day on which contracts were dated even common people (i.e., Romans) calculated the day from dawn to dark.

8. Barth, *Witness to the Word*, 148. Cf. Schlatter, *Der Evangelist Johannes*, 53.

9. Barrett, *John*, 181.

known, even in non-Christian Jewish circles. That Andrew, with the other disciple, heard from John and "followed" (ἀκολουθησάντων) Jesus is not insignificant, for "follow" (and "remain") in the Gospel defines the nature of true discipleship. These two followers are the first disciples of Jesus.

What is interesting is that the second of the two disciples is never introduced. He remains the anonymous one "of the two" (ἐκ τῶν δύο). The anonymity of the second disciple can only be intentional, for it is highly unlikely that the evangelist was unaware of this individual. Since early Christianity, the anonymous disciple has been viewed as a clue that this unidentified disciple was the evangelist himself, who for various reasons decided to remain anonymous. Modern scholarship has outright rejected a close bond between the evangelist and the eyewitness, describing such a theory, in the words of Bultmann, as "purely wishful thinking."[10] But more recent examinations of ancient oral history and historiographic practices have helped secure for the Gospels a place within the practice of eyewitness testimony (see Introduction).

But the connection to eyewitness testimony does not reveal the identity of the anonymous disciple. Besides the historical person of the evangelist, others have proposed that the anonymous disciple in v. 40 is to be understood as "the disciple whom Jesus loved" (13:23; 19:26; 20:2; 21:7, 20; cf. the "other disciple" 18:15; 20:2–5, 8). The theory of "the Beloved Disciple" is much larger than this verse and will be addressed throughout the commentary (see comments on 21:24). Beyond the hypothesis regarding the identity of the anonymous disciple in this verse as well as the Gospel as a whole, it is likely that the evangelist is being quite intentional with the anonymity. Anonymity is itself a narrative tool to develop both plot and character-

ization. As Adele Reinhartz explains, "The absence of a proper name does not consign [the character] to narrative oblivion but simply requires that the readers interact with, analyze, or construct the unnamed characters on a basis other than the proper name," namely, "to focus the readers' attention on the role designations that flood into the gap that anonymity denotes."[11] The challenge is to interpret the "gap that anonymity denotes" with a precision that is pressured by the narrative as a whole.

We can at least surmise the following based upon the function of the anonymous disciple in v. 40. First, the anonymity is intentional and — as we have seen — will be employed again in the narrative. For this reason the function of anonymity, and its relation to the plot and charactization, must continually be addressed. Second, the anonymous disciple is placed at the beginning of the ministry of Jesus and is one of the earliest disciples of Jesus. That the anonymous disciple was a disciple of Jesus before Peter is potentially significant. Third, the intentional use of anonymity in this pericope and in the rest of the Gospel raises the question of the role of the anonymous disciple in the Gospel as a whole, as well as the relationship between the anonymous disciple and the evangelist; a relation that can only remain mysterious at this point in the narrative.

1:41 The first thing he did was find his brother, Simon, and said to him: "We have found the Messiah!" (which is translated Christ) (εὑρίσκει οὗτος πρῶτον τὸν ἀδελφὸν τὸν ἴδιον Σίμωνα καὶ λέγει αὐτῷ, Εὑρήκαμεν τὸν Μεσσίαν [ὅ ἐστιν μεθερμηνευόμενον Χριστός]). With the focus still on Andrew, the narrative describes his initial response after transitioning from the Baptist to Jesus. Andrew seeks "his brother" (ἀδελφὸν τὸν ἴδιον), Simon, and declares: "We have found the Messiah!"

10. Bultmann, *John*, 101n.3.
11. Adele Reinhartz, *"Why Ask My Name?" Anonymity and*

Identity in Biblical Narrative (Oxford: Oxford University Press, 1998), 188.

(εὑρήκαμεν τὸν Μεσσίαν). The transliterated term "Messiah" only occurs here and in 4:25, and in both places a translation is provided. The more frequent term is the Greek translation of Messiah, "Christ" (Χριστός). The use of Semitic terms makes apparent the Palestinian-Jewish background of the Gospel, but also the fact that at least some of the implied readers would be of a different background (i.e., Hellenistic) so that an explanation by way of translation was needed.[12] This statement, inclusive of the anonymous disciple, and hence a known entity to Peter, provides a summary of the interaction between Jesus and his first two disciples. The fact that Andrew immediately went to find his brother suggests that this was an enthusiastic exclamation (on "Messiah," see comments on 1:20).[13]

1:42 He led him to Jesus. Looking directly at him Jesus said to him: "You are Simon, son of John, you will be called Cephas" (which is translated Peter) (ἤγαγεν αὐτὸν πρὸς τὸν Ἰησοῦν. ἐμβλέψας αὐτῷ ὁ Ἰησοῦς εἶπεν, Σὺ εἶ Σίμων ὁ υἱὸς Ἰωάννου· σὺ κληθήσῃ Κηφᾶς [ὃ ἑρμηνεύεται Πέτρος]). The verse serves primarily to connect Peter to Jesus, but it should not be missed that Andrew his brother "led" or "brought" (ἤγαγεν) him to Jesus. We can only imply that Peter went willingly, trusting the witness of his brother and hoping for the coming Messiah (cf. 20:29). Each time Andrew is mentioned in the narrative, he is bringing someone to Jesus (6:8–9; 12:22). Though it is clear Andrew, like the rest of Jesus's disciples, grew in his understanding of Jesus, his immediate response to witness to Jesus is worth noting.

The meeting between Jesus and Peter is marked by a divine intensity. Jesus is depicted as "looking directly" (ἐμβλέψας) at Peter, the same understanding gaze as John the Baptist had directed upon Jesus (cf. 1:36). Just as John knew by supernatural means the character and destiny of Jesus, so also Jesus knew of Peter. Jesus addresses Peter by his biological name: "Simon, son of John" (Σίμων ὁ υἱὸς Ἰωάννου). Simon was the most common of all known Jewish male names.[14] As was common in Palestinian Judaism, he was also known by the name of his father (cf. Matt 16:17). But Jesus knows another name that belongs to Simon: "Cephas" (Κηφᾶς). Jesus pronounces, denoted by the future tense "you will be called" (κληθήσῃ), that Simon, son of John, is to be known as "Cephas" (Cf. Mark 3:16). Again, because some of the readers would be unfamiliar with the Semitic term, the narrator translates the word as "Peter." Both the Semitic as well as the Greek term mean "rock," though John is less concerned to explain this than Matthew (see Matt 16:13–20). In this scene the narrative seems more intent to inform the reader about Jesus than Peter, serving as a prelude to vv. 43–51 where Jesus not only sees them but gives a pronouncement about them.

Jesus's pronouncement to Simon Peter marks a point in the narrative at which Jesus takes center stage. Since the concept of a name in the ancient world was not merely a label but the character of a person, and the giving of a new name was an assertion of the authority of the giver (see e.g., 2 Kgs 23:34; 24:17), Jesus's pronouncement reflects the work of Jesus in his disciple. In the OT, God would give a new name to those belonging to him (e.g., Gen 32:28). The scene is not fully explicable by means of the historical circumstances or the narrative context. Jesus, looking intently at Peter, declares him to be his disciple. The same man, named Simon, yet now different and new, is now also called Peter. Peter is a new man, yet not one thing in him made it so. It was only Jesus and his declaration that changed Peter. Something has changed; it is no longer John looking at the Lamb

---

12. See Klink, *The Sheep of the Fold*, 170–72.
13. Cf. McHugh, *John 1–4*, 154–56.

14. Bauckham, *Jesus and the Eyewitnesses*, 85.

of God, it is the Lamb of God looking at the son of John. The strength of the church, with this apostle at the center as the "rock" (Matt 16:18), was not founded upon Peter the man but upon Peter the disciple of Jesus Christ. Thus began the testimony of the apostle Peter.

1:43 On the next day Jesus desired to leave for Galilee, and he found Philip. And Jesus said to him, "Follow me" (Τῇ ἐπαύριον ἠθέλησεν ἐξελθεῖν εἰς τὴν Γαλιλαίαν, καὶ εὑρίσκει Φίλιππον. καὶ λέγει αὐτῷ ὁ Ἰησοῦς, Ἀκολούθει μοι). The designation "on the next day" (τῇ ἐπαύριον) begins a new section. It is now the fourth day of Jesus's ministry (see comments before 2:1). The previous scene had depicted Jesus securing disciples by means of the Baptist's witness; Jesus was the passive recipient. In this scene, Jesus takes the initiative. This disciple, Philip, is the only disciple said in the Gospel to have been called by Jesus. It is grammatically possible that Andrew is the subject and therefore the one who leads Philip to Jesus. However, it is strongly unlikely since Jesus is the subject of the preceding sentence (v. 42b) and because it is difficult to imagine the evangelist ever referring to the travel plans of a disciple. In the Fourth Gospel it is Jesus that the narrative follows, not a disciple. Some commentators favor Andrew as the subject so that all who come to Jesus in this chapter do so because of someone else's witness.[15] The theological value, then, is that the theme of the importance of bearing witness is made emphatic by the evangelist (see comments on 20:29). As important as the theme of witness is in this chapter, it is nevertheless clearly secondary to the foundational activity of God as the true initiator, as explained by the prologue.

The scene hides as much as it reveals. We are told that Jesus "desired" (ἠθέλησεν) to go to Galilee, yet no reason is given. Nor is any explanation pro-vided regarding the place where Jesus met Philip or whether Jesus had any previous knowledge of Philip. But one thing is clear: Jesus is inviting Philip to become his disciple (see related comments on 1:37). Jesus has gone from more generic questions (cf. v. 38: "What do you seek?") to a specific and focused command. Philip was now a follower of Jesus Christ.

1:44 Now Philip was from Bethsaida, from the city of Andrew and Peter (ἦν δὲ ὁ Φίλιππος ἀπὸ Βηθσαϊδά, ἐκ τῆς πόλεως Ἀνδρέου καὶ Πέτρου). Like v. 40, where the narrator provides information regarding Andrew, here Philip is introduced to the reader. The name of the city of Philip's origin, "Bethsaida" (Βηθσαϊδά), literally means "Fishers Home." Bethsaida was on the northeast shore of Lake Gennesaret in the territory of Herod Philip the Tetrarch (cf. Josephus, *Ant.* 18.28; *J.W.* 2.168; 3.7). The mystery around the connection between Philip and Jesus is partially alleviated in v. 44. Since Philip is from the same city as Andrew and Peter, and Andrew was a disciple of John the Baptist, it is possible that they were already socially connected. Even if the nature of their connection cannot be delineated, v. 44 suggests a connection between them.

Philip is mentioned in all lists of the twelve apostles, always in fifth place after Simon, Andrew, James, and John (Matt 10:3; Mark 3:18; Luke 6:14; Acts 1:13). The Synoptics mention Philip but give no further information about him. John brings Philip forward on a number of occasions, often in moments where Philip is confused or misunderstands Jesus (e.g., 6:7; 12:21 – 22; 14:8 – 9). As Morris suggests, "Some of the apostles were undoubtedly men of great ability, but Philip compels us to realize that others were perfectly ordinary people. Jesus had (and has) use for such followers."[16]

---

15. See, for example, Carson, *John*, 157 – 58.

16. Morris, *John*, 142.

1:45 Philip found Nathanael and said to him, "We have found the one about whom Moses wrote in the Law and the Prophets, Jesus, the son of Joseph, from Nazareth (εὑρίσκει Φίλιππος τὸν Ναθαναὴλ καὶ λέγει αὐτῷ, Ὅν ἔγραψεν Μωϋσῆς ἐν τῷ νόμῳ καὶ οἱ προφῆται εὑρήκαμεν, Ἰησοῦν υἱὸν τοῦ Ἰωσὴφ τὸν ἀπὸ Ναζαρέτ). Just as Andrew is important, especially as a link to Peter, so also Philip is important as a link to Nathanael. The story of this connection brings the scene to a conclusion and, in a very real way, serves as the climax of the entire pericope. When Philip speaks, he does so in the first person plural: "We have found" (εὑρήκαμεν), which reflects that he identifies himself with the growing group of disciples around Jesus. Other than his presence among the fishermen in 21:2 (which adds the information that he came from Cana), this is the only occurrence of Nathanael in the Gospel. Since Nathanael means "God has given," many have posited that this scene is allegorical and that an ideal disciple is meant. There is, however, no need for such a conclusion. Everything depicted in the narrative is as real as the other scenes. Even more, Nathanael, though less common, is a recognizeable name in first-century Judaism.[17] Suggestions that Nathanael is really Matthew (whose name has a similar meaning) or Bartholomew (whose name is only a nickname) lack any credible evidence. When John wants to detect symbolic significance in such names, he provides a translation (e.g., 9:7). It also neglects that Jesus had many followers outside the Twelve. In this sense, if Nathanael represents anything, he does not represent a future apostle but rather the average follower of Jesus.

While Andrew declared to his brother Peter in v. 41 that "we have found" the Messiah, Philip declares to Nathanael that "we have found the one about whom Moses wrote in the Law and the Prophets." Andrew spoke of the Messiah, but Philip speaks of the object of the writings of Moses and the prophets. Although both the Law and the Prophets spoke about "the one" within their own corpus, the terms together serve as an inclusive reference to the entire Old Testament. This is, of course, the position held by the Gospel: Jesus fulfills the OT Scriptures (cf. 5:39; see also 2:17, 22; 7:37 – 39; 12:15 – 16; 20:9). There are several likely candidates in mind in the Law (e.g., Gen 49:10; Num 24:17; Deut 18:15, 18 – 19) and the Prophets (e.g., Isa 11:1; Jer 23:5 – 6; Zech 3:8).[18]

1:46 And Nathanael said to him, "What good thing is able to come from Nazareth?" Philip said to him, "Come and see" (καὶ εἶπεν αὐτῷ Ναθαναήλ, Ἐκ Ναζαρὲτ δύναταί τι ἀγαθὸν εἶναι; λέγει αὐτῷ Φίλιππος, Ἔρχου καὶ ἴδε). The narrative now turns its attention to the final member of the first disciples. Nathanael responds to Philip's exclamative statement with a skeptical question concerning Nazareth. It was certainly not a famous city; there is no evidence that it was ever mentioned before the NT. The question suggests that Nathanael cannot conceive of "the one" coming from such an insignificant place like Nazareth. Nathanael would not be the last to speak derogatorily of Jesus's place of origin, for years later Christians would be belittled by being described as the "Nazarene sect" (Acts 24:5).

Ultimately, Nathanael's skepticism arises "out of a stubborn provincialism in reverse that refuses to see anything great or glorious in that which is familiar or close to home."[19] Nazareth is offensive in the same way that the reader was shocked to be told that the "Word became flesh." Philip's response echoes Jesus's answer in v. 39. Clearly Philip, with a short-sighted and limited estimation of Jesus's person,

---

17. Bauckham, *Jesus and the Eyewitnesses*, 87.
18. Cf. McHugh, *John 1 – 4*, 158 – 59.

19. Michaels, *John*, 129.

did not understand the fullness of what he invited Nathanael to "come and see." Yet its repetition in the narrative forms a contrast between each occurrence so that in both situations, with full or partial understanding, Jesus is deemed worthy of attention.

1:47 Jesus saw Nathanael coming to him and he said concerning him, "Behold, a true Israelite, in whom there is no deceit" (Εἶδεν ὁ Ἰησοῦς τὸν Ναθαναὴλ ἐρχόμενον πρὸς αὐτὸν καὶ λέγει περὶ αὐτοῦ, Ἴδε ἀληθῶς Ἰσραηλίτης ἐν ᾧ δόλος οὐκ ἔστιν). Nathanael, not fully deterred by his skepticism, responded to Philip's invitation and headed toward Jesus. What Jesus "saw" (εἶδεν) when Nathanael was coming toward him was more than just another inquiring follower interested in him; he saw a seeker of God. Philip invited Nathanael to come and "see," but it was Nathanael himself that was the object in view. Jesus gives a public declaration regarding Nathanael, denoted by "behold" (ἴδε), and describes him as a "true Israelite" (ἀληθῶς Ἰσραηλίτης). The term "Israelite" occurs nine times in the NT: five in Acts as a formal address to assembled Jews (2:22; 3:12; 5:35; 13:16; 21:28); three times in Paul when he is emphasizing his racial and religious credentials (Rom 9:4; 11:1; 2 Cor 11:22); and here in John. When prefaced by the attributive adverb "true" (ἀληθῶς), it affirms the devotion of Nathanael to the God of Israel.[20] Nathanael, the true Israelite, is described further as one "in whom there is no deceit" (ἐν ᾧ δόλος οὐκ ἔστιν). The use of the term "deceit" (δόλος) parallels and expands "true" (ἀληθῶς). Nathanael is a true Israelite without pretense.

1:48 Nathanael said to him, "How do you know me?" Jesus answered and said to him, "I saw you while you were still under the fig tree before Philip called you" (λέγει αὐτῷ Ναθαναήλ, Πόθεν με γινώσκεις; ἀπεκρίθη Ἰησοῦς καὶ εἶπεν αὐτῷ, Πρὸ τοῦ σε Φίλιππον φωνῆσαι ὄντα ὑπὸ τὴν συκῆν εἶδόν σε). Nathanael is wondering by what means Jesus had come to know him. Jesus responds with a cryptic saying that, though apparently satisfactory to Nathanael, has often confused interpreters. Jesus simply states that even before Philip had made things known, Nathanael had been seen by Jesus, specifically under a fig tree. There is no further explanation and no other reference to the incident. The "fig tree" (συκῆ) often served as a symbol of home (e.g., Isa 36:16; Mic 4:4; Zech 3:10). In later times its shade was used as a place for prayer, meditation, and study and could be depicted to symbolize such activity.[21] As a traditional Jewish idiom, the "fig tree" could also signifiy rest as opposed to labor or tranquility as opposed to trouble (e.g., 1 Kgs 4:25; 2 Kgs 18:31). The detail, however, does not appear to have its own symbolic significance other than to highlight the specificity with which Jesus saw Nathanael. Nathanael's response in v. 49 implies not only that Jesus knew Nathanael's physical location but also his spiritual location, the nature of his heart. This is not the only time the Gospel will portray the supernatural awareness and insight of Jesus (cf. 4:16–19).

1:49 Nathanael answered him: "Rabbi, you are the Son of God, you are King of Israel" (ἀπεκρίθη αὐτῷ Ναθαναήλ, Ῥαββί, σὺ εἶ ὁ υἱὸς τοῦ θεοῦ, σὺ βασιλεὺς εἶ τοῦ Ἰσραήλ). Although the exact insight of Jesus is enigmatic to the reader, Nathanael was entirely convinced regarding the identity of Jesus. He answers Jesus's insight with a messianic confession of faith, in sharp contrast to his earlier resistance.[22] The impression made upon Nathanael is revealed by his use of three titles. First, Nathanael addresses Jesus with the honorific title "Rabbi" (ῥαββί), which acccorded the individual with the

---

20. BDAG 44; cf. 8:31.
21. See Keener, *John*, 1:486.

22. Cf. Schnackenburg, *John*, 1:317–18.

highest status as a teacher (see comments on v. 38). Nathanael's skepticism regarding Jesus (cf. v. 46) has subsided as he positions himself as a student of Jesus. But "rabbi" serves primarily to describe himself before Jesus. What he speaks next will describe his belief in his teacher's true identity.

Second, Nathanael declares regarding his teacher: "You are the Son of God" (σὺ εἶ ὁ υἱὸς τοῦ θεοῦ). One might assume that Nathanael bestows a title on Jesus that is part of the expectation of Second Temple Judaism, or more importantly, of the OT. In a general way the OT did expect and predict a "Son of God," and the title is undoubtedly messianic (cf. 2 Sam 7:14; Ps 2:7). From the perspective of Judaism, however, the connection is not quite so obvious. According to McHugh, "there is no clear evidence that in Palestinian Judaism the title 'Son of God' was ever applied to the Messiah even in a metaphorical sense during pre – Christian times," and even where the divine sonship of the Davidic Messiah had been clearly declared, "these OT texts were intended only to affirm the legitimacy of the claim of the line of David to the throne, not to assert that there was some exceptional ontological relationship between God and the monarch."[23] But John sees no such difficulty. And even if Nathanael's words reflect a certain naivete — which would not be the first time (e.g., v. 46: "What good thing is able to come from Nazareth?"), he was right in what he unknowingly confessed. In fact, as the reader of John will shortly come to see, the link between Jesus and God is not merely a messianic relation but also a unique relation of intimacy and oneness (cf. comments on 5:19 – 29). This relation Nathanael could not have understood, even though his words described it perfectly. The messianic predictions, the monarchial promise of the Davidic king, and even the concept of sonship so connected to the nation of Israel (e.g., Exod 4:22 – 23; Deut

1:31; 32:6; Jer 31:9, 20; Hos 11:1) has come to a climactic fulfillment in the person of Jesus. And it is significant that the title has the article: "*The* Son of God" (ὁ υἱὸς τοῦ θεοῦ). "The Son" — *the* promised Messiah, *the* descendant of David, *the* true Israel — is Jesus. Even a partial suggestion, shackled to Judaism's limited expectations, roused Nathanael to a confession of faith.

Third, Nathanael declares regarding his teacher: "You are King of Israel" (σὺ βασιλεὺς εἶ τοῦ Ἰσραήλ). Like "Son of God," the title "King of Israel" is not entirely obvious. Apart from texts which refer to Israel's monarch, the term "King of Israel" appears twice in the OT, in Zephaniah 3:15 and Isaiah 44:6, as a description of Yahweh, King of Israel. Nowhere in the OT is the term used of the predicted messiah. It is only used once in the OT Pseudepigrapha (Pss. Sol. 17:42), in a text that clearly envisions a military leader to revolt against Rome. The title is also entirely absent from the Qumran literature. Yet it occurs twice in John, here and in 12:13, alongside the synonymous though ironic "King of the Jews" in chapters 18 – 19. Thus, like the former title, "King of Israel" is vague regarding its antecedent referent but quite clear in regard to its subsequent referent. What Nathanael almost certainly saw was a political and militaristic king; what he could not see was the actual nature of Jesus's kingdom, which was "not of this world" (18:36).

1:50 Jesus answered and said to him, "Because I told you that I saw you under the fig tree you believe. You shall see greater things than these" (ἀπεκρίθη Ἰησοῦς καὶ εἶπεν αὐτῷ, Ὅτι εἶπόν σοι ὅτι εἶδόν σε ὑποκάτω τῆς συκῆς πιστεύεις; μείζω τούτων ὄψῃ). Jesus acknowledges Nathanael's confession of faith but resituates it accordingly. Jesus's answer is more of a statement than a question. Nathanael responded to Jesus because of a miracle; such faith,

23. McHugh, *John 1 – 4*, 162.

though real, is inferior to the faith that truly sees (i.e., needs no signs; cf. 4:48; 14:11).[24] The misunderstanding so pervasive in Nathanael and in all the first disciples is rooted in a sightless reading of the Scriptures and signs. The repeated statement "come and see" (v. 39) echoes in the mind of the reader. Nathanael has come, but has he truly seen? Jesus's response is not a criticism; rather, it is a promise. Jesus promises that Nathanael shall see "greater things than these" (μείζω τούτων).[25] Jesus is not casting doubt on Nathanael's faith, only on the nature of his sight. It might be significant that Nathanael is the first disciple in the Gospel who is explicitly said to "believe." Several disciples have "come"; now it is time to learn how to "see." "Entry into the relationship of a disciple is not only the result but also the beginning of seeing what is to be seen in Jesus."[26] Jesus now goes on to explain the kind of vision he promises.

1:51 And he said, "Truly, truly I say to you, you will see heaven open and the angels of God ascending and descending upon the Son of Man" (καὶ λέγει αὐτῷ, Ἀμὴν ἀμὴν λέγω ὑμῖν, ὄψεσθε τὸν οὐρανὸν ἀνεῳγότα καὶ τοὺς ἀγγέλους τοῦ θεοῦ ἀναβαίνοντας καὶ καταβαίνοντας ἐπὶ τὸν υἱὸν τοῦ ἀνθρώπου). Jesus prefaces his statement with an introductory confirmation: "Truly, truly, I say to you" (ἀμὴν ἀμὴν λέγω ὑμῖν). The Greek word "truly" (ἀμήν) is the translation of an Aramaic/Hebrew word that means "to confirm." It was used to indicate one's consent or assent to words uttered by someone else. The use of the term by Jesus to introduce his own speech is unique; there is no known Jewish use by a person introducing his own statement, for it was always used to affirm the statement of another. Although this is the first use of the term in John, it is also quite common in the Synoptics, but only on the lips of Jesus and again only to introduce his own statements. In view of the associations of the term, it almost certainly has religious significance. It would be uttered by a person who stands before God, speaking things only God can affirm or bring to pass. The fact that Jesus prefaces his own statements in this way implies that Jesus identifies himself with the words and with the God to whom he appeals.[27] As Ladd explains, "Jesus's usage is without analogy because in his person and words the Kingdom of God manifested its presence and authority."[28] Since Jesus is the Word, his statements are by definition "the word of the Lord." For this reason, Jesus can and must preface his statements in a similar manner to those from God in the OT: "Thus saith the LORD" (KJV) or "This is what the LORD says" (NIV). Thus, in all four Gospels Jesus prefaces his statements and teachings, especially those of significance, with what we have translated as "truly" (ἀμήν), what can only be called an authoritative preface. An interesting and unexplainable fact is that while the Synoptics only ever have a single "truly," John always has two. Whatever is to follow must, therefore, be important.

Following the authoritative preface, Jesus now speaks. It is fitting that after all the questions, testimonies, and confessions regarding Jesus's messiahship from others, Jesus for the first time speaks about himself. Jesus's statement breaks all messianic categories and expands the horizon regarding what Jesus's disciples are invited to "come and see."

---

24. Barrett, *John*, 186.

25. Since "these" (τούτων) is preceded by a comparative adjective, "greater than" (μείζω), it is a genitive of comparison.

26. Barth, *Witness to the Word*, 153. Cf. J. H. Bernard, *A Critical and Exegetical Commentary on the Gospel according to St. John*, 2 vols., ICC (New York: Charles Scribner's Sons, 1929), 1:65.

27. Klaus Berger, *Die Amen-Worte Jesu. Eine Untersuchung zum Problem der Legitimation in Apokalyptischer Rede*, BZNW 39 (Berlin: Walter de Gruyter, 1970), 18–28.

28. George Eldon Ladd, *Jesus and the Kingdom: The Eschatology of Biblical Realism* (New York: Harper & Row, 1964), 163.

Although contextually the statement is a final response to Nathanael, the statement itself is plural: "You (plural) will see" (ὄψεσθε). Thus, this authoritative statement is an address to all the disciples, both in the early ministry of Jesus and in the history of the church. The entire statement echoes Jacob's vision of a ladder or "stairway resting on the earth, with its top reaching to heaven, and the angels of God were ascending and descending on it" (Gen 28:12). Jesus's statement, however, is not entirely controlled by the imagery of Jacob's vision, for it makes a necessary and important distinction, even development, regarding the person and work of God and the nature of God's revelation.

Jesus declares, "You will see heaven open" (ὄψεσθε τὸν οὐρανὸν ἀνεῳγότα). In John, the verb "see" is regularly used as a promise that the disciples will be given some spiritual insight (cf. 11:40; 16:16, 17, 19). Although John rarely speaks of "heaven," when it occurs it is found in passages that speak of rebirth through water and Spirit (ch. 3) and of Jesus as the life-giving bread from heaven (ch. 6). The perfect participle, "open" (ἀνεῳγότα), leaves the length of the vision undefined but can hardly mean any one particular vision or a recurrent one.[29] The disciples will "see" (i.e., experience) Jesus in all his works and in his entire person. Jesus is heaven open. As we saw in the prologue, Jesus is the one who reveals the Father (1:18). What is unique about Jesus is not only his sonship or that he is God or intimate with the Father, but also that he provides for some to "see" God. Jesus will later declare that "the one who sees me has seen the Father" (14:9). This emphatic statement declares that Jesus is (and always was) the opening of heaven. The nature of this opening, this vision, is not to be sought entirely behind one statement but in Jesus's

person and work, which the rest of the Gospel will explicate.

Jesus also declares that they will see "the angels of God ascending and descending" (τοὺς ἀγγέλους τοῦ θεοῦ ἀναβαίνοντας καὶ καταβαίνοντας). The allusion to Jacob's vision in Genesis 28:12 is neither as direct or unmistakable as is often assumed. In the new context, there is no stairway or ladder reaching to heaven, no vision of the Lord, no covenant promise, and — surprisingly — no Jacob. In the original context, there were no angels ascending and descending on Jacob. He was not the bearer of the heavenly power but, like the disciples here, the one whose eyes were opened to that power in the vision granted to him.[30] This is not to deny an allusion but only to make clear that *the allusion is meant to be radically redefined in its new context and for its new subject.* Jacob saw a vision; the disciples saw the Word-become-flesh.[31] The statement of God is now in the form of a person.

Thus, it is not insignificant that the angels will be seen ascending and descending "upon the Son of Man" (ἐπὶ τὸν υἱὸν τοῦ ἀνθρώπου). The title "Son of Man" has been notoriously difficult for interpreters to explain. Though its background and, therefore, meaning, is difficult to determine,[32] it was clearly Jesus's favored self-designation. The title echoes its earlier use in Daniel 7:13–14, which describes one who, clothed by God with heavenly glory, is to exercise God's rule on earth. The two visions echoed here from Genesis 28 and Daniel 7 fit uniquely together, with aspects taken from each. The reference to heaven opening is reminiscent of the visions themselves and symbolizes the power and love of God being revealed in Jesus. The ascending and descending angels over Jesus represent the "glory" to be displayed in Jesus's ministry

---

29. Schnackenburg, *John*, 1:321.
30. Cf. Michaels, *John*, 136.

31. Ridderbos, *John*, 94.
32. See McHugh, *John 1–4*, 170–75.

(cf. 1:14). It reflects that God is with Jesus from the beginning of his ministry to the end. Finally, the "Son of Man" brings power, glory, and kingdom together in the person of Jesus. The explication of the title "Son of Man" is not completed, however, for the person of Jesus is intimately connected to his work — a work done in obedience and unto death. This is the grand irony, clearly misunderstood by the disciples even at the end of Jesus's ministry yet central to the Gospel account.

Theology in Application

The first and foundational response of the Christian to the gospel of Jesus Christ is "come and see." The ministry of Jesus is about his person, which includes his work as "the Lamb of God." Jesus has moved from the object of the Baptist's ministry to the subject of the Gospel. The identity of Jesus as the gate of heaven, the revelation of God, has become central to his person. Worship and religion are now entirely defined by him.

The Gospel as a Return to God

The first recorded action of Jesus in the Gospel is that he "turned" toward those following him (v. 38). The term serves a technical function in the OT by evoking instinctively the insistent prayers for the "return of God" to his people: "Turn, O Lord! How long?" (e.g., Ps 90:13 NRSV). It was the normal word for the return of God to Israel and for the return of Israel to God. The moment the two Israelites turned from the Baptist toward Jesus, he turned toward them, toward his people, answering the long-standing prayers echoed throughout the Psalms and redeeming the promises made in Zechariah and Malachi at the end of the Old Testament. The cry, "How long?" has been changed into an invitation: "Come and see."

The church proclaims a God who has returned. Christmas is the celebration of the advent of Christ, and Easter is the celebration of the successful completion of his return. The Christian seeks God not in some mystical place but in the person of Jesus Christ. Discipleship is displayed by those who "come and see," that is, who return to God and seek him through Jesus.

God Is the True Initiator

The gospel offers a return to God, but before we ever sought him he turned toward us. God has always been and will always be the initiator. As important as the theme of witness is in chapter 1, it is clearly secondary to the foundational activity of God as the true initiator. The prologue has already depicted the creative activity of God in the calling of the Baptist (1:6); thus it should be no surprise that in the first scene after the Baptist, God, now in the person of Jesus, is again described as taking the initiative. The "desire" of Jesus to go to Galilee is rooted in his overarching desire to come "to what belongs to him" (1:11).

As much as the Christian is a person who is seeking after God, it has always been God who first sought us. Just as Nathanael is loaded with naive bias regarding what God can and will do, so is the contemporary Christian. We are blind to our own sin, our own situation, our own self-righteousness. We are blind without God. As Calvin reminds us, "When we are not even thinking of Christ we are observed by him; and this needs be so, that He may bring us back when we have withdrawn from him."[33] Just as Jesus the Word came to his own without being called and was not recognized by his own creation when he arrived, so also will his ministry be to people (then and now) who do not recognize him and do not see a need for him. Yet Jesus still comes.

"Come and See"

Jesus's first statement to interested followers was "come and see." The ministry of Jesus is so intimately connected to his own person that it almost entirely defines Christian discipleship and evangelism. Ironically, all the disciples, but especially Nathanael, reflected a lack of sight regarding Jesus. The same blindness potentially exists for us. We have come, but have we truly seen? Each of the disciples had "come"; now it was time to learn how to "see." "Entry into the relationship of a disciple is not only the result but also the beginning of seeing what is to be seen in Jesus."[34] Only a disciple of Jesus who has come and seen him will be able to truly see.

The mission of the church can be simply stated in Jesus's first statement to his interested followers: "Come and see." God has returned to broken humanity in the person of Jesus, all life hangs in the balance, and we are blind to the state of disrepair. The only thing we can do is come and see Jesus. To come and see is not to have arrived but to be in a posture of discipleship; it is to be at a place where one can view Jesus at all times and where one has complete access to God through Christ. "Come and see" is not a completed task but a constant striving of the Christian. "Come and see" is a conviction held by an interested follower or new believer when their spiritual life is just beginning. It is also a conviction held firmly at the end of one's life when their earthly life is near completion. It serves as a summary of what it means to be Christ centered.

The True Israelite

In the climactic scene of the first disciples, Jesus describes Nathanael as a "true Israelite" (v. 47). The statement is clearly a public declaration and therefore serves as a guide to those who "come and see." Jesus is neither using the term merely to define Nathanael ethnically or nationally nor as a proclamation that Nathanael had arrived spiritually. Rather, Jesus credits Nathanael with having the inner disposition of a true worshipper of God. Jesus's words echo Psalm 32, in which happiness comes to

33. Calvin, *John 1–10*, 42.   34. Barth, *Witness to the Word*, 153.

the worshipper of God who is open before God with his sin and accepts forgiveness from God. Thus, Jesus commends Nathanael as a member of the true Israel of God (cf. Gal 6:16), comprised of those who worship their Lord with full awareness of their sin and full allegiance to his authority. It is the Israel of God that the Baptist came to prepare for purification, now made manifest in Jesus, the one called the Lamb of God, who takes away the sin of the world (1:29, 36). And surrounding this Lamb will be "true Israelites," eventually from every nation and people, robed in white, and declaring: "Salvation belongs to our God" (Rev 7:9 – 10). This is the posture that Jesus "saw" in Nathanael. Nathanael was a seeker of God, and God was to be sought in and only in Jesus.

The posture of Nathanael, the "true Israelite," is the posture Jesus should see in all true Christians. The church seeks to model itself as the true Israel, those who are found entirely in the death, resurrection, and ascension of Jesus Christ. Like Nathanael, God seeks not perfect obedience or perfect understanding but the perfection of Jesus Christ, now offered to all who "come and see." The gospel demands a full admission of sin and a full submission to Christ. This is the posture of worship, and it is the position in which grace and mercy are received and by which the throne of God becomes a place of grace that can be confidently approached (Heb 4:16).

Jesus, the Revealer

The one who sees Jesus sees God (1:18, 51). Jesus's climactic statement to Nathanael reiterated what the prologue declared: through Jesus we can see God. Just as the word of Jesus is "thus saith the Lord," so also the mission of Jesus is access to God. Jesus is the one who reveals the Father. What is unique about Jesus is not only his sonship or that he is God or in intimate relation with the Father but that he provides for some to "see" God. A person, not a place, is *Bethel*, the "house of God." The Fourth Gospel moves the story of redemption drastically forward and subordinates the sacred past to the coming of Jesus Christ. Jacob's vision of God in Genesis 28 is realized by the disciples, by the church. Jacob saw a vision; the disciples saw the Word-become-flesh. The dwelling place of God is fully realized in "the Son of Man."

The church declares Christ to be the source and solution, for Christ is the revealer of God. There is no God talk without Christ. All talk of religion, all talk of spirituality or spiritual things, all talk of God or gods is nothing if it is not rooted in and mediated by and through Christ. Our discipleship is rooted in Christ as well as our evangelism. To speak of God without Christ might be socially more acceptable, but it is entirely unchristian. Without the "Son of Man," the rest of men cannot know God.

CHAPTER 4

John 2:1 – 11

Literary Context

The careful and lengthy introduction to Jesus by means of a prologue (1:1 – 18) and a two-pericope introduction to the narrative proper (1:19 – 51), along with the careful articulation of the completion of the first "week" of the ministry of Jesus, has emphasized that in the person of Jesus the Creator is now with his creation. The focus can now transition to the work of God in the world. This pericope is the first recorded work. This first work serves as a "sign" to the unseen realities also at work and to that which the work will ultimately accomplish.

→ **III. The Beginning of Jesus's Public Ministry (2:1 – 4:54)**
    A. The First Sign: The Wedding at Cana (2:1 – 11)
    B. The Cleansing of the Temple: The Promise of the Seventh Sign (2:12 – 25)
    C. Nicodemus, New Birth, and the Unique Son (3:1 – 21)
    D. The Baptist, the True Bridegroom, and the Friend of the Bridegroom (3:22 – 36)
    E. The Samaritan Woman, Living Water, and True Worshippers (4:1 – 42)
    F. The Second Sign: The Healing of the Royal Official's Son (4:43 – 54)

Main Idea

The arrival of Jesus transforms the world and all its activities. During a wedding celebration, Jesus transposes the purposes and plans of humanity with the will and wisdom of the Father, and, with a reversal of grace, transforms a failing celebration into the celebration of the wedding of God. Jesus, the faithful Son and true bridegroom, is making preparations for his bride, the Church.

Translation

(See next page.)

John 2:1–11

1a	Setting	**On the third day there was a wedding**
b	Place	in Cana of Galilee,
c	Character Entrance	and **the mother of Jesus was there.**
2a		And **Jesus and his disciples were also invited to the wedding.**
3a	Problem	When the wine was gone,
b		**the mother of Jesus said to him,**
c	Assertion	*"They have no more wine."*
4a	Conflict:	**Jesus said to her,**
b	Interrogative Challenge	*"What does this have to do with me, woman?*
c	Basis	*My hour has not yet come."*
5a	Resolution (5–8)	**His mother said to the servants,**
b	Response/Command	*"Do whatever he tells you."*
6a	Aside	And **there were in that place six stone water jars,**
b	Description	placed there for the Jewish purifiction,
c	Description	each holding twenty to thirty gallons.
7a	Reaction to 5	**Jesus said to them,**
b	Command #1	*"Fill the water pots with water."*
c	Reaction	And **they filled them to the brim.**
8a		Then **he said to them,**
b	Command #2	*"Now draw some out*
c	Command #3	*and bring it to the master of the banquet."*
d	Reaction	And **they brought it to him.**
9a	Conclusion (9–11)	And when the master of the banquet tasted the water
b		that had been turned into wine,
c	Reaction to 9b	**he did not know from where it had come,**
d	Aside/Contrast	though the servants who had drawn the water knew.
f	Reaction	Then **he called for the bridegroom.**
10a		And **he said,**
b	Assertion: Social Norm	*"Everyone brings out the good wine first and then*
c	Sequence	*the cheaper wine after the guests have had too much to drink,*
d	Contrast	*but you have kept the good wine until now."*
11a	Interpretation of Scene	**This Jesus did in Cana of Galilee as the beginning of the signs,**
b	Result of 11a (#1)	and **he revealed his glory,**
c	Result of 11a (#2)	and **his disciples believed in him.**

Structure and Literary Form

Unlike the previous pericopae, which serve as the introduction to the narrative proper and have unique structural designators, this is the first pericope in the Gospel that corresponds to the basic story form (see Introduction). The *introduction/setting* is established in vv. 1 – 3. The *conflict* is quickly presented in v. 4, with the response of Jesus creating the climactic moment of the pericope. The *resolution* is provided in vv. 5 – 8, including the response to and aftermath of Jesus's statement. Finally, the *conclusion/interpretation* is provided in vv. 9 – 11 and serves to explain the result of the activities, with v. 11 offering a closing summary regarding the meaning of the pericope and its relation to the rest of the Gospel.

Exegetical Outline

➡ **A. The First Sign: The Wedding at Cana (2:1 – 11)**
    1. Invitation to a Wedding in Cana (vv. 1 – 3)
    2. Jesus, his Mother, and a Shortage of Wine (v. 4)
    3. From Purification Water to Celebratory Wine (vv. 5 – 8)
    4. The First Sign of Jesus's Glory (vv. 9 – 11)

Explanation of the Text

Although the Gospel of John begins with a prologue which serves to guide and direct the reader, at the level of the narrative's development the entire first chapter (1:1 – 51) has functioned as an introduction to the Gospel and to Jesus. This introduction explained the context into which Jesus entered, the witness provided for him by the Baptist, and his functional identity as the revelation of God. Paralleling the creative work of God at creation, God was now present with his people, creatively and powerfully at work in the world. The entire first chapter of the Gospel has projected the creative "first week" of the Creator as he enters his creation.

IN DEPTH: Jesus's First Week

A directional clue matching this creation theme is suggested in the narrative itself[1] as the evangelist appears to structure the opening to the narrative proper by designating certain days. While John does not stress the collective nature of the days, they might be taken to refer to the first full week of the ministry of Jesus. The structure of days appears to be the following:

DAY 1: 1:19 – 28
DAY 2: 1:29 – 34 ("on the next day")
DAY 3: 1:35 – 42 ("on the next day")
DAY 4: 1:43 – 51 ("on the next day")
DAY 6: 2:1 – 11 ("on the third day," i.e., two days later)

---

1. Cf. Morris, *John*, 114: "The framework unobtrusively suggests creative activity."

We have already explored the significance of the designations of "day" as they appeared in the narrative. As we approach the last occurrence, however, it is necessary to surmise the intention of the "week" displayed throughout the first three pericopae of the narrative proper. We argued above that the refraction of Genesis 1:1 – 5 in 1:1 – 5, as well as the developing new creation motif established throughout the prologue (see comments on 1:17), implies that the "week" in 1:19 – 2:11 is to be seen as parallel to the creation week, which also took six days! Several commentators have minimized the "week" imagery because it is six, not seven, days. Usually, then, the "days" merely serve to progress the narrative through the natural historical circumstances. Warnings about symbolic parallels must be heeded, for clearly an arbitrary connection cannot be allowed. However, John certainly intended to communicate by means of the six days. Other commentators who try to extend the six days to seven in order to get a true "week" fail to do justice to the narrative details. The days can only be counted as six days.[2]

The strong connection to Genesis, and specifically to creation, thus far in the Gospel suggests that the first six days of Jesus's ministry are to be seen as parallel to the first six days of creation. Jesus, the one through whom all things were created and by whom new creation takes place, is beginning his creative activity in human history. In a very real way, the first six days of the work of Jesus at the beginning of his ministry are equivalent in nature and force to the first six days of the work of God at the beginning of time. This is not the time for rest (day seven); it is the time for work. The symbolic significance need not be carried too far, with every detail serving as a direct and corresponding allusion. The importance is not that there is a perfect match point for point but that the allusion *and its differences* express something (cf. 1:51).[3] Just as John has retold creation in light of Jesus and made him the pinnacle of the act of creation, so also has John taken man, the one made in God's image on the sixth day of creation, and retold the creation story in light of Jesus and made Jesus the pinnacle of creation.

The creation of man was literally renewed at the incarnation — in Jesus, the Word-become-flesh (1:14). Jesus is the image of God, the true revealer of the Father (1:18). The focus of John is on the sixth day, the creation of the God-man; the remainder of the Gospel is focused on the sixth day of creation, awaiting the seventh day, the day of rest, to arrive. Although he is announced to the reader in 1:14 and through the imagery of the six-day "week," he will only partially

---

2. Contra Carson, *John*, 168.
3. Cf. Johannes Willemse, *Het Vierde Evangelie. Een Onder-* *zoek naar Zijn Structuur* (Hilversum-Antwerpen: Brand, 1965), 153.

be introduced to the world until he is officially introduced in 19:5, when the world—Rome (i.e., Pilate)—declares: "Behold, the man!" This is the sixth day, when the image of God is made known to his creation. But he is not ruling over his creation, even though he is dressed like a king (19:2–3). For they have yet to see what Nathanael and the other disciples (and the reader) have been told, that he is no mere man but is in fact the "Son of Man" (1:51).

2:1 On the third day there was a wedding in Cana of Galilee, and the mother of Jesus was there (Καὶ τῇ ἡμέρᾳ τῇ τρίτῃ γάμος ἐγένετο ἐν Κανὰ τῆς Γαλιλαίας, καὶ ἦν ἡ μήτηρ τοῦ Ἰησοῦ ἐκεῖ). The narrator introduces the scene by informing the reader of a wedding that was taking place in Cana of Galilee (on the significance of "the third day," see the sidebar "Jesus's First Week"). The favored location is Khirbet Qana, which is located about nine miles north of Nazareth (Josephus, *Life* 86.207).[4] Though some try to deduce a symbolic significance in Cana, the only significance that can be deduced is that it serves as a narrative place marker, since the first section of the Gospel story begins and ends in Cana (cf. 4:43–45, 54). It is not Cana but "a wedding" that is most determinative for the context of the pericope. It is interesting that the scene is set without Jesus being mentioned; the only character mentioned is the mother of Jesus. Her identity, however, is entirely defined by Jesus: "the mother of Jesus" (ἡ μήτηρ τοῦ Ἰησοῦ). She is never named in the Gospel.

2:2 And Jesus and his disciples were also invited to the wedding (ἐκλήθη δὲ καὶ ὁ Ἰησοῦς καὶ οἱ μαθηταὶ αὐτοῦ εἰς τὸν γάμον). The narrator adds that Jesus and his disciples were also invited to the wedding. Based upon chapter 1, the disciples accompanying Jesus are probably the five already mentioned: Andrew, Simon Peter, Philip, Na-

thanael, and the anonymous disciple (1:35). There is no mention in the Gospel of the arrival of other disciples, though by 6:67 the narrator can speak of "the Twelve" without giving any indication when and from where the other seven came. That Jesus, his mother, and Jesus's disciples were all invited to the wedding suggests the wedding was for a relative or close friend of the family, especially since Jesus's mother bears some responsibility for the shortage of wine at the wedding (v. 3). It might also be significant that one of the disciples, Nathanael, originated from Cana (cf. 21:2).

Several aspects of first-century wedding ceremonies are assumed in this statement and need explanation. Wedding ceremonies were always accompanied by celebratory feasts and were important in Jewish culture. The importance of wedding celebrations caused many rabbis to excuse a wedding party from conflicting religious festival obligations.[5] According to the custom, wedding celebrations normally lasted seven days. The guests in attendance were usually connected in a social manner. For example, depending on the wealth of the family, entire towns could be invited. Even more, people who disliked the wedding family would be obliged to attend the wedding, since refusing to attend was socially inappropriate. This makes an invited person, like Jesus, difficult to define in relation to the wedding family. And since it was common for a scholar to be invited to a wed-

---

4. Carson, *John*, 168.

5. Keener, *John*, 1:498.

ding, it is also possible that Jesus's invitation was connected to his growing recognition as a public teacher. This might also explain the attendance of his disciples, since they would have been included with their teacher.[6]

2:3 When the wine was gone, the mother of Jesus said to him, "They have no more wine" (καὶ ὑστερήσαντος οἴνου λέγει ἡ μήτηρ τοῦ Ἰησοῦ πρὸς αὐτόν, Οἶνον οὐκ ἔχουσιν). After being introduced to the characters in vv. 1–2, we are now being prepared for the source of the conflict: the wedding celebration is running out of wine. Although wine was a standard part of daily life in the ancient Mediterranean world, Jewish literature makes clear that wine was an important part of festive occasions, especially at weddings.[7] Since weddings in the first century were not about two people but about two families, the social dynamics were more comprehensive and intense. For this reason, to run out of wine during the wedding celebration was likely to have caused a loss of family honor and status.[8] The anarthrous "wine" (οἴνου) might suggest that the wine was entirely gone, rather than just running out. Thus, the situation is dire.

The lack of wine at the wedding is connected to the mother of Jesus. The narrative not only gives no indication regarding the reason Jesus's mother is involved, it also does not explain what options she had besides turning to Jesus. Various proposals have been offered for her connection to the wedding ceremony (e.g., a relative of the family) and her reason for going to Jesus (e.g., it was the oldest son's responsibility in the absence/death of Joseph). None, however, are anything but conjecture, and

several go well beyond any reasonable reconstruction. Although it is impossible to reconstruct his mother's intentions, the narrative's grammar might indicate that rather than commanding Jesus, she appears to be softly telling Jesus of the celebration's plight in the hope that he might intervene.[9] It is worth reiterating, however, that the narrative has not made the mother of Jesus the point of the story. Her lack of a name is itself support of this. However the plot's conflict arrived at the feet of Jesus, it is there now.

2:4 Jesus said to her, "What does this have to do with me, woman? My hour has not yet come" ([καὶ] λέγει αὐτῇ ὁ Ἰησοῦς, Τί ἐμοὶ καὶ σοί, γύναι; οὔπω ἥκει ἡ ὥρα μου). Jesus's response to his mother's statement has long plagued interpreters. The confusion is usually compounded by the reconstructed intention behind his mother's actions. But v. 3 only seems to posit that Jesus's mother merely presented the problem respectfully before her son, with only cultural expectations prodding some sort of response.[10] It is in light of this enigmatic exchange that we turn to the response of Jesus. In order to explore the meaning of this verse, there are three exegetical difficulties that need to be explained.

First, the use of "woman" (γύναι) by Jesus to address his mother. In our contemporary context, the term seems harsh or disrespectful. BDAG, for example, lists this occurrence as an example of a rare but possible use in which there is "a tone of disrespect" (cf. Matt 15:28; Luke 22:57), but the term is generally not disrespectful but respectful, even affectionate, meaning something like "ma'am"

---

6. Ibid., 1:499.

7. Ibid., 1:500. First-century wine was not merely unfermented grape juice but did contain alcohol. It was not, however, given an artificially increased alcoholic content through distillation and was also mixed with water, often two or four parts water for one part wine.

8. Cf. Bruce J. Malina and Richard L. Rohrbaugh, *Social-Science Commentary on the Gospel of John* (Minneapolis: Fortress, 1998), 70–71.

9. See McHugh, *John 1–4*, 179.

10. Ritva H. Williams, "The Mother of Jesus at Cana: A Social-Science Interpretation of John 2:1–12," *CBQ* 59 (1997): 679–92 (686).

today.[11] Much of this depends on Jesus's intention. The term is never addressed to a mother by a son in all known Greek or Jewish literature, so there is no known context from which to compare its use here. It would be easy to understand the term as imposing a severe separation between Jesus and his mother if it were not for Jesus's use of the term toward his mother from the cross at a moment filled with empathy and love (see 19:26). However, the term's normal use demands that it be seen to function at least minimally as a distancing mechanism, even if it is enveloped — more clearly in 19:26 and possibly even in 2:4 — within a healthy and loving relationship between mother and son. The fact that the narrator uses "mother" three times in 2:1–11 (four if we included v. 12) suggests that Jesus's use of "woman" be viewed as significant to the narrative's presentation.[12] This choice of word must be drawing attention away from her blood relationship with Jesus. This need not be a distancing that denies the mother her son but locates it in the larger context of a much greater and more foundational relationship between the unique Son and the Father. The unseen forces that the prologue has already revealed explain that Jesus's relationship to his mother is not entirely defined by cultural norms. This very word, without excluding a respectful response to his mother, portrays Jesus as a step beyond, all the while not being indifferent.

Second, the ambiguous idiom: "What does this have to do with me?" (τί ἐμοὶ καὶ σοί). Jesus responds to his mother with a peculiar idiom that rigidly translates the dative construction as "what to me and to you?" This Greek phrase is an idiomatic expression found in the OT (Josh 22:24; 2 Sam 16:10; 1 Kgs 17:18; 2 Kgs 3:13) as well as in the NT, though in the latter it is always used by demons to Jesus (Matt 8:29; Mark 1:24; 5:7; Luke 4:34; 8:28). What can be clearly determined from the use of the idiom's range of uses is that it is intending to serve as a distancing response by one party to a request or expectation from another party.[13] The level of distancing can range from hostility to simple disengagement with even the latter carrying some degree of reproach, all of which depend on the nuances of the context and even the tone of voice.[14] Along this spectrum, the response from Jesus in this scene is almost certainly in the range of simple disengagement. Jesus's response serves as a nuanced form of refusal intending to communicate a divergent view.[15] While the next statement explains the reason for Jesus's divergence (the "hour"), v. 5 suggests that the refusal was neither entirely hostile nor received in an entirely negative manner by Jesus's mother. We must consider the reason for Jesus's coming as an explanatory context for this scene (see 3:16). As much as his plans (to be explained below) differ from his mother's, Jesus — the very expression of the love of God — would certainly be able to incorporate into his mission to the world the situation of the people (especially his mother) with whom he now dwells.

Third, the important concluding statement: "My hour has not yet come" (οὔπω ἥκει ἡ ὥρα μου). In many ways, the entire difficulty of the verse rests with this final statement. The meaning of this concluding statement is bound up with the meaning of the term "my hour" (ἡ ὥρα μου).

11. BDAG 209.

12. As suggested by Christian P. Ceroke, "The Problem of Ambiguity in John 2,4," *CBQ* 21 (1959): 316–40 (320).

13. See Edward W. Klink III, "What Concern is That to You and to Me? John 2:1–11 and the Elisha Narratives," *Neot* 39 (2005): 273–87.

14. Schnackenburg, *John*, 1:329.

15. Brown, *John*, 1:99.

IN DEPTH: "Hour"

The term "hour" (ὥρα) in John is a technical term that is generally assumed to refer to the death of Jesus on the cross (4:21, 23; 5:25, 28; 7:30; 8:20; 12:23, 27; 13:1; 16:2, 4, 21, 25, 32; 17:1). The term first occurs at 2:4; the occurrences before 12:23 depict the hour in the future, whereas after 12:23 the hour is depicted as being immediate. The term has a technical and established use in the Gospel. As much as it is intimately and directly connected to the death of Jesus, it is also connected to Jesus in a much broader sense — not only at the point of the cross but also his going to the Father and his glorification. That is, the death of Jesus is only its beginning. The hour never came to its conclusion during the life of Jesus,[16] for its true completion is rooted in the life of Jesus beyond this world — the life of Jesus rooted in the cosmological plot of the Gospel's narrative depiction.

By declaring to his mother that it was not "the hour," Jesus does not claim an inability to act but an inability to act in a full way. While the great moment he had been called to had not fully arrived, it had, by his very presence, already begun. This is the distance Jesus forces between his mother and himself. His plan, his agenda, had already been determined. In fact, the very reason Jesus could (and did!) respond to his mother's implied request was because he could do something. What he had come to do had begun, and it was starting to show forth. The narrative does not reveal to us if his mother knew this, but we find out that Jesus would act in a manner fully consistent with his mission yet to come. What appears to be the acquiescence of a first-century son to his mother was more accurately the response of the "unique Son" to the Father. The cosmological plot has made certain that we not only see the distance but also understand it. Our cautious reconstruction of the intentions of Jesus and his mother in this difficult verse has left us with a beautiful Johannine irony: although his mother wanted the wedding to reach its end without embarrassment, Jesus, thinking of a much grander wedding feast, knew that embarrassment (the cross) is required for it to reach its ultimate conclusion.

2:5 His mother said to the servants, "Do whatever he tells you" (λέγει ἡ μήτηρ αὐτοῦ τοῖς διακόνοις, Ὅ τι ἂν λέγῃ ὑμῖν ποιήσατε). The response of Jesus's mother suggests that Jesus's refusal was neither entirely hostile nor was received in an entirely negative manner. Jesus's statement in v. 4 is best viewed as a distancing response, not a rebuke or even a rejection. As much as the statement of Jesus transforms the meaning and significance of the immediate wedding crisis, the person of Jesus remains constant enough for his mother to assume he will respond to her need. It would not be a stretch to assume that Jesus's person emitted the very essence of grace and love, something especially noticed by his mother. She may not have known what he would do, as the grammar suggests (the verb is in the subjunctive mood), but she does assume he will do something. The response of the

---

16. Cf. Ridderbos, *John*, 105 – 6.

Son of Man to a man-made dilemma was both distancing yet embracing. The mother of Jesus, even if not fully understanding the cosmological vision and mission of her son, had come to understand his vision for those around him. His ultimate submission to the will of the Father does not negate his concern for his siblings (1:12). The narrative depicts with great detail the ability of the Word to "dwell" with his creation and yet to remain the God of creation.

2:6 And there were in that place six stone water jars, placed there for the Jewish purification, each holding twenty to thirty gallons (ἦσαν δὲ ἐκεῖ λίθιναι ὑδρίαι ἓξ κατὰ τὸν καθαρισμὸν τῶν Ἰουδαίων κείμεναι, χωροῦσαι ἀνὰ μετρητὰς δύο ἢ τρεῖς). The narrator, pulling back from the focused discussion, gives a fuller picture of the scene by mentioning that conveniently located nearby were six jars of water. There are two important details regarding these water jars. First, they were made from "stone" (λίθιναι). Clay water jars that had not been fired in a kiln could become unclean, and when this occurred it was required that they be destroyed (Lev 11:33). Stone water jars, however, did not become unclean (m. Kelim 10:1). Second, they were "placed there for the Jewish ceremonial purification" (κατὰ τὸν καθαρισμὸν τῶν Ἰουδαίων κείμεναι). The "tradition of the elders" held that the Jews were not to eat until they gave their hands a ceremonial washing (Mark 7:3 – 4). This tradition involved the servants pouring water over the hands of every guest before the meal. The larger the number of guests, the larger the amount of water needed.

While the previous scene was dominated by an awkward situation, this scene is filled with wonderful coincidences. The jars are both permanently clean and intimately tied to purification. Yet they become useful for what would initially be taken as an entirely different purpose: as wine jars. The vessels used to contain the requirements for purification were now to contain celebratory drink. The relation between purity and celebration find an uncanny connection to the person and work of Jesus. The stated crisis at this wedding is being refracted to envisage the greater crisis — and both find their solution in this one act of Jesus. This wedding in Cana, this need for wine, and this moment in time simultaneously reflect something much greater and more important. To take the symbols (e.g., the six water pots) too rigidly misses the intersection of the cosmological and historical strands of the plot so central to the deep structure of the Gospel's narrative.[17] At one and the same time, Jesus was providing a way out.

2:7 Jesus said to them, "Fill the water pots with water." And they filled them to the brim (λέγει αὐτοῖς ὁ Ἰησοῦς, Γεμίσατε τὰς ὑδρίας ὕδατος. καὶ ἐγέμισαν αὐτὰς ἕως ἄνω). The story returns to Jesus, who gives directions to the servants regarding the six water pots nearby. Relating well with what we argued above, this verse makes clear that v. 4 cannot be taken as a pure refusal to act. Interestingly, the narrative only emphasizes the amount of water the servants were ordered to pour: "To the brim" (ἕως ἄνω). Nothing about the transfer from water to wine is mentioned. "The reader knows, without being told in so many words, that the water — and in such quantities! — has been changed into wine."[18] The moment of transformation from water to wine is avoided because it is eclipsed by a much greater transformation. The imagery is just too potent. In the presence of Jesus, a collection of pure (stone) water jars for the ceremonial washing of many people serves to herald the fulfillment ("to the brim") of the entire ceremonial purification of

---

17. We prefer to see the symbolism stemming from the deep narrative structures, not beneath every "stone" jar.

18. Bultmann, *John*, 117 – 18.

Second Temple Judaism. In the person and work of Jesus, the purification jars and their water become useless, only suitable to contain celebratory wine.

2:8 Then he said to them, "Now draw some out and bring it to the master of the banquet." And they brought it to him (καὶ λέγει αὐτοῖς, Ἀντλήσατε νῦν καὶ φέρετε τῷ ἀρχιτρικλίνῳ· οἱ δὲ ἤνεγκαν). The use of the word "draw out" (ἀντλήσατε) is awkward since it is normally used to refer to drawing water from a well and not from a jar or vessel (cf. 4:7, 15). The awkward word serves to emphasize that the water of purification is "now" (νῦν) *something to drink*. The implication is far reaching: true purification is no longer in reference to external things (e.g., hands and pots) but is entirely internal. And the source of purification is not from the tradition of the elders but "from God" (1:13). The Christian life according to John is drinking and eating what Jesus provides (cf. 6:51 – 58).

Jesus ordered the servants to bring the wine to the master of the banquet. The "master of the banquet" (ἀρχιτρίκλινος) was almost certainly not a servant, as in the chief servant, but was probably one of the invited guests, selected to oversee and preside over the celebration. This was common to both Greeks and Jews.[19] This command from Jesus could be understood to serve two purposes. First, to announce that the wine once lacking is now in abundance. The celebration may continue without embarrassment. Second, to get approval of the new wine from the master of the banquet, who was the person in charge of not merely the supply but also the quality of the drink and effects of the drink for the purpose of regulation. Although the reader is aware that the purification water is now wine, it

was time for the master of the banquet, and thereafter the crowd, to be served this new wine.

2:9 And when the master of the banquet tasted the water that had been turned into wine, he did not know from where it had come, though the servants who had drawn the water knew. Then he called for the bridegroom (ὡς δὲ ἐγεύσατο ὁ ἀρχιτρίκλινος τὸ ὕδωρ οἶνον γεγενημένον, καὶ οὐκ ᾔδει πόθεν ἐστίν, οἱ δὲ διάκονοι ᾔδεισαν οἱ ἠντληκότες τὸ ὕδωρ, φωνεῖ τὸν νυμφίον ὁ ἀρχιτρίκλινος). This verse begins the scene of the pericope in which the story is brought to its conclusion and the interpretation of the story is provided (vv. 9 – 11). After the servants brought the wine, following the orders of Jesus, the master of the banquet was obviously surprised in regard to the wine. He "did not know from where" (οὐκ ᾔδει πόθεν) it had come. The question regarding the origin of the wine is primarily because of its quality, as v. 10 reveals.

It is ironic that the master of the banquet, the person who should have the most knowledge of and authority over the wine for the wedding, knew less than the servants. The surprise caused the master of the banquet to call for the bridegroom. The two characters so central to the actual wedding are made only secondary in this story.[20] The pericope has reversed who is important at the wedding; rather than involving from the start the master of the banquet and the bridegroom, the narrative began immediately with Jesus. The reversal is stark. What was unknown to the characters themselves is that at this wedding Jesus was ultimately fulfilling the role of the master of the banquet and the bridegroom (v. 10).[21] The image is loaded with

---

19. Keener, *John*, 1:514. Cf. Barrett, *John*, 192 – 93.

20. See Edward W. Klink III, "The Bridegroom at Cana: Ignorance is Bliss," in *Character Studies in the Fourth Gospel: Literary Approaches to Sixty Figures in John*, ed. Steven A. Hunt, D. Francois Tolmie, and Ruben Zimmermann, WUNT 314

(Tübingen: Mohr Siebeck, 2013), 233 – 37.

21. Ruben Zimmermann, *Christologie der Bilder im Johannesevangelium: Die Christopoetik des vierten Evangeliums unter besonderer Berücksichtigung von Joh 10*, WUNT 171 (Tübingen: Mohr Siebeck, 2004), 208 – 15.

significance of the wedding *par excellence* and the new wine to be served to the wedding party of the true bridegroom (Rev 19:7–9).

2:10 And he said, "Everyone brings out the good wine first and then the cheaper wine after the guests have had too much to drink, but you have kept the good wine until now (καὶ λέγει αὐτῷ, Πᾶς ἄνθρωπος πρῶτον τὸν καλὸν οἶνον τίθησιν, καὶ ὅταν μεθυσθῶσιν τὸν ἐλάσσω· σὺ τετήρηκας τὸν καλὸν οἶνον ἕως ἄρτι). The final statement by a character in the story is made by the master of the banquet to the bridegroom and is intended to express the meaning and significance of the entire pericope. As in other Gospel stories, the greatness of what happened is emphasized by a demonstration of acclamation by the public.[22]

The statement by the master of the banquet is one of surprise regarding what he claims is the reversal of a customary practice. According to the master of the banquet, the best wine is served first, followed by the cheaper wine, assumingly once the palate has become numb to the lessening quality.[23] A powerful implication is suggested when the master of the banquet gives the bridegroom credit for what Jesus has done. Such an ironic depiction demands that Jesus be seen as fulfilling the role of the bridegroom. As John will make clear soon enough, Jesus is the true bridegroom (3:29; cf. Mark

2:19–20). Thus, this final statement between the master of the banquet and the bridegroom summarizes perfectly the situation that has come into being with the arrival of Jesus and his work.[24]

2:11 This Jesus did in Cana of Galilee as the beginning of the signs, and he revealed his glory, and his disciples believed in him (Ταύτην ἐποίησεν ἀρχὴν τῶν σημείων ὁ Ἰησοῦς ἐν Κανὰ τῆς Γαλιλαίας καὶ ἐφανέρωσεν τὴν δόξαν αὐτοῦ, καὶ ἐπίστευσαν εἰς αὐτὸν οἱ μαθηταὶ αὐτοῦ). The final verse of the pericope is a summarizing interjection by the narrator. The deep significance of the pericope requires a bit of interpretive guidance. It is important to note that the same precision of insight that was presented by the prologue is also to be attributed to the narrator. The narrator will weave the prologue's interpretive wisdom and explanatory insight throughout the narrative proper. The narrator explains that this miraculous work of Jesus was the start of the "signs" of Jesus. The anarthrous "beginning" (ἀρχὴν) is best understood not as "the first" but "a beginning," or more loosely, "an inauguration of the signs yet to come."[25] That the signs are referred to as "beginning" suggests the writer knows of them as a specific set of events and about which more shall be heard.[26] The message of the Gospel is intimately connected to several "signs."

IN DEPTH: "Signs"

Miracles in John are often described as "works" (ἔργα) of Jesus (e.g., 5:36; 9:3; 10:32, 37; 14:10). These "works" make visible both the character and the power of God and that in Christ he is active in a unique way. Yet there is an even

22. Cf. Bultmann, *John*, 118.

23. The narrative's depiction of drinking wine and drunkenness is being descriptive and not prescriptive for the reader. While the appropriate consumption of alcohol is not condemned in Scripture, it is clear that drunkenness is (see Eph

5:18). The biblical reader would have to go to other texts in Scripture to determine the proper use of alcohol.

24. Ridderbos, *John*, 108.

25. BDF § 292; McHugh, *John 1–4*, 186–87.

26. Michaels, *John*, 153.

more potent term for miracles in John that confronts us in this pericope: "sign" (σημεῖον). As Barrett explains, "This is one of the most characteristic and important words of the Gospel."[27] Like John's use of "Word" (λόγος), John has chosen a deeply biblical term that has nonbiblical associations. In classical Greek, for example, "sign" referred to a distinguishing mark, a token, or a signal. But in the OT (LXX), its meaning often became linked to a special part of the prophetic activity: "No mere illustration, but a symbolical anticipation or showing forth of a greater reality of which the σημεῖον [the "sign"] is nevertheless itself a part."[28] In this later biblical sense the term is innately eschatological, but for John — in contrast to the more future-oriented use of the term in the Synoptics — the eschatological reality is already present.

There is debate over the number of "signs" in John. There are six miracles that the Gospel specifically identifies as "signs" (2:1 – 11; 4:43 – 54; 5:1 – 18; 6:1 – 15; 9:1 – 41; 11:1 – 57).[29] Interpreters have spilled a lot of ink trying to determine where the seventh, implicit sign is located, if at all, and how to determine the seventh sign.[30] Although we will explore the nature of John's "signs" as we progress throughout the narrative, it is interesting to note that the first of the six stated "signs" occurs in the same pericope as the last of the six stated "days," another term about which there has been much debate. Similar to John's use of the six "days," the six "signs" serve alongside their individuality as a corporate unit, unfolding throughout the remainder of the Gospel. It is not surprising, though, that on the sixth "day," when the image of God is made known to his creation, the "signs" have their "beginning." We should expect, then, for the implicit seventh sign not to be hidden in the middle of John somewhere but to be fully manifested only at the end, at the transition point between work and rest, alongside the implicit seventh day (for a summary of the identification of the seventh sign, see comments before 20:1).

The signs function as the means by which Jesus "revealed his glory" (ἐφανέρωσεν τὴν δόξαν αὐτοῦ). The signs "point us to something beyond themselves,"[31] so that the images pressed upon the reader by the narrative regarding Jesus reflect who he is and what he can (and will) do. These signs, then, express what the prologue and introduction have foretold: "We beheld his glory" (1:14) and "You will see heaven open ... upon the Son of Man" (1:51). Said another way, "What you just saw, that was the glory of God, and his name is Jesus." In this sense, the signs are the aftershock of "God with us." Their purpose is fulfilled in the disciples, who after seeing the signs "believed in him"

27. Barrett, *John*, 75.
28. Ibid., 76.
29. On the Gospel's explicit identification of the "signs," see Köstenberger, *A Theology of John's Gospel*, 324 – 35.
30. For a brief survey, see Köstenberger, *Theology of John*, 324 – 35.
31. Morris, *John*, 163.

(ἐπίστευσαν εἰς αὐτὸν). They did not believe in the signs themselves but in the one to whom they pointed. Ultimately, this is exactly what John wants for the reader, since his last reference to "signs" is in the concluding purpose statement of the Gospel: "These [signs] have been recorded that you may believe" (20:30 – 31).

Theology in Application

The God of creation is at one and the same time intimately involved with his creation and wholly other. The arrival of the "Son of Man" (1:51) creates a cognitive dissonance that reflects both aspects of the Creator in creation. Even more, it reflects by means of the love of God the good news that the separation between God and humanity is being restored in the person and work of Christ but on his terms. This is the good news: God is working by his means, his power, and for his purposes. Let us rejoice and be glad in it!

The Mission of the Son from the Father

The strong bond of family relations between Jesus and his mother was rightly qualified by means of the strong bond of family relations between Jesus, the unique Son, and his Father (v. 4). The nature of separation was merely correction, as Jesus carefully located his response to his mother within the loving confines of the will of his Father. Only God can incorporate all our needs (imagined and real) into his own will and mission, ultimately bringing to himself all the glory (v. 11). The distance Jesus placed between himself and his mother was an expression of the love of God.

The church is constantly redefining itself by means of the strong bond of family relations it has with the Father through Christ and guided by the Holy Spirit. By nature, the Christian is distanced from not merely the world but even himself, his old self. The call of the Christian is constantly to work at establishing the will and wisdom of God as the plumb line for every human plan and purpose. Placing God at the center is ultimately the best, self-seeking decision a Christian can make. It is to have "thy will be done" as the backdrop of every thought and as the motor of every decision. In the end, it is to embrace a Christ-centered posture.

God's Timing

God is never late or hurried. God is compassionate and gracious, slow to anger, abounding in love (Ps 103:8). Jesus's emphatic statement for the timing of God, "the hour," made certain that all things be viewed as part of God's schedule and on God's timeline. The actual "hour" for John is inclusive of everything the death and resurrection of Jesus will bring. All clocks set their time by this "hour." It is the center of all activity and the source of all movement in any direction. According to John, however, even when this "hour" was future it was not entirely inactive. The Creator had always been extending his love to creation. The OT proclaims the various moments before the "hour," depicting the "hour" as both mandatory and marvelous. It is in Jesus that the "hour" becomes the climactic moment of God's love, the culminating hour in the long history of God's expression of love to the world. And all God's initial expressions of love, taking the form of Jewish customs, feasts, and every religious institution, find their fulfillment in Jesus.

The True Master of the Banquet, the True Bridegroom

From the moment the wedding started, the actual characters in the story were eclipsed by Jesus. The narrative suggests as much by turning to the actual master of the banquet and bridegroom at the end of the pericope. The master of the banquet was not a servant but an honored guest; Jesus, in contrast, was just one of the guests. The bridegroom was the person being celebrated; Jesus, in contrast, was just one of those bestowing honor. Yet it was Jesus who in the end became the honored guest and the person being celebrated. The irony reaches its climax when the master of the banquet gives the credit for the superior wine to the bridegroom. The silence of the bridegroom is deafening — the name of Jesus shouts through the silence.

The world is full of people being honored and celebrated, speaking to each other with praise or even to themselves in words of self-promotion. Yet there is only one person who deserves to be honored and celebrated: Jesus Christ. He is the true master and bridegroom of the church, the one through whom all things came into being (1:3) and through whom all things find their meaning. The church reserves its worship for God through Christ alone. There is no other name, no other person, no other truth besides Jesus and what he brings.

From Purification Water to Celebratory Wine

Everything about those jars of water for Jewish purification speaks of Judaism and the old covenant. Yet their value was entirely changed in the presence of Jesus. The moment he arrived, true cleansing had no need for ceremonial jars made of purified stone. Rather, their use was relegated to serving as containers for celebratory wine. Purification water was transformed into wine for celebration, not for cleansing. The church is in no need of purification jars made of purified stone; rather, the church needed and received a greater purification that has come through, ironically, a man made in the form of a jar of clay (2 Cor 4:7).

The narrative has guided the reader to grasp the significance and imagery it projected. Three things can be highlighted. First, based upon the "hour" of Jesus (v. 4) and that the good wine was kept "until now" (v. 10), along with the Gospel's clear connection to the Old Testament, *Jesus's person and work is depicted as the fulfillment of God's activity in the world*. Yet the miracle of water to wine is at the same time a distancing "not yet" and a "taste" of the good that has already broken through with Jesus.

Second, based upon the amount (v. 6) and quality (vv. 9–10) of water turned to wine, along with the implicit connection to the OT motif of the abundance of wine as characteristic for the coming kingdom of God (e.g., Amos 9:13–14; cf. Gen 49:11), *Jesus's person and work is depicted as the full blessing of God's activity in the world.*[32] As Isaiah declared: "The Lᴏʀᴅ Almighty will prepare a feast of rich food for all peoples, a banquet of aged wine … the finest of wines…. In that day they will say, 'Surely this is our God; we trusted in him, and he saved us. This is the Lᴏʀᴅ, we trusted in him; let us rejoice and be glad in his salvation'" (Isa 25:6, 9).

Third, based upon the narrative tension between his role at the wedding and the master of the wedding and the bridegroom (vv. 8–10), along with the implicit connection to the biblical motif of the wedding of God (Rev 19:7–9; cf. Matt 22:1–14), *Jesus's work is to be understood in light of and in preparation for the wedding par excellence.* We stated above that the role Jesus played in this wedding was ultimately the role of the master of the banquet. But the narrative suggests even more. The narrative's depiction of the anonymous bridegroom, the recipient of the praise of the master of the banquet, is suggesting (and made explicit in 3:29) that Jesus is the bridegroom, whose role as the true bridegroom is bursting through the narrative's significance and imagery.

The Wedding of Cana Became the Wedding of God

The details of the pericope are careful to express specifically how Jesus is the center of and meaning behind this wedding in Cana of Galilee, and that his meaning ultimately extends to something much grander: the wedding of God. The wedding in Cana of Galilee, with its wedding party waiting to have their hands washed and their wine replenished, is like the world who has not known that the God of creation is the way, the truth, and the life (14:6). The church, the bride of Christ, has enjoined herself to the true bridegroom and awaits the real celebration to begin. The church's existence in this world is like being one of the servants in the wedding who knows who the true bridegroom is but is surrounded by people who are unaware. The church, seeing the unseen, must now navigate itself as both a witness to the wedding of God and as a faithful partner awaiting reunion with her bridegroom. Thus, at one and the same time, the church is blessed with the promise of glory and committed to participate in the mission of the Son from the Father.

---

32. Cf. Klink, "What Concern is That to You and to Me?" 282.

John 2:12 – 25

Literary Context

The narrative moves from a wedding in Cana to the temple in Jerusalem at Passover. The narrative's careful depiction of Jesus in the previous pericope (2:1 – 11), with the imagery of purification followed by celebratory imagery, now confronts the reader as they watch Jesus enter into the temple. While he was willing to maintain his "guest" status at the wedding, he is not willing to remain a guest at the temple, his "Father's house." All of this is set in the context of the revelation of his "glory" (2:11), the theme ending the previous pericope and now pressuring this entire scene.

III. The Beginning of Jesus's Public Ministry (2:1 – 4:54)

   A. The First Sign: The Wedding at Cana (2:1 – 11)

➡ **B. The Cleansing of the Temple: The Promise of the Seventh Sign (2:12 – 25)**

   C. Nicodemus, New Birth, and the Unique Son (3:1 – 21)

   D. The Baptist, the True Bridegroom, and the Friend of the Bridegroom (3:22 – 36)

   E. The Samaritan Woman, Living Water, and True Worshippers (4:1 – 42)

   F. The Second Sign: The Healing of the Royal Official's Son (4:43 – 54)

Main Idea

God the Father shall accept no other sacrifice than Jesus, the true Passover lamb and true temple of God. Only in Jesus can a person be reconciled to God and dwell with him. The business of the church is to sell nothing but the gospel of Jesus Christ, which is the crucified Lamb of God who alone can remove the sin and the shame of the world. Only those who receive this gospel, purchased for them by Christ, can dwell in the house of God.

Translation

(See pages 174–75.)

John 2:12–25

12a	Setting (12–14)	**After this Jesus, …**
b	Company	with his mother, his brothers and sisters, and his disciples,
c	Action	**… went down**
d	Place	into Capernaum,
e	Action	and **they remained there for a few days.**
13a	Event	**The Passover of the Jews was near,**
b	Reaction/Place	and **Jesus went up to Jerusalem.**
14a	Result/Place	And **he found in the temple**
b	Problem	those who were selling oxen and sheep and doves, and
c	Problem	others seated exchanging money.
	Conflict (15–17)	
15a	Reactions to Problem: #1	Making a whip out of cords,
b	Reactions to Problem: #2	**he drove them all from the temple,**
c		including the sheep and oxen,
d	Reactions to Problem: #3	and **he poured out the coins of those exchanging money**
e	Reactions to Problem: #4	and **overturned the tables.**
16a	Reactions to Problem: #5	And **to those who sold doves he said,**
b	Command	*"Get these out of here!*
c	Rebuke	*Stop making my Father's house*
d	Comparison	*a house of business!"*
17a	Aside/Climax of Conflict	**His disciples remembered that it is written:**
b	OT Quotation	"Zeal for your house will consume me." (Ps 69:9a)
18a	Resolution (18–22)/	Then **the Jews answered and said to him,**
	Character Entrance	
b	Interrogative Challenge	*"What sign can you show us to prove that you do these things?"*
19a	Retort	**Jesus answered and said to them,**
b	Prophetic Irony/Condition of 22	*"Destroy this temple and in three days I will raise it."*
20a	Response	**Then the Jews said,**
b	Rhetorical Question	*"It took forty-six years for this temple to be built,*
c		*and in three days you will raise it?"*
21a	Aside: Explanation of 19b	**He was speaking concerning the temple of his body.**
22a		Then
b	Temporal Circumstance	when he was raised from the dead,
c	Recollection of 19	**his disciples remembered that he said this,**
d	Result #1	and **they believed the Scripture and**
e	Result #2	the message which Jesus had spoken.
23a	Conclusion/Interpretation (23–25)	And
b	Time	while he was in Jerusalem during the Passover at the feast,
c	Assertion	**many believed in his name,**
d	Circumstances	when they were seeing the signs which he was doing.
24a	Contrast to 23c	But **Jesus did not entrust himself to them**
b	Basis	because he knew them all.

| 25a | Explanation #1 | For **he did not need a witness concerning humanity,** |
| b | Explanation #2 | For **he knew what was in humanity.** |

Structure and Literary Form

The basic story form (see Introduction) of this pericope centers around the conflict and resolution of the temple cleansing at Passover. The *introduction/setting* is established in vv. 12 – 17, explaining the significant time (Passover) and location (temple) of the actions of Jesus in order to establish the context for the encounter with the authorities that immediately follows. Jesus's aggressive actions in the temple (vv. 15 – 17) are not the conflict of the pericope but serve to express the forces at work in the actual conflict: the temple and its authority. The *conflict* is expressed by the brief dialogical exchange between Jesus and "the Jews" in vv. 18 – 20. Although not a technical dialogue (such as Jesus's dialogue with Nicodemus), it serves a related function in this pericope (see Introduction). The *resolution* is provided by the narrator in vv. 21 – 22, serving to guide the reader to the ironic sign to which Jesus points and by which the meaning is derived from Jesus's response to the Jews. Finally, vv. 23 – 25 provide the *conclusion/interpretation* of the pericope, carrying forward the conflict of the macrolevel plot of John that was first introduced in the prologue.

Exegetical Outline

➡ **B. The Cleansing of the Temple: The Promise of the Seventh Sign (2:12 – 25)**

   1. The House of God and a House of Business (vv. 12 – 17)

   2. A Challenge of Temple Authority (vv. 18 – 20)

   3. The True Temple, the Body of Jesus (vv. 21 – 22)

   4. Jesus's Witness to the Nature of Humanity (vv. 23 – 25)

Explanation of the Text

This pericope is connected to a particular issue that has the potential of eclipsing the actual meaning intended by the text: the chronology of the cleansing of the temple. The differences in wording and setting between John and the Synoptics has caused much confusion regarding this incident (cf. Matt 21:12 – 13; Mark 11:15 – 17; Luke 19: 45 – 46). While Michaels is not wrong when he writes, "Such discussions belong either to canonical criticism or to the study of the historical Jesus. They are outside the scope of a commentary on any one Gospel,"[1] his statement ignores the eclectic nature of exegesis, in

---

1. Michaels, *John,* 158.

which intra- and extratextual insights are needed to explain a text. In John there is only one temple cleansing; but that to which John witnesses demands that the possibility of two temple cleansings be addressed (and such possibilities affect what the text might be saying). The judgment of this commentary is that John speaks about a different (and earlier) temple cleansing than the Synoptics. The two-cleansing construction, we will argue, handles better not only the differences between the Gospels and their cleansings but also the nuances within the Fourth Gospel itself.

IN DEPTH: John and the First Temple Cleansing

The general consensus has been that there was only one temple cleansing that happened near the end of Jesus's ministry as recorded in the Synoptics. The earlier placement by John was considered to have more to do with theological than historical concerns.[2] But to argue that John is not concerned with details is to ignore his detailed account of the historical realities surrounding Jesus. Even more, to assume that the single-cleansing hypothesis simplifies the matter is to ignore the distinctions between the Gospels. The complexity of a cross-Gospel reconstruction demands that we hold loosely to either position (on Gospel comparison and reconstruction, see Introduction).[3] The suggestion of this commentary is that two temple cleansings provide the more comprehensive solution to this long-standing issue.

Several interpreters have been preferential to two cleansings based upon historical data;[4] we would like to offer support to that position based upon sociological data. Richards has made a sociological observation regarding honor/shame that adds a further dimension to the temple incident.[5] To begin we must understand social relations in the first century: "The culture of the first-century world was built on the foundational social values of honor and dishonor."[6] It is almost certain that during the first century, all people — from the most powerful to the most average person — regarded honor and shame (or dishonor) as their primary axis of value. For this reason, honor was a desired and contested form of currency, like financial currency in the modern Western world. Just as money can be gained or lost in the marketplace today, so also could honor be gained or lost. Honor could be won or lost in public confrontations or so-

2. For a succinct argument for a single cleansing, see Witherington, *John's Wisdom*, 85 – 86.

3. Cf. Luther, *John*, 22:219: "But even if it happened three times, that would not be heresy."

4. For example, Morris, *John*, 166 – 69; Carson, *John*, 177 – 78; Köstenberger, *John*, 111; Craig L. Blomberg, *The Historical Reliability of John's Gospel: Issues and Commentary* (Downers Grove, IL: InterVarsity Press, 2001), 87 – 91; Darrell L. Bock, *Luke*, 2 vols., BECNT (Grand Rapids: Baker, 1996), 2:1576 – 77.

5. E. Randolph Richards, "An Honor/Shame Argument for Two Temple Clearings," *TrinJ* 29 (2008): 19 – 43.

6. David A. deSilva, *Honor, Patronage, Kinship & Purity: Unlocking New Testament Culture* (Downers Grove, IL: InterVarsity Press, 2000), 23.

cial contexts, situations familiar to the Gospels. As Richards explains, "What we often read as an innocent quest for knowledge, 'Teacher, what must I do to inherit eternal life?' (Luke 10:25), was usually a challenge for honor. Either by a question or an action, someone was making a claim to have additional honor. Since honor was a limited good, an increase in honor came by being drained, so-to-speak, from another."[7] When a challenge has been posed, the challenge demands some sort of response. The lack of a response was also considered a response. It was up to the bystanders to decide the recipient of honor: the challenger or the person challenged.[8]

A significant issue, and one especially pertinent for our pericope, was the beginning honor of the challenger. Not just anyone could make a legitimate claim to honor. For example, if one's status was far below the honor claimed, those whose honor should have been at risk could merely ignore the challenge. This nonresponse was itself a shaming, and it could only be done if the challenger was not a serious contender, something recognized by the bystanders. This is the situation likely at play in John's cleansing of the temple. Jesus claimed honor by his actions in the temple. It was a claim to a very high honor (at least prophetic honor, if not divine honor). The argument is that the "Jews" responded to his challenge by asking for a sign (v. 18). What happens next is significant: Jesus's statement was deemed unsatisfactory and the challenge by the Jews is assumed to have been victorious. The leaders treated Jesus's answer with disdain and contempt — they shame him, so much so that the Gospel does not even deem it necessary to echo the sentiment from the perspective of the crowd.[9] Even the comment by the narrator serves as evidence that Jesus's challenge was deemed a failure in the historical events.[10]

This analysis coincides with our depiction of the plot of John with its historical and cosmological strands. Although they coalesce in the person of Jesus, the strands of the plot are still distinct at numerous levels. So much so that while the narrator is cluing the reader into the fact that Jesus *is* providing a sign, the very same sign was deemed inadequate by the Jews — and even by the disciples *until* the resurrection. With every other social challenge in John, the response of the crowd is provided by the narrator (and always in Jesus's favor); in this scene, the crowd does not answer because there was no need for them

---

7. Richards, "An Honor/Shame Argument for Two Temple Clearings," 31.

8. deSilva, *Honor, Patronage, Kinship & Purity*, 29. Cf. Bruce J. Malina, *The New Testament World: Insights from Cultural Anthropology*, 3rd ed. (Louisville: Westminster John Knox, 2001), 33 – 36.

9. Richards, "An Honor/Shame Argument for Two Temple Clearings," 33.

10. Ibid., 33 – 34.

to do so. According to Richards, this explains other scenes in John in which Jesus is depicted as being connected to the public shame inflicted as a result of the temple-cleansing challenge (e.g., 7:4, 32, 50 – 52).[11] The second (Synoptic) cleansing, then, at the level of reconstructing the ministry of Jesus, was merely the final proof that Jesus had not received shame. Further challenges would be futile since they could only ascribe shame. The authorities now needed to take more drastic measures; they needed to adjust from social to physical punishment. The Synoptics tell us that the authorities "began looking for a way to kill him, for they feared him" (Mark 11:18). They feared him because he could not be controlled; he did not play by the rules. In their estimation, he was shameless. This is not merely a significant clue for a reconstruction of the ministry of Jesus but a powerful insight regarding the ironic interaction between the Word and the world depicted in this pericope.

2:12 After this Jesus, with his mother, his brothers and sisters, and his disciples, went down into Capernaum, and they remained there for a few days (Μετὰ τοῦτο κατέβη εἰς Καφαρναοὺμ αὐτὸς καὶ ἡ μήτηρ αὐτοῦ καὶ οἱ ἀδελφοὶ [αὐτοῦ] καὶ οἱ μαθηταὶ αὐτοῦ, καὶ ἐκεῖ ἔμειναν οὐ πολλὰς ἡμέρας). "After this" (μετὰ τοῦτο; or elsewhere with the plural: μετὰ ταῦτα) occurs frequently in John as a connective between narratives (cf. 3:22; 5:1, 14; 6:1; 7:1; 11:7, 11; 19:28, 38). This connective is imprecise, giving no indication of the timing of the events being summarized. The narrator takes care to establish the people traveling with Jesus, a surprising fact since his mother is not mentioned again until 19:25 – 27, and his brothers are mentioned again only in 7:3 – 5. "His brothers and sisters" (οἱ ἀδελφοὶ [αὐτοῦ]) is best understood to be referring to the biological children of Mary and Joseph, to his legal siblings.[12] The nominative plural can refer to either all brothers or both brothers and sisters, with the latter option the most likely (cf. Matt 13:55 – 56; Mark 6:3).

Since Capernaum (the modern site is Tell Hum) was near the Sea of Galilee, to travel from Cana to Capernaum would naturally require a descent, thus the narrator describes that they "went down" (κατέβη). The trip from Cana to Capernaum was about sixteen miles. That Jesus and his fellow travelers stayed "for a few days" (οὐ πολλὰς ἡμέρας) suggests that there was not a long interval between the wedding they had just attended and the Jewish Passover. It is possible that John makes mention of this interlude in Capernaum, in agreement with the Synoptics (Matt 4:13; Luke 4:31), because Capernaum served as a home base for Jesus (e.g., Matt 9:1: "His own town").

2:13 The Passover of the Jews was near, and Jesus went up to Jerusalem (Καὶ ἐγγὺς ἦν τὸ πάσχα τῶν Ἰουδαίων, καὶ ἀνέβη εἰς Ἱεροσόλυμα ὁ Ἰησοῦς). The narrator, still introducing the scene and its setting, states that the "Passover of the Jews" (τὸ πάσχα τῶν Ἰουδαίων) was at hand. The Jewish Passover commemorated the great deliverance of the people

11. Ibid., 35 – 37. Richards's insights regarding the honor/shame dimension of the temple cleansings are helpful, but not all his responses to the alternative theory are without problems.

12. See Richard Bauckham, *Jude and the Relatives of Jesus in the Early Church* (Edinburgh: T&T Clark, 1990), 5 – 44.

from Egypt (Exod 12). The qualification, "of the Jews," is common in John; the narrator elsewhere offers explanatory comments for non-Jewish readers. These qualifications, however, are not entirely consistent, for some advanced Jewish details are left unqualified, while some are applied to basic Jewish details that might even be known to the non-Jew.[13] The "Passover" takes place three times in John at 2:13–23, 6:4, and 11:55 (cf. 19:14), suggesting that the ministry of Jesus took place for at least two years (hence, the typical understanding of a three-year ministry of Jesus). Such chronological precision (unique to John) should be taken into account as we consider the timing of the temple cleansing provided by the Fourth Gospel. The Passover serves to frame not merely this pericope (vv. 13, 23) but also the Gospel as a whole (19:14).

2:14 And he found in the temple those who were selling oxen and sheep and doves, and others seated exchanging money (Καὶ εὗρεν ἐν τῷ ἱερῷ τοὺς πωλοῦντας βόας καὶ πρόβατα καὶ περιστερὰς καὶ τοὺς κερματιστὰς καθημένους). This verse provides the final details regarding the setting of the pericope. The narrator depicts within the temple precincts — almost certainly the outermost court, the court of the gentiles — the business of the Jewish sacrificial religion. It is likely that the animal merchants would set up booths to meet the needs of people traveling from afar to offer sacrifices in the temple. And since many were probably from all over the Roman world, there were also some currency traders, providing foreigners with currency conversions.

The most significant detail is that this was occurring in the temple. The term becomes significant in this pericope, since its two primary NT forms both occur here. The term for "temple" (ἱερόν) that the narrator uses in vv. 14–15 is best understood to

refer generally to "the whole temple precinct with its buildings, courts, etc."[14] This serves to explain the narrator's depiction of the geographical circumstances in the pericope. The other term for "temple" (ναός), however, is primarily used to denote the dwelling place of God. It can be used comprehensively to refer to the whole temple precinct, but it does so with the emphasis on "dwelling," not physical structure. This becomes significant since the term Jesus uses in v. 19 (followed by the Jews in v. 20 and the narrator in v. 21) is "temple" (ναός).

In the first-century Mediterranean world, corporate entities such as "the temple" and "the palace" were more than simply structures or locations for certain kinds of activities. They were invested with a social significance and therefore were personified and viewed as moral persons. "They had ascribed honor just as did any family or individual and could be insulted, cursed, hated, and dishonored. By dishonoring the temple, one also dishonored all of its personnel, from high priest down, including the One who commanded its construction and occasionally dwelled there — God."[15] For this reason, the narrative events about to be described as happening in this place are personal at numerous levels.

2:15 Making a whip out of cords, he drove them all from the temple, including the sheep and oxen, and he poured out the coins of those exchanging money and overturned the tables (καὶ ποιήσας φραγέλλιον ἐκ σχοινίων πάντας ἐξέβαλεν ἐκ τοῦ ἱεροῦ, τά τε πρόβατα καὶ τοὺς βόας, καὶ τῶν κολλυβιστῶν ἐξέχεεν τὸ κέρμα καὶ τὰς τραπέζας ἀνέτρεψεν). The narrator describes with graphic detail the response of Jesus to what he found in the temple courts. Only John notes that he was "making a whip" (ποιήσας φραγέλλιον). Such on-the-spot ingenuity reflected the dire necessity of

13. See Klink, *The Sheep of the Fold*, 152–84.
14. BDAG 470.

15. Malina and Rohrbaugh, *John*, 79.

the situation. Although "them all" (πάντας) refers primarily to the men, denoted by the masculine, since the term for "whip" (φραγέλλιον) implies that it is the sort used for driving cattle, "them all" can include both merchants and their animals.[16] This scene includes no unnecessary detail for John: the sacrificial Lamb himself replaces the sacrificial animals in the temple. The specific inclusion of the "sheep and oxen" is to make clear that a full cleansing was needed; all blood (of man or animal) was deemed inadequate and tarnished save one. In light of their removal, the strong handling of their equipment makes clear that Jesus's concern is not with trade itself but the location of this trade: "in the temple" (v. 14). The imagery is again significant. Jesus was attacking explicitly the corruption that had turned the sacrificial system into a business and attacking implicitly the failings of the sacrificial system itself.

2:16 And to those who sold doves he said, "Get these out of here! Stop making my Father's house a house of business!" (καὶ τοῖς τὰς περιστερὰς πωλοῦσιν εἶπεν, Ἄρατε ταῦτα ἐντεῦθεν, μὴ ποιεῖτε τὸν οἶκον τοῦ πατρός μου οἶκον ἐμπορίου). After removing the men and their larger animals, the comment to the dove sellers seems less necessary. Yet it is in his final statement to the dove sellers that Jesus gives the reason for his whole action: the abuse of his Father's house. The negation with a present imperative, "stop making" (μὴ ποιεῖτε), is used to stop action that is already taking place.[17] We are not to see this statement as occurring following the removal of all traders except for the dove sellers. Rather, Jesus's words "are to be read as more or less simultaneous with his actions."[18] By giving the reasoning last, John has made sure that

we grasp the explanation as a commentary on the action of judgment already accomplished.

The force of Jesus's statement comes when he sets his Father's "house" in opposition to a "house of business" (οἶκον ἐμπορίου). Since the Greek phrase is a descriptive (or epexegetical) genitive, it is often translated as simply "market place," which does not allow the English reader to see the play on the word "house" (οἶκος).[19] The play on "house" makes the place, not the activity, the focus of attention. In contrast to the Synoptics' cleansing, Jesus here is not objecting to their dishonesty (cf. Mark 11:17: "a den of robbers") but to their presence. The contrast is sharpened when Jesus describes the temple as "my Father's house." Although this is the first occurrence of "my Father" by Jesus, it is anything but foreign in light of the prologue (1:14, 18). This subtle hint to the onlookers (since faithful Jews would have probably felt comfortable using the phrase) is a clear reminder of the source of the authority that Jesus has for his action (see Isa 56:7; Zech 14:21).[20]

2:17 His disciples remembered that it is written: "Zeal for your house will consume me" (ἐμνήσθησαν οἱ μαθηταὶ αὐτοῦ ὅτι γεγραμμένον ἐστίν, Ὁ ζῆλος τοῦ οἴκου σου καταφάγεταί με). While this statement by the narrator might seem to be intended to explain the actions of Jesus, they are better understood to be shedding light on the conflict to come. It is difficult to know if this statement is suggesting the disciples remembered the OT text at that moment or only later. In light of v. 22 and 12:16, this is almost certainly a later, reflective statement. Until this verse, the disciples were entirely unimportant to the scene. This intervention by the narrator serves to provide an interpretive transition to the Scripture they remembered.

---

16. Barrett, *John*, 197.
17. See Moulton, *Grammar*, 1:22–26.
18. Michaels, *John*, 159–60.

19. Cf. Wallace, *Greek Grammar*, 79–81.
20. McHugh, *John 1–4*, 205.

The Scripture, then, becomes the interpretive grid through which the actions of Jesus are to be understood.

The Scripture the disciples remembered is from Psalm 69:9. The larger context of this quotation brings clarity to its use in this pericope. The psalmist declares in v. 7 that it is on account of God that "shame [dishonor] covers my face," and in v. 8 he states, "I am a foreigner to my own family, a stranger to my own mother's children." The emphasis on the unique relation to God and the distance between his mother's offspring connects directly to how Jesus is depicted thus far in the Gospel. The psalmist is declaring that the people were reviling God by their worship, and his public protest has caused them to begin to revile him as well. The people do not understand the protest, "and they attack the suppliant for suggesting that they are attacking Yhwh or because they infer admission of personal sin."[21] Thus, the use of Psalm 69:9 depicts both what Jesus intended *by* his actions (i.e., a pure temple; a right relationship with God for the people) and what Jesus received *from* his actions (i.e., shame) in the temple.[22] In this way the setting and context of the pericope is introduced. God in the person of Jesus has just entered his temple, declared it unclean, and has prepared to receive its shame *himself*.

2:18 Then the Jews answered and said to him, "What sign can you show us to prove that you do these things?" (Ἀπεκρίθησαν οὖν οἱ Ἰουδαῖοι καὶ εἶπαν αὐτῷ, Τί σημεῖον δεικνύεις ἡμῖν, ὅτι ταῦτα ποιεῖς;). The conflict of the pericope is forcefully introduced to the reader. Although the Jews appear without explanation, their intentions are clear after the narrator's inclusion of Psalm 69:9. They are the revilers who both revile God and will shame Jesus. The commotion caused by the cleansing in the court forced the authorities to present themselves. The authorities that appear, "the Jews" (οἱ Ἰουδαῖοι), are those that the Gospel has already introduced as the representatives of Judaism (see comments on 1:19) and frequent opponents of Jesus. The Jews are asking for Jesus to authenticate his enacted claim by a "sign" (σημεῖον). Their demand is clear: "We are the authorities of the temple, so by what higher authority do you claim the right to act as you have?" This question addresses the issue out of which the conflict of the pericope will find resolution.

2:19 Jesus answered and said to them, "Destroy this temple and in three days I will raise it" (ἀπεκρίθη Ἰησοῦς καὶ εἶπεν αὐτοῖς, Λύσατε τὸν ναὸν τοῦτον καὶ ἐν τρισὶν ἡμέραις ἐγερῶ αὐτόν). Without hesitation, Jesus directly states the proof of his authority. The content of the sign is made clear by the grammar. The imperative "destroy" (λύσατε) is best understood as a conditional imperative. The idea is that "if X, then Y will happen," but by stating the conditional aspect of the mood the force of the imperative risks becoming eclipsed.[23] And it is only when both forces, conditional and imperatival, are held together that the prophetic irony is fully expressed. The proof of the sign is conditionally dependent on the destruction of the "temple," his body, and fulfilled when it is "rebuilt," his resurrection, three days later (cf. vv. 21 – 22). At the same time, however, the command to destroy the temple (i.e., his body) is itself part of the very plan of the Father for the Son; Jesus's command is itself a prophetic command pointing toward "the hour" of the cross (cf. 12:27, 32 – 33).

21. John Goldingay, *Psalms*, 3 vols., BCOT (Grand Rapids: Baker, 2006 – 8), 2:344.

22. Richards, "An Honor/Shame Argument for Two Temple Clearings," 34.

23. Wallace, *Greek Grammar*, 489 – 91. Cf. BDF § 387.2.

Interestingly, the real "sign" given to the Jews—and the disciples as well (cf. v. 22)—is here declared: the destruction of "this temple" and its resurrection "in three days," that is, the death and resurrection of Jesus Christ. In the Gospel, the death and resurrection of Jesus cannot be separated; they are one unified event—his "glorification" (cf. 1:14; 2:11; 7:39; 12:23). Since six "signs" are explicitly as such, the "sign" about which Jesus explicitly foretells here must be the seventh and final sign by which Jesus "revealed his glory" (2:11). It is the final and conclusive proof of Jesus's identity and authority (for a summary of the identification of the seventh sign, see comments before 20:1). Thus, the death and resurrection of Jesus is the ultimate temple cleansing, and the temple of his body is a full replacement of the temple of the Jews.

2:20 Then the Jews said, "It took forty-six years for this temple to be built, and in three days you will raise it?" (εἶπαν οὖν οἱ Ἰουδαῖοι, Τεσσαράκοντα καὶ ἓξ ἔτεσιν οἰκοδομήθη ὁ ναὸς οὗτος, καὶ σὺ ἐν τρισὶν ἡμέραις ἐγερεῖς αὐτόν;). Although the narrator will explain below that by means of his statement Jesus is referring to himself, we must not miss that Jesus's statement taken on its own is referring to the real temple. Only this explains the response of the Jews and therefore the need for the narrator to give an explanation. To fault the Jews for taking Jesus's statement too literally is to misunderstand the message of the pericope. The rhetorical force of John is dependent upon this truly referring to one thing and yet also to another. For this reason, the Jews heard correctly what Jesus was saying and responded with a response intended to reject the sign as well as to shame the challenger.

This rhetorical question by the Jews is itself a statement. It makes what would have been deemed an insurmountable defense of their position and status. According to Josephus, the reconstruction of the temple began in the eighteenth year of King

Herod, 20–19 BC (*J.W.* 1.21). Forty-six years from the commencement of the work would suggest that it was around AD 27–28 when the Jews made this statement. Such a statistic would have crushed the validity of Jesus's statement. To interpret this as anything other than a defeating counterclaim by the Jews is to misunderstand the pericope. Interpreters often speak about the overly rigid (mis)understanding of the Jews at this point. But Jesus is talking about the temple, and they do hear him correctly. In this scene, the temple is nevertheless eclipsed by *the* temple (1:14), and both need to be kept in view. The reader is supposed to see two temples, not one, with the former now rendered entirely obsolete. And the reader is supposed to have heard a valid defense of the old temple. Quite simply, the misunderstanding is not to understand that the Jews are defending the wrong temple.

2:21 He was speaking concerning the temple of his body (ἐκεῖνος δὲ ἔλεγεν περὶ τοῦ ναοῦ τοῦ σώματος αὐτοῦ). The resolution of the conflict is so significant (and complex) that the narrator interjects the necessary explanation. Comments by the narrator that provide necessary insight are common in John (e.g., 6:64, 71; 7:5, 39; 11:13, 51–52; 12:6, 33; 20:9). In every instance they serve to add insight to the scene at hand, even to the historical details. This is precisely how this comment by the narrator is functioning. The conclusion of the dialogue between Jesus and the Jews ends with the official counterresponse to Jesus's proof or sign. The statement by the Jews and the absence of a response by Jesus are fully intended to signify that Jesus lost the challenge. In a culture built on the foundational social values of honor and shame, Jesus was shamed. Jesus did not respond because no response was warranted; in the eyes of the temple authorities, in the eyes of any bystanders, and even in the eyes of the disciples—as v. 22 will explain—Jesus was shamed. This is the only honor contest recorded in the Gospels where the verdict was not declared — and perhaps more significantly — where Jesus was not (publicly) victorious.[24] Such a conclusion is not based entirely upon sociological insights or even the silence of the narrative but by the explanation provided by the narrator. The narrator provides the necessary ("unseen") insight that no one else saw: Jesus was not referring to the Jewish temple but to the temple of his body.

This statement, then, serves as a defense of Jesus's honor and implicitly serves to show that Jesus received shame in the eyes of everyone else present — even his disciples (cf. v. 22). As Richards explains, "John's defense of Jesus's honor is correct, but the appeals to other evidence indicate what the initial verdict was. Jesus lost the honor contest. He was shamed (unfairly, John argues)."[25] It could be said that it was not merely unfair; it was wrong. Admittedly, however, Jesus did offer evidence that could not be proven until after his resurrection. But only after the resurrection did that become clear to the disciples, and only with this statement is that beginning to be made clear to the reader.

2:22 Then when he was raised from the dead, his disciples remembered that he said this, and they believed the Scripture and the message which Jesus had spoken (ὅτε οὖν ἠγέρθη ἐκ νεκρῶν, ἐμνήσθησαν οἱ μαθηταὶ αὐτοῦ ὅτι τοῦτο ἔλεγεν, καὶ ἐπίστευσαν τῇ γραφῇ καὶ τῷ λόγῳ ὃν εἶπεν ὁ Ἰησοῦς). The narrator makes one final statement regarding the conflict of the scene in order to provide the necessary resolution. The narrator begins by connecting what the reader was being guided to understand with the eventual conclusion drawn by the disciples. The proof Jesus offered as a sign to the Jewish authorities, his death and resurrection, served as proof, as the final "sign" regarding this event, carrying with it all the necessary sig-

nificance. Although it had already begun to make sense, it was only at that "hour" when it would all come together (cf. 2:4), when the words and deeds of Jesus came to make sense of all things. It was only "when he was raised from the dead" (ὅτε ἠγέρθη ἐκ νεκρῶν) that the disciples gained full understanding. For the disciples "remembered" (ἐμνήσθησαν) what Jesus had said and therefore came to place their trust in both "the Scripture" (τῇ γραφῇ) and "the message" (τῷ λόγῳ) Jesus had spoken. The Scripture in view is almost certainly Psalm 69, though it is not wrong for the term to include the Gospel's awareness of the larger context of the Scriptures (cf. 5:39).

What is important to see is that the disciples had come to see as authoritative and complementary the word of God and the Word of God. The "memory" of the disciples, therefore, was not in regard to something different but to the same thing, which they only later saw as having begun well before they could understand it.

2:23 And while he was in Jerusalem during Passover at the feast, many believed in his name, when they were seeing the signs which he was doing (Ὡς δὲ ἦν ἐν τοῖς Ἱεροσολύμοις ἐν τῷ πάσχα ἐν τῇ ἑορτῇ, πολλοὶ ἐπίστευσαν εἰς τὸ ὄνομα αὐτοῦ, θεωροῦντες αὐτοῦ τὰ σημεῖα ἃ ἐποίει). The pericope ends with a few verses that provide some interpretive conclusions. The narrator explains that many people celebrating Passover in Jerusalem believed "in his name" (εἰς τὸ ὄνομα αὐτοῦ), being founded on "the signs" (τὰ σημεῖα) he was performing. But two things are perplexing. First, since only one sign is recorded (2:11), to what other signs is the narrator referring? While there is no doubt that the author of the Gospel intends for us to understand that there were many other signs that Jesus performed (cf. 20:30–31; 21:25),

24. Richards, "An Honor/Shame Argument for Two Temple Clearings," 35.

25. Ibid.

it is probably best understood as emphasizing the fact that Jesus performed numerous other miracles and that his words and deeds were a constant sign of sorts.

Second, and related to the first, did the "many" truly understand the signs? Perhaps this answers our initial question. What the many thought they "were seeing" (θεωροῦντες) they were likely not understanding. The disciples become primary evidence on this point. The suggestion of this verse, then, is not that the crowds understood Jesus, in sharp contrast to the temple authorities; rather, it is claiming in fact that they did not understand him. Just as the temple authorities were blinded by their own agenda and understanding of God, so also were the people. The prologue has already informed us of this irony (see 1:11).

2:24 But Jesus did not entrust himself to them because he knew them all (αὐτὸς δὲ Ἰησοῦς οὐκ ἐπίστευεν αὐτὸν αὐτοῖς διὰ τὸ αὐτὸν γινώσκειν πάντας). What was implied in v. 23 is made explicit here. Jesus knew what they did not know — he knew them! Even if creation has forgotten its Creator, the Creator has not forgotten his creation. It is significant that "Jesus did not entrust himself" (αὐτὸς Ἰησοῦς οὐκ ἐπίστευεν). This sense of "trust" or "faith" is rarely used in this sense in the NT (e.g., Luke 16:11; Rom 3:2; 1 Cor 9:17; Gal 2:7; 1 Thess 2:4; 1 Tim 1:11; Titus 1:3). The contrast between Jesus and those interested in him highlights two things. The first is correct understanding. With spiritual fervor in their hearts, faithful Jews arrived in Jerusalem to meet with God and, in the midst of their festival, began to include Jesus within their religious excitement. They do not know the "name" about which they speak because they do not know

the true Passover, the true temple, the true sacrificial Lamb, or even the true God. And for this very reason they do not — even cannot — know him. True faith must reside on Jesus, the Word of God. The subjectivity of their faith means that Jesus cannot entrust himself to them — he cannot let their distortion be the object of their faith.

The second is true discipleship. The true disciple has a correct belief in Jesus. Just as the Jews were correct to hear in Jesus's words a reference to the real temple yet wrong in their understanding of the true temple, so also did the "many" believe in Jesus without truly believing in Jesus. The assumption is that not all belief in Jesus corresponds to the belief required: not all have been given the "right" (ἐξουσία) to believe (1:12). The right to "become" (γενέσθαι) children of God requires the creative force of God *ex nihilo* (see comments on 1:12). Such children are a new creation, those not of this world (17:6, 16), who have received the spiritual new birth from above (3:1–11).

2:25 For he did not need a witness concerning humanity, for he knew what was in humanity (καὶ ὅτι οὐ χρείαν εἶχεν ἵνα τις μαρτυρήσῃ περὶ τοῦ ἀνθρώπου· αὐτὸς γὰρ ἐγίνωσκεν τί ἦν ἐν τῷ ἀνθρώπῳ). The pericope ends with what serves as a commentary on Jesus's interaction with humanity, rooted strongly in the prologue's preparatory description of the Light in the darkness. Rather than speaking from beyond human history, as in the prologue, we are now receiving from the narrator an explication of the state of the darkness of humanity. To make sure that we do not miss the depth of spiritual blindness, the Gospel is about to introduce to us a person who exemplifies the problem Jesus knows concerning humanity: Nicodemus.

Theology in Application

From the moment of his arrival, the person and work of Jesus have been depicted in the Gospel as the locus of divine revelation and the dwelling place of God. In this pericope, the true house of God enters the temple in Jerusalem and speaks of its fulfillment in him. Interestingly, Jesus makes this bold declaration not in the holy of holies, but in the court of the gentiles. This is itself a "sign" that "God loved the world" (3:16).

Jesus is the Temple and the Passover

The Gospel has not portrayed Jesus as merely analogous to the temple but as its full replacement. Although the new mode of worship has not yet been depicted (cf. ch. 4), the new place of worship is now fully defined in Jesus. Christ is the temple of God, and only through Christ can a person find God (cf. 14:1 – 7). The Fourth Gospel anticipates the temple typology found in Paul, who declares that the church is the body of Christ, the realization of God's promise to dwell among his people (Col 1:18). Also anticipated is Revelation, where the union between Christ and the people of God finally comes to fruition in the new Jerusalem, when God's people are fully with God in the city of God (Rev 21:3).

The cleansing of the temple is the replacement of a system that was "trading" what it did not have (the true removal of sins) for what it should not want (personal profit). Purification was God's business; there could be no business partners in this deal. Our churches and our lives are no different. Our "religious" activities are nothing if they are not Christ centered, that is, centered upon his cross and resurrection and the significance of his work for our lives. God is not to be found in any religious practice or place; he is found only through Christ. Anything else is trading on grace, an offense that God himself deems worthy to remove.

The Importance of the Word of God

This pericope emphasizes that the disciples made connections between what they were seeing and hearing in Jesus and what had been recorded in the Scriptures (vv. 17, 22). These are not insignificant comments. Verse 22 even suggests that the disciples were putting their faith in the Scriptures; that is, they were beginning to trust the proof that, though attested long ago, was only now being made manifest. The disciples had come to see as authoritative and complementary the word of God and the Word of God. Although God has fully and decisively revealed himself in *the* Word, his Son, he had always revealed himself through his word, the Scriptures. The Scriptures, then, are depicted as revealing in their subject matter the person and work of Jesus Christ.

This should encourage the Christian in two ways. First, it should remind us that the Bible's meaning and significance is found ultimately in Christ. God had planned (and worked) from the beginning to bring together all things in Christ. For this reason, the meaning of the Bible is entirely christocentric. Second, we would do well to follow the exhortation of Luther, who argued that the emphasis on the Scriptures in this pericope exhorts us "to hear, believe, and accept God's Word gladly...."[26] Verse 22 makes it especially clear that to entrust ourselves to the message of Scripture is similar to entrusting ourselves to the message of Jesus. The Christian is exhorted by the narrator's comment "to meditate industriously and continually on Scripture."[27] The ministries of our churches and the direction for our lives should be founded entirely on the Word of God.

A Passion for Christ

We get a glimpse of what motivated Jesus's response in the temple in v. 17: zeal for the house of God. Jesus was passionate for God's house, and he would not let it be made a marketplace or to offer things it did not have the authority to sell (i.e., the removal of sin). The memory of the disciples was not merely to the past, making sense of Jesus's actions, but also to the future, making sense of all appropriate religious zeal. If we truly have "the mind of Christ" (1 Cor 2:16), then we are to be passionate for the things that Christ is passionate for. Since God can be concerned with nothing higher than his own glory, then we too must be passionate for his glory, which is only made visible in his Son, Jesus Christ (1:18). By definition, then, the Christian has a passion for Christ and for the things of Christ. The Christian sees his or her own life eclipsed by Christ, becoming a slave — to use Paul's language again — to the things of righteousness, in place of sin (Rom 6:17 – 18). As the children of God (1:12), we begin to model our Father, enjoying what God enjoys and avoiding what God avoids, simply because we have found the love of God and guidance of the Holy Spirit so rewarding — so right — that in Christ everything makes sense.

The Celebration of Shame: From Wine to Whip

The clue to understanding the pericope above is to grasp the honor/shame conflict between the Jews and Jesus. The narrator does not want us to miss that Jesus actually lost the conflict with the Jews. Everyone knew it: the Jews, the crowd, even the disciples. Jesus lost! Such a statement sounds like it is not the story the Gospel of John was telling until we realize that "Jesus lost" is the story of the gospel — "Jesus lost" is the good news. We can too easily become like the Jews or the Pharisees or the disciples who think Jesus is their king according to their standards (e.g., military leader; financial provider). No — Jesus lost; it could be no other way. Jesus was

---

26. Luther, *John*, 22:229.   27. Calvin, *John 1 – 10*, 54.

shamed. In his temple, at his Passover, in his city, by Jewish leaders who should be serving and honoring him — by his own creation, Jesus received shame.

But this is the good news. This is God in the person of Jesus declaring through Psalm 69 that "shame covers my face" (v. 7) and that the insults of the people had fallen upon him (v. 9b). In Jesus, God entered his corrupt and negligent temple, declared it unclean, and received its shame. This is the very thing he should not have done and in light of his holiness could not have done — but he did! The contrast between the two pericopae in chapter 2 of John is stark: Jesus has gone from the master of the celebratory banquet to the shameful charlatan. The scene has moved from the Lord of the wine to the servant of the whip, and in neither case was he rightfully recognized. This is the gospel: "For the joy set before him he endured the cross, scorning its shame" (Heb 12:2). For this reason we, the children of God, exhort one another to "fixing our eyes on Jesus," the one who authored true fellowship with God and perfected our wandering faith (Heb 12:2). To live in this gospel is to celebrate shame, holding fast to what he lost, which is our gain. We too now understand that if we are reviled because of the "name of Christ," we are blessed, for like Jesus in the temple, "the Spirit of glory and of God rests" on us (1 Pet 4:14).

John 3:1 – 21

Literary Context

The narrative moves from a public encounter with the temple authorities at Passover to a private encounter with a representative from the temple at night. But the issues are just as heated and just as important. This scene is best viewed as part of a larger and progressing conflict between Jesus and the ruling authorities, between God and the world. Although the arrival of Jesus, the Light, exposes the evil and darkness of the world, it is also a Light that can embrace the darkness. In this pericope, Jesus speaks as the true teacher, guiding even the religious elite to grasp the significance of his authoritative person and gracious work.

III. The Beginning of Jesus's Public Ministry (2:1 – 4:54)
   A. The First Sign: The Wedding at Cana (2:1 – 11)
   B. The Cleansing of the Temple: The Promise of the Seventh Sign (2:12 – 25)
→ **C. Nicodemus, New Birth, and the Unique Son (3:1 – 21)**
   D. The Baptist, the True Bridegroom, and the Friend of the Bridegroom (3:22 – 36)
   E. The Samaritan Woman, Living Water, and True Worshippers (4:1 – 42)
   F. The Second Sign: The Healing of the Royal Official's Son (4:43 – 54)

Main Idea

Jesus is the representative of God who challenges and shames the darkness of the world with its system of religion. Yet Jesus is also the manifestation of the love of God that meets the very challenge he initiated and receives upon himself the shame that belonged to the world.

Translation

(See pages 189–191.)

Continued on next page.

John 3:1–21

1a	Character Entrance	Now **there was** **a man**
b	Description	who was one of the Pharisees,
c	Identification	whose name was Nicodemus,
d	Apposition to "a man"	a ruling official from the Jews.
2a	Setting	**He came to him at night**
b	Initiation of Challenge Dialogue	and **said to him,**
c	Hyperbolic Assertion	*"Rabbi, we have become aware that you are a teacher*
d	Ironical Description	*who has come from God,*
e	Explanation	*for no one is able to perform the signs you do*
f	Condition	*unless God were with him."*
3a	Counterchallenge	**Jesus answered and said to him,**
b	Amen Formula	*"Truly, truly I say to you,*
c	Condition	*unless a man is born new,*
d	Inference	*he is not able to see the kingdom of God."*
4a	Counterchallenge	**Nicodemus said to him,**
b	Question of Means	*"How is a man able to be born*
c	Circumstance	*when he is old?*
d	Question of Ability	*He is not able to enter into his mother's womb …*
e	Circumstance	*a second time,*
f		*… is he?"*
5a	Counterchallenge	**Jesus answered,**
b	Amen Formula	*"Truly, truly I say to you,*
c	Condition	*unless a man is born*
d	Sphere of Origin/OT Allus.	*from water and spirit,*
f	Inference	*he is not able to enter into the kingdom of God.*
6a	Explanation of Sphere of Origin	*That which is born of flesh is flesh,*
b	Contrast	*and that which is born of spirit is spirit.*

Continued from previous page.

7a	Challenge of Knowledge	You should not be surprised that I say this to you,
b	Summary of 5–6	'You must be born new.'
8a	Explanatory Metaphor of 5–7 /	The wind blows wherever it wants.
b	Allusion: Ezek 37	You hear its sound,
c	Contrast to 8a–b	but you do not know from　　where it comes and
d		where it is going.
e	Conclusion of Metaphor (8a–d)	So it is with everyone born of the Spirit."
9a	Confused Counterquestion	**Nicodemus answered and said to him,**
b		"How can these things be?"
10a	Final Challenge	**Jesus answered and said to him,**
b	Defeat of Nicodemus	"You are the teacher of Israel
c		and you do not know these things?
11a	Amen Formula	Truly, truly I say to you,
b	Victory Speech (11–15)	we speak what we know and
c		we testify to what we have seen, and
d	Indictment of Nicodemus	you do not receive our testimony.
12a	Condition	If I have spoken to you about earthly things
b	Inference	and you do not believe,
c	Interrogative Inference	how will you believe
d	Condition	if I speak of heavenly things?
13a	Basis for Jesus's Authority	And no one has gone up into heaven
b		except　the one who came down from heaven,
c	Allusion: Dan 7	the Son of Man.
14a	Explanation/Allusion: Num 21:4–9	For just as Moses lifted up the snake in the wilderness,
b	Comparison/Son of Man's Work	it is also necessary for the Son of Man to be lifted up.
15a	Purpose	In order that all who believe in him may have eternal life."

16a	Narrator's Explanation (16–21)	For **in this way God loved the world,** and
b	Result	so he gave the unique Son
c	Purpose	in order that all who believe in him might not be destroyed but
d	Contrast	have eternal life.
17a	Expansion of 16	For **God did not send his Son into the world**
b	Purpose (–)	in order to condemn the world, but
c	Purpose (+)	in order to save the world
d	Agency	through him.
18a	Promise	**The one who believes in him will not be condemned,**
b	Contrast	but **the one who does not believe is already condemned,**
c	Basis	for he has not believed in the name of the unique Son of God.
19a	Conclusion	**This is the verdict:**
b	Event	**the Light has come into the world**
c	Reaction	and **humanity loved the darkness rather than**
d	Contrast	**the Light,**
e		←
f	Basis	for their deeds were evil.
20a	Explanatory Sequence #1	For **all who practice evil hate the light**
b	Explanatory Sequence #2	and **do not come toward the Light,**
c	Purpose	in order that their deeds may not be exposed.
21a	Contrast	But **the one who does the truth comes toward the Light,**
b	Purpose	in order that his deeds may be made manifest
c	Result	as having been accomplished in God.

Structure and Literary Form

This is the first substantial dialogue in the narrative proper, and it is a *social challenge dialogue*, which takes the form of an informal debate intending to challenge the honor and authority of one's interlocutor (see Introduction). In reference to this pericope, Barrett is correct when he observes that "narrative is in this section reduced to a minimum."[1] However, such a statement too easily divorces the dialogues from the narrative movement and emplotment of the Gospel as a whole. This is not a tangent for John; this is a necessary element in the developing story of Jesus.

Exegetical Outline

➡ **C. Nicodemus, New Birth, and the Unique Son (3:1 – 21)**
　　1. Nicodemus's Provocative Introduction (vv. 1 – 2)
　　2. First Verbal Exchange: "Born New" (vv. 3 – 4)
　　3. Second Verbal Exchange: "Born from Water and Spirit" (vv. 5 – 10)
　　4. Jesus's Victory Announcement: The Cross (vv. 11 – 15)
　　5. Narrator's Commentary (vv. 16 – 21)

Explanation of the Text

After a compelling scene in the temple in Jerusalem at Passover in which Jesus challenged not merely the temple authorities but also the entire religious system of Judaism, the narrative moves to a more private but just as animated dialogue between Jesus and one of the temple authorities. This first dialogue, a social challenge, carries forward the plot's depiction of the person and work of Jesus in relation not merely to religious authority, but to the foundation of the entire Jewish religion (i.e., the replaced "grace" of 1:16).

It is important to note that two transitions occur from the previous pericope to this one, both of which are a move from general to specific. First, the narrative moves from "the Jews" in a corporate sense to an individual Jew, though still a rul-

ing official. Second, the narrative moves from "humanity/man" (2:25) in a corporate sense to an individual man. Thus, all the tension in the prologue between the Light and the darkness or God and the world is also present in this scene when Jesus confronts a representative of the opponents of God. Nicodemus embodies broken religion and broken humanity. The prologue has set the context not merely for the Gospel as a whole but even for its intricate parts.

This larger context provides insight into the nature and scope of this pericope. The scene with Nicodemus is usually considered to be a more innocent teaching moment, somehow removed from the conflict so present in the previous scenes. Nicodemus is often described as "a sincere inquirer

---

with limited belief."[2] In fact, commentaries are nearly unanimous on this point.[3] The general reconstruction goes something like this: Nicodemus comes to Jesus with a genuine openness, acknowledging that Jesus is credentialed by God. He seems to be guilty of nothing more than befuddlement before a confusing revelation, a befuddlement the reader can easily understand! At the end, Nicodemus does not argue with Jesus or depart in protest. He simply throws up his hands, asking helplessly, "How can this be?"[4]

But in light of the developing context of the Gospel as well as the qualification that the dialogue between Jesus and Nicodemus is in the form of a social challenge — an informal debate that is a challenge for honor and authority — the above reconstruction is misguided. As we will explain below, the encounter between Jesus and Nicodemus is part of the larger conflict between Jesus and the religious authorities, that is, between God and humanity.

3:1 Now there was a man who was one of the Pharisees, whose name was Nicodemus, a ruling official from the Jews (Ἦν δὲ ἄνθρωπος ἐκ τῶν Φαρισαίων, Νικόδημος ὄνομα αὐτῷ, ἄρχων τῶν Ἰουδαίων). The use of "man" (ἄνθρωπος) in an unusual expression is almost certainly intended to link this pericope with the closing words of the previous pericope (2:25). The insight given in 2:25, and more importantly 1:11, regarding the nature of humanity ("a man") gives insight into the dialogue between Jesus and this "man." This man is described as having the name Nicodemus, being from the party of the Pharisees, and having the position of one of the ruling officials of the Jews. In

one sense, he is no different than any other man (2:25); in another sense, however, he is a distinct representative of the ruling authorities of the religion of God.

The narrative introduction to Nicodemus establishes for the reader the context out of which and the force with which the interaction with Jesus will take place. Verse 1 gives us three pieces of information that need explaining. First, his religious-political party: Nicodemus is a Pharisee. The Pharisees have been introduced previously and need little explanation here (see comments on 1:24). The Pharisees were strict and precise in regard to the law (Josephus, *J.W.* 2.162). One of the distinguishing marks of the Pharisees was commitment to "the traditions of the elders" as supplementing or amending biblical law (cf. Josephus, *Ant.* 13.297; Mark 7:1 – 13). In general, however, the Pharisees had only popular support and indirect authority, for they were neither politically connected nor aristocratic.

Second, his position and status: Nicodemus is a ruling official. This might seem to conflict with the party with which he is aligned, because the Pharisees were rarely associated with the ruling elite. In the Gospel, however, "the Pharisees" does not usually denote the Pharisaic party in general but the small number of wealthy aristocratic Pharisees who belonged to the ruling elite. This can be seen when John describes the ruling group as "the high priests and the Pharisees" (7:32, 45; 11:47, 57; 18:3). This suggests that Nicodemus comes from an elite family, and fits Josephus's depiction of some of the Pharisees being "distinguished men" (*Ant.* 20.201 – 2). Barrett suggests, however, that John did not distinguish clearly between Jewish parties.[5]

2. Don Williford, "John 3:1 – 15 — *gennêthênai anôthen*: A Radical Departure, a New Beginning," *RevExp* 96 (1999): 451 – 61 (453).

3. Cf. Gabi Renz, "Nicodemus: An Ambiguous Disciple? A Narrative Sensitive Investigation," in *Challenging Perspectives on the Gospel of John*, ed. John Lierman, WUNT 2.219 (Tübingen: Mohr Siebeck, 2006), 255 – 83.

4. Sandra M. Schneiders, "Born Anew," *ThTo* 44 (1987): 189 – 96 (190).

5. Barrett, *John*, 204.

Such an awkward collection suggests instead to him that the author has mistakenly fused Jewish parties and affiliations for rhetorical purposes. Another possibility, however, is that Nicodemus is a unique case. The third piece of information explains that this latter option is more accurate.

Third, his family connections: he has been given the name Nicodemus. Standing between the description of this "man" as a Pharisee and a ruling official is his name, that is, "the name given to him" (ὄνομα αὐτῷ). Commentators often draw attention to the fact that "Nicodemus" was a common Greek name.[6] But even though it was a common Greek name, it was a rare name among Palestinian Jews of the first century. Bauckham has recently shown that sources reveal only four Palestinian Jews between 330 BC and AD 200 had the name Nicodemus, and all four belonged to the same family: the Gurion family.[7] After reconstructing the Gurion family and seeing the clear connection between Gurion and the name Nicodemus, Bauckham concludes that Nicodemus was a member of "a single, very wealthy, very prominent Jerusalem family of Pharisaic allegiance."[8] The very name Nicodemus, which means "conqueror of the people," along with the military meaning behind the name Gurion suggests that "the family's unusual and distinctive names are those appropriate to military heroes. So it may be that the first Gurion or the first ... Nicodemus was a successful general in the Hasmonean period, won the name in the first place as a laudatory nickname, and received landed estates as a reward for his distinguished service."[9]

As member of the Gurion family, Nicodemus was both a Pharisee and a ruling official of the Jews, one of the ruling elite. He was wealthy, powerful, and born into an honorable and influential aristocratic family who, along with the high priests, composed the ruling group of first-century Judaism. Nicodemus, then, was a rare Jew, combining elements from the popular pietist movement of the Pharisees (he is a "teacher," 3:10) with the wealthy and aristocratic ruling class of Judaism (he is a wealthy patron, 19:39). Such a position places Nicodemus at the very center of Judaism, as the most representative voice possible. Contra Barrett, John was not forcing foreign elements together "in order to portray Nicodemus as a representative Jew," for Nicodemus, in light of his heritage and social-religious status, was already qualified to be the representative Jew *par excellence*. With this context in mind, we see Nicodemus, the perfect representative of the Jews, facing Jesus, the perfect representative of God. In this way, the narrator establishes the social-religious and theological context for this social challenge dialogue.

3:2 He came to him at night and said to him, "Rabbi, we have become aware that you are a teacher who has come from God, for no one is able to perform the signs you do unless God were with him" (οὗτος ἦλθεν πρὸς αὐτὸν νυκτὸς καὶ εἶπεν αὐτῷ, Ῥαββί, οἴδαμεν ὅτι ἀπὸ θεοῦ ἐλήλυθας διδάσκαλος· οὐδεὶς γὰρ δύναται ταῦτα τὰ σημεῖα ποιεῖν ἃ σὺ ποιεῖς, ἐὰν μὴ ᾖ ὁ θεὸς μετ' αὐτοῦ). The narrator briefly sets the stage for the challenge dialogue by describing the time at which Nicodemus approached Jesus: "at night" (νυκτός). Since every occurrence of "night" in John has negative associations (see 9:4; 11:10; 13:30; 21:3), it is likely that the "impression" the narrator is intending to create to set the context is derived from the cosmic depiction of darkness first established in the prologue (see Introduction). This is not to deny that the real Nicodemus approached Jesus when it was "night." In fact, the sociological evidence would suggest

6. BDAG 673.
7. Bauckham, *Jesus and the Eyewitnesses*, 88.
8. Bauckham, "Nicodemus and the Gurion Family," in *Testimony of the Beloved Disciple*, 137 – 72 (161).
9. Ibid., 162.

that an evening event would have allowed for the dialogue to be even more public in nature.[10] It is simply to suggest that in view of the prologue's projection of the two-strand plot of John it is likely that John is pleased to have "night" impress itself upon both the historical circumstances and symbolic (cosmological) realities at play in this encounter.

Nicodemus's opening statement to Jesus, with its honorific language, is common for a challenge dialogue. The opening address was often filled with praise for the opponent, even though it frequently turned out to be a form of self-promotion for the one who gave it.[11] This opening address is a formal initiation to a social challenge dialogue. All the titles and statements reflect a recognizable form of honorific flattery, without any sense of genuineness until the dialogue continues. In the least it shows that Nicodemus takes Jesus to be a worthy interlocutor with whom he must engage.

The courteous title "Rabbi" (Ῥαββί) bestows upon Jesus the status of a professional teacher of Judaism (see comments on 1:38). The professional teaching status of Jesus is strengthened when Nicodemus also refers to Jesus as a "teacher" (διδάσκαλος). The terms in the context of first-century Judaism were connected to the spiritual guides of the people, the "scribes," who were the only teachers of the people in matters of religion since it was deemed that the age of prophecy had ended and the will of God could only be known by a serious study of the Scriptures.[12] Thus, on the lips of Nicodemus, the term suggests that Jesus is to be viewed as a religious authority to the highest degree.

If this were not enough, Nicodemus also describes this "teacher" as one who "has come from God" (ἀπὸ θεοῦ ἐλήλυθας). This is not a normal OT expression for a divine messenger ("send" is the more usual verb: cf. 1 Sam 15:1; 16:1; Isa 6:8; Jer 1:7). The preposition "from" (ἀπό) is regularly used in John to denote someone's place of origin (1:44, 45; 7:42; 11:1; 12:21; 19:38; 21:2) and is used by both John (13:3) and the disciples (16:30) when referring to the heavenly origin of Jesus. The perfect "has come" (ἐλήλυθας) suggests an abiding presence and is frequently found on the lips of Jesus himself (5:43; 7:28; 8:42; 12:46; 16:28; 18:37).

The plain sense of these words is that Nicodemus is positing Jesus "as a new and heaven-sent interpreter of the Law and the prophets," which rests uncomfortably with what Nicodemus should have known in regard to the one who would be a "prophet like Moses" (Deut 18:15 – 19).[13] The uncomfortableness forces other commentators to nuance the strength of Nicodemus's statement, showing how it is different from the details in Deuteronomy 18. Yet in the context of a social challenge dialogue, the language need not be interpreted so mechanically. Rather, the honorific language is intentionally echoing through the "prophet like Moses" motif in order to provide a show of wits and provocation. Nicodemus is initiating a "verbal contest with an *ad hominem* orientation."[14] With a creative maneuver, Nicodemus jabs at Jesus in a manner that on the surface sounds entirely complimentary, but at the deeper level — at the level of Scripture (for which Jesus supposedly serves as a teacher) and religious authority (which Jesus is supposedly assuming for himself) — is combative hyperbole, intending to challenge the very things it claims: Jesus's warrant to serve as a teacher and religious authority.

This entire challenge is set in the context of a growing tension between Jesus and "the Jews" (see

---

10. F. P. Cotterell, "The Nicodemus Conversation: A Fresh Appraisal," *ExpTim* 96 (1985): 237 – 42 (238).

11. Brant, *Dialogue and Drama*, 129.

12. McHugh, *John 1 – 4*, 223.

13. Ibid., 224.

14. Ward Parks, *Verbal Dueling in Heroic Narrative: The Homeric and Old English Traditions* (Princeton: Princeton University Press, 1990), 6.

comments on 1:19). Nicodemus suggests as much in two ways. First, he claims to speak on behalf of others: "We have become aware" (οἴδαμεν). This serves to heighten the conflict in light of the context. "While some say this is who you are, we do not buy it!" There is no need to see the "we" as either a literary intrusion by the evangelist or a sign that Nicodemus is "betraying a touch of swagger or nervousness."[15] Rather, it connects this dialogue — this dispute — with what has come before and what is certain to follow. The "we" reflects a real conflict with the Jewish authorities, of which Nicodemus is an official member (v. 1). This also makes sense of Nicodemus's final statement regarding the signs Jesus performs that warrant that God is with him; this serves as the grand finale of Nicodemus's combative hyperbole.

At one level, Nicodemus's opening address describes accurately what the common people are perceiving in Jesus's activities (cf. 2:23). But on another level, it is exactly what "the Jews" need to confront, since the shame they tried to attribute to Jesus during the temple cleansing incident seems to have not affected him (see comments before 2:12). What was needed was a more direct and formal shaming. For this the Jews selected one of their most prominent ruling officials, a member of one of the most honorable and influential families that enjoyed a long history of "conquering" enemies of Judaism. Nicodemus is a man who was not only aristocratic but was also a Pharisee, with whom Jesus, who was known for associating with one version of the pietist movement (i.e., John the Baptist) might find familiarity. Thus the social challenge dialogue has been formally initiated.

3:3 Jesus answered and said to him, "Truly, truly I say to you, unless a man is born new, he is not able to see the kingdom of God" (ἀπεκρίθη

Ἰησοῦς καὶ εἶπεν αὐτῷ, Ἀμὴν ἀμὴν λέγω σοι, ἐὰν μή τις γεννηθῇ ἄνωθεν, οὐ δύναται ἰδεῖν τὴν βασιλείαν τοῦ θεοῦ). Without the larger context of the social challenge, Jesus's statement appears inconsistent. The connection is not in the words themselves but in their illocutionary intent; that is, in what they functionally intend to communicate. What appears to be disconnected is actually an immediate and forceful response to the challenge. We should not take this as an inappropriate flexing of the muscles by Jesus but as a righteous response rooted in the authority of God. If Jesus can claim the authority of God in the Jerusalem temple, certainly he can claim that same authority in a social challenge with one of the temple authorities.

Jesus begins his response to Nicodemus with an authoritative preface that connects the speaker with God himself (see comments on 1:51). Jesus declares that a man must be born "new" (ἄνωθεν). This term and our chosen translation are particularly important. While there are three possible meanings of the term, only two adverbial functions are possible here: 1) an adverb of time: *again*; or 2) an adverb of place: *from above*.[16] Even though Nicodemus understands the adverb to be functioning temporally (v. 4), clearly Jesus is intending for it to function as an adverb of place. The intentional duality of this adverb has long been noted and seemed to force a difficult interpretive choice. Even if we would agree that Nicodemus did not fully understand what Jesus was meaning, he certainly heard correctly. Therefore our translation of the term must allow for this duality of meaning, since it has to mean both "again" and "from above" in v. 3. To select one of the options is to misunderstand v. 3. The intentional ambiguity of this adverb is part of the plot. In this case, the adverb is doing something that requires both its meanings to be

15. Carson, *John*, 187.

16. Cf. Schnackenburg, *John*, 1:367 – 68; Mark Edwards, *John*, BBC (Malden, MA: Blackwell, 2004), 46.

cooperatively in play. Nicodemus was both entirely correct in what he heard and at that very same moment dead wrong.

The context of the challenge dialogue adds a further significance to the function of this adverb. The "exploitation of divergent meanings of a single word" is a common — even necessary — part of a social challenge dialogue.[17] It is not only an appropriate counter to the interlocutor, but it also serves the facilitation of meaning in the developing dialogue. But Jesus is not just playing dialogue games, for his use of "again/from above" (ἄνωθεν) corresponds directly to the attack initiated by Nicodemus. In v. 2, Nicodemus used a combative hyperbole that mockingly linked Jesus to the "prophet like Moses" in Deuteronomy 18. For Nicodemus, nothing could have been further from the truth. Yet the reader knows that Jesus actually is, according to Philip in 1:45, "the one about whom Moses wrote in the Law and the Prophets." The irony is stark. Nicodemus crafts a statement so theologically lofty that it was intended to be an obvious mockery and rebuke. Yet the one to whom it was addressed was entirely worthy of the statement. Even Nicodemus's intended exaggeration of acclaim could not surpass or be denied Jesus.

The result of this new birth would be the ability "to see the kingdom of God" (ἰδεῖν τὴν βασιλείαν τοῦ θεοῦ). While a Jew like Nicodemus might have primarily understood the kingdom to occur entirely at the end of the age, John (as well as the Synoptics) announces that the kingdom of God has already been inaugurated in the person and work of Jesus. The very fact "to see" is mentioned here echoes back to 1:51, where Jesus declared to his disciples that they "will see heaven open and … the Son of Man." "Seeing" God (1:18) or the kingdom of God (3:3) is entirely dependent upon Jesus.

IN DEPTH: Kingdom of God

The kingdom of God is a common motif in the Synoptics, but in John it is only mentioned in this pericope (3:3, 5; cf. 18:36 which also refers more generically to the kingdom). Although it is frequently assumed that the OT/Judaism understood the kingdom of God to be less a territory (realm) and more the sovereign rule of God (reign), this is not entirely accurate. The Jewish understanding of the kingdom was multifaceted and cannot be defined entirely by "reign," even if that is the larger, categorical meaning.[18]

3:4 Nicodemus said to him, "How is a man able to be born when he is old? He is not able to enter into his mother's womb a second time, is he?" (λέγει πρὸς αὐτὸν [ὁ] Νικόδημος, Πῶς δύναται ἄνθρωπος γεννηθῆναι γέρων ὤν; μὴ δύναται εἰς τὴν κοιλίαν τῆς μητρὸς αὐτοῦ δεύτερον εἰσελθεῖν καὶ γεννηθῆναι;). Nicodemus responds with a counter-question that is often taken as affirmation that he misunderstood the ambiguous adverb. Brant suggests that it is an open question whether Nicodemus "is insensible to Jesus's intended meaning" or whether he is actually engaging in the social challenge dialogue and "trying to foul Jesus by accusing him of crossing the bounds of truth and thereby

17. Brant, *Dialogue and Drama*, 127.

18. Jonathan T. Pennington, *Heaven and Earth in the Gospel of Matthew*, NovTSup 126 (Leiden: Brill, 2007), 255.

violating the rules of play."[19] That is, does Nicodemus's response reflect confusion (misunderstanding) or rebellion (a further challenge based upon the rules of dialogue)? It is most likely a mixture of both. Nicodemus's categories were being annihilated, and his only response is rebellion — made manifest in a counterquestion that fails to provide an adequate response and merely serves to move the plot of the dialogue forward. Nicodemus has yet to understand what the reader has already heard in the prologue about "new birth" (1:13).[20]

3:5 Jesus answered, "Truly truly I say to you, unless a man is born from water and spirit, he is not able to enter into the kingdom of God" (ἀπεκρίθη Ἰησοῦς, Ἀμὴν ἀμὴν λέγω σοι, ἐὰν μή τις γεννηθῇ ἐξ ὕδατος καὶ πνεύματος, οὐ δύναται εἰσελθεῖν εἰς τὴν βασιλείαν τοῦ θεοῦ). Prefacing his response to Nicodemus's counter with another authoritative preface, Jesus declares that a person must be born "from water and spirit" (ἐξ ὕδατος καὶ πνεύματος). Several things require explanation to interpret this prepositional phrase. First, the grammar of the phrase demands that the two terms be understood in relation to each other. The fact that this phrase is taken to be an explanation of "again/from above" (ἄνωθεν) demands that the birth spoken of here is singular, not plural.

Second, the terms need to be explained by means of both their background (OT) and their foreground (John). Although the full construction is not found in the OT, "the ingredients are there."[21] With the creation motif so strong in John, it is significant that the OT begins with the statement, "The *Spirit* of God was hovering over the *waters*" (Gen 1:2; emphasis mine). More specifically, Jeremiah, Ezekiel, and Daniel had all seen the destruction of Jerusalem and its temple and yet

envisaged the restoration of the city and its temple. Ezekiel specifically spoke of a renewal of Israel which cleansed the people with clean water from all uncleanness and gave them a new heart and a new spirit (Ezek 36:24 – 28). Following Ezekiel 36 is the resurrection of a new people (Ezek 37) and the building of a new temple (Ezek 40 – 48). Thus Ezekiel, whose influence will also be seen in John 4 together with a score of other OT passages (e.g., Ezek 11:16 – 20; Jer 31:31 – 34) is fully adequate to account for the phrase "born of water and spirit."

The use of "water" and "spirit" by the Gospel itself also shows a similar swath of impressions that speak to the broader motif of cleansing, restoration, and newness. "Water" in John evokes images either of cleansing (9:7; 13:5) or of sustaining life by the quenching of thirst (4:10 – 14; 6:35; 7:37 – 38) and is even directly connected to "the Spirit" in 7:39. "Spirit" in John can be either the "life-giving" Spirit (6:63) or the agent of purification (1:33). While this includes the capital-S "Spirit," he is not the specific referent of "spirit" here at 3:5. The phrase "water and spirit" refers to the work of the Trinitarian God, which includes the Father, Son, and Holy Spirit. The Spirit has a central role in this cleansing, but the cleansing would be entirely incomplete without the Son. Thus, "born from water and spirit" is referring to a radical new birth that yields a cleansing and renewal that is not merely from God — "from above" — but is the full manifestation of what God had promised long ago. This new birth is an eschatological birth, the cleansing and renewal *par excellence*. It is so overwhelmingly rooted in God that it can only be described as "from above" and explained with various OT images. Nicodemus is not only directed "to see" it (v. 3) but is invited "to enter" (εἰσελθεῖν). In Jesus what God promised has now been fulfilled. And in

---

19. Brant, *Dialogue and Drama*, 129.
20. See Bultmann, *John*, 137.

21. Carson, *John*, 194.

Jesus both spiritual realities and physical realities of the kingdom coalesce.

3:6 "That which is born of flesh is flesh, and that which is born of spirit is spirit" (τὸ γεγεννημένον ἐκ τῆς σαρκὸς σάρξ ἐστιν, καὶ τὸ γεγεννημένον ἐκ τοῦ πνεύματος πνεῦμά ἐστιν). This further statement by Jesus serves to reinforce the radical nature of the cleansing and renewal from God. The concept of flesh is not to be simplistically imported from the apostle Paul, for in John "flesh" is merely the body and its limitations, which is sharply contrasted to the source of the children of God, which is supernatural and entirely from the outside of a person (cf. 1:12 – 13). The point is quite simple: "flesh" and "spirit" are different spheres of reality, each producing offspring like itself.[22] "Neither can take to itself the capacity of the other."[23] While the contrast is clear, it is only at the center of the contrast, at the point of their interrelation, that the gospel is presented. The one who speaks these words is the one who became flesh. Standing before Nicodemus and now confronting the reader is the "spirit"-become-flesh. It is for this reason that the prologue so intimately connected this new birth to Christ's person and work.

3:7 "You should not be surprised that I say this to you, 'You must be born new'" (μὴ θαυμάσῃς ὅτι εἶπόν σοι, Δεῖ ὑμᾶς γεννηθῆναι ἄνωθεν). In the context of the social challenge, Jesus presses further his response to the rebuke and mockery initiated by Nicodemus. Since interlocutors would often employ divergent meanings of a single word, it is likely that "water" and "spirit" (v. 5) and "flesh" (v. 6) have served to diminish Nicodemus's ability to respond. Again, this is not an inappropriate aggression but an authoritative response to the initiating aggressor and a leader of Judaism. For this

reason, Jesus reinforces his rebuke of Nicodemus and silences any kind of response. Interestingly, Jesus's restatement of what has surprised Nicodemus is stated this time with a plural "you" (ὑμᾶς). Jesus was well aware that the one to whom he was speaking was merely the figurehead, so he speaks through him to all who have ears to hear. Jesus is not merely involved in a social challenge with one ruling official but with Judaism — indeed, with the world. Nicodemus (and those he represents) was wrong to claim in 3:2, "we know" (οἴδαμεν); the prologue has already made clear that "the world did not know him" (1:10). What the prologue foretold Jesus has now made fully known. The challenge dialogue has been turned back upon the interlocutor. Now Nicodemus is forced to face his true challenger: God himself.

3:8 "The wind blows wherever it wants. You hear its sound, but you do not know from where it comes and where it is going. So it is with everyone born of the Spirit" (τὸ πνεῦμα ὅπου θέλει πνεῖ, καὶ τὴν φωνὴν αὐτοῦ ἀκούεις, ἀλλ᾽ οὐκ οἶδας πόθεν ἔρχεται καὶ ποῦ ὑπάγει· οὕτως ἐστὶν πᾶς ὁ γεγεννημένος ἐκ τοῦ πνεύματος). Jesus explains why Nicodemus should not be surprised about new birth in the form of an analogy regarding wind. Interpreters usually discuss how this "verse is complicated" by the use of the word "wind/spirit" (πνεῦμα), with some focusing on the (physical) wind and others the Spirit.[24] The answer to this "complication" is found in the context of the social challenge. By giving an analogy that is able to exploit the flexibility of the word "wind/spirit" (πνεῦμα), Jesus not only provides a powerful explanation of the nature of new birth but does so in the form of an appropriate counter befitting the dialogue. The style is not to be dismissed as inappropriate or unneeded. In its first-century context,

22. Michaels, *John*, 185.
23. Hoskyns, *Fourth Gospel*, 215.
24. Morris, *John*, 195.

a social challenge dialogue was based on both principle and poetics. Jesus is showing himself to be the definitive Word.

The analogy is empowered by the contrastive traction between the two. The meaning is found not in the point of reconciliation between differences but in the one thing that both wind and spirit have in common: the mysterious, the unseen. The further apart the two might appear only enhances what they have in common, and this is exactly what Jesus stresses. The wind cannot be controlled; it contains its own power. The wind can be heard and even recognized, but it cannot be known or analyzed. Its activities, though active in and around us, are wholly other. It is at one and the same time a part of our experience and yet totally beyond us and entirely outside of what we can know and do. "So it is" (οὕτως) with the "spirit." Jesus's comparison is not between "wind" and lowercase "spirit," but he has creatively necessitated that the term refer to the uppercase "Spirit." For only *the* Spirit is able to provide new birth. The creative use of "spirit/wind/Spirit" (πνεῦμα) allows Jesus to explain forcefully the mysterious power and activity of the Spirit. Just as "life" is "in the Word" (1:4), so also are *spirit*ual things empowered "by the Spirit." The one "born of the Spirit" (ὁ γεγεννημένος ἐκ τοῦ πνεύματος), therefore, is nothing less than a mysterious, supernatural creation of God (cf. 1:12 – 13). Just as "water and spirit" in v. 5 was echoing Ezekiel 36, so here the playful use of the term "wind/spirit/Spirit" echoes Ezekiel 37, where the dead have "breath put in them" (v. 10). This is the nature of the new birth about which Jesus speaks.

3:9 Nicodemus answered and said to him, "How can these things be?" (ἀπεκρίθη Νικόδημος καὶ εἶπεν αὐτῷ, Πῶς δύναται ταῦτα γενέσθαι;). Nicodemus gives a second and final response to Jesus,

again in the form of a question. In the context of a social challenge, this is not best viewed as an "incredulous question"[25] but as a counter toward his interlocutor. It is likely that Nicodemus's question is rejecting the terms.[26] But even then, such a counter is more a move out of desperation than a competent countering statement. This question is the last and definitive statement of Nicodemus — a shockingly impotent conclusion in a social challenge dialogue. Before Jesus, silence suits him better. The historical situatedness of Nicodemus as a Pharisee and ruling official as well as his family heritage as "the conqueror" makes the scene all the more telling. The representative of the Jews is silenced before the representative of God.

3:10 Jesus answered and said to him, "You are the teacher of Israel and you do not know these things?" (ἀπεκρίθη Ἰησοῦς καὶ εἶπεν αὐτῷ, Σὺ εἶ ὁ διδάσκαλος τοῦ Ἰσραὴλ καὶ ταῦτα οὐ γινώσκεις;). Jesus brings the challenge around full circle and, after receiving the honorific title mockingly bestowed upon him from Nicodemus, takes away from Nicodemus the title Nicodemus would have claimed for himself: "the teacher of Israel" (ὁ διδάσκαλος τοῦ Ἰσραὴλ). With the definite article, the title is an appropriate mockery of this God challenger who has spoken out of turn and claimed for himself a title and position that does not belong to him. The true teacher, the definitive Word of God, is the one to whom that office has already been given. While this might be viewed as hyperbole in a social challenge, the prominence of Nicodemus might suggest that Nicodemus is not far removed from this position. Jesus provides a crushing counter that completes the dialogue. In one sense, it is a rebuke of Nicodemus's inability to see what the prophets had foretold in the Old Testament (see examples above). In another sense, it is

---

25. Carson, *John*, 198.

26. Brant, *Dialogue and Drama*, 129.

a rebuke of Nicodemus's vainglory, his inappropriate posture toward himself and toward God. Thus, the one who thought he was coming to shame the shameless has received the shame; the one who thought he was the teacher has become the student. Although the Gospel will give us insights into Nicodemus's response, the silence from Nicodemus is deafening. Nicodemus became the very proof of Jesus's point; he was not only defeated by an argument, he became the argument.

3:11 "Truly, truly I say to you, we speak what we know and we testify to what we have seen, and you do not receive our testimony" (ἀμὴν ἀμὴν λέγω σοι ὅτι ὃ οἴδαμεν λαλοῦμεν καὶ ὃ ἑωράκαμεν μαρτυροῦμεν, καὶ τὴν μαρτυρίαν ἡμῶν οὐ λαμβάνετε). Jesus began his counter to Nicodemus with an authoritative preface (see comments on 1:51) and in the same manner he begins what can be described as his victory speech. This verse begins what in the context of a social challenge dialogue is "the vaunting at the end of a battle."[27] But in contrast to a social challenge between equals, from the start the reader has known that this was no true challenge. Thus, this is no egotistical vaunt of a fortunate winner, but the I AM, "the Maker of all things." These postvictory comments, therefore, were rightfully his from the beginning.

After the authoritative preface, Jesus makes a strong statement that is filled with first-person plurals: "We speak what we know" (ὃ οἴδαμεν λαλοῦμεν); "we testify to what we have seen" (ὃ ἑωράκαμεν μαρτυροῦμεν), and "you [pl.] do not receive our testimony" (τὴν μαρτυρίαν ἡμῶν οὐ λαμβάνετε). On the surface, the "we" of Jesus is a perfect counter to the "we" of Nicodemus (v. 2). But more is clearly intended by the "we" spoken by Jesus. In light of the context of the Gospel, Jesus is referring to what he uniquely has seen and heard,

what is uniquely his to know as "the unique Son." He is the one who has descended from heaven (v. 13) and has seen heaven (cf. 5:19 – 20). "If the claim refers to the testimony that only Jesus can make on the basis of what he has seen in heaven, then not even his disciples in the future can say '*we* testify to what *we* have seen,' only that Jesus testified to what *he* had seen."[28] This is a "we" of authoritative testimony (see comments on 1:14). The "intention is not to refer to any other persons along with the speaker, but to give added force to the self-reference … the plural intensifies the authority expressed."[29] Only Jesus can speak this way; there is no other person that can speak as such. Even the testimonies of the disciples are all derivative, whereas the testimony of Jesus is the very fountainhead of Christian revelation. Thus, the testimony and message of Jesus is connected to his presence with God as a person of God. Jesus is *the* "thus says the Lord." And it is interesting to note that the "you" that does not receive Jesus's testimony is plural. Although it includes with Nicodemus the Jewish authorities he represents, it extends well beyond them (i.e., the world; cf. 1:10 – 11).

3:12 "If I have spoken to you about earthly things and you do not believe, how will you believe if I speak of heavenly things?" (εἰ τὰ ἐπίγεια εἶπον ὑμῖν καὶ οὐ πιστεύετε, πῶς ἐὰν εἴπω ὑμῖν τὰ ἐπουράνια πιστεύσετε;). Jesus's return to the first person "I have spoken" (εἶπον) is not to be contrasted with the authoritative "we" in v. 11, but should be seen as synonymous. His reversion is merely to bring into focus the specific dialogue he had been having with Nicodemus. Jesus presents a contrast that, by putting it in the form of a question, he deems is beyond what Nicodemus is able to grasp. The contrast is between "earthly things" (τὰ ἐπίγεια) and "heavenly things" (τὰ ἐπουράνια). It is

27. Brant, *Dialogue and Drama*, 130.
28. Bauckham, *Jesus and the Eyewitnesses*, 378.
29. Ibid., 372 (emphasis original).

common for commentators to see the latter as contrasting the "higher teaching,"[30] or if not a contrast at least a difference "of degree."[31] But the Gospel up to this point has been careful to show the careful coalescence of these things ultimately being made manifest in Jesus. To conclude that "earthly things" cannot contain or allude to anything "spiritual" would require that Jesus had not yet said anything "earthly," since his first words to Nicodemus were "from above." Yet Jesus himself claims that he had been speaking of "earthly things." Thus, "earthly" must refer to that which takes place here, to that which is connected to and related to the flesh — including the very fleshly presence of Jesus; yet it also includes the new birth that is offered to humanity. The "heavenly things," then, would be not merely what has been inaugurated with the arrival of Jesus but the things that will arrive at the consummation of history, namely, heaven and the full-blown kingdom of God.[32] The difference between the two conditional clauses lends support for this reading.[33] The message of Jesus (and the Gospel), therefore, is not abstract and otherworldly but is fleshly and about the real, physical world.

3:13 "And no one has gone up into heaven except the one who came down from heaven, the Son of Man" (καὶ οὐδεὶς ἀναβέβηκεν εἰς τὸν οὐρανὸν εἰ μὴ ὁ ἐκ τοῦ οὐρανοῦ καταβάς, ὁ υἱὸς τοῦ ἀνθρώπου). The authority that belongs to Jesus, an authority that gives him the right to speak of "earthly" and "heavenly" things, is an authority rooted in his heavenly origin. The "and" (καὶ) connects this verse to v. 12 and explains the nature of Jesus's authority. The negative statement, "no one has gone up into heaven" (οὐδεὶς ἀναβέβηκεν εἰς τὸν οὐρανὸν), reinforces the importance of "belief" in Jesus. Jesus is the authoritative one in both his po-

sition "with God" and in his person as God (1:1); he is "the way ... the truth ... the life" (14:6). Although Jesus's language makes it sound as if he had already "gone up to heaven," it need not be taken so mechanically; the solution is not found in appealing to the perspective of the evangelist or to the flexible use of "except" (εἰ μή).[34] This is the voice of one who speaks of the historical and cosmological realities in a coalescing manner. Speaking historically, we would say that Jesus has not yet ascended; yet the moment we speak cosmologically we are required to say that Jesus has always been and will always be defined as the one who was "in the beginning ... with God" (1:1) and "from above" (v. 3). There is no need to pit them against one another, for the prologue has given us a vision of the things "unseen" that find their coalescent meaning in the incarnate Jesus.

His concluding title for himself, "the Son of Man" (ὁ υἱὸς τοῦ ἀνθρώπου), is used for a second time in the Gospel (see comments on 1:51). In this occurrence, however, it is not angels who are "going up and coming down," but the Son of Man himself. With these words, Jesus reinforces the note of impossibility and human limitation which has dominated the dialogue with Nicodemus from the start, while at the same time transcending it with a clear exception: "no one ... except" me![35] This statement confirms what the prologue declared in 1:18: only the "unique Son" can "reveal" the Father, for "no one [else] has ever seen God." The language of ascent/descent is ultimately referring to the divine work of redemption accomplished by (and in) the Son of Man.

3:14 "For just as Moses lifted up the snake in the wilderness, it is also necessary for the Son of Man to be lifted up" (καὶ καθὼς Μωϋσῆς ὕψωσεν

---

30. Morris, *John*, 197.
31. Schnackenburg, *John*, 1:378.
32. Cf. Carson, *John*, 199.
33. See Wallace, *Greek Grammar*, 690–99, especially 698.
34. For a defense of the latter, see Carson, *John*, 199–200.
35. Michaels, *John*, 194.

τὸν ὄφιν ἐν τῇ ἐρήμῳ, οὕτως ὑψωθῆναι δεῖ τὸν υἱὸν τοῦ ἀνθρώπου). At this point, the essential and functional significance of Jesus could not be more heavenly. With this second occurrence of "the Son of Man" and with clear connections to the divine magnificence and authority so evident in the prologue, Jesus concludes his postvictory comments with a shocking twist — with the gospel. This concluding statement gives further clarification to what has come before, namely, "new birth" and the effective power of "water and spirit." This time, however, Jesus does not speak with "earthly/heavenly" language but by allusion to an Old Testament narrative. Jesus uses the gracious provision of refuge and new life depicted in Numbers 21:4 – 9 as a parabolic portrayal of his work and provision.

Several points of comparison are intended to be made. First, it is clear in Numbers 21 that the Israelites were not appropriately postured before God. They grew impatient (v. 4) and spoke directly against God and his assigned leader, Moses, freely rebuking God in a manner that reflected their own pride (v. 5). Just as the Israelites mocked and rebuked God, Nicodemus mocked and rebuked Jesus. By using this narrative, Jesus was making a parallel to what was so obvious in his conversation with Nicodemus as well as to something so obvious in the very nature of humanity: enacted rebellion and sin before God.

Second, it is clear in Numbers 21 that Moses served as the intercessor between the Israelites and God. It was only to Moses that the people could turn for relief from their suffering and their situation (v. 7), and it was only through Moses that the suffering was reversed and relationship was restored. Jesus's statement in v. 14 makes this comparison clear by making an explicit connection between the "redemptive" work of Moses and the redemptive work of Christ. There are, however, two important differences. First, the work of Moses was clearly depicted in Numbers 21:8 to be not his own doing but the gracious work of God simply funneled through him. In contrast, as much as God the Father is still entirely behind the work of Christ (cf. 3:16), it is also clear that Jesus is entirely behind the work as well. Second, the work of Moses involved something outside of himself (e.g., a staff), whereas the work of Christ necessarily involves himself, his own "flesh" (1:14). Moses's lifting of the staff was temporary; what was needed was an intercessor who could provide a permanent "lifting" of the staff (i.e., the cross).

It is the differences between Numbers 21 and Jesus, however, that are the ground for his message to Nicodemus, serving to present the irony of the gospel. Jesus, though victorious over Nicodemus, can only truly win when he loses — when he is killed and declared the defeated. That is, *the finale of Jesus's postvictory speech is his ultimate defeat* and an ultimate victory for Nicodemus. Jesus's own carefully selected term, "lifted up" (ὑψωθῆναι), conveys a rich duality of meaning. In the context of the cross (the historical strand of the plot), the verb is able to speak of death, suffering, and defeat. But in its larger context (the cosmological strand of the plot), the verb is also able to speak of exaltation in majesty and glorification (cf. Acts 2:33). In this one word, the message of the gospel is presented. It is only in his humiliation that Jesus can be exalted and glorified. And it is at the center of this irony that humanity receives eternal life "from above" — from Jesus. To look at Jesus is to understand the necessity of the exalted Son of Man on a cross, to understand how a crucified God can become for the world the greatest thing imaginable.

3:15 "In order that all who believe in him may have eternal life" (ἵνα πᾶς ὁ πιστεύων ἐν αὐτῷ ἔχῃ ζωὴν αἰώνιον). Jesus concludes with a purpose summary of his work and person, denoted by "in order that" (ἵνα) with the subjunctive "may have" (ἔχῃ). In light of v. 14, this statement carries with it all the weight of the plight of humanity as well as the exaltation of the crucified God. It can only be offered after the cross, and it can only be received by those "who believe in him" (ὁ πιστεύων ἐν αὐτῷ). The nature of this life is "eternal life" (ζωὴν αἰώνιον). The addition of the qualifier "eternal" occurs here for the first time in the Gospel and is only ever used to qualify "life." Since the prologue already defined life by means of the Word, its qualification here is necessarily related. The phrase "eternal life" speaks not merely about the quantity of life (i.e., life forever) but also the quality of life.[36] Eternal life is life in Christ.

This concludes the final statement by Jesus. Although the majority of translations imply that Jesus is speaking to the end of v. 21, the expression and tone change, and the apparent change to past tense strongly suggests that the narrator takes over in v. 16 (see below). One reason why vv. 13–15 are often considered not to be Jesus's words is because they seem disconnected from what has come before. But when understood as the end of the social challenge dialogue, these final words, belonging to Jesus by right of his victory, are remarkable. *At the moment when Jesus could be heralding the honor due to him, he announces his impending shame.* And it is by Jesus's shame that Nicodemus can become victorious, albeit in a manner quite different than expected. Thus Jesus, the winner of the social challenge, claims that his true honor (the exaltation) can only come through shame (the cross). Such an explanation bridges this pericope with what has come before. While the proof of Jesus's victory will only be in the resurrection (cf. 2:18–19), the power of his victory must go through the cross (shame). The strange irony with which Jesus ends his dialogue with Nicodemus needs to be explained by the narrator regarding its meaning and significance.

3:16 For in this way God loved the world, and so he gave the unique Son in order that all who believe in him might not be destroyed but have eternal life (Οὕτως γὰρ ἠγάπησεν ὁ θεὸς τὸν κόσμον, ὥστε τὸν υἱὸν τὸν μονογενῆ ἔδωκεν, ἵνα πᾶς ὁ πιστεύων εἰς αὐτὸν μὴ ἀπόληται ἀλλ᾽ ἔχῃ ζωὴν αἰώνιον). This verse begins an extended reflection by the narrator. Because ancient texts did not use anything like quotation marks, the exact point of this transition is disputed. Some have suggested the voice of Jesus stopped at v. 12 and the narrator began at v. 13, but not only is the dialogue best viewed as extending through v. 15 but the language in vv. 13–15 is strongly linked to Jesus elsewhere. For example, the title "Son of Man" is reserved for Jesus's lips alone in the Gospel (12:34 is no exception). A similar argument demands that vv. 16–21 are best viewed as the words of the narrator/evangelist; for example, the expression "unique Son" is only used by the evangelist (1:14, 18; cf. 1 John 4:9), and Jesus does not normally refer to his Father as "God" (ὁ θεός).

It also seems clear that vv. 16–21 echo again the great themes of the prologue. Some examples include the following: (1) the term "world," used only once since the prologue, occurs five times in these verses; (2) "light" occurs five times in these verses — its first appearance since the prologue; and (3) "unique Son" occurs only outside the prologue in these verses. As we discussed in regard to the prologue, it was common in classic prologues that the narrator of the prologue "would continue to comment on the action of subsequent scenes."[37] We have already seen as much since the beginning of the narrative proper. In several pericopae thus far, the narrator has been guiding the reader to understand an action as a "sign" (2:11) or to understand the words of Jesus and their correct in-

36. Cf. B. F. Westcott, *The Epistles of St. John* (London: Macmillan, 1982), 215.

37. Hooker, "Beginnings and Endings," 186.

terpretation by the disciples (2:17, 21 – 22), and we will see such explanatory "intrusions" later as well (e.g., 3:31 – 36). For this reason, it is imperative that we not detach vv. 16 – 21 from vv. 1 – 15. This is not a digression or mere meditation but a necessary interpretation of the dialogue that has just taken place; it is where the narrator gives us fuller insight into the meaning and significance of the events being testified to. By this, the evangelist "provided members of his audience with the vital information that would enable them to comprehend the plot, and to understand the unseen forces ... which were at work in the story."[38] This interpretation by the narrator reveals the "unseen" motivation behind all of God's actions: love.

The narrator begins by giving insight into God's actions: "For in this way God loved the world (Οὕτως γὰρ ἠγάπησεν ὁ θεὸς τὸν κόσμον). This is the first occurrence of "God" (θεὸς) since the prologue. The "for" (γὰρ) is best understood as an explanatory conjunction, serving to introduce the narrator's comments (cf. 4:8; 6:64; 7:5; 13:11; 20:9).[39] The term translated "in this way" (οὕτως) is more often taken as an adverb of degree, which serves as a "marker of a relatively high degree": "God so loved the world" or "God loved the world so much."[40] But although οὕτως can indicate high degree when individually modifying adjectives, adverbs, and adverbial phrases, when it occurs in combination with ὥστε it serves rather to refer retrospectively and is best translated "in this way."[41] Thus, the grammatical construction of v. 16 serves not only to separate vv. 16 – 21 from what has come before but even facilitates a retrospective analysis and interpretation of what has come before. This not only provides further warrant for seeing v. 16 as the beginning of a narrator comment but also

guides the reader to see that the statement being made in v. 16 is a retrospective summary intended to provide explanation.

What does the narrator explain? Quite simply, that the motivation behind the words and actions of Jesus, who is the Word of God, is God's love for the world. In case the reader was confused by Jesus's concluding statement to Nicodemus, the narrator explains it in its larger (cosmological) context with a theological proposition: everything Jesus does and says is rooted in the love of God. This is the first occurrence of "love" in the Gospel, and it is rather shocking that the object of God's love is "the world" (τὸν κόσμον). Nowhere else in this Gospel or anywhere else in the NT is God explicitly said to "love" (ἀγαπάω) the world (on "world," see comments on 1:10). Although the prologue implied as much, it is only after Jesus had been depicted among the darkness of the world that the narrator thought it time to reveal the deeper intentions of God. What made God come? What made God embrace human weakness and suffering? What made God endure mockery and shame? The answer is his love for the world — the very ones for whom he was enduring and suffering shame!

In light of the grammatical construction discussed above (οὕτως ... ὥστε), although ὥστε would individually function as a result conjunction ("so that" or "with the result that"), in combination with οὕτως it now adds something more or less parallel to the earlier referent.[42] In this way, v. 16 gives retrospective interpretation of what has come before in the form of two parallel statements, both speaking about the same thing. The former, denoted by οὕτως, gives the general explanatory declaration. This happened because of God's love for the world. The latter, denoted by ὥστε, gives

---

38. Ibid., 186.
39. Wallace, *Greek Grammar*, 673.
40. BDAG 742, definition 3.

41. Robert H. Gundry and Russell W. Howell, "The Sense and Syntax of John 3:14 – 17 with Special Reference to the Use of οὕτως ... ὥστε in John 3:16," *NovT* 41 (1999): 24 – 39.
42. Ibid., 35.

explanatory nuance to the former: God's love is made manifest in what and who he gave to the world. God gave to the world the "unique Son" (τὸν υἱὸν τὸν μονογενῆ). The giving of the Son by God is the very expression of his love. The love of God is not floating in abstraction but embodied in human "flesh."

The purpose of the love of God, of the giving of the unique Son, is that "all who believe in him might not be destroyed but have eternal life" (ἵνα πᾶς ὁ πιστεύων εἰς αὐτὸν μὴ ἀπόληται ἀλλ' ἔχῃ ζωὴν αἰώνιον). Although impending destruction in judgment is what is coming upon the darkness, a persistent theme in John (cf. 5:22 – 30; 8:15 – 16; 12:31, 47 – 48; 16:11), the provision offered is life. Since v. 16 is a retrospective explanation, giving meaning to what was declared previously, it is not surprising to see "life" mentioned again (see comments on 1:15). The statement of Jesus to Nicodemus is being given a cosmological commentary by the narrator. Along with the prologue we can now see that the mission of the Son is also the mission of God, and the mission field is the world, the darkness, humanity. In light of Jesus's challenge with Nicodemus, such language rebukes an impotent religious system and offers a way beyond the darkness of humanity.

3:17 For God did not send his Son into the world in order to condemn the world, but in order to save the world through him (οὐ γὰρ ἀπέστειλεν ὁ θεὸς τὸν υἱὸν εἰς τὸν κόσμον ἵνα κρίνῃ τὸν κόσμον, ἀλλ' ἵνα σωθῇ ὁ κόσμος δι' αὐτοῦ). Since v. 16 gave the explanatory overview, the rest of the narrator's comments give further clarification and application. The first clarification is to explain what the sending of the Son was *not* intending to accomplish. The purpose of the unique Son, denoted by the twofold use of "in order to" (ἵνα), was not "to condemn" (κρίνῃ) but "to save" (σωθῇ).

This is the first occurrence out of seven of "the

Son" (τὸν υἱὸν) absolutely, that is, without any qualification (cf. 3:36; 5:19; 6:40; 8:36; 14:13; 17:1). The various titles of Jesus presented thus far have found their most natural home: the Son of God (cf. 20:31). Although later Jesus will declare that he came to condemn (see 9:39), the narrator is here describing the specific love-based sending of the Son. While condemnation is unavoidable (cf. v. 18), it is not what the love of God seeks to bring about. Condemnation is, rather, what is natural to (as the inevitable result of) darkness. What initiated the "sending" is love, not condemnation. This is not to deny a place for condemnation but to say that the sending of the Son is rooted in the love of God. This clarification sheds further light on the social challenge with Nicodemus. The intention of Jesus was not to gain his own honor at the expense of Nicodemus but to gain honor for Nicodemus at the expense of his own.

3:18 The one who believes in him will not be condemned, but the one who does not believe is already condemned, for he has not believed in the name of the unique Son of God (ὁ πιστεύων εἰς αὐτὸν οὐ κρίνεται· ὁ [δὲ] μὴ πιστεύων ἤδη κέκριται, ὅτι μὴ πεπίστευκεν εἰς τὸ ὄνομα τοῦ μονογενοῦς υἱοῦ τοῦ θεοῦ). The narrator transitions from speaking about "the world" to "the one." As much as the whole world is in need of Jesus, only "the one who believes in him" may receive what he offers. The present-tense substantival particle, "the one who believes" (ὁ πιστεύων), is commonly used in soteriological contexts, speaking of the appropriate response and posture of the child of God. Although the whole world is already condemned (in darkness), there is at the same time a way through which "the one who believes" may be exonerated. And this exoneration, this love of God, is only possible for those who believe "in the name of the unique Son of God" (εἰς τὸ ὄνομα τοῦ μονογενοῦς υἱοῦ τοῦ θεοῦ). As discussed earlier, someone's "name" in the ancient world did not merely function as a label but said something about the character of the person (see comments on 1:12). With the additional insight of God's intention in sending the Son, the "name" now contains within it God's love for the world (v. 16).

3:19 This is the verdict: the Light has come into the world and humanity loved the darkness rather than the Light, for their deeds were evil (αὕτη δέ ἐστιν ἡ κρίσις, ὅτι τὸ φῶς ἐλήλυθεν εἰς τὸν κόσμον καὶ ἠγάπησαν οἱ ἄνθρωποι μᾶλλον τὸ σκότος ἢ τὸ φῶς, ἦν γὰρ αὐτῶν πονηρὰ τὰ ἔργα). The narrator concludes his comment in vv. 19–21 by casting the same cosmological vision developed in the prologue, with the addition of further explanations. By now, however, the reader has also gained numerous insights from the historical strand of the plot already unfolding. The narrator makes a declarative statement with the significant term "verdict" (κρίσις), which could be translated as "judgment" but more generally speaks of the judicial process that includes and culminates in a verdict. Thus, our use of "verdict" implies an ongoing judicial process.[43] The prologue described the darkness of the world, but v. 19 explains it. The world manifested its darkness by its self-love and selfishness, both of which necessarily excluded God, for God should be loved and obeyed. It was only when the love of God came, when "the light" came "into the world," that the darkness saw itself by means of contrast. It was only in the Light that humanity could see that it was in darkness (1:4–5).

3:20 For all who practice evil hate the light and do not come toward the Light, in order that their deeds may not be exposed (πᾶς γὰρ ὁ φαῦλα πράσσων μισεῖ τὸ φῶς καὶ οὐκ ἔρχεται πρὸς τὸ φῶς, ἵνα μὴ ἐλεγχθῇ τὰ ἔργα αὐτοῦ). The reason the darkness does not "recognize" the Light (1:5) is because it hates the light. And its hate is rooted in its pride; it does not want its deeds exposed. Without the light, darkness feels safe, although in reality it has already been condemned (v. 18). Not to come to the Light, then, is true disbelief.[44]

3:21 But the one who does the truth comes toward the Light, in order that his deeds may be made manifest as having been accomplished in God (ὁ δὲ ποιῶν τὴν ἀλήθειαν ἔρχεται πρὸς τὸ φῶς, ἵνα φανερωθῇ αὐτοῦ τὰ ἔργα ὅτι ἐν θεῷ ἐστιν εἰργασμένα). The narrator concludes with the contrast to v. 20, with one significant difference. Rather than avoiding the Light, the one who does truth comes toward the Light. The title "the one who does the truth" (ὁ ποιῶν τὴν ἀλήθειαν) is in part a contrast with the evildoer; yet it might also be an expression that describes "the one who believes." If this is the case, then "to do the truth" is to keep the faith.[45] While the evildoer finds the Light shameful, the one who does the truth embraces the Light as the place to escape shame. While the evildoer embraces who he is, the one who does truth embraces who Christ is. Finally—and this is the significant difference between the person described in v. 20 and that of v. 21—while the actions of the evildoer reflect who he is, the actions of the one who does truth reflect who God is. The purpose, denoted by "in order that" (ἵνα), is that his deeds may be made manifest "as having been accomplished in God" (ὅτι ἐν θεῷ ἐστιν εἰργασμένα). Although "through God" might seem to make more sense, "in God" (ἐν θεῷ) is more comprehensive, for the Christian life is rooted "in him" (v. 16).

---

43. BDAG 569.
44. Schnackenburg, *John*, 1:407. Cf. Hoskyns, *Fourth Gospel*, 208.

45. Cf. Barrett, *John*, 218.

Theology in Application

The arrival of Jesus has sparked a wide range of challenges, from the hesitant disciples of John the Baptist to the challenging authorities of the established Jewish religion. In this pericope, the teacher of Israel — Nicodemus — is forced to become a student, and the reader participates in a social challenge that forces upon them the choice between evil and truth, darkness and light, and a love of self and the love of God.

The Challenge of God

The context of the social challenge not only gives important insight into the details of the dialogue between Jesus and Nicodemus but also serves to set the challenge in its larger cosmological context. Like Nicodemus, the world has approached God with all its sinful pride and declared itself to be the judge of its Creator and King. Like Nicodemus, the world has crafted for itself a position of control and power that directly confronts the God of the universe. And when this world speaks of God, like Nicodemus it naively builds vaulted cathedrals and writes poetic words that simply "expose" its own darkness, its own inability to see and understand God. In his dialogue with Nicodemus, Jesus takes the challenge on directly and reverses the challenge initiated by Nicodemus so that Nicodemus's own words turn back upon him. In the same way, God uses the darkness of the world and the shame we so quickly conceal in our pride to be the means by which we perform exactly what God wanted us to do and in the exact manner. What the world thought was a victory over Jesus at the cross became the very victory of Christ and his moment of exaltation. We crown him with thorns, and he wears them with honor! We beat him to our own benefit! The gospel — the good news — is that God has taken on our challenge, allowed us to speak in mocking hyperbole of him in our pride, and has used that for his own glory and our ultimate good.

The Love of God

It is in the very midst of a social challenge, when God has been confronted by the full, pompous brokenness of humanity, that God declared his love for the world. In one sense, this was a strange place for God to declare it, for it was wholly undeserved. Yet there was, at the same time, no better place. For it is in the deepest depth of sin that God's love in the form of the cross of Jesus Christ makes the most sense. It is in darkness that light is most necessary and most magnificent. Ultimately, then, it was love that made God engage and counter humanity's sinful, self-righteous challenge. God did not leave us to ourselves but came to us, extended himself to us in the form of his Son, and given us newness of life.

Oh world, embrace the love of God! Oh church, make the love of God the foundation of all life! Just as Christ during his postvictory speech over Nicodemus — when victors would traditionally declare their own brilliance and success — preferred to announce his own defeat and shame for our gain, so also we, the children of God, in moments when we appear victorious need to declare to the world the true source of our success and real reason for our life: the love of God shown in Christ. The love of God is not something to hide but to proclaim. It is not something about which we find embarrassment, for it is the embarrassment of God that makes love possible. The love of God, therefore, cannot be portrayed as abstract or vague, for in and through Jesus it is the most personal, the most "fleshly" attribute known of God.

Humanity Exposed

It was only when the Light arrived in the darkness that the darkness was exposed as darkness. And the response of the darkness to the Light made manifest its dark quality, for it did not want to be exposed. Ironically, evil is aware of its own shame, and it knows exactly what to do to stay in the dark. As the Light of humanity (1:4), Jesus has exposed the darkness of humanity. While the world speaks naively of "goodness" and "morality," for the Christian human sinfulness and depravity are the true norm and plumb line of human existence. For this very reason, the Christian does not deny in any way their own sinfulness but wears it as a badge — not for their own honor but as proof of the work of God in one's life. To speak of goodness or morality without Christ is to speak as a non-Christian; for the Christian is first and foremost a sinner who has been worked on by God. That is, to speak of a general morality is to speak without God and to speak about one's own honor. The Christian finds their honor and significance in Christ, which means he or she finds acceptance and true identity as a child of God not in spite of their sin but by means of it. The motto of the Christian is "but of God" (1:13). Such a motto provides the needed contrast in regard to the old self ("but") as well as the source of the newness of life ("of God"). Anything else is self-righteousness and idolatry.

The One Who Does the Truth

The connection between faith and behavior is located in the person and work of Jesus Christ. The reason the darkness does not "recognize" the Light (1:5) is because it hates the light. And its hate is rooted in its pride: it does not want its deeds exposed. Evil is always aware of its innate shame. Without the Light, the darkness feels safe, even though it has already been condemned (v. 18). Not to come to the Light, then, is true disbelief. The one who does the truth is the one who believes rightly about self and God. The one who does the truth knows who he is and who God is, and finds in the light the only repellant for the shame that naturally belongs to them. While the evildoer finds the light shameful, the one who does the truth embraces the light as the place to escape shame. While the evildoer embraces who he is, the believer embraces who Christ is.

It is for this reason that Christ is at once repulsive and attractive. He is repulsive because he demands a full acknowledgement of our true sin-laden selves. Yet he is attractive because he offers a "new birth." It is so new — so different, so alien — that it can only come from God. But the attraction takes away what is repulsive. This does not mean that the Christian is able to disassociate from sin, only that sin is now different; sin is now exposed for what it is. In the light of Christ, sin becomes repulsive, something to avoid. Once in this light, the darkness becomes a place of cursing not blessing. Ultimately, then, doing the truth is a response to the love of God. To do the truth is truly to believe.

John 3:22 – 36

Literary Context

After an intense conflict with an official representative of the Jewish authorities, Jesus continues his ministry. In light of the last three pericopae (2:1 – 3:21), the ministry of Jesus is now surrounded by a much larger context. Every scene depicts more clearly what the prologue described: the world does not recognize Jesus (1:5), but Jesus recognizes the world (2:25). In this scene, however, the confusion comes more from the inside, from some of the disciples of John the Baptist. With the help of the narrator (vv. 31 – 36), John the Baptist makes his final appearance in the Gospel and utters his most significant exhortation to his followers regarding the person of Jesus and the nature of life and ministry with him.

III. The Beginning of Jesus's Public Ministry (2:1 – 4:54)
   A. The First Sign: The Wedding at Cana (2:1 – 11)
   B. The Cleansing of the Temple: The Promise of the Seventh Sign (2:12 – 25)
   C. Nicodemus, New Birth, and the Unique Son (3:1 – 21)
→   **D. The Baptist, the True Bridegroom, and the Friend of the Bridegroom (3:22 – 36)**
   E. The Samaritan Woman, Living Water, and True Worshippers (4:1 – 42)
   F. The Second Sign: The Healing of the Royal Official's Son (4:43 – 54)

Main Idea

The identity of the Christian is entirely defined by Jesus, and all Christian service must be submitted to the service he already offered. For this reason, Jesus challenges not only the identity of the religious and political institutions of the world but also the identity of all Christian ministries. The task of the Christian minister is to proclaim this news in such a way that even when using their own words, it is an entirely other "Word" that is heard.

Translation

John 3:22–36

22a	Setting (22–24)	**After this Jesus and his disciples went into the Judean countryside,**
b	Circumstances	where he was spending time with them and
c		baptizing.
23a	Simultaneous Action	And **John was also baptizing in Aenon near Salem,**
b	Basis	because there was plenty of water,
c	Reaction to 22–23b	and **people were coming and being baptized.**
24a	Aside	(For John had not yet been put into prison.)
25a	Conflict (25–26)	**Then a discussion arose between John's disciples and a Jew regarding purification.**
26a	Reaction to "discussion"	And **they came to John and said to him,**
b	Honorific Address	"Rabbi,
c	Description of 26a	the one who was with you on the other side of the Jordan,
d	Description of 26a	the one to whom you have been bearing witness,
e	Entreaty	look,
f	Assertion	he is baptizing and everyone is going to him."
27a	Resolution (27–30)/Response	**John answered and said,**
b	Maxim	"A man is not able to receive anything
c		except what is given to him from heaven.
28a	Reiteration of J. B.'s Identity	You yourselves can testify concerning me that I said,
b	Restatement of 1:20	'I am not the Christ, but I am sent before him.'
29a	Explanatory Analogy	The one who has the bride is the bridegroom,
b	Contrast	but the friend of the bridegroom,…
c	Description	who attends to and listens for him,
d		…greatly rejoices
e	Circumstance	when he hears the voice of the bridegroom.

f		*This, ...*
g	Exclamation	*then,*
h	Declaration	*... is my joy;*
i	Conclusion of Analogy	*it has been fulfilled.*
30a		*He must become greater;*
b		*I must become less."*
31a	Conclusion/Interpretation (31–36)	**The one who comes from above is above all;**
b	Contrast	**the one who is from the earth belongs to the earth,**
c	Consequence	**and speaks as one from the earth.**
d	Inclusio with 31a	**The one who comes from heaven is above all.**
32a	Action of Witness	**The one who has seen and heard bears witness to this,**
b	Rejection of Witness	and no one receives his witness.
33a	Contrast	**The one who receives his witness certified that God is truthful.**
34a	Expansion of 31 (34–35)	For
b	Contrast to 31b,c	**the one whom God has sent speaks the words of God,**
c	Basis	for God gives to him the Spirit without measure.
35a	Assertion (basis for 34b and 35b)	**The Father loves the Son,**
b	Result	and has given everything in his hand.
36a	Exhortation	**The one who believes in the Son has eternal life,**
b	Warning	**but the one who rejects the Son will not see life,**
c	Basis	for the wrath of God remains upon him.

Structure and Literary Form

This pericope corresponds to the basic story form (see Introduction). The *introduction/setting* is established in vv. 22 – 24, explaining the place and people involved, both of which center upon John the Baptist. In vv. 25 – 26 the *conflict* is revealed by means of an argument involving John's disciples and another Jew. The argument focuses upon the issue and gives it specific clarity for which resolution is made necessary. The *resolution* is given directly and forcefully in vv. 27 – 30 through a speech by John the Baptist. Finally, vv. 31 – 36 provide the *conclusion/interpretation* of the pericope, not merely by an implicit response by the crowd or an interlocutor but by the commentary of the narrator. Like the prologue, the narrator's comments serve not only to explain the immediate scene but also to make connections to the developing message of the Gospel.

Exegetical Outline

➡ **D. The Baptist, the True Bridegroom, and the Friend of the Bridegroom (3:22 – 36)**
   1. Introduction to the Baptism of Jesus (vv. 22 – 24)
   2. Baptism Controversy (vv. 25 – 26)
   3. The Bridegroom and the Friend of the Bridegroom (vv. 27 – 30)
   4. Narrator's Commentary (vv. 31 – 36)

Explanation of the Text

The common supposition that this pericope, or part of it, is out of place does not need to be explored. These conjectural suggestions neither rest on solid foundations nor make better sense of the larger context.[1] The pericope makes sense just as and exactly where it stands. This is the fourth successive pericope to point out ways in which Jesus fulfills and surpasses Judaism: 2:1 – 11 (true purification), 2:12 – 25 (true temple), and 3:1 – 21 (true birth). It also serves to frame the first three chapters of the Gospel: 1:1 – 5 introduce Jesus as "the Word" and 3:31 – 36 give a conclusive definition to "the words" Jesus is in the process of speaking.[2] The narrative has been guiding the reader to

see Jesus correctly and to make the correct biblical connections. Everything we have read so far has entrusted us to the narrative and to the narrator who is witnessing not only to the work and person of Christ in the past but also to the work of God in the present. The Gospel of John is well aware that we, the readers, are to be included with those in the "darkness" (20:30 – 31).

3:22 After this Jesus and his disciples went into the Judean countryside, where he was spending time with them and baptizing (Μετὰ ταῦτα ἦλθεν ὁ Ἰησοῦς καὶ οἱ μαθηταὶ αὐτοῦ εἰς τὴν Ἰουδαίαν γῆν, καὶ ἐκεῖ διέτριβεν μετ᾽ αὐτῶν καὶ ἐβάπτιζεν). The narrative signals to the reader the transition to a

---

1. Cf. Dodd, *Historical Tradition*, 279 – 87.

2. Michaels, *John*, 212.

new pericope with the phrase "after this" (μετὰ ταῦτα), giving no indication of the timing of the events (cf. 2:12). Sometime after Jesus's encounter with Nicodemus, which took place around Jerusalem (see 2:23), Jesus and his disciples left the city proper and went out into the rural parts of Judea, "the Judean countryside" (τὴν Ἰουδαίαν γῆν).[3] After two intense conflicts, Jesus has now moved away from the city with his disciples and is described as "spending time" (διέτριβεν) with them. The point is not to conjecture about the nature of their time, as interesting as it would be to know what Jesus said or did with his disciples, but to be reminded that God had "made his dwelling" among them (1:14).

After informing the reader that Jesus spent time with his disciples, the narrative adds that he was also "baptizing" (ἐβάπτιζεν). This almost add-on statement has raised more than a few questions, most notably: *Why* was Jesus baptizing and *what* did this baptism signify? The "why" cannot be deferred to 4:1–2, where the narrator explains that it was not Jesus who was baptizing but the disciples (see comments on 4:2), because the third-person singular verb explicitly connects the baptism to Jesus. That is, although Christ did not physically perform the baptism (according to 4:2), he is still named as the author of the baptism. This verse provides a thematic introduction to the impending scene.

While supporters of John the Baptist might see a distinction, even competition, between the two baptisms (John's and Jesus's), for the Gospel there has always been only one baptism, and it was always and only a baptism from above, involving the Spirit and performed by Jesus, the true Baptist.[4] For this reason, it is best to view the forthcoming comment in 4:2 not as an attempt to separate Jesus

from the act of baptism but as an attempt to show that the similarity between those who are doing the baptizing, John the Baptist and the disciples of Jesus, is founded upon Jesus, who is authorizing true baptism on both accounts.[5] This is why "he was baptizing" (ἐβάπτιζεν) had to be third-person singular, and why baptism in the church is always done in the name of Jesus (Acts 10:48; cf. Matt 28:19). It becomes imperative, then, that one not understand the statement "Jesus was baptizing" to be subsumed under the already existing baptism of John, as is common when viewing the events from within linear history. While it is true in one sense that John's baptism came first, in another and more important sense Jesus/God was already well at work before John—from "the beginning" (1:1), or as John explained, "because he was prior to me" (1:30). And since John's own beginning has already been rooted in the work of God (see comments on 1:6), it would be entirely inaccurate to view even the smallest part of John's ministry as conflicting with and not serving under the ministry of God through Jesus Christ. John's baptism was never cleansing in and of itself, and it is no coincidence that John is never even called "the Baptist" in the Fourth Gospel, for he cannot be the true Baptist (see comments on 1:33).

Thus, the historical chronology is misleading if it divides or disassociates John in any way from Jesus. In no real way is John any less a disciple than "the disciples" present with Jesus. And in no real way is John's baptism any different from theirs.[6] To view John's baptism with the historical lens alone misconstrues the overt cosmological coalescence taking place at this unique point in redemptive history. John *is* only because Jesus was, is, and will be. There is no need for John to stop baptizing, or Jesus (through his disciples) to stop baptizing, for

---

3. See BDAG 1093–94.
4. Cf. Augustine, *John*, 15.4.100.
5. Helpful here is Aquinas, *John*, 1:207–8.
6. Cf. Chrysostom, *John*, 29.1.100.

that matter. Baptism is not the problem; John is not the problem. Rather, it is simply that Jesus is necessary. For this reason, everything can and must carry on as before. The difference is that Jesus is now present. And his presence changes everything, even when it looks the same to the natural eye. In cooperation with 4:2, this verse makes clear that Jesus is the Baptizer, even if he was not physically performing the baptisms.

3:23 And John was also baptizing in Aenon near Salem, because there was plenty of water, and people were coming and being baptized (ἦν δὲ καὶ ὁ Ἰωάννης βαπτίζων ἐν Αἰνὼν ἐγγὺς τοῦ Σαλείμ, ὅτι ὕδατα πολλὰ ἦν ἐκεῖ, καὶ παρεγίνοντο καὶ ἐβαπτίζοντο). The narrative now shifts to John, who is described as baptizing in Aenon near Salem. The "also" (καὶ) intends to portray the baptisms as happening simultaneously. Although the location names taken together would mean "spring (fountain) near peace," the narrative is mentioning them only so as to explain why baptisms are being performed there: "Because there was plenty of water" (ὅτι ὕδατα πολλὰ ἦν ἐκεῖ). The site is probably modern Ainun ("little fountain"), which has many springs in the region. Even more, this location lies east of Mount Gerizim and the ancient Shechem, the leading center of the Samaritans.[7] Even though Jesus's ministry was clearly underway, two indicative verbs explain that people were continually "coming" (παρεγίνοντο) and "being baptized" (ἐβαπτίζοντο) by John.

3:24 (For John had not yet been put into prison.) (οὔπω γὰρ ἦν βεβλημένος εἰς τὴν φυλακὴν ὁ Ἰωάννης). The introduction and setting of the pericope is concluded with a brief parenthetical statement. Since this event has not been told by the Gospel, this narrative aside assumes the readers were aware of not only John the person but even

(at least some of) the events of his life. The snippet of information given by John is more substantially explained by the Synoptics (Matt 14:1–12; Mark 1:14; 6:14–29; Luke 3:19–20). It is warranted to assume that the Fourth Gospel was written with readers in mind who were aware of the other Gospels already (especially Mark). John may have written to avoid confusion or contradiction, or more simply to connect his witness to what had already been witnessed by the other Gospels.

Since the Gospel is concerned primarily with the person and work of Jesus, such a comment must develop the portrait of Jesus in some way. Two reasons for the comment can be posited. First, the Gospel is giving further details (not stated in the Synoptics) regarding what happened between the temptation of Jesus and the arrest of John. Such an inclusion suggests that the Gospel is much concerned with chronology and especially with the events that took place at the beginning of Jesus's ministry. This supports the view of this commentary that it is likely that the Fourth Gospel's placement of the temple cleansing is not loosely attached to the chronological happenings of Jesus, moved forward in the life of Jesus for theological reasons, but is directly reflecting what did in fact take place.

Second, the Gospel is showing the symbiotic relationship between the work of John and of Jesus. The narrative has created an *inclusio* in the first three chapters around the witness of John, serving to highlight the nature of Jesus's ministry coming out of the OT and first-century Judaism. It also serves to highlight the Baptist and his unique role to Christ. This is not merely a chronological overlap but a symbiotic relationship that is rooted in the same work of the same God. While each has his own part to play, they are both significant in and of themselves and are both reflective of the unity of the work of God done through Jesus Christ. The

---

7. Keener, *John*, 1:576.

pericope will continue to explain this unique symbiotic relationship in what follows.

3:25 Then a discussion arose between John's disciples and a Jew regarding purification (Ἐγένετο οὖν ζήτησις ἐκ τῶν μαθητῶν Ἰωάννου μετὰ Ἰουδαίου περὶ καθαρισμοῦ). This statement begins the conflict of the pericope (vv. 25 – 26). The details of the "discussion" (ζήτησις), which could also be translated as "debate" or "argument," are not given. It could have been anything from a formal debate to nothing more than a mild discussion over a particular issue.

The discussion is between John's disciples and an anonymous Jewish (or "Judean") male. The prepositional phrase translated "between John's disciples" (ἐκ τῶν μαθητῶν Ἰωάννου) could be understood to contain a partitive genitive, and thus be translated "between *some of* John's disciples," but it is best viewed as referring to John's disciples as a whole (i.e., "out of John's disciples"). Apparently, there was discussion regarding purification, which just happened to "arise" (ἐγένετο) in the presence of John the Baptist. The significance of ἐγένετο throughout the prologue makes it difficult not to see significance here. Since this is the last occurrence of the Baptist in the Gospel, the occurrence of "came/made/arise" (ἐγένετο) here potentially forms a potent *inclusio*. The Baptist is about to announce what the narrative has already been showing the reader: the Gospel has always been about what God is doing (and Jesus in particular), not the Baptist (who is merely a witness). Thus, the reason for mentioning the dispute is to bring focus on purification, not on the disciples of John or the unnamed Jew. They, like the reader, are to be directed to the true meaning and source of purification. The Baptist, in what will be his final appearance, is a witness to something other, and for

this to be made clearer it is time for his presence to be removed.

3:26 And they came to John and said to him, "Rabbi, the one who was with you on the other side of the Jordan, the one to whom you have been bearing witness, look, he is baptizing and everyone is going to him" (καὶ ἦλθον πρὸς τὸν Ἰωάννην καὶ εἶπαν αὐτῷ, Ῥαββί, ὃς ἦν μετὰ σοῦ πέραν τοῦ Ἰορδάνου, ᾧ σὺ μεμαρτύρηκας, ἴδε οὗτος βαπτίζει καὶ πάντες ἔρχονται πρὸς αὐτόν). In some way, the discussion between John's disciples and the unidentified Jew connected itself to the nearby and seemingly parallel ministry of Jesus. The disciples of John (and perhaps the unidentified Jew as well) come to the Baptist and offer a concern regarding Jesus. They address the Baptist as "Rabbi" (Ῥαββί), a term that except for this use is only applied to Jesus in the Gospel. Such a title is clearly honorific, indicating to the reader that these disciples claim allegiance to him. The narrative has allowed the reader to feel the palpable tension that was stirring around the disciples of John regarding the person and ministry of Jesus.

It is possible to interpret the statement of the disciples as arising out of jealousy or envy against Jesus in support of the Baptist. But "one must not attempt to give a psychological interpretation of the disciples' report to John."[8] John's disciples state unequivocally that John is witness to another, and a witness by nature points to something or someone other. The implicit problem, therefore, is not with Jesus but with the witness. What is a witness to do when the object of the witness has arrived? What is the nature of a witness? This is the conflict that has been placed at the feet of the witness, the prophet-apostle (see comments on 1:15). John has declared who he is not (see comments on 1:20); now in his last act of witnessing he must explain who he is.

8. Bultmann, *John*, 171.

3:27 John answered and said, "A man is not able to receive anything except what is given to him from heaven" (ἀπεκρίθη Ἰωάννης καὶ εἶπεν, Οὐ δύναται ἄνθρωπος λαμβάνειν οὐδὲ ἓν ἐὰν μὴ ᾖ δεδομένον αὐτῷ ἐκ τοῦ οὐρανοῦ). With the conflict placed before John the Baptist, his response serves to bring resolution to the plot of the pericope (vv. 27 – 30). The resolution the Baptist provides, however, has not always satisfied interpreters. What is given? To whom is it given? How does this explain the issue raised by John's disciples? Carson is right to note that John casts his response in the form of an aphorism or a maxim.[9] But the point is not that the Baptist is being general, vague, or cryptic but that he is speaking directly at misunderstanding (see 1:5). The Baptist declares prophetically that there is another perception that is needed — a perception "from heaven." By this statement, the Baptist has performed the task to which he was called. It is not insignificant that "man" (ἄνθρωπος) is used here, for in perfect symbiosis with 1:6, the "man who was sent from God" has completed his task as witness. At this moment the Baptist speaks with insights similar to the prologue, situating this scene into the carefully crafted two-strand plot of the Gospel.

3:28 "You yourselves can testify concerning me that I said, 'I am not the Christ, but I am sent before him'" (αὐτοὶ ὑμεῖς μοι μαρτυρεῖτε ὅτι εἶπον [ὅτι] Οὐκ εἰμὶ ἐγὼ ὁ Χριστός, ἀλλ᾽ ὅτι Ἀπεσταλμένος εἰμὶ ἔμπροσθεν ἐκείνου). In order to explain his position and purpose from a heavenly perspective, the Baptist reiterates what he had already declared: he is not the Christ (see comments on 1:20). By beginning with the emphatic "You yourselves" (αὐτοὶ ὑμεῖς), the Baptist makes clear that his followers are themselves recipients of his negative revelation — what he is not! — so that just

as he can "witness" about Christ, they too can witness or "testify" (μαρτυρεῖτε) about him.[10]

From the first moment the Baptist began his ministry (according to the Fourth Gospel), his message has been about another. The entire statement is loaded with emphatics and is intended to rebuke his disciples, demote himself, and promote another. John's disciples had conflated the witness with the one witnessed to, and in so doing had confused the message with the messenger. The difference between John and his disciples in v. 29 is not that one knew of Jesus and the others had not, for both knew of Jesus and his activity. Rather, the difference was what they knew about themselves. John had seen himself, his true identity, whereas John's disciples had not. The Baptist's embrace of Christ directly corresponded to his negation of self ("I am not …"). It was only at the point of his "not" that the Baptist could truly be who he was supposed to be, a messenger for the message and a witness to the true "I AM."

3:29 "The one who has the bride is the bridegroom, but the friend of the bridegroom, who attends to and listens for him, greatly rejoices when he hears the voice of the bridegroom. This, then, is my joy; it has been fulfilled" (ὁ ἔχων τὴν νύμφην νυμφίος ἐστίν· ὁ δὲ φίλος τοῦ νυμφίου, ὁ ἑστηκὼς καὶ ἀκούων αὐτοῦ, χαρᾷ χαίρει διὰ τὴν φωνὴν τοῦ νυμφίου. αὕτη οὖν ἡ χαρὰ ἡ ἐμὴ πεπλήρωται). In order to explain who he is in relation to Christ, the Baptist employs the analogy of a wedding. The analogy is even more fitting in light of the Gospel's employment of this theme earlier in 2:1 – 11, especially since in that pericope it was clear that at the Cana wedding Jesus was the true bridegroom, connecting the details of the pericope to the larger work of God in redemptive history (cf. Mark 2:19 – 20; Matt 25:1 – 13).

---

9. Carson, *John*, 211.

10. See Wallace, *Greek Grammar*, 348 – 50.

The Baptist uses the wedding analogy to state that he is the true friend of the bridegroom. While a historical reconstruction of his "position" in first-century weddings cannot be provided with exactness, it is likely that the "friend" (φίλος) of the bridegroom was the *shoshbin*, which is only partially comparable to a contemporary "best man" since it was much more extensive and official.[11] The "friend" would be chosen with more forethought than the "master of the banquet," who was usually one of the invited guests and was selected to oversee and preside over the celebration on the day it began (see comments on 2:8). The "friend" was a highly honored position who had numerous, important functions at the wedding, including serving as witness, contributing financially, having a prominent place in the festivities, and providing general oversight and arrangement for the ceremony. He possibly even served as the agent of the bridegroom.[12] This was the role of the friend of the bridegroom, the role that John the Baptist performed for Jesus.

Besides the wedding analogy, the Baptist's words also provide important insight regarding the scene at hand. By claiming that "the one who has [i.e., holds] the bride is the bridegroom" (ὁ ἔχων τὴν νύμφην νυμφίος ἐστίν), the Baptist is asserting that the very fact "everyone" is converging on Jesus is itself evidence that Jesus is the bridegroom of his bride — his people. The wedding analogy not only extends to God in Christ but also to the people of God in Israel and, ultimately, in the church. The OT clearly depicts Israel as the bride of the Lord: "'In that day,' declares the LORD, 'you will call me "my husband"; ... I will betroth you to me forever'" (Hos 2:16 – 23; cf. Isa 62:5). Interestingly, it was the duty of the "friend" to provide assistance

to the bride as well, including the tasks of ensuring that the bride was bathed, appropriately dressed and adorned, and publicly escorted from her father's house to her new home.[13] In this sense, John the Baptist was the true friend of the bridegroom, who not only performed preparatory work for the bridegroom but also assisted the bride, the people of God, to be ready to receive the bridegroom. The ministry of the Baptist, then, can be viewed as a time of prewedding purification (reflected in the rite of baptism), ensuring that God's people are appropriately dressed and adorned before they are introduced to the bridegroom.

Ironically, then, the concern the disciples of John had for their teacher was entirely misplaced. It would be like a bride who was concerned that the best man of the bridegroom was not getting any attention at the wedding. Unlike his disciples, the Baptist knew his purpose and the role he played in the wedding between God in Christ and his people, the church, among whom he was a fortunate benefactor and for whom he was a servant. For this reason, he can state that he "greatly rejoices" (χαρᾷ χαίρει; the use of the cognate dative is a rare emphatic form in Greek), for the presence of the bridegroom yields a blessing of which he is part.[14] The fullness of what God has promised has been made manifest. It would be a mistake, however, to fully equate the Baptist's joy with the "fulfillment" of his specific task.[15] The Baptist's satisfaction is not merely in what he accomplished for God but what God is accomplishing for him. At the same time that he was serving God, God was serving him. In a sense, the best thing the Baptist could do was hear and respond to his own witness. In this pericope, the Baptist shows the appropriate

---

11. Cf. M. Zimmermann and R. Zimmermann, "Der Freund des Bräutigams (Joh 3,29): Deflorations- oder Christuszeuge?," *ZNW* 90 (1990): 123 – 30.

12. Keener, *John*, 1:579 – 80.

13. McHugh, *John 1 – 4*, 251.

14. Cf. Schlatter, *Der Evangelist Johannes*, 108.

15. Contra Barrett, *John*, 223; Carson, *John*, 212.

posture of a Christian minister, who must witness and receive the witness simultaneously.[16]

3:30 "He must become greater; I must become less" (ἐκεῖνον δεῖ αὐξάνειν, ἐμὲ δὲ ἐλαττοῦσθαι). The Baptist's last words in the Fourth Gospel provide a universal summary of the purpose behind his sending from God (1:6) and a universal statement for all messengers of the message. The central term is "must" (δεῖ), which posits a divine necessity. Just as surely as God requires that a person "must" be born new (3:7) and that the Son of Man "must" be lifted up (3:14), so God requires that Jesus "must" come first and John the Baptist (or any other believing disciple) second.[17] The strong contrast between "he" (ἐκεῖνον) and "I" (ἐμὲ) does not create a tension but is a natural reflection of the symbiosis between the witness and his object, in which "the one is fulfilled and made good by the other."[18]

It is in this way that John the Baptist departs from the story the Fourth Gospel tells. There is no need to tell, like the Synoptics (cf. Matt 14:1 – 12), the end of the Baptist's life and career, for it was at this moment that he had already given of himself. Regarding the "increase" language, it must not be taken too rigidly as if Jesus needed to increase (in glory, for example). Rather, to increase for Jesus means he becomes the one who gives, and to decrease for the Baptist means he becomes the one who receives.[19] Jesus is now not only the object of the witness but also the sole witness himself — for he, like the Baptist, was sent from God to make the Father known (1:18; 3:16). Even more, Jesus not only provides a better baptism than John, but he also provides a better witness (cf. 3:32). The conflict initiated by the disciples of John has now been explained to the reader. Jesus was never the problem; he was the solution.

3:31 The one who comes from above is above all; the one who is from the earth belongs to the earth, and speaks as one from the earth. The one who comes from heaven is above all (Ὁ ἄνωθεν ἐρχόμενος ἐπάνω πάντων ἐστίν· ὁ ὢν ἐκ τῆς γῆς ἐκ τῆς γῆς ἐστιν καὶ ἐκ τῆς γῆς λαλεῖ. ὁ ἐκ τοῦ οὐρανοῦ ἐρχόμενος [ἐπάνω πάντων ἐστίν]). This verse begins an extended reflection by the evangelist. We have already seen a narrator "intrusion" in 3:16 – 21 and should be less surprised to see one again (see comments on 3:16). There are enough stylistic similarities with 3:16 – 21 (e.g., words spoken about Jesus in the third person) and the prologue to convince the reader that it is again the narrator who is speaking. By these asides, the narrator "provided members of his audience with the vital information that would enable them to comprehend the plot, and to understand the unseen forces … which were at work in the story."[20]

In light of the preceding context in which the disciples of John contrasted Jesus and the Baptist, the narrator's intrusion also provides an explanatory contrast, though this time with the "unseen" meaning and significance about which the disciples of John were blind. As much as it appeared on the surface that Jesus and John were similar, the narrator explains that they are quite the opposite. Jesus is described as "the one who comes from above" (Ὁ ἄνωθεν ἐρχόμενος), which in whole or in part echoes several other statements in the Gospel, especially 3:13 (see comments on 3:13; cf. 1:15, 27; 3:7; 6:14; 11:27; 12:13). His origin "from above" connects directly to what was revealed about Jesus in the prologue and should be used to support the force and meaning here. His origin defines who he

---

16. Cf. Calvin, *John 1 – 10*, 81; Luther, *John*, 22:441 – 46.
17. Michaels, *John*, 220.
18. Hoskyns, *Fourth Gospel*, 224.
19. Augustine, *John*, 14.5.95.
20. Hooker, "Beginnings and Endings," 186.

is in every way. Like a genealogical statement, this insight gives context to his identity. But it also describes his authority, for because he "comes from above" he "is above all" (ἐπάνω πάντων ἐστίν). The exact identity and authority of Jesus cannot be determined or fully imagined; it can only be given an approximation by means of contrast.

Thus, the narrator provides the contrast with the phrase, "The one who is from the earth" (ὁ ὢν ἐκ τῆς γῆς). In contrast to a heavenly origin, which is unlimited, an earthly origin is limited by definition. The term "earth" (γῆ) is not used in John in a derogatory manner, unlike the Gospel's use of "world" (κόσμος), which can often carry negative connotations (see comments on 1:10). The point is not to declare the earthly as valueless but to show its subordination to the heavenly, both in origin and in type. Whatever its value, that which is earthly is finite and limited. By referring to one who "speaks" (λαλεῖ) in an earthly manner, the narrator makes a clear allusion to John the Baptist, giving the "unseen" analysis regarding a comparison between Jesus and the Baptist. Although the Baptist had already "spoken earthly" about the real difference between himself and Jesus (cf. 1:32 – 34), the narrator explains it even further. The difference cannot be contained or explained by a historical contrast but can only be portrayed in cosmological categories. Thus, v. 31 ends its short *inclusio* with a repetition of its opening clause, making emphatic the unsurpassed difference between Jesus and John, a difference in both origin and type.

3:32 The one who has seen and heard bears witness to this, and no one receives his witness (ὃ ἑώρακεν καὶ ἤκουσεν τοῦτο μαρτυρεῖ, καὶ τὴν μαρτυρίαν αὐτοῦ οὐδεὶς λαμβάνει). The one from above, Jesus, is in a superior position based upon his place of origin, which from the very start of the

Gospel has been defined as "in the beginning" and "with God" (1:1). He is described with the perfect tense as having "seen" (ἑώρακεν) and with the aorist tense as having "heard" (ἤκουσεν). Although the difference in tenses is almost impossible to gauge, since the context of the communication is between the Father and the Son, it is likely that a theological distinction is in play. The distinction might be that while the perfect denotes a "seeing" that is entirely unique to the Son as the one who reveals the Father (1:18), the aorist denotes a "hearing" that is more self-revelatory and therefore more global (a constative or comprehensive aorist), in which what is heard is the very Word himself, who is now made visible to all.[21] With Augustine, we might say that although in one sense the Son hears the Father (8:26), in another sense what the Son hears can be nothing other than himself, since the Son is the only Word the Father speaks.[22] Beyond this intra-Trinitarian construction (including the Spirit in v. 34), the overall point is clear: the unique origin of Jesus gives him (and makes him) the final "Word" of God and the perfect "witness" to the things of God. It is not merely the baptism of John that has been surpassed; even his witness was incomplete. Yet, as the plot of the prologue has already revealed, the Son's witness is not received. Not to receive him is not to receive his witness (1:11; 3:11); the Word is his word.

3:33 The one who receives his witness certified that God is truthful (ὁ λαβὼν αὐτοῦ τὴν μαρτυρίαν ἐσφράγισεν ὅτι ὁ θεὸς ἀληθής ἐστιν). Similar to the prologue, universal rejection is immediately followed by an offer of reception (cf. 1:10 – 12; 3:20 – 21). The person who accepts his testimony "certifies" (ἐσφράγισεν) or "gives attestation to" the witness regarding God, like a seal certifies the document upon which it is placed.[23] This certification

---

21. Cf. BDF § 342.2.
22. Augustine, *John*, 14.8.97.
23. BDAG 980.

is a sort of witness "from below," reflecting the veracity of the witness "from above"; the Word from God is acknowledged as the word for humanity. The certification reflects not the truthfulness of the witness but the truthfulness of the object of the witness, namely, God. This passage echoes directly 1 John 5:10: "Whoever believes in the Son of God accepts this testimony. Whoever does not believe God has made him out to be a liar, because they have not believed the testimony God has given about his Son." In both cases, not to believe in the Son is to deny God himself and to make God a liar. In contrast, God is "truthful" (ἀληθής), that is to say, he is the truth (14:6; cf. 8:26). Since God *is* truth, we can offer him no more acceptable worship than the faithful confession that he is true.[24]

3:34 For the one whom God has sent speaks the words of God, for God gives to him the Spirit without measure (ὃν γὰρ ἀπέστειλεν ὁ θεὸς τὰ ῥήματα τοῦ θεοῦ λαλεῖ, οὐ γὰρ ἐκ μέτρου δίδωσιν τὸ πνεῦμα). The Father and the Son are so identified that just as the response to the Son is a response to the Father, so also the "Word" (λόγος) is the very "words" (ῥήματα) of God. It is as God that Jesus is given unlimited access to the Spirit, who is God. The phrase "without measure" (οὐ ἐκ μέτρου) is found nowhere else in the Greek language, but must mean something like the opposite of the nonnegated form, "without using a measure."[25] Although the subject of the final clause is unexpressed, it is clearly God who is implied, since he is the stated subject of the previous clause.

For this reason, we have included the implied subject "God" in our translation, helping the reader to see that Jesus is the one God sent, through whom God speaks, and to whom he gives the Spirit. To suggest that it is the Son who gives the Spirit to believers in this way not only makes little

sense of the context but also dangerously imputes the "measureless" Spirit to believers in a way that lacks biblical warrant and theological precision. As Ephesians 4:7 explains, each believer is given according to the measure of Christ's gift (κατὰ τὸ μέτρον τῆς δωρεᾶς τοῦ Χριστοῦ). Thus, the warrant or guarantee for the truthfulness of God's witness, Jesus, is the Spirit.

3:35 The Father loves the Son, and has given everything in his hand (ὁ πατὴρ ἀγαπᾷ τὸν υἱόν, καὶ πάντα δέδωκεν ἐν τῇ χειρὶ αὐτοῦ). If the gift of the Spirit beyond limits was not enough, the narrator informs us that "everything" (πάντα) belongs to the Son. The perfect "has given" (δέδωκεν) enforces the permanence of Christ's ownership. A nearly identical statement is made in 13:3. The Father's love for the Son, mentioned elsewhere in the Gospel (10:17; 15:9; 17:23 – 26), demands that he give him all things "that the Son should be such as the Father is."[26] This is a form of self-love which, in contrast to everything humanity has ever known, is entirely worthy. By this point, the reader has been so engulfed in the intra-Trinitarian relationship provided by the narrator that the comparison between Jesus and the Baptist has long seemed trivial.

3:36 The one who believes in the Son has eternal life, but the one who rejects the Son will not see life, for the wrath of God remains upon him (ὁ πιστεύων εἰς τὸν υἱὸν ἔχει ζωὴν αἰώνιον· ὁ δὲ ἀπειθῶν τῷ υἱῷ οὐκ ὄψεται ζωήν, ἀλλ' ἡ ὀργὴ τοῦ θεοῦ μένει ἐπ' αὐτόν). In a fitting climax, the narrator expands the cosmological commentary to all its readers. The narrator speaks about life in the Son through belief (or the lack thereof); these themes were discussed in the earlier narrator intrusion. In fact, this statement is best viewed as a summary of what was stated in more detail previously (see

---

24. Calvin, *John 1 – 10*, 83 – 84.
25. BDAG 644.

26. Augustine, *John*, 14.10.98.

comments on 3:16 – 21). It is worth noting that while 3:16 – 21 spoke of those who reject the Son as already "condemned," here those who reject the Son continue beneath "the wrath of God" (ἡ ὀργὴ τοῦ θεοῦ).[27] Logically, if the Son is the love of God, to not receive the love of God is to receive his wrath by definition. Just as the love of God is personally defined by the Son, so also is the wrath of God. "God's wrath is not some impersonal principle of retribution, but the personal response of a holy God who comes to his own world...."[28]

In today's culture, it is popular to proclaim a God of love but less popular to proclaim a God of wrath. Not only does the Gospel of John disallow such a distinction, but so also does the nature of God himself — the immeasurable love of God is a necessary response to the equally immeasurable wrath of God. The use of the present tense "remains" (μένει) suggests that what is portrayed historically (in linear time) as something to occur at the end of time is cosmologically already in play, with no need for the two times to be collapsed. This is denoted by the grammar itself. The one who believes "has" eternal life (present tense), while the one who rejects the Son "will not see" life (future tense). Bultmann is right when he states that this "conclusion is less a promise than a warning."[29] In this way, the narrator intrusion ends, providing not only a commentary on the state of the disciples of John but for all potential seekers of God.

Theology in Application

The arrival of Jesus has sparked a wide range of challenges and questions, but the scene shift from an intense challenge dialogue with Nicodemus to a puzzling question from the disciples of John forces upon the reader a deeper question regarding the identity of God's opponents. It was clear that Nicodemus was on the wrong side of the challenge. But John's disciples had committed themselves to his ministry and stood in agreement with his witness to Jesus. And yet, the conflict posited by this pericope between John the Baptist and Jesus found its source not in the Baptist or in Jesus but in the disciples of John. Somehow a concern for good things turned into a concern for self. It is to this issue that the Fourth Gospel turns and employs its authoritative narrative to ensure that the reader not merely be exposed to the light emanating from Jesus but also to the darkness contained in humanity.

Jesus Must Increase

Augustine is right when he suggests that to increase for Jesus means he becomes the one who gives. Everyone else can only decrease, that is, become the recipient of what he offers. At the wedding, the bride (the church) is only concerned with her bridegroom (Jesus); all the other guests, even our parents who brought us to this day (Abraham, Moses, David, the prophets, even the Baptist) all fade away as the bride approaches the bridegroom. No one else matters — and no one else should. The

27. This is the only occurrence of "wrath" in the Gospel.
28. Carson, *John*, 214.
29. Bultmann, *John*, 166.

wedding analogy uses the pinnacle of human relationship to highlight the unique bond between Jesus and his church (corporately and individually), but it also highlights the necessity for complete monogamy. The Christian is exhorted to commit oneself to fidelity to Jesus even when the world provides its own select offerings. To receive from another, to unite oneself with another partner, is not merely adulterous but exhibits a lack of faith, for it reveals that the person does not really think that Jesus is "above all" (v. 31) and does not really have "everything" to offer (v. 35).

The God Who Is True

The reason why Jesus must increase is because he is our access to the God who is truthful (v. 33). This pericope gives grand insight into the God of the universe, not only in regard to his heavenly origin and universal authority (vv. 31 – 32, 35) but also in regard to the wonderful mysteries of the Trinitarian God. The Son is in a position that is unique (v. 32). He is in full and unhindered communion with the Spirit and has been given everything the Father can give, including the love of the Father. The Father does not do anything without the Son, and the Spirit is entirely defined by his empowerment of the Son. This mystery is the cause of the beauty of the universe and depicts in human words the glory of God that cannot be grasped by the human mind. The marital union between the church and Christ is merely a symptom of the perfect union between the Father, Son, and Spirit. And the "life" offered to us through the Son (v. 36) is life in the Trinitarian God. May this be the fulfillment of our "joy" (v. 29)!

The Message and the Messenger

The Christian message is at its core very personal. It involves the whole person — not merely his mind but also his life. The ministry of the Christian intrudes on all areas of life. For that reason, the Christian must make sure that the message he proclaims is the gospel *of* Jesus Christ and not some other, potentially attractive "good news." The way this becomes confusing is when the gospel gets mixed with the symptoms of the gospel. Examples abound, and each would need to be subjectively explored, but the point is that the message is not the messenger. The Christian life is not about getting God into your story, but about getting your life into God's story. To confuse your story with God's is to confuse the gospel, to confuse the message with the messenger. It is, like the disciples of the Baptist, to begin to sense conflict when Jesus is around — when the commands and demands of Jesus feel restrictive and unnecessary. The moment that this happens, the center has moved. Remember, brothers and sisters, you are not the center, God is.

The Christian Vocation

John the Baptist was at one and the same time the "friend" of the bridegroom as well as a member of the "bride," the people of God. The Christian has a similar calling as John's. He or she is to proclaim the good news of Jesus Christ throughout the world (Matt 28:18 – 20). This is the task of the friend of the bridegroom. Yet, each Christian needs to maintain an appropriate balance between serving Christ (as the "friend") and being served by Christ (as part of the "bride"). Even more, both positions are necessary for the Christian life — to be appropriately involved in the wedding of God. An absentee bride or friend of the bridegroom is ruinous for a wedding. Not only must the Christian see the need for both sides of the Christian life — the passive and the active — but also the inadequacy of either one on its own.

The friend of the bridegroom is fully defined by his service to the bride and the bridegroom. In a sense, his work is self-benefitting, for his joy is found in the bridegroom (v. 29) and his service benefits his own body, the church. Like the Baptist, the friend's entire mission is centered upon what is needed for the bridegroom. In contemporary culture, it can become easy to think and act like a consumer, to focus our affections on what we desire and what makes us comfortable and happy. A friend of a bridegroom knows that this day — every day — is the day of the bridegroom. The friend knows who he is and who the bridegroom is and finds fulfillment in nothing else (v. 29). The friend of the bridegroom lives in his own witness, which has Jesus Christ as its object and eternal life as its promise.

John 4:1 – 42

Literary Context

The narrative thus far has centered upon how the beginning of Jesus's ministry fulfills and surpasses Judaism: 2:1 – 11 (true purification), 2:12 – 25 (true temple), 3:1 – 21 (true birth), and 3:22 – 36 (true baptism and witness). The previous pericope brought to conclusion an *inclusio* the narrative had created around the witness of John the Baptist, serving to highlight the nature of Jesus's ministry coming out of the OT and entering directly into the Second Temple Judaism of his day. The scenery has now changed, as Jesus moves not merely beyond Jerusalem (cf. 3:22) but also beyond "Israel," that is, Judaism. The Creator of the world has not merely come to his creation; he is moving through it. In this scene, the same Jesus is in one sense confronting a very different opponent (a Samaritan woman) from a very different context (non-Jewish/pagan). In another sense, however, Jesus is confronting the very same opponent (humanity) from a very familiar context (a world in darkness).

III. The Beginning of Jesus's Public Ministry (2:1 – 4:54)
   A. The First Sign: The Wedding at Cana (2:1 – 11)
   B. The Cleansing of the Temple: The Promise of the Seventh Sign (2:12 – 25)
   C. Nicodemus, New Birth, and the Unique Son (3:1 – 21)
   D. The Baptist, the True Bridegroom, and the Friend of the Bridegroom (3:22 – 36)
➡ **E. The Samaritan Woman, Living Water, and True Worshippers (4:1 – 42)**
   F. The Second Sign: The Healing of the Royal Official's Son (4:43 – 54)

Main Idea

In the person of Jesus, the entire world is confronted with the inadequacy of its resources and the overabundant riches of the gift of God, which is international in scope and cross-cultural in character. It is at each person's place of need, where they hunger and thirst, that God seeks and satisfies them with a food and drink no one could have imagined, rooted in the divine mission of the Trinitarian God. The appropriate response to God can be nothing less than true worship.

Translation

(See pages 228–32.)

Structure and Literary Form

This is the second substantial dialogue in the narrative proper, and it is a *rhetorical challenge dialogue*, which takes the form of a creative discussion of antitheses rather than a challenge or conflict over an exchange of ideas. A rhetorical challenge does not intend to advance an argument but to intensify conflict between two parties that have already agreed to disagree. The goal is not invitation but exclusion (see Introduction). It is in the form of a rhetorical challenge dialogue that the plot of the Gospel advances, especially as the reader takes into account the larger literary context.

Exegetical Outline

➡ **E. The Samaritan Woman, Living Water, and True Worshippers (4:1 – 42)**
  1. Jesus's Return to Galilee through Samaria (vv. 1 – 6)
  2. First Verbal Exchange: Jesus's Provocative Request for Water (vv. 7 – 9)
  3. Second Verbal Exchange: "Living Water" (vv. 10 – 12)
  4. Third Verbal Exchange: Well of Eternal Life (vv. 13 – 15)
  5. Fourth Verbal Exchange: The Woman and Her Husbands (vv. 16 – 18)
  6. Fifth Verbal Exchange: True Worship and Worshippers (vv. 19 – 24)
  7. Sixth Verbal Exchange: The Confession of Christ (vv. 25 – 26)
  8. Interlude: Jesus's Disciples, True Food, and the Harvest (vv. 27 – 38)
  9. "The Savior of the World" (vv. 39 – 42)

John 4:1–42

1a Introduction (1–3) — Jesus became aware that
b Content — the Pharisees had heard
c — that Jesus was gaining and baptizing more disciples than John
d — Although in fact it was not Jesus who baptized, but his disciples.
2a Aside (see 3:22) — Although in fact it was not Jesus who baptized, but
b Clarification — his disciples.

3a Departure (Place) — He left Judea,
b Destination (Place) — and went back again to Galilee.
4a Setting (4–6) — Now he had to go through Samaria
5a Place — So he came to a village in Samaria
b Identification — called Sychar,
c Description — near the piece of land
d Significance of Land — which Jacob gave to Joseph,
e Relationship — his son.

6a Assertion (basis of 6b–d) — Jacob's well was there,...
b Action (Subject) — so Jesus,...
c Description — who had become tired from the journey,
d (Predicate) — ...sat down by the well.
e Time — It was about the sixth hour.
7a Character Entrance — A Samaritan woman came to draw water.
b Rhetorical Dialogue (7c–27) — Jesus said to her,
c Entreaty — *"Give me some water to drink."*
8a Aside — (For his disciples had gone into the village
b Purpose — in order to purchase food.)

9a Response — Then the Samaritan woman said to him,
b Clarifying Question — *"How is it that you,...*
c Identification — *a Jew,...*
d — *...ask for a drink from me,*
e Identification — *a Samaritan woman?"*
f Intensifying Aside — (For Jews do not associate with Samaritans.)

Continued on next page.

10a	Response	Jesus answered and said to her,
b	Condition #1 (what)	"If you knew the gift of God and
c	Condition #2 (who)	who it is that said to you,
d		'Give me some water to drink,'
e	Inference	you would have asked him
f	Inference	and he would have given you
g	OT/NT Allusion	living water."
11a	Confused Response	The woman said to him,
b	Respectful Address	"Sir,
c	Assertion	you do not have a bucket
d	Assertion	and the well is deep.
e	Inferring Question	From where, then, will you obtain this living water?
12a	Interrogative Rebuke	You are not greater than our father Jacob, ...
b	Description	who gave us the well, and
c		drank of it himself, and his sons and his livestock,
d		. . . are you?"
13a	Response	Jesus answered and said to her,
b	Maxim	"Everyone who drinks this water will be thirsty again.
14a	Contrast	But whoever drinks the water that I will give to him will never thirst,
b	Basis	for the water I will give to him will become in him a well of water
c	OT Allusion	springing up into eternal life."
15a	Response	The woman said to him,
b	Address	"Sir,
c	Imperatival Rebuke	give me this water,
d	Hyperbolic Result	so that I may not be thirsty or come here to draw water."
16a	Counterresponse	He said to her,
b	Imperatival Rebuke	"Go, call for your husband and come back here."
17a	Defensive Response	The woman answered and said to him,
b	Retort	"I do not have a husband."
c	Response	Jesus said to her,
d	Affirmation	"You spoke correctly that you do not have a husband.
18a	Explanation #1	For you have had five husbands,
b	Explanation #2	and the man whom you now have is not your husband.
c	Emphatic Restatement of 18a	This you have said is true."

Continued from previous page.

19a	Intrigued Response	**The woman said to him,**
b	Respectful Address	*"Sir,*
c	Sincere Assertion	*I see that you are a prophet.*
20a	Assertion	*Our fathers worshipped*
b	Place	*on this mountain,*
c	Contrasting "worship"	*and you claim that the place where it is necessary to worship is …*
d	Contrasting Place	*… in Jerusalem."*
21a	Declaration	**Jesus said to her,**
b	Command	*"Believe me,*
c	Affectionate/Distancing Address	*woman,*
d	Basis of 21b	*because the hour is coming*
e	Negation 20b	*when you will worship the Father neither on this mountain*
f	Negation of 20d	*nor in Jerusalem.*
22a	Assertion	*You worship what you do not know;*
b	Emphatic Contrast	*we worship what we do know,*
c	Basis	*for salvation is from the Jews.*
23a	Reassertion of 21d (Not yet)	*But an hour is coming*
b	Oxymoron (Already)	*and now is*
c	Contrast of "worship" to 20a, c	*when the true worshippers will worship the Father*
d	Sphere	*in Spirit and truth,*
e	Explanation	*for this is the kind of worshippers the Father seeks.*
24a	Assertion (Basis of 24b)	*God is Spirit,*
b	Consequence	*and his worshippers must worship in Spirit and truth."*
25a	Ironic Response	**The woman said to him,**
b	Assertion	*"I know that Messiah is coming*
c	Aside	*(called Christ).*
d	Expectation	*When he comes, he will proclaim everything to us."*
26a	Response	**Jesus said to her,**
b	Confession & Correction to 25 (Scene Shift to Disciples)	*"I am he, the one speaking to you."*

Continued on next page.

27a	Character Reentrance	Just then his disciples came
b	Reaction to Scene	and were surprised that he was speaking with a woman.
c		But no one said,
d	Unspoken Reaction #1	"What do you seek?" or
e	Unspoken Reaction #2	"Why are you speaking with her?"
	(Return to Woman's Response)	
28a	Reactions to 26b: #1	Then the woman left her water jar
b	Reactions to 26b: #2	and went into the city
c	Reactions to 26b: #3	and said to the people,
29a	Invitation	"Come,
b	Declaration	see a man who told me everything that I did.
c	Interrogative Assertion	This is not the Christ, is it?"
30a	Reaction to 28–29	They came out of the town
b		and came toward him.
	(Interlude 31–38/Reshift to Disciples)	
31a	Simultaneous Action to 30	In the meantime his disciples urged him saying,
b	Ironic Comparison to Woman	"Rabbi, eat."
32a	Response	But he said to them,
b	Rejection of 31b via Metaphor	"I have food to eat that you know nothing about."
33a	Confused Response	Then the disciples were saying to one another,
b	Further comparison to Woman	"Could someone have brought him something to eat?"
34a	Continuation of Metaphor	Jesus said to them,
b	Source	"My food is to do the will of the one who sent me and
c	of Jesus's food	to finish his work.
35a	Comparison to 1st c. agriculture	Do you not say that there are still four months
b	to describe spiritual reality	and then the harvest comes?
c	Exhortation	Behold, I say to you,
d	Commandment	lift up your eyes and look
e	Source of food for Disciples	at the fields that are already white for the harvest.
36a	Description of harvester's role	The harvester is receiving payment
b		gathering crop for eternal life,
c	Result	and
		so that the sower might rejoice together with the harvester.
37a		For in this the saying is true that one is the sower and
b	Explanation	the other is the harvester."

Continued from previous page.

38a	Role of Disciples as Harvesters	*I sent you to harvest that for which you have not labored.*
b		*Others have labored,*
c		*and you have entered into their labor."*
	(Refocus to Samaritans/	
	Conclusion of Scene 39–42)	
39a	Result of 39b, a "harvest"	And **from that city many of the Samaritans believed in him**
b	Cause, a "harvester"	because of the word of the woman who testified,
c	Testimony	*"He told me everything that I did."*
40a		When the Samaritans came to him,
b	Request	**they were asking him to remain with them,**
c	Result #1	and **he remained there two days.**
41a	Result #2	And **many more believed**
b	Cause	because of his word.
42a	Climax of Scene	And **they were saying to the woman,**
b	Assertion	*"We no longer believe because of your message,*
c	Explanation	*for we have heard*
d		*and we know*
e	Climactic Declaration	*that this man is truly the Savior of the world."*

Explanation of the Text

It has been common for interpreters to construct a controlling motif of a betrothal scene that, much more than an "impression" (see Introduction), is viewed as a technical "type-scene" taken from the Old Testament. Since 1981, Alter's detection of a "betrothal type-scene" in biblical narratives has had an overwhelming effect on the interpretation of the dialogue between Jesus and the Samaritan woman.[1] Although some of Alter's thesis is helpful in its analysis of this pericope and supports the wedding (2:1 – 11) and bridegroom (3:29) imagery that has already been made explicit, its imposing presence has raised more than a few problems. First, while there are several "betrothal" images that Alter and others have been right to notice, the motif cannot be determined or applied exegetically with anything close to certitude.[2] Second, the methodological concerns mentioned above are ultimately a problem with the betrothal type-scene construct itself. The error began with Alter, who wrongly clustered the biblical narrative repetitions of betrothal into a technical type-scene.

Helpful here is Arterbury, who argues that even ancient exegetes read the OT narratives that Alter cites not as depictions of betrothal but as depictions of the ancient custom of hospitality.[3] The ancient customs Alter recognizes as a pattern in the OT texts, including some aspects of betrothal, take place within the broader social context of hospitality. Alter overemphasizes the male/female relationship in those texts and misses the more central host/guest relationship emphasized by ancient authors. He also makes a "grossly exaggerated" link between wells (water) and betrothals, when references to travelers stopping at wells for assistance in ancient hospitality narratives are commonplace, and he misplaces the necessary link between hospitality and betrothal, with the latter serving as a subset of the former.[4]

This commentary, therefore, will argue that the motif (or "impression") controlling the dialogue between Jesus and the Samaritan woman is not a technical type-scene of "betrothal" but the more general concept of "hospitality," and that this controlling motif plays an important role in giving definition to the rhetorical challenge dialogue.[5] We suggest that the larger social category of hospitality, a recognized Mediterranean custom in ancient cultures, is guiding the reader in John 4 (see especially comments on vv. 23 and 40). Rather than emphasizing the male/female dimension central to betrothal, hospitality emphasizes the narrative's explicit tension, that is, the host/guest tension between a Samaritan and a Jew (and ultimately the host/guest tension between the world and God). The focus is less on the male/female relation and more on the identity of the guest and the responsiveness of the host. The social context of the scene provides for an ironic twist. The innate tension between a Samaritan and a Jew, traditionally reinforced by means of a rhetorical challenge (an encounter), has morphed into a demand for

1. Robert Alter, *The Art of Biblical Narrative* (New York: Basic Books, 1981).

2. See Danna Nolan Fewell and Gary A. Phillips, "Drawn to Excess, or Reading beyond Betrothal," *Semeia* 77 (1995): 23 – 58; Teresa Okure, *The Johannine Approach to Mission: A Contextual Study of John 4:1 – 42*, WUNT 2.31 (Tübingen: Mohr Siebeck, 1988), 87 – 88. Cf. Moloney, *John*, 121.

3. Andrew E. Arterbury, "Breaking the Betrothal Bonds: Hospitality in John 4," *CBQ* 72 (2010): 63 – 83.

4. Ibid., 76. There are several instances where the offer of a daughter in marriage was a show of hospitality to the guest on the part of the host.

5. See Kasper Bro Larsen, *Recognizing the Stranger: Recognition Scenes in the Gospel of John*, BIS 93 (Leiden: Brill, 2008), 124 – 41.

hospitality between a host and her guest. Yet a grand irony takes place in this strange, tension-filled encounter, when the supposed host (the Samaritan woman) becomes the surprise guest before the generous hospitality of the true host (Jesus).

4:1 Jesus became aware that the Pharisees had heard that Jesus was gaining and baptizing more disciples than John (Ὡς οὖν ἔγνω ὁ Ἰησοῦς ὅτι ἤκουσαν οἱ Φαρισαῖοι ὅτι Ἰησοῦς πλείονας μαθητὰς ποιεῖ καὶ βαπτίζει ἢ Ἰωάννης). Because Jesus has moved from the Judean countryside to Samaritan territory (3:22; 4:4), the narrative gives a brief introduction to the scene change in vv. 1 – 3. Some commentators separate this introduction from the rest of the pericope or consider it to be an editorial insertion intending to make sense of the change in venue.[6] But the reoccurrence of the Pharisees is not an awkward intrusion but serves to highlight the plot's continual interest in Jesus's opponents, who in this case appear to be watching and taking note, even if from a distance. If the Pharisees took great interest in the work of the Baptist (cf. 1:19, 24), how much more the activities of Jesus, who not only had recently cleansed the temple and survived the challenge with Nicodemus but was now the greater threat, gaining and baptizing more disciples than John (cf. 3:26). This comment, therefore, connects this pericope with what has come before, moving the plot forward. By reminding the reader of the larger conflict between Jesus and "the Jews," the encounter with the Samaritan woman serves as an ironic twist: the further Jesus moves from Jerusalem, the less combative are his encounters.

4:2 Although in fact it was not Jesus who baptized, but his disciples (— καίτοι γε Ἰησοῦς αὐτὸς οὐκ ἐβάπτιζεν ἀλλ'οἱ μαθηταὶ αὐτοῦ —). In an aside, the narrator makes clear that Jesus did not perform the baptisms; his disciples did. For a full discussion of the meaning of this verse and the important clarification it makes, see the comments on 3:22. Its occurrence here and not in 3:22 is to ensure that the reader is aware that the Pharisees' interest in all unapproved religious activities has centered entirely upon Jesus, under whom all his disciples are actively ministering (John and his disciples included). Even the "revival" work taking place in Judea (3:22) and involving a large-scale ministry of the Baptist has been tied to the person of Jesus, who is no longer in Judea but in Samaria (vv. 3 – 4).

4:3 He left Judea, and went back again to Galilee (ἀφῆκεν τὴν Ἰουδαίαν καὶ ἀπῆλθεν πάλιν εἰς τὴν Γαλιλαίαν). What is often the first information given regarding the context is reserved for the end of the introduction to the new scene. Although v. 1 explains that Jesus left Judea for Galilee after he heard about the Pharisees, we are given no details regarding the specific concern(s) Jesus might have had or the reason for his departure. Certainly there is nothing in the narrative that suggests that he was "troubled" by this knowledge and took flight "to avoid the Pharisees' questions."[7] If he were trying to avoid conflict, he had failed to do so at this point in the Gospel. A clue to Jesus's departure might be implied by the word "left" (ἀφῆκεν), which normally carries the meaning "abandoned" (cf. v. 28 in regard to the woman's waterpot). Such a move is an abandonment of Judea, a temporary but vivid rebuke of his opponents, who after several encounters are only growing in their darkness-filled reproach of the light.[8] What had begun in the outermost court of the temple, the court of gentiles (cf. 2:14), was now taking place in the land of the gentiles, in Samaria. This was the kind of tangent

6. For example, McHugh, *John 1 – 4*, 262.

7. Michaels, *John*, 231 – 34.

8. Cf. Morris, *John*, 224.

or coincidence that is grafted quite naturally into the original plan of God.

4:4 Now he had to go through Samaria (ἔδει δὲ αὐτὸν διέρχεσθαι διὰ τῆς Σαμαρείας). Since the route normally followed by Jewish travelers heading north from Judea to Galilee passed through Samaria, Jesus "had" (ἔδει) to go through Samaria. Interpreters are often split between viewing this verb as expressing personal convenience (the shortest route from Judea to Galilee) and divine compulsion (the divine will for Jesus). Those that look to Josephus to support the view that the shortest route was through Samaria (*Ant.* 20.118; *J.W.* 2.232; *Life* 269) often ignore the context of his discussions, which involve the pilgrimage to Jerusalem (not from Jerusalem) for religious reasons.[9]

The Gospel has already made clear that the activities of Jesus are founded upon something greater than circumstance (cf. 2:4), and the term "had" (ἔδει) is particularly important in John for the eschatological necessity of God's plan, especially in regard to the saving work of Jesus (3:7, 14, 30; 9:4; 10:16; 12:34; 20:9). The Gospel has already used words as conceptual markers (see comments on 1:17). For the Fourth Gospel, therefore, the word "had" (ἔδει) connotes the cosmological mission of the Son and demands that the reader see the creative work of God in the world. In a very real sense, the OT and the developing mission of God explain that Jesus "had" to go through Samaria. Jesus is the Light to the world, the one through whom "all peoples on earth will be blessed" (Gen 12:3).

IN DEPTH: Samaritans

The Samaritans are difficult to define with precision.[10] Most of our information comes from the NT itself; extra-canonical sources are either of a relatively late date or must be sifted through strong Jewish propaganda, which tends to overemphasize their paganism. Even the origin of the Samaritans is not without debate. Although some of the tensions between Jews and Samaritans will be brought to light in the dialogue, it is worth noting that there was a high level of hatred and distrust between the two people groups. The Samaritans were most likely descendants of the undeported Northern Kingdom and foreign colonists brought in from Babylon and Media by the Assyrian conquerors of Samaria (see 2 Kgs 17:24 – 41).[11] The Samaritans adapted the worship of the God of Israel with the gods of Babylon, which created direct theological confrontation with the Jewish religion. If that were not enough of a reason for hatred between Jews and Samaritans, by the early first century there had already been around two centuries of conflict and strife between the groups, with both sides committing violent war crimes against the other. For this reason, the very mention of "Samaria" in v. 4 is intended "to evoke unease with the readers."[12] The reader is

---

9. Okure, *Johannine Approach to Mission*, 84.

10. See Gerard S. Sloyan, "The Samaritans in the New Testament," *Horizons* 10 (1983): 7 – 21. Cf. Keener, *John*, 1:591 – 601.

11. Brown, *John*, 1:170.

12. J. Eugene Botha, *Jesus and the Samaritan Woman: A Speech Act Reading of John 4:1 – 42*, NovTSup 65 (Leiden: Brill, 1991), 103.

expected to be aware of the sharp conflict existing at numerous levels between the two groups. This explains the expectation of a rhetorical challenge rather than a social or legal challenge. The encounter between these two was normally avoided at all costs, and when unavoidable it warranted merely a public repudiation of the other group for the establishment of their own.

4:5 So he came to a village in Samaria called Sychar, near the piece of land which Jacob gave to Joseph, his son (ἔρχεται οὖν εἰς πόλιν τῆς Σαμαρείας λεγομένην Συχὰρ πλησίον τοῦ χωρίου ὃ ἔδωκεν Ἰακὼβ [τῷ] Ἰωσὴφ τῷ υἱῷ αὐτοῦ). Because he traveled through Samaria, he happened to come upon a certain "village" (πόλιν) in the region of Samaria. The most significant piece of information is the inclusion that it is "near the piece of land" (πλησίον τοῦ χωρίου) connected to Jacob. The importance of the mention of "Samaria" and "Sychar" was to highlight the geographical context; the mention of "Jacob" provides a different kind of map — it connects the place within the history of God and his people. The setting for this encounter is not merely first-century Samaritan soil but ground upon which God has been toiling for centuries. In this sense, the entire biblical story becomes part of the map for this scene.

4:6 Jacob's well was there, so Jesus, who had become tired from the journey, sat down by the well. It was about the sixth hour (ἦν δὲ ἐκεῖ πηγὴ τοῦ Ἰακώβ. ὁ οὖν Ἰησοῦς κεκοπιακὼς ἐκ τῆς ὁδοιπορίας ἐκαθέζετο οὕτως ἐπὶ τῇ πηγῇ· ὥρα ἦν ὡς ἕκτη). The narrator situates the reader's gaze more intently over the map of the biblical story by mentioning the presence of Jacob's well. Though not mentioned in the OT, it was apparently known in the first century. The setting recalls three well-known biblical incidents in which a man met a prospective bride

at a well: (1) when Abraham's servant met Rebekah on behalf of Isaac (Gen 24:1 – 27), (2) when Jacob met Rachel (Gen 29:1 – 12), and (3) when Moses met Zipporah (Exod 2:15 – 21). This has led some interpreters to read the remainder of this pericope through the lens of a technical "betrothal" type-scene. But the images portrayed by the narrative are intending to "impress" upon the reader the larger map of the biblical story alongside the first-century cultural customs of hospitality.

The narrator gives the reason for stopping at Jacob's well: Jesus "had become tired from the journey" (κεκοπιακὼς ἐκ τῆς ὁδοιπορίας). Such a statement provides a potent insight into the humanity of the Word-become-flesh. Jesus's fatigue, however, does not merely fit into the timing and place of his rest but expresses the very essence of his mission. The mission of the Son is not merely reflected in where he goes and what he says but even in what he endures.[13] "It was about the sixth hour" (ὥρα ἦν ὡς ἕκτη), which suggests it was around noon. In light of the map of the biblical story suggested above, the setting of this scene creates a powerful image. In the middle of the day, on soil upon which God had already worked, the Christ sat at the well of Jacob. The sun of the day was beating down on the Son, who himself is light in a world that is overtaken by darkness. As much as this "piece of land" was significant for the Jewish people, the impending encounter would make this property significant to the whole world (v. 42).

13. Cf. Calvin, *John 1 – 10*, 89.

4:7 A Samaritan woman came to draw water. Jesus said to her, "Give me some water to drink" (Ἔρχεται γυνὴ ἐκ τῆς Σαμαρείας ἀντλῆσαι ὕδωρ. λέγει αὐτῇ ὁ Ἰησοῦς, Δός μοι πεῖν). A woman who is a native of the region of Samaria came to the well upon which Jesus rested. "Samaritan" (ἐκ τῆς Σαμαρείας) is to be understood as functioning adjectivally with "woman" (γυνὴ) and is not to be locating her from the city of Samaria, which lay several miles to the northwest.[14] It is all but certain that by mentioning the region of Samaria as the origin of this woman and not her particular village, the narrator is imputing to her all the vitriol properly basic to the broken human relations between her people and the Jews. This unnamed woman is known only by her origin from an enemy people.

When used for a request rather than a command, the aorist imperative, "give" (Δός), is best taken as a polite command. Even though the imperative is spoken by a superior to an inferior, as in this case from a Jewish male to a Samaritan woman, the context serves to soften the command.[15] It is not just the tone of the statement that is interesting, for as the dialogue will reveal the request is surprising at numerous levels. But the dialogue has begun, and Jesus has initiated it with the Samaritan woman.

4:8 (For his disciples had gone into the village in order to purchase food.) (οἱ γὰρ μαθηταὶ αὐτοῦ ἀπεληλύθεισαν εἰς τὴν πόλιν, ἵνα τροφὰς ἀγοράσωσιν). Although the larger religious and social context of the encounter between Jesus and the Samaritan woman had already been established by the narrative, an explanation was needed regarding why the request was made to the Samaritan woman and not to one of Jesus's disciples, which would have been normal practice for students of a

teacher in the ancient world. The narrator informs us that they had gone into the village to buy food. Thus, Jesus was left alone. Apparently the woman had come alone as well, even though it was likely that women more frequently went to gather water in groups. If her isolation is connected to a consequence of her public shame, as several interpreters have suggested, the narrative gives no indication (see vv. 16 – 18).

4:9 Then the Samaritan woman said to him, "How is it that you, a Jew, ask for a drink from me, a Samaritan woman?" (For Jews do not associate with Samaritans) (λέγει οὖν αὐτῷ ἡ γυνὴ ἡ Σαμαρῖτις, Πῶς σὺ Ἰουδαῖος ὢν παρ᾽ ἐμοῦ πεῖν αἰτεῖς γυναικὸς Σαμαρίτιδος οὔσης; [οὐ γὰρ συγχρῶνται Ἰουδαῖοι Σαμαρίταις]). Rather than rejecting directly the request, the woman seems to receive Jesus's polite command and turn it back on his position as the superior with a clarification question that illustrates her surprise and serves as a cutting rejoinder.[16] In a sense, the woman's surprise at Jesus's engagement with her serves to soften the nature of this rhetorical challenge. Although the surprise is ultimately rooted in the long-lasting conflict between Jews and Samaritans, to which the narrator's comment adds further warrant, it is probably also based upon the fact that a man was speaking like this to a "Samaritan woman" (γυναικὸς Σαμαρίτιδος οὔσης), considered in rabbinic tradition to be the lowest of the low.[17] The question and the narrator's comment presuppose much of the tension between Jews and Samaritans we have already discussed (see comment on 4:4). The use of the term "associate" (συγχρῶνται) by the narrator does not merely refer to the history of strife between the two groups but is probably intended to

---

14. Barrett, *John*, 231 – 32.
15. Wallace, *Greek Grammar*, 487 – 88.
16. Okure, *Johannine Approach to Mission*, 95.

17. According to one Jewish dictum, "The daughters of the Samaritans are [deemed unclean as] menstruants from the cradle" (m. Nid. 4:1).

include also the numerous particulars of ritual purity that separate Jews from Samaritans.[18]

4:10 Jesus answered and said to her, "If you knew the gift of God and who it is that said to you, 'Give me some water to drink,' you would have asked him and he would have given you living water" (ἀπεκρίθη Ἰησοῦς καὶ εἶπεν αὐτῇ, Εἰ ᾔδεις τὴν δωρεὰν τοῦ θεοῦ καὶ τίς ἐστιν ὁ λέγων σοι, Δός μοι πεῖν, σὺ ἂν ᾔτησας αὐτὸν καὶ ἔδωκεν ἄν σοι ὕδωρ ζῶν). Jesus receives the woman's surprise and rejoinder and counters them both: the surprise is greater than you can imagine, and the response is the opposite it would be if you truly knew the one with whom you speak! Such a counter by Jesus bends the rules of the rhetorical challenge, as Jesus is only challenging her posture and not her party. It is through a rhetorical challenge that the mission of the Son becomes most clear, for only through Jesus can the "dividing wall of hostility" be broken (see Eph 2:14 – 18). Jesus's counter is in regard to the misunderstanding of identity the Samaritan woman has raised. It is not that Jesus does not know who he is (and therefore is acting inappropriately); it is the woman who does not know who Jesus is — and she, therefore, is the one acting inappropriately. His identity is Jewish, and his appearance is one of a thirsty and helpless traveler; yet the truth is that he is the unique Son, the very expression of the love of God.

Jesus makes clear that she is unaware of "the gift of God" (τὴν δωρεὰν τοῦ θεοῦ). This mysterious phrase is given several possibilities by interpreters. The term "gift" (δωρεά) occurs eleven times in the NT and always denotes a "graciously offered" gift of God, four times with reference to the Spirit (Acts 2:38; 10:45; 11:17; Heb 6:4; cf. Acts 8:17 – 20).[19]

Since the Spirit was prominent in the previous pericope, it is likely that "the gift" includes the Spirit. Yet since the gift is "of God" (τοῦ θεοῦ), with the subjective genitive making emphatic that God the Father is the giver of the gift, then "the gift" is rooted in the Trinitaran identity of God. "The gift of God" is salvation ("eternal life") culminating in the gift of the Spirit, given by both the Father who initiated this divine action and the Son who serves as the agent of this divine activity.[20]

The gift, however, is given more explicit definition by the phrase "living water" (ὕδωρ ζῶν). While several symbolic or metaphorical interpretations have been suggested, rooted in first-century climate,[21] the phrase is clearly connected to the culminating work of God promised in the OT. A clear example is in Jeremiah 2:13, where the Lord brings a complaint against Israel: "My people have committed two sins: They have forsaken *me, the spring of living water*, and have dug their own cisterns, broken cisterns that cannot hold water" (emphasis mine). Significant here is that God is described as the spring of living water (cf. Jer 17:13; Ps 36:9). Yet even after rebuking the people for rejecting him, God offers hope: "The days are coming … when I will bring my people Israel and Judah back from captivity and restore them …" and "I will make a new covenant" (see Jer 30:3; 31:31 – 34). "In OT terms, this declaration is truly breath-taking: the people that had abandoned the very fountain of living water are promised a future superior to everything that Moses gave."[22] A similar declaration of restoration is given by Ezekiel. God will cleanse his people with "clean water" and will "put my Spirit in you" (Ezek 36:25 – 27). He will cause water to flow out of the sanctuary in the new Jerusalem to bring life to the dried-up land *even beyond* Judah's

---

18. Cf. David Daube, "Jesus and the Samaritan Woman: The Meaning of συγχράομαι," *JBL* 69 (1950): 137 – 47.

19. McHugh, *John 1 – 4*, 269.

20. Cf. Okure, *Johannine Approach to Mission*, 97 – 98.

21. Dale C. Allison Jr., "The Living Water (John 4:10 – 14; 6:35c; 7:37 – 39)," *SVTQ* 30 (1986): 143 – 57.

22. McHugh, *John 1 – 4*, 275.

borders (Ezek 47:1 – 12; cf. Zech 13:1; 14:8; Joel 2:28 – 29; 3:18). Such prophecy portrays the blessing of God that floods from Jerusalem into the surrounding countries — even the region of Samaria! And this blessing is not just rooted in the OT, for as Revelation 7:16 – 17 declares: " 'Never again will they hunger; *never again will they thirst*. The sun will not beat down on them,' nor any scorching heat. For *the Lamb* at the center of the throne will be their shepherd; '*he will lead them to springs of living water*' " (emphasis mine). And Revelation 21:6: "He said to me, 'It is done. I am the Alpha and Omega, the Beginning and the End. *To the thirsty I will give water without cost from the spring of the water of life*' " (emphasis mine).

Thus, the "living water" in the context of Jacob's well on a sun-beating day is rest and satisfaction — eternal life — rooted in the Trinitarian God — Father, Son, *and Spirit* — and mediated by Jesus Christ, his person and work. It is inclusive of everything the prophets could foretell and the Apocalypse could describe. It is perfect provision from God, with God, and for God. It is what Calvin summarizes as "the whole grace of renewal."[23] Even in his human fatigue and thirst, Jesus was fully satisfied. It was the Samaritan woman, competent enough to gather water for Jesus, who was the one in true need.

4:11 The woman said to him, "Sir, you do not have a bucket and the well is deep. From where, then, will you obtain this living water?" (λέγει αὐτῷ ἡ γυνή, Κύριε, οὔτε ἄντλημα ἔχεις καὶ τὸ φρέαρ ἐστὶν βαθύ· πόθεν οὖν ἔχεις τὸ ὕδωρ τὸ ζῶν). The woman clearly does not understand the significance of the things about which Jesus spoke. The reason might be because "water" was such a common physical object that she did not think it signified anything more complex. Or perhaps she was unfamiliar with such a metaphorical/theological use of "water," since the Samaritans did not accept

the prophets as canonical. Whatever the reason, she is confused on two fronts: the logistics of obtaining the water about which Jesus speaks and, more implicitly, why he is offering her water when he began the encounter asking for it. Beyond her confusion, however, the woman addresses Jesus with a respectful title, "Sir" (Κύριε), which she will apply to him two more times with increasing respect (vv. 15, 19). Jesus has already bent the rules for what should have been a rhetorical challenge, and the woman seems to have noticed.

4:12 "You are not greater than our father Jacob, who gave us the well, and drank of it himself, and his sons and his livestock, are you?" (μὴ σὺ μείζων εἶ τοῦ πατρὸς ἡμῶν Ἰακώβ, ὃς ἔδωκεν ἡμῖν τὸ φρέαρ καὶ αὐτὸς ἐξ αὐτοῦ ἔπιεν καὶ οἱ υἱοὶ αὐτοῦ καὶ τὰ θρέμματα αὐτοῦ;). Even beyond the seemingly impossible retrieval of water about which Jesus speaks, the Samaritan woman notices that he speaks quite strangely about himself and what he can provide. She likely finds it ironic that he speaks in this manner as he rests on the very well of Jacob, a father claimed by both Jews and Samaritans (cf. Josephus, *Ant.* 11.341). The occurrence of "our father" (τοῦ πατρὸς ἡμῶν) is a turning point in the dialogue because the Samaritan woman has now found a topic agreeable to both parties.

With what is probably another cutting rejoinder, the woman chides Jesus not simply for forgetting his personal Jewish heritage (by speaking to a Samaritan), but for forgetting the roots of Jews (and Samaritans) as a whole. Her question assumes a negative answer, denoted by the use of "not" (μὴ), since it would be inconceivable for a person to consider themselves to be greater than the patriarchs. The negation is not merely denying that Jesus is anything like the great one of the past but also anything like the coming great one. Only one person in the Torah could fit this description, the

23. Calvin, *John 1 – 10*, 92.

one who after having "nothing to draw with" gave Israel "living water" at Rephidim (Exod 17:1 – 7) and Kadesh (Num 20:2 – 13), where "water gushed out, and the community and their livestock drank" (Num 20:11). The Samaritan woman is implicitly asking — even while disbelieving — if Jesus is the prophet like Moses (Deut 18:15 – 19).[24] But the coming prophet would be great like Jacob; therefore it was worth pressing the past comparison: If Jacob drank from this well, as well as his sons and livestock, how is it that you find this well and its water inadequate?

4:13 Jesus answered and said to her, "Everyone who drinks this water will be thirsty again" (ἀπεκρίθη Ἰησοῦς καὶ εἶπεν αὐτῇ, Πᾶς ὁ πίνων ἐκ τοῦ ὕδατος τούτου διψήσει πάλιν). Jesus's response is simple and the proof directly apparent: everyone who drank from this well — Jacob included — was never truly satisfied; shortly after drinking, they needed to drink its water again. By describing it with the emphatic "this water" (τοῦ ὕδατος τούτου), Jesus locates its purpose and therefore its limitation. "This water" is not the same as the water "I will give" (v. 14). Jesus already speaks past this moment and this day (and even physical water) to speak of the life that is to come.

4:14 "But whoever drinks the water that I will give to him will never thirst, for the water I will give to him will become in him a well of water springing up into eternal life" (ὃς δ᾽ ἂν πίῃ ἐκ τοῦ ὕδατος οὗ ἐγὼ δώσω αὐτῷ, οὐ μὴ διψήσει εἰς τὸν αἰῶνα, ἀλλὰ τὸ ὕδωρ ὃ δώσω αὐτῷ γενήσεται ἐν αὐτῷ πηγὴ ὕδατος ἁλλομένου εἰς ζωὴν αἰώνιον). Jesus had already shown the limitations of "this water" and Jacob's well; it was time to describe the greater water that "I will give" (ἐγὼ δώσω). Unlike Jacob's water, those who drink this water "will never thirst" (οὐ μὴ διψήσει εἰς τὸν αἰῶνα). The

phrase translated as "never" (εἰς τὸν αἰῶνα) can also be translated as "into eternity," but is usually translated as "indefinitely, always, forever," or in this case with the negation, "never."[25] The emphasis is on permanent satisfaction from thirst.

Although he is speaking of "water," it is not water found anywhere known to humanity. It is water "from God," given only by Jesus Christ. This water is so potent that Jesus explains that it will plant itself in the person in such a way that they become the location in which it dwells — a well out of which this water will be "springing up into eternal life" (ἁλλομένου εἰς ζωὴν αἰώνιον). The participle "springing up" (ἁλλομένου), translated as "welling up" by the NIV, is used of quick movement by living beings, such as jumping (e.g., after being healed, cf. Acts 3:8), and is used nowhere else of the action of water. It can also be used to emphasize quick movement emanating "from a source." Both nuances of the word can be connected to the Spirit, as well as its use in the LXX, even though no such indication is given here (see comments on 7:37 – 39). The emphasis here is that the "springing up" leads to "eternal life," which is a central theme in John's Gospel (see comments on 3:15). This is the fulfillment of what the OT has long foretold: "With joy you will draw water from the wells of salvation" (Isa 12:3) and "Come, all you who are thirsty.... Listen ... and you will delight in the richest of fare.... Surely you will summon nations ..." (Isa 55:1 – 5).

4:15 The woman said to him, "Sir, give me this water, so that I may not be thirsty or come here to draw water" (λέγει πρὸς αὐτὸν ἡ γυνή, Κύριε, δός μοι τοῦτο τὸ ὕδωρ, ἵνα μὴ διψῶ μηδὲ διέρχωμαι ἐνθάδε ἀντλεῖν). Unaware of both the specifics and the grandeur about which Jesus speaks, the Samaritan woman at least knows she wants this water. Her response to him, however, is likely a bit playful and probably also includes a chiding: "Hey dreamer, this water sounds good to me!" As attractive as his words sound, she is unable to see that to which he speaks. In her hands was an actual bucket, and her throat was dry; the thirst about which Jesus spoke was too ethereal — she was unable to see the Word behind the flesh.

4:16 He said to her, "Go, call for your husband and come back here" (Λέγει αὐτῇ, Ὕπαγε φώνησον τὸν ἄνδρα σου καὶ ἐλθὲ ἐνθάδε). With these words, Jesus began to touch on a topic that was hardly ethereal. It was part of the woman's daily, tangible life and would serve as a handle for the remainder of the dialogue. Although she does not know or understand Jesus, he understands and knows her. Since the Samaritan woman had just uttered what is probably to be viewed as a closing retort, bringing the conversation either to a standstill or a conclusion,[26] Jesus applies a new and strategic tactic — he makes the conversation personal. This tactic is not intended to shame the woman — what would have been expected in a rhetorical dialogue — but to draw her in and help her understand about that which he speaks. And this is "a remarkable example of his compassion — when she would not come to Him voluntarily he draws her almost unwillingly."[27]

4:17 The woman answered and said to him, "I do not have a husband." Jesus said to her, "You spoke correctly that you do not have a husband" (ἀπεκρίθη ἡ γυνὴ καὶ εἶπεν αὐτῷ, Οὐκ ἔχω ἄνδρα. λέγει αὐτῇ ὁ Ἰησοῦς, Καλῶς εἶπες ὅτι Ἄνδρα οὐκ ἔχω). While the woman was probably thinking Jesus strange up to this point in the dialogue and by her questions putting him on the defensive, her response here suggests she is now on the defensive. Her response, "I do not have a husband" (Οὐκ ἔχω ἄνδρα), was probably intended to thwart any fur-

ther investigation. But Jesus quickly turns her defense tactic into his own strategy. He commends her for speaking correctly, though he changes her words so that "husband" (Ἄνδρα) is emphasized (moving it from last to first place in word order). Her life and her sin is exposed — which is exactly what the water of salvation was intended to quench: "On that day a fountain will be opened ... to cleanse them from sin and impurity" (Zech 13:1).

4:18 "For you have had five husbands, and the man whom you now have is not your husband. This you have said is true" (πέντε γὰρ ἄνδρας ἔσχες, καὶ νῦν ὃν ἔχεις οὐκ ἔστιν σου ἀνήρ· τοῦτο ἀληθὲς εἴρηκας). Jesus presses her statement by emphasizing her husband, specifically the "five" (πέντε) husbands she has had, excluding the man to whom she is currently living with but not married to. The repeated emphasis on having said what is "true" (ἀληθὲς) or what is "correct" (καλῶς) in the previous verse serves to heighten her sensitivity to good judgments, to truth, to reality. Jesus has been speaking what is truth; he has been shining light in a dark place. In this moment, he was shining his light into the darkness of a woman's soul.

The exact sin of the woman must be extracted carefully. The verse says nothing about her being a prostitute, as is commonly assumed. If anything, the opposite is implied; she is a victim of an abusive system where husbands can freely divorce their wives, leaving a woman used and helpless so that even her most recent "man" will not marry her. Others argue that nothing in the narrative suggests that the woman's sin is being exposed, only the omniscience of Jesus.[28] While it is true that the narrative is not showing a narrow interest in the sin of the woman, the reader of John would be mistaken to claim it is absent. The Fourth Gospel has been quite keen to expose the sin of its characters, and

---

26. Cf. Okure, *Johannine Approach to Mission*, 103.
27. Calvin, *John 1 – 10*, 94.

28. See Okure, *Johannine Approach to Mission*, 110 – 13; cf. Ridderbos, *John*, 160 – 61.

Jesus himself is also shown to be aware of "what was in humanity" (2:25). Furthermore, to focus exclusively on what the narrative is stating about Jesus harmfully minimizes the significance of Jesus's statement about the woman's personal life. The omniscience of Jesus is no less an implication from the text than the exposed sinfulness of the woman. Even more, the woman's pronouncement of Jesus as a prophet (v. 19) suggests not only that Jesus has special insight about her but that the insight is connected to his status as a religious man of God (cf. v. 29). Finally, the OT images projected by the symbolism of the "well of water" (v. 14) are loaded with images of cleansing from sin (cf. Zech 13:1). Rather than being a "secondary interpretation,"[29] the sin of the woman is an essential component in the dialogue, serving to describe the tension and separation between the two historical parties (Jews and Samaritans) and the two cosmological parties (God and humanity).

4:19 The woman said to him, "Sir, I see that you are a prophet" (λέγει αὐτῷ ἡ γυνή, Κύριε, θεωρῶ ὅτι προφήτης εἶ σύ). Direct insight into the woman's life yields fresh insight regarding the person of Jesus. The vocative need not mean more than "Sir" (Κύριε), as it surely meant in vv. 11 and 15, but at this point in the dialogue it might now be bending toward its deeper meaning: "Lord."[30] The Samaritan woman deems Jesus to be "a prophet" (προφήτης), which probably suggests he is a prophetic "seer," but also that he is competent to speak about spiritual things (cf. 9:17). The Synoptics

show that this was the most general verdict pronounced by people when they saw a man of God at work, being applied to both John the Baptist (Matt 14:5; Mark 11:32; Luke 1:76) and Jesus (Matt 21:11, 46; Luke 7:16). Although the noun is anarthrous, the woman was probably only describing Jesus as a prophet in general, not as "the (messianic) prophet" of Deuteronomy 18:15, especially in light of v. 25. The woman has become intrigued by the man of God standing before her.

4:20 "Our fathers worshipped on this mountain, and you claim that the place where it is necessary to worship is in Jerusalem" (οἱ πατέρες ἡμῶν ἐν τῷ ὄρει τούτῳ προσεκύνησαν· καὶ ὑμεῖς λέγετε ὅτι ἐν Ἱεροσολύμοις ἐστὶν ὁ τόπος ὅπου προσκυνεῖν δεῖ).

The Samaritan woman has begun to recognize that Jesus is able to speak to spiritual things. Her dialogue with Jesus has changed from cutting rejoinders to serious interest. She has not, however, come to join his side. She clearly sees a difference between her people, "our fathers" (οἱ πατέρες ἡμῶν) and Jesus's, designated by the emphatic "you (pl.) claim" (ὑμεῖς λέγετε). If it was difficult for the Samaritan woman to grasp Jesus's claim about a superior water and well, it would be even more puzzling for her to get around the differences separating Samaritans and Jews, who worship in different places and therefore worship differently. The woman has raised one of the most controversial topics between Jews and Samaritans, with the latter rejecting Jerusalem and building their own temple on Mt. Gerizim, a rival temple.[31] How can

---

29. Okure, *Johannine Approach to Mission*, 111.

30. Barrett, *John*, 236.

31. Mt. Gerizim was the scene of the blessing of the people of God when they came into the promised land (Deut 11:29; 27:12). The Samaritans believed that an altar was commanded to be set up on this mountain (Deut 27:4 – 7), though the MT more correctly reads in Deuteronomy 27: 4 "Mount Ebal." They also believed that Abraham's offering of Isaac took place on this Mt. Gerizim as well as the encounter between Abraham and

Melchizedek. Since the patriarchs were so linked with Gerizim, the Samaritans argued the same should be so for the faithful people of God — the Samaritans. The disagreement is rooted in the portions of Scripture each party considers valid. While the Hebrew Bible/Old Testament as a whole refers strongly to Jerusalem, the Samaritans hold as valid only the Torah — the first five books of Moses — which does not mention Jerusalem as the explicit place where worship (in the temple) is to be located.

Jesus raise such spiritual things with her when they do not agree on the starting premises?

The rhetorical dialogue between Jesus and the Samaritan woman seems to adjust at this point. As much as Jesus continues to employ elements of a rhetorical challenge to her, they function less to describe the separation between a Jew and a Samaritan and more to describe the separation between a holy and righteous God and his sinful creation. The remainder of the rhetorical distinctions befitting such a dialogue is now between God and the world — both Jew and gentile — as Jesus announces the mode by which God and humanity must relate. Surprisingly, Jesus has taken a rhetorical challenge, the form of dialogue with the least assumptions of engagement or agreement, and is turning it into an invitation — a witness, all the while maintaining the distinctions that exist between God and the world.

4:21 Jesus said to her, "Believe me, woman, because the hour is coming when you will worship the Father neither on this mountain nor in Jerusalem" (λέγει αὐτῇ ὁ Ἰησοῦς, Πίστευέ μοι, γύναι, ὅτι ἔρχεται ὥρα ὅτε οὔτε ἐν τῷ ὄρει τούτῳ οὔτε ἐν Ἱεροσολύμοις προσκυνήσετε τῷ πατρί). The response Jesus gives to the Samaritan woman's statement in v. 20 is shocking. Jesus proclaims a worship that is not defined by Samaritans *or* Jews. By addressing her as "woman" (γύναι), Jesus is not speaking derogatorily to her but, just as he spoke to his mother, is using it respectfully and possibly affectionately even if with a sense of distancing (see comments on 2:4). What he is about to offer her suggests she is the recipient of his affection.

Jesus tells the woman to "believe" (πίστευέ) him, which is without parallel in John and is often taken as an asseverative, an idiom expressing solemnly the truth of what one is about to say (i.e., "I tell you the truth"). But this need not exclude the overtones of the imperative. Similar to when Jesus

says "truly, truly," much more is implied (see comments on 1:51). This is at least an implicit command to believe (similar to the polite command of a superior in 4:7), which at the cosmological level has much more force. The command to believe is hardly language for volunteers. When God speaks with an imperative, a looser sense is grammatically possible but theologically improbable. While she may choose not to believe, such a decision will have consequences. Such consequences give an "unseen" force to the command that the reader is able to feel. Jesus is not just asking for a generic belief but a belief nuanced by the dative pronoun "in me" (μοι). Ironically, she is not merely being exhorted to believe him, that is, believe what he says to her, but to believe "in him" that *he* is the thing about which he speaks. In light of this, it is not surprising that Jesus again mentions the "hour" (ὥρα), which serves in the Gospel as a technical term to refer to the death of Jesus on the cross (see comments on 2:4).

It is important to note that although Jesus addresses her individually, the people about whom he speaks are plural: "you (all) will worship" (προσκυνήσετε). It is ironic that as the Samaritan stood beside the well — located neither in Jerusalem nor on Mt. Gerizim — she had never been closer to the place where God is worshipped. For she was standing before the true temple of God and the true revelation of the Father (cf. 1:18; 2:21).

4:22 "You worship what you do not know; we worship what we know, for salvation is from the Jews" (ὑμεῖς προσκυνεῖτε ὃ οὐκ οἴδατε· ἡμεῖς προσκυνοῦμεν ὃ οἴδαμεν, ὅτι ἡ σωτηρία ἐκ τῶν Ἰουδαίων ἐστίν). Focusing more directly on the topic of worship, Jesus gives definition to the nature and origin of true worship. The grammar of the verse is significant. The use of plural pronouns by Jesus in v. 21 continues here, with the "you" (ὑμεῖς) and "we" (ἡμεῖς) functioning emphatically, setting Samaritans and Jews in sharp contrast. Of note is that Jesus applies a neuter relative pronoun not only to the Samaritans but also to the Jews and "what" (ὅ) they worship, for even though the Jews "know" (οἴδαμεν) "what" they worship, they do not know "who" he is, for they do not yet have knowledge of the Father through the Son (1:18).

There is one important distinction Jesus makes: "Salvation is from the Jews" (ἡ σωτηρία ἐκ τῶν Ἰουδαίων ἐστίν). The word "salvation" (σωτηρία) occurs nowhere else in John and provides an ironic twist to the scene: salvation is "from" the Jews and yet it has gone "to" no other people. The centuries-old conflict between the Jews and the Samaritans shows the Jews to be acting without any concern for the salvation of the world. They have embraced the "I will bless you" declared to Abraham and have forgotten that in response they were to "be a blessing" to others (Gen 12:2 – 3). This is why it is significant that salvation is "from" (ἐκ) the Jews and not "in" or "by" them. The rhetorical challenge is providing helpful insights, revealing how Jesus is supporting the distinctions between the two parties and simultaneously breaking the traditional mold by showing that both parties are ultimately inadequate. As much as Jesus must embrace his Jewishness, for salvation is from the Jews, he is also correcting what it means to be Jewish. He is the true Jew, through whom all people on earth will be blessed (Gen 12:3). Jesus is the "blessing" given to the Jews, and it is through the Jewish Jesus that the rest of the world is blessed (see comments on v. 42).

4:23 "But an hour is coming and now is when the true worshippers will worship the Father in Spirit and truth, for this is the kind of worshippers the Father seeks" (ἀλλὰ ἔρχεται ὥρα, καὶ νῦν ἐστιν, ὅτε οἱ ἀληθινοὶ προσκυνηταὶ προσκυνήσουσιν τῷ πατρὶ ἐν πνεύματι καὶ ἀληθείᾳ· καὶ γὰρ ὁ πατὴρ τοιούτους ζητεῖ τοὺς προσκυνοῦντας αὐτόν). By restating the connection of worship to the "hour" (ὥρα), Jesus is making the cross the central component of worship. That the "hour" is simultaneously "coming" (ἔρχεται) and "now is" (νῦν ἐστιν), though an oxymoron, reflects the paradoxical intrusion of the cosmological into the historical first introduced in the prologue. It is not merely a rhetorical device; it is detailing the overlap between God's time (beyond time) and humanity's time (linear time). In the same way, the man who is speaking this is not only standing with this Samaritan woman but has always been with God (1:1).

The cross is central to worship because it fosters "true worshippers" (οἱ ἀληθινοὶ προσκυνηταὶ). In the eyes of God, it is neither Jew nor Samaritan (i.e., gentile); the designation of choice is "true worshipper," which is nothing less than a new race. True worshippers must be "children of God" (1:12), and when God's children speak of "Father" they do not think of their natural ancestry but of their cosmological ancestry rooted in their heavenly Father. Everything other than this "true worship" was either proleptic or pagan.[32] True worshippers "will worship the Father" (προσκυνήσουσιν τῷ πατρὶ). McHugh creatively describes the dative here as a "liturgical dative."[33] Those the Father loved (3:16) will respond by worshipping him. And just as Jesus mediated the love of the Father to the world, so also does Jesus mediate true worship to the Father. This presents a stark contrast with the neuter "what" (ὅ) worshipped by both Samaritans and Jews in v. 22. It is not a "what," not even "God," but the Father who is to be worshipped. Worship is only "true" when it is correctly directed at the Father. And the more the Father is made central, the more Jesus becomes central. Such are the unifying distinctions of the Trinitarian God.

It is not merely worship that makes central the

---

32. Cf. Calvin, *John 1 – 10*, 100.

33. McHugh, *John 1 – 4*, 315. Cf. Wallace, *Greek Grammar*, 171 – 73.

Father by the Son, for such worship must be done "in Spirit and truth" (ἐν πνεύματι καὶ ἀληθείᾳ). This phrase has been given a lot of attention. The preposition "in" (ἐν) governs both nouns; they are not two separate characteristics of appropriate worship. The conjunction "and" (καὶ) is not functioning epexegetically (i.e., "that is") but is simply a connective conjunction. Thus, the two nouns must be taken together to make sense of the phrase.

Several interpreters argue that "Spirit" (πνεύματι) refers to the spirit of a person (i.e., the human spirit), so that the contrast is between the right place of worship and the right attitude, "in their inner self, with their mind, their feelings, and their will engaged in activity."[34] But the Spirit, drenching the pages of the Fourth Gospel and already made central to the renewal about which Jesus speaks, is the Spirit of God. The Spirit will shortly be described as the "Spirit of truth" (14:17; 15:26; 16:13). Even more, "it would be foolish to ask what the Spirit contributes to worship as distinct from what truth contributes."[35] Spirit and truth describe the manner in which one receives the "gift of God" and drinks the "living water" Jesus provides (v. 10). The Christian life, therefore, is Trinitarian by nature: "True worship is paternal in focus (the Father), personal in origin (the Son), and pneumatic in character (the Spirit)."[36]

After all this focus on the manner in which the Christian accesses God, v. 23 ends with the shocking declaration that it is actually the Father who "seeks" (ζητεῖ) such worshippers. The verb carries more the sense of "demands" or "asks for," though the idea of "seeking" or "searching" is to be maintained as well and is used in this primary sense elsewhere in John (cf. 18:4).[37] This statement echoes the purpose of the Gospel (20:30 – 31).[38]

4:24 "God is Spirit, and his worshippers must worship in Spirit and truth" (πνεῦμα ὁ θεός, καὶ τοὺς προσκυνοῦντας αὐτὸν ἐν πνεύματι καὶ ἀληθείᾳ δεῖ προσκυνεῖν). Worship is done in "Spirit and truth" because God's essential nature is Spirit. This not only explains the manner in which God must be worshipped but also explains the contrast with place. True worship must be spiritual in nature; the only temple allowed is the body of Jesus. In a real way, everything that God does is befitting his nature. In view of what has already been described as coming from God, the declaration that God is Spirit alludes to the life-giving activity of God. This necessarily restricts worship to the nature and character of God, yet it also expands worship, for it posits God as the true source and "fountain" of such worship (cf. v. 14). For this reason, this kind of worship is not an option but a necessity, denoted by "must" (δεῖ). In vv. 21 – 24, the verb "worship" (προσκυνεῖν) is spoken seven times by Jesus — a significant number.

4:25 The woman said to him, "I know that Messiah is coming (called Christ). When he comes, he will proclaim everything to us" (λέγει αὐτῷ ἡ γυνή, Οἶδα ὅτι Μεσσίας ἔρχεται, ὁ λεγόμενος Χριστός· ὅταν ἔλθῃ ἐκεῖνος, ἀναγγελεῖ ἡμῖν ἅπαντα). From the Samaritan woman's perspective, Jesus is speaking with messianic allusions and connotations. It has frequently been suggested that the woman's use of the term "Messiah" (Μεσσίας) is a reference to the *Taheb*, the restorer of Deuteronomy 18:18, the Samaritan equivalent to the Jewish messiah. But there is no clear evidence for this reconstruction. The narrator's explanatory addition of "called Christ" (ὁ λεγόμενος Χριστός) reflects the varied terms used for this identity; the variations in

---

34. McHugh, *John 1 – 4*, 121.

35. Brown, *John*, 1:180. "Spirit and truth" is probably a hendiadys, a single complex idea expressed by two words, similar to "grace and truth" in 1:17.

36. Mark W. G. Stibbe, *John*, Readings: A New Biblical Commentary (Sheffield: JSOT Press, 1993), 64.

37. Schnackenburg, *John*, 1:439; cf. BDAG 428.

38. Barrett, *John*, 238.

definition were even more extensive. At most we can be certain that both Jews and Samaritans had messianic conceptions, with several important differences between them.[39] Jesus's statements about a coming "hour" and his matching the expectation of a teacher may have guided her insight. She likely had no concern beyond this vague information because this messiah would "proclaim" (ἀναγγελεῖ) everything, that is, "explain" what is to come. The scene is drenched with irony: a Samaritan woman is explaining messianic expectations to the Messiah.

4:26 Jesus said to her, "I am (he), the one speaking to you" (λέγει αὐτῇ ὁ Ἰησοῦς, Ἐγώ εἰμι, ὁ λαλῶν σοι). Jesus's statement is emphatic and strongly impressionistic. With the careful choice of words, "I am he" (Ἐγώ εἰμι), which adds an emphatic "I" and has no "he" in the Greek ("I, I am"), Jesus speaks in the style of the God of the OT (on informal "I am" statements, see comments on 8:58).[40] The self-revelation God gave to Moses through a bush in Exodus 3 has now been spoken to a Samaritan woman through the incarnate God. Jesus's response is both a correction and a revelation. So much of what the Samaritan woman believed was wrong or incomplete. She had been waiting for a "what" (v. 22), yet all the while *the* "who" was standing before her. His revelation is his correction, for there is no need to adjust her messianic theology. He only needs to announce his presence. The irony of v. 25 has been traded for a new irony: the Jewish Messiah announces his presence in Samaria to a Samaritan woman in the middle of a rhetorical challenge. It is equivalent to the birth of the King of kings in a stable! This verse ends the rhetorical challenge proper. The rest of the pericope draws the encounter to a close by providing the necessary resolution and interpretation to the scene.

4:27 Just then his disciples came and were surprised that he was speaking with a woman. But no one said, "What do you seek?" or "Why are you speaking with her?" (Καὶ ἐπὶ τούτῳ ἦλθαν οἱ μαθηταὶ αὐτοῦ, καὶ ἐθαύμαζον ὅτι μετὰ γυναικὸς ἐλάλει· οὐδεὶς μέντοι εἶπεν, Τί ζητεῖς; ἤ, Τί λαλεῖς μετ᾽ αὐτῆς;). The dialogue scene changes upon the return of the disciples from their trip to purchase food (cf. v. 8). The narrator describes them arriving "just then" (ἐπὶ τούτῳ), a phrase which functions temporally to explain that they arrived immediately following the concluding revelation of Jesus.[41] The disciples "were surprised" (ἐθαύμαζον), with the imperfect tense suggesting that their surprise was more than momentary. They were shocked to see him "speaking with a woman" (μετὰ γυναικὸς ἐλάλει). It is often suggested that it was considered undesirable for a rabbi to speak with a woman (m. ʾAbot 1:5), and certainly the fact that she was a Samaritan only caused more surprise.

The narrator informs us of the two unspoken questions that surfaced from their surprise. To the woman they wanted to ask: "What do you seek?" (Τί ζητεῖς;); to their teacher they wanted to ask: "Why are you speaking with her?" (Τί λαλεῖς μετ᾽ αὐτῆς;). Even though the disciples are unaware of the issues raised by the dialogue, their questions serve to make more resolute the dialogue's message. The verb "seek" (ζητεῖς) is significant, for it was the same verb used to describe the action of God in v. 23. The reader has been guided to see that while the woman did not know what she was seeking, God was seeking her.

---

39. See Keener, *John*, 1:619–20.

40. See the connection between this statement and the motif of hospitality in Arterbury, "Breaking the Betrothal Bonds," 81–82.

41. Cf. BDF § 235.5.

4:28 Then the woman left her water jar and went into the city and said to the people (ἀφῆκεν οὖν τὴν ὑδρίαν αὐτῆς ἡ γυνὴ καὶ ἀπῆλθεν εἰς τὴν πόλιν καὶ λέγει τοῖς ἀνθρώποις). The narrator returns to the Samaritan woman and her response to the correction and revelation of Jesus. She is described as leaving her water jar and returning to her city to share her news with the people. The imagery is potent. The narrative's focus on the abandoned water jar reflects the abandonment of Samaritan water for a wholly different kind of water (v. 14). For just feet away from Jacob's well, she had been introduced to a wholly other drinking source. It is also important to note that the narrator includes the disciples of Jesus in the aftereffects of the dialogue (v. 27) before giving the final response of the Samaritan woman (v. 28). The narrator probably intends to make clear that all people, not just the Samaritans, are in need of what the Samaritan woman had just received.

4:29 "Come, see a man who told me everything that I did. This is not the Christ, is it?" (Δεῦτε ἴδετε ἄνθρωπον ὃς εἶπέν μοι πάντα ὅσα ἐποίησα· μήτι οὗτός ἐστιν ὁ Χριστός;). The Samaritan woman does not merely show the effect Jesus had on her; she also proclaims it. In a sense, she has become like the earliest followers of Jesus, using nearly identical language: "Come, see" (cf. 1:39, 46). The woman invites them to meet "a man" (ἄνθρωπον) who "told me everything that I did" (εἶπέν μοι πάντα ὅσα ἐποίησα). This "pardonable exaggeration" describes how deep and personal was her encounter with Jesus.[42] She speaks not as a theologian — she never really did have good theology; rather, she speaks as a witness to someone whom she did not understand but who had under-stood her. It is important to note that the Samaritan woman concludes with a question that, with this particular negative particle "not" (μήτι), expects a negative answer or at least communicates serious hesitation.[43] The effect is not necessarily to challenge the possibility that he is the Messiah but to introduce a possibility not considered before.[44] In a way, the Samaritan woman left the rhetorical challenge with Jesus and entered an entirely different rhetorical challenge, one involving the possibility of a Jewish Messiah for the Samaritans. Having watched Jesus broach a sensitive topic, the Samaritan woman carefully poses an exhortative rhetorical question to her own people.[45] This was no ploy, however, but the question everyone needed to answer for themselves.

4:30 They came out of the town and came toward him (ἐξῆλθον ἐκ τῆς πόλεως καὶ ἤρχοντο πρὸς αὐτόν). The effect of the Samaritan woman's witness was positive. In just two verses, she enters the town, and the townspeople come out of it. The Samaritan woman had become a witness and proves that it is not the quality of the witness that ultimately matters but the object of the witness.

4:31 In the meantime his disciples urged him saying, "Rabbi, eat" (Ἐν τῷ μεταξὺ ἠρώτων αὐτὸν οἱ μαθηταὶ λέγοντες, Ῥαββί, φάγε). The scene changes from the effects of Jesus on the Samaritan woman and her village to the disciples, who in their faithful search for food have missed the provision Jesus already provided. The uncommon phrase "in the meantime" (ἐν τῷ μεταξὺ) makes explicit the direct overlap between the two scenes the narrative is moving between. The scene involving vv. 27 – 38 serves as an interlude that propels forward the central theme of the dialogue. The contrast is filled

---

42. Morris, *John*, 241.

43. According to BDF § 427.2, the negative particle expresses the sense as "that must be the Messiah at last, perhaps this is the Messiah."

44. Michaels, *John*, 259.

45. Bultmann, *John*, 193, suggests the woman formulated the question from the point of view of the townspeople.

with irony and bears witness to the inability of all (Samaritans and Jews alike) to view Jesus and his provision through their own lenses (cf. 1:5). The Samaritan woman saw a "prophet"; the disciples saw a "rabbi" (Ῥαββί).

4:32 But he said to them, "I have food to eat that you know nothing about" (ὁ δὲ εἶπεν αὐτοῖς, Ἐγὼ βρῶσιν ἔχω φαγεῖν ἣν ὑμεῖς οὐκ οἴδατε). The ignorance exhibited by the disciples in v. 31 is now directly addressed by Jesus. They both speak of food but mean something very different. The whole expression "I have food to eat" (Ἐγὼ βρῶσιν ἔχω φαγεῖν) is a metaphor that depicts the sustenance and nourishment he owns and provides in his very person as the source of "living water" and as "the bread of life" (6:35). Without ever denying that even the Word-become-flesh needs food, Jesus shows the symptoms of one who finds their sustenance in God.

4:33 Then the disciples were saying to one another, "Could someone have brought him something to eat?" (ἔλεγον οὖν οἱ μαθηταὶ πρὸς ἀλλήλους, Μή τις ἤνεγκεν αὐτῷ φαγεῖν;). The disciples are completely confused. They have missed the dialogue with the Samaritan woman and have been "in the meantime" in search of food (v. 31). When Jesus speaks of having food already he confuses his disciples, and rightly so. We do not want to be too dismissive of the disciples at this point. The Samaritan woman showed the same confusion. In the context of a well, Jesus spoke about water; in the context of a search for food, Jesus speaks about already having food. Jesus uses real food to speak about something more real, for he is speaking in "parabolic language" in order to move the minds of his disciples beyond themselves (and their stomachs) to the unseen.[46]

4:34 Jesus said to them, "My food is to do the will of the one who sent me and to finish his work" (λέγει αὐτοῖς ὁ Ἰησοῦς, Ἐμὸν βρῶμά ἐστιν ἵνα ποιήσω τὸ θέλημα τοῦ πέμψαντός με καὶ τελειώσω αὐτοῦ τὸ ἔργον). If the disciples had misunderstood Jesus before, this statement only made things more complicated. Jesus is not merely thinking about some sort of spiritual food — water from rocks and manna — but about something much greater, much more cosmic. Even the different term used here for "food" (βρῶμά), in comparison with "food" (βρῶσιν) in v. 32, is often used to denote a special connotation of nourishment, something more than the mere physical substance, though the differences are best nuanced by the larger context.[47] This verse only makes sense when we remember that the prologue taught the reader to see the unseen and to look beyond the historical to the cosmological. Without denying the necessity of food, Jesus is using properly basic nourishment to convey something even more basic and nourishing.

It is important to note that Jesus aligns his needs with "the one who sent me" (τοῦ πέμψαντός με). Jesus is so exclusively defined by the Father and his "sending" that even food is made subsidiary. That is why Jesus claims to do another's "will" (θέλημα) and "work" (ἔργον), terms used exclusively in the Fourth Gospel for the Father's work of salvation. It is never the work of Jesus or his disciples; it is always the work of the Father (cf. 17:4). Jesus is so dependent on the Father that the Father's will and work is food to him, and he is actually hungry for it, actually craving its accomplishment (cf. Deut 8:3). Jesus's "life" was sustained ultimately by God.

4:35 "Do you not say that there are still four months and then the harvest comes? Behold, I say to you, lift up your eyes and look at the fields that are already white for the harvest" (οὐχ ὑμεῖς

46. Hoskyns, *Fourth Gospel*, 246.

47. BDAG 184, gives the meaning, "Nourishment of a transcendent nature."

λέγετε ὅτι Ἔτι τετράμηνός ἐστιν καὶ ὁ θερισμὸς ἔρχεται; ἰδοὺ λέγω ὑμῖν, ἐπάρατε τοὺς ὀφθαλμοὺς ὑμῶν καὶ θεάσασθε τὰς χώρας ὅτι λευκαί εἰσιν πρὸς θερισμόν ἤδη). Jesus turns from his unique food (as the unique Son) and speaks now to the rest of the Father's children about their food: the will and work of God. By describing the fields as "white" (λευκαί) for the harvest, Jesus is describing them as ready to be harvested. There should be no delay. The two-imperative phrase, "Lift up your eyes and look" (ἐπάρατε τοὺς ὀφθαλμοὺς ὑμῶν καὶ θεάσασθε), and a third if we include "behold" (ἰδοὺ), are exhorting a certain kind of vision, the same kind that is hungry, but not for bread alone, or thirsty, but unsatisfied without "living water." Jesus is now speaking directly about what the prologue depicted as the "unseen." What they cannot see is that Jesus can already now "see" a horde of Samaritans coming down the road toward him.[48] They are Samaritans satisfied from their recent meal at midday (cf. v. 6), yet still hungry. It is another exhortation to "come and see" (cf. 1:46). They have come but have not yet seen.

4:36 "The harvester is receiving payment and gathering crop for eternal life, so that the sower might rejoice together with the harvester" (ὁ θερίζων μισθὸν λαμβάνει καὶ συνάγει καρπὸν εἰς ζωὴν αἰώνιον, ἵνα ὁ σπείρων ὁμοῦ χαίρη καὶ ὁ θερίζων). This type of sowing and harvesting is unique not only in the lack of delay but also in regard to unity: the sower does not get replaced by the harvester but cooperates in unity (cf. Deut 28:33; Judg 6:3; Mic 6:15). Interpreters debate the identity of the "sower" and the "harvester," but Jesus is not only silent on the issue but locates them in such a unified fashion that the differences coalesce into one grand "work."[49] This grand work was promised through the prophet Amos:

"The days are coming … when the reaper will be overtaken by the plowman and the planter by the one treading grapes" (9:13). This reality, depicted by a crop so rich that the work of the sower and harvester overlaps, is portrayed by John as the "already" present eschatological harvest. The result of this harvest — the food it produces — is "for eternal life" (εἰς ζωὴν αἰώνιον). What is harvested are people (e.g., Samaritans) for whom eternal life is given. God hungers and thirsts for the world he loves (3:16).

4:37 "For in this the saying is true that one is the sower and the other is the harvester" (ἐν γὰρ τούτῳ ὁ λόγος ἐστὶν ἀληθινὸς ὅτι Ἄλλος ἐστὶν ὁ σπείρων καὶ ἄλλος ὁ θερίζων). Jesus now applies his statements above more directly to the disciples, again with what appears like another proverbial statement. Although the eschatological harvest is at hand and has unified the crop from beginning to end, it should not remove all distinctions so that those who harvest have forgotten their role and their purpose. Even if they are after the same result, sowing and harvesting are different tasks.

4:38 "I sent you to harvest that for which you have not labored. Others have labored, and you have entered into their labor" (ἐγὼ ἀπέστειλα ὑμᾶς θερίζειν ὃ οὐχ ὑμεῖς κεκοπιάκατε· ἄλλοι κεκοπιάκασιν, καὶ ὑμεῖς εἰς τὸν κόπον αὐτῶν εἰσεληλύθατε). With v. 37 in mind, Jesus presses upon his disciples their unique entrance into this grand "work." With emphasis Jesus declares, "I sent you" (ἐγὼ ἀπέστειλα ὑμᾶς), placing the disciples into their position by means of the "will" and purpose of God. It is a position that is simultaneously honorific and humbling in the magnitude of "labor" that has been done by "others." As much as the referent of "others [who] have labored" is

---

48. Cf. Brown, *John*, 1:182; McHugh, *John 1 – 4*, 292.

49. Cf. Moloney, *John*, 144; Schnackenburg, *John*, 1:451; McHugh, *John 1 – 4*, 293.

cryptic and tempting, the point is not to survey salvation history in all its specifics but to press upon the disciples their role and identity. Whatever the specifics, the disciples "have entered into" (εἰσεληλύθατε) their labor, a verb which allows for their distinctive role all the while portraying their work as part of the unified eschatological work of God.[50]

Jesus is not intentionally speaking past his disciples, even if we note misunderstanding and irony in the foreground and allusions to larger theological themes in the background. He is revealing the Father (1:18), especially his "will" and "work." He is also revealing the gospel and is including them as recipients of its nourishing food and its joyous harvest. While the disciples were plodding through a Samaritan village looking for food to feed their "rabbi," he was already offering food from the eschatological harvest of God to a Samaritan woman. The disciples had gone to a Samaritan village to buy food, when instead they should have gone there to provide it — not their own provision, of course, but the harvesting of what had already been sown. The narrator has carefully crafted this teaching in the center of the actual "harvesting" of the Samaritan woman by Jesus, allowing the disciples — and the reader — to "see" what a harvest looks like (v. 35).

4:39 And from that city many of the Samaritans believed in him because of the word of the woman who testified, "He told me everything that I did" (Ἐκ δὲ τῆς πόλεως ἐκείνης πολλοὶ ἐπίστευσαν εἰς αὐτὸν τῶν Σαμαριτῶν διὰ τὸν λόγον τῆς γυναικὸς μαρτυρούσης ὅτι Εἶπέν μοι πάντα ὅσα ἐποίησα). The narrative's return to the Samaritans directly after the didactic interlude between Jesus and his disciples not only brings the Samaritan woman pericope to a dramatic close but also serves to explain in material terms what the interlude had

spoken of in abstraction. With the verb "believed" (ἐπίστευσαν) and the preposition "in" (εἰς), the idea communicated is that they "put their faith in" him. The preposition "because of" (διὰ) is functioning causally so that the "word" of the woman facilitated their belief. Ultimately, however, the "word" of the Samaritan woman is subservient to the "word" of Jesus (see v. 41). Although "the word" (τὸν λόγον) could be translated more softly as "the message," it is hard not to see the use of this particular term in light of the prologue, making emphatic that the message of the woman was entirely centered on the definitive Word — Jesus Christ. The message of the woman is identical to what she was recorded as saying earlier (see comments on v. 29). What is important is that the narrative prefaces her statement with the important term "testified" (μαρτυρούσης). This is an important term in the Fourth Gospel (see comments on 1:7) and serves to portray the task of the Christian disciple.

4:40 When the Samaritans came to him, they were asking him to remain with them, and he remained there two days (ὡς οὖν ἦλθον πρὸς αὐτὸν οἱ Σαμαρῖται, ἠρώτων αὐτὸν μεῖναι παρ' αὐτοῖς· καὶ ἔμεινεν ἐκεῖ δύο ἡμέρας). The witness of the Samaritan woman turned into a host of Samaritan "followers." The estrangement between Jew and Samaritan has entirely dissolved into the request of students to a teacher; their actions suggest they were coming to become his disciples, which is why they want him to remain with them (cf. 1:37 – 39). The rhetorical challenge has been reversed. Rather than a long-established opposition in which conflict is merely to reestablish socially antithetical positions, the reverse has taken place. The two sides have centered upon Jesus, in whom they find a unity.

While the actions of the Samaritans showed

true hospitality, the actions of Jesus reflected those of a true prophet (cf. the expectations between a host and a visiting prophet in Did. 11:4 – 5; cf. John 12:2). Jesus was a prophet in word and deed (cf. v. 19). In the gracious providence of God, Jesus displayed for the Samaritans the prophet God had promised them. The hospitality of the Samaritans to Jesus is simply (if unknowingly) a response to the gracious hospitality of the Word-become-flesh who "came to what belongs to him" (1:11).

4:41 And many more believed because of his word (καὶ πολλῷ πλείους ἐπίστευσαν διὰ τὸν λόγον αὐτοῦ). The narrative explains that at the gathering between Jesus and the Samaritans who came to him, "many more" (πολλῷ πλείους) put their faith in him. In a similar manner to the woman, the many believed "because of his word" (διὰ τὸν λόγον αὐτοῦ). While the message — the "word" — was the same in that it was centered upon Jesus, from Jesus it was a first-person message, an autobiographical statement. The witness of the Samaritan woman was always secondary to the witness of the Word himself, who is the first-order witness to the Father (1:18).

4:42 And they were saying to the woman, "We no longer believe because of your message, for we have heard and we know that this man is truly the Savior of the world" (τῇ τε γυναικὶ ἔλεγον ὅτι Οὐκέτι διὰ τὴν σὴν λαλιὰν πιστεύομεν· αὐτοὶ γὰρ ἀκηκόαμεν, καὶ οἴδαμεν ὅτι οὗτός ἐστιν ἀληθῶς ὁ σωτὴρ τοῦ κόσμου). Even the Samaritans detect the mediated nature of the woman's "message" (λαλιὰν) and acknowledge that her word has been eclipsed by the true Word. The term "message" (λαλιὰν) is distinct from "word" (λόγος) and means something much less sublime — characteristic "talk" in general or even "chatter" in classical Greek.[51] Such a state-

ment, then, not only reveals the first-order status of Jesus's message — she spoke, but he proclaimed the word — but also the success of the woman's message. A successful witness works so that they become entirely secondary, even unnecessary, in the presence of God, the object of their witness. This is not, however, to eliminate the necessity of the second-order witness. Indeed, the woman's word brought the Samaritans to the word of Jesus, so that faith is ultimately "because of his word" (v. 41).[52] This is what the Samaritans confess. They declare with two perfect tense verbs to "have heard" (ἀκηκόαμεν) and "know" (οἴδαμεν) who Jesus is. A mediatory witness at this point would be both unnecessary and cumbersome. With a term that echoes the confidence of the prologue, the Samaritans declare that "this [man]" (οὗτός) is the Savior (cf. 1:2).

The witness of the Samaritan woman and self-attesting witness of Jesus is that he is "the Savior of the world" (ὁ σωτὴρ τοῦ κόσμου). The qualification that he "truly is" (ἐστιν ἀληθῶς) not only confirms the reliability of the object of their faith but also serves as the beginning of their own confession, their own witness. The phrase "Savior of the world" has been analyzed by interpreters from the perspective of the Samaritans — what they believed based upon their context and theology.[53] Like the declaration of John the Baptist regarding the "Lamb of God" (see comments on 1:29), the title means much more than the Samaritans could have imagined. The term cannot be defined by the *Taheb* (cf. v. 25) and the context of the Samaritans but must be defined by Jesus and the context of his mission from the Father. If anything, this pericope has declared that Jesus is more than the *Taheb*. Yet something quite shocking has also been revealed, especially as it relates to the Jews. In a very real

51. BDAG 583.
52. See Bultmann, *John*, 201.

53. See Craig R. Koester, "'The Savior of the World' (John 4:42)," *JBL* 109 (1990): 665 – 80.

sense, Jesus is even more than the Jewish Messiah. Even in the OT, where God is sometimes described as "Savior," it is usually applied to his saving work for his own people. The grand scope of the mission of God and of his harvest demands that Jesus be known with the comprehensive title, "Savior of the world." And thus the pericope ends, with the Jewish Messiah receiving hospitality from a host of Samaritans who sit at his feet in the region of Samaria.[54]

Theology in Application

If Jesus sparked controversy among the Jews, one could only have imagined the reaction to him by the Samaritans. But what required the most imagination had little to do with the Samaritans and everything to do with God. The seeking God, the Savior of the world, was pursuing true worshippers, for he is worthy of true worship and he had enacted a plan for true worship through his Son. Jesus's tension-filled dialogue with the Samaritan woman showed that the conflict between the Jews and Samaritans was only symptomatic of the deeper conflict between God and the world he had made. Yet in the providence of God, the "whole grace of renewal" [55] had arrived in the person and work of Jesus, because of whom all hunger may be satiated and all thirst quenched. For this reason, the reader of the Fourth Gospel is exhorted not only to eat and drink but also alongside Jesus to announce to the world the meal he alone can offer and the God who alone can provide it. It is harvest time!

"If You Knew the Gift of God ..."

In his dialogue with the Samaritan woman, Jesus quickly made clear that she did not "know" what she thought she knew. Alongside her were the disciples, Jesus's intimate followers, who were equally naive to who Jesus was and to what he was doing. Jesus transcended the context and "messianic" theology of the Samaritans and demanded they "come and see" the true God. Jesus also transcended the Jewish context and messianic theology of his disciples and demanded they "look" at the harvest fields. Like the Samaritan woman, the reader is being exhorted to hear the voice of the Word and consider the nature of his or her "messianic" assumptions. Am I worshipping a "what" or a "who" (v. 22), a god of my own making or "the God of Abraham, the God of Isaac and the God of Jacob," that is, Jesus Christ (Exod 3:6)? And like the disciples, the reader is exhorted to hear the call to embrace the mission of God, to see the ripe fields and to participate in the harvest of God. The Christian is aware that what they once thought about God and about themselves was biased, self-benefitting, and wrong and is reminded to make God and his written Word the rule and guide for self-reflection and the call to duty (mission).

---

54. Hendrikus Boers, *Neither on This Mountain nor in Jerusalem: A Study of John 4*, SBLMS 35 (Atlanta: Scholars Press, 1988), 199. Cf. Lesslie Newbigin, *The Light Has Come: An Exposition of the Fourth Gospel* (Grand Rapids: Eerdmans, 1982), 56.

55. Calvin, *John 1 – 10*, 92.

The Hospitable God

The Samaritan woman showed a surprising sensitivity to the enemy of her people and her gender. Although not without cutting rejoinders, through her reactions of surprise at his less-than-attacking conversation with her, the narrative portrayed her as one more trained to receive rebuke than to give it. In the region surrounding this well, Jesus was the guest and she was the host. Yet from the start, he was serving as the host and she the guest. Even at the end of the pericope, when Jesus remained with his new Samaritan followers, although he stayed in their homes and ate their food, it was he who was giving them the truly satisfying meal to eat and water to drink. He had replaced their local well with the well of eternal life.

The Christian, then, no matter the region in which he lives, is living under the hospitality of the God of Jacob's well. Such a picture makes the local expression of the body of Christ, the local church, a true home, an embassy in a foreign or familiar land. Patriotic songs are sung not to honor the fathers of our land but "our Father." And differences of skin color, accents, ethnicities, economic and social classes, education, and gender are not erased but embraced under the umbrella of the hospitable God. Moreover, the Christian extends the hospitality of God to the world around them, drinking water with foreigners from local taps that cannot ultimately satisfy and showing those people the true water of the hospitable God.

Whom the Father Seeks

The Samaritan woman was introduced to the God who "seeks," a term that describes the two sides of God. He is a God that demands a certain kind of worshipper and a certain kind of worship and will not stand for anything below his standard. He is God, we are not; this must be the foundation of our relationship with God. He can and must be sought as he is, not as we want him to be. He must be "sought" as the Father, through Jesus Christ, and in the power of the Holy Spirit. Yet in his mercy and love, he does not just allow himself to be sought; God seeks us. He sent his Son to find us — to drink our water and to eat our food — so that he can be found by us and give to us his water and his food. The Christian knows that it is not only true that "we love because he first loved us" (1 John 4:19); it is also true that we sought him because he first sought us.

The "Jewish Messiah" is the Savior of the World

When the Samaritans heard "Jewish Messiah," they became defensive, thinking only of themselves. When the Jews heard "Jewish Messiah," they became offensive, thinking only of themselves. According to this pericope, when God speaks about the "Jewish Messiah," he is thinking about the whole world. The term is a rebuke not only to those who are not Jewish but also to those who are. It is a term that announces that God loves the whole world, and has sent his son to save it. "Jewish Messiah" is in many ways a summarizing title of the entire Gospel, designating from where the world's rescuer would arise (Israel) and his mission (he would save the world from their sins). The church, even the most gentile local expression, worships the Jewish Messiah — not because they are or must become Jewish but because they are part of the world over which the Jewish Messiah is declared "Savior."

True Worship

Christian worship is done in no other temple than the temple of the body of Jesus Christ. It is done through the crucified and resurrected body of Jesus Christ. A church's worship hour is eternally connected to the "hour" of Christ. True worship is Christ centered and cross centered, since the cross creates the appropriate worshippers — a new race of worshippers that are neither Jew nor Samaritan. True worship is ultimately Trinitarian in that it is directed to the Father, mediated through the Son, and empowered and directed by the Holy Spirit. It is the true worship of a "whom" (not a "what"), through a "whom," and by a "whom." This is worship "in Spirit and truth": paternal in focus (Father), personal in origin (Son), and pneumatic in character (Spirit).[56]

Such worship, however, is not merely spiritual and therefore disembodied. In sharp contrast, worship done through the body of Christ is only rightly done in the body of Christ, a fitting expression of the local church. The local church does not replace a mountain or a city but is the place of a living expression of worship "in Spirit and truth." It is the real body of Christ, the place of the real presence of the Holy Spirit, and the real worshippers the Father seeks. Jesus is not calling us to worship in abstraction, but to worship in "Spirit" and in "truth" in the local church.[57]

The Mission of the Church

The church, like the Jewish disciples of Jesus, can too easily concoct an "ecclesial Messiah" and forget that he came for the entire world! To the church our Lord proclaims, "*Behold*, I say to you, lift up your *eyes* and *look* at the fields that are already white for the harvest" (v. 35). We are too easily concerned with feeding ourselves and forget the harvest that is ripe for picking. At the same time that Jesus exhorts them to work the harvest, however, he reminds them that they are not the only or even primary harvesters. Like a farmer at the time of harvest who feels excitement for the task and a humility in regard to the result, so also a Christian ought to be bent toward serving in the mission of God but simultaneously humbled by the opportunity and by the results of the labor which are in no way their own.

---

56. Cf. Stibbe, *John*, 64.
57. Helpful here is Jim Samra, *The Gift of Church: How God* Designed the Local Church to Meet Our Needs as Christians (Grand Rapids: Zondervan, 2010).

O church, lift up your eyes and look at the fields! Hear the call of God and bring true water to the thirsty and true food to the hungry — bring Jesus to the world. May we embrace the mission of our seeking God and seek the lost, not only around the globe but even around the corner. Lord, let us be conduits of your hospitality for the world, a hospitality that offers no greater security, peace, and comfort than Jesus Christ, your Son.

John 4:43 – 54

Literary Context

The scene shifts from the region of Samaria to Cana in Galilee, the same place where Jesus previously turned water into wine. This return to Cana serves as an intentional *inclusio* and completes the narrative's depiction of the beginning of Jesus's public ministry. The narrative has spoken about what is to take place because of the arrival of Jesus: real purification in the true temple (ch. 2), true birth (ch. 3), and true worship (ch. 4). But in so doing, the Gospel has spoken much about "an hour [that] is coming" and not as much about what "now is" (4:23). In this pericope, the Fourth Gospel switches from "is coming" to "now is" by showing how the actions of Jesus are the manifestations of the things to which Jesus has been pointing. It is not just about what Jesus will do, it is also about what he is already doing and about the "life" he has come to restore.

III. The Beginning of Jesus's Public Ministry (2:1 – 4:54)
   A. The First Sign: The Wedding at Cana (2:1 – 11)
   B. The Cleansing of the Temple: The Promise of the Seventh Sign (2:12 – 25)
   C. Nicodemus, New Birth, and the Unique Son (3:1 – 21)
   D. The Baptist, the True Bridegroom, and the Friend of the Bridegroom (3:22 – 36)
   E. The Samaritan Woman, Living Water, and True Worshippers (4:1 – 42)
   F. The Second Sign: The Healing of the Royal Official's Son (4:43 – 54)

Main Idea

True belief in God occurs when the things the person sought for themselves get eclipsed by the God who alone can provide them. The appropriate response to Jesus is one that learns to find meaning and life not merely in what he gives but in who he is. Jesus is the true provider of life, the source of which is found in the fact that "he lives." And it is because he lives that the Christian may begin to live.

Translation

John 4:43–54

43a	Introduction & Setting (43–46)	After the two days
b	Departure	**he went from there**
c	Place	into Galilee
44a	Aside	For **Jesus himself testified**
b	Ironic Contrast	that a prophet has no honor in his own homeland.
45a	Arrival	When he came into Galilee,
b	Reaction to Arrival	**the Galileans welcomed him.**
c	Basis #1	**They had seen all what he did in Jerusalem at the Passover feast,**
d	Basis #2	for **they also had been there.**
46a	Reassertion of 45a	Then **he came again into Cana of Galilee,**
b	Significance of "Cana" (Inclusio)	where he turned water into wine.
c	Character Entrance	And **there was a royal official**
d	Description: Father of a sick son	whose son was sick
e	Place	in Capernaum.
47a	Conflict (47)	When this man heard that Jesus had come out of Judea into Galilee
b	Sequence #1	**he came to him**
c	Sequence #2	and **was begging him**
d	Purpose	to come down and heal his son,
e	Explanation	for **he was about to die.**
48a	Resolution (48–51)/Response	Then **Jesus said to him,**
b	Condition	*"Unless you see signs and wonders,*
c	Inference (Rebuke)	*you will never believe."*
49a	Response	**The royal official said to him,**
b	Respectful Address	*"Lord,*
c	Entreaty	*come down before my child dies."*
50a	Response	**Jesus said to him,**
b	Command	*"Go,*
c	Declaration	*your son lives."*
d	Reaction #1	**The man believed the word**
e	Description (object of belief)	which Jesus spoke to him
f	Reaction #2	and **he left.**
51a		While he was on his way down
b	Climax of Resolution	**his servants met him**
c	Confirmation of 50c	reporting that his son was alive
	Conclusion & Interpretation (52–54)	

Continued on next page.

Continued from previous page.

52a	Question	Then **he inquired from them about the time at which he began to improve;**
b	Answer	**they said to him,**
c	Confirmation of 50c	*"The fever left him yesterday at the seventh hour."*
53a	Reaction	Then **the father knew that this was the exact time at which Jesus said to him,**
b	Recollection	*"Your son lives,"*
c	Result	and **he and his entire household believed.**
54a	Summary Interjection: 2nd Sign	**This was the second sign Jesus did**
b	Time	when he came from Judea into Galilee.

Structure and Literary Form

This pericope corresponds to the basic story form (see Introduction). The *intro-duction/setting* is established in vv. 43 – 46, explaining the transition from the region of Samaria to Galilee and describing the people around whom the plot's conflict will focus. In v. 47 the *conflict* is revealed when the official addresses Jesus with the problem of his son's health. The *resolution* is provided in vv. 48 – 51 with the important contextualization provided by the rejoinder of Jesus to the official's request, together with his positive response. Finally, vv. 52 – 54 serve as the *conclusion/interpretation* by explaining the result of the activities, the unique timing of the healing, and the official's response to Jesus. In v. 54 the narrator closes the scene by announcing that it was the second sign of Jesus, which connects the pericope to the larger witness of the narrative.

Exegetical Outline

➡ **F. The Second Sign: The Healing of the Royal Official's Son (4:43 – 54)**

1. The Honorless Prophet Returns to Galilee (vv. 43 – 46)

2. Royal Official's Dying Son (v. 47)

3. "Your Son Lives" (vv. 48 – 50)

4. The "Sign" of Life (vv. 51 – 54)

Explanation of the Text

This pericope has been a notorious crux for interpreters because of its placement and its similarity to the Synoptic tradition. It is often suggested that vv. 43 – 45 defy the narrative's natural sequence. Dodd suggests that this awkward transition is evidence that "the Samaritan episode is intruded here into what was originally a single and continuous journey from Judaea to Galilee."[1] But such a conclusion is based on subjective judgments about logical flow and consistency and makes no better sense of the larger context, let alone the pericope. In fact, the specific mention of the return to Cana in Galilee at 4:46 serves as a narrative marker, forming an *inclusio* with 2:1 — what we called the beginning of the narrative proper (with all of chapter 1 serving as an introduction; see comments before 1:19). The *inclusio* ends at 4:54, which ends what can be described as the beginning of Jesus's public ministry. Jesus's first disciples were Jewish and most naturally close to him (2:11); his latest were likely gentile and naturally estranged (4:53). The beginning of his ministry is depicted as cosmic in scope, just as the place from whence he ultimately came (1:1).

4:43 After the two days he went from there into Galilee (Μετὰ δὲ τὰς δύο ἡμέρας ἐξῆλθεν ἐκεῖθεν εἰς τὴν Γαλιλαίαν). Connecting with the previous pericope, the narrator explains that after staying with the Samaritans for two days Jesus left and went into Galilee. Yet this verse also connects with 4:3, in which Jesus was on his way to Galilee after leaving Judea. The narrative is fond of interweaving scenes with others, allowing the one to inform and to be informed by the other (see comments on 4:38 – 39).

4:44 For Jesus himself testified that a prophet has no honor in his own homeland (αὐτὸς γὰρ Ἰησοῦς ἐμαρτύρησεν ὅτι προφήτης ἐν τῇ ἰδίᾳ πατρίδι τιμὴν οὐκ ἔχει). The narrator offers an aside that helps explain the scene that follows, denoted by the use of "for" (γὰρ). This is presented as something once said, not necessarily at this time, but in his teaching as remembered and recorded by his followers (cf. Matt 13:57; Luke 4:24).[2] The explanatory force it gives to the scene is by way of contrast between what had just been made manifest about this "prophet" in Samaria and the reception of his prophetic status "in his own homeland" (ἐν τῇ ἰδίᾳ πατρίδι). The exact identity of "homeland" (πατρίς) is important to the pericope since it serves as a contrast. Although there are several interpretive suggestions that often try to secure the exact soil being referred to, it is clear by the larger context that the location of Galilee is inclusive of the land of the Jews.[3] In comparison to the region of Samaria, Galilee is related to the region of Judea/Jerusalem, and the Fourth Gospel as a whole makes clear that the theme of rejection embraces the whole of the Jewish nation (cf. 12:36 – 43).

It is worth noting that Jesus declares that in his homeland he receives no "honor" (τιμὴν). This noun occurs nowhere else in the Gospel, for when John declares the kind of honor due, he prefers to use the term often translated "glory" (δόξα). This is likely another example of the narrative's use of irony. Although he will be accepted by those in Galilee (v. 45), "It was dependent on the wonder arising from their sight of the signs, not on a realization that Jesus was indeed the Christ, the Savior of the world. Their very acceptance of him was in

---

1. Dodd, *Historical Tradition*, 238.
2. Michaels, *John*, 271.

3. John W. Pryor, "John 4:44 and the *Patris* of Jesus," *CBQ* 49 (1987): 254 – 63 (263).

its own way a rejection."[4] For this reason, while the suggestion by Lightfoot that the "homeland" (πατρίς) of Jesus is not earth but heaven is slightly overstated, he does explain well the true origin of Jesus.[5] Jesus is not of this world (cf. 8:23); he came from elsewhere — "from heaven" (6:38), and that is where he will return (14:2).

4:45 When he came into Galilee, the Galileans welcomed him. They had seen all that he did in Jerusalem at the Passover feast, for they also had been there (ὅτε οὖν ἦλθεν εἰς τὴν Γαλιλαίαν, ἐδέξαντο αὐτὸν οἱ Γαλιλαῖοι, πάντα ἑωρακότες ὅσα ἐποίησεν ἐν Ἱεροσολύμοις ἐν τῇ ἑορτῇ, καὶ αὐτοὶ γὰρ ἦλθον εἰς τὴν ἑορτήν). The narrator explains that although the Galileans welcome Jesus, their motivations were drenched with their own self-interest. They had seen "all that he did" (ὅσα ἐποίησεν) in Jerusalem "at the feast" (ἐν τῇ ἑορτῇ), which can only be the Passover feast narrated in 2:13 – 25. We do not know what things they saw him do, but the narrator uses their shallow intentions as an important detail that reflects both their misunderstanding and, by implication, the true identity of Jesus. The Galileans "had seen" (ἑωρακότες) with the same level of inaccuracy as the disciples of Jesus (cf. 4:35), and their hospitality toward Jesus proves again the truly hospitable one must be God (see comments on 4:40). The *hapax legomenon* "welcomed" (ἐδέξαντο) is a far cry from the term for "acceptance" (λαβεῖν) John normally uses when designating genuine reception (e.g., 1:12; 5:43).

4:46 Then he came again into Cana of Galilee, where he turned water into wine. And there was a royal official whose son was sick in Capernaum

(Ἦλθεν οὖν πάλιν εἰς τὴν Κανὰ τῆς Γαλιλαίας, ὅπου ἐποίησεν τὸ ὕδωρ οἶνον. καὶ ἦν τις βασιλικὸς οὗ ὁ υἱὸς ἠσθένει ἐν Καφαρναούμ). The transition from Samaria to Galilee is rhetorically important for the narrator, who intentionally links 2:1 – 11, which narrates the first sign, with this pericope and the second sign (see v. 54), not merely with the geographical reminder but also with a reminder of the miracle that took place.[6]

The narrator has already established the larger context surrounding this scene, but since this verse ends the introduction and setting of the pericope, the primary characters and the pertinent issues they bring to the scene need to be explained. The reader is introduced to "a" certain man (τις) who is a "royal official" (βασιλικός). Although the qualifier is simply the adjective "royal," the context makes clear that this man was not of royal blood but an official of the king, that is, of the royal house — hence, a "royal official." This man was almost certainly an official serving Herod Antipas, who although was not technically a king was popularly treated as one (cf. Mark 6:14).[7] It is impossible to know if the official was a Jew or a gentile. While the geography was initially more important for this scene than the ethnicity of this particular official, a unique presentation of the expanding mission of Jesus is put before us if he is a gentile. For in John 3, new life is offered to the Jews, in 4:1 – 42 to the Samaritans, and now here to the gentiles.[8] Whatever his ethnicity, however, what is stated as important is that his son was sick. For this reason, he approaches a certain Jew named Jesus, who is in actuality *the* "royal official."

---

4. Cf. Morris, *John*, 254.

5. R. H. Lightfoot, *St. John's Gospel* (Oxford: Oxford University Press, 1956), 35.

6. See Joost Smit Sibinga, "The Shape of a Miracle Story: A Respectful Analysis of John 4:43 – 54," *NovT* 45 (2003): 222 – 36 (223).

7. See A. H. Head, "The βασιλικὸς in John 4.46 – 53," *JSNT* 23 (1985): 69 – 72.

8. Ibid., 71.

4:47 When this man heard that Jesus had come out of Judea into Galilee he came to him and was begging him to come down and heal his son, for he was about to die (οὗτος ἀκούσας ὅτι Ἰησοῦς ἥκει ἐκ τῆς Ἰουδαίας εἰς τὴν Γαλιλαίαν ἀπῆλθεν πρὸς αὐτὸν καὶ ἠρώτα ἵνα καταβῇ καὶ ἰάσηται αὐτοῦ τὸν υἱόν, ἤμελλεν γὰρ ἀποθνῄσκειν). The identity of the man as a royal official is quickly eclipsed by his identity as a father. For upon hearing about the arrival of Jesus into Galilee, the man immediately went to him, denoted by the aorist participle "when … heard" (ἀκούσας), which is to be translated as contemporaneous to the controlling historical present, "had come" (ἥκει).[9] The trip from Capernaum to Cana was approximately twenty-five miles by a road which climbs around 1,350 feet.[10] Such an arduous journey adds tone to the narrator's description when he says the father "was begging" (ἠρώτα) Jesus to come and heal his son, for the imperfect tense with verbs of asking denotes incomplete action and therefore is to be viewed as strengthened in its force.[11] The imminent death of the son, denoted by the present tense "to die" (ἀποθνῄσκειν), has motivated the father to search for life, and he turns to Jesus. Interestingly, while Jesus asks potential disciples to "come and see" (cf. 1:39), here he is asked to "come and heal." The plot's conflict has been presented to Jesus in dramatic fashion.

4:48 Then Jesus said to him, "Unless you see signs and wonders, you will never believe" (εἶπεν οὖν ὁ Ἰησοῦς πρὸς αὐτόν, Ἐὰν μὴ σημεῖα καὶ τέρατα ἴδητε, οὐ μὴ πιστεύσητε). While the narrator tells us that Jesus responded to the royal official, "to him" (πρὸς αὐτόν), Jesus himself speaks in the plural: "Unless you (all) see" (ἴδητε). Fitting what we argued above, the royal official has been classified

by Jesus as part of a larger group, those from his homeland who have seen and heard about him. This royal official, or more specifically, this father with all his paternal sensibilities, is guilty of using Jesus for his own purposes. The criticism is not against signs in total, for what is about to happen *is* the second sign. Rather, Jesus is criticizing belief that is founded on the witness itself and not on the object of the witness, as well as belief that stems from wrong motivations. That is why Jesus declares with the emphatic negative subjunctive, "you will never believe" (οὐ μὴ πιστεύσητε). Jesus's intention is not to reject completely this man and the people he represents, only the kind of belief the man initially displayed toward Jesus. Before resolving this one man's conflict, Jesus addresses a much larger problem.

4:49 The royal official said to him, "Lord, come down before my child dies" (λέγει πρὸς αὐτὸν ὁ βασιλικός, Κύριε, κατάβηθι πρὶν ἀποθανεῖν τὸ παιδίον μου). The royal official speaks past Jesus's public denouncement of unbelief and pleads with Jesus to come and heal his son. The aorist imperative "come down" (κατάβηθι) is best taken as a polite command. It is normally used when an inferior addresses a superior, denoted by the vocative "Lord" (Κύριε), functioning more like a request. He is a royal official, so he knows how to address an authority. But he speaks not as a royal official but as a father when he speaks — not about "his son" (αὐτοῦ τὸν υἱόν) as in v. 47 — but about "my child" (τὸ παιδίον μου), a term that is an expression of affection. While his belief was in theory much like the people Jesus addressed in v. 48, this was no theoretical exercise. This was more like a prayer, and Jesus was the one to whom this royal official, the father of a dying son, was praying.[12]

---

9. Wallace, *Greek Grammar*, 624 – 25.
10. McHugh, *John 1 – 4*, 318.

11. BDF § 328; Moulton, *Grammar*, 3:64 – 65.
12. Cf. Michaels, *John*, 279.

4:50 Jesus said to him, "Go, your son lives." The man believed the word which Jesus spoke to him and he left (λέγει αὐτῷ ὁ Ἰησοῦς, Πορεύου· ὁ υἱός σου ζῇ. ἐπίστευσεν ὁ ἄνθρωπος τῷ λόγῳ ὃν εἶπεν αὐτῷ ὁ Ἰησοῦς καὶ ἐπορεύετο). Without explanation, he commands the royal official to depart, denoted by the imperative, "Go" (Πορεύου), and announces that his son "lives," (ζῇ), a present tense that contains within it a future sense (hence, many translations use the future: "will live"). The verb "to live" serves as a perfect counter to previously imminent death, yet it also touches upon the important theme of "life" presented by the Gospel as presently available (cf. 20:31). Jesus, the true king, commanded this royal official, and he obeyed. Interestingly, the royal official and father is now described merely as "the man" (ὁ ἄνθρωπος). The narrative is quite specific regarding the belief of the man, that he believed "the word which Jesus spoke" (τῷ λόγῳ ὃν εἶπεν). There was no sign. There was only the word of the Word. And this man believed. This verse serves as the conclusion to the resolution of the plot.

4:51 While he was on his way down his servants met him, reporting that his son was alive (ἤδη δὲ αὐτοῦ καταβαίνοντος οἱ δοῦλοι αὐτοῦ ὑπήντησαν αὐτῷ λέγοντες ὅτι ὁ παῖς αὐτοῦ ζῇ). This verse begins not only the conclusion to the pericope but also the necessary interpretation. With nothing but the word of Jesus as collateral, the royal official begins the descent from Cana to Capernaum toward his son. Before he could even reach his home, his servants met him along the way and "reported" (λέγοντες) that his son was alive, using the exact word Jesus used: he "lives" (ζῇ).

4:52 Then he inquired from them about the time at which he began to improve; they said to him, "The fever left him yesterday at the seventh hour" (ἐπύθετο οὖν τὴν ὥραν παρ᾽ αὐτῶν ἐν ᾗ κομψότερον ἔσχεν· εἶπαν οὖν αὐτῷ ὅτι Ἐχθὲς ὥραν ἑβδόμην ἀφῆκεν αὐτὸν ὁ πυρετός). The joyous confirmation was still so intimately tied to the initial pronouncement by Jesus that the royal official "inquired" (ἐπύθετο) from his servants about the exact time his son "began to improve" (κομψότερον ἔσχεν), with the exactness of the change made emphatic by the ingressive aorist. The servants, who had been attending closely to every need of the royal official's son, were able to say with a high degree of certainty when the reversal of the son's condition began, when the fever subsided, namely, "the seventh hour," that is, about 1:00 p.m. (on the Jewish time system, see comments on 1:39).

4:53 Then the father knew that this was the exact time at which Jesus said to him, "Your son lives," and he and his entire household believed (ἔγνω οὖν ὁ πατὴρ ὅτι ἐν ἐκείνῃ τῇ ὥρᾳ ἐν ᾗ εἶπεν αὐτῷ ὁ Ἰησοῦς, Ὁ υἱός σου ζῇ, καὶ ἐπίστευσεν αὐτὸς καὶ ἡ οἰκία αὐτοῦ ὅλη). What sounded like a natural question to ask of the servants was loaded with significance. And the details the father heard were not further confirmation regarding his son, but confirmation regarding the unique Son. Although he had acted like a father with his focused concern for his child, this is the first time the narrative describes him as "the father" (ὁ πατὴρ) and not as the royal official. It is not in his official capacity but in his familial role as a father that God met "this man" through the person and work of Jesus. The narrative explicitly softens the man's position as a royal official ("man," "father") to implicitly suggest that it was Jesus who is the true royal official, sent from the true Father. The father's recollection of the pronouncement of Jesus, "Your son lives" (Ὁ υἱός σου ζῇ), results in belief. And although the narrative is silent on the specifics, the royal official then led his household to the same realization he had come to, and to the same conclusion: Jesus was to be "believed" (ἐπίστευσεν).

4:54 This was the second sign Jesus did when he came from Judea into Galilee (Τοῦτο [δὲ] πάλιν δεύτερον σημεῖον ἐποίησεν ὁ Ἰησοῦς ἐλθὼν ἐκ τῆς Ἰουδαίας εἰς τὴν Γαλιλαίαν). The final verse of the pericope contains a summarizing interjection by the narrator, who weaves the prologue's wisdom and explanatory insight throughout the narrative proper. By referring to this miracle as the "second sign" (δεύτερον σημεῖον), the pericope is given all the weight of the Johannine signs, which we defined earlier as the symbolical anticipation or showing forth of a greater reality (see comments on 2:11). None of this should surprise the reader of John thus far. The moment one leaves the prologue, the reader has already been sensitized to see that which lies beyond. And not surprisingly, the author of the prologue will continue to narrate the "unseen forces" to the reader along the way.

Theology in Application

Even in his homeland, Jesus is confronted by the darkness that envelopes the world he created. And his light is not merely intended to contrast himself from the darkness of the world but to declare to the world what is the way, the truth, and in this pericope in particular, the life (cf. 14:6). In an encounter with the desperate father of a dying son, Jesus not only rebukes the public for their misguided belief in him but describes by his actions the nature of true belief. In this pericope, the readers of the Fourth Gospel are exhorted to explore the nature of their faith, the motivations behind their search for God, and their willingness to trust the Word of the Lord.

God in Our Homeland

Jesus's dictum about the inability of a prophet to receive honor in his own homeland (v. 44) reveals the innate difficulty for humanity to see beyond itself. Amidst all its failings, the unfailing perseverance of a person is most successfully evidenced in their inability to distrust themselves to the lack of their own better judgment. The world in which we live is shaped — and therefore limited — by our context, our opinions, our imaginations, and most dangerously, our needs. And it is not merely the world that is shaped by our context, opinions, and imaginations, it is also our thinking about God. What the Galileans saw in Jesus was not who he truly was; it was who they selfishly wanted him to be. They thought themselves to be healthy, when in truth they were already dead. This is why Jesus speaks right past that father to the crowds, right past the concern of that father to the concern of his Father.

The Christian is reminded by this pericope, and especially the exhortative commentary by Jesus, to live with an appropriate posture of self-critique, knowing that what seems natural and readily apparent is actually only knowing in part (1 Cor 13:12). Before he even introduced himself to Jesus, the royal official was fully known by God. So it is with us. Let us then come to Jesus as he knows us, and let him explain how we might know him and the Father as revealed by him (1:18).

The God of Signs and Wonders

The kind of belief this pericope displays for the reader is one that is firmly rooted in the person and work of Jesus. Jesus is not rebuking the failing faith we all might have but a faith that is resting on inappropriate objects, that is, faith that is inappropriately motivated. Are we motivated to believe in a "god" who does things for us in the manner we deem most appropriate? Or is our belief rooted in the God who declares "I AM," to which we are to respond, "Yes, you are!" (Exod 3:14). Are we motivated to believe in a "god" in whom we derive pleasure? Or is our belief in the God in whom pleasure is entirely redefined and established? Let us not believe as the Galileans but as the children of God. Let us worship God not for the wonders he can perform but for the wonder that he is. A God who is worthy of worship even when there is no "sign," and even when our request goes unanswered — even still he is to us our God, the true sign and wonder.

The Word of the "Word"

Although the royal official, like the Galileans, wanted signs and wonders as proof, Jesus gave him only one thing: his word. No visible angels, no flaming bush, no fire in the sky to lead him home, no star above his son's bed — just the word of the Word. And the narrative is specific in announcing to the reader that the royal official "believed" it. The man believed the word of Jesus, that is, he trusted in who he is and what he said he would do. The contemporary Christian has no other calling than to trust in his word. Do you believe Jesus is who he says he is? Do you believe he will do what he says he will do? Then go!

"He Lives"

The centrality of the concept of "life" in the Fourth Gospel that began in the prologue (1:4) is given further development in this pericope. The life of the royal official's son serves to signal to the reader the life that Jesus created (1:3) and has come to restore (20:31). Jesus is the life, and all life must be located in his person and work. For this reason, the narrative's carefully constructed transition from the "royal official" to the "father" of a "son" in v. 54 should echo in the minds of the reader another Father and his Son, and another death experience and resurrection of a Son to life.

John 5:1 – 18

Literary Context

This pericope begins a new section in the Gospel. Jesus's public ministry is well underway and as he increasingly becomes the center of attention he is required to explain — to confess — his identity and intentions. Up until now Jesus has been working primarily with individuals, but in this section of the Gospel his ministry begins to engage with more corporate entities, both followers and dissenters. This healing is the third sign of Jesus (cf. 6:2; 7:31).

➡ **IV. The Confession of the Son of God (5:1 – 8:11)**

    A. The Third Sign: The Healing of the Lame Man on the Sabbath (5:1 – 18)

    B. The Identity of (the Son of) God: Jesus Responds to the Opposition (5:19 – 47)

    C. The Fourth Sign: The Feeding of a Large Crowd (6:1 – 15)

    D. The "I AM" Walks across the Sea (6:16 – 21)

    E. The Bread of Life (6:22 – 71)

    F. Private Display of Suspicion (7:1 – 13)

    G. Public Display of Rejection (7:14 – 52)

    H. The Trial of Jesus regarding a Woman Accused of Adultery (7:53 – 8:11)

Main Idea

In a world filled with confusion about God and religious superstition, Jesus stands as the direct reflection and primary agent of the personal and powerful work of God. Jesus is both the promise of true wellness and the warning against something much worse. The only appropriate response can be to stop sinning and to start believing.

Translation

(See pages 266–67.)

John 5:1–18

1a	Introduction & Setting (1–5)	After these things
b	Event	**there was a festival of the Jews,**
c	Action	and **Jesus went up**
d	Place	**to Jerusalem.**
2a	Geographic Setting	And **there is in Jerusalem near the Sheep Gate a pool,**
b	Aside	which in Aramaic is called Bethesda,
c	Description	which has five porticoes.
3a	Further Description	**In these were lying a great multitude of the sick—**
b	Apposition #1	**the blind,**
c	Apposition #2	**the lame,**
d	Apposition #3	**the paralyzed.**
5a	Character Entrance	And **a certain man was there**
b	Description	who was lame for thirty-eight years.
6a	Conflict (6–10)	
b	Basis of 6c	When Jesus saw him lying there, and learned that he had already been like that for a long time,
c	Action	**he said to him,**
d	Question	*"Do you want to become well?"*
7a	Response	**The lame man answered him,**
b	Address	*"Sir,*
c	Problem	*I have no one to put me into the pool*
d	Circumstance	*when the water stirs up;*
e		
f	Expansion	*while I am coming,*
g		*another goes down before me."*
8a	Response	**Jesus said to him,**
b	Series of Commands: #1	*"Rise,*
c	Series of Commands: #2	*pick up your mat, and*
d	Series of Commands: #3	*walk."*
9a	Immediate Result	And **at once the man became well,**
b	Reaction	and **he took his mat and walked.**
c	Setting/Escalating Conflict	But **on that day it was the Sabbath.**

10a	Character Entrance	Then **the Jews were saying to the man**
b	Description	who had been healed,
c	Climax of Conflict/Basis of 10d	*"It is the Sabbath,*
d	Rebuke/Narrative Irony	*and it is not lawful for you to carry your mat."*
11a	Resolution (11–15)/Response	But **he answered them,**
b	Deflection of Blame	*"The one who made me well said to me,*
c		*'Pick up your mat and walk.'"*
12a	Response	**They answered him,**
b	Question	*"Who is the man who said to you,*
c		*'Pick up and walk?'"*
13a	Assertion	But **the man did not know who he was,**
b	Explanation	for **Jesus became invisible in the crowd in that place.**
14a	Setting Change (14a, b)	After these things
b		**Jesus found him in the temple**
c		and **said to him,**
d	Pronouncement	*"Behold, you have become well.*
e	Command	*Sin no longer,*
d	Purpose	*so that nothing worse may happen to you."*
15a	Ironic Reaction	**The man went and reported to the Jews that Jesus was the one who made him well.**
16a	Conclusion & Interpretation (16–18)	And **for this reason the Jews were persecuting Jesus,**
b	Basis	because he was doing these things on the Sabbath.
17a	Response to 16	But **Jesus answered them,**
b	Confession & Declaration	*"My Father ...*
c	Contrasting Irony to 16	*... is working up to the present,*
d	Unity of Father & Son's "Work"	*and I too am working."*
18a	Reaction	And **for this reason the Jews were seeking to kill him**
b	Intensification	even harder,
c	Basis #1	not only because he broke the Sabbath, but also
d	Basis #2	because he called God his Father,
e	Result	making himself equal with God.

Structure and Literary Form

This pericope corresponds to the basic story form (see Introduction). The *introduction/setting* is established in vv. 1 – 5, explaining the location, setting, and people around whom the plot's conflict will focus. The *conflict* in this pericope in vv. 6 – 10 is more multifaceted than the previous story units, for it not only involves the healing of the lame man but also the controversy of healing on the Sabbath. It is probably best to view the healing of the lame man as the rising conflict, with the climax of the conflict centering upon the Sabbath controversy. The *resolution* in vv. 11 – 15 removes the healed man from the tension and places the conflict directly at the feet of Jesus. Finally, vv. 16 – 18 serve as the *conclusion/interpretation* by ending the pericope with a description of the Jews' intentions regarding Jesus. It also closes the pericope with a confession that sets a trajectory for Jesus's later public engagement and connects the pericope to the larger witness of the narrative.

Exegetical Outline

➡ **A. The Third Sign: The Healing of the Lame Man on the Sabbath (5:1 – 18)**
  1. A Man Lame for Thirty-Eight Years (vv. 1 – 5)
  2. Get Up — Even on the Sabbath! (vv. 6 – 10)
  3. Sin No Longer (vv. 11 – 15)
  4. The Work of God, Father and Son (vv. 16 – 18)

Explanation of the Text

Bultmann states plainly the problem raised by several interpreters: "The present order of chs. 5 and 6 cannot be the original one."[1] Not only does Bultmann note the problem, he even corrects the arrangement of John's narrative in his commentary, arguing that the original order must have been chapters 4, 6, 5, 7. But there are two reasons why we should be comfortable with the order as we have it. First, there is absolutely no textual evidence that argues against the narrative order as we have it. Second, in order to correct what is seen as a problem at the level of historical sequencing, a new problem is created at the level of the literary

sequencing.[2] Not only was historical narration allowed a level of freedom and flexibility in the ancient world, a freedom in the amount and ordering of its contents (cf. 20:30: "Many other miracles … not recorded in this book"), but narration was also written with a particular literary sequencing in mind, a sequencing that was intended to communicate to the reader by means of its specific order. The received order makes good narrative sense, as we shall see below.

5:1 After these things there was a festival of the Jews, and Jesus went up to Jerusalem (Μετὰ

---

1. Bultmann, *John*, 209. Cf. Schnackenburg, *John*, 2:5 – 9; Bernard, *John*, 1:171.

2. Cf. Michaels, *John*, 286.

ταῦτα ἦν ἑορτὴ τῶν Ἰουδαίων, καὶ ἀνέβη Ἰησοῦς εἰς Ἱεροσόλυμα). "After these things" (Μετὰ ταῦτα) loosely connects this pericope to the previous one and functionally may mean little more than, "The next thing I would like to tell is this" (see comments on 2:12).[3] The narrator explains that Jesus returned to Jerusalem for "a festival of the Jews" (ἑορτὴ τῶν Ἰουδαίων). No indication is given as to which festival is taking place; the anarthrous "a festival" almost emphasizes the anonymity. This is the only occurrence of an unnamed festival in the Gospel, which normally names the festival in question: 2:23; 6:4; 11:55 – 56 (Passover); 7:2 (Tabernacles); and 10:22 (Dedication/Hanukkah). Since festivals in John are often linked thematically to the events at hand, the lack of reference in this pericope suggests there is no innate or necessary connection.

5:2 And there is in Jerusalem near the Sheep Gate a pool, which in Aramaic is called Bethesda, which has five porticoes (ἔστιν δὲ ἐν τοῖς Ἱεροσολύμοις ἐπὶ τῇ προβατικῇ κολυμβήθρα ἡ ἐπιλεγομένη Ἑβραϊστὶ Βηθζαθά, πέντε στοὰς ἔχουσα). The specific scene of this pericope takes place at a pool near the Sheep Gate. The specifics provided reflect the awareness John had of Jerusalem and its geography.[4] Some have argued that the present-tense verb "is" (ἔστιν) implies that the Gospel was written before Jerusalem was destroyed, hence before AD 70, but this is not demanded from the verb.[5] Rather than intending directly to communicate a historical fact, the employment of this common verb is best understood to be inviting the reader "to visualize the scene as it unfolds."[6]

While the exact site is difficult to confirm, several scholars suggest the twin pools beneath St.

Anne's Monastery.[7] The pools were as large as a football field and about twenty feet deep. The "five porticoes" (πέντε στοὰς) represent a porch on each of the four sides and one separating the pools, perhaps separating men and women. Porticoes, like public baths in the ancient world, were open to the public and were gathering places for beggars and other people.

5:3 In these were lying a great multitude of the sick — the blind, the lame, the paralyzed (ἐν ταύταις κατέκειτο πλῆθος τῶν ἀσθενούντων, τυφλῶν, χωλῶν, ξηρῶν). The pools were filled with a large number of the sick, described by three descriptive terms. The second term, "the lame" (χωλῶν), refers primarily to a disability rooted in physical inability (i.e., an improperly functioning body part); the third term, "the paralyzed" (ξηρῶν), refers primarily to a disability rooted in disease (e.g., the term can also mean "withered").[8]

The reason nearly all translations move from v. 3 to v. 5 is because what is labeled as v. 4 (which is really vv. 3b – 4) in some manuscripts is clearly not original, not only because of its absence from the earliest and best witnesses but also because the manuscripts that do contain it have an unnatural diversity of variant forms.[9] According to the NIV in a note, the foreign verse reads after "the paralyzed": " — and they waited for the moving of the waters. From time to time an angel of the Lord would come down and stir up the waters. The first one into the pool after each such disturbance would be cured of whatever disease he had." With the abundance of evidence that pagan religion regularly used healing shrines with water as a regular component, it is not unlikely that this tradition is rooted in folk

---

3. Michaels, *John*, 286.

4. On the name and location of this place, see Barrett, *John*, 251 – 53. Cf. Carson, *John*, 242.

5. See J. A. T. Robinson, *The Priority of John* (Oak Park, IL: Meyer-Stone, 1987), 70.

6. Michaels, *John*, 288.

7. The following is adapted from Keener, *John*, 1:636 – 37.

8. Cf. BDAG 685; 1093.

9. Metzger, *Textual Commentary*, 179.

legend, possibly even a popular Jewish tradition.[10] Although such folk practices would not have been supported by the Jewish establishment, Theissen is probably correct when he suggests that in this scene "Jesus is in competition with ancient healing sanctuaries."[11] Even beyond its origin, this foreign addition was almost certainly added to explain v. 7.

5:5 And a certain man was there who was lame for thirty-eight years (ἦν δέ τις ἄνθρωπος ἐκεῖ τριάκοντα [καὶ] ὀκτὼ ἔτη ἔχων ἐν τῇ ἀσθενείᾳ αὐτοῦ). In the midst of this great multitude of the sick at this grand place of healing was an un-named man, "a certain man" (τις ἄνθρωπος), with an unnamed sickness. Although the sickness is not named, v. 8 suggests that he is unable to walk, thus our translation "lame" (ἀσθενείᾳ). The only thing the narrator deems worthy to describe is the length of his lameness: thirty-eight years. The insight into the length of the man's ailment, especially in light of the absence of other, more key information, suggests that the duration is significant — "it had taken away all hope of a cure."[12] Since the Israelites wandered in the desert before reaching the promised land for thirty-eight years (Deut 2:14), it is often suggested that John is making an intentional allusion to the punishment for their unbelief. But while John may not be unmindful of such an allusion, it is unlikely that such a precise allusion is primarily in mind. This completes the first scene of the plot, the introduction and setting of the pericope.

5:6 When Jesus saw him lying there, and learned that he had already been like that for a long time, he said to him, "Do you want to become well?"

(τοῦτον ἰδὼν ὁ Ἰησοῦς κατακείμενον, καὶ γνοὺς ὅτι πολὺν ἤδη χρόνον ἔχει, λέγει αὐτῷ, Θέλεις ὑγιὴς γενέσθαι;). The narrator describes not only that Jesus "saw" (ἰδὼν) him, but that he "learned" (γνοὺς) of his condition, probably by hearing it from another. The implications are potent. Jesus was walking through a great multitude of sick people gathered around what was superstitiously considered to be a sacred place of healing, unrecognized by the sick as the Creator of the universe, the Life (1:3 – 5).

Jesus asks the man a loaded question: "Do you want to become well?" (Θέλεις ὑγιὴς γενέσθαι;). Although it had been the royal official who initiated conversation with Jesus (4:47 – 48), this is not the first time Jesus has taken the initiative to help someone (recall the Samaritan woman). But interpreters disagree regarding the intention of the question.[13] What issue is Jesus raising with the anonymous lame man? The suggestions offered are varied, including that it is a rebuke, a test of his willingness, or a straightforward question. The variety of suggestions is probably best summarized by admitting with Haenchen that the question is "odd" or at least seems as such to the reader.[14] The solution to the intention of this question cannot be found in the answer given by the lame man in v. 7, as if that explained the hidden context out of which the question arose, for he had no clue with whom he was speaking (v. 13). A special divine insight into the man (his psyche?) is disallowed by the narrative itself, which explains that Jesus "came to know" about this man's condition from others. Even the suggestion by Thomas that the term

10. For a helpful defense of this, see Steven M. Bryan, "Power in the Pool: The Healing of the Man at Bethesda and Jesus's Violation of the Sabbath (Jn. 5:1 – 18)," *TynBul* 54 (2003): 7 – 22, especially 8 – 12.

11. Gerd Theissen, *The Miracle Stories of the Early Christian Tradition*, trans. Francis McDonagh, ed. John Riches (Philadelphia: Fortress Press, 1983), 51.

12. Calvin, *John 1 – 10*, 119.

13. See Jeffrey L. Staley, "Stumbling in the Dark, Reaching for the Light: Reading Character in John 5 and 9," *Semeia* 53 (1991): 55 – 80, especially 58 – 59.

14. Haenchen, *John*, 1:255.

"well" (ὑγιής) carries a Johannine double meaning—both "wellness" and "wholeness"—is disallowed by the narrative, since in 7:23 two different words are used to describe those exact meanings: "Because I made the whole (ὅλον) man well (ὑγιῆ)."

The question is odd because it almost ignores the context so carefully established by the narrative and in which Jesus was standing. It was precisely his desire to become well that had him in that spot, the pool of healing.[15] But because Jesus had "learned" about the man and was therefore aware of the place of healing in which he was standing, the question has to mean more. The key might not be in the word "well" but in a word that has become foundational to the Gospel, "become" (γενέσθαι). This word from the prologue onward has been a central term ("came/made/became" [ἐγένετο/ γίνομαι]) that expresses the creative work of God in the world. The fact that it is a common Greek word cannot deny its significant use by the Gospel at numerous key junctures (see comments on 1:17). By this term, the reader is able to see into the question with the cosmological insight of the prologue. Jesus is really pursuing the man for healing, but he is also pursuing something much grander.

5:7 The lame man answered him, "Sir, I have no one to put me into the pool when the water stirs up; while I am coming, another goes down before me" (ἀπεκρίθη αὐτῷ ὁ ἀσθενῶν, Κύριε, ἄνθρωπον οὐκ ἔχω ἵνα ὅταν ταραχθῇ τὸ ὕδωρ βάλῃ με εἰς τὴν κολυμβήθραν· ἐν ᾧ δὲ ἔρχομαι ἐγὼ ἄλλος πρὸ ἐμοῦ καταβαίνει). The lame man answers Jesus's question with respect, denoted by calling him, "Sir" (Κύριε), but responds in a manner that suggests he

thinks of Jesus as a simple passerby who is taken with the man and his plight. The lame man responds to Jesus's question from within his own categories and capabilities and misses the significance of the question about true wellness. It is likely that his language, denoted by the emphatic pronoun, "while I am coming" (ἐν ᾧ δὲ ἔρχομαι ἐγώ), is an implicit request by manipulation.[16] The reader is meant to be struck by the irony. The "one"—the "man" (ἄνθρωπον)—that the lame man needs is standing before him, but the manner of help he will provide is entirely different.

The lame man is fully admissive that he needs help—"I have no one" (ἄνθρωπον οὐκ ἔχω)—but he thinks the solution is in the water just a few feet away with the (magical) stirring that is believed to heal the sick. This verse strongly implies the man believes in some form of superstition and magic, as noted above (see comments on v. 3). It was quite common for a group or individual to believe in magic alongside institutional religion.[17] What is significant is that the lame man, like others who held to magic, is convinced that the water was infused with an impersonal power that was still very much *from* God. In the very city of Jerusalem, in the shadow of the temple, the response of the lame man in this verse "points to an understanding of God as one whose power sometimes operated as an impersonal force occasionally found within the water."[18] It was this that the lame man and the great multitude of sick were waiting for, the magical actions of the God of Israel. This impersonal—even magical—power of God is an important connection between the lame man and the Jewish authorities with whom Jesus is about to come into conflict.

---

15. Cf. L. Th. Witkamp, "The Use of Traditions in John 5.1–18," *JSNT* 25 (1985): 19–47 (23).

16. Michaels, *John*, 293.

17. Helpful here is David E. Aune, "Magic in Early Christianity," in *Aufstieg und Niedergang der römischen Welt: Geschichte und Kultur Roms im Spiegel der neueren Forsc-*

hung, ed. Wolfgang Haase (Berlin: Walter de Gruyter, 1980), II.23.2.1507–57, who argues that magic was so intertwined with religion that it was "virtually impossible" to distinguish them (1516).

18. Bryan, "Power in the Pool," 14.

In their view, the God they claim to know and the power they believe he enacts are not directly connected, for the power is accessible independent of the direct working of God.

5:8 Jesus said to him, "Rise, pick up your mat, and walk" (λέγει αὐτῷ ὁ Ἰησοῦς, Ἔγειρε ἆρον τὸν κράβαττόν σου καὶ περιπάτει). The confusion spewing from the lame man's mouth is more imaginary than the magical stirring of the healing water, so Jesus without delay gives a threefold command to the lame man. The Word spoke to the man with the same powerful word that made all creation. The abruptness of Jesus's command echoes the proclamation that the lame will "leap like a deer" (Isa 35:6). They leap because the Word has spoken. The separation held by the lame man between God and God's power is coalesced in the person standing before him. By including the command to pick up "your mat" (τὸν κράβαττόν σου), which was a poor man's bed that could be used as a stretcher, Jesus is establishing for the lame man a new functioning identity.[19] He no longer needs to rest his lame body on a mat; all he needs now are soles for his feet. What once carried the man is now to be carried triumphantly by him.[20]

5:9 And at once the man became well, and he took his mat and walked. But on that day it was the Sabbath (καὶ εὐθέως ἐγένετο ὑγιὴς ὁ ἄνθρωπος, καὶ ἦρεν τὸν κράβαττον αὐτοῦ καὶ περιεπάτει. Ἦν δὲ σάββατον ἐν ἐκείνῃ τῇ ἡμέρᾳ). Without delay, denoted by "at once" (εὐθέως), the lame man was no more; the sickness that had made him lame for thirty-eight years was immediately abolished. Noticeably, the narrative no longer calls him "the lame man" (ὁ ἀσθενῶν) but simply "the man" (ὁ ἄνθρωπος). Fitting the question Jesus raised, the narrator claims the man "became well" (ἐγένετο

ὑγιής). The use of the significant term "became" (ἐγένετο) is no reflection of the man's faith but is instead a reflection of the one who made him well and all that this act signifies concerning him. This man was confronted by *the* man, the final judge, Creator of the universe, the Son of Man—a sign of heaven (cf. 1:51). While waiting for the power of a pool, the lame man was confronted in Jesus by *the personal* power of God.

What appears like the resolution to the conflict regarding a lame man is given the penultimate position at the end of v. 9 when the narrator notes that this healing was performed on the Sabbath. Several interpreters mistakenly separate vv. 1–9b from vv. 9c–18, as if the healing miracle and the Sabbath controversy are different events. They are most certainly not distinct events that were poorly edited, nor is this a scene change. The same "God confusion" believed by the great multitude of sick is to be made manifest by "the Jews" in what follows. For this reason, what is described in v. 9 is a reflection of the rising conflict, a strategy common to narrative emplotment (see Introduction). The real conflict of the plot includes both geography (the pool of healing) and chronology (the Sabbath).[21]

5:10 Then the Jews were saying to the man who had been healed, "It is the Sabbath, and it is not lawful for you to carry your mat" (ἔλεγον οὖν οἱ Ἰουδαῖοι τῷ τεθεραπευμένῳ, Σάββατόν ἐστιν, καὶ οὐκ ἔξεστίν σοι ἆραι τὸν κράβαττόν σου). The conflict of the pericope (vv. 6–10) reaches its climax as the chronological placement of the healing gets added to the controversy. The characters known as "the Jews" return to the scene, initiating a dialogue with the "healed" man (see comments on 1:19). The ease with which the healed man and the Jews are included together in the narrative should reflect how the narrative's introduction of the Sab-

19. BDAG 563.
20. Cf. Ridderbos, *John*, 186.

21. Contra Tom Thatcher, "The Sabbath Trick: Unstable Irony in the Fourth Gospel," *JSNT* 76 (1999): 53–77.

bath is not "to change the story's direction," contra Michaels, but to bring together the two "God confusions" into a coalesced problem.[22] The presence of the healed man brings into focus the misperception of an impersonal power of God that Jesus is confronting in both the healed man and the Jews. Even though the healed man now walks, he does not yet truly see; and even though the Jews are the teachers of God, they are still in need of being taught. It is in this way that the pericope climaxes in v. 10.

While the geographic placement (the pool of healing) was more implicit in the pericope, the chronological placement is made explicit. The Jews focus specifically on the day by saying directly, "It is the Sabbath" (Σάββατόν ἐστιν), with "Sabbath" moved forward in the word order for emphasis. The Sabbath regulation is stated clearly: "It is not lawful for you to carry your mat" (οὐκ ἔξεστίν σοι ἆραι τὸν κράβαττόν σου). Based upon the developing oral tradition, it is likely that such a regulation was justified (cf. m. Shabbat 7:2).[23] In this pericope, the focus is only indirectly on the Sabbath and its laws, for its direct focus is the God of the Sabbath. The main theme of what follows is not "the violation of the Sabbath" but the violation of the personal power of God.[24]

5:11 But he answered them, "The one who made me well said to me, 'Pick up your mat and walk'" (ὁ δὲ ἀπεκρίθη αὐτοῖς, Ὁ ποιήσας με ὑγιῆ ἐκεῖνός μοι εἶπεν, Ἆρον τὸν κράβαττόν σου καὶ περιπάτει). In response to their rebuke of his Sabbath-breaking action, the healed man reflects the blame away from himself and places it on his healer, who told him to do it. There is no need to offer a psychological evaluation of the man's response. He did do as he was commanded by Jesus, whether or not he was aware of what day it was (cf. v. 8). It is important to note that while the Jews excuse the man for following his healer's orders, they will not excuse Jesus for following his Father's orders (cf. vv. 17 – 18).

5:12 They answered him, "Who is the man who said to you, 'Pick up and walk?'" (ἠρώτησαν αὐτόν, Τίς ἐστιν ὁ ἄνθρωπος ὁ εἰπών σοι, Ἆρον καὶ περιπάτει;). The Jews move quickly from the healed man to Jesus. There is a surprising irony surrounding this scene. The healing of a man lame for thirty-eight years is eclipsed in the mind of the Jews by the Sabbath — one day drowns out thirty-eight years! The Jews see a violation, not a miracle. Implicit is their blindness to their own "God confusion." A man who sits by a pool, waiting for a magical stirring of pool waters goes unquestioned for years (decades) but is questioned on the same day when his healing occurs on the Sabbath. The narrative is begging the reader to ask the right questions about God. Where and when is God expected to work his power? How is God's power connected to who he is? Apparently, a magical healing pool is considered under the umbrella of God, only as long as it is not done on the Sabbath!

5:13 But the man did not know who he was, for Jesus became invisible in the crowd in that place (ὁ δὲ ἰαθεὶς οὐκ ᾔδει τίς ἐστιν, ὁ γὰρ Ἰησοῦς ἐξένευσεν ὄχλου ὄντος ἐν τῷ τόπῳ). The commotion of the crowd around him, however, caused the healed man to miss the opportunity to identify the person who had healed him. The narrator explains that because of the surrounding crowd, Jesus was able to "became invisible" (ἐξένευσεν), a verb that can imply a turning of the head to dodge or avoid something.[25] By describing the crowd "in that place" (ἐν τῷ τόπῳ), the narrator is bringing the narrative back to the opening description of "that place," the healing pool and great multitude of sick

22. Cf. Michaels, *John*, 295.
23. See Keener, *John*, 1:641 – 43.
24. Contra Brown, *John*, 1:210.
25. BDAG 307; Barrett, *John*, 255.

(vv. 2 – 3), in order to connect the topic with a very different "place" — the temple.[26]

5:14 After these things Jesus found him in the temple and said to him, "Behold, you have become well. Sin no longer, so that nothing worse may happen to you" (μετὰ ταῦτα εὑρίσκει αὐτὸν ὁ Ἰησοῦς ἐν τῷ ἱερῷ καὶ εἶπεν αὐτῷ, Ἴδε ὑγιὴς γέγονας· μηκέτι ἁμάρτανε, ἵνα μὴ χεῖρόν σοί τι γένηται). After an undisclosed amount of time, denoted again by "after these things" (μετὰ ταῦτα), the narrator records how Jesus found the healed man in the temple. The temple is a logical place for Jesus to be during a Jewish festival; he may have been heading to the temple when he stopped by the great multitude of sick lying near the healing pool, which is just north of the temple. The temple is also a logical place for the healed man to be drawn toward, especially after he had just been divinely healed! Beyond all the logic, the fact that Jesus "found" (εὑρίσκει) the healed man suggests it is not a chance encounter. Jesus frequently "finds" the people he is looking for (cf. 1:43, and especially 9:35).

After the pronouncement "you have become well" (ὑγιὴς γέγονας), repeating the verb so central to this Gospel (bringing back into focus Jesus's original question and the deep sense his question was intending to probe; see comments on v. 6), Jesus gives his fourth and final command to the healed man: "Sin no longer" (μηκέτι ἁμάρτανε). While the present imperative can view the prohibition as an ongoing process and could be translated as "stop sinning," yet since it primarily views action from an internal point of view it is more commonly used for general precepts, "for habits that should characterize one's attitude or behavior — rather than in specific situations."[27] It is therefore best translated as a general prohibition. This helps avoid an interpretation that is searching for a specific disease-causing sin in the life of the healed man rather than a general command against sin. Following the prohibition against sin, an appeal is added: "So that nothing worse may happen to you" (ἵνα μὴ χεῖρόν σοί τι γένηται). This purpose-result clause warns the healed man of greater consequences from his sin if he does not heed Jesus's prohibition.

This verse has raised more than a few questions. It is the first time sin is directed at a particular person and the first time sin is mentioned since 1:29, where Jesus was described as the one who would take away the "sin of the world." While some have tried to press from this prohibition and purpose-result clause a direct connection between sin and consequence (in this case, illness), it can only be done so in light of the rest of the teaching of Scripture. It is clear that sin has its consequences and that sickness (and death) can be one of its consequences, but this verse is not addressing directly this issue.

In light of this larger context of wellness, the issue of sin Jesus is addressing is not to be confined to a deed done on one day but is sin rooted in habits that characterize a person, the kind of sin that is detrimental to true wellness. For behind all the concern for geography and chronology in this pericope, there was a "God confusion" that entirely misunderstood the personal nature of the power of God. The healed man truly believed God could and did heal, but he was looking for it in the depersonalized magical waters rooted in superstition and folklore. In the same way, the Jews truly believed that God could and did heal. But when they were confronted with a real healing, they raised no questions regarding the divine origin of Jesus's power but focused entirely on the perceived Sabbath violation. In a manner similar to the superstition of the multitude of the sick, "The Jews think Jesus capable of accessing God's power outside the

---

26. Michaels, *John*, 296 – 97.

27. Wallace, *Greek Grammar*, 721,

will of God … independent of the direct working of God."[28]

It is with this context in mind that Jesus's prohibition and subsequent warning is to be explained. The sin Jesus is concerned with is defined elsewhere by the Fourth Gospel as "the unwillingness to believe that Jesus is the one in whom God — the Father — is revealed and through whom God's power works."[29] For example, in 8:24 and 16:9, sin is defined as not believing in Jesus. And in 15:24, it is made even clearer: "The essence of sin is to see the power of God at work through Jesus and yet refuse to acknowledge that power as evidence of the self-revealing action of God in Jesus."[30] Thus, the command to stop sinning is an admonition against the sin of unbelief, which in this case manifests itself by regarding God's power as operating in impersonal independence from the working of God, a problem for both the healed man and the Jews. Our interpretation is in no way limiting the immediate consequences of sin but following the Gospel narrative by locating the deep root of sin as a rejection of God (idolatrous "God confusion"). The immediate consequences of sin are merely a symptom of the larger sin problem. Jesus has a concern for the man that extends far beyond flesh and bones; it is a concern that the man's healed condition might be "worse" than the first (cf. Matt 12:45).

5:15 The man went and reported to the Jews that Jesus was the one who made him well (ἀπῆλθεν ὁ ἄνθρωπος καὶ ἀνήγγειλεν τοῖς Ἰουδαίοις ὅτι Ἰησοῦς ἐστιν ὁ ποιήσας αὐτὸν ὑγιῆ). The depiction by the narrator does not paint the healed man favorably, as if he now believed or moved closer to belief. Even with his own body as evidence, the healed man represents a particular response to the Gospel

that replaces the power of God with impersonal and superstitious religion and fails to believe in Jesus, the personal manifestation of the power of God. It is in this way that the conflict of the pericope comes to a resolution. Verses 14 – 15 are part of the resolution because they bring completion to the "become well" theme that began in v. 6 at the beginning of the conflict.

5:16 And for this reason the Jews were persecuting Jesus, because he was doing these things on the Sabbath (καὶ διὰ τοῦτο ἐδίωκον οἱ Ἰουδαῖοι τὸν Ἰησοῦν, ὅτι ταῦτα ἐποίει ἐν σαββάτῳ). The Jews take the report from the healed man and announce by their actions their condemnation of him. The narrator's comments describe their response as in process, denoted by the imperfect tense "were persecuting" (ἐδίωκον), which might even suggest it had become a fixed policy at this stage in Jesus's ministry. There is no denial of his power, only the charge that it took place illegally, "on the Sabbath" (ἐν σαββάτῳ). For the first time in the Gospel, the ministry of Jesus, which until now has been primarily centered upon individuals, is turning public — and hostile (see 1:11).

5:17 But Jesus answered them, "My Father is working up to the present, and I too am working" (ὁ δὲ Ἰησοῦς ἀπεκρίνατο αὐτοῖς, Ὁ πατήρ μου ἕως ἄρτι ἐργάζεται, κἀγὼ ἐργάζομαι). Although there is no statement made by the Jews, Jesus "answered" (ἀπεκρίνατο) them according to their condemnatory actions.[31] Jesus's answer is both a confession and a declaration. His reference to "my Father" (Ὁ πατήρ μου) would have probably sounded strange to the Jews but is perfectly at home in the Fourth Gospel (see 1:18). He had spoken of "my Father" once before when he said in the temple, "Stop

---

28. Bryan, "Power in the Pool," 16.
29. Ibid.
30. Ibid.

31. Interpreters have too quickly let the overabundance of Sabbath controversy in the Synoptics eclipse the message of this pericope (see Mark 2:28). The real issue in this scene was not the Sabbath but God.

making my Father's house a house of business!" but it did not register (2:16). This time it does, and they are beginning to grasp its implications (cf. v. 18).[32]

Jesus explains that his Father "is working up to the present" (ἕως ἄρτι ἐργάζεται), with no indication that the time has come or soon will come for work to stop. The idea that God "rested" after creating the world in six days (Gen 2:2 – 3) should not be interpreted to mean that God is now inactive. God not only created the whole world; he also sustains it. In this sense, "breaking" the Sabbath is not only lawful for God; it is necessary. From what can be determined from Jewish exegesis, it is likely that this declaration by Jesus to the Jews would have been quite understandable, fitting comfortably alongside the current exegesis of God's Sabbath rest.[33] The "resting" of God was comfortably defined as an anthropomorphism, for God has never ceased his creative and sustaining activity.

It is not just God who has been working, for Jesus can also claim, "I too am working" (κἀγὼ ἐργάζομαι). The emphatic pronoun "I too" (κἀγὼ) not only equates Jesus's work with God's but also equates Jesus with God (cf. v. 18). Although the Jews do not have the reader's insight from the prologue that Jesus is the one through whom all things were made (1:3), he too must also be working. Jesus's inclusion of himself is not without mystery, for it is difficult to know the exact interrelation of their coparticipatory "work." Even still, Jesus's primary point is clear: both the Father and the Son are at work. Thus, Jesus is not violating the Sabbath but "is acting as God's agent to do what no one denied God could do on the Sabbath."[34] Whatever issues were raised regarding the Sabbath have been trumped by this theological explanation of the work of God, the Father and the Son. In light of this pericope, then, the working that Jesus is doing must include the healing of the lame man on the Sabbath and should also be understood to incorporate his entire mission and ministry.

It is important to note that the "present" working of God speaks directly against the false conception that God's power can be disassociated from his person. This false belief made it possible from the lame man's perspective for there to be a healing pool that had only a loose association with God and according to the Jews for Jesus to use God's power contrary to God's will. This verse, therefore, is a specific rejection of the assertion that Jesus had access to God's power (as evidenced by the healing) but applied it in an inappropriate manner (i.e., on the Sabbath). Bryan offers this interpretive translation: "My Father has not set his power loose in the world to be accessed as an independent force; if his power is at work in the world, it is because my Father is personally at work."[35] The Jews were confronted with a stark reality. The entire event surrounding the healed man was not only directly connected to the person of Jesus but also connected — and necessarily so — to God himself.

5:18 And for this reason the Jews were seeking to kill him even harder, not only because he broke the Sabbath, but also because he called God his Father, making himself equal with God (διὰ τοῦτο οὖν μᾶλλον ἐζήτουν αὐτὸν οἱ Ἰουδαῖοι ἀποκτεῖναι, ὅτι οὐ μόνον ἔλυεν τὸ σάββατον ἀλλὰ καὶ πατέρα ἴδιον ἔλεγεν τὸν θεόν, ἴσον ἑαυτὸν ποιῶν τῷ θεῷ). By their actions, the Jews show that they fully understand what Jesus is communicating about himself and at the same time have revealed an entirely inadequate understanding of God. By misunderstanding Jesus, the Jews are by definition misunderstanding — even rejecting — God, who is ironically the one they are attempting to defend.

---

32. Michaels, *John*, 301.
33. Barrett, *John*, 256.
34. Craig S. Keener, "Is Subordination within the Trin-

ity Really Heresy? A Study of John 5:18 in Context," *TrinJ* 20 (1999): 39 – 51 (41).

35. Bryan, "Power in the Pool," 20.

Their concerns over the Sabbath have long dissipated, for this Sabbath breaker was more than just licentious in their eyes. He was blasphemous and therefore deserving of death. While the author continues to unfold for the reader the historical events surrounding the life and ministry of Jesus, the cosmological insights provided by the prologue prepared the reader for such statements by Jesus (cf. 1:1, 14, 18) and such a reaction to him (1:11). Only now, however, are the insights being viewed for the first time in three dimensions and in color.[36] Ironically, the very people that "were seeking to kill him" (ἐζήτουν αὐτὸν ἀποκτεῖναι) happen to be the same ones for whom he came to die.

Theology in Application

In an encounter with a man lame for nearly four decades, Jesus probes the nature of true wellness and the problem of real sin, all the while confronting the religious superstitions and false conceptions about God so common in the fallen world. In this pericope, the reader of the Fourth Gospel is exhorted to explore the nature of wellness, the consequences of sin, and more importantly, the right questions about who God is and the kind of work he is doing.

Religious Superstition and Our Conception of God

By interlocking two different interlocutors by means of an identical problem, this pericope made manifest the ease with which humans can make God to be something he is not or to connect something to God that is not from him. Both the lame man and the Jews were guilty of disconnecting God from his power. This ironic disconnect in the shadow of the temple in Jerusalem is too common a problem in the church today. This pericope is urging the reader to ask the right questions about God.[37] Where and when is God expected to work his power? How is God's power connected to who he is? Any answer to those questions that removes the work of Jesus is immediately false. In a real way, this passage is encouraging us, the church, to be self-critical, to put ourselves to the test by taking captive "hollow and deceptive philosophy" that depends on "[our own] human tradition and the elemental spiritual forces of this world rather than on Christ" (Col 2:8). It is because we believe in Christ that we distrust ourselves, knowing full well that we continually need him even as he continually works (v. 17).

Sin and Afflictions

This pericope raises the unavoidable question of the afflictions caused by personal sin. Although we argued that Jesus's command to "sin no longer" (v. 14) was

---

36. See Peder Borgen, "Creation, Logos and the Son: Observations on John 1:1 – 18 and 5:17 – 18," *ExAud* 3 (1987): 88 – 97.

37. See A. W. Tozer, *The Knowledge of the Holy: The Attributes of God: Their Meaning in the Christian Life* (New York: Harper & Row, 1961), 1.

speaking more generally about habitual and characteristic sin that produces consequences in eternity, this in no way divorces our current afflictions from our sin. In fact, if we were to separate our afflictions from our sin, we would be committing the same "God confusion" believed by the healed man and the Jews. In a very real way, our afflictions are a direct effect of our sin, even if we cannot precisely define the cause and effect. But our response is not overly to examine sources and symptoms but to be disciplined by our afflictions as by God. Calvin encourages this response: "First, then, we must acknowledge that it is God's hand that strikes us and not imagine that our ills come from blind fortune. Next, we should ascribe this honour to God, that as He is indeed a good Father He has no pleasure in our sufferings and therefore does not treat us harshly unless He is displeased with our sins."[38] In hindsight, Jesus's interaction with the lame man and the Jews is filled with paternal love, and as we look back on our afflictions, we are likely to see the same paternal love embracing our moments of suffering. For this reason, we are exhorted by the Lord himself: "Sin no more!"

The Personal Power of God

In this pericope, Jesus is portrayed as a coparticipant in the work of God; a work now best described as the work of the Father and the Son. A correct conception about God locates the true work that God is doing in the person of Jesus Christ and therefore in the work he has accomplished for the world on the cross. To speak of God in a generic or "spiritual" sense is not to speak of the God of the Bible. The work of God is so intertwined with the work of the Son that Jesus is the personal power of God. Where and how is God working? Quite simply, he is working through the work initiated by Jesus Christ, which he himself will finish upon his return.

Let the church check itself to ensure it has not taken on a "work" that is not of God, that is, not rooted in and commanded by Jesus Christ. Even more, let the church check itself to ensure it has not excluded a "work" that Christ did perform simply because it seems less spiritual. The calling of the church is to embrace the work of Christ as their Great Commission (Matt 28:18 – 20), a work that is from the Father and empowered by the Spirit (20:21 – 23).

---

38. Calvin, *John 1 – 10*, 122.

CHAPTER 11

John 5:19 – 47

Literary Context

The healing of the lame man and the Sabbath controversy clearly raised the issue of the identity of Jesus and his relation to God the Father. This "God confusion" was the pervasive problem reflected in the assumptions of both the lame man and the Jews. In this pericope, Jesus stops to address this God confusion. What becomes important to notice is how the more Jesus addresses humanity's confusion about God, the more humanity's confusion about itself comes to light. It is time for the Word to make a declarative statement about himself, including specific insights regarding his identity, his relation to the Father, and his credibility and in so doing providing insight into the state of humanity.

IV. The Confession of the Son of God (5:1 – 8:11)
    A. The Third Sign: The Healing of the Lame Man on the Sabbath (5:1 – 18)
➡   **B. The Identity of (the Son of) God: Jesus Responds to the Opposition (5:19 – 47)**
    C. The Fourth Sign: The Feeding of a Large Crowd (6:1 – 15)
    D. The "I AM" Walks across the Sea (6:16 – 21)
    E. The Bread of Life (6:22 – 71)
    F. Private Display of Suspicion (7:1 – 13)
    G. Public Display of Rejection (7:14 – 52)
    H. The Trial of Jesus regarding a Woman Accused of Adultery (7:53 – 8:11)

Main Idea

Jesus is so intimately connected to the Father that there is nothing God has ever done in history (e.g., the Baptist; Scripture) or in himself (the Trinity) that is exclusive of Jesus. Everything God has ever said and done is now in his hands. To reject Jesus is not only disbelief in God but is also a revealing depiction of the true object of humanity's faith — the self.

Translation

John 5:19–47

Then Jesus answered and said to them,

19a   Monologue
   Unity of Father & Son: 19c–24
b   Amen Formula — *"Truly, truly I say to you,*
   Antithetical Parallelism 19c–f
c   Negative Assertion — *(a) the Son is not able to do anything by himself,*
d   Exception — *(b) except what he sees the Father doing;*
e   Basis — *(b') since whatever he does,*
f   Positive Assertion — *(a') the Son likewise does these things.*

20a   Explanation (of 19) #1 — *For*
b   Assertion — *the Father loves the Son*
c   Consequence (of 20b) #1 — *and shows him all that he does,*
d   Consequence (of 20b) #2 — *and he will show him works greater than these,*
e   Result — *so that you may be amazed.*

21a   Explanation (of 19) #2 — *For*
b   Comparison — *just as the Father raises the dead and gives them life,*
c   Assertion — *so also does the Son give life to whom he desires.*

22a   Explanation (of19) #3 — *For*
b   Assertion — *the Father judges no one,*
c   Contrast — *but has given all judgment to the Son,*
23a   Purpose — *in order that all may honor the Son*
b   Comparison — *just as they honor the Father.*
c   Inference of 23a, b — *The one who does not honor the Son does not honor the Father*
d   "who sent …" #1 (Source) — *who sent him.*
24a   Amen Formula — *Truly, truly, I say to you,*

b	Simultaneous Action #1	the one who hears my word and
c	Simultaneous Action #2	believes in the one ...
d	"who sent ..." #2 (Source)	who sent me
e	Result of 24b, c	... has eternal life and
f	Result of 24b, c	does not come into judgment, but
g	Restatement	has passed from death into life.

Sufficiency of the Son: 25–29

25a	Amen Formula	Truly, truly I say to you,
b	Assertion (Not Yet)	an hour comes and
c	Oxymoron (Already)	now is
d	Event	when the dead will hear the voice
e	Allusion to John 20:31	of the Son of God and
f	Result of 25d	those who hear will live.

26a	Basis #1 (Source of life)	For just as the Father has life in himself,
b	Comparison	so also he has given to the Son to have life in himself.
27a	Basis #2 (Authority to judge)	And he has given authority to him to make judgment,
b	Basis (Allusion to Dan 7:14)	because he is the Son of Man.
c		

28a	Command	Do not be amazed at this,
b	Basis (Restatement of 25b)	because an hour comes
c	Sequence #1	in which all
29a	Sequence #2	who are in graves will
		hear his voice
		and come out,
b	Expansion of 28c (Condition)	those who have done good things
c	Result of 24 and 29b	to a resurrection of life,
d	Expansion of 28c (Condition)	but those who have practiced evil
e	Result of 29d	to a resurrection of judgment.

Insufficiency of the Son 30–31

30a	Exclamation	I am not able to do anything by myself;
b	Progression #1	Just as I hear
c	Progression #2/Illustration	I judge,
d	Assertion (quality of "judgment")	and my judgment is righteous,
e	Basis	because I do not seek my will but
f	Contrast	the will of the one
g	"who sent ..." #3 (Source)	who sent me.

Continued on next page.

Continued from previous page.

31a	Condition	*If I testify concerning myself,*
b	Inference/Illustration #2 of 30a	*my witness is not sufficient.*
	Sufficiency of Father & Son (32–40)	
32a	Alternative Witness (the Father)	*There is another*
b	Description	*who testifies concerning me,*
c	Exclamation/Contrast to 31b	*and I know that the witness that he testifies concerning me is sufficient.*
	Expansion of 32:33–39	
33a	Coparticipatory Witness #1: J.B.	*You have sent to John,*
b	Progression	*and he has testified to the truth.*
34a	Rejection (Insufficiency of John)	*I do not receive the witness from a man,*
b	Contrast	*but I say these things*
c	Purpose	*in order that you might be saved.*
35a	Explanation of 33, 34	*John was the lamp that burned and shined,*
b	Reaction	*and you wanted to rejoice in his light for a time.*
36a	Contrast/Coparticipatory Witness #2: the Works	*But I have a witness greater than that of John,*
b	Basis	*for the works that the Father has given to me …*
c	Purpose	*so that I might complete them,*
d	Assertion	*which I am doing,*
e	Restatement of 32	*… testify concerning me*
f	"[who] sent …" #4 (Source)	*that the Father has sent me.*
37a	Coparticipatory Witness #3: the Father	*And the Father …*
b	"who sent …" #5 (Source)	*who sent me*
c	Restatement of 32, 36d	*… has himself testified about me.*
d	Rebuke #1	*You have neither heard his voice at any time*
e	Rebuke #2 /	*nor seen his form.*
	Allusion: 1 Chron 16:11; Ps 27:8	
38a	Rebuke #3	*Nor do you have his word*
b	Basis of 37d–38b	*remaining in you,*
c		*because you do not believe the one*
d	"whom he sent" #6 (Source)	*whom he sent.*

39a	Coparticipatory Witness #4: Scripture	You search the Scriptures,
b	Basis	because you think in them you have eternal life,
c	Ironic Contrast to 39a, b	and yet those witnesses are about me.
40a	Rebuke #4	And you are not willing to come to me
b	Purpose	in order to have life.
	Insufficiency of Humanity: 41–44	
41a	Explanation of 37d–40	For
b	Assertion	I do not receive recognition from humanity.
42a	Contrast	But I know you
b	Emphatic Rebuke	that you do not have the love of God in yourselves.
43a	Action/Source	I have come in the name of my Father
b	Reaction	and you do not receive me.
c	Condition (Contrast to 43a)	If another comes in his own name,
d	Contrast to 43b	you will receive him.
44a	Interrogative Rebuke	How can you believe
b	Condition #1	when you receive recognition from one another and
c	Condition #2	do not seek recognition from the Only God?
	Conclusion of Monologue: 45–47	
45a	Exclamation	Do not think that I will accuse you before the Father.
b	Ironic Warning	The one who accuses you is Moses,
c	Object of Faith	in whom you have placed your hope.
46a	Explanation of 45 / Condition	For if you believed Moses,
b	Inference	you would believe me,
c	Inference	
d	Basis	for he wrote about me.
47a	Contrast to 46	But
b	Condition	since you do not believe
c	Content: i.e., Scripture	what he wrote,
d	Concluding Interrogative Rebuke	how will you believe my words?"

Structure and Literary Form

This is the first substantial monologue in the narrative proper. A monologue (see Introduction) is similar to a dialogue in that it is set in the context of an engagement and conflict, but rather than engaging point for point it allows for a lengthy argument. A monologue can contain elements of rhetoric, challenge, and conflict, but it does so in a sustained presentation.

Exegetical Outline

This pericope is so intertwined — compare vv. 21–22 with vv. 26–27 — that there are several possible ways it could be divided. Yet there are distinctions in emphasis that suggest the pericope should be broken into three sections, even though the first two (vv. 19–24 and vv. 25–29) have a clear thematic overlap.

➡ **B. The Identity of (the Son of) God: Jesus Responds to the Opposition (5:19–47)**
   1. Like Father, like Son (vv. 19–24)
   2. Life and Judgment of the Son (vv. 25–29)
   3. Witnesses to the Son (vv. 30–47)
       a. The Insufficiency of Jesus's Witness (vv. 30–32)
       b. The Witness of John the Baptist (vv. 33–35)
       c. The Witness of the Works of Jesus (v. 36)
       d. The Witness of the Father (vv. 37–38)
       e. The Witness of Scripture (vv. 39–40)
       f. The Insufficiency of Human Recognition (vv. 41–47)

Explanation of the Text

The importance of this pericope is often missed because it is eclipsed by the more well-known speeches of Jesus to come (e.g., the "bread of life" and "I am" sayings). But this pericope turns the focus directly on Christ and serves to propel the message of the narrative forward. "Nowhere else in the Gospels do we find our Lord making such a formal, systematic, orderly, regular statement of His own unity with the Father, His divine commission and authority, and the proofs of His Messiah-

ship, as we find in this discourse ... it seems one of the deepest things in the Bible."[1]

5:19 Then Jesus answered and said to them, "Truly, truly I say to you, the Son is not able to do anything by himself, except what he sees the Father doing; since whatever he does, the Son likewise does these things" (Ἀπεκρίνατο οὖν ὁ Ἰησοῦς καὶ ἔλεγεν αὐτοῖς, Ἀμὴν ἀμὴν λέγω ὑμῖν, οὐ δύναται ὁ υἱὸς ποιεῖν ἀφ᾽ ἑαυτοῦ οὐδὲν ἐὰν μή τι βλέπῃ τὸν

---

1. John Charles Ryle, *Expository Thoughts on the Gospels, St. John*, 3 vols. (London: James Clarke, 1957), 1:283.

πατέρα ποιοῦντα· ἃ γὰρ ἂν ἐκεῖνος ποιῇ, ταῦτα καὶ ὁ υἱὸς ὁμοίως ποιεῖ). By prefacing his response with "truly, truly" (Ἀμὴν ἀμὴν), Jesus signals that his forthcoming statement is significant (see comments on 1:51). But the narrator's own preface to Jesus's statement, "Then Jesus answered and said" (Ἀπεκρίνατο οὖν ὁ Ἰησοῦς καὶ ἔλεγεν), is an unusually solemn introduction and with Jesus's opening words clearly highlight the importance of what follows.[2] By these prefaces, the tension developing throughout the Gospel is forcing itself upon this monologue. This is no abstract sermon; this is a contextualized explanation of God by his Word — his representative (1:18) and agent (5:17) — to the world. Even more, it is not only a deconstruction of what the Jews had believed, fitting the historical plot of the Gospel, it is also a construction of what all should believe, fitting the cosmological plot of the Gospel (see comments before 1:1).[3]

Jesus begins with a potent combination of a negation and an affirmation in antithetical parallelism. Jesus claims that the Son can do nothing "by himself" (ἀφ᾽ ἑαυτοῦ), but qualifies this with an "except" (ἐὰν μή) clause to communicate that he can only do "what he sees the Father doing" (τι βλέπῃ τὸν πατέρα ποιοῦντα). The affirmation follows immediately, directed by the causal conjunction "since" (γάρ).[4] Whatever the Father does, the Son also does "in the same way" (ὁμοίως). The point of tension between the negation and affirmation is what is emphasized: the activity of the Son is entirely defined by the activity of the Father. The limitation of the Son is so intimately connected to the unimaginable limitlessness of the Father that the point is less *what* the Son cannot do than it

is the one *with whom* he does it. The limitations placed on Jesus by the Arians so long ago misplaced the point of contrast in the statement. If the Son is limited, then so is the Father.

Just as the prologue declared that only the Son could "see" the Father (1:18), so now Jesus explains that such sight is not merely passive but active so that the Son may speak and act in accord with the Father (on "sight" in John, see comments on 20:29). The expression of their united relation helps explain their differences, for the Son does "likewise" (ὁμοίως), which in this context does not mean "in the same way."[5] This close relation between the Father and Son is not meant to blur their distinctions; the Father is the Father, and the Son is the Son. But their actions, wills, and purposes find agreement between them. While Bultmann presses against a reading like ours that sees in Jesus's words an ontological depiction, what he calls "speculative Christology," he is wrong to claim that the meaning of the existence of Christ can only be derived from those who see and hear him.[6] The Fourth Gospel comfortably goes through the ontological origin of Jesus in order to explain his physical actions and words.[7] And the Gospel is speaking *not from* those who see and hear *but to* them; the people from whom he speaks are persons of the triune God. With the introduction provided by the prologue, the reader is alerted to the depth of the subject matter to which the Gospel refers.

5:20 "For the Father loves the Son and shows him all that he does, and he will show him works greater than these, so that you may be amazed" (ὁ γὰρ πατὴρ φιλεῖ τὸν υἱὸν καὶ πάντα δείκνυσιν αὐτῷ

---

2. Peter W. Ensor, *Jesus and His 'Works': The Johannine Sayings in Historical Perspective*, WUNT 2.85 (Tübingen: Mohr Siebeck, 1996), 217.

3. See Augustine, *John*, 18.8.120.

4. To translate the conjunction as explanatory, i.e., "for," would soften the intentional antithetical parallelism.

5. Ridderbos, *John*, 193.

6. Bultmann, *John*, 249.

7. See Marinus de Jonge, *Jesus: Stranger from Heaven and Son of God* (Missoula, MT: Scholars Press, 1977), 150, 166.

ἃ αὐτὸς ποιεῖ, καὶ μείζονα τούτων δείξει αὐτῷ ἔργα, ἵνα ὑμεῖς θαυμάζητε). The antithetical parallelism is now followed by the thrice-repeated explanatory "for" (γὰρ).[8] The ministry of Jesus is rooted in and empowered by the love of the Father. The present-tense "loves" (φιλεῖ) suggests a continual, habitual love. Love has already been described as the unseen motivation behind all God's actions for the world (see comments on 3:16); now it is also included in the relations between the persons of God. This is manifested in the Son's intimate union with the Father, who "shows" (δείκνυσιν) the Son "all" (πάντα) he does, again described as continual and habitual by the present tense.

Beyond the ontological reality this depicts in regard to the union between the Father and Son, it provides a robust rebuke of those who would see any disconnect between what Jesus is doing (e.g., on the Sabbath) and what God is doing. God is not only still working he has work still to do. Evidence of this is not merely the ontological status between the Father and the Son but the future manifestation of "works" (ἔργα) even "greater than these" (μείζονα τούτων), denoted by the genitive of comparison. These works, which will be given some description below, will result in an "extraordinary impression" of amazement, given emphasis by the emphatic "you" (ὑμεῖς).[9] There is no need to wonder about the work of the Father since it is now clear that the Father's work is to be done by the Son; in fact, these are the works the Son has already been doing. The disassociation of the work of Jesus from the work of the Father explains Jesus's warning to the lame man (cf. 5:14) and gives the immediate context for this monologue.

5:21 "For just as the Father raises the dead and gives them life, so also does the Son give life to whom he desires" (ὥσπερ γὰρ ὁ πατὴρ ἐγείρει τοὺς νεκροὺς καὶ ζῳοποιεῖ, οὕτως καὶ ὁ υἱὸς οὓς θέλει ζῳοποιεῖ). With a second explanatory "for" (γὰρ), Jesus speaks even more directly about the freedom given to him to heal — to restore life — a freedom found in the restorative nature of God. What was believed about God is being impressed as equally and irrevocably true about Jesus (cf. Deut 32:39; 1 Sam 2:6; 2 Kgs 5:7). It is the disassociation, the "God confusion," that is being challenged and rebuked. Jesus is not working beside God, serving in a subsidiary manner when needed; he is participating "just as" (ὥσπερ) the Father in the restoration of life itself. The sonship of Jesus is becoming central to the functional identity of Jesus and the message of the Gospel (cf. 20:31).

It is important to note that the Son gives life "to whom he desires" (οὓς θέλει ζῳοποιεῖ). While the Son is doing what the Father does, this statement suggests that a certain amount of autonomy belongs to the Son. It is the Son alone who gives life, and he is entirely free in his selection, reflected in his selection of one sick man out of a great multitude (cf. 5:6). The one-sidedness and subjectivity of the "desire" or "will" of Jesus shows the capacity of Christ's power. It connects the reception of life with the counsels of infinite wisdom and love and shows its independence from external factors such as genealogical descent (as from Abraham).[10]

5:22 "For the Father judges no one, but has given all judgment to the Son" (οὐδὲ γὰρ ὁ πατὴρ κρίνει οὐδένα, ἀλλὰ τὴν κρίσιν πᾶσαν δέδωκεν τῷ υἱῷ). With a third and final explanatory "for" (γὰρ),

---

8. There are actually four occurrences of "for" (γὰρ), but since the first in v. 19 functions causally in the antithetical parallelism and not explanatorily as in vv. 20–22, the implied structural significance is primarily rooted in the three explanatory clauses.

9. BDAG 444.
10. Westcott, *John*, 86.

Jesus declares that the Son, not the Father, is the judge. Such a statement would have unnerved the Jewish opponents. Some Jews believed God would delegate judgment in some matters, but it was clearly judgment in a limited sense.[11] This statement emphasizes the final phase of the mission of the Son. For although the Son was not sent to condemn the world, a judgment has already begun and belongs entirely to the Son who was sent (see 3:17–18). Only in 1:1 has language been used that was so obviously declaring the divinity of Jesus.

5:23 "In order that all may honor the Son just as they honor the Father. The one who does not honor the Son does not honor the Father who sent him" (ἵνα πάντες τιμῶσι τὸν υἱὸν καθὼς τιμῶσι τὸν πατέρα. ὁ μὴ τιμῶν τὸν υἱὸν οὐ τιμᾷ τὸν πατέρα τὸν πέμψαντα αὐτόν). After three explanatory statements (vv. 20–22), Jesus now gives the purpose behind the functional roles of the Son: "In order that all may honor the Son" (ἵνα πάντες τιμῶσι τὸν υἱόν). The Son not only functions like the Father, but receives honor "just as" (καθὼς) the Father receives honor. Such a statement does not mean that we honor the Son as if he was the Father but that we honor the person of the Son in the same way as we honor the person of the Father. This returns us to the beginning of the Gospel where we wrestled with the definition of "God." This verse is "pressuring" the reader to see the Trinitarian subject matter in view, where "God" must be understood to at least include the Father and the Son, who are different in function but equal in "honor."

What is at stake, according to Jesus, is not merely a correct understanding of Jesus but a correct understanding of the Father. Even beyond the ontological depiction of the identity of God (see comments on 1:1), this statement serves to rebuke the Jews who disassociated Jesus from God. Such "God confusion" is nothing less than heretical. To get Jesus wrong is to get God wrong, for God is fully presented by the Son. As much as this Gospel is about Jesus Christ, its most foundational subject matter is the triune God (cf. 20:31).

5:24 "Truly, truly, I say to you, the one who hears my word and believes in the one who sent me has eternal life and does not come into judgment, but has passed from death into life" (Ἀμὴν ἀμὴν λέγω ὑμῖν ὅτι ὁ τὸν λόγον μου ἀκούων καὶ πιστεύων τῷ πέμψαντί με ἔχει ζωὴν αἰώνιον, καὶ εἰς κρίσιν οὐκ ἔρχεται ἀλλὰ μεταβέβηκεν ἐκ τοῦ θανάτου εἰς τὴν ζωήν). The first section of Jesus's monologue begins and ends with the authoritative preface of Jesus, imposing significance and authority on the summative statement to follow. In light of what has been declared about the Son (vv. 19–23), Jesus can now proclaim what only he can offer: the soteriological conclusion of his person which is nothing less than true life. The unity of the Son and Father are made explicit even in the invitation Jesus gives. The person who responds is the one "who hears" (ὁ … ἀκούων) Jesus's word and "believes" (πιστεύων) in the God — the Father — who sent him. (The absence of a second article for the second participle serves to coordinate the features of this single two-fold description.) Responding to the message — "the word" (τὸν λόγον) — of Jesus is also believing in God the Father! The real distinctions between the persons of God find a cooperative and necessary solidarity in the triune identity of God. Such revelation only magnifies further the God-confused error of the healed man and the Jews in the previous pericope (5:1–18).

Hearing and believing in the triune God leads to nothing less than true life, that is, "eternal life" (ζωὴν αἰώνιον). This life is what the hearer/believer "has" (ἔχει), which, as discussed above (cf. v. 21), suggests it is a present reality. Jesus qualifies the aspects of "life" by claiming that the believer "does

---

11. Keener, *John*, 1:651.

not come into judgment" (εἰς κρίσιν οὐκ ἔρχεται) and "has passed from death to life" (μεταβέβηκεν ἐκ τοῦ θανάτου εἰς τὴν ζωήν). Both of these aspects speak right through the present to the future. This is the first occurrence of "death" (θανάτου) in the Gospel and serves to qualify the status of those al-

ready described as "darkness" (1:5; 3:19). The prologue has foretold the "unseen" by explaining that "in him was life" (1:4), and here Jesus declares it himself. The judge and the giver of life has just declared that he is also the only one who can remove judgment and death.

IN DEPTH: Eschatology in John

Many modern interpreters have so imputed to the Gospel of John a "realized eschatology" that the futuristic eschatology of this pericope seem out of place. As instructive as language like "futuristic eschatology" and "realized eschatology" are for interpreters, proponents of both views have a tendency to speak past the other. Even more, such an antithesis is altogether missing from the Gospel. In fact, for John the promise of a future eschatology is the best argument for the reality of a present eschatology. The present state of the "eternal life" Jesus gives need not deny its future implications or reality, just as a future reality need not deny its present implications. As is common in the Gospel of John, Jesus can speak of the gift of life in the present without diminishing in any way the glorious aspects of life to come. The very fact that he will be life and judge in the future (vv. 28 – 29) is proof that he is serving as life and judge in the now.

5:25 "Truly, truly I say to you, an hour comes and now is when the dead will hear the voice of the Son of God and those who hear will live" (ἀμὴν ἀμὴν λέγω ὑμῖν ὅτι ἔρχεται ὥρα καὶ νῦν ἐστιν ὅτε οἱ νεκροὶ ἀκούσουσιν τῆς φωνῆς τοῦ υἱοῦ τοῦ θεοῦ καὶ οἱ ἀκούσαντες ζήσουσιν). A new section in the monologue begins as Jesus transitions from life to judgment, a theme only hinted at above. The transition is also marked with Jesus's authoritative preface, now familiar to the reader. As we saw in 4:23, an "hour" (ὥρα) is simultaneously "coming" (ἔρχεται) and "now is" (νῦν ἐστιν), though an oxymoron, reflects the paradoxical intrusion of the cosmological into the historical first introduced in the prologue. It is not merely a rhetorical device; it is detailing the overlap between God's time (beyond time) and humanity's time (linear time) and

fits well with the present/future eschatological tension running through this pericope.

As helpful as it is to understand that Jesus is speaking about the overlap of future things into the present, there is mystery regarding the things to which he refers. Just as the "hour" is and is coming, so also "the dead" must refer to a much more complex understanding of death, moving freely across the spiritual-physical continuum. If the identity of God is not limited in the spiritual-physical continuum, then neither can his work and its effects be limited. What is future is what Jesus is announcing, that the dead "will hear the voice of the Son of God and ... live" (ἀκούσουσιν τῆς φωνῆς τοῦ υἱοῦ τοῦ θεοῦ καὶ ζήσουσιν). The overlap between present and future is centralized upon Jesus, the Word, whose "word" gives life. God speaks, and restoration happens; the previous two pericopae and their primary characters prove this. It is significant that Jesus refers to himself as "the Son of God" (τοῦ υἱοῦ τοῦ θεοῦ) in contrast to his preferred title, the Son of Man. In view of John's declared aim in writing, "That you may believe that Jesus is the Christ, the Son of God" (20:31), the sparing use of "the Son of God" is noteworthy.[12] This monologue serves as a foundation for the rest of the Gospel.

5:26 "For just as the Father has life in himself, so also he has given to the Son to have life in himself" (ὥσπερ γὰρ ὁ πατὴρ ἔχει ζωὴν ἐν ἑαυτῷ, οὕτως καὶ τῷ υἱῷ ἔδωκεν ζωὴν ἔχειν ἐν ἑαυτῷ). The explanatory "for" (γὰρ) signals that Jesus is explaining the source and power behind the life that the Son provides. The restorative life the Son provides comes from the very life of God, both Father and Son. "Just as" (ὥσπερ) the Father has "life in himself" (ζωὴν ἐν ἑαυτῷ), so also does the Son, matching the "unseen" foretold by the prologue (1:4). "Life" is the possession of God, echoing a standard theme from the OT (Gen 2:7; Deut 30:20; Job 10:12; 33:4; Pss 16:11; 36:9). Life is functionally and ontologically so attached to God that it is simply "in him," both the Father and the Son.

It is important to note that the Father "has given to the Son" (τῷ υἱῷ ἔδωκεν) to have life in himself. Such language is theologically intriguing, for while the Son is frequently in the Gospel dependent upon the Father, in regard to "life" he is also entirely and individually capable (cf. v. 21). This basic word — "life" — also includes some mystery. We are not told exactly what the term means, but what we are told is quite clear: "Life" is *in* the Son. Just as Jesus reveals the Father, so also does he make known and make possible life. All mystery regarding the divine and life itself finds their answer in Jesus, who incorporates them all in his flesh, through which he explains and imparts them to humanity.[13]

5:27 "And he has given authority to him to make judgment, because he is the Son of Man" (καὶ ἐξουσίαν ἔδωκεν αὐτῷ κρίσιν ποιεῖν, ὅτι υἱὸς ἀνθρώπου ἐστίν). The Father has not only given "life" to the Son but has also given him "authority" (ἐξουσίαν) "to make judgment" (κρίσιν ποιεῖν).[14] Just as v. 26 was building on v. 21, so also v. 27 is building on v. 22. In the earlier two verses, the significance was the similarity between the Father and Son; vv. 26–27 emphasize the power and "authority" that rightfully is to be exercised by the Son.[15] Life and judgment (and its authority) *now* belong to and are made manifest in the Son. As much as it also involves the Father, what is significant is that it belongs in practice to the Son. The Old Testament echoes are now resounding in christological tones without ever denying their original referent. In vv. 19–24 Jesus declares who he is; in vv. 25–29 Jesus declares what belongs to him.

The reason why this authority has been given to him is "because he is the Son of Man" (ὅτι υἱὸς ἀνθρώπου ἐστίν). Interpreters often draw attention to the fact that the title is anarthrous (both nouns), which suggests to some a minimized concept ("*a* son of man"). But it seems unlikely that precisely at the place where Jesus is declared to be the eschatological judge that he would leave the usage of a title he has already applied to himself (cf. 1:51) and apply an entirely different usage as an explanation of his qualification as *the* judge.[16] Fitting with the authority given to Jesus, the title "Son of Man"

---

12. Morris, *John*, 282.

13. See Marianne Meye Thompson, "The Living Father," *Semeia* 85 (1999): 19–31.

14. BDAG 839–40. Other translations morph the noun "judgment" into a verb: "to judge" (NIV) or "to execute judgment" (NASB).

15. Michaels, *John*, 318.

16. One grammatical explanation might be the function of a predicate nominative (see comments on 1:1). It is also worth noting that both the LXX and Theodotion, Greek versions of the OT, preserve the anarthrous construction in Daniel 7:13.

conveys complete power, glory, and rule (see Dan 7:13 – 14). For this reason, our translation includes the definite article. It is "because" (ὅτι) Jesus is *the* Son of Man that the Father gives to him life and the authority for judgment.

5:28 "Do not be amazed at this, because an hour comes in which all who are in graves will hear his voice" (μὴ θαυμάζετε τοῦτο, ὅτι ἔρχεται ὥρα ἐν ᾗ πάντες οἱ ἐν τοῖς μνημείοις ἀκούσουσιν τῆς φωνῆς αὐτοῦ). Jesus declares that something in the future will provide credibility about what he speaks, an "hour" (ὥρα) when "all who are in graves will hear his voice" (πάντες οἱ ἐν τοῖς μνημείοις ἀκούσουσιν τῆς φωνῆς αὐτοῦ). This will be proof that judgment and life belong to the voice — the Word, for this is *the* end, when present and future collide. And standing at the center will be Jesus Christ, the Son of Man. Just as a dying boy from afar heard the healing voice of Jesus, and a lame man's legs heard the command to rise, so also will the dead in their graves respond to the voice of Christ. The eschatological language and imagery of this scene demand that all the eschatological prophecies regarding the "hour" of "the Son of Man" of Daniel 7:13 – 14 have begun their fulfillment in Jesus: the execution of judgment (vv. 22, 27 = Dan 7), the establishment of God's kingdom (vv. 22, 27 = Dan 7), and above all, the resurrection prophecy which leads to eternal life (vv. 25, 28 – 29 = Dan 12:1 – 2).[17] None of this denies a future aspect; it simply demands that such work belongs entirely to Jesus.

5:29 "and come out, those who have done good things to a resurrection of life, but those who have practiced evil to a resurrection of judgment" (καὶ ἐκπορεύσονται, οἱ τὰ ἀγαθὰ ποιήσαντες εἰς ἀνάστασιν ζωῆς, οἱ δὲ τὰ φαῦλα πράξαντες εἰς ἀνάστασιν κρίσεως). Those in the graves will respond to the voice "and come out" (καὶ ἐκπορεύσονται), proving that the life they possess (past and present) belongs to the one who speaks. This is followed by a declaration of one of two resurrections, proving that the authority to judge them also belongs to the one who speaks. This verse does not speak only in regard to unbelievers, but speaks of the resurrection in the last days.[18] Jesus is the Life and the Judge, for the one "without [whom] not one thing came into existence" (1:3) will be the same one through whom the dead are given their resurrected status.

Verse 29 has caused confusion for some over what appears to be the significant role of works in contrast to faith. But the problem is caused by the imputation of a false antithesis between faith and works. Beyond the counsel provided by the rest of Scripture, a few important questions might be asked. If Jesus is easily viewed as the Life, why is it difficult to see him also as Judge? Even more, why is it difficult to reconcile that *the Life that he is* is an equal match to *the Judge that he is*? These questions demand the reader view that Jesus's judgment of our deeds is less the foundation of the believer's salvation and more an invitation and exhortation to embrace the true life that he brings. It is also worth noting what Jesus will himself declare about the work of the believer (see comments on 6:28 – 29). When asked what must be done to do the works God requires, Jesus declared: "This is the work of God: to believe in the one who sent me" (6:29).

5:30 "I am not able to do anything by myself; Just as I hear I judge, and my judgment is righteous, because I do not seek my will but the will of the one who sent me" (Οὐ δύναμαι ἐγὼ ποιεῖν ἀπ᾽ ἐμαυτοῦ οὐδέν· καθὼς ἀκούω κρίνω, καὶ ἡ κρίσις

---

17. Stefanos Mihalios, *The Danielic Eschatological Hour in the Johannine Literature*, LNTS 436 (London: T&T Clark, 2011), 177.

18. Contra Barrett, *John*, 263.

ἡ ἐμὴ δικαία ἐστίν, ὅτι οὐ ζητῶ τὸ θέλημα τὸ ἐμὸν ἀλλὰ τὸ θέλημα τοῦ πέμψαντός με). Although the judgment theme is still present, this verse begins a new section, one in which Jesus begins to describe the inadequacy of his self-judgments. After such lofty statements about what he can do, this shifts in a different direction. This third section of the monologue returns full circle to the theme of the first section, where Jesus's ability was necessarily limited to the Father. Here Jesus reconnects the very actions previously declared to be solely his (vv. 26 – 27) to be united with the very intentions of the Father. The Son's submitted position to the Father gives warrant to the work he does and gives expression to the identity of God.

5:31 "If I testify concerning myself, my witness is not sufficient" (ἐὰν ἐγὼ μαρτυρῶ περὶ ἐμαυτοῦ, ἡ μαρτυρία μου οὐκ ἔστιν ἀληθής). Jesus's dependence on the Father is not only displayed by what he can (or cannot) do but also by what he declares about himself. As part of the identity of God, Jesus is the judge of the world, but he is not the judge of himself. Jesus claims "my witness is not sufficient" (ἡ μαρτυρία μου οὐκ ἔστιν ἀληθής). For the importance of "witness" in John, see comments on 1:7. The word translated "sufficient" (ἀληθής) has as its basic meaning "true" (cf. NIV), though it can also be translated as "valid" (HCSB). But Jesus is not declaring that his witness is untrue or false, nor is he claiming that it is invalid (see comments on 8:14). Rather, he is declaring with v. 30 and in the context of the rest of the pericope that even if it is true and valid it is still not "sufficient" on its own. At a functional level, this conclusion by Jesus might be rooted in the legal principles of the OT that two or three witnesses are required for a matter to be established (cf. Deut 19:15). But in light of this context, it might also be referring to the ontological insufficiency of Jesus's self-witness. Jesus is so dependent on the Father that the Son is unable to provide a witness for himself; the witness of Jesus must be rooted in the Father (and empowered by the Spirit). It is only when Jesus's self-witness is rooted in the Trinitarian identity of God that it can be declared "valid" and "true."

5:32 "There is another who testifies concerning me, and I know that the witness that he testifies concerning me is sufficient" (ἄλλος ἐστὶν ὁ μαρτυρῶν περὶ ἐμοῦ, καὶ οἶδα ὅτι ἀληθής ἐστιν ἡ μαρτυρία ἣν μαρτυρεῖ περὶ ἐμοῦ). Jesus counters the insufficiency of his self-witness by incorporating "another" (ἄλλος) witness, which can only be the Father. Again we translated the word as "sufficient" (ἀληθής) in place of "true" (its more basic meaning) or "valid" because it is not more true or valid than Jesus's self-witness but because when incorporated with Jesus's witness it is sufficient. Although some suggest that this is the first mention of the Father's witness to Jesus, the prologue made God (the Father) so central in the establishment of the witness of the Baptist that his witness was ultimately from the Father (see comments on 1:6).[19] Each of the witnesses to be described below will be depicted in such a way that their sufficiency is rooted in the identity of the triune God. This serves to transition from the insufficiency of Jesus's self-witness to the four coparticipatory witnesses: John the Baptist (vv. 33 – 35), the works of Jesus (v. 36), the Father (vv. 37 – 38), and Scripture (vv. 39 – 40).

5:33 "You have sent to John, and he has testified to the truth" (ὑμεῖς ἀπεστάλκατε πρὸς Ἰωάννην, καὶ μεμαρτύρηκεν τῇ ἀληθείᾳ). The first of four coparticipatory witnesses is John the Baptist (vv. 33 – 35). The Gospel emphasized that the

---

19. Cf. James Montgomery Boice, *Witness and Revelation in the Gospel of John* (Grand Rapids: Zondervan, 1970), 80.

Baptist was "sent from God" (1:6), signifying God's recognition of John as a witness to Jesus, but Jesus emphasizes, denoted by the emphatic "you" (ὑμεῖς), that the Jews also recognized his witness since they had an envoy "sent to John" (ἀπεστάλκατε πρὸς Ἰωάννην), with the perfect tense verb suggesting the permanent recognition of John as a witness to Jesus (cf. 1:19 – 28).[20] Thus, the Baptist's witness to Jesus is an established datum; from both perspectives John the Baptist was a witness to Jesus.[21] The second use of the perfect tense, "he has testified" (μεμαρτύρηκεν), gives permanence to his witness. The object of "the truth" (τῇ ἀληθείᾳ) to which John witnessed is still being developed as the Gospel unfolds (cf. 14:6).

5:34 "I do not receive the witness from a man, but I say these things in order that you might be saved" (ἐγὼ δὲ οὐ παρὰ ἀνθρώπου τὴν μαρτυρίαν λαμβάνω, ἀλλὰ ταῦτα λέγω ἵνα ὑμεῖς σωθῆτε). As much as John's witness was important to God (1:6) and to Jesus (vv. 33, 35), it is ultimately insufficient in itself, since it is "from a man" (παρὰ ἀνθρώπου). Its humanity simply suggests that it is not "from above"; that is, Jesus is independent of human witness. Even more, John's witness required its own witness — the Spirit, as John himself admitted (1:31 – 32). Jesus did not need a witness to humanity (2:25), and they could not offer a complete and independent witness to him. In spite of its limitations, John was the voice in the wilderness, proclaiming to the world what had just been revealed to him (cf. 1:23; 3:27). In this way, John served not God but humanity, proclaiming what he had just seen "from above" to those who were directly beside him "from below."

5:35 "John was the lamp that burned and shined, and you wanted to rejoice in his light for a time" (ἐκεῖνος ἦν ὁ λύχνος ὁ καιόμενος καὶ φαίνων, ὑμεῖς δὲ ἠθελήσατε ἀγαλλιαθῆναι πρὸς ὥραν ἐν τῷ φωτὶ αὐτοῦ). In spite of his insufficiency, Jesus gives his own witness to the efficacy of John's witness and the manner in which it served those to whom John witnessed. This verse grounds John's witness in the coparticipatory witness of God, for John could only reveal what he had been given (from God!).

Jesus's depiction of John's witness and its effects are categorized with symbols that give loose but potent "impressions" as a means of explaining its purpose. Jesus explains that John was the "lamp" (ὁ λύχνος), which probably refers to a common and portable lamp. The definite article with "the lamp" suggests that John was not just any lamp but a divinely ordained lamp. Unlike Jesus's light/witness, John's had run its course: he served "for a time" (πρὸς ὥραν). And as further proof that John's witness was recognized by those to whom he witnessed (cf. v. 33), Jesus claims with the emphatic pronoun, "*You* wanted to rejoice in his light" (ὑμεῖς δὲ ἠθελήσατε ἀγαλλιαθῆναι ἐν τῷ φωτὶ αὐτοῦ), which is probably an allusion to the fervor that surrounded John during his ministry. Such a statement is as much a rebuke of the Jews/the people as it is a depiction of the Baptist's ministry. For the same disconnect between God and his activities evident in the God-confused theology of the lame man and the Jews in 5:1 – 18 probably also manifested itself in the stir surrounding the ministry of John. In a sense Christ declares, "You rejoiced in the witness of John and missed entirely the object of his witness — me!"

5:36 "But I have a witness greater than that of John, for the works that the Father has given to me so that I might complete them, which I am doing, testify concerning me that the Father has sent me" (ἐγὼ δὲ ἔχω τὴν μαρτυρίαν μείζω τοῦ Ἰωάννου· τὰ γὰρ ἔργα ἃ δέδωκέν μοι ὁ πατὴρ ἵνα

---

20. Lincoln, *Truth on Trial*, 78.   21. Barrett, *John*, 264.

τελειώσω αὐτά, αὐτὰ τὰ ἔργα ἃ ποιῶ, μαρτυρεῖ περὶ ἐμοῦ ὅτι ὁ πατήρ με ἀπέσταλκεν). The second of four coparticipatory witnesses is the works of Jesus (v. 36). While the Baptist is working for the Father (1:6), God in the person of Jesus is also working. As significant as the witness of John was, it was not as great as the Son's own witness, denoted with the emphatic pronoun "I" (ἐγὼ). Ultimately, they are the Father's works given to Jesus so that "I might complete them" (τελειώσω αὐτά). And at their completion, the sending of the Son by the Father is declared. The greater weight of Jesus's own witness is that it (and therefore he) is intimately connected to the Father and the one through whom the works are accomplished; the Baptist can claim neither of those unions. The works are so surrounded by the Father (i.e., given by and completed for) that the Son serves as an intermediary. The "works" of Jesus, therefore, must be understood to refer to Jesus's entire mission.

5:37 **"And the Father who sent me has himself testified about me. You have neither heard his voice at any time nor seen his form"** (καὶ ὁ πέμψας με πατὴρ ἐκεῖνος μεμαρτύρηκεν περὶ ἐμοῦ. οὔτε φωνὴν αὐτοῦ πώποτε ἀκηκόατε οὔτε εἶδος αὐτοῦ ἑωράκατε). The third of four coparticipatory witnesses is the Father (vv. 37–38). The connection between v. 36 and vv. 37–38 is so apparent that "and" (καὶ) might also carry the meaning "and so," serving not to introduce a new testimony but to draw a conclusion.[22] While it cannot be denied that the witness of the works of Jesus and the witness of the Father are intimately connected, this does not mean that they cannot serve as independent witnesses. As we said above, each of the witnesses will be described in such a way that their sufficiency is rooted in the identity of the triune God (see comments on v. 32).

Jesus declares that the same "sending" Father who surrounded the witness of Jesus "has himself testified" (ἐκεῖνος μεμαρτύρηκεν), made emphatic by the redundant pronoun "himself" (ἐκεῖνος). The perfect tense suggests that the witness of the Father is both past and present. Suggestions for the reference (e.g., Scripture, Jesus's baptism) fail to do justice to the context and—more importantly—to the comprehensive witness of the Father. At the historical level, this would suggest the revelation of redemptive history, but in light of the cosmological level this must also include "all life, in and from the beginning onwards, when rightly understood, has borne witness, as the activity of the Father, to the Lord."[23] But as Jesus goes on to declare, the witness of the Father was not received.

5:38 **"Nor do you have his word remaining in you, because you do not believe the one whom he sent"** (καὶ τὸν λόγον αὐτοῦ οὐκ ἔχετε ἐν ὑμῖν μένοντα, ὅτι ὃν ἀπέστειλεν ἐκεῖνος τούτῳ ὑμεῖς οὐ πιστεύετε). Not only is his face and voice absent from them, but so is his "word" (τὸν λόγον), that is, the message of God. Such a statement is a wholesale rebuke of their response to their own heritage (cf. Josh 1:8–9) and their own spiritual history (cf. Ps 119:11)—everything they are attempting to protect by their aggression against him. Their response(s) to Jesus are symptomatic—"because" (ὅτι) of their unbelief, for if they truly believed in the message of God, they would have believed "the one whom he sent" (ὃν ἀπέστειλεν ἐκεῖνος τούτῳ). Again the witness of the Father is tied to the Son without ever denying the Father his own permanent witness.

5:39 **"You search the Scriptures, because you think in them you have eternal life, and yet those witnesses are about me"** (ἐραυνᾶτε τὰς γραφάς,

---

22. See BDAG 95: "To introduce a result that comes from what preceded."

23. Lightfoot, *John*, 147.

ὅτι ὑμεῖς δοκεῖτε ἐν αὐταῖς ζωὴν αἰώνιον ἔχειν· καὶ ἐκεῖναί εἰσιν αἱ μαρτυροῦσαι περὶ ἐμοῦ). The fourth of four coparticipatory witnesses is Scripture (vv. 39–40). Jesus rebukes his listeners for not recognizing him as the subject matter of their own Scriptures. The present-tense verb "search" (ἐραυνᾶτε) could be an imperative, but the context demands a rebuke, not a command. The verb "search" implies a "careful or thoughtful effort to learn something,"[24] and possibly reflects a technical rabbinic term for professional biblical study and exposition.[25] Jesus is speaking to those who know *where* to look, just not for *what* or *whom*. They maintain a competent method and hold to an inspired content, but are blinded to the true subject matter of the Scriptures by their confusion about God (cf. 5:1–18) and unbelief (cf. v. 38).

5:40 "And you are not willing to come to me in order to have life" (καὶ οὐ θέλετε ἐλθεῖν πρός με ἵνα ζωὴν ἔχητε). Jesus continues his rebuke by pressing their logic to its ironic conclusion. The importance they place on the Scriptures stops at the end of its pages. That they are "not willing" (οὐ θέλετε) or lack "desire" to come to Jesus is reflective of the state of their hearts, not the nature of the Scriptures. They are finding exactly what they "desire." Ultimately, they do not truly believe the very thing they have placed at the center of their faith.

5:41 "For I do not receive recognition from humanity" (Δόξαν παρὰ ἀνθρώπων οὐ λαμβάνω). After completing his survey of his four witnesses, Jesus returns to the insufficiency theme with which he began: the insufficiency of human recognition (vv. 41–47). If Jesus's self-witness is insufficient in isolation from the identity of the triune God (see

comments on v. 31), the same God who supports the four supporting witnesses (see comments on v. 32), how much more insufficient is the recognition of humanity? While the word "recognition" (Δόξαν) is often translated as "praise" or "glory" (e.g., NRSV; NASB), in this context it must be referring to what BDAG defines as "recognition of status or performance."[26]

5:42 "But I know you, that you do not have the love for God in yourselves" (ἀλλὰ ἔγνωκα ὑμᾶς ὅτι τὴν ἀγάπην τοῦ θεοῦ οὐκ ἔχετε ἐν ἑαυτοῖς). What the Jews do not know is countered by what Jesus knows. The declaration, "But I know you" (ἀλλὰ ἔγνωκα ὑμᾶς), made emphatic with the perfect tense, is the manifestation of the light shining in the darkness of humanity (cf. 1:5) and reveals the logic of the entire monologue. What does Jesus know? He knows that humanity does not possess a love for God.[27] For as the Gospel has already declared, they love not God but themselves (cf. 3:19). For this reason, Jesus counters not only their inadequate knowledge of God but also their inadequate love. Rather than coming to condemn (3:17), Jesus came to manifest the love of God with all the benefits to humanity included (3:16).

5:43 "I have come in the name of my Father and you do not receive me. If another comes in his own name, you will receive him" (ἐγὼ ἐλήλυθα ἐν τῷ ὀνόματι τοῦ πατρός μου καὶ οὐ λαμβάνετέ με· ἐὰν ἄλλος ἔλθῃ ἐν τῷ ὀνόματι τῷ ἰδίῳ, ἐκεῖνον λήμψεσθε). The irony existing between humanity's love for self over God and God's love for humanity over self continues to stand behind Jesus's statement. They claim to love God, but they do not; proof of this is that when he comes to them they do not receive him. The coming of Jesus could

---

24. BDAG 389.
25. Barrett, *John*, 267.
26. BDAG 257.

27. The context demands the phrase be taken as an objective genitive (i.e., "you do not love God").

not be any more drenched in the identity of the triune God. Yet the people could not be any more drenched in their own imaginative "god." The result is that the legitimate one who comes "in the name of my Father" (ἐν τῷ ὀνόματι τοῦ πατρός μου) is passed over for "another" who comes "in his own name" (ἐν τῷ ὀνόματι τῷ ἰδίῳ). The phrase "in the name" (ἐν τῷ ὀνόματι) simply means "in the authority of," so that the person who comes does so in the authority of the person he represents. Interpretive guesses regarding the identity of "another" (ἄλλος) are misguided, for the point of contrast is not between those who come but the "name" in which they come. The contrast is that the unique Son (1:14), who has a name above all names (Phil 2:9 – 10), comes in the name of his Father alone, whereas those who must only remain nameless — "another" — come proudly bearing their incompetence.

5:44 "How can you believe when you receive recognition from one another and do not seek recognition from the Only God?" (πῶς δύνασθε ὑμεῖς πιστεῦσαι, δόξαν παρὰ ἀλλήλων λαμβάνοντες καὶ τὴν δόξαν τὴν παρὰ τοῦ μόνου θεοῦ οὐ ζητεῖτε;). Jesus asks a pointed question that cuts to the heart of the matter. The aorist "believe" (πιστεῦσαι) should probably be taken as an ingressive aorist, stressing the beginning of belief, and could be understood to be saying: "How can you (even) begin to believe?" The limitation according to Jesus is that they receive recognition from another and not from God. Jesus's statement again contains a potent contrast. While the source of their recognition is "from one another" (παρὰ ἀλλήλων), kept anonymous so as to depict the nature of its worth, the source of recognition they neglect is "from the Only God" (παρὰ τοῦ μόνου θεοῦ), a phrase that alludes to the monotheistic roots of Judaism (Deut 6:4). It serves as a rebuke of the faithless, human religious system they are choosing to recognize over God. The term "Only" is so central it serves as a part of the title, hence the capitalization — the Only God — which may also explain the absence of "God" (θεοῦ) in some early manuscripts.[28] Rather than embracing God alone as the standard, humanity has embraced themselves, that is, their condition of darkness and their skewed perception of reality. This statement is virtually a definition of sin: the only thing they "recognize" or find worthy is themselves.

5:45 "Do not think that I will accuse you before the Father. The one who accuses you is Moses, in whom you have placed your hope" (μὴ δοκεῖτε ὅτι ἐγὼ κατηγορήσω ὑμῶν πρὸς τὸν πατέρα· ἔστιν ὁ κατηγορῶν ὑμῶν Μωϋσῆς, εἰς ὃν ὑμεῖς ἠλπίκατε). The monologue begins its conclusion when Jesus makes clear that denying "the Only God" is not merely a betrayal of Jewish monotheism, it is a betrayal of Moses. This is a potent maneuver because Moses would have been perceived as part of those from whom they "seek recognition," probably even the fountainhead of the authority in whose "name" they come. Jesus is the judge (v. 22), but Moses is "the accuser" (ὁ κατηγορῶν). By describing Moses as the one in whom they have placed "hope" or "confidence,"[29] Jesus is challenging the object of their "faith." In whom have they put their trust — themselves, their religious tradition, their forefathers? Faith or belief is central to the message of the Gospel of John (cf. 20:31). In challenging their faith, then, Christ is ultimately declaring himself to be the necessary object of their faith.

5:46 "For if you believed Moses, you would believe me, for he wrote about me" (εἰ γὰρ ἐπιστεύετε

---

28. Cf. Metzger, *Textual Commentary*, 180.

29. BDAG 319.

Μωϋσεῖ, ἐπιστεύετε ἂν ἐμοί, περὶ γὰρ ἐμοῦ ἐκεῖνος ἔγραψεν). After declaring by implication that he is to be the object of their faith, Jesus offers Moses as a positive example. The very message of Moses had Jesus as its object, "for he wrote about me" (περὶ γὰρ ἐμοῦ ἐκεῖνος ἔγραψεν). Jesus's argument could not be clearer. Though they placed their hope in Moses, they do not believe what he says. By this statement, Jesus critiques not only their reading of Scripture but also their heart. A specific OT passage is not in view here; rather, Jesus is declaring himself to be the ultimate and fullest subject matter or "the whole panorama" of the OT Scriptures.[30] Jesus must be understood to be "the end and the soul of the Law."[31]

5:47 "But since you do not believe what he wrote, how will you believe my words?" (εἰ δὲ τοῖς ἐκείνου γράμμασιν οὐ πιστεύετε, πῶς τοῖς ἐμοῖς ῥήμασιν πιστεύσετε;). The logical conclusion can only be that if Moses — their object of hope — is not believed, certainly Jesus will not be believed. Jesus is not pitting Moses's writings against his own words but showing the unchangeable correspondence between the two. As long as the Jews do not understand that the Scriptures of Moses taught the same faith that Jesus demands of them, he would always remain to them a stranger.[32] With this question, Jesus concludes his monologue. The question, though at one level rhetorical, is also a real question about the quest for belief.

Theology in Application

In response to some serious distortions in his opponent's theology of God and his work, Jesus stops and explains who he and his Father are and what they are doing. What begins as a statement on Christology and theology proper carries over into a statement on the nature of humanity and their love for self in place of God. In this pericope, the reader of the Fourth Gospel is exhorted to combat distorted theology with a proper understanding of the Father and the Son, come to grips with the eschatological role of the Son, and respond in faith to the witnesses to the Son.

The Identity of the Triune God

The very first verse of the Gospel declared that Jesus is God (1:1), and the end of the prologue introduced the important relation between the Father and the Son (1:18). In this pericope, the relationship between Father and Son is given more explanation, including the roles given by the Father to the Son. In the context of the Gospel, this serves as a response to the Jews who challenged Jesus and his activity. Jesus shows that they completely misunderstand who he is and therefore who God is. Without denying anything about the Father, in this monologue Jesus declares that not only is everything that God will do being done by Jesus, the Son, but that such authority has already been "given" to him.

The question often asked of this Gospel, whether it is Christocentric or theocen-

30. Hoskyns, *Fourth Gospel*, 276.
31. Calvin, *John 1–10*, 143.
32. Ridderbos, *John*, 207.

tric, is entirely misguided.[33] The Fourth Gospel would never make such a distinction, for not only could the Father and Son not be divided in such a manner but both are essential to the identity of God. To make such a choice is to make the same God-confused mistake of the lame man and the Jews in 5:1 – 18. The Christian need not choose between the Father and the Son, for the Father has already made the choice on our behalf and chosen Christ (i.e., "he has given"; vv. 22, 26, 27). By this the church is exhorted to make its worship and praise of God entirely Christ centered, which according to John is the only way to incorporate into such worship and praise the Father himself (which must also be empowered by the Spirit).

High Christology

Alongside the unity of the Father and Son (and as we will see, the Spirit), the work of the triune identity of God has been given to the Son (vv. 22, 26, 27). Jesus gives life to whom he desires (v. 21). He has been given the authority to be the eschatological judge (vv. 22, 27, 29). He is the recipient of honor (v. 23), for he is resurrection life for the dead, and life itself is in him (vv. 25 – 26). He will speak, and the dead in their graves will listen, for he is the Son of Man and will function as such at the end of human history (v. 28). This is who God is and therefore who Jesus is. In contrast to the low view of Jesus depicted by those around him, especially his opponents, the Gospel portrays him as the highest of the high — the King of kings and Lord of lords.

This Jesus is the head of the church, the one through whom we pray and worship. The church is commanded to worship this God in the person of Jesus Christ and no other. While the world waits until the end of human history to acknowledge the Son of Man who *is coming*, the church acknowledges the Son of Man who *now is*. None of our kings, presidents, or prime ministers can compare. Our God, made known in Jesus Christ, is alone our king; even as we respect the king of our land, we trust in a very different king — the true judge and the only one who can give the good life, and eternal life. Our love of God and our commitment to his message will be directly reflected by the degree to which Christ is at the center of all we do and say.

The Accommodation of God

The witnesses to the Son also bear witness to the accommodation of God, that is, the manifestation of God's grace exhibited in the extension of himself toward us. Jesus did not need a witness concerning himself, and certainly the sending Father knew the one he was sending. It was the world that did not know or recognize Jesus — God himself. But for the good of you and me, for our salvation (v. 34), God established witnesses so as to assist our naivete, our inward focus, and our inability

---

33. See C. K. Barrett, "Christocentric or Theocentric? Observations on the Theological Method of the Fourth Gospel," in *La Notion Biblique de Dieu*, ed. J. Coppens, BETL 41 (Leuven: Leuven University Press, 1976), 361 – 76.

to believe that which we cannot see. Before the grace of God could even be embraced by our true faith, God was already accommodating himself and his message to us. Before we even knew what the love of God was, God was already bestowing his love upon us.

The Subject Matter of Scripture

With his instruction to his Jewish challengers, Jesus gives to the reader the hermeneutical key for reading the Scriptures, the Old Testament: they were written "about me" (vv. 39, 46). This is neither the position of the human author nor the suggestion of the professor of hermeneutics; it is, rather, an instruction from the Lord. The Bible — yes, even the Old Testament — is about Jesus. To read the Old Testament in another way is, according to Jesus, to read the Old Testament like disbelieving Jews. It is unfortunate that the divide is so wide between the covenantal and dispensational methods of interpretation (at least in practice). It is also unfortunate that terms like "literal" have become more political than practical. Jesus is the fullest and ultimate subject matter of Scripture. This does not imply that it speaks about him only implicitly, but that which the Old Testament is speaking about is and has always been about Jesus. To read the Bible in another manner is to read as a non-Christian.

The Love ~~of Self~~ of God

The response of the Jews toward the Scriptures and Jesus was symptomatic of a deeper problem, which Jesus confronted directly: a love of self. In a shocking moment, the God of the universe declared to the Jews not only that he knows them but also that he knows that "you do not have the love of God in yourselves" (v. 42). For as the Gospel has already declared, they love the darkness, not the light (3:19). For this reason, Jesus counters not only their inadequate knowledge of God but also their inadequate love. Rather than coming to condemn, Jesus came to manifest the love of God (3:16 – 17). This is the conflict humanity has caused: while God loves us, we love ourselves. The Gospel of John portrays what the apostle Paul also confessed: "What a wretched man I am! Who will rescue me from this body that is subject to death? Thanks be to God, who delivers me through Jesus Christ our Lord!" (Rom 7:24 – 25). Humanity becomes part of the world's greatest irony: while we loved ourselves, God loved us, and while we would sacrifice everything else for ourselves, God sacrificed himself for everyone else. Embracing this irony is the act of conversion. It reorients the person toward God and away from the world, causing us to turn from ourselves to God, even as the apostle Paul also confessed: "For from him and through him and for him are all things. To him [not self!] be the glory forever! Amen" (Rom 11:36).

John 6:1 – 15

Literary Context

With the public ministry of Jesus in full swing, Jesus is not just drawing the attention of the Jewish authorities, he is also attracting the general populace. In this section of the Gospel, Jesus declares who he is in word and deed, and the narrative is careful to show the variety of responses to him. Day-to-day life in Israel, with its festivals and rituals, carries on in much the same way all the while the God of Israel has made himself known, already working on behalf of his bewildered people. By offering what is implied by the narrative to be his fourth sign, Jesus declares the true food for humanity and the wonderful hospitality of God.

IV. The Confession of the Son of God (5:1 – 8:11)
    A. The Third Sign: The Healing of the Lame Man on the Sabbath (5:1 – 18)
    B. The Identity of (the Son of) God: Jesus Responds to the Opposition (5:19 – 47)
    C. The Fourth Sign: The Feeding of a Large Crowd (6:1 – 15)
    D. The "I AM" Walks across the Sea (6:16 – 21)
    E. The Bread of Life (6:22 – 71)
    F. Private Display of Suspicion (7:1 – 13)
    G. Public Display of Rejection (7:14 – 52)
    H. The Trial of Jesus regarding a Woman Accused of Adultery (7:53 – 8:11)

Main Idea

When humanity did not know for what it was hungry, Jesus came to the world, becoming the host in a strange land of darkness and providing true food that satisfies every desire. The church must recognize Jesus as he is, not as it wants him to be, allowing the Prophet and the King to be what he also came to be: the one who serves.

Translation

John 6:1–15

1a	Introduction & Setting (1–4)	After these things
b	Action	**Jesus went to the other side**
c	Place	of the Sea of Galilee,
d	Explanation	that is, of Tiberias.
2a	Character Entrance	**A large crowd was following him,**
b	Basis	because they were seeing the signs
c	Description	which he was ✍
		performing on the sick.
3a	Sequence of Action #1	**Jesus came to a mountain**
b	Sequence of Action #2	and **was sitting there with his disciples.**
4a	Historical & Theological Context	And **it was near the Passover,**
b	Explanation	the feast of the Jews.
5a	Conflict (5–9)	Then
b	Sequence of Action #1	Jesus lifted his eyes and
c	Sequence of Action #2	saw a large crowd
d	Description	coming toward him,
e	Reaction	and **he said to Philip,**
f	Rhetorical Question	*"From where shall we buy bread*
g	Rhetorical Purpose	*so that these people may eat?"*
6a	Aside (6a–c)	But **he said this**
b	Actual Purpose	in order to test him,
c	Basis (Character's Thoughts)	for **he knew what he was going to do.**
7a	Response #1	**Philip answered him,**
b	Subject (Ironic Misunderstanding)	*"Bread …*
c	Monetary Value	*worth two hundred denarii*
d	Assertion (Insufficient Resources)	*… would not be enough*
e	Result	*so that each could receive*
f	Adverbial Phrase	*(even) a tiny amount."*
8a	Response #2	**One of his disciples,**
b	Identification	Andrew,
c	Association	the brother of Simon Peter,
d		**… said to him,**
9a	Ironic Misunderstanding	*"Here is a child*
b	Description of Circumstance	*who has five barley loaves and*
c		*two fish,*
d	Question	*but what are these for so many?"*
10a	Resolution (10–13)/Response to 7–9	**Jesus said,**
b	Imperatival Rebuke #1	*"Prepare the people to sit down for a meal.*
c	Setting	*There was a large field in that place,*
d		*so the men sat down,*
e		*about five thousand in number."*
11a	Sequence #1	Then **Jesus took the bread**
b		and
c	Sequence #2	after giving thanks

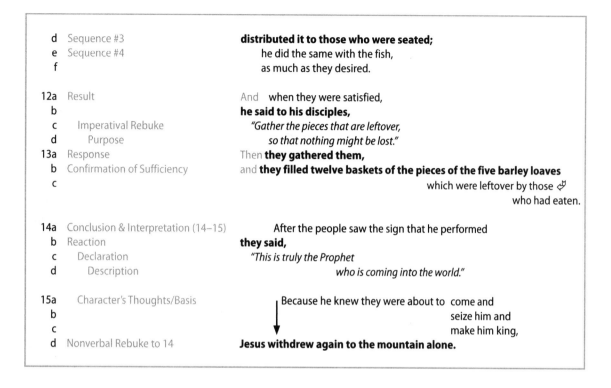

d	Sequence #3	**distributed it to those who were seated;**
e	Sequence #4	he did the same with the fish,
f		as much as they desired.
12a	Result	And when they were satisfied,
b		**he said to his disciples,**
c	Imperatival Rebuke	*"Gather the pieces that are leftover,*
d	Purpose	*so that nothing might be lost."*
13a	Response	Then **they gathered them,**
b	Confirmation of Sufficiency	and **they filled twelve baskets of the pieces of the five barley loaves**
c		which were leftover by those who had eaten.
14a	Conclusion & Interpretation (14–15)	After the people saw the sign that he performed
b	Reaction	**they said,**
c	Declaration	*"This is truly the Prophet*
d	Description	*who is coming into the world."*
15a	Character's Thoughts/Basis	Because he knew they were about to come and
b		seize him and
c		make him king,
d	Nonverbal Rebuke to 14	**Jesus withdrew again to the mountain alone.**

Structure and Literary Form

This pericope corresponds to the basic story form (see Introduction). The *intro-duction/setting* is established in vv. 1 – 4, explaining the location, setting, and people around whom the plot's conflict will focus. The *conflict* is established in vv. 5 – 9 and centers around the large crowd's need of food and the humorously sparse amount of resources. The *resolution* occurs in vv. 10 – 13 when Jesus takes the sparse resources and provides food for the entire crowd with some left over. Finally, the *conclusion/ interpretation* is provided in vv. 14 – 15 with the description of the people's response to Jesus and Jesus's response to the intentions of the crowd, which serves to connect the message of the pericope to the larger witness of the narrative.

Exegetical Outline

➡ **C. The Fourth Sign: The Feeding of a Large Crowd (6:1 – 15)**

　　1. Jesus on a Mountain at Passover (vv. 1 – 4)

　　2. From Where Shall We Buy Bread? (vv. 5 – 9)

　　3. The Hospitality of Jesus (vv. 10 – 13)

　　4. He is the Prophet, Make Him a King! (vv. 14 – 15)

Explanation of the Text

Chapter 6 has been called "the Grand Central Station of Johannine critical issues"[1] and "a kind of summary of the Gospel of John and its riddles."[2] The chapter as a whole is filled with a plethora of historical, literary, and theological issues and debates. While we will not address all the issues, they are lurking below the surface of our discussion. This is also the only miracle of Jesus apart from the resurrection that is recorded in all four Gospels. The concern of this commentary is not to conjecture the reason for this or to reconstruct the event between the four accounts, but to interpret the miracle through the interpretive lens of the Fourth Gospel (see Introduction).[3] While this pericope is significant on its own, it is also thematically connected to the dialogue between Jesus and his disciples to follow (6:25–71). Thus, this pericope begins one of the most important moments in the confession of the Son of God.

6:1 After these things Jesus went to the other side of the Sea of Galilee, that is, of Tiberias (Μετὰ ταῦτα ἀπῆλθεν ὁ Ἰησοῦς πέραν τῆς θαλάσσης τῆς Γαλιλαίας τῆς Τιβεριάδος). John moves the story forward and signals to the reader that a new section has begun by his repeated use of "after these things" (Μετὰ ταῦτα), without giving any indication in regard to the precise timing of events (see comments on 2:12; cf. 5:1). The name of the sea is given two genitive titles, with the second functioning in apposition to the first, providing an additional name by which the body of water is known: "the Sea of Gaililee, that is, (the Sea) of Tiberias" (τῆς θαλάσσης τῆς Γαλιλαίας τῆς Τιβεριάδος). Al-

though traditionally or popularly known as "Galilee," the sea was named "Tiberias" around AD 20 by Herod Antipas in honor of Emperor Tiberias (cf. Josephus, *Ant.* 18.36). John uses only the latter title elsewhere (cf. 6:23), even though it might not have been the established name during Jesus's ministry.[4]

6:2 A large crowd was following him, because they were seeing the signs which he was performing on the sick (ἠκολούθει δὲ αὐτῷ ὄχλος πολύς, ὅτι ἐθεώρουν τὰ σημεῖα ἃ ἐποίει ἐπὶ τῶν ἀσθενούντων). Jesus was not alone on this journey, for the narrator adds that "a large crowd" (ὄχλος πολύς) was following him "because" (ὅτι) they were seeing the signs he had been performing. The events in this verse are described with imperfect tenses, which suggest that the miracles of Jesus and "the following" had continued for some time so that interest in what he could do had become well established. It is significant that the narrator describes the miracles of Jesus as "the signs" (τὰ σημεῖα); not only has the term already been established as significant for John (see comments on 2:11) but it is about to come into prominence once again (cf. 6:30).

6:3 Jesus came to a mountain and was sitting there with his disciples (ἀνῆλθεν δὲ εἰς τὸ ὄρος Ἰησοῦς, καὶ ἐκεῖ ἐκάθητο μετὰ τῶν μαθητῶν αὐτοῦ). Upon crossing the Sea of Galilee, Jesus and his disciples arrived at "the mountain" (τὸ ὄρος), which could also just refer to a "hillside," though the article is suggestive of more. Alongside v. 4, it is likely that the narrator's setting of the scene is intended

1. Paul N. Anderson, "The *Sitz im Leben* of the Johannine Bread of Life Discourse and Its Evolving Context," in *Critical Readings of John 6*, ed. R. Alan Culpepper, BIS 22 (Leiden: Brill, 1997), 1–59 (1).

2. Johannes Beutler, "The Structure of John 6," in Culpepper, *Critical Readings of John 6*, 115–27 (115).

3. For the relationship of this pericope with the Synoptics, see Brown, *John*, 1:236–50.

4. Barrett, *John*, 272–73.

to echo the scene at Mt. Sinai with Moses, who will be alluded to shortly in vv. 31–33.

6:4 And it was near the Passover, the feast of the Jews (ἦν δὲ ἐγγὺς τὸ πάσχα, ἡ ἑορτὴ τῶν Ἰουδαίων). This is the second of three Passovers reported in John (2:13, 23; 6:4; and 11:55/19:14; see comments on 2:13). All three occurrences of the Passover point either directly to the death of Jesus (first and second) or occur in the context of the death itself (third). The Jewish Passover celebrated the past event of the exodus from Egypt, but it also provided the ground of hope for a present deliverance and for the arrival of a present deliverer.[5] This fact explains much of the excitement to be displayed in v. 15 by the Jews, who try to force Jesus to become king.[6] But there is more, for the Passover feast involved the eating of a lamb and bread. Rather than a mere chronological reference, this detail, together with the mention of the "mountain" in v. 3, governs the entire narrative of chapter 6 and establishes Moses and the Passover as the historical-theological backdrop of what is to come.[7] In this way, the setting of the pericope has been established by the narrator.

6:5 Then Jesus lifted his eyes and saw a large crowd coming toward him, and he said to Philip, "From where shall we buy bread so that these people may eat?" (ἐπάρας οὖν τοὺς ὀφθαλμοὺς ὁ Ἰησοῦς καὶ θεασάμενος ὅτι πολὺς ὄχλος ἔρχεται πρὸς αὐτὸν λέγει πρὸς Φίλιππον, Πόθεν ἀγοράσωμεν ἄρτους ἵνα φάγωσιν οὗτοι;). The pericope transitions from the introduction and setting to the conflict as Jesus notices the crowd of people coming toward him. With precision of detail, the narrative describes Jesus "lifting his eyes" (ἐπάρας τοὺς ὀφθαλμοὺς) with what is likely an ingressive aorist, which emphasizes the initiation of the ac-

tion. Reminiscent of a similar construction in 4:35 where Jesus exhorts his disciples to "lift up your eyes and look at the fields," so now it is Jesus who "lifts his eyes," that is, is attentive to the needs of the people around him. Since Philip came from the nearby town of Bethsaida (cf. 1:44), he would be one most able to secure food in that region.

6:6 But he said this in order to test him, for he knew what he was going to do (τοῦτο δὲ ἔλεγεν πειράζων αὐτόν, αὐτὸς γὰρ ᾔδει τί ἔμελλεν ποιεῖν). The narrator offers a necessary explanatory intrusion, which is common in the Gospel (see comments on 3:16). According to the narrator, Jesus asked this "in order to test him" (πειράζων αὐτόν). For Jesus "knew" (ᾔδει) what he was going to do, with the pluperfect tense suggesting he had known the entire time. Such an intrusion is not merely to explain what Jesus was doing with Philip but also serves to guide the reader to see the intentions behind the surface of the story. In light of the Moses motif cast in vv. 3–4, the word "test" (πειράζων) creates an "impression" (see Introduction) that fits nicely with the exodus "testings" of Israel (e.g., Exod 15:25; 16:4; Deut 8:2, 16; cf. Judg 3:1–4; cf. Abraham in Gen 22).

6:7 Philip answered him, "Bread worth two hundred denarii would not be enough so that each could receive (even) a tiny amount" (ἀπεκρίθη αὐτῷ ὁ Φίλιππος, Διακοσίων δηναρίων ἄρτοι οὐκ ἀρκοῦσιν αὐτοῖς ἵνα ἕκαστος βραχύ τι λάβῃ). With an entirely different "bread" in mind, Philip responds with a realistic situation of the food, which also made a mockery of the question. Since a Roman denarius is the daily wage of a worker, "two hundred denarii" (Διακοσίων δηναρίων) would be about a half-year's labor.[8] As much as the test was failed by Philip, Jesus is not shown to rebuke the

---

5. Hoskyns, *Fourth Gospel*, 281.
6. Carson, *John*, 269.
7. Cf. Ridderbos, *John*, 210.
8. BDAG 223.

answer — even though he "knew" that it was a misunderstanding. The answer would not be spoken by Jesus, for in a matter of moments he would reveal the answer with his own hands.

6:8 One of his disciples, Andrew, the brother of Simon Peter, said to him (λέγει αὐτῷ εἷς ἐκ τῶν μαθητῶν αὐτοῦ, Ἀνδρέας ὁ ἀδελφὸς Σίμωνος Πέτρου). Although Jesus directed the question at Philip, Andrew, noted again as the brother of Simon Peter (cf. 1:40, 42), speaks on his own accord to Jesus. With the inclusion of Andrew's insight, the verse suggests that all Jesus's disciples are equally as bewildered as Philip.

6:9 "Here is a child who has five barley loaves and two fish, but what are these for so many? (Ἔστιν παιδάριον ὧδε ὃς ἔχει πέντε ἄρτους κριθίνους καὶ δύο ὀψάρια· ἀλλὰ ταῦτα τί ἐστιν εἰς τοσούτους;). Andrew notices in the midst of the large crowd "a child" (παιδάριον), a term which only occurs here in the NT. As a diminutive, it suggests the child is young. The only food the child is carrying is two "fish" (ὀψάρια), another diminutive which can mean "tidbit,"[9] and five barley loaves, a cheap bread which Philo describes as "a foodstuff ... of somewhat doubtful merit, suited for irrational animals and men in unhappy circumstances" (*Spec. Laws* 3.57). Thus, while Philip looked at the size of the crowd, Andrew looks at the amount of food on hand; the general consensus is offered by Andrew on both counts: "But what are these for so many?" (ἀλλὰ ταῦτα τί ἐστιν εἰς τοσούτους;). Jesus's question is given a rhetorical retort by the disciples for not taking into consideration the amount of people and the sparse resources.[10] This concludes the conflict of the pericope, with the hunger of a large crowd left at the feet of Jesus, along with a mild rebuke from his own disciples.

6:10 Jesus said, "Prepare the people to sit down for a meal. There was a large field in that place, so the men sat down, about five thousand in number" (εἶπεν ὁ Ἰησοῦς, Ποιήσατε τοὺς ἀνθρώπους ἀναπεσεῖν. ἦν δὲ χόρτος πολὺς ἐν τῷ τόπῳ. ἀνέπεσαν οὖν οἱ ἄνδρες τὸν ἀριθμὸν ὡς πεντακισχίλιοι). The resolution of the conflict begins with a directive from Jesus. Without revealing any concern about the large amount of people or the small amount of resources, Jesus instructs his disciples to have the people be seated *for a meal*. There is no hesitation in the narrative account; the rebuke of the disciples toward their generous-but-naive teacher is given a shocking rejoinder when he gives them orders to prepare the people to eat! Although the verb is usually in reference to a table at which to eat, the narrator notes that this meal would be served on "a large field" adjacent to Jesus and his disciples. The narrator concludes by giving insight into the number of men who sat down, denoted by using an accusative of respect, "with reference to number" (τὸν ἀριθμὸν): "about five thousand" (ὡς πεντακισχίλιοι).[11] In light of the switch from "the people" (τοὺς ἀνθρώπους) to "the men" (οἱ ἄνδρες), the number is probably exclusive of women and children, such as the child who provided the barley loaves and fish. Thus the actual number of people could have been well over ten thousand.

6:11 Then Jesus took the bread and after giving thanks distributed it to those who were seated; he did the same with the fish, as much as they desired (ἔλαβεν οὖν τοὺς ἄρτους ὁ Ἰησοῦς καὶ εὐχαριστήσας διέδωκεν τοῖς ἀνακειμένοις, ὁμοίως καὶ ἐκ τῶν ὀψαρίων ὅσον ἤθελον). Without explaining how the food was secured from the child, the narrator explains that Jesus took the bread and the fish and proceeded to distribute it to the large crowd.

---

9. BDAG 746.
10. See Augustine, *John*, 24.1.158.

11. Wallace, *Greek Grammar*, 203–4.

The details depict the beginning aspects of a meal: the receiving of the substance, a prayer of thanks (a common element in Jewish meals), and the distribution of the food. It is striking that Jesus is described as the one who "distributed" (διέδωκεν) the food; the narrator is explicitly connecting the act and therefore the responsibility of the distribution of food to Jesus. Jesus could not delegate this task, for only he could provide the food for the people.[12] It is also important to note that the people to whom the bread and fish were supplied are described as receiving "as much as they desired" (ὅσον ἤθελον). The large crowd, for which over a half year of labor was required to feed, was being given a lavish banquet that was not just satisfactory, it was entirely fulfilling. The scene impresses upon the reader the image of Jesus as the host who offers generous hospitality (see comments before 4:1 and on 4:23, 40). In light of the coming references that are so often interpreted in regard to the Eucharist, the hospitality motif of this pericope is often missed.[13]

6:12 And when they were satisfied, he said to his disciples, "Gather the pieces that are leftover, so that nothing might be lost" (ὡς δὲ ἐνεπλήσθησαν λέγει τοῖς μαθηταῖς αὐτοῦ, Συναγάγετε τὰ περισσεύσαντα κλάσματα, ἵνα μή τι ἀπόληται). Jesus, the host, fed the massive crowd, and the narrator explains that "they were satisfied" (ἐνεπλήσθησαν). The command to gather the leftovers "so that nothing might be lost" (ἵνα μή τι ἀπόληται) cannot be easily explained. Some suggestions have centered on the imagery denoted by the term "gathered," suggesting that Jesus is symbolizing the gathering of God's people, the church.[14] Although it is difficult to be exact, it is probably best to draw from this verse the "impres-

sion" gained from the earlier allusions to Moses, and with Moses the manna in the wilderness, about which the Israelites were given orders for days of gathering. However, even more certain than faithfulness to Jewish custom or allusion is Jesus's faithfulness to his mission, for which he will shortly announce he will "lose none" (6:39). Jesus is taking care to be faithful to do the "works" of the Father (cf. 5:36) and is making sure that each of these "works" are done with the precision and accuracy the Father would expect.

6:13 Then they gathered them, and they filled twelve baskets of the pieces of the five barley loaves which were leftover by those who had eaten (συνήγαγον οὖν, καὶ ἐγέμισαν δώδεκα κοφίνους κλασμάτων ἐκ τῶν πέντε ἄρτων τῶν κριθίνων ἃ ἐπερίσσευσαν τοῖς βεβρωκόσιν). The resolution to the conflict of the pericope is given a dramatic conclusion. The bountiful leftovers declare to those present — as well as to the reader — that though the meal may have been symbolic, it was not merely symbolic.[15] The symbolism of the "twelve baskets" (δώδεκα κοφίνους) cannot be easily explained. On the surface, it serves to reinforce the provision of Jesus and the satisfaction of those who ate — there was more than they could "desire." The deeper significance might simply be that the twelve baskets "make visible the great future inaugurated in Jesus's coming and work … under the image of the host presiding over and providing an abundant meal.…"[16] The suggestion that the twelve baskets signify the twelve tribes of Israel is a possible "impression" in light of the Mosaic background of this pericope.[17] But a referent much closer to the narrative might be the intended symbol instead. In light of the disciples' mild rebuke of Jesus for his

---

12. Contra Bultmann, *John*, 213.

13. See Gail R. O'Day, "John 6:1–15," *Int* 57 (2003): 196–98. Cf. Bultmann, *John*, 213.

14. See Michaels, *John*, 350.

15. Barrett, *John*, 276.

16. Ridderbos, *John*, 213.

17. Carson, *John*, 271.

initial question, there remains for each disbelieving disciple their own basket of leftovers to carry. While impossible to verify, such a suggestion connects with the introduction of Jesus's disciples as "the Twelve" for the first time in the Gospel a short time later at v. 67, as well as to the importance of this pericope as an introduction and trajectory for all chapter 6 — especially the end where the belief of the disciples is in particular focus. If our suggestion is warranted, such a playful rebuke is a fitting picture of the mission of the disciples to come, which will entail the distribution of the bread of life to the world.[18]

6:14 After the people saw the sign that he performed they said, "This is truly the Prophet who is coming into the world" (Οἱ οὖν ἄνθρωποι ἰδόντες ὃ ἐποίησεν σημεῖον ἔλεγον ὅτι Οὗτός ἐστιν ἀληθῶς ὁ προφήτης ὁ ἐρχόμενος εἰς τὸν κόσμον). As the pericope comes to a close, the narrator provides the necessary conclusion and interpretation for the reader. The narrator describes what the people — several thousand of them — saw as a "sign" (σημεῖον), which for this Gospel becomes the fourth sign (cf. 2:11; 4:54; 6:2 in reference to 5:1 – 18). But while the readers are expected to recognize correctly the sign (see comments on 2:11), the crowd for whom the sign was performed mistakenly applied it to themselves and to their own God-confused dreams and priorities. The narrator provides a conclusion and interpretation with

an irony that has become common to the Gospel. Their declaration by itself is absolutely true; Jesus is the Prophet who is coming into the world (Deut 18:15). The narrative wants us to agree with the declaration: the Prophet has arrived! But it does not want our response to be the same.

6:15 Because he knew they were about to come and seize him and make him king, Jesus withdrew again to the mountain alone (Ἰησοῦς οὖν γνοὺς ὅτι μέλλουσιν ἔρχεσθαι καὶ ἁρπάζειν αὐτὸν ἵνα ποιήσωσιν βασιλέα ἀνεχώρησεν πάλιν εἰς τὸ ὄρος αὐτὸς μόνος). Although the crowd was correct in what they declared (unknowingly) about Jesus, what they imported into that role and therefore onto Jesus became their error. For the crowd, Jesus as the Prophet was a warrior-king (see comments on 1:20 – 21). Therefore, they intended to make Jesus king so that he would lead Israel to political dominance over the world (i.e., Rome). Jesus's response is a visible rebuke of their distorted messianic theology, in which God works for their purposes and not his own. For the Jews (and the whole world), the hospitality of God involved fulfilling their own human plans and desires.[19] But the true host showed his hospitality by following not the will of humanity but the will of the Father. The rest of chapter 6 will make this clear. Jesus withdrew to an isolated place, "because he knew" (οὖν γνοὺς) what they intended — because he knew humanity (cf. 2:24 – 25).

---

18. Cf. Aquinas, *John*, 2:9.

19. Cf. Calvin, *John 1 – 10*, 149 – 50.

Theology in Application

After explaining his identity with words (a monologue), in this pericope Jesus declared his identity by his actions. In the most reported miracle in early Christianity, Jesus confesses his true identity. As Augustine explains, "For since Christ is Himself the Word of God, even the act of the Word is a word to us."[20] In this pericope the reader of the Fourth Gospel is exhorted to answer correctly the question Jesus asked Philip, believing that Jesus, the Prophet-King, is the hospitality for the world, providing more than any can desire.

Jesus Lifted His Eyes

The grammatical emphasis placed on the "lifting" of Jesus's eyes to see the large crowd coming toward him is a remarkable showing of the interest of God for humanity, even those for whom Jesus was merely a pawn in their own God-confused dreams. The narrative is careful to describe how Jesus was aware of the crowd's felt needs and was himself the source of provision. That alone is remarkable. Yet what is even more remarkable is not that Jesus could, but that he would. If it is remarkable to think that the God who had just been mildly rebuked by two of his disciples would carry on and feed the whole crowd, it is even more remarkable that the Creator has been shunned every moment in human history since its inception and yet would come, all the while receiving in the flesh the rebukes of their sinfulness. To say with the narrator that God loves the world (3:16) is not to speak into abstraction but to be on the other end of his eyes which he graciously lifted to see us.

The Host and His Hospitality

The eucharistic imagery that so frequently covers discussion of this pericope can easily eclipse the other motif so carefully described by the narration: hospitality. Eucharistic images are noticeably absent from this scene (especially in comparison to the Synoptics). Instead, the Gospel is explicitly showing the service of a host and the nature of his hospitality. The crowd did not come to him because he would feed them; they came because he was healing the sick. This is exactly what God does, made manifest by Jesus in the Fourth Gospel. Jesus exercises better hospitality than the bridegroom at the wedding in Cana (2:1 – 11), offers hospitality to the Samaritan woman by offering her "living water" (4:1 – 42), offers hospitality to his disciples when dining with them by washing their feet (13:1 – 17), and offers hospitality when he invites his followers fully to inhabit the dwelling that he shares with God (cf. 14:2 – 3; 15:1 – 10). Since "hospitality is one of the dominant metaphor fields for

---

20. Augustine, *John*, 24.2.158.

evoking the incarnate presence of God-with-us," the Fourth Gospel makes clear that Jesus is the grace-filled host of God, and we — the readers — are the invited guests (cf. Isa 25).[21]

The rejoinder to the disciples, then, is not merely an exhortation to embrace the hospitality of Jesus for themselves but to fully embrace his earlier command to "lift your eyes and look at the fields" (4:35). The basket that each carries at the pericope's end serves as a tangible reminder of the miraculous provision of Jesus and the duty they now need to perform. In a real way, Christian ministry is emulating the hospitality of Jesus, inviting people to enter the hospitality of God and serving as an intermediary host until God himself embraces them.

Jesus Is the Prophet, Priest, and King

The church has long spoken of Jesus as fulfilling the OT roles of prophet, priest, and king, two of which are mentioned in this pericope (see vv. 14 – 15). The misunderstanding of the crowd should not cause us to miss the clear agreement the narrative displayed toward those titles. Yes, he is the Prophet and the King, but no, not in the manner the crowd thinks. Despite their confusion, the "showing" Jesus displayed in this pericope declares him to be the Prophet and King. As Augustine can exclaim, "Thanks be to Him. He has fulfilled by Himself what was promised in the Old Testament."[22] Jesus is introducing in word and deed the manner of his prophetic and kingly reign; but rather than being served as a king, he serves food to the crowd. And as the Gospel will shortly declare, his public declaration as king takes place upon the cross (cf. 19:2 – 3). Yet it is exactly this king — the Crucified King — that we must worship. The cross, which begins his priestly act, shows the kind of king that he is, fulfilling everything he promised as the Prophet. With Augustine we must also say: Thanks be to God!

21. O'Day, "John 6:1 – 15," 198.   22. Augustine, *John*, 24.5.159.

John 6:16 – 21

Literary Context

The feeding of the large crowd (6:1 – 15) declared by means of "showing" that Jesus, as the true host for humanity, was providing a kind of hospitality only he can provide, symbolized by his serving of food to the people out of the meager lunch of a young child. Following directly on the heels of this "showing" is a "telling" pericope in which Jesus offers a direct confession about himself. This pericope serves as an interlude between the feeding miracle (6:1 – 15) and the revelation that Jesus is the bread of life (6:22 – 71), allowing the Gospel to declare with emphasis the identity of the Son of God as he made it known to his disciples. This entire section of the Gospel (5:1 – 8:11) is focused on the confession of the Son of God, and this pericope is directly at its center.

IV. The Confession of the Son of God (5:1 – 8:11)
- A. The Third Sign: The Healing of the Lame Man on the Sabbath (5:1 – 18)
- B. The Identity of (the Son of) God: Jesus Responds to the Opposition (5:19 – 47)
- C. The Fourth Sign: The Feeding of a Large Crowd (6:1 – 15)
- → **D. The "I AM" Walks across the Sea (6:16 – 21)**
- E. The Bread of Life (6:22 – 71)
- F. Private Display of Suspicion (7:1 – 13)
- G. Public Display of Rejection (7:14 – 52)
- H. The Trial of Jesus regarding a Woman Accused of Adultery (7:53 – 8:11)

Main Idea

Jesus is the "I AM," the voice behind the unconsumed burning bush in Exodus 3, the one who walks across the stirring sea, who speaks on behalf of God in the first person. The presence of Jesus silences our fear and exposes our need to receive him in his fullness.

Translation

John 6:16–21

16a	Introduction & Setting (16–17)	As evening came
b	Sequence #1	**his disciples went down to the sea.**
17a		and
b	Sequence #2	after getting into the boat
c	Sequence #3	**they were going to the other side of the sea to Capernaum.**
d	Progression of Time	And **darkness had already come**
e	Absence of Main Character	and **Jesus had not yet come to them.**
18a	Conflict (18–19)	And **the sea began stirring**
b	Basis	when a strong wind blew.
19a	Circumstance	When they had rowed about three or three-and-a-half miles
b	Reentrance of Main Character	**they saw Jesus**
c	Simultaneous action #1	walking on the sea and
d	Simultaneous action #2	coming close to the boat,
e	Reaction	and **they were afraid.**
20a	Resolution/Response to 19e	But **he said to them,**
b	Confession	*"I* AM;
c	Command	*do not fear!"*
21a	Conclusion/Reaction	Then **they were willing to receive him into the boat,**
b	Arrival to Destination	and **immediately the boat came to the land**
c		to which they were going.

Structure and Literary Form

This pericope corresponds to the basic story form (see Introduction). The *introduction/setting* is established in vv. 16 – 17, explaining the location, setting, and people around whom the plot's conflict will focus, even noting the absence of Jesus. The *conflict* in this pericope in vv. 18 – 19 centers around the fear of the disciples who are on a stormy lake, upon which they see Jesus walking on the sea toward them. The *resolution* occurs in v. 20 when Jesus speaks to them, presents himself, and addresses their fear. Finally, v. 21 offers the *conclusion/interpretation* of the pericope with the description of the disciples' response to Jesus and the conclusion of their journey.

Exegetical Outline

→ **D. The "I** AM**" Walks across the Sea (6:16 – 21)**

    1. The Disciples Depart without Jesus (vv. 16 – 17)

    2. Jesus Walks on the Stirring Sea (vv. 18 – 19)

    3. The Encounter with (the Son of) God (v. 20)

    4. The Disciples Receive Jesus (v. 21)

Explanation of the Text

This short pericope not only has a functional significance in chapter 6 and a central location in a large section of the Gospel (5:1 – 8:11), but it is also loaded with content. It is one of the most popular miracles and a significant confessional statement by Jesus. Our explanation of the pericope must keep in balance all these factors.

6:16 As evening came his disciples went down to the sea (Ὡς δὲ ὀψία ἐγένετο κατέβησαν οἱ μαθηταὶ αὐτοῦ ἐπὶ τὴν θάλασσαν). The narrative transitions from the large crowd, from which Jesus removed himself (cf. 6:15), to the disciples at the end of the day, who make their way to the sea, that is, the Sea of Galilee. The temporal reference, "As evening came" (Ὡς δὲ ὀψία ἐγένετο), serves as a transitional marker to signal that a new scene has begun.[1] The absence of Jesus will be explained below (v. 17). Reflecting continuity with the previous pericope, this verse answers the implied question in regard to the location of the disciples at the end of the feeding miracle.[2]

6:17 and after getting into the boat they were going to the other side of the sea to Capernaum. And darkness had already come and Jesus had not yet come to them (καὶ ἐμβάντες εἰς πλοῖον ἤρχοντο πέραν τῆς θαλάσσης εἰς Καφαρναούμ. καὶ σκοτία ἤδη ἐγεγόνει καὶ οὔπω ἐληλύθει πρὸς αὐτοὺς ὁ Ἰησοῦς). The disciples are described as getting into the boat and beginning their journey across the sea on their way to Capernaum. The narrator concludes the introduction of the pericope with a slightly odd statement that emphasizes the absence of Jesus. In a literary sense, the narrator is setting up the story to come for the reader. Yet it is the awkwardness that directs the reader toward what is central for the narrator: the disciples are alone, for Jesus is not with them. Such a statement bridges well with the conflict shortly to be introduced. The narrator's use of "darkness" (σκοτία) echoes back to its use in 1:5, adding further to the conflict of the scene the disciples' inability to recognize Jesus (see 6:19).

6:18 And the sea began stirring when a strong wind blew (ἥ τε θάλασσα ἀνέμου μεγάλου πνέοντος διεγείρετο). The conflict of the pericope is introduced as the narrator notes that as the disciples were on their way across the sea, a strong wind came upon them so that the sea "began stirring" (διεγείρετο), with the imperfect functioning as an ingressive.[3] There is abundant evidence of the suddenness of storms on the Sea of Galilee, which is likely what occurred on this occasion.[4]

6:19 When they had rowed about three or three-and-a-half miles they saw Jesus walking on the sea and coming close to the boat, and they were afraid (ἐληλακότες οὖν ὡς σταδίους εἴκοσι πέντε ἢ τριάκοντα θεωροῦσιν τὸν Ἰησοῦν περιπατοῦντα ἐπὶ τῆς θαλάσσης καὶ ἐγγὺς τοῦ πλοίου γινόμενον, καὶ ἐφοβήθησαν). The conflict of the pericope reaches its climax not when the sea waters were stirred but when the disciples' categories were stirred as they watched Jesus walking on the water toward their boat. According to the narrator, they had already traveled twenty-five or thirty *stadia* (σταδίους); a *stadion* was the length of a Roman stadium, which was about 197 meters or about 607 feet.[5] When one *stadion* is multiplied by twenty-five or thirty, the total distance the disciples had travelled in their

1. Beutler, "Structure of John 6," 119.
2. Michaels, *John*, 354.
3. Wallace, *Greek Grammar*, 544 – 45.
4. Barrett, *John*, 280.
5. BDAG 940.

boat was between 2.87 and 3.45 miles, hence our translation, "about three or three-and-a-half miles." Thus, they had already gone a good distance across the sea before coming into contact with Jesus.

After rowing three or more miles across the sea, the narrator describes how the disciples "saw Jesus walking on the sea" (θεωροῦσιν τὸν Ἰησοῦν περιπατοῦντα ἐπὶ τῆς θαλάσσης). Contra Bernard, the statement must mean more than Jesus was walking "beside the sea shore."[6] The language used and the distance from shore is making the unavoidable claim that Jesus was walking directly on the surface of the water. Such a miraculous act is simultaneously a declaration, a statement without words, and the disciples "would have recognized an epiphany of the one true deity."[7] From "the beginning" the Spirit of God was "hovering over the waters" (Gen 1:2); here the Son of God was walking over the face of the waters. Even more, with nearly identical language in the LXX, Job declares that God alone "treads on the waves of the sea" (Job 9:8). What the disciples "saw" was nothing less than the Creator in control of his creation. There are no categories that adequately describe or contain such an event. Only the absorption of this category into the identity of God can explain *what* happened and *about whom* it speaks. At that moment, the sound and feel of the waves grew strangely mute; they were undoubtedly in the presence of God. The narrative's depiction of the conflict concludes with an unsurprising response of the disciples: "And they were afraid" (καὶ ἐφοβήθησαν), much like Moses in Exodus 3:6. Like Moses, the disciples were in the unquantifiable presence of God, and as with Moses it would be God who would speak first.

6:20 But he said to them, "I AM; do not fear!" (ὁ δὲ λέγει αὐτοῖς, Ἐγώ εἰμι, μὴ φοβεῖσθε). Excluding a host of explanatory details, the narrator describes how the approaching Jesus arrives and addresses his disciples. Jesus speaks to his disciples with a phrase that could be translated more simply as a phrase of common speech, "It is I" (Ἐγώ εἰμι) rather than with the sacred divine formula for the name of God, "I AM."[8] Some interpreters surmise for this historical event that Jesus is speaking in common idiom and is simply trying to identify himself as someone known to the disciples, without any intention of making a christological statement.[9] But nothing in this historical event is common, for Jesus speaks as he stands firmly atop a stirring sea. In John specifically, the statement "I AM" (Ἐγώ εἰμι) has a central status in the identification of Jesus, the personal expression of God (cf. 4:26; 6:35; 8:58).[10] With this clear intention of the Gospel, situated within the context of Scripture and in the immediate context of a theophanic appearance, Jesus's words must be taken as anything but common. Standing where only God can stand, Jesus declares what only he can claim: "I AM," the one of the unconsumed burning bush (Exod 3) who alone can walk on the waves of the sea (Job 9:8). In this context, then, the command of Jesus, "Do not fear" (μὴ φοβεῖσθε), is a gracious response of hope and promise to his confused and fearful disciples.[11]

6. Bernard, *John*, 1:186. Even worse is the position of Doron Nof, Ian McKeague, and Nathan Paldor, "Is There a Paleolimnological Explanation for 'Walking on Water' in the Sea of Galilee?" *J Paleolimnol* 35 (2006): 417–39, who offer a "scientific" explanation by suggesting that "there is a substantial chance" that a thin layer of ice thick enough to support human weight could form on top of salty and warm spring water below (417).

7. Keener, *John*, 1:673.
8. See Brown, *John*, 1:252. Cf. Haenchen, *John*, 1:280.
9. See Michaels, *John*, 357.
10. Cf. Bultmann, *John*, 215–16.
11. Gail R. O'Day, "John 6:15–21: Jesus Walking on Water as Narrative Embodiment of Johannine Christology," in *Critical Readings of John 6*, 149–59 (155).

6:21 Then they were willing to receive him into the boat, and immediately the boat came to the land to which they were going (ἤθελον οὖν λαβεῖν αὐτὸν εἰς τὸ πλοῖον, καὶ εὐθέως ἐγένετο τὸ πλοῖον ἐπὶ τῆς γῆς εἰς ἢν ὑπῆγον). The conclusion of the pericope and its interpretive guidance provided for the reader is difficult to determine. The narrative gives little insight into the details that followed the encounter with Jesus and his entrance into the boat. Only two things are given an explanation. First, the disciples "were willing to receive him into the boat" (ἤθελον λαβεῖν αὐτὸν εἰς τὸ πλοῖον). This statement suggests the narrator wants to show the disciples' receptive reaction to Jesus. Nothing further is explained, like whether he actually entered the boat or rather walked the entire way across the lake. The important fact was how the disciples responded to him.

Second, the narrator explains that "immedi-ately the boat came to the land to which they were going" (εὐθέως ἐγένετο τὸ πλοῖον ἐπὶ τῆς γῆς εἰς ἢν ὑπῆγον). Without any notice or explanation, the boat — with the disciples inside (and presumably Jesus) — arrives at its intended destination. This does not suggest that they magically arrived but simply that no further activities took place. There need not be a new miracle, which Barrett finds in connection with Psalm 107:23 – 32, where God calms the waves of the sea and "guided them to their desired haven" (v. 30).[12] Rather, the land simply serves to bring closure to the chaotic scene.[13] It might even be better (and warranted) to translate the adverb as "soon" (εὐθέως). In this way, the narrator concludes the pericope, providing circumstantial details in regard to the trip they had taken in the boat and the revelation they had received about God in the first person.

Theology in Application

In the center of an important section of the Gospel, as Jesus is beginning to be noticed by friends and foes, Jesus takes the opportunity to make himself known to his disciples and, therefore, to the readers through the Gospel's witness. In what is a moment of both wonder and worship, the Gospel declares in God's own words the identity of the Son. In this pericope, the reader of the Fourth Gospel is exhorted to encounter the "I AM," the one of the unconsumed burning bush (Exod 3) who alone can walk on the waves of the sea (Job 9:8).

Walking across the Stirring Waters

The archetypical symbol of water, connected to everything from creation to cleansing, is a dominant motif in the ancient world and the OT and is particularly significant in the Gospel of John. With this in view, there is a striking comparison between this pericope and its stirring waters and 5:1 – 18, in which the lame man (and a great multitude of the sick) huddle around so-called magical waters because they believe within them is the healing power of God. They believed that God, or at least his power, was in some way contained within the waters — precisely at the point where the waters stir. But neither God nor his power were contained in those

---

12. Barrett, *John*, 281. 13. Cf. Augustine, *John*, 24.7.163.

waters. God and his power were entirely located in the person of Jesus, who walked across the surface of the stirring waters of the Sea of Galilee toward his disciples. Not only does the water fail to contain any power of God, but the water of the stirring sea failed to control God as he effortlessly walked across its surface with its waves only serving to wash his feet. Moses asked God to remove the water (cf. Exod 14); Jesus can walk directly over it. All the potent imagery of water in the OT has been placed "at the feet" of Jesus, the feet that approached the disciples in their boat. The church is to kneel at the feet of Jesus, the feet that walk on water.

God in First Person

The voice in the burning bush (Exod 3) is the voice of Jesus Christ, who treads the waves of the sea. We have already been told Jesus reveals the Father (1:18), and in this pericope he speaks for him directly. Amidst all the interest in religion and spirituality, it is imperative that Jesus be understood as the only true spokesperson for God. God has spoken in the first person, the person of Jesus Christ. The church has heard the Word of God and thus declares that there is no other person through whom one can be saved (Acts 4:12). This is spoken not by our own authority but by God's own. We are the children of the first person, the one who came through the storm of our darkness to address us, announcing to us the thing we needed most: himself in the first person.

No Fear

In the presence of God, fear is both natural and unwarranted. In comparison to us and our reality, God is terrifying; yet when God is embraced there is no safer place. Psalm 46 serves as almost a commentary on the command of Jesus: "Do not fear" (6:20). The psalmist declares that the presence of God creates a safe place; nations and kingdoms are rising up, yet at the mere sound of God's voice the earth melts (Ps 46:6). In the presence of God the command is clear: "Be still [or, "cease striving"] and know that *I am* God" (v. 10, emphasis added). Jesus commands his disciples not to fear because his presence had already announced by the psalmist: "The Lord Almighty is with us" (Ps 46:11). The command extends beyond the psalms or the Sea of Galilee and enters the heart of the Christian, for whom God is present through the Son and his Spirit, and for whom the mere voice of the Lord is a constant support. Be still, Christians, for the Lord is with us.

Receive Him!

The vagueness of the narrative in regard to the events following the encounter with Jesus makes emphatic what *was* described: the reception of Jesus by his disciples. They were confused and scared, yet they were willing to receive him. They welcomed Jesus even though he could not have been less defined and explainable. They did the only thing they could do: trust him, which was the same thing they had to do when he first said to them, "Come and see" (cf. 1:39, 46).

The call of the Christian and the task of discipleship can be described quite simply as having the same objective: trusting in the inexplicable and all-consuming God made known in Jesus Christ. Without all questions being answered and doubts being solved, the Christian trusts in the God who need say nothing more than "I AM" in order to calm our fears. The Water-Walker has come and stands before the whole world, declaring as he did to his disciples on the stirring sea, "I AM." Will you receive him? Is there truly any other "I" that should take precedence?

John 6:22 – 71

Literary Context

This lengthy pericope in the form of a dialogue has been anticipated through the previous two pericopae: the feeding of the large crowd (6:1 – 15) and the encounter with the "I AM" on the sea (6:16 – 21). From the beginning of the Gospel, Jesus has been intimately connected to God (cf. 1:1), and the previous pericope gave a vivid demonstration of the unity of God and Jesus, the "I AM" in the burning bush and on the sea. As much as this pericope completes the larger picture of chapter 6, it also propels the Gospel's narrative forward, forcing the reader to confront the person of Jesus as the fullness of God. Jesus has confessed in dramatic fashion his true identity; he will now challenge his interested followers to see if they are willing to accept him as he truly is.

IV. The Confession of the Son of God (5:1 – 8:11)
- A. The Third Sign: The Healing of the Lame Man on the Sabbath (5:1 – 18)
- B. The Identity of (the Son of) God: Jesus Responds to the Opposition (5:19 – 47)
- C. The Fourth Sign: The Feeding of a Large Crowd (6:1 – 15)
- D. The "I AM" Walks across the Sea (6:16 – 21)
- ➡ **E. The Bread of Life (6:22 – 71)**
- F. Private Display of Suspicion (7:1 – 13)
- G. Public Display of Rejection (7:14 – 52)
- H. The Trial of Jesus regarding a Woman Accused of Adultery (7:53 – 8:11)

Main Idea

Jesus is not only the source of life; he is also its substance. The mystery of the metaphor of eating his flesh and drinking his blood is comfortably solved in the simplicity of belief in him and his work on the cross. As the bread of life, Jesus offers himself as the satisfying gift of God and offers a challenge against human pride and disbelief.

Translation

(See pages 318–23.)

Structure and Literary Form

This is the third substantial dialogue in the narrative proper, and it is a *social challenge dialogue*, which takes the form of an informal debate intending to challenge the honor and authority of one's interlocutor (see Introduction). Although a few interpreters define it technically as a dialogue, for the majority of interpreters this identification has little to no effect. Structural analyses deal almost exclusively with Jesus's statements, almost certainly because the statements of Jesus are so important and hotly debated. But the dialogical structure into which those statements are placed by the narrative are also important and are strikingly similar to the dialogue with the Samaritan woman, with both having six verbal exchanges surrounded by a closing and opening scene. The dialogical form of this pericope needs to be given its due interpretive authority (see comments on v. 49).

Exegetical Outline

➡ **E. The Bread of Life (6:22 – 71)**
    1. The Crowd Pursues Jesus (vv. 22 – 24)
    2. First Verbal Exchange: "When Did You Come Here?" (vv. 25 – 27)
    3. Second Verbal Exchange: The Work of God (vv. 28 – 29)
    4. Third Verbal Exchange: God Gave You Bread, Not Moses (vv. 30 – 33)
    5. Fourth Verbal Exchange: Jesus Is the Bread, Not Manna (vv. 34 – 40)
    6. Fifth Verbal Exchange: "I Am the Living Bread" (vv. 41 – 51)
    7. Sixth Verbal Exchange: Life in the Flesh and Blood of Jesus (vv. 52 – 59)
    8. The Crowd Deserts Jesus (vv. 60 – 71)
        a. The Offense of Some "Disciples" (vv. 60 – 66)
        b. The Confession of the "Twelve" (vv. 67 – 71)

John 6:22–71

22a	Setting (22–24)	On the next day
b	Character Reentrance (Crowd)	the crowd …
c	Description	that had been with him on the other side of the sea
d	Object of Perception #1	… saw that there was no other small boat there except one, and
e	Object of Perception #2	that Jesus had not entered into the boat with his disciples, but
d	Object of Perception #3	his disciples departed alone.
23a	Aside	But some boats came from Tiberias
b		near the place where they had eaten the bread
c		after the Lord had given thanks.
24a		When …
b		therefore … the crowd saw that neither Jesus nor his disciples were there,
c	Circumstance	
d	Inferential Action	they stepped into the boats
e		and went to Capernaum
f	Purpose	for the purpose of seeking Jesus.
25a	1st Interlocution (25–27)	When they found him on the other side of the sea,
b		they said to him,
c	Address	"Rabbi,
d	Question	when did you come here?"
26a	Response	Jesus answered to them and said,
b	Amen Formula	"Truly, truly, I say to you,
c	Rebuke	you do not seek me
d	(–) Basis #1	because you saw signs but
e	(+) Basis #2	because you ate of the bread and
d	(+) Basis #3	had your stomachs filled.
27a	Exhortation	Do not work for the food that perishes, but
b	Contrast	for the food that endures into eternal life,
c	Source	which the Son of Man will give to you.
d	Basis	For on him the Father has placed his seal."
28a	2nd Interlocution (28–29)	Then they said to him,
b	Clarifying Question	"What must we do
c	Purpose	in order to perform the works of God?"

29a	Response	**Jesus answered and said to them,**
b	Answer	"This is the work of God:
c	Apposition	to believe in the one he has sent."
30a	3rd Interlocution (30–33)	Then **they said to him,**
b	Interrogative Demand	"What sign will you do,
c		then,
d	Result	so that we may see and
e		believe in you?
f	Restatement of 30b	What will you perform?
31a	Explanatory Basis of 30	Our fathers ate manna in the wilderness
b		just as it is written,
c	OT Quotation	'Bread from heaven has been given
d	Purpose	for them to eat.'" (Exod 16:4; Ps 78:24)
32a	Retort	Then **Jesus said to them,**
b	Amen formula	"Truly, truly I say to you,
c	Counterassertion to 31	Moses did not give you bread from heaven, but
d	Contrast	my Father gives you the true bread from heaven.
33a	Explanation	For the bread of God is he
b	Description	who came down from heaven and
c		gives life to the world."
34a	4th Interlocution (34–41)	Then **they said to him,**
b	Address	"Sir,
c	Sarcastic Entreaty	give us this bread always."
35a	Retort	**Jesus said to them,**
b	Confession	"I am the bread of life.
d	Promise #1/Allusion: Isa 55	The one who comes to me will never go hungry,
e	Promise #2/Allusion Isa 55	and the one who believes in me will never be thirsty.
36a	Contrast	But
b	Recollection: John 1:5; 5:37–38	as I said to you,
c	Concession	you have seen me
d	Rebuke	and yet you do not believe.
37a	Explanation of 35–36	All that the Father gives to me will come to me,
b	Result	and the one who comes to me I will never cast away.
38a	Basis of 35–37	For I have come down from heaven
b	(–) Purpose	not to do my own will but
c	(+) Purpose/Contrast	the will of the one who sent me.

Continued on next page.

Continued from previous page.

39a	Expansion #1 of 38	*And* this is the will of the one who sent me,
b	(−) Description	that I might not lose any out of all that he has given to me but
c	(+) Description	will raise them on the last day.
40a	Expansion #2	*For* this is the will of my Father,
c	Descriptive Sequence #1	that all who see the Son and believe in him will have eternal life, and
d	Descriptive Sequence #2	I myself will raise him on the last day."
41a	Redescription of "Crowd"	**The Jews . . .**
b	Reaction/Allusion: Exod 16:2	**. . . were grumbling about him**
c	Basis	because he said,
d		"I am the Bread
e		that has come down from heaven."
42a	5th Interlocution (42–51)	And **they said,**
b	Rhetorical Question #1	"Is this not Jesus,
c	Relationship	the son of Joseph,
d	Descriptive Assertion	whose father and mother we know?
e	Rhetorical Question #2	How can he now say,
f		'I have come down from heaven?'"
43a	Retort	**Jesus answered and said to them,**
b	Rebuke/Allusion: Exod 16: 7–8	"Stop grumbling among yourselves.
44a	Inference	No one can come to me
b	Condition	unless the Father who sent me draws him,
c	Promise	and I will raise him on the last day.
45a	Explanation	It is written in the prophets,
b	OT Quotation	'They will all be taught by God.' (Isa 54:13)
c	Fulfillment of Prophecy	All who heard and learned from the Father come to me.
46a	Continued Explanation	Not that any person has seen God
b	Exception	except the one
c	Source	who is from God,
d	Contrast to 46a	he has seen the Father.
47a	Amen Formula	Truly, truly I say to you,
b	Restatement of 40b–d	the one who believes has eternal life.
48a	Re-confession of 35b	I am the bread of life.

49a	Explanation	Your fathers ate manna in the wilderness
b	(–) Result	and died.
50a	Contrast	This is the bread
b		who has come down from heaven
c	(+) Result	so that a person may eat from it and not die.
51a	Climactic Confession	I am the living bread
b	Source	who has come down from heaven.
c	Promise	Whoever eats this bread will live forever,
d	Explanation	and the bread …
e	Future Event	which I will give
f	Allusion: Jn.1:14 and OT	… is my flesh
g	Advantage	for the life of the world."
52a	6th Interlocution (52–59)	Then the Jews …
b	Reaction/Allusion: Exod 17:2	… began to argue with one another saying,
c	Interrogative Challenge	"How is he able to give us his flesh to eat?"
53a	Retort	Then Jesus said to them,
b	Amen Formula	"Truly, truly I say to you
c	Condition #1	unless you eat the flesh of the Son of Man and
d	Condition #2/OT Allusion	drink his blood,
e	Inferential Rebuke	you have no life in yourselves.
54a	Restatement	The one who eats my flesh and drinks my blood has eternal life,
b	Result	and I will raise him on the last day.
55a	Explanatory Declarations	For my flesh is real food,
b		and my blood is real drink.
56a	Promise	The one who eats my flesh and drinks my blood …
b	Result: Mutual Indwelling	… remains in me and
c		I in him.
57a	Explanatory Comparison	Just as the living Father sent me
b		and I live
c	Basis	because of the Father,
d	Parallel Comparison to 57a, b	so the one who eats me will also live
e	Parallel Basis to 57c	because of me.

Continued on next page.

Continued from previous page.

58a	Concluding Summary	*This is the bread*
b	Source	*that came down from heaven,*
c	Comparison	*not as the fathers who ate and*
d	Result	*died,*
e	Promise	*the one who eats this bread will live forever."*
59a	Context	**He said these things**
b		while he was teaching in a synagogue in Capernaum.
60a	Reaction to Jesus (60–71)	Then
b	Character Reentrance	after many of his disciples had heard
c	Response	**they said,**
d	Rejection of Jesus	*"This message is offensive! Who is able to accept it?"*
61a	Character Thoughts	After Jesus had seen in himself that his disciples were grumbling concerning this
b	Response	**he said to them,**
c	Interrogative Challenge	*"Does this offend you?*
62a	Interrogative Inference	*Then, what*
b	Condition	*if you see the Son of Man*
c		*ascending to where he was*
d	Allusion to John 1:2	*before?*
63a	Explanatory Rebuke of 60d	*The Spirit is giving life,*
b		*the flesh cannot help anything;*
c		*the words…*
d		*which I have spoken to you*
e		*…are spirit and are life.*
64a	Inference	*But there are some of you*
b		*who do not believe."*
c	Aside	For **Jesus had known from the beginning**
d	Present Description	who they are that do not believe and
e	Future Allusion	who it is who will hand him over.

65a	Concluding Reponses to 60d	**And he said,**
b	Basis (63)	*"For this reason*
c	Restatement of 63	*I told you that no one is able to come to me*
d	Exception	*unless it has been given to him*
e	Source	*from the Father."*
66a	Concluding Reaction/Rejection	**From this time many of his disciples fell away**
b		and **were no longer following him.**
67a	Transition	Then **Jesus said**
b	Character Reentrance	to the Twelve,
c	Interrogative Challenge	*"You do not want to leave also,*
d	Emphatic Restatement	*do you?"*
68a	Response	**Simon Peter answered to him,**
b	Address	*"Lord,*
c	Rhetorical Question	*to whom shall we go?*
d	Confession #1	*You have the words of eternal life.*
69a	Confession #2	*And we have believed*
b		*and have known that you are the Holy One of God."*
70a	Response	**Jesus answered to them,**
b	Interrogative Challenge	*"Have I not chosen you,*
c		*the Twelve,*
d	Declaration	*yet one of you is the devil?"*
71a	Concluding Aside/Identification	**He was speaking about Judas,**
b	Relationship	son of Simon of Iscariot,
c	Explanation	for **he was about to hand over Jesus,**
d	Concession	even though he was one of the twelve.

Explanation of the Text

We stated earlier that John 6 has been called "the Grand Central Station" of critical issues in John and a summary of numerous interpretive issues related to the Gospel as a whole (see comments before 6:1). One issue has been so frequently raised in regard to this pericope that we must address it briefly here: the institution of the Lord's Supper, the Eucharist, or the "sacrament."[1]

IN DEPTH: Eucharistic Imagery in the Fourth Gospel

Unlike the Synoptics, John does not give an account of the Lord's Supper. For this reason, alongside what is often taken as strong eucharistic imagery of the pericope (especially vv. 52 – 59), numerous interpreters have debated the manner in which this pericope incorporates a sacramental theology. How one interprets (or even recognizes) the eucharistic imagery is almost entirely dependent upon the author assumed by the interpreter. For example, those who see the sacramental meaning directly in the text consider the author to be writing to a late first-century Johannine "church" audience where such practices are already developed. In contrast, others consider any sacramental meaning to be blatantly anachronistic. One might try to hold them both in tension, like Carson, who has in view primarily the ostensible historical context but would secondarily be willing to say that "it is hard to imagine that the Evangelist, writing several decades after the institution of the Lord's supper, could produce these words without noticing that many readers, even if they understood the passage aright, would in all likelihood detect some parallels with the eucharist."[2]

Rather than choosing between Jesus and the evangelist or trying to mediate between them on historical grounds, this commentary intends to incorporate them both within the confines of the ontology of Scripture (see Introduction), which interprets the words of the divine agent (author) in cooperation with the human agent (author). This allows — no, demands — that one not choose between Jesus and his "Jewish" context or the evangelist and his "Christian" context. That is, we should not be forced to choose between whether the imagery is alluding to the motif of manna in the Old Testament (Jewish) or to the rite of the Eucharist in the early Christian movement (Christian). Rather, in light of the purview of the divine author, the images make "impressions" (see Introduction; cf. comments on 1:14; 6:11) upon the reader that reverberate across the entire

---

1. On "sacrament" in the interpretation of John, see Paul N. Anderson, *The Christology of the Fourth Gospel: Its Unity and Disunity in the Light of John 6*, WUNT 2.78 (Tübingen: Mohr Siebeck, 1996), 112 – 14.

2. Carson, *John*, 279 – 80.

canon, with the manna in Exodus and the Eucharist in 1 Corinthians serving as the appropriate interpretive background from which Jesus comes and is made known. As Augustine explains in regard to manna and the Lord's Supper, "In the signs they were diverse; in the thing which was signified they were alike."[3] As Jesus explained regarding Moses, "He wrote about me" (5:46).

6:22 On the next day the crowd that had been with him on the other side of the sea saw that there was no other small boat there except one, and that Jesus had not entered into the boat with his disciples, but his disciples departed alone (Τῇ ἐπαύριον ὁ ὄχλος ὁ ἑστηκὼς πέραν τῆς θαλάσσης εἶδον ὅτι πλοιάριον ἄλλο οὐκ ἦν ἐκεῖ εἰ μὴ ἕν, καὶ ὅτι οὐ συνεισῆλθεν τοῖς μαθηταῖς αὐτοῦ ὁ Ἰησοῦς εἰς τὸ πλοῖον ἀλλὰ μόνοι οἱ μαθηταὶ αὐτοῦ ἀπῆλθον). After what can be described as a sort of interlude (6:16 – 21), the narrative now returns to the crowd with whom chapter 6 began. The crowd that had completely misunderstood Jesus after the miraculous feeding (cf. 6:14 – 15) was now looking for him again, with intentions the reader is almost certainly supposed to assume are inappropriate. The phrase, "On the next day" (Τῇ ἐπαύριον), suggests that after Jesus's escape from them, the following day they sought to find him again, likely to make him king (cf. 6:15). But instead of finding him, they discovered only the "small boat" (πλοιάριον), from which they concluded that Jesus had crossed the sea without a boat or his disciples. The confusing sense of the verse should not deter the reader from gathering the important details. The crowd is aware that Jesus departed and is convinced he did so separately and without a boat. The point of the narrator may simply be to confirm by means of the crowd the events told in the previous pericope (6:16 – 21).

6:23 But some boats came from Tiberias near the place where they had eaten the bread after the Lord had given thanks (ἄλλα ἦλθεν πλοῖα ἐκ Τιβεριάδος ἐγγὺς τοῦ τόπου ὅπου ἔφαγον τὸν ἄρτον [εὐχαριστήσαντος τοῦ κυρίου]). The narrator adds what appears to be isolated information to explain how the necessary transportation had arrived for a certain number of "the crowd" to continue their pursuit of Jesus (cf. v. 24). Several details are not provided by the narrator, suggesting that the reader is given a mere sketch of what really happened so as to make sense of where the narrative is going. As much as we have further questions for the narrator and other interests in the vague description of the events that transpired, we as readers must not get sidetracked from the narrative's guiding intention.

6:24 When therefore the crowd saw that neither Jesus nor his disciples were there, they stepped into the boats and went to Capernaum for the purpose of seeking Jesus (ὅτε οὖν εἶδεν ὁ ὄχλος ὅτι Ἰησοῦς οὐκ ἔστιν ἐκεῖ οὐδὲ οἱ μαθηταὶ αὐτοῦ, ἐνέβησαν αὐτοὶ εἰς τὰ πλοιάρια καὶ ἦλθον εἰς Καφαρναοὺμ ζητοῦντες τὸν Ἰησοῦν). The narrator concludes the crowds' search for Jesus by describing how after not finding him or his disciples (and by implication being convinced that he had crossed the sea), they enter the boats themselves and pursue Jesus. The use of the purpose participial phrase, "for the purpose of seeking Jesus" (ζητοῦντες τὸν Ἰησοῦν), calls to mind the seeking

---

3. Augustine, *John*, 26.12.171. Cf. Calvin, *John 1 – 10*, 170.

(and finding) done by the first disciples (cf. 1:41, 45). The narrator has set up the dialogue to come, which is centered upon the crowd's pursuit of Jesus and what they think he represents, which will be contrasted with the true identity of Jesus.

6:25 When they found him on the other side of the sea, they said to him, "Rabbi, when did you come here?" (καὶ εὑρόντες αὐτὸν πέραν τῆς θαλάσσης εἶπον αὐτῷ, Ῥαββί, πότε ὧδε γέγονας;). The first verbal exchange of the dialogue (vv. 25–27) begins when the crowd finds Jesus "on the other side of the sea" (πέραν τῆς θαλάσσης). The crowd addresses Jesus as "Rabbi" (Ῥαββί), which is reminiscent of Jesus's first disciples revealing their interest in Jesus (cf. 1:38, 49). Although it serves as an honorific title that accorded the individual with the highest status as a teacher, it does not reveal the nature of their intended discipleship, which up to this point has been motivated more by hunger than humility (cf. 6:1–15).

6:26 Jesus answered to them and said, "Truly, truly, I say to you, you do not seek me because you saw signs but because you ate of the bread and had your stomachs filled" (ἀπεκρίθη αὐτοῖς ὁ Ἰησοῦς καὶ εἶπεν, Ἀμὴν ἀμὴν λέγω ὑμῖν, ζητεῖτέ με οὐχ ὅτι εἴδετε σημεῖα ἀλλ' ὅτι ἐφάγετε ἐκ τῶν ἄρτων καὶ ἐχορτάσθητε). Jesus calls their spiritual bluff and directly addresses the source of the "seeking," their stomachs, reflective of their selfish desires and passions.[4] Although they "saw" (εἴδετε) signs, they did not comprehend them (cf. 2:11). The crowd wanted a king (cf. 6:15), one to take care of their physical needs, not the Prophet (cf. 6:14), who would condemn their sinfulness and announce the plan of God. The "signs" of Jesus according to the Gospel were pointing beyond themselves, past the earthly and physical to the heavenly and eternal. The signs challenge those who see them, for they are material testimony to the identity of Jesus. Thus, encountering one of Jesus's signs can lead to a foreshortening of one's sight, a lowering of one's eyes from the true object of the sign to its mere symptoms (the miracle). Properly perceived, however, the signs draw one's eyes directly to Jesus, deepening and strengthening belief in him. In this way, signs are truly gracious gifts to those who correctly see, and like curses of hindrance to those who do not.[5]

6:27 "Do not work for the food that perishes, but for the food that endures into eternal life, which the Son of Man will give to you. For on him the Father has placed his seal" (ἐργάζεσθε μὴ τὴν βρῶσιν τὴν ἀπολλυμένην ἀλλὰ τὴν βρῶσιν τὴν μένουσαν εἰς ζωὴν αἰώνιον, ἣν ὁ υἱὸς τοῦ ἀνθρώπου ὑμῖν δώσει· τοῦτον γὰρ ὁ πατὴρ ἐσφράγισεν ὁ θεός). What the crowd did not "see" or understand from the sign was the distinction between the temporary and the eternal, that is, the distinction between the Jesus they wanted and his true status as the Son of Man, sent from the Father. Rebuking the shallow "god of their stomachs," Jesus provides the deep answer to their question, which they unknowingly asked as implied by the phrase, "When did you come here?" He states that they should not "work for" (ἐργάζεσθε) food that "perishes" (τὴν ἀπολλυμένην) but rather for the food "that endures into eternal life" (τὴν μένουσαν εἰς ζωὴν αἰώνιον). This food that endures into eternal life is equivalent to "a well of water springing up into eternal life" (4:14). This is what the crowd should pursue, and this is what Jesus alone can provide. The word "work" is not suggesting that we merit eternal life

---

4. Jo-Ann A. Brant, *John*, PCNT (Grand Rapids: Baker Academic, 2011), 120, suggests that Jesus's words were an insult, since to state that a person is ruled by their stomachs is according to Greco-Roman literature to call them a fool.

5. Stephen Fowl, "John 6:25–35," *Int* 61 (2007): 314–16.

by works but is exhorting the crowd to apply themselves to the food that matters.

The verse goes on to declare that what is worked for is what the Son of Man "will give to you" (ὑμῖν δώσει). The antecedent of "which" (ἣν) is unclear. It could be referring to either "the food" or "eternal life." The ambiguity only serves to highlight that both the food and the eternal life come directly from him in the form of a gift. As much as there is a strange paradox created between the command to "work" and the fact that what is obtained is ultimately "given" by Jesus, the two statements ultimately find agreement in Christ.[6]

Jesus offers confirmation of this when he declares that on him the Father "has placed his seal" (ἐσφράγισεν). The verb implies that Jesus has been marked with a seal as a means of identification, suggesting not only that the one sealed is endued with the authority of the one who sent him but also that the sender (the Father) is directly connected with the one sealed (the Son).[7] In the ancient world, a seal was a mark of ownership. It is probably not referring to a particular act of sealing (e.g., the baptism in the Synoptics, or more likely for John, the descent of the Spirit in 1:33 – 34) but to the seal upon his whole person and activity. In this way, the first verbal exchange of the challenge dialogue ends, with Jesus, fully aware of what is in humanity (cf. 2:24 – 25), responding to their self-focused question with the truest answer he could give.

6:28 Then they said to him, "What must we do in order to perform the works of God?" (εἶπον οὖν πρὸς αὐτόν, Τί ποιῶμεν ἵνα ἐργαζώμεθα τὰ ἔργα τοῦ θεοῦ;). The second verbal exchange of the dialogue (vv. 28 – 29) focuses more directly on the challenge Jesus presents to the crowd's misguided pursuits. The crowd responds to Jesus's statement by asking for clarification and further explanation about how to do these "works." The phrase "to perform the works of God" or "to work the works of God" (ἐργαζώμεθα τὰ ἔργα τοῦ θεοῦ) is emphatic in that both the verb and the direct object bear the sense of "work." In spite of all the shocking things Jesus revealed — that he is the Son of Man, that the Father has placed his seal upon him, and that he can provide *eternal life* — it is surprising to see the focus land merely on the "works." The reason is clear. They misunderstood Jesus's rebuke regarding the inappropriate *object* of their work. Jesus is not inventing a new mode of work for his followers but is confronting the idolatrous object(s) of their current work.[8] Their blindness in regard to self is being revealed by the dialogue. In the context of the dialogue, the crowd's misguided focus on their duties and not Christ's takes the form of a rhetorical grumbling, a cry of the victim who has been accused undeservedly. The Son of Man has just declared who he is and what he can do, and all they can think about (and see) is themselves and what they can do.

6:29 Jesus answered and said to them, "This is the work of God: to believe in the one he has sent" (ἀπεκρίθη ὁ Ἰησοῦς καὶ εἶπεν αὐτοῖς, Τοῦτό ἐστιν τὸ ἔργον τοῦ θεοῦ, ἵνα πιστεύητε εἰς ὃν ἀπέστειλεν ἐκεῖνος). Jesus responds to their question by changing their plural "the *works* of God" (τὰ ἔργα τοῦ θεοῦ) to "the *work* of God" (τὸ ἔργον τοῦ θεοῦ), about which he then provides the definitive answer: belief in Jesus. Jesus's statement is in the form of a subjunctive with the conjunction often translated as "that/in order that" (ἵνα), which in this context is best taken as introducing an epexegetical clause explaining the preceding "this" (τοῦτό) and is fittingly translated as an infinitive.[9] It is important to note that the verb "believe" (πιστεύητε) is

---

6. Cf. Calvin, *John 1 – 10*, 154.
7. BDAG 980.

8. Cf. Carson, *John*, 284.
9. Cf. Wallace, *Greek Grammar*, 476.

in the present tense; believing in Jesus is less an *act* of faith and more a *life* of faith.[10]

The singular work of the Christian is faith in the Son who was sent from the Father. The Trinitarian nature of the Christian faith could not be more pervasive. Any work *for* God must involve faith in *his* Son. The Gospel has heralded this message since the prologue (see 1:18). The duties and responsibilities of humanity are entirely eclipsed by this one task of trusting in the person and work of the Son.[11] It is likely for this reason that Jesus kept the word "work" alongside the call to faith in his response to the crowd's question. There is a work to be done, but it belongs to God, both Father and Son (see comments on v. 44). Faith, then, is to trust in the work of God accomplished in Jesus Christ.

The separation of faith from works, fitting so nicely alongside Paul's letter to the Romans, is not to deny a place for works. Rather, it is to place works beneath and subordinated to faith so that true "works" *for* Jesus may be deemed impossible outside of faith *in* Jesus. Belief in Jesus is the structural category into which all other works are placed and function.[12] Even the value of a particular "work" is deemed worthy and acceptable only if it occurs by faith in Christ (cf. 5:28 – 29).[13] In this way, faith becomes the only work of God for the Christian, for by it we possess the Son, obtaining the right to become children of the Father (1:12) and are therefore graciously governed by his Spirit. Only within this Trinitarian identity may the Christian be freed from the demands of God so as to properly respond to the commands of God. And this is what the crowd could not see by focusing entirely upon themselves. Ironically, their rhetorical grumbling in the form of a question was itself

proof that they were "working" to an entirely different end.

6:30 Then they said to him, "What sign will you do, then, so that we may see and believe in you? What will you perform?" (εἶπον οὖν αὐτῷ, Τί οὖν ποιεῖς σὺ σημεῖον, ἵνα ἴδωμεν καὶ πιστεύσωμέν σοι; τί ἐργάζῃ;). In a third verbal exchange of the dialogue (vv. 30 – 33), the crowd presses Jesus to do the sign he mentioned in the first verbal exchange and the "work" he explained in the second verbal exchange. The crowd is pleading — note the emphatic "you" (σύ) — for a sign to confirm the things about which Jesus speaks, including his own person. Even their final question, asked in the form of a futuristic present, "What will you perform?" (τί ἐργάζῃ;), utilizes a verb that could also be translated as "work." He claims to be the "Sent One"; they are now demanding that he match that claim with action — with a sign. Their questions are not symptoms of interest but the jabs of a challenge (cf. Mark 15:32).[14] The social challenge is well underway.

6:31 "Our fathers ate manna in the wilderness just as it is written, 'Bread from heaven has been given for them to eat' " (οἱ πατέρες ἡμῶν τὸ μάννα ἔφαγον ἐν τῇ ἐρήμῳ, καθώς ἐστιν γεγραμμένον, Ἄρτον ἐκ τοῦ οὐρανοῦ ἔδωκεν αὐτοῖς φαγεῖν). The challenge from the crowd is supported by biblical proof and the example of Moses. Their logic proceeded something like the following. If the God-ordained activity of Moses warranted a sign, certainly the prophet-like-Moses of Deuteronomy 18 would give an even greater sign. *If* this is *the* Prophet, giving not just perishing food but something "eternal," he would prove himself to be the giver of even more and greater bread. The feed-

10. Barrett, *John*, 287.

11. Cf. Luther, *John*, 23:23.

12. As Calvin explains, "Faith excludes neither love nor any other good work, but contains them all within itself" (*John 1 – 10*, 155).

13. See Augustine, *John*, 25.12.164.

14. Michaels, *John*, 368.

ing of five thousand men can only have been the appetizer, signaling that the true meal was still to come. From this point on in the dialogue, the focus is markedly on the manna miracle and its motifs.[15]

It is important to note that the crowd uses biblical reasoning in their challenge to Jesus. Nowhere else in the Gospel do we find anyone but Jesus or the narrator/author quoting Scripture in this way. The biblical quotation is taken from both Exodus 16 and Psalm 78. The emphasis of the crowd seems to be primarily on the phrase, "from heaven" (cf. Ps 78:24), which is why the feeding of the five thousand men seems to be an unsatisfactory sign for them. Bread "from heaven" has a strong biblical heritage (cf. Ps 105:40; Neh 9:15), and Jewish literature suggests that Jews believed there would be an end-time recurrence of God's provision of bread from heaven.[16] Jesus had fed them "from below"; in their opinion, it was time for him to make good on his confession and feed them "from above," as Moses had done and promised would happen.

6:32 Then Jesus said to them, "Truly, truly I say to you, Moses did not give you bread from heaven, but my Father gives you the true bread from heaven" (εἶπεν οὖν αὐτοῖς ὁ Ἰησοῦς, Ἀμὴν ἀμὴν λέγω ὑμῖν, οὐ Μωϋσῆς δέδωκεν ὑμῖν τὸν ἄρτον ἐκ τοῦ οὐρανοῦ, ἀλλ᾽ ὁ πατήρ μου δίδωσιν ὑμῖν τὸν ἄρτον ἐκ τοῦ οὐρανοῦ τὸν ἀληθινόν). Beginning his statement with his authoritative preface (see comments on 1:51), Jesus counters their biblical reasoning and reconstructed tradition of the promise of God. He rejects outright that Moses actually gave bread "from heaven" — a remarkable negation (challenge!) of what would have been a saturated biblical logic. It is not Moses who gave bread to them, "but my Father" (ἀλλ᾽ ὁ πατήρ μου). This rebuttal of the crowd's claim of tradition

demands that the true agent of manna was never Moses but the God of Moses. In sharp contrast to the rabbinic argument that Moses was the "first redeemer," and the assumption that followed that the Prophet would be the "second redeemer" (cf. 2 Bar. 29:8), Jesus declares that there had always been only one redeemer, and it was not Moses. This is a hermeneutical correction to the crowd's reading of Scripture.

Alongside this correction is another, more theological correction: it was not Moses but the Father who gives them "the true bread from heaven" (τὸν ἄρτον ἐκ τοῦ οὐρανοῦ τὸν ἀληθινόν). Just as Moses was seen in place of God, the true giver, so also the substance of bread (manna) was seen in place of the "true bread" (which will be explained in v. 33). This is an even more remarkable correction, for it is one thing to correct the crowd when they assert Moses as the giver, thus allowing God (inappropriately) to become merely implicit and therefore secondary. But it is quite another for Jesus to claim that the physical bread was also falsely asserted as the primary bread. There is no need to try to explain this exegetical maneuver based upon Jewish exegesis or typology, even if traits of such maneuvers are present,[17] just as no solution could be offered to explain Jesus's correction of the temple to the Jewish authorities in 2:12 – 25. This time, however, there is no interpretive assistance provided by the narrator (cf. 2:21 – 22).

Beyond the insight already provided by the prologue and the developing narrative, the only possible clue is in the present-tense verb "gives" (δίδωσιν). It can quite easily be taken as a historic present and thus be referring to the bread that God gave through Moses. But why the present tense when the aorist, for example, would be more effective?

---

15. Cf. Ridderbos, *John*, 226.
16. Köstenberger, "John," 446. Cf. Hoskyns, *Fourth Gospel*, 293 – 94; Barrett, *John*, 288 – 89.

17. Cf. Peder Borgen, *Bread from Heaven: An Exegetical Study of the Concept of Manna in the Gospel of John and the Writings of Philo*, NovTSup 10 (Leiden: Brill, 1965), 61 – 69.

The answer must be that Jesus spoke in the present intentionally so as to communicate about a "giving" in the present. In this way, the sense would be something like this: "But my Father *is giving you at this moment* the true bread from heaven."[18] Although our translation cannot maintain both senses, the reader is to hear the echoes from them both in Jesus's words. For this reason these words of Jesus — this remarkable declaration — is not merely a rebuke but is also the manifestation of the long-awaited promise of God's provision.

6:33 "For the bread of God is he who came down from heaven and gives life to the world" (ὁ γὰρ ἄρτος τοῦ θεοῦ ἐστιν ὁ καταβαίνων ἐκ τοῦ οὐρανοῦ καὶ ζωὴν διδοὺς τῷ κόσμῳ). Jesus then declares that he is the true bread: "For the bread of God is he" (ὁ γὰρ ἄρτος τοῦ θεοῦ ἐστιν). The opening phrase could be taken attributively ("*This* is the bread of God that …"), but while grammatically possible the context presses us to take the phrase predicatively ("*He* is the bread of God …"). The personalization of the bread is not only accurate but rhetorically powerful, fitting the forthcoming dialogue (cf. vv. 53 – 58).

If there was any doubt about the present status of "gave" in v. 32, it has now been answered. The "bread of God" is the more precise, more direct way of referring to the "bread of heaven"; it is not a different thing. Jesus is and has always been the bread that God would give to his people, the long-awaited promise now being fulfilled. This bread has arrived in a similar manner to the bread already eaten by the Israelites, but there are several important differences. First, like the manna this bread also "came down from heaven" (ὁ καταβαίνων ἐκ τοῦ οὐρανοῦ), but in a manner unique from what

the Israelites received. The Israelites had to wait each day for a fresh arrival of bread, whereas this bread has already come down. Second, while the manna was given to sustain life, so also this bread "gives life to the world" (ζωὴν διδοὺς τῷ κόσμῳ). But the "life" this bread gives is life *par excellence* (see comments on 1:4 and 3:15), and the recipient is no longer Israel alone but the entire "world" (cf. 4:42). In this third verbal exchange of this dialogue, Jesus has declared that "my Father" is the true provider, that he is the true bread, and that "life" itself, not the mere satiation of hunger, is the true provision.

6:34 Then they said to him, "Sir, give us this bread always" (Εἶπον οὖν πρὸς αὐτόν, Κύριε, πάντοτε δὸς ἡμῖν τὸν ἄρτον τοῦτον.). The fourth verbal exchange of the dialogue (vv. 34 – 40) centers more directly around this bread of God. The ambiguity of Jesus's words mixed with their distorted perception of God directed the crowd to bread and not *the* bread. The crowd, like the world, has become so accustomed to that which is perishing that they are unable to make sense of that which is eternal (cf. v. 27).

After taking into account the rebuke Jesus gave the crowd in the third verbal exchange, the crowd's address to Jesus, "Sir" (Κύριε), though dressed in a respectful form, is anything but polite. Under a cloak of polite expression, the crowd speaks to Jesus with sarcastic daggers in a manner similar to Nicodemus (see comments on 3:2) and thus moves the social challenge forward.[19] Their language, "this bread" (τὸν ἄρτον τοῦτον), also betrays their intentions. They realize Jesus is speaking beyond the manna of Moses, so they beckon him — challenge him — to produce it. Even the grammar suggests a mockery is in play with the strange combination

18. See John McHugh, "'In Him was Life': John's Gospel and the Parting of the Ways," in *Jews and Christians*, ed. J. D. G. Dunn; WUNT 66 (Tübingen: Mohr Siebeck, 1992), 123 – 58 (especially 138).

19. Cf. Neyrey, *John*, 123 – 28. When the pericope is taken as a monologue and not in its dialogical form, the crowd's request is often taken as respectful. Cf. Ridderbos, *John*, 228.

of the aorist imperative, "give" (δός), which deemphasizes duration and repetition, and the adverb, "always" (πάντοτε), which is clearly durative. They had asked him for a general sign in the previous verbal exchange (v. 30), which he was able to deflect by his rebuke. How could he now avoid "proving" himself to them after making such cavalier statements?

6:35 Jesus said to them, "I am the bread of life. The one who comes to me will never go hungry, and the one who believes in me will never be thirsty" (εἶπεν αὐτοῖς ὁ Ἰησοῦς, Ἐγώ εἰμι ὁ ἄρτος τῆς ζωῆς· ὁ ἐρχόμενος πρός με οὐ μὴ πεινάσῃ, καὶ ὁ πιστεύων εἰς ἐμὲ οὐ μὴ διψήσει πώποτε). Jesus's response to the crowd's cloaked retort is one of the most famous declarations of our Lord in the Gospel, even in the entire canon. Almost no explanation is needed in regard to the confession, "I am the bread of life" (Ἐγώ εἰμι ὁ ἄρτος τῆς ζωῆς), for the entire dialogue has provided the needed background and foreground of the title. Jesus is — and has always been — the true bread. Moses did not and could not give this bread, nor did he or this crowd even consider the "enduring bread of eternal life" that was to come and is now here (cf. v. 27). The crowd mockingly asks Jesus for this "magical" bread that trumps the famous bread of Moses, and Jesus offers himself. What was insightfully implied in v. 33 has now been shouted in explicitness.

The true disciple of the bread of life is the one who "comes" (ὁ ἐρχόμενος) and "believes" (ὁ πιστεύων), with the latter term serving as an insightful commentary on the former. To come to Jesus is to believe in him, and both of these are defined by the motif of eating that drenches this entire dialogue. For this reason Jesus can claim that the disciple who comes to/believes in him will no longer "go hungry" (πεινάσῃ) or "be thirsty" (διψήσει), for they have fully embraced Christ as the source and sustenance of life. The motif of thirst recalls Jesus's dialogue with the Samaritan woman (see 4:14). By combining hunger and thirst in the metaphor of the bread of life, Jesus embodies in his person all promises of satisfaction and satiation. Jesus is the recipe for the soul. While it is clear that the remainder of the dialogue will explicate further this confession, it is also clear that the Gospel as a whole (and all Scripture) is part of the necessary interpretive matrix into which this confession is fit (e.g., Isa 55:1 – 3, 6 – 7, 10).

"I am the bread of life" is the first of seven *formal* "I am" statements in the Gospel, each containing "I am" (Ἐγώ εἰμι) and a predicate. The "bread of life" predicate serves to convey the absolute necessity of Christ by linking the most basic and foundational needs of human life to his person and work.[20] In a manner not yet fully described, the phrase signifies that in Jesus there is an eternal sufficiency in which there is no want.[21] In Jesus there is an "eating" that provides deep rest for one's whole being, "even if all about me should go to pieces."[22]

IN DEPTH: "I Am" Statements

In the Gospel of John, Jesus makes seven *formal* "I am" statements, each containing "I am" (Ἐγώ εἰμι) and a predicate. The other six (with some variations) are as follows: "I am the light of the world" (8:12), "I am the gate" (10:7, 9),

---

20. Morris, *John*, 323 – 24; Carson, *John*, 301.
21. Augustine, *John*, 25.14.165.

22. Luther, *John*, 23:44.

"I am the good shepherd" (10:11, 14), "I am the resurrection and the life" (11:25), "I am the way and the truth and the life" (14:6), and "I am the true vine" (15:1, 5). These "I am" statements are rooted in the OT (especially Exod 3:6, 14; 20:2) and communicate the self-revelation of God.[23] Their occurrence in John develops further the revelation of the identity of God by means of the Son. These seven "I am" statements, therefore, are emphatic descriptions of the person and ministry of Jesus and cumulatively form a detailed picture of Jesus Christ.

John employs a number of other "I am" statements that are without a predicate (see comments on 8:58). These *informal* "I am" statements also communicate the self-revelation of God but not in a manner that is to be equated with the seven formal "I am" statements. While all the "I am" statements locate Jesus in the divine identity of God, the informal statements do not identify Jesus as a particular individual (i.e., "light of the world") but serve to give insight to the *particular qualifications* of Jesus.[24] When informal "I am" statements are used, the narrative context of the statement directs the reader to the particular qualification in view.

6:36 "But as I said to you, you have seen me and yet you do not believe" (ἀλλ᾽ εἶπον ὑμῖν ὅτι καὶ ἑωράκατέ [με] καὶ οὐ πιστεύετε). The grand offer of Christ is immediately and strongly contrasted with what Jesus reveals about the unreceptive crowd. His claim to have already communicated this is not necessarily suggesting it occurred earlier in this dialogue (e.g., in v. 26) but in words spoken to other disbelievers (possibly 5:37 – 38), representing the innate disbelief of a world in darkness (1:5). Jesus decries that although they "have seen" (ἑωράκατέ) him, made emphatic with the perfect tense, they still do not believe. Their disbelief is highlighted by the contrastive conjunction "and yet" (καὶ ... καὶ),[25] which implicitly offers judgment on the crowd. This crowd has seen and heard God in the flesh, and yet the encounter has aroused not their faith but their curiosity, physical appetites, and political

ambitions.[26] Even worse, they have given challenge to the very God for whom they claim to be looking.

6:37 "All that the Father gives to me will come to me, and the one who comes to me I will never cast away" (Πᾶν ὃ δίδωσίν μοι ὁ πατὴρ πρὸς ἐμὲ ἥξει, καὶ τὸν ἐρχόμενον πρὸς ἐμὲ οὐ μὴ ἐκβάλω ἔξω). In order that the crowd's disbelief not be viewed as their own possession, Jesus offers a counter by placing their disbelief fully within the sovereign domain of God. That is, rather than rejecting God, in a real way God had already rejected them. "All" (Πᾶν) is neuter and singular and thus is referring not to individuals but to "a general quality" of persons.[27] In this context, the quality is not their own but that which only the Father can give. The second part of the verse, which seems to emphasize more the individual's responsibility, is not contradicting the first part. The Son is not welcoming

23. Bultmann, *John*, 225 – 26; Barrett, *John*, 291 – 92.
24. Carson, *John*, 340.
25. BDF § 444.3.
26. Carson, *John*, 290.
27. BDF § 138.1.

beyond what the Father is giving, but is matching in detail — note the move from collective to individual, "the *one* who comes" (τὸν ἐρχόμενον) — a responsiveness coordinated with the Father's. Even more, the statement, "I will never cast away" (οὐ μὴ ἐκβάλω ἔξω), strengthened by the emphatically negated subjunctive, declares that those the Father *brings in* the Son will *keep in*.[28] The final three verses of this verbal exchange will explain the nature of this coordination between the Father and the Son (vv. 38 – 40).

6:38 "For I have come down from heaven not to do my own will but the will of the one who sent me" (ὅτι καταβέβηκα ἀπὸ τοῦ οὐρανοῦ οὐχ ἵνα ποιῶ τὸ θέλημα τὸ ἐμὸν ἀλλὰ τὸ θέλημα τοῦ πέμψαντός με). The reason for the Son's coordinated effort with the work of the Father is because his entire mission is defined by the Father. The Son who "came down from heaven" (καταβέβηκα ἀπὸ τοῦ οὐρανοῦ) is performing the tasks given to him by "the one who sent me" (τοῦ πέμψαντός με). The "coming" of Jesus is rooted in and a subset of the "sending" by the Father. For this reason the Son claims to do "not my own will but the will" (τὸ θέλημα τὸ ἐμὸν ἀλλὰ τὸ θέλημα) of his Father. There can be no severing the Father from the Son. Jesus is not merely describing the ontological and functional unity between himself and his Father but is also rebuking the crowd for even considering to pit the provision of God for his people against the provision provided through the Son. Even the presence of the Son, which is strengthened by the perfect tense, "I have come down" (καταβέβηκα), gives force to Jesus's location on earth and, therefore, further warrant for its direct connection to the mission "from heaven" (ἀπὸ τοῦ οὐρανοῦ).[29]

6:39 "And this is the will of the one who sent me, that I might not lose any out of all that he
has given to me but will raise them on the last day"** (τοῦτο δέ ἐστιν τὸ θέλημα τοῦ πέμψαντός με, ἵνα πᾶν ὃ δέδωκέν μοι μὴ ἀπολέσω ἐξ αὐτοῦ ἀλλὰ ἀναστήσω αὐτὸ [ἐν] τῇ ἐσχάτῃ ἡμέρᾳ). Jesus continues to explain the coalescence of the Father and Son with a formal description. "This is the will of the one who sent me" (τοῦτο δέ ἐστιν τὸ θέλημα τοῦ πέμψαντός με) contains a substantival participle that is functioning as a subjective genitive, which could also be translated, "This is *what* the one who sent me wills."[30] The will for the Son is that "I might not lose any out of all that he has given to me" (πᾶν ὃ δέδωκέν μοι μὴ ἀπολέσω ἐξ αὐτοῦ). This verse provides further insight into Jesus's earlier statement that he "will never cast away" (v. 37). Just as it is within the will of God that some be given to the Son, so also it is within the will of God that the Son not lose those he has received (cf. 6:12).

Rather than losing them, it is the will of the Father that the Son "will raise them on the last day" (ἀναστήσω αὐτὸ [ἐν] τῇ ἐσχάτῃ ἡμέρᾳ). We have already been told that a future day (or "hour") is coming for which Jesus is the assigned agent of the resurrection of life and judgment (5:28 – 29). The expression here is further confirmation that the Gospel is familiar with a futuristic eschatology. Even more, it demands that the bread of life is not merely ephemeral but is solid food that is connected to an ultimate and final reality.[31] The metaphorical language previously used is merely the sign used to depict a true substance, the present and future reality centered upon Christ.

6:40 "For this is the will of my Father, that all who see the Son and believe in him will have eternal life, and I myself will raise him on the last day" (τοῦτο γάρ ἐστιν τὸ θέλημα τοῦ πατρός μου, ἵνα πᾶς ὁ θεωρῶν τὸν υἱὸν καὶ πιστεύων εἰς αὐτὸν

---

28. See Wallace, *Greek Grammar*, 468 – 69.
29. Cf. Schnackenburg, *John*, 2:47.
30. Cf. Wallace, *Greek Grammar*, 619 – 21.
31. Morris, *John*, 326.

ἔχῃ ζωὴν αἰώνιον, καὶ ἀναστήσω αὐτὸν ἐγὼ [ἐν] τῇ ἐσχάτῃ ἡμέρᾳ). The fourth verbal exchange concludes with Jesus giving his final explanatory comments. The "one who sent me" (vv. 38 – 39) is now explicitly stated as "my Father" (τοῦ πατρός μου). And those "given" by the Father and kept secure by the Son are those "who see the Son and believe in him" (ὁ θεωρῶν τὸν υἱὸν καὶ πιστεύων εἰς αὐτὸν). The inclusion of "seeing" suggests that the one who believes has the vision to recognize who the Son is — God's agent and representative. The crowd saw signs which Jesus performed but could not really see him (cf. v. 26). But he will be seen, if not now, at the "hour" of the *eschaton*, when as he promises with an emphatic first-person pronoun, "I myself will raise him" (ἀναστήσω αὐτὸν ἐγὼ). Jesus concludes the fourth verbal exchange of the dialogue with a rebuke. It is centered upon his identity as the Son who functions entirely within the will of his Father from first ("the beginning"; 1:1) to last ("on the last day"; 6:40).

6:41 The Jews were grumbling about him because he said, "I am the bread that has come down from heaven" (Ἐγόγγυζον οὖν οἱ Ἰουδαῖοι περὶ αὐτοῦ ὅτι εἶπεν, Ἐγώ εἰμι ὁ ἄρτος ὁ καταβὰς ἐκ τοῦ οὐρανοῦ). The fifth verbal exchange of the dialogue (vv. 41 – 51) moves the social challenge in a slightly different direction, for the crowd begins to reveal (at least among themselves) their utter rejection of the claims made by Jesus and therefore of Jesus himself (v. 42). Without being given any recourse to their reasoning, the Jews are clearly opposed to the claims Jesus has made, probably not only in regard to himself but also in regard to the claims he made for God (his Father).

An interesting change also occurs in the narrator's title for the character that had been called "the crowd" (ὁ ὄχλος). For the first time in this peri-cope — almost out of nowhere — the narrator calls Jesus's interlocutors "the Jews" (οἱ Ἰουδαῖοι) and will maintain this title throughout the rest of the dialogue (cf. v. 52). There is no evidence of a change of scene or historical situation; in fact, quite the contrary, the dialogue attends to details and issues rooted in its earlier parts. The change in description must be viewed as having a literary (and rhetorical) function for the narrator. The Gospel frequently uses the title "the Jews" for leaders or spokespersons who are hostile to Jesus (see comments on 1:19), very much fitting the tenor of this social challenge. But what is its specific nuance here?

A visible clue can be derived from the narrator's choice of words regarding the reaction of "the Jews" to Jesus's claims. According to the narrator, the Jews were "grumbling" (Ἐγόγγυζον), a term which depicts a manner of expression done "in low tones of disapprobation," that is, disapproval or condemnation.[32] The term has a significant past, particularly in regard to the Israelites — the Jews — who exhibited their unbelief by "grumbling" against Moses and Aaron, their representatives before God (Exod 16:2). The Jews, like their forefathers, were rejecting God's agent and therefore were rejecting God himself. As Hoskyns describes it, by their grumbling "they preserve the genuine succession of unbelief."[33]

6:42 And they said, "Is this not Jesus, the son of Joseph, whose father and mother we know? How can he now say, 'I have come down from heaven?'" (καὶ ἔλεγον, Οὐχ οὗτός ἐστιν Ἰησοῦς ὁ υἱὸς Ἰωσήφ, οὗ ἡμεῖς οἴδαμεν τὸν πατέρα καὶ τὴν μητέρα; πῶς νῦν λέγει ὅτι Ἐκ τοῦ οὐρανοῦ καταβέβηκα;). The message of Jesus was so shocking that the "Jews" begin to deduce from what they assumed about Jesus in order to evaluate his statements against his person. He speaks like he has just

---

come down from heaven, denoted by the inclusion of "now" (νῦν), which is to be contrasted with the properly basic knowledge that he came from the home and lineage of a known and earthly family, as the son of Joseph. Jesus's words are so evidently claiming a divine heritage that the crowd asks what is clearly a rhetorical question since they already know his father and mother. They do so in order to rebuke his visionary statements and theophanic self-descriptions. The question is loaded with irony for the reader, who knows the true Father of Jesus (cf. 1:1 – 2, 14, 18).

6:43 Jesus answered and said to them, "Stop grumbling among yourselves" (ἀπεκρίθη Ἰησοῦς καὶ εἶπεν αὐτοῖς, Μὴ γογγύζετε μετ᾽ ἀλλήλων). Even though the Jews were not speaking to him but among themselves, Jesus silences their grumbling. This is a unique moment in the dialogue where Jesus responds to what they said among themselves, not to him. As Moses declared to the grumbling Jews in the wilderness, "[the LORD] has heard your grumbling.... You are not grumbling against us, but against the LORD" (Exod 16:7 – 8), so also Jesus "hears" the grumblings of the Jews. This time, however, God, not Moses, confronts the grumbling Jews directly.

6:44 "No one can come to me unless the Father who sent me draws him, and I will raise him on the last day" (οὐδεὶς δύναται ἐλθεῖν πρός με ἐὰν μὴ ὁ πατὴρ ὁ πέμψας με ἑλκύσῃ αὐτόν, κἀγὼ ἀναστήσω αὐτὸν ἐν τῇ ἐσχάτῃ ἡμέρᾳ). Jesus begins to rebuke the Jews, clarifying further exactly who he is. Moses only told the Jews in the wilderness that God heard their grumbling (Exod 16:7); Jesus declares what the Father was thinking about it. This verse is commonly used as a prooftext in debates regarding election, and in many ways rightly so. We would be wrong, however, to miss this as a

further rebuke of the Jews, not only of the forefathers but also their contemporaries.

Even more explicitly than vv. 37 – 40, where Jesus makes connection between the will and giving of the Father to those who believe, Jesus declares that "no one can come to me unless the Father ... draws him" (οὐδεὶς δύναται ἐλθεῖν πρός με ἐὰν μὴ ὁ πατὴρ ἑλκύσῃ αὐτόν). The key verb, "draw" (ἑλκύσῃ), implies that "the object being moved is incapable of propelling itself or in the case of persons is unwilling to do so voluntarily."[34] While theologians will often posit that such a drawing can be resisted, there is not one example in the NT of the use of this verb where the resistance is successful.[35] The statement plainly depicts the inability of a person to "come" (ἐλθεῖν) to Jesus "unless" (ἐὰν μὴ) the Father directly acts in an intervening manner. God is the only acting agent. Such language is stark and even offensive, certainly to the Jews at the time and to a large amount of readers of the Gospel today. Yet it cannot be explained away. Without any real argument, Jesus presents God as the primary agent of salvation, just as he had already made clear that the Father is the one who enacts belief as part of his gift and will (vv. 37 – 40). In this way, Jesus offers a preemptive strike against any and all arguments presented by the Jews. They came as followers (cf. vv. 22 – 24) but have now been challenged to rethink the object of their allegiance (cf. v. 26).

6:45 "It is written in the prophets, 'They will all be taught by God.' All who heard and learned from the Father come to me" (ἔστιν γεγραμμένον ἐν τοῖς προφήταις, Καὶ ἔσονται πάντες διδακτοὶ θεοῦ· πᾶς ὁ ἀκούσας παρὰ τοῦ πατρὸς καὶ μαθὼν ἔρχεται πρὸς ἐμέ). Jesus gives further explanation to his comment in v. 44, this time with the help of the Old Testament. Claiming to speak from the "prophets" (plural), Jesus quotes from Isaiah 54:13:

---

34. BDAG 318.   35. Morris, *John*, 328.

"All your children will be taught by the LORD, and great will be their peace." This prooftext serves to make clear that if one comes to Jesus, one has "heard" (ἀκούσας) and "learned" (μαθὼν) from the Father. These two terms are best viewed as synonyms. What cannot be missed is the necessary connection between the teaching from the Father and the coming to Jesus. This connection and the use of Isaiah make three important claims.

First, as an explanation of what he previously said (v. 44), Jesus makes clear that the intention had always been that God would be the primary agent of belief. It is not only God who propels a person toward Christ (v. 44), but also God who provides the primary instruction. Belief in Christ is enacted by the agency of God who "draws" and "teaches" his children, ultimately being made known personally through Jesus Christ (cf. v. 46). As Augustine explains, "The Son spoke, but the Father taught."[36]

Second, by using this prophecy Jesus is declaring that this reality is being fulfilled in his person. Jesus is "the teaching God," instructing his people directly. There is no longer an intermediary, such as Moses, Aaron, or any kind of priest, for the Word of instruction has arrived. To reject Christ, as the Jews were doing, is proof that the teaching one upholds has not been given by God. Anything that is actively opposed to Christ or passively void of Christ is by definition not instruction from God. The reader is exhorted to be Christ centered, since this is the only subject matter God teaches his children.

Third, this statement serves as a first-order rebuke of the Jews, who reject the teaching of the one they claim to be hoping for (cf. 6:14); yet it also serves to locate them outside the people of God since they do not take part in what was promised to God's "children." Although Jesus does not include the second half of Isaiah 54:13, "and great will be

[your children's] peace," in the context of the dialogue and the earlier connection to the Jews' forefathers, the implication is strong. These children have not yet found peace, for instead of seeking the satisfaction of their souls, they are pleased merely to satisfy their stomachs (vv. 26 – 27).

6:46 "Not that any person has seen God except the one who is from God, he has seen the Father" (οὐχ ὅτι τὸν πατέρα ἑώρακέν τις εἰ μὴ ὁ ὢν παρὰ τοῦ θεοῦ, οὗτος ἑώρακεν τὸν πατέρα). Jesus explains further our second point from v. 45 that he is the fulfillment of the presence of the "teaching God." Some have suggested that this verse is a parenthetical intrusion by the narrator; however, not only is there no such change of speaker signaled to the reader, but when viewed from Jesus's own lips the statement is profound. By beginning with a negation, Jesus is clarifying any possible misunderstanding regarding the teaching presence of God. The teaching of God is not in isolation from his Son, that is, some kind of mystical, direct revelation from God to an individual person, but is centered upon and mediated through him. Jesus is the teaching presence of God, the living narration of God, the ultimate spokesperson for God. The warrant for this claim is that he is the only one who is "from God" (παρὰ τοῦ θεοῦ) and "has seen the Father" (ἑώρακεν τὸν πατέρα), which was first declared to the reader in the prologue (1:18). There is no hearing, learning, or seeing other than through Jesus Christ. The Jews' rejection of Christ in favor of "God" is a *non sequitur*, for to reject Christ *is* to reject God.

6:47 "Truly, truly I say to you, the one who believes has eternal life" (ἀμὴν ἀμὴν λέγω ὑμῖν, ὁ πιστεύων ἔχει ζωὴν αἰώνιον). Jesus now states more firmly a confession about himself that in the logical flow of the last few verses is rooted in

---

36. Augustine, *John*, 26.8.170.

the Trinitarian identity of God. By beginning with the authoritative preface (see comments on 1:51), Jesus is speaking as God and on God's behalf. Jesus brings his discussion of God and belief full circle by concluding that this belief produces eternal life. In a movement from eternal God to eternal life, the person who believes in Christ is already receiving everything that has been announced: hearing, learning, and seeing the Father through Christ. Believing is now referred to absolutely, with no mention of "in me" or "in God" by Jesus.[37] The reason is because one cannot make such distinctions. Belief in God is belief in the one he sent, Jesus Christ, and belief in Christ is belief in God. If it is real belief, both God and Christ are being believed. Such a statement silences the earlier request of the crowd for a sign so that they might believe (v. 30). The very question revealed the answer and serves to explain why Jesus turned their seeking on its head and initiated his challenge.

6:48 "I am the bread of life" (ἐγώ εἰμι ὁ ἄρτος τῆς ζωῆς). The fifth verbal exchange has moved so powerfully from Jesus to God and back to Jesus that with simplicity and rhetorical precision Jesus restates his claim as the bread of life (see comments on v. 35). This title of Jesus provides the theme of the entire dialogue, and after several necessary and combative verbal exchanges, Jesus declares it again to press further the significance of his person and work.

6:49 "Your fathers ate manna in the wilderness and died" (οἱ πατέρες ὑμῶν ἔφαγον ἐν τῇ ἐρήμῳ τὸ μάννα καὶ ἀπέθανον). Following his restated claim, Jesus provides a three-verse summary (vv. 49 – 51) that serves to conclude the fifth verbal exchange. It is unfortunate that many commentators project a section break after v. 48.[38] It is here where the awareness of the dialogue guides the reader to see the structure of the pericope. These last three

verses are essential commentary to the restated claim of Jesus and speak directly into the message Jesus has been presenting against the Jews. Jesus is still responding to their grumbling "origin" question of vv. 41 – 42, with his response giving engaged attention and making direct allusion to the issues raised in those verses. Not until v. 52 will the dialogue adjust its focus.

The earlier conflict between Jesus the bread and the bread of Moses is now readdressed with new insights, for Jesus's claim to be "the bread of life" is now unavoidably linked to the divine provision and agency of God himself. Jesus *is* the offering of God, the provision for his people, *the* bread, and this has always been the case — both for the forefathers in the wilderness and their contemporaries, the crowd/Jews. What Jesus declares in vv. 48 – 51 is essential to what he will declare in the final verbal exchange. It is he whom God has always given to his people, and he is the bread that needs to be eaten. The proof of this was made manifest at the time of the forefathers. They "ate manna" (ἔφαγον τὸ μάννα) and still "died" (ἀπέθανον). The logic is that bread was not truly life sustaining, otherwise the forefathers would not have died. Their death certifies that manna was insufficient and that it was not the final offering of bread from heaven.

6:50 "This is the bread who has come down from heaven so that a person may eat from it and not die" (οὗτός ἐστιν ὁ ἄρτος ὁ ἐκ τοῦ οὐρανοῦ καταβαίνων ἵνα τις ἐξ αὐτοῦ φάγῃ καὶ μὴ ἀποθάνῃ). The final offering of bread, the one competent to bestow true life, is Jesus himself. In contrast to the manna, "This is the bread" (οὗτός ἐστιν ὁ ἄρτος) from which "you may eat and not die" (φάγῃ καὶ μὴ ἀποθάνῃ). The subjunctives denote the possibility of life offered in the bread and the possibility offered to the "person" (τις) who partakes. In line

---

37. Cf. Ridderbos, *John*, 234.

38. See Borgen, *Bread from Heaven*, 86 – 87.

with v. 49, death is now depicted as surmountable. The words Jesus used earlier, "believe" and "come to me" (vv. 35, 37, 44, 47), are now fully contained in the imagery of "eating," just as who he is and what he offers is now contained in the imagery of "bread." This demands that we interpret this imagery as flowing from the semantics of the preceding dialogue and not by a later, sacramental context.[39] But it also suggests that "eating" is not intended to swallow the semantic meaning of "believe" and "come" but to contribute to our understanding of what the terms actually entail.[40]

6:51 "I am the living bread who has come down from heaven. Whoever eats this bread will live forever, and the bread which I will give is my flesh for the life of the world" (ἐγώ εἰμι ὁ ἄρτος ὁ ζῶν ὁ ἐκ τοῦ οὐρανοῦ καταβάς· ἐάν τις φάγῃ ἐκ τούτου τοῦ ἄρτου ζήσει εἰς τὸν αἰῶνα· καὶ ὁ ἄρτος δὲ ὃν ἐγὼ δώσω ἡ σάρξ μού ἐστιν ὑπὲρ τῆς τοῦ κόσμου ζωῆς). After speaking of "the bread" in the third person, he now speaks of it in the first person: "I am the living bread" (ἐγώ εἰμι ὁ ἄρτος ὁ ζῶν). But instead of his previous confession, "the bread of life," he now says in a synonymous manner that he is "the living bread," a nuance that reflects the presence and permanence of the "life" that he now offers and eternally is. The manna-bread that came down has been replaced and fulfilled by the man-bread who has also come down.

This "living bread" is given so that a person may "eat" (φάγῃ). As much as this imagery is still alluding to the manna in the wilderness, it is also referring to something just as edible and presently available through Jesus Christ — for only he can give eternal life. More shocking is the final statement, that "the bread which I give is my flesh" (ὁ ἄρτος δὲ ὃν ἐγὼ δώσω ἡ σάρξ μού ἐστιν). The dialogue has been moving in this direction since the

beginning of chapter 6. The feeding, the manna, the eating, *the* bread, which is now revealed to be "my flesh," is the exact depiction provided in the prologue of the fleshly body of Jesus (1:14). Since "flesh" is conceptually linked to sacrifice — the cross (see comments on 1:14) — its use here explains the nature of God's provision through Jesus.

Such a statement has easily surpassed the manna of the Jews, but it must not be limited by the Eucharist (the Lord's Supper).[41] Both "breads" are representative of *the* bread. They are signs that signify something beyond themselves, pointing outward from their position in salvation history. The Gospel has been working to explain the theological, metaphysical, and religious significance of Jesus's "flesh" — as *the man* (embracing humanity and the world; cf. 1:14), as *the temple* (mediating between God and the world; cf. 2:12 – 25), and now as *the living bread* (conquering death and offering life in his person). The feeding of the large crowd was just the starter, for the meal Jesus offers is for "the world" (τοῦ κόσμου). This is all part of the will of God, the drawing of his people, motivated by his love for the world (3:16). With this robust declaration, the fifth verbal exchange concludes.

6:52 Then the Jews began to argue with one another saying, "How is he able to give us his flesh to eat?" (Ἐμάχοντο οὖν πρὸς ἀλλήλους οἱ Ἰουδαῖοι λέγοντες, Πῶς δύναται οὗτος ἡμῖν δοῦναι τὴν σάρκα [αὐτοῦ] φαγεῖν;). The sixth and final verbal exchange of the dialogue (vv. 52 – 59), carrying the force of the preceding verbal exchanges, gives a final depiction of the shocking statement made by Jesus in v. 51. The dialogue has offered a true challenge to the Jews, who are depicted by the narrator as initiating an argument among themselves. The ingressive imperfect, "began to argue" (Ἐμάχοντο), is a strong term that depicts a heated dispute. The

---

39. Ridderbos, *John*, 235.
40. Cf. Michaels, *John*, 390.

41. See Ridderbos, *John*, 236 – 38.

arguing, however, is not taking place between the Jews as if they are debating the issue among themselves with a mixture of opinions for or against but is to be viewed as an intensification of the "grumbling" of v. 41. The uniformity of their collective question confirms their agreement to the contrary. Like their forefathers, who not only "grumbled" (Exod 16:2) but also "argued with Moses" so as to put God to the test (Exod 17:2), these Jews argue and test Jesus.[42] Their question is a final challenge in the form of a mocking rebuke and is rooted in their unbelief. Ironically, however, their question is actually important and provides Jesus with a final explanation about eating his flesh, the living bread.

6:53 Then Jesus said to them, "Truly, truly I say to you unless you eat the flesh of the Son of Man and drink his blood, you have no life in yourselves" (εἶπεν οὖν αὐτοῖς ὁ Ἰησοῦς, Ἀμὴν ἀμὴν λέγω ὑμῖν, ἐὰν μὴ φάγητε τὴν σάρκα τοῦ υἱοῦ τοῦ ἀνθρώπου καὶ πίητε αὐτοῦ τὸ αἷμα, οὐκ ἔχετε ζωὴν ἐν ἑαυτοῖς). Without any retraction or nuance, and introduced with his authoritative preface (see comments on 1:51), Jesus reiterates his earlier statement (v. 51) in a more robust manner. Jesus states even more explicitly that it is his flesh that is to be eaten, including this time the insight that it is the flesh "of the Son of Man" (cf. v. 27), thus combining in his person the baseness of the flesh of humanity with the loftiness of the Son of Man (see comments on 1:51).

Even more than eating, Jesus adds a further, participatory requirement that they must "drink his blood" (πίητε αὐτοῦ τὸ αἷμα). If eating flesh was shocking, drinking blood was outright offensive and especially abhorrent to Jews who were explicitly forbidden to partake of blood (cf. Gen 9:4).[43] Jesus had become more than a mystery to

the Jews; he was now unavoidably scandalous. While several suggest that "blood" is suggestive of life, since the two concepts are associated in parts of the OT (e.g., Lev 17:11, 14; Deut 12:23), the biblical evidence as a whole clearly suggests that "blood" is conceptually related to and reflective of "death."[44] In combination with "flesh" and in light of the preceding verbal exchange in which sacrifice and the cross were implied, the language here is intentionally directed toward the sacrificial death of Christ. In some manner, then, the benefits of the cross of Christ are received by means of eating and drinking the flesh and blood of Jesus. We would be mistaken to think that this is entirely spiritual, for clearly Jesus had real flesh and blood and would really die. Even more, there is real life bestowed to the person who partakes. In light of the failure of the forefathers, this final stage of the challenge of Jesus consists in surrendering one's own life and laying hold of another's.

6:54 "The one who eats my flesh and drinks my blood has eternal life, and I will raise him on the last day" (ὁ τρώγων μου τὴν σάρκα καὶ πίνων μου τὸ αἷμα ἔχει ζωὴν αἰώνιον, κἀγὼ ἀναστήσω αὐτὸν τῇ ἐσχάτῃ ἡμέρᾳ). Jesus restates the same message, though this time positively and with clear first-person reference: "my flesh" (μου τὴν σάρκα) and "my blood" (μου τὸ αἷμα). The continuing reference to Christ's raising the believer on the last day must be important (cf. vv. 39, 40, 44). There is also an interesting switch in the Greek term used for "eating." Instead of using the term for "eat" (ἐσθίειν) used in v. 53, here another term for "eat" (τρώγειν) is used. While the terms have a high degree of overlap, if anything the latter term is more aggressive — more actively or more audibly eaten — so that some suggest the translation, "munch" or "gnaw."[45] There is

42. Cf. Schnackenburg, *John*, 2:60.
43. See Brant, *John*, 124.
44. Alan M. Stibbs, *The Meaning of the Word "Blood" in Scripture* (London: Tyndale Press, 1947).
45. See BDAG 1019. Cf. Bernard, *John*, 1:210.

no reason to deny a distinction between the two terms, even if it is minute. The change suggests a rhetorical thrust, a forceful explication of the reality of the eating being depicted.

6:55 "For my flesh is real food, and my blood is real drink" (ἡ γὰρ σάρξ μου ἀληθής ἐστιν βρῶσις, καὶ τὸ αἷμά μου ἀληθής ἐστιν πόσις). Jesus had already declared that the food that filled their bellies was not true food, for it was not food "that endures into eternal life" (v. 27). Rather, Jesus describes his food using the adverb "real" (ἀληθής). This is not to be taken as literalizing the food, for Jesus is speaking about something to which food only signifies; yet neither can it be taken as mere metaphor, since something is being signified that is best depicted with the imagery of food.[46] Rather, and with more nuance, Jesus is declaring that the food he gives — that the food he is — is real, that is, it fulfills the ideal, archetypal function of food and drink, for its caloric effects secure eternal life. No other food was as qualitatively real as his food, for nothing and no one else can provide eternal life — not the food given to the large crowd (6:1 – 15), or the manna of Moses, or any other food humanity can discover or invent for itself. His food, his body, is the real food; his drink, his blood, is the real drink. Such pointed language directs our minds to his body and blood, that is, to the cross.

6:56 "The one who eats my flesh and drinks my blood remains in me and I in him" (ὁ τρώγων μου τὴν σάρκα καὶ πίνων μου τὸ αἷμα ἐν ἐμοὶ μένει κἀγὼ ἐν αὐτῷ). Jesus gives further explanation to eating his flesh and blood when he describes it as a mutual indwelling: those who eat and drink remain in him, and he in them. It is the eating and drinking that makes possible this coparticipatory union. The term "remain" (μένει) is one of the central terms in the Gospel; the Father "remains" in

the Son (14:10), the Spirit "remains" upon Jesus (1:32 – 33), and believers "remain" in Christ and he in them (15:4). The term is depicting a coparticipatory existence, where the "being" of the believer is determined or regulated by Jesus.[47] It is nothing less than a depiction of an intimate relationship. The apostle Paul considers himself to have shared so deeply in Christ that the crucifixion of Christ was in a real way also his death, with his life being lived (empowered) by Christ in him (Gal 2:20). This is the first appearance of this concept in the Gospel; later in the Gospel Jesus will give further explanation concerning this mutual indwelling (see 8:31 – 32; 14:20; 15:4 – 10; 17:21 – 23).

6:57 "Just as the living Father sent me and I live because of the Father, so the one who eats me will also live because of me" (καθὼς ἀπέστειλέν με ὁ ζῶν πατὴρ κἀγὼ ζῶ διὰ τὸν πατέρα, καὶ ὁ τρώγων με κἀκεῖνος ζήσει δι' ἐμέ). The concept of life which has been so central to the dialogue thus far continues to be prominent in this further explanation by Jesus. Just as Jesus is the living bread (v. 51), so also is the Father now described as the "living Father." The life that Jesus provides is connected to the Trinitarian identity of God from Father through Son and — as we will soon see — in cooperation with the Spirit (cf. 14:17). The statement draws on what Jesus has already stated in 5:21 – 30 (see comments on 5:24). The Son, the representative of the Father (1:18), is to be eaten, but the meal was produced by the very fullness of God.

6:58 "This is the bread that came down from heaven, not as the fathers who ate and died, the one who eats this bread will live forever" (οὗτός ἐστιν ὁ ἄρτος ὁ ἐκ τοῦ οὐρανοῦ καταβάς, οὐ καθὼς ἔφαγον οἱ πατέρες καὶ ἀπέθανον· ὁ τρώγων τοῦτον τὸν ἄρτον ζήσει εἰς τὸν αἰῶνα). This verse concludes Jesus's statement in the sixth verbal ex-

---

46. Cf. Michaels, *John*, 399.

47. Cf. Barrett, *John*, 300.

change with the Jews and serves as a summary of the entire dialogue. By returning to the third person and with the use of "this" (οὗτός), which has no proper antecedent, Jesus ends by summarizing his message. In short, Jesus offers the Jews real food and real life. To reject this offer would be to reject God himself. Through Jesus, God has personally rebuked the "grumbling" and "arguing" people to whom he showed such great love in the wilderness. No longer! Out of this context and heritage comes the challenge Jesus has launched against the Jews (and — even more — against the reader and the world; cf. v. 51). All their questions have now been answered (vv. 42, 52). It is now time for the Jews to respond. Will they eat this bread and live? The answer will be revealed by the narrative shortly (v. 61).

6:59 He said these things while he was teaching in a synagogue in Capernaum (Ταῦτα εἶπεν ἐν συναγωγῇ διδάσκων ἐν Καφαρναούμ). The dialogue comes to a close with a brief intrusion by the narrator, who provides closure by revealing where the event took place. The reader had already been informed that the location was Capernaum (v. 24); the new insight here is that the dialogue occurred "in a synagogue while he was teaching" (ἐν συναγωγῇ διδάσκων). Although John often begins a new section with the setting, it is not uncommon for the setting to bring a section to a close (cf. 8:20). There is historical evidence that synagogue services allowed such exchanges, all the more if the lectionary reading on that day was Exodus 16.[48] But such specific evidence is not needed, for Jesus's presence in a synagogue, surrounded by a swarming crowd interested in the wrong things, became the perfect context for him to offer his divine challenge. In fact, Jesus will later declare when confronted by the high priest about his teaching that he spoke

"openly to the world," teaching "in synagogues and the temple, where all the Jews come together," saying nothing in secret (18:19 – 20). In this synagogue on this day, it was not the Jews who came to speak to God, it was God who came to speak to them — in the form of a social challenge.

6:60 Then after many of his disciples had heard they said, "This message is offensive! Who is able to accept it?" (Πολλοὶ οὖν ἀκούσαντες ἐκ τῶν μαθητῶν αὐτοῦ εἶπαν, Σκληρός ἐστιν ὁ λόγος οὗτος· τίς δύναται αὐτοῦ ἀκούειν;). With the dialogue concluded, the narrator now turns to the reaction of those present. Those responding to Jesus here transitions from the "crowd/Jews" to "many of his disciples" (Πολλοὶ ἐκ τῶν μαθητῶν αὐτοῦ). This transition suggests that the dialogue scene has shifted its focus more narrowly from the crowd in general and the Jewish opponents of Jesus to a circle of "disciples," more inclusive than the Twelve (cf. v. 67). By the standards of first-century Judaism, they were disciples of a rabbi.

This larger circle of disciples is no less offended than the Jews when confronted by his teaching. They call Jesus's message "offensive" (Σκληρός), a term which refers by itself to something "hard" or "unpleasant" but in relation to people is something that "pertains to causing an adverse reaction because of being hard or harsh."[49] These "disciples" can only ask in disgust, "Who is able to accept it?" (τίς δύναται αὐτοῦ ἀκούειν;).

6:61 After Jesus had seen in himself that his disciples were grumbling concerning this he said to them, "Does this offend you?" (εἰδὼς δὲ ὁ Ἰησοῦς ἐν ἑαυτῷ ὅτι γογγύζουσιν περὶ τούτου οἱ μαθηταὶ αὐτοῦ εἶπεν αὐτοῖς, Τοῦτο ὑμᾶς σκανδαλίζει;). The narrator introduces Jesus's response to these "disciples" by revealing that Jesus was aware of their thoughts, denoted by the awkward prepositional

---

48. See Carson, *John*, 299 – 300.

49. BDAG 930.

phrase, "in himself" (ἐν ἑαυτῷ). The phrase serves to highlight the supernatural awareness of Jesus — an insight regarding Jesus that has been seen previously (v. 43; cf. 1:47–48; 2:24–25; 4:18). These "disciples" respond in a manner conspicuously similar to the response of the Jews to Jesus and of their forefathers to God (see comments on vv. 41, 43). While it is likely that the eating of his flesh and drinking of his blood is the most blatant source of offense, it is best to include around it the entirety of Jesus's message.[50]

6:62 "Then, what if you see the Son of Man ascending to where he was before?" (ἐὰν οὖν θεωρῆτε τὸν υἱὸν τοῦ ἀνθρώπου ἀναβαίνοντα ὅπου ἦν τὸ πρότερον;). Jesus offers another question, though this one is more difficult to interpret, since the apodosis is not given (i.e., the "if" clause is not followed by a "then" clause, thus requiring the inclusion of "what" to make a complete thought). It is likely that Jesus is pressing further his first question in order to say, "Would you still be offended?" The combination of "if" (ἐὰν) and the subjunctive, "see" (θεωρῆτε), refers to the future.[51] Because the ascension is lacking in the Gospel (besides the implied version in 20:17), some interpreters suggest the "ascending" here refers to Jesus's exaltation on the cross (in a similar manner as found in 3:14). But this seems to work against the context of the pericope with the focus on Jesus's person and work as the Son of Man, as well as the message Jesus has been declaring about himself since the Gospel's inception (see 1:51).

When we recall the prologue, the reader is then able to see the referent behind the words, "Where he was before" (ὅπου ἦν τὸ πρότερον). He, the Word, "was in the beginning with God" (1:2). It

is the Word, descended from the Father, who will "ascend" to his rightful place again. Such a statement coalesces perfectly with the emphasis of the pericope on the "descending" of the Son, the bread of life (cf. vv. 33, 38, 41–42, 50–51, 58). It is not, then, that these "disciples" are rejecting the cross; it is rather that they are rejecting God himself. For this reason, the Word confronts these so-called disciples with his full identity and challenges them to reconsider. Jesus seems to be saying, "If you reject me and my words, what will you do if (and when) you see me as I truly am in glory, ascending to my rightful place of power and authority? What, then, would you do with your unbelief and offense?"[52]

6:63 "The Spirit is giving life, the flesh cannot help anything; the words which I have spoken to you are spirit and are life (τὸ πνεῦμά ἐστιν τὸ ζῳοποιοῦν, ἡ σὰρξ οὐκ ὠφελεῖ οὐδέν· τὰ ῥήματα ἃ ἐγὼ λελάληκα ὑμῖν πνεῦμά ἐστιν καὶ ζωή ἐστιν). Pressing further his challenge against their unbelief and offense, Jesus gives commentary on their state of rebellion. Jesus declares that the Spirit, which can only be the Holy Spirit, "is giving life" (ἐστιν τὸ ζῳοποιοῦν). The participle serves to highlight aspectual force, which in this case is the present, even ongoing, occurrence of the giving of life (cf. 2 Cor 3:6).[53] This is contrasted with the emphatic, double-negative denial of "the flesh" (ἡ σὰρξ), which is spoken of as helpless; it "cannot provide anything" (οὐκ ὠφελεῖ οὐδέν).[54] The concept of flesh is not to be simply imported from the apostle Paul, for in John "flesh" is merely the body and its limitations. The point is quite simple: "flesh" and "spirit" are different spheres of reality, each producing offspring like itself.[55] "Neither can take to itself the capacity of the other."[56] This verse has

50. Bultmann, *John*, 445.
51. BDF § 373.1.
52. Ridderbos, *John*, 245–46.
53. Cf. Wallace, *Greek Grammar*, 647–48.
54. BDAG 1107.
55. Michaels, *John*, 185.
56. Hoskyns, *Fourth Gospel*, 215.

many similarities to what Jesus said to Nicodemus (see comments on 3:6).

Thus, when Jesus declares that "the words" (τὰ ῥήματα) he has spoken to these so-called disciples "are spirit and are life" (πνεῦμά ἐστιν καὶ ζωή ἐστιν), he rebukes them by way of reminder that he is the one who gives life (5:21), he is the assigned Judge (5:22), and it is the Father alone who wills belief (cf. v. 37–39, 44). Interpreters who have relied heavily on a eucharistic interpretation of this pericope have difficulty with this verse and usually disassociate this section (vv. 60–71) from the preceding verses because it does not match the emphasis placed on the "flesh" of Jesus.[57] But that confuses the "flesh" in general with *the* flesh of Jesus Christ, which is the unique flesh that provides for our "flesh" the beginnings of eternal life (see especially the comments on v. 51). The contrast, then, is not entirely between all flesh and spirit, but between the "flesh" of dying humanity and the living flesh of Jesus, the flesh of the bread of life — the flesh of the crucified God.[58] It is in the person of Jesus where our flesh, which he himself bore, becomes united with his life.

6:64 "But there are some of you who do not believe." For Jesus had known from the beginning who they are that do not believe and who it is who will hand him over (ἀλλ᾽ εἰσὶν ἐξ ὑμῶν τινες οἳ οὐ πιστεύουσιν. ᾔδει γὰρ ἐξ ἀρχῆς ὁ Ἰησοῦς τίνες εἰσὶν οἱ μὴ πιστεύοντες καὶ τίς ἐστιν ὁ παραδώσων αὐτόν). Jesus adds to his rebuke its logical conclusion: "There are some of you" (εἰσὶν ἐξ ὑμῶν τινες) who do not believe. Just as he revealed himself to them, so also does he now reveal to them their true selves, similar to how he earlier unmasked the unbelief of "the crowd" (v. 36), of "the Jews" in Jerusalem (5:38), and even earlier of Nicodemus and those he represented (3:11–12).[59] The more Jesus

became an offense (vv. 60–61), the more visible their unbelief. That only "some" and not all are declared such is not merely a gentler statement but a sign of hope that there is the possibility of change.

The narrator provides an explanatory intrusion, something common to the reader by now, which provides an important insight: none of this was a surprise to Jesus. The one who knows the nature of humanity (cf. 2:24–25) also knows the nature of these followers. The narrator explains that Jesus had known of these disbelievers "from the beginning" (ἐξ ἀρχῆς), a phrase that harks back to 1:1, which implied that the Word partook of the eternal counsels of God.[60] It is strange that the narrator inserts here the future betrayal of Jesus by one of his disciples. Just as Jesus knew in the past that some disciples would not believe in the present, so also he knows in the present that a certain disciple will reveal his unbelief in the future. The allusion to Judas here also serves as an allusion to the cross, the very thing "some of" these disciples are rejecting.

6:65 And he said, "For this reason I told you that no one is able to come to me unless it has been given to him from the Father" (καὶ ἔλεγεν, Διὰ τοῦτο εἴρηκα ὑμῖν ὅτι οὐδεὶς δύναται ἐλθεῖν πρός με ἐὰν μὴ ᾖ δεδομένον αὐτῷ ἐκ τοῦ πατρός). Jesus concludes his postdialogue conversation with the so-called "disciples" with a statement that reemphasizes a fundamental theme of the entire pericope: the primary agent of faith is the Father. Referring back to what he said in vv. 37–39, 44, Jesus declares "no one is able to come to me" (οὐδεὶς δύναται ἐλθεῖν πρός με), that is, have faith in or believe in him, unless "it has been given to him" (ᾖ δεδομένον αὐτῷ). This latter phrase is conveyed with a perfect passive participle that nearly bursts with theological significance. Faith is not just a general gift but is

---

57. E.g., see Brown, *John*, 1:300–303.
58. Cf. Luther, *John*, 23:166.

59. Cf. Michaels, *John*, 409.
60. Barrett, *John*, 305.

a specific gift, something upon which the Christian is utterly dependent. From start to finish there is no such thing as an independent Christian. Without the Father, there would be no children. It is the Father who must give the "right" (1:12); salvation is "from God" (1:13). In a real way, this is the ultimate rebuke of Jesus to his interlocutors in this challenge dialogue. They lose not only because of their own lack of faith but also because the Father was, quite simply, against them from the start.

6:66 From this time many of his disciples fell away and were no longer following him (Ἐκ τούτου [οὖν] πολλοὶ ἐκ τῶν μαθητῶν αὐτοῦ ἀπῆλθον εἰς τὰ ὀπίσω καὶ οὐκέτι μετ᾽ αὐτοῦ περιεπάτουν). After Jesus brings further clarity to his message to the crowd of Jews, the so-called disciples conclude their interest in him. The verse is filled with peculiar language. "From this time" (Ἐκ τούτου) could also be translated as "for this reason"; in fact both senses are likely to be simultaneously intended. The so-called disciples deny their rabbi by their actions. While the verb "following" (περιεπάτουν) could also be translated as "walking," in the context of first-century Judaism the term stands for the act of a follower, that is, a disciple.[61] To walk no longer with one's teacher was to resign formally from his instruction and disassociate from his message.

> ## IN DEPTH: Discipleship in John
>
> The prologue declared that Jesus "came to what belongs to him, and his own people did not receive him" (1:11) and the rest of the Gospel depicts the constant struggle and even rejection of Jesus by those who met and sometimes even followed him. As this pericope reveals, Jesus and his teachings are not easily accepted by the world in its sinful pride and self-righteousness. Quite simply, the gospel of Jesus Christ is a foreign language to the human heart, and more often than not its message is offensive and rejected (6:60). Jesus even explains that this offense is not merely the work of humanity but is the work of the Spirit (6:63–65). The power of the gospel is not merely the message it communicates but also the life it creates in a person.
>
> The Gospel of John depicts in full color the challenge of being a disciple of Jesus. The church today experiences this weekly as it presents the same gospel message of Jesus to the world and receives a similar response: "This message is offensive! Who is able to accept it?" (6:60). For some people, this is their reaction at the first hearing; for others, the full reality of the gospel's claim on their life and its opposition to the values of this world do not become apparent until they have already followed Jesus for some time and participated in the local church. When an apparent disciple falls away from the church and the gospel message, the Gospel of John serves as a reminder that even during Jesus's ministry some of his disciples stopped following him.

---

61. Schlatter, *Der Evangelist Johannes*, 182–83.

6:67 Then Jesus said to the Twelve, "You do not want to leave also, do you?" (εἶπεν οὖν ὁ Ἰησοῦς τοῖς δώδεκα, Μὴ καὶ ὑμεῖς θέλετε ὑπάγειν;). Jesus now turns from the wider circle of disciples (cf. v. 60) to his more intimate disciples, whom the Gospel describes for the first time as "the Twelve." In a question this form of negation, "not" (Μὴ), produces either "a strong deprecatory tone ... or puts a suggestion in the most tentative and hesitating way."[62] The former is more likely here. The context builds the dramatic force of this question, for the disciples have witnessed in detail the challenge presented to the Jews and then to the wider circle of disciples. And it is the same challenger that now poses a loaded question to them.

6:68 Simon Peter answered to him, "Lord, to whom shall we go? You have the words of eternal life" (ἀπεκρίθη αὐτῷ Σίμων Πέτρος, Κύριε, πρὸς τίνα ἀπελευσόμεθα; ῥήματα ζωῆς αἰωνίου ἔχεις). Simon Peter, known in the Synoptics for being outspoken (cf. Matt 16:22), speaks on behalf of the Twelve with words that serve as a confession of allegiance and belief. His return question to Jesus, "Lord, to whom shall we go?" (Κύριε, πρὸς τίνα ἀπελευσόμεθα;), is to be viewed in sharp contrast to the response of the so-called disciples who had already left, that is, "fell away" (v. 66). Quite simply, the Twelve believe Jesus, for as Peter explains, "You have the words of eternal life." With these words, Peter reveals a true grasp of Jesus's message and an awareness of what is at stake — life itself (see comments on v. 53).

6:69 "And we have believed and have known that you are the Holy One of God" (καὶ ἡμεῖς πεπιστεύκαμεν καὶ ἐγνώκαμεν ὅτι σὺ εἶ ὁ ἅγιος τοῦ

θεοῦ). Peter adds to the confession of the Twelve by declaring with two perfect-tense verbs — "we have believed and have known" — that Jesus is "the Holy One of God" (ὁ ἅγιος τοῦ θεοῦ). The disciples had from early on been more than willing to see Jesus as the Messiah (cf. 1:41, 45, 49), but now they see him and their understanding of "Messiah" as something more. There are no parallels for this title in Judaism.[63] Rather, rooted in the words of Jesus himself, "the Holy One of God" is *the* emissary, the one who came descending and ascending, the "I AM," the "bread of life," the revelation of God, the Judge and the life, the Son of Man. Peter is confessing what he has been "given" to see and believe. It is to all of this that the Gospel has been serving as witness. In Jesus is found everything God wants to do and is doing.

6:70 Jesus answered to them, "Have I not chosen you, the Twelve, yet one of you is the devil?" (ἀπεκρίθη αὐτοῖς ὁ Ἰησοῦς, Οὐκ ἐγὼ ὑμᾶς τοὺς δώδεκα ἐξελεξάμην, καὶ ἐξ ὑμῶν εἷς διάβολός ἐστιν;). After such a lofty confession the reader might have expected Jesus to embrace the Twelve with joy, but even to them (not just to Peter) a challenge of sorts ensues. With the stroke of one forceful rhetorical question, Jesus not only reminds them that they were "chosen" (ἐξελεξάμην) by him but also declares their faith to be still lacking — for "one of you is the devil" (ἐξ ὑμῶν εἷς διάβολός ἐστιν). What v. 71 will explain is that Judas, "the one," will serve as a pawn for Satan, who so operates behind failing humans that his malice becomes theirs.[64] By combining the chosen eleven with "the one," Jesus positions the sovereign work of God on both sides of faith. Not only were the Twelve sovereignly elected by God to have faith, but even the unfaithfulness of

---

62. Moulton, *Grammar*, 1:193.

63. The only other occurrences of the title in Scripture are in the Synoptics (Mark 1:24; Luke 4:34), where it is spoken by a demon!

64. Carson, *John*, 304. Cf. Barrett, *John*, 307: "Satan has made Judas his ally, a subordinate devil." See also Mark 8:33, where Jesus calls Peter "Satan" after a similarly robust confession.

Judas is to be subsumed under the election of God, even if for a contrary task.

6:71 He was speaking about Judas, son of Simon of Iscariot, for he was about to hand over Jesus, even though he was one of the twelve (ἔλεγεν δὲ τὸν Ἰούδαν Σίμωνος Ἰσκαριώτου· οὗτος γὰρ ἔμελλεν παραδιδόναι αὐτόν, εἷς [ὢν] ἐκ τῶν δώδεκα). The narrator concludes the pericope with an explanatory intrusion that serves to explain Jesus's com-

ments and connect the scene and its message to the developing plot of the Gospel. This information only serves to make explicit what had already been implied (see comments on v. 64). The one behind whom the devil will act is "Judas" (Ἰούδαν), modified by two genitives providing his family name and place of origin, "son of Simon of Iscariot" (Σίμωνος Ἰσκαριώτου).[65] This statement provides a reality check for the reader by putting flesh on Jesus's rebuke of and insight into the human condition.

Theology in Application

In a scene reminiscent of Moses and the Israelites in the wilderness, Jesus stands with a horde of followers who want to make him their king. But their vision of him — of God — was drenched with sinful illusions. So Jesus initiates a challenge to his followers, and through his self-revelatory confession challenges not only the "God" the crowd claims to seek but also their self-righteousness. In this pericope the reader of the Fourth Gospel is exhorted to examine the object of their worship, and even more to see life itself as founded upon the work of God through the Son. While the length of the pericope might prohibit the preacher from handling all fifty verses at once, the overall message should at least be maintained in the context of the dialogue and its movement.

Who (or What) Are You Following?

This pericope contains some of the most theological and christological statements of Jesus in the entire Gospel, even in all four Gospels. And on their own they need to be studied and reflected upon. But when viewed in the context of a social challenge dialogue, these statements serve as a rebuke of the reader and all humanity for the objects of our worship. The pericope shows the self-focused infatuation of the crowd and their self-interest in Jesus. Yet Jesus cuts right to the heart of the matter — the food their stomachs crave versus real food for their souls. The rest of the dialogue revolves around this distinction.

In the context of the dialogue over real food, another issue is clearly presented to us: our stomachs (i.e., our desires and passions) cannot be trusted. Our desires are self-seeking, rooted in our skewed perception of what is real and what really matters. The gods of this world are perishing; they are figments of our fallen and limited

---

65. See Brown, *John*, 1:298; Barrett, *John*, 308.

imaginations. Peter may not have fully understood "the Holy One of God" (v. 69), but he at least phrased the right question: "Lord, to whom shall we go?" As Luther explained, this is the message of the Christian church to itself and to the world, declaring in our hearts that he will satisfy us and testifying to the world about the satisfaction we have found in Christ alone.[66]

The Argument from Election

This pericope contains some of the clearest and strongest statements by Jesus that God is the primary agent of salvation. But what might be most significant is that these statements are not just isolated propositions but are used as an argument against the crowd and the Jews in the midst of the social challenge. Jesus is careful to explain to the crowd and the Jews that it is not they who reject God, but God who has preemptively already rejected them. "Unless it has been given to him from the Father" (v. 65), no one can come to Jesus. Such a statement demands that the potential for belief be removed from the individual, for faith is a gift from the Father alone. Just as there is no independent fetus or infant, so also from start to finish there is no such thing as an independent Christian. Without the Father, there simply would be no children. It is the Father who must give the "right" (1:12). It cannot be given from the blood of humanity or the desire of the flesh or the will of a person; it must be "from God" (1:13). In the context of the social challenge, the role of rejection has been reversed. It is not the crowd/Jews/disciples who are rejecting Jesus; rather, it is God rejecting them.

The uncomfortable feelings or philosophical objections that this raises are foreign to the Gospel of John; in its pages, God is depicted in an unqualified manner as having sovereign control alongside the apparent freedom of the individual.[67] While the philosopher may have to spend some time developing categories for such a reality, the theologian may be able to speak something similar to Luther: "Would you expect a prince to divulge all his plans and decisions to his people and confide all his policies to his subjects? Should a general reveal, make known, and publish his tactics and strategy in an encampment? That would be some army and business! And yet we fools, in the devil's name, will not believe God unless He has previously initiated us into the why and the wherefore of His doctrines!"[68] Jesus said clearly that "you have no life in yourselves" (v. 53). While this does not lead to an inappropriate form of fideism, it should lead to a carefully crafted view of "faith," not only in regard to its source but also in regard to its substance.

---

66. Luther, *John*, 23:194.

67. According to Calvin, *John 1 – 10*, 162, "every man's faith is an abundant witness to the eternal predestination of God, so that it is sacrilege to inquire further."

68. Luther, *John*, 23:81.

Eat His Flesh and Drink His Blood: The Centrality of the Cross

Amidst all the debate regarding eating the flesh and drinking the blood of Jesus, one thing should not be missed: the centrality of the cross. By combining into one cumulative metaphor the concepts of hunger and thirst and the bread of life alongside overtly sacrificial images of his flesh and blood (terms that evoke the entire system of sacrifice and atonement in the OT), Jesus declares his person and his work to be the embodiment of all promises of satisfaction. The imagery of the cross is so rich in this pericope that the entire Pauline corpus is needed as a commentary.

The Grumbling of God's People

The pericope was carefully crafted so as to reflect inappropriate expressions of disbelief or dissatisfaction in God through allusions to the Israelites in the wilderness as they complained and argued with Moses and, therefore, with God (see comments on v. 41). As Hoskyns describes it, by their grumbling against Jesus in this pericope, "They preserve the genuine succession of unbelief."[69] Like their forefathers, the Jews were opposing God himself. The rebuke by Christ serves to exhort the reader to avoid bringing against God any categories of unbelief, including elements of arrogance or human wisdom. So often we think we have words for God, or we would like him to hear how we think he should view a situation — often our own situation, so as to get a different result. Yet our actions clearly reveal our unbelief in him; we do not believe that he is capable, proficient, powerful, or loving. With God, the Christian learns to chastise his or her own reason, not for the sake of ignorance but out of a holy fear of God, and to commit to trust him more than we trust ourselves. To grumble against God is to place oneself at the center. This is neither reality nor the mark of Christian discipleship. The disciple of Jesus willingly declares, "Be Thou my Vision," and really means it; not because the Christian has no intellect or foresight, but because his reason and foresight have found their true source and substance.

A Matter of Life and Death

When Jesus speaks of eating his flesh and blood, he speaks of the transfusion of his life for theirs. The Gospel begins and ends with this focus on life. This pericope summarizes everything God wants to declare about Jesus ("that you may believe that Jesus is the Christ"; 20:31a) and everything God wants to offer to the reader ("that … you may have *life* in his name"; 20:31b). This pericope challenges human identity at its most foundational level. But it is also a remarkable offer of an unimaginable gift — the life of God exchanged for the lifelessness of humanity. This pericope and the Gospel as a whole are not dealing with trifles or playing with allusions to the

---

69. Hoskyns, *Fourth Gospel*, 295.

Lord's Supper by means of signs and symbols but are speaking about life and death, the present moment and eternity. And through the witness of the narrative of this Gospel, the God of the universe rebukes the sinful rebellion and self-righteousness of the reader (Jew or not!) and challenges them to embrace his Son by faith, a work of gracious "drawing" he has already begun. How does the reader respond to this life and death challenge of God?

15

John 7:1 – 13

Literary Context

After the departure of some "disciples" of Jesus (not the "Twelve") because of the offensive nature of Jesus's message (6:60), the Gospel continues to show the kind of responses the message and ministry of Jesus yields. Since the beginning of the Gospel, the narrative has been depicting the dramatic interaction between light and darkness, God and the world (1:5). In this pericope, conflict is not far away but right at home, with the very people with whom Jesus should have found the most connection and support — his own kin. Yet it is where things seem most congruent that the true contrast between Creator and creation is made known by the Gospel.

IV. The Confession of the Son of God (5:1 – 8:11)
   A. The Third Sign: The Healing of the Lame Man on the Sabbath (5:1 – 18)
   B. The Identity of (the Son of) God: Jesus Responds to the Opposition (5:19 – 47)
   C. The Fourth Sign: The Feeding of a Large Crowd (6:1 – 15)
   D. The "I AM" Walks across the Sea (6:16 – 21)
   E. The Bread of Life (6:22 – 71)
➡   **F. Private Display of Suspicion (7:1 – 13)**
   G. Public Display of Rejection (7:14 – 52)
   H. The Trial of Jesus regarding a Woman Accused of Adultery (7:53 – 8:11)

Main Idea

Jesus is the true tabernacle, the fulfillment of the world's hopes and joys, whose faithful obedience to the Father is the source of true brotherhood in the family of God. In Jesus, the good things of God are being expressed as grace replacing grace.

Translation

(See next page.)

John 7:1–13

1a Introduction and Setting (1–2) And **after these things Jesus was spending time in Galilee.**
b Place of Avoidance **He chose not to spend time in Judea,**
c Basis/Circumstances because the Jews were seeking to kill him.

2a Context But **the Jewish Feast of Tabernacles was near.**
Conflict (3–5)
3a Character Reentrance **His brothers said to him,**
b Hyperbolic Requests *"You should   leave here*
c Place of Avoidance *and   go to Judea,*
d Hyperbolic Result *so that your disciples may see the works*
e *that you do.*
4a Explanation *For no one who seeks to be in public acts in secret.*

b Condition *If you are doing these things,*
c Inferential Rebuke *show yourself to the world."*
5a Narrator's Aside For **not even his brothers were believing in him.**
6a Resolution (6–9)/Response Then **Jesus said to them,**
b Cryptic Retort *"My time has not yet arrived,*
c Contrast *but your time is always ready.*
7a Explanation *The world is unable to hate you,*
b Contrast *but it does hate me,*
c Basis *because I testify against it*
d Contrast to 3d, e *that its works are evil.*
8a Concluding Counterrebuke *You go up to the Feast.*
b Contrast *I will not go up to this Feast,*
c Basis *because my time has not yet been fulfilled."*

9a After he said these things,
b Jesus's Reaction #1 **he remained in Galilee.**
Conclusion (10–13)
10a Contrast to 9b But
b Jesus's Brothers' Reaction after his brothers went up to the Feast,
c Jesus's Reaction #2 **he also went up,**
d Manner/Contrast to 4a not publicly but in secret.

11a Reaction of Jews Then **at the Feast the Jews were seeking him and saying,**
b Question *"Where is that man?"*

12a Reaction of Crowd Among the crowd
b Escalating Intrigue **there was great whispering concerning him.**
c **Some said,**
d (+) Response *"He is good."*
e **Others said,**
f (−) Response *"No, rather he is leading the crowd astray."*
13a **No one . . .**
b Qualification to 12 though,
c Manner of Reaction **. . . would say anything publicly about him**
d Basis for fear of the Jews.

Structure and Literary Form

This pericope corresponds to the basic story form (see Introduction). The *introduction/setting* is established in vv. 1 – 2, explaining the location, setting, and people around whom the plot's conflict will focus. In vv. 3 – 5 the response of the family of Jesus to his ministry and reputation is the *conflict* of the pericope. In vv. 6 – 9 the counterresponse by Jesus serves to bring *resolution* to the conflict. Finally, vv. 10 – 13 offer the *conclusion/interpretation* of the pericope, including a closing summary of the varied responses of the Jewish crowd to Jesus, which helps establish this pericope in the larger trajectory and plot of the narrative.

Exegetical Outline

→   **F. Private Display of Suspicion (7:1 – 13)**
    1. The Feast of the Jews (vv. 1 – 2)
    2. The Ridicule of Jesus by His Brothers (vv. 3 – 5)
    3. The Response of Jesus to His Brothers (vv. 6 – 9)
    4. The Reluctance toward Jesus because of the Jews (vv. 10 – 13)

Explanation of the Text

The message and ministry of Jesus was no longer a secret. Jesus had become suspicious to many of those around him. In fact, as this scene depicts, the suspicion had trickled down to those who were closest to him. It is important to keep in view the developing plot of the narrative. The private display of suspicion is not mere background material but insight into the deeper reality of the unfolding story; the more the light shines, the more the darkness is revealed for what it truly is (cf. 1:5).

7:1 And after these things Jesus was spending time in Galilee. He chose not to spend time in Judea, because the Jews were seeking to kill him (Καὶ μετὰ ταῦτα περιεπάτει ὁ Ἰησοῦς ἐν τῇ Γαλιλαίᾳ· οὐ γὰρ ἤθελεν ἐν τῇ Ἰουδαίᾳ περιπατεῖν, ὅτι ἐζήτουν αὐτὸν οἱ Ἰουδαῖοι ἀποκτεῖναι). The narrator transitions the reader from the previous scene, denoted by "after these things" (μετὰ ταῦτα; see comments on 2:12), by aligning the story with the movements of Jesus. Jesus is described as "spending time" (περιεπάτει) in Galilee, a verb which could also be translated as "walking around" or just "walking." The term is best taken as a general description of his movements in a large region. No information is given regarding the activities in Galilee; the reference is given so as to explain the upcoming interaction between Jesus and his family in regard to his visit to Judea.

The narrator does add, however, an important piece of information: Jesus "chose not" (οὐ γὰρ ἤθελεν) to spend time in Judea because of the Jews. The statement depicts the divine agency involved in Jesus's movements in and around Judea, and the narrator introduces it here with theological sensitivity, setting the scene for the reader. Jesus "chose not" to spend time in Judea "because the Jews were seeking to kill him" (ὅτι ἐζήτουν αὐτὸν οἱ Ἰουδαῖοι ἀποκτεῖναι). Here, as in chapter 5, "the Jews" are the religious authorities in Jerusalem (see comments on 1:19). The conflict introduced in the previous pericopae has not subsided but increased so that Jesus is now, in some manner, a wanted man.

7:2 But the Jewish Feast of Tabernacles was near (ἦν δὲ ἐγγὺς ἡ ἑορτὴ τῶν Ἰουδαίων ἡ σκηνοπηγία). The narrator concludes the introduction and setting of the pericope by placing the upcoming scene in the context of the Feast of Tabernacles (or Booths), one of the most sacred Jewish holidays (Josephus, *Ant.* 8.100; m. Sukkah 5:1), occurring about six months after Passover (cf. 6:4). The holiday lasted seven days, from the 15th to the 21st of Tishri (September-October). A special day with a festival assembly marked the eighth day (the 22nd of Tishri).[1] The Feast became associated with the eschatological hopes of the people and was likely for this reason filled with joyous celebration.[2] The term we translated "Tabernacles" (ἡ σκηνοπηγία) is the combination of two words that could also be translated as "the setting up of tents" or "the construction of huts."[3] In light of the "tabernacling" presence of Jesus, the detail of the Feast of Tabernacles establishes for the reader both the historical and cosmological context of the scene. The qualification that the holiday is "Jewish" (τῶν Ἰουδαίων) is not new to John (see comments on 2:13).

7:3 His brothers said to him, "You should leave here and go to Judea, so that your disciples may see the works that you do" (εἶπον οὖν πρὸς αὐτὸν οἱ ἀδελφοὶ αὐτοῦ, Μετάβηθι ἐντεῦθεν καὶ ὕπαγε εἰς τὴν Ἰουδαίαν, ἵνα καὶ οἱ μαθηταί σου θεωρήσουσιν [σοῦ] τὰ ἔργα ἃ ποιεῖς). The conflict of the pericope is introduced with the arrival of Jesus's brothers (οἱ ἀδελφοὶ αὐτοῦ), whom the narrator has already briefly introduced (see comments on 2:12), and who will be described in v. 5 as not believing

in Jesus. While this is not technically a dialogue, this short verbal exchange between Jesus and his brothers strongly parallels a social challenge (see Introduction). The issue addressed is not raised for debate but to challenge the honor and authority of the interlocutor. It is common for such challenges to involve both irony and the playful use of words. The narrator has already informed the reader that Jesus had testified that a prophet has no honor in his own homeland (4:44), and Jesus's own brothers were about to prove the point by mocking his person and ministry.

The brothers of Jesus appeal to him with an aorist imperative of request (an entreaty or polite command), which is often used to speak to a superior and which is translated here as "you should leave here" (Μετάβηθι ἐντεῦθεν).[4] In the context of the verbal exchange, the imperative of request serves to mock the perceived public status of Jesus. This is made clear by the playful use of the words "your disciples" (οἱ μαθηταί σου) and "the works" (τὰ ἔργα) that Jesus does, which are used by the brothers as combative hyperbole that intend to challenge the very things it claims. When they saw him coming, Jesus's brothers spoke about Jesus in a similar way to how Joseph's brothers spoke about him: "Here comes that dreamer!" (Gen 37:19).

7:4 "For no one who seeks to be in public acts in secret. If you are doing these things, show yourself to the world" (οὐδεὶς γάρ τι ἐν κρυπτῷ ποιεῖ καὶ ζητεῖ αὐτὸς ἐν παρρησίᾳ εἶναι. εἰ ταῦτα ποιεῖς, φανέρωσον σεαυτὸν τῷ κόσμῳ). The brothers of Jesus do not merely give an exhortation with the intention of mockery; they even add an explanatory rebuke. Offering an interpretation of the intentions of Jesus to become a public figure, Jesus's brothers describe him as one who "seeks to be in public" (ζητεῖ αὐτὸς ἐν παρρησίᾳ εἶναι). The word

1. Barrett, *John*, 310.
2. Ridderbos, *John*, 257.
3. BDAG 928.
4. Cf. Wallace, *Greek Grammar*, 487–88.

"public" (παρρησία) is used nine times in John and in this context carries the sense of acting "openly" (7:13; 11:54; 18:20). By making such a simplified interpretation of Jesus's ministry and actions, his brothers describe him as one seeking attention for himself.

The brothers conclude by offering a closing rebuke to their mockery of his actions. Beginning with a first-class conditional clause that assumes the fact to be truth, "If you are doing these things" (εἰ ταῦτα ποιεῖς), the brothers offer another combative hyperbole that implies the exact opposite of what it actually claims. Even more, they end their challenge by crowning Jesus with unconcealed hyperbole in the form of another imperative of request: "Show yourself to the world" (φανέρωσον σεαυτὸν τῷ κόσμῳ). Such a grandiose statement was certainly intended to offer an over-the-top mockery of his ministry and self-identity. Yet with irony only detected by the reader of the Gospel, the statement intended to be a rebuke founded upon the impossible could not have been more accurate. Jesus had come to show himself to the world, though in a very different manner than what his brothers could have imagined.

7:5 For not even his brothers were believing in him (οὐδὲ γὰρ οἱ ἀδελφοὶ αὐτοῦ ἐπίστευον εἰς αὐτόν). The narrator ends the conflict of the pericope with an important commentary on the brothers of Jesus. This comment provides insight into the verbal exchange that just took place. The more traditional interpretation of the brotherly exchange assumes a positive challenge to Jesus.[5] But the narrator's comment, as readers of the Gospel have come to expect, must be understood as penetrating into the "unseen" context, giving insight into their response to Jesus. The unbelief of the broth-

ers is not due merely to a misunderstanding (i.e., a partial faith). Rather, they are dead wrong, and damagingly so, as Jesus will shortly declare by word and deed.

7:6 Then Jesus said to them, "My time has not yet arrived, but your time is always ready" (λέγει οὖν αὐτοῖς ὁ Ἰησοῦς, Ὁ καιρὸς ὁ ἐμὸς οὔπω πάρεστιν, ὁ δὲ καιρὸς ὁ ὑμέτερος πάντοτέ ἐστιν ἕτοιμος). After placing the conflict at the feet of Jesus, the plot of the pericope transitions to the resolution. Jesus responds with a cryptic statement in regard to his "time" (καιρός) that is not easy to interpret; yet within the framework of a challenge dialogue, the play on words is not only expected but understandable. Interpreters are correct to avoid giving the term "time" (καιρός) inappropriate lexical freight, though the term can be said to reflect qualitative (rather than quantitative) emphasis.[6] Befitting the social-challenge context of the statement in which words are used playfully for rhetorical purposes, Jesus makes a statement that addresses his brothers' exhortation, while at the same time addresses a much larger issue, one understood only in light of the deeper cosmological plot unfolding in the Gospel.

In light of this, therefore, without denying a different nuance in meaning, the use of "time" by Jesus must be viewed as comparable to his use of the term "hour" (see comments on 2:4; cf. 7:30; 8:20; 13:1; 17:1). The latter is a technical term in John that summarizes the eschatological action of God being realized in Jesus's person and work.[7] At the same time, it is appropriate — based upon the different terms and the immediate context — to assume a difference in meaning. While "time" is likely connected to "the hour," it is not the same thing. The former emphasizes God's work in Jesus

---

5. This is even suggested by Neyrey, *John*, 136–37, who uses the challenge/riposte model for interpreting the scene.

6. James Barr, *Biblical Words for Time*, SBT 33 (London: SCM Press, 1962), 121.

7. Ridderbos, *John*, 258.

as a whole and not merely the climactic moment of the cross. Such a distinction helps to make sense of v. 7.

The larger issue Jesus addresses is the public display of the Son that is part of his mission from the Father. Ironically, while Jesus disagrees with his brothers' words, he does not disagree with their intentions. That is, while he will not acquiesce to his brothers' exhortation, he will receive in full the exact result their combative hyperbole was hoping to induce: shame and suffering in the form of a public rebuke. In this way Jesus's statement offers a rejoinder that, without any combative hyperbole, could not be perceived by the brothers, but was intended to act as a distancing mechanism. Just as Jesus distanced himself from his mother (see comments on 2:4), so also he now separates himself from his brothers. And in so doing, Jesus aligns himself directly with the Father.

Jesus declares to his brothers: "But your time is always ready" (ὁ δὲ καιρὸς ὁ ὑμέτερος πάντοτέ ἐστιν ἕτοιμος). Such a statement serves as a rejoinder to the combative hyperbole and evil intentions of Jesus's brothers, making clear that their posture toward him is equivalent to their posture toward God. That is, there is nothing that God is doing that directly involves them. Ironically, the only connection between them and God at this point is, like Joseph's brothers, in their unwittingly fulfilling God's perfect purposes by their destructive naivete (cf. Gen 50:20).

7:7 "The world is unable to hate you, but it does hate me, because I testify against it that its works are evil" (οὐ δύναται ὁ κόσμος μισεῖν ὑμᾶς, ἐμὲ δὲ μισεῖ, ὅτι ἐγὼ μαρτυρῶ περὶ αὐτοῦ ὅτι τὰ ἔργα αὐτοῦ πονηρά ἐστιν). Jesus continues his rejoinder to his brothers by making a connection between them and "the world" (ὁ κόσμος). This is the first time in the Gospel where "the world" is spoken of not as the object of God's love (cf. 3:16, 17; 4:42;

6:33, 51) but as God's enemy. The criterion used to depict ontological equality between Jesus's brothers and the world, namely, the "inability" (οὐ δύναται) of the world to hate them, is the exact same criterion Jesus will use to prove who his true brothers/disciples really are (15:19).

Jesus adds that the world hates him "because I testify against it that its works are evil" (ὅτι ἐγὼ μαρτυρῶ περὶ αὐτοῦ ὅτι τὰ ἔργα αὐτοῦ πονηρά ἐστιν). Such a statement serves to counter that made to him by his brothers that Jesus should let those in Judea "see the works that you do" (v. 3) and "show yourself to the world" (v. 4). By this final rejoinder, Jesus declares that his own brothers' evil intentions serve as proof that his presence is a witness against them. In what can only be a divine mystery, it is only when Jesus separates himself from his brothers that he can truly love them; it is only when he distinguishes himself from them that he can truly make possible their familial reunification.

7:8 "You go up to the Feast. I will not go up to this Feast, because my time has not yet been fulfilled" (ὑμεῖς ἀνάβητε εἰς τὴν ἑορτήν· ἐγὼ οὐκ ἀναβαίνω εἰς τὴν ἑορτὴν ταύτην, ὅτι ὁ ἐμὸς καιρὸς οὔπω πεπλήρωται). Jesus ends his response to his brothers just as they had initiated their rebuke toward him: with a command. Jesus's command, however, is not derived from his own evil intentions but is a response to — even a rebuke of — the evil intentions of his brothers. Jesus reiterates, though this time with different but parallel language, that "my time has not yet been fulfilled" (ὁ ἐμὸς καιρὸς οὔπω πεπλήρωται). It is not just physical separation that Jesus is commandingly describing, not even just a difference in purpose or function, but a difference so cosmologically rooted that Jesus can only depict it with prophetic-like language (i.e., "fulfilled").

It is important to note that Jesus calls the Feast of Tabernacles "this Feast" (τὴν ἑορτὴν ταύτην). The description is a bit awkward in the context, and for that reason, exegetically significant. Schnackenburg is close when he suggests, "His saying 'to *this* feast' carries the underlying thought that he will be going to another feast," but wrong when he suggests that the other feast is the next Passover, the Passover of his death.[8] Rather, what makes this statement remarkable is that the implied other feast is the same feast, the Feast of Tabernacles! The contrast Jesus makes suggests that there is a distinction between the Feast of Tabernacles and the true tabernacle — Jesus himself. If the natural union between Jesus and his brothers can be shown to have real distinctions, so also can the natural union between Jesus the Jew and Judaism be seen to have real distinctions. Said another way, just as the prologue foretold of the true brotherhood of the children of God (1:12 – 13), it also foretold of "grace in place of grace" (1:16) and the fulfillment of the things of Moses by the person of Jesus Christ (1:17).

7:9 After he said these things, he remained in Galilee (ταῦτα δὲ εἰπὼν αὐτὸς ἔμεινεν ἐν τῇ Γαλιλαίᾳ). The resolution of the pericope closes with a concluding comment by the narrator. The narrator explains that Jesus "remained" (ἔμεινεν) in Galilee, with the assumption that his brothers left to go to the Feast (see v. 8). This verse serves as a double-edged sword for the reader, both to alleviate as well as to bring focus to the narrative tension. The tense verbal exchange comes to a fitting close by Jesus rebuking and then removing the challengers, his brothers, from his presence. However, in the very next verse Jesus does what he said he was not going to do; he goes to the Feast. While we will deal with the apparent dilemma in the next verse, it is important to note the importance of v. 9. The very fact that the narrator appears contradictory demands not only that we explain the exegetical

tension (see v. 10) but also that we take notice of the progression. Jesus declared himself to be entirely distinct from his brothers, and this comment by the narrator locates that statement in reality. What comes next must be seen as working with an intentionality that can only be explained in light of the contrast.

7:10 But after his brothers went up to the Feast, he also went up, not publicly but in secret (Ὡς δὲ ἀνέβησαν οἱ ἀδελφοὶ αὐτοῦ εἰς τὴν ἑορτήν, τότε καὶ αὐτὸς ἀνέβη, οὐ φανερῶς ἀλλ᾽ ἐν κρυπτῷ). The conclusion and interpretation of the pericope begins with a shocking twist. After separating himself from his brothers and "this Feast" (v. 8), Jesus ultimately goes up to the Feast. The twist is introduced with "but after" (Ὡς δὲ), which serves to differentiate Jesus from his brothers and transition the reader to the new state of affairs. This verse, however, raises two important questions that we must address in turn. First, how are we to explain the apparent contradiction with v. 8? Second, what is the significance of going "not publicly but in secret"?

How are we to explain the apparent contradiction with v. 8? We must begin with the distinction Jesus himself alerts us to in v. 8 when he calls the Feast of Tabernacles "this Feast" (τὴν ἑορτὴν ταύτην). Such an awkward description must be exegetically significant. He is not *going* to a different Feast but *speaking* of the Feast in a disparaging manner.

This distinction, however, cannot be expressed in merely historical terms. The distinction between "this Feast" and Jesus's participation in it has its point of tension in the person and work of Jesus himself. The Feast of Tabernacles was a joyous celebration, primarily because it was associated with the eschatological hopes of the people. But these eschatological hopes were resting so innately on the

8. Schnackenburg, *John*, 2:141.

shoulders of the work of the Son that for Jesus "this Feast" was different *without* him. The Feast that his brothers attended was, according to the cosmological nature of the work of Christ revealed by the Gospel, a different Feast altogether.[9] For the Gospel of John this is a real distinction, one made in the prologue and, arguably, pressuring the reader by the distinctive nuance in vv. 8 and 10. This might explain on the historical level why Jesus arrived at the Feast with apparently little concern for missing half or more of the festivities and ceremonies and functioned in no real way as a normal participant. Simply stated, he could not be a normal participant at the Feast, for he is the tabernacle, the thing to be celebrated, the fulfillment of the eschatological hopes.[10] Ironically, while the Jews were busy erecting their tabernacles in order to participate in the eschatological ceremonies of their God, God himself was "tabernacling" (1:14) in the midst of his people![11] Yet Jesus went "not publicly but in secret" (οὐ φανερῶς ἀλλ᾽ ἐν κρυπτῷ), offering a clear contrast between the honor-seeking display requested by his brothers and the shame-bearing display assigned to him by the Father (cf. 3:14).

7:11 Then at the Feast the Jews were seeking him and saying, "Where is that man?" (οἱ οὖν Ἰουδαῖοι ἐζήτουν αὐτὸν ἐν τῇ ἑορτῇ καὶ ἔλεγον, Ποῦ ἐστιν ἐκεῖνος;). The narrator moves toward the conclusion of the pericope by describing the reaction to the mystery of Jesus and the question of his presence. The narrator reveals that "the Jews," that is, the religious authorities who were trying to kill him in v. 1, "were seeking him" (ἐζήτουν αὐτὸν). The verb is best taken to mean a hostile search; they are watching for him and hoping to catch him. It is only as the chapter progresses that these influ-

ential opponents become more clearly defined as the Pharisees (7:32, 47–48) and members of the Sanhedrin (7:26, 32, 45, and 48).[12] The use of "that man" (ἐκεῖνος) is probably to be taken as derogatory in this context (cf. 5:11–12).

7:12 Among the crowd there was great whispering concerning him. Some said, "He is good." Others said, "No, rather he is leading the crowd astray" (καὶ γογγυσμὸς περὶ αὐτοῦ ἦν [πολὺς] ἐν τῷ ὄχλῳ· οἱ μὲν ἔλεγον ὅτι Ἀγαθός ἐστιν, ἄλλοι [δὲ] ἔλεγον, Οὔ, ἀλλὰ πλανᾷ τὸν ὄχλον). It is not just "the Jews" who are interested in Jesus; even "among the crowd" (ἐν τῷ ὄχλῳ) there is interest regarding him. The narrator describes the crowd's great "whispering" (γογγυσμός), a term which in this context is used to depict a more general behind-the-scenes talk, not the negative depiction used earlier in the Gospel for the Jews (cf. 6:41, 61).[13]

It is likely that the words used to describe the content of the crowd's whispering, however, are not to be taken as generic summaries but specific and theologically loaded responses to Jesus. For example, the verb "leading astray" (πλανᾷ) could quite naturally be linked to the accusation against a divisive seducer in Deuteronomy 13:6–10. This might explain the logic of those who are seeking to kill Jesus (v. 1). Even the depiction of Jesus as "good" (ἀγαθός) is more than a casual compliment, for it reflects the "goodness of God" motif also in Deuteronomy, and this implies that Jesus is a reflection of the character of God and, therefore, the agent of the blessings and goodness of God himself (cf. Mark 10:18; Luke 18:19).[14]

7:13 No one, though, would say anything publicly about him for fear of the Jews (οὐδεὶς μέντοι παρρησίᾳ ἐλάλει περὶ αὐτοῦ διὰ τὸν φόβον τῶν

---

9. See Westcott, *John*, 117.
10. See Augustine, *John*, 29.9.182.
11. Cf. Hoskyns, *Fourth Gospel*, 310.
12. Schnackenburg, *John*, 2:143.

13. BDAG 204.
14. Jane Heath, "'Some Were Saying, "He Is Good"'" (John 7.12b): 'Good' Christology in John's Gospel," *NTS* 56 (2010): 513–35.

Ἰουδαίων). While all these cosmological realities of the eschatological work of God in Christ during "this" Feast of Tabernacles affect the crowd and their participation in the ceremonies, they could not be directly acted upon "for fear of the Jews" (διὰ τὸν φόβον τῶν Ἰουδαίων). Such language, used elsewhere in the Gospel (cf. 9:22; 19:38; 20:19), depicts the conflict at the historical level of the plot of John. The narrator states emphatically that "no one" (οὐδεὶς) would say anything publicly, marking the high point of the hostility at this point in the narrative.

Theology in Application

In a scene that reveals the growing and publicly-manifested conflict between Jesus and those around him, Jesus receives a private rebuke by those who should have been on his side, his own brothers. The verbal exchange between Jesus and his brothers serves to highlight the depth and nature of the conflict. And with the Feast of Tabernacles as the context for this engagement, the true nature of Jesus's ministry and the magnitude of his presence are made glaringly clear to the reader.

The Brothers of Jesus and the Family of God

The stark contrast between the natural affinity between brothers in the ancient world and the rejection — not just lack of reception — displayed between Jesus and his brothers allows the reader to see the depth of the conflict between the darkness and the light (1:5). What makes this conflict most shocking is that it is the last place one would have expected to find it. One may fight against the whole world, but one's family would be the last to be reckoned as the enemy. Yet in the family of Jesus the war was inevitable. The reason was made clear in v. 7: Jesus's brothers were not *really* his brothers; they belonged to the family of the world. They shared the same biological mother, but they were not children of the same Father.

The Christian finds no greater kinship than in the family of God. It is one's Father, the heavenly Father, who alone gives ultimate definition to "family." There is only one blood relation that ultimately matters — the blood of Christ. This is not to disparage biological families but simply to take heed of their fallibility and shaky foundation. This pericope exhorts us to align ourselves to our brother, Jesus Christ. When we are separated from him, it is not Christ who separated from us, it is we who have separated from him. Ironically, when the world or even our biological families begin to hate us on account of Christ, it is then that we know that we are home, residents of the family of God.

He Is Good

Jesus can be only one of two things: either he is a deceiver or he is "good" (v. 12). There is no in between and no other option. With Jesus you are either his brother or his challenger. There is no second-cousin relationship to Jesus. He is no mere acquaintance. This is because he is and makes manifest God himself and all the good things that God has promised. Jesus is the one who fulfills all the things of God. Every good thing God ever wanted to do he is doing in Jesus Christ. As Paul declares: "For no matter how many promises God has made, they are 'Yes' in Christ" (2 Cor 1:20). This is what some of the crowd in v. 12 were beginning to understand, even if they were too scared to say it aloud (v. 13). The church, however, should shout and proclaim aloud the "Yes!" of Jesus. It cannot but speak, for it has seen and received the love of God. Jesus is the good — yes, "He is good."

The "Tabernacling One" in Place of the Tabernacle

This pericope describes with careful precision how Jesus is "tabernacling" with his people in the midst of the great religious ceremonies and festivities of the Feast of Tabernacles (see 1:14). The Gospel of John crafts the encounter with such rich theological imagery and imagination that the reader is forced to see in the stark contrast the true tabernacle made present by Jesus's person and work. Even more, they are to see how Jesus the tabernacle functions as the real fulfillment of the eschatological hopes and joyous celebration of the traditional Feast. All this depicts with explicit commentary what the prologue had foretold: Jesus is the grace in place of grace. The gracious work of God in the Old Testament — and it *was* grace — is so eclipsed by the gracious work of God in Jesus that it is a full replacement of grace (see comments on 1:16 – 17). This is why the Feast of Tabernacles is not celebrated by Christians, for it is eclipsed by another Feast, called a "love feast" by early Christians (i.e., the Lord's Supper). At this feast, the food is Christ's body and the drink is Christ's blood, and the thing that is joyously celebrated is the glorious cross and the indestructible resurrection from the dead and the eschatological hopes awaiting his certain return. With this in view, the building of dingy tabernacles or booths around Jerusalem pales in comparison with the true temple of God, the church, who are the living expressions of the grace of God.

John 7:14 – 52

Literary Context

The narrative moves from a private encounter between Jesus and his suspicious brothers outside of Judea to a public encounter with the disbelieving Jews at the center of Judea. More than just a geographical center, the encounter takes place in the center of Jerusalem at the temple, which served as the center of Judaism, in the middle of the Feast of Tabernacles. It is at this place and time of worship that Jesus, the Word, provides an important response to the growing animosity expressed toward him. Meanwhile, the Jews further reveal their opinion of him, his ministerial activities, and ultimately his Father.

IV. The Confession of the Son of God (5:1 – 8:11)

    A. The Third Sign: The Healing of the Lame Man on the Sabbath (5:1 – 18)

    B. The Identity of (the Son of) God: Jesus Responds to the Opposition (5:19 – 47)

    C. The Fourth Sign: The Feeding of a Large Crowd (6:1 – 15)

    D. The "I AM" Walks across the Sea (6:16 – 21)

    E. The Bread of Life (6:22 – 71)

    F. Private Display of Suspicion (7:1 – 13)

➡   **G. Public Display of Rejection (7:14 – 52)**

    H. The Trial of Jesus regarding a Woman Accused of Adultery (7:53 – 8:11)

Main Idea

Jesus is the true provision of God, "the Tabernacling One," whom the world cannot understand or accept because they have rejected his Father and their God. Neither can they accept the disciples of Jesus, whose thirst is quenched by the Spirit of God and whose lives bear witness to the "unseen" reality of God.

Translation

(See pages 362–65.)

Structure and Literary Form

This is the fourth substantial dialogue in the narrative proper, and it is a *social challenge dialogue*, which takes the form of an informal debate intending to challenge the honor and authority of one's interlocutor (see Introduction). This dialogue is looser than the previous three dialogues, for not only does it involve an initial, multifaceted verbal exchange involving a complex set of rotating interlocutors (e.g., "the Jews" and "the crowd"), but it also contains at its conclusion a second multifaceted verbal exchange that occurs between the Jewish authorities themselves. By presenting the dialogue by means of both public and private verbal exchange, the dramatic nature of the encounters is given emphasis.

Exegetical Outline

➡ **G. Public Display of Rejection (7:14 – 52)**

    1. The Authority of Jesus (7:14 – 24)

        a. Scene Introduction: Temple, Tabernacles, and Timing (v. 14)

        b. First Verbal Exchange: The Source of Jesus's Teaching (vv. 15 – 19)

        c. Second Verbal Exchange: The Source of Jesus's Miracles (vv. 20 – 24)

    2. The Identity of Jesus (7:25 – 36)

        a. Third Verbal Exchange: The Nature of Jesus's Origin (vv. 25 – 29)

        b. Narrator's Interlude: Control in Confusion and Confrontation (vv. 30 – 32)

        c. Fourth Verbal Exchange: The Nature of Jesus's Mission (vv. 33 – 36)

    3. The Spirit of Jesus (7:37 – 44)

        a. Final Exhortation of Jesus: The Promise of the Spirit (vv. 37 – 38)

        b. Narrator's Interlude: The Interpretation of Jesus's Statement (v. 39)

        c. Final Reaction of the Crowd (vv. 40 – 44)

    4. The Internal Divisions of Unbelief (7:45 – 52)

        a. First Verbal Exchange: Jewish Authorities Challenge the Temple Police (vv. 45 – 46)

        b. Second Verbal Exchange: Jewish Authorities Challenge the Crowd (vv. 47 – 49)

        c. Third Verbal Exchange: Nicodemus Challenges the Jewish Authorities (vv. 50 – 52)

John 7:14–52

14a	Introduction & Setting	When the Feast was already half over,
b	Sequence #1	**Jesus went to Jerusalem**
c	Sequence #2	and **began to teach.**

(1st Interlocution with Jesus)

15a	Character Reentrance	**The Jews were amazed and asked,**
b	Interrogative Challenge	*"How does this man know the Scriptures*
c	Means	*without having been trained?"*

16a	Retort	**Jesus answered them and said,**
b	Assertion	*"My teaching is not mine but*
c	Contrasting Source	*belongs to the One who sent me.*

(Source of Jesus's Teaching)

17a	Condition	*If anyone chooses to do his will,*
b	Inference	*he will learn about the teaching,*
c	Source	*whether it originates from God or*
d	Alternative	*I speak on my own initiative.*

18a	Condition	*The one who speaks on his own initiative …*
b	Inference	*… seeks his own glory,*
c	Contrasting Condition	*but the one who seeks the glory of the one who sent him,*
d	Contrasting Inference #1	*this one is true*
e	Contrasting Inference #2	*and there is no falsehood in him.*
19a	Counterchallenge	*Has not Moses given you the law?*
b	Rebuke	*And yet no one among you does the law.*
c	Escalating Question	*Why are you trying to kill me?"*

(2nd Interlocution with Jesus)

20a	Character Reentrance	**The crowd answered,**
b	Accusation	*"You have a demon.*
c	Counterchallenge	*Who is trying to kill you?"*
21a	Retort	**Jesus answered and said to them,**
b	Counterchallenge	*"I did one deed*
c		*and you are all amazed.*

22a	Informal Argument	*For this reason*
b	Assertion	*Moses has given you circumcision*
c	Parenthetic	*(though it did not come from Moses, but*
d		*from the patriarchs),*
e	Purpose	*and you circumcise a man on the Sabbath.*

23a	Condition	*If a person can receive circumcision on the Sabbath*
b	Result	*so that the law of Moses is not broken,*
c	Inferential Interrogative	*why are you angry with me*
d	Basis	*because I healed the whole man on the Sabbath?*

24a	Rebuke	*Stop judging by outward appearance,*
b	Command	*but make the right judgment."*

	(3rd Interlocution with Jesus)	
25a	Character Entrance	Then **some of the people of Jerusalem were saying,**
b	Interrogative Recognition	*"Is this man not the one they are trying to kill?"*
26a	Wonder	*And here he is, speaking in public,*
b		*and no one is saying anything to him.*
c	Interrogative Rebuke of the Jews	*Can it be that the authorities have truly come to know*
d	Identity	*that this man is the Christ?*
27a	Rebuke of Jesus	*But we know where this man is from;*
b	Basis/Temporal Condition	*when the Christ comes,*
c	Inference	*no one will know where he is from."*
28a	Retort	Then **Jesus cried out and said,**
b	Simultaneous Action	*while teaching in the temple,*
c	Ironic Rebuke to 27b, c	*"You know me*
d		*and you know where I am from.*
e	Contrast of Expectations	*However, I have not come here for myself,*
f	Assertion	*but the one who sent me is true,*
g	Escalating Rebuke	*whom you do not know.*
29a	Contrast to 28g	*I know him,*
b	Basis (Origin)	*because I am from him and he sent me"*
	(Narrator's Interlude)	
30a	Reactive Intention #1	After this **they were trying to seize him,**
b	Contrast	yet **no one laid a hand upon him,**
c	Basis	*because his hour had not yet come.*
31a	Reaction #2	But **many from the crowd believed in him and said,**
b	Temporal Condition	*"When the Christ comes,*
c	Interrogative Interference	*he will not do more signs …*
d	Comparison	*than those that this man did,*
e		*… will he?*
32a	Reaction #3	**The Pharisees heard the things the crowd was whispering concerning him,**
b	Result	and **the high priests and Pharisees sent the temple police to arrest him.**
	(4th Interlocution with Jesus)	
33a	Response to 30–32	Then **Jesus said,**
b	Explanatory Sequence #1	*"I am only with you for a little longer,*
c	Explanatory Sequence #2	*and then I go to the one who sent me.*
34a	Predictive Reaction to 33c	*You will seek me*
b	Result	*and you will not find me,*
c	Basis/Rebuke	*and where I am you are unable to come."*
35a	Response	Then **the Jews said to themselves,**
b	Confused Question	*"Where does this man intend to go that we cannot find him?*
c	Counter–Rebuke #1	*Does he intend to go to those who are dispersed among the gentiles, and*
d	Counter–Rebuke #2	*teach the gentiles?*

Continued on next page.

Continued from previous page.

36a	Mockery of Jesus	*What is this statement that he said,*
b	Restatement of 34	*'You will seek me*
c		*and you will not find me,*
d		*and where I am you are unable to come?'"*
	(Jesus's Concluding Exhortation)	
37a	Context	On the last and greatest day of the Feast,
b	Action	**Jesus stood up and cried out saying,**
c	Condition	*"If anyone is thirsty,*
d	Inferential Exhortation	*let him come to me and drink.*
38a	Explanation/Condition	*The one who believes in me …*
b	Connection to OT & NT	*just as it is written in* ⤷ *Scripture,*
c	Inference	*… streams of living water will flow from within him."*
39a	Narrator's Aside	**But this he said about the Spirit,**
b	Description	which the ones who believed in him were about ⤷ to receive.
c	Explanation	**For the Spirit was not yet [given],**
d	Basis	because Jesus had not yet been glorified.
40a		After hearing his words,
b		**some from the crowd said,**
c	Crowd's Reaction #1 (+)	*"This man is truly the Prophet."*
41a		**Others said,**
b	Crowd's Reaction #2 (+)	*"This man is the Christ."*
c		And **still others said,**
d	Crowd's Reaction #3 (–)	*"How can the Messiah come out of Galilee?*
42a	Question of Origin	*Does not the Scripture say the Christ will come out of the seed of David, and*
b	Location	*out of Bethlehem,*
c	Description	*the town where David* ⤷ *was from?"*
43a	Result of Different Reactions	Then **a division broke out among the crowd**
b	Basis	because of him.
44a	Reactive Intention	**Some of them wanted him to be arrested,**
b	Contrast	but **no one laid a hand upon him.**
	(1st Interlocution without Jesus)	
45a	Character Entrance	Then **the temple police came to the high priests and the Pharisees,**
b		and **they said to them,**
c	Interrogation	*"Why did you not bring him in?"*
46a		**The temple police answered,**
b	Response	*"A man has never spoken like this."*
47a	(2nd Interlocution without Jesus)	Then **the Pharisees responded to them,**
b	Rebuke of Temple Police	*"Surely you have not also been deceived?*
48a	Contrast of Peers	*Surely no one …*
b	Identification	*from among the rulers or*
c	Identification	*the Pharisees*
d		*… believed in him?*

49a	Rebuke of Crowd	*But **this crowd that cannot understand the law—they are accursed!"***
	(3rd Interlocution without Jesus)	
50a	Character Reentrance	**Nicodemus …**
b	Reference to John 3	the one who came to Jesus earlier,
c	Ironic Description: Peer of 48	who was one of their own,
d		**… said:**
51a	Interrogative Challenge	*"Does our law condemn a man*
b	Condition #1	*without first hearing from him and*
c	Condition #2	*understanding what he is doing?"*
52a	Retort	**They answered and said to him,**
b	Interrogative Rebuke	*"Surely you also are not from Galilee?*
c	Imperatival Rebuke	*Search and see that a prophet does not arise from Galilee."*

Explanation of the Text

This lengthy and multifaceted dialogue is best viewed as a complete whole, even though several important parts could be looked at individually, especially, for example, the section on the Spirit (vv. 37–39). The narrative provides the reader with an interactive display not only of the conflict that has been centering upon Jesus but also the growing conflict among the people themselves, with both the crowd and the Jewish authorities in heated exchanges. Even the temple police are unable to remove themselves from the conflict. It is for this reason that the entire dialogue, vv. 14–52, must be viewed as single unit, offering for the reader a kaleidoscopic perspective on the nature of events initiated by the light now shining in the darkness (1:5).

7:14 When the Feast was already half over, Jesus went to Jerusalem and began to teach (Ἤδη δὲ τῆς ἑορτῆς μεσούσης ἀνέβη Ἰησοῦς εἰς τὸ ἱερὸν καὶ ἐδίδασκεν). This verse serves as an introduction to the entire scene and dialogue that follows. The narrator introduces the scene to the reader by means of the fashionably late arrival of Jesus. The timing of Jesus's arrival is not stated definitively. The phrase we translated "when the Feast was

already half over" (Ἤδη δὲ τῆς ἑορτῆς μεσούσης) could imply it was about the middle of the feast but could also simply mean that the Feast was well underway by the time Jesus arrived. In typical Johannine irony, while the Jews were busy erecting their tabernacles or booths in order to participate in the eschatological ceremonies of their God, God himself arrived to "tabernacle" among them (see comments on 7:8, 10).

Jesus does not merely present himself, he also "began to teach" (ἐδίδασκεν), denoted by an ingressive aorist. In the context of the Feast, such an action was a clear statement of his position and authority. It is no surprise that his action was challenged (v. 15). The topic of his teaching is not mentioned, though the source is about to be revealed (vv. 16–17). It is less the topic and more the fact of instruction that interests the narrative; at this moment the Word of God was heralding the word of God for the people of God — in the very center of Judaism.

7:15 The Jews were amazed and asked, "How does this man know the Scriptures without having been trained?" (ἐθαύμαζον οὖν οἱ Ἰουδαῖοι λέγοντες, Πῶς οὗτος γράμματα οἶδεν μὴ μεμαθηκώς;). The teaching of Jesus stirs a reaction from "the Jews" (see comments on 1:19) with whom, along with the crowd, Jesus begins a dialogue. This first verbal exchange (vv. 15 – 19) is between Jesus and the Jewish authorities. In response to the teaching of Jesus, the Jewish authorities ask a question that in a first-century context is a forensic charge against Jesus, calling into question his status as a teacher and therefore the validity of his teaching.[1] The reaction of the Jews to Jesus's teaching, expressed in the statement, they "were amazed" (ἐθαύμαζον), is not to be interpreted as a positive thing. To them Jesus was an uneducated nobody who holds no formal (elected) office and has had no formal (accredited) training. His behavior was a clear and present threat to the establishment and its traditions. Even the designation, "this man" (οὗτος), is to be viewed as contemptuous.[2] The actual question they ask is entirely rhetorical, with the communicative intent of demeaning and challenging the authority of the person.

7:16 Jesus answered them and said, "My teaching is not mine but belongs to the One who sent me" (ἀπεκρίθη οὖν αὐτοῖς [ὁ] Ἰησοῦς καὶ εἶπεν, Ἡ ἐμὴ διδαχὴ οὐκ ἔστιν ἐμὴ ἀλλὰ τοῦ πέμψαντός με). Jesus responds to the accusation by revealing the source of his teaching, which carries with it an authority and validity that devastatingly trumps the teaching succession and authority of any ordained rabbi. Jesus has no need to claim the authority of "the Jews," for he can claim the authority of God. The warrant is connected to "the One who sent me" (τοῦ πέμψαντός με), a phrase echoed throughout the Gospel and connected to the entire mission of God (see comments on 5:19 – 23). Grammatically it is worth noting that Jesus emphasizes his own teaching, "*my* teaching" (Ἡ ἐμὴ διδαχὴ), for the sole purpose of undercutting his right to claim

it as his own ("it is not mine" [οὐκ ἔστιν ἐμὴ]). This is the exact opposite of what would have been the expected practice within the authority-seeking context of rabbinic tradition.

7:17 "If anyone chooses to do his will, he will learn about the teaching, whether it originates from God or I speak on my own initiative" (ἐάν τις θέλῃ τὸ θέλημα αὐτοῦ ποιεῖν, γνώσεται περὶ τῆς διδαχῆς πότερον ἐκ τοῦ θεοῦ ἐστιν ἢ ἐγὼ ἀπ' ἐμαυτοῦ λαλῶ). Jesus presses further his response to the cutting question of the Jews and undercuts the foundation of the question itself. The issue is less the verifiability of the messenger and more the *veritas* of the message, the truthfulness it proclaims and represents. The Jews challenge the ability of Jesus to teach; Jesus challenges the ability of the Jews to hear.[3] The criterion listed for ascertaining the origin and therefore the truthfulness of the message is "to do his [God's] will" (τὸ θέλημα αὐτοῦ ποιεῖν). The only other place this phrase is used is in 9:31, where the man born blind says that God only listens "to the godly man who does his will." In some way, there is a connection between God and the person who seeks and lives for God, a kind of life that flows "from the fear and reverence of God."[4] This is not, as Bultmann notes, an initial ethical demand (which is universally evident) that leads toward faith but an outworking of the process of belief.[5] While distinctions in emphasis can be made between the one who does the "will of God," "the one who does the truth" (3:21), and the one who does "the work of God" (6:29), it is best to view them all as pointing to the same subject matter.[6]

7:18 "The one who speaks on his own initiative seeks his own glory, but the one who seeks the

1. Neyrey, *John*, 140; Brant, *John*, 136.
2. Morris, *John*, 359.
3. Ibid., 360.

4. Calvin, *John 1 – 10*, 186.
5. Bultmann, *John*, 274.
6. Cf. Augustine, *John*, 29.6.184 – 85.

glory of the one who sent him, this one is true and there is no falsehood in him" (ὁ ἀφ᾽ ἑαυτοῦ λαλῶν τὴν δόξαν τὴν ἰδίαν ζητεῖ· ὁ δὲ ζητῶν τὴν δόξαν τοῦ πέμψαντος αὐτόν, οὗτος ἀληθής ἐστιν καὶ ἀδικία ἐν αὐτῷ οὐκ ἔστιν). Pressing even further the reversal of qualifications and credentials, the true teacher from God is one who seeks not his "own glory" (τὴν δόξαν τὴν ἰδίαν) but "the glory of the one who sent him" (τὴν δόξαν τοῦ πέμψαντος αὐτόν). The word translated "glory" means "honor as enhancement or recognition of status or performance."[7] It is the opposite of self-effacement and humility. It is saying, "I must become greater, he must become less," a ghastly antithesis to the message of the Baptist (3:30). Ultimately, the contrast is between the one who is "true" (ἀληθής), that is, faithful and reliable, and one who is "false" (ἀδικία), a term that is often contrasted or described as at enmity with truth and is frequently used to depict unrighteousness and wickedness.[8]

7:19 "Has not Moses given you the law? And yet no one among you does the law. Why are you trying to kill me?" (οὐ Μωϋσῆς δέδωκεν ὑμῖν τὸν νόμον; καὶ οὐδεὶς ἐξ ὑμῶν ποιεῖ τὸν νόμον. τί με ζητεῖτε ἀποκτεῖναι;). After responding to the challenge the Jews presented to him and his teaching authority, Jesus now turns the table and offers a challenge in return. In the form of a rhetorical question followed by a statement that begins with a contrastive conjunction, "and yet" (καί), Jesus turns them against themselves by comparing their reception of the law of Moses with their obedience to it. Jesus then declares that they are trying to kill him, exposing their intention regarding him as a violation of the law of Moses. With a shocking reversal, Jesus uses the royal diadem of the Jewish authorities (Jewish tradition and the Mosaic

law) and made it a noose for them to place tightly around their own necks. In this way, the first verbal exchange of the dialogue is concluded.

7:20 The crowd answered, "You have a demon. Who is trying to kill you?" (ἀπεκρίθη ὁ ὄχλος, Δαιμόνιον ἔχεις· τίς σε ζητεῖ ἀποκτεῖναι;). The second verbal exchange of the dialogue continues to center upon Jesus, but a second interlocutor is introduced: "the crowd" (ὁ ὄχλος). This is no mere "lifelike touch" by the narrator,[9] but a carefully crafted, dialogical presentation of the complex and interrelated responses to Jesus at the Feast. If anything, the narrator presents this dialogue more dramatically, focusing less on one issue and more on the variety of conflicts and confusions stemming from the ministry of Jesus.

The crowd declares Jesus to have "a demon" (δαιμόνιον), which is probably meant to suggest he is out of his mind or crazy (cf. 10:20: "He has a demon and is insane"). The change in interlocutor is not meant to suggest that the latter did not track with or is unaware of the previous argument; it shows instead that the animosity of the verbal exchange is moving in a different direction. This is not a new dialogue but a development of it. Their charge is stated strongly so as to forcefully challenge what they deem to be slanderous words by Jesus.[10] In a sense, the crowd is defending the Jewish authorities against Jesus. Any contrast between the Jewish authorities and the crowd is slowly dissipating; in fact, by the end of the Gospel even the Jews and the Romans — the whole world! — become a single, condemning voice against Jesus (19:15). In this way, then, the crowd offers a second challenge to Jesus.

7:21 Jesus answered and said to them, "I did one deed and you are all amazed" (ἀπεκρίθη Ἰησοῦς

7. BDAG 257.
8. Cf. Barrett, *John*, 318; BDAG 20.
9. Bernard, *John*, 1:262.
10. Brant, *John*, 137.

καὶ εἶπεν αὐτοῖς, "Ἓν ἔργον ἐποίησα καὶ πάντες θαυμάζετε). Jesus's response does not address their question and accusation made against him but reverses the challenge in the form of a charge against them. Jesus refutes their challenge not in principle but in practice — their own practice! Jesus reminds them of their response to one particular "deed" (ἔργον), which in light of v. 23 can only be the healing of the man lame for thirty-eight years (5:1–18). He raises this miracle as key evidence for the case he is about to make against them.

7:22 "For this reason Moses has given you circumcision (though it did not come from Moses, but from the patriarchs), and you circumcise a man on the Sabbath" (διὰ τοῦτο Μωϋσῆς δέδωκεν ὑμῖν τὴν περιτομήν—οὐχ ὅτι ἐκ τοῦ Μωϋσέως ἐστὶν ἀλλ᾽ ἐκ τῶν πατέρων—καὶ ἐν σαββάτῳ περιτέμνετε ἄνθρωπον). This verse offers the main thrust of Jesus's argument. Jesus argues from the agreed to the disputed, an established rhetorical practice. To fulfill biblical commandments, there were times when it was necessary to override other biblical commandments. That is, according to the requirements of the law itself, some commandments were to take precedence over other commandments. Jesus offers the need for circumcision on the Sabbath as the prime example.

The argument is not stated that clearly, however, for the opening phrase, which we translated as "for this reason" (διὰ τοῦτο), does not easily fit.[11] Such an awkward expression, not uncommon to John (see comments on 7:10), is likely to be exegetically significant. By being linked to the first clause, the phrase serves to explain a legal precedent that is intentionally designed to extend beyond itself. Moses gave the Jews circumcision and the right to circumcise on the Sabbath in spite of the law pre-

cisely for this reason: "that it should be a type and anticipation of that greater and entire healing by the Christ, which also of necessity displaces the Sabbath."[12] Jesus's argument, therefore, is a rebuke of the Jewish interpretation of the law. For the intention of Moses, made manifest in the precedence given to circumcision over the Sabbath, was to show that the law was ordained to life, and Jesus's activity on the Sabbath was not breaking the law but fulfilling it.

7:23 "If a person can receive circumcision on the Sabbath so that the law of Moses is not broken, why are you angry with me because I healed the whole man on the Sabbath?" (εἰ περιτομὴν λαμβάνει ἄνθρωπος ἐν σαββάτῳ ἵνα μὴ λυθῇ ὁ νόμος Μωϋσέως, ἐμοὶ χολᾶτε ὅτι ὅλον ἄνθρωπον ὑγιῆ ἐποίησα ἐν σαββάτῳ;). Jesus now draws out the implication of the argument he presented in v. 22: if there are exceptions to the Sabbath law, then there is a greater, more foundational basis for actions performed on the Sabbath. Interpreters frequently notice that this principled argument from lesser to greater, the "light to heavy" argument, was common to Judaism, and is likely in play here. However, after v. 22 the scope of the argument is no longer between the laws of Moses, but between the law of Moses and the law of Christ (Gal 6:2; cf. 1 Cor 9:21). That is, the law of Moses was merely the shadow of the image itself (Christ), the true subject matter of the law of Moses.

There is also an intentional lesser-to-greater contrast between the physical act done to one part of the body (circumcision) and the physical act of healing "the whole man" (ὅλον ἄνθρωπον). Rather than offering a sentimental liberalizing of a harsh and impractical law, Jesus is describing the redemptive purpose of God to which the law had

---

11. Severino Pancaro, *The Law in the Fourth Gospel: The Torah and the Gospel, Moses and Jesus, Judaism and Christianity according to John*, NovTSup 42 (Leiden: Brill, 1975), 163–64.

12. Hoskyns, *Fourth Gospel*, 316.

always been pointing.[13] Ironically, the Jews were right to focus on Jesus; they just did so without the Bible (the law).

7:24 "Stop judging by outward appearance, but make the right judgment" (μὴ κρίνετε κατ᾽ ὄψιν, ἀλλὰ τὴν δικαίαν κρίσιν κρίνετε). The second verbal exchange concludes with a recapitulation and clarification by Jesus.[14] The crowd rightly saw the exception of the law of Moses, but they could not see its fulfillment. The present imperative, "Stop judging" (μὴ κρίνετε), urges a reversal of their current practices, whereas the aorist imperative, "Make the right judgment" (τὴν δικαίαν κρίσιν κρίνετε), directs urgent attention to the specific example.[15] The aorist imperative also contains a cognate accusative (i.e., a direct object that comes from the same lexical root as the verb) which gives the entire clause more emphasis.[16]

It is important to hear this concluding exhortation as less a critique of hermeneutics and more a critique of faith. Since the term we translated as "outward appearance" (ὄψιν) can also refer to the "face" of a person (e.g., 11:44),[17] the rebuke creates an "impression" that reminds the reader of the cosmological (unseen) forces shaping the narrative and the ultimate goal of this Gospel: that Jesus might be recognized as he truly is (20:31).

7:25 Then some of the people of Jerusalem were saying, "Is this man not the one they are trying to kill?" (Ἔλεγον οὖν τινες ἐκ τῶν Ἱεροσολυμιτῶν, Οὐχ οὗτός ἐστιν ὃν ζητοῦσιν ἀποκτεῖναι;). This verse begins a new section in the pericope. The focus has moved from the authority to the identity of Jesus. The narrator introduces yet another interlocutor in what we have already described as a multifaceted dialogue. This time the interlocutor

is described as "some of the people of Jerusalem" (τινες ἐκ τῶν Ἱεροσολυμιτῶν), which likely refers to local residents and not pilgrims. It is worth asking why the narrator would distinguish this group from "the crowd" in general. If "the Jews" (first verbal exchange, vv. 14–19) present to the reader the *theological* issues at stake, and "the crowd" (second verbal exchange, vv. 20–24) presents to the reader the *faith* issues at stake, then "the people of Jerusalem" (third verbal exchange, vv. 25–29) present to the reader the *political* issues at stake. The Jerusalemites did not instigate the challenge to Jesus, but they clearly knew about and understood it, as their statement makes clear. The political issue at stake is the one that had already been revealed to the reader (5:18; 7:19), but its mention here presses it again into the scene at hand. The focus on "this man" (οὗτός) serves to introduce the theme of this section of the pericope (vv. 25–36).

7:26 "And here he is, speaking in public, and no one is saying anything to him. Can it be that the authorities have truly come to know that this man is the Christ?" (καὶ ἴδε παρρησίᾳ λαλεῖ καὶ οὐδὲν αὐτῷ λέγουσιν. μήποτε ἀληθῶς ἔγνωσαν οἱ ἄρχοντες ὅτι οὗτός ἐστιν ὁ Χριστός;). The Jerusalemites are surprised that the authorities are not responding to Jesus. The term we translated as "in public" (παρρησίᾳ) can also be used for a person who is acting with boldness, confidence, or fearlessness.[18] The Jerusalemites find this to be a strange irony. They even offer a concluding rebuke of the Jews in the form of a question: Have the authorities actually come to believe in him? This concluding question not only gives the reader further insight into the social challenge taking place but serves as a rebuke not of Jesus only but especially of the authorities. The term that begins

13. Barrett, *John*, 321.
14. Pancaro, *Law in the Fourth Gospel*, 166.
15. Morris, *John*, 363.
16. Wallace, *Greek Grammar*, 189–190.
17. BDAG 746.
18. BDAG 781.

the concluding question, "Can it be" (μήποτε), is a "marker of inquiry" that in this context levels a judgment against their own Jewish leadership.[19] Such a rebuke, however, is not true misalignment but only serves to strengthen and motivate the growing forces opposed to Jesus. The Jerusalemites reflect such a prominent disbelief that they have actually rebuked their own authorities for their inaction against "this man."

7:27 "But we know where this man is from; when the Christ comes, no one will know where he is from" (ἀλλὰ τοῦτον οἴδαμεν πόθεν ἐστίν· ὁ δὲ Χριστὸς ὅταν ἔρχηται οὐδεὶς γινώσκει πόθεν ἐστίν). The confidence with which the people of Jerusalem can rebuke their own leadership is further revealed as they provide their own answer to the question of the potential messianic identity of Jesus. With irony that could not be made clearer to the reader of the Gospel thus far, the Jerusalemites are against Jesus because, in contrast to the true Christ, "We know where this man is from" (τοῦτον οἴδαμεν πόθεν ἐστίν). There is no need to try to explicate the messianic assumptions of the Jerusalemites or first-century Jews in general, for the point of contrast is not between one expectation versus another but between heaven and earth itself. At this point, the reverberations from the prologue are crying out to the reader, who is well aware that Jesus *is* the Word-become-flesh, the light of humanity, the one "from above," who was "in the beginning" with God. The cosmological identity of Jesus, so visible to the reader, remains completely veiled to the Jerusalemites. The one these interlocutors call "this man" the reader has been told is "God" from the very beginning of the Gospel (1:1).

7:28 Then Jesus cried out and said, while teaching in the temple, "You know me and you know where I am from. However, I have not come here for myself, but the one who sent me is true, whom you do not know" (ἔκραξεν οὖν ἐν τῷ ἱερῷ διδάσκων ὁ Ἰησοῦς καὶ λέγων, Κἀμὲ οἴδατε καὶ οἴδατε πόθεν εἰμί· καὶ ἀπ' ἐμαυτοῦ οὐκ ἐλήλυθα, ἀλλ' ἔστιν ἀληθινὸς ὁ πέμψας με, ὃν ὑμεῖς οὐκ οἴδατε). In light of another response by Jesus without anyone speaking directly to him (e.g., 6:43, 61), along with the significant use of the verb translated "cried out" (ἔκραξεν), which always introduces a saying of importance (1:15; 7:37; 12:44), Jesus's response to the Jerusalemites gives the impression of a prophet.[20] The verb "calls attention to the importance and the solemnity of what follows."[21] This is further supported by the narrator's comment that this was said "in the temple." In the historical context this was a cryptic response by Jesus to the strong opinions of Jews from Jerusalem. But in the narrative context it was never meant to be cryptic, for in light of the cosmological context revealed by the Gospel this statement is a rebuke of their unbelief and the prideful opposition to Jesus that it breeds.

Jesus responds to their ironic statement with his own irony-filled rebuke. In one sense — the historical sense — they can name and locate his ancestral lineage. At the same time, however, and in a very different sense — the cosmological sense — they have no idea who he is or whose ancestral lineage they have challenged by their unbelief. The reader is expected to understand the paradox, even if it would have bypassed the Jerusalemites. For with a contrastive conjunction, "however" (καὶ), Jesus announces what the people of Jerusalem do not know, something he has explained elsewhere: the submission of himself for another (cf. 5:19).[22] The cryptic language Jesus uses to refer to his Father — "the one who sent me" (ὁ πέμψας με); the one who

---

19. BDAG 648.
20. Morris, *John*, 366.
21. Michaels, *John*, 452.
22. Schnackenburg, *John*, 2:147.

"is true" (ἔστιν ἀληθινὸς) — and his mission — "I have come" (ἐλήλυθα) — is intended to magnify the blindness and the lack of knowledge presumed by the Jerusalemites. What the people of Jerusalem think they know about Jesus has become the very evidence that proves there is another they do not know: God himself. Jesus said the same thing to the Samaritans three chapters earlier (4:22). And as the Gospel will make clear, not to know God is not to know Jesus. It is here where the Gospel's timely use of significant words becomes important. In contrast to the God who "is true," everything they have spoken is by implication a lie.

7:29 "I know him, because I am from him and he sent me" (ἐγὼ οἶδα αὐτόν, ὅτι παρ᾽ αὐτοῦ εἰμι κἀκεῖνός με ἀπέστειλεν). The confusion regarding the identity of Jesus is rooted in the Jerusalemites' confusion about God. It is not just that they do not know God but that without Jesus they *cannot* know God. Only the Son can claim emphatically about the Father, "I know him" (ἐγὼ οἶδα αὐτόν). And the reason is just as clear: the Son is from the Father and has been sent by him. The Gospel could not make any clearer the message it has already declared from the beginning (1:18) and will proclaim to its end (20:31) regarding the role and mission of Jesus Christ, the Son of God. With this closing statement of Jesus, the third verbal exchange comes to an end.

7:30 After this they were trying to seize him, yet no one laid a hand upon him, because his hour had not yet come (Ἐζήτουν οὖν αὐτὸν πιάσαι, καὶ οὐδεὶς ἐπέβαλεν ἐπ᾽ αὐτὸν τὴν χεῖρα, ὅτι οὔπω ἐληλύθει ἡ ὥρα αὐτοῦ). The narrator intrudes between the third and fourth verbal exchange to give three different reactions to the claims made by Jesus, both of which serve to advance the con-

flict portrayed by the narrative.[23] The narrator first explains that Jesus's statements resulted in the immediate attempt to capture him. Jesus had made absolute claims that required a serious response (cf. 5:18). Yet the narrator also explains that no one was able to lay "a hand" (τὴν χεῖρα) on him. The reason was "because his hour had not yet come" (ὅτι οὔπω ἐληλύθει ἡ ὥρα αὐτοῦ). No historical details are given — and none are needed. The only stated reason is the explanation of the "hour" (ἡ ὥρα), a significant term in the Gospel (see comments on 2:4). The reason is not grasped at the historical level of events but only at the cosmological level. Jesus had just made clear that the people do not know God; the narrator makes clear that the people cannot stop God.

7:31 But many from the crowd believed in him and said, "When the Christ comes, he will not do more signs than those that this man did, will he? (Ἐκ τοῦ ὄχλου δὲ πολλοὶ ἐπίστευσαν εἰς αὐτόν, καὶ ἔλεγον, Ὁ Χριστὸς ὅταν ἔλθη μὴ πλείονα σημεῖα ποιήσει ὧν οὗτος ἐποίησεν;). The second statement by the narrator is in regard to the public reaction to Jesus's claims. According to the narrator, many people from among "the crowd" (τοῦ ὄχλου) were beginning to believe in him. This belief, however, was anything but the type of belief heralded by the Fourth Gospel. Comparing the number of "signs" (σημεῖα) performed by Jesus with the presumed number of signs expected to be performed by "the Christ" (Ὁ Χριστὸς) when he comes, the crowd suggests by their question that the true Messiah will do more signs than "this man," clearly a derogatory term in this pericope. The irony is thick. The person and work of Jesus are eclipsed by a messianic delusion; it is a similar kind of confusion about God the Gospel portrayed earlier (cf. 5:1–18).

---

23. On the function of "after this" (οὖν), see A. T. Robertson, *A Grammar of the Greek New Testament in the Light of*

Historical Research (Nashville: Broadman, 1934), 1191.

7:32 The Pharisees heard the things the crowd was whispering concerning him, and the high priests and Pharisees sent the temple police to arrest him (Ἤκουσαν οἱ Φαρισαῖοι τοῦ ὄχλου γογγύζοντος περὶ αὐτοῦ ταῦτα, καὶ ἀπέστειλαν οἱ ἀρχιερεῖς καὶ οἱ Φαρισαῖοι ὑπηρέτας ἵνα πιάσωσιν αὐτόν). The third statement by the narrator is in regard to the official reaction to Jesus's claims, the response of the Jewish authorities. The narrator explains that the crowd was "whispering" (γογγύζοντος), a term that has been used negatively in the Gospel (cf. 6:41, 61) but is here merely a depiction of the behind-the-scenes discussion among those present (see comments on 7:12). The authorities were forced into action.

The narrator reveals what must be considered quite significant: both the Pharisees and the high priests responded to the whisperings. In short, while the Pharisees would have been closer to the people and more aware of their issues (see comments on 1:24), the "high priests" (οἱ ἀρχιερεῖς) were in the position of power. They were members of the leading priestly families, the "court" of the high priest, with the majority aligning with the party of the Sadducees — not the Pharisees (cf. Acts 5:17; Josephus, *Ant.* 20.199).[24] The narrator has given significance before to the combination of political parties (see comments on 3:1), so the inclusion here also intends to reflect the cumulative challenge facing Jesus. The narrator adds that the response of the Pharisees and high priests was the order to the temple police to arrest Jesus. The term we translated as "temple police" (ὑπηρέτας) more generally refers to a person who functions in a subordinate capacity, in this case in a religious context. While the term could be translated as "guards" or "officers," their function here is best described as "temple police," since they served both within the temple precincts and outside it for the purpose of maintaining public order.[25]

In this brief narrator intrusion, the Gospel shows that these three types of responses to Jesus's radical claims were limited in their ability to grasp Jesus. The first was physically unable to capture him (v. 30), the second was spiritually unable to believe in him (v. 31), and the third was unable to arrest him (v. 32), as vv. 45–46 will explain. In this way the narrator put this social challenge into its larger, cosmological context.

7:33 Then Jesus said, "I am only with you for a little longer, and then I go to the one who sent me" (εἶπεν οὖν ὁ Ἰησοῦς, Ἔτι χρόνον μικρὸν μεθ᾽ ὑμῶν εἰμι καὶ ὑπάγω πρὸς τὸν πέμψαντά με). The fourth verbal exchange begins differently from the others. In the first three, Jesus's interlocutors were the first to make a challenging statement, but in this final verbal exchange Jesus speaks first to the actions of the religious authorities with a political statement of his own. This statement of Jesus focuses not on his origin but on his mission (cf. vv. 25–29). Jesus declares that his mission is only for "a little longer" (Ἔτι χρόνον μικρόν), a statement which excludes the temple police or the powers above them from controlling what happens to him and when. In a sense, the treatment of Jesus is entirely in the hands of another authority, the God these people have failed to recognize (cf. v. 28). Jesus uses language befitting the cosmological insights already given to the reader by the prologue, language the Gospel will use from now on with more regularity.

7:34 "You will seek me and you will not find me, and where I am you are unable to come" (ζητήσετέ με καὶ οὐχ εὑρήσετέ [με], καὶ ὅπου εἰμὶ ἐγὼ ὑμεῖς οὐ δύνασθε ἐλθεῖν). In light of his unique identity and

---

24. Barrett, *John*, 324.

25. See Gary Manning Jr., "The Temple Police: Double Agents," in *Character Studies in the Fourth Gospel*, 388–96.

mission, Jesus now defines for his opponents the issue separating them. And the difference could not be more personal, for Jesus's statement makes a clear contrast between "I" and "you," denoted by means of grammatical emphasis. Jesus defines this contrast by means of his identity and mission from the Father. He cannot be contained or grasped by them, for he — God — has always been inaccessible to them. When Jesus states that he goes where they "are unable to come" (οὐ δύνασθε ἐλθεῖν), he is not speaking of a definitive place, but to the distinction between persons. Stated simply, "Jesus's opponents are of a different order."[26] Ironically, the God they seek to defend can only be known through the one they are attacking (1:18). Thus, Jesus's words are less a description of present circumstances and more a judgment from above.

7:35 Then the Jews said to themselves, "Where does this man intend to go that we cannot find him? Does he intend to go to those who are dispersed among the gentiles, and teach the gentiles?" (εἶπον οὖν οἱ Ἰουδαῖοι πρὸς ἑαυτούς, Ποῦ οὗτος μέλλει πορεύεσθαι ὅτι ἡμεῖς οὐχ εὑρήσομεν αὐτόν; μὴ εἰς τὴν διασπορὰν τῶν Ἑλλήνων μέλλει πορεύεσθαι καὶ διδάσκειν τοὺς Ἕλληνας;). The indirect nature of this final verbal exchange, with no actual dialogue presented from one interlocutor to the other, strongly emphasizes the "I" and "you" distinction mentioned above. This strange dialogue happens without any direct crossfire, but with one cosmological statement followed by an internal discussion in response. The audience is now simply described as "the Jews," which brings this multifaceted dialogue around full circle. The Jews respond with a myriad of questions that are intended to rebuke Jesus and reinforce their group's solidarity.

The statement by Jesus sounded like a riddle to those who heard him. The Jews clearly misunderstand the departure of Jesus; they have no categories appropriate to his identity or mission. Revealing their complete ignorance, they mockingly suggest that he might be speaking of a trip "to those who are dispersed among the gentiles" (εἰς τὴν διασπορὰν τῶν Ἑλλήνων). The Greek word for "dispersion" in the LXX frequently refers to the Jews who are no longer living in Israel and are living among gentiles, the heathen peoples of the world (e.g., Deut 28:25; 30:4; Jer 34:17), as well as to the dispersed people as a whole (e.g., Isa 49:6; Ps 147:2).[27] Thus, the Jews mockingly suggest that Jesus must be leaving Jerusalem for other Jews, possibly that he might then find a more favorable hearing. Even more, they suggest that Jesus will *also* be teaching gentiles — an abhorrent idea for the Jews. This comment serves as a further rebuke and rejection of the ministry and message of Jesus. If this final statement was intended to suggest Jesus would work with the gentiles, it serves less as a judgment and more as a prophecy.[28] What they deem to be too fantastic of a possibility, that any Jew — and surely not the Messiah — would intend to go and teach the gentiles (i.e., the world) is exactly what Jesus and his disciples, the church, intend to do.

7:36 "What is this statement that he said, 'You will seek me and you will not find me, and where I am you are unable to come?'" (τίς ἐστιν ὁ λόγος οὗτος ὃν εἶπεν, Ζητήσετέ με καὶ οὐχ εὑρήσετέ [με], καὶ ὅπου εἰμὶ ἐγὼ ὑμεῖς οὐ δύνασθε ἐλθεῖν). The Jews conclude their mockery of Jesus by repeating what he said in v. 34 in the form of a question. The forced anonymity that Jesus's opponents continually placed throughout the dialogue on "this man" (vv. 15, 25, 26, 27, 31, 35) did not help them dilute the effect that the specificity of his words was

---

26. Morris, *John*, 370.
27. Barrett, *John*, 325.

28. Hoskyns, *Fourth Gospel*, 319.

having on them. As Strachan describes it, "Sarcasm, however, often conceals a deep perplexity. The speakers are still haunted by Jesus's words."[29]

7:37 On the last and greatest day of the Feast, Jesus stood up and cried out saying, "If anyone is thirsty, let him come to me and drink" (Ἐν δὲ τῇ ἐσχάτῃ ἡμέρᾳ τῇ μεγάλῃ τῆς ἑορτῆς εἱστήκει ὁ Ἰησοῦς καὶ ἔκραξεν λέγων, Ἐάν τις διψᾷ ἐρχέσθω πρός με καὶ πινέτω). The dialogue has reached its climax at this point, with vv. 37 – 39 serving as a final exhortation by Jesus followed by an essential commentary by the narrator, who gives important details regarding the final exhortation of Jesus. While the four verbal exchanges above were described as starting about halfway through the Feast (v. 14), the narrator explains that this final statement takes place "on the last and greatest day of the Feast" (Ἐν δὲ τῇ ἐσχάτῃ ἡμέρᾳ τῇ μεγάλῃ τῆς ἑορτῆς). The Feast of Tabernacles concluded with a special festival day (see comments on 7:2), which the narrator clearly intends to emphasize. This final day, the eighth day,[30] was the climactic day of the Feast and would have been viewed as such by all in attendance.

Because the narrative immediately follows this important contextual detail with Jesus's invitation to drink, a connection between the two must be exegetically significant. It is not just chronology being presented to the reader but deep symbolism, rooted in the symbol-laden Feast of Tabernacles. The connection is likely to be rooted in the critical ritual of the water-drawing ceremony, including the procession from the pool of Siloam to the temple in which both people and priests marched, after which the priests would pour out water and wine at the base of the altar.[31] The water-drawing ceremony was not only part of the celebration of the Feast but was also connected to the provision (and securing) of rain. Since the Feast directly precedes the rainy season, this concluding ceremony was an expression of dependence on the divine miracle of rain — an essential component of life itself.[32] Interestingly, like the confused superstition surrounding the healing pools of 5:1 – 18, numerous Jewish teachers and traditions made rain dependent upon the Feast and its festivities, possibly even primarily by means of the water-drawing ceremony.[33]

To impress further upon the reader this significance, the narrator describes not only the potent words of Jesus but even his intentional action: "Jesus stood up and cried out" (εἱστήκει ὁ Ἰησοῦς καὶ ἔκραξεν). In a moment hard to fathom in the presence of such a sacred feast and ceremony, God himself stood to address his people. Such a statement is not mere speech but can only be described in the language used of the prophets of God (see comments on v. 28). For the first time a prophet did not preface his address with, "Thus says the Lord," for this prophet was *the* Prophet, the Word-of-God-become-flesh. And "this Feast" (see 7:8) and water-drawing ceremony belonged in their entirety to him.

Before dealing with the actual statement of Jesus, which occurs in the next verse (v. 38), we must first address a debated issue of its interpretation. The punctuation of the statement in question is difficult to define with precision. The punctuation is important because it serves to explain from whom the streams of living water flow, whether the believer or Christ. There are two primary options: 1) the "traditional interpretation" places a full stop at the end of v. 37 and therefore understands the believer to be the source of living water; 2) the "christological interpretation" places only a comma

---

29. R. H. Strachan, *The Fourth Gospel: Its Significance and Environment* (London: SCM, 1941), 200.

30. Cf. Bultmann, *John*, 302; Barrett, *John*, 326.

31. Keener, *John*, 1:722.

32. Ibid., 1:723.

33. Ibid., 1:723 – 24.

at the end of v. 37, with the full stop not coming until right before the Scripture statement; it thus understands Christ to be the source of living water. While there are several mediating positions, these two options dominate the history of interpretive discussion.[34]

Option (1), the traditional interpretation, is the preferred interpretation. What is certainly to be viewed as the beginning of the narrator's intrusion is this transitional statement, "But he said this" (τοῦτο δὲ εἶπεν), found at the beginning of v. 39. As Fee helpfully notes, this is a stylistic feature in John, five times interrupting Jesus's statements (2:11; 6:6; 6:71; 12:33; 21:19), once interrupting Caiaphas's statement (11:51), and once interrupting Judas's statement (12:6). In each instance, the formula refers specifically to a saying which immediately precedes it.[35] Thus, vv. 37 – 38 are best understood to be the voice of Jesus, with v. 39 alone being the voice of the narrator. The traditional interpretation in no way denies that Christ is the mediating source of living water but appropriately places the believer *in relation to* Jesus and *his* benefits. As we will argue below, the emphasis placed on the Spirit in the believer is not for the purpose of eclipsing Christ but to assert that the spectacular presence of God the Spirit, mediated through the glorification of God the Son (sent by God the Father), has eternal ramifications for the believer. To pit the believer against Christ is to miss not only the clear invitation of this pericope but also the entire message of the Gospel.

Jesus begins by declaring emphatically, "If anyone is thirsty, let him come to me and drink" (Ἐάν τις διψᾷ ἐρχέσθω πρός με καὶ πινέτω). Much of this echoes what Jesus said to the Samaritan woman (see comments on 4:10 – 14). But in light of the context of this statement — in the shadow of the

temple at the pinnacle of the Feast of Tabernacles on the day of the water-drawing ceremony — such a statement offers an even more robust eschatological declaration. At the point in the ritual where God was beckoned to provide water, the most necessary substance for his people and for life itself, Jesus stands and declares himself to be not only the provision but also the provider.

7:38 "The one who believes in me, just as it is written in Scripture, streams of living water will flow from within him" (ὁ πιστεύων εἰς ἐμέ, καθὼς εἶπεν ἡ γραφή, ποταμοὶ ἐκ τῆς κοιλίας αὐτοῦ ῥεύσουσιν ὕδατος ζῶντος). This verse continues the final exhortation of Jesus and makes an important connection between Jesus and Scripture. First, the "streams of living water" are, according to Jesus, given specifically to "the one who believes in me" (ὁ πιστεύων εἰς ἐμέ). Jesus is claiming that the believer is precisely a believer because he believes in *him*. One cannot simply distinguish a believer from Christ, for Christ is the object of belief, the very ground for qualifying as a believer.

Second, Jesus connects his final exhortation to Scripture's promise. Attempts to determine the specific text of Scripture have proved fruitless, since "the Scripture" Jesus envisages is at the macrolevel of Scripture adopted from a number of places. In light of the contextual significance provided by the narrator (v. 37), it is more likely that the biblical allusions are intended to be funneled through not just possible textual parallels but the "impressions" (see Introduction) created by the specific social-religious context of the climactic day of the Feast of Tabernacles, with its water-drawing ceremony happening at the center of Jerusalem in the shadow of the temple. This context, together with Jesus's promise of the Spirit, should give us some insight into the kind of text(s) in mind. For

---

34. For an overview, see Brown, *John*, 1:320 – 21.

35. Gordon D. Fee, "Once More — John 7[37 – 39]," *ExpTim* 89 (1978): 116 – 18 (116).

example, while not exclusively a reference to Nehemiah 8–9, in which the Israelites return after the exile and are pictured obeying Deuteronomy 31:10–11 and therefore celebrating the Feast of Tabernacles, the connection in Nehemiah 9:20 between manna/water (thirst) and the Spirit serves to make Jesus the ultimate fulfillment.[36] Or in Revelation 21:6, where Jesus declares, "It is done. I am the Alpha and the Omega, the Beginning and the End. To the thirsty I will give water without cost from the spring of the water of life." This end-of-history exhortation parallels not only the language of vv. 37–38 but also the larger context and message of John's Gospel — Jesus is the fulfillment, for his standing before the people and crying out this message on this significant day is itself a statement of finality: "It is done!"

It is in the context of these rituals and eschatological promises that this final statement must be understood: "Streams of living water will flow from within him" (ποταμοὶ ἐκ τῆς κοιλίας αὐτοῦ ῥεύσουσιν ὕδατος ζῶντος). With these words Jesus offers the fulfillment of Judaism — and of life itself — in a very personal way. The phrase we translated as "from within him" (ἐκ τῆς κοιλίας αὐτοῦ) often refers to the "belly" or "stomach," but in this context is referring in a metaphorical manner to the inner "organ of nourishment," specifically to the "seat of inward life."[37] This divine blessing is not to be wished and prayed for superstitiously in traditional rituals at the end of the Feast of Tabernacles but is provided directly through "the Tabernacling One" (cf. 1:14) standing before them.

7:39 But this he said about the Spirit, which the ones who believed in him were about to receive. For the Spirit was not yet [given], be-cause Jesus had not yet been glorified (τοῦτο δὲ εἶπεν περὶ τοῦ πνεύματος ὃ ἔμελλον λαμβάνειν οἱ πιστεύσαντες εἰς αὐτόν· οὔπω γὰρ ἦν πνεῦμα, ὅτι Ἰησοῦς οὐδέπω ἐδοξάσθη). After this final and climactic exhortation of Jesus, the narrator gives the meaning of this significant statement. The key is provided when the narrator explains that the subject matter of Jesus's statement of vv. 37–38 is the Spirit. This clarifies what is meant by the phrase "living water," which occurred both in this dialogue (v. 38) as well as in Jesus's dialogue with the Samaritan woman (4:10–11). The narrator speaks from a postresurrection perspective (see 2:21–22), and the statement contains the cosmological insights of the unseen, reminiscent of the prologue's cosmic vision. And in this case it is also a post-Pentecost perspective, since the timing of this event in the narrative is explained by means of the coming of the Spirit in real, historical time.

The final statement by the narrator is awkward and complex, but need not be confusing. The narrator describes the Spirit as "not yet" (οὔπω), to which some add the word "given." But our translation will not add that interpretive implication because the point is not the timeline of the Spirit but the powerful manifestation of the Spirit as just described by Jesus. To speak of the Spirit as nonexistent or inactive is to misunderstand the third person of the Trinity. In a sense, the point is not to describe when the Spirit meets the world, but when believers are given the grace to meet the Spirit. And none of this was possible until Jesus was "glorified" (ἐδοξάσθη). The narrator, then, takes the reader to the cross. Ironically, the original audience on this last and greatest day of the Feast of Tabernacles would, for very different reasons, move closer to taking Jesus to the very same place.

---

36. Other possible OT connections can be found in Num 20:11; 24:6–9; Prov 4:23; 5:15; Isa 12:3; 44:3; 49:10; Ezek 36:25–27; 47:1–12; Joel 3:18; Amos 9:11–15; Zech 13:1; 14:8. See Carson, *John*, 326–27.

37. BDAG 550–51.

7:40 After hearing his words, some from the crowd said, "This man is truly the Prophet" (Ἐκ τοῦ ὄχλου οὖν ἀκούσαντες τῶν λόγων τούτων ἔλεγον, Οὗτός ἐστιν ἀληθῶς ὁ προφήτης). After this final exhortation, the narrative reveals the public reaction to Jesus and his message. The general public has a mixed reaction to Jesus that is portrayed as doubtful at best. One portion of the crowd responded with the strongly affirming adverb "truly" (ἀληθῶς) and called him "the Prophet" (ὁ προφήτης). The crowd seems convinced that Jesus is the Prophet (see comments on 1:21). John the Baptist was once questioned in regard to this title (1:21), as was Jesus earlier in the narrative (6:14). Here, however, the crowd is convinced not by what he did — his "signs" — but by what he had to say — his "words" (τῶν λόγων).

7:41 Others said, "This man is the Christ." And still others said, "How can the Messiah come out of Galilee?" (ἄλλοι ἔλεγον, Οὗτός ἐστιν ὁ Χριστός· οἱ δὲ ἔλεγον, Μὴ γὰρ ἐκ τῆς Γαλιλαίας ὁ Χριστὸς ἔρχεται;). The narrator tells us that another section of the crowd considered Jesus to be "the Messiah" (ὁ Χριστός; see comments on 1:20; cf. 1:40 – 41). We can only surmise that Jesus's message of the Spirit sparked eschatological connections for the crowd that suggested to them that Jesus was more than a prophet or a forerunner of the Messiah. Others in the crowd, however, responded negatively by questioning how the Messiah could come "out of Galilee" (ἐκ τῆς Γαλιλαίας). Since Jesus was reckoned to be a Galilean, some thought that he was apparently disqualified to be the Messiah.

7:42 "Does not the Scripture say the Christ will come out of the seed of David, and out of Bethlehem, the town where David was from?" (οὐχ ἡ γραφὴ εἶπεν ὅτι ἐκ τοῦ σπέρματος Δαυὶδ, καὶ ἀπὸ Βηθλέεμ τῆς κώμης ὅπου ἦν Δαυίδ, ὁ Χριστὸς ἔρχεται;). The negative question in v. 41 is given an appropriate response in v. 42. The section of the crowd that questions Jesus gives warrant for their concern over his origin by resting on the authority of "the Scripture" (ἡ γραφὴ). The qualifications Jesus apparently fails to meet include the following: 1) the Christ must be a descendent of David, and 2) the Christ must be born in Bethlehem, the ancestral home of David (see Mic 5:2; cf. Ps 89). The reader cannot avoid seeing stark irony in every part of the crowd's reflections. Jesus has already rebuked what he has seen of their interpretation of Scripture (cf. 5:45 – 47); the narrator allows the reader to come to the same conclusion in this instance. Jesus *was* from the line of David and from the town of Bethlehem. But the narrator leaves this correction to the Synoptic Gospels, the rest of the biblical canon, and early Christian tradition. For this Gospel, Jesus is not merely from Bethlehem; he is "from above" (cf. 3:1 – 15).

7:43 Then a division broke out among the crowd because of him (σχίσμα οὖν ἐγένετο ἐν τῷ ὄχλῳ δι᾽ αὐτόν). The mixed reactions of the crowd — where Jesus is anything from the Prophet/Christ (for whom they have been waiting) to a fraud (who needed to be exposed) — created among the crowd a "division" (σχίσμα). This term occurs at other key points in the narrative (see also 9:16; 10:19). To the reader this division is understood to be a natural consequence of Jesus's person and work: the chaos of the darkness (1:5), the superstition and God-confusion underpinning their theology, and the absence of the true object of worship in their religion.

7:44 Some of them wanted him to be arrested, but no one laid a hand upon him (τινὲς δὲ ἤθελον ἐξ αὐτῶν πιάσαι αὐτόν, ἀλλ᾽ οὐδεὶς ἐπέβαλεν ἐπ᾽ αὐτὸν τὰς χεῖρας). The mixed reaction to Jesus in theory was also reflected in practice. While some wanted him to be contained by the authorities, probably those who considered him to be a fraud stirring up trouble during the Feast of Tabernacles, no one touched him. The narrator described the same result in light of earlier attempts to seize Jesus, and the reason can only be the same: "Because his hour had not yet come" (v. 30).

7:45 Then the temple police came to the high priests and the Pharisees, and they said to them, "Why did you not bring him in?" (Ἦλθον οὖν οἱ ὑπηρέται πρὸς τοὺς ἀρχιερεῖς καὶ Φαρισαίους, καὶ εἶπον αὐτοῖς ἐκεῖνοι, Διὰ τί οὐκ ἠγάγετε αὐτόν;). The scene transitions from the discussion among the general public to the internal discussion among the Jewish leadership. This is what we described above as the second multifaceted verbal exchange, again involving a complex set of rotating interlocutors. It consists of three exchanges. In this first exchange of vv. 45–46, the Jewish authorities demand an answer for the lack of response to Jesus by the temple police, almost certainly in light of their command earlier for Jesus to be arrested (v. 32).

7:46 The temple police answered, "A man has never spoken like this" (ἀπεκρίθησαν οἱ ὑπηρέται, Οὐδέποτε ἐλάλησεν οὕτως ἄνθρωπος). The temple police offer only one response in their own defense: "A man has never spoken like this" (Οὐδέποτε ἐλάλησεν οὕτως ἄνθρωπος). Whatever incompetence this reveals about their role as temple police only magnifies their competence as witnesses to "the otherness" of Jesus. Again, the "words" of Jesus are highlighted as significant (cf. v. 40). There is no mention of the chaotic crowd, or the political ramifications that might result from their inability to act, or even the escape of Jesus; the only thing that stopped them was his word (cf. 11:1–4). The first verbal exchange ends, according to the narrative presentation of it, more as a witness to Jesus than as a controlling move by the Jewish leadership.

7:47 Then the Pharisees responded to them, "Surely you have not also been deceived?" (ἀπεκρίθησαν οὖν αὐτοῖς οἱ Φαρισαῖοι, Μὴ καὶ ὑμεῖς πεπλάνησθε;). In response the Pharisees shame the temple police by aligning them with the fickle actions of the crowd. In later rabbinic literature the term "deceiver" was a significant title given to those accused of being heretics and was the specific accusation made against Jesus by later Judaism. The narrative reveals that the true interlocutor is Jesus. This is supported by the significant term "deceived" (πεπλάνησθε), which suggests that the ultimate opponent is not the ones tempted by the so-called deceiver, but the accused deceiver himself, Jesus (see comments on 7:12). This is the beginning of the second verbal exchange (vv. 47–49).

7:48 "Surely no one from among the rulers or the Pharisees believed in him?" (μή τις ἐκ τῶν ἀρχόντων ἐπίστευσεν εἰς αὐτὸν ἢ ἐκ τῶν Φαρισαίων;). This question, expecting a negative answer, must be grasped for all its significance by the reader. What was intended to be an argument to support the rebuke of the incompetent temple police and fickle crowd serves an entirely different end. In light of vv. 50–52, this statement is blatantly ironic and serves again to witness in the exact opposite direction intended by its speaker(s).

7:49 "But this crowd that cannot understand the law—they are accursed!" (ἀλλὰ ὁ ὄχλος οὗτος ὁ μὴ γινώσκων τὸν νόμον ἐπάρατοί εἰσιν). The second verbal exchange ends like the first, with a cultural shaming of the interlocutor, the crowd, who is rebuked by the leadership for not being able to "understand" (γινώσκων) the law, a term which could more simply be translated as "know" but in this context reflects not just factual knowledge but application.[38] While the temple police were rebuked for being incompetent employees, the crowd is rebuked for being incompetent Jews, for which they are pronounced as cursed.[39]

---

38. BDAG 200.

39. Cf. Bultmann, *John*, 310.

7:50 Nicodemus, the one who came to Jesus earlier, who was one of their own, said: (λέγει Νικόδημος πρὸς αὐτούς, ὁ ἐλθὼν πρὸς αὐτὸν τὸ πρότερον, εἷς ὢν ἐξ αὐτῶν). The third verbal exchange (vv. 50–52) begins with the reappearance of Nicodemus, whom the narrator describes with intentional precision. Nicodemus is not only the same person who challenged Jesus earlier (3:1–15), but he is also "one of their own" (εἷς ὢν ἐξ αὐτῶν), that is, an insider among the Jewish leadership. If the significance of his statement is to be grasped, our discussion of Nicodemus's person and rank in 3:1–15 is extremely important here (see comments on 3:1). Nicodemus is a prestigious Jewish authority and challenger of Jesus.

7:51 "Does our law condemn a man without first hearing from him and understanding what he is doing?" (Μὴ ὁ νόμος ἡμῶν κρίνει τὸν ἄνθρωπον ἐὰν μὴ ἀκούσῃ πρῶτον παρ᾽ αὐτοῦ καὶ γνῷ τί ποιεῖ;). On the surface this could be taken as a simple concern that the law not be abused, a concern for justice. But in light of the context, Nicodemus's question is anything but a mere concern for legal principle and practice. As v. 52 will confirm, it is hardly received as a legal footnote by the rest of the Jewish leadership, who respond with an equally loaded question connecting Nicodemus to Jesus.

Interestingly, Nicodemus does not just suggest giving Jesus a hearing but also suggests "understanding what he is doing," with the verb "understanding" (γνῷ) serving as a fitting counter to the charge of the Jewish leadership against the crowd in v. 49 that they did "understand" (γινώσκων) the law. The same negligence displayed by the crowd in understanding the *word* of God (the law) that gave the Jewish leadership warrant to curse them is being applied to the Jewish leadership by one of their own because of the negligence they display in understanding the *Word* of God.

7:52 They answered and said to him, "Surely you also are not from Galilee? Search and see that a prophet does not arise from Galilee." (ἀπεκρίθησαν καὶ εἶπαν αὐτῷ, Μὴ καὶ σὺ ἐκ τῆς Γαλιλαίας εἶ; ἐραύνησον καὶ ἴδε ὅτι προφήτης ἐκ τῆς Γαλιλαίας οὐκ ἐγείρεται). The Jewish leaders respond strongly to Nicodemus with a question that expects a negative answer, thus serving to mock his idea and by implication the person who said it. The sharp rebuke is significant in two ways. First, by drawing a preposterous connection between Nicodemus and Jesus in relation to place of origin, the Jewish leadership heaps upon Nicodemus cultural shame, since by implication his comments were interpreted to be favorable toward Jesus. This is clearly a combative rebuke, a comment befitting a social challenge. In this way, Nicodemus is separated from the Jewish leadership by his fellow authorities. There is no need for us to surmise what Nicodemus intended to do, for the Jewish leadership interprets his intentions for the reader.

Second, such a preposterous rebuke would only work if the exact opposite were in fact true. Only if Nicodemus was known not to be from Galilee would the accusation befit the scene at hand. Thus, it is only because the Jewish leadership knows full well that Nicodemus is not a Galilean that such a comment could serve as a rebuke and chastisement. This implicitly matches at least in part the interpretation of Nicodemus presented in 3:1–15, where he is understood to be a well-known, wealthy, powerful, and influential leader at the center of Judaism. He was certainly not from such an unimportant territory as Galilee. In his first appearance in the Gospel Nicodemus was a challenger of Jesus; in this appearance he is a challenger of his own Jerusalem colleagues, the Jewish leadership.

In contrast to Nicodemus, the Jewish authorities close the scene with their own answer to the Jesus question. They present a double-imperative statement, "Search and see" (ἐραύνησον καὶ ἴδε), which is meant to summarize their interpretation of Scripture in regard to the activities (the "signs") of Jesus. It is interesting to note that they direct Nicodemus to what (they think) is *not* in Scripture rather than what is.[40] Even more, their statement is misguided, because some prophets *did* arise out of Galilee (e.g., Jonah, who was from Gath Hepher, a few miles north of Nazareth in Galilee; 2 Kgs 14:25). And according to Keener, later rabbinic traditions liked to emphasize that prophets had arisen from every tribe and sometimes every city in Israel (e.g., b. Sukkah 27b).[41] While the Jewish leaders might have been intending to refer to "the Prophet" and not just any prophet, the presentation made by the narrative is clear enough. Their ignorance is not merely at the historical level — forgetting a detail from their own Scripture — but is an error of cosmological proportions. Again, the parallels to the Nicodemus narrative are telling; it was to Nicodemus that Jesus first declared that he — and that which he had to offer — was "from above" (3:3).

This third and climactic verbal exchange at the end of a lengthy social challenge offers a strong message to the reader. What had begun as a dialogue between Jesus and a diverse set of interlocutors ended with an internal dialogue within the leadership of Judaism. While any interpretation of Nicodemus's words in this exchange must also include his actions at the crucifixion narrated later (19:38 – 40), the narrative seems to suggest a positive assessment here. We can only guess that Nicodemus's public support of Jesus must have been viewed as a betrayal of his family and its well-known historical heritage (again, see comments on 3:1). At the same time, it is hard not to surmise that Nicodemus was beginning to embrace a new family with an even greater heritage. The message of "new birth" (3:3) that Jesus had declared to him earlier may have forged within him an understanding of a more prestigious identity in the "kingdom of God" (3:5) as one who had been given "the right to become children of God" (1:12).[42]

Theology in Application

In a scene loaded with ceremonial and political significance, the complex verbal exchange presented by this pericope magnifies the provision of Christ and the challenge confronting his person and ministry in the world. Jesus is presented simultaneously as the provision and provider of life itself in the context of the ceremony of the Feast of Tabernacles and as a clear and present danger to the established religion of Judaism. While the length of the pericope might be difficult for some to preach or teach as a whole, the message should at least be maintained in the context of the dialogue and its movement, for the dialogical drama of the pericope adds important depth and focus to the presentation of Jesus and his work, especially with its climactic and surprising ending.

---

40. Michaels, *John*, 475.
41. Keener, *John*, 1:734.

42. Cf. Nicolas Farelly, "An Unexpected Ally: Nicodemus's Role within the Plot of the Fourth Gospel," *TrinJ* 34 (2013): 31 – 43 (40).

Jesus, the Provision of God

The stage upon which this scene is dramatized is the center of the Feast of Tabernacles, a symbol-laden holiday that was connected to the spiritual and daily life of every Jew. It was in this symbolic context on the "last and greatest day of the Feast" (v. 37) that Jesus prophetically declared himself to be the provision of God. There could be no confusion regarding his claim; at that moment Jesus was eclipsing what God had previously ordained as appropriate worship and religion. At that moment, God was fulfilling with the reality to which the ceremony was only able to point. When Jesus stood up to speak at the pinnacle of the ceremony, the God and promises of the Old Testament coalesced in his person and work.

The church declares that Jesus is the provision of God, the source and meaning of true life. This is a declaration to all people that the thirst of our souls can only be satisfied by Jesus Christ. There is no other solution — Jesus has a monopoly on truth and life (14:6).

My Teaching Is Not Mine

If Christ can claim that his teaching does not belong to him but to "the one who sent" him (v. 16), how much more must the Christian declare likewise? If Christ can disassociate himself from what he received from the Father, how much more must the Christian? What do we have that we did not receive (1 Cor 4:7)? We do not have a theology, a ministry, a baptism; that church we attend is not "our church." No! They all belong to our Father, who in his grace and mercy allows us to participate in them for our good and his glory. When we do speak of "our church," "our ministry," or "our doctrine," we must do so with caution. With Luther we should be willing to say, "It is mine and yet it is not mine; for it is God's, the heavenly Father's. But at the same time it is I who proclaim and espouse such doctrine."[43] This is the example set for us by Christ, who created the world and yet would not claim his mission to restore the world as something that belonged to him alone.

The Spirit of Jesus

The narrator reveals to the reader what had been mysterious before, that the "streams of living water" that would "flow from within" are nothing less than the gift of the Holy Spirit. Christ's statement in vv. 37 – 38 reflects the deep symbiosis between the fulfillment and satisfaction Jesus provides and the gift of the indwelling Holy Spirit. The unity between the Father and the Son is only matched by the unity between the Son and the Spirit. And the recipient of these expressions of the love

---

43. Luther, *John*, 23:224.

and power of the Trinitarian God is the believer, who becomes a child of the Father, a brother to the Son, and a temple of the Holy Spirit.

Such truth is not easily articulated, for it speaks of the cosmological reality that this Gospel is slowly unfolding before the reader. The Spirit is not an add-on or a bonus feature but is the manifestation of everything Christ will accomplish for the world. And this fact is filled with irony. The location of the Spirit is not in the temple and mediated by priests but is in the very being of the Christian. Even more, this experience of the Spirit is not celebrated once a year at a special feast but daily in the life of the believer. And finally, the source of the Spirit is not the joyous feast of a glorious holiday but comes by means of the suffering and death of Christ on the cross. Ironically, the Spirit is our receipt that Christ has died in our stead and that we have been given new life in him.

"Make the Right Judgment"

In v. 24 Jesus concludes his rebuke of the crowd by saying, "Stop judging by outward appearance, but make the right judgment." Jesus was not merely addressing their poor application of Scripture, but a poorly founded faith — a faith defined entirely by the historical and not the cosmological. There is no easy way to define "the right judgment," for in many ways such a phrase summarizes the message of the entire Bible concerning the actions of the person made new in Christ. Augustine is correct when he explains that "it requires great labor in this world" to adopt right judgments about life and its activities — God, self, humanity, good, evil, etc.[44] Calvin writes in this regard, "Judgment will never be right unless it is formed from the truth of reality. For as soon as personality comes into it, eyes and senses are focused on that and the truth immediately disappears."[45]

The goal of the Christian, then, is to be rooted in the truth (Jesus, the gospel) and to express that truth in the life one is given to live. This requires a healthy and God-centered self-criticism that burns with the call to repentance and is drenched with the declaration of forgiveness. It involves looking into the "face" of Jesus and his word rather than our human-forged mirrors (see comments on v. 24). It involves the full body of Christ, through whom the Spirit of Jesus is already at work.

"The Conqueror of the People"

The pericope ends with a clear twist. The chief challenger of Jesus in chapter 3 becomes his only defender in chapter 7. The historical connections between Nicodemus and the Gurion family are difficult not to suggest. Nicodemus was a man born into a prestigious and heroic family. He was a descendent of a successful general in

---

44. Augustine, *John*, 30.7.188.   45. Calvin, *John 1 – 10*, 191.

the Hasmonean period and was surrounded by the laudatory praise of honor that came with his social status. He was a man who has connections in both religious parties — both of whom were against Jesus in this scene. And he had come to "understand" Jesus in a new way (see comments on v. 51). The narrative does not give us the details of his new status but only relates his significant and surprising action — a brief glimpse at the new status of Nicodemus more fully perceived in chapter 19.

Nicodemus, with the Baptist, joins a short list of people in this Gospel who were challenged by the authorities on account of Jesus. The "conqueror of the people," from the great military family called Gurion, had just waged a new war, but this time against his own people. Why? Because this descendent of a general had just lost the war he had been primed to fight long before his birth and was now receiving — by means of a "new birth" (3:3) — orders to wage a very different war. He was still fighting for his people and for Judaism, but this time not with weapons made by human hands but with the gospel of Jesus Christ; not with sword and shield but with the cross and by the Spirit. So too the Christian! The reader of this Gospel is coming to know full well that this challenge between God and the world also involves them and their lives. The Christian must come to "understand" that true life is death to self (Luke 9:23), and the battle to be fought is not done with our strength but in the weakness of God displayed on the cross.

John 7:53 – 8:11

Literary Context

The narrative moves from an intense dialogue between Jesus and a complex array of interlocutors to a heated scene involving legal and religious politics regarding a woman, who is presumed guilty of adultery, and Jesus, who is presumed guilty of insurrection and heresy. This is the final scene of the section of the Gospel entitled "the Confession of the Son of God" (5:1 – 8:11), in which the authoritative establishment of Judaism finally comes to understand that neither cultural shaming nor legal challenge will stifle the radical ministry activity of Jesus.

IV. The Confession of the Son of God (5:1 – 8:11)
  A. The Third Sign: The Healing of the Lame Man on the Sabbath (5:1 – 18)
  B. The Identity of (the Son of) God: Jesus Responds to the Opposition (5:19 – 47)
  C. The Fourth Sign: The Feeding of a Large Crowd (6:1 – 15)
  D. The "I AM" Walks across the Sea (6:16 – 21)
  E. The Bread of Life (6:22 – 71)
  F. Private Display of Suspicion (7:1 – 13)
  G. Public Display of Rejection (7:14 – 52)
➡ **H. The Trial of Jesus regarding a Woman Accused of Adultery (7:53 – 8:11)**

Main Idea

Jesus is the true Judge of humanity, "the one without sin," who receives on behalf of the world the condemnation of his own law. This is the grace and love of the gospel. The only acceptable response is to live under the gracious law of Christ, which seeks the promotion of justice and the demotion of sin.

Translation

(See next page.)

John 7:53–8:11

	Introduction & Setting (7:53–8:2)	
53a	Departure of Antagonists	And then **each went to his home.**
1a	Departure of Protagonist	Then **Jesus went to the Mount of Olives.**
2a		And
b	Time	early in the morning
c	Action	**he came again to the temple,**
d	Reaction	and **all the people came to him,**
f	Reaction	and **he sat down and was teaching them.**
3a	Conflict (3–6c)	Then **the scribes and the Pharisees led a woman**
b	Description	who had been caught in adultery
c	Action	and **they placed her in the midst of the people.**
4a		**They said to him,**
b	Hyperbolic Address	"Teacher,
c	Accusation	this woman has been caught in the act of adultery.
5a	Interpretation of OT Law	And in the law Moses commanded us to stone such women.
b	Interrogative Challenge	What …
c		then,
d		… do you say?"
6a	Narrator's Aside	**They were saying this**
b	Communicative Intention	with the purpose of testing him,
c	Purpose	in order that they might have grounds ✍ to accuse him.
	Resolution (6d–8)	
d	Reaction #1	But **Jesus bent down**
e	Reaction #2	and **began writing on the ground with his finger.**
7a		But
b	Escalation of Circumstances	when they continued to question him,
c	Counterchallenge	**he stood up and said to them,**
d	Condition	"Let the one without sin among you …
e	Inferential Imperative	… be the first to throw a stone at her."
8a	Resumed Action of 6d, e	And **again Jesus bent and wrote on the ground.**
	Conclusion (9–11)	
9a		After hearing this
b	Reaction	**they began to leave**
c	Manner of Departure: Defeat /	one by one,
d		beginning with the older ones,
e	Resulting Setting	and **he was left alone,**
f		and **the woman was there in the midst.**
10a		But **Jesus stood up and asked her,**
b	Address	"Woman,
c	Rhetorical Questions	where are they?
d		Has no one condemned you?"
11a	Response	**She said,**
b		"No one, sir."
c	Response	Then **Jesus said,**
d	Gracious Action	"Then neither do I condemn you;
e	Concluding Commands	go,
f		and from now on sin no longer."

Structure and Literary Form

This pericope corresponds to the basic story form (see Introduction). The *introduction/setting* is established in 7:53 – 8:2, explaining the location, setting, and people around whom the plot's conflict will focus. In 8:3 – 6a the *conflict* of the pericope is set before Jesus, centering upon a woman, adultery, and the law of Moses. In 8:6b – 8 the conflict is given *resolution* by a single statement of Jesus framed by a symbolic action of Jesus. Finally, 8:9 – 11 offer the *conclusion/interpretation* to the pericope of the woman accused of adultery, with a clear depiction of the gospel of Jesus Christ made possible by the authoritative activities of the true Judge.

Exegetical Outline

➡ **H. The Trial of Jesus regarding a Woman Accused of Adultery (7:53 – 8:11)**

　　1. Teaching in the Temple (7:53 – 8:2)
　　2. The Law of Moses and Adultery (vv. 3 – 6a)
　　3. The Finger of God (vv. 6b – 8)
　　4. The Law of Christ (vv. 9 – 11)

Explanation of the Text

Since this pericope is strongly questioned in regard to its connection to the original version of the Gospel of John, many view it as an *addendum*, a later addition to the Gospel narrative (see below). Yet in spite of this text-critical mystery, this pericope plays a significant role in the developing narrative, serving as a conclusion to several burgeoning is-sues in chapter 7 and as the climactic episode to the section, "The Confession of the Son of God" (5:1 – 8:11), by clearly showing to the Jewish authorities the authority of Jesus. As the received and contemporary form of the Gospel today, the story guides the reader to see in climactic fashion the confession of Jesus and his mission to the world.

IN DEPTH: The Text-Critical Problem of 7:53 – 8:11

This pericope is famous for several reasons. The pleasant reason is that it is one of the most dramatic displays of the grace of God in the Bible, famously entitled, "The Pericope of the Woman Caught in Adultery." But there is also a more difficult reason that needs to be addressed, for it is very possible that this pericope was not in the original version of the Gospel of John but was added later at an undeterminable time and for an unknown reason. There are several text-critical, interpretive, and pastoral issues that need to be addressed.

The text-critical evidence is strong: this pericope was almost certainly not in the original version of the Gospel of John.[1] The external evidence has been explored so thoroughly that we need only summarize the evidence here:

1. The pericope is entirely absent from all pre-fifth century AD manuscripts.
2. When it does appear, it is located in ten different places in the manuscript traditions (e.g., after John 7:36, 44, 52, 21:25, and Luke 21:38).[2]
3. The pericope contains a large and consistent number of non-Johannine literary features.[3]
4. The pericope is not dealt with in early patristic writings up to the fourth century; moreover, no Greek church father prior to the twelfth century comments on it.

The above evidence strongly suggests that this pericope does not belong to the original Gospel. This is hardly an answer, however, but rather an entirely new question. For nearly every contemporary Bible — even if the text is given double brackets or italics or a smaller font — contains this pericope, thereby declaring to today's reader that it is part of the Gospel of John. If contemporary Christians were reading one of the early papyrus copies of John (such as $\mathfrak{P}^{66}$), we could more easily move beyond this pericope. It exists, however, and even if it did not commonly occur until the eighth century, it has been for the last thirteen hundred years a present and cherished pericope. For this reason, we must offer a fitting response to this issue; not only one that meets the standards of textual criticism, but also one that is appropriate for a text that has been cherished for centuries by the church.

Since the pericope cannot be confirmed by textual criteria, the primary means of solidifying support for the pericope has been by historical criteria. The argument goes as follows. Since the pericope can be shown to be ancient (rooted in the oral tradition that supplied our Gospels with raw materials) and authentic (matching the criteria used to determine what in the Gospels Jesus truly did and said), the text is deemed appropriate for Christian use and reflection. Its insertion into the Gospel of John suggests that earlier Christians deemed it likewise. It is used in every contemporary Christian tradition, sometimes without mention of its secondary and unoriginal status, and is generally considered to be, in the words of Bridges, "A benign expansion of the canon."[4]

But how "benign" can an interpolation (i.e., an unoriginal insertion) to Scripture be? The majority of interpreters seem to rest comfortably on its probable

---

1. Metzger, *Textual Commentary*, 187 – 89.

2. Cf. Chris Keith, "Recent and Previous Research on the *Pericope Adulterae* (John 7.53 – 8.11)," *CBR* 6 (2008): 377 – 404.

3. See Poythress, "Testing for Johannine Authorship," 361 – 62.

4. Carl B. Bridges, "The Canonical Status of the *Pericope Adulterae* (John 7:53 – 8:11)," *SCJ* 11 (2008): 213 – 21 (220).

historical foundation.[5] But even if we knew it was true, we would not know how to interpret it. Stories are not free-floating scenes for interpretation but are intentional parts of larger narratives that provide literary context. A pericope does not just belong to the historical Jesus of historical reconstruction and validation but to a canonical Gospel of the church (see Introduction).

An analogy for comparison raised by a few scholars is the Apocrypha. Bridges compares the pericope *positively* to the Old Testament Apocrypha. While the New Testament Apocrypha often conflict with the portrait of Jesus in the canonical Gospels, the OT Apocrypha "expand the canonical OT in ways agreeable to, or at least not hostile to, its theology."[6] Such a designation for Bridges is only meant to refer to content (that it may belong to John), not to its inspiration. The preacher, then, may use it, but should do so with caution, "not basing whole sermons on the passage, using it (if at all) as an illustration, and verbally footnoting it as a doubtful passage."[7] The distinction between content and canon is almost certainly a Protestant distinction, for Catholics have a creedal commitment to hold the two together.

In contrast, Köstenberger compares the pericope *negatively* to the NT Apocrypha. Agreeing that inspiration does not extend to the pericope, Köstenberger argues that canonical status should not extend to it either. By comparing it to the NT Apocrypha, Köstenberger makes a derogatory judgment regarding the pericope, attempting to remove it not only from preaching in the church but also from inclusion in the main body of translation, even within double brackets.[8]

Our response to the pericope, then, must weigh in the balance all these issues pressing around it. We must be honest with the text-critical evidence, which strongly denies the possibility that the pericope is original to the Gospel. At the same time, the pericope *is* in our Bibles, and the people in the pew are hardly cognizant of textual criticism and are only minimally deterred from double brackets, smaller font, or italics. The pericope has a long-standing presence in the heritage of the church which must be respected, even trusted to some degree. In our opinion, the place where this becomes most important is in the practice of the local church. The text critic can deny the text its authority, but the church cannot so freely do so — not with a thirteen-hundred-year history. It is also unfair to expect the pastor to exclude the passage from the preaching schedule when it is included in the biblical text (in both critical editions and lay

5. See Gary M. Burge, "A Specific Problem in the New Testament Text and Canon: The Woman Caught in Adultery (John 7:53 – 8:11)," *JETS* 27 (1984): 141 – 48 (148).

6. Bridges, "The Canonical Status of the *Pericope Adulterae*," 220.

7. Ibid., 221.

8. Köstenberger, *John*, 248.

versions). It seems best, therefore, to treat the text pastorally in the church in the same manner as it is treated text critically in the academy: to treat its content fully and freely in a manner that matches its double bracketed or italicized nature. That is, we need not deny the significance of its content even if we have questions about its origin. Three reasons make this clear.

First, without trying to minimize the evidence, we must at least admit that textual criticism is as much an art as it is a science, and the evaluation of the text's validity is at best only a (very) educated guess. While this is one of the largest and most difficult text-critical issues in the NT, there are several texts (e.g., verses, phrases, or even single words) that have a dubious history that cannot be determined with specificity, texts that have an admittedly double-bracketed or italicized character. Even most of our earliest manuscripts of the NT are a few centuries removed from the originals. This is not to undermine the text-critical endeavor or its conclusions, but to place them in their context.

Second, since the texts (i.e., verses, etc.) that have a more certain dubious character are omitted from our contemporary Bibles, the presence of this text, even in double-bracketed or italicized form, is itself an argument in favor of approving its use. The thirteen-hundred-year use and application of this text in the church becomes a kind of ecclesial argument, trusting in some limited capacity in the Spirit-guided decisions of the church and, behind the scenes, the providence of God. And in a real way, the text-critical decision to show hesitancy regarding this pericope does not mute providence but cooperates with it.

Third, it might be worth reflecting on the connection between the question of the pericope's origin and the nature of its inspiration. Even Bridges, who viewed the addition of the pericope positively, was hesitant to speak of its inspired status. But as Webster warns, a theological appeal to a foundational theory in order to provide the grounds for the status and interpretation of a "text" is likely to go "well beyond the limits which theology ought to set for itself."[9] That is, while biblical scholars tend to root the authority of the Bible on its material nature and therefore its human origin, theologians are more likely to root the authority of the Bible on its functional nature and therefore its divine origin. "The leading theme of any account of inspiration must be ἀπὸ θεοῦ (from God): inspiration is not primarily a textual property but a divine movement and therefore a divine moving."[10] The theologian is concerned that a material approach in isolation from the theological function of the Bible is controlled by a deistic assumption that is foreign to the nature of Scripture "in so far as the biblical text can itself become a revelatory agent by virtue of an act of divine inspiration in

---

9. Webster, *Word and Church*, 71.   10. Webster, *Holy Scripture*, 36.

the past."[11] Thus, our definition of biblical inspiration will either impede (for the materialist) or expand (for the functionalist) the pericope's canonical status and interpretive authority. Without denying material concerns, our approach must include functional concerns as well.

For these reasons our approach will be to exegete the pericope like any other in the Gospel, including it within the content of the Gospel and as part of the larger argument of the narrative. As we will try to show, there is good evidence within the narrative itself (internal material evidence) that this pericope serves an important role at this point in the Gospel. Although the material evidence of textual criticism gives warrant to describe (and therefore demote) this pericope as an *addendum* — a distinguishable addition of the whole that leaves the character of the original unchanged — there is functional evidence to claim this pericope is part of our Bibles and therefore must be treated accordingly.[12] The approach of this commentary will be to rely on the functional warrant for the pericope's inclusion without denying the material concerns. The material concerns are not muted but express themselves by relativizing or constraining the functional authority of the pericope in question.

Using an analogy, this pericope should be treated as a text on probation, given full membership without loss of rights or privileges, yet serving as if on an extended apprenticeship (which has lasted now for thirteen-hundred years). Just as a person on probation is prohibited from serving in certain authoritative capacities, so also might this text be prohibited from making its own contribution to a doctrine or theological issue. It can be used in collaboration with other pericopae in a secondary and supportive role but should not serve in an independent and isolated position of authority for the church. Such an approach allows it to function according to its verifiable nature without denying material concerns. While it is recommended that the pastor or teacher declare the (material) probationary status of this pericope to the church, to take away its full (functional) rights and privileges, in our opinion, only does more harm than good and only causes more confusion than certainty.

7:53 And then each went to his home ([Καὶ ἐπορεύθησαν ἕκαστος εἰς τὸν οἶκον αὐτοῦ). The narrative transitions from v. 52 to v. 53 by showing the departure of the "high priests and Pharisees" (including Nicodemus) after the dialogue at the end of the last pericope. It might also be inclusive of all the people of Jerusalem — "the crowd" — with 8:1 – 2 depicting the return of normality in Jerusalem after the celebration of the Feast of Tabernacles. The narrative closes the previous scene emphati-

---

11. Ibid.
12. Calling it an *addendum* is to make an even more posi-

tive materialist judgment than calling it an excursus or not dealing with it at all.

cally, thus highlighting the final verbal exchange between the Jewish leadership and Nicodemus. It therefore left some explanatory details regarding the conclusion of the Feast for this pericope. It is mentioned here simply to show that a new encounter is about to take place. It is an abrupt transition and often viewed as evidence of its interpolation, but its abruptness is not entirely strange to John.

8:1 Then Jesus went to the Mount of Olives (Ἰησοῦς δὲ ἐπορεύθη εἰς τὸ Ὄρος τῶν Ἐλαιῶν). This verse is unique in John, for it is the only place that the Mount of Olives is mentioned in the Gospel, a location more commonly mentioned in the Synoptics. The Mount of Olives was located near Jerusalem, so Jesus had not travelled far from the celebration of the Feast. Interestingly, the Mount of Olives may have been Jesus's primary residence (see Luke 21:37). Thus, while the crowd went to their homes, Jesus went to his.

8:2 And early in the morning he came again to the temple, and all the people came to him, and he sat down and was teaching them (Ὄρθρου δὲ πάλιν παρεγένετο εἰς τὸ ἱερόν, καὶ πᾶς ὁ λαὸς ἤρχετο πρὸς αὐτόν, καὶ καθίσας ἐδίδασκεν αὐτούς). The crowd's interest in Jesus at the Feast had not subsided, nor had the political concerns regarding Jesus led to a change in public opinion. Rather, early the next morning Jesus was in the temple "again" (πάλιν), teaching all the people — just as he had done upon his arrival at the Feast (7:14). The content of the teaching is not provided by the narrator. In this scene it is not the content of Jesus's message but his actions that are important for interpretation (see vv. 6b, 8).

By mentioning "all the people" (πᾶς ὁ λαὸς), the narrator introduces the immediate audience for the situation with the woman accused of adultery, ex-

plaining the identity of the group in whose midst she will stand (v. 3). This is also an important detail in regard to the stoning of an idolater under Jewish law, which required that the witnesses should raise their hands against the sinner first, followed by the hands of "all the people" (Deut 13:9; 17:7).[13] This concludes the introduction and setting of the pericope.

8:3 Then the scribes and the Pharisees led a woman who had been caught in adultery and they placed her in the midst of the people (ἄγουσιν δὲ οἱ γραμματεῖς καὶ οἱ Φαρισαῖοι γυναῖκα ἐπὶ μοιχείᾳ κατειλημμένην, καὶ στήσαντες αὐτὴν ἐν μέσῳ). The conflict of the pericope is introduced in dramatic fashion. The teaching of Jesus was interrupted by the Jewish authorities who had with them a woman accused of adultery. The Pharisees are well known to the reader (see comments on 1:24), but this is the first and only mention of "the scribes" (οἱ γραμματεῖς) in the Gospel. While scribes could often be members of the party of the Pharisees, they are not to be equated. Scribes occupied a skilled and important profession in Judaism, functioning as a combination of roles: lawyer, ethicist, theologian, catechist, and jurist.[14] For the purpose about to be explained by the narrative, the presence of the scribes along with the Pharisees is warranted. Their presence makes formal the legal proceedings about to take place.

Beside the formality of their purposeful entrance, the scribes and Pharisees are quickly eclipsed by the unnamed person they forcefully brought with them. Like several significant characters in the Gospel, this woman is unnamed. Her name becomes a title that describes her actions — befitting the focus on actions in this pericope. The narrator describes her as "a woman who had been caught in adultery" (γυναῖκα ἐπὶ μοιχείᾳ

---

13. Chris Keith, *The Pericope Adulterae, the Gospel of John, and the Literacy of Jesus*, NTTSD 38 (Leiden: Brill, 2009), 163.

14. Carson, *John*, 334; Morris, *John*, 780.

κατειλημμένην).[15] The description is vague. It is possible that she was caught in the act of adultery, a requirement if her stoning was to have appropriate evidence, but the narrative does not reveal such detail. It is also just as probable for the reader to assume that the entire situation is a setup, given the character of the Jewish leadership displayed thus far. Even beyond this woman, why Jesus? No reason is given why the Pharisees do not try again to arrest him (cf. 7:30, 32, 44), which they apparently had ample reason to do (cf. 5:16, 18).[16]

Great care must be taken to grasp the true conflict of this pericope. The pericope is often given a title that focuses on the woman, usually in regard to the crime of adultery. There is some warrant for this. But how we define her is significant. The narrator's description need not mean anything more than that she has been *accused* of adultery, just as the description of the entrance of the Jewish authorities need not mean they had good intentions or were honestly concerned with the law (and v. 6 will make clear that this was not the case). Whatever the evidence was against the woman, the judgment has not yet been given. And the need for and expectation of judgment has been laid literally at the feet of Jesus. At this moment Jesus was being challenged, not with words but with action. As much as the woman had been "led" (ἄγουσιν) and "placed" (στήσαντες) before Jesus — terms that depict the treatment of a prisoner — in this pericope it is Jesus who is on trial as the named defendant.

8:4 They said to him, "Teacher, this woman has been caught in the act of adultery" (λέγουσιν αὐτῷ, Διδάσκαλε, αὕτη ἡ γυνὴ κατείληπται ἐπ᾽ αὐτοφώρῳ μοιχευομένη). The legal proceedings begin with the accusation against the woman, that she "has been caught" (κατείληπται) commit-

ting adultery, with the perfect tense verb making the charge certain. According to Jewish law, such an accusation would require eyewitnesses, which are implied by the additional detail that the act of adultery was witnessed while "in the act" (ἐπ᾽ αὐτοφώρῳ), a term only used here in the NT that matches the specific requirement of the law that the adulterers must "be found" (Deut 22:22).

The scribes and Pharisees call Jesus "Teacher" (Διδάσκαλε), a word befitting the legal proceeding into which Jesus has now been included. The only other group that uses that title for Jesus is comprised of his disciples (cf. 1:38; 11:28; 13:13, 14; 20:16). The narrator in 1:38 even uses the title "Teacher" to interpret the title "Rabbi." In light of the intentions of the scribes and Pharisees shortly to be revealed (v. 6), such a title recalls Jesus's dialogue with Nicodemus, who spoke with cloak-and-dagger intentions by means of the same courteous title. In the context of first-century Judaism, the title of "Teacher" was connected to the spiritual guides of the people, the "scribes," who were the only teachers of the people in matters of religion and therefore religious law (see comments on 3:2). The use of the title here, then, is politically loaded, matching their true intentions about to be revealed.

8:5 "And in the law Moses commanded us to stone such women. What, then, do you say?" (ἐν δὲ τῷ νόμῳ ἡμῖν Μωϋσῆς ἐνετείλατο τὰς τοιαύτας λιθάζειν· σὺ οὖν τί λέγεις;). After describing the crime of the woman, the scribes and Pharisees give strong commentary regarding the law. They state emphatically that "Moses commanded us" (ἡμῖν Μωϋσῆς ἐνετείλατο), which serves as a forceful and coercive expectation of the result they desire — her death. The woman is again unnamed. This time she is even spoken of derogatorily, "such women"

---

15. See Gail R. O'Day, "John 7:53 – 8:11: A Study in Misreading," *JBL* 111 (1992): 631 – 40 (632).

16. Michaels, *John*, 495.

(τὰς τοιαύτας), reflecting that her identity is now defined representatively by a notorious group: adulterers.

The commentary by the scribes and Pharisees contains a significant omission. The law to which they refer states clearly that both the woman and the man are to be stoned (Lev 20:10; Deut 22:22). It is also worth noting a significant addition. The law is not as specific as the scribes and Pharisees suggest regarding the manner of execution. Stoning is only prescribed for the guilty pair when the woman is "a virgin pledged to be married" (Deut 22:23 – 24). But the man is not present. It is therefore hard not to see the unfolding scene as an intentional lynching of the woman.[17] The scribes and Pharisees conclude their case with a question addressed to Jesus: "What, then, do you say?" (σὺ οὖν τί λέγεις;). There is no need for us to try to reconstruct the outcome of Jesus's possible responses. The intent was to twist and slander from the start, and they would have used any data provided. The question is ironic, for the one they are trying to set up is the Judge (5:22).

8:6a They were saying this with the purpose of testing him, in order that they might have grounds to accuse him (τοῦτο δὲ ἔλεγον πειράζοντες αὐτόν, ἵνα ἔχωσιν κατηγορεῖν αὐτοῦ). The conflict is given a conclusion by the narrator, who makes the scribes and Pharisees' intentions clear so that the reader not misunderstand the unfolding drama. The narrator reveals that the intentions of the scribes and Pharisees were focused on Jesus (not the woman) in order to test him. Quite simply, they were seeking grounds "to accuse him" (κατηγορεῖν αὐτοῦ). Jesus had neither been sought out for guidance nor to serve as a member of the scribal authorities; Jesus was the one on trial. And

the accusation against the woman was to serve as a pretext for a greater accusation against Jesus.

8:6b But Jesus bent down and began writing on the ground with his finger (ὁ δὲ Ἰησοῦς κάτω κύψας τῷ δακτύλῳ κατέγραφεν εἰς τὴν γῆν). The resolution offered to the conflict by Jesus is communicated by means of an action. After lowering or situating himself nearer to the ground,[18] Jesus "began writing" (κατέγραφεν), with the beginning of the action given emphasis by an ingressive imperfect.[19] He did not write on paper but "on the ground" (εἰς τὴν γῆν), a general term that in this context is referring to the dirt or sand.[20] Jesus did not write with pen but "with his finger" (τῷ δακτύλῳ), denoted by a dative of means (instrumental dative).[21]

It is at this point that the history of interpretation takes a strong detour, focusing entirely on what Jesus was writing in the dirt. This unique response by Jesus has led to scores of interpretive guesses. Was he writing a response from Scripture, like one or all of the Ten Commandments? Or was he writing a response regarding the accusers, like their own sins (so Jerome)? Or was his writing intended to display a rhetorical response, like for a space of silence or to create a dramatic effect?[22] But such an approach — a focus on the *what* — misunderstands not only the action of Jesus but also the movement of the pericope.

The focus of the pericope is not on *what* Jesus wrote on the ground but *that* he wrote on the ground. The narrator has already been shown to be speaking through action and symbolism. The emphasis was not on the content of Jesus's teaching but on the act of him teaching (v. 2); not on any detailed content about the unnamed woman and the accusation against her (Where was the man?

17. Morris, *John*, 782.
18. BDAG 575; LSJ 1012.
19. Wallace, *Greek Grammar*, 544 – 45.
20. BDAG 196.
21. Wallace, *Greek Grammar*, 162 – 63.
22. See Keith, *The Pericope Adulterae*, 11 – 21.

Who are the witnesses?) but on the symbolic action displayed through her treatment (v. 3). The narrator's description of Jesus's action of writing on the ground is no less intentional or symbolic here. The narrator is crafting an image for the reader — an "impression" (see Introduction) — that is its own communication. Helpfully, the reader is not left alone to determine the symbolism. The key is in the additional phrase "with his finger" (τῷ δακτύλῳ).[23] Our interpretation of this key phrase and the contextualization of this act must wait until the full response of Jesus has been examined, especially since the act is repeated in v. 8.

8:7 But when they continued to question him, he stood up and said to them, "Let the one without sin among you be the first to throw a stone at her" (ὡς δὲ ἐπέμενον ἐρωτῶντες [αὐτόν], ἀνέκυψεν καὶ εἶπεν αὐτοῖς, Ὁ ἀναμάρτητος ὑμῶν πρῶτος ἐπ᾽ αὐτὴν βαλέτω λίθον). The description of the scene by the narrator suggests that the continued questioning by the scribes and Pharisees intensified the dramatic nature of the encounter. Rising from the ground, Jesus makes only one statement. Jesus speaks a command in the third person, which can easily get confused in English with a permissive idea: "Let the one … throw a stone" (βαλέτω λίθον).[24] But it is not a request; it is a forceful command. Who is qualified to throw a stone at this woman, that is, to judge her? One qualification characterizes this person: "The one without sin" (Ὁ ἀναμάρτητος). This comparative adjective is used with an elative sense, which means it is not technically making a comparison but expressing a quality that by means of the adjective is intensified.[25]

The force of the command, then, is that Jesus is commanding judgment to take place by a sinless one — literally, one who is entirely without sin. This is not a denial or rejection of the law, for the statement only demands that this single qualification be met "first" (πρῶτος). It is, rather, a demand for the right — even perfect — execution of the law. This statement spoke past the legal maneuvering right into the heart of the scribes and Pharisees, who at that moment could not sidestep their own law or Lawgiver. These are the only words spoken by Jesus in response to the public scene at hand.

8:8 And again Jesus bent and wrote on the ground (καὶ πάλιν κατακύψας ἔγραφεν εἰς τὴν γῆν). The resolution concludes with this final, framing comment by the narrator, who again describes Jesus bending down and writing on the ground. The action itself, let alone the narrative's repetitive emphasis of it, is striking to say the least. The parallel with v. 6b is potent, especially in light of the two components that are missing. First and more obvious, the tool for writing, "with his finger" (τῷ δακτύλῳ), is not mentioned. Second and undetectable in English translation, the lexical form of the term for "writing" is different. In v. 6b, "writing" (κατέγραφεν) contains a prefix not found in the verb used in v. 8's "writing" (ἔγραφεν). The significance is not that the words mean different things; they are, in fact, functionally synonymous. Rather, they signal to the reader that a more important symbolic connection is being communicated. It is worth stating that we are not just interpreting the action of an event but the narrator's depiction (i.e., his interpretation) of the event, which supplied the emphatic focus on Jesus's "finger."

It is the term "finger" that forges the connection, for according to Exodus 31:18/Deuteronomy 9:10, the Ten Commandments were written by "the finger of God." The argument for this connection is twofold.[26] First, in the context of the scene as whole and in v. 5 specifically, Jesus is being challenged to stand opposed to Moses in his assessment of

---

23. Cf. Ridderbos, *John*, 289.
24. See Wallace, *Greek Grammar*, 485 – 86.
25. Ibid., 300.
26. See Keith, *The Pericope Adulterae*, ch. 8.

the required punishment regarding one of the Ten Commandments. For this reason, the mention of "finger" intentionally places Jesus in Moses's position, even more, eclipsing the legal authority of Moses with that of Jesus.

Second and more directly, the two lexical forms of the term for "writing" that appear in vv. 6b and 8 are a perfect match to Exodus 32:15 (LXX); the two different lexical forms (one containing the prefix) with synonymous meanings occur in the same pericope referring specifically to the writing of the law given to Moses on stone tablets. Given the fact that the prefixed form of "writing" (κατέγραφεν) only occurs here in the NT, the intentional connection to Exodus 32:15 is only strengthened. In light of the allusion to the finger/writing of the Ten Commandments by God in the Old Testament, the symbolic significance of the action of Jesus, then, is that he himself is the author of the law, and his finger is the very "finger of God." When the scribes and Pharisees challenge Jesus with the legality of the law of God, they are speaking directly to its author.[27]

8:9 After hearing this they began to leave one by one, beginning with the older ones, and he was left alone, and the woman was there in the midst (οἱ δὲ ἀκούσαντες ἐξήρχοντο εἷς καθ᾽ εἷς ἀρξάμενοι ἀπὸ τῶν πρεσβυτέρων, καὶ κατελείφθη μόνος, καὶ ἡ γυνὴ ἐν μέσῳ οὖσα). The conclusion and interpretation of the pericope begins with a description by the narrator of the aftermath of Jesus's statement and further symbolic action. Without any continued confrontation, the crowd — presumably both the scribes and Pharisees as well as "all the people" (v. 2) who had come to hear Jesus teach — "began to leave" (ἐξήρχοντο), denoted by an ingressive imperfect that conveys the nature of their departure.

The narrator adds two further details regarding this departure. First, they left "one by one" (εἷς καθ᾽ εἷς). Second, they left "beginning with the older ones" (ἀρξάμενοι ἀπὸ τῶν πρεσβυτέρων). These descriptions emphasize the "dramatic and ceremonious" nature of the departure (cf. Ezek. 9:6).[28]

The narrator carefully describes the two people that remain: Jesus and the woman. Jesus is described as "alone" (μόνος) to emphasize the fact that only he met his own qualification; only he was "the one without sin" (v. 7). The woman is also described carefully as still "in the midst" (ἐν μέσῳ), which we left awkwardly translated so as to match its earlier use and to allow the narrative to return dramatically to her person and presence. She had not moved an inch, and yet everything around her had changed dramatically. The only constant was Jesus, who was still kneeling just above the ground upon which he had written — at her level.

8:10 But Jesus stood up and asked her, "Woman, where are they? Has no one condemned you?" (ἀνακύψας δὲ ὁ Ἰησοῦς εἶπεν αὐτῇ, Γύναι, ποῦ εἰσιν; οὐδείς σε κατέκρινεν;). Just as Jesus rose to address the legal experts, he now rises to address the accused. By addressing her as "woman" (Γύναι), Jesus is doing nothing more impersonal or harsh than he did to his own mother (see 2:4; 19:26). In fact, its use in this context is fitting. The normal use of the term demands that it be seen to function at least minimally as a distancing mechanism, even if it is enveloped within a healthy and loving relationship (see comments on 2:4). Even though Jesus has already come to the defense of this woman, he is not technically on her side. He alone is "the one without sin." The title, "woman," depicts brilliantly how Jesus can embrace our sinfulness without the slightest hint of capitulation. According to his own

---

27. Cf. Augustine, *John*, 33.5.117. As Keith explains, "Jesus is shown here to be the author for whom Moses himself was only the delivery person" (*The Pericope Adulterae*, 190).

28. Michaels, *John*, 499.

qualification (v. 7), Jesus is the perfect Judge (5:22). Jesus asks the woman two questions that are difficult to interpret. Is this true surprise or gentle sarcasm?[29] Jesus's statement in v. 11 makes clear the woman is not innocent. The questions focus the reader's attention on his status as the Judge and on his authority to render a judgment in regard to her and her sinfulness.

8:11 She said, "No one, sir." Then Jesus said, "Then neither do I condemn you; go, and from now on sin no longer" (ἡ δὲ εἶπεν, Οὐδείς, κύριε. εἶπεν δὲ ὁ Ἰησοῦς, Οὐδὲ ἐγώ σε κατακρίνω· πορεύου, [καὶ] ἀπὸ τοῦ νῦν μηκέτι ἁμάρτανε]). The woman's answer is simply an acknowledgement of the direction of Jesus's questions: there is no other Judge. This is not a statement of faith but simply a statement of fact. Jesus would have to explain his judgment.

The pericope ends with a final, two-part statement by Jesus. First, Jesus declares that he does not condemn her. Here, as in v. 10, Jesus speaks of condemnation in a legal sense. In this statement is found the paradox of the gospel of Jesus Christ. For since the one who wrote the law is also the judge that presides over it, everything in between — freedom and condemnation, life and death — is under his authority (5:26 – 27; cf. Luke 4:18 – 19; 5:24).[30]

This explains, then, the second part of Jesus's statement. Jesus sends the woman away — free, but not without qualification. Since he is still Judge, she must live accordingly. She must live as one under the law of God (and of Christ; cf. Gal 6:2). As will shortly be announced in the pericope to follow, true freedom is found in Christ (8:31 – 38), which serves as further evidence that this pericope fits comfortably where it sits. It is in this way that the pericope presents its conclusion and interpretation.

Theology in Application

In this short and text-critically disputed pericope, the grace of the gospel of Jesus Christ is dramatically displayed in regard to a woman accused of adultery. What begins as a trial of an unnamed woman becomes a trial of Jesus, and what starts in the law of Moses becomes entirely about the law of Christ. In this pericope the reader of the Fourth Gospel is exhorted to sit under Jesus the Judge, who is both the author of the law and the authority over it, and to view their sin in light of his person and work.

Jesus the Judge

This pericope declares the legal status and functional authority of Jesus. Jesus is the "finger" of God, the true Judge, and his law — the law of Christ — is the foundation for all humanity (Gal 6:2). The concern of the scribes and Pharisees regarding adultery was eclipsed by Christ the Judge's concern for all sin. Christ is concerned with the deep-rooted and selfish sins inside every person. The gospel of Jesus Christ is not self-help instruction but the good news about real sin, the sin for which only God can help.[31] That is why the author of Hebrews can exhort us to entrust ourselves

---

29. See Brown, *John*, 1:334.
30. Ridderbos, *John*, 291.

31. Cf. Luther, *John*, 23:316 – 17.

to Jesus, our high priest. "For we do not have a high priest who is unable to empathize with our weaknesses, but we have one who has been tempted in every way, just as we are — yet he did not sin" (Heb 4:15). That is why, then, the courtroom of God our Judge is described as containing "the throne of grace," so that we may approach "with confidence" and "receive mercy and find grace to help us in our time of need" (Heb 4:16). The church lives under this law of Christ, under the ruling authority of this high-priestly Judge, under whom even the most demanding law of God is drenched in the grace of the cross of Christ. This law then is freedom, not burden, and we have moved away from slavery to sin and been propelled by grace to embrace this righteousness (Rom 6:15 – 23).

The Law of Christ and Human Authority

This pericope describes the divine foundation for all law and dealing with sin. It emphasizes the "finger of God" behind all the legal proceedings of humanity. This is in no way a repudiation of the legal authority of humans or human institutions but is instead an explanation of the source and nature of that authority. The law of Christ is intended to pervade all human authority, serving in, around, and through the justice displayed to those around us.

It is in the church that this kind of authority makes itself more prominently known. The church is even more concerned with true justice but expresses it in two unique ways. First, the Christian expects justice not just of others but first and foremost of oneself. Justice is what God requires, and the judging authority given to humans and their institutions is entirely derivative. Second, the Christian locates the justice (of God) within the grace (of God).[32] This is what makes the cry for justice by the Christian — individual or institution — look so different, so Christian; it does not come from selfish motives but "from above" and does not stand by human hands but by the "finger" of God.

"Sin No Longer"

The concluding exhortation of Jesus to the woman accused of adultery is a command to "sin no longer" (v. 11). It is a gracious command to live life in freedom. The gospel of Jesus Christ proclaims a remarkable paradox. The author of the law of God and the Judge of humanity is also the one who receives the punishment. The giver of life embraces death for us; "the one without sin" becomes sin for us. This is grace and love — this is good news. For this reason the Christian strives to embrace the law, the law of Christ, in every way. To do this is to submit to sin no longer and instead to submit to Christ.[33] The exhortation of Christ, then, calls out to the reader as it did the woman by looking forward to the glorious future, all the while looking back to

---

32. Cf. Hoskyns, *Fourth Gospel*, 571.   33. Cf. Calvin, *John 1 – 10*, 209.

the humble memory of the past. It sees, then, the law of the gospel of Christ in all things and behind every aspect of life, for Jesus Christ is the same yesterday, today, and forever (Heb 13:8).

The Reliability of the Bible

The actual (textual) science used to offer a level of confident certainty in the original form of the Bible can undercut that confidence for those whom such technical issues are a cause for fear. This need not be the case. The pastor or teacher should use this text to reaffirm the reliability of the Bible, using the human fingerprints across every page of the Bible to discuss its natural integrity and truthfulness. This is not time for a lesson in textual criticism. The issues surrounding this pericope demand that the pastor speak about inspiration, about canon, about the human authorship of Scripture, and yet also about providence, about church history and tradition, and about the divine authorship of Scripture. A paradox similar to the gospel discussed above occurs here: mere humans wrote words that are the very Word of God. This requires some analysis and explanation from the academic but it also requires some reflection and adjudicating from the pastor-shepherd. The goal of such a discussion would not be absolute certainty but appropriate faith in a trustworthy object we know today as the Bible.

John 8:12 – 59

Literary Context

This pericope begins a new section in the Gospel. In spite of the overall coherence of the Gospel narrative, with each section serving as part of a unified whole, the confession of the Son of God of the previous section (5:1 – 8:11) intensifies in this section into a more formal controversy, the controversy over the Son of God (8:12 – 10:42). Jesus has revealed who he is; at this point in the story, the Gospel will depict the more formal interaction and intentionally negative conflict between Jesus and "the Jews." The dialogues turn from social challenges (over honor) to legal challenges (over law). The forensic patterns of this section, with themes of interrogation and judgment, serve to interconnect each pericope in the section.[1] Jesus has officially made public who he is; this section will depict the aftermath of this announcement and its ramifications among the Jewish authorities.

→ **V. The Controversy over the Son of God (8:12 – 10:42)**

    A. "The Light of the World": The Accusations of Jesus the Judge (8:12 – 59)

    B. The Fifth Sign: The Testimony of the Blind Man (9:1 – 41)

    C. The Shepherd and the Sheep (10:1 – 21)

    D. The Son of the Father (10:22 – 42)

Main Idea

As the Judge of humanity, Jesus serves as the plaintiff who charges the world guilty of sin and declares it convicted to death. Yet as the Savior of the world, Jesus takes the sin of the world upon him and fulfills in his body the death that the world deserves. True discipleship is the transfer from darkness to the "light of life," from enslavement to freedom, and from slave to sons and daughters.

---

1. For a similar analysis, see Lincoln, *Truth on Trial*, 97. Cf. Dodd, *Interpretation*, 354 – 62.

Translation

John 8:12–59

12a	1st Interlocution (12–20)	**Jesus spoke to them again saying,**
b	Confession/Allusion: OT	*"I am the light of the world.*
c	Condition	*The one who follows me …*
d	Result	*… will never walk in darkness but*
e	Contrast	*will have the light of life."*
13a	Character Reentrance	Then **the Pharisees said to him,**
b	Rejoinder	*"You are testifying concerning yourself.*
c	Resulting Challenge	*Your witness is not true."*
14a	Surrejoinder	**Jesus answered and said to them,**
b	Concessive Condition	*"Even if I testify concerning myself,*
c	Inference	*my witness is true,*
d	Basis	*because I know from where I came and where I go.*
e	Contrast	*But you do not know from where I come and where I go.*
15a	Cryptic Explanation	*"You judge according to the flesh,*
b	Contrast	*I am not judging anyone.*
16a		*But*
b	Concessive Condition	*even if I judge,*
c	Inference	*my judgment is true,*
d	Basis	*because I am not alone, but*
e	Contrast	*I and the one who sent me,*
f	Identification	*the Father.*
17a		*But even*
b	Emphatic Concession	*in your law*
d	Emphatic Rebuttal	*it has been written that the testimony of two men is true.*
18a	Explanation: 1st Witness	*I am the one who testifies concerning myself,*
b	Explanation: 2nd Witness	*and the one who sent me …*
c	Identification	*the Father,*
d		*… testifies concerning me."*
19a	Retort	Then **they said to him,**
b	Interrogative Demand	*"Where is your Father?"*
c	Jesus's 1st Verdict	**Jesus answered,**
d	Declaration	*"You neither know me nor my Father.*
e	Condition	*If you knew me,*
f	Inference	*you would also know my Father."*
20a	Narrator's Aside	**He spoke these words**
b	Simultaneous Action	while teaching
c	Location	by the treasury in the temple,
d	Assertion	and **no one seized him,**
e	Basis	because his hour had not yet come.

21a	2nd Interlocution (21–30)	Then **again he said to them,**
b	Assertion	*"I am going away*
c	Descriptive Reaction	*and you will seek me,*
d	Warning/Allusion: Ezek 3:16–21	*and you will die in your sin.*
e	Declarative Challenge	*Where I am going you are not able to come."*
22a	Character Reentrance	Then **the Jews said,**
b	Mocking Rejoinder	*"Surely he will not kill himself,*
c		*because he said,*
d	Restatement of 21e	*'Where I am going you are not able to go?'"*
23a	Interchanging Surrejoinder	And **he said to them,**
b	Declaration of Origin	*"You are from below;* A
c	Contrast	*I am from above.* B
d	Declaration of Origin	*You are from this world;* A
e	Contrast	*I am not from this world.* B
24a	Restatement of 21d	*I just said to you that you will die in your sins;*
b	Explanation	*for*
c	Condition	*unless you believe that I am,*
d	Inferential Warning	*you will surely die in your sins."*
25a	Rejoinder	Then **they said to him,**
b		*"Who are you?"*
c	Surrejoinder	**Jesus said to them,**
d	Confession/Allusion: OT/NT	*"[I am] what I said to you at the beginning.*
26a	Judgment	*I have many things to say and to judge concerning you,*
b	Reliability of Origin	*but the one who sent me is true,*
c	Assertion	*and the things I have heard from him I declare to the world."*
27a	Narrator's Aside	**They did not know that he was speaking to them about the Father.**
28a	Jesus's 2nd Verdict	Then **Jesus said to them,**
b	Temporal Condition	*"When you have lifted up the Son of Man,*
c	Inference	*then you will know that I am,*
d	Declaration	*and I do nothing on my own,*
e	Contrast	*but I declare the things*
f	Authentication of Reliability	*just as the Father taught me.*
29a	Explanation of 28f	*The one who sent me is with me.*
b		*He has not left me alone,*
c	Basis	*for I always do the things that are pleasing to him."*
30a	Narrator's Aside	While he was saying these things,
b	Result	**many believed in him.**
31a	3rd Interlocution (31–47)	Then **Jesus said to the Jews**
b	Description	**who had believed in him,**
c	Condition	*"If you remain in my word,*
d	Progressive Inference #1	*you are truly my disciples."*
32a	Progressive Inference #2	*Then you will know the truth,*
b	Progressive Inference #3	*and the truth will set you free."*
33a	Rejoinder	**They answered him,**
b	Assertion of Identity	*"We are the seed of Abraham*
c	Entailment	*and we have never been enslaved to anyone.*
d	Interrogative Challenge	*How can you say,*
e	Restatement of 32b	*'We will become free?'"*

Continued on next page.

Continued from previous page.

34a	Surrejoinder	**Jesus answered to them,**
b	Amen Formula	*"Truly, truly I say to you,*
c	Critique of 33 (Condition)	*everyone who sins …*
d	(Inference)	*… is a slave to sin.*
35a	Explanation (35–38)	*And the slave does not remain in the house forever;*
b	Contrast	*the son remains forever.*
36a	Condition	*If then the Son has set you free,*
b	Inferential Answer to 33e	*you will be free indeed.*
37a	Concession to 33b	*I know that you are the seed of Abraham.*
b	Contrast	*Yet you are seeking to kill me,*
c	Basis	*because there is no place in you for my word.*
38a	Action	*I am declaring to you what I have seen*
b	Source	*in the presence of the Father,*
c	Descriptive Reaction	*and you do what you have heard from your father."*
39a	Countercritique	**They answered and said to him,**
b	Reiteration of 33b	*"Abraham is our father."*
c	Countercritique	**Jesus said to them,**
d	Condition	*"If you are the children of Abraham,*
e	Inference	*you would do the works of Abraham.*
40a	Contrast to 39e	*But now you seek to kill me,*
b	Description	*a man who has spoken the truth to you*
c	Source	*which I heard from God.*
d	Contrast to 40a	*This Abraham did not do.*
41a	Emphatic Contrast to 39b	*You do the works of your father."*
b	Argumentative Maneuver	Then **they said to him,**
c	Assertion	*"We have not been born as illegitimate children.*
d	Reassertion of Identity	*We have one Father,*
e	Description	*God."*
42a	Critique of 41c–e	**Jesus said to them,**
b	Condition	*"If God were your Father,*
c	Inference	*you would love me,*
d	Basis #1	*for I came from God*
e	Basis #2	*and am now present.*
f	Explanation	*For I have not come on my own,*
g	Source	*but he sent me.*
43a	Rhetorical Question	*Why do you not understand my language?*
b	Answer: Basis	*Because you are unable to hear my word.*
	(Jesus's 3rd Verdict)	
44a	Contrasting Source	*You belong to your father,*
b	Identification	*the devil,*
c	Consequence	*and you want to do your father's desire.*
d	Description #1	*He was a murderer from the beginning,*
e	Description #2	*and does not stand in the truth,*
f	Basis	*because there is no truth in him.*

g	Circumstantial Condition	When he speaks a lie,
h	Inference	he speaks from his own supply,
i	Basis #1	because he is a liar and
j	Basis #2	the father of lies.
45a	Contrast to Devil	But
b	Basis	because I speak the truth,
c	Description of Reaction	you do not believe me!
46a	Rhetorical Question #1	Who among you convicts me of sin?
b	Condition	If I am speaking the truth,
c	Rhetorical Question #2	why do you not believe me?
47a	Answer (Condition)	The one who belongs to God …
b	Answer (Inference)	… hears the words of God.
c	Basis of 47	The reason you do not hear is because you do not belong to God!"
48a	4th Interlocution (48–59)	**The Jews answered and said to him,**
b	Interrogative Accusation #1	"Are we not right in saying that you are a Samaritan and
c	Interrogative Accusation #2	have a demon?"
49a	Rejoinder	**Jesus answered,**
b	Denial of Accusations	"I do not have a demon,
c	Basis for Denial #1	but I honor my Father,
d	(Contrast) #2	and you dishonor me.
50a	Basis for Denial #3	But I do not seek my glory,
b	(Contrast) #4	but there is one who seeks it and
c		who judges.
51a	Amen Formula	Truly, truly I say to you,
b	Condition	if a person keeps my word,
c	Inferential Warning	he will never see death."
52a	Surrejoinder	Then **the Jews said to him,**
b	Escalating Accusation	"Now we know that you have a demon.
c	Basis for Accusation #1	Abraham died, and the prophets,
d	(Contrast) #2	yet you say,
e	Restatement of 51	'If a person keeps my word,
f		he will never taste death.'
53a	Rhetorical Question	Surely you are not greater than our father Abraham,
b	Description	who died?
c	Assertion	The prophets also died.
d	Interrogative Accusation	Whom do you make yourself out to be?"
54a	Rejoinder	**Jesus answered,**
b	Condition	"If I glorify myself,
c	Inference	my glory is nothing.
d	Vindicatory Critique #1	The one who glorifies me is my Father,
e	Description	whom you say is your God.
55a	Expansion of Critique	And you do not know him,
b	Contrast	but I know him.
c		And
d	Condition	if I said that I did not know him,

Continued on next page.

Continued from previous page.

e	Inference	*I would be a liar like you,*
f	Contrast #1	*but I know him*
g	Contrast #2	*and keep his word.*
56a	Vindicatory Critique #2	*Your father Abraham was overjoyed*
b	Content (Basis)	*that he was to see my day,*
c		*and he saw and rejoiced."*
57a	Surrejoinder	Then **the Jews said to him,**
b	Interrogative Countercritique	*"You are not yet fifty years old*
c		*and you have seen Abraham?"*
58a	Climactic Rejoinder	**Jesus said to them,**
b	Amen Formula	*"Truly, truly, I say to you,*
c	Context	*before Abraham was [born],*
d	Confession of Identity	*I am."*
59a	Condemnatory Reaction	Then **they picked up stones**
b	Purpose	*in order to throw at him,*
c		but **Jesus was concealed**
d	Departure	and **went out from the temple.**

Structure and Literary Form

This is the fifth substantial dialogue in the narrative proper, and it is a *legal challenge dialogue*, which takes the form of a formal debate (see Introduction). The purpose is not to challenge the honor or authority of one's interlocutor but to debate a principle, idea, or law as part of a forensic case. The dialogue is framed by two significant statements by Jesus, which by its conclusion reduces his opponents to silence and displays his mastery of the legal challenge.

Exegetical Outline

➡ **A. "The Light of the World": The Accusations of Jesus the Judge (8:12 – 59)**

1. First Accusation: The Charge against Inappropriate Belief (vv. 12 – 30)

    a. First Verbal Exchange: The Authority and Judgment of the Son (vv. 12 – 20)

    (1) Charge: "I Am the Light of the World" (v. 12)

    (2) Responses: The Witness of the Father and Son (vv. 13 – 18)

    (3) Verdict: "You Know neither Me nor My Father" (vv. 19 – 20)

    b. Second Verbal Exchange: The Origin of the Son (vv. 21 – 30)

    (1) Charge: "You Will Die in Your Sin" (v. 21)

    (2) Responses: "You Are from the World; I Am Not from This World" (v. 22 – 27)

    (3) Verdict: "You Will Know That I Am" (vv. 28 – 30)

2. Second Accusation: The Charge against Illegitimate Origin (vv. 31 – 59)

   a. First Verbal Exchange: The Identity of the People of God (vv. 31 – 47)

      (1) Charge: True Disciples Abide in my Word (vv. 31 – 32)

      (2) Responses: Abraham and the Father (vv. 33 – 43)

      (3) Verdict: "You Belong to Your Father, the Devil" (vv. 44 – 47)

   b. Second Verbal Exchange: The Counterclaim by the Jews: Heresy! (vv. 48 – 59)

      (1) Charge: "You are a Samaritan and Have a Demon" (v. 48)

      (2) Responses: "Before Abraham Was [Born], I Am" (vv. 49 – 58)

      (3) Verdict: The Attempted Stoning of Jesus (v. 59)

Explanation of the Text

The previous pericope, 7:53 – 8:11, depicted Jesus as the true Judge, a final statement regarding the identity of the Son of God. In this scene, "the Judge" begins to enact his judgment by making two formal charges against his opponents, who like before are made up of a multifaceted group of people (the Pharisees and "the Jews"). Up until now Jesus has been the defendant, the one being challenged by the religious leaders and by intrigued followers; the narrative depicted the light by means of the darkness's inability to recognize it (1:5). But beginning in this scene, the Light becomes the plaintiff, offering his own challenge to the imposing darkness. This is no mere honor challenge but an issue of the heart and soul, which the narrative will depict in creative detail by means of a formal legal challenge.

8:12 Jesus spoke to them again saying, "I am the light of the world. The one who follows me will never walk in darkness but will have the light of life" (Πάλιν οὖν αὐτοῖς ἐλάλησεν ὁ Ἰησοῦς λέγων, Ἐγώ εἰμι τὸ φῶς τοῦ κόσμου· ὁ ἀκολουθῶν ἐμοὶ οὐ μὴ περιπατήσῃ ἐν τῇ σκοτίᾳ, ἀλλ᾽ ἕξει τὸ φῶς τῆς ζωῆς). The context for this statement and the entire dialogue to follow is related to what has come before, made clear by the first word in the Greek,

"again" (Πάλιν), though the text-critical concerns regarding the previous pericope make the connection complex. The majority prefer to connect this pericope with chapter 7, which places this scene at the end of the Feast of Tabernacles.[2] But the significant role played by the crowd in chapter 7, mentioned eight times there, is absent in chapter 8.[3] In contrast, in this scene, as in 7:53 – 8:11, Jesus is confronted by his adversaries, the Jewish authorities. And like 7:53 – 8:11, the forensic procedures of a trial and the depiction of Jesus as the plaintiff and judge are emphasized from the beginning, befitting a close link between 8:11 and 8:12. After his final statement on the last and greatest day of the Feast of Tabernacles, followed by a definitive action in the temple after the Feast, Jesus now begins to enact his divine right as the ultimate authority and judge of the world (cf. 5:22 – 27).

The scene begins with a magnificent statement by Jesus: "I am the Light of the world" (Ἐγώ εἰμι τὸ φῶς τοῦ κόσμου), which serves as an evocation of judgment.[4] In legal contexts, an "evocation" is when a judge is deprived of his jurisprudence (legal authority) for the purpose of conferring to another judge the authority and power of decision. Such a claim intentionally replaces the authority to

---

2. Cf. Michaels, *John*, 476.

3. Morris, *John*, 386.

4. Cf. Lincoln, *Truth on Trial*, 84.

judge of the Jewish authorities, a claim to which the Pharisees will quickly respond.

The statement itself is the second of seven formal "I am" statements in the Gospel of John (see comments on 6:35). Interpreters who try to explain the "light" metaphor by means of the Feast of Tabernacles,[5] or worse by means of some other ancient religious comparison, fail to do justice to the force of the phrase.[6] Not only does the metaphor of light have a strong biblical heritage (see e.g., Exod 13:21 – 22; 14:19 – 25; Pss 27:1; 119:105; Prov 6:23; Ezek 1:4, 13, 26 – 28; Isa 49:6; 60:19 – 22; Hab 3:3 – 4), but it was given a foundational introduction in the prologue and will continue to be expressed throughout the Gospel (e.g., 9:5). Unlike the first formal "I am" statement (6:35), this second one is without any immediate thematic preparation in the narrative (e.g., the feeding of a large crowd; the bread of life discourse). It is, rather, part and parcel of the primary theme of the entire Gospel, having been thematically introduced in the prologue.[7] Jesus calls himself the Light not in the context of the Jewish celebration of the Feast of Tabernacles but in the context of the mission of God to the world. Such language impresses upon the reader the Son's creative activity at the beginning of time, that in him "was life, and the life was the light of humanity" (1:4) as well as the conflict into which the Son entered: "The light shined in the darkness, and the darkness did not recognize it" (1:5).

It is with the context established by the prologue in mind that the reader is expected to interpret the second claim of Jesus, pitting those who "walk in darkness" (περιπατήσῃ ἐν τῇ σκοτίᾳ) against those who have through Jesus "the light of life" (τὸ φῶς τῆς ζωῆς). The difference is not in their person or work but in the person and work of Jesus. He is the light, the giver of life; without him all activity ("walking") is helplessly shrouded in darkness. In the prologue, "darkness" was introduced as an interlocutor (see comments on 1:5). It is therefore fitting that Jesus describes those opposed to him as darkness. Before even starting to engage with him, his opponents have already been exposed and defeated. It is significant that Jesus claims to be the light of the world, matching ironically the declaration made about him by the Samaritans (4:42). This is no "moderate and reasonable claim"; it is a political statement with cosmic ramifications.[8] This kind of politic requires the categories of the cosmological strand of the Gospel's plot.

In the context of the conflict dialogue, this opening statement by Jesus makes a formal claim regarding the plaintiff's own identity that demands he be viewed not merely as the accuser but also as the judge. At the same time the statement serves as a formal charge against those who oppose Jesus.[9]

8:13 Then the Pharisees said to him, "You are testifying concerning yourself. Your witness is not true" (εἶπον οὖν αὐτῷ οἱ Φαρισαῖοι, Σὺ περὶ σεαυτοῦ μαρτυρεῖς· ἡ μαρτυρία σου οὐκ ἔστιν ἀληθής). The exchange of responses begins with a rejoinder by the Pharisees, who have become in this Gospel professional antagonists of Jesus. While they have normally plotted against him silently (5:16, 18; 7:30, 32), spoken about him to each other (7:11, 45 – 49), or even spoken about him but not to him while in his presence (6:41 – 42, 52; 7:15, 35 – 36), here the Pharisees confront him directly.[10]

The rejoinder of the Pharisees is a legal chal-

---

5. For example, see Beasley-Murray, *John*, 127.

6. Even Keener, *John*, 1:739, is hesitant to see a relevant connection. Cf. Barrett, *John*, 335 – 36.

7. See J. Gerald Janzen, "'I Am the Light of the World' (John 8:12): Connotation and Context," *Enc* 67 (2006): 115 – 35.

8. Luther, *John*, 23:319 – 20.

9. See Beasley-Murray, *John*, 104.

10. Michaels, *John*, 479.

lenge to Jesus's claim based upon the law of Moses that required multiple witnesses in criminal cases (Deut 17:6; 19:5). Such a counter is an attempt to undermine his entire claim because of its lack of testimonial support. Since he is testifying in regard to himself, his testimony, based upon their interpretation, cannot be "true" (ἀληθής).

8:14 Jesus answered and said to them, "Even if I testify concerning myself, my witness is true, because I know from where I came and where I go. But you do not know from where I come and where I go" (ἀπεκρίθη Ἰησοῦς καὶ εἶπεν αὐτοῖς, Κἂν ἐγὼ μαρτυρῶ περὶ ἐμαυτοῦ, ἀληθής ἐστιν ἡ μαρτυρία μου, ὅτι οἶδα πόθεν ἦλθον καὶ ποῦ ὑπάγω· ὑμεῖς δὲ οὐκ οἴδατε πόθεν ἔρχομαι ἢ ποῦ ὑπάγω). Jesus offers a lengthy surrejoinder (vv. 14 – 18) that serves to discredit the rejoinder of the Pharisees. As much as the form of Jesus's surrejoinder fits the pattern of a forensic response, it is not entirely supported by legal counterarguments. Jesus's language is somewhat cryptic and must be interpreted within the cosmological framework already established by the Gospel, including the cosmological statement of v. 12.

Jesus's claim here might seem to contradict what he said in 5:31: "If I testify concerning myself, my witness is not sufficient." But there is an important distinction that each statement is making. In 5:31, Jesus was describing his dependence on the Father in a manner that disallowed him from having an identity independent or outside of the identity of God. The Son is so dependent on the Father that he is unable to provide a witness for himself; the witness of Jesus must be rooted in the Father (and empowered by the Spirit). But that does not mean that Jesus's self-witness, when rooted in the Trinitarian identity of God, is not therefore valid and "true." Thus, at one and the same time, Jesus's self-witness

is valid in its Trinitarian identity and insufficient alone. Said another way, it is the interdependence of the Father, Son, and Spirit that qualifies Jesus to have an independent ground for truth. In this way, Jesus gives the warrant for his truthful witness by rooting his witness in the context of his participatory identity in the Trinitarian God: "Because I know where I came from and where I go" (ὅτι οἶδα πόθεν ἦλθον καὶ ποῦ ὑπάγω). Jesus has already declared that his truth is founded upon the fact that "the one who sent [him] is true" (7:28). By definition Jesus is the Word of God.

8:15 "You judge according to the flesh, I am not judging anyone" (ὑμεῖς κατὰ τὴν σάρκα κρίνετε, ἐγὼ οὐ κρίνω οὐδένα). Jesus continues his surrejoinder by expressing again the paradox of his authoritative function. Even though he has already stated that he is the Judge (5:22 – 27) and will say as much in the verse to follow (v. 16), Jesus here claims what might seem contradictory: "I am not judging anyone" (ἐγὼ οὐ κρίνω οὐδένα).[11] The explanation must be found in the contrast: "You judge according to the flesh" (ὑμεῖς κατὰ τὴν σάρκα κρίνετε). Judgment according to "the flesh" is a reference to the limited perspective of the person who judges.[12] This is the only time in the Gospel this term is used as a qualifier. In this Gospel, "flesh" is not evil but limited and is to be contrasted with that "from above" (3:3).[13] The judgment of Jesus, then, is different in kind (not degree) from the judgment of the Pharisees. The judgment of Jesus is a subtext of the cosmological mission of the Son, who came simultaneously as Judge (v. 16; cf. 9:39) and Savior of the world (4:42).

8:16 "But even if I judge, my judgment is true, because I am not alone, but I and the one who sent me, the Father" (καὶ ἐὰν κρίνω δὲ ἐγώ, ἡ κρίσις

11. See Brown, *John*, 1:345, for a helpful analysis of the judgment of Jesus in John.

12. Calvin, *John 1 – 10*, 212.
13. Barrett, *John*, 339.

ἡ ἐμὴ ἀληθινή ἐστιν, ὅτι μόνος οὐκ εἰμί, ἀλλ᾽ ἐγὼ καὶ ὁ πέμψας με πατήρ). The proper judgment can only be made by Jesus because his judgment is "true" (ἀληθινή) and because it is rooted in the one who is true — God the Father, who is "the eternal standard of rightness beyond which there is no appeal."[14] For Jesus, the Judge is none other than the Son "in the bosom of the Father" (1:18), who bears an authority rooted in the Trinitarian identity of God. The statement "I am not alone" (μόνος οὐκ εἰμί) expresses in one statement the entire philosophy of Jesus's ministry. The activity of the Son is defined by his relation to the Father, just as the activity of the Father is made known by his relation to the Son (1:18). And it is out of this mysterious and glorious relation that the love of God is bestowed upon the world (3:16).

8:17 "But even in your law it has been written that the testimony of two men is true" (καὶ ἐν τῷ νόμῳ δὲ τῷ ὑμετέρῳ γέγραπται ὅτι δύο ἀνθρώπων ἡ μαρτυρία ἀληθής ἐστιν). After giving what was clearly an untraditional counterargument to the Pharisees in vv. 14 – 16, Jesus concludes his surrejoinder in vv. 17 – 18 by claiming to have met their legal requirements (cf. v. 13). While impossible to see in the English, the location of "But" (δὲ) is in an emphatic position. Combined with the phrase "your law" (τῷ νόμῳ   τῷ ὑμετέρῳ), the distance between Jesus and the Pharisees, or human authority and the authority of God, is given prominence. Jesus had earlier claimed that Moses gave "you the law" (7:19), and here he simply calls it their own. But to prove that the author is not inconsistent with what he wrote, Jesus shows the interrelation between their law and his word. By calling it "your law" and yet showing its facilitation of his word, Jesus further establishes his teaching while rebuking their misunderstanding of the law. These laws

were conceived out of Jesus's true and just nature, and through them he serves to instruct, and in this case to convict, his people.

8:18 "I am the one who testifies concerning myself, and the one who sent me, the Father, testifies concerning me" (ἐγώ εἰμι ὁ μαρτυρῶν περὶ ἐμαυτοῦ καὶ μαρτυρεῖ περὶ ἐμοῦ ὁ πέμψας με πατήρ). Jesus now offers the two, qualified witnesses. He offers himself and "the one who sent me" (ὁ πέμψας με), the Son and the "Father" (πατήρ). These witnesses frame creation itself (John 1:1 – 3) and provide an insurmountable surrejoinder. Jesus speaks of himself with one of several informal "I am" (ἐγώ εἰμι) statements in the Gospel, which serve to give insight into the *particular qualifications* of Jesus (see comments on 6:35). Here the statement offers a climactic declaration of the authority and truthfulness of Jesus's testimony. With this closing statement, the exchange of responses between the plaintiff (Jesus) and the defendants (the Pharisees) concludes.

8:19 Then they said to him, "Where is your Father?" Jesus answered, "You neither know me nor my Father. If you knew me, you would also know my Father" (ἔλεγον οὖν αὐτῷ, Ποῦ ἐστιν ὁ πατήρ σου; ἀπεκρίθη Ἰησοῦς, Οὔτε ἐμὲ οἴδατε οὔτε τὸν πατέρα μου· εἰ ἐμὲ ᾔδειτε, καὶ τὸν πατέρα μου ἂν ᾔδειτε). The verdict begins with a final interjection by the Pharisees. The question, "Where is your Father?" (Ποῦ ἐστιν ὁ πατήρ σου), which for the reader must be seen as originating "according to the flesh" (v. 15), serves as a demand that Jesus bring forth the witness to whom he appeals.[15] It could be taken as a legitimate request, if the Pharisees are thinking of his human "father," or it could be intentionally mocking his preferred title for God, with whom he claimed to have a special re-

---

14. Ibid.   15. Brant, *John*, 143.

lationship. Either way, Hoskyns is correct to call it "doubly blasphemous," since it is arrogantly ignorant of both the Father and the Son.[16] Jesus uses their interjection as a perfect setup for the declaration of his verdict, "You neither know me nor my Father" (Οὔτε ἐμὲ οἴδατε οὔτε τὸν πατέρα μου).

8:20 He spoke these words while teaching by the treasury in the temple, and no one seized him, because his hour had not yet come (Ταῦτα τὰ ῥήματα ἐλάλησεν ἐν τῷ γαζοφυλακίῳ διδάσκων ἐν τῷ ἱερῷ· καὶ οὐδεὶς ἐπίασεν αὐτόν, ὅτι οὔπω ἐληλύθει ἡ ὥρα αὐτοῦ). The narrator concludes the first verbal exchange by explaining how the encounter came to a close. There is no clear significance to the mention of the location, "By the treasury" (ἐν τῷ γαζοφυλακίῳ); if anything, it serves to locate this heated dispute in a populated and significant place in the temple. Even in the domain of the Jewish authorities,[17] Jesus could not be "seized" (ἐπίασεν), for "his hour" (ἡ ὥρα αὐτοῦ) had not come (see comments on 2:4; 7:6, 30). By this the narrator gives emphasis to the authority of Jesus.

8:21 Then again he said to them, "I am going away and you will seek me, and you will die in your sin. Where I am going you are not able to come" (Εἶπεν οὖν πάλιν αὐτοῖς, Ἐγὼ ὑπάγω καὶ ζητήσετέ με, καὶ ἐν τῇ ἁμαρτίᾳ ὑμῶν ἀποθανεῖσθε· ὅπου ἐγὼ ὑπάγω ὑμεῖς οὐ δύνασθε ἐλθεῖν). The second verbal exchange of the first accusation begins with a second evocation of judgment, a charge against the defendants: "You will die in your sin" (ἐν τῇ ἁμαρτίᾳ ὑμῶν ἀποθανεῖσθε). The prepositional phrase "in your sin" (ἐν τῇ ἁμαρτίᾳ) could be functioning as a locative ("in a state of sin") or as an instrumental ("by reason of your sin"). Barrett suggests that the singular "sin" focuses attention

upon the cardinal sin of rejecting Jesus.[18] The absence of further explanation regarding the reason gives emphasis to the judgment itself. Jesus's statement strongly parallels Ezekiel 3:16 – 21, where God gives authority to his agent for the judgment of his people.[19]

While no explanation is added to the judgment, the Judge himself is given a fuller description. Jesus frames this judgment with the stark contrast between the Judge and the accused. The Judge is "going" (ὑπάγω), and the accused will be seeking him in vain. The reason is that "where I am going you are not able to come" (ὅπου ἐγὼ ὑπάγω ὑμεῖς οὐ δύνασθε ἐλθεῖν). Jesus's statement, identical to an earlier statement (see comments on 7:34), presents a contrast between "two antagonistic realities" that are directly opposed to one another (cf. 7:34).[20] The full significance of this statement will be explained in the exchange of responses to follow. Since the term we translated as "going" (ὑπάγω) generally refers to the death of Jesus in the Gospel and therefore to his subsequent return to the Father, it is likely that the cross is the final statement of judgment of Jesus's opponents.

8:22 Then the Jews said, "Surely he will not kill himself, because he said, 'Where I am going you are not able to go?'" (ἔλεγον οὖν οἱ Ἰουδαῖοι, Μήτι ἀποκτενεῖ ἑαυτόν, ὅτι λέγει, Ὅπου ἐγὼ ὑπάγω ὑμεῖς οὐ δύνασθε ἐλθεῖν;). The exchange of responses begins with a private rejoinder by "the Jews," who are the most prominent opponents of Jesus in the Gospel (see comments on 1:19). The rejoinder intends to challenge the claim of Jesus in a slanderous manner. Similar to the Gospel's fourth dialogue (7:14 – 52), this dialogue also involves a complex set of rotating interlocutors, with the different set

---

16. Hoskyns, *Fourth Gospel*, 332.
17. Morris surmises that this location was near the specific hall where the Sanhedrin met (*John*, 394).
18. Barrett, *John*, 340.

19. See Daniel I. Block, *The Book of Ezekiel: Chapters 1 – 24*, NICOT (Grand Rapids: Eerdmans, 1997), 139 – 50.
20. Hoskyns, *Fourth Gospel*, 334.

of interlocutors acting as markers for the main divisions of the pericope.[21]

The Jews respond with a statement that gives the misleading appearance of misunderstanding in order to mock and distort and thereby challenge what Jesus said.[22] The question they ask expects a negative answer and is made emphatic with the term translated as "surely" (Μήτι).[23] Yet their suggestion serves to slander Jesus, since suicide in Judaism was abhorred and considered to be the act of an insane person (cf. Josephus, *J.W.* 3.375). The question was never intended to be realistic but to make a rhetorical statement regarding the sanity of Jesus. Again the irony of the cross is at play (see 10:18).[24]

8:23 And he said to them, "You are from below; I am from above. You are from this world; I am not from this world" (καὶ ἔλεγεν αὐτοῖς, Ὑμεῖς ἐκ τῶν κάτω ἐστέ, ἐγὼ ἐκ τῶν ἄνω εἰμί· ὑμεῖς ἐκ τούτου τοῦ κόσμου ἐστέ, ἐγὼ οὐκ εἰμὶ ἐκ τοῦ κόσμου τούτου). Jesus offers a surrejoinder to the Jews that explains his earlier statement, making clear that he and his opponents are "two antagonistic realities" that are directly opposed to one another.[25] Jesus does not ignore their question but receives it according to its intention — a slander — and offers his own counter by means of two constrastive parallels, the "from below/from above" parallel and the "from this world/not from his world" parallel. There is no need to determine if the below/above reference is Greek or Jewish in background, for the prologue already introduced the cosmological mission of the Son.[26] By comparing the two parallels, the distinction is clear. Jesus and the Jews belong to two different worlds. The origin of Jesus is rooted

in the identity of God, whereas the origin of "the Jews" is rooted in the identity of darkness, sin, and death (v. 21; cf. 1:5). The reader continues to learn the significance of rebirth "from above" (3:1 – 11); such a renewal of origin is needed to overcome our natural state of darkness "from below."

8:24 "I just said to you that you will die in your sins; for unless you believe that I am, you will surely die in your sins" (εἶπον οὖν ὑμῖν ὅτι ἀποθανεῖσθε ἐν ταῖς ἁμαρτίαις ὑμῶν· ἐὰν γὰρ μὴ πιστεύσητε ὅτι ἐγώ εἰμι, ἀποθανεῖσθε ἐν ταῖς ἁμαρτίαις ὑμῶν). Jesus continues his surrejoinder by explaining his opening charge against the defendants (v. 21), making a direct connection between himself and their sin-related death. They will surely die, "If [they] do not believe that I am" (ἐὰν μὴ πιστεύσητε ὅτι ἐγώ εἰμι). The third-class conditional clause, which presents the fulfillment as uncertain though likely, offers a hint of hope to the Jews.[27] However, with the indicative in the apodosis, "You will surely die" (ἀποθανεῖσθε), the negative result if the condition is not met is made emphatic.[28] Interestingly, while the sin mentioned in v. 21 was singular, now it is plural, "sins" (ταῖς ἁμαρτίαις), even as Jesus repeats what he had previously said. The parallel statement with this single distinction suggests that they be viewed as synonymous in meaning. If anything, the move from singular to plural serves rhetorically to emphasize "that unbelief is the fountain and cause of all evils."[29]

According to Jesus, the content of belief is that "I am" (ἐγώ εἰμι). While the phrase by itself could be translated "I am he," the Greek in this context does not appear to fit that normal expression. The

21. Lincoln, *Truth on Trial*, 82.

22. Neyrey, *John*, 155.

23. BDAG 649.

24. According to Bultmann, the Jews "unwittingly become prophets" (*John*, 348). Cf. Origen, *Gospel of John*, 190.

25. Hoskyns, *Fourth Gospel*, 334.

26. See Barrett, *John*, 341.

27. Wallace, *Greek Grammar*, 696.

28. Cf. Brown, *John*, 1:347.

29. Calvin, *John 1 – 10*, 215.

expression is intentionally obscure, as the response by the Jews will reflect in v. 25. Several interpreters suggest the meaning of the expression is its parallel in Isaiah 40 – 55 (see 41:4; 43:10, 13, 25; 46:4; 48:12), where God discloses himself in the repeated declaration, "I am he." It is likely that there is an intentional connection being made between Jesus and Yahweh in the OT. What is clear is that Jesus speaks with one of several informal "I am" statements in the Gospel, which serve to give insight into the *particular qualifications* of Jesus (see comments on 6:35; cf. 8:18). Here the statement qualifies Jesus as the agent of God who mediates life and death, befitting this context where he is presented as the authority and judge of humanity. At this moment, Jesus implies what he will shortly make explicit: "No one comes to the Father except through me" (14:6). The condition Jesus demands is unavoidably clear; the only escape from sin and its consequence of death is belief in Jesus. The disciples of Jesus will soon restate this assertion (Acts 4:12).

8:25 Then they said to him, "Who are you?" Jesus said to them, "[I am] what I said to you at the beginning" (ἔλεγον οὖν αὐτῷ, Σὺ τίς εἶ; εἶπεν αὐτοῖς ὁ Ἰησοῦς, Τὴν ἀρχὴν ὅ τι καὶ λαλῶ ὑμῖν). The Jews offer a second, follow-up rejoinder to Jesus's surrejoinder in the form of a question: "Who are you?" (Σὺ τίς εἶ;). The question is rooted in Jesus's obscure statement in v. 24, in which he gave the condition of the content of belief that "I am" (ἐγώ εἰμι). Jesus had just spoken to the Jews with the "I am" of the Son of God. The Greek word order of their rejoinder makes the "you" emphatic, which serves alongside the first rejoinder as a rebuke and challenge: "You, who are you to be saying such things."[30] Using an analogy Jesus himself will use

(v. 43) the Jews probably recognized the language (the "I am" from the OT; cf. Exod 3), but they could not make sense of it. If they do not know the Father, as Jesus will declare later in the dialogue, they cannot know the Son. The reader, in sharp contrast, knows enough to answer the question, which is exactly what the Gospel expresses as its purpose (20:31).

Jesus offers a second surrejoinder to their question with a clear answer that not only will fit well with v. 26 and carries over from v. 24 the implied "I am," but is also richly theological.[31] The term "the beginning" (Τὴν ἀρχὴν) makes an "impression" (see Introduction) upon the reader that is missed by "the Jews," for the term speaks not merely of the "beginning" of Jesus's ministry but also — and simultaneously — about Jesus the Creator, the one who was with God "in the beginning" (1:1 – 3). Just as the "I am" is both present (in the flesh; 1:14) and timeless ("in the beginning"; 1:1), so also does the verb "I said" suggest both the present speaking of Jesus and the eternal Word. This is no mere creative use of double meaning by the evangelist but a depiction of the coalescence of the historical and cosmological strands of the Gospel's plot in the person and work of Jesus. Jesus was at the creation of the world what he had publicly claimed to be since the beginning of his ministry; it was who he was at that very moment, standing before the Jews.[32]

8:26 "I have many things to say and to judge concerning you, but the one who sent me is true, and the things I have heard from him I declare to the world" (πολλὰ ἔχω περὶ ὑμῶν λαλεῖν καὶ κρίνειν· ἀλλ᾽ ὁ πέμψας με ἀληθής ἐστιν, κἀγὼ ἃ ἤκουσα παρ᾽ αὐτοῦ ταῦτα λαλῶ εἰς τὸν κόσμον). Jesus continues to respond to their question — not to its content

---

30. Morris, *John*, 398.

31. On the text-critical issue, see Metzger, *Textual Commentary*, 191.

32. Hoskyns, *Fourth Gospel*, 336.

but to its rhetorical rebuke and challenge directed at him. Jesus does not speak in the form of a sermon, but "seeing that He is preaching to the deaf," he declares that God will vindicate that about which he speaks.[33] Jesus responds with a judgment "concerning" (περὶ) them. The actions of the Jews are themselves proof of his first accusation against them: the charge against unbelief (vv. 12 – 30). In his function as Judge, Jesus cannot overlook such conduct. The judgment of Jesus must be understood in light of his mission from the Father, who is true (i.e., is reliable and authentic; cf. 1:9) and speaks to — and therefore through — the Son. Jesus's mission, therefore, is legal proof of Jesus's person and words, serving as a legal contract that involves the whole world.

8:27 They did not know that he was speaking to them about the Father (οὐκ ἔγνωσαν ὅτι τὸν πατέρα αὐτοῖς ἔλεγεν). The exchange of responses between the Jews and Jesus is concluded by an explanatory intrusion by the narrator, not uncommon in John (cf. 2:11; 3:16), in which the reader is given key information for interpreting the previous encounter. Quite simply, the Jews did not catch the allusion or, more importantly, the subject matter of Jesus's message about the Father. Unlike the reader, who has been given cosmological insight from the prologue, "the Jews" are blind to things (and persons) about which Jesus speaks. The pause created by the narrator concludes the responses; all that is left is for Jesus to announce his verdict.

8:28 Then Jesus said to them, "When you have lifted up the Son of Man, then you will know that I am, and I do nothing on my own, but I declare the things just as the Father taught me" (εἶπεν οὖν [αὐτοῖς] ὁ Ἰησοῦς, Ὅταν ὑψώσητε τὸν υἱὸν τοῦ ἀνθρώπου, τότε γνώσεσθε ὅτι ἐγώ εἰμι, καὶ ἀπ᾽ ἐμαυτοῦ ποιῶ οὐδέν, ἀλλὰ καθὼς ἐδίδαξέν με ὁ

πατὴρ ταῦτα λαλῶ). The second verbal exchange concludes with Jesus's verdict, beginning with a sovereign statement that offers the final, forensic proof of the present courtroom-like proceedings of this legal challenge. Interestingly, it is not proof that Jesus will provide; "the Jews" themselves will yield this proof!

Jesus prophesies that the proof will be established: "When you have lifted up the Son of Man" (Ὅταν ὑψώσητε τὸν υἱὸν τοῦ ἀνθρώπου). This statement is a direct match to what Jesus said to Nicodemus (cf. 3:14). The use of the term "lifted up" (ὑψώσητε) conveys a rich duality of meaning. In the context of the cross (the historical strand of the plot), the verb speaks of death, suffering, and defeat. But in its larger context (the cosmological strand of the plot), the verb also speaks of exaltation in majesty and glorification (cf. Acts 2:33). In this one word, the message of the Gospel is presented; it is only in his humiliation that Jesus can be exalted and glorified.[34] Ironically, it is in the very act of the crucifixion of Jesus by "the Jews," those Jesus describes as performing the execution ("When *you* have lifted up . . ."), that Jesus is exalted, that is, given the place of honor belonging to Son. The statement is a paradox, combining the most humiliating and cruel act the ancient world could devise (crucifixion) with a title (the "Son of Man"; see comments on 1:51) that incorporates all the power, glory, and authority of God himself. By these words Jesus declares the heart of the Christian message: the Judge has decided to receive upon himself the guilt of the defendant.

This remarkable statement by Jesus is supported by two important additions. First, this event will reveal the identity of Jesus. For as Jesus declared, "Then you will know that I am" (τότε γνώσεσθε ὅτι ἐγώ εἰμι). That the understanding occurs "then" is significant; the Son is revealed at the cross. While

---

33. Calvin, *John 1 – 10*, 217.

34. Cf. Michaels, *John*, 491 – 92.

the world intends the cross to be the world's final word against Jesus, in reality it will be God's final word about Jesus, the coronation of Jesus as the divine authority and Judge.[35] Yet further, this coronation will also declare him Savior of the world (4:42).

Second, this event will make known the relationship of the Son to the Father. The cross will confirm Jesus's participation and role in the cosmological mission of God: "And I do nothing on my own, but I declare the things just as the Father taught me" (καὶ ἀπ᾽ ἐμαυτοῦ ποιῶ οὐδέν, ἀλλὰ καθὼς ἐδίδαξέν με ὁ πατὴρ ταῦτα λαλῶ). Jesus does nothing on his own; what the Father tells him he speaks (see v. 18; cf. 3:34; 5:30; 6:38). As the Gospel will explain, even the specifics of Jesus's ministry are facilitated by the providential will of the Father.

8:29 "The one who sent me is with me. He has not left me alone, for I always do the things that are pleasing to him" (καὶ ὁ πέμψας με μετ᾽ ἐμοῦ ἐστιν· οὐκ ἀφῆκέν με μόνον, ὅτι ἐγὼ τὰ ἀρεστὰ αὐτῷ ποιῶ πάντοτε). The last words of the verdict that Jesus speaks emphasize the intimate communion between the Father and the Son — an issue that will lead directly into the second accusation (vv. 31 – 59). Jesus explains that "the one who sent me (ὁ πέμψας με), a phrase repeated so often that it might be considered a title for Jesus, is "with me" (μετ᾽ ἐμοῦ). Jesus participates within the intimate unity of the divine identity of God. Even in his humanity Jesus has never ceased to be "in the beginning with God" (1:2). The relationship is reciprocal; the Father never leaves the Son, and the Son "always" (πάντοτε) does what pleases the Father. The relationship between the Father and the Son within the divine identity of God is expressed not only by means of presence but also by means of action.

8:30 While he was saying these things, many believed in him (Ταῦτα αὐτοῦ λαλοῦντος πολλοὶ ἐπίστευσαν εἰς αὐτόν). The narrator again (cf. v. 20) concludes the verbal exchange by explaining how the encounter came to a close. The narrator's insight becomes for the reader as much a question as it does a statement, since Jesus himself did not always trust such expressions of belief (cf. 2:23 – 25; see comments on 2:24), nor does the remainder of the dialogue express confidence that the belief of these "Jews" was genuine. In the context of this dialogue, the message is clear for the reader: true belief is belief in the Father through the Son. It is in this way that the second verbal exchange between Jesus and the Jews (vv. 21 – 30) comes to a conclusion within the larger section of Jesus's first accusation as Judge against inappropriate belief (vv. 12 – 30).

8:31 Then Jesus said to the Jews who had believed in him, "If you remain in my word, you are truly my disciples" (Ἔλεγεν οὖν ὁ Ἰησοῦς πρὸς τοὺς πεπιστευκότας αὐτῷ Ἰουδαίους, Ἐὰν ὑμεῖς μείνητε ἐν τῷ λόγῳ τῷ ἐμῷ, ἀληθῶς μαθηταί μού ἐστε). The dialogue transitions to the second accusation of Jesus (vv. 31 – 59), which contains another two verbal exchanges between Jesus and his opponents. The narrator explains the context out of which the first verbal exchange arises. Jesus offers a charge to an unstated number of Jews "who had believed in him" (τοὺς πεπιστευκότας αὐτῷ). There is no warrant for seeing a disconnect between v. 30 and v. 31. In light of the forensic context, "belief" takes on a particularly legal force. Impressed by his appeal to God as witness, some of "the Jews" are prepared to accept his claim.[36] For this reason Jesus will now turn and define the nature of true belief.[37]

The first verbal exchange of the second accusation begins with another evocation of judgment,

---

35. Cf. Bultmann, *John*, 350 – 53.
36. Motyer, *Your Father the Devil*, 157.

37. Jerome H. Neyrey, *An Ideology of Revolt: John's Christology in Social-Science Perspective* (Philadelphia: Fortress, 1988), 43.

a charge against the defendants: "If you remain in my word, you are truly my disciples" (Ἐὰν ὑμεῖς μείνητε ἐν τῷ λόγῳ τῷ ἐμῷ, ἀληθῶς μαθηταί μού ἐστε). The conditional response of the true disciple is to "remain" (μείνητε), a central term in the Gospel (see comments on 6:56). The term communicates the sense of "presence," a permanent residing in a specific location.[38] Just as the Father "remains" in the Son (14:10) and the Spirit "remains" upon Jesus (1:32 – 33), so also must believers "remain" in the Son and he in them (6:56; 15:4). The term is depicting a coparticipatory existence, where the "being" of the believer is determined or regulated by Jesus. It is the depiction of an intimate relationship.

The true disciple is the one who remains "in my word" (ἐν τῷ λόγῳ τῷ ἐμῷ). In a very important sense, Jesus's "word" is his teaching; yet to "remain in my word" is more than what the NIV translates as "hold to my teaching." Jesus will refer to his "word" several times in this chapter (vv. 37, 43, 51, 52, 55). But it is more than Jesus's intellectual property; it must incorporate the sense of coparticipatory presence. That is, it must include a spiritual dimension (cf. 5:37, 38). The use of the significant term "word" (λόγος), a term made foundational to the person of Christ in the prologue (see comments on 1:1), demands that we not limit the intentionally robust "impression" (see Introduction) it is expected to make upon the reader. To "remain" in "my word" is ultimately to remain in "the Word." In this sense, the "word" is not merely the message of Jesus but also his person and his work. In contrast to the Jews in 5:38, it is taking personal and permanent residence in the spiritual presence of God mediated through the Son and shortly to be empowered and facilitated by the Spirit. It is the mode of existence for the Christian.

8:32 "Then you will know the truth, and the truth will set you free" (καὶ γνώσεσθε τὴν ἀλήθειαν, καὶ ἡ ἀλήθεια ἐλευθερώσει ὑμᾶς). Jesus continues his charge with the addition of a guarantee. For the one who truly believes and is a true disciple, they "will know the truth" (γνώσεσθε τὴν ἀλήθειαν). The prologue has already explained that grace and "truth" are part and parcel of a relationship with the Son, which when taken together speak of God's original expression of covenantal faithfulness to his people, which has now been transcended by Christ (see comments on 1:14). "Truth" is not only a philosophical concept but is also relational, denoting true knowledge of God. The truth to be known is that Jesus is the saving mission of God, the one through whom grace and "truth" have come (1:17), who is the authoritative expression of the Father and his love for the world.[39] In short, the "truth" is the gospel of Jesus Christ.

Jesus continues by saying that this truth "will set you free" (ἐλευθερώσει ὑμᾶς). The term "freedom," which only occurs in this context in John (vv. 33, 36), is not best defined by Stoic or rabbinic definitions. In this context, it is defined by being contrasted with sin (v. 34), which suggests that the "freedom" about which Jesus speaks is equivalent to salvation. The truth, which centers upon the person and work of Jesus, is liberating. Again, this liberation is not philosophical or rooted in politics, but is a spiritual freedom. Nor is this kind of freedom based on the original freedom of humanity, the authentic self of man, but a freedom that belongs entirely to God.[40] It is the kind of liberation that can only come from a birth "from above" (3:3); it is liberation that flows out of the eschatological birth "from water and spirit" (3:5).

8:33 They answered him, "We are the seed of Abraham and we have never been enslaved

---

38. BDAG 630 – 31.
39. Barrett, *John*, 344.
40. Cf. Bultmann, *John*, 436.

to anyone. **How can you say, 'We will become free?'** ᵉ" (ἀπεκρίθησαν πρὸς αὐτόν, Σπέρμα Ἀβραάμ ἐσμεν καὶ οὐδενὶ δεδουλεύκαμεν πώποτε· πῶς σὺ λέγεις ὅτι Ἐλεύθεροι γενήσεσθε;). The exchange of responses begins with a rejoinder by Jesus's opponents, who are clearly baffled by the suggestion that they are not already free. Although the narrator leaves undefined the particular identity of this respondent,[41] he has been careful to depict with literary precision the multifaceted group that opposes Jesus, both in this dialogue and in the previous one (7:14 – 52; see comments before 7:14). The silence on the particulars is best viewed as an intentional focus on the larger opponent of this dialogue, the Jewish authorities, who in this particular verbal exchange represent the people of God under the old covenant.

Jesus's opponents respond with strong opposition to Jesus's claim in vv. 31 – 32: "We are the seed of Abraham and we have never been enslaved to anyone" (Σπέρμα Ἀβραάμ ἐσμεν καὶ οὐδενὶ δεδουλεύκαμεν πώποτε). The Jewish authorities offer a rejoinder that declares their identity as the "seed of Abraham," which is a title that makes a claim that is something akin to divinely established royalty. It is a claim that is rooted in Old Testament Scripture and founded upon centuries of the proven faithfulness of God. As biblical as this title might sound, it is profoundly mistaken, as the opponent's second statement makes clear.

The opponents add a second claim: "We have never been enslaved to anyone" (οὐδενὶ δεδουλεύκαμεν πώποτε). Interpreters often explain the misunderstanding of this statement in this way: " 'The Jews' seem to misunderstand Jesus's words about freedom and take them in a political sense."[42] This is usually followed by a necessary correction

based upon political standards that make clear that such a boast is inappropriately founded, since the Jewish people were enslaved by Egypt, Babylonia, and then Rome. But the Jews were not thinking in mere political terms. They too were thinking of a spiritual reality. The Jews were not oblivious to their own history — and neither was Jesus. Rather, the Jews are giving what might be described as an internal definition of freedom, so that "in spite of political oppression they think of themselves as free sons of Abraham, who have never inwardly bowed to foreign rule."[43] The claim by the Jews is not in regard to physical-political slavery but to their monotheism: "They have never served any being other than God; indeed, to serve another 'divine' being would be tantamount to slavery."[44] It is important to see how the counterclaim of the Jews raises an important, clarifying question: "How can you say, 'We will become free?' " (πῶς σὺ λέγεις ὅτι Ἐλεύθεροι γενήσεσθε;). The counterclaim by the Jews, then, suggests that the Jews understand Jesus's statement to be violating or transgressing the boundaries of biblical monotheism.

8:34 Jesus answered to them, "Truly, truly I say to you, everyone who sins is a slave to sin" (ἀπεκρίθη αὐτοῖς ὁ Ἰησοῦς, Ἀμὴν ἀμὴν λέγω ὑμῖν ὅτι πᾶς ὁ ποιῶν τὴν ἁμαρτίαν δοῦλός ἐστιν [τῆς ἁμαρτίας]). Jesus begins his surrejoinder with an authoritative preface (see comments on 1:51) that signifies the importance of what follows. Jesus gives further explanation to his charge of enslavement, claiming that slavery is defined not by a person's "seed" but by a person's "sin" (τὴν ἁμαρτίαν). If someone sins, Jesus states clearly, that person is "a slave to sin" (δοῦλός ἐστιν [τῆς ἁμαρτίας]; the objective genitive serves as the direct object of the

41. See Debbie Hunn, "Who Are 'They' in John 8:33?" *CBQ* 66 (2004): 387 – 99.

42. Brown, *John*, 1:355.

43. Schnackenburg, *John*, 2:207.

44. Adele Reinhartz, "John 8:31 – 59 from a Jewish Perspective," in *Remembering for the Future: The Holocaust in an Age of Genocide*, ed. John K. Roth and Elisabeth Maxwell, 3 vols. (New York: Palgrave, 2001), 2:787 – 97 (793).

noun "slave"). Jesus demands his opponents define their "freedom" not only by means of their relation to God but also by means of their relation to sin. In this way, while the Jewish people are distinct from the world according to their Abrahamic nature, they are identical to the world according to their human nature. They too are enslaved to sin. The very law of God that made them a unique people in the world should have also revealed to them their similarity to the world; it should have been through the law that they became "conscious of [their] sin" (Rom 3:20).

8:35 "And the slave does not remain in the house forever; the son remains forever" (ὁ δὲ δοῦλος οὐ μένει ἐν τῇ οἰκίᾳ εἰς τὸν αἰῶνα· ὁ υἱὸς μένει εἰς τὸν αἰῶνα). In the form of a metaphor or an illustration (cf. 10:6; 11:9),[45] Jesus explains the difference between a "slave" and a "son" (υἱός); the son has a permanent residence in the household, that is, the family, but the slave does not. The statement is significant beyond its analogy to the Jews. For it speaks not of "sons" but "the son" (ὁ υἱὸς) who remains "forever" (εἰς τὸν αἰῶνα), and in this Gospel the primary referent of "son" is Jesus Christ. Jesus is "the Son of God" (ὁ υἱὸς τοῦ θεοῦ; cf. 20:31); the ones for whom he came are more simply designated as "children of God" (τέκνα θεοῦ; cf. 1:12). The distinction is important (cf. Gal 3:16). Thus, "the son" serves as both an analogy for the adoption of the people of God and as a direct reference to Jesus. Since the reference to Jesus is only made clear in v. 36, the term "son" is translated lowercase so as to preserve the analogy.

8:36 "If then the Son has set you free, you will be free indeed" (ἐὰν οὖν ὁ υἱὸς ὑμᾶς ἐλευθερώσῃ, ὄντως ἐλεύθεροι ἔσεσθε). The referent of "son" is clearly Jesus when he claims that it is only the Son that can offer true freedom — freedom "indeed"

(ὄντως). By this statement Jesus declares to his opponents that there is a freedom that does not yet belong to them. It is a freedom that belongs to the Son and that only he can give. It is a freedom that is unknown not only to the world but even to the descendants of Abraham — a freedom from the tyranny of sin.[46] The freedom that Jesus offers is liberation from enslavement to self-interest and the devil; it is a freedom that turns slaves into sons and those of the household of the devil into eternal members of the household of the Father.

8:37 "I know that you are the seed of Abraham. Yet you are seeking to kill me, because there is no place in you for my word" (οἶδα ὅτι σπέρμα Ἀβραάμ ἐστε· ἀλλὰ ζητεῖτέ με ἀποκτεῖναι, ὅτι ὁ λόγος ὁ ἐμὸς οὐ χωρεῖ ἐν ὑμῖν). After clarifying their definition of "freedom" (vv. 34–36), Jesus now clarifies their definition of "the seed of Abraham." Just as Jesus can acknowledge the uniqueness of the Jewish people in the plan of God and yet still declare them to be enslaved to sin, so also can Jesus acknowledge that they are born of "the seed of Abraham" and yet still need a "new birth" (cf. 3:3–5). The need is made visible by the actions of the Jews. Their attempts to kill Jesus prove the point. Their actions are similar to the suicidal actions of an insane person, with "the seed" trying to kill "the Seed." The reason for this spiritual insanity is that "there is no place in you for my word" (ὁ λόγος ὁ ἐμὸς οὐ χωρεῖ ἐν ὑμῖν). Just as the use of "the word" (ὁ λόγος) in v. 31 signified the sense of coparticipatory presence, here it implies that Jesus's opponents want nothing to do with the person and work of Jesus. The contrast between these Jews and their father Abraham is being made clear, for Abraham was aware of what he had received from above, causing his vision not to go inward toward himself but forward toward Christ (see Heb 11:10, 16).

---

45. Cf. Michaels, *John*, 507.

46. Hoskyns, *Fourth Gospel*, 339.

8:38 "I am declaring to you what I have seen in the presence of the Father, and you do what you have heard from your father" (ἃ ἐγὼ ἑώρακα παρὰ τῷ πατρὶ λαλῶ· καὶ ὑμεῖς οὖν ἃ ἠκούσατε παρὰ τοῦ πατρὸς ποιεῖτε). Jesus contrasts the lack of presence between Jesus and his opponents ("no place in you for my word") with the coparticipatory presence between the Father and the Son. Jesus spoke in the previous verbal exchange (vv. 21 – 30) of the intimate relation he has with the Father (v. 29). Here he explains that his message finds its source and origin in his relation to his Father.

Jesus presents by implication a sharp contrast when he compares "the Father" under whose authority he acts with "the father" under whose authority the Jews act. Neither "F/father" is connected to a possessive noun. As a result, all the emphasis falls on the fatherhood itself as the decisive origin, background, and standard for each.[47] In a sense, the actions and character of the "S/son" reveals the nature of the "F/father." The rhetorical force of Jesus's statement demands that his opponents define their "father" and therefore the nature of their origin and kinship.

8:39 They answered and said to him, "Abraham is our father." Jesus said to them, "If you are the children of Abraham, you would do the works of Abraham" (Ἀπεκρίθησαν καὶ εἶπαν αὐτῷ, Ὁ πατὴρ ἡμῶν Ἀβραάμ ἐστιν. λέγει αὐτοῖς ὁ Ἰησοῦς, Εἰ τέκνα τοῦ Ἀβραάμ ἐστε, τὰ ἔργα τοῦ Ἀβραὰμ ἐποιεῖτε). The Jews reiterate what they already stated in v. 37 that Abraham is their father. Such a response suggests they discern the paternity challenge of Jesus. Abraham was their father; he was *the* patriarch and the matter was beyond dispute. Their lack of understanding, however, reminds the reader of the overlap between legal and social challenges, where the engagement involved the creation of creative

possibilities — not for empty purposes but to make emphatic the higher realities.

Jesus responds with a simple counterargument: if you were "children" (τέκνα) of Abraham, you would "do the works of Abraham" (τὰ ἔργα τοῦ Ἀβραὰμ ἐποιεῖτε). That is, if their origins were truly founded upon Abraham, they would do what he did. By implication, the opponents are being declared to be outside the family of Abraham. The logic for this is not rooted in a distinction between the terms "seed" (σπέρμα) and "children" (τέκνα), for the terms here are interchangeable, but rather in the distinction that exists between one's heritage and one's actions. While the Jews are "naturally" descendants of Abraham, there is something more significant about them that is unnatural — they are unspiritual. Because of this they are neither the true "seed" nor the true "children" of Abraham. Ultimately, the bloodline that is significant is not Abrahams's but Christ's.

8:40 "But now you seek to kill me, a man who has spoken the truth to you which I heard from God. This Abraham did not do" (νῦν δὲ ζητεῖτέ με ἀποκτεῖναι, ἄνθρωπον ὃς τὴν ἀλήθειαν ὑμῖν λελάληκα ἣν ἤκουσα παρὰ τοῦ θεοῦ· τοῦτο Ἀβραὰμ οὐκ ἐποίησεν). Jesus again offers them proof by showing the disconnection between the heritage they claim and their actions. Interestingly, Jesus compares himself to Abraham as "a man" (ἄνθρωπον) who listens to God and responded to what he heard by doing it. That is, while Jesus speaks about life, the Jews seek his death. Clearly God would not command this! Nor would Abraham respond in this way. The implication is becoming clearer. Their actions betray the identity they claim for themselves.

8:41 "You do the works of your father." Then they said to him, "We have not been born as

---

47. Ridderbos, *John*, 311.

illegitimate children. We have one Father, God"
(ὑμεῖς ποιεῖτε τὰ ἔργα τοῦ πατρὸς ὑμῶν. εἶπαν [οὖν]
αὐτῷ, Ἡμεῖς ἐκ πορνείας οὐ γεγεννήμεθα· ἕνα πατέρα
ἔχομεν τὸν θεόν). The implication of their actions
according to Jesus is that their works — their murderous intentions (vv. 37, 40) — betray the identity
of their true father.[48] At this point the father is not
named (until v. 44), serving as an emphatic contrast
with the Father who has already been named.

Correctly interpreting Jesus's rebuke of their
ancestry, his opponents respond with a strong protest: "We have not been born as illegitimate children" (Ἡμεῖς ἐκ πορνείας οὐ γεγεννήμεθα). While
the phrase might be translated as "not born of for-
nication" (NASB), in this context they are speaking about their heritage and the legitimacy of their
birthright and lineage as the people of God.[49] The
emphatic "we" (Ἡμεῖς) is intended to be self-referential to direct attention to their claim of origin.
Even the next phrase is focused on their identity,
not the identity of Jesus.[50] Not until v. 48 do the
Jews turn and attack the identity of Jesus. The
reader is expected to see the clear contrast between
the claim of the Jews to be legitimate children and
the very different claim made by the prologue regarding the true "children of God" (1:12).

After stating who they are not, Jesus's opponents
make a further claim of identity: "We have one
Father, God" (ἕνα πατέρα ἔχομεν τὸν θεόν). The
transition from Abraham as father (v. 39) to God
as Father is not entirely clear. The Old Testament
rarely referred to God as Father, though it was implied in certain depictions of God as Creator (Deut
32:6; Isa 64:8; Jer 3:4), in his covenant relationship
with Israel (Jer 3:19; Mal 2:10; cf. Jub. 2:20; 19:29),
and in his rule and kingship over them (Isa 63:16;
Ps 89:27; 2 Sam 7:14). "Jesus's description of his adversaries as children of an alien father would be to

their minds the most offensive accusation he could
advance against them."[51] It is quite possible, therefore, to interpret the statement by the Jews as an
argumentative maneuver; Jesus can try to disassociate them from Abraham, but he certainly cannot
disassociate them from God.

**8:42 Jesus said to them, "If God were your Fa-
ther, you would love me, for I came from God
and am now present. For I have not come on my
own, but he sent me"** (εἶπεν αὐτοῖς ὁ Ἰησοῦς, Εἰ
ὁ θεὸς πατὴρ ὑμῶν ἦν, ἠγαπᾶτε ἂν ἐμέ, ἐγὼ γὰρ ἐκ
τοῦ θεοῦ ἐξῆλθον καὶ ἥκω· οὐδὲ γὰρ ἀπ' ἐμαυτοῦ
ἐλήλυθα, ἀλλ' ἐκεῖνός με ἀπέστειλεν). But Jesus is
not persuaded by their divine trump card. Their
actions deserve to be betrayed not only as a disassociation from Abraham but also as a separation from God. The evidence is their treatment of
Jesus. Rather than trying to kill him (cf. vv. 37, 40),
they should "love" (ἠγαπᾶτε) him. The term "love"
does not intend to refer to emotional or personal
affection but to allegiance, commitment, even obedience. Jesus reveals to his opponents the cosmological "unseen" of the prologue and the mission of
Father who sent the Son (1:9–10). Ironically, in the
exact manner that God loved the world, the world
hated God (3:16).

**8:43 "Why do you not understand my language?
Because you are unable to hear my word"** (διὰ τί
τὴν λαλιὰν τὴν ἐμὴν οὐ γινώσκετε; ὅτι οὐ δύνασθε
ἀκούειν τὸν λόγον τὸν ἐμόν). This statement by
Jesus — a question followed by an answer — is significant because of the use of two related words
that are distinct. The term "language" (λαλιὰν)
here refers to the way someone speaks, as in their
dialect or accent (cf. Matt 26:73). The question can
be translated, "Why do you not understand what
I say?" This is in contrast to "word" (λόγον), an

48. Motyer, *Your Father the Devil*, 192–94.
49. Cf. BDAG 854.
50. Cf. Schnackenburg, *John*, 2:212.
51. Ridderbos, *John*, 313.

important term in this dialogue (see comments on v. 31). Here it refers to the content of what someone says. Thus, it is a contrast between the *way* one speaks (their style) and *what* one speaks (their subject matter). Jesus is arguing that his opponents cannot make sense of his style of speech because they are unable "to hear" (ἀκούειν) its subject matter. The term "hear" was defined earlier by Jesus as an act of belief in which one responds to God (see comments on 5:24). A similar meaning is clearly intended in this context.[52] The very accommodation of God to them in the person of Jesus becomes to them a rebuke. With this closing statement, this lengthy exchange of responses between Jesus and his opponents concludes.

8:44 "You belong to your father, the devil, and you want to do your father's desire. He was a murderer from the beginning, and does not stand in the truth, because there is no truth in him. When he speaks a lie, he speaks from his own supply, because he is a liar and the father of lies" (ὑμεῖς ἐκ τοῦ πατρὸς τοῦ διαβόλου ἐστὲ καὶ τὰς ἐπιθυμίας τοῦ πατρὸς ὑμῶν θέλετε ποιεῖν. ἐκεῖνος ἀνθρωποκτόνος ἦν ἀπ᾽ ἀρχῆς, καὶ ἐν τῇ ἀληθείᾳ οὐκ ἔστηκεν, ὅτι οὐκ ἔστιν ἀλήθεια ἐν αὐτῷ. ὅταν λαλῇ τὸ ψεῦδος, ἐκ τῶν ἰδίων λαλεῖ, ὅτι ψεύστης ἐστὶν καὶ ὁ πατὴρ αὐτοῦ). The first verbal exchange of the second accusation concludes with the verdict of Jesus. The verdict makes explicit what for rhetorical purposes Jesus kept implicit during the change of responses: "You belong to your father, the devil" (ὑμεῖς ἐκ τοῦ πατρὸς τοῦ διαβόλου ἐστὲ). The statement is grammatically flexible but is best understood by viewing the two genitives as appositional, with the genitive case communicating belonging.[53]

Jesus declares that his opponents find their origin and identity in the person and work of the devil. This is not only a guilty verdict but a declaration of evil. According to Jesus, they "want to do" (θέλετε ποιεῖν) the desires of their father. And their father's nature and desires are the definition of evil, against which the reader is expected to contrast the nature of Jesus. The contrast is evident in the three descriptions of the devil. First, the devil is described as a murderer "from the beginning" (ἀπ᾽ ἀρχῆς). In contrast, Jesus is not associated with death but "life" (1:4), the one who has "life in himself" (5:26) and is "life" (14:6), who has no beginning (1:1). Second, the devil is described as one who does not "stand" (ἔστηκεν) in the truth (emphasized with the perfect tense) because "there is no truth in him" (οὐκ ἔστιν ἀλήθεια ἐν αὐτῷ). In contrast, Jesus has his origins in "the one who ... is true" (v. 26), and he is "the truth" (14:6). Third, the devil speaks lies, has his own supply of lies,[54] and bears the title "the father of lies" (ὁ πατὴρ αὐτοῦ) — an awkward phrase (more rigidly, "the father of it") in which the antecedent of the pronoun, "lie" (ψεῦδος), may be supplied.[55] In contrast, Jesus has only spoken "truth" (v. 40) which he received from his Father's supply (v. 38), and he is the Father's Son (1:14). The illegitimate origin of the opponents of Jesus has been expressed with the most graphic and offensive terminology possible in this context, using the most biblical depictions of evil recorded in Scripture.

8:45 "But because I speak the truth, you do not believe me!" (ἐγὼ δὲ ὅτι τὴν ἀλήθειαν λέγω, οὐ πιστεύετέ μοι). In contrast to the lies of the devil, their father, Jesus speaks the truth. According to Jesus, the verdict is given validity by the irony of their response to him. It proves the affiliation of his opponents with this "liar." Jesus does not say "although" I speak the truth you do not believe me,

52. Cf. Bultmann, *John*, 317.
53. Cf. BDF § 268.2.
54. See BDAG 467.
55. Cf. Bultmann, *John*, 318–19.

but "because" (ὅτι).[56] Jesus and his interlocutors are in contradictory camps and are opponents by nature. The cost of freedom is to know the truth — not merely about God but also about self (v. 32). It was a choice between a life of freedom and the death of sin (v. 24). They chose instead to believe the devil's very first lie: "You will surely not die" (Gen 3:4).[57]

8:46 "Who among you convicts me of sin? If I am speaking the truth, why do you not believe me?" (τίς ἐξ ὑμῶν ἐλέγχει με περὶ ἁμαρτίας; εἰ ἀλήθειαν λέγω, διὰ τί ὑμεῖς οὐ πιστεύετέ μοι;). As the verdict of Jesus comes to a close, Jesus the Judge challenges his defendants with two rhetorical questions. Using language common to a courtroom ("convicts" [ἐλέγχει]), Jesus challenges them to prove him wrong, with the full knowledge that they cannot do so. This question makes a remarkable claim about the sinlessness of Jesus, establishing his perfect qualifications and "perfect confidence"as the Judge of this trial.[58] As Morris notes, what is remarkable is not simply that there was no sin to behold but that Jesus made the claim at all.[59]

At the same time, in this context such a claim is not primarily about him but his Father. He is claiming that there is no evidence to show that he is not faithfully declaring what he received from his Father (v. 38). This explains how the second rhetorical question offers a corollary rebuke that serves as further warrant: "The sinless truth is right in front of you, and yet you reject it!" Godet surmises that this second question was probably "followed by a pause sufficient to give opportunity to whoever should wish to accuse Him to be heard … No one opens his mouth."[60] Jesus had declared their origin to be illegitimate and their ancestral heritage to be insufficient as the people of God. There was nothing left for them to say.

8:47 "The one who belongs to God hears the words of God. The reason you do not hear is because you do not belong to God!" (ὁ ὢν ἐκ τοῦ θεοῦ τὰ ῥήματα τοῦ θεοῦ ἀκούει· διὰ τοῦτο ὑμεῖς οὐκ ἀκούετε, ὅτι ἐκ τοῦ θεοῦ οὐκ ἐστέ). Jesus concludes his verdict and the verbal exchange by providing the answer to his own questions above. This concluding statement is in the form of a syllogism, working cooperatively with what Jesus already explained in v. 44.[61] Since they belong to the devil, they do not belong to God. They are, quite simply, illegitimate children. The ancestral heritage they claim for themselves is a lie from the devil. As the reader has long known, the true "children of God" (1:12) find their origin "not from blood, nor from the desire of the flesh, nor from the will of a husband, *but from God*" (1:13). Everything about them is distorted and unnatural. They are outsiders to God, his kingdom, and his promises. They are blinded by "the god of this age" (2 Cor 4:4) and dead in their own sin. A clearer and more damning conclusion is hardly conceivable. And yet the reader cannot forget that these opponents of Jesus, intentionally unnamed in this verbal exchange, are the epitome of those Jesus came to save and the object of God's love (3:16).

8:48 The Jews answered and said to him, "Are we not right in saying that you are a Samaritan and have a demon?" (Ἀπεκρίθησαν οἱ Ἰουδαῖοι καὶ εἶπαν αὐτῷ, Οὐ καλῶς λέγομεν ἡμεῖς ὅτι Σαμαρίτης εἶ σὺ καὶ δαιμόνιον ἔχεις;). The second verbal exchange of the second accusation of this formal conflict dialogue begins with a twist. In the first three verbal exchanges, Jesus was the aggressor,

---

56. Morris, *John*, 412.
57. Michaels, *John*, 521.
58. Calvin, *John*, 229.
59. Morris, *John*, 412.

60. Godet, *John*, 677.
61. Richard A. Bondi, "John 8:39 – 47: Children of Abraham or of the Devil?" *JES* 34 (1997): 473 – 98 (482).

offering his own challenge to his accusers. In this final verbal exchange the Jewish authorities, designated again as "the Jews," try to regain control of the conflict. The narrative gives no reason for this adjustment; the reader can only assume that the plaintiff has made his final statement and the Judge his final verdict. This section begins with the reintroduction of "the Jews," who here assume the role of the plaintiff.

The charge of the Jews is in the form of a rhetorical question that serves as a statement to which Jesus is expected to respond. The opening phrase of the question begins with an idiomatic expression in Greek, "Are we not right in saying" (Οὐ καλῶς λέγομεν ἡμεῖς), which gives the impression that this was a common opinion concerning Jesus among the Jewish authorities.[62] Jesus declared "the Jews" to be outsiders to God (cf. vv. 23, 47), and the Jews reciprocate by declaring Jesus to be an outsider to Judaism.

The Jews declare Jesus to be "a Samaritan" (Σαμαρίτης) and to "have a demon" (δαιμόνιον ἔχεις). This declaration has a significant relation to the response of the Jews to the verdict of Jesus where they were speaking not of physical-political slavery but monotheism (v. 33). By implication, then, the Jews were counterclaiming that Jesus was violating or transgressing the boundaries of biblical monotheism. While it is possible simply to interpret this opening verse as "an ancient version of name-calling devoid of specific content,"[63] its inclusion in a formal legal challenge makes this unlikely.

But there is more evidence to consider. It is not just the individual names that are important but the significance derived from their combination.

According to Reinhartz, both insults are associated with heresy in ancient sources (see Ps 106:36 – 37; Jub. 19:28 – 29).[64] For example, Psalm 106:36 – 37 draws a parallel between the Israelite's worship of idols and the sacrificing of their sons and daughters to demons. And in later Jewish literature, the devil is considered to be at work in those who worship other gods (Jub. 19:28 – 29). The connection is most clearly seen in Justin Martyr's address to the emperor of Rome, who connects the origin and work of Samaritans to demons.[65] By claiming Jesus is *both* a Samaritan and possessed by a demon, the Jews are effectively calling him a heretic, "accusing him of straying from the one true God."[66] This, then, is the charge that initiates the fourth verbal exchange.

8:49 Jesus answered, "I do not have a demon, but I honor my Father, and you dishonor me" (ἀπεκρίθη Ἰησοῦς, Ἐγὼ δαιμόνιον οὐκ ἔχω, ἀλλὰ τιμῶ τὸν πατέρα μου, καὶ ὑμεῖς ἀτιμάζετέ με). Jesus makes a rejoinder to the charge made by "the Jews," strengthened in force by the emphatic pronouns. Jesus only addresses the charge of demonic oppression, not the charge of being a Samaritan. It is possible that the charge of demon possession is a foundational charge, viewed as the underlying cause of all heresy and idolatry, whether by a Samaritan, a gentile, or even a Jew. At the same time, the Gospel has already made clear that Jesus has an identity that is rooted in the divine identity of God and that he is proclaiming a message that fits neither the Jewish nor Samaritan mode of worship (cf. 4:23). Thus, Jesus is not ignoring the charge of being a Samaritan[67] but eclipsing it in his very person, rooted in his divine identity as the Son of God

---

62. Michaels, *John*, 522.
63. Reinhartz, "John 8:31 – 59 from a Jewish Perspective," 793.
64. Ibid.

65. Justin Martyr, *Writings of Saint Justin Martyr*, trans. T. B. Falls (New York: Christian Heritage, 1948), 61 – 62.
66. Reinhartz, "John 8:31 – 59 from a Jewish Perspective," 793.
67. Contra Lincoln, *John*, 274.

and Son of Man. For this reason he does not need to defend who he is but only what he is doing, connecting it to the authority of God and not the devil.

Jesus's concern is not with the specifics of the charge, but with its implication. Jesus contrasts his behavior with theirs: "I honor my Father, and you dishonor me" (τιμῶ τὸν πατέρα μου, καὶ ὑμεῖς ἀτιμάζετέ με). Again the depiction of the Father as "my Father" (τὸν πατέρα μου) serves to separate the Jews from "their" God. But there are two significant contrasts that Jesus communicates. The first contrast is between two opposing actions communicated by the use of related verbs: "I honor . . . you dishonor" (τιμῶ . . . ἀτιμάζετέ). According to Jesus, his actions are the exact opposite of a heretical or demon-possessed person, for his actions "honor" God. Jesus epitomizes what it means to honor God; indeed, it is only through the person and work of Jesus that any person can give honor to God.

This is why Jesus can make a second contrast, one between the Father and the Son. As the representative of the Father, dishonoring Jesus is equivalent to dishonoring God. Jesus makes this clear, as recorded earlier in the Gospel (5:23). In essence, their claim against Jesus is self-refuting. The moment they raised their accusatory finger toward Jesus, they accused the very God they wrongly thought they were serving and defending.

8:50 "But I do not seek my glory, but there is one who seeks it and who judges" (ἐγὼ δὲ οὐ ζητῶ τὴν δόξαν μου· ἔστιν ὁ ζητῶν καὶ κρίνων). By seeking the "honor" of his Father, Jesus explicitly denys himself "my glory" (τὴν δόξαν μου), which by implication suggests that there is glory that belongs to and is due him. Just as the active work of Jesus is defined by the Father, so is his passivity also a reflection of his submission to the Father. Jesus states with rhetorically implicit language how "there is one" who will be concerned on behalf of Jesus; the Father himself will vindicate Jesus and

disprove the charges made against him and has by implication already judged in favor of his Son against his accusers, the Jews. The ambiguity in the Gospel regarding who is the judge between the Son and the Father — the judgment of the Son is not done in isolation from the Father (cf. vv. 15 – 16), and the Father never judges except through the Son (5:22 – 27) — serves to emphasize the intimate and functional identity of the Father and the Son. The charge against the Son *is* a charge against the Father.

8:51 "Truly, truly I say to you, if a person keeps my word, he will never see death" (ἀμὴν ἀμὴν λέγω ὑμῖν, ἐάν τις τὸν ἐμὸν λόγον τηρήσῃ, θάνατον οὐ μὴ θεωρήσῃ εἰς τὸν αἰῶνα.). Jesus continues his rejoinder to the charge of the Jews with another statement that starts with an authoritative preface (see comments on 1:51), signifying the importance of what follows. Having declared his vindication from the Father, Jesus turns and offers hope to his accusers. The condition is centered again on the "word" (λόγον) of Jesus. The phrase "keeps my word" (τὸν ἐμὸν λόγον τηρήσῃ) is best viewed as synonymous with the phrase used by Jesus in v. 31, "remain in my word." Unless a person joins Jesus, embraces fully his person and work, the only verdict available to them will be one that falls against them, declared by the Father himself. That verdict is "death" (θάνατον). Yet Jesus offers hope, as he has done before (see comments on v. 28). The person who embraces Jesus "will never see death" (θάνατον οὐ μὴ θεωρήσῃ εἰς τὸν αἰῶνα), a phrase filled with grammatical emphases. To "see death" is to experience death. To "never" see death, then, is to experience eternal life — the very reason the Father sent the Son (3:16).

8:52 Then the Jews said to him, "Now we know that you have a demon. Abraham died, and the prophets, yet you say, 'If a person keeps my word, he will never taste death'" (εἶπον [οὖν] αὐτῷ οἱ

Ἰουδαῖοι, Νῦν ἐγνώκαμεν ὅτι δαιμόνιον ἔχεις. Ἀβραὰμ ἀπέθανεν καὶ οἱ προφῆται, καὶ σὺ λέγεις, Ἐάν τις τὸν λόγον μου τηρήσῃ, οὐ μὴ γεύσηται θανάτου εἰς τὸν αἰῶνα). The Jews offer a surrejoinder that seeks to discredit and rebuke the rejoinder of Jesus. The Jews repeat Jesus's statement almost verbatim with the exception of the change from "see" death to "taste" (γεύσηται) death, a change of little significance. The Jews offer a theological criticism of Jesus's statement, claiming he contradicts God and his previous "word." According to their logic, if these great "word"-bearers of God like Abraham and the prophets "died" (ἀπέθανεν), so then must they! In effect, they claim, "Your declaration, Jesus, is entirely false, and your own words bear witness to our charge against you. You are a heretic! Anyone who would claim to be superior to Abraham and all the prophets is under the influence of the powers of darkness."

8:53 "Surely you are not greater than our father Abraham, who died? The prophets also died. Whom do you make yourself out to be?" (μὴ σὺ μείζων εἶ τοῦ πατρὸς ἡμῶν Ἀβραάμ, ὅστις ἀπέθανεν; καὶ οἱ προφῆται ἀπέθανον· τίνα σεαυτὸν ποιεῖς;). The Jews continue their surrejoinder by pressing against Jesus the implications of their logic. They begin with a slanderous question that expects a negative answer. Their question, with the language of "our father Abraham" (τοῦ πατρὸς ἡμῶν Ἀβραάμ), is nearly identical to the one posed by the Samaritan woman (4:12) with regard to "our father Jacob," both of which are probably uses of the exclusive "we."[68] The question then does not only intend to deny Jesus his claim to be the representative of God but to exclude Jesus from the very God he claims to represent.

The Jews try to corner Jesus by questioning the merit of his identity and affiliation. He claims not to be demon possessed, so now the Jews attempt to remove from him his affiliation with Abraham or the prophets — his Jewish identity. So they ask him in the form of an idiomatic question, "Whom do you make yourself out to be?" (τίνα σεαυτὸν ποιεῖς;).[69] Similar language was used in 5:18 when the Jews were trying to kill Jesus because he was "making himself" (ἑαυτὸν ποιῶν) equal with God.

8:54 Jesus answered, "If I glorify myself, my glory is nothing. The one who glorifies me is my Father, whom you say is your God" (ἀπεκρίθη Ἰησοῦς, Ἐὰν ἐγὼ δοξάσω ἐμαυτόν, ἡ δόξα μου οὐδέν ἐστιν· ἔστιν ὁ πατήρ μου ὁ δοξάζων με, ὃν ὑμεῖς λέγετε ὅτι θεὸς ἡμῶν ἐστιν). At this point in the exchange the reader can feel the irony dripping from the Jews' rebukes of Jesus. Not greater than Abraham? Is that how you speak to the "I AM?" Make yourself to be something? Do you know he is the one who "made" all things? Yet Jesus responds to their attacks from the perspective of his office as the Son of the Father.[70] Jesus again turns down an opportunity to assert his own glory (cf. v. 50), rejecting a glory that finds its source in him alone. Rather, the Father is "the one who glorifies me" (ὁ δοξάζων με). Yet the Jews claim him as their God (cf. v. 41).

The overlap is intended as a point of contention. The one the Jews call "our God" is the one Jesus calls "my Father." Jesus again defers judgment to the Father (v. 50), the one to whom both sides should be willing to defer judgment. The reader knows full well that only Jesus's claim is true; the Son was "in the beginning with God" and "is in the bosom of the Father" (1:2, 18). The Jews can claim to speak of "our God," but when they exclude Jesus they demonstrate that they are excluded from God. Their questions to Jesus in v. 53 are turned back

---

68. See Wallace, *Greek Grammar*, 398.
69. Cf. Bruce, *John*, 203.
70. Cf. Calvin, *John 1–10*, 233.

upon them: "Since you have rejected the messenger of God, who do you think you are?"

8:55 "And you do not know him, but I know him. And if I said that I did not know him, I would be a liar like you, but I know him and keep his word." (καὶ οὐκ ἐγνώκατε αὐτόν, ἐγὼ δὲ οἶδα αὐτόν. κἂν εἴπω ὅτι οὐκ οἶδα αὐτόν, ἔσομαι ὅμοιος ὑμῖν ψεύστης· ἀλλὰ οἶδα αὐτὸν καὶ τὸν λόγον αὐτοῦ τηρῶ). Jesus presses further this point of contention between "your God" and "my Father." While judgment ultimately resides in the Father, truth clearly belongs to the Son, and Jesus calls the statement by the Jews what it is: a lie. Truth has been at stake in this entire dialogue, and the Jews have already been declared to be enslaved to what is untrue (cf. v. 32). For this reason, Jesus cannot leave the entire defense of his identity and purpose to God's future vindication on his behalf, since truth — and life — are at stake.

Jesus's declaration that the Jews do not know the Father has one potent implication: God cannot be "your God" (v. 54). The different Greek words for "know" (ἐγνώκατε/οἶδα) are not meant to signify a different kind of knowing.[71] They intend to serve a rhetorical emphasis that visibly distinguishes true knowledge from false knowledge. The prologue has already explained in 1:10 that "the world did not know him" (ὁ κόσμος αὐτὸν οὐκ ἔγνω); the reader can now see what that looks like in practice.

In sharp contrast is Jesus, who is the truth (14:6) and speaks the truth. He cannot deny his knowledge of the Father, nor can he affirm the knowledge of God claimed by his opponents. They are the liars. And their claims — not his — are entirely untrue. The proof Jesus offers is simple: "I keep his word" (τὸν λόγον αὐτοῦ τηρῶ). Just as true disciples will keep and remain in Jesus's word (v. 31),

so also does Jesus keep and remain in his Father's word.

8:56 "Your father Abraham was overjoyed that he was to see my day, and he saw and rejoiced" (Ἀβραὰμ ὁ πατὴρ ὑμῶν ἠγαλλιάσατο ἵνα ἴδῃ τὴν ἡμέραν τὴν ἐμήν, καὶ εἶδεν καὶ ἐχάρη). Jesus not only rejects their claim to be aligned with God but also rejects their claim to be aligned with Abraham. The statement is not straightforward. In some manner, Jesus declares that Abraham was purposefully looking forward to the time of Jesus with triumphant joy.

The statement raises two interpretive questions.[72] First, what does Jesus mean by "my day" (τὴν ἡμέραν τὴν ἐμήν)? Although it is possible that the "day" is in the future — perhaps a reference to the "second coming," for example — the verbal exchange almost demands that "my day" refers to the present moment, the moment when "the Word became flesh." The "day" of Jesus does not merely refer to his appearance in a chronological sense but primarily to the eschatological day now inaugurated in the coming of the Son of Man. In some manner, "Abraham knew that he was not himself the fulfillment of the saving will of God, not the yard-stick for judging the greatness of divine revelation; he looked forward to the fulfillment in the Messiah, and welcomed the day when he himself would be judged by one greater than himself."[73] Just as the Jews muted the christological sensibility of Moses by distorting the meaning of the law of Moses (cf. 5:45 – 47), so now the Jews distort the promise of Abraham by muting the christological sensibility of Abraham.

Second, when did Abraham's rejoicing take place? Just as the "day" is not specific but general and stated with an intentional ambiguity, so also

---

71. Cf. Barrett, *John*, 351; Brown, *John*, 1:514.

72. For a survey of options, see Keener, *John*, 1:766 – 68; Michaels, *John*, 530 – 32.

73. Bultmann, *John*, 326.

is the nature and timing of Abraham's rejoicing. The faith of Abraham, his christological sensibility, rooted in the promise made by God, became for him his source of hope and joy. As Calvin says, "Faith has its degrees of seeing Christ."[74] So Abraham saw Christ and rejoiced from afar (cf. Gen 17:19; 21:6). The Jews tried to take back the judicial controls from Jesus, claiming Abraham as their primary witness and God as their judge.[75] But it was to Jesus whom Abraham had long been witnessing; and it was Jesus for whom vindication would come from God.

8:57 Then the Jews said to him, "You are not yet fifty years old and you have seen Abraham?" (εἶπον οὖν οἱ Ἰουδαῖοι πρὸς αὐτόν, Πεντήκοντα ἔτη οὔπω ἔχεις καὶ Ἀβραὰμ ἑώρακας;). The Jews challenge Jesus's argument with a mocking question, rhetorically serving as a rebuke. It is interesting that the Jews use the age of fifty years as a baseline rather than something closer to his probable age, something closer to thirty (cf. Luke 3:23). While some have tried to find significance behind the use of "fifty," it is best taken as a rounded number, well above the age of Jesus so as to expose the absurdity of his argument.

8:58 Jesus said to them, "Truly, truly, I say to you, before Abraham was [born], I am" (εἶπεν αὐτοῖς Ἰησοῦς, Ἀμὴν ἀμὴν λέγω ὑμῖν, πρὶν Ἀβραὰμ γενέσθαι ἐγὼ εἰμί). And with the brilliant timing that masterful irony requires, the narrative returns to Jesus who confesses the very absurdity of the argument the Jews used to mock him. Beginning again with an authoritative preface (see comments on 1:51), Jesus proclaims, "Before Abraham was [born], I am." Several aspects of this statement require explanation.

This is one of several informal "I am" statements in the Gospel (see comments on 6:35), which serve to give insight into the *particular qualifications* of Jesus. In light of the point of debate in this verbal exchange of the legal challenge, especially in regard to the promise of Abraham, the qualification highlighted by this informal "I am" statement seems to center on the arrival — the "day" (v. 56) — of the eschatological redeemer promised and sent by God the Father.[76] Jesus is the long-awaited redeemer of God promised long ago to Abraham. The Jews said as much with the intention to slander; God said the same thing with the intention to love (3:16).

The one the Jews just mocked as being less than fifty years old is the ageless one, the one through whom time has its origin (1:3). Jesus offers the insurmountable rejoinder of his own person to the charge of the Jews. The Jews tried to locate the origin of their charge against Jesus in Abraham; Jesus responded by locating the origin of Abraham in himself. Jesus's statement is intentionally unfinished, primarily because the statement is expected to be grasped by the listener/reader as an allusion to the identity of God (Exod 3).[77] But the unfinished statement could have been finished by the Jews quite easily: "I am the God of Abraham, the God of Isaac, and the God of Jacob." This verse parallels the Gospel's first verse, "And the Word was God" (1:1).[78] And it was said not to explain what was "unseen" to the reader (as in the prologue) but to explain what was being seen in the "flesh" at that very moment by the Jews.

8:59 Then they picked up stones in order to throw at him, but Jesus was concealed and went out from the temple (ἦραν οὖν λίθους ἵνα βάλωσιν ἐπ᾽ αὐτόν· Ἰησοῦς δὲ ἐκρύβη καὶ ἐξῆλθεν ἐκ τοῦ ἱεροῦ). Just as the narrator concluded the first

---

74. Calvin, *John 1 – 10*, 234.
75. Cf. Schnackenburg, *John*, 2:221.
76. Cf. Ridderbos, *John*, 323.

77. See Carson, *John*, 342 – 44, who suggests Jesus's statement is more reflective of Isa 40 – 55 (cf. Isa 41:4; 43:13).
78. Cf. Morris, *John*, 535.

verbal exchange of this lengthy dialogue (v. 20), so now the narrator explains how the final verbal exchange came to a close. And like v. 20, as much as the Jews wanted to stone him, they were unable to, for the text cryptically claims that he "was concealed" (ἐκρύβη) and left the temple (cf. 5:13). The concealment of Jesus is almost certainly supernatural, probably for the same reason stated in v. 20 that "his hour had not yet come."

According to the pattern of legal challenge dialogues, the narrator's depiction of events serves as the final declaration regarding the accused. Just as Jesus stated that the actions of the Jews betray their true identity (cf. vv. 41–42), so now their actions betray their verdict against Jesus. They believe that he is guilty of a capital crime.[79] Deuteronomy 13 prescribes death by stoning for anyone who sought to lead Israel astray. The reader, however, is well aware of the irony of their self-righteous judgment, a judgment that they did not have the authority to make. It was Jesus who was the judge in this pericope, yet on display here is the remarkable truth that Jesus did not come to judge the world but to save it (3:17).

Theology in Application

As the narrative begins a new section, "The Controversy over the Son of God" (8:12–10:42), Jesus initiates a challenge of his own. Jesus has some accusations to make against his accusers, rooted not merely in the authority of his own person but in an authority given to him by his Father. In the first legal challenge of the Gospel, it is not merely the Jewish authorities who are challenged by Jesus or even the contemporaries of the "historical" Jesus but the contemporary reader who is challenged with the nature of true freedom and discipleship. While the length of the pericope might be difficult for some to preach or teach as a whole, the message should at least be maintained in the context of the dialogue and its movement, for the dialogical drama of the pericope adds important depth and focus to the presentation of Jesus and his work.

The Judgment of Jesus

The rhetorical precision with which this pericope is crafted serves to confront the reader with the overwhelming fact that Jesus is the Judge. The legal challenge serves as a perfect subgenre to communicate the force of God's authority. The reader — not just the historical opponents of Jesus — is confronted in a personal way by the authority of God. The charge of Jesus is a charge against the world, against any person who has claimed what rightfully belongs to God alone.

The two accusations of Jesus apply not only to these first-century Jews but also to the contemporary reader. First, the people of God are those who believe in the Son of God. There is no generic belief or spirituality appropriate for God our Father.

---

79. Reinhartz, "John 8:31–59 from a Jewish Perspective," 794.

It is, rather, belief that is specific to his Son, Jesus Christ. Any other "belief" is inappropriate belief; it is unbelief.

Second, the people of God are those who belong to the bloodline of Jesus Christ. There is something significant and unique about God's relationship to Israel.[80] Yet that uniqueness was distorted by Jesus's first-century opponents, who had prematurely declared themselves as the manifestation of the inheritance promised by God to Abraham. But even Israel's emancipation from slavery was but a foretaste of true freedom — freedom from sin and death. This "the Jews" could not see. They were blinded by the darkness of their own self-righteousness. But by God's grace, a Light had come.

Light of the World

The entire conflict dialogue begins with the formal declaration of Jesus, "I am the Light of the world" (v. 12). The metaphor of light is so central to this Gospel that its occurrence here is significant. The imagery has already been filled with the significance of creation itself (1:1 – 5), so its use in this pericope imposes a similar force upon the reader. The metaphor of light and darkness speaks to one of the most basic senses of a person — sight. All our day-to-day movements are guided by light, a resource God provides to the whole world by means of the sun. But in his Son he has provided a more robust light. In view of his light, the day is not conceived by means of twenty-four hours but by the "day" Abraham had in view when he first heard the promise of God (v. 56).

Christ has commanded that we follow him, and he has promised that if we do, he will guide us away from darkness and into true life. God revealed this promise long ago through the psalmist: "Your word is a lamp for my feet, a light on my path" (Ps 119:105). The "word" Jesus beckoned us to "keep" and "remain in" was his own (vv. 31, 37, 43, 51). It is in this way that Jesus is "the light of life" (v. 12). It is also in this way that the promise of Jesus becomes an exhortation to respond to the grace of God. It is only when I am charged as guilty that I can receive the verdict of grace from God. That is the irony of the gospel. It is only when I admit to being what I am not supposed to be that I can be declared what I do not deserve to be. And this new reality — new creation (2 Cor 5:17) — becomes the path upon which I am intended to walk.

"I Am"

No other pericope in John contains as many "I am" statements as this one. The legal challenge pitted two of these against each other: the "I am" of the world versus

---

80. Helpful here is R. Kendall Soulen, *The God of Israel and Christian Theology* (Minneapolis: Augsburg Fortress, 1996).

the "I am" of the Son. The "I am" of the world claimed for itself and by itself, whereas the "I am" of the Son claimed nothing for himself or by himself (v. 14). The "I am" of the world was founded upon itself, but the "I am" of the Son was founded upon the Father: "Because I am not alone, but I and the one who sent me, the Father" (v. 16). As the pericope revealed, however, the world's concern was never about the "I am" of the Son; it was always about the "I am" of the world. Jesus revealed that the darkness of sin has blinded the world to itself and therefore to God "so that they cannot see the light of the gospel that displays the glory of Christ, who is the image of God" (2 Cor 4:4).

The Christian, however, the one born "from above" (3:3, 5), speaks not the "I am" of the world but rather the "I am" of the Son. The Christian's only claim is, "I am his!" As the apostle Paul explains, the emphasis must be placed on Christ: "For what we preach is not ourselves, but Jesus Christ as Lord, and ourselves as your servants for Jesus' sake. For God, who said, 'Let light shine out of darkness,' made his light shine in our hearts to give us the light of the knowledge of God's glory displayed in the face of Christ" (2 Cor 4:5 – 6). Christ says "I am," and the Christian responds with the claim, "Yes, you are!" Christ is the "I am," and we are his servants, true disciples (v. 31), the "children of God" (1:12).

Sin and Death

In the midst of a plethora of legal language and points of law stretching across centuries of biblical history, the dispute between Jesus and "the Jews" centered on the one primary issue of sin. No other word better depicts the "darkness" that the Gospel speaks about so often. And if the cause of darkness is sin, the effect of darkness is death. Before the courtroom scene had even begun, the defendants — the Jews — had already been declared guilty, for they were already judged to "die in your sin" (vv. 21, 24). They were, like the whole world around them (v. 23), stricken with the state of sin. But they, like the whole world around them, could not see it. The Jews enacted what is theoretically true of us all: the light shined but "the darkness did not recognize it" (1:5).

Against all human reasoning, the Christian allows Christ to be their mirror; the "law of Christ" guides us to "become conscious of our sin" (Gal 6:2; Rom 3:20). This was always the intention of God for his people "so that every mouth may be silenced and *the whole world* held accountable to God" (Rom 3:19; emphasis added). That is, this is the gospel, the motivation of God's love for the world, the reason the Father sent the Son (3:16). This pericope begins with a focus on sin and death, but by its conclusion the focus is exclusively on Christ. It focuses on Christ because he took our sin upon himself and fulfilled in himself the death we deserved. Sin and death dissipate in the presence of Christ, who absorbs them both on our behalf, like darkness in the presence of light. For "he was pierced for our transgressions; he was crushed for our iniquities … [because of] judgment he was taken away … an offering for sin" (Isa 53:5, 8, 10).

Freedom, Truth, and Discipleship

An important distinction needs to be made between the biblical depiction of freedom and the contemporary use of the term.[81] The OT understood freedom in very concrete terms. The emphasis on freedom offered by the exodus narrative and beyond was not, surprisingly, freedom from slavery. The Bible expects slavery in the sense that all people will serve something (cf. Rom 6). Freedom in the Bible is not a contrast between freedom and slavery but between an inappropriate master (Pharaoh; sin) and an appropriate master — God (cf. Exod 9:14). It was freedom *for* something more than freedom *from* something. The freedom about which the exodus is the paradigmatic instance is liberation from degrading bondage for the endless service of the God who remembers his covenant, redeems from exile and oppression, and gives commandments through which the people of God are sanctified. This is the biblical notion of freedom about which Jesus speaks. If you are not a disciple of Jesus (v. 31), then by implication you serve the tyrant of sin (vv. 21, 24, 34).

The gospel of Jesus Christ is not just about who a person was, a sinner dying in their sins (vv. 21, 24), but also about who a person can become. In this pericope, God declares that the person who believes becomes a "true disciple" (v. 31), is defined by truth (v. 32), is free from sin (vv. 32 – 36), and is given an eternal inheritance into the family of God (v. 35). These are large-scale biblical ideals, beginning all the way back with Abraham and finding ultimate expression in and through Jesus Christ. True discipleship is freedom *from* self-interest and the devil and freedom *for* God. This is what Jesus means when he offers us "the light of life" (v. 12).

---

81. Helpful here is Richard Bauckham, *God and the Crisis of Freedom: Biblical and Contemporary Perspectives* (Louisville: Westminster John Knox, 2002).

John 9:1 – 41

Literary Context

In this pericope the narrative transitions from a formal courtroom scene in the temple (8:12 – 59) to a more informal scene of a preliminary hearing. Here an expert witness, one who has personal experience (and therefore expertise) of the defendant (Jesus) and the particular crime of which he is being accused (healing on the Sabbath) is examined by legal officials.[1] The conflict initiated in the previous pericope has made one thing clear to "the Jews": Jesus is a threat. Questions surrounding him no longer concern his identity; they now entirely focus on his extermination. Even though Jesus's presence only frames the pericope, the dialogical exchange between several different characters serves to highlight his person and work. The reader is being guided to "see" the meaning and significance of the mission of the Son of Man and to believe in him.

V. The Controversy over the Son of God (8:12 – 10:42)

    A. "The Light of the World": The Accusations of Jesus the Judge (8:12 – 59)

→   **B. The Fifth Sign: The Testimony of the Blind Man (9:1 – 41)**

    C. The Shepherd and the Sheep (10:1 – 21)

    D. The Son of the Father (10:22 – 42)

Main Idea

From birth every person is blind to the light of the world and separated from God. True blindness goes much deeper than the eyes; it is a disease that creates blindness to oneself. For the Christian, however, blindness becomes the channel of belief,

---

1. The larger section of 8:12 – 10:42, of which this pericope is part, is unified and controlled by forensic patterns and themes of interrogation and judgment which structure the narrative presentation and give guidance to the interpretation of each pericope. Cf. Lincoln, *Truth on Trial*, 97; Dodd, *Interpretation*, 354 – 62.

the posture of worship. True belief is expressed not in spite of blindness but by means of it, manifesting the "works of God" in the Christian whose own story testifies to the one who can truly heal.

Translation

John 9:1–41

	Scene 1	
1a	Introduction & Setting	And
b		as he was passing by,
c	Character Entrance: Blind Man	**he saw a man who had been blind from birth.**
2a	Character Reentrance	**His disciples asked him saying,**
b		*"Rabbi,*
c	Question/Assumed Cause	*who sinned,*
d	Assumed Transgressors	*this man or his parents,*
e	Assumed Consequence (of 2c)	*that he was born blind?"*
3a	Response	**Jesus answered,**
b	Negative Answer	*"Neither this man nor his parents sinned,*
c	Positive Answer	*but **this happened***
d	Purpose	*so that the works of God might be made manifest*
e	Passive Agency	*in him.*
4a	Exhortation	*We must work the works of the one who sent me*
b	Duration	*as long as it is day;*
c	Contrasting Time	*night is coming*
d	Result	*when no one is able to work.*
5a	Circumstance	*While I am in the world,*
b	Pronouncement	*I am the light of the world."*
6a		After he said these things,
b	Progressive Action #1	**he spit on the ground,**
c	Progressive Action #2	**made mud with the saliva,**
d	Progressive Action #3	and **applied his clay to the eyes.**
7a		Then **he said to him,**
b	(Command) #4	*"Go, wash in the pool of Siloam"*
c	Aside	(which is called "Sent").
d	Reaction	So **he went and washed,**
e	Result	and **returned seeing.**
	Scene 2	
8a	1st Interlocution (8–12)	Then
b	Character Entrance	**the neighbors and those who had seen him previously as a beggar were** ↵ **saying,**
c	Question	*"Is this man not the one who used to sit and beg?"*

Continued on next page.

Continued from previous page.

9a		**Some were saying,**
b	Speculated Answer	*"This is he."*
c		But **others were saying,**
d	Speculated Answer	*"No, but he is similar to him."*
e		Then **he said,**
f	Real Answer	*"I am he."*
10a		Then **they were saying to him,**
b	Question of Means	*"How were your eyes opened?"*
11a		**He answered,**
b	Answer	*"The man …*
c	Identification	*called Jesus*
d		*… made mud and touched my eyes and said to me,*
e		*'Go to Siloam and wash.'*
f		*So I went and after washing I received sight."*
12a	Response	And **they said to him,**
b	Question	*"Where is this man?"*
c	Response	**He said,**
d		*"I do not know."*
13a	2nd Interlocution (13–17)	**They led the formerly blind man**
b	Character Reentrance	to the Pharisees.
14a	Narrator's Aside: Context	Now **it was the Sabbath on the day Jesus made the mud and opened his eyes.**
15a	Interrogation	Then **the Pharisees also asked him how he received sight.**
b		And **he said to them,**
c	Answer	*"He placed mud on my eyes and I washed and I see."*
16a		**Some of the Pharisees were saying,**
b	Response #1	*"This man is not from God,*
c	Basis	*because he did not keep the Sabbath."*
d		But **others were saying,**
e	Response #2	*"How can a sinful man do such signs?"*
f	Result	and **there was a division among them.**
17a	Continued Interrogation	Finally **they said again to the blind man,**
b	Question	*"What do you say concerning him,*
c	Basis	*because he opened your eyes?"*
d		**He said,**
e	Answer	*"He is a prophet."*
18a	3rd Interlocution (18–23)	**The Jews still did not believe that he was blind and had received sight**
b	Condition	until they called
c	Character Entrance	the parents of the formerly blind man.
19a	Continued Interrogation	**They asked them saying,**
b	Question of Identity	*"Is this your son,*
c		*whom you say was born blind?*
d	Inferential Question of Means	*How …*
e		*then*
f		*… can he now see?"*
20a		**His parents answered and said,**
b	Answer of Identity	*"We know that he is our son and*
c	Answer of Birth Condition	*that he was born blind."*

21a	Contrasting Situation	"But
b		how he now can see
c	Ignorance	we do not know,
d		or
e		who opened his eyes
f	Ignorance	we do not know.
g		Ask him,
h	Credibility of Son's Testimony	he is old enough,
i		he will speak for himself."
22a	Narrator's Aside	**His parents said these things**
b	Basis	because they feared the Jews,
c	Explanation	**for already the Jews had agreed**
d	Condition (Content)	that … if anyone who confessed ⌅
		that he is the Christ,
e	Inference (Content)	… they would be expelled from the synagogue.
23a	Continued Explanation	For this reason
b		**his parents said,**
c		"He is old enough, ask him."
24a	4th Interlocution (24–34)	Then **they called the man**
b		who was blind
c	Continued Interrogation	a second time
d		and **said to him,**
e	Imperatival Indictment	"Give glory to God.
f	Confessional Basis	We know that this man is a sinner."
25a	Response	**He answered,**
b	Confession of Ignorance	"I do not know
c		if he is a sinner.
d		
e	Counterconfession to 24f	One thing I do know:
f		I was blind
g		but now I see."
26a	Continued Interrogation	Then **they said to him,**
b		"What did he do to you?
c		How did he open your eyes?"
27a		**He answered them,**
b	Interrogative Mock #1	"I already told you
c	Interrogative Mock #2	and you did not hear.
d	Interrogative Mock #3	What do you want to hear again?
e	Interrogative Rebuke	Do you also want to become his disciples?"
28a	Manner of Reaction	**They reviled him and said,**
b	Escalating Indictment	"You are a disciple of this man,
c	Challenge of Authority	but we are disciples of Moses.
29a	Explanatory Basis (+)	We know that God has spoken to Moses,
b	Explanatory Basis (−)	but we do not know where this man is from."
30a	Retort	**The man answered and said to them,**
b	Mocking Astonishment	"Why,
c		there is something remarkable about this;

Continued on next page.

Continued from previous page.

d		*you do not know where he is from,*
e	Counterindictment	*yet he opened my eyes.*
31a	Counterexplanatory Basis	*We know that God does not listen to sinners,*
b	Contrasting Circumstance	*but*
d	Condition #1	*if a man is God-fearing and*
c	Condition #2	*does his will,*
e	Inferential Rebuke	*he listens to this man.*
32a	Emphatic Context	*From the beginning of time*
b	Premise #1	*it has not been heard that someone opened the eyes of a man born blind.*
33a	Premise #2	*If this man were not from God,*
b	Inferential Conclusion	*he could do nothing."*
34a	Retort	**They answered and said to him,**
b	Counterindictment	*"Every part of you was born in sin,*
c		*and you are teaching us?"*
d	Rejection of Testimony	And **they cast him out.**

Scene 3

35a	Character Reentrance	**Jesus heard that he had been cast out,**
b	1ˢᵗ Interlocution (35–38)	and **after finding him he said to him,**
c	Question	*"Do you believe*
d	Title	*in the Son of Man?"*
36a	Response	**He answered and said,**
b	Question	*"And who is he,*
c	Title	*sir,*
d	Purpose	*that I may believe in him?"*
37a	Response	**Jesus said to him,**
b	Answer:	*"You have seen him;*
c	Confession	*he is the one speaking with you."*
38a	Response	So **he said,**
b	Confession	*"I believe,*
c	Contrasting Title to 36c	*Lord."*
d	Reaction	And **he worshipped him.**
39a	2ⁿᵈ Interlocution (39–41)	**Then Jesus said,**
b	Purpose	*"For judgment*
c	Declaration	*I came into this world,*
d	Result	*so that the blind may see and*
e	Contrasting Result	*those who see may become blind."*
40a	Character Reentrance	**Some of the Pharisees …**
b	Description	*who were with him and heard him say these things*
c	Response	**… said to him,**
d	Interrogative Mock	*"Are we also blind?"*
41a	Retort	**Jesus said to them,**
b	Condition	*"If you were blind,*
c	Inference	*you would not have sin,*
d	Contrast	*but*
e	Circumstantial Condition	*since you say that you can see,*
f	Climactic Indictment	*your sin remains."*

Structure and Literary Form

This is the sixth substantial dialogue in the narrative proper, and it is a *legal challenge dialogue* that takes the form of a formal debate (see Introduction). The purpose is not to challenge the honor or authority of one's interlocutor, but to debate a principle, idea, or law as part of a forensic case. Although this pericope is best defined as a dialogue, it is unique in form for two reasons.[2] First, the dialogue includes (and is based upon) a succinct miracle story that occurs at the beginning of the pericope. It is not a miracle story with a basic story form, but more like a pronouncement story, that is, a brief, undetailed story used to set up a significant statement by Jesus.[3] Second, this dialogue actually consists of an exchange of dialogues, which means that while it will function overall like the other dialogues in the Gospel, in its parts it contains more creative variety. That is, since the dialogical exchanges are presented in the mode of the *interrogation of a witness*, at times the dialogue will resemble a social challenge, even though its overall form establishes it as a legal challenge.[4]

Exegetical Outline

➡ **B. The Fifth Sign: The Testimony of the Blind Man (9:1 – 41)**

    1. The Healing of the Man Blind from Birth (vv. 1 – 7)

        a. Blindness and Sin: "Rabbi, Who Sinned?" (vv. 1 – 2)

        b. Blindness and "the Works of God" (vv. 3 – 5)

        c. Jesus Heals the Blind Man (vv. 6 – 7)

    2. The Judgment of Jesus *In Absentia*: Preliminary Hearing in the Sabbath Healing Case (vv. 8 – 34)

        a. First Verbal Exchange: The Blind Man and the Neighbors (vv. 8 – 12)

        b. Second Verbal Exchange: The Blind Man and the Jewish Authorities, Part 1 (vv. 13 – 17)

        c. Third Verbal Exchange: The Blind Man's Parents and the Jewish Authorities (vv. 18 – 23)

        d. Fourth Verbal Exchange: The Blind Man and the Jewish Authorities, Part 2 (vv. 24 – 34)

    3. The Confession of the Blind Man (vv. 35 – 41)

        a. First Verbal Exchange: Jesus Encounters the Blind Man (vv. 35 – 38)

        b. Second Verbal Exchange: Jesus Judges the Pharisees (vv. 39 – 41)

---

2. The uniqueness of this pericope is not only its dialogical form but also its literary artistry, for which it has long been recognized. See Dodd, *Interpretation*, 357; Leithart, *Deep Exegesis*, 168; Larsen, *Recognizing the Stranger*, 151.

3. Staley, "Stumbling in the Dark," 64.

4. See Parsenios, *Rhetoric and Drama in the Johannine Lawsuit Motif*, 1 – 47.

Explanation of the Text

This pericope is particularly famous because of the focus given to it by J. L. Martyn and the significance he attributed to it for revealing the circumstances of the Johannine community. The approach of this commentary is opposed to Martyn's theory (see Introduction). Our explanation below will not engage with Martyn's influential interpretation except briefly at v. 22, the key verse for his theory.

9:1 And as he was passing by, he saw a man who had been blind from birth (Καὶ παράγων εἶδεν ἄνθρωπον τυφλὸν ἐκ γενετῆς). The pericope begins with a brief setting for the miracle and dialogue to follow. The narrator introduces the scene by describing Jesus as the implied subject of the temporal participle, "as he was passing by" (παράγων). The participle communicates almost nothing about timing or circumstances surrounding this event. Jesus is probably still in Jerusalem, even if no longer in the temple (cf. 8:59). The opening statement nevertheless does work well with the closing of the previous pericope (Jesus "went out from the temple . . . and was passing by").[5]

Since the dialogue is centered upon the healing of a blind man, the few details the narrator provides are significant for the dialogue to follow. The notable detail provided here is that the man was blind "from birth" (ἐκ γενετῆς), a term used nowhere else in the NT. The term is a Greek expression (not Semitic, which preferred the phrase, "from the mother's womb") that emphasizes the causation of the ailment. The man has been blind "from the hour of birth," making the miracle even more remarkable (cf. v. 32).[6]

9:2 His disciples asked him saying, "Rabbi, who sinned, this man or his parents, that he was born blind?" (καὶ ἠρώτησαν αὐτὸν οἱ μαθηταὶ αὐτοῦ λέγοντες, Ῥαββί, τίς ἥμαρτεν, οὗτος ἢ οἱ γονεῖς αὐτοῦ, ἵνα τυφλὸς γεννηθῇ;). The plight of the central character, the unnamed blind man, is raised by the disciples, who use his condition to ask Jesus, their "rabbi" (Ῥαββί), a theological question. The disciples have not been mentioned by the narrative since 6:70 and are unquestionably "the Twelve," the usual (even if unmentioned) companions of Jesus. Even before the miracle occurs, the disciples interject a theological question, which leads to a pronouncement-like statement from Jesus.[7] Such a narrative maneuver not only reveals the emphasis of the periocope on the dialogue but also serves to interconnect the miracle to the surrounding dialogue.

The disciples assume that the blindness of the man is a result of sin, denoted by the result clause "that he was born blind" (ἵνα τυφλὸς γεννηθῇ). Their question regarding the congenital blindness of the man is an exploration of the connection between sin and physical deformity. There are several OT texts (e.g., Exod 20:5; Ps 89:32) and later rabbinic texts (b. Shabbat 55a: "There is no death without sin and no suffering without iniquity") that infer such a connection.[8] But taken cumulatively, the evidence from the ancient world is not so clear. As Kelley notes after a survey of Jewish and Greco-Roman literature, "Not all (or even most) such anomalies would have been experienced as 'suffering' or understood as chastisement from the gods. Indeed, birth defects were attributed to a

---

5. Schnackenburg, *John*, 2:240.

6. John Painter, "John 9 and the Interpretation of the Fourth Gospel," *JSNT* 28 (1986): 31 – 61 (34). Cf. Barrett, *John*, 356; Brown, *John*, 1:371.

7. Staley, "Stumbling in the Dark," 65.

8. Cf. Malina and Rohrbaugh, *John*, 169 – 70.

range of causes that varied according to the deformity and its interpreter."[9]

9:3 Jesus answered, "Neither this man nor his parents sinned, but this happened so that the works of God might be made manifest in him" (ἀπεκρίθη Ἰησοῦς, Οὔτε οὗτος ἥμαρτεν οὔτε οἱ γονεῖς αὐτοῦ, ἀλλ' ἵνα φανερωθῇ τὰ ἔργα τοῦ θεοῦ ἐν αὐτῷ). Jesus's response does not rule out a theory, but places it emphatically in the hands of God, not the man or his parents. Such a claim removes neither the man nor his parents from the guilt or consequences of sin, but simply undergirds what they have done with what God has done, even in spite of them.

Before exploring the reason provided by Jesus, we must address the theodicy problem this statement raises. For many interpreters this places the blame directly, rather than indirectly, on God. As David Rensberger explains, "Despite a hopeful beginning, as theodicy this is really worse yet. It seems to say that God did not even blind the man for his entire lifetime in order to punish some wrongdoing; he did it merely to show off his power by finally sending Jesus around to heal him."[10] The problem is not solved by suggesting, based upon the "so that" (ἵνα) clause, that Jesus offers only the purpose of the problem, not the cause (result).[11] Not only does the grammatical difference create only a minimal theological distinction, but it also suggests that Jesus is not answering the question; or, as Ridderbos writes, it "subsumes suffering under a totally different viewpoint."[12] But Jesus has already connected sin to consequence (see comments on 5:14), and it seems more likely that Jesus is not avoiding the true cause (result) but stating

the cause with profound directness. Without denying that the man or his parents had a sinful connection to this blindness, Jesus emphasizes that the man's blindness was in the control of God. The mystery of this connection demands that we be restrained when we impute guilt to either a person or God.[13]

Jesus declares that this happened so that "the works of God might be made manifest in him" (φανερωθῇ τὰ ἔργα τοῦ θεοῦ ἐν αὐτῷ). The plural "works" of God is striking. Why is one incident of blindness connected to a plurality of works? Interpreters are often forced to choose between the coming miracle of Jesus and the burgeoning spiritual life of the blind man. But even the addition of "in him" (ἐν αὐτῷ) does not intend to describe the work but to show that they are "made manifest" (φανερωθῇ) — note the passive verb — or testified to through his person. The anonymous blind man becomes a primary witness of the works of God. He is not the work per se but one part of the ensemble on display. Thus, the statement as a whole is best defined more generally as part of something like a pronouncement story (see comments above), which must be understood as entailing (and explained by) all of vv. 3–5. The reader brings to this pericope what Jesus has already explained about "the work(s) of God" (see comments on 6:28–29), which finds its expression in belief in Jesus. Just as Jesus structurally frames this dialogue, in a similar manner he is also the frame of the problem of evil and sin.

9:4 "We must work the works of the one who sent me as long as it is day; night is coming when no one is able to work" (ἡμᾶς δεῖ ἐργάζεσθαι τὰ

---

9. Nicole Kelley, "The Theological Significance of Physical Deformity in the Pseudo-Clementine *Homilies*," *PRSt* 34 (2007): 77–90 (78).

10. David Rensberger, *Johannine Faith and Liberating Community* (Philadelphia: Westminster, 1988), 43–44.

11. See Brown, *John*, 1:371.

12. Ridderbos, *John*, 333.

13. Cf. Calvin, *John 1–10*, 239.

ἔργα τοῦ πέμψαντός με ἕως ἡμέρα ἐστίν· ἔρχεται νὺξ ὅτε οὐδεὶς δύναται ἐργάζεσθαι). The centrality of Jesus in v. 3 and in v. 5 (see comments below) causes confusion here when he continues his statement with an emphatic first-person plural: "We must work the works of the one who sent me" (ἡμᾶς δεῖ ἐργάζεσθαι τὰ ἔργα τοῦ πέμψαντός με). What is the meaning, and who is the referent of "we?"[14] The Gospel will draw a clear connection between the "work" of Jesus and the "work" of his disciples (see 14:12). But even there the clear connection functions under a necessary and recognizable distinction between the "works" of each party (see comments on 14:12 – 13).

For this reason, it is best to take this occurrence as another example of the use of the "we" of authoritative testimony (see comments on 3:11). Bauckham prefers to describe this occurrence as an associative "we," not only because he sees the occurrence in 3:11 as unique but also because the "we" of authoritative testimony is not intended "to refer to any other persons along with the speaker but to give added force to the self-reference."[15] In this context, however, the "work" of the disciples is not only future but is also entirely derivative. Further, in light of the forensic patterns and themes of interrogation and judgment, along with the already established authority of Jesus the Judge, the "we" of authoritative testimony is better equipped to handle the force of the self-reference; it adds "a sense of augmented authority ... by a speaker who is in some sense superior to those he addresses."[16] This is not to deny the future role of the disciples (again, see 14:12) but to make sense of the statement in its surrounding context in which the role of God and Jesus is emphasized.

What strengthens the focus on Jesus is the urgency with which the statement is made ("we must" [ἡμᾶς δεῖ]). Pronouncement statements tend to speak in generalities, so there is probably no need here to find a specific referent for "day" (ἡμέρα) and "night" (νὺξ). The imagery recalls the creation imagery of the prologue, which is a developing motif in this pericope (cf. vv. 1, 6). It is in this broader context that Jesus's statement here must be understood. Jesus speaks of the cosmological mission of the Father sending the Son, which the prologue first introduced to the reader (see comments before 1:1). Again, this is not to deny the historical mission into which the church will join (an associative "we" sense), but to subjugate it under the more cosmic mission of the light into the darkness. As much as the statement starts with a "we," its significance resides in that it ends with a "me." The narrative may make the timing and task of this "work" (and even the eventual coworkers) undefined and cryptic, but the primary worker is clear enough.[17]

9:5 "While I am in the world, I am the light of the world" (ὅταν ἐν τῷ κόσμῳ ὦ, φῶς εἰμι τοῦ κόσμου). The conclusion of Jesus's pronouncement-like statement is nearly identical to his statement in 8:12, though without the emphatic and formal "I am" statement. Jesus is not intending to make the same formal statement but to put it in a functional context. And the function is about to be performed by the sign itself, towards which this proclamation points (vv. 6 – 7).[18] The qualification, "while I am in the world" (ὅταν ἐν τῷ κόσμῳ ὦ), makes clear that the primary agent of the work is Jesus without denying that the work will continue after his departure. The light metaphor is again intended to take the reader through the Gospel's prologue

---

14. The text-critical evidence supports the cryptic nature of the statement. See Metzger, *Textual Commentary*, 194.

15. Bauckham, *Jesus and the Eyewitnesses*, 372.

16. Ibid. Bauckham admits that the Greek usage of "we"

and "I" cannot be defined with precision. Cf. Moulton, *Grammar*, 1:86.

17. See Augustine, *John*, 44.6.247.

18. Schnackenburg, *John*, 2:242.

to creation itself: "In the Word … was the light of humanity" (1:4). At this moment, the solution to the anonymous blind man's predicament rests comfortably in the hands of Jesus.

9:6 After he said these things, he spit on the ground, made mud with the saliva, and applied his mud to the eyes (ταῦτα εἰπὼν ἔπτυσεν χαμαὶ καὶ ἐποίησεν πηλὸν ἐκ τοῦ πτύσματος, καὶ ἐπέχρισεν αὐτοῦ τὸν πηλὸν ἐπὶ τοὺς ὀφθαλμούς). After the statement by Jesus, the narrator returns and gives only a few details about the miracle (vv. 6 – 7). There is no transition from the conversation with the disciples to the blind man, no geographic depiction of how the two parties approached each other, and no information about the nature of conversation between the blind man and Jesus. There is just the action of Jesus.

The action of Jesus involved making a mixture of "mud" (πηλὸν) and "saliva" (πτύσματος), which Jesus "applied" (ἐπέχρισεν) to the blind man's eyes. Several interpreters make the "saliva" the focus, suggesting that the use of saliva would have been viewed as problematic to the Jewish authorities (for it may have suggested an association with magical practices) or as a symbol of religious authority.[19] Historical explanations can only explain Jesus's actions as superstitious and prescientific.[20] A better solution is to understand Jesus's actions as symbolic, as a communication through recognizeable actions. Moreover, a detail often missed is that it is not the saliva that the narrator highlights; rather, it is the "mud" that is mentioned twice by the narrator. The saliva is simply mentioned to explain how the mud was applied.

But there is something more. The narrator places what appears to be a stray pronoun "his" (αὐτοῦ) immediately after "he anointed" (ἐπέχρισεν), which most interpreters and translations believe to refer to the blind man (cf. NIV; NASB). However, the possessive pronoun "his" sits directly before "mud," thereby separating it from the "implied" presence of the blind man at the conclusion of the verse. It is not uncommon in the Gospel for the pronoun to precede the head noun it modifies (see vv. 14, 21; cf. 4:47; 6:53). Although this makes the most grammatical sense, it does make for somewhat of an awkward sentence. Yet in this way the narrator describes the mud as "his mud" (αὐτοῦ τὸν πηλὸν), that is, as the mud of Jesus. In light of the already established creation motif in the Gospel, the reader is encouraged to understand "his mud" to be a reference to the creation of humanity from the earth (Gen 2:7; cf. Job 4:19; 10:9, where the same term is used in the LXX).[21] The awkwardness created by the grammatical sense nudges the reader to see the intended allusion, a maneuver we have seen in this Gospel before (see comments on 2:4). The moment described by the narrator is not between a miracle worker and an ailing blind man, but between the Creator and "his" creation.

9:7 Then he said to him, "Go, wash in the pool of Siloam" (which is called "Sent"). So he went and washed, and returned seeing (καὶ εἶπεν αὐτῷ, Ὕπαγε νίψαι εἰς τὴν κολυμβήθραν τοῦ Σιλωάμ [ὃ ἑρμηνεύεται Ἀπεσταλμένος]. ἀπῆλθεν οὖν καὶ ἐνίψατο, καὶ ἦλθεν βλέπων). After applying the softened mud to the blind man's eyes, Jesus commands him to go wash in the pool of Siloam. Probably within Jerusalem's walls at the time, the Pool of Siloam was surrounded by four porches and was well known, especially since it was often used during the Jewish festivals.[22] But the reason for this command is not entirely clear. No specific historical or social-religious significance explains Jesus's command. If anything, the reason might be more simple than often assumed; the act of washing was

19. Carson, *John*, 363 – 64.
20. See Keener, *John*, 1:779 – 81.
21. Schlatter, *Der Evangelist Johannes*, 225.
22. Keener, *John*, 1:781.

part of the ritual practice of Judaism and therefore may have served as a sign to the authorities. The detail is best understood to conclude the miracle and connect it to the events that will transpire in v. 8.

The narrator focuses not on the historical significance but on the lexical significance of this specific pool. In light of the creation motif, the narrator perhaps wants to "impress" the reader with the conceptual relation between this pool "which is translated as 'Sent'" (ὃ ἑρμηνεύεται Ἀπεσταλμένος) and Jesus, the one who "sent" the blind man and who was himself "sent" by the Father (v. 4). There is no need to develop a large-scale thematic significance to the term.[23] Much of the narrator's selective recounting is for the purpose of emphasis. Yet the Gospel's concern with etymology in this verse "attests to the symbolic character of the healing miracle."[24] Although the reader will not hear from Jesus again until v. 35, the narrator has made certain that the reader will not forget that the entire dialogue to follow is framed by the power and authority of his person — the Creator, the "I AM," the "light of humanity," the "Sent One."

9:8 Then the neighbors and those who had seen him previously as a beggar were saying, "Is this man not the one who used to sit and beg?" (Οἱ οὖν γείτονες καὶ οἱ θεωροῦντες αὐτὸν τὸ πρότερον ὅτι προσαίτης ἦν ἔλεγον, Οὐχ οὗτός ἐστιν ὁ καθήμενος καὶ προσαιτῶν;). The pericope transitions to a new section that functions like a preliminary hearing, that is, an evidentiary hearing that determines whether there is sufficient evidence to warrant a trial. In the four verbal exchanges of this section of the dialogue, there are three different interlocutors with the blind man serving as the primary witness. The first interlocutor (vv. 8–12) is simply described as his "neighbors" (γείτονες) — those who had known him as a blind man who had to beg for survival. Their question, which expects an affirmative answer, is intended to determine the identity of "this man," who again remains anonymous, even to his "neighbors."

9:9 Some were saying, "This is he." But others were saying, "No, but he is similar to him." Then he said, "I am he" (ἄλλοι ἔλεγον ὅτι Οὗτός ἐστιν· ἄλλοι ἔλεγον, Οὐχί, ἀλλὰ ὅμοιος αὐτῷ ἐστιν. ἐκεῖνος ἔλεγεν ὅτι Ἐγώ εἰμι). The narrator reveals the whispering among those who had previously known the man born blind. Like the people of Jerusalem in regard to Jesus (cf. 7:25–27), the neighbors are confused regarding the identity of the one who is no longer the blind man but "the healed man."[25] The fact that something about him is "similar" (ὅμοιος) demands that something else is entirely different. The narrator leaves his old-to-new identity rhetorically implicit by simply referring to him with pronouns.

The blind man interrupts the dizzying exchange with the potent statement, "I am he" (Ἐγώ εἰμι). Most interpreters are quick to describe it as Brown does, as "a purely secular use of the phrase."[26] But Morris is right when he admits that the phrase "creates an effect strangely similar to what it would have on Jesus's lips."[27] The reader cannot help but see how the blind man is already representing Jesus to some degree. The noticeable difference displayed in the blind man has little to do with him

23. Contra Bruce Grigsby, "Washing in the Pool of Siloam — A Thematic Anticipation of the Johannine Cross," *NovT* 27 (1985): 227–35.

24. William M. Wright IV, *Rhetoric and Theology: Figural Reading of John 9*, BZNW 165 (Berlin: Walter de Gruyter, 2009), 165.

25. As described by Bultmann, *John*, 333.

26. Brown, *John*, 1:373. Barrett, *John*, 359, even warns against assuming it "was necessarily to John a religious formula."

27. Morris, *John*, 548. On "impressions," see Introduction.

and everything to do with Jesus. Even the response of the blind man testifies to something beyond itself, to something "unseen."

9:10 Then they were saying to him, "How were your eyes opened?" (ἔλεγον οὖν αὐτῷ, Πῶς [οὖν] ἠνεῴχθησάν σου οἱ ὀφθαλμοί;). Those who recognized the blind man now address him for the first time and ask him to explain how it is that he can now see. The passive verb, "were opened" (ἠνεῴχθησάν), assumes that the restoration of his vision was provided for him. The focus of the exchange now centers upon a single topic: "How" did this happen? Or more importantly, by whom did this happen?

9:11 He answered, "The man called Jesus made mud and touched my eyes and said to me, 'Go to Siloam and wash.' So I went and after washing I received sight" (ἀπεκρίθη ἐκεῖνος, Ὁ ἄνθρωπος ὁ λεγόμενος Ἰησοῦς πηλὸν ἐποίησεν καὶ ἐπέχρισέν μου τοὺς ὀφθαλμοὺς καὶ εἶπέν μοι ὅτι Ὕπαγε εἰς τὸν Σιλωὰμ καὶ νίψαι· ἀπελθὼν οὖν καὶ νιψάμενος ἀνέβλεψα). The blind man responds by describing what he knows, matching almost perfectly the account provided by the narrator in v. 6. The blind man gives to his questioners the name of the man, but in a style that suggests unfamiliarity: "The man called Jesus" (Ὁ ἄνθρωπος ὁ λεγόμενος Ἰησοῦς).[28]

9:12 And they said to him, "Where is this man?" He said, "I do not know" (καὶ εἶπαν αὐτῷ, Ποῦ ἐστιν ἐκεῖνος; λέγει, Οὐκ οἶδα). In regard to his location, however, the blind man is uninformed. The first verbal exchange (vv. 8 – 12) ends with the focus having turned dramatically to Jesus as the source of the miracle. But because the blind man was the recipient of the miracle, he must also remain at the center of attention, that is, as the primary witness.

The significant (and mysterious) relationship between "knowing" and "seeing" has been officially established for the reader (cf. vv. 35 – 38).[29]

9:13 They led the formerly blind man to the Pharisees (Ἄγουσιν αὐτὸν πρὸς τοὺς Φαρισαίους τόν ποτε τυφλόν). The second verbal exchange (vv. 13 – 17) begins with a transition from the informal interrogation of the blind man by his neighbors to a more formal interrogation by the Pharisees, who in this scene are representative of the Jewish authorities (see comments on 1:19, 24). The narrator describes how those who knew the blind man "led" (Ἄγουσιν) him, the same term used in 8:3 to describe the treatment of the woman who had been caught in adultery. Although the blind man is not on trial, the language is suggestive of the treatment of a prisoner, serving to increase the intensity of the interrogation. And like the pericope of the woman accused of adultery, the reader understands that two people — not one — are being judged in the proceedings that are to follow.

9:14 Now it was the Sabbath on the day Jesus made the mud and opened his eyes (ἦν δὲ σάββατον ἐν ᾗ ἡμέρᾳ τὸν πηλὸν ἐποίησεν ὁ Ἰησοῦς καὶ ἀνέῳξεν αὐτοῦ τοὺς ὀφθαλμούς). The narrator adds an important detail that also intensifies the scene. When the healing took place, "it was the Sabbath" (ἦν σάββατον). The narrator does not explain the significance, but the reader is expected to understand, since a nearly identical dilemma occurred in the healing of the lame man in 5:1 – 18. The offense is that Jesus "made the mud" (τὸν πηλὸν ἐποίησεν) on the Sabbath, which would later be declared as a violation of Sabbath law in the Talmud (b. Shabbat 108b). But more generally, since "kneading" was on a list of thirty-nine

---

28. See Leithart, *Deep Exegesis*, 165; cf. Augustine, *John*, 44.8.247.

29. Wright, *Rhetoric and Theology*, 169.

activities forbidden on the Sabbath (m. Shabbat 7:2; cf. 24:3), Jesus's interaction with the blind man was by definition a sacrilege.[30]

Like the healing of the lame man, the narrator delayed informing the reader about the occurrence of the healing on the Sabbath (cf. 5:9).[31] Such information not only explains why the local townspeople who knew the blind man took him to the authorities (v. 13) but also serves to intensify the interrogation and explain the symbolic dialogue to follow.[32] The delayed information thrusts Jesus into the spotlight. Similar to the eclipse of the adulterous woman led before Jesus, the blind man is more fittingly described as guilty by association; it is no surprise that in both pericopae the codefendant with Jesus remains anonymous.

9:15 Then the Pharisees also asked him how he received sight. And he said to them, "He placed mud on my eyes and I washed and I see" (πάλιν οὖν ἠρώτων αὐτὸν καὶ οἱ Φαρισαῖοι πῶς ἀνέβλεψεν. ὁ δὲ εἶπεν αὐτοῖς, Πηλὸν ἐπέθηκέν μου ἐπὶ τοὺς ὀφθαλμούς, καὶ ἐνιψάμην, καὶ βλέπω). The Pharisees, the second interlocutor, now begin a more formal interrogation. While the neighbors and those who knew him asked a related question, it was rooted more in the possibility of the healing (v. 10); this question is primarily concerned with the legality of the healing.

This is the fifth occurrence (vv. 2 [2x], 11, 14, 15) of the term "mud" (Πηλὸν), which reminds the reader of its allusion to creation and the Creator. The reader is expected to recall the innate connection between the Sabbath (the seventh day) and the creation imagery, having remembered that what the Pharisees thought was the seventh day was only the sixth day; it was not yet "the hour" for rest (see

comments before 2:1). A similar confusion was exhibited by the Jewish authorities with the healing of the lame man (5:1 – 18).

9:16 Some of the Pharisees were saying, "This man is not from God, because he did not keep the Sabbath." But others were saying, "How can a sinful man do such signs?" and there was a division among them (ἔλεγον οὖν ἐκ τῶν Φαρισαίων τινές, Οὐκ ἔστιν οὗτος παρὰ θεοῦ ὁ ἄνθρωπος, ὅτι τὸ σάββατον οὐ τηρεῖ. ἄλλοι [δὲ] ἔλεγον, Πῶς δύναται ἄνθρωπος ἁμαρτωλὸς τοιαῦτα σημεῖα ποιεῖν; καὶ σχίσμα ἦν ἐν αὐτοῖς). The Pharisees respond to the account given by the blind man with a mixture of conclusions that, according to the narrator, swing from a statement of accusation to a statement of credulity — a response matching the first interlocutors (v. 9; cf. 7:25 – 27).

The Greek word order is unusual, giving emphasis to the anonymous title used for Jesus, rigidly translated: "He is not from God — this man!" (Οὐκ ἔστιν οὗτος παρὰ θεοῦ ὁ ἄνθρωπος). The statement seems to make a dual statement — he is not from God, he is simply a man.[33] But "others" (ἄλλοι) are not so convinced. True, he is "a sinful man" (ἄνθρωπος ἁμαρτωλὸς) — for who else would heal on the Sabbath — but his actions are clearly recognizable as "signs" (σημεῖα). The OT was well aware of the tension created by "a prophet" who could perform signs but who taught a subject matter that was idolatrous and leading people astray (Deut 13:1 – 5). The different interpretations of the actions of Jesus created "a division" (σχίσμα) among the Pharisees, a reaction the readers have seen before (see 7:43). The reader is required to make their own judgment regarding the "fifth sign" of Jesus (on "signs," see comments on 2:11).

---

30. Cf. Morris, *John*, 550.

31. Contra Thatcher, "The Sabbath Trick," 60, the purpose is to dramatically deflect the reader's focus from the blind man to Jesus.

32. Cf. Wright, *Rhetoric and Theology*, 172.

33. Barrett, *John*, 360. Cf. Paul D. Duke, *Irony in the Fourth Gospel* (Atlanta: John Knox, 1985), 120.

9:17 Finally they said again to the blind man, "What do you say concerning him, because he opened your eyes?" He said, "He is a prophet" (λέγουσιν οὖν τῷ τυφλῷ πάλιν, Τί σὺ λέγεις περὶ αὐτοῦ, ὅτι ἠνέῳξέν σου τοὺς ὀφθαλμούς; ὁ δὲ εἶπεν ὅτι Προφήτης ἐστίν). In a perplexing move, the Pharisees come back to the blind man with a second question, almost as if he (the witness) was expected to resolve the disagreement (like a judge). The only warrant suggested by their question was the blind's man more intimate connection to Jesus ("because he opened your eyes" [ὅτι ἠνέῳξέν σου τοὺς ὀφθαλμούς]). While it is impossible to reconstruct the historical dimensions of the interrogation proceedings or the motivation behind their second question, it was almost certainly intended to force a compliant answer that matched the majority of the Pharisees — "He is a fraud, a liar, an idolater!" But for whatever reason, the blind man does not capitulate.

But of even more significance is how for the reader the question becomes a perfect setup for the interpretation the blind man offers. The blind man states in two Greek words what might be viewed as a moment of proclamation, "He is a prophet" (Προφήτης ἐστίν). The narrative reveals no hesitation; just a statement of fact. There is no need to evaluate the theology of the blind man, which Michaels calls "characteristically simple."[34] The man's blurry vision of Jesus presses the reader to fill in the gaps, to see what is being shouted by implication, knowing full well that the Gospel will flesh out the fullness of Jesus both later in this pericope (vv. 35 – 38) as well as in the Gospel as a whole. With the blind man's statement, the second verbal exchange (vv. 13 – 17) concludes.

9:18 The Jews still did not believe that he was blind and had received sight until they called the parents of the formerly blind man (Οὐκ ἐπίστευσαν οὖν οἱ Ἰουδαῖοι περὶ αὐτοῦ ὅτι ἦν τυφλὸς καὶ ἀνέβλεψεν, ἕως ὅτου ἐφώνησαν τοὺς γονεῖς αὐτοῦ τοῦ ἀναβλέψαντος). The third verbal exchange (vv. 18 – 23) begins with a more aggressive and personal cross-examination involving the blind man's parents. The Pharisees have been replaced in the account by the "Jews" (see comments on 1:19). The unexplained exchange of the Pharisees by the Jews suggests that the Gospel views them to some degree as synonymous; they are two different but related subgroups under the Jewish authorities. The Jews "called" (ἐφώνησαν) for the parents of the blind man, a term that reflects a subpoena-like summoning of the parents to the judicial hearing. The reason for the subpoena was that "the Jews still did not believe" (Οὐκ ἐπίστευσαν οὖν οἱ Ἰουδαῖοι) the facts of the miracle and wanted to verify the account. The use of the term "belief" reinforces a significant concept for the Gospel. The summoning of the blind man's parents reveals the social power wielded by the Jewish leadership, who has control of the legal investigation.[35]

9:19 They asked them saying, "Is this your son, whom you say was born blind? How then can he now see?" (καὶ ἠρώτησαν αὐτοὺς λέγοντες, Οὗτός ἐστιν ὁ υἱὸς ὑμῶν, ὃν ὑμεῖς λέγετε ὅτι τυφλὸς ἐγεννήθη; πῶς οὖν βλέπει ἄρτι;). The Jews ask the parents two questions regarding their son. The first question was to confirm his relation to them and that he was truly born blind. The situation could be alleviated if cross-examination proved that their son had never been blind. The emphatic "you say" (ὑμεῖς λέγετε), however, suggests that the authorities already have reason to believe that the parents will testify to exactly that, even if it implies that some will hold them responsible for their son's birth condition (v. 2).[36]

34. Michaels, *John*, 552.
35. Keener, *John*, 1:787.
36. Michaels, *John*, 553.

The second question is less obvious in its intention, simply because it has little to do with the parents. They are clearly the authorities regarding his birth, but they can say nothing authoritatively about his healing. This question does not seek further information. Rather, the second question is an authoritative and threatening challenge to the parents, intended publicly to embarrass them and to display their testimony as unreliable and deceptive. It was an example of "badgering the witness," except the parents had no legal defense team of their own.

9:20 His parents answered and said, "We know that he is our son and that he was born blind" (ἀπεκρίθησαν οὖν οἱ γονεῖς αὐτοῦ καὶ εἶπαν, Οἴδαμεν ὅτι οὗτός ἐστιν ὁ υἱὸς ἡμῶν καὶ ὅτι τυφλὸς ἐγεννήθη). The parents respond to the first question, confirming the identity of their son and that he was blind from birth. This answer springs from what they "know" (Οἴδαμεν); they know their son and they know the details of his blindness from his birth. This statement confirms that a miracle has taken place.

9:21 "But how he now can see we do not know, or who opened his eyes we do not know. Ask him, he is old enough, he will speak for himself" (πῶς δὲ νῦν βλέπει οὐκ οἴδαμεν, ἢ τίς ἤνοιξεν αὐτοῦ τοὺς ὀφθαλμοὺς ἡμεῖς οὐκ οἴδαμεν· αὐτὸν ἐρωτήσατε, ἡλικίαν ἔχει, αὐτὸς περὶ ἑαυτοῦ λαλήσει). The parents are less competent regarding the second question. Their answer not only is intended to separate them from any right or access to that kind of information but also to give themselves legal separation from their son. The first separation is the simplest, which the parents make certain with the emphatic, twice-stated, "We do not know" (οὐκ οἴδαμεν).

The second separation requires more legal posi-

tioning. In response to the social-religious threat by the Jewish authorities, the parents distance themselves from the situation involving their son in the form of two arguments. The first argument is that he is a reliable witness (i.e., he meets the legal-age requirement). With an imperative of request, "Ask him" (αὐτὸν ἐρωτήσατε), used by an inferior when addressing a superior, the blind man's parents defer to their son. The statement that "he is old enough" (ἡλικίαν ἔχει) is an idiom which expresses that a person is of the legal age to speak on his own behalf.[37] The second argument is that their son is a competent witness. The final statement, "He will speak for himself" (αὐτὸς περὶ ἑαυτοῦ λαλήσει), communicates that their son is cognitively competent enough to reason with.[38]

9:22 His parents said these things because they feared the Jews, for already the Jews had agreed that if anyone who confessed that he is the Christ, they would be expelled from the synagogue (ταῦτα εἶπαν οἱ γονεῖς αὐτοῦ ὅτι ἐφοβοῦντο τοὺς Ἰουδαίους, ἤδη γὰρ συνετέθειντο οἱ Ἰουδαῖοι ἵνα ἐάν τις αὐτὸν ὁμολογήσῃ Χριστόν, ἀποσυνάγωγος γένηται). The exchange of responses between the Jews and the blind man's parents is concluded by an explanatory intrusion by the narrator, not uncommon in John (cf. 6:6, 64, 71; 8:27), in which the reader is given key information for interpreting the previous encounter.[39] The inclusion of this detail offers a climax to the progressing dialogue. Interpreters have long noticed the centrality of this section of the pericope (vv. 18–23), not only because it is framed by the two encounters with the Jewish officials but also because according to some it is the center of the chiastic structure of the pericope.[40] But not only does the forensic pattern of the dialogue warn against too precise of a center, but such an interpretation often tends to prioritize this

---

37. Barrett, *John*, 361.
38. Morris, *John*, 433.

39. Cf. Staley, "Stumbling in the Dark," 67.
40. See Leithart, *Deep Exegesis*, 161–71.

pericope over and against the Gospel as a whole, as we will discuss below.

The narrator reveals that the parents "feared the Jews" (ἐφοβοῦντο τοὺς Ἰουδαίους). This statement merely serves to confirm the growing hatred and murderous intentions of the Jews against Jesus that has been developing in the Gospel. This was not a top secret detail, for not only did "the crowd" already "fear the Jews" (7:13), but even "the people in Jerusalem" were aware of the threat against Jesus's life (see 7:25). The reader is being directed to see this historical conflict as a subset of the cosmological conflict between light and darkness (1:5).

The narrator explains that the source of the parents' fear is an "already" (ἤδη) existing socio-religious "decree" — "the Jews had agreed" (συνετέθειντο οἱ Ἰουδαῖοι) that offenders would "be expelled from the synagogue" (ἀποσυνάγωγος γένηται). This statement has been made famous by the influential proposal of J. L. Martyn, for whom this verse is the entry point for a two-level reading of the Gospel (see Introduction).[41] Martyn argues that since formal excommunications did not occur between Jews and Christians until late in the first century, this narrative aside refers to an issue contemporary with the writing of the Gospel in the late first century and is superimposing it upon the narrative half a century earlier in the life of the historical Jesus. It does this to depict how the contemporary Jesus followers of the Johannine community are responding to a similar crisis with their own set of "Jews." For Martyn this is confirmed by the two other uses of the technical term "expelled from the synagogue" (ἀποσυνάγωγος; 12:42; 16:2) and by the formal confession of "the Christ" (Χριστόν), which is also "clearly" a later development. For this rea-

son, then, the term "expelled from the synagogue" (ἀποσυνάγωγος) functions as an (intentionally) anachronistic clue to the reader for separating the traditional-historical material (i.e., the time of Jesus) from the edited material (i.e., the time of the Johannine community).

Much has been written in response to Martyn's proposal that need not be surveyed here, for it has to do with important hermeneutical concerns (see Introduction).[42] But there are several historical issues that must briefly be addressed.[43] First, there is almost unanimous agreement that there is no connection between the "decree" of 9:22 and the proposed referent by Martyn (the Birkat Haminim). There is no verifiable event to which this so-called technical term, "expulsion from the synagogue" (ἀποσυνάγωγος), can be connected, which means this verse is not alerting the reader to something outside the historical time of the ministry of Jesus depicted by the narrative.

Second, evidence surrounding the time of Jesus demonstrates that there were always intra-Jewish conflicts — disputes between religious authorities and alleged heretics — within common Judaism. The description provided by the narrator, then, is a portrait of a basic (and therefore common) use of power by the Jewish authorities to combat theological and political threats to the institution of Judaism.

Third, and directly related to v. 22, there is rabbinic evidence that the family of the alleged heretic and even the people of his town of origin would be guilty by association if they received him as one of their own, that is, did not respond to him in accord with the religious authorities. According to Neale, "The fierceness of the punishment for the

---

41. Martyn, *History and Theology in the Fourth Gospel.*

42. See Klink, *The Sheep of the Fold*, 127–47, for an analysis of 9:22.

43. See Edward W. Klink III, "Expulsion from the Synagogue: Rethinking a Johannine Anachronism," *TynBul* 59

(2008): 99–118; idem, "The Over-Realized Expulsion in the Gospel of John," in *John, Jesus, and History: Vol. 2; Aspects of Historicity in John*, ed. Paul N. Anderson, Felix Just, and Tom Thatcher; SBLSymS 44 (Atlanta: SBL Press, 2009), 175–84.

mesith [heretic] or those who tolerate his activity is remarkable. Judicially both the perpetrator and those who tolerate the crime are the subject of extreme punishment."[44] This would explain why the Jewish authorities would approach the blind man's parents, why the parents "feared the Jews," and why they tried to disassociate themselves from their own son. This might also explain why his neighbors "led" him to the authorities (v. 13) — they were protecting themselves from being accessories to a crime. As much as their response can be viewed as harsh, it might possibly be an attempt to protect their other children and even their town of origin from the punishment of the Jewish authorities. They have already tried to kill Jesus (5:18; 7:1, 19, 25; 8:37, 40); they are now threating anyone — friends, family, even those who live in the same village — who might join his movement, that is, "who confessed that he is the Christ."

9:23 For this reason his parents said, "He is old enough, ask him" (διὰ τοῦτο οἱ γονεῖς αὐτοῦ εἶπαν ὅτι Ἡλικίαν ἔχει, αὐτὸν ἐπερωτήσατε). The narrator concludes with a comment that confirms the reason for the parent's action. The Gospel is not primarily concerned with the parents' state of belief but with their role in this judicial hearing.[45] For the narrator's purposes, they not only confirmed that a healing miracle occurred but serve to show the legal intentions and aggression of the Jewish authorities. The blind man has been cross-examined; as the parents themselves said, he is the one most intimately connected to the healer. Unfortunately, the offending fact of the case has become personal, since the blind man is the "fact." So to him the proceedings must return.

9:24 Then they called the man who was blind a second time and said to him, "Give glory to God. We know that this man is a sinner" (Ἐφώνησαν οὖν τὸν ἄνθρωπον ἐκ δευτέρου ὃς ἦν τυφλὸς καὶ εἶπαν αὐτῷ, Δὸς δόξαν τῷ θεῷ· ἡμεῖς οἴδαμεν ὅτι οὗτος ὁ ἄνθρωπος ἁμαρτωλός ἐστιν). The fourth verbal exchange (vv. 24 – 34) begins with a transition from the parents of the blind man to the blind man himself. The narrator reminds the reader that this is the "second time" (ἐκ δευτέρου) he is examined by the Pharisees. This time, however, he was not "led" to the Pharisees (v. 13) but more formally subpoenaed or summoned by them ("called" [Ἐφώνησαν]). The Pharisees offer a formal declaration regarding Jesus that is prefaced with a command for truthfulness: "Give glory to God" (Δὸς δόξαν τῷ θεῷ). The preface is something like an "oath formula" used before offering testimony or a confession of guilt (cf. Josh 7:19).[46] And in a trial or interrogation context it can even be a demand for a confession of wrong, a call to repentance.[47]

The declaration is in the form of a judgment. The statement is made emphatic with the stated subject, "We know" (ἡμεῖς οἴδαμεν), which suggests they reject the witness of the blind man and his parents who both claim not "to know" the truth about Jesus (cf. vv. 12, 21). After hearing the evidence and firsthand accounts, the Pharisees now can reveal the official position of the Jewish authorities: "This man is a sinner" (οὗτος ὁ ἄνθρωπος ἁμαρτωλός ἐστιν). Even though the blind man provided his healer's name (v. 11), the Pharisees do not use it, just as they do not use the testimony he provided. In light of the significance of the name of Jesus revealed in the prologue (1:12), their avoidance of it is symptomatic of their unbelief.

44. D. Neale, "Jesus was a *Mesith*? Public Response to Jesus and his Ministry," *TynBul* 44 (1993): 89 – 101 (91).

45. Contra Cornelis Bennema, *Encountering Jesus: Character Studies in the Gospel of John* (Milton Keynes: Paternoster, 2010), 140.

46. Brown, *John*, 1:374.

47. Keener, *John*, 1:790.

They state in general terms that Jesus is a "sinner" (ἁμαρτωλός), offering no evidence for a judgment that leads away from the implications suggested by not only the blind man (v. 17) but even a selection of their own (v. 16). By silencing all such implications, along with the name (identity) of the accused man, the Pharisees intended to force the hand of the blind man regarding the person who had healed him.

9:25 He answered, "I do not know if he is a sinner. One thing I do know: I was blind but now I see" (ἀπεκρίθη οὖν ἐκεῖνος, Εἰ ἁμαρτωλός ἐστιν οὐκ οἶδα· ἓν οἶδα, ὅτι τυφλὸς ὢν ἄρτι βλέπω). The blind man responds in a climactic and surprising manner, especially in light of the threatening statement made toward him (and his parents) by the Pharisees. By claiming ignorance regarding Jesus's status as a sinner ("I do not know" [οὐκ οἶδα]), the blind man defers to the status and expertise of the religious authorities. Yet there is "one thing" (ἓν) about which the blind man claims to know with certainty: "I was blind but now I see" (τυφλὸς ὢν ἄρτι βλέπω). The blind man's response is nothing less than a contrast of "knowledge." In the forensic context, it was a direct counter and therefore a challenge to the judgment made by the Jewish authorities, a refusal to submit to the demand placed upon him.

9:26 Then they said to him, "What did he do to you? How did he open your eyes? (εἶπον οὖν αὐτῷ, Τί ἐποίησέν σοι; πῶς ἤνοιξέν σου τοὺς ὀφθαλμούς;). The counterconfession of the blind man received a very strange response by the Pharisees. The force with which the "oath formula" placed a demand to recant upon the blind man would have led the reader to expect the authorities to counter with equal force. Unless the further questions are to be taken as a trick intended to cause him to contra-

dict his previous testimony, they serve to expose the Pharisees' surprise at the blind man's confident confession. He has not been swayed by the social-religious pressure.

9:27 He answered them, "I already told you and you did not hear. What do you want to hear again? Do you also want to become his disciples?" (ἀπεκρίθη αὐτοῖς, Εἶπον ὑμῖν ἤδη καὶ οὐκ ἠκούσατε· τί πάλιν θέλετε ἀκούειν; μὴ καὶ ὑμεῖς θέλετε αὐτοῦ μαθηταὶ γενέσθαι;). The blind man responds to the Pharisees' two questions with two of his own that serve as a rebuke. He not only reminds them that they have already heard his testimony (see v. 15), but he accuses them of not paying attention ("you did not hear" [οὐκ ἠκούσατε]). By implication, their ears might need to be restored to hear God's Word (see comments on v. 31), just as his sight needed to be restored to see God's world. He has already explained the "what" and "how"; what he wants to know from them is "why" they continue to press him.

The blind man's first question to the authorities, "What do you want to hear again?" (τί πάλιν θέλετε ἀκούειν;), mocks their repeated questioning. It has become clear that their interest in Jesus and the healing miracle contains broader implications. The blind man's second question offers a potential solution to the "why" question: "Do you also want to become his disciples?" (μὴ καὶ ὑμεῖς θέλετε αὐτοῦ μαθηταὶ γενέσθαι;). Even though the question expects a negative answer, its rhetorical force is intended to be suggestive. The emphatic "do you also want" (καὶ ὑμεῖς θέλετε) might suggest that the blind man views himself as in some sense a disciple.[48]

9:28 They reviled him and said, "You are a disciple of this man, but we are disciples of Moses" (καὶ ἐλοιδόρησαν αὐτὸν καὶ εἶπον, Σὺ μαθητὴς εἶ

---

48. Cf. Michaels, *John*, 559.

ἐκείνου, ἡμεῖς δὲ τοῦ Μωϋσέως ἐσμὲν μαθηταί). The narrator explains that the Pharisees respond by speaking abusively to the blind man ("they reviled him" [ἐλοιδόρησαν αὐτὸν]), which probably summarizes a number of statements made against his person and his standing in the community. They follow this assault with a judgment that matches the implication from v. 27, emphatically calling him a disciple of Jesus, though again without stating his name (cf. v. 24). In contrast, they declare themselves with equal emphasis to be disciples of Moses ("but we are disciples of Moses" [ἡμεῖς δὲ τοῦ Μωϋσέως ἐσμὲν μαθηταί]). The Pharisees make a hard and fast distinction between Jesus and Moses that is intended to refute the authority of Jesus. But the reader is well aware that Moses himself was on the side of Jesus (see 5:45 – 46).

9:29 "We know that God has spoken to Moses, but we do not know where this man is from" (ἡμεῖς οἴδαμεν ὅτι Μωϋσεῖ λελάληκεν ὁ θεός, τοῦτον δὲ οὐκ οἴδαμεν πόθεν ἐστίν). The ignorance of this further statement by the Pharisees is easily recognized by the reader. The theme of "knowledge" is drenching the dialogue (vv. 12, 21, 25), with the religious leaders again emphasizing what they think they know. The ignorance of the Pharisees is magnified when they declare that "God has spoken to Moses" (Μωϋσεῖ λελάληκεν ὁ θεός), which is probably reflective of Exodus 33:11. It is the Son alone who "knows" God (1:18). Their ignorance is highlighted by their dismissal of his origin ("but we do not know where this man is from" [τοῦτον δὲ οὐκ οἴδαμεν πόθεν ἐστίν]).The reader is well aware that Jesus is "from above" (3:3, 5, 31), that his origin is "in the beginning with God" (1:2), and therefore from God. Their dismissive attitude toward Jesus is in truth dismissive of God.

9:30 The man answered and said to them, "Why, there is something remarkable about this; you do not know where he is from, yet he opened my eyes" (ἀπεκρίθη ὁ ἄνθρωπος καὶ εἶπεν αὐτοῖς, Ἐν τούτῳ γὰρ τὸ θαυμαστόν ἐστιν ὅτι ὑμεῖς οὐκ οἴδατε πόθεν ἐστίν, καὶ ἤνοιξέν μου τοὺς ὀφθαλμούς). The blind man responds with his longest speech of the dialogue (vv. 30 – 33). Beginning with a conjunction that is best translated as an interrogative, "why" (γὰρ), the blind man offers his astonishment at the conclusion arrived at by the religious leaders.[49] The grammar of the sentence is significant. Like several times in this dialogue, the phrase, "you do not know" (ὑμεῖς οὐκ οἴδατε), highlights the Pharisees' lack of knowledge. The conjunction "that" (ὅτι) could be translated as a direct object clause but is best translated as signaling a coordinating apposition.[50] With rhetorical emphasis, he declares their conclusion to be "a remarkable thing" (τὸ θαυμαστόν), a thing of amazement. The evidence from the miracle that Jesus performed is such glaring evidence that to reject it becomes a miracle of its own.[51]

9:31 "We know that God does not listen to sinners, but if a man is God-fearing and does his will, he listens to this man (οἴδαμεν ὅτι ἁμαρτωλῶν ὁ θεὸς οὐκ ἀκούει, ἀλλ᾽ ἐάν τις θεοσεβὴς ᾖ καὶ τὸ θέλημα αὐτοῦ ποιῇ τούτου ἀκούει). The blind man counters the extrabiblical reasoning of the religious leaders with some of his own. The verb "we know" (οἴδαμεν) mimics and mocks the twice-repeated claim of his interlocutors (vv. 24, 29).[52] The blind man reasons theologically that God does not "listen to" (ἀκούει) the person who sins but does to the one who is "God-fearing" (θεοσεβὴς) and "does his will" (τὸ θέλημα αὐτοῦ ποιῇ). The former term is only used here in the NT and is probably best defined by the second trait of someone who obeys

---

49. BDF § 452.2.
50. See Wallace, *Greek Grammar*, 458 – 59.

51. Cf. Morris, *John*, 437 – 38.
52. Michaels, *John*, 561.

God. As Bultmann suggests, the two traits are expressed best by Micah 6:8: "To love mercy, to act justly, and to walk humbly with your God."[53] The blind man's reasoning that God does not hear the sinner is in one sense an appropriate judgment from Scripture (Isa 1:15; Pss 66:16 – 20; 109:7; Prov 15:29). There is an undeniable separation between God and humanity which ironically is more often depicted in Scripture by a different sense — sight (as it will be at the end of this dialogue [vv. 39 – 41]). At the same time, however, God is not limited by the inadequacies of humanity, for he certainly can and has heard the cry of the sinner. The gospel of Jesus Christ is rooted in this fact.

9:32 "From the beginning of time it has not been heard that someone opened the eyes of a man born blind" (ἐκ τοῦ αἰῶνος οὐκ ἠκούσθη ὅτι ἤνοιξέν τις ὀφθαλμοὺς τυφλοῦ γεγεννημένου). Using an uncommon expression, "from the beginning of time" (ἐκ τοῦ αἰῶνος), the blind man speaks emphatically about the uniqueness of what has happened to him. The expression would be hyperbolic were it not directed to Jesus, the one by whom time itself was created (1:3). Playing on the verb "hear," the blind man declares that such a miracle, the healing of a man born with blindness, "has never been heard" (οὐκ ἠκούσθη).[54]

9:33 "If this man were not from God, he could do nothing" (εἰ μὴ ἦν οὗτος παρὰ θεοῦ, οὐκ ἠδύνατο ποιεῖν οὐδέν). Though stated negatively for rhetorical purposes, the logical conclusion is that God is with Jesus. The reader knows what the blind man is only putting together in part. The work of the Son is not only rooted in his connection to the Father but is rooted in his being the cause of creation. With one prepositional phrase ("from God" [παρὰ θεοῦ]), the blind man summarizes the cosmological mission of the Son from the Father.

9:34 They answered and said to him, "Every part of you was born in sin, and you are teaching us?" And they cast him out (ἀπεκρίθησαν καὶ εἶπον αὐτῷ, Ἐν ἁμαρτίαις σὺ ἐγεννήθης ὅλος, καὶ σὺ διδάσκεις ἡμᾶς; καὶ ἐξέβαλον αὐτὸν ἔξω). After the lengthy closing testimony by the blind man, the Pharisees offer a strong *ad hominem* rejoinder. Using an adjective that emphasizes the degree of completeness ("every part of …" [ὅλος]), the religious leaders declare his entire person unclean. By this they offer their own logical conclusion: "You were born blind, blindness is a result of sin, therefore by definition you are sinful." This is, however, the exact deduction the disciples were making when they first saw the blind man (v. 2). Only now does the meaning of Jesus's response to his disciples (vv. 3 – 5) make sense. God is not a mere solution to the things of this world; he is also creation's very source.

The fourth verbal exchange concludes with the cryptic statement by the narrator that "they cast him out" (καὶ ἐξέβαλον αὐτὸν ἔξω). From where did they cast him? No specific setting has been provided by the narrator. The only logical connection is the threatened expulsion from the synagogue mentioned in v. 22. The testimony of the blind man has forced the Jews to excommunicate him. We can only surmise that this comment by the narrator describes how the Jewish authorities have declared him to be a social-religious outcast, a heretic (in the divisive sense), and placed him in a position of shame and exclusion.[55] In this way the preliminary hearing of the Sabbath case ends, with the primary witness becoming a codefendant and ultimately being declared guilty for aligning himself with Jesus.

---

53. Bultmann, *John*, 337.
54. Cf. Michaels, *John*, 563.
55. Cf. Painter, "John 9 and the Interpretation of the Fourth Gospel," 39.

9:35 Jesus heard that he had been cast out, and after finding him he said to him, "Do you believe in the Son of Man?" (Ἤκουσεν Ἰησοῦς ὅτι ἐξέβαλον αὐτὸν ἔξω, καὶ εὑρὼν αὐτὸν εἶπεν [αὐτῷ], Σὺ πιστεύεις εἰς τὸν υἱὸν τοῦ ἀνθρώπου;). The final section of the pericope (vv. 35–41) begins with the return of Jesus, who has been absent since v. 7. In lieu of the elaborate forensic proceedings that have just taken place, it is surprising that the narrator does not give any indication of where, how, or why Jesus returned. The focus is on the continued dialogue. In the first verbal exchange of this final section (vv. 35–38), Jesus approaches the blind man.

The reader is immediately struck by the narrator's choice of words: "Jesus *heard*" (Ἤκουσεν Ἰησοῦς) about the blind man's excommunication. Using a word that reverberates with the blind man's proverb, "We know that God does not listen to sinners" (v. 31), the depiction of Jesus "hearing" serves as confirmation of the actions of the blind man — who "feared God" more than "the Jews" (v. 22). Moreover, Jesus not only "heard" about him but "found him," in a manner similar to the Father not only loving the world but sending his Son to it (3:16).

Jesus asks the man a surprising question: "Do you believe in the Son of Man?" (Σὺ πιστεύεις εἰς τὸν υἱὸν τοῦ ἀνθρώπου;). The stated subject, "you" (Σὺ), makes the question emphatic, matching the emphatic questioning from the Pharisees (cf. vv. 28, 34).[56] The reader is aware that an ironic twist has occurred; the one who has been responding to questions about Jesus by others is now being asked a question by Jesus himself. The reader is aware of the significance of the question (on "believe in," see comments on 1:12). In a pericope controlled by forensic patterns and themes of interrogation

and judgment, the title "Son of Man" declares all the power, glory, and rule of God that resides in the person of Jesus, the ultimate Judge (see 1:51; 5:27; cf. Dan 7:13–14). The blind man has already been judged by the Jewish authorities, but the judgment about to be made eclipses their judgment. At the same time, this title declares that Jesus is the revelation of God.[57] At this moment the blind man is intended to "see" with much more than his eyes; he is being asked to see with his faith. Like all who become disciples of Jesus, the formerly blind man is in need of even more sight; he must "come and see" (cf. 1:39, 46).

9:36 He answered and said, "And who is he, sir, that I may believe in him?" (ἀπεκρίθη ἐκεῖνος καὶ εἶπεν, Καὶ τίς ἐστιν, κύριε, ἵνα πιστεύσω εἰς αὐτόν;). The response of the blind man to Jesus's question reveals that he has not yet connected the Son of Man with Jesus, his healer. Jesus's question had certainly been prompted by what had already taken place, and the blind man was prepared to concede the connection. The belief Jesus pursues is a belief that recognizes who Jesus truly is.[58] The term translated "sir" (κύριε) does not yet mean "Lord" in this context, though the reader is intended to feel the movement toward the latter (see comments on v. 38).

9:37 Jesus said to him, "You have seen him; he is the one speaking with you" (εἶπεν αὐτῷ ὁ Ἰησοῦς, Καὶ ἑώρακας αὐτὸν καὶ ὁ λαλῶν μετὰ σοῦ ἐκεῖνός ἐστιν). Jesus declares in the perfect tense, "You have seen him" (ἑώρακας αὐτὸν), to indicate that the two kinds of vision — physical and spiritual — have now completely come together. It is fair to say that this moment of sight has less to do with the eyes and more to do with faith — for at this mo-

---

56. Michaels, *John*, 565.

57. See Francis J. Moloney, *The Johannine Son of Man*, 2nd ed.; BSR 14 (Rome: LAS, 1978), 149–59.

58. Cf. Bultmann, *John*, 338.

ment the blind man was truly seeing God (see comments on 14:9; cf. 1:18).

It is important to note that in both clauses Jesus speaks about himself in the third person ("him" [αὐτὸν] and "the one speaking" [ὁ λαλῶν]). In light of the context of seeing beyond physical sight, the third person suggests that Jesus is to be known beyond his physical presence. This in no way denies the theological significance of the physicality of Jesus (see comments on 1:14) but expresses that the significance of Jesus extends far beyond those who "see" him with their eyes (see 20:29).

9:38 So he said, "I believe, Lord." And he worshipped him (ὁ δὲ ἔφη, Πιστεύω, κύριε· καὶ προσεκύνησεν αὐτῷ). The moment the blind man's physical and spiritual sight came together upon the person of Jesus, the "sir" (κύριε) of v. 36 changed to "Lord" (κύριε). The word is identical, but its meaning has entirely changed. The reason is that the faith of the blind man had found its object. Jesus says "I am"; the disciple must respond with "I believe" (Πιστεύω). And as the narrator reveals, true confession finds expression in only one response: worship.[59] The blind man is now removed from the view of the reader; his witness has been offered and received. The fifth sign and its interpretation are now complete.

9:39 Then Jesus said, "For judgment I came into this world, so that the blind may see and those who see may become blind" (καὶ εἶπεν ὁ Ἰησοῦς, Εἰς κρίμα ἐγὼ εἰς τὸν κόσμον τοῦτον ἦλθον, ἵνα οἱ μὴ βλέποντες βλέπωσιν καὶ οἱ βλέποντες τυφλοὶ γένωνται). The second verbal exchange of the final scene of the pericope (vv. 39 – 41) has Jesus standing alone, making what is like a sermon that encapsulates the scene and dialogue that just transpired. By beginning with "for judgment" (Εἰς κρίμα), the accent is on the negative assertion being made, not the positive one.[60] At this moment the defendant stands and takes his rightful place as the Judge, and as presented by the narrative his audience becomes the whole world. The narrative has already presented the love of God for the world (3:16 – 17, 21), but not without forecasting the judgment to come (3:18 – 20).[61]

Using the analogy of the healing of the blind man, Jesus declares that just as the blind are given sight (by the Light), so also "those who see may become blind" (οἱ βλέποντες τυφλοὶ γένωνται). Jesus speaks as the revealer of God (1:18), addressing no particular group or individual. Everyone is faced with the question that Jesus's statement imposes upon them: Do you have blindness or sight?[62] From the prologue onward, the Gospel has depicted the inability of the darkness to recognize the light (1:5). But the scandal is not simply that the darkness cannot see the light, but also that it cannot see itself for what it is. *The foundational irony of the gospel is not that God became human but that humanity thought they had become God.* For this reason they were blind, and for this reason the true God, the Word who actually was God (1:1), came to manifest the truth about himself and his world. He alone is "the light of life" (8:12) and "freedom" (8:32 – 36); anything else is "slavery to sin" (8:34) and existence in a state of blindness. Here Jesus declares the fulfillment of the judgment of God promised through the prophets (see Isa 6:10; see comments on 12:38 – 40).[63]

9:40 Some of the Pharisees who were with him and heard him say these things said to him, "Are

---

59. Cf. Leithart, *Deep Exegesis*, 164.

60. Michaels, *John*, 573.

61. See Wright, *Rhetoric and Theology*, 188.

62. Bultmann, *John*, 341.

63. J. Duncan M. Derrett, "John 9:6 read with Isaiah 6:10; 29:9," *EvQ* 66 (1994): 251 – 54. Cf. J. M. Lieu, "Blindness in the Johannine Tradition," *NTS* 34 (1988): 83 – 95.

we also blind?" (Ἤκουσαν ἐκ τῶν Φαρισαίων ταῦτα οἱ μετ' αὐτοῦ ὄντες, καὶ εἶπον αὐτῷ, Μὴ καὶ ἡμεῖς τυφλοί ἐσμεν;). Without any explanation as to how or why only "some of the Pharisees" (ἐκ τῶν Φαρισαίων) were "with him" (μετ' αὐτοῦ), the narrator states that after hearing Jesus's declaration they ask an incredulous question that expects a negative answer. The very fact that they have to ask the question is evidence of their blindness. The Pharisees embody the condemnation about which Jesus has been speaking.[64]

9:41 Jesus said to them, "If you were blind, you would not have sin, but since you say that you can see, your sin remains" (εἶπεν αὐτοῖς ὁ Ἰησοῦς, Εἰ τυφλοὶ ἦτε, οὐκ ἂν εἴχετε ἁμαρτίαν· νῦν δὲ λέγετε ὅτι Βλέπομεν· ἡ ἁμαρτία ὑμῶν μένει). Jesus responds to their question with an answer that penetrates beneath their (spiritual) blindness to the sinful foundation upon which it rests. If they "were blind" in the sense that they had judged themselves

and had been illuminated by the light, they would "not have sin" in the sense that they would not be guilty of sin.[65] But since they claim they can see, they are in reality blind to the depth of their own sinfulness (cf. Prov 26:12).[66] The fact that their sin "remains" (μένει) — a verb more commonly used positively in John (see comments on 15:5) — suggests that they are pronounced guilty before God (cf. 3:36).

The motif of sight and blindness centers upon the illusion "that one can manage without Jesus as the light of the world."[67] For this reason Jesus declares that only those who are blind can be made (by the Son) to see. One need not look for blindness as if it can be procured, for one already has it — just like the blind man, from birth. The disciples' opening question "Who sinned?" (v. 2) was prophetic in regard to the issue at hand. Just like the blind man, before someone can claim "I believe" (v. 36), they must first declare, "I am a sinner!"

Theology in Application

In what may be defined as the climactic forensic scene in the section, "The Controversy over the Son of God" (8:12 – 10:42), Jesus displays his authority as Judge in both deed (vv. 1 – 7) and word (vv. 35 – 41). The intervening dialogue then serves as a perfect depiction of the blindness of his opponents (who belong to "the world") who are in need of a spiritual vision that only Jesus can provide (vv. 8 – 34). Through this pericope the readers are challenged to examine themselves and the question of their own spiritual blindness. While the length of the pericope might be difficult for some to preach or teach as a whole, the message should at least be maintained in the context of the dialogue and its movement, for the dialogical drama of the pericope adds important depth and focus to the presentation of Jesus and his work.

True Blindness and True Sight

This pericope makes an important claim about the nature of blindness and sight. What is clear is that true sight is ironically contingent on having true blindness.

---

64. Morris, *John*, 442.
65. Carson, *John*, 378.

66. Cf. Aquinas, *John*, 2:182.
67. Ridderbos, *John*, 351.

When Jesus declares that only those who are blind can truly see (vv. 39–41), he declares that there is a blindness that is innate to fallen humanity that is necessary to Christian existence. Blindness, then, is central to the confession of each individual Christian, who testifies concerning himself, "It is I, not Christ, who is the sinner!" (v. 31). This type of blindness is actually a new manner of seeing in which a person is able to see themselves as they truly are. This blindness, therefore, is blindness to the deception that innately distorts human nature. It is the illusion of self. Those who think they can see are in actuality oblivious by an innate self-delusion that imposes upon them a deep and serious blindness. However, those who know they are blind — who know who they truly are as those who have sinned against a holy God — are in actuality seeing with a clarity that is unhindered by physical limitations. It is seeing not merely with physical eyes but with the eyes of faith. This is the sight of those who say "I believe" (v. 38) and can truly "give glory to God" (v. 24). These are the true "God-fearers" who "do the will" of God (v. 31).

"The Works of God"

The concept of "work" is often shunned by the Christian, who immediately thinks of the apostle Paul's declaration that "it is by grace you have been saved, through faith ... not by works" (Eph 2:8–9). Yet Jesus speaks unhesitatingly about work — "the works of God." Jesus was sent by the Father to do these works — works like the one made manifest in the blind man. While it is clear that the primary worker is Christ, the church derives from him a calling to work that is basic to the Christian life. It is time that John — not just Paul — define for the Christian the nature of the Christian vocation. For as John will shortly explain, the Christian is expected to perform the work that Christ has already been doing (14:12). Christ may be the light of the world (v. 5), but the church, like the moon, is to reflect his light to a world in utter darkness.

The Nature of Christian Witness

This pericope presents a vivid picture of the nature of Christian witness, with the blind man serving as a model witness in the face of social and religious pressure. But it is important to note that the blind man's testimony was undeniably affected by the situation of his blindness with which the narrative began. Jesus admitted to his disciples that the blindness of the man happened for a purpose: "So that the works of God might be made manifest in him" (v. 3). The reader is to be reminded that their own situation in life, inclusive of not only gifts and talents but also hardship and suffering, is an essential piece of what God may intentionally use to create for himself a witness through their person. What may be described as God's common grace to the world is that he allows Christians to suffer and endure hardship right alongside those who do not know God, those blind to their own self-deception. The God who is working "in all things" (Rom 8:28) is more than capable of making a way for his disciples to witness to him in oncology departments and funeral homes, not just in church sanctuaries. The Christian is exhorted to let their whole life become a Christian witness and to allow the unique circumstances into which God has already placed them to become part and parcel of their regular ministry, testifying to the world in a very personal way about a very personal God.

The Trial Motif

The forensic patterns that direct the story of the blind man and shape this entire section of the Gospel impress upon the reader the lawcourt imagery stretching across the Bible. The numerous connections to Eden in this pericope (cf. vv. 4 – 6, 14) remind us that from the beginning humanity has been guilty before the holy God. This pericope defines the arrival of Jesus as intended for judgment (v. 39), showing that the true Judge has arrived to enact it; the light of the world has come to reveal the darkness and uncover sin. In a very important way, however, the narrative's depiction of the progressing threats against Jesus leading to his eventual trial, conviction, and death become a powerful description of how the judge of the world (5:27) will ultimately apply to himself the penalty for sin. The Son of God receives in his own person the wrath of God the Father. At the same time, however, this pericope asks interrogation questions of the reader: "Do you understand the origin and effects of sin?" (v. 2); "Do you have blindness or sight?" (v. 39); and ultimately, "Do you believe in the Son of Man?" (v. 35). These are not mere rhetorical questions but questions that concern life and death.

John 10:1 – 21

Literary Context

This pericope begins the last message of Jesus to the general public; the final two pericopae of this section (10:1 – 21; 10:22 – 42) conclude the controversy over the Son of God (8:12 – 10:42). The last two chapters in John have highlighted in robust, forensic tones the judicial conflict between Jesus and the Jewish authorities. In chapter 8, Jesus engaged with his accusers in a formal courtroom scene in the temple; in chapter 9, a judicial hearing took place with a key witness, a man born blind, seeking to secure evidence with which to declare Jesus guilty as charged. But the Gospel has already made clear to the reader that Jesus is not the defendant but the final authority and judge of the world (7:53 – 8:11). Time for debate and verbal exchange has come to an end. At this moment, Jesus takes his rightful place of judgment with the authority given to him by the Father (5:22) and makes his own indictment against those who oppose him. Yet he still offers an invitation to those who would join him.

V. The Controversy over the Son of God (8:12 – 10:42)

   A. "The Light of the World": The Accusations of Jesus the Judge (8:12 – 59)

   B. The Fifth Sign: The Testimony of the Blind Man (9:1 – 41)

➡   **C. The Shepherd and the Sheep (10:1 – 21)**

   D. The Son of the Father (10:22 – 42)

Main Idea

Jesus is the Door and Good Shepherd of the sheep, the access to God and the provision from God. There is now one flock and one shepherd, the full expression of the love of the Father and the Son to the world. Because Christ is my shepherd, I shall not want.

Translation

John 10:1–21

	Monologue	
1a	Amen Formula	*"Truly, truly I say to you,*
b	Jesus's Illustration (1–5)	*the one who does not enter the courtyard of the sheep*
c	Entry	*through the door but*
d	Contrast	*goes up by another way …*
e	Predication of Identity	*… is a thief and robber.*
2a	Contrast	*But the one who enters …*
b	Entry	*through the door*
c	Predication of Identity	*… is a shepherd of the sheep.*
3a	Resulting Sequence #1	*To this one the doorkeeper opens (the door),*
b	Resulting Sequence #2	*and the sheep hear his voice,*
c	Resulting Sequence #3	*and he calls his own sheep by name*
d	Resulting Sequence #4	*and leads them out.*
4a	Circumstance	*When he has led out all his own,*
b	Resulting Sequence #5	*he goes on ahead of them,*
c	Resulting Sequence #6	*and his sheep follow,*
d	Basis	*because they know his voice.*
5a	Contrast to 4c	*But they will never follow a stranger,*
b		*but will run away from him*
c	Basis	*because they do not know the voice of the stranger."*
6a	Narrator's Aside (6)	**Jesus spoke this illustration,**
b		but **they did not understand what he was saying to them.**
7a	Jesus's Interpretation (7–18)	Again **Jesus said,**
b	Amen Formula	*"Truly, truly I say to you,*
c	Confession of Identity	*I am the door of the sheep.*
8a	Contrasting "Entries"	*All whoever came before me were thieves and robbers,*
b	Contrasting Reaction	*but the sheep did not listen to them.*
9a	Restatement of 7c	*I am the door;*
b	Promise (Condition)	*whoever enters through me …*
c	Promise (Inference)	*… will be saved and will come in and go out and find ⅌ a pasture.*
10a	Warning	*The thief does not come*
b	Purpose	*except to steal and kill and destroy;*
c	Contrast to "thief"	*I came*
d	Purpose	*in order that they may have life and*
e		*may have it in abundance.*
11a	Confession of Identity	*I am the good shepherd.*
b	Declaration of Job Description	*The good shepherd lays down his life*
c	Beneficiary	*for the sheep.*

12a	Contrast to the "good shepherd"	*The hired worker is neither the shepherd nor*
b		*the one who owns the sheep.*
c		
d	Circumstantial Condition	*When he sees the wolf coming*
e	Inference	*he releases the sheep and flees*
f	Parenthetic Result	*—and the wolf seizes and scatters them—*
13a	Basis #1	*because he is a hired worker and*
b	Basis #2	*it does not matter to him about the sheep.*
14a	Contrast to "hired help"	*I am the good shepherd,*
b		*and I know what are mine*
c		*and mine know me.*
15a	Comparative Basis of 15c	*Just as the Father knows me*
b		*I also know the Father,*
c	Restatement of 10c–12	*and I lay down my life for the sheep.*
16a	Additional Declaration	*And I have other sheep*
b	Description	*that are not from this courtyard.*
c	Sequence #1	*It is necessary for me to lead them also,*
d	Sequence #2	*and they will hear my voice,*
e	Sequence #3 (Ezek 34:11)	*and there will be one flock,*
f		*one shepherd.*
17a		*For this reason*
b	Result of 15c	*the Father loves me,*
c	Basis	*because I lay down my life,*
d	Purpose	*in order that I may receive it.*
18a	Explanatory Expansion of 17	*No one takes it from me,*
b		*but I lay it down by myself.*
c		*I have authority to lay it down,*
d		*and I have authority to receive it again.*
e	Source of Authority	*This I received from my Father."*
19a	Narrator's Commentary	**Again a division broke out among the Jews**
b	Basis	*because of these words.*
20a	Negative Reaction	**Many of them said,**
b	Accusation	*"He has a demon and is insane.*
c		*Why listen to him?"*
21a		**Others said,**
b	Inferential Conclusion	*"These words are not from one who is demon possessed.*
c	Premise	*A demon-possessed man cannot open the eyes of a blind man."*

Structure and Literary Form

This is the second substantial monologue in the narrative proper. A monologue (see Introduction) is similar to a dialogue in that it is set in the context of an engagement and conflict, but rather than engaging point-for-point, it allows for a lengthy argument. A monologue can contain elements of rhetoric, challenge, and conflict, but it does so in a sustained presentation.

In light of the contextual significance of the monologue, it is necessary to place this speech by Jesus within the forensic and judicial context of the preceding pericopae (chs. 8–9). It is ultimately in chapter 10 where the forensic patterns and themes of interrogation and judgment reach their climax. Unlike the trial before the Sanhedrin as recorded in the Synoptics (Matt 26:57–68; Mark 14:53–65; Luke 22:66–71), the Fourth Gospel does not record Jesus's trial before the leaders of Israel. For John, the trial of Jesus extends throughout the entire Gospel.[1]

The structure of the pericope has long been a matter of debate. Most common is the assumption that the pericope contains two main parts, vv. 1–5 and vv. 7–18, with each being followed by a transition. Most also see the latter section as a sort of interpretation of the former. Much of this is rooted in the assumption that vv. 1–5 contain a parabolic "illustration" that is given an applied interpretation in vv. 7–18 (see comments on v. 6).

Exegetical Outline

→ **C. The Shepherd and the Sheep (10:1–21)**

    1. An "Illustration": The Door, the Shepherd, and the Sheep (vv. 1–5)

    2. Narrator's Commentary (v. 6)

    3. The Interpretation of the "Illustration" (vv. 7–18)

       a. "I Am the Door of the Sheep" (vv. 7–10)

       b. "I Am the Good Shepherd" (vv. 11–18)

    4. Narrator's Commentary (vv. 19–21)

Explanation of the Text

It is common for interpreters to suggest that this pericope is disconnected from the preceding literary context. Usually this is based upon the assumption that the previous context was the Feast of Tabernacles, which was introduced in chapter 7 and served as a dominant backdrop for the heated verbal exchange of 7:14–52, making the reference to the Feast of Dedication in 10:22 both awkward and out of place.[2] But we have already argued that the Feast of Tabernacles ceased to serve as the contextual backdrop for the narrative in chapter 8 (see comments on 8:12), with the forensic procedures and rhetorical engagement of a trial serving as the new contextual guide. The connection is actually quite apparent. Not only do the narrative details align with one another, as in v. 21 where the blind man is again referred to, but the messages of both pericopae nicely coalesce. After exposing

1. See Parsenios, *Rhetoric and Drama in the Johannine Lawsuit Motif*, 1–2. Cf. Jan G. Van der Watt, *Family of the King: Dynamics of Metaphor in the Gospel according to John*, BIS 47 (Leiden: Brill, 2000), 388; Lincoln, *Truth on Trial*, 171.

2. See Schnackenburg, *John*, 2:276–78. Cf. Beasley-Murray, *John*, 165–67.

the shoddy shepherding of the religious authorities in regard to the blind man (and his parents), the reader has been prepared to see the identity and practice of the Good Shepherd.

10:1 "Truly, truly I say to you, the one who does not enter the courtyard of the sheep through the door but goes up by another way is a thief and robber" (Ἀμὴν ἀμὴν λέγω ὑμῖν, ὁ μὴ εἰσερχόμενος διὰ τῆς θύρας εἰς τὴν αὐλὴν τῶν προβάτων ἀλλὰ ἀναβαίνων ἀλλαχόθεν ἐκεῖνος κλέπτης ἐστὶν καὶ λῃστής). A new section begins without any introduction or setting, only the authoritative preface of Jesus that the reader has seen before (see comments on 1:51). While the preface serves to transition to the monologue of Jesus, it is "never used abruptly to introduce a fresh topic, out of connection with what has gone before.... It always has reference to something that has been said already, which is expanded or set in a new light."[3] The context of this monologue, then, is an extension of chapter 9, the scene where the blind man and his parents were poorly shepherded by the Jewish leadership. After such gross neglect and self-seeking posturing, Jesus offers an authoritative address to the flock.

Jesus begins with an "illustration" that is difficult to classify but significant to the interpretation of the entire pericope (see comments on v. 6). The "illustration" employs agrarian language and describes a context common to first-century shepherds. The term "courtyard" (αὐλὴν) describes "an area open to the sky, frequently surrounded by buildings, and in some cases partially by walls."[4] This courtyard may have been bordered by family homes, serving as a sheep pen or corral for the one or more families who owned and had access to the courtyard. The scene depicted, therefore, is familial and private. This is not a public courtyard; it was restricted and private property.

Befitting such a courtyard, there was only one point of entry, a "door" (θύρας), or more fitting to this agrarian context, a "gate." Our translation, however, will maintain the more general translation "door" so as to maintain the theologically significant image that will reoccur later in the pericope (v. 9). The private and personal nature of this sheep pen helps explain the stated concern regarding who enters and the nature of their access. There is only one access point—the door. The one who "goes up by another way" (ἀναβαίνων ἀλλαχόθεν), that is, climbs over the fence, can be only "a thief and robber"—or more emphatically—"that one is a thief and robber" (ἐκεῖνος κλέπτης ἐστὶν καὶ λῃστής). The demonstrative pronoun makes two titles that are synonymous representative of a single figure.[5]

10:2 "But the one who enters through the door is a shepherd of the sheep" (ὁ δὲ εἰσερχόμενος διὰ τῆς θύρας ποιμήν ἐστιν τῶν προβάτων). In contrast to the negative entrance of the "thief and robber" over the fence is the positive entrance of "a shepherd of the sheep" (ποιμήν τῶν προβάτων) through the door. The contrast is intentional and clear. The courtyard is private and familial and ultimately belongs to the shepherd of the sheep.

10:3 "To this one the doorkeeper opens (the door), and the sheep hear his voice, and he calls his own sheep by name and leads them out" (τούτῳ ὁ θυρωρὸς ἀνοίγει, καὶ τὰ πρόβατα τῆς φωνῆς αὐτοῦ ἀκούει, καὶ τὰ ἴδια πρόβατα φωνεῖ κατ' ὄνομα καὶ ἐξάγει αὐτά). It is not for the "thief and robber" but for the "shepherd" (made emphatic with the dative pronoun, "to this one" [τούτῳ]) that "the doorkeeper" (ὁ θυρωρὸς) opens the door. It is not precisely clear how the "doorkeeper" is to be understood. It is possible that by mentioning

3. Bernard, *John*, 2:348.
4. BDAG 150.
5. Beasley-Murray, *John*, 169. On the individual titles, see Barrett, *John*, 369.

the doorkeeper the flock is depicted as quite large, since small flocks would not need such a guard or undershepherd.[6] But what is clear is that the presence and action of the doorkeeper serves to confirm that the shepherd who enters the courtyard is the natural and rightful shepherd of the flock. Not only are the intentions of this shepherd different from the "thief and robber," but he has been given the authority to enter what already belongs to him.

It is not just the shepherding assistant that recognizes this shepherd; it is also the sheep. The sheep are said to "hear his voice" (τῆς φωνῆς αὐτοῦ ἀκούει), which conveys that the sound of the shepherd's voice is recognizable to them. They might be brute beasts, but they know the one who tends to them; he is not foreign or new but familiar. Moreover, the shepherd is described as calling to "his own sheep by name" (τὰ ἴδια πρόβατα κατ᾽ ὄνομα).[7] They are his sheep and he knows their name. Like Adam in the garden, he gives them each a name — a sign of authority and intimacy (Gen 2:19 – 20) that is expressed in his leadership over them when he "leads them out" (ἐξάγει αὐτά).

10:4 "When he has led out all his own, he goes on ahead of them, and his sheep follow, because they know his voice" (ὅταν τὰ ἴδια πάντα ἐκβάλῃ, ἔμπροσθεν αὐτῶν πορεύεται, καὶ τὰ πρόβατα αὐτῷ ἀκολουθεῖ, ὅτι οἴδασιν τὴν φωνὴν αὐτοῦ). This shepherd is described as leading out the sheep that belong to him. The language is significant. The phrase "all his own" (τὰ ἴδια πάντα) explains his special relationship to the sheep and that his activity involves every single sheep. Furthermore, the term "led out" (ἐκβάλῃ) is the same word used to describe the expulsion of the formerly blind man from the synagogue by the Jewish leadership (9:34). The contrast between the shepherd and the "thief and robber"

is clear: one leads the sheep in the direction they should go, while the other dismisses the sheep for his own selfish purposes. The shepherd remains with his sheep, going "ahead of them" (ἔμπροσθεν αὐτῶν) — not driving them but directing them by his voice, a voice "they know" (οἴδασιν). As Jesus said earlier (6:37), the one who comes to him he will never "cast away" (ἐκβάλω ἔξω).

10:5 "But they will never follow a stranger, but will run away from him because they do not know the voice of the stranger" (ἀλλοτρίῳ δὲ οὐ μὴ ἀκολουθήσουσιν ἀλλὰ φεύξονται ἀπ᾽ αὐτοῦ, ὅτι οὐκ οἴδασιν τῶν ἀλλοτρίων τὴν φωνήν). Again a contrast is made between the shepherd who is known and the one who is not, in this case, "a stranger" (ἀλλοτρίῳ). The illustration does not attempt to develop or further identify the "thief and robber" but to depict how the shepherd of the sheep can be distinguished from others by their flock.[8] The "stranger" is almost entirely undefined; his identity is only given definition by his negative relation to the sheep. The sheep do *not know* his voice and therefore they will *not remain* with him. What drives the sheep away is not the command of the "stranger" but merely his alien presence.

10:6 Jesus spoke this illustration, but they did not understand what he was saying to them (Ταύτην τὴν παροιμίαν εἶπεν αὐτοῖς ὁ Ἰησοῦς· ἐκεῖνοι δὲ οὐκ ἔγνωσαν τίνα ἦν ἃ ἐλάλει αὐτοῖς). As is common in John, in the middle of the monologue by Jesus the narrator interjects and offers important commentary for the reader. The narrator explains that Jesus was speaking in the form of what we are describing as an "illustration" (τὴν παροιμίαν), a term that has resulted in much scholarly discussion. The term is translated in most lexicons as a proverb,

---

6. Morris, *John*, 447.
7. The language of "his own" (τὰ ἴδια) strongly alludes to the prologue (1:11).

8. Cf. Ridderbos, *John*, 355.

figure of speech, or a saying.[9] It occurs three times in the Fourth Gospel (10:6; 16:25, 29) and once in 2 Peter (2:22). In 2 Peter 2:22, it refers more simply to a well-known proverb or saying, but in the Fourth Gospel it bears a more complex meaning that can be described as a veiled or symbolic saying, "a brief communication containing truths designed for initiates."[10] In 16:25, for example, Jesus declares that he has been speaking "in illustrations" or "figuratively" (ἐν παροιμίαις), that is, in veiled or symbolic speech, but he will shortly speak "plainly" (παρρησίᾳ). Thus, the Gospel itself makes clear that this term, and therefore vv. 1 – 5 as a whole, is being used in this pericope with intentional symbolism.[11]

The discussion surrounding the term we translated "illustration" often centers upon whether vv. 1 – 5 should be interpreted according to the genre of an allegory or a parable. If declared an allegory, each of its elements demands to be interpreted, whereas if declared a parable, only one or two main points are assumed to be intended, not a point-for-point correspondence.[12] There is, however, a natural overlap between parable and allegory that demands that we not make too tight of a distinction.[13] In light of the uncertainty surrounding the Gospel's use of this term, we have chosen to translate the term as "illustration." This translation is a broad designation that avoids loading the term with preconceived notions that may be foreign to it, without limiting the figurative-symbolic imagery and parabolic-allegorical functions common to this "proverb, figure of speech, and saying" genre.

As much as Jesus's monologue speaks directly into a historical situation in the first century, the interpretation he is about to provide relies less on the historical background of sheep and shepherds and more on the canonical-cosmological background of "the sheep" and "the Shepherd."[14] This is almost certainly why the narrator explains to the reader that the listeners of Jesus "did not understand" (οὐκ ἔγνωσαν) what he was talking about. As much as Jesus was speaking through symbolic illustration, "the distinction lies in His hearers, and not in the various methods of teaching which he adopted."[15]

10:7 Again Jesus said, "Truly, truly I say to you, I am the door of the sheep" (Εἶπεν οὖν πάλιν ὁ Ἰησοῦς, Ἀμὴν ἀμὴν λέγω ὑμῖν ὅτι ἐγώ εἰμι ἡ θύρα τῶν προβάτων). The applied interpretation of the "illustration" (vv. 1 – 5) begins in vv. 7 – 10 with the first of two statements by Jesus. Beginning with an authoritative preface (see comments on 1:51), Jesus declares, "I am the door of the sheep" (ἐγώ εἰμι ἡ θύρα τῶν προβάτων). This statement is the third of seven formal "I am" statements in the Gospel of John (see comments on 6:35). Similar to the first "I am" statement, this third statement is set in a context that has already been given thematic preparation in the narrative by means of the "illustration."

It is significant that Jesus uses the "I am" metaphor to explain an "illustration" that is also a

---

9. Cf. Kim E. Dewey, *"Paroimiai in the Gospel of John," Semeia* 17 (1980): 81 – 99; F. Hauck, *TDNT* "παροιμία," 5:854 – 56.

10. BDAG 780.

11. Unfortunately, much of the discussion of this so-called Johannine parable has been dominated by the parable in the Synoptics. According to Klyne Snodgrass, "In the technical sense there are no parables in John" (*Stories with Intent: A Comprehensive Guide to the Parables of Jesus* [Grand Rapids: Eerdmans, 2008], 22).

12. For an overview of the issues, see Reinhartz, *Word in the World*, 48 – 70.

13. Cf. Dan Otto Via Jr., *The Parables: Their Literary and Existential Dimension* (Philadelphia: Fortress, 1967), 2. Cf. G. B. Caird, *The Language and Imagery of the Bible* (London: Duckworth, 1980), 167.

14. According to Gary T. Manning Jr., *Echoes of a Prophet: The Use of Ezekiel in the Gospel of John and in Literature of the Second Temple Period*, JSNTSup 270 (London: T&T Clark, 2004), 100 – 135, vv. 1 – 9 are dependent primarily on Numbers 27, and vv. 10 – 16 are dependent primarily on Ezekiel 34.

15. Hoskyns, *Fourth Gospel*, 370.

parabolic metaphor. Such a maneuver locates the primary meaning of the illustration not in a reconstructed agrarian context or in the history-of-religions context of the shepherd imagery but in the person and work of Jesus himself. Since the illustration focused immediately on access to the courtyard of the sheep, Jesus declares himself to be "the door" of the sheep, that is, not only the primary or only point of access but also the one who mediates all access to the sheep. No one else has the right to exercise care over the sheep, and no one else has the right to manage the flock.[16] The formal "I am" statement shows how Jesus is uniquely qualified to control access to the sheep, not merely to care for them but also to protect them.

10:8 "All who ever came before me were thieves and robbers, but the sheep did not listen to them" (πάντες ὅσοι ἦλθον [πρὸ ἐμοῦ] κλέπται εἰσὶν καὶ λῃσταί· ἀλλ᾽ οὐκ ἤκουσαν αὐτῶν τὰ πρόβατα). Befitting the contrast emphasized by the illustration, Jesus compares himself to other, potential candidates. Jesus declares that "all who came before me" (πάντες ὅσοι ἦλθον [πρὸ ἐμοῦ]) were thieves and robbers, a statement that Morris rightly describes as "strangely comprehensive."[17] It is usually taken as strange because it would seem to incorporate not just the corrupt religious leaders of Jesus's own day (as exemplified in ch. 9) but also the legitimate shepherds raised up earlier by God, such as Moses, Isaiah, and Jeremiah, who served faithfully under the old covenant. Interpreters often try to alleviate the tension by relying on the historical imagery of the illustration. By understanding "before me" to be spatial rather than temporal, the phrase would then refer to those who might come to the sheep

before the shepherd arrived in the morning (i.e., thieves and robbers).[18]

While it is fair to suggest that the statement has a more intentional focus on the corrupt first-century religious leaders of Jesus's day, the statement must also be seen to be describing the cosmological contrast between the mediating work of Jesus and all others. Bultmann writes that this further explanation asserts "the exclusiveness and the absoluteness of the revelation" provided by Christ.[19] This means that there is and has never been access to God other than through Christ. Rather than being a statement about the first century alone, this is a cosmological interpretation of the history of religious teaching. While this need not include as "thieves and robbers" the faithful OT prophets, since they were true heralds of Christ, even the "shepherding" of Moses and the other OT prophets was insufficient in and of itself; they were temporary shepherds who shepherded through a veil which is only removed in the presence of the true shepherd (2 Cor 3:7 – 18). The "exclusiveness and absoluteness" of Christ not only supplements previous shepherding but fulfills it.

10:9 "I am the door; whoever enters through me will be saved and will come in and go out and find a pasture" (ἐγώ εἰμι ἡ θύρα· δι᾽ ἐμοῦ ἐάν τις εἰσέλθῃ σωθήσεται καὶ εἰσελεύσεται καὶ ἐξελεύσεται καὶ νομὴν εὑρήσει). After offering the cosmological contrast between the true entry point and the false (or incomplete) entry points, Jesus restates his unique status as "the door." Barrett and Keener helpfully offer a survey of the use of the expression in ancient sources, but the meaning must be defined by Jesus's own qualification.[20] This is especially significant because as much as

---

16. Cf. Ridderbos, *John*, 356.

17. Morris, *John*, 450.

18. Cf. Michaels, *John*, 582 – 83.

19. Bultmann, *John*, 376. Against Bultmann, however, the source of this truth is not Gnosticism but the Old Testament itself.

20. Barrett, *John*, 371 – 73; Keener, *John*, 1:797 – 813. Some of the options include: (1) a door to heaven (cf. Gen 28:17; 1 En. 72 – 75); (2) eschatological salvation (cf. Odes Sol. 17:6 – 11; 42:15 – 17); and (3) entering the kingdom of God (cf. Matt 7:13 – 14).

shepherding imagery is used, the significant term "will be saved" (σωθήσεται), which is hardly used in the Fourth Gospel (only here and 3:17; 12:47), is the guide to the explanation of the metaphor of the door. It is significant because it is "strangely comprehensive," similar to what we saw in v. 8. The term demands to be taken to concern the entire work of Christ that the Gospel is in process of unfolding. Jesus is not just the shepherd, but the way, the truth, and the life (14:6). This language of salvation connected with the imagery of sheep peacefully and freely living to the full in the pasture can best be explained by Psalm 23.

10:10 "The thief does not come except to steal and kill and destroy; I came in order that they may have life and may have it in abundance" (ὁ κλέπτης οὐκ ἔρχεται εἰ μὴ ἵνα κλέψῃ καὶ θύσῃ καὶ ἀπολέσῃ· ἐγὼ ἦλθον ἵνα ζωὴν ἔχωσιν καὶ περισσὸν ἔχωσιν). Jesus concludes his first of three statements by stating again the contrast. Unlike the shepherd who offers true life, the thief can only offer death, with the three-fold depiction serving as an emphatic summary of the nature of the destruction.[21] The imagery uses words that create an impression of the slaughtering of animals; the reverse of the work of the true shepherd who declares that his purpose in coming is the giving of life; indeed, that they "may have (life) in abundance" (καὶ περισσὸν ἔχωσιν). Such a qualification defines "life" less as a *degree* of existence and more as a *kind* of existence. This shepherd does not just preserve life; he creates it afresh in an unparalleled way. Jesus gives life its meaning. By these words, Jesus offers "paradise" to those once condemned to death (cf. Luke 23:43) — not merely to those in the first century but also to the contemporary reader of the Gospel.

10:11 "I am the good shepherd. The good shepherd lays down his life for the sheep" (Ἐγώ εἰμι ὁ ποιμὴν ὁ καλός· ὁ ποιμὴν ὁ καλὸς τὴν ψυχὴν αὐτοῦ τίθησιν ὑπὲρ τῶν προβάτων). The applied interpretation of the "illustration" (vv. 1 – 5) continues in vv. 11 – 16 with the second of two statements by Jesus. Jesus declares, "I am the good shepherd" (Ἐγώ εἰμι ὁ ποιμὴν ὁ καλός). This statement is the fourth of seven formal "I am" statements in the Gospel of John (see comments on 6:35). Similar to some of the previous "I am" statements (v. 7), this fourth statement is set in a context that has already been given thematic preparation in the narrative by means of the "illustration."

We discussed above (v. 7) that it was significant that Jesus uses the "I am" metaphor to explain an "illustration" that is also a parabolic metaphor. Such a maneuver locates the primary meaning of the illustration not in a reconstructed agrarian context or in the history-of-religions context of shepherd imagery but in the person and work of Jesus himself. This becomes all the more important as we are forced to reconcile the fact that Jesus is both the door (or gate) and the shepherd. No explanation of the "illustration" can make sense with historical, agrarian logic how one person can be both the door and the shepherd. But this paradox is essential to the Fourth Gospel. In the economy of God, the door is not an inanimate object or mere periphery; the door is the access point to God and therefore entirely under his control. Never before has one person been a door and a shepherd, but never before had the Word become flesh (1:14). It is for this reason that we defined vv. 1 – 5 as an "illustration" and not more technically as a parable or allegory, for this illustration depicts realities controlled not by a recognizable historical

---

21. Although the immediate context applies "thief" to the Jewish religious authorities, the Gospel — and certainly the rest of Scripture — warrants its application to Satan/the devil, espe-cially in light of the cosmological strand of the Gospel's plot. Contra Keener, *John*, 1:812.

correspondence regarding any one man, but a cosmological correspondence regarding the Son of Man, through whom heaven has opened (1:51).[22]

The title "good shepherd" (ὁ ποιμὴν ὁ καλός) is a declaration that Jesus is the shepherd *par excellence*. This declaration is not only intended to contrast Jesus with the "bad" shepherds of the Jewish authorities in chapter 9 but also serves as the fulfillment of the long-awaited "shepherd" promised in the Old Testament. Jesus's words fulfill what God promised through the prophet Ezekiel: "I myself will tend my sheep and have them lie down ... I will shepherd the flock with justice" (Ezek 34:15 – 16). In this sense this shepherd is "good," for he is not only the "one shepherd, my servant David" (Ezek 34:23), but he is also the ideal shepherd, matching the superb quality of the promised shepherding.

What makes this shepherd "good" is the kind of shepherding he is able to perform for his sheep: "The good shepherd lays down his life for his sheep" (ὁ ποιμὴν ὁ καλὸς τὴν ψυχὴν αὐτοῦ τίθησιν ὑπὲρ τῶν προβάτων). On the historical level of the "illustration," such a statement speaks to this shepherd's willingness to put his life at risk for his sheep, facing all predators that may try to harm the sheep. But something much more is intended. In the context of the Gospel the language is loaded. When Jesus explains that the shepherd "lays down" (τίθησιν) his life, the referent can only be to his sacrificial death on the cross. This applied interpretation is not derived from the OT or any other source — its background is the cross of Christ, which in narrative time is still in the foreground.[23] This is made all the more clear when it is described as being "for" (ὑπὲρ), that is, "on behalf of," the sheep, a preposition that denotes purpose (see comments on 6:51).

10:12 "The hired worker is neither the shepherd nor the one who owns the sheep. When he sees the wolf coming he releases the sheep and flees — and the wolf seizes and scatters them — " (ὁ μισθωτὸς καὶ οὐκ ὢν ποιμήν, οὗ οὐκ ἔστιν τὰ πρόβατα ἴδια, θεωρεῖ τὸν λύκον ἐρχόμενον καὶ ἀφίησιν τὰ πρόβατα καὶ φεύγει — καὶ ὁ λύκος ἁρπάζει αὐτὰ καὶ σκορπίζει –). Pressing further the contrast emphasized by the illustration, Jesus compares negatively the good shepherd to a "hired worker" (ὁ μισθωτὸς), who is employed to care for things he neither bears full responsibility for nor owns. In the ancient world, the "hired worker" was viewed in a derogatory sense, those who acted for pay, not from loyalty or friendship.[24] For that reason when the hired worker is personally threatened, he saves himself, leaving the sheep in harm's way. The very moment the hired worker is needed is the exact moment he fails to perform. Even with good intentions, he is primarily self-interested; there is no personal connection with the sheep.[25]

10:13 "Because he is a hired worker and it does not matter to him about the sheep" (ὅτι μισθωτός ἐστιν καὶ οὐ μέλει αὐτῷ περὶ τῶν προβάτων). Jesus gives the reason for the hired worker's actions. The sheep do not "matter to him" (μέλει αὐτῷ), that is, they are no care or concern of his.[26] The sheep are to the hired worker a means to an end and an expendable means if the self-benefiting end in view is threatened. This is neither a "good" hired worker nor a real shepherd, serving as a stark contrast to the Good Shepherd Jesus Christ.

10:14 "I am the good shepherd, and I know what are mine and mine know me" (Ἐγώ εἰμι ὁ ποιμὴν ὁ καλός, καὶ γινώσκω τὰ ἐμὰ καὶ γινώσκουσί με τὰ ἐμά). The direct antithesis to the disinterested hired

---

22. See Augustine, *John*, 46.3.256.
23. Cf. Barrett, *John*, 374 – 75.
24. Keener, *John*, 1:814 – 15.
25. Cf. Schnackenburg, *John*, 2:296.
26. BDAG 626.

worker is the Good Shepherd, who has a personal connection with his sheep. By restating the "I am" title, Jesus establishes afresh the contrast between himself and any other so-called shepherd. More than simply being concerned with his sheep — which is already far beyond the care of the hired worker, the Good Shepherd can claim to "know" (γινώσκω) his sheep, even more, to claim them as his own and to be claimed by them. There is a mutual knowledge between the Good Shepherd and his sheep that defines the nature of their coexistence. This kind of knowledge does not blur the line between sheep and shepherd, but fastens them together in an appropriate manner, whereby the Shepherd provides for and loves his sheep, and the sheep respond in gratitude, faith, and obedience to their Good Shepherd.[27]

10:15 "Just as the Father knows me I also know the Father, and I lay down my life for the sheep" (καθὼς γινώσκει με ὁ πατὴρ κἀγὼ γινώσκω τὸν πατέρα· καὶ τὴν ψυχήν μου τίθημι ὑπὲρ τῶν προβάτων). Jesus explains further the reciprocal relationship between the shepherd and his sheep by comparing the relationship between the Father and himself, the Son. The unity (again, not without distinction — as the Gospel has already made clear) between the Father and the Son becomes a partial analogy of the unity between the Shepherd and his sheep. It is, quite simply, an intimate union, different persons and different roles that form a holy and unique relationship.

It is significant to note that the Father is now a necessary part of the imagery of the shepherd and the sheep. This adds confirmation that the interpretive context of the illustration is not merely the historical, agrarian context of the first century but also the cosmological context of God and the world. Indeed, this is needed to explain why Jesus

somewhat awkwardly restates what he had already said in v. 11 that "I lay down my life for my sheep." Not only is it now stated with a first-person pronoun ("my life" [τὴν ψυχήν μου]), but it is propelled by the loving relationship between the Father and the Son.[28] Without real clarity, the restatement suggests that the love between the Shepherd and his sheep is dependent upon the love between the Father and the Son. "It is as if He said that it is no more possible for Him to be oblivious of us than for the Father to reject or neglect him."[29] There is no need to speculate but simply to note that what we have received from the Good Shepherd is deeply (even if mysteriously) rooted in the Trinitarian God.

10:16 "And I have other sheep that are not from this courtyard. It is necessary for me to lead them also, and they will hear my voice, and there will be one flock, one shepherd" (καὶ ἄλλα πρόβατα ἔχω ἃ οὐκ ἔστιν ἐκ τῆς αὐλῆς ταύτης· κἀκεῖνα δεῖ με ἀγαγεῖν, καὶ τῆς φωνῆς μου ἀκούσουσιν, καὶ γενήσονται μία ποίμνη, εἷς ποιμήν). What is remarkable about this shepherd is not merely the kind of shepherd that he is but also the magnitude of his flock. Jesus declares that he has "other sheep" (ἄλλα πρόβατα) that are not from this courtyard. This parenthetic-like comment, almost forcing itself between v. 15 and v. 17, offers a depiction of the expression of love that exists between the Father and Son and to the world.[30]

In the historical context of first-century Judaism, Jesus's words must be taken to refer beyond the "courtyard" of Judaism to the gentile world — befitting the universal scope of the mission of Jesus that the Gospel has long declared in regard to the whole "world" (cf. 1:29; 3:16; 4:42). This is more than a gentile mission; it is the unifying work of the Good Shepherd, who brings together those

---

27. Barrett, *John*, 376.
28. Cf. Morris, *John*, 455.
29. Calvin, *John 1–10*, 266.
30. Michaels, *John*, 588.

who have always belonged to him. For these "other sheep" likewise "will hear" the Shepherd's voice (v. 3), for this is the shepherd who has been assigned by God "to lead" (ἀγαγεῖν) them.

Jesus's statement is an overt reference to Ezekiel 34, where God declares that he will "search" for his sheep and look after them (v. 11) and join together all his sheep into "one flock" (v. 23) under his servant David.[31] What is significant is that Ezekiel 34 refers to the unification of Israel and Judah, which Jesus now extends to include not merely Jews but also gentiles. That is, Jesus is using the historically rooted plot of the Old Testament to speak about the cosmological realities he is initiating in his mission to the world.[32]

Jesus concludes his statement with a play on words that cannot be produced in English: "one flock, one shepherd" (μία ποίμνη, εἷς ποιμήν). The words "flock" (*poimnē*) and "shepherd" (*poimēn*) are so similar in the Greek — the same six letters with only the last two in a different order — that the reader has to look closely to see the difference. Its rhetorical effect highlights that the unity of the sheep (Jew and gentile — as the people of God!) finds its origin in the person of the Shepherd. John's depiction of the sheep of the Shepherd fits comfortably beside the apostle Paul's depiction of the church's unity "in Christ" (Gal 3:26 – 29).

10:17 "For this reason the Father loves me, because I lay down my life, in order that I may receive it" (διὰ τοῦτό με ὁ πατὴρ ἀγαπᾷ ὅτι ἐγὼ τίθημι τὴν ψυχήν μου, ἵνα πάλιν λάβω αὐτήν). The reason v. 16 is not a parenthetical comment inserted between v. 15 and v. 17 is because its message is part and parcel of the essential and eternal relationship between the Father and the Son.[33] Just

as the person of the Son is defined by the Father, so is his work — a cosmological work not confined to the first century or the first recipients of the gospel, the Jews. The "reason" the Father loves the Son is because of his redemptive work, bringing to fruition what God had longed planned — one Davidic shepherd over one dependent flock (Ezek 34).

The causal ("because") sense seems to be that the Father's love is grounded, at least in part, upon the unifying work of the Son. It is almost as if the Shepherd all along has been the Father, with the work of the Son making possible that which was prophesied in the prophets that there to be many children (sheep) under one Father (the shepherd) — something the Fourth Gospel itself has already announced (1:12). This might explain why Jesus makes a close connection between the cross and the resurrection with the purpose clause "in order that" (ἵνα), suggesting that the cross was from the beginning more about life than death. This, then, is part of the mystery of the gospel (Eph 6:19). Just as God is not merely one person but three persons, so also the role of shepherd is uniquely and necessarily shared by both the Father and Son. And just as the cross is historically the epitome of death, so it is at the same time also the source of life — not only for Jews but also (and mysteriously) for the gentiles.

10:18 No one takes it from me, but I lay it down by myself. I have authority to lay it down, and I have authority to receive it again. This I received from my Father" (οὐδεὶς αἴρει αὐτὴν ἀπ' ἐμοῦ, ἀλλ' ἐγὼ τίθημι αὐτὴν ἀπ' ἐμαυτοῦ. ἐξουσίαν ἔχω θεῖναι αὐτήν, καὶ ἐξουσίαν ἔχω πάλιν λαβεῖν αὐτήν· ταύτην τὴν ἐντολὴν ἔλαβον παρὰ τοῦ πατρός μου). At the core of the mystery of the gospel is this ab-

---

31. Cf. Mavis M. Leung, *The Kingship-Cross Interplay in the Gospel of John: Jesus' Death as Corroboration of His Royal Messiahship* (Eugene, OR: Wipf & Stock, 2011), 119 – 47.

32. See Andreas J. Köstenberger, "Jesus the Good Shepherd

Who Will Also Bring Other Sheep (John 10:16): The Old Testament Background of a Familiar Metaphor," *BBR* 12 (2002): 67 – 96, for a helpful analysis of the OT texts.

33. Barrett, *John*, 377.

solute and certain claim by Jesus. Even in his death, Jesus is not a passive recipient but the initiator, the one in complete control. This is no Shepherd who falls to thieves or wolves while trying to defend his sheep — a martyr who can save his sheep but not himself. No! Death is not something this shepherd *might* face; it is the very thing he must face — and willingly so. That is, what makes this shepherd and this act of shepherding so mysterious and remarkable is that *death is the means by which he saves his sheep.* For this shepherd does not guard the sheep from those on the outside, but from the sheep themselves. And this shepherd will not carry a wooden staff but a wooden cross. And the food and drink these sheep receive from this shepherd is not found in a field or stream but in his body and blood. That is why Jesus, the Good Shepherd, speaks of his shepherding so strongly. For Jesus is fulfilling what God promised through the prophets long ago that "I will save my flock" (Ezek 34:22). And this salvation is made possible only at the cross.

It is significant that Jesus claims to have the authority over his own death and resurrection. In general throughout the NT, the resurrection of Jesus is referred to as an act of God the Father (e.g., Acts 2:24; Rom 1:4). The tension is only on the surface, for not only does the Gospel describe a necessary and beautiful interdependence between the Father and the Son, but even here what Jesus can claim "to receive" (λαβεῖν) on his own authority is at the same time what he "received" (ἔλαβον) from his Father. The reason is rooted in the unity of the Father and the Son (cf. 10:30). That is why this shepherd is the Good Shepherd, because he died for his sheep — not out of necessity but out of love (3:16).

10:19 Again a division broke out among the Jews because of these words (Σχίσμα πάλιν ἐγένετο ἐν τοῖς Ἰουδαίοις διὰ τοὺς λόγους τούτους). At the conclusion of Jesus's monologue, the narrator offers an explanation and commentary of the reaction that transpired. Jesus's statements led to a "division" (Σχίσμα), a term used elsewhere in the Gospel to depict the controversial nature of Jesus's message (7:43; 9:16). That the division occurred "among the Jews" (ἐν τοῖς Ἰουδαίοις) might suggest that "the Jews" (see comments on 1:19) being referred to in this instance extend beyond the Jewish leadership to a listening and interested — even if divided — crowd. The statement is somewhat ironic, for while the message of Jesus spoke of the divine fulfillment of the long-divided nation of Israel, its hearing resulted in a new division, though this time in regard directly to the person of Jesus.

10:20 Many of them said, "He has a demon and is insane. Why listen to him?" (ἔλεγον δὲ πολλοὶ ἐξ αὐτῶν, Δαιμόνιον ἔχει καὶ μαίνεται· τί αὐτοῦ ἀκούετε;). The narrator concludes the pericope by providing insight into the negative (v. 20) and positive (v. 21) reactions to the message of Jesus. The charge that Jesus "has a demon" (Δαιμόνιον ἔχει) and "is insane" (μαίνεται) is not two but one charge; insanity was regarded as symptomatic of demon possession.[34] The accusation of demonic possession is not a new charge against Jesus (cf. 7:20; 8:48, 52). It is also not a coincidence that the only occasions in the Gospel when the word "demon" appears is when the Jews are accusing Jesus of being demon possessed. The tone and content of the reaction of those rejecting Jesus appears to be growing in intensity (cf. 9:16). Such a reaction shows the misunderstanding between the cosmologically rooted invitation of the Light of humanity (1:4) and the historically rooted darkness into which he has been sent (1:5).

The careful reader will hear something familiar in the final question of those who reject Jesus

---

34. Barrett, *John*, 377.

("Why listen to him?" [τί αὐτοῦ ἀκούετε;]). In the "illustration" (vv. 1 – 5), the most apparent important characteristic of the sheep was their ability to listen to the shepherd. The sheep were described with threefold emphasis as those who "hear his voice" (v. 3), "know his voice" (v. 4), and "do not know the voice of a stranger" (v. 5). What was intended to be a rhetorical question serving as a rebuke has become a revealing statement. The very fact that the Jews are uninterested in his voice declares that they neither hear him nor know him, and worse, that he is to them a stranger.

10:21 Others said, "These words are not from one who is demon possessed. A demon-possessed man cannot open the eyes of a blind man" (ἄλλοι ἔλεγον, Ταῦτα τὰ ῥήματα οὐκ ἔστιν δαιμονιζομένου·

μὴ δαιμόνιον δύναται τυφλῶν ὀφθαλμοὺς ἀνοῖξαι). But some had a positive reaction to Jesus or at least a more positive interpretation of his actions. Not only is the message of Jesus taken by some to be uncharacteristic of a demon-possessed person, but the ability of Jesus to heal a blind man (ch. 9) is also taken to be reflective of not evil but good. A demon causes illness; it does not heal it.[35] Yet the reader cannot disregard what is left unsaid: "They say what Jesus is not, but they make no attempt to say what he is."[36] In the end some of the Jews are confronted with the evidence of the fifth sign (9:1 – 41) and this explanatory monologue by Jesus (10:1 – 21), and they must make their own verdict regarding the claims of this shepherd and their status as the sheep of his flock.

Theology in Application

In this section, "The Controversy over the Son of God" (8:12 – 10:42), Jesus is initially depicted as the Judge, bringing an indictment against unbelief, but here in this pericope he is depicted as the Good Shepherd, offering an invitation to true belief. Just as the bronze serpent lifted up to save the Israelites from the wrath of God was both judgment and salvation (cf. 3:14 – 15), so also is Jesus both Judge and Shepherd, the bookends of history, the meaning of life and death. Jesus alone is both the Door and the Shepherd, simultaneously offering access to the Father and provision from the Father. Through this pericope the readers are invited to respond in obedience to the voice of the true and long-awaited Shepherd of God.

The Lord Is My Shepherd

This pericope presents one of the most significant portraits of the person and work of Christ in the entire Bible. Christ is described in comprehensive ways as both the entry point into the people of God and the caregiver of the church. The depiction is not vague but focused: the caregiving of Christ includes the giving of himself for the church. This is the kind of shepherd we have in Christ.

This pericope declares the fulfillment of Psalm 23, itself an "illustration" of Christ's administration of the new covenant and his personal relation with the

---

35. Cf. Schnackenburg, *John*, 2:303.

36. Morris, *John*, 458.

church, his flock. In a real sense, John 10:1 – 21 is an interpretation of the illustration presented by Psalm 23:[37] Christ is my Shepherd; I shall not want! Christ makes me lie down in green pastures, he leads me beside quiet waters, for Christ refreshes my soul. Christ guides me along the right paths for his name's sake. Even though I walk through the darkest valley (cf. John 1:5) I will fear no evil, for Christ is with me; Christ's rod and staff, they comfort me. Christ has prepared a table for me in the presence of my enemies. Christ has anointed my head with oil; my cup overflows. Surely goodness and love will follow me all the days of my life (i.e., "life in his name" [John 20:31]), and I will dwell in the house of the Lord forever (v. 16: "And there will be one flock, one shepherd").

The Shepherding of the Shepherd

It is not just the image of the Shepherd that is significant for the church but the nature of the shepherding. This pericope depicts not merely a shepherd who is willing to risk himself for the protection of his sheep but a shepherd who intentionally "lays down" his life for his sheep (vv. 15, 17, and 18). That is, this pericope declares that the shepherding of this shepherd is rooted in and springs from the cross. This shepherd is not one who is merely willing to die; on his own accord he must die. For this shepherd is not one who might have to save the life of his sheep if a thief or wolf happen to approach, but he must save the life of his sheep — for they are already dead (Rom 5:12)! This shepherd is giving life to his sheep. This is a very different kind of shepherd and therefore a very different kind of shepherding.

The Door of the Sheep

The theological ramifications of the Shepherd make clear why the Shepherd must also be the Door of the sheep (v. 7). The Gospel of John has already explained that Jesus is the access point to God, in whose name and authority the children of God have access to the Father (1:12). For since there is no other shepherd under heaven and earth by which the sheep must be saved (Acts 4:12), there can therefore be no other door by which the "green pastures" can be gained (Ps 23:2).

The witness of the Christian church is not about a generic "god" but the God made known personally in the person and work of Jesus Christ. We can discuss "God" and "spirituality" with all of our neighbors and not even come close to introducing them to the Father, who is only made known in Jesus Christ. "God" is fine, "spirituality" is even better, but Jesus is offensive. For the Christian, rather, the offense is *not* to proclaim Christ and him crucified (1 Cor 2:1 – 5). The offense is that

---

37. See Brevard S. Childs, *The Church's Guide for Reading Paul: The Canonical Shaping of the Pauline Corpus* (Grand Rapids: Eerdmans, 2008), 193.

God loved the world — the world that hated him — and came not to condemn but to save (3:16 – 21). The offense is that we would hate our neighbors enough *not* to tell them that they are dying and that God loves them. God has not just provided a shepherd for his sheep, he has also provided a door for those who are still goats (Matt 25:31 – 46).

The Sheep of God

The wonderful focus this pericope gives to the Shepherd can almost eclipse the beautiful description of the sheep of God that it also presents. While Jesus offers a rebuke against false shepherds, he also offers an invitation to the world — Jew and gentile — to enter his fold and become his sheep. The metaphor of the shepherd and his sheep is an image of the gospel, the good news, where God lovingly extends himself to the world, offering salvation and new life (20:31).

The sheep of God, however, are not merely to be recipients of God's love but respondents to it. The thematic response of the sheep in this pericope is that they "hear" and "know" the voice of the Shepherd and that they "follow" as he "leads" and "goes ahead of them" (vv. 3 – 5). The image of the sheep to the Shepherd is directive for the Christian. The sheep must respond to the Good Shepherd, and this response manifests itself in a life of submission and obedience. Having received grace, we must respond with gratitude, manifested in faith, hope, and love (1 Cor 13).

John 10:22 – 42

Literary Context

This pericope concludes the last message of Jesus to the general public; the final two pericopae of this section (10:1 – 21; 10:22 – 42) serve to close the section entitled "The Controversy over the Son of God" (8:12 – 10:42). The forensic themes and judicial procedures of this section began from the perspective of the Jewish authorities with Jesus as the defendant (ch. 8) and the one against whom evidence was mounted (ch. 9), but from the perspective of the reader Jesus had already been declared the ultimate authority (5:22) and the judge of the world (7:53 – 8:11). It is in this concluding pericope where the foundational issue of the relationship between Jesus and the Father is made known. There is no longer room for indecision; Jesus must either be declared a blasphemer or become the object of belief. As the Jewish authorities make their final declaration regarding the person and work of Jesus, the reader is also expected to decide their verdict regarding God and to respond to the invitation of his Son.

V. The Controversy over the Son of God (8:12 – 10:42)
- A. "The Light of the World": The Accusations of Jesus the Judge (8:12 – 59)
- B. The Fifth Sign: The Testimony of the Blind Man (9:1 – 41)
- C. The Shepherd and the Sheep (10:1 – 21)
- **D. The Son of the Father (10:22 – 42)**

Main Idea

God has assigned Jesus, his Son, to be the ruler of his people, fulfilling the mission of God to the world. In Jesus, God represents his own people, caring for their every need and fighting on their behalf. The response of the church is belief, which is the posture of worship for the Christian.

Translation

John 10:22–42

22a	Introduction & Setting (22–23)	**Then came the Feast of Dedication**
b	Place	in Jerusalem.
c	Time	**It was winter.**
23a	Action	And **Jesus was walking**
b	Location	in the temple
c	Location	in the portico of Solomon.
24a	1st Interlocution (24–30)	Then
b	Character Reentrance	**the Jews surrounded him and said to him,**
c	Interrogative Mock	*"How long will you take away our life?*
d	Condition	*If you are the Christ,*
e	Challenge	*say it clearly to us."*
25a	Rejoinder	**Jesus answered them,**
b	Accusation	*"I spoke to you*
c		*and you did not believe.*
d	Declaration	*The works …*
e	Description	*which I do in my Father's name*
f		*… testify concerning me.*
26a	Escalating Accusation	*But you do not believe,*
b	Basis	*because you do not belong to my sheep.*
27a	Contrast	*My sheep listen to my voice,*
b	Reciprocation	*and I know them,*
c	Result #1	*and they follow me."*
28a	Result #2	*And I give them eternal life,*
b	Result #3	*and they will never be destroyed,*
c	Result #4	*and no one can take them out of my hand.*
29a	Syllogism: Premise	*That which my Father has given to me is greater than all,*
b	Syllogism: Premise	*and no one is able to take [it] out of my Father's hand.*
30a	Syllogism: Conclusion	*I and the Father are one."*
31a	2nd Interlocution (31–39)	**Again the Jews picked up stones**
b	Nonverbal Surrejoinder	in order to stone him.
32a	Rejoinder to the Jews' Reaction	**Jesus answered them,**
b	Declaration	*"I have shown you many good works*
c	Source	*from the Father.*
d	Counterchallenge	*For which of these works do you stone me?"*
33a	Surrejoinder	**The Jews answered him,**
b	Counterchallenge	*"We are not stoning you about good works, but*
c	Accusation	*for blasphemy,*
d	Basis	*because you …*
e	Derogatory Identification	*a man,*
f	Ironic Accusation	*… make yourself to be God."*

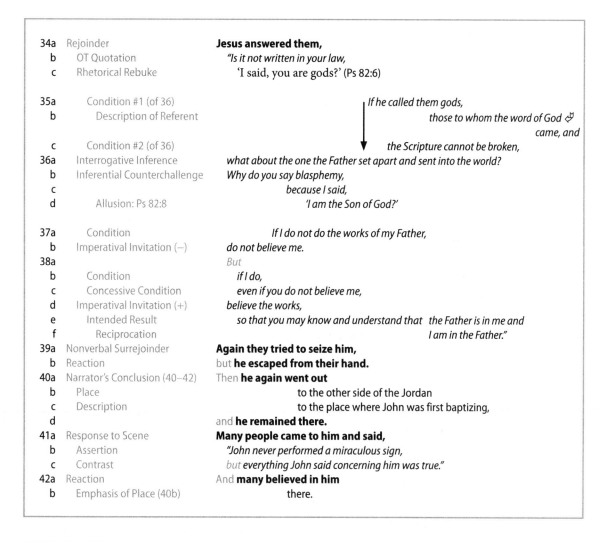

34a	Rejoinder	**Jesus answered them,**
b	OT Quotation	*"Is it not written in your law,*
c	Rhetorical Rebuke	'I said, you are gods?' (Ps 82:6)
35a	Condition #1 (of 36)	If he called them gods,
b	Description of Referent	those to whom the word of God ↵ came, and
c	Condition #2 (of 36)	the Scripture cannot be broken,
36a	Interrogative Inference	*what about the one the Father set apart and sent into the world?*
b	Inferential Counterchallenge	*Why do you say blasphemy,*
c		*because I said,*
d	Allusion: Ps 82:8	*'I am the Son of God?'*
37a	Condition	If I do not do the works of my Father,
b	Imperatival Invitation (–)	do not believe me.
38a		*But*
b	Condition	if I do,
c	Concessive Condition	even if you do not believe me,
d	Imperatival Invitation (+)	believe the works,
e	Intended Result	so that you may know and understand that the Father is in me and
f	Reciprocation	I am in the Father."
39a	Nonverbal Surrejoinder	**Again they tried to seize him,**
b	Reaction	but **he escaped from their hand.**
40a	Narrator's Conclusion (40–42)	Then **he again went out**
b	Place	to the other side of the Jordan
c	Description	to the place where John was first baptizing,
d		and **he remained there.**
41a	Response to Scene	**Many people came to him and said,**
b	Assertion	*"John never performed a miraculous sign,*
c	Contrast	but *everything John said concerning him was true."*
42a	Reaction	And **many believed in him**
b	Emphasis of Place (40b)	there.

Structure and Literary Form

This is the seventh and final substantial dialogue in the narrative proper, and it is a *social challenge dialogue*, which takes the form of an informal debate intending to challenge the honor and authority of one's interlocutor (see Introduction). It is almost certainly significant that this is the seventh dialogue in the Gospel of John. The number seven has a rhetorical significance frequently employed by the Gospel, for example, the seven "signs" (see 2:11) and the seven formal "I am" statements (see 6:35). It is also important to note how the larger contextual force of these dialogues highlights the dialogical nature of the interaction between the darkness and the light (1:5). With the first (3:1 – 21) and last dialogue falling under the pattern of a challenge dialogue, the entire public ministry of Jesus is framed by the conflict between the Word and the world.

Exegetical Outline

→ **D. The Son of the Father (10:22–42)**

    1. Narrator's Introduction (vv. 22–23)

    2. First Verbal Exchange: "I and the Father Are One" (vv. 24–30)

    3. Second Verbal Exchange: Blasphemy or Belief? (vv. 31–39)

    4. Narrator's Conclusion (vv. 40–42)

Explanation of the Text

In this pericope the reader is given interpretive guidance by the narrator by means of the historical and theological symbolism of the Feast of Dedication (see comments on vv. 22–23), which highlights and expresses the significance of the challenge dialogue.

10:22 Then came the Feast of Dedication in Jerusalem. It was winter (Ἐγένετο τότε τὰ ἐγκαίνια ἐν τοῖς Ἱεροσολύμοις· χειμὼν ἦν). The pericope begins with a prefatory comment by the narrator (vv. 22–23), who uses a term that can mean "renewal" or "rededication" (τὰ ἐγκαίνια) but is referring here to what is called the Feast of Dedication.[1] This description of the setting of the dialogue serves as an introduction to the scene at hand and an interpretive guide for the reader. It is an interpretive guide because the details of the setting do not merely depict both the historical as well as the cosmological contexts (see comments before 1:1). The narrator is normally quite direct with the symbolic significance of the Feasts and their interpretive role in the Gospel. Only once is a feast left unnamed (5:1). The normal purpose of the mention of a feast is to highlight its symbolism rooted in its social-religious context (cf. the Feast of Tabernacles, 7:2, 14; see comments on 7:37), expressing the historical and cosmological forces at work in the narrative. To understand the Feast

of Dedication, we must explain the significance of the time and place so intentionally revealed by the narrator.

The Feast of Dedication was the commemoration of the rededication of the temple by Judas Maccabaeus ("Judas the Hammer") in 165 BC. This was in response to the assault on the Jews and Judaism in 167 BC by the Syrian king, Antiochus Epiphanies, who claimed to be deity ("God-manifest"), who attacked Jerusalem and polluted the temple, ultimately sacrificing swine on the temple altar to a pagan god. In response the people, led by Maccabaeus, overthrew their oppressor, recaptured the temple, and rededicated it to God on 25 Kislev (the lunar month that coincides with December).[2] The Jewish people celebrated the rededication for eight days, and it was decreed that this Feast of Dedication (Hanukkah) should be held every year at the same time (1 Macc 4:36–59). The festival was also called the Feast of Lights, because of the lamps and candles that were lit to celebrate the feast, symbols used because the right to worship "appeared to us" or "shone upon us" (Josephus, *Ant.* 12.316–25). The Festival commemorated national deliverance, a political victory over Hellenistic (pagan) forces at a time when God's temple, God's people, and God himself were being challenged. It was the last and greatest deliverance of Israel that the Jews had known; in their minds, it was close to a second exo-

---

1. See Brown, *John*, 1:402.

2. Carson, *John*, 391.

dus. The Feast of Dedication was the celebration of the memory that "the sovereign God, against all human probabilities, wrought deliverance for his people, brought them out of darkness, and enabled them to offer real worship."[3]

The symbolic significance of the Feast of Dedication, a religious and national holiday, has several correspondences to Jesus (e.g., hero, Light, God-manifest).[4] Ironically, the Jews reject Jesus even though he is God's agent, Israel's true hero who has been "sent" by God. Even more, he is sanctified ("set apart") just as the new altar was (v. 36), for in his very person not just the altar but the entire temple (and sacrificial system) is replaced and renewed (cf. 2:12–25).

10:23 And Jesus was walking in the temple in the portico of Solomon (καὶ περιεπάτει ὁ Ἰησοῦς ἐν τῷ ἱερῷ ἐν τῇ στοᾷ τοῦ Σολομῶνος). The narrator concludes his introduction to the dialogue by giving more details about the location of Jesus and his walking in a specific section of the temple. The "portico of Solomon" (τῇ στοᾷ τοῦ Σολομῶνος) was the most external court of the temple which was surrounded by magnificent covered colonnades or cloisters on all four sides.[5] These porticoes were open on the inside, facing the temple, but closed on the outside, thus making it a likely place for Jesus to find some cover from the "wintry weather."[6] Ironically, in the midst of the celebration of the faithfulness of God in the past to his people and to his temple, God himself is "walking in the temple" (περιεπάτει ἐν τῷ ἱερῷ). Jesus, the fulfillment of all the religious and national hopes of Israel, is walking in their midst — "dwelling" or "tabernacling" among them (1:14).

10:24 Then the Jews surrounded him and said to him, "How long will you take away our life? If you are the Christ, say it clearly to us" (ἐκύκλωσαν οὖν αὐτὸν οἱ Ἰουδαῖοι καὶ ἔλεγον αὐτῷ, Ἕως πότε τὴν ψυχὴν ἡμῶν αἴρεις; εἰ σὺ εἶ ὁ Χριστός, εἰπὲ ἡμῖν παρρησίᾳ). The first verbal exchange of the dialogue between Jesus and the Jewish authorities (see comments on 1:19) begins with a remarkably strong depiction by the narrator of the actions of the Jews. The term "surrounded" (ἐκύκλωσαν) is almost certainly intended to communicate that the Jews "encircled" Jesus with hostile intent.[7] It is difficult not to see a connection to Psalm 118 in this confrontation: "They surround me on every side, but in the name of the LORD I cut them down.... The stone the builders rejected has become the cornerstone" (vv. 11, 22). Even more, and befitting the Feast of Dedication/Lights: "The LORD is God, and he has made his light shine upon us. Bind the festal sacrifice with cords, up to the horns of the altar" (v. 27 ESV). Before the Jews can get a chance to ask Jesus who he is, the narrator tips his hat in the direction of the psalmist's declaration. The command to "bind" refers to the tying of a sacrificial lamb as preparation to its being sacrificed.[8] The true hero of Israel has returned to cleanse and rededicate the temple, but this hero comes not like a "hammer" but as a lamb — the Lamb of God (1:29).

The Jews ask a question that is difficult to translate: "How long will you take away our life?" (Ἕως πότε τὴν ψυχὴν ἡμῶν αἴρεις;). The statement is awkward, causing the majority of English translations to translate it as an idiom (e.g., the NIV reads, "How long will you keep us in suspense?"). But while this idiomatic translation might make sense in the context, there is not a shred of evidence that

---

3. Morris, *John*, 459.

4. See Keener, *John*, 1:822.

5. Cf. Brown, *John*, 1:402; Keener, *John*, 1:823.

6. It is possible that the statement, "It was winter" (χειμὼν ἦν), conveys to the reader an ethos of conflict, functioning as

much as a cosmological reference as it is a historical reference (see comments on 3:2; cf. 13:30).

7. BDAG 574.

8. Goldingay, *Psalms*, 3:364.

the phrase ever had such an idiomatic meaning in biblical, classical, or Hellenistic Greek.[9] Some have argued that modern Greek retains something of the idiom, but the sense there is not suspense but annoyance (i.e., "How long will you annoy [vex, trouble] us in this way?").[10] But even this sense of the idiom, while possibly fitting the context, is only a hypothesis regarding the Greek. Although the idiom cannot be translated with precision, certainly it was stated with hostile intent. Yet this idiom expresses something that has already been declared by the Gospel to be rigidly literal: Jesus is (literally) the one who has "life in himself" (5:26), just as the prologue announced at the Gospel's beginning that "in the Word was life" (1:4).

The second statement made by the Jewish authorities employs the force of the hostile first question to demand a specific answer regarding his identity. The emphatic statement, "If *you* are the Christ, say it clearly to us" (εἰ σὺ εἶ ὁ Χριστός, εἰπὲ ἡμῖν παρρησίᾳ), seeks clarification, probably because Jesus has been speaking in several metaphors, using such things as bread, light, doors, and shepherds as imagery to convey his message. That the Jews refer here to Jesus's past teaching provides warrant for seeing the idiom in their first question as also coming from his previous teaching. This question is focused on the self-perception of Jesus. Does he think he is the "Christ"—a loaded term for first-century Judaism and the Gospel (see comments on 1:20). They demand that he tell them "clearly" (παρρησίᾳ), that is, "plainly," perhaps even without the use of his metaphors (on speaking "clearly," see 7:26; 18:20). In the developing context of the Gospel, their demand is less concerned with "who" he thinks he is and more with "what" he plans to do. They know who Jesus thinks he is; their concern is what his religious-political strategy

might be. For his actions will determine what they must do with him.

10:25 Jesus answered them, "I spoke to you and you did not believe. The works which I do in my Father's name testify concerning me" (ἀπεκρίθη αὐτοῖς ὁ Ἰησοῦς, Εἶπον ὑμῖν καὶ οὐ πιστεύετε· τὰ ἔργα ἃ ἐγὼ ποιῶ ἐν τῷ ὀνόματι τοῦ πατρός μου ταῦτα μαρτυρεῖ περὶ ἐμοῦ). Jesus responds to the hostility with a substantial rejoinder (vv. 25–30). According to Jesus, the assumption that he had been cryptic was incorrect. It is not that he did not speak clearly, it was that they did not listen, which he describes as a malfunction not of the ears but of the heart ("you did not believe" [οὐ πιστεύετε]).

In one sense it could be argued that Jesus never spoke to the Jews directly about being "the Christ" (ὁ Χριστός), for he never used the term himself; he only claimed the title when it was said in his presence (cf. 4:25–26). In another sense, however, Jesus could not have been more clear and open about his identity as the Christ. Everything he did and said was rooted in or descriptive of his identity as the unique Son, the Son of Man. That is why Jesus connects emphatically what he has said about himself with what he has done—"the works which *I* do" (τὰ ἔργα ἃ ἐγὼ ποιῶ)—because he cooperates in perfect harmony with the Father. The Son may do a "work," but it is done "in my Father's name" (ἐν τῷ ὀνόματι τοῦ πατρός μου), that is, not just with the authority of the Father but quite literally as a "work" of the Father. In this way, Jesus's "works" are ontologically the works of the Father and therefore function as testimonies to the identity of the Son. This is no crude circular argument but the ontological and functional relationship between the Father and the Son—the Trinitarian God (cf. v. 30). And this circularity demands that when the Jews do not hear what Jesus is saying, they are by their

9. Cf. Michaels, *John*, 596; Barrett, *John*, 380.
10. Brown, *John*, 1:403; Morris, *John*, 461. Cf. Alexander

Pallis, *Notes on St. John and the Apocalypse* (Oxford: Oxford University Press, 1926), 23–24.

own self-incriminating "works" being declared deaf to God himself. By this Jesus reverses the accusation and places it back upon the Jews.

10:26 "But you do not believe, because you do not belong to my sheep" (ἀλλὰ ὑμεῖς οὐ πιστεύετε, ὅτι οὐκ ἐστὲ ἐκ τῶν προβάτων τῶν ἐμῶν).

It is significant that Jesus repeats the charge that the Jews do not believe, again made emphatic by the stated pronoun. It is important to note that the issue Jesus is addressing by this emphasis on "unbelief" is not the inability of the Jews to conceive of a suffering Christ instead of a nationalistic or political Christ. Rather, the issue Jesus addresses is a spiritual issue; it is about the nature of God and the expression of God by means of the Son. The issue is not merely intellectual, as if further study would clear things up. We should not think that the Jews understood God but had a hard time fitting Jesus into the already established Jewish belief system. Rather, the very fact that the Jews rejected Jesus was proof of their rejection — no, unbelief — of God himself. There is no God without Jesus, and there is no belief in God without believing in Jesus. Just as the Father works through the Son (v. 25), so also it is the Son that makes the Father known (1:18).

In the same vein Jesus also can declare, "You do not belong to my sheep" (οὐκ ἐστὲ ἐκ τῶν προβάτων τῶν ἐμῶν). There is no connection to God without Jesus, and therefore there is no participation in the people of God without Jesus. Jesus here returns to the sheep metaphor introduced in the previous pericope (10:1 – 21). Just as everything the Son does (and is) belongs to the Father (v. 25), so also must the sheep belong to the Shepherd, who is none other than Jesus (cf. 10:11). There is no other mode of existence, and there is no other access point or "door" to God (10:7). There is an unavoidable trace of election implied by this statement that serves to make clear that it is not just the disbeliever who rejects God but also God who rejects the disbeliever.[11] This challenge is ultimately not between Jesus and the Jews, but God and the Jews.

10:27 "My sheep listen to my voice, and I know them, and they follow me" (τὰ πρόβατα τὰ ἐμὰ τῆς φωνῆς μου ἀκούουσιν, κἀγὼ γινώσκω αὐτά, καὶ ἀκολουθοῦσίν μοι).

Jesus repeats what he stated in the previous pericope regarding the intimate relationship between the Shepherd and his sheep (see comments on 10:3 – 5). There is a significant difference, however, that is important to note. In 10:1 – 21 the emphasis was placed on the sheep's knowledge of the shepherd (10:4); now the emphasis is placed on the Shepherd's knowledge of the sheep: "and I know them" (κἀγὼ γινώσκω αὐτά).[12] While there was certainly an implied mutual knowledge in the previous pericope (cf. 10:14), the primary focus was the sheep's recognition of the Shepherd. The reversed emphasis here serves to carry forward the rebuke of the Jews. It is not just their (passive) inability to recognize him as their shepherd; it is also his (active) rejection of them as his sheep. Not only are the Jewish authorities declared incompetent as shepherds (10:1 – 21), but they are now no longer even able to call themselves sheep!

10:28 "And I give them eternal life, and they will never be destroyed, and no one can take them out of my hand" (κἀγὼ δίδωμι αὐτοῖς ζωὴν αἰώνιον, καὶ οὐ μὴ ἀπόλωνται εἰς τὸν αἰῶνα, καὶ οὐχ ἀρπάσει τις αὐτὰ ἐκ τῆς χειρός μου).

Jesus here declares what only he can offer his sheep: "eternal life" (ζωὴν αἰώνιον). What makes this gift of life significant is that it is invincible; that is, it cannot be destroyed or taken by another. It belongs to Christ and to those

---

11. On the issue of election or "Johannine predestination," see Bultmann, *John*, 362; Ridderbos, *John*, 369; Calvin, *John 1 – 10*, 272.

12. Cf. Morris, *John*, 463.

to whom he gives it. The phrase, "they will never be destroyed" (οὐ μὴ ἀπόλωνται εἰς τὸν αἰῶνα), is accentuated not only by the emphatic negative subjunctive, which is "the strongest way to negate something in Greek,"[13] but also by the prepositional phrase we simply translated as "never" (εἰς τὸν αἰῶνα), which strengthens further the already robust subjunctive negation.[14] This gift can neither be destroyed nor can anyone "take them" (ἁρπάσει αὐτά), with the neuter pronoun referring back to "the sheep" (τῶν προβάτων) in v. 26, which is also neuter grammatically. The Good Shepherd watches over the sheep. He was described in the previous pericope as the one from whom no sheep could be taken because he has authority given to him by the Father (10:18). The gift of eternal life is given to these sheep, not by a mere "hired worker" (10:13) but by Jesus, the Good Shepherd.

10:29 "That which my Father has given to me is greater than all, and no one is able to take [it] out of my Father's hand" (ὁ πατήρ μου ὃ δέδωκέν μοι πάντων μεῖζόν ἐστιν, καὶ οὐδεὶς δύναται ἁρπάζειν ἐκ τῆς χειρὸς τοῦ πατρός). Jesus again connects his "work" and authority to the Father. The verse, however, is filled with text-critical and translation difficulties. The core of the difficulty concerns whether the relative pronoun is (1) neuter and translated as "that" (ὅ), or (2) masculine and translated as "who" (ὅς).[15] The difference in translation would be as follows:

1. "*That which* my Father has given me is greater than all things, and no one is able to take [it] out of my Father's hands."

2. "My Father, *who* has given [them] to me, is greater than all, and no one is able to take [them] out of my Father's hands."

While several interpreters and the majority of translations select reading (2), almost always because of what appears to be a more natural contextual fit,[16] the text-critical evidence is strongly in favor of reading (1).

The difference in meaning is important to clarify. In reading (2), the implied object is the sheep, whom the Father has given to Jesus. The sheep are not merely secure in the hand of Jesus but also in the hand of the Father. The sheep, then, are firmly and safely located in both the Father and Son's hands. In reading (1), however, the implied object is more inclusive. While it includes the "sheep," as v. 28 made clear,[17] it must also include everything the Father has elsewhere been described as having given to the Son, including authority, judgment, and life itself (5:22 – 27). Thus, it is not just the sheep that are in the Father's hand, as reading (2) might be taken to mean, but authority, judgment, and life itself, under which the sheep are firmly and securely selected to dwell. What the Father gave to the Son was not merely sheep but his Sonship and everything that goes with it![18] In contrast to reading (2), it is not the Father who is being described as "greater than all," but *that which* the Father has given to the Son — not merely the sheep but the life-giving authority and power to sustain and protect them that properly belongs to the Son.

For this reason v. 29 is not adding to the "hand" of v. 28 a further supporting "hand" around the sheep, but showing how the hand of the Son has been given authority and power from the hand of the Father, which now includes the gift of eternal life abundantly bestowed upon the sheep. Said another way, the hand of the Son *is* the hand of the Father; to speak of one is to simultaneously speak of the other. Whatever is attributed to the Father is

---

13. Wallace, *Greek Grammar*, 468.

14. Barrett, *John*, 381.

15. See Metzger, *Textual Commentary*, 198 – 99; Barrett, *John*, 381 – 82.

16. Cf. Ridderbos, *John*, 370.

17. Michaels, *John*, 600.

18. Cf. Augustine, *John*, 48.6.267.

also to be attributed to the Son. This has been the Gospel's depiction of the work of Jesus all along (see comments on 1:18). This distinction makes even stronger Jesus's claim that no one can destroy or steal the sheep from his hand (v. 28), because it makes clear that it is never two hands but one — note the term "hand" (τῆς χειρὸς) is always singular. It is the Son that protects the sheep, but it is the Father who empowers the Son. The Son's hand holds and empowers the sheep just as the Father's hand holds and empowers the Son.

This response of Jesus (vv. 25–30) therefore is almost entirely about the Shepherd, not the sheep. Jesus mentioned the sheep, but only to rebuke the claims of the Jewish leadership. Thus, reading (1) also actually fits best the context of the social challenge. The debate does not concern the security of the sheep but the authority of the Shepherd and therefore is directly about the messianic identity of Jesus, which the questions in v. 24 made clear. While these verses are often taken to give comfort to the sheep and rightly so, it is only because it speaks less of the sheep and more of the Shepherd. It speaks less about what we have received and more about the one who gives it to us. And it speaks less about our connection to "the Christ" and more about the connection between "the Christ" and the Father. This explains the force of Jesus's concluding statement in v. 30.

10:30 "I and the Father are one" (ἐγὼ καὶ ὁ πατὴρ ἕν ἐσμεν). Jesus concludes his response to the Jews with a rich theological statement of what in the immediate context refers to the ontological and functional unity between the Father and the Son. What the Gospel declared in the opening verse regarding their ontological relationship — "the Word was God" (1:1) — is here stated similarly as a determinative reality of that relationship.

Jesus has given the Jews a syllogistic response to their challenge: (a) I have the authority to protect the sheep; (b) the authority I have has been given to me by my Father; therefore, (c) the Father and I are doing the same work.[19] Jesus has already declared himself to be coworking with God (5:17), which the Jews interpreted rightly as a claim that he was "making himself equal with God" (5:18). This time, however, the integrated nature of their cooperation is being stressed. The work of the Father and Son are so intertwined that it can only be one work. In the same way, the identity of the Father and Son are so intertwined that they must be described as one God, without denying their distinction as persons. In this way, the first verbal exchange comes to an end with one of the most elevated and divine statements in all of Scripture being used as a rebuke of the disbelief of the Jewish authorities.

10:31 Again the Jews picked up stones in order to stone him (Ἐβάστασαν πάλιν λίθους οἱ Ἰουδαῖοι ἵνα λιθάσωσιν αὐτόν). A comment by the narrator provides a transition from the first to the second verbal exchange. "Again" (πάλιν) refers back to the previous attempt at stoning (8:59; cf. 5:18). Jesus's statement to the Jews in the first verbal exchange gave the Jews only two options: either declare Jesus a blasphemer or believe in him; they chose the former. According to the law, blasphemy was to be punished by stoning (Lev 24:16). This description of the Jews' intentions sets the context and explains the force of the second verbal exchange.

10:32 Jesus answered them, "I have shown you many good works from the Father. For which of these works do you stone me?" (ἀπεκρίθη αὐτοῖς ὁ Ἰησοῦς, Πολλὰ ἔργα καλὰ ἔδειξα ὑμῖν ἐκ τοῦ πατρός· διὰ ποῖον αὐτῶν ἔργον ἐμὲ λιθάζετε;). Jesus offers a verbal rejoinder to the wordless actions of the Jews.

---

19. Cf. Michaels, *John*, 600.

It is a defense or, more accurately, an explanation of his actions that serves to challenge their interpretation of and response to him. Jesus claims to have "shown" (ἔδειξα) his good works, a term that suggests that he has offered demonstrations of proof regarding his identity and intention.[20] His proof is "good works" (ἔργα καλὰ), with the qualification "good" expressing "deeds of power and moral excellence, resulting in health in well-being."[21] That is, these works are "good" in that they signify the salvific character of the works and, therefore, authenticate the one who performs them. It is not just that these works are "good" but also that they are "from the Father" (ἐκ τοῦ πατρός). The unity between Jesus and the Father made clear in the first verbal exchange (vv. 24 – 30) was intended to explain the purity and power of his actions. That is why Jesus can ask a question that serves as a strong rejoinder. Which of these "works" is to serve as counterevidence to the testimony stemming from the "good works" themselves?

10:33 The Jews answered him, "We are not stoning you about good works, but for blasphemy, because you, a man, make yourself to be God" (ἀπεκρίθησαν αὐτῷ οἱ Ἰουδαῖοι, Περὶ καλοῦ ἔργου οὐ λιθάζομέν σε ἀλλὰ περὶ βλασφημίας, καὶ ὅτι σὺ ἄνθρωπος ὢν ποιεῖς σεαυτὸν θεόν). The Jews offer a very different interpretation of Jesus's works, declaring them to be a blasphemous claim, one in which a mere man declares himself to be God. The interpretation is more than just an interpretation of his works, but is a direct response to his statement in v. 30 — "I and the Father are one" — which is why they immediately picked up stones. While this is the first time the Jews publicly charge Jesus with blasphemy, the narrator already informed us of their earlier interpretation of his actions in 5:18. Twice before, when similar interpretations of

his actions occurred, Jesus explained that he was not "making himself" to be anything but allowing the Father's works to speak for him (cf. 5:19 – 23; 8:54 – 55).[22]

10:34 Jesus answered them, "Is it not written in your law, 'I said, you are gods?'" (ἀπεκρίθη αὐτοῖς [ὁ] Ἰησοῦς, Οὐκ ἔστιν γεγραμμένον ἐν τῷ νόμῳ ὑμῶν ὅτι Ἐγὼ εἶπα, Θεοί ἐστε;). Jesus responds to the Jews' interpretation of his action with his own interpretation of the "Jewish" Scriptures. The thrust of Jesus's response centers upon an argument rooted in an applied interpretation of Psalm 82. Jesus prefaces his exegetical argument with the statement, "Is it not written in your law" (Οὐκ ἔστιν γεγραμμένον ἐν τῷ νόμῳ ὑμῶν). By this statement, Jesus does not intend to distance himself from the law, as if it was the law "of the Jews" — no; it is his law! (See comments on 8:17.) Rather, his statement intends to highlight the connection between the Jews and the law they already claim as authoritative so that the forthcoming argument from Scripture hits forcefully.

Jesus quotes from Psalm 82:6, "I said, you are gods" (Ἐγὼ εἶπα, Θεοί ἐστε). The meaning of the phrase and its use in this pericope is almost entirely dependent on the original intended addressees of Psalm 82. There are three traditional options that all find representative support in early Judaism: option (1), "gods" refers to *angelic powers* who had authority over the nations but misused it; option (2), "gods" refers to *the people of Israel* at the giving of the law; and option (3), "gods" refers to *the judges of Israel* who had been given authority over the people but failed to administer it with justice. There is just not enough textual evidence to support option (1), even if it was given this application by early Judaism. In Psalm 82, the "gods" can only be a title for humans. Ultimately, the argument for

20. Schnackenburg, *John*, 2:309.
21. Barrett, *John*, 383.

22. Michaels, *John*, 602.

the choice between options (2) and (3) is strongly dependent on Jesus's own words in v. 35.

10:35 "If he called them gods, those to whom the word of God came, and the Scripture cannot be broken"

(εἰ ἐκείνους εἶπεν θεοὺς πρὸς οὓς ὁ λόγος τοῦ θεοῦ ἐγένετο, καὶ οὐ δύναται λυθῆναι ἡ γραφή). Jesus offers a contextual clue when, after restating the key phrase from Psalm 82:6, he provides an explanatory clause that unpacks what he understood by "gods," namely, "those to whom the word of God came" (πρὸς οὓς ὁ λόγος τοῦ θεοῦ ἐγένετο).[23] The expression "those to whom the word of God came" lacks any specific reference to the Sinai theophany and therefore to Israel in general, contra option (2), and can be only secondarily applied to that event. Rather, Psalm 82 addresses the judges of Israel, those against whom God will render his own "judgment" (v. 1) for defending the unjust and showing partiality to the wicked (v. 2). These "judges" should have ruled in the entirely opposite manner. They should have defended the weak and the fatherless and rescued the weak and the needy (vv. 3 – 4). Through the Psalm, then, God declares judgment on those assigned to be judges in language that echoes the prologue (John 1:5): "The 'gods' know nothing, they understand nothing. They walk about in darkness" (Ps 82:5). For this reason the Judge declares a guilty verdict on these judges: "I said, 'You are "gods" … But you will die like mere mortals; you will fall like every other ruler' " (vv. 6 – 7).

In light of the explanatory clause Jesus provided, in Psalm 82 God is judging the judges of Israel, those who had been given an exalted title ("gods") in order to reflect the significance of their position. Just as God addresses the king as "my son" (Ps 2:7),

so he addresses those in the office of judge (leader, authority) as "gods," "sons of the Most High" (Ps 82:6), which serves as an expression of their power and authority that they received from God himself.[24] These judges have failed the people of Israel and, even worse, God himself. They have failed to be worthy representatives of him. For this reason, they shall no longer be known primarily as "gods" but as "mere mortals," who are not only declared guilty by the very justice system they were supposed to uphold by means of their assigned office but will also receive its greatest punishment: death.

Jesus's use of Psalm 82 finds remarkable agreement with this entire section of the Gospel (8:12 – 10:42), which has employed forensic themes and judicial procedures to depict Jesus's rebuke of the Jewish authorities for their failed leadership and to present Jesus as the true authority and leader of Israel. The previous pericope presented Jesus as the true Shepherd (10:1 – 21) in contrast to the failed shepherding of the Jewish authorities (ch. 9). This pericope presents Jesus as the true Judge of Israel and the only one who is deserving of the office (and title) of "god," in contrast to the failed contemporary rulers of the Jewish people. The irony is stark. Jesus is not only the intended replacement of these judges but also a perfect fulfillment of their office.

With the force of Jesus's exegesis of Psalm 82, Jesus adds, "and the Scripture cannot be broken" (καὶ οὐ δύναται λυθῆναι ἡ γραφή). The term "broken" (λυθῆναι) is not defined and is rarely used of Scripture (cf. 7:23), but it is also intelligible. It means Scripture cannot be shown to be erroneous and that its specifics are to the detail proven true.[25] Thus, it not only serves to reinforce the emphatic "your law" of v. 34 but also to declare Scripture

---

23. In agreement with Jerome H. Neyrey, " 'I Said: You are Gods': Psalm 82:6 and John 10," *JBL* 108 (1989): 647 – 63, who writes, "The chief clue to a special reading of Ps. 82:6 lies in 10:35" (654).

24. Goldingay, *Psalms*, 2:567.
25. Morris, *John*, 468.

everlasting in its authority and applicability, right down to this very moment in the ministry of Jesus.[26]

10:36 "what about the one the Father set apart and sent into the world? Why do say blasphemy, because I said, 'I am the Son of God?'" (ὃν ὁ πατὴρ ἡγίασεν καὶ ἀπέστειλεν εἰς τὸν κόσμον ὑμεῖς λέγετε ὅτι Βλασφημεῖς, ὅτι εἶπον, Υἱὸς [τοῦ] θεοῦ εἰμι;). Jesus now lays out the implication of his exegetical argument and applied use of Psalm 82 in the form of a rhetorical question that addresses the charge of blasphemy. If the judges in the OT were given offices that merited the title "gods," is it not both logical (per exegesis) and appropriate (per application) for the Father to create another office that receives the title?[27]

The force of the argument is not just that a human office (judge or ruler) was worthy of the title "god" but that God himself had established a system that broke down the strict dichotomy erected between God and humanity. The history of the OT "witnesses to a series of individuals who served as God's representatives, including judges, prophets, priests, and kings."[28] These individuals filled these offices by means of God's Spirit in order to accomplish a particular task or proclaim a particular word.[29] By these already-established offices from the OT "we find a paradigm of union between the divine and the human, no matter how qualified or limited it may have been."[30]

Jesus's argument, then, is a claim to be filling another office divinely authorized by God. While the majority of interpreters believe Jesus is presenting an *a fortiori* argument ("from lesser to greater"),[31] the explicit *a fortiori* element is missing ("how

much more …") and the description of Jesus in v. 36 is not described in relation to "those to whom the word of God came" in v. 35.[32] As Ridderbos keenly notes, "If in this argument Jesus's purpose was to justify his claim to his unique relationship to God as his Father from Scripture … how could Jesus … appeal to that which was qualitatively less?"[33] The argument of vv. 34–36, therefore, is intended to disassociate himself from the claim of blasphemy by connecting his divine office to the already established "divine" offices from the Old Testament. God does not feel diminished in his rights or honor by identifying himself with special representatives, nor does it cause him concern to address them with the honorific title, "god." The Jews had been wrong about God before (see comments on 5:39), and here Jesus provides a further example.

In this way, Jesus concludes his interpretive argument from Psalm 82 with the counterquestion that defends his unique office as "the Son of God" (Υἱὸς [τοῦ] θεοῦ). The psalmist closed with a request to God, "Rise up, O God, judge the earth, for all the nations are your inheritance" (Ps 82:8). The words of Jesus are the fulfillment of this psalm. God has risen and presented ("set apart") his Son to the world. In this way Jesus, the Son of God, is the true Judge, the ultimate representative of God, and the final mediator between humanity and God. Ironically, at the same time the Jewish nation is celebrating the Feast of Dedication by remembering the heroes of Israel who have represented them and redeemed them from the enemy, the greatest hero and representative Israel (and the world!) would ever have was standing among them, though he was being dishonored and charged with blas-

---

26. Michaels, *John*, 603.

27. Cf. Augustine, *John*, 48.9.269.

28. Köstenberger, "John," 466.

29. See Stephen L. Homcy, "'You are Gods'? Spirituality and a Difficult Text," *JETS* 32 (1989): 485–91 (489).

30. Ibid.

31. For example, see Brown, *John*, 1:410.

32. Ridderbos, *John*, 374.

33. Ibid.

phemy. But the Jews would get what they prayed for in Psalm 82:8; God had sent his Son to "judge the earth" — but not before he would save it (cf. 3:17 – 21).

10:37 "If I do not do the works of my Father, do not believe me" (εἰ οὐ ποιῶ τὰ ἔργα τοῦ πατρός μου, μὴ πιστεύετέ μοι). After making a biblical argument for his divine office, Jesus offers his "works" (τὰ ἔργα) alongside this interpretive proof as something more tangible. Jesus returns to the argument he made in the first verbal exchange (see comments on v. 25), uniting himself both functionally and ontologically with the Father. Just as the office of the OT judges were rooted in God, so Jesus's "works" and his office — his entire ministry and the character of his person — are also grounded in the Father. After rebuking them by declaring them unbelievers in v. 26, this verse serves as an extension of grace, an invitation to believe the evidence in front of them.

10:38 "But if I do, even if you do not believe me, believe the works, so that you may know and understand that the Father is in me and I am in the Father" (εἰ δὲ ποιῶ, κἂν ἐμοὶ μὴ πιστεύητε, τοῖς ἔργοις πιστεύετε, ἵνα γνῶτε καὶ γινώσκητε ὅτι ἐν ἐμοὶ ὁ πατὴρ κἀγὼ ἐν τῷ πατρί). Jesus again restates his invitation to the Jews, this time positively, but now with an even stronger invitation centered upon the foundational truth of the Gospel: the relation between the Father and the Son. The ultimate goal is that the Jews would not disbelieve the ontological and therefore functional unity of the Father and the Son. Functional in the sense introduced by the Gospel thus far that Jesus is the only access to God (1:18) and the manifestation and expression of the Father's love for the world (3:16). Jesus's stated hope is that the Jews would truly know this truth. Jesus emphasizes this knowledge by repeat-ing the same Greek word "to know" in two different tenses, aorist and present, which we translated as "know and understand" (γνῶτε καὶ γινώσκητε). The translation signifies that the former (aorist) is referring to the act of knowing whereas the latter (present) is referring to the continuing progress in understanding.[34]

10:39 Again they tried to seize him, but he escaped from their hand (Ἐζήτουν [οὖν] πάλιν αὐτὸν πιάσαι· καὶ ἐξῆλθεν ἐκ τῆς χειρὸς αὐτῶν). The second verbal exchange is concluded with an explanatory statement by the narrator, who describes how the Jews "again" (πάλιν) rejected his invitation (and him) and tried to arrest him. The attempt was unsuccessful as before and certainly for the same reason (see comments on 7:30). In the same manner that it began (v. 31), the second verbal exchange comes to an end.

10:40 Then he again went out to the other side of the Jordan to the place where John was first baptizing, and he remained there (Καὶ ἀπῆλθεν πάλιν πέραν τοῦ Ἰορδάνου εἰς τὸν τόπον ὅπου ἦν Ἰωάννης τὸ πρῶτον βαπτίζων, καὶ ἔμεινεν ἐκεῖ). The pericope is concluded by the narrator (vv. 40 – 42), who begins by describing how Jesus left Jerusalem, the location that served as the contextual backdrop for this entire section of the Gospel (8:12 – 10:42). While these verses will make sense of the beginning of chapter 11 and the location of Jesus at the time of Lazarus's death (11:1, 3, 5), these concluding verses (vv. 40 – 42) are more naturally connected to "went out" (v. 40) than to what follows. Furthermore, the two trips of Jesus "on the other side of the Jordan" (cf. 3:26) serve as bookends to the public ministry of Jesus.[35] These verses, then, serve as a clear break in the construction of the narrative, completing the fifth section of the Gospel.

---

34. Porter, *Verbal Aspect*, 328.

35. Michaels, *John*, 609.

10:41 Many people came to him and said, "John never performed a miraculous sign, but everything John said concerning him was true" (καὶ πολλοὶ ἦλθον πρὸς αὐτὸν καὶ ἔλεγον ὅτι Ἰωάννης μὲν σημεῖον ἐποίησεν οὐδέν, πάντα δὲ ὅσα εἶπεν Ἰωάννης περὶ τούτου ἀληθῆ ἦν). The narrator reminds the reader of the importance of the Baptist's ministry described earlier in the Gospel (1:6 – 8, 15; 1:19 – 34; 3:22 – 36). This Gospel is only briefly concerned with the historical life of the Baptist; his importance is found in that to which he witnesses. By returning to the Baptist, the reader is reminded of the message of the Baptist and exhorted to hear afresh his witness and the titles for Jesus that emerged at the Gospel's start from the Baptist's ministry: "Lamb of God" (1:29), "Messiah" (1:41), "Son of God" and "King of Israel" (1:48). It is not what the Baptist did, no "sign," but what he said that was important. Jesus would do the "signs"; the Baptist merely pointed to Jesus. In many ways the Gospel itself, like the Baptist, is to be remembered by the reader as simply pointing to Jesus and his signs (cf. 20:31).

10:42 And many believed in him there (καὶ πολλοὶ ἐπίστευσαν εἰς αὐτὸν ἐκεῖ). The narrator concludes a section on "controversy" — a section filled with rejections of Jesus — with a significant statement. The departure from Jerusalem and return to where the ministry began might look like a failure when in reality it had been a success. A good number of people ("many") believed in Jesus, and this is what the narrator wants the reader to understand.

Theology in Application

As the fifth section of the Gospel comes to a close, the reader has seen a progressive reversal. The forensic themes and judicial procedures have shifted the direction of their attention from the adjudication of Jesus by the Jewish leadership to the adjudication of the Jewish leadership by Jesus. It is the Jews, not Jesus, who have been negligent of their duties to God's people — and to God himself. The "Controversy over the Son of God" has been reversed against the accusers. It is the Jewish leadership with whom God is angry; indeed, it is the Jewish authorities who are guilty of blasphemy — denying God the Son his divine identity. Through this pericope, the readers are invited to respond appropriately to the true ruler of God's people and to believe (not blaspheme!) the Son of God.

The Feast of Dedication and the Hero of God's People

The narrator was careful to craft the pericope through the interpretive lens of the symbolic significance of the Feast of Dedication, which was the celebration of God's redemptive activity in Israel's past and a foretaste of God's redemptive activity in Israel's future. There was something very different, however, at this Feast of Dedication. Unbeknownst to the Jews, the greatest hero Israel would ever know was at the festival, participating with his people. There was no need to remember "Judas the Hammer," for Jesus the Son was present; he is the one who is just as much Hero of heroes as he is King of kings and Lord of lords. Even more, this hero was not merely significant for this holiday but is the fulfillment of all holidays — he is the fulfillment of Judaism, even more, of the entire human race (the new Adam!). In and through this one person, creation itself was being "renewed." Since that day, his people, Christians, those from every tribe and tongue have also celebrated the restoration of God's temple and religious renewal. But this time it is not through only one Feast: the Lord's Supper. For in Jesus all the feasts and festivals of the Old Testament find their meaning. Jesus is, for example, both the Passover lamb and the one who renewed the temple, the mediation point between God and humanity. No longer are there eight days of lights to celebrate, for there is only one light — the light of the world (8:12).

Christ is the Leader (the Judge) of the People of God

Christ is the promised one of God who fills the unique office that God himself established. In the past God had established offices that mediated between God and humanity — kings and prophets and judges. God was breaking down the barrier that separated God from his people. But the barrier was never entirely broken down, for the offices could never be truly fulfilled — until now. Jesus has been given an office from the Father that encompasses and surpasses all previous offices. Jesus was "set apart" (v. 36) by the Father and sent into the world to accomplish the mission of God. This is not to deny that there are still offices of mediation (see 20:21), but simply to say that the mediation of Christ is the *fulfillment* of all past mediation and the *foundation* of all future mediation. Jesus, the Son of God, is the true Judge, the ultimate representative of God, and the final mediator between humanity and God. Even still, the church yet awaits the final fulfillment, the blessed hope, and prays to their Lord, "Rise up, O God, judge the earth, for all the nations are your inheritance" (Ps 82:8).

The Unity of the Father and the Son

When Jesus declared that he was the Son of God (v. 36), he was claiming that everything God wanted to do or say was being accomplished in his person. The prologue made this clear from the beginning (1:18). Christ is the only one who can see God, the only one who is in perfect, intimate relationship with God, and the only one who can make him known. After seven dialogues, each of which gave further clarification to the unique role and intimate relation of the Son to the Father, Jesus finally declares this reality in full: "I and the Father are one" (v. 30). Such a statement requires an understanding of the Trinitarian identity of God, an identity rooted in the meaning and beginning of life itself.

22

John 11:1 – 57

Literary Context

This pericope begins a new section in the Gospel. The reader has seen the confession of the Son of God (5:1 – 8:11) and the ensuing controversy over the Son of God (8:12 – 10:42) and is given in this section of the Gospel a dramatic conclusion to the public ministry of Jesus (11:1 – 12:50). At the literary level, there is a strong break at 10:42, with the final verses of chapter 10 serving as a large *inclusio*, with the public ministry of Jesus beginning and ending with the witness of the Baptist (1:19 – 10:42).[1] At the same time, the clear connections with what has just occurred makes certain that the narrator uses these two final chapters to conclude Jesus's public presence. Jesus is done speaking publicly; his last public acts will sufficiently display who he is (his person) and what he is about (his work). In this pericope, Jesus's message centers upon a significant miracle, the sixth sign (cf. 11:47), which serves as a clear demonstration of the truth already declared in the Gospel that it is the Son who gives life (cf. 5:21). In this way, the public receives further visible evidence of his invisible nature, and the reader receives greater insight into the unique Son of God.

> → **VI. The Conclusion of Jesus's Public Ministry (11:1 – 12:50)**
> **A. The Sixth Sign: The Death and Resurrection of Lazarus (11:1 – 57)**
> B. The Anointing of Jesus (12:1 – 11)
> C. The Royal Entrance of Jesus into Jerusalem (12:12 – 19)
> D. "The Hour has Come": The Final Public Statement of Jesus (12:20 – 50)

Main Idea

Jesus is the resurrection and the life, the one who has defeated death and who uses the sufferings of sin for his good purposes and glory. God demonstrates his love in this in that while the world was dying to sin, Christ gave it life.

---

1. Carson, *John*, 403.

Translation

John 11:1–57

Continued on next page.

1a	Introduction & Setting (1–16)	**There was a man who was sick,**
b	Character Entrance	Lazarus
c	Location	from Bethany,
d	Description	from the village of Mary and Martha,
e	Relationship	her sister.
2a	Aside	**It was Mary**
b	Description	who had anointed the Lord with perfume and
c		had wiped his feet with her hair,
d	Relationship	whose brother,
e		Lazarus,
f		… was sick.
3a	Character Entrance	**Then the sisters sent to him saying,**
b		*"Lord,*
c	Manner of Relationship	*we want you to know that the one whom you love …*
d	Relating Situation	*… is sick."*
4a	Response	After hearing this
b		**Jesus said,**
c	Purpose (–)	*"This sickness is not for the purpose of death but*
d	Purpose (+)	*for the glory of God,*
e	Result	*so that the Son of God may be glorified through it."*
5a	Aside: Manner of Relationship	**Jesus loved Martha and her sister and Lazarus.**
6a	Counterintuitive Reaction	However,
b		when he heard that Lazarus was sick,
c	Delay	**he remained in the place where he was**
d	Duration	two days.
7a	Character Reentrance	Then after this
b		**he said to the disciples,**
c	Cohortative	*"Let us go*
d	Redescription of Location	*to Judea again."*

Continued from previous page.

8a	Counterrecommendation	**The disciples said to him,**
b		"Rabbi,
c		the Jews are now seeking to stone you,
d		and you are going there again?"
9a	Response	**Jesus answered,**
b	Illustration	"Are there not twelve hours
c	Time	during the day?
d	Condition	If a person is walking in the day
e	Inference	he will not stumble,
f	Basis	because he sees the light of this world.
10a	Contrast	But
b		if a person walks in the night
c		he will stumble,
d		because the light is not in him."
11a	Continued Response	**He said this,**
b		and **after this said to them,**
c		"Lazarus …
d	Manner of Relationship	our friend,
e	Assertion	… has fallen asleep,
f	Intended Reaction	but I am going
g	Purpose	in order to wake him up."
12a	Counterrecommendation	Then **the disciples said to him,**
b		"Lord,
c	Condition	if he sleeps
d	Inference	he will be better."
13a	Narrator's Aside	But **Jesus had been speaking about his death,**
b		but **they thought he was speaking about natural sleep.**
14a	Clarifying Response	So then **Jesus said to them plainly,**
b		"Lazarus is dead.
15a	Assertion	And I rejoice for you
b	Basis	that I was not there,
c	Purpose	in order that you might believe.
d	Cohortative	But let us go to him."
16a	Character Entrance	Then **Thomas** …
b	Identification	(called Didymus)

c   Response   "... said to his fellow disciples:

d   Ironic Agreement   "Let us go also

e   Expected Result   in order that we may die with him."

17a   Arrival   After he arrived,

b   Conflict (17–37)   Jesus found that Lazarus had already been in the tomb

c   Amount of Time   for four days.

18a   Geographical Context   Bethany was near Jerusalem,

b   distance   about two miles away.

19a   Character Entrance   And many of the Jews had come to Martha and Mary

b   Purpose   in order to comfort them in regard to their brother.

20a   Reaction   Then Martha ...

b   Circumstance   when she heard that Jesus was coming,

c   ... went out to meet him,

d   Contrasting Reaction   but Mary was remaining in the house.

21a   Then Martha said to Jesus,

    "Lord,

b   Condition   if you had been here,

c   my brother would not have died.

d   Indirect Rebuke

22a   Contrast   But

b   Concessive Condition   even now

    I know that ... whatever you ask God,

c   Inadequate Confession   ... God will give to you."

23a   Response   Jesus said to her,

b   Correction   "Your brother will rise."

24a   Response   Martha said to him,

b   Mistaken Agreement   "I know that he will rise

c   Time   in the resurrection in the last day."

25a   Response   Jesus said to her,

b   Declaration of Identity   "I am ...

    ... the resurrection and

c   Spheres   the life.

d   The one who believes in me ...

e   Promise (Condition)   ... will live,

f   Promise (Inference)   even if he dies.

g   Concessive Condition

26a   Expansion of Promise   And everyone who lives and

b   believes in me ...

c   Inference   ... will never die.

Continued on next page.

Continued from previous page.

d	Interrogative Invitation	*Do you believe this?"*
27a	Response	**She said to him,**
b	Affirmative Answer	*"Yes,*
c		*Lord,*
d	Confession	*I have believed that you are the Christ,*
e	Apposition	*the Son of God*
f	Description	*who has come into the world."*
28a	Transition to Mary	And after she had said this,
b	Manner of Action	**she went and quietly called Mary,**
c		her sister,
d		saying,
e	Assertion	*"The teacher is here and*
f		*is calling for you."*
g		
29a		And
b		when she heard that,
c	Reaction	**she got up quickly and went to him.**
30a	Narrator's Aside	But **Jesus had not yet come to the village,**
b		but **was still at the place**
c		where Martha had met him.
31a	Character Reentrance	Then **the Jews …**
b	Description	who had been with her in the house and comforting her
c		**… saw that Mary got up quickly and went out,**
d	Reaction	**they followed her,**
e	Assumption	thinking that she was going to the tomb
f	Purpose	in order to weep there.
32a	Arrival	When Mary came where Jesus was,
b		after seeing him
c	Reaction	**she fell at his feet,**
d	Response	saying to him,
e		*"Lord,*
f	Condition	*if you were here*
g	Indirect Rebuke	*my brother would not have died."*

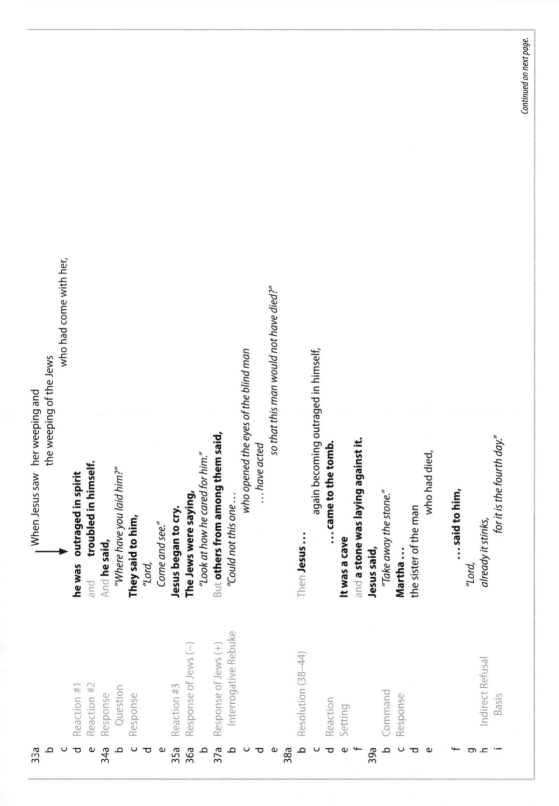

33a		When Jesus saw her weeping and
b		the weeping of the Jews
c		who had come with her,
d	Reaction #1	he was **outraged in spirit**
e	Reaction #2	and **troubled in himself.**
34a	Response	And **he said,**
b	Question	*"Where have you laid him?"*
c		**They said to him,**
d	Response	*"Lord,*
e		*Come and see."*
35a	Reaction #3	**Jesus began to cry.**
36a	Response of Jews (−)	**The Jews were saying,**
b		*"Look at how he cared for him."*
37a	Response of Jews (+)	But **others from among them said,**
b	Interrogative Rebuke	*"Could not this one . . .*
c		*who opened the eyes of the blind man*
d		*. . . have acted*
e		*so that this man would not have died?"*
38a	Resolution (38—44)	Then **Jesus . . .**
b		again becoming outraged in himself,
c		**. . . came to the tomb.**
d	Reaction	**It was a cave**
e	Setting	and **a stone was laying against it.**
f		**Jesus said,**
39a	Command	*"Take away the stone."*
b	Response	**Martha . . .**
c		the sister of the man
d		who had died,
e		**. . . said to him,**
f		*"Lord,*
g	Indirect Refusal	*already it stinks,*
h	Basis	*for it is the fourth day."*
i		

Continued on next page.

Continued from previous page.

40a	Response	**Jesus said to her,**
b	Interrogative Warning	*"Did I not say to you*
c		*that . . .*
d		*. . . you will see the glory of God?"*
41a	Reaction	**They took away the stone.**
b	Prayer	**Then Jesus lifted his eyes upward and said,**
c	Familial Address	*"Father,*
d	Gratitude	*I thank you*
e	Basis	*that you have heard me.*
42a	Assertion	*I knew that you always hear me,*
b	Contrast	*but I said this for the crowd standing around,*
c	Intended Result	*so that they might believe that you sent me."*
43a	Manner of Progression	After he said these things,
b		**Jesus shouted in a loud voice,**
c	Address	*"Lazarus,*
d	Command	*come out!"*
44a	Reaction	**The man who had died came out,**
b	Description	his hands and feet wrapped with strips of cloth, and
c	Description	with a cloth wrapped around his face.
d		**Jesus said to them,**
e	Command	*"Unwrap him and let him go."*
45a	Conclusion (45–57)	Then **many of the Jews . . .**
b	Character Reentrance	those who had come with Mary and
c		had seen what he did,
d		**. . . believed in him.**
46a	Reaction #1	But **some of them went**
b	Character Reentrance	to the Pharisees
c		and
d	Reaction #2	**reported to them what Jesus had done.**
47a	Character Reentrance	Then **the high priests** and
b	Progression of Reaction (46a)	**the Pharisees assembled a meeting of the council and said,**
c	Question of Exasperation	*"What are we doing,*
d	Basis	*because this man is doing many signs?*

48a	*If we allow him to continue like this,*	Condition
b	*everyone will believe in him,*	Religious Inferential Fear
c	*and the Romans will come and take away both our place and our nation."*	Political Inferential Fear
49a	But **one of them …**	Character Entrance
b	Caiaphas,	Identification
c	who was the high priest that year,	Description
d	**… said to them,**	
e	*"You do not understand anything.*	Ironic Rebuke
50a	*You are not considering that it is better for you*	Explanation
b	*that* one man should die for the people,	Description of "it"
c	not the whole nation perish."	
51a	**He said this not by himself,**	Narrator's Intrusion (51–53)
b	but	
c	as high priest that year	
d	**he prophesied that Jesus would die**	Ironic Prophecy
e	for the nation. And not only	Beneficiary
52a	for the nation, but also	Contrast
b	in order to gather together into one the scattered children of God.	Purpose
53a	So **from that day they planned to kill him.**	Climax of Reaction (46a)
54a	Therefore **Jesus** **no longer traveled openly among the Jews,**	Reaction
b	but **went away from there to the region near the country,**	Contrast
c	to a city called Ephraim,	Place
d	where he remained with the disciples.	Description
55a	**The Passover of the Jews was near,**	Escalating Context
b	and **many went up to Jerusalem from the country before the Passover**	
c	in order to purify themselves.	Purpose
56a	**They were seeking Jesus,**	Escalating Plot (56–57)
b	and **as they stood in the temple spoke with one another,**	
c	*"What do you think?*	Rhetorical Question
d	*Surely he is not coming to the Feast?"*	Answer
57a	But **the high priests and the Pharisees had given an** **order**	Basis for 56d
b	that … he should report it,	Description of "order"
c	if anyone knew where he was,	
d	in order that they could arrest him.	Purpose

Structure and Literary Form

This pericope corresponds to the basic story form, although it could have been given a much more complicated structure with its dual-rising conflict and resolution (see Introduction).[2] The *introduction/setting* is established in vv. 1–16, explaining the location, setting, and people around whom the plot's conflict will focus. In vv. 17–37 the *conflict* (or conflicts) of the pericope is placed in front of Jesus, having a dual focus: the death of Lazarus and the crisis of faith among those present (Lazarus's sisters as well as some of "the Jews"). In vv. 38–44 the conflict(s) is given *resolution* by the resurrection of Lazarus and the exhortation for a "resurrection of belief" given to Lazarus's sisters.[3] Finally, vv. 45–57 offer the *conclusion/interpretation* to the pericope by placing it within the context of Jesus's public ministry, with a detailed description of the (prophetic) response of the Jews toward this sixth "sign" of Jesus.

Exegetical Outline

→   **A. The Sixth Sign: The Death and Resurrection of Lazarus (11:1–57)**

   1. The Death of Lazarus, Belief, and the Glory of God (vv. 1–16)

   2. "I am the Resurrection and the Life": The Dialogue between Mary and Martha and Jesus (vv. 17–37)

   3. The Resurrection of Lazarus, Belief, and the Glory of God (vv. 38–44)

   4. The (Prophetic) Response of the Jews to the Sign of Jesus (vv. 45–57)

Explanation of the Text

The depth and beauty of this pericope has unfortunately made it fodder for biblical critics, especially source critics, who have difficulty accepting it without reconciling it with the rest of the biblical tradition.[4] This is almost certainly because this story is only found in the Gospel of John, which to some already makes it suspect, but also because it is the most spectacular miracle in all four Gospels. Why does it not appear in the other three Gospels? A good amount of comparative work has already tried to find the material links between this pericope and other biblical material, primarily in the Synoptic Gospels,[5] but also in the Johannine tradition.[6] While there is some value to these questions

---

2. See Wilhelm Wuellner, "Putting Life Back into the Lazarus Story and Its Reading: The Narrative Rhetoric of John 11 as the Narration of Faith," *Semeia* 53 (1991): 113–32. Cf. Brendan Bryne, *Lazarus: A Contemporary Reading of John 11:1–46*, ZSNT (Collegeville, MN: Liturgical Press, 1991), 24–28.

3. Several interpreters conclude that the pericope ends at v. 44 for form-critical reasons. Cf. Mark W. G. Stibbe, "A Tomb with a View: John 11.1–44 in Narrative-Critical Perspective," *NTS* 40 (1994): 38–54 (especially 39–42). Cf. Francis J. Moloney, "Can Everyone Be Wrong? A Reading of John

11.1–12.8," *NTS* 49 (2003): 505–27.

4. See Alan J. Torrance, "The Lazarus Narrative, Theological History, and Historical Probability," in *The Gospel of John and Christian Theology*, 245–62.

5. See Dodd, *Historical Tradition*, 228–32; cf. Morris, *John*, 473–76.

6. See Wendy E. Sproston North, *The Lazarus Story within the Johannine Tradition*, JSNTSup 212 (Sheffield: Sheffield Academic Press, 2001).

and comparisons, there is no perfect solution. The material history (i.e., sources, tradition) of this pericope is as removed from the reader (and interpreter) as the power needed to raise Lazarus from the dead (on method, see Introduction). This miracle is not entirely unique in John but comfortably fits within the developing narrative as the climactic sixth sign, a capstone for the previous five signs and the narrative's cornerstone for the seventh and final "sign" of the Gospel (see comments before 20:1).

11:1 There was a man who was sick, Lazarus from Bethany, from the village of Mary and Martha, her sister (Ἦν δέ τις ἀσθενῶν, Λάζαρος ἀπὸ Βηθανίας, ἐκ τῆς κώμης Μαρίας καὶ Μάρθας τῆς ἀδελφῆς αὐτῆς). The pericope starts with an introduction of the primary characters in the story. The narrator describes Lazarus as a man "who was sick" (ἀσθενῶν), without giving any indication of the nature of the sickness. The uniqueness of this miracle in the four Gospels has led several scholars to connect this Lazarus to the Lazarus in Luke's parable of the rich man and Lazarus (16:19 – 31), but the lack of any thematic connection and the popularity of the name makes this highly unlikely.[7]

It is important to note that the narrator moves quickly from the sick Lazarus, the person the action of the pericope will focus upon, to Mary and Martha. Even more, while v. 2 will make the family connection between Lazarus and the sisters, here the family connection is only made between Mary and Martha. The focus of the story is surprisingly on the sisters — not Lazarus — and especially on Mary in this verse, who is listed as the primary relation both here and in v. 2 in reference to Lazarus.

The appearance of the sisters in another Gospel (Luke 10:38 – 42) might explain the initial focus on them by the narrator, for it may already be assumed that they were known by the reader.[8]

The narrator also centers this story on the location of these related characters, "Bethany" (Βηθανίας), placing both Lazarus and the sisters in relation to this particular "village" (τῆς κώμης). The village of Bethany, which is on the east side of the Mount of Olives and about two miles from Jerusalem (see v. 18), has not been mentioned in the Gospel before and must be distinguished from the Bethany of 1:28 (and alluded to in 10:40 – 42).[9]

11:2 It was Mary who had anointed the Lord with perfume and had wiped his feet with her hair, whose brother, Lazarus, was sick (ἦν δὲ Μαριὰμ ἡ ἀλείψασα τὸν κύριον μύρῳ καὶ ἐκμάξασα τοὺς πόδας αὐτοῦ ταῖς θριξὶν αὐτῆς, ἧς ὁ ἀδελφὸς Λάζαρος ἠσθένει). The narrator adds a parenthetical statement in his introduction to explain further the identity of the Bethany family, especially Mary. The focus on Mary is likely because of the dramatic encounter between her and Jesus recorded in the Synoptics. The accounts can only be hesitantly compiled, for while the setting (Bethany) fits the account in Mark 14:3 – 9 (= Matt 26:6 – 13), the actions (specifically the wiping of the feet) fit the account in Luke 7:36 – 50. It is best to assume that the Fourth Gospel was written with readers in mind who were aware of the other Gospels (see comments on 3:24).

The connection of this previous encounter between the previously anonymous Mary and Jesus is more than a little significant for the story about to be told. Rather than being a meaningless addition

---

7. Richard Bauckham, "The Bethany Family in John 11 – 12: History or Fiction?" in *Testimony of the Beloved Disciple*, 173 – 89 (174).

8. See Adele Reinhartz, "From Narrative to History: The Resurrection of Mary and Martha," in *"Women Like This"*:

New Perspectives on Jewish Women in the Greco-Roman World, ed. Amy-Jill Levine; SBLEJL 1 (Atlanta: Scholars Press, 1991), 161 – 84.

9. Schnackenburg, *John*, 2:321.

or even a "clumsy introduction,"[10] the narrator has established for the reader the intimate relational connection between Jesus and the Bethany family, specifically with both sisters (Luke 10:38 – 42), and especially Mary (Mark 14:3 – 9; Matt 26:6 – 13), who was heralded for her devotion (Mark 14:9). The upcoming request of the sisters in the next verse is no naive request, but the prayer of devoted and exemplary disciples. This explains why v. 1 moved so quickly from Lazarus to focus on Mary (and her sister, Martha). The response of Jesus, not merely the plight of Lazarus, will move to center stage.

11:3 Then the sisters sent to him saying, "Lord, we want you to know that the one whom you love is sick" (ἀπέστειλαν οὖν αἱ ἀδελφαὶ πρὸς αὐτὸν λέγουσαι, Κύριε, ἴδε ὃν φιλεῖς ἀσθενεῖ). The intimate relationship between Jesus and the Bethany family implied by vv. 1 – 2 is made certain in v. 3. The narrator explains that "the sisters" (αἱ ἀδελφαὶ) sent a message to Jesus to inform him of their brother's sickness. The family clearly has close ties to Jesus, evidenced not only by the assumption that they could communicate their situation to Jesus but also by their access to him.

While the title "Lord" (Κύριε) could be simply translated as "sir," the intimacy between Jesus and the family suggests that the sisters are relating to him in a manner that extends beyond polite respect. The word translated more loosely as "we want you to know" (ἴδε) is often merely translated as "behold" or "look," but in this context is "arousing the attention" of Jesus in an emphatic way and therefore can be expressed this way in light of the context.[11] This "message is an indirect request that Jesus should come and heal the sick man."[12] The sisters are speaking with affectionate reverence to Jesus, beckoning him to "see" their plight.

Interestingly, the sisters do not speak of their brother by his name, Lazarus, but as "the one whom you love" (ὃν φιλεῖς). While some have taken this phrase to help identify the Beloved Disciple and potentially the author of the Gospel of John (see Introduction), the designation has a clear narrative function here. In light of vv. 1 – 2, the statement reflects the real and intimate relationship between Jesus and Lazarus and, even more, between Jesus and the Bethany family. The entire Gospel has depicted the love that God has in general for the.00 world (cf. 3:16), but in this moment and for the first time in the Gospel, an individual is described as being loved by God. The narrative is carefully revealing to the reader that the sickness of Lazarus is only part of the conflict of the pericope, for the conflict now also includes the love of God and the nature of its expression.

11:4 After hearing this Jesus said, "This sickness is not for the purpose of death but for the glory of God, so that the Son of God may be glorified through it" (ἀκούσας δὲ ὁ Ἰησοῦς εἶπεν, Αὕτη ἡ ἀσθένεια οὐκ ἔστιν πρὸς θάνατον ἀλλ' ὑπὲρ τῆς δόξης τοῦ θεοῦ, ἵνα δοξασθῇ ὁ υἱὸς τοῦ θεοῦ δι' αὐτῆς). After receiving the message from the sisters, Jesus offers a response that overlaps significantly with what he said earlier to his disciples in regard to the man born blind (see comments on 9:3). Like 9:3, Jesus sees the plight of the Bethany family in a different way and entirely through the lens of "purpose." While the function of the preposition "for the purpose of" (πρὸς) could be result and not purpose (with BDAG preferring the former), the difference is slight at best and the meaning only established in view of the larger context.[13] The larger sense seems to be less that the sickness "would not lead to death" and more "is not for the purpose of death." The fact that Lazarus does die might further suggest

---

10. Barrett, *John*, 387.
11. BDAG 468.
12. Bultmann, *John*, 397.
13. BDAG 874; cf. Wallace, *Greek Grammar*, 380.

that the meaning of this phrase was less result and more purpose. In other words, Jesus speaks less about the conclusion of the sickness and more about the *intention* of the sickness. And this important interpretation of the sickness of Lazarus will be necessary to explain the actions of Jesus to follow.

What is the intention of the sickness? Two things become clear. First, it is not about death but "the glory of God" (τῆς δόξης τοῦ θεοῦ). Just as the first sign was intended to reveal "his glory" (2:11), and the prologue claims a vision of "his glory" (1:14), so also the plight of Lazarus and the Bethany family is intended to make known, reveal, and magnify the glory of God. In light of its OT context, "glory" is "the manifestation of God's being, nature and presence" (see comments on 1:14).[14] In many ways, then, Jesus not only foreshadows what he is about to make manifest through the plight of Lazarus but also what all who believe are intended to see when they look at his creation, and more specifically, when they look at Jesus (cf. 20:31).

Second, it is not about Lazarus but about the "Son of God" (ὁ υἱὸς τοῦ θεοῦ). The glory of God is ultimately exhibited by and expressed in "the Son of God," so that when one gives glory to the Son the entire Trinity is glorified. By this statement the reader is again reminded that everything God wanted to do and to show has been placed at the feet of the Son, the one through whom the Father is known (1:1; cf. Heb 1:1 – 2).

11:5 Jesus loved Martha and her sister and Lazarus (ἠγάπα δὲ ὁ Ἰησοῦς τὴν Μάρθαν καὶ τὴν ἀδελφὴν αὐτῆς καὶ τὸν Λάζαρον). In light of the previous statement, this description of the love

of Jesus for the Bethany family is remarkable, for it demands that the reader not see the purpose of God — even displayed through the plight of Lazarus — as outside the intention with which God loves the world and the people in it.[15] The fact that the narrator adds this parenthetical statement gives support to reading v. 4 as a claim by Jesus to embrace and include within his mission and purpose the difficulties of life, even death. With the narrator's direction the reader is corrected from a possible misinterpretation of v. 4 and v. 6.[16]

11:6 However, when he heard that Lazarus was sick, he remained in the place where he was two days (ὡς οὖν ἤκουσεν ὅτι ἀσθενεῖ, τότε μὲν ἔμεινεν ἐν ᾧ ἦν τόπῳ δύο ἡμέρας). Without any explanation, the narrator describes how Jesus, even after hearing about Lazarus's plight, stayed where he was "two days" (δύο ἡμέρας). It is significant that the motive for the delay is not stated. It is common for interpreters to reconstruct the reasons motivating the delay. Yet there is little warrant for basing an interpretation upon possible but entirely unknown (and unstated) variables.

For this reason v. 5 — which reminds the reader of the love of Christ for those involved in this crisis — is so significant, especially coming between v. 4 and v. 6 as it does. Quite simply, if God is intentional with the event of sickness and death, he can also be intentional with his response to such events. The mode in which God works, even if different than expected, must not be attributed to incompetence or insensitivity but as befitting his greater purposes, even if unseen.[17] In a moment of crisis, the "however" of God (v. 6) is not to be believed more than the "love" of God (v. 5).

---

14. Dodd, *Interpretation*, 206.

15. While there is an interesting change in the Greek word for love between v. 3 "love" (φιλεῖς) and v. 5 "loved" (ἠγάπα), we would be wrong to make too strong of a distinction in meaning as many have been prone to do. The Gospel uses the

two words in what is generally an interchangeable manner (see comments on 21:15).

16. Cf. Barrett, *John*, 390.

17. See Calvin, *John 11 – 21*, 3: "Christ is the unique mirror of divine grace."

11:7 **Then after this he said to the disciples, "Let us go to Judea again"** (ἔπειτα μετὰ τοῦτο λέγει τοῖς μαθηταῖς, Ἄγωμεν εἰς τὴν Ἰουδαίαν πάλιν). After the two-day delay, Jesus announced to his disciples that it was time to go back to Judea. The double note about time, "then" (ἔπειτα) and "after this" (μετὰ τοῦτο), places emphasis on the delay.[18] Jesus mentions "Judea" not "Bethany" because it was in the general region of Judea that Jesus had encountered severe opposition (7:1).

11:8 **The disciples said to him, "Rabbi, the Jews are now seeking to stone you, and you are going there again?"** (λέγουσιν αὐτῷ οἱ μαθηταί, Ῥαββί, νῦν ἐζήτουν σε λιθάσαι οἱ Ἰουδαῖοι, καὶ πάλιν ὑπάγεις ἐκεῖ;). Aware of the intention of the Jews to bring the ministry (and influence) of Jesus to an end, the disciples offer advice to Jesus that serves as a counter to his just-announced plan. For the last time in the Gospel, the disciples address Jesus as "Rabbi" (Ῥαββί), an honorific title (see comments on 1:38) that the reader cannot help but see as nearsighted. The Gospel does not want the reader to believe in a "rabbi" but in "the Christ, the Son of God" (20:31). It is not merely his title that will be expanded but his intention. Rather than avoiding the murderous intentions of the Jews in Judea, it was for this very reason that Christ came to the world. In a unique twist, the narrative places before the reader a paradoxical comparison: the death Jesus is about to remove from the body of Lazarus he will not do for himself. In fact, as the reader is beginning to grasp, it is only by means of Jesus's death that true life can ever be given, not just to Lazarus or his sisters or the disciples, but to the whole world. While the death of Lazarus will give Jesus the opportunity to prove he loves the Bethany family (v. 5), the death of Jesus will give God the opportunity to prove he loves the whole world (cf. 3:16).[19]

11:9 **Jesus answered, "Are there not twelve hours during the day? If a person is walking in the day he will not stumble, because he sees the light of this world"** (ἀπεκρίθη Ἰησοῦς, Οὐχὶ δώδεκα ὧραί εἰσιν τῆς ἡμέρας; ἐάν τις περιπατῇ ἐν τῇ ἡμέρᾳ, οὐ προσκόπτει, ὅτι τὸ φῶς τοῦ κόσμου τούτου βλέπει). Jesus responds to the misguided concern of his disciples with an illustration that explains what the disciples are misunderstanding.[20] In the ancient world, time was much less precise and counted generally by the amount of daylight, which for both Jews and Romans was divided into twelve equal "hours" which occupied the whole period between sunrise and sunset.[21] The illustration therefore depicts the time, established naturally — by God — for a person to move, work, and live. Outside of that time, that is, at night, movement is hindered (even dangerous) and therefore limited (see v. 10; cf. 9:4).

11:10 **"But if a person walks in the night he will stumble, because the light is not in him"** (ἐὰν δέ τις περιπατῇ ἐν τῇ νυκτί, προσκόπτει, ὅτι τὸ φῶς οὐκ ἔστιν ἐν αὐτῷ). Jesus concludes the illustration by describing the inability of a person who attempts to walk in the night. Again, the reason that is given employs a play on words: "The light is not in him" (τὸ φῶς οὐκ ἔστιν ἐν αὐτῷ). Rather than saying the person "has no light" (an external condition), Jesus declares that the light is not "in him" (an internal condition). The real issue, according to this play on words, is the internal condition of the person, the darkness of the person. In this way, the reader is reminded of the state of humanity de-

---

18. Morris, *John*, 480.
19. Cf. Hoskyns, *Fourth Gospel*, 400.

20. We use the designation "illustration" loosely, for no specific description is given by the narrator (see comments on 10:6).
21. Cf. Morris, *John*, 480.

clared by the prologue and the centrality of Jesus as "the light of humanity" (1:4 – 5).[22]

By this statement Jesus has not only redefined the solution but also redefined the problem. The problem is not the Jews or the threat of death, just as the sickness — even death — of Lazarus is not the real problem. The real problem is the cosmological problem that the ministry of Jesus as a whole was addressing, the solution to which was found in his body, his flesh (1:14). Ironically, the disciples (and all Christians) could not be more secure as they enter life-threatening situations (e.g., Judea), than when they are right where they are supposed to be: "In him." The love of Christ (v. 5) is not to be defined by our location in regard to danger and death but by our location in regard to Christ, befitting his purposes and his glory (v. 4).

11:11 He said this, and after this said to them, "Lazarus, our friend, has fallen asleep, but I am going in order to wake him up" (ταῦτα εἶπεν, καὶ μετὰ τοῦτο λέγει αὐτοῖς, Λάζαρος ὁ φίλος ἡμῶν κεκοίμηται, ἀλλὰ πορεύομαι ἵνα ἐξυπνίσω αὐτόν). Jesus now gives the specific reason for their return to Judea. The fact that Lazarus is referred to as "our friend" (ὁ φίλος ἡμῶν) by Jesus reinforces the established relationship between Jesus and the Bethany family (cf. v. 3), for even the disciples consider him a friend. According to Jesus, Lazarus has "fallen asleep" (κεκοίμηται), which in the ancient world was used metaphorically to speak of death. In the NT, the term is used four times to speak of literal sleep and fourteen times to speak of death.[23] The multiple senses of "sleep" and "wake up" (ἐξυπνίσω) are about to be explained in the verses to follow.

11:12 Then the disciples said to him, "Lord, if he sleeps he will be better" (εἶπαν οὖν οἱ μαθηταὶ αὐτῷ, Κύριε, εἰ κεκοίμηται σωθήσεται). The disciples clearly misunderstand Jesus's statement regarding Lazarus. He is not taking a nap; he is dead. The disciples are almost offering encouragement to Jesus, suggesting that the rest will do him good. What is significant, however, is not merely what the disciples say, but the way in which their statement offers an interpretation of Jesus's statement. The disciples obviously interpreted Jesus's statement as less severe than death. While they were clearly confused at a medical level, they were hardly wrong in their interpretation of what Jesus had said. The plain sense and tone of Jesus's statement must have expressed not dire concern but the description of something that can (and would!) be overcome. Jesus would "wake" Lazarus from his rest. In that sense, the disciples understood Jesus perfectly.

11:13 But Jesus had been speaking about his death, but they thought he was speaking about natural sleep (εἰρήκει δὲ ὁ Ἰησοῦς περὶ τοῦ θανάτου αὐτοῦ. ἐκεῖνοι δὲ ἔδοξαν ὅτι περὶ τῆς κοιμήσεως τοῦ ὕπνου λέγει). The narrator intrudes again and offers another significant parenthetical statement, as in v. 5, which guides the reader to the correct interpretation of the scene and its meaning. It is common for interpreters to highlight what the disciples got wrong, specifically the misinterpretation of the word that can mean both "sleep" and "death."[24] But the confusion is not to be unexpected, and the exchange might be better viewed as another example of Jesus's playful and rhetorical use of words. The narrator is helping the reader to understand Jesus, not the disciples, making sure that the significance of what was just said be applied correctly to what is about to take place.[25]

The significance of this clarification of what Jesus understands to be happening with Lazarus

---

22. Bultmann, *John*, 399.
23. Morris, *John*, 481.

24. Cf. Hans Förster, "Johannes 11:11 – 14 — ein typisches johanneisches Missverständnis?" *NovT* 53 (2011): 338 – 57.
25. Contra Brant, *John*, 173.

is vitally important for the reader. While the use of "sleep" for death was not a Christian invention, for it is also found in ancient secular writings, it was much more characteristic of Christians.[26] When Jesus described Lazarus's condition, he used a word that embraced the historically perceived condition of Lazarus with the cosmological vision of the Son of Man, about whom the prologue declared, "In the Word was life" (1:4). Augustine suggests the same when he writes, "It was in reference to His own power that He spoke of him as sleeping."[27] To the disciples (and to the honest reader), Lazarus's status had separated him from his sisters and placed him in the custody of that which comes after this life, but to Jesus Lazarus had not even come close to leaving the Son's custody or domain, for the Father has given the authority of life and death to the Son (5:22 – 29).

11:14 So then Jesus said to them plainly, "Lazarus is dead" (τότε οὖν εἶπεν αὐτοῖς ὁ Ἰησοῦς παρρησία, Λάζαρος ἀπέθανεν). By beginning with "so then" (τότε οὖν), the narrative shows the chronological progression of the dialogue, helping the reader make sense of the change in Jesus's explanation.[28] The narrator's introduction to Jesus's statement is itself evidence that Jesus had spoken at first to the disciples in a rhetorically significant expression or mode. The use of the adverb "plainly" (παρρησία) confirms that Jesus had previously spoken to the disciples with intentional symbolism (see comments on 10:6). In a sense, Jesus first spoke with regard to the cosmological plot involving Lazarus but now speaks at the level of the historical plot. That is why the narrator's instruction in v. 13 is so important for the reader, for it explains what Jesus had in mind; it explains the

connection Jesus was making between his person and life and death.

11:15 "And I rejoice for you that I was not there, in order that you might believe. But let us go to him" (καὶ χαίρω δι᾽ ὑμᾶς, ἵνα πιστεύσητε, ὅτι οὐκ ἤμην ἐκεῖ· ἀλλὰ ἄγωμεν πρὸς αὐτόν). This is a remarkable statement by Jesus that is entirely dependent on our interpretation of the previous verses. Taken on its own, even in context, it is marked by a certain degree of harshness. Even though Jesus is not glad that Lazarus is dead, his ability to rejoice in it for the sake of others, as if Lazarus's death were a means to an end, is difficult to understand. Attempts to explain the grammar or to provide an alternate sense of the words fail to provide an adequate solution.[29] Jesus's statement can only be understood when one apprehends what he has already implied about death; namely, that death is not the end and is not supposed to be viewed as such. Like the plight of the blind man in 9:1 – 3, Jesus speaks with a cosmological vision that demands the subordination of all human circumstance and reality. Clearly Jesus is not using Lazarus for another end — he loves Lazarus (v. 5). At the same time, Jesus the Word, the one through whom all things were made (1:3), is in absolute control of all things, unbound by circumstance and time — even life and death — and cannot help but see the work of God and the value of God in all things.

Our interpretation is given merit by Jesus's exhortation to his disciples, "Let us go to him" (ἄγωμεν πρὸς αὐτόν). The choice of words is striking. Jesus does not suggest a return to Lazarus's sisters but specifically "to him," as if he were not dead but still living.[30] This prepositional phrase explains the manner in which Jesus has been addressing the

26. Morris, *John*, 481.
27. Augustine, *John*, 49.9.273.
28. BDAG 1012.
29. See Stephen Voorwinde, *Jesus's Emotions in the Fourth Gospel: Human or Divine*, LNTS 284 (London: T&T Clark, 2005), 162 – 68.
30. Cf. Michaels, *John*, 623; Barrett, *John*, 393; Hoskyns, *Fourth Gospel*, 401.

entire Lazarus plight. The tension depicted by this pericope between death and love in vv. 4 – 6 and death and life in vv. 11 – 14 is solved in the person and work of Jesus (cf. Rom 8:38 – 39). It is worth noting that this verse offers unparalleled insight into a source of joy for God. With this verse, the reader learns that the faith his disciples place in him is what brings joy to God. God rejoices when we trust him.

11:16 Then Thomas (called Didymus) said to his fellow disciples: "Let us go also in order that we may die with him" (εἶπεν οὖν Θωμᾶς ὁ λεγόμενος Δίδυμος τοῖς συμμαθηταῖς, Ἄγωμεν καὶ ἡμεῖς ἵνα ἀποθάνωμεν μετ' αὐτοῦ). The introduction and setting of the pericope concludes with this important statement by Thomas. The disciple named Thomas is known more for his doubting than his courageous belief (see comments on 20:24 – 29). The narrator's explanatory addition of "called Didymus" (ὁ λεγόμενος Δίδυμος), which means "twin," is almost certainly the provision of his nickname and the name by which he was more generally known. There is no need to speculate regarding his twin, as though his nickname would not make sense on its own; his twin may well have had nothing to do with Jesus and his public following.[31] As implied by the scene, Thomas is "one of the Twelve" (20:24), and his exhortation to "his fellow disciples" (τοῖς συμμαθηταῖς), a term that only occurs here in the NT, is probably intended to reflect the feeling of the entire group.[32]

Thomas's statement serves as a reminder to the reader that the disciples' original concern was that the place where Lazarus had died and the place to where they must now go — Judea — was the same place where the Jews were even now trying to kill Jesus (cf. v. 8). In one sense, the statement completely overlooks what Jesus had just finished saying in regard to the plight of Lazarus that even death was under the authority of the Son of Man. Yet in another sense, the statement is a faithful response to the "rejoicing" of Jesus in v. 14. Thomas is motivated to respond to Jesus in a fitting manner, even if it involves loss. While such a response is honorable and a sign of vigorous faith (v. 14), it is clearly misguided in one important way. It is not their lives but the life of Jesus that is to suffer loss. By speaking beyond what he himself could see or understand, Thomas exhorts all believers to believe in Christ, even when such belief extends beyond oneself.[33] In this way the introduction and setting of this lengthy pericope comes to an end.

11:17 After he arrived, Jesus found that Lazarus had already been in the tomb for four days (Ἐλθὼν οὖν ὁ Ἰησοῦς εὗρεν αὐτὸν τέσσαρας ἤδη ἡμέρας ἔχοντα ἐν τῷ μνημείῳ). The conflict of the pericope begins the moment Jesus arrives on the scene. For all the details not provided by the narrator, the insight regarding the four days Lazarus had already spent in the tomb is significant. The four days will not only become significant as the narrative develops, but they also confirm that Lazarus is truly dead. Lazarus is not simply sick or near death; he is already in the process of decay (cf. v. 39). There is no room for the "swoon theory" here.

11:18 Bethany was near Jerusalem, about two miles away (ἦν δὲ ἡ Βηθανία ἐγγὺς τῶν Ἰεροσολύμων ὡς ἀπὸ σταδίων δεκαπέντε). The geographic details are given so as to explain the visit of many Jews in v. 19. Yet it also serves to locate Jesus near Jerusalem, the place where Jesus's ministry will find its conclusion. According to the narrator, Bethany was a distance of "fifteen" (δεκαπέντε) *stadia* (σταδίων); a *stadion* was the length of a Roman stadium,

---

31. Bauckham, *Jesus and the Eyewitnesses*, 105.
32. Cf. Morris, *John*, 483.

33. Thomas is courageous in faith with Jesus beside him (ch. 11); he will be much less so when Jesus is absent (ch. 20).

which was about 197 meters or about 607 feet.[34] Thus, Bethany was between 1.7 and 1.85 miles from Jerusalem, hence our translation "about two miles away."

11:19 And many of the Jews had come to Martha and Mary in order to comfort them in regard to their brother (πολλοὶ δὲ ἐκ τῶν Ἰουδαίων ἐληλύθεισαν πρὸς τὴν Μάρθαν καὶ Μαριὰμ ἵνα παραμυθήσωνται αὐτὰς περὶ τοῦ ἀδελφοῦ). This verse provides further context for the conflict of the pericope. The disciples had already voiced their concern about returning to Judea because of the threats against Jesus's life (v. 8), and the narrator's depiction of the presence of "the Jews" reminds the reader of the Gospel's larger conflict regarding Jesus. In light of the Gospel's depiction of "the Jews" as antagonists and opponents of Jesus (see comments on 1:19), their more favorable and neutral presence here is important to note. At the level of the narrative, the presence of "the Jews" connects Jesus and the Lazarus event to the Jewish authorities later in the pericope (see vv. 45–46). But their presence also helps situate the ministry of Jesus in its very Jewish context, magnifying the tension that Jesus had already created in and around Jerusalem.

The narrator explains that the Jews had come for the purpose of comforting the family. It was required in first-century Judaism that the deceased be buried on the day of death (cf. the immediate burial of Ananias and Sapphira in Acts 5:5–6, 10), which was followed by six further days of mourning (for a total of seven), known as *shiva* (i.e., "seven days"), during which the bereaved family would remain at home while others came to supply food and express sympathy.[35] "The Jews," in spite of all their failings thus far in the Gospel, are depicted as faithful to their religious tradition and to

their friends/neighbors by attending to the needs of Martha and Mary.

11:20 Then Martha, when she heard that Jesus was coming, went out to meet him, but Mary was remaining in the house (ἡ οὖν Μάρθα ὡς ἤκουσεν ὅτι Ἰησοῦς ἔρχεται ὑπήντησεν αὐτῷ· Μαριὰμ δὲ ἐν τῷ οἴκῳ ἐκαθέζετο). The narrative now turns its attention to the sisters of Lazarus, who will be involved in a significant dialogue with Jesus for the remainder of the scene (vv. 17–37). The narrator offers an interesting insight into the sisters by describing their response to the news that Jesus was arriving at their home. Our translation of the verb "went out to meet" (ὑπήντησεν) treats it as an ingressive rather than a constative aorist, which places the focus of the description on the detailed response of Martha.[36]

Some interpreters have argued that the reason Martha left the house and went to Jesus is because he was hiding outside of the village for fear of "the Jews" and waiting for a safe escort to her home. This interpretation often highlights v. 30 as further evidence that Jesus was afraid to go to the house because of the Jews. But not only does this response find no comparison in the rest of the Gospel's portrayal of Jesus's concerns and fears, but it also disregards the rebuke Jesus had just given to his disciples for their own such fears (vv. 8–10). The reason Jesus did not go to the home is because it was not time for ceremonial and religious mourning (see comments on v. 30). Martha's response is rather a reflection of her devotion to Jesus. Although it would have been expected according to religious custom for Martha to remain in her home and let Jesus come to her and express his sympathy, she paid him great respect by going out to greet him, even at the cost of offending those who had already come to her and her sister. In the ancient

---

34. BDAG 940.
35. Keener, *John*, 2:842.

36. See Wallace, *Greek Grammar*, 558.

world one would honor a person by meeting them as they approached and conducting them to their destination.[37]

In what is probably intended to be a form of contrast, while Martha had departed to meet Jesus, Mary "was remaining" (ἐκαθέζετο) in the house, a verb which can also be translated as "was sitting."[38] The point of contrast need not be taken to mean that Mary's faith or commitment to Jesus was inferior, for Mary was clearly following protocol in regard to the religious and ceremonial procedures following the death of her brother.[39] What's more, Mary is quick to respond to Jesus in vv. 29 – 31, which might suggest she had not even heard of Jesus's arrival. But this does not mean that a contrast was not implied.[40] As the interaction to follow will reveal, both sisters were dealing with the reality of death and the nature of grief at different levels. Perhaps more importantly, both sisters will also deal with Jesus differently, and Jesus was about to address them both in a manner that befitted not only their needs but also his person and work.

11:21 Then Martha said to Jesus, "Lord, if you had been here, my brother would not have died" (εἶπεν οὖν ἡ Μάρθα πρὸς τὸν Ἰησοῦν, Κύριε, εἰ ἦς ὧδε οὐκ ἂν ἀπέθανεν ὁ ἀδελφός μου). The respect Martha paid to Jesus by going out to greet him is counterbalanced by her first-recorded words for him. While several interpreters take her statement as "an expression of faith,"[41] by speaking in the form of a conditional statement Martha is actually offering an indirect rebuke, especially when examined using speech act theory.[42] Conditional sentences are often employed to communicate *indirectly* what

would be harsh if communicated directly; the protasis (the if-clause) serves as "a mitigator or politeness marker."[43] What Martha was implicitly saying to Jesus was, "Lord, you should have been here!"

11:22 "But even now I know that whatever you ask God, God will give to you" ([ἀλλὰ] καὶ νῦν οἶδα ὅτι ὅσα ἂν αἰτήσῃ τὸν θεὸν δώσει σοι ὁ θεός). For the interpreters who take v. 21 as an expression of faith, this verse is "puzzling,"[44] primarily because in v. 39 Martha will not express the high faith these words might imply. But by taking v. 21 as an indirect rebuke of Jesus, this verse offers further clarification. Martha's statement is correct in what it affirms. Jesus has real and current — "even now" (καὶ νῦν) — access to God; about this Martha is certain ("I know" [οἶδα]). However, Martha's statement is incorrect about what it implicitly denies, for it fails to reflect true faith *in* Jesus, the Son of God. By using "generic God" language as she stands before God the Son, Martha reveals an inadequate understanding of Jesus Christ, the one to whom God has given authority to render judgment, because he is the Son of Man (5:27).

11:23 Jesus said to her, "Your brother will rise" (λέγει αὐτῇ ὁ Ἰησοῦς, Ἀναστήσεται ὁ ἀδελφός σου). In the context of a rebuke, Jesus begins his response to Martha. Without correcting her confusion, Jesus speaks on the authority he has received from the Father. Although several translations have "will rise again," the addition of "again" — a word not in the Greek — attempts to clarify what is clearly an ambiguous statement, as Martha's interpretation of it makes clear (v. 24). The ambiguity is not intended to be a play between final resurrection, as Martha

---

37. Keener, *John*, 2:843.

38. BDAG 492.

39. Cf. Ridderbos, *John*, 394.

40. Cf. Bultmann, *John*, 401.

41. Morris, *John*, 487. See also Schnackenburg, *John*, 2:329; Carson, *John*, 411 – 12.

42. Helpful here is R. A. Young, "A Classification of Conditional Sentences Based on Speech Act Theory," *GTJ* 10 (1980): 29 – 49.

43. Ibid., 42. Cf. Wallace, *Greek Grammar*, 703.

44. Morris, *John*, 487.

takes it, and the immediate resurrection of Lazarus about to transpire, but is intended as a statement that encompasses both. Jesus himself — in the eternally established power and authority of his person as the Son of Man — is resurrection (v. 25).

11:24 Martha said to him, "I know that he will rise in the resurrection in the last day" (λέγει αὐτῷ ἡ Μάρθα, Οἶδα ὅτι ἀναστήσεται ἐν τῇ ἀναστάσει ἐν τῇ ἐσχάτῃ ἡμέρᾳ). Jesus's words are again mistakenly understood (see vv. 11 – 14). Martha believes that Jesus speaks on the linear-historical level about the resurrection at the end of human history, a belief common in Judaism (though a point of debate between Pharisees and Sadducees; cf. Mark 12:18 – 27; Acts 23:8; Josephus, *J.W.* 2.163). By these words Martha is finding solace in the promise of God that he will right all things in the end. One might even say that Martha's words, "I know" (Οἶδα), contain an undertone of dissatisfaction.[45] Was this to be Martha's comfort, her solace "from above?" Not at all! Jesus was not offering solace in the final resurrection, as grand and true as that may (and should) be, but in his person, as his next words will make clear.

11:25 Jesus said to her, "I am the resurrection and the life. The one who believes in me will live, even if he dies" (εἶπεν αὐτῇ ὁ Ἰησοῦς, Ἐγώ εἰμι ἡ ἀνάστασις καὶ ἡ ζωή· ὁ πιστεύων εἰς ἐμὲ κᾶν ἀποθάνῃ ζήσεται). Like with the disciples' misunderstanding of his depiction of the death of Lazarus (cf. v. 14), Jesus now speaks to Martha plainly: "I am the resurrection and the life" (Ἐγώ εἰμι ἡ ἀνάστασις καὶ ἡ ζωή). This is the fifth of seven formal "I am" statements in the Gospel, each containing "I am" (Ἐγώ εἰμι) and a predicate (see comments on 6:35; cf. 8:58). These seven "I am" statements are emphatic descriptions of the person

and ministry of Jesus and cumulatively form a detailed picture of Jesus Christ.

In the context of Jesus's discussion with Martha, the occurrence of the "I am" statement is significant. Jesus does not say he will provide resurrection and life, but that he *is* resurrection and life. The combination of "resurrection and life" is also important. Since the former is more generally applied to the future (cf. v. 24) and the latter more generally applied to the present, their combination here demands that they both maintain an eschatological and present application. For example, "life" must now be understood to be "an eschatological phenomenon,"[46] just as "resurrection" can no longer be confined to the resurrection "in the last day." The two predicates, resurrection and life, speak to the same subject matter; "by a paradoxical mode of expression they remove the concepts of death and life into another sphere, for which human death and human life are only images and hints."[47] That is, Jesus's statement here is only defined by the cosmological strand of the Gospel's plot introduced by the prologue: "In the Word was life" (1:4). For this reason, "What to the Jews is a future hope is to Christians a present reality."[48]

The connection between this paradoxical existence of resurrection and life and the Christian is located in faith in Jesus. Jesus offers this mode of existence to "the one who believes in me" (ὁ πιστεύων εἰς ἐμέ). Here Jesus claims for himself the authority over life and death given to him by the Father (cf. 5:21 – 29). It is important to note that this resurrection and life are both coming and not yet; as Jesus explained it, "An hour *comes and now is* when the dead will hear the voice of the Son of God and those who hear will live" (5:25). In this way, "belief" in Jesus is faith placed in the person of Jesus, so that Jesus is both the promise of the provi-

---

45. Ibid., 396.
46. Bultmann, *John*, 403.

47. Ibid.
48. Hoskyns, *Fourth Gospel*, 402.

sion of God for the future and the present reality of the provision of God. This is a paradoxical intrusion of the cosmological into the historical without contrast or contradiction.[49]

11:26 "And everyone who lives and believes in me will never die. Do you believe this?" (καὶ πᾶς ὁ ζῶν καὶ πιστεύων εἰς ἐμὲ οὐ μὴ ἀποθάνῃ εἰς τὸν αἰῶνα· πιστεύεις τοῦτο;). After explaining the limitation of physical death (the historical), Jesus now explains the benefit of spiritual life (the cosmological): "Everyone who lives and believes in me will never die" (πᾶς ὁ ζῶν καὶ πιστεύων εἰς ἐμὲ οὐ μὴ ἀποθάνῃ εἰς τὸν αἰῶνα). While the first of the two parallel statements, "even if he dies," is straightforward (found in v. 25), this second parallel statement oddly includes the phrase "everyone who lives" (ὁ ζῶν) instead of merely assuming that those who might believe would logically be alive. The reason is that the "life" of those who "believe in" Jesus is an entirely different life. It is not just that the Christian is given a different *degree* of life (more life — eternal life) but that they are given a different *kind* of life — a different life altogether.

The Christian life is life without the constraints of death. "Faith in Jesus does not make humans immortal. What it does bring about is that from this moment on they no longer live under the power of death."[50] The powerlessness of death over the believer is described with a redundant and emphatic expression that denies death its position of authority ("will never die" [οὐ μὴ ἀποθάνῃ εἰς τὸν αἰῶνα]; cf. 8:51). All such authority — over life and death itself — has been given by the Father to the Son, Jesus Christ (5:21 – 29). For this reason, belief in Jesus is the act of submitting to the authority of the Son of God, the creator of all things (1:3). This belief entails finding one's end (death) secured in

Jesus (both present and future) and one's beginning (life) renewed and redefined in Jesus so that one is "free indeed" (8:36), unencumbered by the slavery of sin, having received the full rights of sonship in the house of God forever (8:34 – 35).

It is in light of the foregoing context that Jesus's concluding question to Martha must be understood. The rebuke of Martha, even if only indirect (v. 21), is now seen by the reader to be a categorical misunderstanding. It was not Jesus's *presence* that was the issue, as if had he been there this would not have happened. No, what was important was his *position* of authority over life and death, a position not confined by distance (a journey to Bethany) or time (four days in the tomb). Martha had made Jesus merely a divine steward. This was not only a misunderstanding regarding Jesus, but it was inappropriate belief in God. Faith in God *is* faith in Christ. For this reason Jesus concludes his robust declaration, the fifth "I am" statement, with a rejoinder in the form of a question to Martha — and to the reader: "Do you believe this?" (πιστεύεις τοῦτο;). The question is really asking, "Do you believe in me?" That is, Jesus asks Martha whether she believes in his person and work.

11:27 She said to him, "Yes, Lord, I have believed that you are the Christ, the Son of God who has come into the world" (λέγει αὐτῷ, Ναί, κύριε· ἐγὼ πεπίστευκα ὅτι σὺ εἶ ὁ Χριστὸς ὁ υἱὸς τοῦ θεοῦ ὁ εἰς τὸν κόσμον ἐρχόμενος). Martha responds with a collection of emphatics. The "Yes, Lord" (Ναί, κύριε) reveals the personal nature of her claim. What is slightly out of place is the perfect tense, "I have believed" (ἐγὼ πεπίστευκα), which is less fitting as a response than a present-tense verb would have been, which is why several versions translate it as a present ("I believe"; e.g., NIV; NRSV; ESV).

---

49. As Ridderbos explains, "This is not a 'spiritualization' of the resurrection — see the sequel! — nor does the resurrection become a timeless datum that is therefore cancelled out or

meaningless as a future event" (*John*, 397).

50. Ibid.

The perfect gives force to the confession without demanding that Martha had already come to believe this about Jesus. (For a similar confession by Peter, see 6:69.) It is best to view Martha's confessional statement as entirely focused on Jesus. In fact, Martha's confession matches nearly word for word the confession that the Gospel desires for all of its readers (see 20:31). The additional element of Martha's confession, "who has come into the world," is clearly not unique to the Gospel as a whole. In fact, this addition is a core message of the entire Gospel from the prologue onward (e.g., 1:15, 27, 30; 4:25; 6:14; 12:13).[51]

11:28 And after she had said this, she went and quietly called Mary, her sister, saying, "The teacher is here and is calling for you" (Καὶ ταῦτα εἰποῦσα ἀπῆλθεν καὶ ἐφώνησεν Μαριὰμ τὴν ἀδελφὴν αὐτῆς λάθρᾳ εἰποῦσα, Ὁ διδάσκαλος πάρεστιν καὶ φωνεῖ σε). The narrative transitions from Martha to her sister Mary. After finishing her discussion with Jesus, Martha returns and informs Mary that Jesus has arrived. The narrator explains that Martha spoke to Mary "quietly" (λάθρᾳ), that is, privately or without others being aware.[52] This may suggest that Martha was trying to draw Mary away from the ceremonial and religious mourning procedures she would have been expected to participate in. Martha calls Jesus "the teacher" (Ὁ διδάσκαλος), a term which might be a mere synonym for "rabbi" (see comments on 3:2). It may also be significant that Jesus is described as "calling" (φωνεῖ) or "summoning" Mary. The narrator does not give us a reason but simply describes how Jesus had not yet entered the village (v. 30). The narrator is careful to depict Jesus as outside of the ceremonial and religious mourning, for

Jesus alone is the one who authorizes death and its ceremonies.

11:29 And when she heard that, she got up quickly and went to him (ἐκείνη δὲ ὡς ἤκουσεν ἠγέρθη ταχὺ καὶ ἤρχετο πρὸς αὐτόν). The narrator's language suggests that Mary responded to her sister's message without delay, as if she were getting up while Martha was still speaking. Although their responses to Jesus occur at different times (and in slightly different ways), clearly both respond in a timely manner. The contrast between the sisters' encounters with Jesus is at least in part intended to depict the ongoing ceremonial and religious mourning taking place at their home and its distance from Jesus.

11:30 But Jesus had not yet come to the village, but was still at the place where Martha had met him (οὔπω δὲ ἐληλύθει ὁ Ἰησοῦς εἰς τὴν κώμην, ἀλλ᾽ ἦν ἔτι ἐν τῷ τόπῳ ὅπου ὑπήντησεν αὐτῷ ἡ Μάρθα). The narrator again reminds the reader of the distance between Jesus and the ceremonial and religious mourning, explaining that Jesus had not yet entered the village but was still located where Martha had earlier met him. This statement is not intended to describe Jesus as timid and fearful of "the Jews" (see comments on v. 20), for certainly Jesus is not tempted to embrace a fear of the death and life he upholds by his own authority.

11:31 Then the Jews, who had been with her in the house and comforting her, saw that Mary got up quickly and went out, they followed her, thinking that she was going to the tomb in order to weep there (οἱ οὖν Ἰουδαῖοι οἱ ὄντες μετ᾽ αὐτῆς ἐν τῇ οἰκίᾳ καὶ παραμυθούμενοι αὐτήν, ἰδόντες τὴν Μαριὰμ ὅτι ταχέως ἀνέστη καὶ ἐξῆλθεν,

---

51. See Andrew C. Brunson, *Psalm 118 in the Gospel of John: An Intertextual Study on the New Exodus Pattern in the Theology of John*, WUNT 2.158 (Tübingen: Mohr Siebeck, 2003), 240–57.

52. BDAG 581.

ἠκολούθησαν αὐτῇ, δόξαντες ὅτι ὑπάγει εἰς τὸ μνημεῖον ἵνα κλαύσῃ ἐκεῖ). The departure of Mary from the ceremonial mourning attracted the attention of the other mourners, the Jews, who had come to comfort the Bethany family (see v. 19). The narrator describes how the Jews, upon noticing the quickness of Mary's departure, suppose that she was moving the ceremonial mourning from her house to the tomb of Lazarus. Since family tombs were frequently near family residences,[53] it is likely that they considered her immediate departure to the tomb as an intentional and formal development in the ceremony (cf. Wis 19:3).

11:32 When Mary came where Jesus was, after seeing him she fell at his feet, saying to him, "Lord, if you were here my brother would not have died" (ἡ οὖν Μαριὰμ ὡς ἦλθεν ὅπου ἦν Ἰησοῦς ἰδοῦσα αὐτὸν ἔπεσεν αὐτοῦ πρὸς τοὺς πόδας, λέγουσα αὐτῷ, Κύριε, εἰ ἧς ὧδε οὐκ ἄν μου ἀπέθανεν ὁ ἀδελφός). When Mary reaches Jesus, she says the exact same thing her sister Martha had said. As with Martha, this statement is an implicit chastisement of Jesus for not doing what he alone can do (see comments on v. 21). And similar to Martha, Mary combines her indirect rebuke of Jesus not with further words of faith in "God" (see v. 22) but with action. According to the narrator, "after seeing him" (ἰδοῦσα αὐτὸν) Mary "fell at his feet" (ἔπεσεν αὐτοῦ πρὸς τοὺς πόδας). The action must only be interpreted with extreme caution as either "greater devotion"[54] or as nothing more than "the first step of faith, from which her sister advanced."[55] With what is probably an equally confused confession, Mary says with action what Martha said with words that Jesus is the God-connected solution (see v. 22).[56] With her words she indirectly rebukes him, yet by her actions she overtly worships him.

11:33 When Jesus saw her weeping and the weeping of the Jews who had come with her, he was outraged in spirit and troubled in himself (Ἰησοῦς οὖν ὡς εἶδεν αὐτὴν κλαίουσαν καὶ τοὺς συνελθόντας αὐτῇ Ἰουδαίους κλαίοντας, ἐνεβριμήσατο τῷ πνεύματι καὶ ἐτάραξεν ἑαυτόν). Just as Jesus responded to the words of Martha with a formative statement of his own, he likewise responds to Mary's actions. While v. 32 said nothing of Mary "weeping" (κλαίουσαν), here the narrator says that both Mary and "the Jews" were weeping in the presence of Jesus. With Mary at his feet weeping, the narrator describes the response of Jesus, which is notoriously difficult to interpret. Not only is it difficult to know exactly *what* Jesus was doing — the terminology is rare and difficult to define — but it is also difficult to know *why* he responded in such a manner. We must address these issues in turn.

First, what was the response of Jesus? The verb we've translated as "was outraged" (ἐνεβριμήσατο) is used in two basic ways: 1) as an expression of anger or displeasure, and 2) as an expression of emotion.[57] While option (2) is common in English translations ("deeply moved" [ESV, NASB, NIV, RSV]; "groaned" [KJV, RV]; "sighed heavily/deeply" [NEB]; "deeply touched" [GNB]; "greatly disturbed" [NRSV]), in German translations option (1) is the dominant translation, established by Luther's translation of the verb as "angry" (*ergrimmen*). Because the verb is unusual, it is difficult to know how to translate it, especially in this context, and even more so in regard to Jesus, the one who "loves" (v. 5). But the term cannot be flattened in a manner that makes a more comfortable (i.e., less angry) Jesus. In the majority of contexts in which it occurs, the verb expresses anger or displeasure,

53. Keener, *John*, 2:845.
54. Barrett, *John*, 398.
55. Bultmann, *John*, 405.
56. Stibbe, "A Tomb with a View," 47.
57. BDAG 322.

that is, option (1).[58] This is almost unanimously agreed upon by interpreters.[59] The only problem, then, is how to make sense of this in the context of the Lazarus story.

This is not to say, however, that option (2) does not have warrant, for certainly Jesus's reaction could be taken as more about grief than anger. It is a mistake to make too large of a distinction between anger and grief, since these are not contradictory emotions. They are in fact components of each other (cf. Mark 3:5).[60] Since neither of the verb's meanings can be denied the term in this context, both can rightly find their place in the narrative development. Even if we might want to give more priority to one of the meanings, we should not be surprised to see the Gospel intending for the term to have multiple senses simultaneously (on "impressions," see Introduction). While our translation of the verb gives a slight priority to anger, it attempts also to express the emotional response of the grief of Jesus.

Second, *why* did Jesus respond in this manner? Usually the answer to this question is partly resolved by the interpreted sense of the verb, whether it refers to grief or anger. Is Jesus responding to the grief of the sisters (and perhaps the Jews as well),[61] or is he angry at death and the sin that caused it and perhaps also the unbelief that is the root of all sin? At the level of the meaning of the verb, the "impressions" it creates allows for both possibilities; certainly the pericope suggests a more complex "impression" than an either/or decision allows.[62] This is not to be vague in our interpretation but to allow the pericope, and the entire Gospel narrative, to explain the nature of Jesus's reaction.

Since the narrator prefaces the response of Jesus

with the twice-stated "weeping" of Mary and the Jews, certainly Jesus's response is in part a coparticipatory response. At that moment, Jesus, the second person of the Trinity, was embracing the circumstances and plight of his people. Such a moment is commentary on the prologue's declaration that "the Word became flesh," when the Word took on the sinful and broken condition of the world and when the Light had come to live in the darkness (see comments on 1:14). At the same time, however, the larger context of the Gospel would also suggest that Jesus was not just sharing the grief of his people but "was outraged" at the condition of sin and disbelief. The insight the reader has been given by the prologue, with the historical and cosmological strands of the Gospel's plot, gives direction to understanding the reaction of Jesus. At that moment, the Lord saw not only what Mary and the Jews saw — physical death — but what God saw: spiritual death and the effects of sin. The tomb of Lazarus was not the only place of death; the whole world was a tomb-in-waiting.

11:34 And he said, "Where have you laid him?" They said to him, "Lord, Come and see" (καὶ εἶπεν, Ποῦ τεθείκατε αὐτόν; λέγουσιν αὐτῷ, Κύριε, ἔρχου καὶ ἴδε). Jesus begins to act upon his anger and grief by asking for the location of the tomb where Lazarus was laid. While it is not apparent to whom "they said" (λέγουσιν) refers, it likely refers to the two sisters of Jesus, who would be responsible for the burial of their brother, though the immediate context also allows for it to be some of the Jews with Mary (v. 33). The response to Jesus, "Come and see" (ἔρχου καὶ ἴδε), intriguingly recalls Jesus's first words to his disciples in 1:39.[63]

---

58. Brown calls this its "basic meaning" (*John*, 1:425).

59. See Beasley-Murray, *John*, 192 – 93.

60. Geoff Walters, *Why Do Christians Find It Hard to Grieve?* (Exeter: Paternoster, 1997), 30.

61. There is nothing in the narrative that would suggest the "weeping" of the Jews is hypocritical.

62. Cf. Carson, *John*, 416.

63. J. S. Randolph Harris, "John 11:28 – 37," *Int* 63 (2009): 402 – 4 (403).

11:35 Jesus began to cry (ἐδάκρυσεν ὁ Ἰησοῦς). In one of the shortest verses in the Bible, Jesus is described by an aorist verb that is probably to be interpreted as an ingressive, which stresses "the beginning of an action or the entrance into a state."[64] The word translated "cry" (ἐδάκρυσεν) is different than the word used to describe the "weeping" (κλαίουσαν) of Mary and the Jews in v. 33. While the latter is often taken to be a bit stronger ("weep" instead of "cry"), in light of Jesus's previously stated response to the situation, the context does not allow for much of a distinction. Since this is the second of three descriptions of the emotional or angry response of Jesus by the narrator, the reader should take note.

11:36 The Jews were saying, "Look at how he cared for him" (ἔλεγον οὖν οἱ Ἰουδαῖοι, Ἴδε πῶς ἐφίλει αὐτόν). The narrator informs us that some of the Jews had their own interpretation of Jesus's response to the plight of Lazarus. The Jews' inference of the love of Jesus for Lazarus is entirely misguided.[65] Certainly the cry of Jesus is partly due to human affection, but it was also much more. They could not even imagine how far and wide the love of Christ is (Eph 1:4–5; Rom 8:38–39).

11:37 But others from among them said, "Could not this one who opened the eyes of the blind man have acted so that this man would not have died?" (τινὲς δὲ ἐξ αὐτῶν εἶπαν, Οὐκ ἐδύνατο οὗτος ὁ ἀνοίξας τοὺς ὀφθαλμοὺς τοῦ τυφλοῦ ποιῆσαι ἵνα καὶ οὗτος μὴ ἀποθάνῃ;). But not all of the Jews had such a positive, even if nearsighted, interpretation of Jesus and his actions. As the narrator allows us to see, several of "the Jews" also considered Jesus's inaction as a failure of sorts, for certainly the one who healed the blind man (the fifth sign) would

be able to have "acted" (ποιῆσαι) in a similar manner with "this man" (οὗτος). While not spoken at Jesus directly, this group of the Jews is indirectly rebuking him in a manner similar to the indirect rebukes of Martha (v. 21) and Mary (v. 32), but with a greater note of skepticism.[66] They think of Jesus not as the light and the life, but "as a thaumaturge" (i.e., a worker of miracles), whose inaction is as much a moral failure as it is ineptitude.[67] In this way the conflict of the pericope concludes.

11:38 Then Jesus, again becoming outraged in himself, came to the tomb. It was a cave and a stone was laying against it (Ἰησοῦς οὖν πάλιν ἐμβριμώμενος ἐν ἑαυτῷ ἔρχεται εἰς τὸ μνημεῖον· ἦν δὲ σπήλαιον, καὶ λίθος ἐπέκειτο ἐπ’ αὐτῷ). The resolution of the pericope begins in a dramatic way and serves as the narrative climax of the pericope.[68] The narrator explains that Jesus "again" (πάλιν) became "outraged" (ἐμβριμώμενος), the term that bore so much significance earlier (see comments on v. 33) that expresses his internal state — "in himself" (ἐν ἑαυτῷ), an angry and emotional response to the situation. The narrator adds that the tomb was a "cave" (σπήλαιον) covered by "a stone" (λίθος). While many private burials used vertical shaft tombs, this cave burial was probably oriented horizontally. The stone would keep animals away from the body.[69] The distance between the family home and the tomb guarded the family and others from ritual impurity.

11:39 Jesus said, "Take away the stone." Martha, the sister of the man who had died, said to him, "Lord, already it stinks, for it is the fourth day" (λέγει ὁ Ἰησοῦς, Ἄρατε τὸν λίθον. λέγει αὐτῷ ἡ ἀδελφὴ τοῦ τετελευτηκότος Μάρθα, Κύριε, ἤδη ὄζει, τεταρταῖος γάρ ἐστιν). The anger and grief

---

64. Wallace, *Greek Grammar*, 558.
65. Schnackenburg, *John*, 2:337.
66. Michaels, *John*, 640.
67. Barrett, *John*, 401.

68. See Otfried Hofius, "Die Auferweckung des Lazarus: Joh 11,1–44 als Zeugnis narrativer Christologie," *ZTK* 102 (2005): 17–34.
69. Brown, *John*, 1:426; Keener, *John*, 2:848.

of Jesus did not paralyze him but propelled him. With what must have been an authoritative tone, Jesus commanded that the stone be removed. Martha, the sister who is known to speak not just act (cf. vv. 21–22), who had obviously joined the group that took Jesus to the tomb, offers a corrective or word of caution to Jesus: "It stinks already" (ἤδη ὄζει). While the implied subject of the verb could also be "he," the strongly established death of Lazarus almost demands that we interpret her description as impersonal (in contrast to Jesus; see comments on v. 15). Martha was speaking about a corpse and the decay of death, which she adds has been in process for four days. The concern for odor suggests that there had been no embalming of the body, even though there are hints of the embalming process (v. 44).[70] Martha's corrective assumes what all the mourners assume: Lazarus was dead. Although they were right about Lazarus, they were dead wrong about Jesus.

11:40 Jesus said to her, "Did I not say to you that if you believe you will see the glory of God?" (λέγει αὐτῇ ὁ Ἰησοῦς, Οὐκ εἶπόν σοι ὅτι ἐὰν πιστεύσῃς ὄψῃ τὴν δόξαν τοῦ θεοῦ;). But Jesus corrects Martha's correction. Jesus reminds Martha of what he had said to her earlier, which must be a summary of what Jesus said to Martha in vv. 25–26. Jesus did not promise to resurrect Lazarus in vv. 25–26; rather, he offered an entirely new (cosmological) definition of "resurrection" and "life," established by faith in his person (see comments on vv. 25–26). Jesus's earlier rebuke of Martha was in regard to her assumption that Jesus's authority (to act) was limited by his presence and that Jesus was not the full manifestation of God. Here Jesus reconnects with his earlier argument in this new context, rebuking Martha for her assumption that Jesus's authority (to act) was limited by

death and that Jesus was not the full manifestation of resurrection and life.

11:41 They took away the stone. Then Jesus lifted his eyes upward and said, "Father, I thank you that you have heard me" (ἦραν οὖν τὸν λίθον. ὁ δὲ Ἰησοῦς ἦρεν τοὺς ὀφθαλμοὺς ἄνω καὶ εἶπεν, Πάτερ, εὐχαριστῶ σοι ὅτι ἤκουσάς μου). The narrator describes how those present at the tomb obeyed Jesus's command and removed the stone covering the grave. As strange as it may have seemed, the narrator gives no indication that there was any pushback beyond that given by Martha (v. 39). The narrator then introduces the first prayer of Jesus in the Gospel, which he prefaces by describing his body movements: "Jesus lifted his eyes upward" (Ἰησοῦς ἦρεν τοὺς ὀφθαλμοὺς ἄνω). The other occurrences of "lifting the eyes" in the Gospel (4:35; 6:5) are intimately connected to the work of the Son. And the last occurrence of the phrase will have as its goal that "the world might believe that you have sent me" (17:1). Such a posture is intended to reflect the magnitude of the moment and the union (ontological and functional) between the Father and the Son and the mission they share. The Father sent the Son for this very moment.

Jesus begins the prayer by addressing his Father, making clear that the "sign" about to take place was connected to both the Son and the Father, because his entire mission is grounded in the mission and nature of the Trinitarian God. Jesus thanks the Father for already having heard him, a statement that is somewhat mysterious since by implication it assumes that all that is left is for God to be thanked. The statement implies that Jesus had already prayed to the Father on behalf of Lazarus. While it is possible that Jesus prayed earlier (and perhaps silently), the lack of a stated prayer (in contrast to the prayer of Jesus in ch. 17) is stark. The Christian is

---

70. Michaels, *John*, 641; cf. Carson, *John*, 417.

so embraced by Christ in faith that the cries of the child of God are also and immediately heard and felt by the Son of God. By recording only the prayer of thanksgiving and not the prayer of supplication, the reader is reminded of the diligent intercession of the Son to the Father on our behalf, even when we do not hear it ourselves (Heb 7:25).[71]

11:42 "I knew that you always hear me, but I said this for the crowd standing around, so that they might believe that you sent me" (ἐγὼ δὲ ᾔδειν ὅτι πάντοτέ μου ἀκούεις· ἀλλὰ διὰ τὸν ὄχλον τὸν περιεστῶτα εἶπον, ἵνα πιστεύσωσιν ὅτι σύ με ἀπέστειλας). Jesus continues the prayer by describing the confidence he has in the Father, who "always" (πάντοτέ) hears him. Such a statement magnifies the intimate union between the Father and the Son, who is in every way "with God" (1:1). As said above (v. 41), if the Father hears the Son, and the children of God are embraced by Christ in faith, then God will also "always" (πάντοτέ) hear our prayers — prayers to the Father, through the Son, and empowered by the Holy Spirit. Just as Jesus has been drawing Mary and Martha into a kind of life that can overcome death (vv. 23–26), so now by his example of prayer he is trying to draw those standing around him into the life of God.

11:43 After he said these things, Jesus shouted in a loud voice, "Lazarus, come out!" (καὶ ταῦτα εἰπὼν φωνῇ μεγάλῃ ἐκραύγασεν, Λάζαρε, δεῦρο ἔξω). The resolution of the pericope ends quickly and dramatically. With a majestic tone and volume, Jesus commands Lazarus to come out of the tomb. According to the narrator, Jesus "shouted" (ἐκραύγασεν) at Lazarus, a term that only in this occurrence depicts Jesus's manner of speech, with every other occurrence of the term directed at

Jesus — primarily used in the Jews' rejection of Jesus later in the Gospel (cf. 18:40; 19:6, 12, 15). When Jesus "shouts," it is for the purpose of giving life; when the Jews "shout," it is for the purpose of taking life.[72] Jesus speaks to Lazarus not as one absent but as one merely "sleeping" (cf. vv. 11–13). Jesus does not use an imperative verb but only an adverb, "come" (δεῦρο), which bears the force of both an imperative (command) and an interjection.[73] In this act Jesus asserts his divine office, for the Father has given the authority of life and death to the Son (5:22–29): "An hour comes *and now is* when the dead will hear the voice of the Son of God and those who hear will live" (5:25).

11:44 The man who had died came out, his hands and feet wrapped with strips of cloth, and with a cloth wrapped around his face. Jesus said to them, "Unwrap him and let him go" (ἐξῆλθεν ὁ τεθνηκὼς δεδεμένος τοὺς πόδας καὶ τὰς χεῖρας κειρίαις, καὶ ἡ ὄψις αὐτοῦ σουδαρίῳ περιεδέδετο. λέγει αὐτοῖς ὁ Ἰησοῦς, Λύσατε αὐτὸν καὶ ἄφετε αὐτὸν ὑπάγειν). And Lazarus came out! The narrator offers a rich description of his reappearance. Instead of calling him Lazarus, the narrator describes him as "the man who had died" (ὁ τεθνηκὼς); although he had once died, denoted by the perfect tense participle, he was dead no longer. The title, then, is entirely ironic and serves as a mockery of death by the Son of God, who speaks and "*the dead will hear*" his voice (5:25).

The irony continues as the narrator describes how "the man who had died" came out dressed in the clothes of a corpse, that is, grave clothes. To prevent premature distortion of tissue, a dead body would be wrapped tightly with shrouds or strips of cloth from head to toe, including the tight wrap around the head and face to keep the mouth

---

71. Cf. Augustine, *John*, 49.19.276.
72. Stibbe, "A Tomb with a View," 50.

73. Barrett, *John*, 403.

closed.[74] The wrapping would have been so tight and comprehensive that Lazarus would have hardly been able to walk; it is probably best to imagine him shuffling or hopping out of the tomb.[75] The image is remarkable. The "man who had died" makes his way out of the tomb in a manner that required great exertion. He is alive and well!

Befitting his renewed state, Jesus commands "them" (αὐτοῖς) — probably the same bystanders who removed the stone from the grave — to "unwrap him and let him go" (Λύσατε αὐτὸν καὶ ἄφετε αὐτὸν ὑπάγειν). Only Christ could resurrect Lazarus's body, but it was appropriate for the bystanders to undress it. He is no longer dead, so the clothes of a grave are now unnecessary, just as the grave is no longer a tomb but a "cave" (σπήλαιον), which might be why the narrator described it as such in v. 38. What was thought to be a tomb was nothing more than a cave in which Lazarus had a four-day "sleep" (cf. vv. 11 – 13). In this way the resolution of the pericope concludes.

11:45 Then many of the Jews, those who had come with Mary and had seen what he did, believed in him (Πολλοὶ οὖν ἐκ τῶν Ἰουδαίων, οἱ ἐλθόντες πρὸς τὴν Μαριὰμ καὶ θεασάμενοι ἃ ἐποίησεν, ἐπίστευσαν εἰς αὐτόν). The conclusion and interpretation of the pericope begins with a description of the responses to the resurrection of Lazarus, the sixth sign. The narrator explains that "many" (Πολλοὶ) of the Jews "believed in him" (ἐπίστευσαν εἰς αὐτόν). This need not be taken to mean that these Jews had true belief (see comments on 2:23), just as this pericope has shown how much more Martha and Mary had still to grasp about the person and work of Jesus. The narrator is showing that the "sign" was recognized by the Jews and that it in some way tickled their faith.

11:46 But some of them went to the Pharisees and reported to them what Jesus had done (τινὲς δὲ ἐξ αὐτῶν ἀπῆλθον πρὸς τοὺς Φαρισαίους καὶ εἶπαν αὐτοῖς ἃ ἐποίησεν Ἰησοῦς). The narrator contrasts the Jews that "believed" with the Jews that "reported" (εἶπαν) to the Pharisees the actions of Jesus. Since the beginning of the Gospel, the "Pharisees" were connected to the authorities in Jerusalem (see 1:19, 24), and the people had long been aware (often motivated by fear; 9:22) that they were to report such incidents to the authorities (cf. 9:13; see also v. 57). The witness of the Jews both for and against Jesus (vv. 45 – 46) does not end here and will later facilitate and even magnify the concern of the Jewish authorities regarding Jesus (see 12:17 – 19).

11:47 Then the high priests and the Pharisees assembled a meeting of the council and said, "What are we doing, because this man is doing many signs?" (συνήγαγον οὖν οἱ ἀρχιερεῖς καὶ οἱ Φαρισαῖοι συνέδριον, καὶ ἔλεγον, Τί ποιοῦμεν, ὅτι οὗτος ὁ ἄνθρωπος πολλὰ ποιεῖ σημεῖα;). Upon hearing the report of the resurrection of Lazarus, an official gathering of the Jewish authorities takes place. The "high priests" (οἱ ἀρχιερεῖς) were members of the leading priestly families, the "court" of the high priest, with the majority aligning not with the Pharisees (see comments on 1:24) but with the party of the Sadducees (see comments on 7:32; cf. 3:1). Their gathering together for a second time suggests that their common enemy — Jesus — is large enough to overshadow the differences that normally stood between them.

The term translated as "a meeting of the council" (συνέδριον), or the "Sanhedrin," refers to the governing council and chief court of the Jewish nation. The Sanhedrin was a ruling council or senate. Although it was limited in authority by the Ro-

---

74. Keener, *John*, 2:850.

75. Contra Bultmann, *John*, 409, along with several others, there is no need to see this as a "minor miracle."

mans (cf. v. 48), it was the highest authoritative and governing body in first-century Judaism. It was the final authority and primary decision-making body in all major administrative and judicial roles in Jewish self-governance.[76] The council was able to be called on short notice and was frequently the place where religious "politics" took place. Since the rest of the Gospel says so little about the Jewish trial of Jesus, it is possible that this "meeting of the council" was the real trial of Jesus, where the decision was made to solve the Jesus problem.[77]

The question asked by the council, presumably one that summarizes the feelings of the entire group, reveals their exasperation toward Jesus. "What shall we do?" (Τί ποιοῦμεν) suggests that the little they have done has not worked (e.g., 7:13, 30, 45 – 52; 9:22). The reason they have failed is clearly stated as "because this man is doing many signs" (ὅτι οὗτος ὁ ἄνθρωπος πολλὰ ποιεῖ σημεῖα). If Jesus's miraculous works had already drawn attention to him, how much more after this latest miracle — the resurrection of Lazarus (see 12:9 – 11)? The glaring absence of his name by the Jewish authorities and in its place the now common designation, "this man," serves to reflect the disdain of Jesus's person. There is no longer the need to make a legal case (e.g., 5:16 – 18), for the case against "this man" had become much more personal.

11:48 "If we allow him to continue like this, everyone will believe in him, and the Romans will come and take away both our place and our nation" (ἐὰν ἀφῶμεν αὐτὸν οὕτως, πάντες πιστεύσουσιν εἰς αὐτόν, καὶ ἐλεύσονται οἱ Ῥωμαῖοι καὶ ἀροῦσιν ἡμῶν καὶ τὸν τόπον καὶ τὸ ἔθνος). The summarized feelings of the council continue, this time with the potential political ramifications. According to the Sanhedrin, "if we allow him"

(ἀφῶμεν αὐτὸν), as in, "if we do not stop him," and he continues to do what he has been doing, two things are likely to happen. First, "everyone will believe in him" (πάντες πιστεύσουσιν εἰς αὐτόν). While this is certainly an exaggeration, it suggests that they truly fear the response of the people to Jesus.

Second, the Romans will "take away both our place and our nation" (ἀροῦσιν ἡμῶν καὶ τὸν τόπον καὶ τὸ ἔθνος). The concern is that the Romans would see the upheaval caused by the heralding of a newly crowned king (see comments on 6:14 – 15), who would probably be viewed in a messianic manner as a warrior-king. Such would be considered a threat to the power and authority of Rome. Although the Jews were officially subordinate to Roman authority, they enjoyed a good amount of religious freedom. Nevertheless, they were not allowed to have their own king; Caesar was their king. Thus, the political ramifications could be severe, even deadly. Rome could come and take away their "place" (τὸν τόπον), which likely refers to their city or more specifically to the temple, and their "nation" (τὸ ἔθνος), which likely refers to the semiautonomous status of the Jewish nation under the Roman Empire. The grammar presses together "place and nation" as a unit, which is not without precedence in Jewish writings (cf. 2 Macc 1:29; 5:19) and which taken together reflects a concern for religious freedom and, more personally (and selfishly), their own power as the ruling council.[78]

11:49 But one of them, Caiaphas, who was the high priest that year, said to them, "You do not understand anything" (εἷς δέ τις ἐξ αὐτῶν Καϊάφας, ἀρχιερεὺς ὢν τοῦ ἐνιαυτοῦ ἐκείνου, εἶπεν αὐτοῖς, Ὑμεῖς οὐκ οἴδατε οὐδέν). The narrator explains how Caiaphas, the high priest, provides a response to the summarized voice given in vv. 47 – 48. The

76. Keener, *John*, 2:1073 – 76; cf. Brown, *Death of the Messiah*, 1:342 – 43.

77. Morris, *John*, 501.
78. Schnackenburg, *John*, 2:348.

narrator's qualification that Caiaphas was high priest "that year" (τοῦ ἐνιαυτοῦ ἐκείνου) does not mean that there was a new high priest every year, since the evidence suggests that high priests were generally in positions for much longer than a year (see comments on 18:13). According to Josephus, while his two predecessors served for only a year or less (*Ant.* 18.35), Caiaphas was high priest for eighteen years (*Ant.* 18.35; 18.95; cf. Luke 3:2).[79] The qualification might simply give emphasis to the significance of "that year" in which Jesus was crucified. It might also strike a note of irony, especially in light of v. 48.[80] With the ruling authority belonging to Rome, Caiaphas — or any high priest — could be easily deposed — like Caiaphas's father-in-law, Annas (18:13). The threefold occurrence of the qualification that Caiaphas was high priest "that year" (vv. 49, 51; 18:13)[81] directs the reader's attention to the eternal high priest about whom the narrator speaks: Jesus Christ, the High Priest (Heb 8:1 – 2). In a real way, "that year" was the year of transition from the old covenant and a temporary priesthood to the new covenant, a better covenant and an eternal priesthood (Heb. 7:22, 24).

The high priest functioned as the chair of the council, held considerable political authority, and according to tradition could break ties in the case of a split vote.[82] Thus, it is not unusual for him to direct the proceedings, as he does here. His statement to the council, with its dual emphatic pronoun and emphatic double negative, is contemptuous,[83] rebuking the Sanhedrin for not taking their logical observations and concerns to their obvious conclusion. As Bultmann suggests, "The words of rebuke with which his proposition is introduced sets the blindness crassly in the light."[84]

11:50 "You are not considering that it is better for you that one man should die for the people, not the whole nation perish" (οὐδὲ λογίζεσθε ὅτι συμφέρει ὑμῖν ἵνα εἷς ἄνθρωπος ἀποθάνῃ ὑπὲρ τοῦ λαοῦ καὶ μὴ ὅλον τὸ ἔθνος ἀπόληται). According to the political wisdom of the high priest, "it is better" (συμφέρει), that is, more advantageous or profitable,[85] for *one* man to "die" (ἀποθάνῃ) than for the *whole* nation to "perish" (ἀπόληται). The statement need not mean that they (the Jewish authorities) need to kill Jesus but simply that they need to direct the attention of Rome away from the nation (with its growing messianic fervor) and toward the one man who is the source of it all.[86] Said another way, Caiaphas, with great "political sagacity,"[87] suggests to the Sanhedrin that they make a Jewish problem look just as much like a Roman problem! Such a maneuver would remove Jewish-Roman tensions and pit both the Jews and the Romans against the one man, Jesus.

11:51 He said this not by himself, but as high priest that year he prophesied that Jesus would die for the nation (τοῦτο δὲ ἀφ' ἑαυτοῦ οὐκ εἶπεν, ἀλλὰ ἀρχιερεὺς ὢν τοῦ ἐνιαυτοῦ ἐκείνου ἐπροφήτευσεν ὅτι ἔμελλεν Ἰησοῦς ἀποθνήσκειν ὑπὲρ τοῦ ἔθνους). The significance of the statement is so great that the narrator inserts an explanatory "intrusion" (cf. 3:16) to ensure the reader grasps its full meaning and irony. The narrator does not just explain the meaning of Caiaphas's statement but describes its true *source* ("he said this not by himself") and its true *nature* ("he prophesied"). The

---

79. See Adele Reinhartz, *Caiaphas the High Priest*, SPNT (Minneapolis: Fortress, 2013), 11 – 51.

80. Keener, *John*, 2:854.

81. Cf. Hoskyns, who writes that this is not "so trivial a piece of information" (*Fourth Gospel*, 411).

82. Keener, *John*, 2:1073 – 75.

83. Morris, *John*, 503.

84. Bultmann, *John*, 410 – 11.

85. BDAG 960.

86. Michaels, *John*, 651.

87. Bultmann, *John*, 411.

narrator is not claiming that Caiaphas was speaking like Balaam's donkey, even if the analogy is in one sense quite appropriate,[88] but that by his own "cognitive processes" (v. 50) Caiaphas's intended and plain-sense meaning actually carried with it a clear and retrievable extended-sense meaning. Using the lens offered by the prologue, Caiaphas spoke by means of the historical strand, whereas the reader is expected to see the cosmological plot also at work.[89]

To make this even more emphatic, the narrator claims Caiaphas "prophesied" (ἐπροφήτευσεν). In one sense this is just a playful use of the traditional understanding of the significant office held by the high priest, who could be regarded as "particularly prophetically endowed."[90] But in another, more important sense the narrator speaks of the use that God would make of this statement, using Caiaphas like an OT prophet who speaks with specificity about what would soon take place! In a remarkable moment, the Jerusalem high priest declares in the voice of a prophet "against his knowledge and intention" that Jesus would *redemptively* die for the nation of Israel (cf. Isa 53:11).[91] The redemptive sense is highlighted by the use of "for" or "on behalf of" (ὑπὲρ), which the Gospel has already used to refer to the sacrificial death of Christ on the cross (see comments on 6:51). Jesus said he would lay down his life "for" the sheep (10:11, 14). Indeed, it was his alone to give; there was no authority (Jewish or Roman) that could take it from him (10:18). Caiaphas, then, was simply repeating what Jesus had himself already "prophesied."

This helps to explain not only the use of the word "prophesy" but also the enigmatic, threefold use of "that year," occurring for a second time here. At "that" moment, Caiaphas the high priest may have been moving his lips, but it was Jesus the high priest who was doing the speaking. The demonstrative "that," used also in the Gospel to refer to two different objects simultaneously (see comments on 7:8), indicates that the transition has begun. It was in "that year" that the high priest was replaced by the eternal high priest. The Gospel is moving us to see that the work of Jesus the high priest is quickly and necessarily headed to the cross.

11:52 And not only for the nation, but also in order to gather together into one the scattered children of God (καὶ οὐχ ὑπὲρ τοῦ ἔθνους μόνον ἀλλ᾽ ἵνα καὶ τὰ τέκνα τοῦ θεοῦ τὰ διεσκορπισμένα συναγάγῃ εἰς ἕν). The narrator continues to express the extended-sense meaning of Caiaphas's "prophecy." The narrator had already shifted the plain-sense focus on political expediency to the extended-sense meaning of salvation;[92] now he shifts again from the plain-sense focus on Israel to the extended-sense referent of the church. The narrator claims that the death of Jesus is not only "for" (see v. 51) the nation of Israel but also for the "children of God" (τὰ τέκνα τοῦ θεοῦ), whom he depicts in the language Jesus used of his sheep in 10:16, sheep who are "scattered" (τὰ διεσκορπισμένα), that is, not yet united in his person and work. The work of Jesus is universal and, as denoted by the purpose clause, is intended to "gather together" (συναγάγῃ) all God's children, both Jew and gentile, into one body, the church. This is, then, the Israel of God (Gal 6:16), and Jesus will be their eternal high priest.[93]

11:53 So from that day they planned to kill him (ἀπ᾽ ἐκείνης οὖν τῆς ἡμέρας ἐβουλεύσαντο ἵνα ἀποκτείνωσιν αὐτόν). The narrator concludes his insights into the meeting chambers of the Sanhedrin

---

88. Morris, *John*, 504.

89. Aquinas writes, "These words have one meaning according to the intention of Caiaphas, and another according to the explanation of the Evangelist" (*John*, 2:254).

90. Keener, *John*, 2:857.

91. Bultmann, *John*, 411.

92. Michaels, *John*, 653.

93. Cf. Ridderbos, *John*, 410.

by revealing their agreement with the political strategy of Caiaphas. Their decision was that "they planned" (ἐβουλεύσαντο) to kill Jesus, almost certainly by using the political strategy suggested by Caiaphas to join hands with the Romans against Jesus. The qualifying demonstrative "that year" (vv. 49, 51) is now being used to qualify a single day ("that day" [ἐκείνης τῆς ἡμέρας]). Little did they know that the plan the Jewish authorities made on that day had always been the plan of God. As Peter would soon say to the Jerusalem crowd in regard to Jesus, "This man was handed over to you *by God's deliberate plan and foreknowledge*; and you, with the help of wicked men, put him to death by nailing him to the cross" (Acts 2:23; emphasis added).

11:54 Therefore Jesus no longer traveled openly among the Jews, but went away from there to the region near the country, to a city called Ephraim, where he remained with the disciples (Ὁ οὖν Ἰησοῦς οὐκέτι παρρησίᾳ περιεπάτει ἐν τοῖς Ἰουδαίοις, ἀλλὰ ἀπῆλθεν ἐκεῖθεν εἰς τὴν χώραν ἐγγὺς τῆς ἐρήμου, εἰς Ἐφραὶμ λεγομένην πόλιν, κἀκεῖ διέτριβεν μετὰ τῶν μαθητῶν). The narrator concludes the pericope by describing the strategy of Jesus, who intentionally avoided being seen by the Jews. Jesus is not running out of fear but is acting by his own authority (10:18) and according to his own schedule — "my hour" (see comments on 2:4). Jesus withdrew with his disciples outside the populated area of Jerusalem to "the country" (τὴν χώραν), specifically to a city called Ephraim on the edge of the desert about twelve miles northeast of Jerusalem.[94]

11:55 The Passover of the Jews was near, and many went up to Jerusalem from the country before the Passover in order to purify themselves (Ἦν δὲ ἐγγὺς τὸ πάσχα τῶν Ἰουδαίων, καὶ ἀνέβησαν πολλοὶ εἰς Ἱεροσόλυμα ἐκ τῆς χώρας πρὸ τοῦ πάσχα ἵνα ἁγνίσωσιν ἑαυτούς). Jesus would not remain away for long, however, for Passover was approaching, which for the Gospel will no longer be background but foreground: the Lamb of God, the cross, and a new exodus. This is the third Passover mentioned by the Gospel (2:13, 23; 6:4). The narrator describes the Jewish traditional and ceremonial practice of traveling to Jerusalem to prepare for Passover. The Passover required self-purification as mandated by the OT (see Num 9:6–12; 2 Chr 30:17–18).[95] Jesus, in sharp contrast, needed no purification (cf. 12:1).

11:56 They were seeking Jesus, and as they stood in the temple spoke with one another, "What do you think? Surely he is not coming to the Feast?" (ἐζήτουν οὖν τὸν Ἰησοῦν καὶ ἔλεγον μετ' ἀλλήλων ἐν τῷ ἱερῷ ἑστηκότες, Τί δοκεῖ ὑμῖν; ὅτι οὐ μὴ ἔλθῃ εἰς τὴν ἑορτήν;). Even the Passover could not eclipse the attention Jesus had drawn. The narrator explains that the travelers were hoping to see Jesus and are even described as continually "seeking" (ἐζήτουν) him, denoted by the imperfect tense verb. The narrator depicts them standing in the temple, in the central and populated area, asking one another if Jesus would make an appearance. While the first question reflects the discussion among the people present, the second question reveals their answer, since the question is asked with the emphatic negation subjunctive, the strongest negation in Greek: "Surely he is not coming to the Feast?" (οὐ μὴ ἔλθῃ εἰς τὴν ἑορτήν).[96]

11:57 But the high priests and the Pharisees had given an order that if anyone knew where he was, he should report it, in order that they could arrest him (δεδώκεισαν δὲ οἱ ἀρχιερεῖς καὶ οἱ Φαρισαῖοι ἐντολὴν ἵνα ἐάν τις γνῷ ποῦ ἐστιν

---

94. Brown, *John*, 1:441.
95. Keener, *John*, 2:858. Cf. Josephus, *J.W.* 1.229; 6.290.
96. Wallace, *Greek Grammar*, 468–69.

μηνύσῃ, ὅπως πιάσωσιν αὐτόν). The reason people could not imagine the appearance of Jesus is because the Jewish authorities had already made it known to the public that the presence of Jesus should be reported so that he could be arrested. In light of the decision of the Sanhedrin, Jesus was now a wanted criminal. The seriousness of the situation is denoted both by the pluperfect tense verb, "had given" (δεδώκεισαν), which carries the element of "lasting consequence,"[97] and by the term "order" (ἐντολὴν), which only occurs here in the Gospel for anything other than a command of God or Christ (cf. 10:18). The authorities had devised a plan for dealing with Jesus, but the reader is well aware that the plan truly belongs to the Lord (see v. 53). The narrator concludes the pericope with a description of the mounting social and religious pressure placed upon Jesus as well as the growing interest in his person and presence. The narrator is transitioning the reader to the final stage of Jesus's journey by connecting the narrative time to Passover, for the remainder of the Gospel takes place in connection with the Passover and the *true* Passover, the death of Christ.

Theology in Application

As the sixth section of the Gospel begins, the reader is given an insider's view on the sixth sign of the Gospel, which displays not only the cosmological identity of Jesus as "the resurrection and the life" but also the intimate love of God for the world. This pericope is a powerful and engaging story that exhorts the reader to see God as he truly is, the one who loves and conquers death because he *is* life, true life. While the length of the pericope might prohibit the preacher from handling it in its entirety, the message should at least be maintained in the context of the full story and its movement.

Sickness, Death, and the Love of God

On the surface this pericope is about the resurrection of a man named Lazarus, who was once dead. But the raising of Lazarus is only part of the miracle — the "sign" — this pericope intends to communicate. The thirty-seven verses (!) leading up to the resurrection are filled with their own significant drama regarding the threat of sickness and death and the greater purpose of God. Earlier in the pericope, the reader is confronted with a paradox: the sickness (and death) of Lazarus was not "for the purpose of death but for the glory of God" (v. 4). Jesus's statement imposes itself upon the reader, demanding that they interpret everything recorded thereafter as divinely purposeful and directed at bringing glory to God. But before such a paradox gets fully explained to the reader, the narrator breaks into the story and makes a remarkable statement about the love of Jesus (v. 5). God's ability to use the sickness and death of Lazarus must be understood as fitting perfectly and purposefully with

---

97. BDF § 347.

his love for Lazarus and his family. Even the delay of Jesus recorded in v. 6 is not to be viewed as a dispassionate response but must be understood in light of the love of God.

The Christian, like the Bethany family, is also loved by Jesus, by God (cf. 3:16). For the same reason, then, the threat and experience of sickness and death for the Christian cannot (must not!) be viewed as a betrayal or contradiction of the love of God for them. If God delays in responding to our crisis (as he did for Lazarus in v. 6), that does not mean he does not love us or is not being purposeful in regard to our plight. This pericope urges the Christian to look for the glory of God in every circumstance, even if (and maybe emphatically so) the result does not appear to meet the demand — our demand. Because "Christ is the unique mirror of the divine grace,"[98] Christians are exhorted by this pericope to claim the life Christ offers over their own standards for life.

The Life (and Death) of the Christian

This pericope presses upon the reader a much more robust understanding of "life." Jesus declares that he is "the resurrection and the life" (v. 26), two terms that speak to the same subject matter, even though one is more often considered to refer to the future and the other to the present. In the person and work of Jesus, life is no longer bound by death, and death no longer may willfully intrude into life. Death is so impotent for the Christian that he or she can actually die and yet still live (v. 25)! The reader of the Gospel is exhorted to believe that death is now "unreal."[99] The Christian shouts with the apostle Paul: "Where, O death, is your victory? Where, O death, is your sting?" (1 Cor 15:55).

For this reason, sickness and death are no longer what they seem. Those "in [Christ]" (v. 10) have an internal security that defeats and mutes all external conditions. "Indeed, it is because the Word became flesh and dwelt among us that the distinction between the physical and the spiritual is blurred and the two become bewilderingly interlocked.... In Jesus, the continuity between *all* degrees of being is complete."[100] The life of the Christian is now entirely in Christ. Divide life into physical and spiritual and you risk a depersonalizing dualism; affirm the indivisible and you endanger the reality of the transcendent. "But the heart of this baffling mystery is simply Jesus."[101] According to the Gospel of John, Jesus *is* life. The life of the Christian, therefore, is no longer defined by his own living but by the life he has in Christ.

---

98. Calvin, *John 11–21*, 3.
99. Ibid., 404.

100. C. F. D. Moule, "The Meaning of 'Life' in the Gospels and the Epistles of St. John," *Theology* 78 (1975): 114–25 (123).
101. Ibid., 125.

The God Who Weeps

This pericope offers the Christian insight into the very heart of God. Jesus may be the Word who was with God in the beginning of time itself, but he is also with his people in their time, experiencing the depth of their pain and weeping with them (vv. 33, 35, 38). Debates over the anger or emotion of Jesus in vv. 33 and 38 can often eclipse the truth that Jesus, the second person of the Trinity, was embracing the circumstances and plight of his people. In a crystal clear picture of grace, the Creator embraced creation and the Light associated with the darkness, although not in a manner that corrupted God but in a manner that depicted clearly the fact that God loves the world (cf. 3:16).

O church, your God is "outraged and troubled" (v. 33) over you, coparticipating in your burdens by being angry and mournful at sickness, death, and sin. The "unmoved mover" (Aristotle) is moved to tears for his people, the shepherd of his sheep (ch. 10). "We do not have a high priest who is unable to sympathize with our weaknesses, but we have one who has been tempted in every way, just as we are — yet he did not sin" (Heb 4:15). Worship the Lord, all his people, for he has come to you, meeting you where you are in your difficulties, embracing the suffering you face just as fully as he embraces you.

The Plan of God

God does not merely embrace with his children the evil they face but uses that same evil for his own good purposes. The response of Caiaphas before the Sanhedrin to the resurrection of Lazarus was filled with rich irony, which the narrator of the Gospel explains to the reader (vv. 49–52). The intentions of the Jewish leadership to kill Jesus fit perfectly within the divine intentions of God, so much so that Caiaphas words were, quite literally, "prophetic." As God explained back in the days of Joseph, "You intended to harm me, but God intended it for good to accomplish what is now being done, the saving of many lives" (Gen 50:20).

The God who created all things also controls all things, even the evil intentions and actions of his enemies. This is your God, Christian, the one in whom you have placed your trust. Your faith is not in the systems and institutions of humanity nor in your own ability to devise a plan, but in the God who controls them all — in the mysterious but gracious plan of God for you and the world. For we know that in all things God works for the good (Rom 8:28), and for this reason we trust in him, no matter the initial forecast.

Do You Believe This?

After Jesus made one of the most cosmological statements in the Gospel, declaring himself to be the resurrection and the life, declaring death itself to be subsumed by life in him (v. 25), he asks Martha a pointed question: "Do you believe this?" (v. 26). At that moment Jesus was not just speaking to Martha but to all the earth: "Do you, O human, believe?" For the Christian this question continually points them to Christ, who must become for them the foundation of their existence, their life. Like Moses declared before the Israelites: "This day I call the heavens and the earth as witnesses against you that I have set before you life and death, blessings and curses. Now choose life, so that you and your children may live" (Deut 30:19). So Jesus declares to the Christian through the Gospel: "I am the resurrection and the life.... Do you believe this?"

John 12:1 – 11

Literary Context

This section of the Gospel, "The Conclusion of Jesus's Public Ministry" (11:1 – 12:50), offers a significant conclusion to the public presence of Jesus. Jesus is done speaking publicly; his last public appearances and actions provide a potent display of his identity (his person) and his mission (his work). The pericope of 12:1 – 11 is intimately related to the previous pericope, the death and resurrection of Lazarus (11:1 – 57), as well as to the pericopae that follow (12:12 – 19; 12:20 – 50). Even at a dinner celebrating the resurrection of Lazarus, the demands and necessity of death do not escape Jesus. In this pericope, "the resurrection and the life" (11:25) is given what is due him, an extravagant and honorific anointing that befits both a king and a corpse.

VI. The Conclusion of Jesus's Public Ministry (11:1 – 12:50)
  A. The Sixth Sign: The Death and Resurrection of Lazarus (11:1 – 57)
➡ **B. The Anointing of Jesus (12:1 – 11)**
  C. The Royal Entrance of Jesus into Jerusalem (12:12 – 19)
  D. "The Hour has Come": The Final Public Statement of Jesus (12:20 – 50)

Main Idea

Jesus is worthy enough to be extravagantly anointed as king on a throne but loving enough to be prepared for death on a cross. Christian discipleship involves humble service to the King, valuing all things and activities by their ability to express honor to Christ.

Translation

John 12:1–11

1a	Introduction & Setting (1–3)	Then **Jesus …**
b	Timing of Festival	six days before the Passover,
c	Place	**… came to Bethany**
d		where Lazarus was,
e	Description of Event	whom Jesus had raised from the dead.
2a	Action	**They made a dinner for him there,**
b	Characters Reentrance (2–3a)	and **Martha was serving,**
c		while Lazarus was one of those reclining at the table with him.
3a	Sequence of Worship #1	Then **Mary took a pound of perfume,**
b	Description	a genuine and expensive oil of nard,
c	Sequence of Worship #2	and **anointed the feet of Jesus**
d	Sequence of Worship #3	and **wiped his feet with her hair.**
e	Result	And **the house was filled from the fragrance of the perfume.**
4a	Contrast to Mary	But
b	Character Entrance	**Judas Iscariot …**
c	Association	one of his disciples,
d	Description	the one who was about to betray him,
e	Conflict (4–6)	**… said,**
5a	Interrogative Rebuke	"Why was this perfume not sold for three hundred denarii and
b	Proposed Counteruse	given to the poor?"
6a	Narrator's Aside	But **he did not say this**
b	Basis	because he was caring for the poor himself but
c	Contrast	because he was a thief,
d	Explanation of 6a–c	and
e		since he was the one who had the money box,
f		**he was taking what was put into it.**
7a	Resolution (7–8)	Then **Jesus said,**
b	Direct Counterrebuke	"Leave her alone;
c	Explanation	it was intended to be kept
d	Purpose	for the day of my preparation for burial.
8a	Explanation Continued	For you will always have the poor with you,
b	Contrast	but you will not always have me."
9a	Conclusion (9–11)	Then **a large crowd of the Jews learned that he was there,**
b	Reaction	and **they came** not only
c	Purpose #1	because of Jesus but also
d	Purpose #2	in order to see Lazarus,
e	Description of Event	whom he had raised from the dead.
10a	Contrasting Reaction	But **the high priests planned**
b	Purpose	to kill Lazarus.
11a		
b		Because of him
c	Basis for 10	**many of the Jews were leaving and**
d		**believing in Jesus.**

Structure and Literary Form

This pericope corresponds to the basic story form (see Introduction). The *introduction/setting* is established in vv. 1 – 3, explaining the location, setting, people, and act (the anointing) around which the plot's conflict will focus. In vv. 4 – 6 the *conflict* of the pericope is directed at Jesus, centering upon the meaning and value of the anointing. In vv. 7 – 8 the conflict is given a *resolution* by a statement of Jesus that explains the prophetic significance of the anointing. Finally, vv. 9 – 11 serve to explain the *conclusion/interpretation* of the activities, both of this scene and the previous one (11:1 – 57), placing them in the context of Jesus's concluding public presence.

Exegetical Outline

➡   **B. The Anointing of Jesus (12:1 – 11)**

     1. Gift for a King (vv. 1 – 3)

     2. But What about the Poor? (vv. 4 – 6)

     3. Preparation for a Corpse (vv. 7 – 8)

     4. The Public Response toward Jesus (vv. 9 – 11)

Explanation of the Text

Because the anointing of Jesus occurs in all four Gospels (cf. Matt 26:6 – 13; Mark 14:3 – 9; Luke 7:36 – 50), the account in John has been heavily compared with the Synoptics, especially since different information and emphases are given in each account.[1] The most difficult issue between the four accounts is that in Matthew and Mark Jesus's head is anointed, whereas in Luke and John Jesus's feet are anointed. It is highly unlikely that the Gospels are describing two different events, but for methodological reasons (see Introduction) our attention will focus only on the account given by the Fourth Gospel.

12:1 Then Jesus, six days before the Passover, came to Bethany where Lazarus was, whom Jesus had raised from the dead (Ὁ οὖν Ἰησοῦς πρὸ ἓξ ἡμερῶν τοῦ πάσχα ἦλθεν εἰς Βηθανίαν, ὅπου ἦν Λάζαρος, ὃν ἤγειρεν ἐκ νεκρῶν Ἰησοῦς). The introduction and setting of the pericope provides the time and location of the scene along with the primary characters. The scene is intentionally connected by the narrator with the previous pericope. After the resurrection of Lazarus, with the Jews now seeking to kill him (11:53), Jesus left Bethany for a city called Ephraim, where he remained with his disciples (11:54). He has now returned to Bethany, probably to the home of the Bethany family since the narrator says he went "where Lazarus was" (ὅπου ἦν Λάζαρος). Morris even prefers to translate the word we translated "then" (οὖν) as "therefore," because the dinner is a celebratory dinner in Jesus's honor (v. 2). Lazarus "was," that is, he

---

1. See J. K. Elliott, "The Anointing of Jesus," *ExpTim* 85 (1974): 105 – 7; Dodd, *Historical Tradition*, 162 – 73.

"was" in a home, surrounded by family and friends, not in a tomb surrounded by death and decomposition. How could this not be a joyous gathering?

The narrator reveals that it was "six days before the Passover" (πρὸ ἓξ ἡμερῶν τοῦ πάσχα). The odd Greek construction is not the most difficult issue surrounding this phrase.[2] In the Gospel of John, the chronology of the crucifixion in relation to the Passover appears different from the Synoptics. Although this interpretive issue will be addressed later (see comments on 13:1 and before 18:28; cf. 19:14), it is significant that the countdown to the "hour" of *the* Passover has begun. It might also be significant that "six days" (ἓξ ἡμερῶν) are specifically mentioned. While interpreters are right to be guarded against loose symbolic interpretations of the "six days,"[3] we cannot forget that "six days" was significant at the beginning of the Gospel, the first "six days" of Jesus's ministry (see comments before 2:1). While this chronology might simply be a time designation in regard to the events surrounding Passover, it also gives emphasis to the last week of Jesus's ministry, just as it did for his first week. Forming what is like an *inclusio*, the reader is being guided to see that it is now the dawn of the seventh day.[4]

12:2 They made a dinner for him there, and Martha was serving, while Lazarus was one of those reclining at the table with him (ἐποίησαν οὖν αὐτῷ δεῖπνον ἐκεῖ, καὶ ἡ Μάρθα διηκόνει, ὁ δὲ Λάζαρος εἷς ἦν ἐκ τῶν ἀνακειμένων σὺν αὐτῷ). The introduction and setting continues by explaining the nature of the event. The term "dinner" or "supper" (δεῖπνον) is used elsewhere in the Gospel only of the Last Supper (13:2, 4; 21:20). In this context, however, it is in reference to a dinner in honor of Jesus, denoted by "for him" (αὐτῷ), reflecting again that this scene is directly related to what has come before (ch. 11). Jesus is being honored by the Bethany family (and others) for his miraculous and loving response to the sickness and death of Lazarus. The fact that Martha, one of Lazarus's sisters, is serving might suggest further that the specific location is the home of the Bethany family, but even if not it makes clear the connection to Jesus's earlier visit to the Bethany family and the radically different circumstance he now finds there. The mention of Lazarus serves to highlight the other "honored" guest, the one whose presence is entirely dependent on the presence of Jesus. What may have begun as a funeral banquet in preparation for his absence had been transformed into a celebratory dinner in his presence.[5] And since the Passover is six days away (v. 1) and the Gospel presents the Passover as beginning on the following Friday evening (13:1; 18:28; 19:31, 42), this celebratory dinner must have been held on the preceding Saturday, the Sabbath (the eve of what Christians now call Palm Sunday).[6]

12:3 Then Mary took a pound of perfume, a genuine and expensive oil of nard, and anointed the feet of Jesus and wiped his feet with her hair. And the house was filled from the fragrance of the perfume (ἡ οὖν Μαριὰμ λαβοῦσα λίτραν μύρου νάρδου πιστικῆς πολυτίμου ἤλειψεν τοὺς πόδας τοῦ Ἰησοῦ καὶ ἐξέμαξεν ταῖς θριξὶν αὐτῆς τοὺς πόδας αὐτοῦ· ἡ δὲ οἰκία ἐπληρώθη ἐκ τῆς ὀσμῆς τοῦ μύρου). The introduction and setting of the pericope concludes with the introduction of Mary, the other sister of Lazarus, who when first introduced by the Gospel was identified by means of this act—the anointing of Jesus (11:2). Mary's action is

2. For a discussion of the phrase, see C. F. D. Moule, *An Idiom Book of New Testament Greek*, 2nd ed. (Cambridge: Cambridge University Press, 1959), 74.

3. See e.g., Michaels, *John*, 663.

4. Cf. Aquinas, *John*, 2:261.

5. Brant, *John*, 179.

6. See Malina and Rohrbaugh, *John*, 207–8. There is no evidence to suggest that this was the Jewish meal called the *Habdalah*, ceremonially performed at the end of the Sabbath.

highly symbolic and therefore requires a detailed analysis, for the remainder of the pericope is dependent upon its meaning.

The narrator's description of the approach of Mary to Jesus is a bit vague; there is no stated announcement of her action or explanatory comment. She silently approaches Jesus and, presumably, kneels at his feet.[7] She brings with her "perfume, a genuine and expensive oil of nard" (μύρου νάρδου πιστικῆς πολυτίμου), a collection of terms not easily defined. It appears that Mary approached Jesus with a perfume that is an "aromatic oil," probably in the form of an ointment.[8] The perfume is described as "genuine" (πιστικῆς), a word which was used by later Greek writers to refer to that which belongs to something "faithful" or "trustworthy" (πίστις), thus, our translation of "genuine," which reflects its pure and unadulterated nature.[9] This is probably why the narrator also adds that the perfume was "expensive" (πολυτίμου). This was no ordinary or generic perfume in the hands of Mary; it was of the highest quality and normally possessed by only the well-to-do in the Mediterranean world.[10]

Mary did not just bring a perfume of the highest quality to Jesus, but she also brought a large amount of it. The word translated as "a pound" (λίτραν), which only occurs in the NT here and in 19:39, is a measure of weight, not volume. It is a term borrowed from Latin (*libra*), which denotes one Roman pound — about 327.45 grams or about twelve ounces of oil.[11] This is therefore a ridiculously lavish amount of such fine perfume to be used all at once, and especially when applied to only one person!

But it is not just the quality and the amount of perfume Mary offers to Jesus, but how she honors him with it that is most significant. With minimal detail, the narrator describes Mary's twofold action. First, she "anointed the feet of Jesus" (ἤλειψεν τοὺς πόδας τοῦ Ἰησοῦ). The act of anointing a person in the ancient world was intended to set them apart in regard to their particular office or role (e.g., as a king or ruler, prophet, or priest) and to establish them with honor and praise. An anointing would almost always involve the person's head, which was the most honorable part of the body.[12] While some have suggested that the anointing of a person's feet is "unparalleled,"[13] and certainly it was quite rare, Coakley has catalogued eight instances from ancient sources, both Greco-Roman and Jewish, that clearly depict the practice of anointing a person's feet.[14] The few and diverse instances confirm two things: the practice was rare and, more importantly, was an "act of extravagance."[15] Its rarity can almost be attributed to its unnaturalness, for as discussed earlier, caring for the feet of another person was the most demeaning task assigned to household servants (see comments on 1:27).

Such an act of anointing would have normally symbolized the anointing of royalty. In the OT, for example, kings or priests would be anointed to mark the beginning of their rule or priesthood (e.g., Exod 28:41; 1 Sam 10:1 – 13; 16:12 – 13).[16] And the use of sweet-smelling ointment or perfume was symptomatic of the office of the king in both the OT and pagan contexts. In 1 Samuel 8:11 – 13, for example, God through Samuel directly connects perfume with service required of a king. This is

---

7. Reinhartz, "From Narrative to History," 179.

8. BDAG 666.

9. BDAG 818.

10. Keener, *John*, 2:863.

11. J. H. Moulton and G. Milligan, *Vocabulary of the Greek Testament* (London: Hodder & Stoughton, 1930; repr., Peabody, MA: Hendrickson, 1997), 377; BDAG 597.

12. Neyrey, *John*, 210.

13. Brown, *John*, 1:451.

14. J. F. Coakley, "The Anointing at Bethany and the Priority of John," *JBL* 107 (1988): 241 – 56 (247 – 48).

15. Ibid., 248.

16. Susan Miller, "Exegetical Notes on John 12:1 – 8: The Anointing of Jesus," *ExpTim* 118 (2007): 240 – 41.

confirmed by the Greek historian Polybius, who recounts how the eccentric Antiochus Epiphanies would have "precious ointments brought in to him" and then records the commentary of an onlooker: "How lucky you are, you kings, to use such scents and smell so sweet."[17] This observation, reflecting perhaps a widely held assumption in the ancient world, when applied to the anointing of Jesus strongly suggests that Mary's act was intended to present Jesus as a royal personage — a king.[18] The historical evidence matches well with the Fourth Gospel, which is keenly interested in the royalty of Jesus (e.g., 1:49; 6:15; 12:13 – 15; 18:33 – 19:3; 19:13 – 22); indeed, the full picture of the enthronement of Jesus is the Son of Man "lifted up" on the cross (3:14; 12:32). This pericope makes Jesus's kingship implicit and private; in the next pericope Jesus's kingship is explicit and public (12:12 – 19). As the reader will come to see, however, this is an ironic king. For just as he is being anointed for his burial (v. 7), so also will he be enthroned as king not with honor but with shame (19:2 – 3) and not on a throne but on a cross (19:19).

Second, Mary "wiped his feet with her hair" (ἐξέμαξεν ταῖς θριξὶν αὐτῆς τοὺς πόδας αὐτοῦ). Rather than using a towel, Mary uses her own hair, shaken loose as a sign of her deep and intimate affection for her Lord.[19] The use of her hair was, similar to the anointing of the feet instead of the head, almost unnatural in the sense that it was undoubtedly to be viewed as a scandalous or taboo expression between a woman and a man.[20] This is not to say that this was a sexual act — not at all! It was, rather, an act that communicated and was directed by something far more significant than gender. Evidence from the ancient world suggests that the lowering of one's hair in this manner could be a sign of extreme gratitude and an expression of humility.[21] Thus, Mary was addressing Jesus not as a man but as *the* King, the one to whom the only appropriate posture was kneeling face down at his feet, anointing him with luxurious and sweet-smelling perfume, and using her own hair to express how much her whole person was in service to the King. Her hands were not soft enough to touch this King; she needed to use the softness of her own hair. In sharp contrast to what King Jesus would receive by the Jewish authorities and Roman guards in John 19, here Mary opens herself to shame to magnify the honor rightly due her Lord.

Finally, the narrator explains that "the house was filled from the fragrance of the perfume" (ἡ δὲ οἰκία ἐπληρώθη ἐκ τῆς ὀσμῆς τοῦ μύρου). This is often interpreted to say that the message of the Gospel will soon spread and fill the whole world.[22] This interpretation is likely influenced by Mark 14:9//Matthew 26:13, often dictated by the controlling comparison with the Synoptics to which we were opposed (see comments before v. 1). But the narrative gives us sufficient information to make sense of this comment by the narrator. Besides a depiction of the extravagance of the act,[23] this detail impresses upon the reader the common connection both in Scripture (Song 1:2) as well as the ancient world between social status/power and scent, thus highlighting the grand royalty of Jesus.[24] Ironically, as v. 7 will explain, what Mary intended for a king Jesus received for a corpse.

---

17. Polybius, *Histories* 26.1.12 – 14.

18. J. Edgar Bruns, "A Note on Jn 12, 3," *CBQ* 28 (1966): 219 – 22.

19. Lincoln, *John*, 338.

20. Keener, *John*, 2:864.

21. Charles H. Cosgrove, "A Woman's Unbound Hair in the Greco-Roman World, with Special Reference to the Story of the 'Sinful Woman' in Luke 7:36 – 50," *JBL* 124 (2005): 675 – 92.

22. See Bultmann, *John*, 415; Hoskyns, *Fourth Gospel*, 414 – 15; Aquinas, *John*, 2:265.

23. Moloney, "Can Everyone be Wrong?," 524.

24. Dominika A. Kurek-Chomycz, "The Fragrance of Her Perfume: The Significance of the Sense Imagery in John's Account of the Anointing in Bethany," *NovT* 52 (2010): 334 – 54

12:4 But Judas Iscariot, one of his disciples, the one who was about to betray him, said (λέγει δὲ Ἰούδας ὁ Ἰσκαριώτης εἷς τῶν μαθητῶν αὐτοῦ, ὁ μέλλων αὐτὸν παραδιδόναι). The conflict of the pericope is introduced by Judas Iscariot, whom the narrator describes almost paradoxically as both one of Jesus's disciples and "the one who was about to betray [Jesus]" (ὁ μέλλων αὐτὸν παραδιδόναι). Judas has only been mentioned once before as both "one of the Twelve" and as "the devil" (6:70–71). In this scene, Judas almost serves as the "anti-narrator," offering a commentary on the activities that distort their substance and truth. He does not speak in anger or rage, but with reasoned pretentiousness asks a question that directly rebukes Mary and indirectly (that is, more politely) rebukes the just-anointed King himself.[25]

12:5 "Why was this perfume not sold for three hundred denarii and given to the poor?" (Διὰ τί τοῦτο τὸ μύρον οὐκ ἐπράθη τριακοσίων δηναρίων καὶ ἐδόθη πτωχοῖς;). Mary's symbolic act, drenched with significance in regard to her slave-like worship of Jesus whom she anointed as the King (v. 3), is thrown out by Judas with one question that focuses only on the economic significance of the act. His concern is that the perfume is worth "three hundred denarii" (τριακοσίων δηναρίων). Since one denarius was what an average worker could make in one day, the perfume was valued by Judas to be the equivalent of one year's wages. Thus, the perfume was beyond extravagant. And shockingly, Mary did not hand it to Jesus to be credited to his bank account but poured it all on his feet! Since it was more than most women would inherit, the gift was like an inheritance, an offering of a slave to her King.[26]

Judas asks why this costly perfume, if it was to be spent, was not turned into cash and "given to the poor" (ἐδόθη πτωχοῖς) instead of being used as anointing oil. The statement makes two interesting assumptions. First, it assumes that the value of the perfume was financial, thus relegating the act of anointing Jesus as superfluous and wasteful. Second, it assumes that there was another office that needed it more than the office of king — the office of the poor. Again, however, this interprets the value of the perfume only by economic standards. Even before we hear the narrator's interpretation of Judas's intentions, we must take note of the distinction between Mary and Judas regarding the value of the perfume. For Mary the perfume was to be *measured by its price of expression*; its value was that it was the most worthy substance with which to anoint Jesus, and its worth was to be equated with the worth of the person upon whom it was placed (making the placement on the feet suggestive that even this luxurious oil was only worth placing there). For Judas the perfume was to be *measured by its purchase price*; its value was found in the amount of dollars with which it could be compared and exchanged.

12:6 But he did not say this because he was caring for the poor himself but because he was a thief, and since he was the one who had the money box, he was taking what was put into it (εἶπεν δὲ τοῦτο οὐχ ὅτι περὶ τῶν πτωχῶν ἔμελεν αὐτῷ ἀλλ' ὅτι κλέπτης ἦν καὶ τὸ γλωσσόκομον ἔχων τὰ βαλλόμενα ἐβάσταζεν). The conflict of the pericope is concluded with an explanatory comment by the narrator. The narrator explains that Judas was not actually interested in the poor, for

---

(esp. 342–44). Cf. David S. Potter, "Odor and Power in the Roman Empire," in *Constructions of the Classical Body*, ed. James I. Porter (Ann Arbor: University of Michigan Press, 2002), 169–89.

25. As Michaels notes regarding Judas, "His abrupt ques-

tion is conspicuously *not* introduced by 'Lord' or 'Rabbi'" (*John*, 669).

26. Keener, *John*, 2:864. While the value of the perfume might suggest that the Bethany family had some wealth, the gift is still nearly beyond description.

his only interest was the perfume itself. The narrator helps the reader understand that while Mary had never truly considered the perfume on its own but had viewed it through the lens of the worth of Jesus, Judas thought only about the perfume itself and its economic value. The narrator further explains that Judas's bias is rooted in his identity as "a thief" (κλέπτης), who as the treasurer, "the one who had the money box" (τὸ γλωσσόκομον ἔχων), was comfortably helping himself to the group's financial resources. Though the text does not say as much, perhaps Judas felt a personal loss when the perfume was given to Jesus in a manner that nullified its financial value. Perhaps Judas may have also seen the value of the perfume by its price of expression, but only if it had been poured into his own purse instead of on the feet of Jesus.

But Judas's question has raised conflict that needs to be resolved. Two issues are made evident. First, *was Mary right* to bestow upon Jesus the honor that she did? Second, *was Mary wrong* to offer such an extravagant gift to Jesus when there are others for whom the gift could be offered, like the poor, as Judas (even if maliciously) suggested? To these questions Jesus now responds.

12:7 Then Jesus said, "Leave her alone; it was intended to be kept for the day of my preparation for burial" (εἶπεν οὖν ὁ Ἰησοῦς, Ἄφες αὐτήν, ἵνα εἰς τὴν ἡμέραν τοῦ ἐνταφιασμοῦ μου τηρήσῃ αὐτό). The resolution of the pericope is provided by Jesus, who responds to both issues of the meaning (v. 7) and value (v. 8) of Mary's act. Jesus responds directly to Judas's question by defending the action of Mary: "Leave her alone" (Ἄφες αὐτήν). Such a statement affirms the symbolic meaning of the act performed by Mary. Jesus then offers an explanation as to why her act was acceptable: "It was intended to be kept for the day of my preparation for

burial" (ἵνα εἰς τὴν ἡμέραν τοῦ ἐνταφιασμοῦ μου τηρήσῃ αὐτό).[27] According to Jesus, the perfume was always intended for Jesus. Yet the reader is left wondering why Jesus suggests that the intention of the act was for the burial and not for his anointing as king. As we discussed above (v. 3), a person was anointed to mark the beginning of their rule, not the end. By offering his own commentary on the symbolic meaning of Mary's act, Jesus provides further insight into the particular (royal) office he is beginning. Mary may have acted as a slave to anoint her King, but it will ultimately be Jesus who must serve the children of God by pouring out his entire inheritance given to him by the Father. In this way, Jesus offers a rejoinder to Judas's question that affirms the royal anointing that Mary bestowed upon him, but not without taking it one step further.

12:8 "For you will always have the poor with you, but you will not always have me" (τοὺς πτωχοὺς γὰρ πάντοτε ἔχετε μεθ' ἑαυτῶν, ἐμὲ δὲ οὐ πάντοτε ἔχετε). After affirming the meaning of Mary's act and even speaking beyond her pious intentions, Jesus now responds to the value of Mary's act, offering a fitting resolution to the conflict. Jesus's statement does not deny the poor their place, but he clearly moves them into a secondary position in his presence. In one sense, this is because there is a shortage of time for giving to Christ, whereas "you will always have the poor with you" (τοὺς πτωχοὺς γὰρ πάντοτε ἔχετε μεθ' ἑαυτῶν). However, more than chronological priority is implied by this comparison, especially when he will later promise his disciples in a similarly paradoxical mode of expression that he will not leave them as orphans, for they will always see him (see comments on 14:18 – 19).[28] What is being communicated is that the primary, even sole, object of devotion is always Jesus Christ. The poor are never an object onto themselves, but

27. Cf. Moloney, *John*, 357.

28. See Augustine, *John*, 50.13.282.

in light of God's character and commands are ideally suited as symptomatic expressions of devotion to Christ. Just as Mary had not considered the perfume on its own but had viewed it through the lens of the worth of Jesus (in contrast to Judas; see v. 6), so also must the disciple of Jesus give full devotion to the one who deserves it above any other — Jesus Christ, our King.

Christ's comment about the poor here does not contradict the entirely Christian concern for the poor taught elsewhere in Scripture. In fact, Jesus's statement assumes the continuing validity of traditional obligations to the poor commanded by the OT, for example in Deuteronomy 15:11: "There will always be poor people in the land. Therefore I command you to be openhanded toward your fellow Israelites who are poor and needy in your land."[29] But ultimately Christian devotion to the poor, as necessary as it is, is a subset of Christian devotion to Christ, the King, who commands his people to serve others. We give to the poor because they are in need; we give to Jesus because we are in need. It is only by means of the latter that we can rightly see ourselves as slaves of Christ and not as fellow royalty. With Calvin we can say that our care for the poor may then become "a sweet savour [fragrance] to God."[30]

12:9 Then a large crowd of the Jews learned that he was there, and they came not only because of Jesus but also in order to see Lazarus, whom he had raised from the dead (Ἔγνω οὖν [ὁ] ὄχλος πολὺς ἐκ τῶν Ἰουδαίων ὅτι ἐκεῖ ἐστιν, καὶ ἦλθον οὐ διὰ τὸν Ἰησοῦν μόνον ἀλλ᾽ ἵνα καὶ τὸν Λάζαρον ἴδωσιν ὃν ἤγειρεν ἐκ νεκρῶν). The conclusion and interpretation of the pericope shifts focus from the intimate details of the celebratory dinner to the public reaction toward Jesus in light of the resurrection of Lazarus. A large crowd of "the

Jews," whom the Gospel has clearly defined as antagonists and opponents of Jesus (see comments on 1:19) and who had earlier been looking for Jesus (11:55 – 56), had become aware of Jesus's location and were making their way toward him. They were not merely coming on account of him, "but also in order to see Lazarus" (ἀλλ᾽ ἵνα καὶ τὸν Λάζαρον ἴδωσιν). Clearly the resurrection of Lazarus (the sixth sign) had become known, and people wanted to see the evidence for themselves. The narrator thus depicts how the public reputation of Jesus is beginning to grow (cf. 12:17 – 18).

12:10 But the high priests planned to kill Lazarus (ἐβουλεύσαντο δὲ οἱ ἀρχιερεῖς ἵνα καὶ τὸν Λάζαρον ἀποκτείνωσιν). The Jewish authorities had already "planned" (ἐβουλεύσαντο) in the meeting chambers of the Sanhedrin to kill Jesus (11:53), but with the growing fame of Jesus centering upon the Lazarus miracle (see v. 11), a further decision was made to kill Lazarus as well, as if the Lord could resurrect those who die by sickness and not by murder.

12:11 Because of him many of the Jews were leaving and believing in Jesus (ὅτι πολλοὶ δι᾽ αὐτὸν ὑπῆγον τῶν Ἰουδαίων καὶ ἐπίστευον εἰς τὸν Ἰησοῦν). Here the reason the Jewish authorities need to kill Lazarus is clearly stated. Everything Lazarus did — every breath, every conversation, every time he recounted being awoken in the dark, cold tomb — was a thorn in the flesh of the Jewish authorities. They needed to silence his (living) testimony. The word translated as "leaving" (ὑπῆγον) is used here with the meaning, to "depart from one's allegiance" (for a similar use, see 6:67).[31] But from the beginning of the Gospel, the reader has been warned not to confuse such beliefs with real belief; belief not in the signs Jesus was doing but in his name (1:12).

---

29. Lincoln, *John*, 339.
30. Calvin, *John 11 – 21*, 28.

31. Cf. Barrett, *John*, 415.

Theology in Application

As the public ministry of Jesus nears its conclusion (11:1 – 12:50), the Gospel gives the reader rich insights into the person and work of Jesus Christ. At this dinner, transformed from funeral banquet to joyous celebration, Jesus is bestowed honor for being "the resurrection and the life" (11:25). But it is not Lazarus's resurrection that will finally defeat death. For as this pericope explains, the lavish honor properly directed at Jesus for the gift of life is simultaneously (and necessarily) preparation for the shame he is about to endure by means of his death. In this pericope the reader of the Fourth Gospel is being directed to the cross and is exhorted to give their full devotion to the one ultimately worthy of our service, Jesus Christ.

Honoring the King and the Corpse

In this pericope Jesus is rightly declared to be the King. And Jesus is a king; he is the King of kings and the Lord of lords, before whom "every knee should bow, in heaven and on earth and under the earth, and every tongue acknowledge that Jesus Christ is Lord, to the glory of God the Father" (Phil 2:10 – 11). As extravagant as Mary's gift was in its context, it is simply not enough, for the whole world — every created thing — ought to bestow him with all the honor and gifts they possess. This is the primary task of the church: to honor Christ, giving God the glory in all things. The chief end of humanity is something like the celebratory dinner in this pericope, "to glorify God and enjoy him forever." It is to have received new life from him (like Lazarus) and to return to him the most that can be given (like Mary) — our most precious and valuable gifts.

But what is remarkable about this pericope is that the emphasis is placed not on Jesus as King but on Jesus as corpse. For Jesus, the anointing was preparation for death, which suggests that he receives his honor not from those he came to serve but from his Father, and not in spite of the cross but because of it. That is, his exaltation can only occur after his humiliation, as the following order suggests: "He humbled himself by becoming obedient to death — even death on a cross! Therefore [i.e., for this reason] God exalted him to the highest place and gave him the name that is above every name" (Phil 2:8 – 9). It is the cross, then, that is the final coronation for this king; the cross is where he will be crowned with thorns and dressed with shame and contempt and ultimately "lifted up." This king's throne is a cross and his castle is a tomb. And when the coronation is over, it will be not one pound but one hundred pounds of perfume — a hundredfold (19:39) — with which this king will be anointed. Jesus is the Son of Man *and* the Suffering Servant, the Sovereign Lord *and* the slain Lamb (Rev 5:6); he is both King and corpse.

The Posture of the Disciple

In a highly symbolic and extravagant act, Mary of Bethany anoints Jesus as King, but she also did so in a manner that rightly expressed her position of servitude (slavery) to her king. Without words, Mary shouted allegiance and humble submission to the Lord, kneeling at his feet and using her hair to anoint them with expensive perfume. Mary displayed the true posture of the Christian disciple. Drenched in the fragrance of Christ, Mary performed what Paul preached: "We are to God the pleasing aroma of Christ" (2 Cor 2:15).

Care for the Poor

It would be a mistake to think that this pericope was suggesting that the poor were not a Christian concern. Jesus's statement in v. 8 assumes that the poor are a fundamental and present issue for God's people (cf. Deut 15:11). Jesus's statement was not intended to release the Christian from such social and ethical concerns; rather, it rightly emphasizes the subject of Christian devotion. A Christian concern for the poor must not be motivated by philanthropy ("love for humanity") but *theophilia* ("love for God"). Or, as it is more commonly known, by charity, the English word derived from the Greek word for "grace" (*charis*).

Augustine is helpful here. In book one of *Teaching Christianity*, Augustine establishes a division between what should be "enjoyed" and what should be "used." Augustine argues that only that which can be loved for its own sake should be the object of our love and devotion.[32] For this reason, as strange as it may sound in contemporary culture, all things other than God — including the poor — are to be "used" and not "enjoyed." This in no way degrades that which is used — hardly! — but rather locates them in their proper place so as to be appropriately attended to. That is, to "use" things is to place them in relationship to God. It is to love things "in the right order, so that you do not love what is not to be loved, or fail to love what is to be loved."[33]

This is significant in two ways, especially in relation to the tension between Jesus and the poor. First, it gives the greatest warrant possible for caring for the poor, which becomes one of the objective ways ("uses") a Christian can show devotion to God. Devotion to the needs of the poor, then, is really and more foundationally devotion to God.[34] Second and at the same time, it allows the Christian to maintain a distinction (a division!) between love for God and love for humanity (philanthropy). It makes clear that the true object of love and devotion, that is, true Christian love and devotion, can only be directed toward God alone. In this way, we can understand how Jesus was not pitting the devotion displayed toward him over and against devotion to the poor, but describing the true object of devotion — even when it is applied simultaneously to the poor. Love and care for the poor, Christian! And when you do, you are bestowing honor where it is ultimately due, at the feet of Jesus.

---

32. Augustine, *Teaching Christianity*, 1.3 – 4.107.   34. Ibid., 1.37.122.
33. Ibid., 1.28.118.

John 12:12 – 19

Literary Context

The Gospel continues in this section, "The Conclusion of Jesus's Public Ministry" (11:1 – 12:50), by continuing to focus on the final public appearances of Jesus. After having moved away from the center of the activity, Jesus now returns to Jerusalem for the last time before his death and resurrection. Jesus was honored as a king at a private dinner party in the previous pericope (12:1 – 11), but here he receives a more public and explicit honoring by a large crowd that is part of a growing interest in him. Yet as this pericope will make clear, the arrival of Jesus is more significant than the enduring crowd and onlookers — even the disciples (cf. v. 16) — are fully aware. For in this scene a very different kind of king arrives in Jerusalem for a very different reason: to offer the world a kind of kingdom that they have never seen before.

VI. The Conclusion of Jesus's Public Ministry (11:1 – 12:50)

    A. The Sixth Sign: The Death and Resurrection of Lazarus (11:1 – 57)

    B. The Anointing of Jesus (12:1 – 11)

→   **C. The Royal Entrance of Jesus into Jerusalem (12:12 – 19)**

    D. "The Hour has Come": The Final Public Statement of Jesus (12:20 – 50)

Main Idea

Jesus is the King of kings, the one who comes in the name of the Lord. The "glory" of King Jesus must be understood not only by his royal entrance into Jerusalem but also by his departure from the grave, his resurrection from the dead.

Translation

John 12:12–19

12a	Introduction & Setting (12–13)	On the next day
b	Character Entrance	**the large crowd …**
c		that had come for the feast
d		**… heard that Jesus was coming**
e	Destination	into Jerusalem.
13a	Progression of Action #1	**They took palm branches**
b	Progression of Action #2	and **went out to meet him,**
c	(Proclamation) #3	and **they shouted,**
d	Allusion: Ps 118:25–27	"Hosanna,
e		blessed is the one who comes in the name of the Lord, even
f		the King of Israel."
	Conflict (14–15)	
14a	Simultaneous Action	**Jesus found a donkey and sat upon it,**
b	Conflation of OT Texts	just as it is written,
15a	Imperative of Comfort	"Do not fear,
b	Address	O Daughter of Zion;
c	Regal Exclamation	behold,
d	Acceptance of 13	your King is coming,
e	Regal Description	seated on a young donkey."
16a	Resolution/Narrator's Aside (16)	**At first his disciples did not understand these things,**
b	Contrast	but
c	Event	when Jesus was glorified
d	Result	**then they remembered that these things had been written about him** and
e		**that they had done these things to him.**
17a	Conclusion (17–19)	Then **the crowd …**
b		that was with him
c	Description of Event	when he called Lazarus from the tomb and
d		raised him from the dead
e	Reaction of "Crowd"	**… was testifying about him.**
18a		For this reason
b	Progressing Reaction	**the crowd went out to meet him,**
c	Basis	because they heard that he had given this sign.
19a	Reaction of the Pharisees	Then **the Pharisees said to one another,**
b	Escalating Exasperation	"You can see that you are accomplishing nothing.
c	Interjection	Look,
d	Hyperbolic Assertion	the whole world is going after him."

Structure and Literary Form

This pericope corresponds to the basic story form (see Introduction). The *introduction/setting* is established in vv. 12 – 13, explaining the location, setting, and people around which the plot's conflict will focus. In vv. 14 – 15 the *conflict* of the pericope is focused upon Jesus, specifically the unique actions he undertakes as he enters Jerusalem past the heralding crowd. In v. 16 the conflict is given a *resolution* by the narrator who offers significant commentary on the connection of the events to Jesus and the postglorification understanding of the disciples. Finally, vv. 17 – 19 serve to explain the *conclusion/interpretation* of the activities, placing them in the context of Jesus's concluding public presence.

Exegetical Outline

➡   **C. The Royal Entrance of Jesus into Jerusalem (12:12 – 19)**
1. Preparations for a King (vv. 12 – 13)
2. The Royal Entrance of the King (vv. 14 – 15)
3. The True Nature of Jesus's Kingship (v. 16)
4. "The Whole World Has Gone After Him": Public Responses to Jesus (vv. 17 – 19)

Explanation of the Text

This pericope, like the previous one (12:1 – 11), occurs in all four Gospels (cf. Matt 21:1 – 11; Mark 11:1 – 11; Luke 19:29 – 38) and is therefore heavily compared with the Synoptics, especially by means of the differences between them. The most important difference between John and the Synoptics is the description of the procurement of the animal to ride found in all three Synoptics, whereas in John the animal is simply "found" (v. 14). It is highly unlikely that the Gospels are describing two different events — in fact, there is evidence to the contrary (see comments on v. 14). However, for methodological reasons (see Introduction), our attention will focus only on the account given by the Fourth Gospel.

12:12 On the next day the large crowd that had come for the feast heard that Jesus was coming into Jerusalem (Τῇ ἐπαύριον ὁ ὄχλος πολὺς ὁ ἐλθὼν εἰς τὴν ἑορτήν, ἀκούσαντες ὅτι ἔρχεται ὁ Ἰησοῦς εἰς Ἱεροσόλυμα). The phrase "on the next day" (Τῇ ἐπαύριον) is a technical transition common in John that informs the reader that a new section of the narrative is beginning (see comments before 1:19; cf. comments on 12:9). Since the events of the previous day occurred on the Jewish Sabbath, Saturday, the arrival of Jesus to Jerusalem must be occurring on Sunday, what Christians now celebrate as Palm Sunday, a holiday on which the church emulates the actions depicted in this pericope and the other three Gospels. This pericope provides the biblical warrant for one of the church's traditional holiday practices, especially since the symbols and actions depicted by this pericope are still used in contemporary Christian worship.

The introduction and setting of the pericope begins with a description of the continued pursuit of

Jesus by "the large crowd" (ὁ ὄχλος πολὺς), which probably includes not only those who had been looking for Jesus after hearing of the resurrection of Lazarus (see 11:55 – 56; 12:9 – 11) but also many more "that had come for the feast" (ὁ ἐλθὼν εἰς τὴν ἑορτήν), that is, for Passover (cf. 12:1). Since very large numbers of people could be expected to come to Jerusalem to celebrate Passover, there may have been a growing messianic fervor surrounding the legends regarding Jesus, as the Pharisees themselves will acknowledge in v. 19.

12:13 They took palm branches and went out to meet him, and they shouted, "Hosanna, blessed is the one who comes in the name of the Lord, even the King of Israel" (ἔλαβον τὰ βαΐα τῶν φοινίκων καὶ ἐξῆλθον εἰς ὑπάντησιν αὐτῷ, καὶ ἐκραύγαζον, Ὡσαννά· εὐλογημένος ὁ ἐρχόμενος ἐν ὀνόματι κυρίου, καὶ ὁ βασιλεὺς τοῦ Ἰσραήλ). The crowd expresses their growing messianic fervor and reveals their interpretation of Jesus dramatically by the preparations they undertake for his arrival. According to the narrator, the large crowd "went out to meet him" (ἐξῆλθον εἰς ὑπάντησιν αὐτῷ), a phrase commonly used in a special and more official sense to signal "the official welcome of a newly arrived dignitary."[1] This phrase is likely reflecting the crowd's favorable reception of Jesus as a dignitary, a phrase which also often carried royal and political overtones.[2] The picture being painted would involve the large crowd "welcoming the person [Jesus] in an elaborate and festive procession accompanied by songs and praises."[3]

The crowd has "palm branches" (τὰ βαΐα τῶν φοινίκων) in their possession, for which there is ample evidence in regard to its symbolism. While there is no OT connection to palm branches and Passover, palm branches would have been imme-

diately recognized by first-century Jews as a religious and political symbol. They were used as a religious symbol during the liturgies of the Feasts of Tabernacles and Dedication, carrying "a special significance in Judaism as a symbol of victory, resurrection, and authority."[4] Thus, religiously the palm branch served as a proleptic proclamation of the future triumph that God would provide for his people.

Palm branches were also used as a national symbol by the Jews. For over one hundred fifty years, they had been directly associated with the Maccabean revolution, when after Simon Maccabeus expelled the Syrian forces from the temple and Jerusalem he was welcomed back to Jerusalem with songs and praises and "palm branches" (βαΐων), celebrating the Jewish triumph over their enemies (1 Macc 13:51). Palms were also used by Simon's brother, Judas Maccabeus, when he rededicated the sanctuary after it had been profaned by the Seleucid ruler Antiochus IV Epiphanes (2 Macc 10:7; cf. 1 Macc 1:59; Josephus, *Ant.* 12.320 – 21), which resulted in the celebration of the Feast of Dedication (which the Fourth Gospel clearly knows [cf. 10:22]). In light of the explicit reference to the Feast of Dedication in 10:22, the symbolic significance of palm branches here for the Gospel of John takes on greater significance.

The significance of this Jewish history — and therefore the symbolic action of the crowd — is evidenced even further and directly connected to the ministry of Jesus in two other ways. First, since either five or six of the disciples had Maccabean names (as well as two of Jesus's brothers), this strongly suggests that Jesus ministered in a region that cherished the national heroes of Israel as a proud people under foreign rule, hoping for

1. Moulton, *Grammar*, 1:14.
2. See Brunson, *Psalm 118 in the Gospel of John*, 188 – 96.
3. Bill Salier, "Jesus, the Emperor, and the Gospel according to John," in *Challenging Perspectives on the Gospel of John*, 284 – 301 (296).
4. Brunson, *Psalm 118 in the Gospel of John*, 216.

ultimate deliverance.[5] Second, surrounding the time of Jesus's ministry there is evidence of Jewish coins that had the image of a palm tree, with some bearing the inscription "for the redemption of Zion."[6] Thus, while the symbolic act of carrying or waving branches would have symbolized for many ancient readers the communication of triumph or royal welcome,[7] by focusing specifically on "palm branches" with its centuries of religious significance and its overtones of Maccabean nationalism, the crowd is officially heralding Jesus as a king. Our analysis does not only make this judgment from historical evidence (Jewish history, literature, and coins) but also from Scripture itself, for according to Revelation 7:9 there will also be a great multitude singing songs and praises to Christ, holding "palm branches in their hands" (φοίνικες ἐν ταῖς χερσὶν αὐτῶν).

As significant as the two symbolic actions of the crowd are to the scene at hand (i.e., going out to meet Jesus and the waving of palm branches), it is what "they shouted" (ἐκραύγαζον) that is given the most narrative emphasis.[8] It is important to note that the heralding of the crowd is derived from Psalm 118:25 – 26, with Psalm 118 originally serving as a king's psalm, celebrating God's kingship and the king's role as Yahweh's representative. It was used in royal processions, emphasizing the central role and leadership of the king.[9] Interestingly, the psalm was delivered out of a crisis, befitting in many ways the context of this scene.[10]

This is also the only citation of Scripture in the Gospel not preceded by a quotation formula (cf. vv. 14 – 15).[11] The crowd makes a threefold proclamation that needs to be analyzed in detail.

First, the crowd shouts "Hosanna" (Ὡσαννά). The term is a Greek transliteration of the Hebrew and Aramaic imperative addressed to God: "Save!" In the context of Psalm 118, the term is an appeal to Yahweh for help, yet it was clearly used as an acclamation in later Jewish tradition and the NT (e.g., Matt 21:9; Mark 11:10),[12] with even the rest of Psalm 118, especially v. 27, reflecting implicitly this allowance in meaning.[13] By the time the Didache was written (late first or early second century), the term in Christian circles was used for praise and was almost entirely an expression of exultation (Did. 10:6). While in the Fourth Gospel the term clearly functions as acclamation, its original nuance should not be lost behind its use as an acclamation: the person being officially welcomed is expected to be the one who will save them.[14] By this one word, the crowd expresses their hopes about Jesus, assuming he is God's light shining upon them (Ps 118:27).

Second, the crowd shouts, "Blessed is the one who comes in the name of the Lord" (εὐλογημένος ὁ ἐρχόμενος ἐν ὀνόματι κυρίου), a statement taken directly from Psalm 118:26, which is intended to "bless" or praise "the one who is coming" to save the people. This latter phrase served in early Christianity as a messianic title, and even the Gospel

5. William R. Farmer, "The Palm Branches in John 12, 13," *JTS* 3 (1952): 62 – 66 (64).

6. Ibid., 63. Cf. Abraham A. Reifenberg, *Ancient Jewish Coins*, 2nd ed. (Jerusalem: Rubin Mass, 1947), 37.

7. Keener, *John*, 2:869.

8. See Leung, *The Kingship-Cross Interplay in the Gospel of John*, 154.

9. Brunson, *Psalm 118 in the Gospel of John*, 23 – 45.

10. Goldingay, *Psalms*, 3:354 – 55.

11. Margaret Daly-Denton, "The Psalms in John's Gospel," in *The Psalms in the New Testament*, ed. Steve Moyise and

Maarten J. J. Menken (London: T&T Clark, 2004), 119 – 37 (126).

12. See Joseph A. Fitzmyer, "Aramaic Evidence Affecting the Interpretation of *Hosanna* in the New Testament," in *Tradition and Interpretation in the New Testament: Essays in Honor of E. Earle Ellis for His 60th Birthday*, ed. Gerald F. Hawthorne with Otto Betz (Grand Rapids: Eerdmans; Tübingen: Mohr Siebeck, 1987), 110 – 18.

13. Brunson, *Psalm 118 in the Gospel of John*, 205.

14. Cf. J. F. Coakley, "Jesus's Messianic Entry into Jerusalem (John 12:12 – 19 Par)," *JTS* 46 (1995): 461 – 82 (473 – 74).

gives evidence of such a meaning and use (see comments on 3:2). Even more, this statement is nearly copyrighted by the Fourth Gospel, with this theme serving as a primary motif of the person and mission of Jesus (e.g., 1:15, 27, 30; 4:25; 6:14; 11:27).[15] While the crowd would have used this statement to honor Jesus out of their more limited, messianic purview, the reader of the Gospel has a more cosmological perspective.

Third, the crowd shouts, "Even the King of Israel" (καὶ ὁ βασιλεὺς τοῦ Ἰσραήλ). This final part of the proclamation is the clearest declaration of the kingly nature of the crowd's interpretation of Jesus. This statement is not original to Psalm 118:26, yet it is added in such a way that it is inseparable from "the coming one." By adding "King of Israel" to the quotation from Psalm 118:16, the crowd clearly identifies Jesus with the royal figure of the psalm, thus evoking the original procession (vv. 25–27) as a model for Jesus's arrival to Jerusalem. The Gospel is clearly interested in the kingship of Jesus. The theme serves as a frame for both the public ministry of Jesus (1:49 and 12:13) as well as the narrative as a whole (18:33, 39; 19:3, 19, 21). Thus the heralding of Jesus as king here is highly significant. In a sense, the crowd is reenacting Psalm 118, proclaiming Jesus as king as he enters Jerusalem. It is in this way that the introduction and setting of the pericope concludes, establishing for the reader a vibrant scene of royal pomp and circumstance.

12:14 Jesus found a donkey and sat upon it, just as it is written (εὑρὼν δὲ ὁ Ἰησοῦς ὀνάριον ἐκάθισεν ἐπ᾽ αὐτό, καθώς ἐστιν γεγραμμένον). The conflict of the pericope must be understood as occurring in the midst of the kingly welcome Jesus is receiving from the large crowd as he approaches Jerusalem. Jesus offers a clear response to the royal acclamation of the crowd by doing two symbolically significant acts.

First, Jesus "found a donkey" (εὑρὼν ὀνάριον). The symbolic meaning of the donkey may be the most important tool for interpreting the nature of Jesus's entrance into Jerusalem and, more specifically, his response to the acclaiming crowd. Many interpreters consider Jesus's use of a donkey to be a correction of the crowd because of the general assumption that "the ass had lowly associations" (cf. Sir 33:24).[16] Since many interpreters assume the crowd's acclamation of king Jesus was drenched in nationalistic expectations, it is often assumed that Jesus chose a donkey with the specific intention of "dampening down" such misguided expectations.[17] If Jesus were to accept the crowd's royal praise, he would have chosen a kingly horse (symbolizing war), not a donkey, a beast of burden (cf. Isa 30:6).

But the biblical and historical evidence does not support this picture of the donkey. While the horse would eventually become symbolic for military power,[18] mules and donkeys have a much earlier and longer heritage as symbols for royalty. Furthermore, as Kinman notes, a "clear example of a Jewish king riding a horse is not to be found in the LXX."[19] As much as donkeys were widely characterized "as the beast of burden *par excellence*" throughout ancient Near Eastern texts, they also served as a mount for people of high standing—nobility and aristocracy, prophets, royalty, and deity.[20] That is, while the donkey on its own is often symbolic of

15. Bultmann, *John*, 404.
16. Morris, *John*, 521.
17. Carson, *John*, 433.
18. See Philippe Germond and Jacques Livet, *An Egyptian Bestiary: Animals in Life and Religion in the Land of the Pharoahs*, trans. Barbara Mellor (London: Thames & Hudson, 2001), 82.
19. Brent Kinman, *Jesus's Entry into Jerusalem: In the Context of Lukan Theology and the Politics of His Day*, AGJU 28 (Leiden: Brill, 1995), 52.
20. Kenneth C. Way, *Donkeys in the Biblical World: Ceremony and Symbol*, HACL 2 (Winona Lake, IN: Eisenbrauns, 2011), 97–100.

a "pack animal," with a rider of high standing the donkey became an intentional symbol of status (e.g., prestige, power, and wealth), most often employed to signify royal status. As Way describes it, "The donkey is, so to speak, the 'Mercedes-Benz' of the biblical world."[21] The fact that the narrator describes Jesus himself as the one who procured a donkey suggests that his choice of animal — and all its symbolic meaning — was part of his response to the crowd. Rather than correcting or rebuking the acclamation of the crowd, Jesus appears to be accepting it, even participating in the crowd's reenactment of the royal proclamation of Psalm 118.

Second, Jesus "sat upon it" (ἐκάθισεν ἐπ᾽ αὐτό). It is not just the presence of the donkey that is suggestive of the image Jesus is presenting but what Jesus did with the donkey — he mounted it. In light of our discussion above, this is a kingly move, matching the royal acclamation of the crowd. Against Coakley, who argued that "Jesus did not intend to ride the donkey at all but was made to do so by enthusiastic followers,"[22] the text clearly depicts Jesus as the agent of action, securing the donkey himself and placing himself upon it. The crowd reenacts the kingly coronation of Psalm 118, and Jesus enters in like manner. In light of the historical and symbolic context of this scene, the image of Jesus riding into Jerusalem mounted on a donkey symbolizes not humility but authority and kingship. Jesus's actions intensify his claim to kingship, evoking the ancient enthronement liturgy of Psalm 118.[23] The symbolic significance of these acts, however, is not left to the assumptions of cultural practices but is intended to correspond to and be explained by an OT Scripture, to which the narrator points the reader. That is, the symbolic meaning of Jesus's responsive act must be understood by means of the message of Zechariah 9, which the narrator sets up authoritatively with the preface "just as it is written" (καθώς ἐστιν γεγραμμένον).

12:15 "Do not fear, O Daughter of Zion; behold, your King is coming, seated on a young donkey" (Μὴ φοβοῦ, θυγάτηρ Σιών· ἰδοὺ ὁ βασιλεύς σου ἔρχεται, καθήμενος ἐπὶ πῶλον ὄνου). Neither this quotation nor the context of Zechariah 9 suggest that this king comes humbly or in peace.[24] There is nothing humble or peaceful about the king's arrival in Zechariah 9, for to those that oppose him this king "will take away her possessions and her destroy her power ... she will be consumed by fire ... will writhe in agony ... for her hope will wither" taking "blood from their mouths" (vv. 4–7). For as this king says, "I will encamp at my temple.... Never again will an oppressor overrun my people, for now I am keeping watch" (v. 8). The "peace" this king secures is an extension of his powerful and authoritative kingship. He "will take away the chariots from Ephraim and the war horses from Jerusalem, and the battle bow will be broken," thereby extending his rule "to the ends of the earth" (v. 10). If there is peace, it is because this king has defeated the enemies by overpowering and overthrowing them. And the humility of this king is that he welcomes his people into his kingdom, under his rule, offering them "salvation" (v. 9), establishing a blood covenant with them (v. 11), shielding them from all further enemies (v. 15), and establishing them "as his flock," dwelling in his land "like jewels in a crown" (v. 16). This king's humility and peace consist in the fact that he is *for* and not *against* the people to whom he comes; yet this makes him no less powerful and authoritative (or even less dangerous), just more righteous and gracious. It is the difference between a king of the law and the King of "grace and truth" (see 1:17). It is out of this context that the Gospel quotes Zechariah 9:9, which

21. Ibid., 87.
22. Coakley, "Jesus's Messianic Entry into Jerusalem," 479.
23. Brunson, *Psalm 118 in the Gospel of John*, 276.
24. Contra Köstenberger, "John," 472.

assumes and summarizes the overall thrust of the entire message of Zechariah 9 with its symbol of the king on his donkey. It is a symbol laden prophecy that Jesus himself has now fulfilled.

The narrator provides a significant scriptural interpretation of Jesus's response to the royal acclamation of the crowd. The opening phrase, "Do not fear" (Μὴ φοβοῦ), is not found in Zechariah 9:9 and is probably a conflation — not uncommon in the NT — from one or more OT texts that echo the theme of Zechariah 9 (e.g., Isa 40:9; Zeph 3:16). The reason there is no fear is because the "shielding" power and authority of the true King has arrived. The phrase commonly occurs in the OT in the contexts of theophanies and announcements of God's reign.[25] The change from "rejoice" in Zechariah 9:9 to "do not fear" serves to emphasize the royal authority of this king, who offers his people a new and more powerful object of devotion and service. The title "O Daughter of Zion" (θυγάτηρ Σιών) is a collective, referring to the entire city of Jerusalem, the city into which Jesus now rides, probably reflective of all his people — the manifestation of an eschatological (cosmological) kingship.[26]

The biblical interpretation of Jesus's royal entrance into Jerusalem perfectly coincides with the next phrase from the quotation: "Behold, your king is coming, seated on a young donkey" (ἰδοὺ ὁ βασιλεύς σου ἔρχεται, καθήμενος ἐπὶ πῶλον ὄνου). By reenacting Zechariah 9, Jesus does not offer a critique of the crowd's nationalistic expectations of a monarchy; rather, he offers the announcement of salvation which he has come to establish by "the blood of my covenant with you" (Zech 9:11). Jesus has not rejected the crowd's royal greeting but embraced it. This is probably a surprise to the reader, who remembers another crowd's earlier attempt to

"seize him and make him king," followed by Jesus's intentional escape to the mountain (see 6:14 – 15). The reason for the change, however, should not be at all surprising; until this moment "his hour had not yet come" (7:30; 8:20; see comments on 2:4). Here Jesus accepts the office of King, but in his own time, as we are about to see, and in his own manner.[27]

As agreeable as Jesus's symbolic kingly entrance into Jerusalem is to the royal acclamation of the crowd, it is not without a certain degree of difference, which centers upon the symbol of the donkey as portrayed in Zechariah 9:9. In Zechariah 9:9, three different terms are used for donkey. The phrase in question is often translated as "riding on a donkey, on a colt, the foal of a donkey" (NIV). Recently Kenneth Way has argued that the three different terms form an intentional string of "donkey terms" that move from general to specific, with the second and third terms adding new information to the preceding term.[28] While, the first term is the general term for "donkey" (חֲמוֹר), the second and third terms add uniqueness to this "donkey" and have nothing to do with the age of the animal. Thus, "Instead of the very popular translations 'donkey,' 'colt,' and 'foal of a donkey' (for חֲמוֹר, עַיִר, and בֶּן־אֲתֹנוֹת), it is suggested that Zion's king is riding on a donkey (חֲמוֹר), but not just any donkey. He is riding on a [male donkey] (עַיִר), but not just any [male donkey]. He is riding on a purebred (בֶּן־אֲתֹנוֹת) [male donkey]."[29] Zion's king, who is now understood to be Jesus, comes not on the usual royal means of transportation associated with military conquest but on a "purebred male donkey," which is the royal mount associated with peace rather than elitism and conquest. That is, Jesus comes as king of a very different sort, and

---

25. Lincoln, *John*, 344.

26. Cf. Brunson, *Psalm 118 in the Gospel of John*, 279; Morris, *John*, 521.

27. Cf. Michaels, *John*, 678.

28. Kenneth C. Way, "Donkey Domain: Zechariah 9:9 and Lexical Semantics," *JBL* 129 (2010): 105 – 14 (106).

29. Ibid., 114.

this distinction needed the biblical and interpretive lens of Zechariah 9 to make sense of the nature of his kingship. This explains why the narrator has to explain the delayed understanding of the disciples (v. 16).

As the scene concludes, the conflict of the pericope is not quite what the reader expected. While "the crowd" is rarely depicted as insightful by the Gospel, Jesus's response to their royal acclamation of him is received with a symbolic act that accepts their declaration. Even still, something deeper and different is communicated by the royal entrance of Jesus, and it required the interpretive assistance of Zechariah 9 to make sense of it. The true nature of Jesus's kingship was so biblically grounded that even those present could not fully grasp it without the insights from Zechariah 9, and then only after Jesus was "glorified" (John 12:16). Our interpretation argues against the common assumption that Jesus rejected the royal acclamation of the crowd. This was no mere priestly entrance but the arrival of the King, the salvation of the world! But even when he accepts the title of King, Jesus is fulfilling a kingship of an entirely different order.

12:16 At first his disciples did not understand these things, but when Jesus was glorified then they remembered that these things had been written about him and that they had done these things to him (ταῦτα οὐκ ἔγνωσαν αὐτοῦ οἱ μαθηταὶ τὸ πρῶτον, ἀλλ᾽ ὅτε ἐδοξάσθη Ἰησοῦς τότε ἐμνήσθησαν ὅτι ταῦτα ἦν ἐπ᾽ αὐτῷ γεγραμμένα καὶ ταῦτα ἐποίησαν αὐτῷ). As the resolution of the pericope begins, the reader is struck by the unique conflict that has been presented. After chapters of Jesus's avoidance of kingship, Jesus now claims what rightfully belongs to him: the acclamation as the King of Israel who has come in the name of the Lord (v. 13). But as correct as the people were in regard to the identity of King Jesus, they were still unable to see the true nature of Jesus's kingship.

For this reason, the narrator intervenes to provide the resolution of the conflict which no one on the scene could have understood, for it required not only an explanation from the past (Zech 9) but also an explanation from that which is yet to come (the death and resurrection of Jesus Christ). Just as a similar intervention by the narrator occurred at the beginning of Jesus's public ministry (cf. 2:12–25, see especially comments on 2:17, 21–22), so also at the end of Jesus's public ministry the narrator is needed to explain the deeper (unseen) significance of Jesus's actions. Like frames around Jesus's public ministry, these pericopae expose the deeper and true person and work of Jesus Christ.

The resolution provided by the narrator is that while at first Jesus's disciples "did not understand these things" (ταῦτα οὐκ ἔγνωσαν), everything changed "when Jesus was glorified" (ὅτε ἐδοξάσθη Ἰησοῦς). This latter phrase is almost certainly synonymous with what the narrator said in a parallel situation in 2:22: "When Jesus was raised from the dead." The Gospel has already made clear that the "glorification" of Jesus, that is, his death and resurrection, was the final act of Jesus's ministry and that even the Spirit was not available until this occurred (see comments on 7:39). It was only after Jesus died and rose again that the disciples were able to understand the deeper meaning of what had just transpired. It was only when God by his Spirit removed the cataracts of distorted human kingship from their eyes that the disciples understood the nature of King Jesus (see comments on 16:13). Ironically, it was only after Jesus finished his ultimate service of sacrifice that they saw his power and glory.

In one sense, the royal entrance of Jesus was grasped by all participants, who with pomp and circumstance reenacted the royal acclamation of the king in Psalm 118. But in another important sense only understood in light of the scriptural lens of Zechariah 9 provided by the narrator, a very different kind of royal entrance was taking place. At that moment, it was only Jesus who knew what kind of king he truly was (the Son of Man; the King of kings), what kind of kingly duty he had to fulfill (the cross), and how inappropriately low were the kingly hopes and expectations of these people, including his disciples. And as Jesus entered Jerusalem that day, only he knew that the throne he was heading toward had a coronation involving a cross and that his "lifting up" was in order to receive shame not honor.[30] In this way the narrator brings resolution to the conflict of the pericope.

12:17 Then the crowd that was with him when he called Lazarus from the tomb and raised him from the dead was testifying about him (ἐμαρτύρει οὖν ὁ ὄχλος ὁ ὢν μετ᾽ αὐτοῦ ὅτε τὸν Λάζαρον ἐφώνησεν ἐκ τοῦ μνημείου καὶ ἤγειρεν αὐτὸν ἐκ νεκρῶν). The conclusion and interpretation of the pericope concerns the responses derived from the crowd's and Jesus's actions during his entrance into Jerusalem. While the narrator's comment seems to suggest that two crowds were present, the Lazarus crowd and another, more general crowd, it is better to see the narrator making a connection between the heralding of Jesus in this scene with the resurrection of Lazarus, the sixth sign (see comments on 12:9). The person and work of Jesus was growing in popularity and magnitude, and the crowd was "testifying" (ἐμαρτύρει) about the other amazing things they had seen and heard.

12:18 For this reason the crowd went out to meet him, because they heard that he had given this sign (διὰ τοῦτο [καὶ] ὑπήντησεν αὐτῷ ὁ ὄχλος ὅτι ἤκουσαν τοῦτο αὐτὸν πεποιηκέναι τὸ σημεῖον). The growing popularity of Jesus, climaxing with the Lazarus miracle, explains why a crowd was present

and willing to greet Jesus not just enthusiastically but also royally. Here the narrator offers commentary on the reenactment of Psalm 118 that the crowd offered to Jesus. The crowd had begun to act out what they believed to be taking place through Jesus. At this point, unfortunately, the crowd's reactions were all hearsay. As correct as the crowd was to see the Lazarus miracle as a sign pointing to the identity of Jesus and his role as king, in light of the Gospel as a whole it is clear that the crowd did not grasp the true nature of Jesus's kingship or the true meaning of his "signs." For as the narrator will explain in 12:37, even after performing these miraculous signs in their presence, the people did not believe in Jesus.

12:19 Then the Pharisees said to one another, "You can see that you are accomplishing nothing. Look, the whole world is going after him" (οἱ οὖν Φαρισαῖοι εἶπαν πρὸς ἑαυτούς, Θεωρεῖτε ὅτι οὐκ ὠφελεῖτε οὐδέν· ἴδε ὁ κόσμος ὀπίσω αὐτοῦ ἀπῆλθεν). After offering the general public's reaction to Jesus, the narrator concludes the pericope with the reaction of the Pharisees, the Jewish authorities. In a loaded statement that must be interpretively paired with Caiaphas's statement following the Lazarus miracle (see comments on 11:49 – 52), the Pharisees speak hyperbolically about the crowd's reaction to Jesus in a manner that is filled with irony. The reaction of the crowd stirs a response of failure (thus far) by the Pharisees in their attempt to kill Jesus (11:53; cf. 7:1).[31] With words of exasperation, the Pharisees become prophets like Caiaphas. Their intended and plain-sense meaning carries with it a clear and retrievable extended-sense meaning, for the one about whom they speak "is truly the Savior of the world" (4:42).

---

30. Cf. Ridderbos, *John*, 424; Aquinas, *John*, 2:272 – 73.

31. See Bultmann, *John*, 419.

Theology in Application

In a public display of pomp and circumstance, in which a large crowd preparing for Passover gathers around Jesus as he enters Jerusalem, hailing him as king of Israel, Jesus receives the royal acclamation of the crowd, much to the surprise of the reader. Jesus's actions not only serve to accept the acclamation of the crowd, but he secures for himself a donkey (a royal mount) and places himself upon it in a manner that can only be described as an act of acceptance in regard to his royal status. But with the insightful and biblically grounded commentary of the narrator, the reader realizes that the actions of Jesus are not easily conflated with the perception of the crowd. While Jesus truly is the King, he is like no other king before him, and he is establishing an entirely different kind of kingdom. In this pericope the reader of the Fourth Gospel is given the proper understanding of the King of kings and is begin exhorted from that perspective alone to offer him the acclamation he is due.

Not a King but the King (or, A King of a Different Sort)

The plot of this pericope offers the reader a remarkable twist: rather than correcting the understanding of the crowd, Jesus accepts it. In fact, in a manner similar to the disciples who were there, had we been there we would have considered Jesus to be accepting our acclamation of him as king of Israel, that is, as the next ruler of the people. But as the narrator carefully explains, as much as Jesus was truly the king of Israel, he was also much more — a king of a different sort. Jesus is not just any king, but by means of the narrator's biblical commentary, Jesus is God himself coming to his people to be their king. With the arrival of Jesus to Jerusalem, it was not just another king in a long line of frail human kings filling the royal office, but God himself who was filling — and fulfilling — the office of King.

Not only is this king different, but so is the nature of his kingship. When Jesus accepts the title of King, he is fulfilling a royal office and kingship of an entirely different order. Jesus has arrived to Jerusalem as King, but his enthronement and the establishment of his rule will be enacted in a manner that is nothing like the kings of the past. For this king (the Son of Man) did not come to be served but to serve (Mark 10:45). And this king could never be exalted by humanity but only by God, who will soon exalt Jesus "to the highest place and give him the name above every name … Jesus Christ is Lord" (Phil 2:9, 11). But this throne cannot be claimed until this king bears the shame of the cross (Heb 12:2).

The "Glory" of the King

The conflict of the pericope is only given resolution when the narrator directs the reader to the "glorification" of Jesus, that is, to the death and resurrection of Jesus. The rule of the King and his royal "glory" is directly connected to his ultimate act of service and humiliation. The throne Jesus had in view as he entered Jerusalem on that day was not a golden chair but a wooden cross, and his "lifting up" was in order to receive shame not honor. King Jesus came not to rule a vassal state under Rome or to direct the political and military activities of the people of Israel; Jesus is King of the whole world, and his kingly authority extends well beyond external interests to the inward natures of his servants. This king came to "save" (Hosanna!) his people from the greatest enemies that humanity would ever know: sin, death, and the wrath of God. Jesus did this by defeating them with his own body, not with a sword but by giving up his spirit (19:30). As Augustine explains, Jesus's royal glorification "was an act of condescension and not promotion; a token of compassion, and not any increase of power."[32] That is why the Jesus we worship is finally depicted as "a lamb, looking as if it has been slain, standing in the center of the throne" (Rev 5:6).

The Christian acclaims King Jesus as the slain lamb, the crucified God, the one who bowed his head and gave up his spirit. But as the Christian knows, this is not weakness but strength; this is not defeat but victory. This is our King's "glory." And for this reason, "God exalted him to the highest place and gave him the name that is above every name, that at the name of Jesus every knee should bow, in heaven and on earth and under the earth, and every tongue confess that Jesus Christ is Lord, to the *glory* of God the Father" (Phil 2:9 – 11; emphasis added). This is our King. This is the one to whom we owe absolute devotion and service. Long live this King! (cf. 1 Sam 10:24).

Palm Sunday

The Christian celebration of Palm Sunday should incorporate the rich biblical and theological perspective provided by the narrator of this pericope. First, it should make clear that Jesus is a very different kind of king and his rule extends both externally and internally. Second, it should make the necessary connection to the Sunday that directly follows: Easter Sunday. The nature of Jesus's kingship is intimately connected to his death and resurrection. Jesus's triumphal entry was for the purpose of defeat and death. Our celebration of this day — and this King — should appropriately declare the true nature and purpose of his royal office.

---

32. Augustine, *John*, 51.4.284.

John 12:20 – 50

Literary Context

This pericope concludes the section of the Gospel entitled, "The Conclusion of Jesus's Public Ministry" (11:1 – 12:50), with a theologically charged speech by Jesus to the large crowd that has had a growing interest in him, a crowd made up not only of Jews but of Greeks. In his last public statement, Jesus makes three significant claims regarding his glorification (the cross), his mission (the purpose of his coming), and his witness (to the Father). In a context of unbelief, Jesus makes a final public exhortation to the crowd about his person and work, that is, about the gospel. This speech summarizes much of what Jesus has already said and what he is about to do, and it serves as a fitting conclusion to his entire public ministry (chs. 2 – 12).

> VI. The Conclusion of Jesus's Public Ministry (11:1 – 12:50)
>   A. The Sixth Sign: The Death and Resurrection of Lazarus (11:1 – 57)
>   B. The Anointing of Jesus (12:1 – 11)
>   C. The Royal Entrance of Jesus into Jerusalem (12:12 – 19)
> ➡ **D. "The Hour has Come": The Final Public Statement of Jesus (12:20 – 50)**

Main Idea

The glorification of the Son of Man, the death of Jesus on the cross, is the climax of the mission of God. Through the cross, victory and life are given to those who believe in him, but defeat and judgment are announced to the world and its ruler who stand against him.

Translation

(See pages 545–48.)

John 12:20–50

20a	Introduction (20–22)	Now there were …
b	Character Entrance	… some Greeks among those who went up
c	Purpose	in order to worship at the Feast.
21a	Character Reentrance	Then they came to Philip,
b	Description	who was from Bethsaida of Galilee,
c		and asked him saying,
d	Address	"Sir,
e	Entreaty	we want to see Jesus."
22a	Reaction #1	Philip came and spoke to Andrew,
b	Reaction #2	Andrew and Philip came and spoke to Jesus.
	Monologue (22–36)	
23a	Response	Jesus answered them saying,
b	Declaration	"The hour has come
c	Purpose	for the Son of Man to be glorified.
	Explanatory Illustration	
24a	Amen Formula	Truly, truly, I say to you,
b	Condition	unless the seed of wheat falls to the ground to die,
c	Inference	it remains alone.
d	Contrast	But
e	Condition	if it dies,
f	Inference	it produces much fruit.
25a	Continued Explanation	The one who loves his life …
	Result	… will lose it,
b	Contrast	and the one who hates his life …
c	Sphere/Place	in this world
d	Result	… will keep it
e	Contrasting Sphere/Place	into eternal life.
	Application of Illustration	
26a	Condition of Service	If anyone serves me,
b	Imperatival Inference	he must follow me,
c		and
d	Condition of Location	where I am
e	Inference	my servant will be there also.

Continued on next page.

Continued from previous page.

f	Restatement of 26b		If anyone serves me,
g	Inference		the Father will honor him.
	Jesus's Public Prayer		
27a	Declaration		Now my soul is troubled,
b	Interrogative Emphasis		and what shall I say?
c	Address		Father,
d	Rhetorical Entreaty		save me from this hour?
e	Contrast		But
f			for this reason
g			I came to this hour.
28a	Address		Father,
b	Entreaty		glorify your name."
c	Character Reentrance	**Then**	
d	Father's Response	**a voice came from heaven,**	
e			"And I have glorified it
f			and I will glorify it again.
29a	Character Reentrance	**Then the crowd . . .**	
b			that had stood there and
c			heard it
d	Crowd's Response		. . . said there had been thunder;
e		**others said an angel had spoken to him.**	
30a	Response	**Jesus answered and said,**	
b			"This voice did not occur for me, but
c	Contrasting Beneficiary		for you.
31a	(–) Description of "hour" (27g)		Now is the judgment of this world,
b	Apposition		now the ruler of this world will be cast outside.
32a	(+) Description of "hour"	**And**	
b	Condition		if I am lifted up from the earth,
c	Inference		I will draw all people to myself."
33a	Narrator's Aside	**He said this to indicate the kind of death he was going to die.**	
34a	Response	**Then the crowd answered,**	
b	Assertion		"We have heard from the law that the Christ remains into eternity.
c	Question #1		How do you say that it is necessary for the Son of Man to be lifted up?
d	Question #2		Who is this Son of Man?"
35a	Response	**Then Jesus said to them,**	
b	Basis of 35d		"The light is among you
c	Duration		just a little longer.

Ref	Function	Text
d	Exhortation	*Walk*
e	Duration	*while you have the light,*
f	Result	*so that the darkness does not overtake you.*
g	Warning	*The one who walks in the darkness does not know where he is going.*
36a	Duration	*While you have the light,*
b	Exhortation	*believe in the light,*
c	Result	*so that you may become sons of the light."*
d	Narrator's Commentary (36d–43)	**Jesus spoke these things**
e	Character Departure	and **he departed and was concealed from them.**
37a		But after he had performed all of his signs before them,
b	Character's Thoughts	**they were not believing in him.**
38a	Prophetic Fulfillment	**This happened in order that the word of Isaiah the prophet might be fulfilled** which said,
b		
c	Address	"Lord,
d	Quotation	who has believed in our message?
e		And to whom has the arm of the Lord been revealed?" (Isa 53:1)
39a		For this reason
b	Result	**they were unable to believe,**
c	Basis	because as Isaiah also said,
40a	Quotation	"He has blinded their eyes
b	Resulting Sequence #1	and hardened their heart,
c	Resulting Sequence #2	so that they cannot see with the eyes and
d	Resulting Sequence #3	understand with their heart and
e		turn,
f	Counterfactual Inference	and I would heal them." (Isa 6:10)
41a	Narrator's Explanation	**Isaiah said these things**
b	Basis	because he saw his glory and
c		has spoken about him.
42a	Character's Thoughts	**Despite that many of the rulers believed in him,**
b		but
c	Basis (Character Reentrance)	because of the Pharisees
d	Contrasting Lack of Action	**they were not confessing,**
e	Purpose	in order that they might not be expelled from the synagogue.

Continued on next page.

Continued from previous page.

43a	Explanation	For **they loved the glory of humanity** rather than
b	Comparison	the glory of God.
44a	Character Reentrance	Then **Jesus cried out and said,**
b	Redeclaration of "Belief"	"The one who believes in me …
c	Result	… does not believe in me but
d	Contrast (Source)	in the one who sent me.
45a	Declaration of Vision	And the one who sees me …
b	Result (Source)	… sees the one who sent me.
46a	Declaration of Purpose	I have come into the world
b		in order that everyone who believes in me might not remain in darkness.
47a	Explanation of Purpose	
	Conjunctive Conditions	If anyone hears my words and
b		does not keep them,
c	Counterintuitive Inference	I am not judging him,
d	Explanation	for I did not come
e	(–) Purpose	in order to judge the world but
f	(+) Purpose	in order to save the world.
48a	Description	The one who rejects me and
b		does not receive my words …
c	Resulting Warning	… has one who judges him;
d	Allusion: Deut 18:18–19	the words themselves …
e		which I have spoken
f	Emphatic Warning	… will judge him on the last day.
49a	Explanation	Because I did not speak from myself, but
b	Contrast	the one who sent me,
c	Identification	the Father,
d	Predication	he has given the command to me
e		what to say and
f	Content	what I speak.
50a	Concluding Statement	
	Premise	And I know that his command is eternal life,
b	Inference	therefore what I speak …
c		just as the Father has spoken to me,
d	Comparison	… so I speak."

Structure and Literary Form

This is the third substantial monologue in the narrative proper and the last public speech of Jesus in the Gospel. A monologue (see Introduction) is similar to a dialogue in that it is set in the context of an engagement and conflict, but rather than engaging point-for-point it allows for a lengthy argument. A monologue can contain elements of rhetoric, challenge, and conflict, but it does so in a sustained presentation.

Not uncommon for a monologue, Jesus's speech is interspersed with two sets of comments/commentary. The narrator's commentary serves to guide the interpretation of the monologue's context and content (vv. 37 – 43), while the brief comments by the crowd during Jesus's speech facilitate the direction of the monologue (vv. 29, 34). Several interpreters split this pericope into various parts, most commonly splitting vv. 20 – 36 from vv. 37 – 50 (or sometimes vv. 37 – 43 from vv. 44 – 50), with some scholars labeling the latter section as an epilogue to the ministry of Jesus.[1] However, this pericope is best understood as a single unit, with each of these parts serving to offer something like a collection of final statements to the reader. While Jesus's monologue (the speech proper) is the primary statement, there is also a secondary statement provided by the crowd (their misunderstanding and unbelieving reaction) as well as the narrator's (biblical) interpretive commentary.

Exegetical Outline

→ **D. "The Hour Has Come": The Final Public Statement of Jesus (12:20 – 50)**
    1. Narrator's Introduction (vv. 20 – 22)
    2. The Glorification of the Son (vv. 23 – 26)
    3. The Mission of the Son (vv. 27 – 36)
    4. Narrator's Commentary: The Unbelief of the People (vv. 37 – 43)
    5. The Witness of the Son (vv. 44 – 50)

Explanation of the Text

Critical scholarship considers this pericope, usually focusing only on vv. 20 – 36 (see discussion above), to be either a composite of originally separate sources or puzzlingly incoherent.[2] But nothing in the pericope requires submission to such source-critical analyses; rather, the textual unit, all of vv. 20 – 50, can be understood as an original whole composed with intentionality and precision.[3] The intentionality of the pericope consists in not merely its own inner coherence, but also that it

---

1. Beasley-Murray, *John*, 206; cf. Brodie, who calls it an epilogue because it "stands apart and summarizes" (*John*, 421).
2. See Bultmann, *John*, 419; Barrett, *John*, 421, 430. Cf. Dodd, *Historical Tradition*, 338 – 43; Smith, *John*, 238.
3. Cf. Kiyoshi Tsuchido, "Tradition and Redaction in John 12:1 – 43," *NTS* 30 (1984): 609 – 19.

is serving as a conclusion to the entire public ministry of Jesus. But as we shall see, it is not merely vv. 44 – 50 that has an epilogue-like function, but all of vv. 20 – 50 functions this way. At the end of his ministry, Jesus makes a final public statement to the "world," both Greeks and Jews.

12:20 Now there were some Greeks among those who went up in order to worship at the Feast (Ἦσαν δὲ Ἕλληνές τινες ἐκ τῶν ἀναβαινόντων ἵνα προσκυνήσωσιν ἐν τῇ ἑορτῇ). The monologue of Jesus begins with the narrator's introduction. The word translated as "now" (δέ) is a frequently occurring marker linking narrative segments,[4] signaling to the reader that what has previously transpired is being continued or developed further. One verse after the Pharisees were quoted as saying, "Look, the whole world is going after him" (12:19), the narrator describes the arrival of some "Greeks" (Ἕλληνές). The narrator explains that these gentiles or non-Jews, probably "Godfearers" (gentiles interested in the Jewish God/religion) or even proselytes (converted gentiles), are present because of "the Feast," that is, Passover (cf. 12:1). Josephus explains that many interested gentiles would attend the Jewish feasts (*J.W.* 6.427).

12:21 Then they came to Philip, who was from Bethsaida of Galilee, and asked him saying, "Sir, we want to see Jesus" (οὗτοι οὖν προσῆλθον Φιλίππῳ τῷ ἀπὸ Βηθσαϊδὰ τῆς Γαλιλαίας, καὶ ἠρώτων αὐτὸν λέγοντες, Κύριε, θέλομεν τὸν Ἰησοῦν ἰδεῖν). The Greeks address Philip respectively, "Sir" (Κύριε), and state their desire to meet with Jesus. The geographic designation for Philip provided by the narrator (see comments on 1:44) suggests that the Greeks may have chosen him because Bethsaida was within proximity to the Greek re-gion (e.g., the Decapolis).[5] Nothing is suggested as to why they want to spend time with Jesus or how they heard about him. In fact, we hear nothing further of the Greeks or even whether their request was granted.[6] The significance is to be seen in their presence not their persons; in this moment the "world" had come to Jesus (12:19). From the beginning of Jesus's ministry, he had invited his disciples to "come and see" (cf. 1:39), and even at the end of his ministry interested disciples come "to see" Jesus.

12:22 Philip came and spoke to Andrew, Andrew and Philip came and spoke to Jesus (ἔρχεται ὁ Φίλιππος καὶ λέγει τῷ Ἀνδρέᾳ· ἔρχεται Ἀνδρέας καὶ Φίλιππος καὶ λέγουσιν τῷ Ἰησοῦ). The narrator concludes the introduction to the monologue by describing how this information, the presence of the Greeks or simply their request for a meeting, had been delivered to Jesus. Little needs to be made of the collaboration between Philip and Andrew, who also is from Bethsaida (cf. 1:44). Quite probably, Philip and Andrew were the most comfortable with the Greek culture and language, and so they were more geographically and culturally related to these Jesus seekers. The specific reason is secondary to the narrative; the lack of detail is itself noteworthy. What is important is that the presence and request of the Greeks (the world!) had reached the ears of the Lord.

12:23 Jesus answered them saying, "The hour has come for the Son of Man to be glorified" (ὁ δὲ Ἰησοῦς ἀποκρίνεται αὐτοῖς λέγων, Ἐλήλυθεν ἡ ὥρα ἵνα δοξασθῇ ὁ υἱὸς τοῦ ἀνθρώπου). The first part of Jesus's three-part monologue (vv. 23 – 26) explains the glorification of the Son. Jesus's initial response is surprising in that it is not addressed

---

4. Cf. BDAG 213.

5. Philip's name is also Greek, but many Jews were given Greek names.

6. Richard L. Jeske, "John 12:20 – 36," *Int* 43 (1989): 292 – 95 (292).

to the Greeks who wanted to meet with him. Jesus "answered" (ἀποκρίνεται) not these particular individuals but the world that has now taken note of him. Jesus's answer is commentary on what Jesus has already done before the world and the one thing he has yet to do — the final and climactic act of his public ministry at the cross.

Jesus declares the arrival of his hour: "The hour has come" (Ἐλήλυθεν ἡ ὥρα). The term "the hour" (ἡ ὥρα) is a technical one in the Gospel (see comments on 2:4), and until this verse it has always been described as in the future. Although intimately connected to the death of Jesus, "the hour" is also connected to Jesus in a much broader sense, not only at the point of the cross but also his going to the Father and his glorification. This explains why, according to Jesus, the arrvial of "the hour" is "for the Son of man to be glorified" (ἵνα δοξασθῇ ὁ υἱὸς τοῦ ἀνθρώπου). The purpose of "the hour," denoted by the purpose clause (ἵνα plus the subjunctive), is the glorification of the Son. This is a strange paradox; the hour of the glorification of Jesus is also (and simultaneously) the hour of his death. This is the "lifting up" or exaltation of the King.[7]

The paradox of "the hour" is explained even further by the title "Son of Man" (ὁ υἱὸς τοῦ ἀνθρώπου). As we saw earlier (see comments on 1:51), the title echoes its earlier use in Daniel 7:13 – 14 and incorporates all power, glory, and rule — all of God — into one person and is manifested throughout one life and ministry. This is the grand irony of the Gospel. The hour of the glorification of the Son of Man (i.e., the King, Creator, and Ruler of all) is made manifest on the cross (i.e., the place of suffering, humiliation, and shame)!

12:24 "Truly, truly, I say to you, unless the seed of wheat falls to the ground to die, it remains alone. But if it dies, it produces much fruit" (ἀμὴν ἀμὴν λέγω ὑμῖν, ἐὰν μὴ ὁ κόκκος τοῦ σίτου πεσὼν εἰς τὴν γῆν ἀποθάνῃ, αὐτὸς μόνος μένει· ἐὰν δὲ ἀποθάνῃ, πολὺν καρπὸν φέρει). Jesus spends the next three verses (vv. 24 – 26) explaining his formal, opening statement. Beginning with an authoritative preface (see comments on 1:51), Jesus offers a brief "illustration," not uncommon in John (see comments on 10:6 and 16:25), as a commentary on the meaning of his opening statement. The illustration is quite simple. For a seed to be effective — to do what a seed is intended to do — it must die, otherwise "it remains alone" (αὐτὸς μόνος μένει), that is, it will remain a seed. But since the *natural* function of a seed is the production of "much fruit" (πολὺν καρπὸν), it must do what might be considered *unnatural*; it must die.

When applied to Jesus, the illustration offers a remarkable explanation of the paradox of the glorification of the Son of Man (v. 23). Three things can be highlighted. First, the illustration serves to make a direct connection between the death of Jesus, the Son of Man, and the life which springs from his death. Just as fruit cannot come into existence without the death of the seed, so also must the unique Son die for the children of God to come into existence. As much as this is a life-for-death paradox, it is logically consistent and interconnected.

Second, the illustration serves to explain the purpose of Jesus's person and work, culminating in his death on the cross. Without taking the analogy too far, especially in relation to the nature of God, we can surmise the following. Just as the seed is to be understood and related according to its purpose, so must we relate to Jesus, the Son of Man, according to his intended purpose, rooted in the larger mission of God (e.g., 3:16). This is not to say that the value of the seed (or the Son) is only defined by its function, but that our relation to the seed (or the Son) is necessarily rooted in its function.

---

7. See Bultmann, *John*, 424.

Third, the illustration offers a significantly different perspective of death. While death is normally unnatural and entirely unproductive, this death (of seed or Son) is quite the opposite in that it becomes the means by which natural things are produced and in great quantity! In a strange sense, reflecting on the illustration, the death of the seed, though still death, becomes known more for its life-producing results than for its death. That is, the seed becomes less eclipsed or replaced and more expanded and reproduced. The farmer does not lose a seed but gains fruit, just as God the Father through the Son gains many children (1:12).

12:25 "The one who loves his life will lose it, and the one who hates his life in this world will keep it into eternal life" (ὁ φιλῶν τὴν ψυχὴν αὐτοῦ ἀπολλύει αὐτήν, καὶ ὁ μισῶν τὴν ψυχὴν αὐτοῦ ἐν τῷ κόσμῳ τούτῳ εἰς ζωὴν αἰώνιον φυλάξει αὐτήν). Jesus's explanation now connects the seed with the fruit, that is, the death of the Son with the life of the children of God. After defining the natural expression or purpose of the seed, Jesus now defines the natural expression or purpose of the "much fruit." The explanation is offered by two antithetically parallel lines, speaking hyperbolically to strengthen the force of the statement.[8] According to Jesus, the seed (the Son) establishes a precedent or an example for the fruit (the disciples) to follow. Just as a seed that loves its own life would fail to produce fruit but also then would fail to understand its true purpose, so also must the fruit know its purpose, one that extends beyond its perceivable self. The children of God owe their life to the Son, which means that the value of their lives is now owed to the Son (the seed); they are not their own, they have been bought for a price. Ultimately, the value of life is to be sought not in its innate, perceived

value — "in this world" (ἐν τῷ κόσμῳ τούτῳ) — but in its extended and purposeful value "into eternal life" (εἰς ζωὴν αἰώνιον).[9]

12:26 "If anyone serves me, he must follow me, and where I am my servant will be there also. If anyone serves me, the Father will honor him" (ἐὰν ἐμοί τις διακονῇ, ἐμοὶ ἀκολουθείτω, καὶ ὅπου εἰμὶ ἐγὼ ἐκεῖ καὶ ὁ διάκονος ὁ ἐμὸς ἔσται· ἐάν τις ἐμοὶ διακονῇ τιμήσει αὐτὸν ὁ πατήρ). Jesus now directly connects the illustration of the seed and the fruit to himself and his disciples. Just as fruit springs from and follows the seed, so also do the disciples come from and therefore should follow the Son. Note the large amount of first-person pronouns used to denote emphasis.[10] The Christian is the one who knows his or her true value and purpose and lives accordingly by following and serving beside the Son. The fruit (Christians) is so organically joined to the seed (Christ) that its very existence is directed by the interrelationship. Hating life — which means to love it rightly (v. 25) — is to live according to the sequence, death-life-obedience.[11] Christian living "cannot be acts of mere self-abnegation. Self must be displaced by another; the endless, shameless focus on self must be displaced by focus on Jesus Christ."[12] This is the kind of life the Father "will honor" (τιμήσει), which probably suggests the confirmation by the Father of participating in the life of the Son (see 14:21, 23; 16:24; 17:22–23).

12:27 "Now my soul is troubled, and what shall I say? Father, save me from this hour? But for this reason I came to this hour" (Νῦν ἡ ψυχή μου τετάρακται. καὶ τί εἴπω; Πάτερ, σῶσόν με ἐκ τῆς ὥρας ταύτης; ἀλλὰ διὰ τοῦτο ἦλθον εἰς τὴν ὥραν ταύτην). The second part of Jesus's three-part monologue (vv. 27–36) explains the mission of the

---

8. Cf. Ridderbos, *John*, 432.
9. See Augustine, *John*, 51.10.285.
10. Morris, *John*, 528.

11. Hoskyns, *Fourth Gospel*, 424.
12. Carson, *John*, 439.

Son. The transition of the monologue is made clear by its new focus: a prayer-like address to God the Father. Jesus had moved from himself (the seed) to the disciples (the "much fruit"), but now he transitions back to himself—the seed that must die! The sequence of death-life-obedience must begin with death, and this Jesus reflects upon in his final public statement.

Jesus declares, "Now my soul is troubled" (Νῦν ἡ ψυχή μου τετάρακται). As much as Jesus was the royal Son of Man, he was also "flesh" (1:14) and therefore fully capable of experiencing the full range of human fear and suffering. The term translated as "soul" (ψυχή) is the same term translated as "life" above (v. 25). What now grips Christ has taken hold of all of him. In this moment the seed—to continue the earlier illustration—is tempted to love his life and not hate it. This is the question Christ is faced with and why he poses it as a question.

12:28 "Father, glorify your name." Then a voice came from heaven, "And I have glorified it and I will glorify it again" (πάτερ, δόξασόν σου τὸ ὄνομα. ἦλθεν οὖν φωνὴ ἐκ τοῦ οὐρανοῦ, Καὶ ἐδόξασα καὶ πάλιν δοξάσω). Jesus now answers his own question: "Father, glorify your name" (πάτερ, δόξασόν σου τὸ ὄνομα). This statement is a perfect depiction of hating your life in this world and loving your life in eternity (v. 25). Jesus speaks with an imperative of request, "glorify your name" (δόξασόν σου τὸ ὄνομα),[13] which highlights the sovereign control and purposes of God the Father. Jesus has already connected the glorification of the Son of Man (v. 23) to "the hour"; now it is revealed that the glorification of the Son is also for the purpose of glorifying the "name" of the Father (see comments on 1:14). The work of the Son is a direct reflection of the Father. The work of the fruit (the Christian)

gives glory to the seed (the Son), just as the Son gives glory to the Father.

In the middle of Jesus's prayer-like statement, a remarkable thing happened. After Jesus offered glory to the Father, the Father spoke "from heaven" (ἐκ τοῦ οὐρανοῦ), confirming that he had been and will again be glorified by the Son. Although the voice declares that Jesus has already participated in the glory of the Son (denoted by the aorist tense, "I have glorified it" [ἐδόξασα]), there is no need to determine a specific point in time when this occurred (e.g., the baptism of Jesus or the transfiguration). Not only does the Gospel offer no suggestions, but it is best to view the glory offered between the Father and Son as part of the very identity of God. In a sense, the aorist tense verb might best be understood as a gnomic aorist, which "does not refer to a particular event that *did* happen, but to a generic event that *does* happen."[14] The name of the Father has been glorified by the entire ministry of Jesus (now spoken of at its end), and it is not yet finished. While the cross is probably to be understood as the climactic glorifying act of the Father by the Son (cf. v. 23), we may still speak of the perpetual glory distributed between Father and Son. But the Father's final remark, "I will glorify it again" (πάλιν δοξάσω), offers confirmation that in this moment of anguish, filled with the decision to love or hate life in this world (v. 25), the Father is confident in the service of the Son; so confident that he predicts it—and his predictions never fail! The last remark by the Father, therefore, points not only to the cross but also to the resurrection.

12:29 Then the crowd that had stood there and heard it said there had been thunder; others said an angel had spoken to him (ὁ οὖν ὄχλος ὁ ἑστὼς καὶ ἀκούσας ἔλεγεν βροντὴν γεγονέναι· ἄλλοι ἔλεγον, Ἄγγελος αὐτῷ λελάληκεν). The narrator

---

13. See Wallace, *Greek Grammar*, 487 – 88.

14. Ibid., 562.

reveals the crowd's interpretation of "the voice." The crowd is described as having been present and listening; some thought it was a natural occurrence — "thunder" (βροντὴν), whereas others thought it was the voice of "an angel" (Ἄγγελος) speaking to Jesus. The crowd's perception was not provided by the narrator for its accuracy — for the reader knows that it was the Father who spoke — but to stress that "the voice" was audible to the human ear and was not a vision or dream. What is important for the narrator is not the understanding of the people but their incomprehension. The people could not make sense of the "voice" of God the Father, even as they did not understand the Word of God, his Son.

12:30 Jesus answered and said, "This voice did not occur for me, but for you" (ἀπεκρίθη καὶ εἶπεν Ἰησοῦς, Οὐ δι᾽ ἐμὲ ἡ φωνὴ αὕτη γέγονεν ἀλλὰ δι᾽ ὑμᾶς). Jesus offers a response to the incomprehension of the crowd even though no question was asked.[15] Jesus explains that the voice was not given for his benefit, "but for you" (ἀλλὰ δι᾽ ὑμᾶς). Interpreters differ over the implications of Jesus's statement. Some understand Jesus's response to imply that the crowd was expected to understand the voice and are therefore at fault for their lack of comprehension. A smaller number think Jesus is referring not to the words at all but to the sound itself — interestingly, the Greek word translated as "voice" (φωνὴ) can also mean "sound." This latter view is the more likely option. Jesus does not deny that the words were intended for him; he rather explains that the Father spoke audibly for all to hear to make clear to the world that the one he addressed was his Son, the Son of God.[16] In a real

sense, the entire audible prayer between Jesus and the Father was *conversationally* private between the Father and the Son (vv. 27 – 28), but *ministerially* public as a witness to the world confirming the mission of the Son of God.

12:31 "Now is the judgment of this world, now the ruler of this world will be cast outside" (νῦν κρίσις ἐστὶν τοῦ κόσμου τούτου, νῦν ὁ ἄρχων τοῦ κόσμου τούτου ἐκβληθήσεται ἔξω). After the Father speaks from heaven to confirm the mission of the Son, the Son now speaks from the earth to declare further his mission, continuing the description of "the hour" (v. 27). In vv. 31 – 32 Jesus explains what he declared in v. 23, "The hour has come for the Son of Man to be glorified." The repeated and emphatic use of the adverb "now" (νῦν) connects this part of Jesus's statement to its beginning (v. 23),[17] but it also magnifies the eschatological nature of the events being described.[18] This verse makes two important claims.

First, Jesus explains that "the hour" of his glorification (v. 23) is also the time for "the judgment of this world" (νῦν κρίσις τοῦ κόσμου τούτου).[19] Although the Gospel has already depicted this judgment as belonging to the Son (see 5:22 – 30), the language used previously seemed to suggest that the judgment would take place at the second coming of the Son, not the first (see 3:17 – 19). At the same time, however, since the Gospel does connect the final judgment of God to Jesus in the present ("now") in both chapters 3 and 5, this connection should not be surprising.

What is important to notice is that the judgment of this world is directly connected to the cross. The cross is simultaneously the "glorification" of Jesus

15. Schnackenburg, *John*, 2:390.
16. Ridderbos, *John*, 437.
17. Cf. Barrett, *John*, 426.
18. George R. Beasley-Murray, "John 12, 31 – 32: The Eschatological Significance of the Lifting Up of the Son of Man,"

in *Studien zum Text und zur Ethik des Neuen Testament: Festschrift zum 80. Geburtstag von Heinrich Greeven*, ed. Wolfgang Schrage, BZNWKAK 47 (Berlin: Walter de Gruyter, 1986), 70 – 81.
19. Cf. Schnackenburg, *John*, 2:390.

and the "judgment" of the world. It is the throne upon which the King of kings is crowned — his glory. Yet it is also the point of decision for the world, either as *the place of their salvation*, in which the cross is the sacrifice of the Lamb of God on their behalf, or *the place of their judgment*, by which they stand already condemned (3:18).

Second, Jesus explains that this judgment will also involve the removal or "casting outside" (ἐκβληθήσεται ἔξω) of "the ruler of this world" (ὁ ἄρχων τοῦ κόσμου τούτου). Michaels is right to describe this as exorcism language, a frequently noted absence in John in comparison to the Synoptics.[20] While the title "the ruler of this world" is only found in John (see also 14:30; 16:11), there are clear precedents elsewhere in the NT (2 Cor 4:4; Eph 2:2). Interestingly, in Revelation 12:7–9 a cosmic "war in heaven" takes place with Satan and his angels in which they are defeated by being "cast out" (ἐβλήθη … ἐβλήθη … ἐβλήθησαν), a term stated three times in one verse. In light of this biblical context, Jesus's statement depicts the cross as "the locus of a cosmic battle, in which Jesus achieves a decisive victory over Satan."[21] While the implications of this are too vast to solve here, what is clear is that the cross is not merely the final work of Jesus's mission, but the ultimate work of God — the mission of God. The ruler of this world is cast out and replaced by a new ruler, the rightful King. The "hour" of the cross is therefore "the dethronement of the Devil from his tyranny over men,"[22] and at the same time ("the hour") the enthronement of the true King, the glorification of the Son of Man.[23]

12:32 "And if I am lifted up from the earth, I will draw all people to myself" (κἀγὼ ἐὰν ὑψωθῶ ἐκ τῆς γῆς, πάντας ἑλκύσω πρὸς ἐμαυτόν). In the previous pronouncement, Jesus said nothing directly about his own role,[24] nor did he speak of the positive aspect of "the hour."[25] But now he addresses both himself and the positive nature of his work with a two-part statement. Jesus begins by describing being "lifted up from the earth" (ὑψωθῶ ἐκ τῆς γῆς), a statement not easily defined. The statement is prefaced with the word "if" (ἐὰν) to connect it to the illustration in v. 24 about the seed that dies in order to produce food. Since the "if" is a bit awkward, some translations translate the word as "when" (e.g., NIV), but this misses the important connection Jesus is making between his person and the seed of v. 24. Even more, the contrast is not just between Jesus and the seed, but also between "to the ground/earth" (εἰς τὴν γῆν) in v. 24 and "from the earth" (ἐκ τῆς γῆς).

The meaning of the change in preposition is rooted in the meaning of the ambiguous verb "lifted up" (ὑψωθῶ). Jesus has used this exact verb twice before, both times in significant moments in his public ministry (and the Gospel narrative). In both occurrences (3:14; 8:28), Jesus describes himself as the Son of Man (see comments on 1:51) without fully explaining the nature of the "lifting up," though the reader has been guided to understand that it is connected to the work of Christ (the cross) and to the person of Christ (his glory).[26] Clearly this "lifting up" is "not simply six feet above the earth."[27]

The verb "lifted up" (ὑψωθῶ) evokes a rich duality of meaning. In the context of the cross (the historical strand of the plot) it speaks of death, suffering, and defeat; but in its larger context (the cosmological strand of the plot), it simultaneously speaks of exaltation in majesty and glorification

20. Michaels, *John*, 695.
21. Judith L. Kovacs, "'Now Shall the Ruler of This World Be Driven Out': Jesus's Death as Cosmic Battle in John 12:20–36," *JBL* 114 (1995): 227–47 (246).
22. Hoskyns, *Fourth Gospel*, 425.

23. Bultmann, *John*, 431.
24. Michaels, *John*, 697.
25. Schnackenburg, *John*, 2:393.
26. Cf. Michaels, *John*, 698.
27. Beasley-Murray, "John 12, 31–32," 75.

(cf. Acts 2:33). In this one word the message of the gospel is presented. It is only in his humiliation that Jesus can be exalted and glorified. The verb creates a paradoxical "impression." In the very same statement Jesus combines the most humiliating and cruel act the ancient world could devise (crucifixion) with a title that incorporates all the power, glory, and authority of God himself (the Son of Man). Interpreters are right, therefore, to see in this one word not only a picture of the cross but also of the resurrection and ascension — the full effect of "the hour" and the glorification of the Son of Man (v. 23).[28]

Jesus then states, "I will draw all people to myself" (πάντας ἑλκύσω πρὸς ἐμαυτόν). The verb "draw" (ἑλκύσω) was used earlier by Jesus to refer to the work of the Father (see comments on 6:44). The term has an identical meaning here, except Jesus is the stated subject or agent of salvation. No difference or conflict is implied; the act is both that of the Father (who sent the Son) and of the Son (who obeyed the Father).[29] The emphasis, however, is not on the total number of objects but on the totality of the subject, the agency of God. While the drawing is not universally applied (not all are drawn), it is universally effective for those who are drawn.[30] The agent of drawing is universal in that the Son of Man, with the Father and the Spirit (through whom the exalted Lord continues his work of judgment and salvation in the world), draws the "children of God" to himself. With the Greeks now coming to Jesus (vv. 20 – 22), "all" the world had truly come.

12:33 He said this to indicate the kind of death he was going to die (τοῦτο δὲ ἔλεγεν σημαίνων ποίῳ θανάτῳ ἤμελλεν ἀποθνῄσκειν). In case the reader was confused in thinking the "glorification" of the Son of Man was to be expressed with splendor, the narrator explains to the reader that the "lifting up" of the Son of Man would occur by means of Roman crucifixion.[31] The narrator's intrusion serves to direct the reader's vision to the final public work of the Son of Man, without losing sight of its meaning. While the reader might float off in grand pursuit of the *meaning* of the death of Jesus, the narrator reminds him to remember the *manner* or "the kind of death" (ποίῳ θανάτῳ) it entailed. The focus here is still on what had to be accomplished; before glory must come suffering and death — the seed must die (v. 24).[32]

12:34 Then the crowd answered, "We have heard from the law that the Christ remains into eternity. How do you say that it is necessary for the Son of Man to be lifted up? Who is this Son of Man?" (ἀπεκρίθη οὖν αὐτῷ ὁ ὄχλος, Ἡμεῖς ἠκούσαμεν ἐκ τοῦ νόμου ὅτι ὁ Χριστὸς μένει εἰς τὸν αἰῶνα, καὶ πῶς σὺ λέγεις ὅτι δεῖ ὑψωθῆναι τὸν υἱὸν τοῦ ἀνθρώπου; τίς ἐστιν οὗτος ὁ υἱὸς τοῦ ἀνθρώπου;). The crowd offers something like an interjection and reply to Jesus's statement regarding his mission. Arguing from the OT, the crowd challenges Jesus's statement by claiming emphatically that "the law" (τοῦ νόμου), that is, Scripture, says something different about "the Christ" (ὁ Χριστὸς), the promised Messiah, and his eternal presence with his people. For the crowd, the term "to be lifted up" (ὑψωθῆναι) implied that he would no longer "remain" (μένει) with his people. Moreover, the crowd was unaware of the identity of "the Son of Man" (οὗτος ὁ υἱὸς τοῦ ἀνθρώπου). Our interpreta-

---

28. See John W. Romanowsky, "'When the Son of Man is Lifted Up': The Redemptive Power of the Crucifixion in the Gospel of John," *Hor* 32 (2005): 100 – 116 (108).

29. Cf. Barrett, *John*, 427. Even the Spirit must (for doctrinal reasons) be included in this (Trinitarian) agency, as the Gospel will shortly explain.

30. Cf. Michaels, *John*, 698 – 99; Beasley-Murray, *John*, 214.

31. Cf. Carson, *John*, 444.

32. Contra Godfrey C. Nicholson, *Death as Departure: The Johannine Descent-Ascent Schema* (Chico, CA: Scholars Press, 1983), 128.

tion of this text, however, is not to be based on the understanding of first-century Jews, for Jesus has already challenged such interpretations by declaring that the Scriptures have long spoken about him (see 5:39 – 47).

The crowd's questions are getting at the two core issues for "the Jews": Why must the Christ die? (question 1), and what kind of messianic figure is the Son of Man? (question 2). The response of the crowd, taken together, summarizes everything Jesus has claimed about himself — from the dialogue with Nicodemus to the present moment. It voices the classic Jewish and the world's objection to the cross.[33] In an applied sense, the final question is not a question at all but a rejection of Jesus: "What kind of Christ is this — a crucified Messiah?" For the crowd, a crucified Messiah is not only nonsensical, but abhorrent and heretical — even unbiblical. The scandal of the cross is meaningless to them, and the paradox that the Christ must suffer "puts an end to their welcome of Jesus as the Messiah of the Jews."[34]

12:35 Then Jesus said to them, "The light is among you just a little longer. Walk while you have the light, so that the darkness does not overtake you. The one who walks in the darkness does not know where he is going" (εἶπεν οὖν αὐτοῖς ὁ Ἰησοῦς, Ἔτι μικρὸν χρόνον τὸ φῶς ἐν ὑμῖν ἐστιν. περιπατεῖτε ὡς τὸ φῶς ἔχετε, ἵνα μὴ σκοτία ὑμᾶς καταλάβῃ· καὶ ὁ περιπατῶν ἐν τῇ σκοτίᾳ οὐκ οἶδεν ποῦ ὑπάγει). Jesus's rejoinder is not as direct as it could have been. Rather, Jesus speaks in a manner he has spoken before regarding the imminent ending of his ministry (cf. 7:33; 9:4 – 5; 11:9; 12:8; see also 13:33; 14:19; 16:16 – 24). Jesus here remains focused on his public ministry, denoted by the phrase "a little longer" (Ἔτι μικρὸν χρόνον), which he will soon define for his disciples (see 16:16 – 19). In a sense, just as the crowd in v. 34 summarized every-

thing Jesus had claimed about himself, Jesus does the same, using images and statements he has used and defined elsewhere to make one final invitation to the world. Jesus first declared a nearly identical invitation-warning in chapter 8 (see comments on 8:12), defining not only his mission (which he is doing again here) but also his judgment against the world for "walking in darkness." Thus, Jesus speaks past their Jewishness and their first-century Palestinian context and declares himself to be the Light (of the world!) shining in the darkness. He is the one who can *see* their condition (their *sin*) and the one who can *save* them from it (as their *Savior*).

12:36 "While you have the light, believe in the light, so that you may become sons of the light." Jesus spoke these things and he departed and was concealed from them (ὡς τὸ φῶς ἔχετε, πιστεύετε εἰς τὸ φῶς, ἵνα υἱοὶ φωτὸς γένησθε. Ταῦτα ἐλάλησεν Ἰησοῦς, καὶ ἀπελθὼν ἐκρύβη ἀπ᾽ αὐτῶν.). Jesus concludes the second part (of three) of his monologue with a final exhortation, a call to "believe in the light" (πιστεύετε εἰς τὸ φῶς). The goal is that the crowd, all who believe, "may become sons of the light" (υἱοὶ φωτὸς γένησθε), a statement that strongly echoes the message of the prologue (see comments on 1:12 – 13).

The second part of Jesus's monologue is concluded by the narrator, who explains that after Jesus finished his rejoinder to the crowd "he departed and was concealed from them" (ἀπελθὼν ἐκρύβη ἀπ᾽ αὐτῶν). While the passive verb "was concealed" (ἐκρύβη) might be understood to be functioning as a reflexive (i.e., "concealed himself"), the equally mysterious and clearly theological use of the same verb in 8:59 suggests that this is an intentionally cryptic description that serves a more functional purpose (see comments on 8:59; cf. 5:13). The narrator describes Jesus in a manner that enacts the very warning he just gave — that he is present "just

---

33. Michaels, *John*, 703.

34. Hoskyns, *Fourth Gospel*, 426.

a little longer" (v. 35). Jesus "was showing by his actions what he had said by his words."[35]

12:37 But after he had performed all of his signs before them, they were not believing in him

(Τοσαῦτα δὲ αὐτοῦ σημεῖα πεποιηκότος ἔμπροσθεν αὐτῶν οὐκ ἐπίστευον εἰς αὐτόν). Between the second and third part of Jesus's final statement, the narrator intrudes to offer a commentary on the response of the people (vv. 37 – 43). His commentary is both a biblical-theological analysis of the divine purposes of God as well as a judgment against unbelief or a lack of confession in Jesus (cf. v. 42). The narrator provides an interpretive reflection not only of the scene at hand but also the public response to the entire ministry of Jesus (denoted by the more generic reference to "them" [αὐτῶν] and the focus on "all of his signs" [Τοσαῦτα αὐτοῦ σημεῖα]).[36] These "signs" that Jesus performed have become a technical term in the Gospel for a miraculous work that points beyond itself to an eschatological reality in regard to the identity of Jesus and the present work of God in the world (see comments on 2:11). Not believing in the signs is tantamount to not believing in God himself. It is likely for this reason that the narrator makes such a sweeping generalization about the people (i.e., "the world") for the first time since the prologue.[37]

12:38 This happened in order that the word of Isaiah the prophet might be fulfilled which said, "Lord, who has believed in our message? And to whom has the arm of the Lord been revealed?"

(ἵνα ὁ λόγος Ἡσαΐου τοῦ προφήτου πληρωθῇ ὃν εἶπεν, Κύριε, τίς ἐπίστευσεν τῇ ἀκοῇ ἡμῶν; καὶ ὁ βραχίων κυρίου τίνι ἀπεκαλύφθη;). The narrator's

commentary begins with a "word" (λόγος) from the prophet Isaiah, whose appearance at the beginning and end of the public ministry of Jesus forms a thematic *inclusio* that locates his ministry within Isaiah's eschatological promises and judgments (see comments on 1:23). Our translation of the Greek, "This happened in order that ... might be fulfilled" (ἵνα πληρωθῇ) is intended to show how the narrator introduces a selection of Isaiah texts that serve as biblical commentary in regard to the fulfillment enacted by the work of Jesus (on the cross) and the public response he received. The narrator begins by quoting from Isaiah 53:1, which in its context fits nicely the circumstances portrayed by the Gospel of John.

From Isaiah 40 onward, the "arm of the Lord" (ὁ βραχίων κυρίου) is the Servant of the Lord (Isa 42:1 – 9; 49:1 – 6; 50:4 – 9), whose ministry, even after apparent failure, had worldwide consequences. The context preceding Isaiah 53:1 fits well with the royal and exaltation motif of John 12: "See, my servant will act wisely; he will be raised and lifted up and highly exalted ... so will he sprinkle many nations; kings will shut their mouths because of him." (Isa 52:13, 15).[38] The emphasis of Isaiah 53:1 is twofold. First, and rooted in the first question, Israel has heard "the message" (τῇ ἀκοῇ) but has refused to believe. Second, and rooted in the second question, the "arm of the Lord" declares that God has promised a restoration for Israel that she could not bring about for herself, which he promised to do for Israel as well as for the nations through his mighty "arm" (cf. Isa 40:10; 48:14; 51:5; 52:10).[39] This divine restoration, however, is accomplished in a shocking and unexpected manner,

---

35. Aquinas, *John*, 2:294.

36. See Willis Hedley Salier, *The Rhetorical Impact of the Sēmeia in the Gospel of John*, WUNT 2.186 (Tübingen: Mohr Siebeck, 2004), 125 – 26. See also Donald E. Hartley, "Destined to Disobey? Isaiah 6:10 in John 12:37 – 41," *CTJ* 44 (2009): 263 – 87 (esp. 278).

37. Cf. Michaels, *John*, 708; Lincoln, *John*, 357.

38. See John N. Oswalt, *The Book of Isaiah: Chapters 1 – 39*, NICOT (Grand Rapids: Eerdmans, 1986), 373 – 81.

39. Köstenberger, "John," 478.

which Isaiah 53 goes on to explain. Therefore, with his quotation the narrator claims that Isaiah 52 – 53 is being fulfilled at the end of Jesus's ministry. By quoting Isaiah 53:1, the narrator not only offers a theological interpretation of the Gospel events but also shows how they match perfectly with what God had always intended.

12:39 For this reason they were unable to believe, because as Isaiah also said (διὰ τοῦτο οὐκ ἠδύναντο πιστεύειν, ὅτι πάλιν εἶπεν Ἠσαΐας). What is implied in v. 38 is stated explicitly in v. 39: faith and the divine activity of God are connected.[40] This is an instance of Scripture interpreting itself, placing the entire human condition and story of human relationship to God under the power and authority of God.[41] While some are concerned that this raises a real problem,[42] for the narrator there is no stated concern. "The unbelief of the Jews is not a problem; it is the precise fulfillment of prophecy."[43] The later debates of predestination, though rightly discussed in light of this pericope, should not be uncritically read into the argument here. For nowhere in the Gospel (or Scripture, for that matter) are the will of God and human freedom pitted against one another or made to be a problem. If it is a problem, it is outside of or on this side of the text. To explain this further, the narrator turns to Isaiah a second time.

12:40 "He has blinded their eyes and hardened their heart, so that they cannot see with the eyes and understand with their heart and turn, and I would heal them" (Τετύφλωκεν αὐτῶν τοὺς ὀφθαλμοὺς καὶ ἐπώρωσεν αὐτῶν τὴν καρδίαν, ἵνα μὴ ἴδωσιν τοῖς ὀφθαλμοῖς καὶ νοήσωσιν τῇ καρδίᾳ καὶ στραφῶσιν, καὶ ἰάσομαι αὐτούς). The narrator now quotes from Isaiah 6:10, which raises the heart of the difficult matter as to why the message of God would bring about the prevention of repentance and the announcement of total destruction (Isa 6:9 – 13). In the context of Isaiah 6, the issue seems to be that more than healing (repentance) is involved in the message.[44] This message becomes "a pure revelation of the character of God and of the human condition."[45] Such a revelation — the truth — could only harden the people to whom it was announced (cf. Isa 3:8, 9; 5:18, 19). But the truth is what Israel (and the world) needed to hear; anything else would make a mockery of both God and the human predicament. Isaiah's purpose, then, was not to be successful in a merely human sense but to be faithful to both God and humanity.[46] For the solution to the human predicament was not available to humanity but needed to come "from above" (see 3:1 – 13; cf. 1:15, 27; 3:31; 6:14; 11:27; 12:13). Thus, it was God who "blinded their eyes" (Τετύφλωκεν αὐτῶν τοὺς ὀφθαλμοὺς) and "hardened their heart" (ἐπώρωσεν αὐτῶν τὴν καρδίαν).

This pericope does not create a new problem but raises an old one. The fundamental problem with humanity was hinted at from the very beginning of the Gospel (1:5, 10 – 11) and is given further elaboration throughout the Gospel, climaxing here at the end of Jesus's ministry.[47] It will shortly be described as partly rooted in human action (v. 43), but here it is also described as rooted (and foundationally so) in divine action. In one sense, then, the application from Isaiah 6 is that this response to

---

40. Cf. Morris, *John*, 536.

41. According to Brian J. Tabb, "Johannine 'fulfillment' is characterized by a dialogical, mutually interpretive relationship between the OT and Jesus" ("Johannine Fulfillment of Scripture: Continuity and Escalation," *BBR* 21 [2011]: 495 – 505 [500]).

42. See Schnackenburg, *John*, 2:414.

43. Hoskyns, *Fourth Gospel*, 428.

44. For a helpful overview of the exegetical issues involving this quotation, see Craig A. Evans, *To See and Not Perceive: Isaiah 6:9 – 10 in Early Jewish and Christian Interpretation*, JSOTSup 64 (Sheffield: Sheffield Academic Press, 1989).

45. Oswalt, *Isaiah*, 189.

46. Ibid., 189 – 90.

47. Salier, *Rhetorical Impact of the Sēmeia*, 126.

Jesus is ultimately a *judgment from God*, allowing the darkness to which they belong to impose itself upon them.[48] In another sense, however, without denying human action (i.e., the failure to believe), the response of the crowd can also be described as an *action of God*; God is the primary cause of their disbelief.

A survey of interpreters reveals that many try to avoid making God look in any way arbitrary or unjust in his actions. This then motivates the search for a human basis for the judgment and therefore results in an interpretation that understands this text as merely a reaction of God to unbelief.[49] But this pericope will not permit the interpreter to take such actions away from the purposes of God. God *is* the cause of the unbelieving response to Jesus, not merely the judge of it.[50] If the depiction of God as the cause of unbelief makes God look unjust, we must look not for resolution in the doctrine of God alone but in the presentation of God provided by his Son, Jesus Christ, who perfectly exemplifies the mercy and grace of God. Jesus is "the unique mirror of the divine grace" (to use Calvin's phrase), and he suspended his own rights for ours and took our shame upon himself.[51]

12:41 Isaiah said these things because he saw his glory and has spoken about him (ταῦτα εἶπεν Ἡσαΐας, ὅτι εἶδεν τὴν δόξαν αὐτοῦ, καὶ ἐλάλησεν περὶ αὐτοῦ). The narrator explains further that Isaiah said what he said "because he saw his glory" (ὅτι εἶδεν τὴν δόξαν αὐτοῦ). In the context of Isaiah 6, the "glory" that Isaiah witnessed was the glory of YHWH (6:1, 3), but here "his glory" (τὴν δόξαν αὐτοῦ) is almost certainly a reference to Christ,

even though he has not been mentioned by name since v. 36. This implication is demanded, not only because the Gospel has already explained that Abraham "saw" Jesus (see 8:56, 58) but also because "glory" has now been applied specifically to Jesus, the Son of Man (v. 23; see also comments on 1:14). And just as Abraham did not see the "day" of Christ in a specific, chronological sense but in the eschatological sense of the coming of the Son of Man (see comments on 8:56), so also did Isaiah's vision depict glory that necessarily included Jesus the Son. That is, the text here makes an explicit judgment regarding the identity of God, describing in the very texture of the pericope's discourse the nature and function of the God of Israel and his relationship to Jesus.[52] Thus, the seemingly ambiguous "his" intentionally portrays the intrinsic relationship between "the LORD" (YHWH) of Isaiah 6:1, 3 and "the Son of Man" (Jesus) of this pericope.

This intra-Scriptural exegesis helps to make sense of the pericope at hand. The "glory" of the Lord is also and more fully the glory of Christ. Indeed, this "glory" revealed to Isaiah was made manifest to the world — especially to the Jews — by the "signs" of Jesus, and these signs according to the narrator in 2:11 were intended to "reveal his glory" (ἐφανέρωσεν τὴν δόξαν αὐτοῦ), with the "his" unavoidably referring to Christ. The narrator has just made an intra-Scriptural connection not merely between the Father and the Son but also between the responses of the people in Isaiah's day and Jesus's day. We can therefore say comfortably that God "blinded" and "hardened" (v. 40) even though it was not fully manifested until Jesus revealed it, just as we can say that Isaiah saw Jesus

---

48. See Calvin, *John 11–21*, 47; Ridderbos, *John*, 444.

49. Cf. Hartley, "Destined to Disobey?," 283–84.

50. Bultmann is helpful here: "The thought that one's actual behavior in an individual instance is determined by the deepest ground of being does not destroy responsibility, but for the first time really awakens it" (*John*, 453).

51. Calvin, *John 11–21*, 3.

52. For a helpful explanation of this, see David S. Yeago, "The New Testament and the Nicene Dogma: A Contribution to the Recovery of Theological Exegesis," *ProEccl* 3 (1994): 152–64.

even though it was not fully manifested in Isaiah. Isaiah and Jesus proclaim the same message of God, now made known as the gospel of Jesus Christ, the one who finally and more fully reveals it (1:18).

12:42 Despite that many of the rulers believed in him, but because of the Pharisees they were not confessing, in order that they might not be expelled from the synagogue (ὅμως μέντοι καὶ ἐκ τῶν ἀρχόντων πολλοὶ ἐπίστευσαν εἰς αὐτόν, ἀλλὰ διὰ τοὺς Φαρισαίους οὐχ ὡμολόγουν ἵνα μὴ ἀποσυνάγωγοι γένωνται). After focusing on the divine action of unbelief, the narrator turns to the human action of unbelief. The general analysis of unbelief is too broad if it is viewed as comprehensive, for "despite" the overall disbelief, "many of the rulers" (ἐκ τῶν ἀρχόντων πολλοὶ), that is, the Jewish authorities, believed in Jesus. The narrator explains that the Jewish authorities who did believe were unable to express that belief fully because they feared rejection from their own people, the Jews. There is no need to interpret this statement under the guidance of the influential proposal of J. L. Martyn regarding the "expulsion from the synagogue" (see comments on 9:22; see also Introduction). The narrator merely describes in practice the tools used to procure "blinding and hardening" (v. 40).[53]

12:43 For they loved the glory of humanity rather than the glory of God (ἠγάπησαν γὰρ τὴν δόξαν τῶν ἀνθρώπων μᾶλλον ἤπερ τὴν δόξαν τοῦ θεοῦ). The narrator concludes his commentary on the public ministry of Jesus with a statement that echoes the commentary he offered of the "believing" Passover crowd at the beginning of his ministry (see 2:23 – 25). The narrator explains that the people "loved" (ἠγάπησαν) the "glory" (τὴν δόξαν)

of humanity more than the glory of God ("loved" meaning "chose" or "preferred"). And the use of "glory" here can mean more simply "recognition" or "approval" as it did in 5:41, though the "glory of God" is almost certainly intended to reflect the more robust sense related to Isaiah's vision in Isaiah 6 and the glory of the Son (cf. v. 23).[54] The "blindness and hardening" (v. 40) of unbelievers is such a distortion of reality that they are drawn to their own perverse and disfigured state of being rather than the healing and restoring power of God. If only they would see themselves in light of the "glory of Christ" as Isaiah did (see Isa 6:5)! This serves as a fitting conclusion to the public rejection of Jesus, offering a penetrating analysis of the human condition first introduced in the prologue (1:5).

12:44 Then Jesus cried out and said, "The one who believes in me does not believe in me but in the one who sent me" (Ἰησοῦς δὲ ἔκραξεν καὶ εἶπεν, Ὁ πιστεύων εἰς ἐμὲ οὐ πιστεύει εἰς ἐμὲ ἀλλὰ εἰς τὸν πέμψαντά με). The third part of Jesus's three-part monologue explains the witness of the Son (vv. 44 – 50). In light of the apparent departure of Jesus in v. 36, this reappearance of Jesus is often viewed as awkward (or worse, as an editorial mistake).[55] But this reappearance by Jesus makes for an emphatic and climactic "final appeal to believe," not only for the crowd listening but also for the reader of the Gospel. Just as the departure and concealment of Jesus was intentionally cryptic (see comments on v. 36), so also is Jesus's reappearance for a final exhortation to the people. The (historical) specifics of the scene are not indicated, and they are made secondary in this instance to the Gospel's rhetorical interests.

Jesus's final statement is prefaced with the prophetic verb "cried out" (ἔκραξεν), a verb used of Jesus's speech before (7:28, 37). The verb is not used

---

53. Cf. Romans 10:9 – 10, where faith and confession are depicted in parallelism.

54. Michaels, *John*, 713.
55. See Lincoln, *John*, 359.

for emotional or irrational cries but with a special sense for inspired speech (see comments on 1:15). With this introduction, the final public statement of Jesus is rendered more emphatic. In a sense, this concluding statement is like an encore, a re-appearance in order to make one final exhortative statement. The "cry" of Jesus here is the cry of the merciful and gracious God, calling the reader — the world — to repentance. Such a call matches the purpose of the entire Gospel (see 20:30 – 31).

Jesus begins with a statement that summarizes much of his preaching and his entire ministry (hitting a theme announced in the prologue, especially 1:18). Everything Jesus has said and done is as the representative of the Father, whom Jesus describes in the theologically robust language as "the one who sent me" (τὸν πέμψαντά με). The term "believe" (πιστεύει) is a central term in the Gospel (see comments on 1:12); to believe in Jesus *is* to believe in the Father. In this verse, Jesus claims that all that he has said and done has been God centered. To be Christocentric is to be focused on the Father. The true object of the Christian's faith is God, and the mode of their faith is Christ (and the empowerment of that same faith is the Spirit). "Christian faith is not a cult of Jesus; it is faith in God."[56]

12:45 "And the one who sees me sees the one who sent me" (καὶ ὁ θεωρῶν ἐμὲ θεωρεῖ τὸν πέμψαντά με). Just as belief in Jesus ultimately finds its object in God, so also Jesus is the ultimate expression of God. The Father and the Son are so intimately connected that Jesus is not only the access point to the Father but also the visible manifestation and presence of God. The prologue has already announced such a relationship (see comments on 1:1, 14), and the entire Gospel has depicted the ministry of the Trinitarian God in the person of Jesus Christ in the world.

Just as the language of "belief" intends to relate the person of Jesus to the person of God the Father, so also is the language of "sending" in vv. 44 – 45 intended to relate the work of the Son to the work of God the Father. By these words, Jesus unites his task and purpose to God himself and exhorts his hearers to listen carefully to the invitation of God made manifest through his "Word" (see comments on 3:16).

12:46 "I have come into the world in order that everyone who believes in me might not remain in darkness" (ἐγὼ φῶς εἰς τὸν κόσμον ἐλήλυθα, ἵνα πᾶς ὁ πιστεύων εἰς ἐμὲ ἐν τῇ σκοτίᾳ μὴ μείνῃ). Jesus now speaks in vv. 46 – 48 with words and themes that are undeniably similar to the narrator's commentary in 3:16 – 19. Since the text makes these statements the words of Jesus, there is no need for fanciful editorial theories.[57] Jesus continues to summarize his teaching by declaring the purpose of his coming into the world, his mission from the Father. Restating what he said earlier (see comments on 8:12), Jesus claims that his purpose for coming was that everyone who believes in him "might not remain in the darkness" (ἐν τῇ σκοτίᾳ μὴ μείνῃ).

12:47 "If anyone hears my words and does not keep them, I am not judging him, for I did not come in order to judge the world but in order to save the world" (καὶ ἐάν τίς μου ἀκούσῃ τῶν ῥημάτων καὶ μὴ φυλάξῃ, ἐγὼ οὐ κρίνω αὐτόν, οὐ γὰρ ἦλθον ἵνα κρίνω τὸν κόσμον ἀλλ' ἵνα σώσω τὸν κόσμον). Jesus here further defines the purpose of his mission, which is really a restatement of what the narrator said earlier in the Gospel (see comments on 3:17 – 18). What initiated the sending of the Son was love (3:16), not judgment, even if judgment is the inevitable result of darkness.[58] What

---

56. Hoskyns, *Fourth Gospel*, 430.
57. Contra Bultmann, *John*, 342 – 47.

58. Hoskyns, *Fourth Gospel*, 430.

is important to notice is how significant it is that the believer both "hears" (ἀκούσῃ) and "keeps" (φυλάξῃ) the words of Jesus, that is, is "living by the Word."[59] Such an explanation befits the end of Jesus's public ministry, in which he has spoken the truth, and it has been rejected. The rejection of the words of Jesus is itself a form of judgment, as v. 48 will make clear.

12:48 "The one who rejects me and does not receive my words has one who judges him; the words themselves which I have spoken will judge him on the last day" (ὁ ἀθετῶν ἐμὲ καὶ μὴ λαμβάνων τὰ ῥήματά μου ἔχει τὸν κρίνοντα αὐτόν· ὁ λόγος ὃν ἐλάλησα ἐκεῖνος κρινεῖ αὐτὸν ἐν τῇ ἐσχάτῃ ἡμέρᾳ). Not only does rejecting the words (message) of Jesus mean that one is rejecting Jesus, but it also means that judgment is inevitable. Jesus's own words will render judgment "on the last day" (ἐν τῇ ἐσχάτῃ ἡμέρᾳ) when "the one who judges," God the Father, gives all judgment to the Son (see comments on 5:22 – 30). Jesus speaks here (and in vv. 49 – 50) as the prophet-like-Moses that was promised in Deuteronomy 18:18 – 19.[60] Jesus had said in 5:45 that Moses was the one who accuses the disbelieving Jews; Jesus now offers verbal allusions to the exegetical proof from Deuteronomy 18. The essence of the statement is that the intimate relationship between God the Father and God the Son is made manifest in the mission, message, and judgment they share.

12:49 "Because I did not speak from myself, but the one who sent me, the Father, he has given the command to me what to say and what I speak" (ὅτι ἐγὼ ἐξ ἐμαυτοῦ οὐκ ἐλάλησα, ἀλλ᾽ ὁ πέμψας με πατὴρ αὐτός μοι ἐντολὴν δέδωκεν τί εἴπω καὶ τί

λαλήσω). Continuing with the theme from Deuteronomy 18, Jesus declares again that he spoke not "from" (ἐξ) himself but what he was commanded to speak. The Trinitarian nature of Jesus's work and ministry is further articulated here; everything Jesus has said in his public ministry is rooted in God himself, just as the faith he intended to produce had God as its object (v. 44). To pit Jesus against God is to misunderstand Jesus *and* to misunderstand God. Jesus has simply obeyed "the command" (ἐντολὴν) of his Father.

12:50 "And I know that his command is eternal life, therefore what I speak, just as the Father has spoken to me, so I speak" (καὶ οἶδα ὅτι ἡ ἐντολὴ αὐτοῦ ζωὴ αἰώνιός ἐστιν. ἃ οὖν ἐγὼ λαλῶ, καθὼς εἴρηκέν μοι ὁ πατήρ, οὕτως λαλῶ). The "command" (ἡ ἐντολὴ) of the Father "is eternal life," echoing again Deuteronomy 18. The commands also connect the act of obedience required of the Son to the Father to the obedience required of the believer to God. This closing exhortation is not harsh but gracious. It is an invitation to life, even more, to eternal life, for "his command *is* eternal life" (ἡ ἐντολὴ αὐτοῦ ζωὴ αἰώνιός ἐστιν). This is *the* command of God that sums up the covenant obligations of the believer.[61]

In this way Jesus concludes his monologue and his final public exhortation to the crowd and the reader. Barrett summarizes well the point of Jesus's final public statement: "Jesus is not a figure of independent greatness; he is the Word of God, or he is nothing at all."[62] Jesus's concluding statement has not only summarized the themes and message of his entire public ministry but prepares his audience for their fulfillment in his death that follows.

---

59. Beasley-Murray, *John*, 217 – 18.

60. See Brown, *John*, 1:491 – 92. Even the terminology used by the LXX fits the language of our pericope.

61. Brown, *John*, 1:492 – 93.

62. Barrett, *John*, 435.

Theology in Application

In his final statement at the end of his public ministry, Jesus summarizes his message and his ministry to the crowd before him, Jews and Greeks — the whole world. This three-part monologue serves as a theological commentary on his public ministry. In this pericope, the reader of the Fourth Gospel hears a final statement from the Lord regarding his mission from the Father and the purpose of the cross and is exhorted to respond by believing in God the Father through the Son, Jesus Christ.

The Fruit of God

The illustration Jesus used in v. 24 not only explains his role as the "seed" but also the origin and life force of the "fruit," that is, the people of God — the church. Just as the natural function of the seed is that it must die, so also the natural function of its fruit is that it must blossom and grow in a manner befitting its seed of origin. The intimate connection between seed and death is also implied between fruit and life. The Christian life is a life originating from the Son of God, the source of our very existence. The church, then, is the fruit of God, produced by his grace and for his glory. As the fruit of God, Christians individually and corporately are to blossom in person and purpose, for "we are God's handiwork, created in Christ Jesus to do good works" (Eph 2:10). This theological truth about our origin by the death of Christ should facilitate our healthy growth "in Christ." For the seed of the gospel "is bearing fruit and growing throughout the whole world — just as it has been doing among you since the day you heard it and truly understood God's grace" (Col 1:6). Therefore, let us water and tend the seed implanted in us, for as Augustine explains, "He has awakened in us a great longing for that sweet experience of his presence within: but it is by daily growth that we acquire it; it is by walking that we grow, and it is by forward efforts that we walk, so as to be able at last to attain it."[63]

The Glorification and Exaltation of the Son

Jesus begins his final statement to the world by declaring that now is the time ("the hour") of his glorification. The glorification of the Son of Man, according to the rest of the Gospel, is the manifestation of all the power, glory, and rule of God in the person and work of Jesus Christ. But the expression of this "glory" is not with a crown but with the cross. This is the grand irony of the gospel. The hour of the glorification of the Son of Man (i.e., the King, Creator, and Ruler of all) is made manifest on the cross (i.e., the place of suffering, humiliation, and shame)! Ultimately, the glory of the Son is for the glory of the Father (v. 28); this glorification involves the Trinitarian identity of God. The exaltation of the Son in majesty and glory occurs

---

when he is "lifted up" on the cross. The power and purposes of God are best displayed in the most humiliating of acts. But this is our God and the fullest expression of the love of God.

The Judgment of This World and the Ruler of This World

The death of Christ is not a defeat but a victory. The cross is not where Jesus is judged but where the world and the ruler of the world are judged. When the world puts Jesus on the cross, it is from its perspective a judgment of Jesus's person and work; in reality, however, the crucifixion of the Son is in fact the exact reverse — it is the judgment of the world. The cross is the pinnacle of this paradox, for it is the throne upon which the King of kings is crowned — his glory. Yet it is also the point of decision for the world, either as *the place of their salvation*, in which the cross is the sacrifice of the Lamb of God on their behalf, or *the place of their judgment*, by which they stand already condemned (3:18). It was the death of Christ "that was the true beginning of a properly ordered state [the kingdom of God] and the complete restoration of the world."[64] The cross is not the defeat of Jesus; it is the victory of God!

This victory is not merely the moral victory of a martyr but the physical and spiritual victory over all opposing forces and powers. By this victory, all humanity is either judged or saved, and all challengers have been defeated — even death itself (1 Cor 15:55). Even Satan, the long-standing opponent of God, is defeated, exorcised from the world he for too long had tried to rule. The mission of God was not merely about the soul of humanity but the entire created order. The ruler of this world is cast out and replaced by a new ruler, the rightful King. The cross is therefore the dethronement of Satan from his tyranny over the world and the enthronement of the true King, Jesus Christ, the Son of Man. In the story John tells — an entirely true story—God wins.

The God Who Blinds Eyes and Hardens Hearts

This pericope raises several questions regarding the sovereignty of God and his active role in sin and salvation. Debates surrounding Calvinism and predestination cannot avoid this difficult text — difficult not merely in regard to what the text means but also because of what it implies in regard to the character of God. The narrator's commentary on the unbelief of the people in vv. 37 – 43 raises numerous theological issues that the church must address with theological sensitivity and wisdom. These issues, all of which center on the nature of God, are not cerebral and abstract but overtly practical regarding the way God works and the ministry of the church (see comments on v. 40). In the least, pastors and church leaders should wrestle long and hard with this text and this issue, but hopefully all Christians would desire to know

---

64. Calvin, *John 11 – 21*, 42.

and respond rightly to God, even the God who is described as the one who blinds eyes and hardens hearts.

The Glory of Humanity vs. the Glory of God

The final public statement of Jesus reveals that there is a battle for allegiance in the human heart between the glory of humanity (self) and the glory of God. Beneath this battle is the temptation to be swayed by the opinions of others, perhaps especially those in power who might be opposed to God — our God (v. 42). This pericope describes this temptation to fear men over God as loving "the glory of humanity rather than the glory of God" (v. 43). While the narrator's commentary ends his analysis of the public ministry of Jesus, it only just begins the analysis the reader must give to the things he or she "loves." Do we love Christ in the midst of public opinion to the contrary? Or are we silent before others about God because he simply does not fit the cultural and political agenda around us? This is not an argument for an insensitive, prideful, and in-your-face Christian proclamation, but for a contextualized presentation of the grace and glory of God that seeks to extend the healing power and loving truth of the gospel to the people with whom we work and live. May our prayer be the same as the prayer of Augustine: "That faith may learn not to blush at His name."[65] And may the church be a healthy dose of salt and light in a decaying and dark world (Matt 5:13 – 16).

---

65. Augustine, *John*, 53.13.295.

John 13:1 – 20

Literary Context

This pericope begins a new section in the Gospel. The public ministry of Jesus has come to an end, and on the eve of "the hour" Jesus gathers his disciples together to address them privately with what is called the farewell discourse (see an overview below). This pericope also serves as the first of a two-part introduction to the farewell discourse, setting the historical and theological context in which Jesus's fourth and most complex monologue will take place. Jesus has spoken of the cross before, but in this scene he enacts the service of the cross for his disciples with the washing of their feet. At this moment the King of kings, the Son of Man, God himself kneels before his disciples to serve them. In this pericope the radical nature of the gospel and the radical response it requires is presented to the reader in dramatic fashion.

VII. The Farewell Discourse (13:1 – 17:26)

→   **A. Introduction: The Love of Jesus (13:1 – 30)**

1. Jesus and the Washing of His Disciples' Feet (13:1 – 20)

2. Jesus Announces His Betrayal (13:21 – 30)

B. The Farewell Discourse (13:31 – 16:33)

1. Prologue: Glory, Departure, and Love (13:31 – 38)

2. I Am the Way and the Truth and the Life (14:1 – 14)

3. I Will Give you the Paraclete (14:15 – 31)

4. I Am the True Vine (15:1 – 17)

5. I Have Also Experienced the Hate of the World (15:18 – 27)

6. I Will Empower You by the Paraclete (16:1 – 15)

7. I Will Turn Your Grief into Joy (16:16 – 24)

8. Epilogue: Speaking Plainly, Departure, and Peace (16:25 – 33)

C. Conclusion: The Prayer of Jesus (17:1 – 26)

Main Idea

Christ is the Servant, the one who must (and did!) wash the feet of every disciple. The only appropriate response is to humbly receive his service and to make his service a Christian "rule of life" for the life of the church and its mission to the world.

Translation

John 13:1–20

1a	Introduction & Setting (1–5)	Now **it was before** the Feast,
b	Description	that is, the Passover.
c	Character Reentrance/Subject	**Jesus,**
d	Character's Thoughts	knowing that his hour had come
e	Purpose	for him to depart from this world
f	Destination	to the Father,
g	Character's Thoughts	having loved his own who were in the world,
h	Predicate of 1c	**he loved them to the end.**
2a		And
b	Context	while a meal was taking place,
c	Character Reentrance/Action	**the Devil had already come into the heart**
d	Character Reentrance	of Judas,
e	Identification	son of Simon of Iscariot,
f	Purpose	in order that he might betray him.
3a	Subject of 4a	**[Jesus]**
b	Character's Thoughts	knowing that the Father has given all things into his hands and
c	Origen	that he had come from God and
d	Destination	was going to God,
4a	Sequence Action/Predicate of 3a	**he got up from the meal**
b		and **removed his garments,**
c		and
		taking a towel,
d		**he wrapped it around himself.**
5a		**Then he poured water into the basin**
b		and **began to wash the feet of his disciples**
c		and **dry them with a towel**
d	Description	which was wrapped around him.
6a	Dialogue (6–11)	Then **he came**
b	Character Reentrance	to Simon Peter.
c		**He said to him,**
d	Address	*"Lord,*
e	Emphatic Question	*are you going to wash my feet?"*

7a	Response	**Jesus answered and said to him,**
b	Rhetorical Rebuke	*"What I do you do not understand now,*
c		*but you will after these things."*
8a	Response	**Peter said to him,**
b	Rejection	*"You shall not wash my feet in all eternity!"*
c	Response	**Jesus answered him,**
d	Condition	*"If I do not wash you,*
e	Inferential, Escalating, Rebuke	*you have no part with me."*
9a	Confused Response	**Simon Peter said to him,**
b	Address	*"Lord,*
c	Imperative	*not only my feet but also*
d		*my hands and*
e		*my head!"*
10a	Responsive Explanation	**Jesus said to him,**
b	Description	*"The one who has been bathed …*
c	Result	*… has no need*
d	Exception	*except to wash his feet,*
e	Contrast	*but he is completely clean.*
f	Proleptic Declaration	*And you are clean,*
g	Contrast	*but not everyone."*
11a	Narrator's Aside	For **he knew the one who was going to betray him;**
b	Basis of 10g	for this reason
c		**he said,**
d		*"not everyone is clean."*
12a	Monologue (12–20)	Then
b	Context	when he had washed their feet and
c		picked up his garments and
d		reclined again,
e		**he said to them,**
f	Question	*"Do you understand what I did to you?*
13a	Premise for 14	*You call me*
b	Title #1	*'the Teacher' and*
c	Title #2	*'the Lord,'*
d	Commendation	*and you speak well,*
e	Basis/Verification	*for that is who I am.*
14a		*Then*
b	Condition	*if I …*
c	Identification (Premise)	*the Lord and the Teacher,*
d		*… have washed your feet,*
e	Inference	*you also ought to wash the feet of one another.*
15a	Explanation	*For I have given an example to you*
b	Purpose	*in order that you might do*
c	Comparison	*just as I did to you.*
16a	Amen Formula	*Truly, truly I say to you,*
b	Illustration	*a slave is not greater than his master,*
c		*nor a messenger greater than the one who sent him.*

Continued on next page.

Continued from previous page.

17a	Condition #1	*If you understand these things,*
b	Inferential Promise	*you are blessed*
c	Condition #2	*if you do these things.*
18a	Qualification	*I am not speaking concerning all of you,*
b	Assertion	*I know those I have chosen,*
c	Contrast to "Chosen"	*but*
d	Purpose (of 18b)—"know"	*in order that Scripture may be fulfilled,*
e	Description	*'The one who eats my bread …*
f	Result	*… has lifted up his heel against me.'* ✥ (Ps 41:9)
19a	Explanation of 18	*I speak to you at this point*
b	Time	*before it happens,*
c	Intended Result	*so that you may believe*
d	Time	*when it happens that I Am.*
	Concluding Exhortation	
20a	Amen Formula	*Truly, truly I say to you,*
b	Description	*the one who receives the one I send …*
c	Result	*… receives me, but*
d	Contrast	*the one who receives me …*
e	Result	*… receives the one who sent me."*

Structure and Literary Form

This pericope is a combination of a basic story unit followed by a dialogue and a monologue. There is a clear three-part structure: a narrative introduction (vv. 1 – 5), a dialogue (vv. 6 – 11), and a monologue (vv. 12 – 20). The narrative has already combined action, dialogue, or monologue in various ways before, either by combining two different kinds of dialogues or prefacing a dialogue or monologue with an action (e.g., 9:1 – 41). While at times action, dialogue, or monologue are only briefly applied by the narrator to move the plot along (e.g., 12:29, 34), in this pericope there is a much more substantial and integrated movement of action-dialogue-monologue.[1] The pericope is introduced in vv. 1 – 5 when Jesus washes his disciples' feet. In vv. 6 – 11 a dialogue occurs between Jesus and Peter that develops out of the preceding action. Finally, in vv. 12 – 20 Jesus offers a monologue response to all the disciples and provides an explanation of the meaning and significance of the foot washing.

---

1. See George Mlakuzhyil, *The Christocentric Literary Structure of the Fourth Gospel* (Rome: Pontifical Biblical Institute, 1987), 117.

Exegetical Outline

→ **1. Jesus and the Washing of His Disciples' Feet (13:1 – 20)**

   a. Jesus Washes His Disciples' Feet (vv. 1 – 5)

   b. Jesus's Dialogue with Peter (vv. 6 – 11)

   c. Jesus Explains His Foot Washing (vv. 12 – 20)

Explanation of the Text

This section of the Gospel, "The Farewell Discourse" (13:1 – 17:26), has a long history of interpretation in regard to its nature and literary form that requires a more official introduction. Several interpretive issues need to be discussed and defined before we examine the details of the text, including the following: What is the farewell discourse, what is its literary structure, and what is its function? This brief overview will facilitate the commentary on all of chapters 13 – 17.

IN-DEPTH: The Farewell Discourse

What is the farewell discourse? In one sense, the farewell discourse is simply another monologue or speech of Jesus (see Introduction), and in the Gospel we have seen three other monologues of Jesus (5:19 – 47; 10:1 – 21; 12:20 – 50). But the farewell discourse is not a typical monologue, for its topics and location in the ministry of Jesus suggest that it has been formed by specific genre conventions that require a more complex definition of its nature. Like the Gospel as a whole, the farewell discourse employs "a composite of various literary forms."[2] A brief discussion of the genre associations employed by the farewell discourse is now in order.

The scholarly consensus is that the farewell discourse exemplifies a well-established literary pattern called a testament. Similar farewell speeches were common in the OT, as in the farewell and blessing of Jacob to his children (Gen 47:29 – 49:33), Joshua's farewell to Israel (Josh 22 – 24), and David's farewell speech (1 Chr 28 – 29). Even more, the entire book of Deuteronomy can rightly be described as Moses's farewell speeches to Israel. The comparisons between Deuteronomy and John's farewell discourse are worthy to note, especially in that both are expressions of their respective covenants between God and his people (Deuteronomy, the old covenant; John, the new covenant).[3] The genre of testament became even more popular in the late biblical and intertestamental

---

2. Parsenios, *Departure and Consolation,* 7.

3. See Aelred Lacomara, "Deuteronomy and the Farewell Discourse (Jn 13:31 – 16:33)," *CBQ* 36 (1974): 65 – 84.

periods (e.g., Testaments of the Twelve Patriarchs). Brown nicely summarizes the originating circumstances of the testament: "The common situation is that of a great man who gathers together his followers (his children, his disciples, or the people) on the eve of his death to give them instructions that will help them after his departure."[4] The genre of John's farewell discourse, therefore, both its form and situation, clearly matches the testamentary literature of "farewell" speeches.[5] But to interpret the farewell discourse requires more than assembling lists of generic parallels between John and testamentary literature. Since the farewell discourse contains other noticeable and "particular pressures" that distinguish it from a traditional testament, we must examine two other generic composites.[6]

One of the primary places where the farewell discourse differs from the traditional testament scene is in its reliance on what Parsenios calls "dynamic movement."[7] In the standard testamentary farewell scenes, there are no exits; the speakers typically wait for death to come to them on a deathbed (see e.g., Gen 49:33). In the Fourth Gospel, by contrast, the entire farewell discourse, stretching from 13:1–18:1, is centered around two dynamic exits, that of Judas at 13:30 and that of Jesus, announced at 14:31 and executed at 18:1. "The exits of Judas and Jesus add a dimension to the Johannine scene ... that differs markedly from the typical testament. These exits are readily recognizable in ancient drama, however, where exits and entrances profoundly affect narrative development."[8] Structurally, the exit of Judas at 13:30 (commanded by Jesus in 13:27) signals to the reader that what follows is the beginning of the farewell discourse, with its conclusion signaled again when Jesus himself exits at 18:1. Exits, therefore, can function as a "dramatic device" for framing or emphasizing a scene or even focusing upon a character (for a specific example of this function, see comments on 14:31). This is not to say that the Gospel of John is a drama — it is a (prose) narrative — but it does have many dramatic modes of narration. Its use of a prologue and frequent application of irony is evidence of the Gospel's participation in ancient dramatic techniques.[9] In a sense, the farewell discourse reflects "bilingualism"[10] in that it shares similarities with the testament genre, and yet it can (and does) speak in several other ancient literary idioms (Jewish and Greco-Roman), with the dramatic device of "exits" being one example.

4. Brown, *John*, 2:598.

5. Cf. Fernando F. Segovia, *The Farewell of the Word: The Johannine Call to Abide* (Minneapolis: Fortress, 1991), 2–20.

6. Ashton, *Understanding the Fourth Gospel*, 445.

7. Parsenios, *Departure and Consolation*, 12.

8. Ibid., 13.

9. P. E. Easterling, "From Repertoire to Canon," in *The Cambridge Companion to Greek Tragedy*, ed. P. E. Easterling (Cambridge: Cambridge University Press, 1997), 226, refers to their frequent and underlying use of dramatic techniques as "the theatricalization of ancient culture."

10. This term is taken from W. D. Davies, "Reflections on Aspects of the Jewish Background of the Gospel of John," in *Exploring the Gospel of John: In Honor of D. Moody Smith*, ed. R. Alan Culpepper and C. Clifton Black (Louisville: Westminster John Knox, 1996), 43–64.

There is another "pressure" particular to the farewell discourse in John compared to the traditional testament: ancient consolation. Consolation literature employed a range of therapeutic methods to console their audience, most commonly because of an impending death. There are three primary consolatory functions.[11] First, a surrogate or replacement is offered to those left by the departing figure; this replacement becomes the means by which the departed figure remains present. In John the replacement is "another paraclete" (14:16), who is the functional presence of Jesus for his disciples (14:18 – 21). Second, the grief is preemptively satiated by being predicted, for only unexpected loss or surprise misfortune can truly leave one unprepared and imbalanced. In John the departure of Jesus and the trials to follow are clearly articulated and explained (15:18 – 16:4). Third, those left by the departing figure are exhorted to stay the course and be responsible in action, since excessive grief can lead to a neglect of one's duties. In John the disciples of Jesus are exhorted to remain and bear fruit (15:1 – 16). Not only does the farewell discourse proper (13:31 – 16:33) offer all three of these consolatory elements, but befitting ancient consolation even further, the entire farewell section of the Gospel (13:1 – 17:26) also contains the opening context of a symbolic meal (13:1 – 30) and a closing "prayer of departure" (17:1 – 26).[12]

What is the literary structure of the farewell discourse? The attempt to determine the literary structure of the farewell discourse has proven more than a little difficult. A primary reason for this is the almost universally held position that the farewell discourse is a highly edited (redacted) text. This axiom is rooted in what is perceived to be clear evidence of poor editorial work when Jesus says "arise, let us depart from here" in 14:31 and then continues his speech until 18:1. Because of this axiomatic literary seam (see comments on 14:31), the farewell discourse is commonly described as containing in reality two discourses: 13:31 – 14:31 and 15:1 – 16:33. But as we already discussed above, we will argue that 14:31 uses a dramatic "exit" device common to the literary milieu of the Fourth Gospel. Moreover, the farewell discourse shows an idiolect and syntactic structure that is consistent and logically functional throughout. For these reasons the farewell discourse (not "discourses") is best treated as a competent literary whole.[13]

While the farewell discourse may confidently be read as a unity and integral whole, the internal organization of the discourse is still difficult to determine

---

11. This is adapted from Paul A. Holloway, "Left Behind: Jesus's Consolation of His Disciples in John 13,31 – 17,26," *ZNW* 96 (2005): 1 – 34.

12. Ibid., 21 – 33.

13. L. Scott Kellum, *The Unity of the Farewell Discourse: The Literary Integrity of John 13:31 – 16:33*, JSNTSup 256 (London: T&T Clark, 2004).

with precision. The discourse's "dynamic movement" exhibited by the "exit" device (see above) strongly suggests that the discourse proper begins at 13:31 and ends at 16:33. The discourse proper is best understood to be framed by a significant introduction (13:1–30) and conclusion (17:1–26), both of which fit the nature of a farewell speech, especially a "consolatory testament" (see above). Finally, the discourse proper cannot easily be given a logical outline, though an exegetically reasonable structure can be suggested. The discourse proper consists of six significant and developing thematic *statements* by Jesus (14:1–14; 14:15–31; 15:1–17; 15:18–27; 16:1–15; 16:16–24) that are framed by what is functionally a prologue (13:31–38) and an epilogue (16:25–33).[14]

Outline for the Farewell Discourse

Prologue (13:31–38)

STATEMENT 1: "I Am the Way and the Truth and the Life" (14:1–14)

STATEMENT 2: "I Will Give You the Paraclete" (14:15–31)

STATEMENT 3: "I Am the True Vine" (15:1–17)

STATEMENT 4: "I Have Also Experienced the Hate of the World" (15:18–27)

STATEMENT 5: "I Will Empower You by the Paraclete" (16:1–15)

STATEMENT 6: "I Will Turn Your Grief into Joy" (16:16–24)

Epilogue (16:25–33)

Statements 1–3 focus on the disciples' relationship to Jesus; statements 4–6 focus on the disciples' engagement with the world. As we discussed above, however, this structural logic is moved and controlled by the macrolevel pressures of the generic features of the farewell discourse, that is, the testament genre, the "exit" device, and ancient consolation, especially in the context of a symbol-laden meal.

What is the function of the farewell discourse? In the larger context of the Gospel, the farewell discourse serves a significant role. Jesus's public ministry has come to an end, so Jesus gathers his intimate disciples around a symbolic meal and instructs them for the last time concerning his person and work and their corporate identity and work as his disciples. Jesus addresses their questions and fears, but he also exhorts them to stay the course, which involves remaining in him by the Spirit. As Jesus's ministry turns toward the cross-resurrection-ascension, Jesus uses the farewell discourse to explain what is to come and where he must go.

Jesus also explains his departure, his "presence-in-absence," in two signifi-

---

14. The logic for a prologue and epilogue framing the discourse proper is not merely the question of where Jesus is going and the affirmation of where he is from (13:31 and 16:28) but also the reaction of Jesus to Peter and to the disciples alike regarding betrayal or abandonment (13:38 and 16:32). See John L. Boyle, "The Last Discourse (Jn 13, 31–16,33) and Prayer (Jn 17): Some Observations on Their Unity and Development," *Bib* 56 (1975): 210–22.

cant ways.[15] First, Jesus is the way to the Father so that his departure is intended to prepare the place where they too will go and the provision of the route that they too will take (14:3 – 6). Thus, his absence is actually for the purpose of his presence, so that the disciples may be present with God eternally. Second, the departure of Jesus actually allows him to be more fully present with his disciples (14:18; 16:7). Only after his departure will he and the Father come and make their home with them (14:23), enabling the disciples to do greater works (14:12), to pray effectively by the use of his name (14:13 – 14; 16:23 – 24), and to be intimately united with him (15:1 – 11), having his peace (14:27) and sharing in his suffering (15:18 – 21) and ultimately his victory (16:33).[16] In both ways, therefore, the things to come are good things, even necessary. It is part of the purposeful plan of God and his continuing mission to the world. On the eve of the new covenant, the farewell discourse, speaking in "covenant-form," functions as the explanation of this transition and a guide to the new dispensation of God and his people.[17]

13:1 **Now it was before the Feast, that is, the Passover. Jesus, knowing that his hour had come for him to depart from this world to the Father, having loved his own who were in the world, he loved them to the end** (Πρὸ δὲ τῆς ἑορτῆς τοῦ πάσχα εἰδὼς ὁ Ἰησοῦς ὅτι ἦλθεν αὐτοῦ ἡ ὥρα ἵνα μεταβῇ ἐκ τοῦ κόσμου τούτου πρὸς τὸν πατέρα, ἀγαπήσας τοὺς ἰδίους τοὺς ἐν τῷ κόσμῳ, εἰς τέλος ἠγάπησεν αὐτούς). The narrative section of the pericope (vv. 1 – 5) serves as an introduction to the rest of the pericope (even to the entire farewell discourse) with a significant and symbol-laden action by Jesus: the washing of his disciples' feet. Since vv. 4 – 5 explain the actions of the foot washing, vv. 1 – 3 function like "a small prologue" that transitions the reader from the public ministry of Jesus

to the private ministry of Jesus and the farewell discourse.[18] This explains why this verse speaks with such a cosmological perspective, for it is almost as if it is looking both backward at what Jesus has done and forward to what Jesus still must do.[19] In just a few sentences (vv. 1 – 3), the narrator reorients the reader to God's love for the world through the Son's person and work and to the cosmological context of the Son's ministry.[20]

After the temporal phrase relating things to the Passover (see comments on 18:28; cf. 12:1; 19:14) that sets the historical and theological contexts for the events to follow, the narrator offers a cosmological commentary on the love of Jesus for his disciples. The narrator describes the affections and intentions of Jesus in light of his awareness of the

---

15. Cf. Ashton, *Understanding the Fourth Gospel*, 456.

16. Cf. Daniel B. Stevick, *Jesus and His Own: A Commentary on John 13 – 17* (Grand Rapids: Eerdmans, 2011), 88.

17. Cf. Rekha M. Chennattu, *Johannine Discipleship as a Covenant Relationship* (Peabody, MA: Hendrickson, 2006).

18. Mary L. Coloe, "Welcome into the Household of God: The Foot Washing in John 13," *CBQ* 66 (2004): 400 – 415.

19. Francis J. Moloney, "The Function of John 13 – 17 within the Johannine Narrative," in *"What is John?" Volume II: Literary and Social Readings of the Fourth Gospel*, ed. Fernando F. Segovia, SBLSymS 7 (Atlanta: Scholars, 1998), 43 – 66 (48).

20. David Gibson, "The Johannine Footwashing and the Death of Jesus: A Dialogue with Scholarship," *SBET* 25 (2007): 50 – 60 (55).

arrival of his "hour" and departure to his Father (see comments on 2:4; 12:23). In a statement that reveals the nature of God toward his people, Jesus is depicted as loving "his own" (τοὺς ἰδίους), not only since the inception of his ministry but also "to the end" (εἰς τέλος). While it is possible to interpret the phrase "to the end" as something more than a chronological statement, as in "completely, finally, to the uttermost, unto death,"[21] in the context of the farewell discourse this love is certainly grounded in something still to come — the cross.[22] This is no abstract declaration but a concrete statement of the epitome of love, the death of God the Son on behalf of the world. That he loved "his own" (τοὺς ἰδίους) must be understood in light of the prologue. Not only does it stipulate that Christ must be received by faith (1:12), but it also shows the strong contrast between the world and Christ. When "his own" people did not know him (1:11), he knew them and was loving them and still loves them.

13:2 And while a meal was taking place, the devil had already come into the heart of Judas, son of Simon of Iscariot, in order that he might betray him (καὶ δείπνου γινομένου, τοῦ διαβόλου ἤδη βεβληκότος εἰς τὴν καρδίαν ἵνα παραδοῖ αὐτὸν Ἰούδας Σίμωνος Ἰσκαριώτου). After the cosmological commentary, the narrator continues the "small prologue" (vv. 1 – 3) by moving into the scene at hand. The scene is left quite vague. The phrase "while a meal was taking place" (δείπνου γινομένου) ushers the reader into an activity already in process. It also makes clear that the foot washing to follow took place during the meal, which calls attention to the peculiarity of Jesus's action, which usually would have taken place before the meal, not after and certainly not during the meal.[23]

If this is the Last Supper (per the Synoptics), it is clearly deemphasized as such and could only be known by implication from later statements, one of which is that this was an evening meal (see 13:30, where Judas departs when "it was night"). As much as the interpreter is itching to compare this "evening meal" with the Last Supper in the Synoptics, great restraint is required. The issue is more than just methodological (see Introduction), for it also involves the unique and legitimate perspective of the Fourth Gospel, which will use this meal as a frame for something else just as deep and just as central to the new covenant (cf. 18:28).

This dinner also involves the active presence of the devil, who is described by the narrator as entering "into the heart" (εἰς τὴν καρδίαν) of Judas for the purpose of instigating the betrayal of Jesus (denoted by the purpose clause [ἵνα with the subjunctive]). The statement is awkwardly stated so that while it is probably saying that the devil put the idea into Judas's heart, it might also be saying that the devil "made up his mind" on the matter. Either way, Judas will fulfill the devil's purpose.[24] The power of this statement is not merely the omniscient commentary provided for the reader but how it functions as an insight into the cosmological plot (the "unseen forces") alluded to by the prologue. Jesus has already declared Judas to be the "devil" (see 6:70), and in this verse their intimate union is displayed in its fullness. In a sense, while Nicodemus was the representative of the Jewish authorities opposed to Jesus (the historical opponents), Judas is the representative of the demonic authorities opposed to Jesus (the cosmological opponents). It is no longer just humanity that opposes and challenges Jesus but also all the satanic powers of the cosmos.

---

21. See Hoskyns, *Fourth Gospel*, 436.

22. Moloney, *John*, 373. Cf. Augustine, *John*, 55.2.300.

23. John Christopher Thomas, *Footwashing in John 13 and*

the Johannine Community, JSNTSup 61 (Sheffield: Sheffield Academic Press, 1991), 83.

24. Michaels, *John*, 723; Carson, *John*, 461 – 62.

13:3 [Jesus] knowing that the Father has given all things into his hands and that he had come from God and was going to God (εἰδὼς ὅτι πάντα ἔδωκεν αὐτῷ ὁ πατὴρ εἰς τὰς χεῖρας καὶ ὅτι ἀπὸ θεοῦ ἐξῆλθεν καὶ πρὸς τὸν θεὸν ὑπάγει). The narrator concludes the "small prologue" (vv. 1 – 3) by making clear that this situation, the cosmic conflict, was neither a surprise to Jesus nor a realistic threat. For Jesus, the implied subject, was "knowing" (εἰδὼς), with the perfect tense expressing that Jesus "had already known." What did he know? Jesus knew that God had given him "all things" (πάντα), with the added expression "into his hands" (εἰς τὰς χεῖρας) serving to make his reception of all things emphatic. The perfect-tense "knowing" (εἰδὼς) in v. 3 here matches the perfect-tense "knowing" (εἰδὼς) of v. 1, creating a frame around the statement regarding the satanic conflict involving Jesus.[25] That is, on both sides of this historical (with Judas) and cosmological (with the devil) conflict is the love *and* power of God. God is not loving but powerless or powerful but unloving; he is simultaneously both. God is the perfection of love and power, made manifest in Jesus — especially as the cross approaches. And all of this, even the conflict still to come, was part of the plan of God, from whom and to whom the Son moves as he fulfills the mission of God.

13:4 He got up from the meal and removed his garments, and taking a towel, he wrapped it around himself (ἐγείρεται ἐκ τοῦ δείπνου καὶ τίθησιν τὰ ἱμάτια, καὶ λαβὼν λέντιον διέζωσεν ἑαυτόν). The love and power of God is here expressed by Christ in the action he performs for his disciples in the middle of the meal. The present-tense verb "he got up" (ἐγείρεται) dramatizes the scene for the reader. At some point during the meal, Jesus gets up and prepares himself to wash the disciples' feet. This is significant, for in Jesus's action the Passover no longer serves as the event in the past that sustains and gives primary meaning to this meal; rather, it is an event that is about to come (the cross). The narrator's detailed attention to the preparation by Jesus is important; by removing his outer garments and dressing in a towel, Jesus puts on the garments of a servant. But this is no normal servant about to perform such a menial task. No, this servant will "lay down" (τίθημι) even his own life by the authority that belongs to him, and he will pick it up by that same authority (cf. 10:17 – 18).[26] Jesus became a servant just like he became a man, not by laying down what he already had (his authority and divinity), but by assuming that which he had not before.[27] Said another way, just as God became a man, so the King became the Servant.

13:5 Then he poured water into the basin and began to wash the feet of his disciples and dry them with a towel which was wrapped around him (εἶτα βάλλει ὕδωρ εἰς τὸν νιπτῆρα καὶ ἤρξατο νίπτειν τοὺς πόδας τῶν μαθητῶν καὶ ἐκμάσσειν τῷ λεντίῳ ᾧ ἦν διεζωσμένος). Like a servant, Jesus prepared the water followed by the washing and drying of his disciples' feet. At this moment the reader is seeing the dramatic entrance of the Son of Man into the plight of humanity. For we would be mistaken to forget that included among the foot-washed disciples was Judas, the hand of Satan, directly opposing Jesus and facilitating his (attempted) destruction.[28] The narrator's restatement of the servant garments of Jesus (cf. v. 4) emphasizes the radical posture of Jesus toward his disciples and the radical nature of the gospel for the world.

The foot washing itself needs to be explored further, both its social-cultural as well as its symbolic significance. First, in the social-cultural context of

---

25. Cf. Michaels, *John*, 724.
26. Ridderbos, *John*, 458 – 59.
27. Augustine, *John*, 55.7.301.
28. Cf. Carson, *John*, 462.

the first century, foot washing was the most demeaning task assigned to household servants, and some historical sources even considered the task too demeaning for servants to have to perform for their masters, for to do such work was to be a slave (see comments on 1:27). But more importantly, the act of foot washing truly was the act of a slave. In scores of Greco-Roman texts, foot washing is equated with slavery, for "footwashing could be used as a synonym for slavery."[29] Never — never! — is this act performed by a superior. As Thomas explains, "Jesus's action remains unparalleled in ancient literature, for no other master (superior) condescends to perform this act for a subordinate."[30] By this act Jesus violates social customs to such a degree that there is no fitting comparison. Yet the reader has only just begun to be prepared for the horrific paradox of the cross.

But foot washing did not only communicate something about the person who performed the washing; it also communicated something about the recipient of the washing. There is historical evidence to suggest that foot washing occurred in contexts of hospitality, which coincides well with the Fourth Gospel's thematic use of hospitality in regard to the ministry of Jesus (see comments before 4:1).[31] Related to hospitality and significant in the context of the farewell discourse (chs. 13–17), foot washing was also preparatory.[32] The act of "footwashing serves to prepare one for a specific task, experience, or relationship."[33] Thus, when Jesus washes his disciples' feet, he is not simply enacting for the disciples who he is; he is enacting *who they are*. By washing the disciples' feet, Jesus prepares

them for the "specific task, experience, and relationship" they are about to begin by means of his death and resurrection — his ultimate act of service.

Second, in the context of the Gospel the foot washing also bears symbolic significance. Scholars have offered several different proposals for the symbolic significance of the foot washing. There are six worth mentioning: (1) an example of humility, (2) a symbol of the Eucharist, (3) a symbol of baptism, (4) a symbol of the forgiveness of sin/cleansing, (5) a sacrament separate from baptism and Eucharist, and (6) a soteriological sign.[34] While the pericope itself will aritculate the symbolic significance of the foot washing, it it important to remember that there should be no forced choice between these six symbolic meanings. Just as *words* were "expected to evoke in hearers' minds shared impressions of people and events and things, and shared ideas, generalities, abstract concepts,"[35] we should also expect *actions* to create symbolically complex "impressions" (see Introduction). This is not to say that the meaning of the foot washing is open-ended, but that the symbolic action should not be constrained by any one symbolic concept or even the social-cultural context of the first century. Its meaning should be kept free to express fully the majestic glory of the Trinitarian God made known in Jesus Christ.

In this way the first section of the pericope concludes (vv. 1–5). In what may be the most symbol-laden, "tight syntactical construction," and "tight concentration of themes" of five verses in the Gospel,[36] the reader has been dramatically introduced and prepared to understand the person and work

29. Thomas, *Footwashing in John 13*, 56.

30. Ibid., 88. Thomas claims that at most a peer might wash an equal's feet, but never a superior.

31. See Coloe, "Welcome into the Household of God," 411–15. Cf. Arland J. Hultgren, "The Johannine Footwashing (13.1–11) as Symbol of Eschatological Hospitality," *NTS* 28 (1982): 539–46.

32. See Mark Thiessen Nation, "Washing Feet: Preparation

for Service," in *The Blackwell Companion to Christian Ethics*, ed. Stanley Hauerwas and Samuel Wells (Malden, MA: Blackwell, 2004), 441–51.

33. Thomas, *Footwashing in John 13*, 59.

34. See Ibid., 11–17.

35. Downing, "Ambiguity, Ancient Semantics, and Faith," 146.

36. Gibson, "The Johannine Footwashing and the Death of Jesus," 53.

of Jesus and to life in the new covenant. The rest of the pericope will explain the complex significance of the foot washing.

13:6 Then he came to Simon Peter. He said to him, "Lord, are you going to wash my feet?" (ἔρχεται οὖν πρὸς Σίμωνα Πέτρον. λέγει αὐτῷ, Κύριε, σύ μου νίπτεις τοὺς πόδας;). The second section of the pericope is a brief dialogue between Jesus and Peter that focuses on the Servant who performed the foot washing (vv. 6 – 11). While the context of this dialogue is the foot washing, few details are given. No other disciples are mentioned, nor is the placement of this encounter made known. The conjunction "then" (οὖν) suggests that Peter was not the first disciple to have his feet washed (contra Augustine), but neither does it imply that he was the last (contra Origen).[37] It is best to understand the dialogue between Jesus and Peter as representative of all the disciples — even of all Christians.

Peter asks Jesus a question that gives emphatic placement to the pronouns, placing them in a sharp contrast: "Lord, are *you* going to wash *my* feet?" (Κύριε, σύ μου νίπτεις τοὺς πόδας;). The question suggests that Peter is scandalized, almost certainly in part by the social-cultural significance of the act Jesus is about to perform. This is not to say that Peter fully understood the sharpness of the contrast, but in light of the full scriptural witness the reader can see it clearly. Ironically, while Peter thinks Jesus is breaking the (socially constructed) rules of service, it is actually Peter who is breaking the rules. For what looks like an objection rooted in modesty is really disobedience and self-righteousness. The careful reader should note that at this moment Peter was actually rejecting the grace of God, the gospel. The "you-me" are not just words; they are the subjects of the work of God, as Jesus is about to make clear.

13:7 Jesus answered and said to him, "What I do you do not understand now, but you will after these things" (ἀπεκρίθη Ἰησοῦς καὶ εἶπεν αὐτῷ, Ὃ ἐγὼ ποιῶ σὺ οὐκ οἶδας ἄρτι, γνώσῃ δὲ μετὰ ταῦτα). Jesus responds to Peter's question with a similar use of emphatic pronouns, probably intended to challenge and rebuke Peter's strong objection: "What *I* do *you* do not understand now" (Ὃ ἐγὼ ποιῶ σὺ οὐκ οἶδας ἄρτι).[38] Jesus's response affirms the scandal recognized by Peter but offers no explanation other than a reference to future understanding ("later" or "after these things" [μετὰ ταῦτα]). The scandal is not just a "thing" but a person; specifically, it is the unique relationship that exists between Christ's "I" and the disciple's "you/me."

What are the "things" to which Jesus is referring? It is best to understand the referent to be not one thing or something that occurs at one moment in time, like the glorification and resurrection of Jesus, but to be the gradual unfolding of the fullness of the revelation of the Son of Man. The foot washing then is just one of several "things" — "illustrations," teachings, even the Spirit (cf. 14:26; 16:13) — that will explain the person and work of Jesus Christ. The explanation to follow, even the entire farewell discourse, is part of this larger process whereby God guides and mediates his "covenant" with the children of God.

13:8 Peter said to him, "You shall not wash my feet in all eternity!" Jesus answered him, "If I do not wash you, you have no part with me" (λέγει αὐτῷ Πέτρος, Οὐ μὴ νίψῃς μου τοὺς πόδας εἰς τὸν αἰῶνα. ἀπεκρίθη Ἰησοῦς αὐτῷ, Ἐὰν μὴ νίψω σε, οὐκ ἔχεις μέρος μετ' ἐμοῦ). Peter increases his objection to Jesus in dramatic fashion. Peter not only prohibits Jesus from washing his feet — made emphatic by the strongest negation in the Greek language, "You shall not" (Οὐ μὴ)[39] — but adds further to

---

37. Augustine, *John*, 56.1.301.
38. Michaels, *John*, 727.

39. See Wallace, *Greek Grammar*, 468, who interprets this negation to rule out "even the idea as being a possibility."

his objection a phrase that negates the idea at all ("in all eternity" [εἰς τὸν αἰῶνα]). The additional phrase is also ironic, since what Jesus is doing (and explaining) is actually effective "in all eternity." In a sense, even though he is still responding to the social-cultural scandal, Peter is swearing an oath "by heaven" (cf. Matt 5:34) without knowing that the one by *whom* he makes this oath is the very same one *against whom* the oath is made.

Jesus offers a stark response to Peter's bold objection that gives insight into the significance of the foot washing. Jesus connects the foot washing to the relational dynamic between the "I-you." The protasis of the conditional statement, "If I do not wash you" (Ἐὰν μὴ νίψω σε), almost certainly refers to something more than just the foot washing, as v. 10 will reveal. To deny any part of the "I-you" relationship is to deny it all, as the apodosis of the conditional statement shows ("you have no part with me" [οὐκ ἔχεις μέρος μετ' ἐμοῦ]). This is not to equate the foot washing with the full washing, as Jesus will shortly explain (v. 10), but simply to say that the foot washing is part of being appropriated into this dynamic relationship with Christ, with God.

13:9 Simon Peter said to him, "Lord, not only my feet but also my hands and my head!" (λέγει αὐτῷ Σίμων Πέτρος, Κύριε, μὴ τοὺς πόδας μου μόνον ἀλλὰ καὶ τὰς χεῖρας καὶ τὴν κεφαλήν). Peter responds with a reversal of sorts — an emphatic response mixed with confusion. Unfortunately, not only does Peter still not understand the nature of the washing about which Jesus speaks, but he still speaks as if what Jesus offers needed modification. Peter is getting closer to understanding the "I-you" dynamic between Christ and himself, but he is still trying to adjudicate the relationship. Peter

has gone from stopping Jesus from serving him at all to commanding Jesus to serve him even more: "But also my hands and my head!" (ἀλλὰ καὶ τὰς χεῖρας καὶ τὴν κεφαλήν). Peter is right about the need for the "I-you" relationship, but wrong about the nature of its dynamic, as if what Jesus offered was not enough or not sufficiently efficacious.

13:10 Jesus said to him, "The one who has been bathed has no need except to wash his feet, but he is completely clean. And you are clean, but not everyone" (λέγει αὐτῷ ὁ Ἰησοῦς, Ὁ λελουμένος οὐκ ἔχει χρείαν εἰ μὴ τοὺς πόδας νίψασθαι, ἀλλ' ἔστιν καθαρὸς ὅλος· καὶ ὑμεῖς καθαροί ἐστε, ἀλλ' οὐχὶ πάντες). Jesus responds to Peter's confusion with a significant expansion of the subject of "washing," making clear that the foot washing is simply one aspect of a much fuller cleansing. This verse is more difficult to interpret in light of the questions raised by its varied manuscript tradition, most notably with the possible addition of the phrase "except … the feet" (εἰ μὴ τοὺς πόδας). But in light of the overwhelming text-critical support for the inclusion of the phrase, as well as the success with which the longer reading can be read in the context of the pericope and the entire Gospel, the longer reading is to be preferred.[40] The manuscript diversity is merely a reflection of the interpretive diversity surrounding this verse.

The meaning of Jesus's statement is strongly dependent on the relationship between two conceptually related and overlapping words: "bathed" (λελουμένος) and "to wash" (νίψασθαι). The words are certainly related (both could be translated as "wash"), but the former is primarily used in a more general manner to refer to the whole body, while the latter is primarily used in a more specific manner to refer to one part of the body, such as the

---

40. See John Christopher Thomas, "A Note on the Text of John 13:10," *NovT* 29 (1982): 46–52; cf. Metzger, *Textual Commentary*, 204.

hands or feet (see T. Levi 9.11; Tob 7:9).[41] Moreover, while the Fourth Gospel frequently uses related or overlapping words synonymously across the narrative (e.g., 21:15 – 17), when they are used together in close proximity (especially in the same verse) there is usually a carefully nuanced distinction or comparison intended between them. But the distinction in this case is most easily understood by means of the literary context. Jesus calls Peter "completely clean" (καθαρὸς ὅλος) *before* he has washed his feet, an action that is not finished until v. 12.[42]

In this verse, therefore, Jesus uses the illustration of bathing and washing to explain the fullness of the cleansings Peter (and every disciple) receives from Christ. The twofold nature of these distinct cleansings needs to be explained. First, the "bath" that results in being "completely clean" is not the foot washing but what has already been applied to the disciples by means of their relationship to Jesus.[43] Jesus speaks of Peter in the perfect tense as "one who has been bathed" (Ὁ λελουμένος). Although this "bathing" can only be in reference to the work Jesus has not yet accomplished — his sacrificial and sin-atoning death on the cross — it is already being applied (proleptically) to Peter. By means of his association with Jesus, Peter already belongs to God.

Second, the "washing," that is, the foot washing, is not what unites Peter to Jesus — for that is already done. Nor is it a full cleansing — for Peter is already "completely clean." It is instead part of the hospitality of God and the necessary preparation for the specific "task, experience, and relationship" of Christian discipleship (see comments on v. 5). The foot washing is not when Jesus unites the disciples to himself, but when he anoints and dedicates them for service to God, appointing them as his disciples. None of this could be accomplished had he not bathed them first, which is why *he* had to be the one to anoint (wash) them — and not their entire body, nothing "except . . . the feet." This makes sense of how Jesus can exhort Peter and the disciples to wash the feet of one another (v. 14). Only Jesus can "bathe" a disciple, but disciples can "wash" (prepare) one another to be coparticipants in the new covenant and the mission of God. But while the foot washing and all its significance is perfectly applicable to Peter (and to the Christian), Jesus ends his dialogue with Peter by hinting that "not everyone" (οὐχὶ πάντες) is clean, that is, "has been bathed" in Christ.

IN DEPTH: The Practice of Foot Washing

So how, exactly, should the foot washing be applied to the Christian, especially when it is distinct from the primary "bath"? The answer to this question is rooted in the interpretation of the act of the foot washing. The following are the three traditional interpretations of the foot washing, followed by their potential applications.[44]

---

41. See Thomas, *Footwashing in John 13*, 97 – 106.

42. Cf. Michaels, *John*, 731.

43. This need not be a reference to water baptism, as several interpreters suggest, but to the cosmological bath received through the death of Christ for the forgiveness of sins (1 John 1:7 – 9; Rev 1:5; 5:9; 19:13).

44. The following is adapted from Ruth B. Edwards, "The Christological Basis of the Johannine Footwashing," in *Jesus of Nazareth: Lord and Christ: Essays on the Historical Jesus and New Testament Christology*, ed. Joel B. Green and Max Turner (Grand Rapids: Eerdmans, 1994), 367 – 83. Cf. Georg Richter, *Die Fusswaschung in Johannesevangelium* (Regensburg: Pustet, 1967).

(1) *Exemplary Interpretation*. The clearest interpretation of the foot washing is that it was intended to be an example to be followed, especially since Jesus specifically commands it as such in v. 15. According to this interpretation, the foot washing is representative of humble service and self-denial.

The application of the exemplary interpretation emphasizes the *moral* aspect of the foot washing. Since the foot washing is representative of humility, it primarily focuses on the humility of Jesus, and only later is it applied to the disciples (vv. 12 – 20). In reference to the element of "washing," the application is in regard to humble service and not as an actual cleansing from impurity; "it represents Jesus's servanthood and not the disciples' impurity."[45] For this interpretation, the foot washing is to be applied by following the example of Jesus and serving in a manner that models his humility and self-denial.

(2) *Christological Interpretation*. This interpretation places the foot washing within the larger movement of the narrative, coming as it does at a turning point in the Gospel in which the act depicts the task, meaning, and application of the cross, the cleansing of the "sins of the world" (cf. 10:17 – 18). This interpretation fits nicely with the work of Christ, whose humility was expressed by his death on the cross (Phil 2:6 – 8).

The application of the christological interpretation emphasizes the *spiritual* aspect of the foot washing. While for some the application is merely the doctrine of Christ, for others an application can be applied to the disciples as well by taking the "illustration" as the interpretive framework. Since the "illustration" depicts the cleansing of the feet alone since the rest of the person is already clean, it can be argued that the foot washing is to be interpreted spiritually to refer to the need for Christians to be cleansed "from the sin contracted through daily life in this world."[46] Carson, for example, compares v. 13 to 1 John 1:9 where the Christian is exhorted continually to confess sin as something like a partial "wash," reflecting dependence on the already accomplished and primary "bath," the atoning sacrifice for sins (1 John 2:1 – 2).[47] This was also the application of Calvin, who argues that "feet … is a metaphor for all the passions and cares by which we are brought into contact with the world … the part in which we are carnal, we crawl on the ground."[48] The foot washing is to be applied by being continually cleansed or renewed from daily sin and the struggle of the flesh. For this interpretation, the foot washing is to be applied by beholding the saving work of Christ on the cross, by depending on its power, and by working at embracing daily its "cleansing" effects.

45. Ridderbos, *John*, 462.
46. Thomas, *Footwashing in John 13*, 105.

47. Carson, *John*, 465 – 66.
48. Calvin, *John 11 – 21*, 59.

(3) *Sacramental Interpretation.* Based upon the prominence of the foot washing in the Gospel, along with the absence of any words of "institution" of the Last Supper (the Eucharist), this interpretation suggests that the foot washing must be functioning sacramentally. Some think it refers directly to the Lord's Supper, but others think it refers to baptism (or some post-baptismal forgiveness or purification practiced by some in the early church); the latter is made more feasible with the removal of the text-critical variant "except his feet." But both of these views interpret the foot washing symbolically in reference to the two sacraments already clearly established elsewhere in the New Testament. For this reason, others suggest that neither of the traditional sacraments, the Lord's Supper and baptism, are in view, but a new and literal sacrament — a third sacrament of foot washing. But there is minimal evidence for this new sacrament, nor much clarity regarding the relationship between a physical foot washing and Jesus's death.

The application of the sacramental interpretation emphasizes the *ceremonial* aspect of the foot washing. Beyond the symbolic interpretations of the foot washing, which find some discussion in the early church, some suggest that the foot washing, especially in light of the command to perform it on one another (vv. 12 – 20), is intended to be performed as a physical ceremony or rite.[49] This view finds some support in the early church and the history of the church (the rite of *Pedilavium*) as a visible sign of grace or sacrament which has Christology as its focus.[50] Proponents argue that this view makes better sense of the rest of the pericope, where the physical practice is commanded to be repeated (vv. 12 – 20). The foot washing is to be applied by the establishment of a foot-washing ceremony, an ordinance or sacrament similar to baptism and the Lord's Supper/Eucharist. For this interpretation, the foot washing is to be applied by practicing it as a ceremony, a sacrament that facilitates the Christian's identification with Jesus (and therefore one another) in his humble service and death.

While each of these three interpretations has exegetical warrant, our interpretation of the foot washing does not view it as an ordinance or sacrament, interpretation (3). This is in part because the debate over whether the foot washing is to be taken literally or symbolically is to create a false dichotomy. As Bauckham explains, "There is no indication that the command is not meant literally, but literal footwashing is a concrete instance of the practice of the humble service in ordinary life."[51] That is, to be literal in this case is also necessarily

49. See Allen Edgington, "Footwashing as an Ordinance," *GTJ* 6 (1985): 425 – 34.

50. See Frank D. Macchia, "Is Footwashing the Neglected Sacrament? A Theological Response to John Christopher

Thomas," *Pneuma* 19 (1997): 239 – 49.

51. Richard Bauckham, "Did Jesus Wash His Disciples' Feet?," in *Testimony of the Beloved Disciple*, 191 – 206 (195).

to be symbolic. To make foot washing an ordinance, a ceremonial practice, is to remove it from its place as one of the daily chores of the Christian life. Rather, our interpretation is rooted in interpretations (1) and (2), since foot washings in their social-cultural context reflected upon both the servant who performed the washing — the emphasis of interpretation (1) — as well as the person who received the washing — the emphasis of interpretation (2). To choose between the washer and the washed is to create another false dichotomy. The foot washing refers both to Jesus and to his disciples, for it is a christological depiction of what Christ has done for us and what we must do in and for Christ.[52] That is, it is both a reflection of the hospitality of God toward us and our preparation for service in the mission of God. The foot washing and its illustration give exegetical warrant for the Christian to apply it morally or spiritually; in fact, to make too much of a distinction between "moral" and "spiritual" applications is to separate two things that belong together.[53]

13:11 For he knew the one who was going to betray him, for this reason he said "not everyone is clean" (ᾔδει γὰρ τὸν παραδιδόντα αὐτόν· διὰ τοῦτο εἶπεν ὅτι Οὐχὶ πάντες καθαροί ἐστε). The second section of the pericope concludes with a commentary by the narrator regarding the hint that Christ gave to Peter in v. 10. The narrator explains that Jesus was talking about "the one who was going to betray him" (τὸν παραδιδόντα αὐτόν), that is, Judas, about whom the reader has already been informed (see comments on v. 2). The reader knows more at this point than Peter and the other disciples, who only know that there is a traitor in their midst.[54]

13:12 Then when he had washed their feet and picked up his garments and reclined again, he said to them, "Do you understand what I did to you?" (Ὅτε οὖν ἔνιψεν τοὺς πόδας αὐτῶν [καὶ] ἔλαβεν τὰ ἱμάτια αὐτοῦ καὶ ἀνέπεσεν πάλιν, εἶπεν αὐτοῖς, Γινώσκετε τί πεποίηκα ὑμῖν;). The third section of the pericope (vv. 12 – 20) is a monologue by

Jesus that offers an explanation of the foot washing and an exhortation to its recipients (see comments on v. 5). The transition to the monologue is denoted by the narrator's depiction of the completion of the foot washing and Jesus's return to his place at the meal. Jesus has made the connection between him and his disciples in vv. 6 – 11 (the "I-you"); now he must explain the connection that also exists between his disciples themselves in vv. 12 – 20.

By way of introduction, Jesus asks the disciples a loaded question: "Do you understand what I did to you?" (Γινώσκετε τί πεποίηκα ὑμῖν;). Jesus already knows the answer to this question, having said as much in v. 7, so his question here is intended to prepare the disciples to perceive something deeper regarding his person and work, which he just "illustrated" for them.

13:13 "You call me 'the Teacher' and 'the Lord,' and you speak well, for that is who I am" (ὑμεῖς φωνεῖτέ με Ὁ διδάσκαλος καὶ Ὁ κύριος, καὶ καλῶς

---

52. J. A. T. Robinson, "The Significance of the Foot-Washing," in *Neotestamentica et Patristica*, ed. W. C. van Unnik, NovTSup 6 (Leiden: Brill, 1962), 144 – 47.

53. Cf. Stevick, *Jesus and His Own*, 48.
54. Cf. Morris, *John*, 550.

λέγετε, εἰμὶ γάρ). Before explaining what he did for them, Jesus reminds them who he is to them. The disciples frequently call Jesus "Teacher" (Ὁ διδάσκαλος), which is equivalent to "Rabbi" (see 1:38) and is a respectful way of addressing a religious instructor and leader. "Lord" (Ὁ κύριος) is a title used to denote anything from general respect (i.e., "sir") to great reverence. The title "Lord" can also speak of the divinity of Jesus, as shown by the use of the title for the resurrected Jesus (20:2, 18, 20, 25, 28), and readers of the LXX would have been quite familiar with the use of "the Lord" in reference to God. In this way Jesus establishes the foundation of his argument.

13:14 "Then if I, the Lord and the Teacher, have washed your feet, you also ought to wash the feet of one another" (εἰ οὖν ἐγὼ ἔνιψα ὑμῶν τοὺς πόδας ὁ κύριος καὶ ὁ διδάσκαλος, καὶ ὑμεῖς ὀφείλετε ἀλλήλων νίπτειν τοὺς πόδας). Jesus then presents his argument based upon the previously established premise. Jesus's argument is clear; if "I," your superior, "washed" (ἔνιψα) your feet, "you … ought to wash" (ὀφείλετε νίπτειν) the feet of one another. Jesus has made a logical connection between what he has done and what he expects his disciples to do, but since what he has done is so illogical — a superior serving an inferior — Jesus needs to support such illogic with a logical argument.

13:15 "For I have given an example to you in order that you might do just as I did to you" (ὑπόδειγμα γὰρ δέδωκα ὑμῖν ἵνα καθὼς ἐγὼ ἐποίησα ὑμῖν καὶ ὑμεῖς ποιῆτε). Jesus now presses the argument to its logical conclusion: "For I have given an example to you" (ὑπόδειγμα γὰρ δέδωκα ὑμῖν), with the perfect-tense verb strengthening the force of the exhortation. The term "example" (ὑπόδειγμα)

can also be translated as "model" or "pattern."[55] In this context the term should not be understood too narrowly but as "a rule of life."[56] That is, the nature of this "example" must be understood within the cosmological framework of the Gospel, in the dynamic relation between Christ's "I" and the disciples' "you." "Only the man whom Jesus has served can see him as the [example] ὑπόδειγμα."[57] It is this illogic — that Christ served us — that provides the reason or purpose ("in order that") to do the same.

13:16 "Truly, truly I say to you, a slave is not greater than his master, nor a messenger greater than the one who sent him" (ἀμὴν ἀμὴν λέγω ὑμῖν, οὐκ ἔστιν δοῦλος μείζων τοῦ κυρίου αὐτοῦ οὐδὲ ἀπόστολος μείζων τοῦ πέμψαντος αὐτόν). Jesus now offers a conclusion to his argument in vv. 16 – 17, beginning with an authoritative preface (see comments on 1:51) that strengthens his exhortation. Following through on the logic of v. 14, if Christ has served, the "master" and "the one who sent," so must the disciples, the "slave" and the "messenger." That is, the "example" of Christ redefines (illogically) the identity of the disciples (i.e., the servants) and motivates (logically) their mission.[58] This exhortation regarding the identity and mission of a disciple of Christ establishes an important foundation for the "sending" the disciples are soon to receive from "the Lord" (see 20:19 – 23), as well as for the mission of all Christians.

13:17 "If you understand these things, you are blessed if you do these things" (εἰ ταῦτα οἴδατε, μακάριοί ἐστε ἐὰν ποιῆτε αὐτά). Jesus concludes his argument by revisiting the "understanding" of the disciples first introduced in v. 12 at the start of the monologue. Jesus is concerned that they understand "these things" (ταῦτα), which must

---

55. BDAG 1037.

56. Ridderbos, *John*, 463.

57. Bultmann, *John*, 475.

58. Cf. Jerome H. Neyrey, "The Footwashing in John

13:6 – 11: Transformation Ritual or Ceremony?," in *The Social World of the First Christians: Essays in Honor of Wayne A. Meeks*, ed. L. Michael White and O. Larry Yarbrough (Minneapolis: Fortress, 1995), 198 – 213.

include "what I did to you" (v. 12), that is, the foot washing, but also the theological explanation that has been provided. The sentence has two conditional clauses, with the former made more certain by the latter, thus making it possible to translate the former in this way: "*Now that* you understand ..."[59] The implication is that the disciples now know these things, which leaves open the question whether they will act on their understanding.[60]

The second conditional clause is much like a promise, for Jesus declares that if they "do these things" they "are blessed" (μακάριοί ἐστε). Helpful here is Brown, who after surveying the use of "blessed" in the OT and NT determines that the term in the NT has come to mean more than good fortune (i.e., happiness) or even future blessing, but something very present: "An eschatological state has been made possible by the heralding of the Kingdom."[61] In short, to understand *and* to do service exemplified by Jesus is to experience the goodness of God, even more, the grace of God. "Blessedness is a divine gift."[62] This explains how God the Son, although he left his superior status to serve his inferiors at the same time acted entirely in character as God himself.[63] In the same way, when a disciple of Jesus serves others, he or she is not experiencing a demotion but a promotion to the kind of "life" God offers his children.

13:18 "I am not speaking concerning all of you, I know those I have chosen, but in order that Scripture may be fulfilled, 'The one who eats my bread has lifted up his heel against me'" (οὐ περὶ πάντων ὑμῶν λέγω· ἐγὼ οἶδα τίνας ἐξελεξάμην· ἀλλ᾽ ἵνα ἡ γραφὴ πληρωθῇ, Ὁ τρώγων μου τὸν ἄρτον ἐπῆρεν ἐπ᾽ ἐμὲ τὴν πτέρναν αὐτοῦ). After finish-

ing his argument (vv. 12–17) Jesus concludes his monologue by revealing more about the betrayer he mentioned earlier (v. 10). These last three verses (vv. 18–20) bring closure to the present pericope and serve as a transition to the next one, offering a fitting conclusion to the first of a two-part introduction to the farewell discourse. The promise Jesus offers is only in effect for "those I have chosen" (τίνας ἐξελεξάμην), a phrase that echoes Jesus's early pronouncements regarding the divine initiative of the mission of God (cf. 6:39, 44). But this statement also repeats almost exactly what Jesus said in 6:70 regarding the disciples who were "chosen" as well as the outsider who works for the devil (see comments on 6:70).

The inclusion of Judas in the intimate events that just transpired, so much so that he would have also had his feet washed by Jesus (cf. v. 12), was not a mistake but part of the plan of God, to which the Scriptures themselves pointed long before. Quoting from the OT, Jesus uses Psalm 41:9 to give commentary on "the one" who has not been "chosen," or at least chosen in a positive sense. The context of shared bread signifies the paradox of intimacy and fellowship between Jesus and his betrayer. The use of the more aggressive Greek word for "eats" (τρώγων) highlights their shared intimacy and hospitality (see comments on 6:54). But this disciple "has lifted up his heel against me" (ἐπῆρεν ἐπ᾽ ἐμὲ τὴν πτέρναν αὐτοῦ), implying rejection and rebellion, a shocking betrayal between intimate friends and colleagues.[64] The specific image in the psalm that Jesus quotes might be that or a horse or mule kicking the person feeding it (cf. Ps 32:9); or a person showing another the bottom of one's foot as an expression of contempt (cf. Mk. 6:11).

59. See Michaels, *John*, 738.
60. Morris, *John*, 552.
61. Brown, *John*, 2:553.
62. Stevick, *Jesus and His Own*, 36.
63. Hoskyns, *Fourth Gospel*, 440.

64. See J. Ramsey Michaels, "Betrayal and the Betrayer: The Uses of Scripture in John 13.18–19," in *The Gospels and the Scriptures of Israel*, ed. Craig A. Evans and W. Richard Stegner, JSNT 104/SSEJC 3 (Sheffield: Sheffield Academic Press, 1994), 459–74.

13:19 **"I speak to you at this point before it happens, so that you may believe when it happens that I am"** (ἀπ᾽ ἄρτι λέγω ὑμῖν πρὸ τοῦ γενέσθαι, ἵνα πιστεύσητε ὅταν γένηται ὅτι ἐγώ εἰμι). Jesus explains that his previous statement is predictive and that its purpose is to facilitate the belief of his disciples when the events transpire as he and Scripture have foretold. What will result ("so that") will be a fuller grasp of the person and work of Jesus Christ. The one who spoke creation into existence (1:3) now speaks about what will take place within it. When this happens the disciples will believe that Jesus is the "I am" (ἐγώ εἰμι). This is one of several informal "I am" statements without a predicate that communicate the self-revelation of God, giving insight to the particular qualifications of Jesus (see comments on 6:35).

13:20 **"Truly, truly I say to you, the one who receives the one I send receives me, but the one who receives me receives the one who sent me"** (ἀμὴν ἀμὴν λέγω ὑμῖν, ὁ λαμβάνων ἄν τινα πέμψω ἐμὲ λαμβάνει, ὁ δὲ ἐμὲ λαμβάνων λαμβάνει τὸν πέμψαντά με). The third section of the pericope, the monologue of Jesus (vv. 12 – 20), concludes with a final exhortation by Jesus, supported by another authoritative preface (see comments on 1:51). Befitting the "sending for service" motif of vv. 14 and 16, Jesus describes the oscillating and intimate relation that exists between himself and his disciples, that is, between the "I-you" (see v. 8). Here the dynamic nature of the "I-you" is most clearly expressed. Just as Jesus is representative of the Father (cf. 1:18), so also are the disciples representative of Jesus. This is the mission of God and therefore also the mission of the church. And this explains why Jesus is the "example," model, and pattern for ministry, the Servant who both serves and sends his servants. The effect of this pronouncement is to place all the preceding verses into the framework of the disciples' mission in the world.[65] Just as Jesus is the agent of God, so also are the disciples agents of Jesus. What this means will need further explanation in the farewell discourse. Here this issue has simply been introduced.

Theology in Application

After the public ministry of Jesus concludes, Jesus gathers his disciples together to offer "his own" (v. 1), the children of God (1:12), further teaching regarding who he is and what he still must do, but also regarding the identity of the disciples and what the disciples are assigned to do. Before teaching the disciples with words, Jesus teaches with action by enacting his service (the cross) for them and anointing his disciples for their service for him, the "specific task, experience, and relationship" of being his disciples in the new covenant. This majestic scene depicts almost beyond the capacity of words the humble service and sacrifice of our Lord and the kind of lord he is — the Servant. It also depicts the nature of Christian discipleship, manifested in Christlike service and sacrifice for the benefit of others. In this way the farewell discourse is provided a robust introduction. The Christian life is depicted by a dramatic "illustration." Through this pericope the reader is challenged to come to

---

65. Michaels, *John*, 744.

grips with the reality and role of Jesus the Servant and is exhorted to embrace a similar reality and role of Christian discipleship, which entails service as a "rule of life."

The Foot Washing of Christ

When Jesus washed the feet of his disciples, he enacted his role as the Servant, a role which he most fully performed by his death on the cross. Jesus, the King of kings, became the Servant, the Servant of servants for all the children of God. The foot washing is the best commentary on the service that Christ performs on the cross, for it explains its paradoxical and indispensable nature in two ways. First, the most superior died for those who are clearly inferior; the inferior — those normally suited only for the role of servant — were in need of this Servant. Second, the paradox and indispensability is not only in regard to humanity but in regard to God, whose very nature is expressed by the Servant, for whom such an act is entirely in character with his divine nature "because God is love" (1 John 4:8) and because it is the very expression of both "grace and truth" (1:17).

But there is more. When Jesus washed the feet of his disciples, he initiated their role as his servants, as those anointed for the specific "task, experience, and relationship" they now have by means of their relationship to Jesus. The foot washing is preparation for service, the initiation of Christian discipleship. This service is performed not only to one another, but also as part of the mission of God to the world, heralding the new covenant and the gospel of Jesus Christ. And since Christ was superior in every way to those whose feet he washed, no Christian may ever claim to be so superior that he or she is above washing the feet of another. According to the "example" of Christ, this means that "the last will be first and the first will be last" (Matt 20:16).

The foot washing by Jesus is to be applied to the Christian as the means by which a person sees Christ as his or her Servant, as the one who enacted the cross on their behalf. Christ has washed your feet! It is also to be applied as an anointing for service, in which we wash the feet of one another, thereby adopting the role of the servant that was exemplified for us by the Servant. This is "literally" to have one's feet washed and to wash one another's feet. To treat the foot washing as a ceremony, rite, or ordinance/sacrament runs the risk of removing it from its place as the manner or mode of Christian discipleship, the "rule of life" for the Christian. In a sense, rather than having the foot washing serve as a reflection of the Christian life, our life is to serve as a reflection of — as the enactment of — the foot washing of Jesus.

But the foot washing is not a mere metaphor. There are two specific applications that should be derived from this text, one passive (receiving the washing of Christ) and one active (following the example of the washing of Christ). First, passively we are to be "spiritually" washed by Christ on a daily basis. This is done by *accepting* the washing Christ performed upon us, which involves sharing in the practices and life of the church — not a full cleansing, for we are already "completely clean" (v. 10). Second, actively we are to be serving others as Christ served us. This is done by *emulating* Christ's washing of us, which involves a heart and mind bent on serving others in a posture of humble service. There is no need to choose between the passive and active applications of this text, since together they serve as the two legs of the Christian walk: "We [serve] because he first [served] us" (cf. 1 John 4:19).

Religious Pride and Gospel Humility

The demand of the gospel is that we need Jesus Christ, the Son of Man, to wash our feet, to serve us. Yet everything in us repels such an idea. In fact, the pride that so easily conceals itself in religion would have us to think the exact reverse — we must serve Christ. But this is what makes the gospel so radical. It is not Christ but we who need to be served. When Peter chastises the attempt of Jesus to wash his feet, what looks like an objection borne of modesty is really disobedience and self-righteousness. At that moment Peter was actually rejecting the grace of God.

The Christian must first learn that according to the gospel, Christ is placed below us to serve us, and the required response is first and foremost obedience. It is not we who are assigned to exalt Christ; that role belongs to Father. After Christ served us, God "exalted him to the highest place and gave him the name that is above every name" (Phil 2:9). Our role is to be served by Christ and to obey his lordship. As Calvin explains, "Until a man renounces his liberty of judging the works of God, however he may strive to honour God, pride will always be latent under the semblance of humility."[66] In this way, even when we are washing the feet of others, we do not serve in the same manner as Christ, for we are simply obeying Christ.

---

66. Calvin, *John 11 – 21*, 57.

27

John 13:21 – 30

Literary Context

This pericope is the second of a two-part introduction to the farewell discourse, setting the historical and theological context in which Jesus's fourth and most complex monologue will take place. In the first part of the introduction (13:1 – 20), Jesus enacted the service of the cross for his disciples with the washing of their feet. In the second part of the introduction Jesus will announce his betrayal, setting into motion the historical (Judas) and the cosmological (Satan) conflict that will only find resolution in his death and resurrection. In this scene Jesus reveals that his "hour" had come and that his battle was not merely with those on the outside, but even with one on the inside, revealing that his person and work confront not only the cosmological opposition of Satan but also the sin that entangles every person, including the reader of the Gospel.

VII. The Farewell Discourse (13:1 – 17:26)

    A. Introduction: The Love of Jesus (13:1 – 30)

        1. Jesus and the Washing of His Disciples' Feet (13:1 – 20)

➡   **2. Jesus Announces His Betrayal (13:21 – 30)**

    B. The Farewell Discourse (13:31 – 16:33)

        1. Prologue: Glory, Departure, and Love (13:31 – 38)

        2. I Am the Way and the Truth and the Life (14:1 – 14)

        3. I Will Give You the Paraclete (14:15 – 31)

        4. I Am the True Vine (15:1 – 17)

        5. I Have Also Experienced the Hate of the World (15:18 – 27)

        6. I Will Empower You by the Paraclete (16:1 – 15)

        7. I Will Turn Your Grief into Joy (16:16 – 24)

        8. Epilogue: Speaking Plainly, Departure, and Peace (16:25 – 33)

    C. Conclusion: The Prayer of Jesus (17:1 – 26)

Main Idea

Even at his betrayal, Jesus communed with his disciples. Christians, "beloved disciples" of Jesus, should find their rest in his person, reclining on his chest and remaining in permanent communion with him and his church.

Translation

John 13:21–30

21a	Introduction & Setting	After he said these things,
b	Character's Emotions	**Jesus was troubled in spirit**
c	Action	and **testified and said,**
d	Amen Formula	*"Truly, truly I say to you*
e	Announcement	*that one of you is going to betray me."*
22a	Reaction	**The disciples looked to one another,**
b	Description	perplexed about whom he was speaking.
23a	Character Reentrance	**One of his disciples ...**
b	Description of "Disciple"	the one whom Jesus loved,
c	Description of Setting	**... was reclining on the chest of Jesus.**
24a	Character Reentrance	Then **Simon Peter ...**
b	Action	**... nodded to this [disciple]**
c		to inquire who it was about whom he was speaking.
25a	Reaction	So **he simply leaned back on the chest of Jesus**
b		and **said to him,**
c	Address	*"Lord,*
d	Question	*who is he?"*
26a	Response	**Jesus answered,**
b	Answer	*"He is the one*
c	Description	*with whom I will dip the piece of bread and*
d		*give to him."*
e	Progression of Scene	Then,
f		after dipping the piece of bread,
g	Action	**he took it**
h	Character Reentrance	and **gave it to Judas,**
i	Identification	son of Simon of Iscariot.
27a	Progression of Scene	After the piece of bread,
b	Character Reentrance/Action	**then Satan entered into him.**
c	Reaction	Then **Jesus said to him,**
d	Command	*"What you are doing, do quickly."*
28a	Response	But **no one ...**
b		among those reclining
c		**... understood why he said this to him.**

Continued on next page.

Continued from previous page.

29a	Explanation	For **some were thinking …**				
b	Basis		since Judas was holding the money box,			
c			**… that Jesus**	**said to**		**him,**
d	Misunderstanding #1	*"Buy what we need for the Feast,"*				
e		**or**		[**spoke to**		**him]**
f	Misunderstanding #2				in order that	he might give 𝒥 something to the poor.
30a	Conclusion of Scene	Then				
b	Progression		after he took the piece of bread,			
c	Departure of Judas	**he went out immediately;**				
d	Historical & Theological Setting	and **it was night.**				

Structure and Literary Form

This pericope is a combination of a basic story form and a dialogue. Unlike the previous pericope (13:1 – 20), which moved in the sequence of action-dialogue-monologue, in this pericope a dialogue (vv. 23 – 26) is framed on both sides by narrative action (vv. 21 – 22 and vv. 27 – 30). What is similar, however, is the combination of action with dialogue, which the reader should understand as working as part of an integrated movement. Jesus introduces the issue of the pericope, followed by the response of the disciples in vv. 21 – 22. In vv. 23 – 26 a dialogue ensues, prompted by Peter, between the Beloved Disciple and Jesus that provides insight into the prophetic and cryptic statement of Jesus. This dialogue is unique in that it is a symbol-laden dialogue with few words. Finally in vv. 27 – 30 the narrator turns his attention to Judas, the betrayer of Jesus, describing his transition from his association with Jesus and the disciples to his new association with Satan. As the second of a two-part introduction to the farewell discourse, the pericope guides the reader to see even more clearly the historical and cosmological context of opposition to Jesus.

Exegetical Outline

➥   **2. Jesus Announces His Betrayal (13:21 – 30)**

   a. The Prophecy of a Betrayer (vv. 21 – 22)

   b. Jesus's Dialogue with the Beloved Disciple (vv. 23 – 26)

   c. The Entrance of Satan and Departure of Judas (vv. 27 – 30)

Explanation of the Text

Since this entire section of the Gospel is replete with interpretive issues, we refer the reader to the first pericope of this section where we provided an overview of the nature (genre), literary structure, and function of the farewell discourse (see comments before 13:1).

13:21 After he said these things, Jesus was troubled in spirit and testified and said, "Truly, truly I say to you that one of you is going to betray me" (Ταῦτα εἰπὼν ὁ Ἰησοῦς ἐταράχθη τῷ πνεύματι καὶ ἐμαρτύρησεν καὶ εἶπεν, Ἀμὴν ἀμὴν λέγω ὑμῖν ὅτι εἷς ἐξ ὑμῶν παραδώσει με). The phrase "after he said these things" (Ταῦτα εἰπὼν) serves as an introductory expression and signals to the reader that this is a new pericope and a new phase in the story.[1] The new phase is introduced further by a summarizing statement by the narrator depicting the emotional condition of Jesus: "Jesus was troubled in spirit" (ὁ Ἰησοῦς ἐταράχθη τῷ πνεύματι). Jesus has been depicted as "troubled" before, with the most revealing example occurring at the death of Lazarus. The use of a related phrase here reveals a similar emotional state, one in which Jesus is filled with deep emotion as the "hour" draws near (see comments on 11:33; cf. 12:27).

Beginning with an authoritative preface (see comments on 1:51), Jesus announces that there is a betrayer among the disciples. Jesus had been prophetically aware of this moment much earlier, as had the reader, who was given specific insight into the betrayal and the betrayer (see 6:64, 71; cf. 12:4; 13:2, 11). The disciples had only been told cryptically that one of them was the devil (see 6:70; cf. 13:18). Like the original announcement, it is best to understand this more direct statement not only as a "prophecy" of what will take place but also as

an accusation against his disciples, those sharing with him in this intimate meal, out of whom would come the betrayer (see comments on 6:70).

13:22 The disciples looked to one another, perplexed about whom he was speaking (ἔβλεπον εἰς ἀλλήλους οἱ μαθηταὶ ἀπορούμενοι περὶ τίνος λέγει). The prophecy and accusation of Jesus caused a stir among the disciples. Taking their eyes away from Jesus, they "looked to one another" (ἔβλεπον εἰς ἀλλήλους). Rather than asking Jesus directly, they remain silent and communicate at first only with their eyes — the first of several "wordless" communications in this pericope.[2] They look to each other as a way of expressing their perplexity regarding the identity of the one about whom Jesus speaks (the prophecy), as well as in regard to themselves (the accusation).[3]

13:23 One of his disciples, the one whom Jesus loved, was reclining on the chest of Jesus (ἦν ἀνακείμενος εἷς ἐκ τῶν μαθητῶν αὐτοῦ ἐν τῷ κόλπῳ τοῦ Ἰησοῦ, ὃν ἠγάπα ὁ Ἰησοῦς). The narrator focuses his attention on one disciple in particular, with whom Jesus will have a short dialogue (vv. 23 – 26). This anonymous disciple is simply described as "the one whom Jesus loved" (ὃν ἠγάπα ὁ Ἰησοῦς) or, more traditionally, "the Beloved Disciple." This is the first of several occurrences of the Beloved Disciple in the Gospel (see also 19:25 – 27, 35; 20:1 – 10; 21:1 – 7, 20 – 24; cf. 1:40; 18:15). The anonymity of the Beloved Disciple can only be intentional, for it is highly unlikely that the evangelist was unaware of this individual. As we discussed earlier, anonymity is itself a narrative tool to develop both plot and characterization (see comments on 1:40). It serves "to focus the readers'

1. Ridderbos, *John*, 468.
2. Michaels, *John*, 748.

3. Cf. Bultmann, *John*, 481.

attention on the role designations that flood into the gap that anonymity denotes,"[4] a gap not to be filled until the Gospel's conclusion (see comments on 21:24; see Introduction).

This first occurrence of the Beloved Disciple does reveal some important details about his identity. First, it is likely that the Beloved Disciple is one of the "Twelve." While the Gospel is not explicit on this point, this is the implicit assumption in this scene and in later appearances in the narrative. This is not to suggest the Gospel is only (or even primarily) concerned with the historical referent, as the next point will make clear.

Second, while the Beloved Disciple is a "real" disciple, by using anonymity the Gospel establishes the Beloved Disciple as not only a figure in history but as a character in the narrative. In this way, the anonymity functions as a literary device that forces the reader to engage with the Beloved Disciple primarily by his narrativized identity. For the reader then, the identity of the Beloved Disciple is not simply *who* he is (*behind* the narrative) but *what* he is (*within* the narrative). The anonymity of the Beloved Disciple depicts the "ideal disciple," one having special access and intimate relationship with Jesus (see comments on 21:24).[5] This in no way minimizes the historical reality of the Beloved Disciple, but creates alongside his historical identity a narrativized identity and role that is significant to the message of the Gospel.

Third, the narrator depicts the Beloved Disciple in "a position that signals a privileged relationship," made clear by the description of him as "reclining on the chest of Jesus" (ἦν ἀνακείμενος ἐν τῷ κόλπῳ τοῦ Ἰησοῦ).[6] While this is not best compared too strictly with the similar language in 1:18 ("Son … in the bosom [chest] of the Father") that relates

Jesus to the Father (a cosmological union), it certainly intends to communicate a deep and mutual commitment between Jesus and his disciple, befitting the ancient context and dining customs (a historical union). For 1:18 makes clear that Jesus's intimate relationship with the Father is intended to provide an intimate relationship between God and all disciples.[7] The unique relationship between Jesus and the Beloved Disciple is not mentioned explicitly here, but it may stem from a personal friendship or even from a relation of kin (see comments on 19:25 – 27). It is important to note that meals in the ancient world did not involve tables with chairs but involved reclining on couches, usually U-shaped (called a *triclinium*) around a low table. Participants would support themselves on their left elbows and eat with their right hands.[8] The position of the Beloved Disciple is not to be understood as resting "on top of" Jesus, but as reclining "by the side of" Jesus. Although our less idiomatic translation helps make the important connection to 1:18, it could mislead the modern reader in regard to physical position.

Fourth, the Beloved Disciple is also in a unique relationship, at least narratively, with Peter (v. 24). Most of the appearances of the Beloved Disciple are in direct connection with Peter and will be noted in the commentary as the narrative progresses. As we will see, this is not to be viewed as a competition but as a depiction of the different roles and kinds of disciples. This is, however, the first of four comparison-like depictions of Peter and the Beloved Disciple (13:22 – 25; 20:3 – 9; 21:7; 21:20 – 23).

Finally, and most obviously, Jesus "loved" (ἠγάπα) this disciple. The Beloved Disciple is not the only one Jesus is said to have loved, for not only is Jesus described as loving Martha and Mary

---

4. Reinhartz, *"Why Ask My Name?,"* 188.

5. Richard Bauckham, "The Beloved Disciple as Ideal Author," in *Testimony of the Beloved Disciple*, 73 – 91.

6. R. Alan Culpepper, *John, the Son of Zebedee: The Life of a Legend* (Minneapolis: Fortress, 2000), 60.

7. Michaels, *John*, 749.

8. See Keener, *John*, 2:915.

(11:5), Lazarus (11:36), and all his disciples (13:1; 15:19), but God himself is described as loving the whole world (3:16).[9] But befitting his role as an "ideal" disciple, this serves to portray the uniquely loving relationship that exists between Jesus and his disciples.

13:24 Then Simon Peter nodded to this [disciple] to inquire who it was about whom he was speaking (νεύει οὖν τούτῳ Σίμων Πέτρος πυθέσθαι τίς ἂν εἴη περὶ οὗ λέγει). The relationship between Peter and the Beloved Disciple is made evident by the response Peter gives to him in regard to Jesus's statement. The narrator describes how Peter "nodded" (νεύει) to the Beloved Disciple; that is, Peter made some kind of motion to him as a signal, probably by inclining his head.[10] As much as the Beloved Disciple is in close communion with Jesus, this nonverbal communication between Peter and the Beloved Disciple suggests that they are similarly in close relationship, for whom words were not even needed.[11] Peter wanted to know "about whom" (περὶ οὗ) Jesus spoke, so he signaled to the Beloved Disciple in order that he might ask Jesus to be more specific.

13:25 So he simply leaned back on the chest of Jesus and said to him, "Lord, who is he?" (ἀναπεσὼν οὖν ἐκεῖνος οὕτως ἐπὶ τὸ στῆθος τοῦ Ἰησοῦ λέγει αὐτῷ, Κύριε, τίς ἐστιν;). In response to the signal given by Peter, the Beloved Disciple "leaned back" (ἀναπεσὼν) toward Jesus, so much so that the narrator claims he was resting "on the chest of Jesus" (ἐπὶ τὸ στῆθος τοῦ Ἰησοῦ). With the combination of the Greek words translated "so" (οὖν) and "simply" (οὕτως), the narrator focuses the reader's attention on the wordless communica-

tion of the Beloved Disciple, who responds to Peter's signal "without further ado," another possible translation in place of "simply" (οὕτως).[12] The nature of this description reveals the kind of intimate closeness the Beloved Disciple is able to express with Jesus. At this moment a disciple of Jesus, a mere man, has immediate and personal access to God himself.

The word translated as "chest" (τὸ στῆθος) in this verse is different from the word translated as "chest" (τῷ κόλπῳ) in v. 23. While the terms are generally synonymous, the difference is certainly intentional, probably serving to strengthen or emphasize the closeness of this disciple to Jesus, for he is literally "on" Jesus (on the use of two related words in close proximity, see comments on 13:10).[13] The Western reader must be immediately reminded that such physical closeness was (and is) quite different in an Eastern context. In many parts of the world today, men walk down the street holding hands as a sign of friendship, not as a sign of homosexuality. This is an especially common practice between two men operating together in a business relationship, reflecting mutual respect and trust. With this in view, the actions of the Beloved Disciple become wordless communication that shows mutual trust and respect, even intimacy, between Jesus and the Beloved Disciple. Thus, when he finally does speak ("Lord, who is he?" [Κύριε, τίς ἐστιν;]), the Beloved Disciple speaks as one who has been given the "right" to ask such questions because he is, quite simply, "in Christ."

13:26 Jesus answered, "He is the one with whom I will dip the piece of bread and give to him." Then, after dipping the piece of bread, he took it and gave

9. Cf. Hoskyns, *Fourth Gospel*, 443.
10. BDAG 670.
11. While several scholars posit a tension in the Gospel between the Beloved Disciple and Peter, this verse suggests the opposite (see comments on 21:20 – 22).
12. See BDAG 742.
13. See Hoskyns, *Fourth Gospel*, 442.

it to Judas, son of Simon of Iscariot (ἀποκρίνεται Ἰησοῦς, Ἐκεῖνός ἐστιν ᾧ ἐγὼ βάψω τὸ ψωμίον καὶ δώσω αὐτῷ. βάψας οὖν τὸ ψωμίον [λαμβάνει καὶ] δίδωσιν Ἰούδᾳ Σίμωνος Ἰσκαριώτου). Befitting this pericope's focus on "wordless" communication, Jesus designates the betrayer not by his name but by his *actions*. Only the narrator gives the name of Judas, son of Simon of Iscariot, to the reader.

Jesus explains that the betrayer is the one "with whom *I* dip" (ᾧ ἐγὼ βάψω), with the first-person pronoun giving emphasis to Jesus's action. This action is made especially significant because of the intimacy of meals in the first-century context. Social gatherings, but especially meals, were intimate affairs. A person did not just eat with anyone. To eat with a person was to show approval and equality. This explains why Jesus was denounced by the Pharisees and scribes for eating with sinners: "This man welcomes [gathers with] sinners and eats with them" (Luke 15:2). Thus, when Jesus announces the betrayal with actions (not words), he too *signals* to those present that the forthcoming actions of Judas are a betrayal.[14] The fact that the narrator, not Jesus, makes Judas the explicitly stated referent suggests that Jesus's wordless signal is intended to depict Judas in a manner similar to the Beloved Disciple as an ideal disciple, although clearly in a negative sense. In this pericope "Judas becomes the archetypal defector."[15] Judas becomes a model in the Fourth Gospel for disbelief, for breaking away from Christian fellowship and intimacy and becoming an agent of Satan (as v. 27 will establish).[16]

13:27 After the piece of bread, then Satan entered into him. Then Jesus said to him, "What you are doing, do quickly" (καὶ μετὰ τὸ ψωμίον τότε εἰσῆλθεν εἰς ἐκεῖνον ὁ Σατανᾶς. λέγει οὖν αὐτῷ ὁ Ἰησοῦς, Ὃ ποιεῖς ποίησον τάχιον). The final section of the pericope (vv. 27–30) begins with the introduction of Satan. Continuing the theme of "wordless" signals, the narrator connects the entrance of Satan "into" Judas with the giving of the piece of bread. This is the only place in the Gospel that Satan is mentioned by name. Interestingly, only the reader is given access to the interpretation of this signal. The "odd expression"[17] of the sharing of bread between Jesus and Judas creates something like a contract or covenant between them, initiated by Jesus, through which Judas was given the right or authority to do what he was going to do. Like the Spirit of God entering those chosen by God in the OT, it was not until that moment— "then" (τότε) — that Satan "entered into" (εἰσῆλθεν εἰς) Judas. This event cannot be described with any greater clarity or precision, for this is a cosmological event that needed the narrator's insight.

Jesus's statement to Judas stems from his authority — "no one takes [my life] from me, but I lay it down by myself" (10:18). As much as Jesus has been serving Judas (e.g., washing his feet), even in the betrayal Judas is technically serving Jesus. The urgency Jesus demands befits the significance of "the hour" in the Gospel (see comments on 2:4). All that has transpired, even the betrayal of Judas, has been rooted in his plan, for everything had already been determined by God himself. Thus, Judas, and even Satan, are in reality servants of the King. This makes sense of Jesus's command to Judas ("do quickly" [ποίησον τάχιον]).

13:28 But no one among those reclining understood why he said this to him (τοῦτο [δὲ] οὐδεὶς

---

14. Cf. Stagg, "The Farewell Discourses: John 13–17," *Rev Exp* 62 (1965): 459–72 (463).

15. Nicholas J. Zola, "'The One Who Eats My Bread Has Lifted His Heel against Me': Psalm 41:10 in 1QH^a 13.25–26 and John 13:18," *PRSt* 37 (2011): 407–19 (418).

16. See William M. Wright IV, "Greco-Roman Character Typing and the Presentation of Judas in the Fourth Gospel," *CBQ* 71 (2009): 544–59.

17. Michaels, *John*, 753.

ἔγνω τῶν ἀνακειμένων πρὸς τί εἶπεν αὐτῷ). The cosmological insight provided to the reader by the narrator is now contrasted with the rest of the disciples who were watching the symbol-laden interaction between Jesus and Judas. The narrator explains that "no one … understood" (οὐδεὶς ἔγνω) the statement Jesus made to Judas. With no awareness of the wordless signal of the dipping of the piece of bread, the disciples appear to be looking for the meaning of Jesus's stated words alone. In this pericope, wordless communication has played a significant role in the narrative. This is true once again here by the narrator's description of the rest of the disciples as "those reclining" (τῶν ἀνακειμένων), a symbolic depiction of their intimate relationship to Jesus.

13:29 For some were thinking, since Judas was holding the money box, that Jesus said to him, "Buy what we need for the Feast," or [spoke to him] in order that he might give something to the poor (τινὲς γὰρ ἐδόκουν, ἐπεὶ τὸ γλωσσόκομον εἶχεν Ἰούδας, ὅτι λέγει αὐτῷ [ὁ] Ἰησοῦς, Ἀγόρασον ὧν χρείαν ἔχομεν εἰς τὴν ἑορτήν, ἢ τοῖς πτωχοῖς ἵνα τι δῷ). The narrator does not merely note the misunderstanding of the disciples but even offers a description of the innocent constructions they concocted to explain the departure of Judas, who had previously been "among those reclining" (v. 28). The disciples knew Judas was the administrator of the common fund (see 12:6), so they assumed by implication that Jesus either told him to purchase what was needed for the Passover Feast or instructed him regarding a religious offering for the poor, which was common during such festivals (cf. Tob 2:2).

13:30 Then after he took the piece of bread, he went out immediately; and it was night (λαβὼν οὖν τὸ ψωμίον ἐκεῖνος ἐξῆλθεν εὐθύς· ἦν δὲ νύξ).

The pericope concludes with the departure of Judas from the intimate communion of Jesus and his disciples. It is of great significance that the narrator again, continuing the theme of "wordless" signals, connects the departure of Judas with the giving of the piece of bread (cf. v. 27). The narrative could not express in more physical (action-based and symbol-laden) terms the contrast between the intimate communion and the betrayal.

Judas physically removes himself from the communion, with the narrative giving it emphasis with the adverb "immediately" (εὐθύς). This departure is hardly just a depiction of the historical plot — that Judas left the room — but also of the cosmological plot of the Gospel, that Judas left the "one flock" and the "one Shepherd" (see 10:16). It is with this in mind that the narrator's concluding description must be understood: "And it was night" (ἦν δὲ νύξ). Without denying that this detail fits nicely with the time of day at which the meal was taking place, the term "night" is never used positively in the Gospel (cf. 3:2; 11:10; 21:3) and impresses upon the reader the symbolic, cosmological realities at play in the action of the Gospel. Even the "night" serves as a "wordless" communication to the reader!

It is important to note that the exit by Judas at v. 30 is part of the "dynamic movement" of the Gospel's farewell discourse, serving as a transitional marker and bringing closure to its two-part introduction (see comments before 13:1). According to Parsenios, an important detail to note from this dramatic exit is that Judas does not leave the meal of his own accord. It is a "forced" exit; Jesus orders Judas to exit. This plot-guiding insight serves two significant functions.[18] First, such an exit sends someone offstage to prepare for future action. In order for Jesus properly to address "his" disciples, Judas the outsider needed to leave. The

---

18. The following is adapted from Parsenios, *Departure and Consolation*, 14 – 16.

plot depended on this symbolic action. Second, involuntary (or "forced") exits remove from the scene a character whose presence would disrupt its natural flow. The reader is, in a sense, readjusted or better prepared for what is about to come (the farewell discourse proper). The significance of this will be made clear at the beginning of the next pericope (see comments on 13:31).

Theology in Application

Jesus gathers his disciples together, washes their feet in a ceremony filled with symbolism of service and sacrifice (the cross), and then prophecies that he is about to be betrayed by one of them! The betrayal reveals not merely who is with Jesus (the "Eleven") but also who is against him — not merely Judas but Satan himself. As the second of a two-part introduction to the farewell discourse, this pericope gives the reader a powerful depiction of the call of discipleship and the demands facing Jesus, not only the external opposition of the prince of darkness, but also the internal opposition from one of "his own" (1:11). Through this pericope the reader witnesses both the historical and cosmological forces at work in the world and is exhorted to be faithful to the end, resting comfortably in the love and on the "chest" of Jesus.

Body (of Christ) Language

This pericope communicates its message with an abundance of nonverbal, symbol-laden actions and gestures that present a robust portrait of the body of Christ. The foot washing of the previous pericope (13:1 – 20) offered one significant symbol-laden act, but this pericope is filled with small, almost unnoticeable acts that communicate rich theological realities. The "look" between disciples (v. 22) and the "nod" Peter gives to the Beloved Disciple (v. 24) communicate a shared identity and cause and express a trust and fellowship that words alone cannot depict. Moreover, the description of the disciples "reclining" together (v. 28) and sharing in a meal together, which included Judas (vv. 26, 27, 30), portrays the intimate fellowship of the disciples of the new covenant, with whom God himself was "dwelling" (1:14).

The church, the people of God, can and must speak with words; the saying, "Preach the gospel, and if necessary use words," is even at its best incomplete, for the gospel is a message that requires words. Yet the truth of the gospel begets a way of life that also speaks. Such "wordless" communication shows the way brothers and sisters in Christ live and work together, trust and share together. They are expressions of the very nature of the Trinitarian God.

The Beloved Disciple

The first appearance of the Beloved Disciple depicts him as an "ideal disciple," having immediate access to and intimate closeness with Christ. It takes all of the apostle Paul's robust theology regarding life "in Christ" to serve as a commentary on the symbolic description of the Beloved Disciple leaning "on the chest of Christ" (v. 25). It should be no surprise that John in his first letter calls the church "the beloved" (Ἀγαπητοί), a term that is minimized by its translation as "dear friends" (NIV; see 1 John 2:7). The Beloved Disciple enjoyed an intimate relationship with the Lord, but so do all disciples have such a relationship with the Lord. God is the lover and we are the loved. The same God who loves the whole world (3:16) simultaneously declares his love to each Christian that each is his "beloved" disciple.

Satan

This is the only pericope in the Gospel that mentions Satan by name. But befitting the cosmological plot of the Fourth Gospel, Satan is a primary character of the darkness, which was introduced to the reader in the prologue (1:5). "Darkness" is abstract; "Satan" is what Scripture uses to express its personal nature. Paul explains this well, "For our struggle is not against flesh and blood, but against the rulers, against the authorities, against the powers of this dark world and against the spiritual forces of evil in the heavenly [i.e., cosmological] realms" (Eph 6:12). Paul and John together teach that Satan opposes Christ and therefore those who belong to Christ. Moreover, Satan is not far removed from the people of God but beside them and, when permitted, "in" them (v. 27). The purpose of this pericope is not to give a full description of Satan but to show how present and active is the darkness. But thanks be to God, the light shines in the darkness (1:5).

Judas and the Christian

Judas must not be viewed as an isolated example but as a common experience in the church. While the gospel is good news, it is not easily swallowed. Scripture warns that the message of Christ is a stumbling block and foolishness (1 Cor 1:23) and that even Satan, "the god of this age," is actively blinding the minds of the world (2 Cor 4:4). But as scary as this is, there is something else frightening in the example of Judas. Judas does not represent disbelief among those on the outside of faith and opposed to Christ but disbelief among the faithful and those on the inside. Judas is a far more threatening figure than Pilate or the Jewish leaders, for he reminds us that on any day some faithful follower sitting among us might turn off the light and stumble out into the darkness.[19]

May this not be you, O reader of this Gospel. May the Spirit of God protect you from such a flight into the "night," into darkness and keep you in Christ, "shielded by God's power" (1 Pet 1:5), in intimate communion with Christ. Hold firm, Christian; hold fast, church.

---

19. David L. Bartlett, "John 13:21–30," *Int* 43 (1989): 393–97 (394).

John 13:31 – 38

Literary Context

This pericope is the first of eight sections of the farewell discourse proper. It functions as a prologue, offering an opening announcement about the person and work of Jesus and the expected response of the reader/hearer. The farewell discourse was given a complex introduction (13:1 – 30) through which the context for this intimate monologue of Jesus is given. At this intimate gathering, after washing the feet of his disciples, Jesus begins to give his final instructions to the children of God, the people of the new covenant. In this part of the farewell discourse, Jesus locates his person and work within the glory of God, formally introduces and explains his departure, and gives a new commandment that serves to demarcate the people of the new covenant from the rest of the world. The disciples — and the readers — are exhorted to make a radical commitment to Jesus and to loving one another, something which Peter himself is exhorted to see as not only difficult but as requiring the work that Christ still must finish.

VII. The Farewell Discourse (13:1 – 17:26)

    A. Introduction: The Love of Jesus (13:1 – 30)

        1. Jesus and the Washing of His Disciples' Feet (13:1 – 20)

        2. Jesus Announces His Betrayal (13:21 – 30)

➡   **B. The Farewell Discourse (13:31 – 16:33)**

        1. Prologue: Glory, Departure, and Love (13:31 – 38)

        2. I Am the Way and the Truth and the Life (14:1 – 14)

        3. I Will Give You the Paraclete (14:15 – 31)

        4. I Am the True Vine (15:1 – 17)

        5. I Have Also Experienced the Hate of the World (15:18 – 27)

        6. I Will Empower You by the Paraclete (16:1 – 15)

        7. I Will Turn Your Grief into Joy (16:16 – 24)

        8. Epilogue: Speaking Plainly, Departure, and Peace (16:25 – 33)

    C. Conclusion: The Prayer of Jesus (17:1 – 26)

Main Idea

Out of Christ's love for Christians they are given the commandment to love one another. Christian discipleship is grounded in the work of God (not one's own work) and is an expression of the nature of God himself.

Translation

John 13:31–38

	Section #1 of "Farewell Discourse"	
31a	Scene Transition	Therefore
b	Context	when he went out
c	Prologue (31–38) of "Discourse"	**Jesus said,**
d	Pronouncement	*"Now the Son of Man is glorified,*
e	Reciprocation	*and God is glorified in him.*
	Explanation of Reciprocation	
32a	Condition	*If God is glorified in him,*
b	Inference #1	*God will also glorify him in himself,*
c	Inference #2	*and immediately he will glorify him.*
33a	Affectionate Address	*Children,*
b	Assertion	*I am with you only a little longer.*
c	Predictive Reaction	*You will seek me,*
d		*and*
e	Comparison	*just as I said to the Jews,*
f	Restatement	*'where I am going you are not able to go,'*
g		*I also say to you.*
34a	Action	*I give a new commandment to you:*
b	Commandment	*love one another.*
c	Comparative Basis	*Just as I loved you,*
d	Commandment	*you also should love one another.*
35a	Means	*In this way*
b	Result	*all people will know that you are my disciples,*
c	Condition	*if you have love for one another.*
36a	Response	**Simon Peter said to him,**
b	Address	*"Lord,*
c	Question of Concern	*where are you going?"*
d	Response	**Jesus answered him,**
e	Place	*"Where I am going*
f	Answer	*you are not able now to follow me,*
g	Temporal Contrast	*but you will follow later."*

Continued on next page.

Continued from previous page.

37a	Response	**Peter said to him,**
b	Address	*"Lord,*
c	Interrogative Challenge	*why am I not able to follow you immediately?*
d	Ironic Counteroffer to 36g	*I will offer my life*
e	Ironic Beneficiary	*on behalf of you."*
38a	Response	**Jesus answered,**
b	Interrogative Counterrebuke	*"Will you offer your life*
c	Ironic Beneficiary	*on behalf of me?*
d	Amen Formula	*Truly, truly I say to you,*
e	Emphatic Rebuke	*the rooster will not crow*
f	Predictive Circumstance	*until you have denied me three times."*

Structure and Literary Form

As the first of eight sections of the farewell discourse, this pericope is part of the fourth (and longest) substantial monologue in the narrative proper. A monologue (see Introduction) is similar to a dialogue in that it is set in the context of an engagement and conflict, but rather than engaging point-for-point it allows for a lengthy argument. A monologue can contain elements of rhetoric, challenge, and conflict, but it does so in a sustained presentation.

This pericope functions like a prologue. The first and last sections of the farewell discourse serve as a frame and *inclusio* for the entire monologue. The logic behind seeing a prologue (13:31 – 38) and an epilogue (16:25 – 33) framing the discourse proper is rooted in the nearly identical content in each pericope, serving to connect the entire monologue together. For not only do both pericopae include the question of where Jesus is going and the affirmation of where he is from (13:31 and 16:28), but also both include the reaction of Jesus to Peter and to the disciples alike regarding betrayal or abandonment (13:38 and 16:32).[1] This first section of the farewell discourse introduces the disciples to Jesus's depiction of life in his person and the covenantal transition that is taking place through his work. In his opening statement Jesus explains the nature of his glory and its most vivid expression: commitment and love.

Exegetical Outline

→ **1. Prologue: Glory, Departure, and Love (13:31 – 38)**

   a. The Glory and Departure of the Son of Man (vv. 31 – 33)

   b. A New Commandment: Love One Another (vv. 34 – 35)

   c. The Prophecy of Peter's Betrayal (vv. 36 – 38)

---

1. Boyle, "The Last Discourse," 217.

Explanation of the Text

Since this entire section of the Gospel is replete with interpretive issues, we refer the reader to the first pericope of this section where we provided an overview of the nature (genre), literary structure, and function of the farewell discourse (see comments before 13:1).

13:31 Therefore when he went out Jesus said, "Now the Son of Man is glorified, and God is glorified in him" (Ὅτε οὖν ἐξῆλθεν λέγει Ἰησοῦς, Νῦν ἐδοξάσθη ὁ υἱὸς τοῦ ἀνθρώπου, καὶ ὁ θεὸς ἐδοξάσθη ἐν αὐτῷ). The "therefore" (οὖν) and the repeated mention of the departure of Judas serves as an intentional literary marker. Judas's "exit draws a sharp line between the scene of the dinner (13:1–29) and the [discourse] that [follows] the dinner until 18:1."[2] The plot depends on this symbolic action (see comments on 13:30), for it prepares the scene (and the reader) for the discourse to follow, which is for Jesus's disciples alone.

Jesus begins his farewell discourse with a lofty statement: "Now the Son of Man is glorified, and God is glorified in him" (Νῦν ἐδοξάσθη ὁ υἱὸς τοῦ ἀνθρώπου, καὶ ὁ θεὸς ἐδοξάσθη ἐν αὐτῷ). The pronouncement echoes several similar statements of Jesus in the Gospel (cf. 8:54; 11:4; 12:23, 28). This is the last time in the Gospel that Jesus refers to himself as the "Son of Man," a significant title that is used to depict the power, authority, and glory displayed in the person and work of Jesus (see comments on 1:51). The "now" (Νῦν) points to the present circumstances, moments after the betrayal, when "present and future are bound together" (see

v. 32),[3] and when the power and authority of the Son of Man have set in motion the ultimate display of his glory—his death and resurrection. "The glorification of Christ is connected with what appears to human understanding as the very opposite of glory."[4] The cross is not shame but glory, a glory that can only be understood through the cosmological vision cast by the prologue. The exaltation of the Son of Man is on the cross. And this glory is not merely the opinion of the Son but also the Father, who is "glorified in" the Son. It is the acceptance of the death of Jesus by the Father, not the assurance of a future vindication or reward, that makes the death not a scandal but the supreme manifestation of glory.[5] Ironically, "an instrument of human cruelty and injustice became a sign of tenderness and victory."[6] The cross then is the authoritative expression of the love of God for the world (3:16).

13:32 "If God is glorified in him, God will also glorify him in himself, and immediately he will glorify him" ([εἰ ὁ θεὸς ἐδοξάσθη ἐν αὐτῷ] καὶ ὁ θεὸς δοξάσει αὐτὸν ἐν αὐτῷ, καὶ εὐθὺς δοξάσει αὐτόν). Jesus continues with an awkward statement that offers further explanation of the Father's confirmation of the glory of the Son.[7] The fivefold "glorification" in vv. 31–32[8] and the mixture of verbal tenses (three aorists followed by two futures) intentionally creates a paradoxical situation where a future event is transposed to the present.[9] The verbal tenses here, especially when interpreted by means of verbal aspect theory, are making an

2. Parsenios, *Departure and Consolation*, 16. Cf. Moloney, *John*, 388.
3. Bultmann, *John*, 523.
4. Morris, *John*, 560.
5. Hoskyns, *Fourth Gospel*, 449–50.
6. Stevick, *Jesus and His Own*, 99.
7. See Peter Ensor, "The Glorification of the Son of Man:

An Analysis of John 13:31–32," *TynBul* 58 (2007): 229–52. On the different senses of "glory," see Aquinas, *John*, 3:35–39.
8. The hymn-like linked set of five clauses about glorifying give further evidence that this opening section of the farewell discourse (vv. 31–38) functions like a prologue.
9. See Schnackenburg, *John*, 3:49–52. Cf. Bultmann, *John*, 524.

"omnitemporal" or "timeless" reference.[10] While the cross is a real, in-time referent in which God is glorified and the resurrection is likely also in view for which glory is "immediately" (εὐθύς) present, the entire sequence simultaneously looks beyond history and the temporal passing of events — the historical plot — to their interpenetration in the cosmological plot of the Gospel. Lyons in reference to the verbal aspect explains that "the situation, or state-of-affairs, that it describes is outside time altogether."[11] The theology of this statement can also be explained: "The glorification of the Son of Man is therefore past, present and future: any logical distinction between these tenses breaks down, since the significance of the Death and of the Coming of the Spirit to the believers, events in time as they are, cannot be limited to their event."[12]

This is not in any way to minimize the historical events; Jesus would die on the cross and would be raised ("immediately") on the third day. It is rather to say with Jesus's own words as recorded in Scripture that the events are inextricably linked together not only by means of the historical event and chronological time, but also (even primarily) by the approval and confirmation of God himself — Father and Son (and Spirit). The Son glorifies the Father and the Father glorifies the Son. For this reason the meaning of the cross and the resurrection/ascension, which can now be viewed as a singular event,[13] are defined primarily by God. What the world saw as "shame" the Son received as "joy" (Heb 12:2), for it was nothing less than the manifestation of the glory of God. In his opening statement Jesus declares the imminent fulfillment

of what he had promised at the beginning of his ministry regarding the Son of Man and the revelation of God (see comments on 1:51).

13:33 "Children, I am with you only a little longer. You will seek me, and just as I said to the Jews, 'where I am going you are not able to go,' I also say to you" (τεκνία, ἔτι μικρὸν μεθ' ὑμῶν εἰμι· ζητήσετέ με, καὶ καθὼς εἶπον τοῖς Ἰουδαίοις ὅτι Ὅπου ἐγὼ ὑπάγω ὑμεῖς οὐ δύνασθε ἐλθεῖν, καὶ ὑμῖν λέγω ἄρτι). Jesus concludes his opening statement regarding the glorification of the Son by setting it in the context of his impending departure. Befitting a farewell speech, Jesus begins the discourse by explaining his departure; a departure intimately connected to work he still must complete. The glorification of Jesus, his death, resurrection, and ascension, is another way of saying that the appointed "hour" has finally arrived and that his departure from this world is imminent.[14] But as much as this is about the Son of God (vv. 31–32), it also involves the children of God (v. 33). For this reason Jesus now turns to them.

As Jesus turns to address his disciples, again befitting the consolatory nature of a farewell speech (see comments before 13:1), God addresses his "children" (τεκνία). Jesus explains that he will be with them "only a little longer" (ἔτι μικρὸν). The reader knows full well that he is going to his death and that this is exactly where God has willed for him to go. Yet the disciples understand his coming in a much more limited (historical) sense and cannot conceive of his departure as a good thing. That is, Jesus knows that what he is about to say will be difficult for them to hear, which is why he

10. See Porter, *Verbal Aspect*, 233. Cf. Carson, *John*, 482–83, 486–87.

11. John Lyons, *Semantics*, 2 vols. (Cambridge: Cambridge University Press, 1977), 2:680.

12. Hoskyns, *Fourth Gospel*, 450. Cf. Dodd, *Interpretation*, 403.

13. See Beasley-Murray, *John*, 246: "The redemptive dying is inconceivable apart from the rising, as the rising is from the dying." Cf. Ensor, "The Glorification of the Son of Man," 233.

14. Fernando F. Segovia, "The Structure, *Tendenz*, and *Sitz im Leben* of John 13:31–14:31," *JBL* 104 (1985): 471–93 (479).

affectionately calls them "children" (cf. 1:12) and why he explains to them what their response to his departure will look like.

Jesus says to the disciples that they will seek him but cannot go where he is going. As Jesus reveals, he had already said this to the Jews on two occasions (7:34; 8:21). As with the first two occurrences of this statement, it is best understood to be reflecting a more complex meaning, making not only a distinction in place but also a distinction in person. To the Jews this was a warning to believe in him before it was too late (8:21: "You will die in your sin"); for the disciples it is more consolatory, serving to let them know ahead of time that a change in his presence and the manner in which they relate to him is about to take place (cf. 14:19; 16:16).[15]

The departure of Jesus is no aimless, blind, or haphazard departure—no "going" out into the darkness of the "night" like Judas (13:30); it is "the deliberate inauguration of the way that is to be followed by the children of light" (14:2, 4, 6).[16] In this instance Jesus simply explains the transition to come. The new mode of existence will also shortly be explained, beginning even in the next pericope (14:1 – 14). Even the disciples are soon to be transitioned into a new mode of existence, worshippers who relate to God "in Spirit and truth" (4:23). This verse, then, serves as a foundational statement for the rest of the farewell discourse, for it introduces the questions and issues that the rest of the discourse will answer and explain.[17]

13:34 "I give a new commandment to you: love one another. Just as I loved you, you also should love one another" (ἐντολὴν καινὴν δίδωμι ὑμῖν, ἵνα ἀγαπᾶτε ἀλλήλους· καθὼς ἠγάπησα ὑμᾶς ἵνα καὶ

ὑμεῖς ἀγαπᾶτε ἀλλήλους). The second part of this pericope (vv. 34 – 35), sandwiched between Jesus's description of his departure and the exhortation to follow him, is this commandment.[18] The phrase "a new commandment"[19] is shoved forward in the Greek sentence, making it emphatic. The dependent-clause subjunctive (ἵνα plus the subjunctive) should probably be understood as an imperatival use of the subjunctive.[20] The content of this command is not entirely "new," for love was a fundamental rule in the life of the OT people of God (cf. Lev 19:18; Luke 10:25 – 27). Even more, Jesus has already initiated this command by means of the foot washing, which serves as the foundational "example" of the source and nature of this love (see comments on 13:14 – 15).

The newness of this love is explained by the second part of Jesus's statement that the source of this love between the disciples is the love of Jesus. The departure of Jesus demands that God's love for the world that Jesus inaugurated now be expressed between the "children," between those who have already experienced his love (as "beloved" disciples). The newness of this love is not that it is an independent love, for Christian love is a subset of and is founded upon the love of God himself; it is "the response to the love of Jesus."[21] The love commandment finds its source in and emulates the love between the Father and the Son (e.g., 8:29; 10:18; 12:49 – 50; 14:31; 15:10).

13:35 "In this way all people will know that you are my disciples, if you have love for one another" (ἐν τούτῳ γνώσονται πάντες ὅτι ἐμοὶ μαθηταί ἐστε, ἐὰν ἀγάπην ἔχητε ἐν ἀλλήλοις). Jesus explains further the purpose of the new commandment of love.

15. Ridderbos, *John*, 475.
16. Hoskyns, *Fourth Gospel*, 450.
17. Schnackenburg, *John*, 3:52 – 53.
18. Cf. Keener, *John*, 2:923.
19. In the Latin Vulgate, "new commandment" is *man-*

datum novum, from which the name "*Maundy* Thursday" is derived, the anniversary of the Last Supper when this new commandment was given.
20. Cf. Wallace, *Greek Grammar*, 476 – 77. Cf. BDF § 394.
21. Bultmann, *John*, 529.

It is not merely a command, it is also the promise of witness. This witness is not only for "all people" (πάντες) but also to signify the identity of the disciples. This love, therefore, becomes the character trait and identity marker of the people of God. "Faith which has accepted the service of love can only be fulfilled in love."[22]

This new love command is "no retrograde and narrow exclusivism" from Jesus's command to love one's neighbor (Mark 12:28 – 31), for the love of God now expressed in and by the people of God becomes the clearest expression of the love of God for the world.[23] Augustine suggests that both commands — to love God and to love neighbor — are found and fulfilled in this one new command.[24] The love of God first expressed by Jesus has now "become flesh" in an even more expansive way and is to go out into every corner of the world through the body of Christ, the church.[25]

13:36 Simon Peter said to him, "Lord, where are you going?" Jesus answered him, "Where I am going you are not able now to follow me, but you will follow later" (Λέγει αὐτῷ Σίμων Πέτρος, Κύριε, ποῦ ὑπάγεις; ἀπεκρίθη [αὐτῷ] Ἰησοῦς, Ὅπου ὑπάγω οὐ δύνασαί μοι νῦν ἀκολουθῆσαι, ἀκολουθήσεις δὲ ὕστερον). The final section of the pericope (vv. 36 – 38) involves a brief dialogue between Peter and Jesus that serves to offer a strong exhortation to all disciples. Peter asks Jesus directly where he is going, this time without the mediation of the Beloved Disciple (cf. 13:24). This is not a question drenched in irony, as the Jews had asked it in 7:35, but a question out of concern.[26]

Jesus's response is almost identical to his statement in v. 33, though here Jesus offers a significant addition: Peter cannot follow "now" (νῦν) but can follow "later" (ὕστερον). By this Jesus holds out an invitation without denying a distinction between himself and Peter. For as Jesus will shortly explain (14:1 – 14), Peter and the disciples will go where Jesus is going, but not at the same time ("the hour") or in the same manner (the cross). Many are the children of God, but there is only one unique Son.

13:37 Peter said to him, "Lord, why am I not able to follow you immediately? I will offer my life on behalf of you" (λέγει αὐτῷ ὁ Πέτρος, Κύριε, διὰ τί οὐ δύναμαί σοι ἀκολουθῆσαι ἄρτι; τὴν ψυχήν μου ὑπὲρ σοῦ θήσω). With bold naivete Peter offers a response to the explanation Jesus gave to his earlier question that functions more like a rebuke, even a challenge. Peter presses against Jesus's departure "now" without him by asking why he cannot "follow ... immediately" (ἀκολουθῆσαι ἄρτι), with the adverb "immediately" (ἄρτι) serving as a direct challenge to Jesus's use of "now" (νῦν) in v. 36.

Peter even claims to be willing to give his life for Jesus, which suggests that he considered Jesus's departure to be a reference to his death. Like Thomas (called Didymus) in 11:16, Peter states his willingness to die for the cause for which Jesus foresees death. But just as Thomas misunderstood the death about which Jesus spoke until the resurrection of Lazarus (see comments on 11:16), so also does Peter misunderstand the death about which Jesus speaks until the resurrection of the Son of God. By this statement Peter fails to understand not only *where* Jesus is going (to the Father) but also *why* he is going (to give life, not to take it).[27] But Peter must abide by the distinction between himself and Christ, the distinction between "now" and "later" (v. 36), "the eschatological distinction which for John is also a spiritual distinction,"[28] the

---

22. Barrett, *John*, 452.
23. Hoskyns, *Fourth Gospel*, 451.
24. Augustine, *John*, 55.2.318.
25. See Bultmann, *John*, 528.

26. Schnackenburg, *John*, 3:55.
27. Cf. Beasley-Murray, *John*, 248.
28. Barrett, *John*, 453.

difference between the historical and the cosmo-logical plot of the Gospel of John.

13:38 Jesus answered, "Will you offer your life on behalf of me? Truly, truly I say to you, the rooster will not crow until you have denied me three times" (ἀποκρίνεται Ἰησοῦς, Τὴν ψυχήν σου ὑπὲρ ἐμοῦ θήσεις; ἀμὴν ἀμὴν λέγω σοι, οὐ μὴ ἀλέκτωρ φωνήσῃ ἕως οὗ ἀρνήσῃ με τρίς). Jesus responds to Peter's rebuke with a strong rebuke of his own. But he is not pushing back against mere overconfidence but against actions that threaten the very purpose for which he came. Peter challenges the unique character and purpose of the departure of Jesus. For Peter's challenge is an attempt (even if only implicitly) to thwart Jesus's mission from the Father and to stop him from drinking the cup the Father has given him to drink.[29] Jesus not only denounces such an action but graciously offers proof of its necessity: Peter's own example of faithlessness.

Jesus responds to Peter's question with a question of his own that speaks volumes when understood in the cosmological context of the Gospel: "Will you offer your life on behalf of me?" (Τὴν ψυχήν σου ὑπὲρ ἐμοῦ θήσεις;), with the word "your

life" thrown forward in the Greek sentence for emphatic focus. The irony is stark; it is Jesus whose life is to be given on behalf of Peter. This statement offers a foundation for understanding discipleship. As much as the disciples are servants of Christ, giving their lives to the service of the Lord, they are first and foremost served by Christ, who gave himself — his life — on their behalf. To reverse this is to misunderstand the gospel.

Jesus concludes his dialogue with Peter and his rebuke of Peter's distortion of the gospel with a statement so significant that he begins it with an authoritative preface (see comments on 1:51). Jesus prophesies that Peter will deny him three times before the rooster crows (fulfilled in 18:15 – 18, 25 – 27). Not only will Peter fail to offer his life on behalf of Jesus, he will even do the exact opposite: he will give up Jesus to save his own life. This statement must have silenced Peter, for even though several of the other disciples speak or ask questions during the rest of the farewell discourse, we do not hear of Peter again until it is over (at 18:10).[30] In this way the pericope concludes what we have described as the prologue of the farewell discourse (13:31 – 38).

Theology in Application

In the first of eight sections of the farewell discourse, Jesus introduces for his disciples what the remainder of the discourse will explain further: his imminent departure, the new love commandment, and the true nature and source of Christian discipleship. Through this pericope the reader listens to Christ's exhortation to follow him and is invited to see how their entire Christian life and mission is founded less upon who they are and what they must do and more upon *who* Christ is and *what* Christ has already done.

29. Ridderbos, *John*, 478.

30. Morris, *John*, 564.

The Glory of the Cross

Jesus begins his farewell discourse with an emphatic description of the glorification of the Son of Man (vv. 31 – 32). In these verses the glory of the Son of Man — a title that itself magnifies the glory of the one who bears it — is expressed in his death on the cross. The cross, which proleptically includes the resurrection and ascension of Christ, is the place where the work and person of the Son, the very purpose of the Son's mission to the world, is affirmed and given its approval. The glory of the cross is so rooted in God that it is beyond time; it is "omnitemporal" because its effects interpenetrate past, present, and future. The cross is the place and time when God fully accommodates himself to his creation, where the light overcomes the darkness and death procures life. The church now sees this place of death and darkness as the manifestation of its life and light. What the world sees as shame the Son receives as "joy" (Heb 12:2). This is the gospel: the cross of Christ is life not death for us, and this "great reversal" is the ultimate expression of God's love for the world (cf. 3:16). That which was "an instrument of human cruelty and injustice became a sign of tenderness and victory."[31]

The Love Commandment

As much as the plan of God had always involved the arrival of Jesus, so also did it always include his departure. The departure of Jesus initiates the fullest expression of the love of God for the world, for in the new covenant Christ's love for the world transitions to the body of Christ's love for the world, beginning with the new commandment to love one another (v. 34). The plan of God had always been to share the love between the Father and the Son with the children of God and ultimately the world. The people of God are not only the recipients of the love of God but also become the expression of the love of God in the world. The Christian life and mission is centered upon and compelled by this new commandment. In this way the Ten Commandments of the Old Testament, and even Jesus's summary of the Ten into two — love of God and neighbor — find their truest expression in this single love commandment. When we love God, we are able to love one another, and when we love one another we love God. These are not the same thing, but they have the same source — the love found among and between the persons of the Trinitarian God. Quite simply: "We love because he first loved us" (1 John 4:19).

Beware the Audacity of Peter

Peter completely misunderstood Christ's message and therefore Christ's mission. He spoke with an authority and with assumptions that depict how easily we, like

---

31. Stevick, *Jesus and His Own*, 99.

Peter, not only misunderstand something about God but also misunderstand something about ourselves. Human nature has the innate sinful ability to think more highly of itself than it should — to think that it can be like God (Gen 3:5). But God in his great mercy teaches Peter — and the reader — not only what he (Jesus) is going to do but even what Peter with his sin-laden condition is going to do. Augustine is right when he says, "The weak man boasted of his willingness, but the Physician has an eye on the state of his health; the one promised; the Other foreknew: the ignorant was bold; He that foreknew all condescended to teach."[32] Christian discipleship therefore may also be defined as learning not to place confidence in human strength.

May the boldness of the church not come from our inappropriately grounded self-confidence but from our trust in the sovereign purposes and plan of God. May we boldly follow the path that Christ has prepared for us to walk. May our security come from abiding in Christ (ch. 15), and may our food be found in his flesh and blood (ch. 6). That is, may we deny self, not Christ, and may we live in his love even when the whole world itself has nothing but hate for us (15:19).

---

32. Augustine, *John*, 66.1.319.

John 14:1 – 14

Literary Context

This pericope is the second of eight sections of the farewell discourse. Surrounded by a prologue (13:31 – 38) and an epilogue (16:25 – 33), the farewell discourse can be divided into six significant and developing thematic statements by Jesus, with each offering comfort and consolation for the disciples from Jesus, befitting the nature of a farewell discourse (see comments before 13:1). These six statements within the farewell discourse offer one long exhortation to stay the course and encouragement that their efforts will be matched by the Trinitarian God himself. In the first of these six statements, Jesus firmly establishes his identity and his relation to the Father, which serves to explain not only the path he must take but also the path his disciples will follow. In this well-known "I am" statement by Jesus, the entire force of the Gospel lands powerfully on his person and work. The disciples — and the readers — are exhorted to consider afresh the magnitude of the person and work of Jesus, in order that they may find their true rest (v. 1) and true home (vv. 2 – 3) and, on the way, their true vocation (vv. 12 – 15).

VII. The Farewell Discourse (13:1 – 17:26)

    A. Introduction: The Love of Jesus (13:1 – 30)

        1. Jesus and the Washing of His Disciples' Feet (13:1 – 20)

        2. Jesus Announces His Betrayal (13:21 – 30)

    B. The Farewell Discourse (13:31 – 16:33)

        1. Prologue: Glory, Departure, and Love (13:31 – 38)

➡   **2. I Am the Way and the Truth and the Life (14:1 – 14)**

        3. I Will Give You the Paraclete (14:15 – 31)

        4. I Am the True Vine (15:1 – 17)

        5. I Have Also Experienced the Hate of the World (15:18 – 27)

        6. I Will Empower You by the Paraclete (16:1 – 15)

        7. I Will Turn Your Grief into Joy (16:16 – 24)

        8. Epilogue: Speaking Plainly, Departure, and Peace (16:25 – 33)

    C. Conclusion: The Prayer of Jesus (17:1 – 26)

Main Idea

Jesus Christ, who alone is the way, the truth, and the life, exhorts his disciples to find through faith in his person and work their true rest, their true home, and their true vocation.

Translation

John 14:1–14

	Section #2 of "Farewell Discourse"	
1a	Exhortation	*"Do not let your heart be frightened.*
b	Command #1	*Believe in God;*
c	Command #2	*believe also in me.*
2a	Basis (2–4)	*In my Father's house there are many rooms.*
b	Condition	*If it were not so,*
c	Interrogative Inference	*would I tell you that I am going to prepare a place for you?*
3a		*And*
b	Condition	*if I go and*
c		*prepare a place for you,*
d	Inference	*I will come again and*
e		*take you with me,*
f	Purpose	*in order that where I am you also may be.*
4a		*And*
b	Location	*where I am going,*
c	Inference	*you know the way."*
5a	Character Reentrance	**Thomas said to him,**
b	Address	*"Lord,*
c	Assertion	*we do not know where you are going.*
d	Question	*How are we able to know the way?"*
6a	Response	**Jesus said to him,**
b	Declaration of Mode	*"I am the way and*
c	Declaration of Reality	*the truth and*
d	Declaration of Source	*the life.*
e	Implicit Inference	*No one comes to the Father*
f	Exception	*except through me.*
	Explanation	
7a	Condition	*If you have known me,*
b	Inference	*you will know my Father also.*
c	Time	*From now on*
d	Assertion #1	*you know him*
e	Assertion #2	*and have seen him."*

Continued on next page.

Continued from previous page.

8a	Character Reentrance	**Philip said to him,**
b	Address	"Lord,
c	Naive Entreaty	show the Father to us,
d	Supposed Result	*and it will be sufficient for us."*
9a	Response	**Jesus said to him,**
b	Premise	"I have been with you for so long a time
c	Interrogative Rebuke	*and* you do not know me,
d		do you,
e	Address	Philip?
f	Restatement of 7d–e	The one who has seen me has seen the Father.
g	Question	How can you say,
h		'Show me the Father?'
10a	Question	You believe
b	Content: Mutual Indwelling	that I am in the Father and
c		the Father is in me,
d		do you not?
e	Assertion	The words that I speak to you I do not speak on my own,
f	Contrast of Source	*but* the Father …
g	Description	who abides in me
h		… does his works.
11a	Command	Believe me
b	Content: Mutual Indwelling	that I am in the Father and
c		the Father is in me.
d	Contrast	*But*
e	Condition	if not,
f	Command	believe
g	Basis: "works"	because of the works themselves.
12a	Amen Formula	Truly, truly I say to you,
b	Description/Condition	the one who believes in me,
c	Result/Inference #1	the works that I do he will also do, and
d	Result/Inference #2	greater works than these he will do,
e	Basis	because I am going to the Father.
13a	Description of "greater works"	*And*
b	Circumstantial Condition	whatever you ask
c	Source	in my name
d	Inferential Promise	I will do this,
e	Result	so that the Father may be glorified in the Son.
	Emphatic Restatement	
14a	Condition	If you ask me anything
b	Source	in my name
c	Inferential Promise	I will do it."

Structure and Literary Form

As the second of eight sections of the farewell discourse, this pericope is part of the fourth (and longest) substantial monologue in the narrative proper. A monologue (see Introduction) is similar to a dialogue in that it is set in the context of an engagement and conflict, but rather than engaging point-for-point it allows for a lengthy argument. A monologue can contain elements of rhetoric, challenge, and conflict, but it does so in a sustained presentation.

This pericope is the first of six statements by Jesus intending to exhort and encourage his disciples. While all of 14:1 – 31 works together (see comments on 14:27 – 29), a transition occurs after v. 14, warranting a section break. In this first statement Jesus reveals the future rest and future work he has established for his disciples, both of which have been founded in the unique identity of Jesus Christ.

Exegetical Outline

➡   **2. I Am the Way and the Truth and the Life (14:1 – 14)**

    a. "I Go and Prepare a Place for You" (vv. 1 – 4)

    b. Not just a Place but a Person — the "I Am" (vv. 5 – 7)

    c. The Father, the Son, and "the Works" in the Name of the Son (vv. 8 – 14)

Explanation of the Text

Since this entire section of the Gospel and "the farewell discourse" proper is replete with interpretive issues, we refer the reader to the first pericope of this section where we provided an overview of the nature (genre), literary structure, and function of the farewell discourse (see comments before 13:1).

14:1 "Do not let your heart be frightened. Believe in God; believe also in me" (Μὴ ταρασσέσθω ὑμῶν ἡ καρδία· πιστεύετε εἰς τὸν θεόν, καὶ εἰς ἐμὲ πιστεύετε). In the first section of the pericope (vv. 1 – 4), Jesus begins by exhorting his disciples to trust him as he explains what is soon to take place. Jesus commands his disciples not to "be frightened" (ταρασσέσθω), a verb which refers to an in-

ward turmoil or confusion.[1] Since the imperative mood is addressing an emotional state, it is best taken as a command to "be in control of yourself."[2] Jesus is addressing their inner person, their "heart" (ἡ καρδία), ministering to his disciples by addressing them from their own point of view.[3]

After commanding them to remove fear from their heart, Jesus commands them to receive in its place the confidence that comes from a more appropriate and worthy foundation and security: belief in God. The two occurrences of "believe" (πιστεύετε) could grammatically have several possible combinations of imperatives and indicatives (e.g., indicative-imperative or imperative-imperative), but are more likely continuing the

---

1. BDAG 990.
2. Wallace, *Greek Grammar*, 440.
3. Aquinas, *John*, 3:47.

imperative force of the previous phrase.[4] It is less likely that an indicative would be sandwiched between two imperatives than three imperatives would be working emphatically together.[5] Jesus is not assuming their belief in God (indicative: "You believe in God") and hoping to add belief in him (imperative: "Believe also in me") — as if belief in God and Jesus could ever be separated (a foreign thought to this Gospel and Scripture as a whole). Rather, Jesus is assuaging their fears by commanding them to believe in God, the one made known and accessible by Jesus Christ, demanding that their belief in God be fully established in him.

14:2a "In my Father's house there are many rooms" (ἐν τῇ οἰκίᾳ τοῦ πατρός μου μοναὶ πολλαί εἰσιν). Jesus then begins to describe the foundation upon which belief in God is built. He starts by using two terms that need to be defined carefully, for they direct much of the discourse to follow: my Father's "house" (οἰκίᾳ) and many "rooms" (μοναὶ). We will discuss them in turn.

The term "house" (οἰκίᾳ) is a spatial metaphor that has already been used in the Gospel to refer to a building where one dwells (cf. 11:31; 12:3). Jesus even used the full phrase "my Father's house" in 2:16 when referring to the physical temple in Jerusalem, though that is not the particular reference in this case. There are three other ways the term can be used. First, befitting its previously mentioned reference to the temple but placing it in this particular context, some have suggested that the imagery in vv. 2 – 3 is referring to a heavenly temple, drawing from an elaborate collection of similar language in the OT and other Jewish literature that portrayed the temple as the eschatological dwelling place of the followers of God.[6] Second, some have interpreted the term in a more personal and spiritual sense to refer to a "family" or "household," a use not foreign to the Gospel (cf. 4:53; 8:35). Third, the more traditional interpretation and the one to be preferred interprets the spatial metaphor as simply referring to the heavenly abode of God and therefore to the promised abode of the children of God. While all three interpretations are dependent on the interpretation given to the second term, "rooms" (μοναὶ), we can already identify difficulties with the first two options: the first interprets the metaphor too tightly (too physically), and the second interprets a clearly spatial metaphor too loosely (too spiritually). In a sense, both interpretations inappropriately fuse the historical and cosmological realities so important to the Gospel.

The term "rooms" (μοναὶ) is also a spatial metaphor and gives further expression to the "house" metaphor discussed above. The Greek term is a cognate of the verb "remain," "abide," or "dwell" (μένω), a significant term in the Gospel (see ch. 15). It generally refers to a dwelling place or, more simply, a room. The common translation "mansions" (KJV), which is filled with inappropriate associations, is based upon the Latin Vulgate's *mansiones*, which more simply refers to "stations" and "resting places."[7] Similar to the previous metaphor, some interpret "rooms" too rigidly, suggesting that there is a series of progressive and temporary steps up which one advances until perfection is ultimately attained (e.g., Origen).[8] But this idea is entirely foreign to the Gospel. A more contemporary interpretation, based on the use of the same term in 14:23, interprets "rooms" too loosely by suggesting it refers to spiritual relationships: "Not mansions in the sky, but spiritual positions in Christ, much

---

4. See Barrett, *John*, 456.

5. Cf. Michaels, *John*, 766.

6. See Steven M. Bryan, "The Eschatological Temple in John 14," *BBR* 15 (2005): 187 – 98.

7. The Latin noun would not have had the connotations of an elaborate or palatial home in the sixteenth century as it does today.

8. See Westcott, *John*, 200.

as in Pauline theology."[9] But to define the Father's "house" and presence by means of the people of God is to reverse the movement of the entire Gospel. No, it is the people of God who one day will be with the Father, just as the Son — the Word — in the beginning was "with God" (1:1).

Without denying the level of complexity presented to us by this verse, it is important that we not miss its overt simplicity. Jesus begins the discourse proper by telling the disciples of their inheritance, and invites them, heirs of the eternal house of God (8:35), to visualize and embrace even now the bountiful blessings offered to the children of God. Jesus depicts how every Christian — man or woman, slave or king in this world — will have a place to dwell with God. The focus of this text is wrongly applied to the "rooms" because of the frequent translation, "mansions." The focus of this text is not merely the place but the person; as Jesus said, each Christian will dwell in *my Father's* house." The good news is not fully manifest at Christmas, when God came to us and dwells with us, but at the new creation when we are taken to God and dwell with him.

14:2b "If it were not so, would I tell you that I am going to prepare a place for you?" (εἰ δὲ μή, εἶπον ἂν ὑμῖν ὅτι πορεύομαι ἑτοιμάσαι τόπον ὑμῖν;). After offering such powerful hope, the phrase that follows in the text of v. 2 is difficult to explain with certainty.[10] The aorist verb "I tell" (εἶπον) could have been translated as referring to a time in the past when Jesus had already spoken about such things, but Jesus never explicitly made such a statement up

to this point in the Gospel. There is a growing consensus, however, that Greek tense does not technically refer to the time of an action. Although it is common to assume that an aorist verb refers to a past-time event, the verbal aspect in this context allows this verb to speak for a present action (i.e., the dramatic aorist).[11] There is a clear and related example of this use of the aorist in 13:31, where Jesus declares with two aorist-tense verbs: "Now (Νῦν) the Son of Man *is glorified* (ἐδοξάσθη), and God *is glorified* (ἐδοξάσθη) in him." Thus, Jesus here asks a question not in reference to a previous teaching (even an implicit one) but as a way of reinforcing and substantiating the statement he just made.[12]

It is significant that Jesus claims to be going "to prepare a place" (ἑτοιμάσαι τόπον) for his disciples. Some interpreters find this statement awkward. If there are already "many rooms," why is there need for preparation? Jesus is not merely going to prepare a place, for the "going" is itself the preparation. The term "going" has become a technical term in the Gospel for the final journey of the mission of the Son. The cross, resurrection, and ascension to the Father *is* the preparation, the provision of permanent dwelling with God.[13] That is how Jesus is never fully departing, for his going is for the purpose of fellowship and communion with God — *eternal* life. That is also why the discourse proper must be viewed as encouraging. This is not to deny a real (i.e., in space and time) "place" (τόπον) that will be occupied by the people of God or to minimize the physical place as anything other than an indisputable and extremely important fact.[14]

---

9. Robert H. Gundry, " 'In my Father's House are many Μοναί' (John 14:2)," *ZNW* 58 (1967): 68–72 (70).

10. Part of the difficulty can be laid at the feet of textual criticism. See Brown, *John*, 2:619–20. Cf. Metzger, *Textual Commentary*, 206.

11. Porter, *Verbal Aspect*, 239. See also Porter, *Idioms*, 20–49.

12. Cf. Bultmann, *John*, 601.

13. Cf. Carson, *John*, 489.

14. The term "place" almost becomes a technical term in the Gospel, appearing at key moments in the narrative in a manner than serves to express significant aspects of the cosmological reality of the person and work of Jesus (e.g., 4:20; 11:48). Cf. James McCaffrey, *The House with Many Rooms: The Temple Theme in Jn. 14, 2–3* (Rome: Biblical Institute Press, 1988), 37–38, 98–109, 185–92.

Rather, it is to say that the "place" is not an end in itself but a symptomatic expression of the reality of life in and with God (see comments on vv. 5–7). Just as the Word was "in the beginning," so shall we be in the end "with God" (1:1).

14:3 "And if I go and prepare a place for you, I will come again and take you with me, in order that where I am you also may be" (καὶ ἐὰν πορευθῶ καὶ ἑτοιμάσω τόπον ὑμῖν, πάλιν ἔρχομαι καὶ παραλήμψομαι ὑμᾶς πρὸς ἐμαυτόν, ἵνα ὅπου εἰμὶ ἐγὼ καὶ ὑμεῖς ἦτε). Jesus presses the logic of his encouragement even further by drawing the following conclusion: his departure is intended to provide a departure for his disciples as well. The third-class condition (ἐὰν plus the subjunctive) is best understood to refer to certain fulfillment.[15] The certainty of Jesus's purposeful departure — the death, resurrection, and ascension to the Father — serves as a guarantee of his return for his disciples, the people of God. Just as certainly and physically as Jesus came to the world, he will come again. And when he comes again, he will "take" or "receive" (παραλήμψομαι) his disciples for this one purpose (denoted by the telic use of ἵνα): that they "may be" (ἦτε) where "I am" (εἰμὶ ἐγὼ). The emphatic "I am," one of several informal "I am" statements (see comments on 6:35), is intended to magnify God as the *place* of dwelling. In a real way, God's ultimate purpose is for us to "be" with the one who simply "is."

Jesus's exhortation to believe and hope-filled encouragement is the groundwork for the doctrine of eschatology.[16] But the Gospel's depiction of this eschatology has two important aspects.[17] First, this is the clearest example of a statement by Jesus regarding his second coming in all four Gospels. Jesus declares here the truth that the church has long proclaimed regarding the return of Christ. Jesus is promising the disciples that he, the Good Shepherd, will come and gather his sheep (ch. 10). Since "the end" is safely grounded in the one who was "in the beginning" (1:1), we may "not let our heart be frightened" but "believe" in the purposeful plan of God (v. 1). This truth — eschatology — is not merely something for which we wait expectantly; it is also something for which we live purposefully.

Second, as much as this eschatological encouragement is future, its meaning is not contained by a future event, for it is grounded in the very personal presence of God. The promise of Jesus is not to leave them and wait for them at the other end but to come back to them, to receive them, and to take them to the place where he is.[18] This aspect of eschatology is significant, for it speaks not merely of the future (the end) but also of the present. Jesus really is speaking of a place — there is a "where" (ὅπου); yet the most important factor is when he speaks of his person — the "who." For the Christian this means that the entire ministry presence of Christ is eschatological, for eschatology properly understood is the manifest presence of Christ, from the incarnation to the new creation.[19] It is for this reason that Jesus will make clear in the discourse to follow that God is present even in his absence. For at this moment the disciples are not merely being informed about the "last things" but about living (eschatologically) in the new covenant.[20]

14:4 "And where I am going, you know the way" (καὶ ὅπου [ἐγὼ] ὑπάγω οἴδατε τὴν ὁδόν). The first

---

15. Cf. Wallace, *Greek Grammar*, 696–97.

16. A common interpretation of Jesus's statement denies a reference to a future coming and understands it to be referring to a "coming" to believers by means of the Spirit/Paraclete. While there is a strong "present" eschatology in this pericope (and the Gospel as whole), it is a mistake to deny a future reference.

17. See Beasley-Murray, *John*, 250–51.

18. Cf. Newbigin, *The Light Has Come*, 179.

19. See Dodd, *Interpretation*, 405.

20. The discussion among interpreters of the Gospel of John regarding future and realized eschatology creates a false dichotomy.

section of this pericope (vv. 1 – 4) is concluded by a final exhortation by Jesus. To reinforce their belief in God and him (v. 1), Jesus reinforces what they already know: the "where" (ὅπου) and "the way" (τὴν ὁδόν). The disciples should know that the place where Jesus is "going" is the cross (and resurrection/ascension). The implication of Jesus's statement is that the "where" (the cross) is also "the way," or the "where" and "the way" are mutually explanatory.[21] Just as Jesus has preparatory work to do to accomplish his purposes, so here he prepares his disciples, involving them in the process that not only serves them but includes them. As Augustine explains, "He is in a certain sense preparing the dwellings by preparing those who are to dwell in them."[22] Ultimately, "the way" (τὴν ὁδόν) contains a necessary ambiguity (of which the readers, not the disciples, should be aware) in that it addresses not a literal road or path or even a set of directions but a (metaphorical) "way" of life, a certain kind of life (see comments on 12:26), or more fully, the goal of human life.[23]

14:5 Thomas said to him, "Lord, we do not know where you are going. How are we able to know the way?" (Λέγει αὐτῷ Θωμᾶς, Κύριε, οὐκ οἴδαμεν ποῦ ὑπάγεις· πῶς δυνάμεθα τὴν ὁδὸν εἰδέναι;). A transition to the second section of the pericope (vv. 5 – 7) is provided and introduced by Thomas's question, who claims not to know either the "where" or "the way." The interrelation between them discussed above (v. 4) demands that knowledge of the one is knowledge of the other; thus, Thomas's dual confusion is truly only a single, even if multifaceted, confusion. That is why Jesus's answer can be a single, multifaceted answer (v. 6). Hoskyns is right to suggest that the narrator does not introduce

this brief dialogue with Thomas simply to record a conversation but "to extract a precise statement of that faith," that "way"/kind/goal of life by which the disciples have access to God.[24]

14:6 Jesus said to him, "I am the way and the truth and the life. No one comes to the Father except through me" (λέγει αὐτῷ ὁ Ἰησοῦς, Ἐγώ εἰμι ἡ ὁδὸς καὶ ἡ ἀλήθεια καὶ ἡ ζωή· οὐδεὶς ἔρχεται πρὸς τὸν πατέρα εἰ μὴ δι' ἐμοῦ). Thomas's question provides the opportunity for Jesus to make one of the most well-known statements in all Scripture. Jesus defines exactly what the "the way" is, and it is not *what* but *who*. Jesus is the way. But Jesus does not just link the way to himself, but also the truth and the life — a threefold expression of his person and work. This is the sixth of seven formal "I am" statements in the Gospel, each containing "I am" (Ἐγώ εἰμι) and a predicate (see comments on 6:35). These seven formal "I am" statements are emphatic descriptions of the person and ministry of Jesus and cumulatively form a detailed picture of Jesus Christ.

It is difficult to define with precision the meaning of this threefold "I am" statement. Noting the contextual focus on "the way," some have suggested that "the way" is the key term, with the other two nouns standing in apposition to explain the first noun.[25] But as much as "the way" has been the leading term thus far in the pericope, in the "I am" statement all three nouns are syntactically coordinated into a multifaceted unity. The development is logical. Jesus had been giving a definition of "the way" that was multifaceted and complex and which found its meaning in his person and work. Thomas's question, then, is not simply about an abstract "way" but about Jesus. Thus Jesus answers not merely about a place or direction but about

21. Cf. Bultmann, *John*, 603.
22. Augustine, *John*, 68.2.323.
23. Cf. Michaels, *John*, 773; Hoskyns, *Fourth Gospel*, 454.
24. Hoskyns, *Fourth Gospel*, 454.

25. See, for example, Ignace de La Potterie, *La Vérité dans Saint Jean*, 2 vols. (Rome: Pontifical Biblical Institute, 1977), 2:254 – 55; Barrett, *John*, 458; Michaels, *John*, 775.

his person. For this reason the definition of each of these nouns — way, truth, life — cannot be left to abstraction but must be grounded directly in Jesus. The entire Gospel is needed to explain Jesus, for these three nouns speak in a language that is rooted more in foreground (Christology) than background (abstract concepts) and are reflective of the grand subject matter of Scripture.[26]

This does not mean, however, that we cannot give any definition to this threefold "I am" statement. It simply means that our definition must guard against truncating or diluting the fullness of the object in view. It also means that the terms cannot be defined in abstraction, for they are cumulatively interdependent and interrelated and present concretely in Jesus who is simultaneously the way, the truth, and the life.[27] With this in mind we can offer a summary of this threefold "I am" statement: as "the way," Jesus is the *mode*; as "the truth," Jesus is the *reality*; as "the life," Jesus is the *source*.

Jesus is "the way" in that he is the (only) *mode* by which the Christian existence and participation in God are made possible and accessible. Jesus fulfills this by means of his death, resurrection, and ascension to the Father. While "the way" for Jesus is quite literal and physical — entailing suffering and death — for the Christian, as we discussed above (v. 4), "the way" is less a road or path and more a "way of life," a goal, or even the mode in which the Christian now functions.[28]

Jesus is "the truth" in that he is the *reality* through which Christian existence and participation in God are confirmed and find their meaning. Jesus fulfills this by embodying the supreme revelation. Jesus is the standard for what is real in this world and true about God, for he is the one who reveals God (1:18). Jesus, the Son of God, says and

does exclusively what the Father has given him to say and do (5:19; 8:29). He is ultimately the perfect expression of God (1:14). For this reason Jesus is the plumb line for all things — seen and unseen, the lens through which the world is to be interpreted and by which it must be judged. He is the gracious extension of light (reality) into a world confined by darkness (distortion).

Jesus is "the life" in that he is the *source* through which Christian existence and participation in God are founded and given their origin. Jesus fulfills this by being the supplier of life and existence, the Creator of all living things — without whom "not one thing came into existence that has been made" (1:3). Jesus is the beginning and was "with God" in the beginning and is God, the second person of the Trinity. Jesus is life itself (1:4), is the one who has life in himself (5:26), is the one who defines life even over death, for Jesus is "the resurrection and the life" (11:25). Since Jesus is "the life," all the dichotomies are broken that have been created between life and death, this life and the life to come, the seen and the unseen.

Jesus destroys the wall that divides humanity from God (the way), denies the falsehood that distorts humanity in relation to God (the truth), and defeats the last and greatest enemy of humanity, death (the life).[29] He is the totality of what God has done, is doing, and will do. This is why Jesus concludes his "I am" statement with such an exclusive summary: "No one comes to the Father except through me" (οὐδεὶς ἔρχεται πρὸς τὸν πατέρα εἰ μὴ δι᾿ ἐμοῦ).[30] This may be the most disturbing claim in all Scripture, and to some this statement is problematic. But as Koester explains, " 'Except' is like a window that lets light into a closed room.... Rather than restricting access to God the word 'except' in-

---

26. Attempts to find a single background prooftext from the OT are doomed to fail, not merely for exegetical reasons but for theological reasons.

27. Hoskyns, *Fourth Gospel*, 455.

28. Cf. Luther, *John*, 24:37.

29. Cf. Calvin, *John 11 – 21*, 76.

30. Schnackenburg calls it "a precise and absolute expression" of the previous statement (*John*, 3:65).

dicates access to God."[31] When Jesus declares that he is "the way and the truth and the life," he offers to humanity — every single person — God's gift to the world. This is the epitome of "good news" and is the opposite of being restrictive or exclusive, for it is true freedom (8:36).

14:7 "If you have known me, you will know my Father also. From now on you know him and have seen him" (εἰ ἐγνώκατέ με, καὶ τὸν πατέρα μου γνώσεσθε· καὶ ἀπ᾽ ἄρτι γινώσκετε αὐτὸν καὶ ἑωράκατε αὐτόν). Jesus concludes his formal "I am" statement with a promise and an invitation.[32] The conditional statement is intended to connect Jesus's person and work with the Father. The disciples' knowledge of the Father in the future is directly connected to their experience of and relationship to Jesus in the present. This is why Jesus commands them to believe not only in him but also in God (v. 1), for the two persons, the Father and the Son, form a single object of faith — God.

Here Jesus does not merely explain to the disciples (via Thomas's question) what they should have known about the Father (and therefore the Son) but also exhorts them to respond — "from now on" (ἀπ᾽ ἄρτι) — to what they now know and have seen of the Father in the person and work of the Son.[33] Everything must be different "from now on," for the revelation of God has been dramatically declared by the Word-become-flesh. The prologue announced that Jesus would reveal the Father (1:18), and "now" the disciples have been told in the most explicit terms that when they see Jesus they are seeing God. "In short, He both exists unchangeably in Himself and inseparably in the

Father."[34] And it is into this perfect union that the Son and the Father (by the Spirit) invite the disciples to share and coexist; the children of God with the unique Son and the Father (1:12, 14, 18). This is "the way and the truth and the life" (v. 6).

14:8 Philip said to him, "Lord, show the Father to us, and it will be sufficient for us" (λέγει αὐτῷ Φίλιππος, Κύριε, δεῖξον ἡμῖν τὸν πατέρα, καὶ ἀρκεῖ ἡμῖν). A transition to the third section of the pericope (vv. 8–14) is introduced by another question, this time from Philip, who correctly interprets in Jesus's statement a connection between "seeing" the Father and the work of Jesus, but in a manner that inappropriately disassociates the Father from the person of Jesus. Jesus is about to strongly rebuke this confusion, for it not only misunderstands how the children of God "see" the Father but more importantly how the children of God relate to the Father through his unique Son, Jesus Christ. In this final section of the pericope, Jesus addresses these confusions. In vv. 9–11 Jesus will rebuke and correct Philip's misunderstanding by showing the inherent unity between the person of the Father and the person of the Son, and in vv. 12–14 Jesus will show even further the inherent connection that now exists between the work of the Father and Son and the work of the children of God.

It is important to note the exact words Philip uses in the question he addresses to Jesus. Speaking on behalf of the disciples as a whole, Philip requests that Jesus "show the Father to us" (δεῖξον ἡμῖν τὸν πατέρα). Was he expecting some theophany comparable to what Moses saw when he similarly requested of God, "Show me your glory" (Exod 33:18)?[35] As

---

31. Craig R. Koester, "Jesus as the Way to the Father in Johannine Theology (John 14:6)," in *Theology and Christology in the Fourth Gospel*, 117–33 (125).

32. There is a difficult textual variant that adjusts the verse so that it becomes a rebuke instead of a promise. See Metzger, *Textual Commentary*, 207.

33. See Hoskyns, *Fourth Gospel*, 455.

34. Augustine, *John*, 70.1.326.

35. Schnackenburg, *John*, 3:68.

Jesus is about to declare, Philip's truncated understanding of "seeing" the Father stifles not only his view of Jesus but also his understanding of Christian existence. Not only does Philip misunderstand how Jesus "shows" the Father but also what a "sufficient" experience of the Father truly is.[36] Philip's question then, especially coming from one who had been with Jesus from the beginning (see 1:43 – 46), reveals not only a limited perspective of Jesus but also a limited perspective of the Christian life.

14:9 Jesus said to him, "I have been with you for so long a time and you do not know me, do you, Philip? The one who has seen me has seen the Father. How can you say, 'Show me the Father?'" (λέγει αὐτῷ ὁ Ἰησοῦς, Τοσούτῳ χρόνῳ μεθ' ὑμῶν εἰμι καὶ οὐκ ἔγνωκάς με, Φίλιππε; ὁ ἑωρακὼς ἐμὲ ἑώρακεν τὸν πατέρα· πῶς σὺ λέγεις, Δεῖξον ἡμῖν τὸν πατέρα;). Jesus responds to Philip's statement with a question that serves as a rebuke. The form of the Greek negation "not" (οὐκ) signals that the question expects an affirmative answer. The question could be translated more like a statement: "I have been with you for so long a time and *still* you do not know me!" The rebuke and the explicit mention of their participation with Jesus "for so long a time" (Τοσούτῳ χρόνῳ) suggests that Philip — and all the disciples — should have known who he was and therefore the one he represents (cf. 1:18). Jesus asks Philip not one rebuking question but two, with the second question pressing further the assumption that Philip should have "known" the connection between Jesus and the Father from his participation "with" (μεθ') Jesus during his earthly ministry.

These two rebuking questions serve as a frame around the central statement by Jesus that summarizes the subject matter of his ministry: "The one who has seen me has seen the Father" (ὁ ἑωρακὼς ἐμὲ ἑώρακεν τὸν πατέρα). Jesus has spoken di-

rectly of this before (see comments on 12:45; cf. 13:20). Jesus is the ultimate expression of God and the visible manifestation of God (1:18). The prologue has already announced such a relationship (see comments on 1:1, 14), and the entire Gospel has depicted the ministry of the Trinitarian God in the person of Jesus Christ in the world. This is why Philip's vision for what was "sufficient" was so insufficient, for life "with him" is "the vision of God."[37] In the person of Jesus, the Father could not have been more fully made known or shown.

14:10 "You believe that I am in the Father and the Father is in me, do you not? The words that I speak to you I do not speak on my own, but the Father who abides in me does his works" (οὐ πιστεύεις ὅτι ἐγὼ ἐν τῷ πατρὶ καὶ ὁ πατὴρ ἐν ἐμοί ἐστιν; τὰ ῥήματα ἃ ἐγὼ λαλῶ ὑμῖν ἀπ' ἐμαυτοῦ οὐ λαλῶ· ὁ δὲ πατὴρ ἐν ἐμοὶ μένων ποιεῖ τὰ ἔργα αὐτοῦ). Jesus now presses Philip and by implication the other disciples (and the readers) with a question that again assumes an affirmative answer. The question is a restatement of the same subject matter: "I am in the Father and the Father is in me" (ἐγὼ ἐν τῷ πατρὶ καὶ ὁ πατὴρ ἐν ἐμοί ἐστιν). The statement in v. 9 emphasized the manifestation of the Father by the Son, whereas here the emphasis is centered upon the relational unity between the Father and the Son.

The twofold use of the preposition "in" (ἐν) speaks unavoidably of the mutuality of the Father and the Son, rooted in what the church has long expressed by its Trinitarian theology.[38] As much as there is a distinction in person between the Father and the Son, there is a clear and essential functional overlap, commonality, and unity. The language here even speaks of a mutual indwelling or mutual interpenetration of the Father and Son, which although might be taken to refer to the

---

36. See Gail R. O'Day, "'Show Us the Father, and We Will Be Satisfied' (John 14:8)," *Semeia* 85 (1999): 11 – 17 (16).

37. Hoskyns, *Fourth Gospel*, 455.
38. See Augustine, *John*, 71.2.328.

divine essence is clearly referring to the mode of revelation, for the Father has revealed himself "in" Jesus.[39] Both the words of the Word as well as his actions reflect the abiding presence of the Father. Everything Jesus *is*, has *said*, and has *done* is itself also an expression not only *of* or *about* the Father but even *by* the Father. While we can differentiate the persons of the Father and the Son, the Father and the Son maintain a functional inseparability through the person and work of the Son.

14:11 "Believe me that I am in the Father and the Father is in me. But if not, believe because of the works themselves" (πιστεύετέ μοι ὅτι ἐγὼ ἐν τῷ πατρὶ καὶ ὁ πατὴρ ἐν ἐμοί· εἰ δὲ μή, διὰ τὰ ἔργα αὐτὰ πιστεύετε). Jesus concludes his focus on the inherent unity of the Father and the Son (vv. 9 – 11) by commanding belief in this unified presence and activity of the Father and the Son. The imperative verb "believe" (πιστεύετέ) demands that Christians submit to this truth, and the subordinating conjunction "that" (ὅτι) stresses that the belief be focused not just on a person but on the proposition of the functional unity of the Father and the Son.[40] That is, Christian belief is located not only in the person of the Son but also in the message of the Son.

Jesus suggests the "works" (ἔργα) of God as an alternate object of belief beyond the word of God. In this Gospel the "works" of Jesus act as "signs" (see comments on 2:11). The works of Jesus point beyond themselves to their true subject matter, the person and work of God made known through Jesus Christ. Both the words and works of Jesus reveal who he is — who God is — and serve as witnesses for belief in God. The works make clear that the Son is "in the Father and the Father is in" him, showing concretely what the prologue announced about the unseen (cf. 5:36; 10:25, 38).

14:12 "Truly, truly I say to you, the one who believes in me, the works that I do he will also do, and greater works than these he will do, because I am going to the Father" (ἀμὴν ἀμὴν λέγω ὑμῖν, ὁ πιστεύων εἰς ἐμὲ τὰ ἔργα ἃ ἐγὼ ποιῶ κἀκεῖνος ποιήσει, καὶ μείζονα τούτων ποιήσει, ὅτι ἐγὼ πρὸς τὸν πατέρα πορεύομαι). Beginning with an authoritative preface (see comments on 1:51), Jesus transitions from the works of the Son of God to the works of the children of God (vv. 12 – 14). Jesus states clearly that "the works that I do he will also do" (τὰ ἔργα ἃ ἐγὼ ποιῶ κἀκεῖνος ποιήσει). This statement is dependent on their belief in Jesus, but it transitions the believer from being a witness of to being a participant in the works of God.[41] In this way Jesus makes a promise to the disciples that is rooted in their position "in Christ" (to use the apostle Paul's terminology). A comparison between the Father-Son and the Son-children is important to note. The Father and Son are mutually indwelling and interpenetrated, whereas the children of God are dependent on the Son. Moreover, the Father and Son share the same essence and function, whereas the children and the Son only share the same function. Faith in Christ is not merely a passive act, it is also active; it is to become a participant in the power and mission of God and in some way to share in the ministry of God through Christ.

Jesus adds to the promise a statement that has raised interpretive confusion: "And greater works than these he will do" (καὶ μείζονα τούτων ποιήσει). From early on in the early church, the "greater works" have been interpreted as the missionary success of the disciples, often including accompanying miraculous works.[42] But certainly the children of God cannot be said to do "greater works"

---

39. Cf. Calvin, *John 11 – 21*, 78.
40. See Morris, *John*, 573.
41. See Bultmann, *John*, 611.

42. See Andreas J. Köstenberger, "The 'Greater Works' of the Believer according to John 14:12," *Did* 6 (1995): 36 – 45. Gordon D. Fee, "John 14:8 – 17," *ExpTim* 43 (1989): 170 – 74.

than the unique Son. The additional promise is enigmatic and must be handled with care, for too often it has been inappropriately used in a manner that actually compares the works of Jesus with the works of believers, pitting them against one another. The clear emphasis of the pericope thus far has been the cooperation and unity first between the Father and the Son and now between the Son and believers. To impose at this juncture a point of comparison would be to misunderstand the statement in a very clear context. Whatever is greater about the works of believers, it is not in spite of Christ but because of him — belief "in me."

The meaning of "greater works" is provided by the statement that immediately follows: "Because I am going to the Father" (ὅτι ἐγὼ πρὸς τὸν πατέρα πορεύομαι). Jesus has already spoken of his departure (cf. 13:31–38), which is the deliberate inauguration of the new mode of existence for the believers, the moment in which the believers themselves are transformed in Jesus by the Spirit (see comments on 13:33). Thus, by specifically mentioning his departure here, Jesus does not in any way separate himself from these "greater works." In fact, as the immediate context has dictated, it is only *in* him and *through* him that these works find their source and power. Thus the comparison was never between the works of Jesus and the works of the disciples, but between the preglorification works of Jesus and the postglorification works of Jesus, with the disciples simply participating in the works of the risen and exalted Lord.

This interpretation is assisted by an earlier statement in the Gospel in which the Father, who is already working through the Son, will show him "works greater than these" (see comments on 5:20; cf. 1:50; 5:22–27). These "greater works" are connected to the time when Jesus is established and ruling as "the Son of Man" — note the comment made to Nathaniel in 1:50: "You shall see *greater things than these*" (emphasis added).[43] The reader should note the remarkable promise made here. They are invited — no, commissioned (cf. Matt 28:18–20) — to participate in the ongoing and powerful ministry of God the Father, the exalted Christ, and the indwelling Holy Spirit. The ministry of the church is truly the work of God in the world.[44]

14:13 "And whatever you ask in my name I will do this, so that the Father may be glorified in the Son" (καὶ ὅ τι ἂν αἰτήσητε ἐν τῷ ὀνόματί μου τοῦτο ποιήσω, ἵνα δοξασθῇ ὁ πατὴρ ἐν τῷ υἱῷ). The necessary connection between Jesus and the disciples in v. 12 is just as necessary here. Jesus continues to describe the "greater works" of believers by describing in more detail the outworking of the power of life and ministry in the era of the exalted Christ. The phrase "whatever you ask in my name" (ὅ τι ἂν αἰτήσητε ἐν τῷ ὀνόματί μου), like the "greater works" statement discussed above, is wrongly interpreted if disassociated from Jesus, as if the one "praying" is the source and the primary agent giving direction and Jesus is the mere resource or supplier and the secondary, dependent agent. Rather, the statement makes two things explicit.

First, the believer is the one doing the "asking," that is, placing himself beneath the primary agency of God. In this sense, the disciple is praying as a "representative" of Jesus,[45] seeking to do what he would be doing if he were present — no, what he *is* doing in and through his disciples by means of his exalted presence through the Spirit, in the same way that the Father *is* working in and through Jesus (v. 10).

43. See Beasley-Murray, *John*, 255. Cf. Christian Dietzfelbinger, "Die Größeren Werke (Joh. 14. 12 f.)," *NTS* 35 (1989): 27–47.

44. Hoskyns, *Fourth Gospel*, 457.
45. Barrett, *John*, 460.

Second, the believer is asking "in my name" (ἐν τῷ ὀνόματί μου), that is, by means of the authority that resides and belongs to Jesus alone. Just as the Father has given authority to the Son, so the disciples of Jesus work not by means of their own authority but under the authority of the Son (see 1:12; 5:27). Since the concept of a "name" in the ancient world is the character of a person (see comments on 1:12), by asking in the name of Jesus the disciples are seeking not themselves but Christ, and their "prayer is to be in accordance with all that that name stands for."[46] In fact, one might say that to ask in the name of Jesus is to deny one's own person and adopt the character of another person — in this case, the Son of God. Thus, such prayer is not done independent of God but is rooted in the power of God and the desires of God, which God will direct through us by his Spirit (cf. 16:13).

This participation of the believer in the life and ministry of the exalted Christ is for one overriding purpose: "So that the Father may be glorified in the Son" (ἵνα δοξασθῇ ὁ πατὴρ ἐν τῷ υἱῷ). Just as

the work of the Father is inextricably intertwined with the Son, so also is the "glory" which is *for* the Father and *in* the Son; the glory is innate to their unity in relation to the godhead but different in relation to their distinct persons.[47] "Glory" means "honor as enhancement or recognition of status or performance."[48] It is the opposite of self-effacement and humility. The identity of the believer — the disciple — is minimized, whereas the identity of God is magnified.

14:14 "If you ask me anything in my name I will do it" (ἐάν τι αἰτήσητέ με ἐν τῷ ὀνόματί μου ἐγὼ ποιήσω). Jesus ends this pericope with a final statement that is intended to make certain or to guarantee the future works of the believers.[49] The prayers of God's workers are not just placed before him and not just asked in Jesus's name but are also, for all intents and purposes, already accomplished in the providential will of God. By this final statement Jesus holds himself accountable for the works of his disciples — that is how interconnected God is to the works of his disciples.

IN-DEPTH: Does God Give Us Whatever We Ask?

It is unfortunate that many use 14:13 – 14 (and 16:23) as an unconditional pledge that every believer's prayer, of whatever content, will be heard and answered by God. Yet the language must be understood in its immediate context. Two things can be stated in this regard. First, the point is not to suggest that the believer has a new and more powerful resource in God, but that Jesus is not withdrawing from them by his departure but in fact by means of his departure is even more present — and more powerfully so! Second, the kind of prayers believers should ask is also presented by this statement. They should pray in a manner befitting the *mission of God* (denoted by the "works" the believer will do in v. 12) and the *character of God* (denoted by the use of "in his name" in v. 13). Prayers expecting results outside of these parameters are not prayers at all but

---

46. Morris, *John*, 574.
47. Cf. Augustine, *John*, 73.4.333.
48. BDAG 257.
49. Cf. Bultmann, *John*, 612.

commands and are outside the bounds of the disciple of Jesus Christ. This final promise is not about the pursuit of self-seeking permission from God but is an invitation to participate in the fullness of life in God through Christ and by the Spirit.

When a Christian prays then, they are agreeing to trust not only in God's sovereign and authoritative *resources* but also in God's perfect and providential *results*. What makes the prayer Christian and not pagan is that God is not used to fulfill the desires of the person who prays, but rather the person who prays submits his or her will to both the power and purpose of God. A Christian prayer is a paradox in that it seeks from God what one simultaneously surrenders to God. Asking from God therefore is also a letting go. It is letting God be God over all things (Rom 11:36), even the things we want (or need) the most.

Theology in Application

In the second of eight sections of the farewell discourse, Jesus makes the first of six statements that explain, encourage, and exhort the disciples as they transition to the era of the new covenant, from life with Jesus to life "in Christ." Through this pericope the reader is exhorted to replace their fear with faith in Jesus, who is the work of God in the world, the one who not only enacts but *is* the way, the truth, and the life.

Faith not Fear

The very first thing Jesus addresses with his disciples in the discourse proper is their fear (v. 1). He commands their fear away, providing the Father and the Son as the more appropriate object of their focus and devotion. The same powerful and authoritative voice that spoke creation into existence now addresses his disciples. Jesus calls them to faith, not fear. But note that this replacement is only possible because Christ has taken our fear upon himself. The only comfort a person can receive is the one that comes from the cross. The reader, no less than the disciples, is to receive and respond to the same, ongoing admonition today to live by faith not fear.

Our Father's House

Heaven is a place (or at least a topic) that still fits comfortably in most of modern culture. Those with minimal religious interest will use the term as a concept for the afterlife, a happy place of peaceful dwelling for those who have died. In this pericope, however, the place about which Jesus speaks is entirely different. It is not a generic place beyond this one but a home, the very home of God the Father and the Son, who not only dwells there but prepares it for the children of God. This "house" belongs to

God and to those — only those — who believe in the Son. For this reason it is a glorious place, not because of us but because of God; it is a home God prepared for us, a home in which we may be with God. This is a cosmological home, the extension of God's grace from this temporal place into eternity.

The danger is that such common talk about a very uncommon thing will secularize it — transfer it from sacred to civil possession, making the dwelling of God a common depiction in cartoons, movies, and common speech — places in which it does not fit or make sense. No, the place about which Jesus speaks is "my Father's house." So we must speak of it as sacred, since God himself not only prepared it with his own hands but paid our debt fully in order to give us access to it. This place, therefore, cannot be secularized, for it is not a common possession. It is a place of grace, the holy of holies, the new creation, our true home. The church needs to recover this sacred place, not only as a future place but as a present hope that guides and directs the manner of our current dwelling.

The Blessing and Burden of John 14:6

Jesus is everything! As the way-truth-life, Jesus is the mode-reality-source of all things for all people. Jesus is the totality of what God has done, is doing, and will do; there is nothing of value in existence that does not come from or move toward Jesus Christ. This is the blessing, the promise of hope for those who believe in Jesus.

The antithesis of this blessing is a corresponding burden. Since Jesus is everything, those who do not have him have nothing. There is no middle ground or position. If this appears exclusive, it is; otherwise Christ would be excluded — and this cannot be! For too long the so-called problem of Christian exclusivism has placed humanity at the center. This is devastating not only to humanity but also to Christ. Christian grace is not an easy grace but an impossible grace which Christ has mediated to us by his person and work. If it is exclusive, it is because it is his alone to give. For this reason it can be inclusive, not without Christ but through him — but him alone, since it remains an impossible grace. The Gospel of John is inclusive in that it wants everyone to believe (20:31), but it is simultaneously exclusive in that it knows that this belief must be mediated through Christ. Jesus is the perfect combination of exclusivity and inclusivity, making impossible grace accessible to every possible person.

The Works of God

This pericope makes an important connection between the work of Christ and the work of the Father (v. 10). Without denying the need to distinguish them based upon an appropriate understanding of the doctrine of the Trinity, the Father and the Son are inseparable in their expression through the work of the Son. But there is more. The "work" of God is also inseparable from the "work" to be done by

Christians (v. 12) — and this is the way it is supposed to be, for Jesus's departure is in fact an intentional continuation of the same work of God. As we discussed above, Jesus magnifies the work to come (i.e., they are "greater works") because the works to come, those that include those who believe, are the works of the risen and exalted Lord in the new era of the new covenant.

O church, you are participating in the power of the risen and exalted Lord and the works of God. You are called to facilitate the work of the kingdom of God, bestowing the blessings of God to the nations by the empowering Spirit of God. You have been commissioned by God to do the work of God in the world. Be faithful!

Christian Prayer

Prayer is not best described as accessing God but as being accessed by God. It is not about power but about submission. It is not about requesting but about submitting. Because the work of God never ceases to be his work, our access to the work of God, as real and effective as it is, is also always secondary. It is significant that the first thing Jesus discusses after articulating the Christian's work of God is prayer (vv. 13 – 14). Prayer may be described as the primary mode of the Christian and their participation in the work of God. That is why the apostle Paul can command that prayer never cease (1 Thess 5:17), for it is both the expression of Christian work and the metaphor for that work. It is passive submission to God in the person of Christ and active service for God in the mission of God. Prayer therefore is the lifeblood of Christian existence, even human existence, and the most properly basic Christian activity.

John 14:15 – 31

Literary Context

This pericope is the third of eight sections of the farewell discourse. Surrounded by a prologue (13:31 – 38) and an epilogue (16:25 – 33), the farewell discourse can be divided into six significant and developing thematic statements by Jesus, with each offering comfort and consolation for the disciples (and the reader) from Jesus, befitting the nature of a farewell discourse (see comments before 13:1). These six statements within the farewell discourse offer one long exhortation to stay the course and encouragement that their efforts will be matched by the Trinitarian God himself. After offering himself to the disciples in the previous pericope, in the second of these six statements Jesus offers the Holy Spirit. Jesus begins to articulate the Christian life after his departure and speaks about living in obedience to the commandments of God in a fallen world that opposes God and is ruled by a different ruler. The disciples — and the readers — are exhorted to begin living in Christ by the Spirit, participating in the mission of God after having received from Christ the peace of God.

VII. The Farewell Discourse (13:1 – 17:26)

    A. Introduction: The Love of Jesus (13:1 – 30)

        1. Jesus and the Washing of His Disciples' Feet (13:1 – 20)

        2. Jesus Announces His Betrayal (13:21 – 30)

    B. The Farewell Discourse (13:31 – 16:33)

        1. Prologue: Glory, Departure, and Love (13:31 – 38)

        2. I Am the Way and the Truth and the Life (14:1 – 14)

➡   **3. I Will Give You the Paraclete (14:15 – 31)**

        4. I Am the True Vine (15:1 – 17)

        5. I Have Also Experienced the Hate of the World (15:18 – 27)

        6. I Will Empower You by the Paraclete (16:1 – 15)

        7. I Will Turn Your Grief into Joy (16:16 – 24)

        8. Epilogue: Speaking Plainly, Departure, and Peace (16:25 – 33)

    C. Conclusion: The Prayer of Jesus (17:1 – 26)

Main Idea

The Christian life is participation in God through Christ and in the Spirit, the Paraclete who guides the believer as the indwelling and eternal presence of God.

Translation

John 14:15–31

	Section #3 of "Farewell Discourse"	
15a	Condition	*"If you love me,*
b	Inference	*you will keep my commandments.*
16a	Assertion	*And I will ask the Father*
b	Result	*and he will give to you*
c	Gift: Character Entrance	*another Paraclete*
d	Purpose	*in order that he will be with you forever.*
17a	Identification of 16c	*The Spirit*
b	Objective Genitive (cf. 14:6)	*of truth,*
c	Description	*which the world is not able to receive,*
d	Basis	*because it does not see or*
e		*know him.*
f	Contrast/Premise of 18	*You know him,*
g	Basis	*because he remains beside you and*
h		*is in you.*
18a	Implicit Inference #1	*I will not leave you as orphans;*
b	Implicit Inference #2	*I am coming to you.*
19a	Time	*After a little while*
b	Assertion	*the world will no longer see me,*
c	Contrast	*but you will see me,*
d	Basis	*because I live you also will live.*
20a	Time/Event	*On that day*
b	Progression of Indwelling #1	*you will know that I am in my Father and*
c	Progression of Indwelling #2	*you are in me and*
d	Progression of Indwelling #3	*I am in you.*
21a	Description (Condition)	*The one who has my commandments and*
b		*keeps them,*
c	Inferential Identification	*this is the one who loves me.*
d	Progression #1	*And the one who loves me will be loved by my Father,*
e	Progression #2	*and I will love him*
f	Progression #3	*and I will reveal myself to him."*
22a	Character Entrance	**Judas …**
b	Description	(not Iscariot)
c	Response	**… said to him,**

d	Address	*"Lord,*
e	Question	*what has happened that you intend to reveal yourself to us and*
f		*not to the world?"*
23a	Response	**Jesus answered and said to him,**
b	Relative Condition	*"If anyone loves me*
c	Progressive Inference #1	*he will keep my word,*
d	Progressive Inference #2	*and my Father will love him,*
e	Progressive Inference #3	*and we will come to him*
f	Progressive Inference #4	*and we will make a dwelling place beside him.*
24a	Contrast	*The one who does not love me …*
b	Inference	*… will not keep my word.*
c	Assertion	*The word …*
d	Description	*that you are hearing*
e	Source	*… is not mine, but*
f	Contrast	*belongs to the one who sent me,*
g	Identification	*the Father.*
25a	Assertion	*I have spoken these things to you*
b	Presence	*while I remain with you.*
		But
26a	Contrasting Presence	*the Paraclete,*
b	Identification	*the Holy Spirit,*
c	Source #1	*whom the Father will send*
d	Source #2	*in my name,*
e	Function #1	*he will teach you all things and*
f	Function #2	*remind you of all the things*
g	Description	*that I said to you.*
27a	Assurance	*Peace I leave with you;*
b	Emphatic Assurance	*my peace I give to you.*
c	Assertion	*I do not give to you*
d	Contrast	*as the world gives.*
e	Exhortation #1	*Do not let your heart be troubled*
f	Exhortation #2	*nor let it be fearful.*
28a	Restatement (Premise of 28d)	*You heard that I said to you,*
b		*'I am going*
c		*and I am coming to you.'*
d	Condition	*If you loved me*
e	Inferential Exhortation	*you would have rejoiced that I am going to the Father,*
f	Basis	*because the Father is greater than I.*
29a	Assertion	*And now I have told you,*
b	Event	*before it happens*
c	Intended Result	*so that …*
d	Temporal Circumstance	*when it does happen,*
e		*… you may believe.*

Continued on next page.

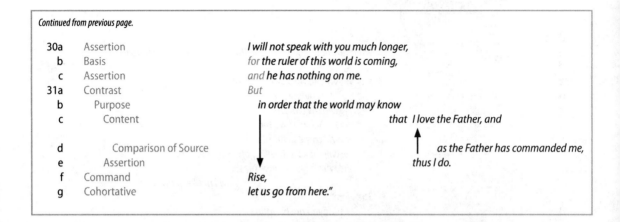

Structure and Literary Form

As the third of eight sections of the farewell discourse, this pericope is part of the fourth (and longest) substantial monologue in the narrative proper. A monologue (see Introduction) is similar to a dialogue in that it is set in the context of an engagement and conflict, but rather than engaging point-for-point it allows for a lengthy argument. A monologue can contain elements of rhetoric, challenge, and conflict, but it does so in a sustained presentation.

This pericope is the second of six statements by Jesus intending to exhort and encourage his disciples. While all of 14:1 – 31 works together (see comments on 14:27 – 29), the warrant for this section is not only the common subject matter throughout — the combination of love and obedience (vv. 15, 21, 23, 31) — but also the way in which the subject manner forms an *inclusio* that frames the entire section (vv. 15, 31). In this second statement, Jesus introduces the Holy Spirit to his disciples and prepares them to participate in God and in their Christian vocation.

Exegetical Outline

➡ **3. I Will Give You the Paraclete (14:15 – 31)**
  a. An Introduction to "Another Paraclete" (vv.15 – 21)
  b. Participation with the Father and the Son in the Spirit (vv. 22 – 24)
  c. The Peace of Christ in the Spirit (vv. 25 – 31)

Explanation of the Text

Since this entire section of the Gospel and "the farewell discourse" proper are replete with interpretive issues, we refer the reader to the first pericope of this section where we provided an overview of the nature (genre), literary structure, and function of the farewell discourse (see comments before 13:1).

14:15 "If you love me, you will keep my commandments" (Ἐὰν ἀγαπᾶτέ με, τὰς ἐντολὰς τὰς ἐμὰς τηρήσετε). A new section in the farewell discourse begins as Jesus develops further what was introduced in the last section concerning the mutuality between God (Father and Son) and the disciples. In this first section of the pericope (vv. 15 – 21), Jesus introduces the common denominator in their mutuality, the promised Holy Spirit. But before introducing the Spirit, Jesus explains that the nature of the relationship between God and his children consists in love and obedience. The pericope starts and ends (v. 31) with this twofold expression of the disciple.

Fellowship and partnership with God is a relationship of love, not only God's love for us, but also our love for God. But love according to this Gospel is never a sentiment or an emotion; it is always moral.[1] Up to this point in the Gospel, the love of God for his people has been dominant; the disciple's love for God has hardly been mentioned,

and even then only implicitly (see 8:42). But from this point onward it becomes the explicit theme. The condition here is not intended to threaten the disciples to respond with love, but properly to define love.[2] The person who loves God "will keep my commandments" (τὰς ἐντολὰς τὰς ἐμὰς τηρήσετε). The Greek emphasizes the pronoun "my" ("*my* commandments") in a way that suggests that even in his physical absence Jesus is the standard for the life of the disciple, for he is the one who fulfilled the law (cf. 8:31). Love for God is always founded upon and directed toward Christ.

14:16 "And I will ask the Father and he will give to you another Paraclete in order that he will be with you forever" (κἀγὼ ἐρωτήσω τὸν πατέρα καὶ ἄλλον παράκλητον δώσει ὑμῖν ἵνα μεθ' ὑμῶν εἰς τὸν αἰῶνα ᾖ). The obedience God requires goes beyond human achievement, so Jesus promises the believer divine assistance. The functional mutuality between the believer and God that results in prayer (see comments on 14:13 – 14) is similarly present between God the Son and God the Father. Jesus "will ask the Father" (ἐρωτήσω τὸν πατέρα) and the Father "will give" (δώσει), befitting the perfect union between the Son's desire and the Father's will. The gift from the Father is "another Paraclete," introduced here for the first time.

IN-DEPTH: The Paraclete

The title "Paraclete" (παράκλητος), often with a definite article ("the Paraclete"; see e.g., 14:26), is difficult to translate and define. Common translations include the following: "Comforter" (KJV), "Advocate" (NRSV; NEB; JB; NIV), "Counselor" (HCS), and "Helper" (NASB; ESV). The term only occurs five times in the NT, all in the Johannine literature (14:16, 26; 15:26; 16:7; 1 John 2:1). Thus there is not

1. Barrett, *John*, 461.

2. Cf. Bultmann, *John*, 612.

much NT data with which to work. Even in the Greek corpus up to the first century but prior to the Fourth Gospel, the term only occurs in fifteen passages.[3] And the search for an equivalent Hebrew term is a lost cause.

While the term is understood to have varied meanings, the traditional scholarly opinion has been that the word has a legal or forensic emphasis; thus the corresponding translation of "advocate."[4] While scholars will admit that the Fourth Gospel does "qualify and add to this particular meaning, *advocate*, so that helper and teacher are functions that provide a further dimension to this forensic one," they are still forcing the term to have a single and determinable primary meaning.[5] Other proposals like the various translations listed above prefer a different but still single and determinable meaning. Indeed, there is a growing push against the legal or forensic definition of the term ("advocate"); the argument is that the same data is better interpreted not for a forensic but a prophetic role or office.[6] Quite simply, the term "has a general meaning which could appear in legal contexts," but even when it did it was used "as a supporter or sponsor."[7]

Translating the term therefore is quite difficult, for it will inevitably force the translator to choose one of the conceptual meanings discussed above as *the* primary meaning. However, the term has a general meaning that overlaps with several potential meanings and almost certainly encapsulates many of those meanings simultaneously, even if certain contexts tend to emphasize one meaning over another. For this reason we will not translate the term by giving it a more limited or selective English translation. Rather, we will simply translate (that is, transliterate) the term as "Paraclete" or "the Paraclete" (ὁ παράκλητος) to avoid limiting or muting aspects of the identity and multifaceted function of the Paraclete that are core to its (his) identity (on "impressions," see Introduction).[8] This approach also assumes that it is not a background that is best suited to determine the meaning of the word (e.g., religious-historical perspectives),[9] but a foreground—the doctrine of the Holy Spirit (see v. 26). The figure and function of the Holy Spirit cannot be defined by the history of religions, for it requires not only sensitivity to the Gospel's own multifaceted portrayal but also the foregrounding depiction from the rest of the biblical canon—the primary source for offering a conceptual interpretation of the Spirit's person and

3. Tricia Gates Brown, *Spirit in the Writings of John: Johannine Pneumatology in Social-Scientific Perspective*, JSNTSup 253 (London: T&T Clark, 2003), 170.

4. See Lincoln, *Truth on Trial*, 113 – 14.

5. Ibid., 114.

6. See BDAG 766, which does not even list "advocate" as a primary meaning of the term.

7. Kenneth Grayston, "The Meaning of PARAKLēTOS," *JSNT* 13 (1981): 67 – 82 (75).

8. Cf. Brown, *John*, 2:1137.

9. For a survey of potential religious backgrounds, see Burge, *The Anointed Community*, 10 – 31; Keener, *John*, 2:954 – 62.

work.[10] While our analysis of the rest of the Gospel will continue to unpack the function of the Paraclete, a general summary of the Paraclete is needed here.

First, the Paraclete is still to come. Jesus will ask the Father and the Father "will send" the Paraclete to the disciples (v. 26). While the church has long wrestled with the procession of the Spirit (i.e., does he come from the Father and the Son?), this verse allows both to be included, even if they have different roles in the coming of the Spirit.[11] This is not to say, however, that the Spirit had not been active up to this point. For if we include the analysis of Paul that "no one can say, 'Jesus is Lord,' except by the Holy Spirit" (1 Cor 12:3), then we must conclude that the Spirit had already been at work.[12] It is significant that the Paraclete can only come when Jesus departs (16:7), for it suggests that his coming is a direct consequence of the saving work of Christ without which he could have no place or function at all. The Paraclete is therefore symptomatic of the era to come in the new covenant and the new life in Christ, the *Spirit*ual life.

Second, the Paraclete has a special relationship to the disciples. Without exception, the functions ascribed to the Spirit are elsewhere in this Gospel assigned to Christ.[13] The disciples (i.e., all believers) will be granted the ability to know and relate to the Paraclete just as they have the privilege of knowing Jesus (14:7, 9). The Paraclete will indwell the disciples and remain with them just as Jesus is to remain in and with the disciples (14:16 – 17, 20, 23; 15:4 – 5; 17:23, 26). The Paraclete as the Spirit of truth (14:17; 15:26; 16:13) will teach and guide the disciples into "all the truth" (16:13), just as Jesus is the truth (14:6; see also 1:14). The Spirit bears witness to Christ (15:26) and glorifies Christ (16:14), just as it is Christ from whom the Paraclete receives what he makes known to the disciples (16:14).

Third, the Paraclete has a unique role in the world to convict the world of sin, righteousness, and judgment (16:8). The world cannot see or accept the Paraclete, just as they could not accept or see Jesus (5:43; 12:48). It is in relation to the world that the Paraclete can be helped by the legal or forensic sense of the term. Not only does the Paraclete witness in relation to Jesus like a defending counsel (15:26; 16:14), but the Paraclete also has an advocacy role in relation to the disciples, aiding the disciples in their witness in the world, since his witness takes place through their own.[14] Even more, the Paraclete or Spirit of truth (see

---

10. This is similar to our discussion on "Word" (see comments on 1:1).

11. Jesus claims in 16:7 to "send" the Spirit, and according to Titus 3:6 the Spirit is poured out "through Jesus Christ." The Spirit is also interchangeably called "the Spirit of God" (Rom 8:11, 14; 1 Cor 2:11) and "the Spirit of Jesus" (2 Cor 3:17; Gal 4:6; Phil 1:19).

12. See James M. Hamilton Jr., "Old Covenant Believers and the Indwelling Spirit: A Survey of the Spectrum of Opinion," *TrinJ* 24 (2003): 37 – 54. Cf. Augustine, *John*, 74.2.334.

13. Morris, *John*, 589.

14. Lincoln, *Truth on Trial*, 113.

v. 17) provides a grounding witness to reality for the disciples, directed at Jesus who *is* the truth (14:6). Thus, the Paraclete empowers the disciples in their witness to the world, continuing the mission of Jesus (20:21 – 22), who was sent by the Father (3:16).

These three aspects of the Paraclete point directly to a close relationship between the Paraclete and Jesus Christ. This conclusion is drawn not merely from the functional parallels mentioned above but from Jesus's own qualification that the Paraclete is "another Paraclete" (ἄλλον παράκλητον). It should not be overlooked that this first occurrence of the title "Paraclete" in the Gospel carefully qualifies him in relation to Jesus. The adjective "another" (ἄλλον) signifies "another of the same kind" in contrast to the other adjective that could have been used, "other" (ἕτερον), which signifies "another of a different kind" (cf. the use of both adjectives in Gal 1:6 – 7).[15] The implication is that Jesus was *also* a Paraclete, just a different Paraclete than the Spirit (see also 1 John 2:1).[16]

This qualification of the Paraclete demands not only that the Paraclete *is* the Spirit but also that the Paraclete is *more than* the Spirit. That is, this adjectival qualification directs us to undersand more fully the nature of the works and persons of God. In this verse the Trinity is not imposed upon the text but springs from it with clarity and force. For here we see how the Son and the Spirit can belong together (as God) and participate in the same work (the mission of God) and yet be different persons and have different assignments or functions, thus allowing for a distinction in purpose, a unity in function, and an equality in essence.[17] And the relationship among the Trinity is gifted to us by means of the Spirit — the Paraclete, for at his departure (cross, resurrection, ascension) Jesus gives us "a share in his filial relationship with the Father by the indwelling of the Holy Spirit."[18] In this way Jesus is never replaced but incorporates into his work the work of the Spirit and shortly thereafter the work of his disciples (see comments on 14:12). As we will soon see, Jesus is not leaving his disciples but magnifying his presence and work among them (see v. 18).[19]

Our discussion above for the linguistic meaning of the title "Paraclete" has now become more complex, not in regard to definition but to expression. For the title not only refers to the Spirit of God but also to the Son of God, Jesus Christ. The title "Paraclete" therefore expresses the intimate presence of God with his people, a presence that formally began with the incarnation and will

15. V. George Shillington, "The Spirit-Paraclete as Jesus's Alter Ego in the Fourth Gospel (John 14 – 16)," *Vision* 13 (2012): 31 – 39 (35).

16. Cf. Ridderbos, *John*, 499.

17. Helpful here is Calvin, *John 11 – 21*, 82.

18. Andreas J. Köstenberger and Scott R. Swain, *Father, Son and Spirit: The Trinity and John's Gospel*, NSBT 24 (Downers Grove, IL: InterVarsity Press, 2008), 147.

19. Cf. Dorothy A. Lee, *Hallowed in Truth and Love: Spirituality in the Johannine Literature* (Eugene, OR: Wipf & Stock, 2012), 95 – 96.

carry on until the new creation. For this reason, the title "Paraclete" *refers to the ministerial office of the Trinitarian God in the world, occupied by both the Son of God and the Spirit of God.* First Jesus and now the Spirit witness to God, speak on behalf of God, console, guide, and teach in the way of God, and help in the work of God. This is why "Paraclete" cannot be translated into any one word or concept, nor can any language — English or otherwise — grasp its fullness. For "Paraclete" is the title of an office of God, the one from which he ministers to the world he loves. It is the term that guarantees that God is present and that nothing — neither death nor life, neither angels nor demons, neither the present nor the future, nor any powers, neither height nor depth, nor anything else in all creation — can separate us from God and his love for us (Rom 8:38 – 39).

According to Jesus the Paraclete had always been the intention of God ("in order that he will be with you forever" [ἵνα μεθ᾽ ὑμῶν εἰς τὸν αἰῶνα ᾖ]). God had always intended a multifaceted sending of himself, the first *and* second Paracletes, initiated and established by the work of the Son and appropriated and maintained by the work of the Spirit. Nothing here denies a future and even greater presence with God in "my Father's house" (see 14:2 – 3), but it does mean that even in our present "dwellings" God is also dwelling intimately with his people, guaranteeing what has been officially inaugurated — eternal life (20:31).[20]

14:17 "The Spirit of truth, which the world is not able to receive, because it does not see or know him. You know him, because he remains beside you and is in you" (τὸ πνεῦμα τῆς ἀληθείας, ὃ ὁ κόσμος οὐ δύναται λαβεῖν, ὅτι οὐ θεωρεῖ αὐτὸ οὐδὲ γινώσκει· ὑμεῖς γινώσκετε αὐτό, ὅτι παρ᾽ ὑμῖν μένει καὶ ἐν ὑμῖν ἐστιν). After introducing the person of the (second) Paraclete, Jesus gives further details

regarding his function. Jesus begins by describing the Paraclete as "the Spirit of truth" (τὸ πνεῦμα τῆς ἀληθείας), a phrase he will repeat later twice (15:26; 16:13). The genitive construction is likely an objective genitive ("the Spirit who communicates truth").[21]

"Truth" is an important concept in the Gospel (1:14; 16:12 – 15) and especially in light of the recent occurrence of Jesus's sixth formal "I am" statement: "I am the way, *the truth*, and the life" (14:6). In light of its connection to Jesus, truth is more than a statement of fact or even a doctrine, for it speaks of the reality of God now accessed *through* Christ and *in* the Spirit. Just as Jesus is the standard for what is real in this world and true about God as the perfect expression of God (see comments on 14:6), the Spirit of truth is the incorporation of this reality, the substance of what is real in this world and true about God as the perfect provision of God. The Spirit of truth therefore serves as the instrument of God that gives "creational realities meaning and existence."[22] Truth finds its source

20. Bultmann calls it "a new history" (*John*, 616).
21. Cf. Barrett, *John*, 463; Brown, *John*, 2:639. Since objective genitives usually require a verbal head noun, it could also be an attributive genitive. See Wallace, *Greek Grammar*, 86 – 88; 116 – 19.

22. Daniel Rathnakara Sadananda, *The Johannine Exegesis of God: An Exploration into the Johannine Understanding of God*, BZNW 121 (Berlin: Walter de Gruyter, 2004), 258 – 59.

in God, the God of truth (cf. Jer 10:10), and is returned to him in witness and expression through the death of Christ who is "the truth" and life in the Spirit of truth. Truth, therefore, is something to be received and obeyed, which is exactly the kind of help the Paraclete intends to offer the disciple.

The possession of this truth by the Spirit of truth according to Jesus is not something "the world" is able to receive (see comments on 1:10). The reason is that the Spirit is alien to the world, for "it does not see or know him" (οὐ θεωρεῖ αὐτὸ οὐδὲ γινώσκει). The Spirit has no personal relationship with the world. The terms "see" and "know" are not to be distinguished; they are referring to the experience of knowing and relating to God, the Spirit.[23] The reality of God is mediated or experienced by the Spirit of truth in such a way that the believer knows and sees it.

How is this experience of the Spirit possible? According to Jesus, it is because "you know him" (ὑμεῖς γινώσκετε αὐτό), which in the Greek makes the subject ("you") emphatic. And how is he known? "Because he remains beside you and is in you" (ὅτι παρ' ὑμῖν μένει καὶ ἐν ὑμῖν ἐστιν). The prepositional phrase "beside you" (παρ' ὑμῖν) is equivalent to "with you" (μεθ' ὑμῶν) in v. 16. The prepositions are not to be played off each other but to be understood to be speaking with their own overlapping perspectives regarding the real presence of the Paraclete "with," "beside," and even "in" the believer. The last prepositional phrase, "in you" (ἐν ὑμῖν), emphasizes the agency of the Spirit in the life of the believer.[24] Using language that expresses presence and agency, Jesus highlights the indwelling nature of the Spirit of truth, the Paraclete.[25]

14:18 "I will not leave you as orphans; I am coming to you" (Οὐκ ἀφήσω ὑμᾶς ὀρφανούς, ἔρχομαι πρὸς ὑμᾶς). The coming of the Paraclete allows Jesus to state without hesitation that he will not leave his disciples as "orphans" (ὀρφανούς), a metaphor that can be used of a slave without a master but is best taken here as referring to children without a father (see 1:12). Moreover, Jesus declares that he — yes, Jesus himself — is "coming" (ἔρχομαι) to them. But about which coming does Jesus speak? Does he speak about a coming after his resurrection, or about his second coming, or about the coming of the Holy Spirit? The context of chapter 14 is important but exacerbates the problem. In 14:3 Jesus speaks of his own coming, the second coming, yet in the immediate and probably most determinative context (vv. 16 – 17) the coming of the Holy Spirit is in view. Is Jesus continuing the concept of the Paraclete's presence or is he returning again to refer to his own coming? There is no reason to think that the developing context of chapter 14 should not be understood cumulatively to refer to the new reality of the new covenant era. The argument for this is the newly established ministerial office of the Paraclete, both the first (Jesus) and the second (Holy Spirit), who cumulatively incorporate the intimate presence of God in the world.

Therefore, all three "comings" can be defended and put into a fitting order. First, the resurrection seems to be in view in v. 20 where Jesus speaks of a knowledge or realization occurring "on that day" (ἐν ἐκείνῃ τῇ ἡμέρᾳ), with the specificity ("that day") demanding that a particular day — the third day — be in view. Indeed, such an interpretation is essential to understanding v. 19 and therefore must be included as part of the "coming." Second, the immediate context cannot have skipped past the Paraclete and the dramatic emphasis on his eternal and intimate presence, not only in vv. 16 – 17 but also in v. 23 where arguably the Father and Son dwell

---

23. Bultmann, *John*, 616. Bultmann refers to these senses as the "super-senses."

24. See Wallace, *Greek Grammar*, 373 – 75.
25. Cf. Luther, *John*, 24:120.

with believers *by means of* the indwelling Holy Spirit. Third, the second coming of Jesus is what Jesus began with in the discourse proper (14:2 – 3), and now after the promise of the Spirit he wanted to remind his disciples that he *too* would be with them, not merely the Holy Spirit (cf. v. 23).[26] And as much as the immediate context is in reference to the Holy Spirit (vv. 16 – 17), Jesus does refer to himself in this verse twice in the first person: "*I* will not leave you … *I* am coming." If Jesus had not linked himself to the Paraclete (the "another Paraclete" of v. 16), we would be forced to choose a single "coming." But since "Paraclete" refers to the multifaceted presence of God with his people, Jesus speaks not merely of himself but of the Trinitarian God, so much so that Jesus will soon explain that the Father and Son will indwell (via the Spirit) the believer (see v. 23).

14:19 "After a little while the world will no longer see me, but you will see me, because I live you also will live" (ἔτι μικρὸν καὶ ὁ κόσμος με οὐκέτι θεωρεῖ, ὑμεῖς δὲ θεωρεῖτέ με, ὅτι ἐγὼ ζῶ καὶ ὑμεῖς ζήσετε). Jesus continues to address this new eschatological life and his own personal presence with his disciples by comparing the (eschatological) experience of the disciples to the world. The departure of Jesus changes his relationship to the world, but not to the disciples, who still "will see" (θεωρεῖτέ) him, with the emphatic pronoun reinforcing the vision experience of the disciples. Once Jesus leaves, the world will no longer see him in the flesh, and they have never known him by the Spirit.[27] Jesus's first remark to his earliest disciples, "Come and see" (cf. 1:39, 46), is now given even greater significance.

Jesus then explains the source of this difference in vision between the world and the disciples: "because I live you also will live" (ὅτι ἐγὼ ζῶ καὶ ὑμεῖς

ζήσετε), with both subjects given emphasis in the Greek. When Jesus states, "I live," he is clearly referring to his resurrection. Therefore the "life" the disciples experience is rooted in the new eschatological life only God can provide. This life is more than flesh and bones, for it is life in the cosmological reality of God. The resurrection of Christ does not merely guarantee that death is defeated but also means that life itself is new (see comments on 6:57).

14:20 "On that day you will know that I am in my Father and you are in me and I am in you" (ἐν ἐκείνῃ τῇ ἡμέρᾳ γνώσεσθε ὑμεῖς ὅτι ἐγὼ ἐν τῷ πατρί μου καὶ ὑμεῖς ἐν ἐμοὶ κἀγὼ ἐν ὑμῖν). Jesus continues to root this new eschatological life founded upon his resurrection in the Trinitarian life of God. Jesus claims emphatically that "on that day" (ἐν ἐκείνῃ τῇ ἡμέρᾳ), that is, on the glorious third day after his death, Resurrection Day, "*you* will know" (γνώσεσθε ὑμεῖς). The verb translated as "know" (γνώσεσθε) is flexible enough to also mean to "realize," "understand," and even "perceive." The focus is less on the experience of their confirmation and more on the source of it — the resurrection of Christ. It is important to note that the focus in vv. 19 – 20 on the resurrection does not intend to eclipse the Spirit. For not only is God appropriated by the indwelling Holy Spirit but even coming to "know" Christ requires an act "by the Holy Spirit" (1 Cor 12:3; see comments on v. 16).

Using again language of mutual indwelling and interpenetration (see comments on 14:10 – 11), Jesus speaks of the new state that will exist between the Father, Son, (Spirit), and the disciples. This is not merely a depiction of life in the kingdom, for this is also a depiction of the kingdom in this life; the cosmological reality to which the Gospel has witnessed is coalescing through Christ and in the

---

26. Cf. Augustine, *John*, 75.1.335.

27. Cf. Morris, *John*, 579.

Spirit into the historical reality of created existence. The resurrection of Jesus inaugurates a new era, so much so that "the day of the resurrection *is extended* in the experience of all who love the Lord" (v. 15).[28]

14:21 "The one who has my commandments and keeps them, this the one who loves me. And the one who loves me will be loved by my Father, and I will love him and I will reveal myself to him" (ὁ ἔχων τὰς ἐντολάς μου καὶ τηρῶν αὐτὰς ἐκεῖνός ἐστιν ὁ ἀγαπῶν με· ὁ δὲ ἀγαπῶν με ἀγαπηθήσεται ὑπὸ τοῦ πατρός μου, κἀγὼ ἀγαπήσω αὐτὸν καὶ ἐμφανίσω αὐτῷ ἐμαυτόν). The first section of the pericope (vv. 15–21) concludes where it began, with love for Christ and obedience to his commandments. In many ways, this expected response matches well the "covenant-form" message of the farewell discourse (see comments before 13:1). As we noted earlier (see comments on v. 15), fellowship and partnership with God is a relationship of love that is expressed through obedience.

The final statement, "and I will reveal myself to him" (καὶ ἐμφανίσω αὐτῷ ἐμαυτόν) perhaps simply refers to the "comings" of Christ, the resurrection and later second coming, for the verb is often used to refer to something "being seen, visible"; yet in context the verb seems to express its other, less physical meaning as well: "Make clear, explain, inform."[29] In light of our interpretation of v. 18 above, it is best to understand the subject matter of the verb to be inclusive of the Spirit. Therefore, it is likely intended to interpret further the previous mutual indwelling and interpenetration language.[30] For as much as this love is fleshly and rooted in this world, it is also beyond the world, rooted in an experience not obtained but by those who have the Holy Spirit. This love is rooted in the very meaning of life, in the person(s) of God. But as much as this involves the Father and the Spirit, Jesus is right to return to himself as the focal point of the revelation of God.[31]

14:22 Judas (not Iscariot) said to him, "Lord, what has happened that you intend to reveal yourself to us and not to the world?" (Λέγει αὐτῷ Ἰούδας, οὐχ ὁ Ἰσκαριώτης, Κύριε, [καὶ] τί γέγονεν ὅτι ἡμῖν μέλλεις ἐμφανίζειν σεαυτὸν καὶ οὐχὶ τῷ κόσμῳ;). A transition to the second section of the pericope (vv. 22–24) is provided and introduced by a reasonable question from one of Jesus's disciples named Judas,[32] whom the narrator makes certain the reader does not confuse with Judas, son of Simon Iscariot, who is no longer with the disciples (cf. 13:30). Although Judas is trying to understand the difference in vision between the disciples and the world, he asks a more specific question about its source. The phrase "what has happened" (τί γέγονεν) is looking for the thing or event that created a distinction between the disciples and the world.

Judas is not merely confused about what happened but also about the intentions of Jesus.[33] Picking up on the verb Jesus used in v. 21 ("reveal" [ἐμφανίζειν]), Judas's question probes further the distinction between the disciples and the world in relation to Jesus. How will his disciples see him but the world will not? Or more accurately, why would he *intend* for this to happen? The question may be rooted in the first-century assumption that the OT predicted a public self-disclosure of the Messiah (e.g., Isa 11; Dan 7; Hab 3:3–15; Zech 9).[34] While the resurrection (and before it, the cross) will be a clear and unmistakably physical manifestation that

---

28. Hoskyns, *Fourth Gospel*, 459 (emphasis added).
29. BDAG 325.
30. Cf. Ridderbos, *John*, 506.
31. See Barrett, *John*, 464.
32. This disciple is only named here in the Gospel. Almost nothing is known about him.
33. See BDAG 628.
34. Cf. Carson, *John*, 504.

will be seen by many (see 1 Cor 15:3 – 70), it will also inaugurate a revelatory experience in which the disciples will "see" God and be seen by God in a way that the world will not experience.

14:23 Jesus answered and said to him, "If anyone loves me he will keep my word, and my Father will love him, and we will come to him and we will make a dwelling place beside him" (ἀπεκρίθη Ἰησοῦς καὶ εἶπεν αὐτῷ, Ἐάν τις ἀγαπᾷ με τὸν λόγον μου τηρήσει, καὶ ὁ πατήρ μου ἀγαπήσει αὐτόν, καὶ πρὸς αὐτὸν ἐλευσόμεθα καὶ μονὴν παρ᾽ αὐτῷ ποιησόμεθα). Jesus's answer to Judas' question (vv. 23 – 24) returns to the relationship of love already mentioned that is uniquely established between the Trinitarian God and his children. It is not love in a generic and abstract sense but love within personal relationship, entailing love and obedience on the part of the disciple (see comments on vv. 15, 21).

The relationship is also experienced not in an abstract sense but in a very tangible manner, for not only will the Trinitarian God (denoted by the first-person plural ["we"]) come to the disciple, but he will also take up residence with them. The noun translated as "dwelling place" (μονὴν) is the same noun used in 14:2 regarding "my Father's house" (see comments on 14:2). While it could be translated as "room," the term is used here to depict the indwelling presence of God in the individual believer. For this reason the "we" not only includes the explicitly mentioned Father and Son but must also imply the Spirit, about whom the rest of Scripture overtly describes as the "indwelling one" of God. Jesus's statement intends to summarize life "in the realm of the Spirit" who "lives in you" (Rom 8:9).[35] This powerful statement is not intended to eclipse or deny that this experience of the presence of God is only the inauguration of something even

greater to come (see comments on 14:2 – 3). The interpreter must constantly maintain a distinction between the eschatological inauguration and the eschatological consummation.

14:24 "The one who does not love me will not keep my word. The word that you are hearing is not mine, but belongs to the one who sent me, the Father" (ὁ μὴ ἀγαπῶν με τοὺς λόγους μου οὐ τηρεῖ· καὶ ὁ λόγος ὃν ἀκούετε οὐκ ἔστιν ἐμὸς ἀλλὰ τοῦ πέμψαντός με πατρός). In light of the depth of the relationship that exists between God and a disciple, the difference Judas was pressing for is now made more manifest. The world has not known or seen God (in the Spirit of God) and therefore does not love or obey God. And to establish more firmly his answer and its authority, Jesus ends by saying that his answer is not his own but belongs to God the Father. The "sending" imagery reminds the reader that this is no chance occurrence but is a result of the mission of God and has been ordained by God. By this Jesus also gives the negative side of his answer — the grace of life with God is not for all but only for those who love and obey — that is, believe in Jesus Christ (cf. 20:30 – 31). In many ways, the difference in vision that Judas noted, the state of the blindness of the world, is itself the judgment it suffers (cf. 9:39).[36]

14:25 "I have spoken these things to you while I remain with you" (Ταῦτα λελάληκα ὑμῖν παρ᾽ ὑμῖν μένων). The third and final section of the pericope (vv. 25 – 31) begins when Jesus transitions from answering the question of Judas to making a final statement of his own. Referring to what he has just spoken to his disciples ("these things" [Ταῦτα]), Jesus reminds his disciples that his presence with them and personal instruction to them is about to come to an end, befitting the function of a farewell discourse (see comments before 13:1).

---

35. Cf. Augustine, *John*, 76.4.338.

36. Bultmann, *John*, 625.

The ministerial "office" of the Paraclete is about to transition from the first Paraclete to "another Paraclete" (v. 16), who will continue to mediate God's presence and personal instruction to the disciples.

14:26 "But the Paraclete, the Holy Spirit, whom the Father will send in my name, he will teach you all things and remind you of all the things that I said to you" (ὁ δὲ παράκλητος, τὸ πνεῦμα τὸ ἅγιον ὃ πέμψει ὁ πατὴρ ἐν τῷ ὀνόματί μου, ἐκεῖνος ὑμᾶς διδάξει πάντα καὶ ὑπομνήσει ὑμᾶς πάντα ἃ εἶπον ὑμῖν [ἐγώ]). The departure of Jesus is not the departure of God, for Jesus mentions for a second time "the Paraclete" (ὁ παράκλητος), who will take his place and fulfill the role of teacher and God's presence for the disciples. This is not to say, however, that the Spirit eclipses the Son but simply to say that the Spirit fills the office of the Paraclete first occupied by Jesus. In every way (and in an even greater way) Jesus is still ministering to his people as only the Son can do. The "transition" from the first to the second Paraclete is not therefore a transition from the ministry of the Son to the Spirit, for the first does not cease to minister when the second comes; rather, they serve their respective roles harmoniously together. The unity between the persons of the Trinity must be applied to their work.

The (second) Paraclete is described explicitly as "the Holy Spirit" (τὸ πνεῦμα τὸ ἅγιον), the traditional title used for the third person of the Trinity. We have already introduced the figure and function of the Spirit/Paraclete (see comments on vv. 16 – 17); here Jesus gives further definition. Jesus adds three aspects here. First, the Spirit was sent by the Father. In the Gospel up until this point, it has been the Son who has been regularly described as being sent by the Father (cf. 3:16). Although we would be theologically negligent if we suggested the Spirit had not been working up to this point (see comments on v. 16), clearly the Spirit is now working in a new way, befitting the start of the newly inaugurated state of existence for the children of God.

Second, the Spirit was sent "in my name" (ἐν τῷ ὀνόματί μου). This is a significant phrase, for it explains that the ministry of the Spirit is not technically a replacement of the ministry of Jesus but a continuation, giving further insight into the use of the title "Paraclete" for both Jesus and the Spirit. "In my name" locates the work of the Spirit within the larger work of Christ, just as the work of Christ is located within the larger mission of the Father. It also demands that the work of the Spirit be understood as facilitating the same work. In this way Jesus never stopped working when he departs and the Spirit comes, for the Spirit's work is also the work of Christ.[37]

Third, the Spirit "will teach" (διδάξει) and "will remind" (ὑπομνήσει) the disciples. One of the primary roles of the Spirit/Paraclete is to teach the disciples (cf. 15:26; 16:13 – 14) and to assist them in their own participation in the mission of God. When Jesus says the Spirit will teach the disciples "all things" (πάντα), he is simply saying "all" that they will need (see comments on 16:13). In a similar way, when Jesus says the Spirit will "remind" the disciples, he is simply referring to what they need to grasp from Christ. The two terms "teach" and "remind" are best understood as synonyms.[38] For the word (message) of the Word was not lacking but fully sufficient, so that the Spirit is not adding to the Word but emboldening it. The Spirit is a living representation of all that Jesus had once spoken, a *creative exposition* of the gospel.[39]

14:27 "Peace I leave with you; my peace I give to you. I do not give to you as the world gives. Do

---

37. Angus Paddison, "Exegetical Notes on John 14:23 – 29," *ExpTim* 118 (2007): 342 – 43.

38. Schnackenburg, *John*, 3:83.

39. Hoskyns, *Fourth Gospel*, 461.

not let your heart be troubled nor let it be fearful" (Εἰρήνην ἀφίημι ὑμῖν, εἰρήνην τὴν ἐμὴν δίδωμι ὑμῖν· οὐ καθὼς ὁ κόσμος δίδωσιν ἐγὼ δίδωμι ὑμῖν. μὴ ταρασσέσθω ὑμῶν ἡ καρδία μηδὲ δειλιάτω). The work of God that is fully and finally expressed by the Spirit allows Jesus to offer his disciples "peace" (cf. 14:1). It is not surprising that a farewell speech would include language of assurance, but what Jesus offers is not mere human tranquility.[40] The "peace" about which Jesus speaks is the peace *of* God *through* Christ and *in* the Spirit. That is, this newly inaugurated state of existence for the disciple involves receiving the peace of Christ, which is an unbroken union with the Father, even in a world filled with continuous strife, persecution, humiliation, and even death.[41] Certainly this fits the OT concept of peace — *shalom* (Num 6:26; Ps 28:11; Isa 54:13; 57:19; Ezek 37:36), but what is being described here is its fulfillment.

Jesus offers peace to his disciples in the two related phrases "peace I leave with you" and "my peace I give to you." While they are generally synonymous, these overlapping statements create a couple of items worthy of note. First, the peace given to the disciples is grounded in and belongs to Christ. It is the peace of Christ that the disciple receives, a peace rooted not merely in his person but also in his work on the cross. Second, the peace that Christ gives to his disciples may now be rightfully described as belonging also to them. The participation of the believer in the life of the Trinitarian God is inclusive of the peace of God. The world, which can neither see God nor relate to God, cannot provide this peace. This is why Christ must repeat what he said in 14:1, adding this time the equivalent addition "nor … be fearful" (μηδὲ δειλιάτω). The believer is to live by means of this peace.

14:28 "You heard that I said to you, 'I am going and I am coming to you.' If you loved me you would have rejoiced that I am going to the Father, because the Father is greater than I" (ἠκούσατε ὅτι ἐγὼ εἶπον ὑμῖν, Ὑπάγω καὶ ἔρχομαι πρὸς ὑμᾶς. εἰ ἠγαπᾶτέ με ἐχάρητε ἄν, ὅτι πορεύομαι πρὸς τὸν πατέρα, ὅτι ὁ πατὴρ μείζων μού ἐστιν). Jesus restates a summary of his message thus far, "going and coming," the inauguration and consummation of the mission of God through his person and work, in order to exhort his disciples to believe in him and his final speech to them. He just exhorted his disciples to trust him in relation to their worldly circumstances (v. 27); now he exhorts them to trust him in regard to his circumstances.

Jesus makes a final argument that "if you loved me you would have rejoiced" (εἰ ἠγαπᾶτέ με ἐχάρητε ἄν) in his departure. Rooting his argument in "love," which has been defined throughout this pericope not as a sentimental expression but as a relational foundation (see comments on vv. 15, 21, 23), Jesus suggests that his departure to the Father should be viewed positively. The one reason Jesus gives for this is "because the Father is greater than I" (ὅτι ὁ πατὴρ μείζων μού ἐστιν). This statement asks the disciple to trust in the person and work of God. If God is greater than Christ who therefore submits himself to the will of God, how much greater is Christ than the disciples? This comparison is not to be interpreted like the ancient heretics, the Arians, who argued that the Son was less than equal to the Father, for from the Gospel's first verse their ontological equality was stressed (1:1; cf. 1:18; 5:16 – 18; 10:30; 20:28).[42] Rather, what is "greater" is the Father's *will*, out of which Christ has been "sent" and to which he has continually been dependent and obedient (cf. 4:34; 5:19 – 30; 8:29; 12:48 – 49). Jesus is not trying to separate the

---

40. Cf. Keener, *John*, 2:982.
41. Hoskyns, *Fourth Gospel*, 461.

42. See Augustine, *John*, 78.1 – 3.340 – 42.

Father from the Son according to their distinct persons but to join them together according to their united work. Jesus is also trying to show that he is returning from where he came for good reason, and that they should understand this by means of their faith-based relation of love with him, and by understanding (and accepting) his good and perfect purposes.

14:29 "And now I have told you before it happens, so that when it does happen, you may believe" (καὶ νῦν εἴρηκα ὑμῖν πρὶν γενέσθαι, ἵνα ὅταν γένηται πιστεύσητε). Jesus concludes his invitation to believe, which began at 14:1, with a statement similar to one he has made before (see 13:19). By understanding what is to come, the disciples should be firmly grounded in the only appropriate object of belief—God. It is interesting that Jesus does not give the converse response; he simply says that when it does happen, "you may believe" (πιστεύσητε). This is not to shame the disciples when later they would exhibit fear (e.g., 20:19) but to show them the "way" out of the fear and the more appropriate object to which they should direct their faith.

14:30 "I will not speak with you much longer, for the ruler of this world is coming, and he has nothing on me" (οὐκέτι πολλὰ λαλήσω μεθ' ὑμῶν, ἔρχεται γὰρ ὁ τοῦ κόσμου ἄρχων· καὶ ἐν ἐμοὶ οὐκ ἔχει οὐδέν). In v. 29 Jesus focused on the positive that "you may believe," but here Jesus introduces the negative experience they are certain to encounter, the experience that will require them to "love" God and "rejoice" in his mission and purposes. The impending departure of Jesus not only sets the stage for the "coming" of the Spirit/Paraclete but also for "the ruler of this world" (ὁ τοῦ κόσμου ἄρχων).

This is the second use of this title in the Gospel (see comments on 12:31; cf. 16:11). In its first oc-

currence, the departure of Jesus was depicted as a cosmic battle in which Jesus defeats Satan, a battle fought and secured by the death of Jesus on the cross. In this context the emphasis is on the imminent initiation of this cosmic battle, one in which Satan, though defeated by the Son of God, will also become an opponent of the children of God (cf. Eph 6:10–17). Later in the discourse, Jesus will give further insight and instruction regarding this spiritual battle. His purpose here is not only to introduce this ruler's more public entrance (not merely his personal "coming" to Judas in 13:27) but also to declare this cosmic opponent of God as defeated even before the battle has begun. Proof of this defeat is not only found in 12:31 where Christ is depicted as judging the world and casting outside "the ruler of the world" but also here in this further statement of Jesus translated "and he has nothing on me" (καὶ ἐν ἐμοὶ οὐκ ἔχει οὐδέν). This idiom often occurs in legal contexts and means something like "he has no claim on me" or "he has nothing over me."[43]

14:31 "But in order that the world may know that I love the Father, and as the Father has commanded me, thus I do. Rise, let us go from here" (ἀλλ' ἵνα γνῷ ὁ κόσμος ὅτι ἀγαπῶ τὸν πατέρα, καὶ καθὼς ἐνετείλατό μοι ὁ πατήρ, οὕτως ποιῶ. Ἐγείρεσθε, ἄγωμεν ἐντεῦθεν). Jesus makes a further statement related to "ruler of this world" and his inability to make a claim on Christ. Jesus explicitly explains to the disciples that he wants the world to know two things, both of which are directly related to the Father and his grand mission. He wants the world to know that "I love the Father" (ἀγαπῶ τὸν πατέρα) and that "I do" (ποιῶ) what the Father has commanded. These two things are best understood as synonyms and reflect the exact two things Jesus expects from the disciples: to love and obey (see comments on vv. 15, 21, 23).

43. Carson, *John*, 508–9.

By this statement Jesus urges the disciples to see that his death is actually for the purpose of victory and his departure is to provide an even more empowering presence. Even though he will shortly depart — in a dramatic and shameful manner — and even though the "ruler of this world" is about to "come," "nothing" has a claim on the mission of God. This is commentary on the "unseen" things introduced by the prologue (see comments before 1:1). At the same time Jesus also exhorts the disciples to do what he himself is already doing (the present-tense verb is probably better translated as "I am doing"). Forming an *inclusio* that frames this pericope, the beginning (v. 15) and end of Jesus's message in this pericope is to love and obey God. And Jesus is "doing" already what he is asking them to do; in fact, his "doing" is making the way for their "doing" (cf. 14:6). In this way Jesus ends this pericope by pointing again to the "way" so that the "truth" can be understood with the hope that "life" can be fully attained. This is what the world *must* know, and it serves as the mission statement of the church (see 20:21; cf. Matt 28:18 – 20).

The pericope concludes with a command by Jesus, "Rise, let us go from here" (Ἐγείρεσθε, ἄγωμεν ἐντεῦθεν), that has convinced modern scholarship that the farewell discourse is highly edited and an out-of-order collection of discourses. We argued earlier, however, that there is warrant for seeing the discourse as a unified whole (see comments before 13:1). While several solutions have been offered that might fit the theological context of the Gospel,[44] few have offered a solution that might explain the literary nature of the statement. Rather than being a literary seam reflecting editorial activity,

what appears to be an out-of-place statement is an intentional literary technique or dramatic device called a "delayed exit" that is common in literature similar to the Gospel of John.

According to Parsenios, the "exit device" would have the following characteristics.[45] First, the argument for this "exit device" operates on a grand level, encompassing the whole narrative. Jesus's exit to death in the Gospel is also "the culmination of thematic preparation."[46] The narrative's development of "the hour" (see comments on 2:4) has been forged by the Gospel into one dramatic moment. Second, the "exit device" is designed to give emphasis to the speaker, offering a demonstration of his power and a focus on his person. "The 'Big Speech' gains its prominence in Greek tragedy very often from a suspension or displacement of the action, which makes the dramatic time in these interludes qualitatively different...."[47] The dramatic device creates something like a pause for the speaker in order to transport the speech to a state above the action. The "exit devices," as summarized by Parsenios, "serve to focus attention on the speakers, lifting them beyond their immediate surroundings.... The delay of the exit need not be seen as a sloppy set of footprints left by people who did not know how to cover their tracks. It is a legitimate literary move."[48]

In the developing flow of the farewell discourse, the pause created by the "exit device" not only gives greater focus to Jesus but also halts momentarily his progression toward death so that Jesus is given the opportunity to offer consolation to his disciples. Befitting the blended genre conventions of the Fourth Gospel's farewell discourse, the "farewell speech" genre also includes these dramatic

---

44. See Dodd, *Interpretation*, 409; Calvin, *John 11 – 21*, 92. See also H. B. H. Bevan, "Does 'Arise, Let Us Go Hence' (John 14:31D) Make Sense Where it Stands?," *JTS* 54 (2003): 576 – 84.

45. The following is adapted from Parsenios, *Departure and Consolation*, 49 – 76.

46. Ibid., 66.

47. Fiona Macintosh, *Dying Acts: Death in Ancient Greek and Modern Irish Tragic Drama* (Cork: Cork University Press, 1994), 94.

48. Parsenios, *Departure and Consolation*, 75.

device of "exits" (13:30 – 31; 14:31; 18:1) not only to focus the discourse on Jesus but also to provide Jesus with the opportunity to include "consolatory discourse" that is both therapeutic and facilitates his presence (see comments before 13:1). With this literary technique the pericope ends, setting up for the disciples one of the most conciliatory and grace-filled pericopae in all of Scripture. The dramatic pause was not intended to separate Jesus from his disciples but to bring them closer, allowing Jesus to share with them one of his most intimate sections of his farewell discourse.

Theology in Application

In the third of eight sections of the farewell discourse, Jesus makes the second of six statements that explain, encourage, and exhort the disciples as they transition to the era of the new covenant, from life with Jesus to life "in Christ" and in the Spirit. Through this pericope the reader is introduced to the Paraclete and is invited to participate directly in the life of the Trinitarian God.

Love and Obedience

This pericope mentioned the combination of love and obedience four times (vv. 15, 21, 23, 31), establishing it as an *inclusio* that framed this entire section of the discourse. Love according to this pericope is not to be understood in a generic and abstract sense, but as that which facilitates the personal relationship between God and his children. In the same way, obedience is symptomatic of love, a sign of recognition and of dependence on God and participation in him — his person, his work, his will, and his ways.

This pericope revealed a shocking reality: God responded in love and obedience first! It was Jesus according to v. 31 who loved and obeyed his Father — and on our behalf. Scripture also describes the love of the Father in this way: "This is love: not that we loved God, but that he loved us and sent his Son as an atoning sacrifice for our sins" (1 John 4:10). In this way our love is made possible. Moreover, our love for and obedience to God participates in the love and obedience he already established by the sending and work of the Son, Jesus Christ. Such a message breathes life into a culture that tries to make love abstract and to separate love from obedience. It also makes sense of the Psalms' description of the goodness and benefit of the law (e.g., "The law of the LORD is perfect, refreshing the soul" [Ps 19:7; cf. Ps 119]). The Christian's relationship to God is founded upon the intersection of love (affection) and obedience (dependence).

The Paraclete

In this pericope we are introduced to the third person of the Trinity, the Holy Spirit, who is defined not only as the Spirit of truth, but as "another Paraclete."

The theology of the Spirit provided by this pericope (and the rest of the farewell discourse) is sorely needed in our churches today. The Spirit is generally the most abused person of God, for he is either underemphasized for fear of abuse or over-emphasized for fear of neglect. Yet the entire Christian life can rightly be described as life in the Spirit. To live in the Spirit is neither to neglect the Father nor to eclipse Christ but to serve, respond to, and participate in them both by means of this divine appropriation. To live in the Spirit is to be Trinitarian. But this is not a Spirit who only works in secret or in supernatural ways, but the Spirit indwelling in us. If the Paraclete is the manifestation of God's presence, as this pericope explains, then the Christian life must be a Spirit-filled life, just as our churches must be Spirit-filled churches. The Spirit must stop being merely a debate over prayer languages and powerful healings and must become the constant reality (individual and corporate) of the Christian life and experience.[49]

Life in God and the Peace of God

The overall goal of this section of the farewell discourse is to invite the Christian into the life of God. The Christian life is participation in God *through* Christ and *in* the Spirit. Christ may be the way/truth/life, but he was sent on behalf of the Father and he is empowered by the Spirit. Thus, the Christian life is overtly Trinitarian, not only in its orthodoxy but also in its orthopraxy. The emphasis on the Spirit/Paraclete in this pericope simply brings to fruition the fullness of life promised in the pro-logue: "In the Word was life" (1:4), and this "life" is participation in the Trinitarian life of God, inaugurated now in the era of the new covenant and ultimately consum-mated at the new creation.

While we are right to speak of this life as a *Spirit*ual life, for this life is expressed in the Spirit, it is not spiritual in a manner that is less than physical. This life requires real dependence, real obedience, and real suffering. It is not only grounded in the flesh, death, and resurrection of Christ, but it is incorporated amidst the difficulties of this world, even the conflict that is ensuing as part of the cosmic battles involving "the ruler of this world" (cf. Eph 6:10 – 17). Our *Spirit*ual life is not best exemplified by some sort of monastic separation from the world but by the peace of God in the midst of suffering and persecution (see 1 Cor 15:55, 57). Peace is an overtly Christian trait. The world, which can neither see God nor relate to God, cannot provide this peace — nor have it. This peace was sent from the Father in the person of Jesus Christ and is applied by the Father and the Son in the person of the Holy Spirit. Life in the inaugurated new covenant is the peace of God. In this newly existing state of Christian existence, we are not defined by our circumstances alone but by our God and for his glory.

---

49. See Kenneth Berding, *Life in the Spirit* (Wheaton: Cross-way, 2011).

31

John 15:1 – 17

Literary Context

This pericope is the fourth of eight sections of the farewell discourse. Surrounded by a prologue (13:31 – 38) and an epilogue (16:25 – 33), the farewell discourse can be divided into six significant and developing thematic statements by Jesus, with each offering comfort and consolation for the disciples (and the reader), befitting the nature of a farewell discourse (see comments before 13:1). These six statements within the farewell discourse offer one long exhortation to stay the course and encouragement that their efforts will be matched by the Trinitarian God himself. After offering himself to the disciples in the previous pericope, in the third of these six statements Jesus invites the disciples to enter fully into the life of the Trinitarian God through his person and work, as assigned by the Father and empowered by the Spirit. This takes place in the mutual "remaining" between the disciples and Jesus. The disciples — and the readers — are exhorted to respond to this invitation to participate in Christ in order to be "fruitful" in the work of God, a work that involves the joy of God and the love of God and of one another.

VII. The Farewell Discourse (13:1 – 17:26)

    A. Introduction: The Love of Jesus (13:1 – 30)

        1. Jesus and the Washing of His Disciples' Feet (13:1 – 20)

        2. Jesus Announces His Betrayal (13:21 – 30)

    B. The Farewell Discourse (13:31 – 16:33)

        1. Prologue: Glory, Departure, and Love (13:31 – 38)

        2. I Am the Way and the Truth and the Life (14:1 – 14)

        3. I Will Give You the Paraclete (14:15 – 31)

➡   **4. I Am the True Vine (15:1 – 17)**

        5. I Have Also Experienced the Hate of the World (15:18 – 27)

        6. I Will Empower You by the Paraclete (16:1 – 15)

        7. I Will Turn Your Grief into Joy (16:16 – 24)

        8. Epilogue: Speaking Plainly, Departure, and Peace (16:25 – 33)

    C. Conclusion: The Prayer of Jesus (17:1 – 26)

Main Idea

Remain in Christ, the true Vine, the source of purposeful fruit and true joy, and the means by which the love of God is embodied in the church and declared to the world.

Translation

John 15:1–17

	Section #4 of "Farewell Discourse" (Illustration 1–8)	
1a	Character: "Vine"	*"I am the true vine,*
b	Character: "Farmer"	*and my Father is the farmer.*
2a	Character: "Branch"	*Every branch*
b	Source/Sphere	*in me*
c	Description	*that does not bear fruit,*
d	Consequence	*he takes it away,*
e	Contrast	*and*
f	Description	*every branch that does bear fruit*
g	Consequence	*he cleans it*
h	Intended Result	*so that it may bear even more fruit.*
3a	Declaration	*You are already clean*
b	Basis	*because of the word*
c	Description	*which I have spoken to you.*
4a	Exhortation	*Remain*
	Source/Sphere	*in me,*
c	Promise	*and I will remain*
d	Sphere	*in you.*
e	Comparison	*Just as a branch cannot bear fruit by itself*
f	Condition	*unless it remains in the vine,*
g	Inference	*so neither can you bear fruit*
h	Condition	*unless you remain*
i	Source/Sphere	*in me.*
5a	Restatement of 1a	*I am the vine;*
b	Identification of Branches	*you are the branches.*
	Application of Illustration	
c	Condition (Subject)	*The one who remains*
d	Source/Sphere	*in me and*
e	Reciprocation	*I in him,*
f	Inference (Predicate)	*he bears much fruit,*
g	Basis	*for . . .*
h	Source	*apart from me*
i		*. . . you can do nothing.*

Continued on next page.

Continued from previous page.

6a	Condition/Contrast to 5c–f	*If a person does not remain*
b	Source/Sphere	*in me,*
c	Sequence of Consequences	*he is thrown outside*
d	Description	*like a branch*
e		*and is dried up;*
f		*and they gather them*
g		*and throw them into the fire*
h		*and they are burned.*
7a	Condition	*If you remain*
b	Source/Sphere	*in me and*
c	Reciprocation	*my word remains*
d	Sphere	*in you,*
e	Promise	*ask whatever you wish,*
f	Result	*and it will happen for you.*
	(Conclusion of Illustration 1–8)	
8a	Manner	*In this way*
b	Assertion	*my Father is glorified,*
c	Description of Manner	*that you bear much fruit and*
d		*become my disciples.*
9a	Comparison	*Just as the Father has loved me,*
b	Basis of 9c	*I have loved you;*
c	Exhortation	*remain in my love*
10a	Condition	*If you keep my commandments,*
b	Promise	*you will remain*
c	Sphere	*in my love,*
d	Comparison	*just as I have kept my Father's commandments and*
e		*remain in his love.*
11a	Basis for 1–10	*I have spoken these things to you*
b	Intended Result	*so that my joy may be in you and*
c	Reciprocal Result	*your joy may be fulfilled.*
12a	Assertion	*This is my commandment:*
b	Description: "Love"	*love one another*
c	Comparison	*just as I have loved you.*
13a	Expansion of "Love" (12b)	*No one has a greater love than this:*
b	Further Description	*that a person lay down his life*
c	Beneficiary	*for his friends.*
14a	Expansion of "Friend" (13c)	*You are my friends*
b	Condition	*if you do what I command you.*
15a	Further Expansion of "Friend"	*I no longer speak to you*
b	Manner/Comparison to "Friend"	*as slaves,*
c	Basis	*because the slave does not know what his master is doing;*

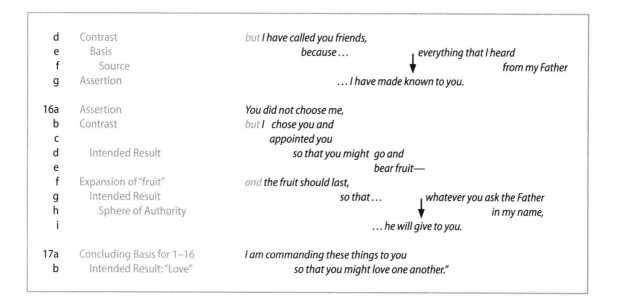

d	Contrast	*but I have called you friends,*
e	Basis	*because . . .* ↓ *everything that I heard*
f	Source	*from my Father*
g	Assertion	*. . . I have made known to you.*
16a	Assertion	*You did not choose me,*
b	Contrast	*but I chose you and*
c		*appointed you*
d	Intended Result	*so that you might go and*
e		*bear fruit—*
f	Expansion of "fruit"	*and the fruit should last,*
g	Intended Result	*so that . . .* ↓ *whatever you ask the Father*
h	Sphere of Authority	*in my name,*
i		*. . . he will give to you.*
17a	Concluding Basis for 1–16	*I am commanding these things to you*
b	Intended Result: "Love"	*so that you might love one another."*

Structure and Literary Form

As the fourth of eight sections of the farewell discourse, this pericope is part of the fourth (and longest) substantial monologue in the narrative proper. A monologue (see Introduction) is similar to a dialogue in that it is set in the context of an engagement and conflict, but rather than engaging point-for-point it allows for a lengthy argument. A monologue can contain elements of rhetoric, challenge, and conflict, but it does so in a sustained presentation.

This pericope is the third of six statements by Jesus in order to exhort and encourage his disciples. The application of the literary technique in 14:31 signals to the reader that 15:1 is a new section. The warrant for this section is not only the thematic development of love that ends at v. 17 as the conclusion of an *inclusio* that began at v. 12, but also the clear transition in subject matter that occurs at 15:18. In this third statement, Jesus invites the disciples to participate in the life of God by "remaining" in him.

Exegetical Outline

➡ **4. I Am the True Vine (15:1–17)**

    a. An Illustration of the Vine, the Farmer and the Branches (vv. 1–8)

    b. Remain in the Love of God (vv. 9–11)

    c. The Love Commandment (vv. 12–17)

Explanation of the Text

Since this entire section of the Gospel and "the farewell discourse" proper are replete with interpretive issues, we refer the reader to the first pericope of this section where we provided an overview of the nature (genre), literary structure, and function of the farewell discourse (see comments before 13:1).

15:1 "I am the true vine, and my Father is the farmer" (Ἐγώ εἰμι ἡ ἄμπελος ἡ ἀληθινή, καὶ ὁ πατήρ μου ὁ γεωργός ἐστιν). In the first section of the pericope (vv. 1–8), Jesus begins with what can be described as an "illustration," not uncommon in John (see comments on 10:6 and 16:25), that employs agrarian language and describes a context common to first-century farmers.[1] Jesus begins this section with the declaration, "I am the true vine" (Ἐγώ εἰμι ἡ ἄμπελος ἡ ἀληθινή). This is the seventh of seven formal "I am" statements in the Gospel, each containing "I am" (Ἐγώ εἰμι) and a predicate (see comments on 6:35; cf. 8:58). These seven formal "I am" statements are emphatic descriptions of the person and ministry of Jesus and cumulatively form a detailed picture of Jesus Christ. The symbolic impression created by the predicate, "the true vine," is almost entirely supported by the OT, which frequently and with great importance used the image of the vine, often for the designation of Israel (e.g., Ps 80:8–16; Isa 27:2–6; Jer 2:21; Ezek 15:2–6; 17:5–10; 19:10–14).[2]

By declaring himself to be the true vine, Jesus is making a significant symbolic connection with the nature and role of Israel. By comparing this title within the progressive portrayal of Israel in the OT

and seeing its radical transformation, two aspects of Jesus's person and work can be articulated. First, this title describes the *condition* of the true vine, how Jesus entered and took upon himself the failure of Israel and the sinful condition of the world. In every occurrence where "vine" is used to represent Israel, it is used to rebuke and judge Israel. For example, Israel is compared to a vine that is only fit to be burned (Ezek 15:2–6), a once fruitful and abundant vine that has been uprooted, thrown to the ground, stripped of its fruit, and consumed by fire (Ezek 19:10–14), or a once choice vine that was planted in a fertile vineyard that produced only bad fruit (Isa 5:1–2). This biblical context of "the vine" of God is immensely significant, for by this title Jesus declares solidarity with this vine and participation in its condition.

Second, this title describes the *quality* of the true vine, how Jesus accomplished everything the Israel-vine was unable to do: he thrives and bears fruit. The qualification "true" is intended to contrast forcefully Jesus with Israel (cf. 10:11).[3] Jesus is the fulfillment of the Israel-vine and the one who completes its mission. The vine imagery does not intend to depict the Eucharist/Lord's Supper[4] or the church.[5] These comparisons can only be tangential to and derived from the clear and necessary comparison between Jesus and Israel, including her role in the mission of God. The Gospel of John has already taken great care to describe how Jesus fulfills and replaces the old covenant persons and institutions of the temple (e.g., ch. 2), sacred places/mountains (e.g., ch. 4), Moses (ch. 5), and the Jewish feasts (e.g., ch. 6);

---

1. Cf. Jan G. Van der Watt, " 'Metaphorik' in Joh 15,1–8," *BZ* 38 (1994): 67–80.

2. Cf. Bernard, *John*, 2:478; Barrett, *John*, 472–73; Keener, *John*, 2:988–93.

3. Keener, *John*, 2:993.

4. See Brown, *John*, 2:672–74; Barrett, *John*, 472–73.

5. See Bernard, *John*, 2:478.

as the true vine Jesus also supersedes Israel as the center and source of God's people. The *places* (i.e., the land, Jerusalem, temple, altar)[6] and the *people* (Israel, Jewish bloodlines, priestly heritage) have been fulfilled and replaced by *one person*: Jesus Christ.

Jesus provides an important addition to his own self-description: "And my Father is the farmer" (καὶ ὁ πατήρ μου ὁ γεωργός ἐστιν). God has always been depicted in the OT as the farmer, Israel's vinedresser (e.g., Ps 80:7 – 15). Just as the Father has always been planting and tending the vine, it was always the Son who was the intended vine. The Father has not stopped tending his vine; it is the Son who has now "become" the vine tended by the Father, that is, sent by the Father (3:16). With this further revelation the same mission of God that began "in the beginning" of the Old Testament is continued, though this time there is perfect communion and obedience between the Vine and the Farmer, the Son and the Father.

15:2 "Every branch in me that does not bear fruit, he takes it away, and every branch that does bear fruit he cleans it so that it may bear even more fruit" (πᾶν κλῆμα ἐν ἐμοὶ μὴ φέρον καρπόν, αἴρει αὐτό, καὶ πᾶν τὸ καρπὸν φέρον καθαίρει αὐτὸ ἵνα καρπὸν πλείονα φέρῃ).

Jesus continues the "illustration" involving the vine (the Son) and the farmer (the Father), but now introduces a new character: "the branch" (τὸ κλῆμα). According to v. 5, the disciples are the branches. The illustration explains the nature of the relationship between the vine, the branches, and the farmer. Two things are important to note regarding this relationship. First, the branches are "in me" (ἐν ἐμοὶ), that is, in the vine. As this pericope will make clear, connection to the vine is essential for the branches' existence

and productivity (see vv. 4 – 7). There is an innate reciprocity that occurs between the vine and the branches: the branches can only produce by their participation *in* the vine, and the vine produces fruit *through* the branches. Second, the farmer tends to the branches based upon their production of "fruit" (καρπόν). Two different levels of production are described, followed by two different kinds of responses by the farmer. For the branch that *does not* bear fruit, the farmer "takes it away" (αἴρει αὐτό). For the branch that *does* bear fruit, the farmer "cleans it" (καθαίρει αὐτὸ) with the result that it might bear even more. Much has been made of the change of verbs and even the exact meaning of the verbs. Both of these issues need to be addressed in turn.

First, while it cannot be seen in English, the Greek verbs are a play on words since both verbs are so similar, with the latter having the addition of a prefix ("takes away ... cleans" [αἴρει καθαίρει]). The terms can be used to describe agricultural work, especially the latter, but the former is not the natural choice and is probably to be understood as awkward or out of place.[7] That is, the verbs were not chosen because they clearly describe the ancient practices of agriculture; on the contrary, they were chosen because they describe well the relationship Jesus and the Father (the vine and the farmer) have with the disciples (the branches). The true subject matter here is not the work of a farmer (historical) but the work of *the* Farmer (cosmological).

Second, and related to the previous point, the tendency to place too much weight on an isolated and unique reading of the verbs is unwarranted. The play on words between the verbs demands that they be read in concert.[8] This is especially the case

---

6. Gary M. Burge, "Territorial Religion, Johannine Christology, and the Vineyard of John 15," in Green and Turner, *Jesus of Nazareth*, 384–96 (392).

7. See Dodd, *Interpretation*, 136.
8. Cf. Ridderbos, *John*, 516.

with the verb "takes away" (αἴρει), which in popular writings over the last century has been commonly translated as "lifts up." This latter interpretation is grounded upon the perceived contradiction that occurs between a branch being "in [Christ]" and yet "taken away" and so has become commonly associated with debates over eternal security.[9] But there is no need to see in this verse a contradiction.

Several things must be explained. First, as we discussed above, the verb "takes away" is not truly an agricultural word. This alone should prohibit a translation that is rooted in agricultural practices. The word can be translated as "lifts up," but to apply to a word its larger range of meaning loosely or without enough contextual support is a lexical fallacy. Second, there is further proof that the meaning of the verb is not to be found in agricultural practices. The subject matter of the illustration, its real referent, is not the relationship between a farmer and his vine but the relationship between God and his people. As we have seen before, it is not background but foreground that is needed to explain the verb. Third, beyond the lexical limitations, the translation "lifts up" manipulates the illustration and pushes its intended symbolism beyond appropriate limits.

Contrary to popular readings, this verse is not about an individual Christian and Jesus, for v. 1 had already made clear that the symbolism is intended to evoke the corporate dimension of the relationship between God and his people. Just as Christ represents all Israel, in the same way he represents all of us. To separate the Christian from Jesus, even for the purpose of explaining moral responsibility or eternal security, is to make a category mistake. According to v. 1, the branches have corporate solidarity with the vine. The fruit of the branches is the fruit of the vine, just as the branches are part of the vine.[10] It is important to note that the word "branch" (κλῆμα) could have just as easily been translated as "vine," contextually viewed as a subset of the vine proper. Without denying a distinction, this verse explains how the vines (branches) *are* the vine. In this verse, "fruit" is not being used as a requirement but as a symptom of faith. Quite simply, since the farmer is the subject of the verbs, it speaks less about the actions of the individual Christian and more about the actions of God. This interpretation makes even further sense in light of the genre of the farewell discourse, which is similar to the "covenant-form" message with its description of corporate relationship with God.

15:3 "You are already clean because of the word which I have spoken to you" (ἤδη ὑμεῖς καθαροί ἐστε διὰ τὸν λόγον ὃν λελάληκα ὑμῖν). After talking about God, Jesus now turns to his disciples and addresses their situation. In order to protect them from wrongly interpreting the illustration, Jesus emphatically reminds them what he has already told them, that they are "already" (ἤδη) clean. Based upon the use of the same statement earlier, Jesus is declaring that the disciples are already "in" him and are already branches in the vine (see comments on 13:10). Jesus explains that this has already happened "because of the word which I have spoken to you" (διὰ τὸν λόγον ὃν λελάληκα ὑμῖν). In this case "the word" must imply the entirety of his message; the term could even have been translated as "message." Jesus is the Word, and his work has been to make God known (1:18). This has been done for his disciples. Here, then, they are simply encouraged to understand their relationship to and identity in him and, as the next verses will make clear, to "remain" in him.

---

9. On the origin of this interpretation, see J. Carl Laney, "Abiding is Believing: The Analogy of the Vine in John 15:1–6," *BSac* 146 (1989): 55–66. Cf. Arthur W. Pink, *Exposition of the*

Gospel of John, 3 vols. (Cleveland: Cleveland Bible Truth Depot, 1929; repr., Grand Rapids: Zondervan, 1975), 805–8.

10. Cf. Newbigin, *The Light Has Come*, 197.

15:4 "Remain in me, and I will remain in you. Just as a branch cannot bear fruit by itself unless it remains in the vine, so neither can you bear fruit unless you remain in me." (μείνατε ἐν ἐμοί, κἀγὼ ἐν ὑμῖν. καθὼς τὸ κλῆμα οὐ δύναται καρπὸν φέρειν ἀφ' ἑαυτοῦ ἐὰν μὴ μένη ἐν τῇ ἀμπέλῳ, οὕτως οὐδὲ ὑμεῖς ἐὰν μὴ ἐν ἐμοὶ μένητε). Thus far Jesus has described the work of God in the disciples — their identity (vv. 1 – 3); now he turns to address the work of God through the disciples — their purpose and function (vv. 4 – 7). The primary theme presented by the "illustration" is stated as a command: "Remain in me" (μείνατε ἐν ἐμοί). The verb "remain" can be understood to mean "dwell," "stay," or even "continue to live."[11] The term has become a technical term in the Gospel (5:38; 6:56; 8:31; 12:36; 14:10, 17, 25), though its meaning and function is fully established in this pericope.[12] Wallace suggests that the aorist imperative is a constative (a solemn command), which stresses the *urgency* of the act: "It is as if the author says, 'Make this your top priority.'"[13] This command serves to introduce the primary category by which the Christian relates and communes with God. This is the foundational manner of Christian existence; this is the nature of salvation. It is what the church has long described and defined by several theological terms, perhaps primarily "union with Christ."

The lack of a verb in the second clause is significant, for it implies that there is such a link between the "remaining" of both subjects that one verb alone will suffice. Jesus commands them to "remain in him" and equally commands the same of himself, that is, he promises to remain in them. Yet the careful reader of the Gospel will realize that he has already been "remaining" or "dwelling"

("tabernacling") with his people (1:14). All that is left is for them to "remain" in union.

In order to make clear that this mutual indwelling is not something the disciples can simply will into being, Jesus distinguishes the cause from the effect by returning to the illustration.[14] The Vine is the cause of this mutually indwelling existence; the effect is fruit produced in — no, through — the branches. Quite simply, and stated emphatically in the Greek, "The branch cannot bear fruit by itself" (τὸ κλῆμα οὐ δύναται καρπὸν φέρειν ἀφ' ἑαυτοῦ). This is not a new topic in the farewell discourse, for Jesus has spoken previously of this mutual indwelling and interpenetration between the Son and Father and the Christian ("I am in my Father and you are in me and I am in you" [14:20]).

15:5 "I am the vine; you are the branches. The one who remains in me and I in him, he bears much fruit, for apart from me you can do nothing" (ἐγώ εἰμι ἡ ἄμπελος, ὑμεῖς τὰ κλήματα. ὁ μένων ἐν ἐμοὶ κἀγὼ ἐν αὐτῷ οὗτος φέρει καρπὸν πολύν, ὅτι χωρὶς ἐμοῦ οὐ δύνασθε ποιεῖν οὐδέν). After introducing the primary theme of the pericope, Jesus connects it again to the illustration by reidentifying the agents in the illustration: Jesus is the vine and Christians are the branches. The farmer (the Father) and the task of pruning are not being neglected; rather, since the primary mode of "remaining" occurs through the Son, only he is mentioned in relation to the disciples. Jesus also reiterates the mutual indwelling of the Son and disciples, using again only one verb, "remain": "The one who remains in me and I in him" (ὁ μένων ἐν ἐμοὶ κἀγὼ ἐν αὐτῷ). In a real way, both Jesus and the disciples can be described as "the one who remains" (ὁ μένων), for it is a mutual remaining.

---

11. BDAG 630 – 31.

12. Cf. Fernando F. Segovia, "The Theology and Provenance of John 15:1 – 17," *JBL* 101 (1982): 115 – 28 (121).

13. Wallace, *Greek Grammar*, 720.

14. Michaels, *John*, 804.

15:6 "**If a person does not remain in me, he is thrown outside like a branch and is dried up; and they gather them and throw them into the fire and they are burned**" (ἐὰν μή τις μένῃ ἐν ἐμοί, ἐβλήθη ἔξω ὡς τὸ κλῆμα καὶ ἐξηράνθη, καὶ συνάγουσιν αὐτὰ καὶ εἰς τὸ πῦρ βάλλουσιν καὶ καίεται). After describing the positive effects of "remaining" in v. 5, Jesus now describes the negative. The antithesis of "remaining" is departing, though it is important to note that the person is not departing on their own volition but is "thrown outside" (ἐβλήθη ἔξω), depicted in a manner that returns again to the "illustration" for explanatory imagery. As we noted in regard to v. 4, the text is careful to distinguish the cause from the effect; just as Jesus is the primary cause of the mutual indwelling, so he is the primary cause of the departing. The same interpretive looseness exemplified by a "popular" reading of v. 2 is often applied here also, and the same warning needs to be appropriated (see comments on v. 2).

15:7 "**If you remain in me and my word remains in you, ask whatever you wish, and it will happen for you**" (ἐὰν μείνητε ἐν ἐμοὶ καὶ τὰ ῥήματά μου ἐν ὑμῖν μείνῃ, ὃ ἐὰν θέλητε αἰτήσασθε καὶ γενήσεται ὑμῖν). Summarizing the premise of the illustration thus far, including both the language of mutual indwelling and "remaining," as well as the use of his "word" in v. 3, Jesus reminds his disciples of the ministerial authority they have "in him." This is rooted in and expands upon what he said to them in chapter 14 regarding the asking of God (see comments on 14:13–14). But here more is explained. This prayer is not asked in isolation but in the intimate, mutually indwelling relationship between Jesus and the disciples. Unique this time is the phrase "and my word remains in you" (καὶ τὰ ῥήματά μου ἐν ὑμῖν μείνῃ), which explains how the prayer, like the relationship, has Christ as

the primary cause. This is because it is created in and guided from the entirety of Jesus's message — his person and work. In light of our union with Christ, "whatever you wish" is not a blank-check prayer but participation in the life and mission of God. It is we who are "doing" the work of Christ (see 14:31), with the mutual indwelling creating a mutually performed work.

15:8 "**In this way my Father is glorified, that you bear much fruit and become my disciples**" (ἐν τούτῳ ἐδοξάσθη ὁ πατήρ μου, ἵνα καρπὸν πολὺν φέρητε καὶ γένησθε ἐμοὶ μαθηταί). The first section of the pericope (vv. 1–8) concludes with Jesus explaining how an appropriate understanding of the identity (vv. 1–3) and purpose or function (vv. 4–7) of the disciples brings glory to God. Jesus said nearly the same thing already in 14:13, with one noticeable difference. In 14:13 the Father was glorified in the Son, whereas here the Father is glorified in the disciples by means of their production of fruit as well as by their establishment as Jesus's disciples. It is not only the Son who glorifies the Father, for so do the children of God. In fact, the mutuality between Jesus and the disciples probably demands that to glorify the Father by our lives is to do so "in the Son" (14:13), for the branch can do nothing by itself apart from the vine (vv. 4–5). This section of the pericope has made clear that fruitlessness is threatened by fire (v. 6) but also robs God of the glory that rightly belongs to him.[15]

15:9 "**Just as the Father has loved me, I have loved you; remain in my love**" (καθὼς ἠγάπησέν με ὁ πατήρ, κἀγὼ ὑμᾶς ἠγάπησα· μείνατε ἐν τῇ ἀγάπῃ τῇ ἐμῇ). In the second section of the pericope (vv. 9–11) Jesus offers insights into the life prepared for his disciples (v. 8) and the fellowship for those who "remain" in him. The illustration Jesus used in vv. 1–8 is never explicitly mentioned

---

15. Carson, *John*, 518.

again, but its subject matter and themes are still at work in the remainder of the pericope.

According to Jesus, the Christian is the recipient of the love of God. As Jesus explains, the very love of the Father for the Son has been distributed to the disciples through Christ. It is for this reason that Jesus commands the disciples to "remain in my love" (μείνατε ἐν τῇ ἀγάπῃ τῇ ἐμῇ), using the same aorist imperative used earlier (see comments on v. 4). The noticeable difference from v. 4 is that the command is not to remain "in me" but "in my love." While these should be understood as generally synonymous, this command highlights not just participation in the person of Jesus but participation in the nature of God — to "dwell," "stay," even "live" in the love of God. In a remarkable and unexplainable way, the relationship between the Father and the Son is the type and origin of the relationship between the Son and his disciples.[16] While access to God is confined to the mediation provided by Jesus, the love of God does not begin with Jesus but finds its source and energy in the love with which God loved the Son for the salvation of the world (3:16).[17] The disciples are the recipients of this Trinitarian love. As much as God is the cause of this relationship (cf. vv. 4, 6, 7), the command to "remain" encourages the disciple to understand their need to respond to this love, a response Jesus is about to explain.

15:10 "If you keep my commandments, you will remain in my love, just as I have kept my Father's commandments and remain in his love" (ἐὰν τὰς ἐντολάς μου τηρήσητε, μενεῖτε ἐν τῇ ἀγάπῃ μου, καθὼς ἐγὼ τὰς ἐντολὰς τοῦ πατρός μου τετήρηκα καὶ μένω αὐτοῦ ἐν τῇ ἀγάπῃ). Jesus now answers the obvious question raised from the previous command: How does a disciple remain in Jesus's love? The answer is that a disciple remains "if you keep my commandments" (ἐὰν τὰς ἐντολάς μου τηρήσητε). Remaining in the love of God is not some mystical experience; it is an active response of obedience. Jesus said almost the same thing earlier, "If you love me, you will keep my commandments" (14:15), though there obedience was the manner in which the disciples showed love for Jesus. Yet even then Jesus suggested such obedience would facilitate the reception of the love of both the Father and the Son (see comments on 14:21). The intersection of love and obedience has been an important theme in the farewell discourse (see 14:15, 21, 23, 31), and it continues to be the two pillars of the Christian life and experience.

Two aspects of these pillars need to be further explained. First, we must be careful not to reverse the order of love and obedience. That is, obedience springs from love and is a response to love, not the reverse. This pericope has been intentional to make God the cause and the disciple the effect (cf. vv. 4, 6, 7); God is the source and the disciples are passive recipients but also active respondents. Reversing the order makes the disciple the active agent, the one to whom God responds, but this is not so. For God demonstrated and initiated his love for us "while we were still sinners" (Rom 5:8). It is never that we obey in order to receive God's love but rather that we obey because we have received God's love. We obey because God is love, and our obedience returns to him what is rightfully his and shared with us through Christ, who exemplified love and obedience to the Father on our behalf (see 14:31).

Second, just as "love" is not defined in abstraction but by the person and work of God through Jesus, so also is "obedience." Our obedience is enabled by our participation in God (by the Spirit) and is guided by his person (the example of Christ). For our obedience is rooted in and springs not from a natural law but from the holiness and

---

16. Hoskyns, *Fourth Gospel*, 476.

17. Ridderbos, *John*, 519.

perfection of God (1 Pet 1:16) that has been imputed to us through the work of Christ, which has now become the standard, the example, the law of Christ to which we submit (1 Cor 9:21; Gal 6:2). In this way the gospel message rebukes a works-based righteousness and offers a salvation that frees us to be slaves of righteous works (Rom 6:18 – 19) as those "created in Christ Jesus to do good works" (Eph 2:10). Christian obedience, therefore, as an expression of who God is (King, Lord, Savior, and Father) and who we are (disciples, brothers and sisters, slaves of Christ, and children of God), becomes the posture of the Christian.

15:11 "I have spoken these things to you so that my joy may be in you and your joy may be fulfilled" (Ταῦτα λελάληκα ὑμῖν ἵνα ἡ χαρὰ ἡ ἐμὴ ἐν ὑμῖν ᾖ καὶ ἡ χαρὰ ὑμῶν πληρωθῇ). The second section of the pericope (vv. 9 – 11) concludes by giving the twofold reason for speaking about these things: so that "my joy may be in you" (ἡ χαρὰ ἡ ἐμὴ ἐν ὑμῖν ᾖ) and "your joy may be complete" (ἡ χαρὰ ὑμῶν πληρωθῇ).[18] The disciples' participation in God involves not only love but "joy." Coming after the expectation of obedience, this statement stresses that the Christian life is not burdensome but blessing. "Joy" was mentioned before in the Gospel (see comments on 3:29) and is rightly defined by Scripture as a whole as, coincidentally, the "fruit" of God's presence by the Spirit (Gal 5:22) and a sign of God's present reign (Rom 14:17).[19] In the Gospel the fulfillment of joy is a common theme (cf. 3:29; 16:24; 17:13) and is always the result of a life that is participating in God through Christ. Just as God's love for us finds its source in the love between the Father and the Son, so also the fulfillment of joy bestowed upon the disciples is according to Jesus, "my joy," which will "be in you." The joy found in

the perfection of the Trinitarian God is deposited into the Christian and, as the next section will explain, is matured and perfected in mutual love between Christians (vv. 12 – 17).[20]

15:12 "This is my commandment: love one another just as I have loved you" (αὕτη ἐστὶν ἡ ἐντολὴ ἡ ἐμή, ἵνα ἀγαπᾶτε ἀλλήλους καθὼς ἠγάπησα ὑμᾶς). The third section of the pericope (vv. 12 – 17) begins (and ends) with a command from Jesus. This is not a summation of the obedience mentioned above that is required to "remain in my love," but it is one of its primary expressions. The commandments (plural) expected to "remain" in Christ's love in v. 10 are here narrowed to one: "Love one another." An identical commandment was given in the discourse's prologue (see comments on 13:34 – 35). The love of God *for* Christians becomes the love of God *between* Christians. The twofold love for God and one another matches the twofold nature of the greatest commandment explained elsewhere by Jesus (Matt 22:34 – 40; Mark 12:28 – 34; Luke 10:25 – 28). Love for both God and humanity, especially (according to this text) for brothers and sisters in Christ, *is* the life of the church. This is not a normal love but one which stems from the love of Christ: "Just as I have loved you."[21]

15:13 No one has a greater love than this: that a person lay down his life for his friends" (μείζονα ταύτης ἀγάπην οὐδεὶς ἔχει, ἵνα τις τὴν ψυχὴν αὐτοῦ θῇ ὑπὲρ τῶν φίλων αὐτοῦ). Speaking to both his own love for his disciples and the disciples' love for others, Jesus declares that the greatest expression of love is when a person "lay down his life for his friends" (τὴν ψυχὴν αὐτοῦ θῇ ὑπὲρ τῶν φίλων αὐτοῦ). The preposition "for" or "on behalf of"

---

18. Boyle, "The Last Discourse," 216, suggests that this verse is "the central verse of the whole Discourse, not merely arithmetically (it is that!), but also thematically."

19. Cf. Keener, *John*, 2:1004.
20. Cf. Hoskyns, *Fourth Gospel*, 477.
21. Cf. Augustine, *John*, 83.3.349.

(ὑπέρ) has already been used in the Gospel to designate the death of Christ on behalf of the disciples (cf. 6:51); its reference here is expanded to include also a parallel (but certainly not an identical) death of the disciple on behalf of another. In many ways this greatest love is also the greatest test of love, one which Jesus was about to take.[22] The recipient of this greatest love is "his friends" (τῶν φίλων αὐτοῦ). There may be a play on the Greek words at work here between "friend" (φίλος) and "love" (φιλέω), since a "friend" is literally "one who is loved." The term "friend" is not intended to evoke too many possibilities or alternatives (e.g., what about "enemies?") but simply to show the giving of one's life for another.[23] In a sense, the one for whom a person would give his life is, by definition, his friend. Christian love therefore proceeds from the recognition of the love of God in the life-giving death of the Son.

"Friendship" was an important category in the ancient world. It could imply a relationship of dependence or equality, or impersonal alliances or of personal bonds of affection, though the lines between these varieties were not rigid. Friendship did not always imply social equality, which might be significant for the friendship between Jesus and his disciples, between whom commands are given in one direction. Yet in spite of this distinction, friendship reflected a kind of equality that facilitated affection and good will.[24]

15:14 "You are my friends if you do what I command you" (ὑμεῖς φίλοι μού ἐστε ἐὰν ποιῆτε ἃ ἐγὼ ἐντέλλομαι ὑμῖν). Jesus now defines further the friendship about which he is speaking. According to Jesus, friendship is evidenced and defined by obedience. Again the combination of love and obedience is used to define proper relationship between God and the children of God (see 14:15,

21, 23, 31). This verse does not suggest that we can merit Christ's friendship by our obedience. Rather, as v. 13 suggested, such friendship requires first and foremost that Christ focus his greatest love upon us, the gift of his life for ours. And as the recipient of such an extension of friendship, what is reciprocated is the giving of ourselves back to God by means of the appropriate response of love and obedience.

15:15 "I no longer speak to you as slaves, because the slave does not know what his master is doing; but I have called you friends, because everything that I heard from my Father I have made known to you" (οὐκέτι λέγω ὑμᾶς δούλους, ὅτι ὁ δοῦλος οὐκ οἶδεν τί ποιεῖ αὐτοῦ ὁ κύριος· ὑμᾶς δὲ εἴρηκα φίλους, ὅτι πάντα ἃ ἤκουσα παρὰ τοῦ πατρός μου ἐγνώρισα ὑμῖν). Jesus continues to explain the nature of the unique friendship between God and his children. As much as obedience looks like a trait of slaves, it is not. For slaves do not know what their master (Lord) is doing. Friends, on the contrary, are fully aware. It is knowledge that distinguishes a friend from a slave, and this knowledge is reflective of relationship. As Jesus has already declared, the disciples are not slaves but "sons" who have been set free by "the Son" (see comments on 8:35 – 36). This sonship, that is, the "right" to become the children of God (1:12), depicts the inaugurated relationship that exists in "my Father's house" (14:2). Just as Abraham was the first to be called the "friend of God" (Isa 41:8; 2 Chr 20:7; Jas 2:23), the one to whom the covenant of God was announced and initiated (Gen 12:1 – 3), so also we, the children of Abraham (Gal 3:7), are also those to whom the new covenant is announced and initiated. None of this removes the hierarchy between God and his children or removes the need for appropriate responses to God; rather, it actually facilitates such

22. Morris, *John*, 598.
23. See Keener, *John*, 2:1004 – 15; Carson, *John*, 521 – 22.
24. Keener, *John*, 2:1006 – 11.

responses as positive, finding their source not merely in law but in love and not merely because of judgment but also because of joy (v. 11).

15:16 "You did not choose me, but I chose you and appointed you so that you might go and bear fruit — and the fruit should last, so that whatever you ask the Father in my name, he will give to you" (οὐχ ὑμεῖς με ἐξελέξασθε, ἀλλ᾽ ἐγὼ ἐξελεξάμην ὑμᾶς καὶ ἔθηκα ὑμᾶς ἵνα ὑμεῖς ὑπάγητε καὶ καρπὸν φέρητε καὶ ὁ καρπὸς ὑμῶν μένῃ, ἵνα ὅ τι ἂν αἰτήσητε τὸν πατέρα ἐν τῷ ὀνόματί μου δῷ ὑμῖν). Again Jesus reiterates what was suggested in v. 13, that he "chose" the disciples, offering his friendship to them, and has "appointed"[25] them to his purposes. The emphatic first-person pronoun and twice-repeated accusative pronouns, "*I* chose you and appointed you" (ἐγὼ ἐξελεξάμην ὑμᾶς καὶ ἔθηκα ὑμᾶς), gives authority to the statement. The relationship between the Father and the disciples (through Christ and by the Spirit) is for good "works," works that will bear lasting "fruit" under the authority of the Father in the name of the Son, the one who is sending his disciples (cf. 14:12).

The authoritative prayers of the disciples as part of the mission of God has been addressed before (see comments on 14:13 – 14; see also v. 7).[26]

15:17 "I am commanding these things to you so that you might love one another" (ταῦτα ἐντέλλομαι ὑμῖν, ἵνα ἀγαπᾶτε ἀλλήλους). The third section of the pericope (vv. 12 – 17) concludes just as it began, with the love commandment forming an *inclusio* that frames its explanation. The statement could be understood as nearly synonymous with or as slightly stronger than its counterpart in v. 12, with the dependent clause (ἵνα plus the subjunctive) focusing more on the intended result. The latter is to be preferred, even if only because of the cumulative force of the argument.

The pericope ultimately ends exhorting an intraecclesial unity that stems from and parallels the intra-Trinitarian unity, inviting the reader through faith in Christ to be taken up into the love of the Father and the Son (by the Spirit).[27] But it is more than an invitation; it is also a command. For this pericope presents the church with the essential criterion for its belonging to and participating in the Vine.[28]

Theology in Application

In the fourth of eight sections of the farewell discourse, Jesus makes the third of six statements that explain, encourage, and exhort the disciples as they transition to the era of the new covenant, from life with Jesus to life "in Christ" and *in* the Spirit. Through this pericope the reader is exhorted to situate themselves in the person and work of Christ, through whom they become participants in the work of God and the very expression of God's love in the world.

Jesus is True Israel

This pericope magnifies the incarnational ministry of Jesus, moving him from his "tabernacling" presence as a human like us to his role as the embodiment of Israel (v. 1). Just as he bore our "flesh" and entered into the sinful condition of humanity,

---

25. See Barrett, *John*, 478.

26. Cf. Schlatter, *Der Evangelist Johannes*, 305; Hoskyns, *Fourth Gospel*, 478.

27. Bultmann describes faith and love as a unity (*John*, 547).

28. Ridderbos, *John*, 522.

so also did he bear the embarrassing condition and record of Israel — a vine that had been uprooted, thrown to the ground, stripped of its fruit, and consumed by fire — and enter into the sinful and failed state of Israel. But in distinction from our individual existence and Israel's corporate existence, Jesus fulfilled to perfection the role of Israel. Jesus restored Israel, becoming the mediator that Israel was always intended to be in him. Thus, Jesus is true Israel. All the old covenant *places* and *people* have been fulfilled and replaced by *one person*, Jesus Christ. Every other vine, including the rich (and biblical!) heritage of Israel, is declared bankrupt and counterfeit in contrast to the true vine of God. In fact, Jesus had always been the intended and true vine, just as the farmer who had been planting and tending his vineyard had always been the Father.

"Remain"

As much as the call to the church is to "go" (the Great Commission of Matt 28:18 – 20 or even John 20:21), there is just as much a call to the Christian to "stay," "abide," and "remain" in Christ. To "remain" is to find one's existence and meaning by means of the provision of Christ. It is to be aware of our dependence and insufficiency, which is a state that the world tries to reverse and deny. This command to "remain" is not a burden but a gift, an opportunity to really live and, ironically, to truly be free. It is to have life as it was designed, in harmony with the Creator. It is in a real sense to dwell in the house of God, to "tabernacle" with God through Christ and by the Spirit, even if a more perfect dwelling is still to come (cf. 14:2). And this command is matched by a promise that if we remain in Christ, he pledges to "remain" with us. To remain, then, is to exist in the grace and love of God.

Christian Fruit

The bearing of fruit is the natural and foundational work of a branch. A fruitless branch is, quite simply, a dead branch. In the same way, the Christian life is branch-like in that it not only needs to be attached to the Vine to survive, but it also is expected to bear fruit. Its purpose is not simply to exist. The Christian's purpose is not simply to exist, to find enjoyment in their private spiritual quest or moral program, but to participate in the fruit-bearing task required throughout God's vineyard. The "fruit" of the Christian is participation in the mission of God through the church and to the world. It need not be limited to one or two Christian works, for God is the one who defines fruit and grows branches in the places he sees fit. All this has been God's plan from the beginning. As the apostle Paul explains, "For we are God's handiwork, created in Christ Jesus to do good works, which God prepared in advance for us to do" (Eph 2:10). Thus, there is an obligation placed upon us to bear fruit. This is in no way a work that merits salvation (cf. Eph 2:8 – 9) but actually the reverse. It is a natural response of those who have already received it.

Trust and Obey ... to Be Joyful in Jesus

God wants us happy, but not with the definition or means by which our cultures often define it. Rather, Jesus exhorts us to "remain" in the Trinitarian love into which we have been invited and placed by obeying his commandments (vv. 9 – 10). This is hardly unfair, for Christ himself did the same thing in response to his Father. Biblical "law" has always been about participating in God and finding true joy in life. That is, obedience is not intended to limit freedom but to provide and facilitate it. The sin that is innate to humanity has distorted that premise since its beginning. The Christian, however, begins to see the unseen, that our freedom is found in a radical commitment to obey the "law of Christ" (1 Cor 9:21; Gal 6:2).

There is a need in our churches today to redefine how we speak about obedience. We obey the commandments of God not to earn or keep our salvation but to experience salvation. Obedience is the response of the person who is saved — not perfect obedience (1 John 1:8) but a knowledge of what sin really is and an (imperfect) desire to live as life truly is in God through Christ and by the Spirit. That is, obedience is to live life in humble submission to our Father as his children. Exhorting obedience is not legalism but grace. It is giving true life to people who truly need it. This focus on obedience should not eclipse grace but magnify it, for our (imperfect) obedience will not only need to be surrounded and supported by grace but in fact finds its source in grace — the obedience of Christ on our behalf. This, therefore, is true joy.

Christian Love and Friendship

The love of God *for* Christians becomes the love of God *between* Christians. This participation in the love of God creates a Christian relationship, a Christian friendship. Such "friends" are not casual acquaintances but are in a life-sharing and life-giving relationship that finds expression in a cumulative life together. In a Christian friendship one life might even be exchanged for another, promoting this cumulative "life" by means of a cumulative love — life and love that begin and end with God and therefore give unity and meaning to everything in between.

This is the biblical vision of the life of the church. Unfortunately, compared to most of our local churches, it is more of a dream than a reality. Can the church recover this kind of community life, where friendship is defined not by one's Facebook status but by our corporate status as sons and daughters who are friends of God — in communion with the Father through the Son and by the Spirit? We must pray to that end! For this vision is the extension of God's love that began in the sending of his Son (3:16). It is to find its embodiment and expression within the church and is to enable the church's mission to the world. God's love is not an option; it is a necessity, a foundation to the very existence of the church and also therefore to its life together.

John 15:18 – 27

Literary Context

This pericope is the fifth of eight sections of the farewell discourse. Surrounded by a prologue (13:31 – 38) and an epilogue (16:25 – 33), the farewell discourse can be divided into six significant and developing thematic statements by Jesus, with each offering comfort and consolation for the disciples (and the reader), befitting the nature of a farewell discourse (see comments before 13:1). These six statements within the farewell discourse offer one long exhortation to stay the course and encouragement that their efforts will be matched by the Trinitarian God himself. In the first three statements, Jesus explains his relationship to the disciples and their future existence in him; in the last three statements Jesus explains the disciples' relation to the world and their future existence in it. In this pericope, the disciples are warned about the hatred of the world and given insight into its source and judgment. The disciples — and the reader — are exhorted to see the work of God in the world, not only God's judgment of the world but his witness to the world by the Spirit and through the disciples.

VII. The Farewell Discourse (13:1 – 17:26)
   A. Introduction: The Love of Jesus (13:1 – 30)
      1. Jesus and the Washing of his Disciples' Feet (13:1 – 20)
      2. Jesus Announces His Betrayal (13:21 – 30)
   B. The Farewell Discourse (13:31 – 16:33)
      1. Prologue: Glory, Departure, and Love (13:31 – 38)
      2. I Am the Way and the Truth and the Life (14:1 – 14)
      3. I Will Give You the Paraclete (14:15 – 31)
      4. I Am the True Vine (15:1 – 17)
➡   **5. I Have Also Experienced the Hate of the World (15:18 – 27)**
      6. I Will Empower You by the Paraclete (16:1 – 15)
      7. I Will Turn Your Grief into Joy (16:16 – 24)
      8. Epilogue: Speaking Plainly, Departure, and Peace (16:25 – 33)
   C. Conclusion: The Prayer of Jesus (17:1 – 26)

Main Idea

The Christian is so united with Christ that they will experience the world's hate of God, through whom its sinful condition has been made known. Yet it is in the world that the Christian is appointed to be a witness to Christ with the Paraclete.

Translation

John 15:18–27

	Section #5 of "Farewell Discourse"	
18a	Condition	*"If the world hates you,*
b	Inferential Command	*know that it hated me before you.*
19a	Condition	*If you were from the world,*
b	Inference	*the world would love you as its own;*
c	Basis	*because you are not from the world, but*
d	Contrast	*I chose you from the world,*
e	Conclusion of 19a–e	*for this reason the world hates you.*
20a	Command	*Remember the word*
b		*which I spoke to you:*
c	Restatement of 13:16	*'A slave is not greater than his master.'*
d	Condition	*If they persecuted me,*
e	Inference	*they will persecute you also.*
f	Condition	*If they obeyed my word,*
g	Inference	*they will obey yours also.*
21a	Contrast	*But they will do all these things to you*
b	Basis	*because of my name,*
c	Basis	*because they do not know the one*
d	Source	*who sent me.*
22a	Condition	*If I had not come and*
b		*spoken to them,*
c	Inference	*they would have no sin.*
d	Contrast	*But now they have no excuse*
e	Reference	*for their sin.*
23a	Description/Condition	*The one who hates me …*
b	Result/Inference	*… also hates my Father.*
24a	Emphatic Restatement	*If I had not done among them the works*
b	of 22–23	*which no one else did,*
c		*they would have no sin.*
d		*But now they have both seen and*
e		*hated me and*
f		*my Father.*

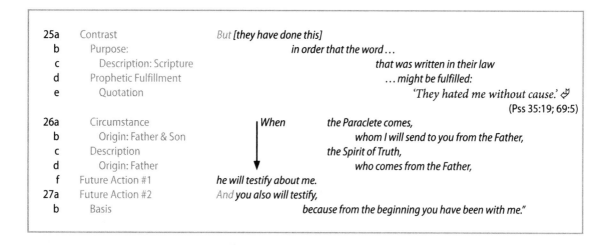

25a	Contrast	*But [they have done this]*
b	Purpose:	*in order that the word …*
c	Description: Scripture	*that was written in their law*
d	Prophetic Fulfillment	*… might be fulfilled:*
e	Quotation	*'They hated me without cause.'*
		(Pss 35:19; 69:5)
26a	Circumstance	*When* the Paraclete comes,
b	Origin: Father & Son	*whom I will send to you from the Father,*
c	Description	*the Spirit of Truth,*
d	Origin: Father	*who comes from the Father,*
f	Future Action #1	*he will testify about me.*
27a	Future Action #2	*And you also will testify,*
b	Basis	*because from the beginning you have been with me."*

Structure and Literary Form

As the fifth of eight sections of the farewell discourse, this pericope is part of the fourth (and longest) substantial monologue in the narrative proper. A monologue (see Introduction) is similar to a dialogue in that it is set in the context of an engagement and conflict, but rather than engaging point-for-point it allows for a lengthy argument. A monologue can contain elements of rhetoric, challenge, and conflict, but it does so in a sustained presentation.

This pericope is the fourth of six statements by Jesus given to exhort and encourage his disciples. The *inclusio* that concluded the last pericope (15:12 – 17) and the change of topic warrants the start of a new pericope here at v. 18. The majority of commentators conclude this pericope at 16:4, in part because the topic of the world's hatred introduced in v. 18 clearly extends through 16:4.[1] But the topic of hatred does not clearly stop at 16:4 either, for there is no clear break from this topic, which extends throughout the discourse. This pericope introduces the *cause* of the persecution; what begins in 16:1 is the explanation of the expected *response* of the disciples.[2]

The farewell discourse as a whole makes an even larger transition here. From 13:31 to 15:17, the focus has been on the relationship between the disciples and Jesus (statements 1 – 3), but from 15:18 to 16:33 the focus transitions to the disciples' engagement with the world (statements 4 – 6).

---

1. See Fernando F. Segovia, "John 15:18 – 16:4a: A First Addition to the Original Farewell Discourse?," *CBQ* 45 (1983): 210 – 30.

2. Carson, *John*, 528.

Exegetical Outline

→ **5. I Have Also Experienced the Hate of the World (15:18–27)**
    a. The Source of the World's Hatred (vv.18–21)
    b. The Judgment against the World (vv. 22–25)
    c. The Witness of the Paraclete (vv. 26–27)

Explanation of the Text

Since this entire section of the Gospel and "the farewell discourse" proper are replete with interpretive issues, we refer the reader to the first pericope of this section where we provided an overview of the nature (genre), literary structure, and function of the farewell discourse (see comments before 13:1).

15:18 "If the world hates you, know that it hated me before you (Εἰ ὁ κόσμος ὑμᾶς μισεῖ, γινώσκετε ὅτι ἐμὲ πρῶτον ὑμῶν μεμίσηκεν). The focus on the love relationship between Jesus and his disciples in the first half of the farewell discourse (statements 1–3) transitions to the hate relationship between the world and the disciples in the second half (statements 4–6; on "the world," see comments on 1:10). The disciples will need to "remain" in him because according to Jesus "the world hates you." But Jesus states this fact in a manner that places him between the disciples and the world. Jesus communicates this by stating it as a condition: If the world hates you, "know that it hated me before you" (γινώσκετε ὅτι ἐμὲ πρῶτον ὑμῶν μεμίσηκεν), with "me" (ἐμὲ) emphatic in form and position. They are not only to "know" that they will be the objects of the world's hate but two further things.[3] First, this hate is not new. Nothing about the world's hate toward them should surprise them or make them expect anything different. Second,

this hate is directed primarily at Jesus and only secondarily at the disciples. The disciples will experience real hate, but it is hate that is rooted in their affiliation with and participation in Jesus. There is a sharp contrast between the disciples and the world — just as the disciples are to be known by their love, the world will be known by its hatred.[4] This response by the world, therefore, should not come as a surprise (cf. 1 John 3:13).

15:19 "If you were from the world, the world would love you as its own; because you are not from the world, but I chose you from the world, for this reason the world hates you" (εἰ ἐκ τοῦ κόσμου ἦτε, ὁ κόσμος ἂν τὸ ἴδιον ἐφίλει· ὅτι δὲ ἐκ τοῦ κόσμου οὐκ ἐστέ, ἀλλ᾿ ἐγὼ ἐξελεξάμην ὑμᾶς ἐκ τοῦ κόσμου, διὰ τοῦτο μισεῖ ὑμᾶς ὁ κόσμος). Jesus defines further the world's hatred toward the disciples. The root of this hate is the disciples' lack of identification with the world. Simply stated, the Christian is no longer "from the world" (ἐκ τοῦ κόσμου), a prepositional phrase that describes to whom the disciples belong and the nature of their identity.[5] They used to be "*from* the world," and they will continue to be "*in* the world" (17:11), but Christ himself — note the emphatic first-person pronoun — "chose" (ἐγὼ ἐξελεξάμην) them *out of* the world. This verb was used earlier to describe

---

3. The verb "know" (γινώσκετε) could be an indicative or imperative, and both moods make sense in the context.

4. Morris, *John*, 602. Cf. Hoskyns, *Fourth Gospel*, 479.

5. Cf. Donald Heinz, "Brief Translation Note on John 15:19," *CTM* 39 (1968): 775.

the works the disciples would perform (see comments on 15:16); here it is used to describe the people they would become.[6]

Again, the prologue's announcement is needed here. While still *in* the world (historical reality), they are at the exact same time no longer *from* the world (cosmological reality). The Christian is so identified "in Christ" that they are now distinguishable from their natural-born origin: they have been born anew "from above" (3:1 – 11). It is "for this reason" (διὰ τοῦτο) that the world hates the disciples. Christ's disciples are now a foreign entity in the world, and the world's antibodies will naturally respond to them in force with intent to destroy.

15:20 **"Remember the word which I spoke to you: 'A slave is not greater than his master.' If they persecuted me, they will persecute you also. If they obeyed my word, they will obey yours also"** (μνημονεύετε τοῦ λόγου οὗ ἐγὼ εἶπον ὑμῖν, Οὐκ ἔστιν δοῦλος μείζων τοῦ κυρίου αὐτοῦ. εἰ ἐμὲ ἐδίωξαν, καὶ ὑμᾶς διώξουσιν· εἰ τὸν λόγον μου ἐτήρησαν, καὶ τὸν ὑμέτερον τηρήσουσιν). To explain this further, Jesus reminds them what he said to them earlier (see comments on 13:16). The identity of the disciples is so grounded in their relation to Christ and his identity that they can be expected to receive similar treatment. The world's treatment of Jesus will continue against his disciples (cf. Acts 9:4: "Saul, Saul, why are you persecuting me?"). The church really is the body of Christ and will physically participate in his real sufferings (cf. Col 1:24). And this treatment is entirely rooted in the world's relationship to Christ; the disciples' relation to the world is derived entirely from their relation to Christ. Using Jesus's examples, some will persecute the disciples (as they did Jesus) and some

will respond in obedience (as they did to Jesus), but all respond ultimately to the person and work of Christ.[7] The call of the Christian is to receive the hate of the world with humility but also with the intention of service.[8]

15:21 **"But they will do all these things to you because of my name, because they do not know the one who sent me"** (ἀλλὰ ταῦτα πάντα ποιήσουσιν εἰς ὑμᾶς διὰ τὸ ὄνομά μου, ὅτι οὐκ οἴδασιν τὸν πέμψαντά με). Jesus concludes the first section of the pericope (vv. 18 – 21) by giving the ultimate, deep-rooted source of the world's hatred of the disciples. Two reasons are given. First, the world rejects the person of Jesus. The phrase "because of my name" (διὰ τὸ ὄνομά μου) is important here. As we discussed earlier (see comments on 1:12), the concept of a "name" in the ancient world was not merely a label but the character of a person. Thus, the world rejects everything the name "Jesus" means and stands for and therefore will do the same to his disciples, the church. The world has rejected the representative of God, Jesus Christ; they will surely do the same to his other representatives.

Second, the world rejects the Father. If the world rejects the representative and the one sent, then they will also reject the one he represents and "the one who sent" (τὸν πέμψαντά). The judgment by Jesus that the world "does not know" (οὐκ οἴδασιν) the Father will be explained in the next section of the pericope (vv. 22 – 25) but primarily refers to the innate enmity between the world and God (cf. 1 John 2:23). The knowledge of God is one of the deep existential issues that the Gospel addresses (see comments on 7:28 – 29; 8:19). And since the knowledge of God is only grasped through the Son

---

6. Barrett, *John*, 480.

7. See Carson, *John*, 525 – 26.

8. See Barnabas Lindars, "The Persecution of Christians in John 15:18 – 16:4a," in *Suffering and Martyrdom in the New Testament*, ed. William Horbury and Brian McNeil (Cambridge: Cambridge University Press, 1981), 48 – 69 (59).

(1:18), the rejection of the Son becomes also the rejection of the Father.[9]

15:22 "If I had not come and spoken to them, they would have no sin. But now they have no excuse for their sin" (εἰ μὴ ἦλθον καὶ ἐλάλησα αὐτοῖς, ἁμαρτίαν οὐκ εἴχοσαν· νῦν δὲ πρόφασιν οὐκ ἔχουσιν περὶ τῆς ἁμαρτίας αὐτῶν). In the second section of the pericope (vv. 22–25) Jesus transitions from the source of the world's hatred to the judgment against the world, and transitions from his disciples' work to his own. Jesus utters two statements that need to be understood in relation to one another: (1) "If I had not come … they would have no sin"; and (2) "now they have no excuse for their sin." The first statement does not claim that sin only became an issue with the arrival of Jesus but rather that sin became most apparent with the arrival of Jesus (see Rom 5:13). The true source and authority for the evaluation and condemnation of sin was not the law of Moses but the law of Christ.[10]

The second statement is best taken as synonymous with the first or as an explanation of the first. The arrival of Jesus made sin known; that is, it made it official that "now they have no excuse." Jesus had spoken this way about judgment and sin before (see comments on 9:39–41) and how the light exposes the evil of the darkness (see comments on 3:18–20). The coming of Jesus inaugurated the judgment of the world. This is what Jesus means when he says he has taken away their "excuse" (πρόφασιν) or their "defense of an action."[11] As the Gospel has been making clear, Jesus is both the prosecuting attorney (Judge) and the defense attorney (sacrifice) for the world (cf. 3:16–21). One either receives the judgment they deserve from Jesus (justice and wrath) or allows Jesus to receive undeservedly the judgment on their behalf (mercy and grace).

15:23 "The one who hates me also hates my Father" (ὁ ἐμὲ μισῶν καὶ τὸν πατέρα μου μισεῖ). By linking himself to the Father, Jesus makes clear that the judgment against the world is no small thing but is the very judgment of God. Jesus is the agent *par excellence*, the representative of the Father (cf. 1:18). When someone hates and therefore rejects Jesus, they are rejecting God himself. The intimate relationship and union between the Father and the Son is one of the primary messages of the Gospel, and Jesus made this exact point earlier, though there it was stated positively (see comments on 13:20).

15:24 "If I had not done among them the works which no one else did, they would have no sin. But now they have both seen and hated me and my Father" (εἰ τὰ ἔργα μὴ ἐποίησα ἐν αὐτοῖς ἃ οὐδεὶς ἄλλος ἐποίησεν, ἁμαρτίαν οὐκ εἴχοσαν· νῦν δὲ καὶ ἑωράκασιν καὶ μεμισήκασιν καὶ ἐμὲ καὶ τὸν πατέρα μου). Jesus restates and summarizes the argument of vv. 22–23. Here Jesus emphasizes not only his presence among them but also the uniqueness of "the works" (τὰ ἔργα) he accomplished. Again Jesus claims that his "works" also contributed to the world's realization of its sin-laden condition. As in v. 22, Jesus claims that the works of Jesus are what inaugurated the judgment of the world. Jesus's "works" are his miracles (e.g., 5:36; 9:3; 10:32, 37; 14:10) and the "signs" (σημεῖα) that were so important to his ministry. These "works" reveal the character and power of God the Father and that in Christ he is active in a unique way. The "signs" of Jesus are distinguishing marks, tokens, or signals, which in the OT were often linked to a special part of a prophet's activity, and in this way are innately eschatological (see comments on 2:11). At the coming of the person of Jesus and the inauguration of his work, the world was witness to

---

9. Cf. Hoskyns, *Fourth Gospel*, 332.
10. Cf. Ridderbos, *John*, 525; Michaels, *John*, 822.

11. BDAG 889.

the prophetic "works" and "signs" of God that gave them no excuse to deny their sin; by these works they were officially declared sinners.

15:25 "But [they have done this] in order that the word that was written in their law might be fulfilled: 'They hated me without cause'" (ἀλλ' ἵνα πληρωθῇ ὁ λόγος ὁ ἐν τῷ νόμῳ αὐτῶν γεγραμμένος ὅτι Ἐμίσησάν με δωρεάν). The second section of the pericope (vv. 22 – 25) concludes with a claim by Jesus that the hate and rejection of God by the world is the fulfillment of Scripture. The quotation appears in slightly different forms in Psalm 35:19 and Psalm 69:5. Jesus speaks through the Psalms to declare the betrayal and treachery of the world and its unprovoked hatred. By using a psalm of a righteous sufferer who faces baseless accusation and persecution, Jesus not only fulfills that psalm by becoming the fullest expression of the righteous sufferer but also fulfills in his person the deliverance from such injustice.[12] The quotation in this context points clearly at the Jews, placing the hatred of God in the personal context first introduced by the prologue (cf. 1:11). Even the qualification "their law" (τῷ νόμῳ αὐτῶν) was used "in order to rivet upon the Jews those scriptures in which they boast themselves so proudly, and then to prove those same scriptures prophetic of their apostasy."[13]

15:26 "When the Paraclete comes, whom I will send to you from the Father, the Spirit of truth, who comes from the Father, he will testify about me" (Ὅταν ἔλθῃ ὁ παράκλητος ὃν ἐγὼ πέμψω ὑμῖν παρὰ τοῦ πατρός, τὸ πνεῦμα τῆς ἀληθείας ὃ παρὰ τοῦ πατρὸς ἐκπορεύεται, ἐκεῖνος μαρτυρήσει περὶ ἐμοῦ). The third section of the pericope (vv. 26 – 27) begins with a reintroduction of the Paraclete. The last two verses of this pericope are not awkwardly inserted here, as some have suggested, but offer the necessary consolation and exhortation to the disciples who have just been informed about the hate they are soon to face from the world. Jesus is departing and the hate of the world is coming. How are the disciples able to face the world and actually continue to perform the works of God in it? These two verses address this very issue and offer a perfect counter to the forecasted hatred of the world (vv. 18 – 19).[14]

This is the third of four occurrences of "Paraclete" in the Gospel (14:16, 26; 15:26; 16:7; cf. 1 John 2:1). It is significant that the Paraclete is mentioned in both halves of the farewell discourse. For while the first three statements of Jesus (14:1 – 15:7) depict the Paraclete's special relationship to the disciples as the manifestation of the presence of God, the last three statements of Jesus (15:18 – 16:24) depict the Paraclete's unique role in the world, involving both the conviction of sin and judgment (for an overview of "the Paraclete," see comments on 14:16). Jesus reintroduces the Paraclete here with a title used before, "the Spirit of truth" (see comments on 14:17), and with similar explanations of the Paraclete's origin (see comments on 14:16). The Spirit/Paraclete is not only the manifest presence of God's person in the world but is also the power of God's work in the world.

Jesus explains that the Paraclete "will testify about me" (μαρτυρήσει περὶ ἐμοῦ). Just as John the Baptist preceded Christ and testified about him (see comments on 1:7), so does the Spirit follow after Christ to testify about him. The language here might give credence to the legal and forensic definition of the term "Paraclete," but as much as the Spirit is clearly related to and part of the witness of the disciples, that is not what is stated here — and for an important reason. The Spirit is not merely facilitating the witness of the disciples,

---

12. Cf. Köstenberger, "John," 493 – 95.
13. Hoskyns, *Fourth Gospel*, 481.

14. Cf. Carson, *John*, 528.

even though he is sent "to you" (ὑμῖν), but offers
his own witness to Christ. It might take place in
and through the disciples (cf. v. 27), but it is the
Spirit's own witness, even as the Father independently testified about Jesus (cf. 5:37–38). Such
language strongly suggests that ultimately God is
the primary and first-order witness to himself. All
other witnesses are secondary and supported by
the foundational witness of God himself.[15] Just as
the "works" of the church are in reality the works of
God (see 14:12–14; 15:4–5), so also is the witness
of the church.

**15:27 "And you also will testify, because from
the beginning you have been with me"** (καὶ ὑμεῖς
δὲ μαρτυρεῖτε, ὅτι ἀπ' ἀρχῆς μετ' ἐμοῦ ἐστε). The
pericope concludes by returning to where it started
in v. 18, with the disciples. As much as the Spirit/
Paraclete is an independent (foundational) witness, Jesus declares to the disciples that "you also
will testify" (καὶ ὑμεῖς δὲ μαρτυρεῖτε). While this
will be further explained later in the discourse (see

16:13–15; cf. Acts 1:8), the lack of specificity here
is important. Jesus introduces the disciples not
only to the persecution they will face but also to the
office to which they are appointed as they join the
mission of God (through Christ and by the Spirit).
The exact nature of this office and the expected
response will be explained in what follows (e.g.,
16:1–15).[16] This verse simply declares the fact of
the future Christian witness.

Jesus connects his disciples' future witness about
him to their current presence with him. Indeed,
they have been with him "from the beginning" (ἀπ'
ἀρχῆς), that is, from the start of his ministry. This
statement gives importance to the disciples' personal participation in Jesus's ministry (cf. the similar requirement for Judas Iscariot's replacement in
Acts 1:22). But it also suggests that the earthly and
historical ministry of Jesus is not eclipsed or superseded by the arrival of the Paraclete. The ministry of the Paraclete and of the church itself as the
body of Christ is the continuation of the ministry
of Jesus (cf. 1 Thess 2:4; 1 John 1:1–2).

Theology in Application

In the fifth of eight sections of the farewell discourse, Jesus makes the fourth of
six statements that explain, encourage, and exhort the disciples as they transition
to the era of the new covenant, from life with Jesus to life "in Christ" and *in* the
Spirit. After transitioning the discourse to the relationship between Christians and
the world, Jesus moves from the Christian love that exists with God and between
other Christians to the hate Christians will receive from the world. Through this
pericope the reader is exhorted to come to understand how their new relationship
to God demands a new relationship to the world and ultimately to the purposes of
God behind it all.

The World Hates God

This pericope peels back the masks of culture(s) and allows the reader to see
the true source of the world's hatred. The world hates God! The arrival of Christ

15. See Augustine, *John*, 92.1.363.

16. Cf. Barrett, *John*, 482.

was the climactic revelation of sin and exposed fully the true nature of the world. Sin is distortion, perverting what is true and good. Sin reverses the standards and measurements, proclaiming evil things to be good and good things to be evil. The good news is not just an announcement about the person of Jesus; it is also an announcement — a true report — regarding the state of the world. The arrival of Jesus inaugurated truth, God-established truth, as the new standard and measurement of life. For this reason the world, enslaved to sin, darkness, falsehood, and evil hates God. For it has been exposed for what it truly is or, more accurately, what it is not. Ultimately, the Christian begins to emulate the Father's love for the world (3:16) even though the world can only hate in return. But the Christian has seen that reaction before, for he or she too has hated God — right up to the moment when he or she saw "truth and grace."

Not "from This World"

One of the clearest symptoms of faith in Christ is the world's hatred. There is a direct connection between God's love and the world's hate. For this reason the Christian life is a paradox, for while one was once *from* the world and still lives *in* the world, they have been also chosen *out of* the world (v. 19). The Christian no longer belongs to the world but to God and therefore are now living in the world as "strangers and aliens" (1 Pet 2:11).

Unlike science-fiction films, however, in this story the "aliens" of God are the natural or normal ones. They are the ones who have been reconnected to their Creator, living as they were designed to live in relationship with God. It is the rest of the world, the nonaliens, who are truly alien — living unnaturally and in opposition to the created order. Ironically, to be not "from this world" is to fit right in — not with the unnaturalness of the world, the brokenness of the creation and its creatures — but with the world as it was created to be ("good") and with the Creator, Jesus Christ (1:3).

Remember . . .

Jesus exhorts his disciples in v. 20 to "remember the word" that he spoke to them. Such a command echoes beyond the first disciples who heard it and demands to be heard today. Christians must constantly be living in the "Word" and on his "word," being guided to see God behind all mighty plans and minute details. Thus, we are being commanded here to remember not only what Jesus once said to his disciples but what Jesus is still saying to his disciples.

The Purposes of God

This pericope explains that the rejection of God and his disciples by the world is not a surprise, for God knew of it and even prophesied about it long before (v. 25).

The Gospel has already explained that God has plans that all other planning is founded upon (see 12:37 – 42). God is never the passive recipient of the will of the world, for his will always precedes and supersedes. Even the crucifixion according to Jesus was done by his permission alone (10:18). This might be difficult to define and explain, but it must be applied. God's purposes will not be thwarted and are accomplished not only through his perfection and love but even despite the world's imperfection and hate. This not only helps us know in whom we place our trust but confirms why it was placed in him in the first place.

The Witness of the Spirit

The Spirit is often discussed in regard to the support and empowerment he gives to the Christian. This is right and good and should continue to be taught. But this pericope reminds us that the Spirit is not merely to be thought of in a utilitarian manner, for he is an independent and foundational witness (and worker) in his own right. Just as the Father is an independent witness to the Son (5:37 – 38), so the Spirit is an independent witness to the Son (v. 26). The theological implications of this are important to note. Such language strongly suggests that ultimately God is the primary and first-order witness to himself. All other witnesses are secondary and supported by the foundational witness of God himself. This truth gives some explanation to the authority of the Gospel itself and to all of Scripture.[17]

---

17. Calvin, *Institutes*, 1:78 – 79.

John 16:1 – 15

Literary Context

This pericope is the sixth of eight sections of the farewell discourse. Surrounded by a prologue (13:31 – 38) and an epilogue (16:25 – 33), the farewell discourse can be divided into six significant and developing thematic statements by Jesus, with each offering comfort and consolation for the disciples (and the reader), befitting the nature of a farewell discourse (see comments before 13:1). These six statements within the farewell discourse offer one long exhortation to stay the course and encouragement that their efforts will be matched by the Trinitarian God himself. In the first three statements, Jesus explains his relationship to the disciples and their future existence in him; in the last three statements Jesus explains the disciples' relationship to the world and their future existence in it. In this pericope, the fifth statement, the disciples are given further insight into the coming Spirit/Paraclete and the empowerment and guidance he will provide for the disciples and the nature of his work in the world.

VII. The Farewell Discourse (13:1 – 17:26)
    A. Introduction: The Love of Jesus (13:1 – 30)
        1. Jesus and the Washing of His Disciples' Feet (13:1 – 20)
        2. Jesus Announces His Betrayal (13:21 – 30)
    B. The Farewell Discourse (13:31 – 16:33)
        1. Prologue: Glory, Departure, and Love (13:31 – 38)
        2. I Am the Way and the Truth and the Life (14:1 – 14)
        3. I Will Give You the Paraclete (14:15 – 31)
        4. I Am the True Vine (15:1 – 17)
        5. I Have Also Experienced the Hate of the World (15:18 – 27)
        6. I Will Empower You by the Paraclete (16:1 – 15)
        7. I Will Turn Your Grief into Joy (16:16 – 24)
        8. Epilogue: Speaking Plainly, Departure, and Peace (16:25 – 33)
    C. Conclusion: The Prayer of Jesus (17:1 – 26)

Main Idea

The ministry of the Paraclete is to convict the world of its sinful and self-righteous existence and to guide the church in its Christian existence. The Spirit is an agent of the love of God for the world and a source of security and empowerment for the church.

Translation

John 16:1–15

	Section #6 of "Farewell Discourse"	
1a	Prefaced Basis for 1b–15	*"I have spoken these things to you*
b	Intended Result	*so that you might not stumble.*
2a	Explanation (2–4a)	*They will exclude you from the synagogue;*
b	Emphasis	*indeed,*
c	Assertion	*an hour is coming*
d	Circumstance	*when everyone who kills you …*
e	Characters' Thoughts	*… will think they are offering a service to ☙ present to God.*
3a	Assertion	*And they will do these things*
b	Basis	*because they have known*
c		*neither the Father*
d		*nor me.*
4a	Restatement of 1a (Inclusio)	*But I have spoken these things to you*
b	Intended Result	*so that …*
c	Circumstance	*when their hour comes,*
d		*… you may remember*
e	Content	*that I spoke to you about them.*
f	Contrast	*But I did not speak these things to you*
g	Time	*from the beginning,*
h	Basis	*because I was with you.*
5a	Declaration of Departure	*But now I go to the one*
b	Destination/Origin	*who sent me,*
c	Rebuke	*and no one is asking me,*
d		*'Where are you going?'*
6a	Contrast	*But*
b	Basis	*because I have spoken these things to you,*
c	Continued Rebuke	*grief has filled your heart.*

7a	Transition to "Paraclete"	*But I tell you the truth,*
b	Assertion	*it is better for you that I go away;*
c	Explanation	*for*
d	Condition	*if I do not go away,*
e	Warning	*the Paraclete will not come to you,*
f	Contrast	*but*
g	Condition	*if I go,*
h	Promise	*I will send him to you.*
8a		*And*
b	Circumstance: Arrival	*when he comes*
c	Resulting Action	*he will convict the world*
d	List of References #1	*concerning sin and*
e	List of References #2	*concerning righteousness and*
f	List of References #3	*concerning judgment;*
9a	Expansion of 8d	*concerning sin*
b	Basis (of 9a)	*because they do not believe in me, and*
10a	Expansion of 8e	*concerning righteousness*
b	Basis (of 10a)	*because I go to the Father and*
c	Result of 10b	*you will no longer see me, and*
11a	Expansion of 8f	*concerning judgment*
b	Basis (of 11a)	*because the ruler of this world has been judged.*
12a	Assertion	*I have much more to say to you,*
b	Contrast	*but you are not able to bear it now.*
13a	Contrast	*But*
b	Circumstance: Arrival	*when he comes,*
c	Title	*the Spirit of truth,*
d	Resulting Action	*he will guide you*
e	Sphere	*in all truth.*
f	Basis (f–h)	*For he will not speak from himself,*
g	Contrasting Sequence #1	*but what he hears he will speak,*
h	Contrasting Sequence #2	*and he will announce to you what is coming.*
14a	Assertion	*He will bring glory to me*
b	Sequential Basis #1	*because he will receive*
c	Source/Origin	*from me and*
d	Sequential Basis #2	*announce it to you.*
15a	Basis for c–e	*All that the Father has is mine;*
b		*for this reason*
c	Restatement of 14b–d	*I said that he will receive*
d		*from me and*
e		*announce it to you."*

Structure and Literary Form

As the sixth of eight sections of the farewell discourse, this pericope is part of the fourth (and longest) substantial monologue in the narrative proper. A monologue (see Introduction) is similar to a dialogue in that it is set in the context of an engagement and conflict, but rather than engaging point-for-point it allows for a lengthy argument. A monologue can contain elements of rhetoric, challenge, and conflict, but it does so in a sustained presentation.

This pericope is the fifth of six statements by Jesus that intend to exhort and encourage his disciples. The pericope can be divided into three sections. The first is established by an *inclusio* by means of the phrase, "I have spoken these things to you" (vv. 1 – 4a).[1] The last two sections are separated by a third use of the phrase, "I have spoken these things to you" (v. 6) and can also be demarcated by their changes in topic: the second (vv. 4b – 6) focuses on the departure of Jesus, while the third (vv. 7 – 15) involves instruction on the work of the coming Paraclete. Following the transition of v. 7, the third section of the pericope can be divided into two further sections regarding the work of the Paraclete: his (negative) ministry of conviction in the world (vv. 8 – 11) and his (positive) ministry of guidance in the church (vv. 12 – 15).

Exegetical Outline

➡   **6. I Will Empower You by the Paraclete (16:1 – 15)**
    a. "An Hour Is Coming" (vv. 1 – 4a)
    b. The True Object of Faith (vv. 4b – 6)
    c. The Ministry of the Paraclete (vv. 7 – 15)
        (1) The Paraclete's Conviction of the World (vv. 7 – 11)
        (2) The Paraclete's Guidance of the Church (vv. 12 – 15)

Explanation of the Text

Since this entire section of the Gospel and "the farewell discourse" proper are replete with interpretive issues, we refer the reader to the first pericope of this section where we provided an overview of the nature (genre), literary structure, and function of the farewell discourse (see comments before 13:1).

16:1 "I have spoken these things to you so that you might not stumble" (Ταῦτα λελάληκα ὑμῖν ἵνα μὴ σκανδαλισθῆτε). The first section of the pericope (vv. 1 – 4a) begins with a phrase that Jesus has used before (cf. 14:25), which serves to demarcate a transition in the discourse. Jesus reminds the disciples of "these things" (Ταῦτα) about which he is speaking as a way to refocus their attention on what he is about to say next. In the immediate context "these things" refers to the hatred of the world

---

1. Cf. Moloney, *John*, 438.

soon to be faced by the disciples. After introducing this coming hate in the last pericope, Jesus now counters it in this pericope with further instruction regarding the coming Paraclete.

Jesus is concerned to reorient his disciples by exhorting them to "remember" (see v. 4a) the farewell speech he is now giving them in the hope "that you might not stumble" (ἵνα μὴ σκανδαλισθῆτε). The term translated "stumble" (σκανδαλισθῆτε) is often translated "go astray" but generally means "to cause to give up the Christian faith," which is how it was used earlier in the Gospel (6:61) as well as throughout early Christian literature (e.g., Did. 16:5). Jesus reminds his disciples that this farewell speech is intended to strengthen and encourage them, not in spite of the difficult circumstances to come but in the midst of them.

16:2 "They will exclude you from the synagogue; indeed, an hour is coming when everyone who kills you will think they are offering a service to present to God" (ἀποσυναγώγους ποιήσουσιν ὑμᾶς· ἀλλ' ἔρχεται ὥρα ἵνα πᾶς ὁ ἀποκτείνας ὑμᾶς δόξῃ λατρείαν προσφέρειν τῷ θεῷ). In light of the previous pericope, Jesus offers penetrating insight into the reality behind the hate the disciples are soon to experience. Jesus begins by describing one application of this hate: exclusion from the synagogue. There is no need to interpret this statement under the guidance of the influential proposal of J. L. Martyn regarding the "expulsion from the synagogue" (see Introduction; see also comments on 9:22). Jesus is simply explaining what the disciples' disassociation from the world will look like in their own towns and religious gatherings. They will be outsiders, even excommunicates.

But Jesus adds further insight to this experience, denoted by the conjunction translated as "indeed" (ἀλλ'), which can be used to strengthen an addi-

tional consideration.[2] Jesus explains that this excommunication at times may involve more than a loss of fellowship, for it could even involve a loss of life. The phrase "an hour is coming" (ἔρχεται ὥρα) seems out of place here. The "hour" is a technical term in the Gospel that has been used to refer to the death of Jesus on the cross (see comments on 2:4), but it is used here in reference to the Jewish authorities. While the term is being used in a different manner, the reader is certainly expected to relate the use of the term here to its more dominant "impression" regarding Jesus's "hour" established throughout the Gospel (on "impressions," see Introduction).

This hour is "when everyone who kills you will think they are offering a service to present to God" (ἵνα πᾶς ὁ ἀποκτείνας ὑμᾶς δόξῃ λατρείαν προσφέρειν τῷ θεῷ). The Jews will "think" (δόξῃ) or "believe" by their reasoning that the death of Christians is a presentation to God of their "service" (λατρείαν), a term which could also be translated as "worship." The link between this "hour" and Jesus's "hour" is made clear by this concluding phrase. For both Jesus and the Jews, death and service are involved, though with very different intentions. While the Jews think their service to God involves taking life from others, Jesus knows that his service to God (the Father) requires that he give his life for others. The irony is stark, and Jesus wants his disciples to grasp it.

16:3 "And they will do these things because they have known neither the Father nor me" (καὶ ταῦτα ποιήσουσιν ὅτι οὐκ ἔγνωσαν τὸν πατέρα οὐδὲ ἐμέ). The reason for these actions is further explained. They "have known" (ἔγνωσαν) neither the Father nor the Son. The statement might imply, according to Bultmann, that the disciples are not even to take offense at their future fate, the hate and killing they will receive from the world, for their actions are completely consistent with their dislocation from God.[3] This verse follows several others that declare not only the intimate relation and union between the Father and the Son (cf. 13:20; 14:7; 15:21, 23) — one of the primary messages of the Gospel — but also the declaration that the rejection of the Son is the rejection of both Father and Son. Repeating what he said in 15:21, Jesus explains that the world will hate and kill God's children because they hate their Father.

16:4a "But I have spoken these things to you so that when their hour comes, you may remember that I spoke to you about them" (ἀλλὰ ταῦτα λελάληκα ὑμῖν ἵνα ὅταν ἔλθῃ ἡ ὥρα αὐτῶν μνημονεύητε αὐτῶν ὅτι ἐγὼ εἶπον ὑμῖν). Jesus concludes the first section of the pericope (vv. 1–4a) by restating the result he hopes to accomplish through his teaching. The repetition of the phrase, "I have spoken these things to you," creates an *inclusio* that frames these four verses and gives them emphatic focus. The frame presented by v. 1 and v. 4a makes clear Jesus's desire that the disciples would "remember" (v. 4a) his instructions so that they "might not stumble" (v. 1). It is likely that "remember" and "not stumble" are to be taken as synonyms; to remember Jesus's teachings is to live under their guidance and protection so as not to stumble.[4]

Again Jesus mentions the "hour," this time calling it "their hour" (ἡ ὥρα αὐτῶν), a phrase we defined above (see comments on v. 2). The qualification "their hour" magnifies the irony that is displayed by the persecution of Christians. What the Jews think is service to God and success is actually a sign of their defeat and symptomatic of the victory of God established at Jesus's "hour." As Jesus explained earlier, their evil intentions are in actuality fulfilling the larger intentions of God (see comments on 15:25). "The hour" has always been a paradox in the Gospel, in which the death of Christ *is* his victory.[5]

16:4b "But I did not speak these things to you from the beginning, because I was with you" (Ταῦτα δὲ ὑμῖν ἐξ ἀρχῆς οὐκ εἶπον, ὅτι μεθ' ὑμῶν ἤμην). The second section of the pericope (vv. 4b–6) gives further insight into Jesus's teaching and is established by an *inclusio* using for a second time the repetition of the phrase "speak/have spoken these things." Jesus explains that he did not provide these specific instructions at first, that is, "from the beginning" (ἐξ ἀρχῆς), a phrase used similarly in 15:27. The disciples have been living *with* Christ; what they need instruction on now is how to live life "*in* Christ" and on how to live by the Spirit/Paraclete in the new covenant. Such a statement reminds the reader of the purpose and significance of the entire farewell discourse.

16:5 "But now I go to the one who sent me, and no one is asking me, 'Where are you going?'" (νῦν δὲ ὑπάγω πρὸς τὸν πέμψαντά με, καὶ οὐδεὶς ἐξ ὑμῶν ἐρωτᾷ με, Ποῦ ὑπάγεις;). The "But now" (νῦν δὲ) suggests that a change is imminent.[6] Jesus has already explained to his disciples that his time with them would only last "a little longer" (13:33). As the discourse moves toward its end, Jesus will speak of the immediacy of his departure. Jesus is about to return to "the one who sent me," a phrase that has been used extensively throughout the Gospel to refer to the Father and serves as a technical title for the mission of the Son (1:33; 4:34; 5:24, 30; 6:38, 39; 7:16, 18, 28, 33; 8:16, 18, 26, 29; 9:4; 12:44, 45, 49; 13:16, 20; 14:24; 15:21; 20:21). The (cosmological) "hour" is only a few (historical) hours away.

The use of the technical title "the one who sent

3. Bultmann, *John*, 556.
4. Cf. Brown, *John*, 2:702.

5. See Newbigin, *The Light Has Come*, 208.
6. Cf. Michaels, *John*, 617.

me" helps make sense of what Jesus says next to the disciples. Jesus explains that the disciples have not asked about the departure of Jesus or, more specifically, "Where are you going?" which suggests they should have. Several interpreters have suggested that this verse directly contradicts 13:36 where Peter asked that very question.[7] But the contradiction is only apparent. The questions asked in 13:36 and in this verse use the same words, but their subject matters are entirely different. In light of the technical title "the one who sent me" and the nearness of his return to the Father, Jesus is rebuking his disciples for failing to grasp the deeper reality of his work and mission. When Peter asked the question in 13:36, he was preoccupied with his own affairs.[8] But the life Jesus is preparing them for requires that they become occupied with God's affairs and engage themselves with the priorities and concerns of his mission. For this reason Jesus rebukes his disciples.

16:6 "But because I have spoken these things to you, grief has filled your heart" (ἀλλ᾽ ὅτι ταῦτα λελάληκα ὑμῖν ἡ λύπη πεπλήρωκεν ὑμῶν τὴν καρδίαν). The second section of the pericope (vv. 4b–6) concludes with the rest of Jesus's rebuke. Jesus explains that "grief has filled your heart" (ἡ λύπη πεπλήρωκεν ὑμῶν τὴν καρδίαν), that is, "grief has pervaded, taken possession of, your heart."[9] Earlier Jesus contrasted peace and joy with a heart filled with grief (14:27). In the context the command was a call to a "belief" that would rejoice "that I am going to the Father" (14:28–29). Jesus was exhorting his disciples to make God the center and to fit themselves into God's mission and purposes. Love of God procures symptoms of faith that include peace, love, and joy in God's purposes

and plans, whereas love of oneself procures symptoms of unbelief, including fear, doubt, and grief.

Jesus rebukes his disciples to unmask the disciples' real object of faith, their understanding of his person and work. In spite of the dangers soon to threaten them, the disciples must have no sense of bereavement at the impending departure of Jesus nor view it as a minimization of God's protection and work. Even the desire for the continuance of the bodily companionship of Jesus enjoyed during his earthly ministry is now a sinful desire, for it displays ignorance or disbelief in the purpose of the death of Jesus and the goal of his mission.[10]

16:7 "But I tell you the truth, it is better for you that I go away; for if I do not go away, the Paraclete will not come to you, but if I go, I will send him to you" (ἀλλ᾽ ἐγὼ τὴν ἀλήθειαν λέγω ὑμῖν, συμφέρει ὑμῖν ἵνα ἐγὼ ἀπέλθω. ἐὰν γὰρ μὴ ἀπέλθω, ὁ παράκλητος οὐκ ἐλεύσεται πρὸς ὑμᾶς· ἐὰν δὲ πορευθῶ, πέμψω αὐτὸν πρὸς ὑμᾶς). The third section of the pericope (vv. 7–15) is not only the most informative collection of verses on the Paraclete but may also be the text with the greatest diversity of interpretations. This verse is the turning point of the pericope, connecting all the way back to 15:18 where the hate and persecution of the disciples was first introduced.[11] Jesus transitions here from the persecution the disciples will experience to the Paraclete who will empower them. This is the last of four occurrences of the "Paraclete" in the Gospel and the fullest and climactic depiction of his ministerial office (for an overview, see comments on 14:16). The emphatic statement "*I tell you the truth*" (ἐγὼ τὴν ἀλήθειαν λέγω ὑμῖν) is probably to be interpreted as equivalent to the authoritative preface Jesus customarily places before significant statements: "Truly, truly, I say to

7. See Carson, *John*, 532–33.
8. Barrett, *John*, 486.
9. Ibid., 486.
10. Hoskyns, *Fourth Gospel*, 483.
11. D. Moody Smith, "John 16:1–15," *Int* 33 (1979): 58–62 (59).

you" (see comments on 1:51). The adjusted preface emphasizes the content of the message to follow.

The foundation of what Jesus is about say to his disciples in vv. 8 – 15 is rooted in the following statement: "It is to your advantage that I go away" (συμφέρει ὑμῖν ἵνα ἐγὼ ἀπέλθω). The verb "it is better" (συμφέρει), that is, to be "advantageous" or "profitable,"[12] has already occurred in the Gospel when Caiaphas applied his political wisdom to the problem of Jesus (see comments on 11:50; cf. 18:14). By using the same term, Jesus offers his own wisdom to the problem confronting his disciples in the world. Ironically, by the providence of God their solutions overlap in the death and departure of Jesus. The two uses of the term create an exegetical connection between the wisdom of man and the wisdom of God at both the historical and the cosmological strands of the Gospel's plot.

Jesus has spoken about the necessity of his departure before (cf. 13:33, 36; 14:2 – 6), but here he connects it directly and with repetitive emphasis to the essential coming of the Paraclete. Two things are made clear. First, the transition from Jesus to the Paraclete is better for the disciples. The transition about which the entire farewell discourse has been addressing portrays the coming of "another Paraclete" as a preferable and even superior state of affairs. The departure of Jesus is not his absence but the magnification of his presence, for the Christian life by the Spirit involves the mutual indwelling and interpenetration of both the Son and the Father (see 14:19 – 20) and a new state of existence between the Trinitarian God and the believer, who is participating already in life that is "eternal" (cf. 20:31).

Second, the departure of Jesus is necessary for the coming of the Paraclete. Jesus makes this clear

with the parallel statements (one negative and one positive) that magnify this necessity. The departure of Jesus initiates and provides for the coming of the Paraclete. In a sense, the transition between the Son and the Spirit, this "departure-coming," forms a unit that can be distinguished (persons of God) but not be separated (purpose of God).[13] For the presence of God with his people, his "tabernacling" (cf. 1:14), also involves and is now accomplished by "another Paraclete," the Spirit. In what might seem like a paradox, the departure of Jesus therefore becomes the promise and guarantee of his presence.[14]

16:8 "And when he comes he will convict the world concerning sin and concerning righteousness and concerning judgment" (καὶ ἐλθὼν ἐκεῖνος ἐλέγξει τὸν κόσμον περὶ ἁμαρτίας καὶ περὶ δικαιοσύνης καὶ περὶ κρίσεως). After transitioning to the Paraclete in v. 7, Jesus now speaks about the twofold ministry of the Paraclete, first his (negative) work in the world (vv. 8 – 11) and second his (positive) work in the church (vv. 12 – 15). In this verse, Jesus summarizes the ministry of the Paraclete in the world. The four weighty terms ("convict," "sin," "righteousness," and "judgment") used by Jesus are difficult to define with precision.[15] Since the last three terms are governed by the first term and are each given a separate verse (vv. 9 – 11), we will deal with them in the corresponding verses below. We must begin by addressing the first and overarching term, "convict" (ἐλέγξει).

Jesus declares that when the Paraclete comes "he will convict the world" (ἐκεῖνος ἐλέγξει τὸν κόσμον). Although the verb can have the more neutral use of "exposing," as it can be rightly understood in 3:20, its more basic use in its eighteen occurrences in the NT presuppose guilt and

---

12. See BDAG 960.

13. See Max Turner, " 'Trinitarian' Pneumatology in the New Testament? — Towards an Explanation of the Worship of Jesus," *AsTJ* 57/58 (2002/2003): 167 – 86 (170 – 77).

14. Schnackenburg, *John*, 3:127.

15. See D. A. Carson, "The Function of the Paraclete in John 16:7 – 11," *JBL* 98 (1979): 547 – 66. Our analysis below relies heavily on Carson's work.

shame.[16] But there is another parallel found earlier in the Gospel. In 8:46 Jesus poses a question to his opponents, "Who among you convicts me of sin?" (τίς ἐξ ὑμῶν ἐλέγχει με περὶ ἁμαρτίας;). The term in 8:46 is in regard to exposing wrong ideas about sin or proving the guilt of sin to a third party. Even more, the translation of the verb as "convict" in 8:46 also bears the sense of "convince," which is how it can also be translated.[17] Since these two verses "bear considerable structural similarities," the overlap at the level of the clause strongly suggests the meaning of "convict" here.[18] In this way the ministry of the Paraclete is given further definition. In regard to all three terms governed by the verb ("sin," "righteousness," and "judgment"), the Paraclete will confront the world with its failure *and* prove its guilt. Whether or not the world recognizes it, the mission of the Paraclete in the "cosmic trial" is to convict the world of its guilt before God.[19]

16:9 "Concerning sin because they do not believe in me" (περὶ ἁμαρτίας μέν, ὅτι οὐ πιστεύουσιν εἰς ἐμέ). After declaring the coming ministry of conviction by the Paraclete, Jesus gives three phrases that further explain the three terms governed by the verb "convict." Jesus has summarized the ministry of the Paraclete in the world (v. 8); now he will explain the nature and outworking of that conviction (vv. 9 – 11). Each of the three phrases is prefaced by a conjunction that could be understood to have either an explicative function (the content of fact) and so translated as "that" (ὅτι) or a causal function (the fundamental ground) and so translated as "because" (ὅτι).[20] The latter is preferred for three reasons. First, it is likely that all three terms are not only equally governed by the verb "convict" (ἐλέγξει) but also coordinated by the repeated conjunction in a parallel manner; all three, therefore, are either explicative or causal. Second, since the second of the three, "righteousness," cannot be given an explicative function, it (and therefore the other two) must be interpreted causally. Third, in light of v. 8 the further explanation in vv. 9 – 11 suggests that Jesus is answering the question as to *why* the Paraclete convicts the world of its sin/righteousness/judgment. The content has already been given; what is needed now is the reason behind it.

Jesus explains that the Paraclete will convict the world concerning "sin" (ἁμαρτίας), a term easily defined by the Gospel. Just as Jesus "takes away the sin of the world" (1:29), so also does the Paraclete convict the world of its sin. The grace of God is that the work of the Spirit is to reveal the sinful condition of the world and the work of the Son is to remove it. The Spirit will convict sin "because they do not believe in me" (ὅτι οὐ πιστεύουσιν εἰς ἐμέ). The reason the Paraclete convicts the world of sin is to make the world aware of its true condition and present need. Sin not only blinds the world to its future condemnation (3:18, 36) but also to its present condition. The Paraclete ministers to the world "because" of the unbelief of its sin and thereby "convicts" (and "convinces") the world to see its need for Christ and for life in his name (20:31). The reader is to see that the conviction of sin by the Spirit is an expression of the love of God and a perfect reflection of the "grace and truth" that he alone can provide (1:17).

---

16. See John Aloisi, "The Paraclete's Ministry of Conviction: Another Look at John 16:8 – 11," *JETS* 47 (2004): 55 – 69, especially 56 – 60, for a helpful summary of the verb's semantic range.

17. Carson, "The Function of the Paraclete in John 16:7 – 11," 558. Cf. A. A. Trites, *The New Testament Concept of Witness*, SNTSMS 31 (Cambridge: Cambridge University Press, 1977), 118 – 20.

18. Aloisi, "The Paraclete's Ministry of Conviction," 60.

19. Lincoln, *John*, 419.

20. Cf. Schnackenburg, *John*, 3:129; Barrett, *John*, 487 – 88.

16:10 "And concerning righteousness because I go to the Father and you will no longer see me" (περὶ δικαιοσύνης δέ, ὅτι πρὸς τὸν πατέρα ὑπάγω καὶ οὐκέτι θεωρεῖτέ με). Jesus explains that the Paraclete will also convict the world concerning "righteousness" (δικαιοσύνης), a term less easily defined.[21] We are helped with defining the term in two, related ways. The first is by assuming symmetry between the force applied to the first and second terms. Thus, just as the Paraclete will convict the world in regard to sin, so also will it convict the world in regard to righteousness. The term is not being used in a positive sense (i.e., a genuine, God-approved righteousness); it is the righteousness displayed by the (sinful) world.

Second, while there are no other occurrences of "righteousness" in the Fourth Gospel with which to compare its use here, the term is used twice in the OT in a clearly negative sense, the first depicting the negative righteousness of the people (Isa 64:6) and the second describing human behavior generally as "righteousness," which is void and empty without the mercy of God (Dan 9:18). These uses in the OT fit nicely with the Gospel's message. Jesus rejects the implied "righteousness" of the Jews, declaring throughout that their temple (ch. 2), their teaching (ch. 3), their worship (ch. 4), and their religious regulations (ch. 5) — to cite just a few examples — are in need of cleansing and must be surpassed and replaced by Jesus and by implication his "righteousness" (cf. Rom 10:3). Thus, the use of "righteousness" (δικαιοσύνης) by Jesus here serves as a summary of the rejection of Jesus displayed by all the opponents of Jesus during his ministry, both Jew and gentile.[22]

The Spirit will convict of righteousness "because I go to the Father and you will no longer see me" (ὅτι πρὸς τὸν πατέρα ὑπάγω καὶ οὐκέτι θεωρεῖτέ με). The causal conjunction "because" (ὅτι) explains that the conviction of the world's righteousness is directly related to the departure of Jesus, a topic already given much explanation (see vv. 4 – 7). The connection is this: just as the presence of Jesus served to convict his opponents in the world, so also will the coming presence of the Paraclete involve a similar conviction. Jesus has previously declared that his coming made sin known (5:22, 24). It is now the Spirit of truth, "another Paraclete," who will perform this task.

This latter point is made clear by the phrase "and *you* will no longer see me," which the reader would have expected to be in the third person ("*they* will no longer see me"), not the second person. The change in subject is potent. The disciples are invited (and expected) to participate in the Spirit's ministry in the world by displaying in their personal and corporate lives the positive righteousness only God can provide. The church, therefore, is to emulate its Lord by incarnating righteousness in its corporate *flesh*.[23]

16:11 "And concerning judgment because the ruler of this world has been judged" (περὶ δὲ κρίσεως, ὅτι ὁ ἄρχων τοῦ κόσμου τούτου κέκριται). Finally, Jesus explains that the Paraclete will convict the world concerning "judgment" (κρίσεως). Again we must assume symmetry: the term here is in reference to the judgment *of the world*. In this sense the term refers not merely to the world's judgment in its rejection of Jesus but to all false judgment, with the judgment against Jesus being the supreme and climactic example. Jesus had previously commanded, "Stop judging by outward appearance, but make the right judgment" (7:24). By these words Jesus was rebuking his opponents/the world for

---

21. See Werner Stenger, "δικαιοσυνη in Jo. XVI 8.10," *NovT* 21 (1979): 2 – 12.

22. Cf. Luther, *John*, 24:341.

23. Cf. Newbigin, *The Light Has Come*, 211; Calvin, *John 11 – 21*, 116.

their spiritual blindness, their wrong assessment of all spiritual things. Befitting the first two clauses, these failed judgments are deeply related to the world's sinful condition and self-righteousness.

The Spirit will convict of judgment "because the ruler of this world has been judged" (ὅτι ὁ ἄρχων τοῦ κόσμου τούτου κέκριται). Again the casual conjunction "because" (ὅτι) explains that the conviction of the world's judgment is directly related to the already established judgment of the ruler of this world. This is the third use of the title "the ruler of this world" in the Gospel (see comments on 12:31; cf. 14:30) and serves to make an emphatic point regarding the judgment of the world in two ways. First, if the "ruler of this world" is susceptible and already defeated, how much more the world he supposedly rules? Second, Jesus declares with the perfect-tense verb that the ruler of this world "has been judged" (κέκριται), that is, although in one sense (in real, historical time) this is a future event, in another sense the "ruler of this world" has already been defeated and judged by God. And as the Gospel has already made clear, the judgment of the world and its ruler will be made official on the cross (see comments on 12:31).

16:12 "I have much more to say to you, but you are not able to bear it now" (Ἔτι πολλὰ ἔχω ὑμῖν λέγειν, ἀλλ᾽ οὐ δύνασθε βαστάζειν ἄρτι). Jesus now transitions to the second part (vv. 12 – 15) of the final section of the pericope. Jesus had just spoken of the (negative) work of the Paraclete in the world; here he will address the (positive) work of the Paraclete in and for the church. Jesus's admission here serves not only as a transition to the next topic but also to make clear that there is so much more he could have explained to them. He claims not to do so, however, because they have reached their limits, being unable to handle it or "to bear it

now" (βαστάζειν ἄρτι). This does not mean, however, that there was more he should have said, as if the disciples' limitation was prohibitive for Jesus. For in another sense Jesus has said everything he needed to say, for even the Paraclete adds nothing new but only brings to remembrance what Jesus has said (see comments on 14:26).[24] This transitional comment gives the reason why Jesus will now speak concerning the instructional guidance God will provide through the ministry of the Paraclete.

16:13 "But when he comes, the Spirit of truth, he will guide you in all truth. For he will not speak from himself, but what he hears he will speak, and he will announce to you what is coming" (ὅταν δὲ ἔλθῃ ἐκεῖνος, τὸ πνεῦμα τῆς ἀληθείας, ὁδηγήσει ὑμᾶς ἐν τῇ ἀληθείᾳ πάσῃ· οὐ γὰρ λαλήσει ἀφ᾽ ἑαυτοῦ, ἀλλ᾽ ὅσα ἀκούσει λαλήσει, καὶ τὰ ἐρχόμενα ἀναγγελεῖ ὑμῖν). Jesus now addresses how the Paraclete will affect the disciples when he comes, referring to him for the third time as "the Spirit of truth" (τὸ πνεῦμα τῆς ἀληθείας). Just as Jesus is the standard for what is real in this world and true about God as the perfect expression of God (see comments on 14:6), the Spirit of truth is the incorporation of this reality, the substance of what is real in this world and true about God as the perfect provision of God (see comments on 14:17; cf. 15:26).

The final occurrence of this title helps contextualize the ministry of the Spirit: "He will guide you in all truth" (ὁδηγήσει ὑμᾶς ἐν τῇ ἀληθείᾳ πάσῃ). The verb "guide" (ὁδηγήσει) or "lead" refers here to instructional assistance, "to assist someone in acquiring information or knowledge."[25] The Spirit of truth will guide the disciples "in all truth" (ἐν τῇ ἀληθείᾳ πάσῃ), a seemingly sweeping claim. The preposition "in" is somewhat awkward and might

---

24. Barrett, *John*, 488.

25. BDAG 690.

explain why some manuscripts replace it with "into" (εἰς); the former is to be preferred, however, even though the difference in meaning is slight.[26] While "into" might suggest that the disciples will come to know the truth "under the Spirit's guidance," "in" (ἐν) also suggests "guidance in the whole sphere of truth," that they will be kept in the truth of God.[27] The truth provided by the Spirit must be connected to Jesus, the truth (14:6), but also to the emphasis on truth expressed throughout the Gospel (e.g., 1:14, 17; 3:21; 4:23 – 24; 8:32, 40, 44 – 46; 14:6; 17:17; 18:37 – 38). That is, this ministry of the Spirit is not guidance "into further new truth, but into the truth concerning that which was concretely and concisely set forth by the Son of God."[28] The truth in which the Spirit will lead and guide the disciples is God's truth, a truth that is not merely received by cognition but also by participation — life in and by the Spirit of truth. The Spirit is not merely a tool for the disciples, a middle-management resource for their spiritual needs, but is himself the truth, like Jesus, guiding the disciples in and through life. This truth is that in which one walks and hopes (cf. Ps 25:5).

The Spirit of truth is not on an isolated mission or one who "will speak from himself" (λαλήσει ἀφ' ἑαυτοῦ), that is, by his own initiative and authority. Rather, his guidance and instruction serves another, just like the first Paraclete, Jesus, taught what he had received from the Father (cf. 3:32 – 35; 7:16 – 18; 8:26 – 29, 42 – 43; 12:47 – 50). The Spirit is not coming "to set up a new kingdom," but rather to continue and extend the kingdom of God already inaugurated by Christ.[29] The Spirit will deliver what he hears and will "announce" (ἀναγγελεῖ) or "report" what is coming. The guidance into "what

is coming" (τὰ ἐρχόμενα) need not be understood to be a futuristic vision, for "the future will not be unveiled in a knowledge imparted before it happens, but it will be illuminated again and again by the word at work in the community."[30] It is important to note that the unity between the three persons of the Trinitarian God finds a parallel unity in their shared message. This message is so constant in the Gospel that it can be presumed that the one revelation of God in Christ is the content of that which the Spirit is to convey to the disciples.[31] This is how Jesus can have much more to say and not have to say it yet (v. 12), for the teachings of Jesus will be extended and completed by the Spirit. The message of Christ is accomplished by Christ *and* the Spirit of Christ; to distinguish their teachings is to divide God against himself.[32]

16:14 "He will bring glory to me because he will receive from me and announce it to you" (ἐκεῖνος ἐμὲ δοξάσει, ὅτι ἐκ τοῦ ἐμοῦ λήμψεται καὶ ἀναγγελεῖ ὑμῖν). Here Jesus reiterates how the ministry of the Spirit and his guidance is the revelation of God in Christ and that this message is entirely Christocentric. Just as the Father was made known by the Son (cf. 1:18), so also the Son is made known by the Spirit. And just as glory is shared and exchanged between the Father and Son (12:27 – 28; 17:1, 5), so also is it between the Son and the Spirit. In fact, this intra-Trinitarian glory is also shared with the disciples, who glorify the Father by their fruit (15:8; cf. 17:22 – 24). The ministry of the Spirit not only extends and cumulatively complements the ministry of Christ but also bestows glory upon him. And the disciples participate in this exchange of glory, first in the flesh of Christ (see comments on 1:14) and now in the Spirit.

---

26. See Metzger, *Textual Commentary*, 210.

27. Barrett, *John*, 489. We should not press the distinction between prepositions too far. Cf. BDF § 218.

28. Hoskyns, *Fourth Gospel*, 485.

29. Calvin, *John 11 – 21*, 121.

30. Bultmann, *John*, 575.

31. Beasley-Murray, *John*, 283.

32. Cf. Morris, *John*, 621, who argues against pitting "the original Jesus" (the so-called historical Jesus) against the teaching of the apostles (i.e., Scripture).

16:15 "All that the Father has is mine; for this reason I said that he will receive from me and announce it to you" (πάντα ὅσα ἔχει ὁ πατὴρ ἐμά ἐστιν· διὰ τοῦτο εἶπον ὅτι ἐκ τοῦ ἐμοῦ λαμβάνει καὶ ἀναγγελεῖ ὑμῖν). Jesus is careful to extend that which is exchanged between the Son and the Spirit to the Father, from whom Christ has received all things, as the Gospel has already made clear (see 3:35; 13:3; cf. 17:10). This section (vv. 7 – 15) brings the pericope to a close with significant instruction regarding the ministerial work of the Paraclete, who is depicted as ministering to the world and the church as part of the cumulative and representative ministry of God the Father, God the Son, and God the Spirit.[33] We argued earlier that "Paraclete" is best understood as a title that refers to the *ministerial office* of the Trinitarian God in the world (see comments on 14:6). The Christ-centered expressions of the Paraclete's ministry to convict the world and guide the church gives insight into the nature of the Christian life in the new covenant.

Theology in Application

In the sixth of eight sections of the farewell discourse, Jesus makes the fifth of six statements that explain, encourage, and exhort the disciples as they transition to the era of the new covenant, from life with Jesus to life "in Christ" and *in* the Spirit. After introducing the disciples to the persecution they will face in the world, Jesus announces the power that will sustain them, the Paraclete, who will not only empower the church in its struggle but personally engage with the world, convicting it of sin, righteousness, and judgment. Through this pericope the reader is exhorted to exchange their grief for the grace to be provided by God through Christ *in* the Spirit.

The Christian "Hour"

This pericope carefully connects the "hour" of Jesus so prominent in the Gospel with the world, both the opponents of Jesus (v. 2) and the disciples. For the disciples, this hour will serve as anchor to help them "remember" the deeper reality behind the persecution they are to face (v. 4a). The "hour" in the Gospel has now broadened to refer to the inauguration of the new covenant, which was established by the death of Christ at his "hour." The newness of this Christian "hour" means that the children of God will receive all the blessings established by the death and resurrection of Christ, yet it also means participation in his sufferings (cf. Col 1:24; 1 Pet 4:13). "The hour" continues to be a paradox in the Gospel, in which the death of Christ *is* his victory. The same is true for the Christian life. Victory is not defined and achieved by military battles and political power but through submission, suffering, and sacrifice. As Jesus prepares the disciples for the persecution to come, he connects this future "hour" to his own "hour" so that they might submit themselves to the pattern of life

---

33. For a helpful reflection on this verse in regard to the equality between the persons of the Trinity, especially the equality of the Spirit, see Augustine, *John*, 100.3 – 4, 386 – 87.

that Christ authored on their behalf. In this way the Christian "hour" is the hour of the cross in every respect (Matt 16:24).

The Presence of God

The departure of Jesus means his presence is not tied to and limited by one time and place but becomes an essential part of human life in every place and in every age.[34] Jesus is not a memorial nor does he belong to the past, for Jesus Christ is the same yesterday, today, and forever (Heb 13:8). Jesus "reminds" the disciples that "they have with them the living Spirit who is the Spirit of the Father and who is also the Spirit of Jesus, the Spirit whose presence is the foretaste of the coming glory. Therefore they do not need to look back but upward and forward."[35] And by this rebuke Jesus intends for them to make him the true object of their faith and to receive through him the Paraclete, the ministerial office of the Trinitarian God in the world. This office is occupied by both the Son and the Spirit of God and is the fullest expression of God's presence and power for the world (see comments on 14:16).[36] Nothing has changed for the Christian today. Christ could not be any more present and protective of the church today if he were present bodily here with us. He still is the Immanuel, "God with us" (cf. Isa 7:14; Matt 1:23), and he will remain as such (Heb 13:8).

Following Christ Is Living in the Spirit

This pericope develops further the close connection between the persons of the Trinity. What is emphasized is clear: following Jesus is to live in the Spirit. As much as they are two different persons, God the Son and God the Spirit, they are so united in their purpose and cumulative functions that faith in the one (Jesus) demands participation in the other (the Spirit). The departure of Jesus is not his absence but the magnification of his presence. In what might seem like a paradox, the departure of Jesus becomes the promise and guarantee of his presence.

The unity between the Son and the Spirit (and also the Father) so carefully communicated by Jesus's speech might help resituate the Spirit in the practical Christian life of the church. It is not a stretch to suggest that in the church today the Spirit can be either underemphasized or overemphasized. One wonders if the latter approach is simply an overreaction to the former. This pericope helps the church to see the necessity of the Spirit in and for the Christian life. To be a Christian is to live in and by the Spirit. The Spirit should be neither assumed nor exaggerated, for he is, quite simply, the tangible substance of the Christian life.

The Christian life is so tied to the Spirit that Christ places all future instruction

34. Newbigin, *The Light Has Come*, 210.
35. Ibid.
36. Cf. Augustine, *John*, 94.5.368.

upon the coming Spirit, who will guide the church into all truth (v. 13). The Spirit of truth, or "the Spirit who communicates truth," is the reality of the fullness of the revelation of God in Christ, leading the church in its response to and expression of what is real about God and the world. The Spirit is not a tool or accessory for the Christian, but the one in whom the Christian walks and hopes (cf. Ps 25:5). The Paraclete's ministry is to guide the church into the new state of existence under the covenant inaugurated by the death, resurrection, and ascension of Jesus to which we are called to set our "minds" (Col 3:1 – 4).

God's Love of and Mission to the World

In the well-known verse of 3:16 we learned that God loves the world; in this pericope we learn how that love is expressed. God does not just speak of love in abstraction. First through the ministry of the Son (in words and signs) and thereafter through the ministry of the Spirit/Paraclete (by conviction), God offers his love to the world by revealing to it its sinful condition and offering his Son as a remedy. As we tried to make clear (cf. v. 8), this ministry is God's. God must be viewed as the primary and first-order minister in and to the world; all other ministry is secondary and supported by the foundational ministry of God, which in the new covenant is ministry in and by the Spirit.

Yet the church is exhorted to participate in God's love of and mission to the world. Just as Christ's righteousness served as a backdrop against which the self-righteousness of the world around him was highlighted and challenged, so also by implication should the church embody and become in their mutual life and love of one another a backdrop of the righteousness of God. The church emulates its Lord not only in sharing in his suffering but also by incarnating in its corporate *flesh* the righteousness it received from God alone, offering a witness to the world that is motivated by and secondary to the Spirit's own ministry. The church is in this way an extension of the love of God and his mission to the world. As much as this can be called a ministry assignment, it is better and more accurately called a lifestyle.

34

John 16:16 – 24

Literary Context

This pericope is the seventh of eight sections of the farewell discourse. Surrounded by a prologue (13:31 – 38) and an epilogue (16:25 – 33), the farewell discourse can be divided into six significant and developing thematic statements by Jesus, with each offering comfort and consolation for the disciples (and the reader), befitting the nature of a farewell discourse (see comments before 13:1). These six statements within the farewell discourse offer one long exhortation to stay the course and encouragement that their efforts will be matched by the Trinitarian God himself. In the first three statements, Jesus explains his relationship to the disciples and their future existence in him; in the last three statements Jesus explains the disciples' relation to world and their future existence in it. In this pericope, the sixth and final statement, the disciples are given the climactic insight into how Christ will turn their grief into joy and how the Father will provide for all their needs in the "name" of the Son.

VII. The Farewell Discourse (13:1 – 17:26)

   A. Introduction: The Love of Jesus (13:1 – 30)

      1. Jesus and the Washing of His Disciples' Feet (13:1 – 20)

      2. Jesus Announces His Betrayal (13:21 – 30)

   B. The Farewell Discourse (13:31 – 16:33)

      1. Prologue: Glory, Departure, and Love (13:31 – 38)

      2. I Am the Way and the Truth and the Life (14:1 – 14)

      3. I Will Give You the Paraclete (14:15 – 31)

      4. I Am the True Vine (15:1 – 17)

      5. I Have Also Experienced the Hate of the World (15:18 – 27)

      6. I Will Empower You by the Paraclete (16:1 – 15)

➡   **7. I Will Turn Your Grief into Joy (16:16 – 24)**

      8. Epilogue: Speaking Plainly, Departure, and Peace (16:25 – 33)

   C. Conclusion: The Prayer of Jesus (17:1 – 26)

Main Idea

The provision of Christ is direct access to and participation in God the Father and permanent joy in place of temporary grief.

Translation

John 16:16–24

	Section #7 of "Farewell Discourse"	
16a	Duration	*"In a little while*
b	Assertion	*you will no longer see me,*
c	Progression of Time	*and* **then**
d	Duration	*after a little while*
e	Assertion	*you will again see me."*
17a	Reaction #1	Then **some of his disciples said to one another,**
b	Question	*"What is this that he is saying to us,*
c		
d	Restatement	*'In a little while*
e		*you will not see me,*
f		*and* **then**
g		*after a little while*
h		*you will see me again,'*
i		*and*
j		*'Because I go to the Father?'"*
18a	Reaction #2	Then **they were saying,**
b	Question	*"What is this that he is saying,*
c	Restatement	*'A little while?'*
d	(Emphatic) Confusion	*We do not know what he is saying."*
19a	Character's Thoughts	**Jesus knew what they wanted to ask him,**
b	Response	and **he said to them,**
c	Question	*"Are you asking one another about this*
d	Basis	*because I said,*
e	Restatement	*'In a little while*
f		*you will not see me, and*
g		*then*
h		*after a little while*
i		*you will see me again?'*
20a	Amen Formula	*Truly, truly I say to you,*
b	Assertion	*you will weep and mourn, but*
c	Contrast	*the world will rejoice;*
d	Assertion	*you will grieve, but*
e	Contrast of Progression	*your grief will become joy.*

Continued on next page.

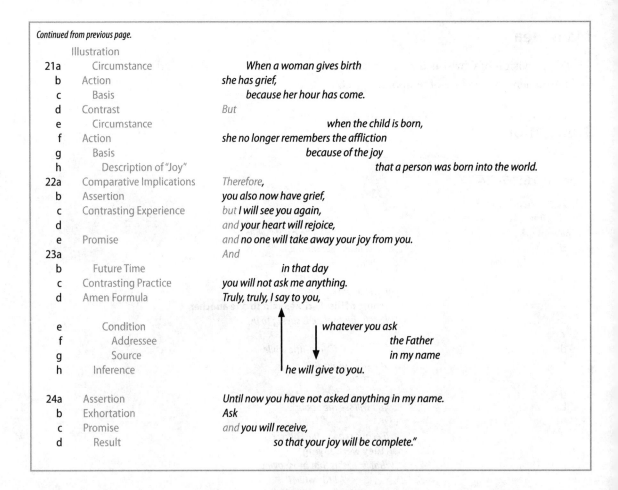

Structure and Literary Form

As the seventh of eight sections of the farewell discourse, this pericope is part of the fourth (and longest) substantial monologue in the narrative proper. A monologue (see Introduction) is similar to a dialogue in that it is set in the context of an engagement and conflict, but rather than engaging point-for-point it allows for a lengthy argument. A monologue can contain elements of rhetoric, challenge, and conflict, but it does so in a sustained presentation.

This pericope is the sixth and final statement by Jesus that intends to exhort and encourage his disciples. The change of topic in v. 16 signals a transition from the previous pericope (16:1 – 15). This new pericope is easily divided into two sections. The first consists of vv. 16 – 18 where Jesus announces again his imminent departure and the disciples reveal their confusion; the second section consists of vv. 19 – 24 where Jesus addresses their confusion and explains how their grief and affliction will shortly turn to joy and great provision.

Exegetical Outline

→ **7. I Will Turn Your Grief into Joy (16:16 – 24)**
   a. Confusion regarding Seeing God (vv.16 – 18)
   b. The Coming Transition from Grief to Joy (vv. 19 – 24)

Explanation of the Text

Since this entire section of the Gospel and "the farewell discourse" proper are replete with interpretive issues, we refer the reader to the first pericope of this section where we provided an overview of the nature (genre), literary structure, and function of the farewell discourse (see comments before 13:1).

16:16 "In a little while you will no longer see me, and then after a little while you will again see me" (Μικρὸν καὶ οὐκέτι θεωρεῖτέ με, καὶ πάλιν μικρὸν καὶ ὄψεσθέ με). The first section (vv. 16 – 18) begins with a transitional verse that signals the start of a new topic and pericope. Jesus makes a statement that is nearly identical with an earlier statement in 14:19 about his imminent departure. While both statements begin the same, they have a clear difference in the manner in which they end and therefore in regard to the deeper subject they address. In 14:19 the statement addressed the ongoing fellowship between Jesus and the disciples and their relational needs (see 14:19 – 24), whereas in this pericope what is addressed is the persecution and grief soon to confront the disciples and their material and emotional needs.[1] Just as he explained in chapter 14, here Jesus will state that his departure is actually in support of all their needs. The topic of "sight" addressed by these two pericopae has shifted from "seeing" the person of Jesus (ch. 14) to "seeing" the work of Jesus (ch. 16), especially in

light of the just completed discussion of the Spirit/Paraclete.

The connection to the Paraclete may also be expressed by the use of two different words for "will see" (θεωρεῖτέ; ὄψεσθέ), something that did not occur in 14:19. While the Fourth Gospel frequently uses related words synonymously across the narrative (e.g., 13:10; 21:15 – 17), when they are used in close proximity (especially in the same verse) there is usually a carefully nuanced distinction or comparison intended between them. In this case the distinction might be made through the use of the second verb "will see" (ὄψεσθέ), which can be used to refer to "inward vision as true apprehension."[2] In this sense, then, the sight that the disciples are to have of Jesus "a little while" after his departure is not in reference to his resurrection or to the second coming of Christ, as some have suggested, but to the "sight" obtained by the coming Spirit. This sight is the cosmological sight or vision of God made possible through the Son, as declared by the prologue (1:18). Christ does not address their loss of him for three days only to depart from them again after his resurrection, nor is he acting as if "a little while" appropriately describes what turned into the rest of their lives (and the last two millennia). Rather, he connects again their participation in him by the Spirit with his departure (see comments on 16:7).[3] Seeing God according to the

---

1. Cf. Ridderbos, *John*, 537.
2. J. Duncan M. Derrett, "Not Seeing and Later Seeing (John 16:16)," *ExpTim* 109 (1998): 208 – 9 (208).
3. Cf. Calvin, *John 11 – 21*, 123.

Gospel is seeing the Father through the Son and in the Spirit.

16:17 Then some of his disciples said to one another, "What is this that he is saying to us, 'In a little while you will not see me, and then after a little while you will see me again,' and 'Because I go to the Father?'" (εἶπαν οὖν ἐκ τῶν μαθητῶν αὐτοῦ πρὸς ἀλλήλους, Τί ἐστιν τοῦτο ὃ λέγει ἡμῖν, Μικρὸν καὶ οὐ θεωρεῖτέ με, καὶ πάλιν μικρὸν καὶ ὄψεσθέ με; καί, Ὅτι ὑπάγω πρὸς τὸν πατέρα;). The interpretive confusion over the kind of "sight" spoken of by Jesus is not felt by biblical interpreters alone, for the disciples also shared their confusion with one another. Their twofold question suggests that they did not understand the nature of this "sight," which we addressed above (v. 16), nor its connection to his departure, which we have also addressed elsewhere (see comments on 16:7). These were real questions that were still present among the disciples regarding the exact nature of life in and by the Spirit. Since the context addressed by the farewell discourse is the Christian life in the new covenant, such prophetic language confuses the disciples. For this reason Jesus is about to make himself even clearer. The inclusion of this question by the narrator is not to rebuke Jesus or his parabolic language but to signal to the reader the importance and comprehensive nature of Jesus's explanation regarding what he is about to inaugurate.

16:18 Then they were saying, "What is this that he is saying, 'A little while?' We do not know what he is saying" (ἔλεγον οὖν, Τί ἐστιν τοῦτο [ὃ λέγει], τὸ μικρόν; οὐκ οἴδαμεν τί λαλεῖ). The repetition of the corporate question of the disciples creates an emphatic transition to Jesus's response, concluding the first section of the pericope (vv. 16 – 18). The repeated question gives focus to their primary

confusion concerning the difficult phrase "a little while" (τὸ μικρόν). At the level of the narrative, these questions serve as a means to bring out further teaching, directing the monologue to address particular issues and the most important concerns. Jesus's six statements have formed a cumulative whole that is difficult to grasp, and the disciples are trying to understand the exact nature of the provision Jesus has been promising them as their hour of persecution approaches.

16:19 Jesus knew that what they wanted to ask him, and he said to them, "Are you asking one another about this because I said, 'In a little while you will not see me, and then after a little while you will see me again?'" (ἔγνω [ὁ] Ἰησοῦς ὅτι ἤθελον αὐτὸν ἐρωτᾶν, καὶ εἶπεν αὐτοῖς, Περὶ τούτου ζητεῖτε μετ' ἀλλήλων ὅτι εἶπον, Μικρὸν καὶ οὐ θεωρεῖτέ με, καὶ πάλιν μικρὸν καὶ ὄψεσθέ με;). The second section of the pericope (vv. 19 – 24) transitions from the disciples' confusion to the clarification of Jesus. As earlier in the Gospel, Jesus was aware of the discussion taking place between the disciples and responds directly to it (see comments on 6:43). Jesus repeats their focus of concern, now stated emphatically for a third time, possibly out of frustration and amazement at their continued misunderstanding and doubt[4] yet also as a way to establish before them his knowledge of their confusion and concern.

16:20 "Truly, truly I say to you, you will weep and mourn, but the world will rejoice; you will grieve, but your grief will become joy" (ἀμὴν ἀμὴν λέγω ὑμῖν ὅτι κλαύσετε καὶ θρηνήσετε ὑμεῖς, ὁ δὲ κόσμος χαρήσεται· ὑμεῖς λυπηθήσεσθε, ἀλλ' ἡ λύπη ὑμῶν εἰς χαρὰν γενήσεται). Jesus begins his response with his familiar authoritative preface (see comments on 1:51). He confirms their fears that something big is going to happen in "a little while." He makes this

---

4. See Michaels, *John*, 842; Ridderbos, *John*, 538.

emphatic with the supplied pronoun "you" (ὑμεῖς) and with the emphatic pairing of verbs, "weep and mourn" (κλαύσετε καὶ θρηνήσετε), which are often used in contexts for mourning over the dead (cf. Jer 22:10). What will cause the disciples to weep and mourn and the world to "rejoice" (χαρήσεται) is the death of Christ. The "world" (ὁ κόσμος) is contrasted with the disciples; just as the world was in conflict with God through Christ (see comments on 1:10), so also is it now in conflict with the children of God.

But Jesus's message changes quickly when he states the emphatic contrast again, but this time with a reversal: "You will grieve, but your grief will become joy" (ὑμεῖς λυπηθήσεσθε, ἀλλ᾽ ἡ λύπη ὑμῶν εἰς χαρὰν γενήσεται). The "obscurity and scandal" of the cross is that it is the opposite of what it first might appear.[5] The paradox is that the cross is the provision of God and the restoration that God had long promised and would soon provide for his disciples. Jesus here does not refer merely to the transition that the resurrection provides (see comments on v. 16) but to life in the Spirit made possible by his death, resurrection, and ascension (departure). The contrast is now able to be described more sharply. What the disciples first received as death and loss, in "weeping and mourning," has itself become the source of their joy. Stated more clearly, in this case death was the necessary precondition for life (see comments on 12:24). And what "the world" first received as victory and "joy" has become itself the source of their defeat. In a real sense, the judgment and death of Christ is the judgment and death of the world (of sin and rebellion against God), and the resurrection of Christ is a resurrection (transformation) for the children of God, a resurrection to life in the Spirit until they are finally received by Christ into the heavenly life he has prepared for them (cf. 14:1 – 6).

16:21 "When a woman gives birth she has grief, because her hour has come. But when the child is born, she no longer remembers the affliction because of the joy that a person was born into the world" (ἡ γυνὴ ὅταν τίκτῃ λύπην ἔχει, ὅτι ἦλθεν ἡ ὥρα αὐτῆς· ὅταν δὲ γεννήσῃ τὸ παιδίον, οὐκέτι μνημονεύει τῆς θλίψεως διὰ τὴν χαρὰν ὅτι ἐγεννήθη ἄνθρωπος εἰς τὸν κόσμον). Jesus offers commentary on his authoritative and prophetic statement by using what can be described as a brief illustration, not uncommon in John (see comments on 10:6 and 16:25). In this illustration, Jesus compares the disciples' coming experience of moving from grief to joy to the experience of a mother who gives birth to a child. Befitting the analogy, the grief is real — and strong, which Jesus describes as "affliction" (τῆς θλίψεως). Even the use of the term "her hour" (ἡ ὥρα αὐτῆς) fits well the analogy of a woman's moment of labor, but also the manner the term was used in the previous pericope (see comments on 16:2, 4a) to depict the future grief and affliction the disciples were to face. But the mother's memory of the affliction is short-lived once the child arrives, for joy takes its place. The reason is "because ... a person was born into the world" (ὅτι ἐγεννήθη ἄνθρωπος εἰς τὸν κόσμον). The reasoning here is quite simple. Just as the gift of a child requires labor, so also does the gift of "true birth" provided by the death of Christ (cf. ch. 3). But as with the birth of a child, the afflictions of labor get absorbed into the larger blessing of the baby. Said another way, the day of the crucifixion can be called "Good Friday" because of Resurrection Sunday.

16:22 "Therefore, you also now have grief, but I will see you again, and your heart will rejoice, and no one will take away your joy from you" (καὶ ὑμεῖς οὖν νῦν μὲν λύπην ἔχετε· πάλιν δὲ

---

5. Hoskyns, *Fourth Gospel*, 487.

ὄψομαι ὑμᾶς, καὶ χαρήσεται ὑμῶν ἡ καρδία, καὶ τὴν χαρὰν ὑμῶν οὐδεὶς αἴρει ἀφ᾽ ὑμῶν). Jesus offers a final comment concerning the disciples' impending grief and joy, claiming that the latter experience will be both definitive and permanent. Jesus's statement here implies that the disciples' grief has already begun, which suggests that their struggle began with the announcement of his impending departure. But Jesus is quick to offer a counter: "But I will see you again" (πάλιν δὲ ὄψομαι ὑμᾶς), reflecting again the transition inaugurated by the resurrection. Yet it also refers to his continual presence with and in them by the Spirit, which he explained earlier with similar language (see 14:19 – 20). The definitive and permanent nature of the disciples' joy is not based upon the absence of any future grief and affliction but by the placement of all grief and suffering into the larger context of the death and resurrection of Jesus Christ.

16:23 "And in that day you will not ask me anything. Truly, truly, I say to you, whatever you ask the Father in my name he will give to you" (καὶ ἐν ἐκείνῃ τῇ ἡμέρᾳ ἐμὲ οὐκ ἐρωτήσετε οὐδέν. ἀμὴν ἀμὴν λέγω ὑμῖν, ἄν τι αἰτήσητε τὸν πατέρα ἐν τῷ ὀνόματί μου δώσει ὑμῖν). This participation in the life of God is reflected not merely in experience (joy) but also in practice, manifested especially in the form of prayer. Jesus offers prayer as an example of what he has been talking about. In "a little while" there will no longer be any need for questions. After beginning with an authoritative preface (see comments on 1:51), Jesus declares that the Christian life will involve direct access to God the Father now officially mediated by Christ — "in my name" (ἐν τῷ ὀνόματί μου) — and that the Father himself "will give" (δώσει) what is asked for. Jesus made a similar statement earlier, and there is no

need to repeat our exegesis here (see comments on 14:13 – 14).

Yet there is one difference worth noting. In 14:13 – 14 it is Jesus who answers the prayer, whereas here it is the Father. The difference may be further highlighted by the different words used for "ask:" "In that day you will not ask (ἐρωτήσετε) me anything" and "Whatever you ask (αἰτήσητε) the Father in my name." (On related words in close proximity, see comments on v. 16.) The distinction seems to be between the questions asked during the life and ministry of Jesus (the first Paraclete; see comments on 14:16) and the questions asked during the ministry of the Spirit (the second Paraclete).[6] This explains why the latter use of "ask" is given an authoritative preface, for by it Jesus declares the new order of life in God.[7]

16:24 "Until now you have not asked anything in my name. Ask and you will receive, so that your joy will be complete" (ἕως ἄρτι οὐκ ᾐτήσατε οὐδὲν ἐν τῷ ὀνόματί μου· αἰτεῖτε καὶ λήμψεσθε, ἵνα ἡ χαρὰ ὑμῶν ᾖ πεπληρωμένη). The pericope concludes with Jesus reminding his disciples that this kind of prayer, prayer to the Father in Jesus's name, had not yet occurred. It could not take place until Christ made such "asking" possible, for this kind of asking reflects the new order of the Christian's participation in the life of the Trinitarian God: prayer *to* the Father *through* the Son and *in* the Spirit.

Jesus ends his sixth and final statement by exhorting his disciples to ask from God. The disciples, by their personal and functional relationship with the Father, will not only receive what they need but be filled with joy. This kind of prayer is fellowship with God (cf. 1 John 1:6 – 7). Jesus ends with a theme that reverberates across the entire farewell discourse: the blessings of those who participate in God. This includes not only joy (15:11)

---

6. Cf. Carson, *John*, 545; Barrett, *John*, 494.

7. Ridderbos suggests it "marks the change of dispensations" (*John*, 540).

but also peace (14:27) and love (15:10), all of which stem from the perfection of God and the life he provides. With this, Jesus offers a climactic conclusion to his six-statement summary of life in the new covenant and participation in the Trinitarian God of Father, Son, and Spirit.

Theology in Application

In the seventh of eight sections of the farewell discourse, Jesus makes the sixth and final statement that explains, encourages, and exhorts the disciples as they transition into the era of the new covenant, from life with Jesus to life "in Christ" and *in* the Spirit. In his final statement, Jesus addresses the disciples' questions and concerns by explaining further how his work will transform their grief into joy and how their life is now in direct relationship to the Father. Through this pericope the reader is exhorted to place their life circumstances into the larger context of their life in God and to enjoy their personal relationship with the Father.

The Cross and Christian Joy

In the Greco-Roman and Jewish world, the cross was a universally recognized symbol of death. It was a place for "weeping and mourning." Yet all that changed when the Father sent his Son to the cross for the purpose of taking upon himself our death. The day Christ died is no longer bad but "Good Friday," just as the cross for the Christian is no longer a symbol of death but a symbol of eternal life. In light of the cross, all grief and affliction is light and momentary, and true joy — though waiting for ultimate consummation in the future — has already begun. The cross has given birth to new life, a life in God that involves fellowship with God and an experience of complete joy. This is not to say that Christianity removes all life's problems; it is simply to say that Christianity explains all life's problems, subjugating the life of the world to the life provided by God. For the future has been safely secured in the past — nailed to the cross.

No More Questions?

This pericope suggests that a transition has occurred from the questions asked of Christ by the disciples and the questions now asked of the Father by the Christian. This is not to say, however, that there are no further questions to be asked (certainly the disciples did not stop asking Christ questions) or that life in the new covenant is without questions. The transition from the old to the new dispensation is not about the removal of questions but about rightly framing the questions by its ultimate subject matter, Jesus Christ.

Jesus's teaching describes the fulfillment of what was promised through the prophet Jeremiah regarding the new covenant: "I will put my law in their minds and write it on their hearts. I will be their God, and they will be my people. No longer will they teach their neighbor, or say to one another, 'Know the LORD,' because they will all know me, from the least of them to the greatest" (Jer 31:33 – 34). This participation in the life of God allows the Christian to "stand beyond the [world]" and to "understand themselves, and thus at the same time everything which the world can bring against them. Their existence has become transparent to them; they have become 'sons of light' (12:36); the anxiety of blindness has been taken away from them, and the future is no longer threatening; they live in an eternal 'today.'"[8] Christians are those who "in that day" will "know the truth" (1 John 2:20), for they have been born from the one who *is* the truth (14:6).

Prayer "in Jesus's Name"

It should come as no surprise to the reader of this Gospel that one of the gifts that the "Word" provides for his disciples is communication with God. Prayer is symptomatic of a relationship with God the Father, secured by the work of God the Son, and facilitated by the ministry of God the Spirit. Thus, when Jesus refers to prayer "in my name" (v. 24), he is speaking of the Trinitarian nature of prayer. There is no need to pray individually to the Son and to the Spirit as if they are not being addressed, for when the Christian addresses the Father they are also speaking to and through the Son and the Spirit. To pray "in Jesus's name" is to pray by means of the access that Christ alone provides and to pray under his authority. It is also to pray "in the Spirit," since the Spirit facilitates and empowers our prayers, at times even speaking on our behalf (Rom 8:26 – 27). Why does our flesh make prayer a burden and not a privilege? May our Christian lives bear the symptoms of having seen and known God the Father through Christ and in the Spirit!

---

8. Bultmann, *John*, 584.

John 16:25 – 33

Literary Context

This pericope is the eighth and final section of the farewell discourse. It functions as an epilogue, offering a concluding commentary on the person and work of Jesus and the expected response of the reader or hearer. After a prologue (13:31 – 38) and six statements (14:1 – 16:24), Jesus now gives a final explanation of his farewell speech and a final exhortation to his disciples. In this part of the farewell discourse, Jesus speaks "plainly" about his return to the Father and encourages the disciples to stay the course in light of his accomplished work. The disciples — and the readers — are exhorted to believe in Christ and his work and to continue to follow him (even if imperfectly), finding peace in his victory over the world.

VII. The Farewell Discourse (13:1 – 17:26)

    A. Introduction: The Love of Jesus (13:1 – 30)

        1. Jesus and the Washing of His Disciples' Feet (13:1 – 20)

        2. Jesus Announces His Betrayal (13:21 – 30)

    B. The Farewell Discourse (13:31 – 16:33)

        1. Prologue: Glory, Departure, and Love (13:31 – 38)

        2. I Am the Way and the Truth and the Life (14:1 – 14)

        3. I Will Give You the Paraclete (14:15 – 31)

        4. I Am the True Vine (15:1 – 17)

        5. I Have Also Experienced the Hate of the World (15:18 – 27)

        6. I Will Empower You by the Paraclete (16:1 – 15)

        7. I Will Turn Your Grief into Joy (16:16 – 24)

➡   **8. Epilogue: Speaking Plainly, Departure, and Peace (16:25 – 33)**

    C. Conclusion: The Prayer of Jesus (17:1 – 26)

Main Idea

In spite of humanity's sinful ignorance and religious pride, Jesus Christ has defeated all sin and evil, the Christian's included, so that the Father may extend his love to them.

Translation

John 16:25–33

	Section #8 of "Farewell Discourse"	
25a	Epilogue (25–33) of "Discourse	*"I have spoken these things to you*
b	Figure of Speech	*in illustrations;*
c	Circumstance	*an hour is coming*
d	Action	*when I will no longer speak to you*
e	Figure of Speech	*in illustrations, but*
f	Contrasting Figure	*will tell you*
g	of Speech	*plainly*
h	Reference	*about the Father.*
26a	Time	*In that day*
b	Assertion	*you will ask*
c	Source	*in my name,*
d	Explanation	*and I am not saying to you*
e	Content	*that I will ask the Father concerning you.*
27a	Basis	*For the Father himself loves you,*
b	Basis	*because you have loved me and*
c		*have believed that I came from God.*
28a	Description of Arrival	*I came from the Father*
b		*and entered into the world;*
c	Description of Departure	*I am leaving the world again*
d		*and going to the Father."*
29a	Response	**His disciples said,**
b	Exclamation (of Ignorance)	*"Behold,*
c		*now you are speaking plainly*
d	Contrast	*and speaking without an illustration.*
30a	Emphasis (of Ignorance)	*Now we know that you know all things and*
b		*have no need for anyone to question you.*
c	Inferential Confession	*For this reason we believe that you are from God."*
31a	Response	**Jesus answered them,**
b	Interrogative Rebuke	*"Now you believe?*

32a	Counterexclamation	*Behold,*
b	Event	*an hour is coming and*
c		*has come*
d	Reaction	*when you will be scattered,*
e		*each to his own home, and*
f		*to leave me alone.*
g	Contrast	*Yet I am not alone,*
h	Basis	*because the Father is with me.*
33a	Assertion	*I have spoken these things to you*
b	Purpose	*in order that …*
c	Source/Sphere	*in me*
d		*… you may have peace.*
e	Contrasting Sphere	*In this world*
f	Assertion	*you will have affliction,*
g	Exhortation	*but be courageous;*
h	Basis	*I have overcome the world."*

Structure and Literary Form

As the eighth of eight sections of the farewell discourse, this pericope is part of the fourth (and longest) substantial monologue in the narrative proper. A monologue (see Introduction) is similar to a dialogue in that it is set in the context of an engagement and conflict, but rather than engaging point-for-point it allows for a lengthy argument. A monologue can contain elements of rhetoric, challenge, and conflict, but it does so in a sustained presentation.

This pericope also functions like an epilogue. The first and last sections of the farewell discourse serve as a frame and *inclusio* for the entire monologue. The logic behind seeing a prologue (13:31 – 38) and an epilogue (16:25 – 33) framing the discourse proper is rooted in the nearly identical content in each pericope, serving to connect the entire monologue together. For not only do both pericopae include the question of where Jesus is going and the affirmation of where he is from (13:31 and 16:28), but also both include the reaction of Jesus to Peter and to the disciples alike regarding betrayal or abandonment (13:38 and 16:32).[1] In his closing statement Jesus reminds the disciples of his impending departure and their impending trials and gives them a final exhortation to believe and find peace in his victorious work.

---

1. Boyle, "The Last Discourse," 217.

Exegetical Outline

→ **8. Epilogue: Speaking Plainly, Departure, and Peace (16:25–33)**

    a. The Christian Faith and the Coming "Hour" (vv. 25–28)

    b. The Misbelief of the Disciples (vv. 29–30)

    c. A Final Exhortation: "I Have Overcome the World" (vv. 31–33)

Explanation of the Text

Since this entire section of the Gospel and "the farewell discourse" proper are replete with interpretive issues, we refer the reader to the first pericope of this section where we provided an overview of the nature (genre), literary structure, and function of the farewell discourse (see comments before 13:1).

16:25 "I have spoken these things to you in illustrations; an hour is coming when I will no longer speak to you in illustrations, but will tell you plainly about the Father" (Ταῦτα ἐν παροιμίαις λελάληκα ὑμῖν· ἔρχεται ὥρα ὅτε οὐκέτι ἐν παροιμίαις λαλήσω ὑμῖν ἀλλὰ παρρησίᾳ περὶ τοῦ πατρὸς ἀπαγγελῶ ὑμῖν). The first section of the pericope (vv. 25–28) begins with a phrase that Jesus has used before (cf. 14:25; 16:1), which serves to demarcate a transition in the discourse. Jesus reminds the disciples of "these things" (Ταῦτα) that he has spoken to them to refocus their attention on what he is about to say next. The discourse transitions here to an epilogue, which offers a summarizing commentary and final exhortation to the disciples.

Jesus explains that he has been speaking to the disciples "in illustrations" (ἐν παροιμίαις). This is the first time Jesus uses this term, which the narrator used in 10:6 for what was best understood as a broadly defined "proverb" or "figure of speech" that employed figurative-symbolic imagery and parabolic-allegorical functions (see comments on 10:6). While the narrator explicitly referred to 10:1–5 as an "illustration," we have argued that there are three other examples of "illustrations" in the Gospel (12:24; 15:1–8; 16:21). Jesus's statement here gives warrant for applying the term "illustration" more generally, not only to other parabolic-allegorical analogies used in his teaching but also in this case to his teaching overall.

Jesus explains that his teaching has been proverbial in nature, or more figurative. Yet this will change at a coming "hour" (ὥρα) when Jesus will speak to the disciples "plainly" (παρρησίᾳ), a term which here refers to "a use of speech that conceals nothing and passes over nothing" (cf. 10:24).[2] According to the rest of the farewell discourse, the "hour" is the new order of Christian existence under the ministerial office of the Paraclete, who will guide the Christian "in all truth" (16:13). Moreover, as Jesus explained, the Spirit is not the teacher, for "he will not speak from himself ... because he will receive from me and announce it to you" (16:13–14). In this way Jesus never ceases to be the teacher, but his instruction is now facilitated by the Spirit of God. Again, the departure of Jesus is depicted as the magnification of his continuing ministry, not the limitation of it. It is only by means of the Spirit therefore that believers can receive fully the words of Jesus and the truth about God (see 1 Cor 2:14). The church can now receive Jesus's words and rightly interpret their true subject

---

2. BDAG 781.

matter in the guidance of the Spirit. The teaching ministry of the contemporary church is also facilitated and actualized by the ministerial office of the Spirit (see comments on 14:16), through whom Jesus, the eternal Word of God, still speaks to his disciples today.

16:26 "In that day you will ask in my name, and I am not saying to you that I will ask the Father concerning you" (ἐν ἐκείνῃ τῇ ἡμέρᾳ ἐν τῷ ὀνόματί μου αἰτήσεσθε, καὶ οὐ λέγω ὑμῖν ὅτι ἐγὼ ἐρωτήσω τὸν πατέρα περὶ ὑμῶν). Jesus clarifies further the new state of existence for the disciples. The reason Jesus will continue to be speaking to them is not simply because the Spirit receives from him and announces to the disciples, but also because even the guidance of the Spirit is done "in my name" (ἐν τῷ ὀνόματί μου), that is, through the mediation of Jesus and by his authority. These themes have already been explained in the discourse (cf. 14:12 – 14; 15:7 – 8, 16; 16:23).

Jesus then clarifies and explains that this process is not a bureaucracy that distances the disciples from God, but rather this process magnifies his presence. That is, the mediation of Christ has so restored fellowship between the Father and the children that the Christian may access the Father directly "in Jesus's name." This is not to remove the need for the Son's mediation, for it is still under his authority ("in his name"), but rather to place the entire Christian life under his functional mediation. The Son always intercedes between the Father and the children of God (see Rom 8:34), but this intercession is in regard to the Christian's status before God, not the ongoing answering of prayer.[3]

16:27 "For the Father himself loves you, because you have loved me and have believed that I came from God" (αὐτὸς γὰρ ὁ πατὴρ φιλεῖ ὑμᾶς, ὅτι ὑμεῖς ἐμὲ πεφιλήκατε καὶ πεπιστεύκατε ὅτι ἐγὼ παρὰ [τοῦ] θεοῦ ἐξῆλθον). Jesus establishes further the real intimacy that exists between the disciples and the Father by stating emphatically (denoted by the pronouns) the reason for this change of relationship: "For the Father himself loves you" (αὐτὸς γὰρ ὁ πατὴρ φιλεῖ ὑμᾶς). This remarkable statement personalizes the love of God for the world (3:16) and shows the fruit of its expression. The love of God is not abstract or theoretical but relational and inviting. This life in God — eternal life — is the result of God's originating love, a love that propelled him to send his Son to the cross.

It is important to note that even here Jesus does not deny that this access is mediated, for he then explains what made the Father's love accessible: "Because you have loved me and have believed that I came from God" (ὅτι ὑμεῖς ἐμὲ πεφιλήκατε καὶ πεπιστεύκατε ὅτι ἐγὼ παρὰ [τοῦ] θεοῦ ἐξῆλθον). Two things are expressed by this statement. First, access to the Father is based upon the reciprocation of love — love that is directed specifically at the Son. Jesus has already explained this statement, revealing that the disciple loves God by obeying his commands (14:21; cf. 14:23). The disciple loves God by the submission of their life to God. Any other response is not love, and any other object is not God. Yet even still, it was not we who loved first (as if his love were contingent upon ours), but God who first loved us (1 John 4:10); our love is merely a response and result of his love. We receive the Father's love by loving the Son, for it is the Son who fully represents God (Col 1:15 – 20) and who makes the Father known (1:18).

Second, access to the Father is based upon belief and, more specifically, belief in the mission of God, the Father's sending of the Son. The Christian life is not only a life of love but also a life of faith — faith

---

3. Ridderbos, *John*, 543. Cf. Schlatter, *Der Evangelist Johannes*, 316.

directed at the appropriate object. Jesus explains that true faith has the Son as its object. Faith/belief is a central term for John (see comments on 1:12) and in this context incorporates not only the person of Jesus but also his work, the mission of God. Just as appropriate love receives God in the fullness of his *person*, so also does appropriate love receive God in the fullness of his *work*. An appropriate faith should ultimately come to understand that Christ's mission sprang from the Father's initial love, which established and now fulfills the circle of love Jesus discussed earlier: (1) God's love for us; (2) our love for one another; (3) our love for God (cf. 15:9 – 16).[4]

16:28 "I came from the Father and entered into the world; I am leaving the world again and going to the Father" (ἐξῆλθον παρὰ τοῦ πατρὸς καὶ ἐλήλυθα εἰς τὸν κόσμον· πάλιν ἀφίημι τὸν κόσμον καὶ πορεύομαι πρὸς τὸν πατέρα). The first section of the pericope (vv. 25 – 28) concludes with a summary by Jesus of "the great movement of salvation."[5] As much as these verses have implied a certain kind of behavior, they have been primarily creedal in orientation, and this verse summarizes the whole package, the sum of what Jesus wants his disciples to understand and believe.[6] The epilogue opens with a potent summary of the new life in God shortly to be secured by Jesus. Jesus not only reminds the disciples of the subject matter of his farewell speech but places it before them so that they might grasp at it, fully understanding and appropriating its message to their own lives. That is, in these four verses Jesus has given a summary of the Christian faith.

16:29 His disciples said, "Behold, now you are speaking plainly and speaking without an illus- tration"** (Λέγουσιν οἱ μαθηταὶ αὐτοῦ, Ἴδε νῦν ἐν παρρησίᾳ λαλεῖς, καὶ παροιμίαν οὐδεμίαν λέγεις). The second section of the pericope (vv. 29 – 30) involves a brief response by the disciples to Jesus's statement. The disciples declare that they now understand. Their declaration is made emphatic by the interjection "behold" (Ἴδε) and by means of expressing positively and negatively the same statement: "You are speaking plainly … without an illustration." This is another example of the Gospel's use of irony (cf. 11:49 – 52), for Jesus had just explained that the "hour" for speaking plainly "is coming" (v. 25) and therefore had not yet come. By this the disciples "forwardly imagine" that they already have perceived the meaning and definition of faith in Christ.[7] What their statement more accurately reveals, however, is not what they believe about Jesus but what they believe about themselves.[8] The mistake is clear and was reflected earlier when they bemoan Jesus's departure (cf. 16:4b – 7), for they have so closely associated themselves and their "Christian" experience to life with the Son that they have not yet prepared themselves to receive the new (and better) life "in the Spirit." For this reason, sadly, much of the farewell discourse is still foreign to them.

16:30 "Now we know that you know all things and have no need for anyone to question you. For this reason we believe that you are from God" (νῦν οἴδαμεν ὅτι οἶδας πάντα καὶ οὐ χρείαν ἔχεις ἵνα τίς σε ἐρωτᾷ· ἐν τούτῳ πιστεύομεν ὅτι ἀπὸ θεοῦ ἐξῆλθες). The disciples' ignorance and self-proclaimed understanding of Jesus's message (even before the "hour") explains why the disciples offer their own creed-like statement. The disciples claim "now" (νῦν) to have an awareness of Jesus's knowledge ("you know all things" [οἶδας πάντα])

---

4. Cf. Augustine, *John*, 102.5.391.

5. Morris, *John*, 630. According to Bultmann, this verse is stated "almost as a doctrinal statement" (*John*, 589).

6. Michaels, *John*, 851.

7. Hoskyns, *Fourth Gospel*, 491.

8. Cf. Barrett, *John*, 497; Calvin, *John 11 – 21*, 131.

and authority, reflected in the somewhat odd statement "(you) have no need for anyone to question you" (οὐ χρείαν ἔχεις ἵνα τίς σε ἐρωτᾷ), supposedly providing them with the warrant and reason to believe that he truly is from God. Their statement is less comprehensive than it could be, though it resembles enough of Christ's own closing statement (v. 28) to suggest that they are claiming a cumulative comprehension to some degree. And their reference to Christ's knowledge appears only slightly more significant than that of the onlookers during his public ministry who were impressed with his authoritative teaching (e.g., 7:45 – 46).

16:31 Jesus answered them, "Now you believe?" (ἀπεκρίθη αὐτοῖς Ἰησοῦς, Ἄρτι πιστεύετε;). The third section of the pericope (vv. 31 – 33) begins with a question[9] that is intended to offer a rebuke and retort to the ignorance-revealing declaration of the disciples. This is not the first time Jesus has responded to a situation with a question (cf. 5:6; 9:35), and here again the question bears a strong rhetorical intention. God has been known to ask questions that probe into the blind ignorance of humanity. God did not ask Adam's location for his own sake, but to offer Adam a moment of self-reflection (Gen 3:9). That is Jesus's intention here: "Do you *really* believe?" Jesus will address their future arrival at knowledge and belief in his concluding prayer (ch. 17); here he is interested more in addressing and rebuking their present ignorance and misbelief.

16:32 "Behold, an hour is coming and has come when you will be scattered, each to his own home, and to leave me alone. Yet I am not alone, because the Father is with me" (ἰδοὺ ἔρχεται ὥρα καὶ ἐλήλυθεν ἵνα σκορπισθῆτε ἕκαστος εἰς τὰ ἴδια κἀμὲ μόνον ἀφῆτε· καὶ οὐκ εἰμὶ μόνος, ὅτι ὁ πατὴρ

μετ᾽ ἐμοῦ ἐστιν). Jesus turns their own self-proclamation against them by revealing that they were right about one thing: he did "know all things" (v. 30; cf. 2:25). Beginning with his own and countering interjection "behold" (ἰδοὺ), Jesus gives the disciples prophetic insight into the reality of their self-declared "belief" in him. Jesus restates the significant coming "hour" (ὥρα) conveniently misplaced by the disciples, but this time declares that the disciples' self-proclaimed allegiance will fail at the moment of crisis, his crucifixion. They will disband from "the Twelve" and "each" (ἕκαστος) will go to their own home, abandoning Jesus entirely. Jesus promised that he would not abandon the disciples (14:18), but the disciples will abandon Jesus at his time of need. At that "hour" their trust in his knowledge and authority (v. 30) will not be confidently resting in his person and work.[10] By these words Jesus rebukes his disciples, but he also reveals to them the true condition of their understanding of the mission of God and the true nature of their faith in him.

In order that the disciples do not mistake Jesus's prediction as a cry for human assistance, Jesus explains that as part of the authorized mission of God, he is not alone "because the Father is with me" (ὅτι ὁ πατὴρ μετ᾽ ἐμοῦ ἐστιν). The work of Jesus is not dependent upon humanity but is performed rather for its benefit, with the Father authorizing the work of the Son and supporting his mission. The most important thing the presence of the Father signifies is that Jesus is right where he is supposed to be, even though not one other person would join him. When the whole world, including the disciples of Jesus, think Jesus had been conquered, the presence of the Father declares the exact opposite.

16:33 "I have spoken these things to you in order that in me you may have peace. In this world you

---

9. The phrase could also be taken as an exclamatory statement: "Now you believe!"

10. Cf. Bultmann, *John*, 592.

will have affliction, but be courageous; I have overcome the world" (ταῦτα λελάληκα ὑμῖν ἵνα ἐν ἐμοὶ εἰρήνην ἔχητε· ἐν τῷ κόσμῳ θλῖψιν ἔχετε, ἀλλὰ θαρσεῖτε, ἐγὼ νενίκηκα τὸν κόσμον). Jesus concludes the pericope and the farewell discourse proper with a statement that summarizes his intentions and offers a final exhortation to his disciples. Using again the phrase with which he began the pericope (v. 25), Jesus declares his purpose: "In order that in me you may have peace" (ἵνα ἐν ἐμοὶ εἰρήνην ἔχητε). Jesus had promised this to the disciples earlier (see comments on 14:27), and he confirms it here at the end of his speech.

Jesus has spoken of this coming affliction before (cf. 16:2), but he probably refers here to the comprehensive nature of the conflict they will face as his disciples in the world (cf. 15:18 – 25). But Christ has something different for them, denoted by the strong adversative "but" (ἀλλὰ); Christ commands them to "stand beyond the world"[11] and the security it offers by being "courageous" (θαρσεῖτε) — "to be firm or resolute in the face of danger or adverse circumstances."[12] The source for this courage is certainly not found in the world nor within the disciples themselves but in the accomplished work of Christ. Said another way, only with the cor-rect object of faith can a person be grounded in a greater and more powerful reality than that which surrounds and threatens him.

What can give the disciples real peace and the courage they need to face the world's afflictions? It is the finished work of Christ, which Jesus announces to his disciples: "I have overcome the world" (ἐγὼ νενίκηκα τὸν κόσμον). This final exhortation is an assertion of his power, making manifest in the historical time-and-space world what had cosmologically always been the case — the darkness could not "recognize" or "overcome" the light (see comments on 1:5). As the Gospel has made clear, the cross is the victory of Christ and the defeat of the world, including "the ruler of this world" (cf. 12:31; 14:30 – 31; 16:8 – 11). This victory belongs not to Christ alone, for it also belongs to his disciples, the children of God, which the prayer to follow will express further (see ch. 17). The cross of Christ is his exultation (cf. 3:14; 8:28; 12:34; cf. Acts 2:33), and the disciples will come to "know" and "believe," in spite of their forthcoming response to the contrary, that Christ alone became at the moment of apparent defeat and death the victor and the giver of life.[13] In this way the pericope concludes, as does the farewell discourse proper.

Theology in Application

In the eighth and final section of the farewell discourse, Jesus gives a final summary of the Christian life in the new covenant and encourages the disciples to understand appropriate belief in him, rooted in his victory over the world. Through this pericope the reader is challenged in the nature of their belief and is exhorted to believe in the victory of Christ.

---

11. Ibid., 584.
12. BDAG 444.

13. Gail R. O'Day, "'I Have Overcome the World' (John 16:33): Narrative Time in John 13 – 17," *Semeia* 53 (1991): 153 – 65 (162).

The Teaching of Jesus

This pericope confirms what the Gospel first declared: Jesus is the Word (1:1), the one who teaches the children of God about the Father (1:18). Jesus's teachings are only magnified "in the Spirit," whose ministry will explain and apply the true subject matter of Jesus's teaching to those who belong to God and participate in the church (cf. 16:13). Jesus is the eternal Word and the final word of God (Heb 1:1 – 2), and the church not only relates to the Father through the Son (and by the Spirit) but also continues to proclaim the same message to the world — the gospel of Jesus Christ. The teaching of the church, therefore, is Christocentric from first to last, for Christ is both the teacher and subject matter of Scripture, the Word of God's Word.

The Love of the Father

Jesus explains that his mediation will facilitate a real and personal relationship between God and the children of God. The love of God for the world (3:16) has been personalized so that God is now both willing and able to love us himself. The love of God is not abstract or theoretical but relational and inviting. Our life in God is the result of God's originating love, a love that propelled him to send his Son to the cross. God is love, and his love is expressed to us, through us, and from us (see 1 John 4:7 – 5:3). God is the great lover, the epitome of love, the most willing to express love, and the most worthy recipient of love. All human love starts and begins with God, and our life of love must find its ultimate grounding in the love of God.

The Condition of Misbelief

The disciples displayed the ignorance of their belief in their brief dialogue with Christ in this periocpe (cf. vv. 29 – 31). The disciples' condition seems to have resulted from a minimization of their own depravity and Christ's real ministry. They thought that Christ was simply the one who would *teach* them and not the one who would *transform* them. Like so many in the Gospel, they did not see the necessity of the cross or the death that needed to occur in their flesh. The question Jesus offered as a response to their ignorance speaks directly to us as well: "Do you now believe?" We also must ask ourselves whether we have eclipsed or minimized any of the particulars of the gospel because of selfish ignorance or pride. We too must ask ourselves if we have confessed and accepted our own need for death, and if we truly seek the power of the resurrection that only comes from being conformed to his death (Phil 3:10).

The Victory of God in Christ

Jesus concluded his farewell speech with a grand declaration of victory. God wins! And his victory is achieved not by the tools of human sin and pride but by a sacrifice of love, the cross. The victory of God was hidden behind the false assumption that power was displayed by killing, not by sacrifice, and that winning was achieved by sustaining one's life, not by giving it as an offering. Yet the death of Christ is the defeat of the world and the ruler of this world and the offer of salvation (i.e., participation in God's victory) to the world.

It is the victory of God that the Christian celebrates, knowing that all enemies (past, present, and future) have already been defeated, even death itself (Hos 13:14; 1 Cor 15:54–55). For this reason when Christians stand with God, they also stand beyond the world, for they understand "everything which the world can bring against them.... The anxiety of blindness has been taken away from them, and the future is no longer threatening..."[14] This is God's victory, but it also belongs to the children of God.

---

14. Bultmann, *John*, 584.

John 17:1 – 26

Literary Context

This pericope serves as a conclusion to the farewell discourse. After gathering his disciples and addressing them privately, Jesus offers a closing prayer to the Father in which he prays for the glory of God, his disciples, and the church. Just as the farewell discourse had an introduction that set the historical and theological context of Jesus's monologue (13:1 – 30), this pericope concludes Jesus's farewell speech by setting the theological (cosmological) context of Jesus's entire ministry and the work God will continue to do. After a lengthy speech directed toward his disciples, Jesus now turns and addresses his Father, the one from whom he came, announcing the completion of his work and praying for its fulfillment in both the present disciples and all future disciples. The disciples — and the reader — are given insight into the plan and provision of God for his church.

VII. The Farewell Discourse (13:1 – 17:26)

    A. Introduction: The Love of Jesus (13:1 – 30)

        1. Jesus and the Washing of His Disciples' Feet (13:1 – 20)

        2. Jesus Announces His Betrayal (13:21 – 30)

    B. The Farewell Discourse (13:31 – 16:33)

        1. Prologue: Glory, Departure, and Love (13:31 – 38)

        2. I Am the Way and the Truth and the Life (14:1 – 14)

        3. I Will Give You the Paraclete (14:15 – 31)

        4. I Am the True Vine (15:1 – 17)

        5. I Have Also Experienced the Hate of the World (15:18 – 27)

        6. I Will Empower You by the Paraclete (16:1 – 15)

        7. I Will Turn Your Grief into Joy (16:16 – 24)

        8. Epilogue: Speaking Plainly, Departure, and Peace (16:25 – 33)

    ➥ **C. Conclusion: The Prayer of Jesus (17:1 – 26)**

Main Idea

Jesus has consecrated his disciples to God so that by their participation in the oneness of the Father and the Son, the church may give him glory, trust in his protection and plan, share in his joy, and facilitate his mission in the world.

Translation

(See pages 707–11.)

Structure and Literary Form

As the conclusion of the farewell discourse, this pericope is part of the fourth (and longest) substantial monologue in the narrative proper. A monologue (see Introduction) is similar to a dialogue in that it is set in the context of an engagement and conflict, but rather than engaging point-for-point it allows for a lengthy argument. A monologue can contain elements of rhetoric, challenge, and conflict, but it does so in a sustained presentation.

This pericope functions as the conclusion to this section of the Gospel, "The Farewell Discourse" (13:1 – 17:26). Befitting the genre of the farewell discourse (see comments before 13:1), the inclusion of a prayer is not uncommon at the end of farewell speeches in the OT and later Jewish literature. For example, Deuteronomy, itself a series of farewell discourses in form, concludes with the Song of Moses in the form of a psalm (ch. 32) and Moses's blessing of the tribes in the form of a prophetic prayer (ch. 33).[1] This prayer is unique, however, because of the person who offers the prayer — the Son of God — and because of the setting of the prayer — Jesus prays that the purposes of God may be perfectly fulfilled through the work he is about to accomplish and later through the work of his disciples. Although the prayer has long been known as "The High Priestly Prayer," at least since the sixteenth century and even in some patristic commentaries (e.g., Cyril of Alexandria), it was best described as "The Prayer of Consecration."[2] For by this prayer Jesus in the presence of his disciples "consecrated Himself to death as the effective sacrifice upon which their sanctification was to depend, and He solemnly dedicated them to the mission which was to be the effective result of His death and resurrection."[3]

The pericope has traditionally been broken into three parts: vv. 1 – 5, 6 – 19, and 20 – 26, often based upon the content of each section: God, the disciples (present), and disciples (future). But the prayer is best divided not by content or ideas alone,[4]

1. See Beasley-Murray, *John*, 293.

2. Westcott, *John*, 236 – 37. Cf. Harold W. Attridge, "How Priestly is the 'High Priestly Prayer' of John 17?" *CBQ* 75 (2013): 1 – 14.

3. Hoskyns, *Fourth Gospel*, 495.

4. See Sadananda, *The Johannine Exegesis of God*, 133 – 34; Michaels, *John*, 857.

John 17:1–26

Conclusion of "Farewell Discourse"

1a	Prayer for Glory (1–8)	
b	Action	After Jesus spoke these things **he lifted his eyes to heaven and said,**
c	Address	"Father,
d	Basis #1 (for 1c, 5a)	the hour has come;
e	Entreaty	glorify your Son,
f	Purpose	in order that the Son may glorify you.
2a	Comparison	Just as you gave to him authority
b	Sphere	over all flesh,
c	Purpose	in order that he might give eternal life to all those
d	Description	who were given to him.
3a	Expansion: "Eternal Life"	This is eternal life:
b	Description	that they know
c	Direct Object #1	you,
d	Identity	the only true God, and
e	Direct Object #2	the one whom you sent,
f	Identity	Jesus Christ.
4a	Assertion	I glorified you on the earth
b	Means	by finishing the work
c	Description	which you gave me to do.
5a	Emphatic Entreaty	And now glorify me,
b	Address	Father,
c	Setting	in your presence with the glory
d	Source of "Glory"	which I had with you
e	Time	before the world was [in existence].
6a	Basis #2 (for 1c, 5a)	I have revealed your name to the people
b	Description	you have given me
c	Source	from the world,
d	Result #1 of 6a	and they have kept your word.
7a	Result #2 of 6a	Now they know …
b	Source	that everything you have given me
c	Source	… is from you.

Continued on next page.

Continued from previous page.

8a	Sequential Basis #1 (of 7)	*Because* the words …
b	Source	which you gave me
c	Sequential Basis #2	… I gave to them, and
d	Sequential Basis #3	they received them and
e		truly understood
f	Source	that I came from you, and
g	Sequential Basis #4	they believed
h	Source	that you sent me.
9a	Prayer: Present Disciples (9–19)	I ask for them,
b	Negative Request	I am not asking for the world but
c	Contrast	for those you have given to me,
d	Basis	for they are yours,
10a	Interchangeable Relationship	and all that belongs to me is yours,
b	Interchangeable Relationship	and what belongs to you is mine,
c	Assertion	and I have been glorified
d	Locative	in them.
11a	Assertion	I am no longer in the world,
b	Contrast	and they are in the world,
c	Imminent Departure	and I am going to you.
d	Address	Holy Father,
e	Entreaty	keep them
f	Locative	in your name
h	Description	which you gave to me,
i	Purpose: / Unity	in order that they … … may be one
j	Comparison	just as we are one.

12a	Contemporaneous Action	While I was with them
b	Progressive Action #1	I kept them
c	Locative	in your name
d	Description	which you gave to me,
e	Progressive Action #2	and I guarded them,
f	Progressive Action #3	and not one of them was destroyed
g	Exception	except the son of destruction,
h	Result/Allusion: Ps 41:9	so that the Scripture might be fulfilled.
13a	Imminent Departure	But now I am coming to you,
b	Assertion	and I say these things
c	Context	while I am in the world
d	Purpose	in order that they may have my joy fulfilled in them.
14a	Restatement of 6–8	I have given your word to them,
b	Reaction	and the world hates them,
c	Basis	because they are not from the world
d	Comparison	just as I am not from the world.
15a	Entreaty (–)	I do not ask that you remove them from the world but
b	Contrast	that you keep them from the evil one.
16a	Restatement of 14	They are not from the world
b	Comparison	just as I am not from the world.
17a	Emphatic Entreaty	Sanctify them in the truth;
b	Basis	your word is truth.
18a	Comparison	Just as you sent me into the world,
b	Proleptic Purpose of 17a	I also sent them into the world.
19a	Allusion to Cross	I sanctify myself
b	Beneficiary	on their behalf,
c	Result	so that they also may be sanctified in truth.

Continued on next page.

Continued from previous page.

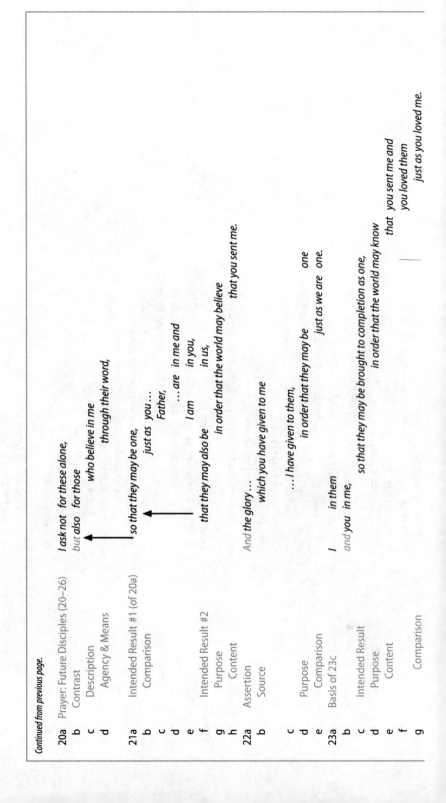

20a	Prayer: Future Disciples (20–26)	I ask not for these alone,
b	Contrast	*but also* for those
c	Description	who believe in me
d	Agency & Means	through their word,
21a	Intended Result #1 (of 20a)	so that they may be one,
b	Comparison	just as you …
c		Father,
d		…are in me and
e		I am in you,
		in us,
f	Intended Result #2	that they may also be
g	Purpose	in order that the world may believe
h	Content	that you sent me.
22a	Assertion	And the glory …
b	Source	which you have given to me
		… I have given to them,
c	Purpose	in order that they may be one
d	Comparison	just as we are one.
23a	Basis of 23c	I in them
b		and you in me,
c	Intended Result	so that they may be brought to completion as one,
d	Purpose	in order that the world may know
e	Content	that you sent me and
f		you loved them
g	Comparison	just as you loved me.

24a	Address	Father,
b	Description	those you have given to me,
c	Entreaty	I desire that they also may be with me
d	Location	where I am,
e	Result	so that they may see my glory
f	Source	which you have given to me,
g	Basis	because you loved me
h	Time	before the creation of the world.
25a	Address	Righteous Father,
b	Contrast	though the world does not know you,
c	Progression #1	I know you,
d	Progression #2	and they know
e	Content	that you sent me,
26a	Progression #3	and I made known your name to them
b	Progression #4	and I will continue to make it known,
c	Intended Result #1	so that the love…
d		with which you loved me
e		in them and
f	Intended Result #2	…may be I in them."

which are difficult to determine in such a unified prayer. Its outline must also be deduced by formal or structural aspects in the text itself, specifically its own threefold indication of whom Jesus is praying for: the glorification of the Father and the Son in v. 1, the disciples whom the Father has given him in v. 9, and those who will believe in him through the preaching of the disciples in v. 20.[5] Not only are each of the sections related developmentally to one another, but they also share five structurally significant features:[6]

1. Each unit begins with what Jesus is praying for (vv. 1, 9, 20).
2. Each has the theme of glory (vv. 1 – 5, 10, 22).
3. Each has an address to the Father partway through the unit (vv. 5, 11, 21).
4. Each mentions the people given to Jesus by the Father (vv. 2, 9, 24).
5. Each has the theme of Jesus's revelation of the Father to humanity (vv. 6, 14, 26: "your name/word").

These structural similarities that interrelate all three parts of the pericope rhetorically support its cumulative message: the double consecration of the mission of God and the mission of the church.[7] Christ's prayer is intimately tied to what has just preceded it — Jesus's introduction to life in the Spirit under the new covenant.[8]

Exegetical Outline

→ **C. Conclusion: The Prayer of Jesus (17:1 – 26)**
    1. Prayer for the Glory of the Father and the Son (vv. 1 – 8)
    2. Prayer for the Present Disciples (vv. 9 – 19)
    3. Prayer for the Future Disciples (vv. 20 – 26)

Explanation of the Text

Since this entire section of the Gospel and "the farewell discourse" proper are replete with interpretive issues, we refer the reader to the first pericope of this section where we provided an overview of the nature (genre), literary structure, and function of the farewell discourse (see comments before 13:1).

17:1 After Jesus spoke these things he lifted his eyes to heaven and said, "Father, the hour has come; glorify your Son, in order that the Son may glorify you" (Ταῦτα ἐλάλησεν Ἰησοῦς, καὶ ἐπάρας τοὺς ὀφθαλμοὺς αὐτοῦ εἰς τὸν οὐρανὸν εἶπεν, Πάτερ, ἐλήλυθεν ἡ ὥρα· δόξασόν σου τὸν υἱόν, ἵνα ὁ υἱὸς δοξάσῃ σέ). In the first section of the pericope (vv. 1 – 8), Jesus prays for the glory of the Father and the Son. The narrator begins by describing the praying posture of Jesus, which has been depicted before (see comments on 11:41). Jesus begins his

---

5. Brown, *John*, 2:748 – 50; Cf. Moloney, *John*, 458 – 59.
6. The following is adapted from Brown, *John*, 2:750.

7. Cf. David Alan Black, "On the Style and Significance of John 17," *CTR* 3 (1988): 141 – 59.
8. Cf. Calvin, *John 11 – 21*, 134.

prayer by addressing the Father, the primary addressee in all three parts of the prayer, addressed six times (vv. 1, 5, 11, 21, 24, 25). Just as the Father sent the Son to focus on the needs of the world, so the Son at the conclusion of his mission to the world returns his focus upon the Father.

Jesus declares that "the hour has come" (ἐλήλυθεν ἡ ὥρα). This is the last intentional occurrence of the term "hour," which has been a technical term in the Gospel (see comments on 2:4). The entire ministry of Jesus has been directed to this moment in time, and now in this prayer of consecration just before the events of the "hour" begin, Jesus places this "hour" before the Father, from whom the Son was sent and for whom all the work of the Son was intended.

After situating the moment of his mission, Jesus prays that the Father provide its ultimate purpose: "Glorify your Son, in order that the Son may glorify you" (δόξασόν σου τὸν υἱόν, ἵνα ὁ υἱὸς δοξάσῃ σέ). Jesus had spoken before of the hour of glorification and had prayed before for glory for the Son and the Father (see comments on 12:23, 28). Jesus does not pray for new glory, but for the consecration of the glory that he already possessed and disclosed (vv. 22 – 24; cf. 1:14) and that he as the Son had consistently given to the Father (11:4, 40).[9] This mutual glorification depends on both parties — the Father glorifies the Son so that the Son may glorify the Father. This "glory" belongs to both the Father and Son not only because of a shared mission, which is now coming to fruition, but also because of a shared identity in the Trinitarian identity of God (cf. 1:1).

17:2 "Just as you gave to him authority over all flesh, in order that he might give eternal life to all those who were given to him" (καθὼς ἔδωκας αὐτῷ ἐξουσίαν πάσης σαρκός, ἵνα πᾶν ὃ δέδωκας αὐτῷ δώσῃ αὐτοῖς ζωὴν αἰώνιον). Jesus continues by establishing the ground for the petition of v. 1. The purpose of the manifestation of God's glory mutually obtained and received by the Father and the Son extends and includes also the children of God, the disciples. God always intended to "[bring] many sons and daughters to glory" (Heb 2:10).[10] This is why Jesus acknowledges in his prayer that the Father gave to him "authority over all flesh," with the term "flesh" (σαρκός) — often translated as "people" (NIV) or "mankind" (NASB) — making an intentional comparison between Jesus's soon-to-be-broken "flesh" (1:14) with the "all flesh" of the world.

The mutual glory of the Father and Son always had as its purpose that the Son "might give eternal life to all those who were given to him" (πᾶν ὃ δέδωκας αὐτῷ δώσῃ αὐτοῖς ζωὴν αἰώνιον). The death of Christ is for the purpose of life, his flesh for "all flesh" — not entirely all but only those "given to him," as the Gospel has mentioned elsewhere (cf. 6:37, 44). By describing the "elect" not by their act of faith but by the action of God, Jesus emphasizes that this entire event is from "above"; not only is the Son's glory and authority given to him by God but so also are those for whom he was sent. In this way, vv. 1 – 2 can be seen to be working closely together. The Son asks the Father to glorify him (v. 1a) because that is the means by which the Son may then glorify the Father (v. 1b); and this "pre-temporal plan" to give all authority to the Son (v. 2a) is the means by which the world may come to faith in the Son and the one who sent him, gaining eternal life (v. 2b).[11] In short, God had always planned to magnify his glory in and extend his life to the world through the person and work of Jesus Christ (cf. Rom 1:1 – 5). This is the gospel:

9. Ridderbos, *John*, 548.
10. Cf. Newbigin, *The Light Has Come*, 226.
11. Carson, *John*, 554 – 55.

the glory of God (both Father and Son) expressed in the gift of eternal life to humanity.[12]

17:3 "This is eternal life: that they know you, the only true God, and the one whom you sent, Jesus Christ" (αὕτη δέ ἐστιν ἡ αἰώνιος ζωή, ἵνα γινώσκωσιν σὲ τὸν μόνον ἀληθινὸν θεὸν καὶ ὃν ἀπέστειλας Ἰησοῦν Χριστόν). Jesus continues his prayer by describing the "gift" of eternal life that is provided by the Son. So what is eternal life? It is the knowledge of God, both the Father and the Son, the latter here specifically referred to as "Jesus Christ." This knowledge is clearly personal, since it involves not merely propositions but persons: "The only true God" (τὸν μόνον ἀληθινὸν θεὸν) and "the one whom you sent" (ὃν ἀπέστειλας). That is, to know God must mean to have received what the prologue announced only the Son could reveal: a vision of God (1:18). And the subject matter of this vision, this gift of knowledge, involves not only the identity or person of God (specifically the Father) but also the work of God (specifically the Son). This is confirmed when Jesus speaks of himself in the third person. For as much as Jesus is the source of this revelation, he is also an essential part of its content. To have eternal life is to know God, that he is the only true God — there is no other — and that he is made known by means of Jesus Christ, whom the Father sent to the world. To know God is to know and participate in his life and his mission, which is the extension of his life to the world, a life with the Father through Christ and in and by the Spirit.[13] This is no double knowledge (Father and Son) any more than fellowship with the Father and with the Son is a double fellowship (see 1 John 1:3). It is one faith in one God.[14]

17:4 "I glorified you on the earth by finishing the work which you gave me to do" (ἐγώ σε ἐδόξασα ἐπὶ τῆς γῆς, τὸ ἔργον τελειώσας ὃ δέδωκάς μοι ἵνα ποιήσω). Jesus rephrases the means by which he glorified the Father, first introduced in vv. 1 – 2, in these two verses (vv. 4 – 5), reversing also the order of glorification. Jesus begins by declaring how he has already glorified the Father: "By finishing the work which you gave me" (τελειώσας ὃ δέδωκάς μοι). Jesus here claims to have "finished" — completed or fulfilled — what he was sent to do. The Father had initiated the now completed work of the Son, an assignment specifically carried out "on the earth" (ἐπὶ τῆς γῆς). Now the Father is expected to finish what he started, to end what he began, restoring what properly belongs to the Son "from above," as the next verse makes clear.

17:5 "And now glorify me, Father, in your presence with the glory which I had with you before the world was [in existence]" (καὶ νῦν δόξασόν με σύ, πάτερ, παρὰ σεαυτῷ τῇ δόξῃ ᾗ εἶχον πρὸ τοῦ τὸν κόσμον εἶναι παρὰ σοί). Jesus addresses the Father with an expectation that can only be grounded in the quality of their persons. The imperative must be handled carefully; it is not a command proper, as if the Son can command the Father, but neither is it best defined simply as a request (to a superior), even though Jesus certainly is submitted to the Father (cf. 5:30). This imperative is rooted in the social dynamics of the Trinity, which remain mysterious to us. It can only be rooted in the Trinitarian identity of God in such a manner that just as the Son completed perfectly what the Father asked of him, the Father will also complete perfectly what the Son now asks. The commands and requests of

---

12. The focus on the Father and Son in these opening verses should not be interpreted to be exclusive of the Spirit. See Francis Watson, "Trinity and Community: A Reading of John 17," *IJST* 1 (1999): 168 – 84 (182).

13. See P. Maritz, "Some Time in John: Tensions between the Hour and Eternity in John 17," *Neot* 41 (2007): 112 – 30.
14. Hoskyns, *Fourth Gospel*, 498.

both persons are entirely satisfied in one another and their interconnected intents and goals.

The command or request is not in regard to the original glory that already belonged to the eternal Son, the preincarnate Son, the Word-before-flesh. This "earlier" glory is not earned but innately and properly belongs to the Son, who both "is God" and was "with God" (1:1). It is the glory bound to the identity of God that the Father and Son share. This is why Jesus can neither command such glory nor merely request it, for it is already and rightfully *his* glory. These two verses (vv. 4 – 5) summarize the cosmological strand of the Gospel's plot, describing how the Son left the glory of God to complete his mission "on the earth" and then will depart and return to his Father the glory of God.[15] It would be theologically inaccurate to think that Jesus's statement implies that the incarnation involved a lessened glory. Rather, Jesus is requesting what already belongs to him. He is asking that the glory that was properly basic to his place in the identity of God "might also be done now in actual accomplishment."[16]

17:6 "I have revealed your name to the people you have given me from the world, and they have kept your word" (Ἐφανέρωσά σου τὸ ὄνομα τοῖς ἀνθρώποις οὓς ἔδωκάς μοι ἐκ τοῦ κόσμου. σοὶ ἦσαν κἀμοὶ αὐτοὺς ἔδωκας, καὶ τὸν λόγον σου τετήρηκαν). Jesus shares with the Father that he has "revealed your name" (Ἐφανέρωσά σου τὸ ὄνομα) to the disciples, fulfilling what the prologue announced the Son would do (1:18). The revelation of the Son is the expression of Jesus's entire ministry — his teachings and his miracles and signs. But what "name" was revealed? Some interpreters choose a particular name, such as "I AM[17]" or "Father,"[18] but there is no need to select just one.

As we discussed earlier, the concept of a "name" in the ancient world was not merely a label but a reference to the character of a person. Thus, what Jesus revealed was not merely the title of God the Father but the full testimony of the person and work of God the Father, which was being manifested through the person and work of his Son. It is not a burning bush (Exod 3) but God himself who has now declared and defined his true identity in the Son.

The recipients of the revelation of God were not haphazardly chosen but were taken "from the world" (ἐκ τοῦ κόσμου) and "given" (ἔδωκάς) by the Father to the Son. This suggests that the mission of God was not performed indiscriminately but with divine intentionality and support. The Son ministered as and to whom the Father assigned (see comments on 6:37 – 38). Moreover, according to Jesus those to whom the Son ministered "have kept your word" (τὸν λόγον σου τετήρηκαν). By paralleling the Father's "giving" with the disciples' "keeping," the activity of both parties are being presented simultaneously as a single divine act. The disciples "kept" because God had (already) "given" (cf. 1:13). The fulfilling mission of the Son is given its climactic depiction in the formation of the children of God.

17:7 "Now they know that everything you have given me is from you" (νῦν ἔγνωκαν ὅτι πάντα ὅσα δέδωκάς μοι παρὰ σοῦ εἰσιν). Jesus acknowledges before the Father that the disciples "now" (νῦν) — that is, "at this time" (the word here serving as a temporal rather than logical indicator) — "know" (ἔγνωκαν) or have come to understand the mission from the Father and through the Son. The significance of knowledge in v. 3 is again expressed here; the disciples have come to a personal knowledge

---

15. Cf. Paul S. Minear, "John 17:1 – 11," *Int* 32 (1978): 175 – 79.

16. Augustine, *John*, 105.8.398.

17. See Brown, *John*, 2:755 – 56; Dodd, *Interpretation*, 417.

18. See Schlatter, *Der Evangelist Johannes*, 319 – 20.

and vision of God the Father through the Son. For this knowledge is specifically in reference to the direct connection between the work of the Son and the Father, since as Jesus says to the Father, "Everything … is from you" (πάντα παρὰ σοῦ εἰσιν). The work of the Son has always been the work of the Father — the work of God. We must understand this statement as part of the larger work of God and not base it on the ability of the disciples at that moment to have already made all the connections between Jesus, God, and their salvation, for certainly at least before the resurrection there was still much confusion.

17:8 "Because the words which you gave me I gave to them, and they received them and truly understood that I came from you, and they believed that you sent me" (ὅτι τὰ ῥήματα ἃ ἔδωκάς μοι δέδωκα αὐτοῖς, καὶ αὐτοὶ ἔλαβον καὶ ἔγνωσαν ἀληθῶς ὅτι παρὰ σοῦ ἐξῆλθον, καὶ ἐπίστευσαν ὅτι σύ με ἀπέστειλας). Jesus concludes this section of the prayer regarding the glory of the Father and Son by confirming that the mission and message of the Father has achieved its purpose. The Father is still the true subject matter of Jesus's mission and message: "The words *you* gave"; "I came from *you*"; "they believed that *you* sent me." The intention of the Son was for God to be "revealed" (ἐξηγήσατο; 1:18), and that is exactly what the Son accomplished. For the disciples have received Jesus's message, which is "the words" (τὰ ῥήματα) from the Father. The subject matter of "*the* Word" (ὁ λόγος) was always "the words" (τὰ ῥήματα) of the Father. But they have also believed in Jesus's mission, which means that they "truly understood that I came from you" (ἔγνωσαν ἀληθῶς ὅτι παρὰ σοῦ ἐξῆλθον). The verb "believed" (ἐπίστευσαν) is intentionally working with "know" (γινώσκωσιν) in v. 3. The intimate connection between knowledge/

understanding and belief/faith in this pericope reminds the reader that God cannot be known without faith, but also that in faith there is such certainty that it can be properly called knowledge.[19] The final prayer of Jesus has functioned like "an operation of divine grace, transforming the shaky faith of the disciples into something firm and lasting."[20]

17:9 "I ask for them, I am not asking for the world but for those you have given to me, for they are yours" (ἐγὼ περὶ αὐτῶν ἐρωτῶ· οὐ περὶ τοῦ κόσμου ἐρωτῶ ἀλλὰ περὶ ὧν δέδωκάς μοι, ὅτι σοί εἰσιν). In the second section of the pericope (vv. 9 – 19), Jesus prays for his present disciples. After speaking in regard to himself, "Jesus now begins intercessory prayer."[21] The "them" (αὐτῶν) Jesus is referring to is the disciples, about whom Jesus had just declared to the Father that he had fully disclosed the name of and words from the Father, which they have truly understood and believed (vv. 6 – 8). Jesus has finished his work as assigned by the Father on behalf of the disciples and now asks the Father for this work to be finalized. Jesus is consecrating his disciples to the plan and purpose of God.

While Jesus uses election language here, it is no different from elsewhere in the Gospel (cf. 6:44; 12:40). But here the point is less the manner in which the disciples were "given" to Jesus and more the fact of it. Jesus's prayer therefore announces the completion of his work and locates the fruit of his work, the disciples, as ultimately belonging to God: "For they are yours" (ὅτι σοί εἰσιν). Jesus's purpose had always been to serve as a mediator between *his* Father and *his* disciples (1:18), and now his mediation was finished. There is no transfer of allegiance implied here and certainly no competition, as the next verse will make clear. The children of God

---

19. Calvin, *John 11 – 21*, 140.
20. Michaels, *John*, 863.
21. Ibid., 864.

belong *to* the Father *through* the Son (and *in* the Spirit). There is no other access to God or mode of Christian discipleship.

17:10 "And all that belongs to me is yours, and what belongs to you is mine, and I have been glorified in them" (καὶ τὰ ἐμὰ πάντα σά ἐστιν καὶ τὰ σὰ ἐμά, καὶ δεδόξασμαι ἐν αὐτοῖς). Jesus speaks here of the interchangeable relationship between "all" (πάντα) things and the Father and the Son. Quite simply, what belongs to the Father also belongs to the Son and vice versa. Jesus is not losing his disciples by securing their relationship with the Father. There is no transfer from the Son to the Father, but rather now there is access to the Father through the Son. Jesus's disciples can be both his and the Father's simultaneously, just as God includes both the Father and the Son (cf. 1:1). The disciples are not then less than the disciples of Jesus but more, for they also are the children of God. In fact, only a disciple of Jesus can be in relationship with the Father. The reader is to see again here the Gospel's concern to present Christ and the disciples' relation to Christ as access to the fullness of God (Father, Son, and Spirit). For just as the disciples approach and have access to the Father only through the Son, so the Father assigned the Son to be the one through whom alone he would approach and have access to us.[22] There is no need to access the Father beyond the Son or to think that God can be found by another means, for according to God's plan Jesus is the way, the truth, and the life (14:6). The person who has the Son has "all that belongs" (τὰ πάντα) to God himself.

Jesus concludes this statement by claiming, "And I have been glorified in them" (καὶ δεδόξασμαι ἐν αὐτοῖς). Referring again to the disciples and his work of mediation, Jesus declares that the completion of his mission from the Father is established in

the disciples (with the perfect-tense verb making the statement emphatic). Jesus has already prayed regarding his glorification (see comments on v. 1), but now he links it explicitly to the work accomplished in the establishment of the disciples. The preposition "in" as part of the phrase "in them" (ἐν αὐτοῖς) is likely locative (rather than instrumental), describing the place in which Christ receives glory. This remarkable statement suggests that God receives glory by the work he performs in his disciples, the church. Just as the flesh of Jesus was the place in and through which the glory of God was made known (see 1:14), so also now will the disciples manifest the glory of God as they bear his name and participate in his mission. By this the church is called to glorify the Son of God. The honor and reputation of Jesus is displayed in the life of the church.[23]

17:11 "I am no longer in the world, and they are in the world, and I am going to you. Holy Father, keep them in your name which you gave to me, in order that they may be one just as we are one" (καὶ οὐκέτι εἰμὶ ἐν τῷ κόσμῳ, καὶ αὐτοὶ ἐν τῷ κόσμῳ εἰσίν, κἀγὼ πρὸς σὲ ἔρχομαι. Πάτερ ἅγιε, τήρησον αὐτοὺς ἐν τῷ ὀνόματί σου ᾧ δέδωκάς μοι, ἵνα ὦσιν ἓν καθὼς ἡμεῖς). Jesus continues to express the completion of his mission by returning to the topic of his departure. But here Jesus speaks paradoxically, referring to his imminent "going" and yet making the seemingly contradictory claim that "I am no longer in the world" (οὐκέτι εἰμὶ ἐν τῷ κόσμῳ). Jesus speaks in the farewell discourse in a timeless manner (16:33),[24] or even in seemingly contrasting ways (cf. 13:33; 17:12). Jesus is not temporally confused but speaks with the authoritative presence and perspective of God even before his departure. "It is as though two discourses have blended together, one that Jesus delivers around the table on

---

22. Cf. Bultmann, *John*, 500.
23. Cf. Lincoln, *John*, 436.

24. O'Day, "'I Have Overcome the World,'" 162.

the night of his betrayal, and one that he delivers from the realm of the Father after the Ascension. Jesus is alternately here and there, before and after, above and below."[25] It is at this moment that Jesus must be interpreted as speaking out of the fullness of the Gospel's two-stranded plot, historical and cosmological (see comments before 1:1). He may be with his disciples, but he has always been "with God" (1:1).

Jesus addresses his Father as "Holy Father" (Πάτερ ἅγιε), a unique title for God in the NT (cf. 1 Pet 1:15 – 16; Rev 4:8; 6:10), though it does occur in Jewish and other Christian writings. In the Gospel as a whole the Spirit is called "holy" three times (1:33; 14:26; 20:22), Jesus is called "holy" once (6:69), and now for the only time the Father is called "holy" here. The rarity of the address is not its most notable quality, for the two terms together combine "awesome transcendence with familial intimacy."[26] While God's holiness in the OT would have created a distance between God and his people, as the "Holy Father" he establishes a remarkable closeness by means of his Son. Beyond the theological truth of the holiness of God to which this title connects and by which it is supported, its use in this context has a specific function. It provides a motive for the request here that the disciples should be protected "in the name" of the Father as well as for the later request for their "sanctification" or "consecration" in vv. 17 – 19, where a verbal form of "holy" is used.[27]

In light of the disciples continuing presence in the world, Jesus asks the Father to preserve the disciples: "Keep them in your name" (τήρησον αὐτοὺς ἐν τῷ ὀνόματί σου). The verb "keep" (τήρησον) requests that God "cause a state, condition, or activity to continue," to keep them unharmed or un-

disturbed.[28] Since "they are in the world," a world that hates them (cf. vv. 14, 15; cf. 15:18 – 21), Jesus asks the Father to protect them. The means of this preservation is the name of the Father, the same name he gave to Jesus. The phrase "in your name" could be understood instrumentally, "by the power of your name,"[29] but is more likely locative. Since the concept of a "name" in the ancient world was not merely a label but referred to the character of a person, Jesus speaks of all that "Holy Father" means, not simply to the uttering of the name (cf. v. 6). Thus, Jesus asks the Father by his very nature to *be* their protection and to *be* their preservation, which was first applied to the Son (protecting and preserving him) and has now been revealed by his own person and work.[30]

This explains why Jesus ends with a petition to share in the communion of the Trinitarian identity of God: "In order that they may be one just as we are one" (ἵνα ὦσιν ἓν καθὼς ἡμεῖς). The disciples by their faith in Christ are being taken into the fellowship and relational unity of the Father and the Son. Jesus has alluded to such relational incorporation before (cf. 10:38; 14:20), but here he finalizes it by his prayer to the Father. In a sense, just as the glory of God can include and be mediated through the disciples (cf. v. 10), so also can God preserve and protect the disciples. The disciples are not being kept by God as outsiders but as those who belong to him, as children with the Father, not as slaves but as adopted "sons and daughters" in the household of God (cf. 1:12 – 14; 8:32 – 36).

17:12 "While I was with them I kept them in your name which you gave to me, and I guarded them, and not one of them was destroyed except the son of destruction, so that the Scripture might be

25. George L. Parsenios, " 'No Longer in the World' (John 17:11): The Transformation of the Tragic in the Fourth Gospel," *HTR* 98 (2005): 1 – 21 (5).

26. Carson, *John*, 561.

27. Schnackenburg, *John*, 3:180.

28. BDAG 1002.

29. Cf. Bultmann, *John*, 503.

30. Cf. Augustine, *John*, 107.6.403 – 4.

fulfilled" (ὅτε ἤμην μετ᾽ αὐτῶν ἐγὼ ἐτήρουν αὐτοὺς ἐν τῷ ὀνόματί σου ᾧ δέδωκάς μοι, καὶ ἐφύλαξα, καὶ οὐδεὶς ἐξ αὐτῶν ἀπώλετο εἰ μὴ ὁ υἱὸς τῆς ἀπωλείας, ἵνα ἡ γραφὴ πληρωθῇ). Jesus continues by saying that he himself "kept" (ἐτήρουν) the disciples "in your name" (ἐν τῷ ὀνόματί σου), suggesting that the nature of the protection to come matches (or began with) the protection Jesus already provided. With his use of the personal pronoun, "*I* kept" (ἐγὼ ἐτήρουν), Jesus emphasizes his agency in their protection, suggesting that their protection is rooted in the revelation he provided — the full testimony of God the Father through the person and work of the Son (see v. 6). Again, the "in" (ἐν) of "in your name" appears significant. Jesus protected the disciples by incorporating them into the fullness of God made known through the Son, by the inclusion of them into his person, and therefore into the Father himself (by the Spirit). Jesus describes his protection more emphatically by including the verb "I guarded" (ἐφύλαξα), often used in military contexts, which is a generally stronger word than "kept" (ἐτήρουν).[31] The emphasis on the work of the Son makes clear that the protection and preservation of the disciples is intimately linked to their salvation, a common depiction in the OT and even by Jesus himself (10:28; cf. 10:29 – 30).[32] As the Gospel will declare to the reader, belief in Christ is about life "in his name" (cf. 20:31).

Jesus does admit to having "lost" one of them, though he uses a play on words that is not easily translated into English or interpreted. According to Jesus "not one of them was destroyed except the son of destruction" (οὐδεὶς ἐξ αὐτῶν ἀπώλετο εἰ μὴ ὁ υἱὸς τῆς ἀπωλείας). The words translated as "destroyed" (ἀπώλετο) and "destruction" (ἀπωλείας) are clearly an intentional play on words and therefore are best translated as such in English, even though in the context the former might be more accurately translated as "perished" or even "lost."[33] The obvious referent of this statement is Judas Iscariot, the betrayer whom Satan indwelled and who departed from the company of the disciples (see 13:21 – 30). The phrase "the son of destruction" (ὁ υἱὸς τῆς ἀπωλείας) could refer either to Judas's character or to his destiny; in the NT the noun is often used to depict eschatological damnation (cf. 2 Thess 2:3).[34] Its use here by Jesus suggests that Judas is an example of the judgment of God in Jesus Christ; that is, it is less that Judas was left unprotected (or lost) by Jesus and more that he was judged by him.[35] This is why Jesus does not name him ("Judas") but classifies him by a name of eschatological judgment.[36] As with the name of God (cf. v. 6, 11) Judas's name, "son of destruction," was more than a label; it was the character of his person as one condemned by God and outside his protection.

In order to make clear that the loss of Judas was not based upon incompetent protection, Jesus adds that his particular departure actually took place "so that Scripture might be fulfilled" (ἵνα ἡ γραφὴ πληρωθῇ). Although no particular "Scripture" (ἡ γραφὴ) is mentioned, Jesus is almost certainly referring to Psalm 41:9, which he referenced at the departure of Judas. Even more, in the larger context of Psalm 41, the statement speaks about how God serves those in need, working behind the situation, faithfully preserving and protecting (see comments on 13:18). The example of Judas actually serves to strengthen the sovereign control of God, declaring its announcement earlier in the biblical record.

---

31. Barrett, *John*, 508.
32. Cf. Lincoln, *John*, 437.
33. BDAG 116.
34. Carson, *John*, 563.

35. A "son" of destruction is one appointed to destruction. Cf. Calvin, *John 11 – 21*, 143.
36. On the narrative role of anonymity, see comments on 1:40.

17:13 "But now I am coming to you, and I say these things while I am in the world in order that they may have my joy fulfilled in them" (νῦν δὲ πρὸς σὲ ἔρχομαι, καὶ ταῦτα λαλῶ ἐν τῷ κόσμῳ ἵνα ἔχωσιν τὴν χαρὰν τὴν ἐμὴν πεπληρωμένην ἐν αὐτοῖς). Jesus states again his impending departure (see v. 11) and reveals the reason for which he speaks (prays) in the presence of his disciples: "That they may have my joy fulfilled in them" (ἵνα ἔχωσιν τὴν χαρὰν τὴν ἐμὴν πεπληρωμένην ἐν αὐτοῖς). Jesus made a nearly identical claim (15:11) and expression (16:24) earlier, and the same meaning should be understood here. "Joy" has been mentioned before in the Gospel (see comments on 3:29) and is rightly defined by Scripture as a whole as the "fruit" of God's presence by the Spirit and a sign of God's present reign (Rom 14:17; Gal 5:22).[37] In the Gospel the fulfillment of joy is a common theme (cf. 3:29; 16:24) and is always the result of a life participating in God through Christ. Here Christ prays that the disciples would receive in their very persons the joy of Christ that can only come from God by the Spirit.

When Jesus says "I say these things" (ταῦτα λαλῶ), he implies that even his prayer to the Father is for the benefit of the disciples. As the eternal Son in perpetual communion with the Father, he has no need of the formal practice of prayer.[38] This prayer then is an "external aid" on behalf of the disciples, so that their minds have something to grasp.[39] It is also part of his mediation and intercession.

17:14 "I have given your word to them, and the world hates them, because they are not from the world just as I am not from the world" (ἐγὼ δέδωκα αὐτοῖς τὸν λόγον σου, καὶ ὁ κόσμος ἐμίσησεν αὐτούς, ὅτι οὐκ εἰσὶν ἐκ τοῦ κόσμου καθὼς ἐγὼ οὐκ εἰμὶ ἐκ τοῦ κόσμου). After speaking on behalf of the disciples to the Father, Jesus restates that he has

given the Father's word to them (see vv. 6 – 8). The phrase "your word" (τὸν λόγον σου) here, like before (vv. 6 – 8), is in reference to the message of God in Christ, the *gospel* of Jesus Christ (cf. Mark 1:1). This message from God and about God is so antithetical to the world that it "hates them" (ἐμίσησεν αὐτούς) just as it hates God. Jesus spoke about this earlier (see comments on 15:18 – 25), where he explained that the hate of the world is a response to the "foreignness" of the disciples because they have been "chosen" from the world and given a new "name" (15:19, 21). Quite simply, the disciples are so incorporated into God through Christ that they are as foreign to the world as Jesus is foreign to it.

17:15 "I do not ask that you remove them from the world but that you keep them from the evil one" (οὐκ ἐρωτῶ ἵνα ἄρῃς αὐτοὺς ἐκ τοῦ κόσμου ἀλλ᾽ ἵνα τηρήσῃς αὐτοὺς ἐκ τοῦ πονηροῦ). Before Jesus restates again the discontinuity between the disciples and the world, he offers a related prayer to the Father. In fact, vv. 14 and 16 form an *inclusio* that emphasizes this request. Jesus begins by making clear that he is not asking for the removal of the disciples from the world. In many respects this is a remarkable statement. First, it confirms that he has no concerns with God's ability to protect the disciples from the world (vv. 11 – 12). Second, it implies that the place to which the disciples are assigned is the world. While this is not their eternal home (see 14:1 – 6), it is the location of their mission, the place where God is still at work through them. The desire of Christians to remove themselves from the world is actually out of step with the purposes and plan of God. The church is neither to withdraw from the world nor partake in it; the church is the Spirit-filled "dwelling" of God and a participant by the Spirit/Paraclete in the *ministerial office* of the Trinitarian God in the world (see comments on

---

37. Cf. Keener, *John*, 2:1004.
38. Barrett, *John*, 509.

39. Calvin, *John 11 – 21*, 144.

14:16; 16:13). While the Son and the disciples are not "from the world," they have both been "sent" to the world (see v. 18; cf. 20:21).[40]

The concern of Jesus is not the removal of the disciples but their protection, for he prays "that you keep them from the evil one" (ἵνα τηρήσῃς αὐτοὺς ἐκ τοῦ πονηροῦ). This is the fourth occurrence of "keep" (τηρήσῃς) in this pericope and the third time some form of protection and provision is requested (cf. vv. 11–12). Here Jesus asks for the Father to protect the disciples from "the evil one" (ἐκ τοῦ πονηροῦ), a term that could also be translated as "evil." While an impersonal "evil" is possible in this context and the context of the Gospel as a whole, there are a couple reasons that suggest that Jesus is referring to a personal evil, the Evil One. First, even when Jesus refers to the world, it is never depicted impersonally. Second, since the protection Jesus seeks for his disciples is still very connected to their location in the world, the "evil one" about whom Jesus speaks is probably to be identified with "the ruler of this world," who has already been mentioned by Jesus three times (12:31; 14:30–31; 16:8–11). In light of other texts from the NT, this is almost certainly a reference to Satan (see comments on 12:31). In many ways this particular request and the spiritual battle it has in view is addressed in 1 John 5:18–20.

17:16 "They are not from the world just as I am not from the world" (ἐκ τοῦ κόσμου οὐκ εἰσὶν καθὼς ἐγὼ οὐκ εἰμὶ ἐκ τοῦ κόσμου). Jesus states again what he said in v. 14, emphasizing the discontinuity between the disciples and the world as well as highlighting the continuity between the disciples and Jesus. Only the word order is different from v. 14, with the phrase "from the world" (ἐκ τοῦ κόσμου) forming an *inclusio* in the Greek word order so that both the children of God and the Son

of God are emphatically denied ontological identification with the world — literally "in" it (v. 11) but not "from" it.

17:17 "Sanctify them in the truth; your word is truth" (ἁγίασον αὐτοὺς ἐν τῇ ἀληθείᾳ· ὁ λόγος ὁ σὸς ἀλήθειά ἐστιν). Jesus now moves toward the conclusion of his prayer for the disciples by consecrating them to the mission of God. First, Jesus prays, "Sanctify them in the truth" (ἁγίασον αὐτοὺς ἐν τῇ ἀληθείᾳ). The verb "sanctify" (ἁγίασον) can mean "to separate, make holy," but in this context refers to the act of consecrating or dedicating a person for a holy task.[41] The same term was used in 10:36 where we translated it as "set apart" (ἡγίασεν) to refer to God's consecration and dedication of Jesus for his mission to the world. As v. 18 is about to explain, the disciples are consecrated here and "set apart" for a related purpose, for God's (continuing) mission to the world.

It is fitting that the disciples are to be sanctified "in the truth" (ἐν τῇ ἀληθείᾳ). By this Jesus requests that the Father immerse the disciples in the revelation of himself in the Son, sanctifying them by sending the Paraclete to them to guide them into all truth (15:13).[42] The disciples are set apart not by their own sanctity or holiness but by that given to them by God through Jesus Christ (see v. 19). That is why Jesus then clarifies what the truth is: "Your word is truth" (ὁ λόγος ὁ σὸς ἀλήθειά ἐστιν). "Word" here probably means more than the written Scriptures (cf. 10:35). It refers to the message from the Father in and of the person and work of Jesus Christ, who sends "the Spirit of truth" (15:26) and is "the truth" (14:16), which he gave to the disciples and they have "received," "understood," and "kept" (see vv. 6, 8). Ultimately this is the promised fulfillment of what was announced in the prologue regarding the provision through Christ of "grace

---

40. Cf. Bultmann, *John*, 508.
41. Cf. BDAG 9–10.

42. Carson, *John*, 566.

and truth" (1:17) and is even the fulfillment of what was announced in the OT.

17:18 "Just as you sent me into the world, I also sent them into the world" (καθὼς ἐμὲ ἀπέστειλας εἰς τὸν κόσμον, κἀγὼ ἀπέστειλα αὐτοὺς εἰς τὸν κόσμον). Jesus now explains the content and purpose of their sanctification, the reason for their being "set apart." The disciples are called to participate in the mission of God in a manner similar to the Son. The phrase "just as" (καθὼς) expresses an equality between the mission of the Son and his disciples. The mission is similar because the sending is similar, but the senders are noticeably different, for the Father sent the Son while the Son sent his disciples. If the sender is different, the roles are different. The mission finds its origin in the Father (3:16) and has been handed to the Son, as Jesus himself explained (cf. 5:22, 26–27). The Son then gives his assignment to his disciples, the church, an assignment that is related but different. Both the unique Son (1:14) and the children of God (1:12) participate in the mission of the Father that consists in expressing God's love and offer of saving life to the world (3:16). But the Son does what *only* the Son can do, and the disciples participate in what is ultimately the work of the Son. In fact, the disciples can do nothing unless Jesus makes it possible, as v. 19 will make clear. Although the church is sent "just as" the Son was sent, the mission of the church is defined by the Son who sent them, from whom the nature and direction of its mission is derived.

17:19 "I sanctify myself on their behalf, so that they also may be sanctified in truth" (καὶ ὑπὲρ αὐτῶν [ἐγὼ] ἁγιάζω ἐμαυτόν, ἵνα ὦσιν καὶ αὐτοὶ ἡγιασμένοι ἐν ἀληθείᾳ). The previous verse can only speak proleptically since the mission man-date requires one further work of Jesus; the mission cannot begin until it is actualized by his death, resurrection, and ascension. Since the sending of the disciples is subsumed under the Son, Jesus concludes his prayer for the disciples by consecrating himself, setting himself apart, so that the mission of God may be fulfilled through his person and only then be continued by the church.[43] When Jesus says "I sanctify myself on their behalf" (ὑπὲρ αὐτῶν [ἐγὼ] ἁγιάζω ἐμαυτόν), he locates the ultimate expression and purpose of his mission as the cross (cf. 6:51). The cross is his exaltation (3:14; 8:28), the ironic place of reversal (11:49–52), the defeat of the ruler of this world (12:31), and the establishment of the church as the finalizing act of the mission of God in the world (v. 18). The self-consecration of Jesus is the ground upon which the church is "sanctified in truth" (ἡγιασμένοι ἐν ἀληθείᾳ), a phrase that echoes v. 17. The second section of the Gospel (vv. 9–19) concludes with Jesus's intercessory prayer for his disciples in a manner that portrays Jesus as the High Priest, consecrating the temple (the church) by the power of his Spirit.[44]

17:20 "I ask not for these alone, but also for those who believe in me through their word" (Οὐ περὶ τούτων δὲ ἐρωτῶ μόνον, ἀλλὰ καὶ περὶ τῶν πιστευόντων διὰ τοῦ λόγου αὐτῶν εἰς ἐμέ). In the third and final section of the pericope (vv. 20–26), Jesus prays for his future disciples. Jesus prays now for the future church, those who will believe "through their word" (διὰ τοῦ λόγου αὐτῶν), which presumes that the present disciples will fulfill the mission given to them by Jesus (v. 18). The "word" (τὸν λόγον) from the Father was given to the present disciples by the Son (v. 14; cf. v. 8), and through the disciples' "word" (τοῦ λόγου) others have come to faith. Such a movement suggests that God has

---

43. Cf. Schnackenburg, *John*, 3:187.

44. See J. Gerald Janzen, "The Scope of Jesus's High Priestly Prayer in John 17," *Enc* 67 (2006): 1–26 (2–6).

always been the author of faith, with the church and its members serving as the ministers through whom one believes (cf. 1 Cor 3:5).[45]

17:21 "So that they may be one, just as you, Father, are in me and I am in you, that they may also be in us, in order that the world may believe that you sent me" (ἵνα πάντες ἓν ὦσιν, καθὼς σύ, πάτερ, ἐν ἐμοὶ κἀγὼ ἐν σοί, ἵνα καὶ αὐτοὶ ἐν ἡμῖν ὦσιν, ἵνα ὁ κόσμος πιστεύῃ ὅτι σύ με ἀπέστειλας). The result or purpose — the three occurrences of "so that/ in order that" (ἵνα) make the goal emphatic — of the mission of the church is a unity that shares in the unity of God and exemplifies its beauty to the world. The unity of the church is not an end in itself, for it is directly related to the unified nature of God. The unity of the church must be understood as analogous to the unity of the Father and the Son.[46] As between the Father and the Son, there is a mutual indwelling or mutual interpenetration between God and the church that gives the church its identity and purpose, something Jesus has spoken of before (see comments on 14:10–11, 20). Without denying the distinction between God and the church, like between the Father and the Son (see comments on 14:10), there is also a shared unity in purpose, in love, and in action.[47] The very existence of the church is a testimony to God's great act of unification, of "reconciling the world to himself in Christ" (2 Cor 5:19).[48]

17:22 "And the glory which you have given to me I have given to them, in order that they may be one just as we are one" (κἀγὼ τὴν δόξαν ἣν δέδωκάς μοι δέδωκα αὐτοῖς, ἵνα ὦσιν ἓν καθὼς ἡμεῖς ἕν). The shared unity between God and the church is not only in purpose, in love, and in action (v. 21) but also in "glory," which like the "word" of God

was given from the Father to the Son and from the Son to the disciples. Jesus began his prayer by asking the Father for the consecration of his original glory which he had before the creation of the world (vv. 1, 5), a glory that is properly basic to his person and place in the identity of God. It is this glory — the glory *of God* — that Jesus now claims to have given the disciples. This glory does not belong to the church but to God from whom it was received and with whom it is shared. Since "glory" is "the manifestation of God's being, nature and presence, in a manner accessible to human experience,"[49] Jesus asks the Father to consecrate the disciples' participation in the fullness of God for the purpose of including them in the personal manifestation of God through Christ, which is again depicted as the great act of unification (cf. v. 21).

17:23 "I in them and you in me, so that they may be brought to completion as one, in order that the world may know that you sent me and you loved them just as you loved me" (ἐγὼ ἐν αὐτοῖς καὶ σὺ ἐν ἐμοί, ἵνα ὦσιν τετελειωμένοι εἰς ἕν, ἵνα γινώσκῃ ὁ κόσμος ὅτι σύ με ἀπέστειλας καὶ ἠγάπησας αὐτοὺς καθὼς ἐμὲ ἠγάπησας). Jesus completes his prayer for the unity of the church by restating some of the major premises of his prayer: the unity between God and the church ("I in them and you in me") and the testimony of this unity to the world ("that the world may know that you sent me"). Here, however, the testimony to the world is not only the *fact* that the Father sent the Son, as in v. 21, but also the love of the Father — for the Son and for the church. That is, the great act of unification, the reconciliation of the world to God in Christ, may have been made possible by the person and work of the Son (the sending), but it is driven by the love of the Father (see 3:16).

---

45. Calvin, *John 11–21*, 147.
46. Barrett, *John*, 512.
47. Cf. Carson, *John*, 568.

48. John E. Staton, "A Vision of Unity — Christian Unity in the Fourth Gospel," *EvQ* 69 (1997): 291–305.
49. Dodd, *Interpretation*, 206.

It is important to note that the final goal of the church is not unity as such, however that might be understood "in the church," but unity "in us" (v. 21), being one "as we are one" (v. 22). Only this can explain the meaning of the statement "so that they may be brought to completion as one" (ἵνα ὦσιν τετελειωμένοι εἰς ἕν). The last phrase could also be translated as "into one" (εἰς ἕν). This perfection does not refer to heaven, for it is also intended to serve as a witness to the world.[50] However, the unity depicted here is not a unity that stems from just "being with one another," nor is it a call to organize and form a united group for friendly and effective coworking.[51] The point here rather is a unity or "in-one-ness" that is established in the unity controlled by, defined by, and shared by the unity of the Father and the Son.[52] This kind of "in-one-ness" cannot be obtained by a human process but can only be an act "from above," a unity that is divine from start to "completion." It is a unity "by the Spirit" not by an organization.[53]

17:24 "Father, those you have given to me, I desire that they also may be with me where I am, so that they may see my glory which you have given to me, because you loved me before the creation of the world" (Πάτερ, ὃ δέδωκάς μοι, θέλω ἵνα ὅπου εἰμὶ ἐγὼ κἀκεῖνοι ὦσιν μετ' ἐμοῦ, ἵνα θεωρῶσιν τὴν δόξαν τὴν ἐμὴν ἣν δέδωκάς μοι, ὅτι ἠγάπησάς με πρὸ καταβολῆς κόσμου). Jesus initiates the conclusion of his prayer by speaking his Father's name. Jesus expresses his "desire" (θέλω) or will for his disciples "that they also may be with me where I am" (ἵνα ὅπου εἰμὶ ἐγὼ κἀκεῖνοι ὦσιν μετ' ἐμοῦ). Jesus is not praying as we pray, but as the Son of God, the Creator of every created thing (1:3), and the one who himself prepared the place "where" he and the disciples will be together (14:2 – 3). He speaks here less as the one who offers prayer and more as the one who answers prayer. Thus, this is not merely a request of the Father but the will of God expressed by the Son. In a real sense, the "dwelling" or "tabernacling" of God with his people (1:14) only begins at the incarnation, for the desire of God is that he may be in the presence of his people forever — eternal life with God.[54]

Jesus's "desire" is not only to dwell with his people but to share with them the glory given to him by the Father ("my glory" [τὴν δόξαν τὴν ἐμὴν]). Jesus first spoke about "glory" in a transferrable way (from the Father to the Son) in vv. 1 – 5; since v. 22 he has been speaking about its transfer from the Son to the disciples. Defining "glory" again as the manifestation of God (see comments on v. 22), Jesus's statement here reiterates his desire to make God known (1:18). There is no need to see a contradiction between v. 22 where Jesus says he has "given" the glory to the disciples and this verse where Jesus desires to do so. What is in view is the glory of the Son already revealed by the person and work of Jesus in this life (v. 22) as well as the full glory of God to be revealed in the life to come (v. 24). In this way, the manifestation of the glory of God has been inaugurated by Jesus and is accessible for those in the new covenant, yet it will only be fully realized and consummated in the full presence of God in the age-to-come.

17:25 "Righteous Father, though the world does not know you, I know you, and they know that

---

50. Cf. Brown, *John*, 2:771.

51. See Don M. Aycock, "John 17 and Jesus's Prayer for Unity," *TTE* 38 (1988): 132 – 44. See also Paul S. Minear, "Evangelism, Ecumenism, and John Seventeen," *ThTo* 35 (1978): 5 – 13.

52. Ridderbos, *John*, 561. Cf. Hoskyns, *Fourth Gospel*, 505.

53. Cf. Constantine Scouteris, "The People of God — Its Unity and Its Glory: A Discussion of John 17:17 – 24 in the Light of Patristic Thought," *GOTR* 30 (1985): 399 – 420 (418).

54. According to Bultmann, the church is to receive this as an exhortation to live "from the future" (*John*, 519).

you sent me" (πάτερ δίκαιε, καὶ ὁ κόσμος σε οὐκ ἔγνω, ἐγὼ δέ σε ἔγνων, καὶ οὗτοι ἔγνωσαν ὅτι σύ με ἀπέστειλας). Jesus addresses his Father again, this time as "Righteous Father" (πάτερ δίκαιε), which is probably parallel to "Holy Father" in v. 11.[55] Since the "righteousness" or "justice" of God is a common theme in the OT, the emphasis here may be the righteous judgments of God made manifest in the conviction of the world (see 16:8–11) and in the blessing of those who believe (v. 24; cf. 1 John 1:9). Such a title declares God victorious and supreme. It serves to situate all people — the world, the disciples, and even the Son — in relation to the knowledge of God, specifically the mission of God: "That you sent me" (ὅτι σύ με ἀπέστειλας). Jesus is the way/truth/life (14:6) who was to make the Father known (1:18); here he declares the state of the knowledge of God — the world does not know God, but the Son does, and he has made God known to the disciples. Jesus has said this before (see comments on vv. 3, 6–8; cf. v. 14), but this verse explains further that there can be no true knowledge of God without Christ. Only the Son can claim regarding the Father, "I know you" (ἐγὼ δέ σε ἔγνων).

17:26 **"And I made known your name to them and I will continue to make it known, so that the love with which you loved me may be in them and I in them"** (καὶ ἐγνώρισα αὐτοῖς τὸ ὄνομά σου καὶ γνωρίσω, ἵνα ἡ ἀγάπη ἣν ἠγάπησάς με ἐν αὐτοῖς ᾖ κἀγὼ ἐν αὐτοῖς). Jesus concludes his prayer by restating much of what he has already said regarding the giving of the Father's "name" to the disciples (see comments on v. 6). This is probably synonymous with their knowledge of God (v. 25), especially since he uses the verb "made known" (ἐγνώρισα) here instead of "revealed" (Ἐφανέρωσά

as in v. 6. Jesus also restates his desire for the disciples to share in the love of God, here specifically described as the love "with which you loved me" (ἣν ἠγάπησάς με). As we discussed in v. 24, Jesus prays for the disciples to participate in the intra-Trinitarian love, a love so divine in essence and reality and so Christocentric that it can be depicted as either "[love] … in them" or "I in them." To know God is to participate in his love, and to receive his love is to share in his person. The love that motivates the Christian life, rules the life of the church, and inspires its ministry in the world is the essential inward love of the Godhead, the love with which the Father eternally loves the Son (cf. 13:34–35; 15:12–17).[56]

There is one thing that Jesus says in this verse that is an addition to his prayer as a whole. Jesus has spoken about what the disciples have known (vv. 6–8) and presently know (vv. 3, 25), but now he also refers to what they will know in the future: "And I will continue to make it known" (καὶ γνωρίσω), a slightly flexible translation of a conjunction and a verb.[57] The prologue declared that Jesus would reveal God the Father (1:18), and here Jesus explains that he will always be *the* "revealer." This is not to exclude the Spirit, who is assigned to guide the church "in all truth" (see 16:13), but to locate the ministry of the Spirit within the (sending) ministry of the Son. This helps make sense of the ministerial office of the "Paraclete" and the relationship between the first (Son) and the second (Spirit) Paraclete (see comments on 14:16). In this way Jesus closes the farewell discourse in a manner that befits the purpose of his coming. He prays that God would be made known and God's people would know the person of God, his glory and his love, sharing in the very life of the Trinitarian God.

55. Cf. Aquinas, *John*, 3:195.
56. Barrett, *John*, 515.
57. Cf. Bultmann, *John*, 521.

Theology in Application

In the conclusion to the farewell discourse, Jesus offers a closing prayer that serves to consecrate the final stage of his mission from the Father but also the mission for which he is commissioning his disciples, the church. Through this pericope the reader is given specific insight into the purposes and plans of God for the church and is exhorted to participate in the church's role in the mission of God through Christ.

The Glory of God

Jesus begins his prayer (v. 1) with a concern for his glory, which is quickly revealed to be the glory of both the Father and Son — the glory of God. Since this prayer intends to consecrate the work Jesus accomplishes, the reader is to understand how the ultimate purpose of God in all things is his own glory. And this glory is primarily provided in the work of the Son. It is in the "flesh" of the Son that the glory of God — the manifestation of God's being, nature, and presence — is made known in a manner accessible to humanity. The glory of God was made possible by the Son, for whom such glory is innate and properly basic, for Jesus shared with the Father in the glory of God before the world even existed (v. 5).

But Jesus declares that the glory of God is shared not only between the Father and Son but also with the church. At the end of his prayer, Jesus prays about the glory he has given to them in order that they might participate in the fullness of God (v. 22). He prays that their faith may turn into sight and they may see the glory of God in Christ (v. 24), which according to Calvin is nothing less than the perfect happiness of the Christian.[58] For the Christian life is about truly participating in God's glory. Even more, this glory is not only received by the church, but the church also manifests the glory of God as they bear his name and participate in his mission (v. 10). Remarkably, this means that God receives glory through us! If the Son's first-order concern was for the glory of God (v. 1), how can the church not also make the glory of God its primary purpose and mission? The church has new life in God through Christ as they participate in the glory of God and receive in themselves the expression of his love. This also then is what they declare to the world. The church becomes the place where the glory of God is revealed to the world as a living testimony to God's glory and love.

Life in God while Living in the World

Jesus's prayer of consecration holds in tension two important aspects of the Christian life: life *in* God and life *in* the world. Jesus makes clear that while his mis-

---

58. Calvin, *John 11 – 21*, 150.

sion concludes with his departure from the world, the church is expected to exist "in the world" (v. 11). In fact, Jesus prays against the removal of the church from the world, but instead prays for its sustenance while living in it (v. 15). Yet it is also clear that while living in the world they are "not from the world" to the same degree that Christ is not from the world (vv. 14, 16). The church is in God (v. 21) and is also physically present in the world — albeit as "foreigners and exiles" in the world (1 Pet 2:11). This is not merely the call of the church; this is its "born new" identity in God through Christ (ch. 3).

What does "life in God while living in the world" look like? Stated briefly, it means that the world does not define or dictate the nature or purpose of the life of the Christian. It means that the life to come impedes upon and directs the life that is. It means that "the god of this world" (2 Cor 4:4) has already been defeated by the God of the world to come and the world that truly is (John 12:31; 14:30; 16:11). And it means at a personal level that our life is not fully our own, for it belongs to God in whom we share life eternal.

The Protection, Plan, and Joy of God

In this pericope Jesus offers an intercessory prayer for the church, revealing several aspects of the work that God will continue to do for his disciples. Three can be summarized. First, the church is to *trust in the protection of God* (v. 11). Jesus asks the Father to protect the church when he prays, "Keep them in your name." Since a "name" in the ancient world referred to the character of a person, Jesus exhorts the Holy Father to be just that to his disciples — the ultimate authority over his own, the children of God (1:12). By this the church is encouraged to trust in God's protection, even when the world in its hatred challenges the church with its own (so-called) authority.

Second, the church is to *submit to the plan of God* (v. 12). Jesus declares that his work was successful in every way, so much so that even the disciple (Judas) who was "destroyed" or "lost" was long before declared as such by Scripture — by God himself. The church is to trust in and submit to God's plan and provision, knowing the one to whom they pray has already "prepared in advance" what his people are to do and be (Eph 2:10).

Third, the church is to *seek the joy that can only be found in God*. Jesus states unequivocally that the joy they should seek is his own ("my joy"), and he prays that it would be "fulfilled in them" (v. 13). The joy offered to the Christian is the joy of Christ, and it does not come to us from the world but from God with whom the Christian participates and is joined (v. 21). This joy then is true and divine joy, springing from the foundation of all that is good and true and right. It therefore is a joy that can never perish, spoil, or fade (1 Pet 1:4). This joy is unaffected by the hatred of the world, untouched by the ruler of this world, and unafraid of the ills of the world. For this joy is Christ's joy, just as we, the church, belong to him and find our meaning in him.

The Unity of the Church

This pericope is frequently used for the promotion of church unity and ecumenical movements, and there are several statements and expressions that promote such a use (see comments on v. 23). But the "unity" portrayed by this pericope is not primarily a unity "in the church" but a unity "in us" (v. 21) and being one "as we are one" (v. 22) — that is, this unity is not within the church itself but between the church and God. Certainly these verses can and should address church unity, but this pericope does more to *explain* church unity than to *exhort* it. For through Christ the church has been united to the relational "in-one-ness" of the Father and the Son. The unity of the church is therefore entirely symptomatic of its participation in God; it is not its own innate unity. The unity depicted here is not a unity that stems from just "being with one another," nor is it a call to organize and form a united group for friendly and effective coworking. The point here rather is a unity or "in-one-ness" that is established in the unity controlled by, defined by, and shared by the unity of the Father and the Son. Just as the love of God finds its expression in and is the source for the church's love for one another (see comments on 13:34; cf. 15:12), so also is the unity within the Godhead in which the church participates through Christ the source and substance of all unifying initiatives within the church.

The Mission of the Church

The prayer of Jesus reveals that the mission of God involves not only the sending of the Son by the Father but also the sending of the church by the Son (v. 21). Although the Son and the church participate in the one mission of God, their roles can be distinguished by the noticeably different senders. The Son performs the Father's assignment whereas the church receives its assignment from the Son. Thus, the church does not duplicate the mission of the Son (e.g., his sacrificial death) — nor can it, but is instead both a result and extension of the mission of Christ to the world. The church is not only created by the mission of God but facilitates it by becoming a living testimony of God to the world.

For this reason Christ, just moments before completing his mission on the cross, offered a prayer of consecration for his church, dedicating it to God the Father for his purposes and protection and entrusting it to the persevering presence of the Spirit/Paraclete. Christ dedicated himself to this very purpose (v. 19) and offers the disciples to God as an extension of his own person and work. The mission of God therefore is neither an option for the church nor an add-on to its already established purpose and program. The mission of God embraces the church, and this pericope exhorts the church to live "sent," like Christ himself.

John 18:1 – 12

Literary Context

This pericope is the first of six pericopae that depicts the events surrounding the sacrificial death of the Son of God. After gathering his disciples and addressing them privately (chs. 13 – 16), followed by a prayer of consecration to the Father on their behalf (ch. 17), Jesus now embraces fully "the hour" and the reason for which he came (see 2:4). In this scene Jesus voluntarily accepts the bonds of the Jewish authorities and Roman soldiers, knowing full well that the "cup" that he must drink is from the Father (v. 11). This pericope begins the climactic moment of the Gospel, the purpose for which the Father sent the Son into the world. The reader is given dramatic insight into the intentionality of Jesus's engagement with the world and the nature of his conflict with those opposing him.

➡ **VIII. The Crucifixion (18:1 – 19:42)**
  A. The Arrest of Jesus (18:1 – 12)
  B. The Jewish Trial and Its Witnesses (18:13 – 27)
  C. The Roman Trial before Pilate (18:28 – 40)
  D. The Verdict: "Crucify Him!" (19:1 – 16)
  E. The Crucifixion of Jesus (19:17 – 27)
  F. The Death and Burial of Jesus (19:28 – 42)

Main Idea

Succeeding where Adam failed, Jesus Christ entered into a garden and surrendered himself to the betrayal of the world, not by force but by his self-surrendered will, in order to drink the cup of suffering from the Father for the salvation of the world.

Translation

John 18:1–12

1a	Introduction & Setting (1–3)	After Jesus had spoken these things,
b	Action	**he went out ...**
c	Character Reentrance	with his disciples
d	Location	**... to the other side of the stream of Kidron**

where there was a garden

into which he and his disciples entered.

2a	Character Reentrance	Now **Judas ...**
b	Description	the one who betrays him,
c	Character's Thoughts	**... also knew the place,**
d	Basis	because Jesus had frequently gathered there with his disciples.
3a	Action	Then **Judas came there,**
b	Character Entrance	after receiving a detachment of soldiers and
c		servants
d	Source #1	from the high priests and
e	Source #2	the Pharisees,
f	List of Items	with lanterns,
g		torches, and
h		weapons.
4a	Conflict (4–9)	Then **Jesus ...**
b	Character's Thoughts	knowing all that was coming upon him,
c	Confrontation	**... went out and**
d		**said to them,**
e	Interrogative Challenge	*"Whom do you seek?"*
5a	Response	**They answered him,**
b	Answer	*"Jesus the Nazarene."*
c	Response	**He said to them,**
d	Declaration	*"I am."*
e	Action	And **Judas ...**
f	Description	the one who betrays him,
g		**... was standing with them.**
6a		
b		When Jesus said to them,
c		*"I am,"*
d	Reaction & Recognition	**they drew back**
e		and **fell to the ground.**
7a	Escalating Confrontation	Then **again he asked them,**
b	Emphatic Challenge	*"Whom do you seek?"*
c	Response	And **they said,**
d	Answer	*"Jesus the Nazarene."*

8a	Response	**Jesus answered,**
b	Restatement of 6c	*"I told you that I am;*
c	Condition	*if you are seeking me*
d	Inference	*then allow these men to depart."*
9a	Narrator's Aside	—so that the word …
b		which he spoke
c	Intended Result: Fulfillment	… may be fulfilled,
d	Restatement of 17:2	*"I have not lost one of those*
e		*which you gave me."*
10a	Resolution (10–11)	Then
b	Character Reentrance	**Simon Peter …**
c	Sequence of Action #1	who had a sword,
d	Description	**… pulled it out**
e	Sequence of Action #2	and **struck the servant of the high priest**
f	Sequence of Action #3	and **cut off his right ear.**
g	Identification	**The name of the servant was Malchus.**
11a		**Then Jesus said to Peter,**
b	Imperatival Rebuke	*"Put the sword in the sheath!*
c	OT & NT Allusion	*The cup …*
d	Source	*which the Father has given to me,*
e	Interrogative Rebuke	*… shall I not drink it?"*
12a	Conclusion	Then **the detachment of soldiers and**
b		**the commander and**
c		**the servants …**
d	Redescription of Source	of the Jews
e	Climactic Reaction	**… arrested Jesus**
f		and **bound him.**

Structure and Literary Form

This pericope corresponds to the basic story form (see Introduction). The *introduction/setting* is established in vv. 1 – 3, explaining the location, setting, people, and even the intention of the people involved (Judas, the servants of the Jews, and the detachment of soldiers) around which the plot's conflict will focus. In vv. 4 – 9 the *conflict* of the pericope is directed at Jesus as he is confronted by the crowd that has come to arrest him. In vv. 10 – 11 the conflict is given a twofold *resolution*, first negatively by Peter and then positively by Jesus, who resolves not only the conflict involving the arresting crowd but also the misguided intention of Peter. Finally, v. 12 serves to explain the *conclusion/interpretation* of the activities, making a connection to the pericope that follows (18:13 – 27).

Exegetical Outline

→ **A. The Arrest of Jesus (18:1 – 12)**
    1. Betrayal in the Garden (vv. 1 – 3)
    2. "Whom Do You Seek?" (vv. 4 – 9)
    3. The Cup from the Father (vv. 10 – 11)
    4. Jesus, Arrested and Bound (v. 12)

Explanation of the Text

It is common for contemporary scholarship to examine this section of the Gospel in relation to the Synoptic Gospels, often for the purpose of delineating literary and theological connections. This is especially the case with the Fourth Gospel, which only has a few pericopae that correspond to the material found in the Synoptics. As we have mentioned earlier, the concern of this commentary is not to conjecture about the shared (or lack of shared) material or to reconstruct an event in light of the four accounts so as to align them into one, but to interpret the trial and death of Jesus (and eventually the resurrection) through the interpretive lens of the Fourth Gospel (on method, see Introduction).[1]

18:1 After Jesus had spoken these things, he went out with his disciples to the other side of the stream of Kidron where there was a garden into which he and his disciples entered (Ταῦτα εἰπὼν Ἰησοῦς ἐξῆλθεν σὺν τοῖς μαθηταῖς αὐτοῦ πέραν τοῦ χειμάρρου τοῦ Κεδρὼν ὅπου ἦν κῆπος, εἰς ὃν εἰσῆλθεν αὐτὸς καὶ οἱ μαθηταὶ αὐτοῦ). A new scene begins as the narrative transitions from the context of the farewell discourse to a new location to which Jesus and his disciples travel. The transition is not only signaled by the location change but also by the "exit" of Jesus. As we discussed earlier,

this "exit" serves as the second of two "dynamic exits" that are readily recognizable in ancient drama, serving to mark narrative development and to frame the previous scene, the farewell discourse proper (see comments before 13:1 and on 14:31). Thus, the "exit" of Jesus is also an entrance — "he entered" (εἰσῆλθεν), the beginning of the end, the start of "the hour" (see comments on 2:4). This is the "exit to death" to which the entire narrative has been building up.[2] The narrative emphasizes Jesus's movement in particular. At this point the disciples are almost no different from the readers, who have been moved into a secondary position and are following Jesus with anticipation and wonder.

The narrator explains the movement of Jesus from the context of a familiar occasion of a festival meal to an isolated and anonymous garden, located on "the other side of the stream of Kidron" (πέραν τοῦ χειμάρρου τοῦ Κεδρὼν), a small and well known brook just to the east of Jerusalem.[3] The unnamed "garden" (κῆπος) clearly serves to establish the historical context of the scene to follow, but more can be argued. The term "garden" makes an intentional "impression" (see Introduction) on the reader that also serves to establish the theological context of the scene, denoted not only by what might be a purposeful anonymity (in contrast to

---

1. On the Synoptics, see Brown, *John*, 2:787 – 804; Beasley-Murray, *John*, 308 – 12; on the genre and historicity of the passion narratives, see Keener, *John*, 2:1068 – 73.

2. Parsenios, *Departure and Consolation*, 50 – 51.
3. Barrett, *John*, 517; Keener, *John*, 2:1076 – 77.

the details of the "stream") but also by means of noting that the Fourth Gospel is the only Gospel that even mentions the arrest taking place in a garden.[4] The Gospel has so clearly applied a Genesis lens to the story it tells that it is difficult not to see the connection between this "garden" and the first garden in Genesis 2:8 – 16.[5]

The argument for this is not only the importance of Genesis for the Gospel but also the significance of "garden," since the Gospel carefully records how Jesus was arrested at a garden as well as how a garden was the place in which he was crucified (19:41) and resurrected (cf. 20:15) — which is specifically recorded as occurring on the first day of the "week" (20:1), making another connection to the Genesis-creation motif (see comments before 2:1).[6] With "garden" being mentioned both before and after the resurrection, it "effectively frames the story of Jesus's passion."[7] This anonymous "garden" therefore is introduced here to prepare the reader for the eventual and full-orbed contrast between the first and second gardens related to the first and second Adams, a theme to be established shortly (see comments on 19:5).[8] As we will soon understand, both gardens saw the production of life and death, but the second reversed the order of the first: *the first garden was the place where death was born out of life; the second garden was the place where life was born out of death.*[9]

18:2 Now Judas, the one who betrays him, also knew the place, because Jesus had frequently gathered there with his disciples (ἤδει δὲ καὶ Ἰούδας ὁ παραδιδοὺς αὐτὸν τὸν τόπον, ὅτι πολλάκις συνήχθη Ἰησοῦς ἐκεῖ μετὰ τῶν μαθητῶν αὐτοῦ). As the narrator's introduction to the pericope (vv. 1 – 3) continues, one of the most significant characters is introduced, Judas, who serves as the antagonist. The narrator is careful to describe Judas in relation to Jesus as "the one who betrayed him" (ὁ παραδιδοὺς αὐτὸν). Since his first appearance, Judas has been described in this way by the narrator (6:71; cf. 12:4) and known as such by Jesus (6:64). But Judas is described not only as the betrayer but as the one who "knew the place" (ἤδει τὸν τόπον), with the place being "a garden" at which Jesus frequently assembled with his disciples.

In light of our analysis of v. 1 and the "impression" created by "garden," the stated emphasis on betrayal again serves to connect this garden with the first garden. Judas is not alone to be called "the one who betrayed God," for since the first man (Adam), that is, since the time of the first garden, the whole world has betrayed him (see 1:11). And like the first betrayal, this betrayal also had Satan working behind the scenes (cf. Gen 3:1 – 5). By positioning the story of Jesus's arrest within the grand story of Scripture, the Gospel displays not merely

---

4. Just as the Synoptics intend the names in the scene (e.g., "Gethsemane" or "Mount of Olives") to signal meaning to the reader, the Gospel of John intends "a garden" to signal meaning to the reader.

5. This is in contrast to the majority of modern interpreters. Contra Brown, *John*, 2:806, the argument is not based on the occurrence of the same Greek word in Genesis 2 and this pericope, but on the motif of "garden" so entrenched in the biblical metanarrative. Brown's linguistic argument against the "garden" motif between Genesis 2 and John has been forcefully challenged by Joachim Schaper, "The Messiah in the Garden: John 19:38 – 41, (Royal) Gardens, and Messianic Concepts," in *Paradise in Antiquity: Jewish and Christian Views*, ed. Markus Bockmuehl and Guy G. Stroumsa (Cambridge: Cambridge

University Press, 2010), 17 – 27, who shows how the different terms for "garden" involved a difference in emphasis but not in concept (20).

6. See also Frédéric Manns, "Le symbolism du jardin dans le récit de la passion selon S Jean," *SBFLA* 37 (1987): 53 – 80; Nicolas Wyatt, " 'Supposing Him to Be the Gardener' (John 20,15): A Study of the Paradise Motif in John," *ZNW* 81 (1990): 21 – 38.

7. Michaels, *John*, 886.

8. Cf. Aquinas, *John*, 3:199.

9. See Brian Brock, "Creation: Mission as Gardening" in *Living Witnesses: Explorations in Missional Ethics*, ed. Andy Draycott and Jonathan Rowe (Nottingham, UK: Apollos, 2012), 57 – 78 (especially 58 – 67).

"a garden" but the biblical garden[10] the place where the world betrayed God. This biblical context makes a garden not only a fitting place for this final betrayal, but also a fitting place for it to be overturned (see 19:41; 20:15). A garden is even a fitting description of the new creation (Rev 21 – 22).

18:3 Then Judas came there, after receiving a detachment of soldiers and servants from the high priests and the Pharisees, with lanterns, torches, and weapons (ὁ οὖν Ἰούδας λαβὼν τὴν σπεῖραν καὶ ἐκ τῶν ἀρχιερέων καὶ [ἐκ] τῶν Φαρισαίων ὑπηρέτας ἔρχεται ἐκεῖ μετὰ φανῶν καὶ λαμπάδων καὶ ὅπλων). Judas's act of betrayal was not done in isolation, for Judas brought with him two different groups of people. The first group is described by a single word which we translated as "a detachment of soldiers" (τὴν σπεῖραν), a term transliterated from the Latin term for a cohort of Roman soldiers, which was one tenth of a legion and therefore about six hundred men,[11] although the actual number of soldiers for any particular detachment could vary widely; often a maniple would be sent consisting of two hundred men.[12] The implication is that the Jewish and Roman authorities were working closely together in this arrest, with the former bringing in the latter as soon as possible, perhaps even well before this day. With passions elevated during Passover, it is likely that the Roman officials happily welcomed the opportunity to work with (and not against) the Jewish authorities to silence a possible rebellion and its leader, a reality supported by the tools (weapons!) they brought with them.[13]

The second group had apparently also been "received" by Judas, this time from the Jewish authorities who sent with him some of their own "servants" (ὑπηρέτας), a term that refers to a person "who functions as a helper, frequently in a subordinate capacity," such as an assistant.[14] In the context of the Gospel, this term often depicts something like the temple police. The implication is that Jesus had been an obvious problem long enough that both the Jews and Romans were willing to cooperate for his demise.[15] Thus, the high priests and the Pharisees sent their subordinates to officially arrest and detain him.

Yet it was Judas, one of Jesus's own disciples, who was at the head of the crowd made up of both Jews and Romans (gentiles), guiding them to the "place" where Jesus was. As in v. 1, Judas is the focus of the narrative, the leader to whom the others belong (denoted by the third-person singular verb "came" [ἔρχεται], which places Judas as the primary agent of the coming to emphasize his leading role). The depiction of Judas leading is especially surprising when a "commander" was also present with the detachment of soldiers (see v. 12). Thus, the "eschatological showdown" in this garden was an intimate betrayal that involved representatively the whole world.[16] With this the introduction and setting of the pericope (vv. 1 – 3) has been provided for the reader.

18:4 Then Jesus, knowing all that was coming upon him, went out and said to them, "Whom do you seek?" (Ἰησοῦς οὖν εἰδὼς πάντα τὰ ἐρχόμενα ἐπ' αὐτὸν ἐξῆλθεν καὶ λέγει αὐτοῖς, Τίνα ζητεῖτε;).

---

10. In this Gospel and Scripture as a whole, "garden" almost becomes a technical term, similar to the term "hour." Cf. Barrett, *John*, 518.

11. BDAG 936.

12. Barrett, *John*, 518; Morris, *John*, 656.

13. With the importance of light and darkness imagery in the Gospel, the double mention of instruments of light may be intended to contrast this group and its artificial light with the one whom the Gospel declares to be the light of the world

(8:12). Cf. Charles Homer Giblin, "Confrontations in John 18, 1 – 27," *Bib* 65 (1984): 210 – 32 (217 – 18); Raymond E. Brown, "The Passion according to John: Chapters 18 and 19," *Wor* 49 (1975): 126 – 34 (127).

14. BDAG 1035.

15. See Keener, *John*, 2:1078 – 80.

16. Wright, "Greco-Roman Character Typing and the Presentation of Judas in the Fourth Gospel," 558.

The narrator now focuses the story back on Jesus and the conflict making its way toward him, explaining that Jesus knew "all that was coming upon him" (πάντα τὰ ἐρχόμενα ἐπ' αὐτὸν). Jesus has already been depicted as knowing the intention and condition of humanity (2:24 – 25; cf. 1:47 – 48; 4:18), and here he is well aware of the coming conflict. The phrase "upon him" may simply refer to the coming conflict, but in light of the cosmological context of the Gospel it may also refer to the larger theological (cosmological) significance of what is being placed "upon him": the sins of the world (1:29). The approaching crowd (and Peter; cf. v. 10) may be thinking that the issue to be faced was a military confrontation or a political or legal battle, but Jesus *knows* that it is the sins of the world and the wrath of God that are shortly to be placed "upon him."

Rather than running or hiding from what he knows is coming, Jesus actually goes out and confronts it directly. In fact it is Jesus who asks the approaching crowd — or mob — if they know their own intentions and agenda. The questions of Jesus in the Gospel usually probe more deeply into the true reality of the scene or person (see comments on 5:6; cf. Gen 3:9). Jesus had asked his disciples almost the same question before (see comments on 1:38): not "whom" but "what do you seek?" (Τί ζητεῖτε). This is a very different "arrest," one with no attempted escape or denial. It is as if the one they seek is in the position of authority, accessible only by his permission and will (see 10:18). The entire scene to follow (vv. 4 – 9) is commentary on the prologue's opening declaration regarding the world: the light shined . . . and the darkness did not recognize or overcome it (1:5).

18:5 They answered him, "Jesus the Nazarene." He said to them, "I am." And Judas, the one who betrays him, was standing with them (ἀπεκρίθησαν αὐτῷ, Ἰησοῦν τὸν Ναζωραῖον. λέγει αὐτοῖς, Ἐγώ εἰμι. εἰστήκει δὲ καὶ Ἰούδας ὁ παραδιδοὺς αὐτὸν μετ' αὐτῶν). The crowd of authorities and soldiers answer the question of Jesus by providing his name, which in the ancient world often involved a person's first name followed by their city of origin (cf. 1:45). No further explanation was needed since the identity of this person was already "on everyone's lips."[17] It is important to note that the narrator mentions again the presence of Judas, describing him for a second time as "the one who betrays" Jesus (cf. v. 2) and depicting him as "standing with them" (εἰστήκει μετ' αὐτῶν). Everyone knew who this was and where he was, for Judas had led the processional (cf. v. 3). The connection made earlier between Judas and Satan (13:2) allows Judas to represent a third authority: the spiritual forces of darkness (cf. Eph 6:11 – 12). Jesus is opposed here by the authorities and powers of Jerusalem, Rome, and the spiritual forces of darkness.

Jesus responds with what has become for the reader a technical title for his person: "I am." While the Greek could be more simply translated as "I am he," even the first-time reader knows full well that more is implied by this statement. It is not the grammatical force of the statement but the force of the Gospel as a whole that allows us to see here what is explicit in every way but the words. This is one of several informal "I am" statements in the Gospel (see comments on 6:35). While all the "I am" statements locate Jesus in the divine identity of God, the informal statements serve to give insight to the *particular qualifications* of Jesus. This informal "I am" statement depicts Jesus's sovereign control over the situation. Jesus not only "knew" their intentions (v. 4) but had also already ordained the situation in such a way that it was not the religious

---

17. Ridderbos, *John*, 576.

leaders or Roman authorities but he, the "I am," who asked the questions and "sanctified" himself for this moment and his purposes (see comments on 17:19).

18:6 When Jesus said to them, "I am," they drew back and fell to the ground (ὡς οὖν εἶπεν αὐτοῖς, Ἐγώ εἰμι, ἀπῆλθον εἰς τὰ ὀπίσω καὶ ἔπεσαν χαμαί). The majestic utterance of Jesus is not only grasped by the reader of the Gospel but was also heard with a mysterious force by the crowd, which according to the narrator "drew back and fell to the ground" (ἀπῆλθον εἰς τὰ ὀπίσω καὶ ἔπεσαν χαμαί). The fact that the narrator connects their response to the informal "I am" statement of Jesus only strengthens our interpretation of it in v. 5. At the sound of his voice, they fell to the ground "as if vanquished by a greater army."[18] The depiction here is not a defensive position, as if Jesus and his band of eleven were about to attack between two to six hundred armed men; the narrator describes an act of fear and reverence, even worship. While this response by the crowd accompanied by a detachment of soldiers makes little sense from a historical perspective, in the cosmological context of the Gospel this was a fitting response, even better than they fully realized (cf. 11:49–52). Hundreds came to take his life, and they could make no claim on him: "They are hopelessly outnumbered by one."[19]

18:7 Then again he asked them, "Whom do you seek?" And they said, "Jesus the Nazarene" (πάλιν οὖν ἐπηρώτησεν αὐτούς, Τίνα ζητεῖτε; οἱ δὲ εἶπαν, Ἰησοῦν τὸν Ναζωραῖον). In what is like a comedic moment, vv. 7–8 repeat nearly the exact sequence of events recorded in vv. 4–6. Did Jesus repeat his initial question while the Jewish leaders and soldiers were still facedown toward the ground? Did they all rise and compose themselves before answering? The narrative gives almost no clarity to these issues, suggesting that something else is in view. By this the narrative emphasizes the authority and independence of Jesus.[20] The repeated question is almost to assist the arresting mob, giving them a chance to reinitiate their intended purpose, now under the guidance of Jesus, the one they came to arrest. Jesus has never been more in control as his arrest, trial, and death are at hand, for it is his "hour" not theirs, and it is according to his authority, not the authority of Jerusalem, Rome, or Satan himself.

18:8 Jesus answered, "I told you that I am; if you are seeking me then allow these men to depart" (ἀπεκρίθη Ἰησοῦς, Εἶπον ὑμῖν ὅτι ἐγώ εἰμι· εἰ οὖν ἐμὲ ζητεῖτε, ἄφετε τούτους ὑπάγειν). Jesus not only restates his identity using the informal "I am" statement (see v. 6) but makes clear that this is his second such statement. This is the third time "I am" has been stated in the narrative, twice by Jesus and once by the narrator. The same sovereign control Jesus exhibited over the encounter with the crowd he now employs in order to disassociate his disciples from his arrest and fate. Jesus had twice directed the crowd to state the person in whom they were interested. Thus, Jesus emphasized their interest in him, "*If* you are seeking *me*" (εἰ οὖν ἐμὲ ζητεῖτε), in order to convince the authorities to let his disciples go. If the greater purpose of the coming of Jesus was to remove the wrath of God from his disciples and place it upon himself, he could certainly do the same with the wrath of the world.

18:9 — so that the word which he spoke may be fulfilled, "I have not lost one of those which you gave me" (ἵνα πληρωθῇ ὁ λόγος ὃν εἶπεν ὅτι Οὓς

---

18. Michaels, *John*, 891.

19. David E. Garland, "John 18–19: Life through Jesus's Death," *RevExp* 85 (1988): 485–99 (486).

20. Cf. Schnackenburg, *John*, 3:225.

δέδωκάς μοι οὐκ ἀπώλεσα ἐξ αὐτῶν οὐδένα). The crowd must have acquiesced to Jesus's demand, for the narrator interjects to explain how Jesus's action to protect his disciples is the fulfillment of his earlier statement, which the narrator here more freely summarizes (see comments on 17:12). The narrator's use of the phrase "so that ... fulfilled" (ἵνα πληρωθῇ) is used elsewhere to describe the fulfillment of an OT Scripture, which suggests that the narrator is placing "the word" (ὁ λόγος) of Jesus on the same level as the word of Scripture.[21] Since the beginning of the Gospel, the scriptural word of God has been equated to Jesus, the Word of God (see 2:22). When Jesus speaks it is "thus says the Lord." In this way the conflict of the pericope (vv. 4–9) has been introduced to the reader. There is a paradox involving this conflict, however, for the sovereign control of Jesus has made clear that the conflict is less what the world is doing to him and more what he is doing for the world.

18:10 Then Simon Peter, who had a sword, pulled it out and struck the servant of the high priest and cut off his right ear. The name of the servant was Malchus (Σίμων οὖν Πέτρος ἔχων μάχαιραν εἵλκυσεν αὐτὴν καὶ ἔπαισεν τὸν τοῦ ἀρχιερέως δοῦλον καὶ ἀπέκοψεν αὐτοῦ τὸ ὠτάριον τὸ δεξιόν. ἦν δὲ ὄνομα τῷ δούλῳ Μάλχος). The resolution of the pericope's conflict (vv. 10–11) begins not with Jesus but with one of his disciples, Peter, to depict with overt clarity the deeper conflict in need of resolution. According to the narrator, acting on his own accord Simon Peter drew "a sword" (μάχαιραν), which would have been more like a short sword or a long knife, and cut off the right ear of one of the servants. Peter's response

suggests that he was less than agreeable with the self-sacrifice of Jesus.

The amount of detail given to this particular action of Peter is worthy of note, especially in regard to Malchus, who is not named in any other Gospel (cf. Luke 22:50). The narrator not only provides the injury sustained and the name of the servant but also says that he was "the servant of the high priest" (τὸν τοῦ ἀρχιερέως δοῦλον). The details, specifically the "right ear" and the servant's connection to the "high priest," may suggest that rather than being an act of defense, Peter's response was an act of defiance. Jewish history (Josephus, *Ant.* 14.366) records a very similar incident, where a high priest was deliberately disqualified from his office by having his ear mutilated.[22] While the high priest would not have been directly disqualified by the mutilated ear of his servant, in an honor/shame culture "he would be seriously and suggestively disgraced by having his servant mutilated in this particular manner."[23]

It may have been a mere coincidence that this particular person and body part was struck by Peter, but the narrator's detail may also intend to reveal that Peter's actions were much more strategic. Even if Peter's response was more clumsy than calculated, it was misguided. If it was a more personal attack, however, it was closer to at least one significant truth. The resolution to this situation would require the mutilation of the servant to the highest religious authority—not Malchus but Jesus, the servant of God the Father, who fulfilled the office of both "the Servant" and the great High Priest (Heb 4:14).[24]

18:11 Then Jesus said to Peter, "Put the sword in the sheath! The cup which the Father has given

21. Cf. Brown, *John*, 2:811.
22. See Garland, "John 18–19," 497; Keener, *John*, 2:1083.
23. David Daube, "Three Notes Having to Do with Johanan ben Zaccai," *JTS* 11 (1960): 53–62 (61).
24. Although Malchus is a common enough name, it is interesting to note that the common Semitic root for Malchus (m-l-k) forms the Hebrew word for "king." At several levels Malchus can be understood to represent Christ.

to me, shall I not drink it?" (εἶπεν οὖν ὁ Ἰησοῦς τῷ Πέτρῳ, Βάλε τὴν μάχαιραν εἰς τὴν θήκην· τὸ ποτήριον ὃ δέδωκέν μοι ὁ πατὴρ οὐ μὴ πίω αὐτό;). Jesus commands Peter to put his sword away and then offers a rebuke in the form of a question that functions more as a statement. The metaphor of the "cup" almost certainly stems from its use in the OT, where it serves as a symbol of suffering in general and can more specifically serve as a symbol of the judgment of God.[25] This "cup" is what the Father "has given" (δέδωκέν) to him. No soldier of Rome or Jewish leader could assign this to him; only the Father can command the Son. In this way Jesus is not arrested by the soldiers but by surrendering himself to them. His obedience to the Father just happened to coincide with the desires of Jerusalem and Rome (even Satan), not because they could enforce such demands but because the Father had given him that exact "cup" to drink. Thus, Jesus's statement dictates to Peter not only the true authority behind his arrest but also its true nature. The "cup" that he must drink is *the* cup of suffering, for the Son is the Suffering Servant whose self-sacrifice allows for the wrath of God to be placed upon him for the salvation of the world (see 3:36).

Earlier Peter had tried to prohibit Jesus from sacrificially serving his body by washing his feet (see comments on 13:38); here Peter tries to prohibit Jesus from sacrificially giving his own body for the more permanent washing. The test of understanding for Peter — and all Christians — is not merely the life of Jesus but also his death. To know Jesus is to know him in his death; his person and

his work cannot be separated. The misunderstanding of Peter is intended to guide the reader to the truth and, more specifically, to the crucifixion of Jesus.[26]

18:12 Then the detachment of soldiers and the commander and the servants of the Jews arrested Jesus and bound him" (Ἡ οὖν σπεῖρα καὶ ὁ χιλίαρχος καὶ οἱ ὑπηρέται τῶν Ἰουδαίων συνέλαβον τὸν Ἰησοῦν καὶ ἔδησαν αὐτόν). The narrator offers a conclusion to the pericope (v. 12) that in the context provides an implicit interpretation of the scene. The narrator lists the entire arresting party, mentioning again the detachment of soldiers and the servants of the Jewish authorities (v. 3). Different from the first list, however, is the inclusion of "the commander" (ὁ χιλίαρχος), a term that means "leader of a thousand soldiers" that was used less rigidly as a technical term for a military commander or tribune of a large group of soldiers.[27] The first list of the arresting party emphasized the force of the group, both Roman and Jewish; but by not mentioning "the commander" until now, the narrator gives greater emphasis here to the authority behind the arrest. But as the careful reader immediately understands, the true authority, the true "commander," was the Father himself.

The pericope thus concludes with a powerful image of the arrest and binding of Jesus. The correct interpretation of this historical scene understands that this binding is the binding of a sacrifice, the self-sacrifice of Jesus (like the binding of Isaac in Gen 22:9). For the reader of the Gospel, therefore, the *conflict* has become the *conquest*.

---

25. See e.g., Pss 11:6; 60:3; Isa 29:9 – 10; 51:17, 21 – 23; 63:6; Jer 25:15 – 29; Ezek 23:31 – 33; Lam 4:21; Zech 12:2; cf. Rev 14:10; 16:19.

26. Cf. Timothy Wiarda, "The Portrayal of Peter and Atonement Theology in the Gospel of John," *BBR* 21 (2011): 507 – 23.
27. BDAG 1084.

Theology in Application

In this pericope what is often called the passion of Jesus Christ is introduced and initiated, beginning the section we've entitled "The Crucifixion of Jesus" (18:1 – 19:42). The narrative depicts with clarity and precision the purpose and authority of Jesus as he is approached by a collection of Jewish and Roman (and satanic) authorities who seek to arrest him. According to the Gospel of John, no external authority arrested and bound Jesus in this garden east of Jerusalem, for Jesus surrendered himself by his own authority and according to his own plan. Through this pericope the reader is introduced to the start of "the hour" (2:4) of Jesus Christ and is given insight into the nature and purpose of his sacrificial death on the cross.

The Biblical "Garden"

The argument discussed above is that the anonymous "garden" in v. 1 makes an intentional "impression" on the reader that connects this garden to the first garden in Genesis 2. This is just the start of the Genesis "garden" motif in the Gospel, a theme that frames Scripture from Genesis to Revelation. When the first Adam brought death into the world in a garden, Jesus, the second Adam, brought life into the world in a garden. This is why the "garden" is so significant to John in chapters 18 – 20, for this garden becomes the place of redemption not revolt, the place of the great reversal, transforming the biblical garden from the place of cursing to the place of blessing — to paradise renewed. For the Gospel of John the betrayal in the garden not only displays the depth of human sin but also the greater depth of the grace and mercy of God. God removed the first Adam from the garden (Gen 3:24), but entered himself as the second Adam to surrender to the curse for the sake of all humanity.

Jesus versus the World

Befitting the first garden and the Genesis lens the Gospel applies to its interpretive telling of the person and work of Jesus, this pericope portrays the cosmic encounter between Jesus and the entire world, represented by the servants of the Jews, a detachment of soldiers from Rome, and even Judas, the representative of Satan and the spiritual forces of darkness. Yet not for a moment did any of the representatives from Rome, Jerusalem, or Satan himself have even an ounce of control over Jesus. On the contrary, from the moment they arrived they were arrested by his authority and bound to the ground by his divine name (v. 6).

From the very beginning of the Gospel, the "world" has been in opposition to Jesus yet unable to comprehend him or overcome him (see comments on 1:5). Even still, it is at the name of Jesus, the "I AM," that every knee should bow and every tongue confess that Jesus is Lord (Phil 2:10 – 11). The church lives under this authority and bears his name, "Christ-ian," and receives his protection so that no one touches the church without the permission of God himself (see ch. 17). The church is not only sent by God into the world but is also sent under the authority of Christ and in the power of the Spirit. Even if only partially, the church now sees the world as Christ saw the mob-like crowd approaching him and engages the world under his authority and by his example of self-sacrifice.

The Plans and Purposes of God

This pericope beckons the reader to see and understand that God is always at work in the world and is always in control. With the rest of Scripture this pericope exhorts belief in the plans and purposes of God, even when the historical circumstances seem dire or seem to lack divine intention. For although the Jews and Romans thought they had performed their duties by capturing Jesus, the very same act was more accurately the perfect performance of the duties of the Son for the Father, not for capturing but for freeing the children of God from the bonds of sin. O church, trust in the plans and purposes of God, no matter how things may at first appear.

Drinking the Cup from the Father

Christ serves as an example for us, for we too should expect to receive from the Father (and the Son) our own cup to drink. Even if for a very different end, we too must be prepared and willing to drink the cup assigned to us by God, to endure the cross that is our burden and our calling (cf. Matt 16:24; Luke 9:23). Christ has set an example for the church, exhorting us to understand that the good life is not to be contrasted with dying or suffering and to believe that the Father's cup, even if full of real suffering, is the most satisfying drink available.

John 18:13 – 27

Literary Context

This pericope continues to depict the events surrounding the sacrificial death of the Son of God. After the surrender of Jesus, he is arrested, bound, and placed before the Jewish authorities for questioning. This makeshift Jewish trial had already been long decided; this was mere formality. But the Gospel's interest is less on the Jewish authorities and their legal procedures and more on the witness of Christ and the witness of his disciple Peter when they are both confronted by the temple authorities. The narrative intentionally contrasts Christ with two significant characters in this pericope: the so-called Jewish high priest and the denial of Peter. The reader is directed to see more fully the nature of Jesus's person and work as the High Priest (cf. Heb 4:14) and the true foundation of Christian discipleship and is exhorted to serve as a faithful witness to Christ in the world.

VIII. The Crucifixion (18:1 – 19:42)

    A. The Arrest of Jesus (18:1 – 12)

➡   **B. The Jewish Trial and Its Witnesses (18:13 – 27)**

    C. The Roman Trial before Pilate (18:28 – 40)

    D. The Verdict: "Crucify Him!" (19:1 – 16)

    E. The Crucifixion of Jesus (19:17 – 27)

    F. The Death and Burial of Jesus (19:28 – 42)

Main Idea

Jesus is the true high priest, the foundation of Christian discipleship, and the motivating source of the church's witness to the world.

Translation

John 18:13–27

13a	Introduction & Setting (13–14)	**They led him**
b	Character Entrance	to Annas first,
c	Basis/Relationship	for **he was the father-in-law**
d	Character Reentrance	of Caiaphas,
e	Description	who was the high priest that year.
14a	Character Description	**Caiaphas was the one who had advised the Jews**
b	Content	that it was better for one man to die
c	Ironic Beneficiary	for the people
15a	Character Reentrance/Action	**Simon Peter was following Jesus,**
b	Character Entrance	together with another disciple.
c	Character's Thoughts	Now **that disciple was known to the high priest,**
d	Action	and **he entered with Jesus**
e	Place: "Court"	into the court of the high priest.
16a	Contrast	But **Peter had to stand at the door outside.**
b	Progression of Action #1	Then **the other disciple . . .**
c		who was known to the high priest,
d	Progression of Action #2	**. . . came out**
e	Progression of Action #3	and **spoke to the doorkeeper**
f	Progression of Action #4	and **brought in Peter.**
17a	Character Entrance	Then **the maid servant at the door said to Peter,**
b	Question	*"Are you also one of this man's disciples?"*
c	Response	**He said,**
d	Peter's 1st Denial	*"I am not."*
18a	Characters Entrance	**The slaves and the servants stood**
b	Place	at a charcoal fire
c	Description	which they had made
d	Basis	because it was cold,
e	Action	and **they were warming themselves.**
f	Contrast to 19	But **Peter was also with them**
g		standing and
h		warming himself.
19a	Simultaneous Action to 18	Meanwhile,
b	Interrogation	**the high priest questioned Jesus**
c	Subject of Interrogation #1	about his disciples and
d	Subject of Interrogation #2	his teaching.
20a	Response	**Jesus answered him,**
b	Answer to Subject #2 (19d)	*"I have spoken openly to the world.*
c	Explanation	*I always taught in the synagogue and*
d	Location	*in the temple,*
e		*where all the Jews come together,*
f		*and I spoke nothing in secret.*

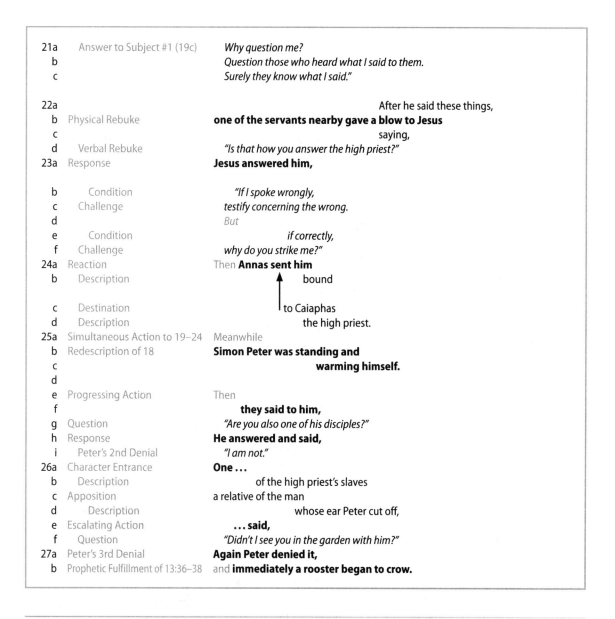

21a	Answer to Subject #1 (19c)	*Why question me?*
b		*Question those who heard what I said to them.*
c		*Surely they know what I said."*
22a		After he said these things,
b	Physical Rebuke	**one of the servants nearby gave a blow to Jesus**
c		saying,
d	Verbal Rebuke	*"Is that how you answer the high priest?"*
23a	Response	**Jesus answered him,**
b	Condition	*"If I spoke wrongly,*
c	Challenge	*testify concerning the wrong.*
d		*But*
e	Condition	*if correctly,*
f	Challenge	*why do you strike me?"*
24a	Reaction	Then **Annas sent him**
b	Description	bound
c	Destination	to Caiaphas
d	Description	the high priest.
25a	Simultaneous Action to 19–24	Meanwhile
b	Redescription of 18	**Simon Peter was standing and**
c		**warming himself.**
d		
e	Progressing Action	Then
f		**they said to him,**
g	Question	*"Are you also one of his disciples?"*
h	Response	**He answered and said,**
i	Peter's 2nd Denial	*"I am not."*
26a	Character Entrance	**One ...**
b	Description	of the high priest's slaves
c	Apposition	a relative of the man
d	Description	whose ear Peter cut off,
e	Escalating Action	**... said,**
f	Question	*"Didn't I see you in the garden with him?"*
27a	Peter's 3rd Denial	**Again Peter denied it,**
b	Prophetic Fulfillment of 13:36–38	and **immediately a rooster began to crow.**

Structure and Literary Form

The structure of this pericope is different than the basic story form (see Introduction). The structure is guided by the trial motif that defines the pericopae leading up to the crucifixion: the Jewish trial (18:13 – 27), the Roman trial (18:28 – 40), and the verdict (19:1 – 16). This pericope contains a brief introduction (vv. 13 – 14) followed by an intercalation, a rhetorical technique that encloses or "sandwiches" one scene in the middle of a different scene (forming an A¹ – B – A² pattern), so that each scene affects the interpretation of the other. The framing scene and the framed (embedded) scene are placed on par with each other, with neither having either logical or chronological priority. Either scene (the framing or the framed) may comment on the other by way of comparison or contrast.[1] Fowler describes their function and relation well: "Intercalation is narrative sleight of hand, a crafty manipulation of the discourse level that creates the illusion that two episodes are taking place simultaneously. In an intercalation neither episode has begun until both have begun, and neither is concluded until both are concluded."[2] By means of the intercalation, the reader is expected to hear the denial of Peter at the very moment Jesus is placing his reputation on Peter's witness.

Exegetical Outline

➡ **B. The Jewish Trial and Its Witnesses (18:13 – 27)**

    1. Jesus Delivered to the Jewish Authorities (vv. 13 – 14)

    2. The First Denial of Peter (vv. 15 – 18)

    3. The Witness of Christ and His Disciples (vv. 19 – 24)

    4. The Second and Third Denials of Peter (vv. 25 – 27)

Explanation of the Text

When one examines the Fourth Gospel, it becomes immediately apparent that the historical details of this pericope are both sparse and confusing, especially in regard to Jewish legal proceedings. Before we analyze the narrative details, we must address the following question: Is this an official trial? A full-scale Jewish trial would have been performed by the Sanhedrin, the Jewish ruling council, as depicted in the Synoptics (see Mark 14:53). This "trial" is not described as occurring before the Sanhedrin but seems to have involved select members of Jerusalem's municipal aristocracy in collaboration with the high priest, probably in order to keep peace between Rome and the people.[3] This is technically more than an interrogation, however, for this trial is clearly driven by political con-

cerns (11:48), not just religious concerns (cf. Mark 14:64). There is no reason to doubt the historicity of the Gospel's account or to challenge the Gospel's depiction of Jewish trials.

18:13 They led him to Annas first, for he was the father-in-law of Caiaphas, who was the high priest that year (καὶ ἤγαγον πρὸς Ἅνναν πρῶτον· ἦν γὰρ πενθερὸς τοῦ Καϊάφα, ὃς ἦν ἀρχιερεὺς τοῦ ἐνιαυτοῦ ἐκείνου). The first section of the pericope (vv. 13 – 14) serves to introduce the reader to the context and characters involved in the Jewish trial of Jesus. These verses have raised confusion regarding the role of Annas and the identity of the "high priest" in v. 19. Because of its importance for the entire pericope, we will address the identity of the high priest here. If Caiaphas was the current high

---

1. James L. Resseguie, *Narrative Criticism of the New Testament: An Introduction* (Grand Rapids: Baker Academic, 2005), 54 – 56.

2. Robert M. Fowler, *Let the Reader Understand: Reader-Response Criticism and the Gospel of Mark* (Harrisburg, PA: Trinity Press International, 1996), 143 – 44.

3. Keener, *John*, 2:1084.

priest, why was Jesus not led before him instead of Annas? And is the high priest who interrogates Jesus in v. 19 Annas or Caiaphas?

The answers to these questions are partially resolved by explaining the identity of Annas and the nature of the high priesthood in first-century Judaism. Annas had been high priest from AD 6 – 15 (Josephus, *Ant.* 18.26 – 35) and was succeeded not only by his son-in-law, Caiaphas, but also by all five of his sons (Josephus, *Ant.* 20.198). Annas was therefore "the patriarch of a high priestly family,"[4] and may have been considered as the "highest" or most influential of the high priests, since the biblical tradition depicted the office of the high priest as lifelong, and it was customary to refer to the entire high-priestly family as "high priests."[5] The narrator is not attempting to be intentionally cryptic here but is simply describing two hearings. The "first" (πρῶτον) with Annas is designated as such, although no record of the hearing is provided, and the second is with Caiaphas, whom the narrator is careful to describe as the high priest "that year" (τοῦ ἐνιαυτοῦ ἐκείνου) or, more simply, "at that time."

Since Caiaphas is the current high priest, it would seem that he is the one who interrogates Jesus beginning in v. 19, the one clearly introduced by the narrator as "the high priest." This is even supported by v. 14, which focuses the reader's attention directly on Caiaphas by reminding the reader of his identity and already important role in the narrative. Yet in v. 24 the narrator explains that after the interrogation with the "high priest," who would logically be Caiaphas, Annas had him sent to Caiaphas. The common divide between interpreters regarding the identity of the interrogator in this scene is often based upon which verse is given

priority: if v. 19, then the interrogator is logically Caiaphas; if v. 24, then the interrogator must be Annas. The argument by this commentator is that this cryptic depiction of the "high priest" bears the marks of intentionality by the narrator, who is directing the reader to see that in this trial neither Annas nor Caiaphas were properly functioning as the high priest, for only Jesus was able to fulfill the requirements of that office.[6]

This judgment regarding the intentionality of the narrative is directed by its own movement and is sensitive to the narrative's bent. Until v. 24 there would be every reason to think the "high priest" interrogating Jesus was Caiaphas, for the text had just stated that Caiaphas was *the* high priest *that year*.[7] Said another way, only Caiaphas is known as the high priest from the text itself; Annas is simply described by his relation (by marriage) to Caiaphas. Only by using other first-century sources do we know that Annas was also a high priest and likely the high-priestly patriarch. Yet v. 24 causes the reader to turn back and reexamine the previous verses with fresh eyes, intentionally forcing a swirl of confusion that demands the reader to ask whether the one doing the questioning the whole time was not Caiaphas but Annas, who is only now sending Jesus on to the *current* high priest. That is, the text forces the reader to ask the question: Who is the high priest? This is no "victimization" of the reader, as suggested by Staley, making the reader "an outsider through his construal of the preceding scene."[8] In contrast, by using this narrative strategy, the rhetorical intention of the narrator is to make the reader "an insider" by allowing the narrative's swirling depiction of the high priest to implicitly portray the ironic confusion between the historical

4. Carson, *John*, 581.
5. See Keener, *John*, 2:1089.
6. Cf. Barrett: "It is difficult to resist the conclusion that the trial narratives have been rewritten by John in order to bring out what, in his opinion, were the points at issue" (*John*, 525).

7. Cf. Michaels, *John*, 903.
8. Jeffrey L. Staley, "Subversive Narrator/Victimized Reader: A Reader Response Assessment of a Text-Critical Problem, John 18.12 – 24," *JSNT* 51 (1993): 79 – 98 (96).

characters, thereby magnifying the cosmological characterization of Jesus that has been developing throughout the Gospel.

This is not to deny that a real high priest (or more likely two of them in turn; cf. Luke 3:2) actually interrogated Jesus. Rather, it is to say that the narrative is more interested in projecting Jesus in his high-priestly actions than it is to chronicle the high priests of first-century Judaism. As the Gospel has done elsewhere before (see comments on 2:10 and 3:1), the narrative has played the historical characters against themselves to establish upfront for the reader the fuller context of the scene about to unfold and the true identity of Jesus.

18:14 Caiaphas was the one who had advised the Jews that it was better for one man to die for the people (ἦν δὲ Καϊάφας ὁ συμβουλεύσας τοῖς Ἰουδαίοις ὅτι συμφέρει ἕνα ἄνθρωπον ἀποθανεῖν ὑπὲρ τοῦ λαοῦ). The introduction to the pericope (vv. 13 – 14) concludes with a brief reintroduction of Caiaphas, preparing the reader for his (apparent) interrogation of Jesus in vv. 19 – 24. Caiaphas was first introduced to the reader near the end of Jesus's public ministry (see comments on 11:49). His importance is not merely his position of authority but the manner in which he used it to direct the strategy of the Jews to kill Jesus (see 11:50 – 52), which the narrator intentionally reminds the reader. By this introduction the reader is not only reminded of the political maneuvering of Caiaphas and the Jewish authorities but of the cosmological maneuvering of God so that the decision of Caiaphas was and continues to be facilitated by the preordained will of God (see comments on 11:53).

18:15 Simon Peter was following Jesus, together with another disciple. Now that disciple was known to the high priest, and he entered with Jesus into the court of the high priest (Ἠκολούθει δὲ τῷ Ἰησοῦ Σίμων Πέτρος καὶ ἄλλος μαθητής. ὁ δὲ μαθητὴς ἐκεῖνος ἦν γνωστὸς τῷ ἀρχιερεῖ, καὶ συνεισῆλθεν τῷ Ἰησοῦ εἰς τὴν αὐλὴν τοῦ ἀρχιερέως). The second section of the pericope (vv. 15 – 18) transitions to Simon Peter who is described as "following" (Ἠκολούθει) Jesus, almost certainly from the garden where he was arrested by the Jewish and Roman authorities. No reason is given for his pursuit of Jesus; the narrator focuses less on what he is thinking and more on what he is about to do. After being rebuked by Jesus, his actions do suggest continued allegiance — an allegiance that is about to be challenged. It is important to note that this section is the first of three sections that perform an intercalation, a rhetorical technique that encloses or "sandwiches" one scene in the middle of a different scene (forming an $A^1 - B - A^2$ pattern), so that each scene affects the interpretation of the other (see comments before v. 13). This section (vv. 15 – 18) is the first of the framing sections (A^1). Our interpretation must read the entire intercalation as interrelated, forming a cumulative whole that provides a unified message.

Although the narrator clearly focuses on Peter (denoted by the singular verb), a second character is also mentioned as being present with Peter — "another disciple" (ἄλλος μαθητής). This is not the first time an anonymous disciple has been mentioned (see comments on 1:40), and although a specific name or title is not given here, many scholars think this disciple is to be identified with "the Beloved Disciple," who was officially introduced in the farewell discourse and appears throughout the end of the Gospel (19:25 – 27, 35; 20:1 – 10; 21:1 – 7, 20 – 24; for an overview of the "Beloved Disciple," see comments on 13:23). As discussed previously, anonymity is itself a narrative tool to develop both plot and characterization. The challenge is to interpret the "gap that anonymity denotes" with a precision that is shaped by the narrative as a whole.[9]

---

9. Reinhartz, *"Why Ask My Name?,"* 188.

In this pericope the anonymous disciple is in a position that signals a privileged relationship to the high priest; according to the narrator he "was known to the high priest" (ἦν γνωστὸς τῷ ἀρχιερεῖ), thus providing him entrance into the high priest's court. The details of this anonymous disciple's relationship are not given and therefore are secondary to the narrative depiction.[10] What is given is the *fact* of his relation, a relation that gives him special access to the events surrounding Jesus. Whether or not they can be equated, this "anonymous disciple" has a privileged relationship with the high priest in a manner similar to the Beloved Disciple's privileged relation to Jesus (see 13:23). Moreover, like the Beloved Disciple this "disciple" is also in a unique relationship with Peter (see 13:24), who is frequently depicted by the Gospel to be in relationship with the Beloved Disciple. And according to the narrator, this disciple is also in relation to Jesus, with whom "he entered" (συνεισῆλθεν) into the court of the high priest.[11]

18:16 But Peter had to stand at the door outside. Then the other disciple, who was known to the high priest, came out and spoke to the doorkeeper and brought in Peter (ὁ δὲ Πέτρος εἱστήκει πρὸς τῇ θύρᾳ ἔξω. ἐξῆλθεν οὖν ὁ μαθητὴς ὁ ἄλλος ὁ γνωστὸς τοῦ ἀρχιερέως καὶ εἶπεν τῇ θυρωρῷ καὶ εἰσήγαγεν τὸν Πέτρον). The contrast between the "anonymous disciple" and Peter is made clear by the narrator, for while that "disciple" is on the inside with Jesus (v. 15), Peter is on the "outside" (ἔξω). The inside-outside language serves a larger, more metaphorical role, defining these two disciples by means of their geographic relation to

Jesus. The "other disciple," who is again depicted by his connection to the high priest, speaks to "the doorkeeper" (τῇ θυρωρῷ), a female (denoted by the gender of the noun), who then gives this disciple permission to bring Peter into the court. The secondary role of Peter is impossible to miss. The detailed description of these two disciples — the anonymous disciple/Beloved Disciple[12] and Peter — serves as a frame for the entire events surrounding the crucifixion of Jesus. From the arrest and trial (v. 15–16) to the morning of Jesus's resurrection (20:2–8), these two disciples serve as direct eyewitnesses and respondents to the climactic work of the Son (see comments on 13:23).

18:17 Then the maidservant at the door said to Peter, "Are you also one of this man's disciples?" He said, "I am not" (λέγει οὖν τῷ Πέτρῳ ἡ παιδίσκη ἡ θυρωρός, Μὴ καὶ σὺ ἐκ τῶν μαθητῶν εἶ τοῦ ἀνθρώπου τούτου; λέγει ἐκεῖνος, Οὐκ εἰμί). The female doorkeeper, here qualified as "the maidservant at the door" (ἡ παιδίσκη ἡ θυρωρός), is a slave girl assigned to the entrance so as to be aware of who entered and exited the premises and to take notice of visitors, permitting entrance only to those who belonged.[13] The phrase "this man" (τοῦ ἀνθρώπου τούτου) probably expresses scorn, not pity.[14] The form of the negation, "not" (Μὴ), causes some to think the question expects a negative answer and is therefore accusatory.[15] Others suggest that the addition of "you also" (καὶ σὺ) changes the question to expect a positive answer and implies that Peter might be a disciple "in addition to" the anonymous disciple.[16] In this context the question simply assumes that Jesus had many disciples

---

10. Cf. Barrett, *John*, 525; Keener, *John*, 2:1090.
11. Cf. Michaels, *John*, 899.
12. This is the last occurrence of the "other/another disciple." While there is no clear evidence that the anonymous "other disciple" and the Beloved Disciple are the same individual, the narrative's employment of their anonymity is certainly intentionally integrated and strongly supports the identification.

13. Keener, *John*, 2:1091.
14. Hoskyns, *Fourth Gospel*, 513.
15. BDF § 427.2. Cf. Morris: "The question suggested a line of escape and Peter gratefully took it up" (*John*, 667).
16. See Barrett, *John*, 526.

and asks if Peter was also one of them.[17] She is the doorkeeper and is making herself aware of the reason for a visitor's entrance.

The focus of this verse, however, is not on the question of the maidservant but on the answer of Peter. In contrast to the Baptist (see 1:20–21), the "I am not" of Peter is a self-focused response, a witness against himself. Although the text does not give the reason for his response, whether it was for protection from harm or embarrassment, Peter was certainly not afraid to deny Christ. He chose instead to fear the question of a maidservant assigned to watch the door: "The voice of a mere woman terrified Peter."[18] In one sense Peter was on the inside, having been given special access to the court of the high priest. Yet when asked about the true High Priest, the one to whom he had also (and more astoundingly) been given access, Peter acts like an outsider, which the next verse makes dramatically clear.

18:18 The slaves and the servants stood at a charcoal fire which they had made because it was cold, and they were warming themselves. But Peter was also with them standing and warming himself (εἰστήκεισαν δὲ οἱ δοῦλοι καὶ οἱ ὑπηρέται ἀνθρακιὰν πεποιηκότες, ὅτι ψῦχος ἦν, καὶ ἐθερμαίνοντο· ἦν δὲ καὶ ὁ Πέτρος μετ᾽ αὐτῶν ἑστὼς καὶ θερμαινόμενος). The second section of the pericope (vv. 15–18) concludes by portraying the outsider status of Peter in a manner that speaks without words. The "impressions" created by the image recounted by the narrator serves as commentary on the words he had just spoken. All the opponents of Jesus were gathered in one place, not only the religious officials (e.g., Annas, Caiaphas) but also "the slaves" (οἱ δοῦλοι), domestic servants of the high priest and temple like the maidservant, and "the servants" (οἱ ὑπηρέται), the "assistants" of the Jewish authorities sent to arrest Jesus (see comments on 18:3). And among them was Peter, warming himself by the fire — an image that is intended to express communion, fellowship, even intimacy; it is an ironic fellowship since just moments before he was attacking the same servants (see 18:10–11)![19] Peter was standing "with them" (μετ᾽ αὐτῶν) and sharing in their warmth and comfort at the same moment (based upon the intercalation) that Jesus (his Lord!) was being treated like an outsider and physically abused.[20] Peter's first witness to Christ was an anti-witness, a denial. But Jesus is not done with Peter; by the Gospel's end he will be warming himself at another "charcoal fire" (see 21:9).[21]

18:19 Meanwhile, the high priest questioned Jesus about his disciples and his teaching (Ὁ οὖν ἀρχιερεὺς ἠρώτησεν τὸν Ἰησοῦν περὶ τῶν μαθητῶν αὐτοῦ καὶ περὶ τῆς διδαχῆς αὐτοῦ). The word translated as "meanwhile" (οὖν) is generally a "marker of continuation of a narrative" (e.g., "then," "so," "now"),[22] but in the context of an intercalation in which the two episodes are taking place simultaneously (see comments before v. 13), the word transitions from one scene to the next in a temporally overlapping manner. As we have already discussed, the narrator's depiction of the high priest's questioning of Jesus is mysterious when read in light of v. 24 and is intentionally crafted so as to depict neither Caiaphas or Annas as the high priest but

---

17. Cf. Bultmann, *John*, 645.

18. Calvin, *John 11–21*, 159.

19. John Paul Heil, *Blood and Water: The Death and Resurrection of Jesus in John 18–21*, CBQMS 27 (Washington, DC: Catholic Biblical Association of America, 1995), 34.

20. Even the statement "because it was cold" (ὅτι ψῦχος ἦν) is hardly just a description of the weather (the historical plot), but is addressing the cosmological plot portrayed by Peter's actions, something portrayed by the Gospel before (cf. 3:2; 10:22; 11:10; 13:30; 21:3).

21. Michaels, *John*, 902.

22. BDAG 736.

rather the one they have arrested and bound, Jesus (see comments on v. 13). Nothing in this "trial" looks official, for this interrogation functions more like a preparatory verdict than a legitimate legal procedure. This "trial" seems less like a proceeding that determines shameful behavior and more like an opportunity to deliver shame. The subject matter of this interrogation is quite general; the high priest questions Jesus about his disciples and his teaching. Particulars are not in view here; this court is evaluating the entire person and work of Jesus.[23]

18:20 Jesus answered him, "I have spoken openly to the world. I always taught in the synagogue and in the temple, where all the Jews come together, and I spoke nothing in secret" (ἀπεκρίθη αὐτῷ Ἰησοῦς, Ἐγὼ παρρησίᾳ λελάληκα τῷ κόσμῳ· ἐγὼ πάντοτε ἐδίδαξα ἐν συναγωγῇ καὶ ἐν τῷ ἱερῷ, ὅπου πάντες οἱ Ἰουδαῖοι συνέρχονται, καὶ ἐν κρυπτῷ ἐλάλησα οὐδέν). The narrator may have started his account by describing what the high priest asked of Jesus, but Jesus is the one who speaks first, befitting the narrative's desire to portray Jesus as the functioning (and rightful) high priest in this scene. Jesus addresses the first of the two issues raised by the high priest: his teaching. Jesus states emphatically, "*I* have spoken openly to the world" (Ἐγὼ παρρησίᾳ λελάληκα τῷ κόσμῳ). The term "openly" (παρρησίᾳ) has been previously used to refer to speaking "in public" (e.g., 7:4, 26; 11:54) and "plainly" or "clearly" (e.g., 10:24; 11:14; 16:25, 29) and is used here to suggest that Jesus has not hidden or distorted his message or his intentions but has shared them openly ("to the world"). The use of "world" here could seem hyperbolic to the questioning high priest, but actually perfectly describes Jesus's intended audience according to the prologue (see 1:10). Jesus explains further that he

has done his teaching in the synagogue (cf. 6:59) and the temple (cf. 5:14; 7:14, 28; 8:20; 10:23), the places Jews would be expected to assemble. This serves as evidence that his teaching ministry was anything but secretive.

18:21 "Why question me? Question those who heard what I said to them. Surely they know what I said" (τί με ἐρωτᾷς; ἐρώτησον τοὺς ἀκηκοότας τί ἐλάλησα αὐτοῖς· ἴδε οὗτοι οἴδασιν ἃ εἶπον ἐγώ). Jesus then addresses the second of the two issues raised by the high priest: his disciples—though in a manner that connects his disciples to his teachings. Since the message of Jesus was intended to result ultimately in the salvation of the world, the true test of the intentions and validity of Jesus's teaching can be witnessed by the fidelity of his disciples.[24] The person and work of Jesus had never been a free-floating abstraction but was a "Word-become-flesh" (1:14) and a message that resulted in the creation of the Father's children (1:12). This is not to suggest that Christ's work can be fully equated with the church but to say that the work of Christ can be witnessed in the existence and therefore the life of the church. It is not insignificant that God through the apostle Paul declares the church to be "the body of Christ" (e.g., 1 Cor 12:27). Just as Jesus is the Word-become-flesh, so the church is the flesh-become-word—declaring the grace, truth, and love of the Father which they received from the Son (and by the Holy Spirit).

Jesus does not respond at all like an accused person at an interrogation, especially in comparison to the submissive and penitent behavior recorded of others who appeared before municipal authorities (see Josephus, *Ant.* 14.172–73).[25] Jesus's response to the high priest is challenging ("Why question me?") and directive ("Question those..."). As we discussed above, in this scene Jesus functions as

---

23. Bultmann, *John*, 646.
24. Hoskyns, *Fourth Gospel*, 514.

25. See Keener, *John*, 2:1093.

the (true) high priest, reversing the authoritative controls and throwing the interrogation back upon his interrogators.

This section is the center section (B) of the intercalation (see comments before v. 13), which means that at the very moment Peter was denying Jesus while sharing in the warmth and fellowship of the temple servants, just some distance away stood Jesus with hands bound inside a chamber with the high priest, claiming that his disciples were reliable witnesses to his teaching and therefore to his identity. The contrast is stark and is intended to penetrate the heart of the reader.

18:22 After he said these things, one of the servants nearby gave a blow to Jesus saying, "Is that how you answer the high priest?" (ταῦτα δὲ αὐτοῦ εἰπόντος εἷς παρεστηκὼς τῶν ὑπηρετῶν ἔδωκεν ῥάπισμα τῷ Ἰησοῦ εἰπών, Οὕτως ἀποκρίνη τῷ ἀρχιερεῖ;). An unnamed "servant" (ὑπηρετῶν), the same term used in the previous pericope for the assistants to the Jewish authorities sent to arrest Jesus (see comments on 18:3), responds to Jesus with a tangible expression of disapproval. The narrator explains that the servant gave "a blow" (ῥάπισμα) to Jesus. The term originally meant a blow with something like a rod, but it can also refer to a strike with an open hand, like a slap in the face.[26] Commentators often discuss the illegality of such a physical response, but in light of the fact that the religious authorities have put God on trial, binding him and demanding that he answer their questions, the blow to the face of the Son of Man is hardly the greatest offense.

The irony, however, is not fully captured by the blow delivered to Jesus, for it is the words of the anonymous servant that more clearly depict the depth of misunderstanding. The reader knows full well that the question should be immediately re-versed and asked of the servant: "Is that how you treat the true High Priest?" It is remarkable that this one question is the only statement any character representing the Jewish authorities and high priest makes in the pericope's depiction of the questioning of Jesus. In this interrogation, Jesus asked the questions.

18:23 Jesus answered him, "If I spoke wrongly, testify concerning the wrong. But if correctly, why do you strike me?" (ἀπεκρίθη αὐτῷ Ἰησοῦς, Εἰ κακῶς ἐλάλησα, μαρτύρησον περὶ τοῦ κακοῦ· εἰ δὲ καλῶς, τί με δέρεις;). Jesus does not leave the falsely attributed abuse without commentary but offers what becomes the final statement of this interrogation. Jesus is not to be judged here as speaking without turning the other cheek. In this moment he speaks as the Judge and Authority (5:22–27), supported by all the authoritative witnesses that have been presented on his behalf, including not only his own works and John the Baptist but also the witnesses of the Father and Scripture (see 5:30–47). What Jesus's response reveals is that the grace of God does not come without truth (1:17). The grace of God is evidenced by the very fact that he even received such questions at all, let alone that he allowed a servant to strike him in the face, and ultimately place him on the cross. The gospel is seen in that Jesus will respond in an equally physical manner to the blow of the Jews, not by giving it back to them but by placing the necessary and justified response upon himself.

18:24 Then Annas sent him bound to Caiaphas the high priest (ἀπέστειλεν οὖν αὐτὸν ὁ Ἄννας δεδεμένον πρὸς Καϊάφαν τὸν ἀρχιερέα). The third section of the pericope (vv. 19–24) concludes with a final comment by the narrator that dramatizes the intentionally ironic depiction of the binding and interrogation of Jesus. As we discussed above

---

26. Morris, *John*, 670.

(see v. 13), up to this point the reader was logically thinking that the "high priest" was the one introduced as such, Caiaphas. This verse intentionally obscures that assumption in a manner that forces the reader to ask the question: Who is the high priest? After watching the narrative unfold, neither Annas nor Caiaphas qualify. Rather it is Jesus, the one bound, arrested, and under interrogation who alone qualifies, not merely because of this scene but because of what the reader has long been told about him (e.g., 5:22 – 27). The reader sees more clearly than ever how carefully the narrative's plot depicts and explains the cosmological realities in, around, and through the unfolding of the historical events.

18:25 Meanwhile Simon Peter was standing and warming himself. Then they said to him, "Are you also one of his disciples?" He answered and said, "I am not" (Ἦν δὲ Σίμων Πέτρος ἑστὼς καὶ θερμαινόμενος. εἶπον οὖν αὐτῷ, Μὴ καὶ σὺ ἐκ τῶν μαθητῶν αὐτοῦ εἶ; ἠρνήσατο ἐκεῖνος καὶ εἶπεν, Οὐκ εἰμί). The fourth section of the Gospel (vv. 25 – 27) returns to Peter again, picking up where it had intentionally concluded before (vv. 15 – 18). This section is the final framing section (A²) of the intercalation (see comments before 18:13). This does not chronologically follow Jesus's statement above (v. 22) but is narratively occurring at the exact same time.[27] The reader is expected to feel the sharpness of the contrast as the text returns to the denial or anti-witness of Peter.

The narrator reminds the reader where Peter was so as to pick up the intercalation from v. 18, standing and warming himself with the very servants of the Jewish authorities who arrested Jesus. One of them asked Peter, now for the second time (cf. v. 17), if he was one of Jesus's disciples. And Peter says "I am not" (Οὐκ εἰμί) for a second time,

acting again as an outsider and anti-witness of Jesus. It is worth noting how none of the speakers are named, which suggests even further that anonymity is a rhetorical strategy of this pericope. The only people who are clearly identified before they speak are Jesus and Peter, for as we discussed above, even the high priest is not directly named before he speaks (see v. 19). In this way the text makes a dramatic and ironic presentation by means of the intercalation: at the same time the real high priest (Jesus) is not treated like one, the real witness (Peter) is not acting like one.

18:26 One of the high priest's slaves, a relative of the man whose ear Peter cut off, said, "Didn't I see you in the garden with him?" (λέγει εἷς ἐκ τῶν δούλων τοῦ ἀρχιερέως, συγγενὴς ὢν οὗ ἀπέκοψεν Πέτρος τὸ ὠτίον, Οὐκ ἐγώ σε εἶδον ἐν τῷ κήπῳ μετ᾽ αὐτοῦ;). The narrative concludes the intercalation between Peter and Jesus with the third and climactic denial by Peter. While the person asking the question is again anonymous, this time an important detail is provided. The questioner is a personal slave of the high priest *and* a "relative" (συγγενής) of Malchus, the man whose ear was cut off by Peter (see 18:10). This was no flippant question; it was more authoritative and personal than the first two. And this questioner personally witnessed Peter represent and defend Jesus in the garden.

18:27 Again Peter denied it, and immediately a rooster began to crow (πάλιν οὖν ἠρνήσατο Πέτρος· καὶ εὐθέως ἀλέκτωρ ἐφώνησεν). Peter's denial need merely be summarized here, for the reader already knows the words Peter would use (cf. vv. 17, 25). After presenting Peter's third and climactic denial of Jesus, the pericope concludes with another temporally overlapping incident, the crow of a rooster. Jesus had specifically foretold Peter that far from sacrificially offering his life on

---

27. Cf. Brown, *John*, 2:827.

behalf of Jesus, he would deny him three times (see 13:36 – 38). And just as the intercalation between Peter and Jesus contrasted their simultaneously occurring responses to questions posed by the temple authorities, so also the moment Peter spoke the last of this threefold denial, "immediately" (εὐθέως) the voice of the rooster was heard. Jesus is not finished

with Peter, as the reinstatement of Peter in the Gospel's epilogue will show (21:15 – 23). The fact that the Gospel ends with Peter's reinstatement suggests that this pericope's depiction of his misunderstanding of Jesus's person and work and his failure to witness to Jesus offers a significant perspective on the nature of Christian discipleship.

Theology in Application

This pericope offers an interpretive description of the Jewish trial of Jesus and a potent exhortation to the reader in regard to the identity of Jesus Christ and the identity of his disciples as witnesses in the world. Like the previous pericope (18:1 – 12), even while being arrested, bound, and questioned, Jesus is in complete control, dictating the terms and guiding his own interrogation. Through this pericope the reader is able to understand the gracious work of the true High Priest and is guided to wrestle with the challenge of Christian discipleship and being a witness for Christ.

The High Priest Who Was Not Treated like One

The rhetorical strategy of this account directs the reader to see Jesus as the legitimate or true High Priest by creating an ironic confusion between the historical characters that ultimately has them working against one another (see comments on v. 13). This narrative maneuver is not for the purpose of entertainment but to provide interpretive guidance to the entire Jewish trial. In this trial the one arrested and bound was (and had always been) in control, dictating the terms. Even his arrest, as the previous pericope explained (18:1 – 12), was more accurately an act of surrender, a sacrificial offering.

What makes the true high priest unique is that his own priestly expectations (and those from the Father) required that he be bound and arrested and eventually crucified. None of this required him to lose his position as the Judge (5:22 – 27); it simply required that his judgment and authority would direct the focus of the world's hate (and even the wrath of God) upon himself. This high priest was not only offering the sacrifice, he *was* the sacrifice. This high priest was the perfect sacrifice, "the Lamb of God" (1:29). While this high priest was not treated like the high priest, he was certainly acting like one.

The Disciple Who Was Not Acting like One

Using the rhetorical technique of intercalation (see comments before v. 13), the narrative displayed the "interrogations" of Jesus and Peter in a manner that had them occurring simultaneously. At the very same moment Jesus was being denied by Peter, Jesus was claiming that his disciples were reliable witnesses to his teaching and therefore to his identity. The contrast is stark and is intended to penetrate the heart of the reader.

Peter exemplifies the paradox of Christian discipleship. Our spiritual life finds its source not in good intentions but in the Good Shepherd, who willingly gave himself for us. The denials of Peter depict with glaring detail how the creation of the children of God was never intended to be based upon the merit of the blood, flesh, or will of humanity but is "from God" alone (1:13). This does not deny what Jesus says to his questioners in v. 21, that the church is to be his witnesses. It is to say rather that our witness cannot stand on its own but can only be a response to what Christ has already done on our behalf. Christian discipleship is not best defined as a work or action done *for* God but as action done *in response to* God and his work.

The Church as the Witness of Christ

As much as discipleship is a response to what God has done, Jesus was serious when he said to his interrogators about his disciples that they "hear" and therefore "know what I said" (v. 21). Such a statement implies that Jesus's disciples are suitable witnesses. This verse is one among many in the Gospel that teaches that the Christian is to be a participant in God's mission to the world.

The witness of the church on behalf of Christ, however, springs not from adequacy but from inadequacy. It is only our "I am not" that allows us to say "I am." Peter forgot what he said earlier in 6:68 – 69: "Lord, to whom shall we go? You have the words of eternal life." For this reason the Christian can answer forthrightly when asked about his association to Christ, "I am," but only because he knows that he is the "I am not" and Jesus Christ alone is *the* "I AM."

CHAPTER

39

John 18:28 – 40

Literary Context

This pericope continues to depict the events surrounding the sacrificial death of the Son of God. Jesus has already been arrested and interrogated by the Jewish authorities; in this pericope he is taken and handed over to the Roman authorities, who perform the equivalent of a Roman trial of Jesus so as to respond to the legal requirements (and political tension) shared between them. The narrative intentionally contrasts Christ with two significant characters and what they represent: "the Jews" (representing the authorities of Judaism) and Pilate (representing the powers of Rome). The reader is guided to understand more fully the authority of Jesus in comparison to the powers of this world both religious and political and is exhorted to see Jesus not only as the true King (and Judge) but also that the "truth" Pilate seeks is not a "what" but a "who."

VIII. The Crucifixion (18:1 – 19:42)

    A. The Arrest of Jesus (18:1 – 12)

    B. The Jewish Trial and Its Witnesses (18:13 – 27)

➡   **C. The Roman Trial before Pilate (18:28 – 40)**

    D. The Verdict: "Crucify Him!" (19:1 – 16)

    E. The Crucifixion of Jesus (19:17 – 27)

    F. The Death and Burial of Jesus (19:28 – 42)

Main Idea

Jesus is the Passover Lamb, the King, and the truth, who became the redemptive sacrifice for the world when he, the Son of Man, was exchanged for the "sons of mankind" in order to release them from their enslavement to sin, death, and the foreign powers of this world.

Translation

John 18:28–40

28a	Introduction & Setting	Then **they led Jesus from Caiaphas**
b	Destination	**to the praetorium.**
c	Time	**It was early**
d	Character's Thoughts	and **they did not want to enter themselves into the praetorium**
e	Purpose	in order that they might not be defiled but
f	Contrast	may eat the Passover.
29a	Character Entrance	Then **Pilate came outside toward them and said,**
b	Question	*"Who brings an accusation against this man?"*
30a	Response	**They answered and said to him,**
b	Condition	*"If this man was not doing evil,*
c	Indirect Verdict: "Guilty of Evil"	*we would not have delivered him to you."*
31a	Response	Then **Pilate said to them,**
b	Command #1	*"You take him yourselves*
c	Command #2	*and judge him*
d	Standard	*according to your law."*
e	Response	Then **the Jews said to him,**
f	Explanation	*"It is not lawful for us to kill anyone."*
32a	Narrator's Aside	**[This happened]**
b	Purpose: Prophetic Fulfillment	*in order that the word of Jesus might be fulfilled,*
c	Description	*which he spoke to indicate what kind of death he ⟳ was about to die.*
33a	Progression of Action #1	Then **Pilate entered again into the praetorium**
b	Progression of Action #2	and **summoned Jesus**
c	Progression of Action #3	and **said to him,**
d	Interrogation (33–38)	*"Are you the king of the Jews?"*
34a	Response	**Jesus answered,**
b	Interrogative Challenge	*"Do you speak this of your own accord*
c		*or did others speak to you about me?"*
35a	Response	**Pilate answered,**
b	Counterquestion #1	*"I am not a Jew, am I?*
c	Perceived State of Affairs	*Your nation and high priests handed you over to me.*
d	Counterquestion #2	*What did you do?"*
36a	Response	**Jesus answered,**
b	Counter State of Affairs	*"My kingdom is not from this world.*
c	Condition	*If my kingdom was from this world,*
d	Inference	*my servants would be fighting*
`	Purpose	*in order that I might not be handed over to the Jews.*
f	Restatement of 36b	*But now my kingdom is not from here."*
37a	Response	Then **Pilate said to him,**
b	Inference	*"So you are a king!"*
c	Response	**Jesus answered,**

Continued on next page.

Continued from previous page.

d	Enigmatic Restatement of 37b	*"You say that*	*I am a king.*
e	Explanatory Reason	*For this reason*	*I was born*
f	Parallel Reason	*and for this reason*	*I came into the world,*
g	Description		*in order that I might testify to the truth.*
h	Result of 37g	*Everyone who hears my voice is from the truth."*	
38a	Conclusion of Interrogation	**Pilate said to him,**	
b	Interrogative Rebuke	*"What is truth?"*	
c		And	
d			after he said this,
e	Reaction to Interrogation	**he went out again to the Jews**	
f		and **said to them,**	
g	Announcement:	*"I find nothing in him that …*	
	Legal Innocence		*… is a basis for a charge.*
39a	Custom	*But it is a custom for you*	
b	Description		*to release one person to you*
c	Circumstance		*on the Passover.*
d	Escalating Question	*Do you want me to release to you,*	
e		*then,*	
f	Ironic Title		*the king of the Jews?"*
40a	Climactic Response	Then **they shouted again,**	
b			saying
c	Exclamation	*"Not this man*	
d	Character Entrance/Alternate	*but Barabbas."*	
e	Narrator's Conclusion	And **Barabbas was a robber.**	

Structure and Literary Form

The structure of this pericope is different than the basic story form (see Introduction). The structure is guided by the trial motif that defines the pericopae leading up to the crucifixion: the Jewish trial (18:13 – 27), the Roman trial (18:28 – 40), and the verdict (19:1 – 16). This pericope contains a brief introduction (v. 28), followed by a narrative structure that has a three-part and interrelated structure similar to the previous pericope (18:13 – 27) that is directed by the back-and-forth movement of the trial's geography (outside-inside-outside).[1] The trial begins outside with a dialogue between the Jewish authorities and Pilate (vv. 29 – 32); it then moves inside for a private discussion between Jesus and Pilate (vv. 33 – 38a); it then moves outside again for a brief, concluding dialogue between the Jewish authorities and Pilate (vv. 38b – 40). Similar to the intercalation of the previous pericope, the three scenes in this pericope are intended to be read with an intentional level of comparison or

---

1. See Moloney, *John*, 493.

contrast. The comparison now is not *temporal* — events occurring simultaneously (see comments before 18:13) — but *geographic*, offering a detailed depiction of the conspiring work of both Jewish and Roman authorities against Jesus, who again is at the center of the action. With a kind of dramatic technique, the narrator "employs the device of two stages upon which the action is exhibited, a front and back stage" (front-back-front).[2] The reader is given direct access into the events of both stages.[3]

Exegetical Outline

→ **C. The Roman Trial before Pilate (18:28 – 40)**
1. Jesus Delivered to the Roman Authorities (v. 28)
2. Pilate and the Jews: "What Accusation Do You Bring?" (vv. 29 – 32)
3. Pilate and Jesus: "What is Truth?" (vv. 33 – 38a)
4. The Negotiation of Jesus (vv. 38b – 40)

Explanation of the Text

IN-DEPTH: The Date of the Crucifixion

There is a pastoral-apologetical issue that has long distracted interpreters of all four Gospels. The Synoptic Gospels seem to reflect a chronological contradiction with the Fourth Gospel in regard to the relation between the death of Jesus and the Passover. In short, the Synoptics are often interpreted in a manner that equates the Last Supper with the Jewish Passover meal (see Mark 14:12), placing the death of Jesus *after* the Passover. In contrast, the Fourth Gospel does not even directly mention the Lord's Supper and suggests that Jesus was crucified at the very time the Passover victims were slaughtered in the temple (see 19:14). When the Jews bring Jesus to Pilate, they are careful not to defile themselves so that they may eat "the Passover" (v. 28), placing the death of Jesus *before* the Passover. Thus, whereas in the Fourth Gospel Jesus is crucified on the day of the Passover sacrifice preceding the evening meal (Friday), in the Synoptics Jesus and his disciples are often understood to be celebrating the Lord's Supper at the Passover meal (Thursday), placing the crucifixion on the day that follows. A survey and analysis of approaches is beyond the scope of this commentary.[4] Our argument is that it is only an apparent contradiction.

2. Dodd, *Historical Tradition*, 96.
3. Duke, *Irony in the Fourth Gospel*, 120.
4. See Brown, *Death of the Messiah*, 2:1351 – 73; John P. Meier, *A Marginal Jew: Rethinking the Historical Jesus*, 4 vols.;

ABRL (New York: Doubleday, 1991), 1:386 – 402; Morris, *John*, 684 – 95. Cf. Barry D. Smith, "The Chronology of the Last Supper," *WTJ* 53 (1991): 29 – 45.

If we begin with the Fourth Gospel, we can see that the date of the crucifixion is anything but an inconsequential detail.[5] The date of the crucifixion is a climactic component of the Gospel's multiform depiction of the sacrificial death of Jesus. A brief overview will be helpful: the prologue describes Jesus as "flesh" (1:14), the Baptist declares Jesus to be "the Lamb of God" (1:29, 36), Jesus declares himself to be the replacement of the temple (2:21), and Jesus commands the eating of his flesh and drinking of his blood (6:51 – 56). By these descriptions of Jesus, the system of atonement rooted in the OT is being applied to his crucified body and sacrificial work. Even more, the role of the Good Shepherd (10:11), the political strategy of Caiaphas (11:51 – 52), the imagery of his public statement (12:4), the humiliation of the foot washing (13:10), and the prayer of consecration (17:19) cumulatively reflect the image of sacrifice. Even the narrative's account of the death of Jesus is filled with detailed allusions that directly connect the crucifixion of Jesus to the Passover and its elements: the unbroken bones of Jesus (19:33 – 36), the hyssop used to give Jesus a drink (19:29), and possibly even the reference to "the sixth hour" (19:14).[6]

For this reason the question regarding the date of the crucifixion cannot be grasped simply by historical analysis situated behind the text, for the entire theological substructure of the Gospel is centered upon the sacrifice on this particular day, "the single most important day in world history … when the great God through his slaughtered Son will make the final and all-fulfilling Passover sacrifice for the sin of the whole world."[7] This is not to minimize the real exegetical "question" but to challenge the focus of the question traditionally asked. We must begin with what is (emphatically) clear in the narrative before moving to what is unclear. The biggest and most traditional "constant" in the exegetical equation is the assumed relation between the Last Supper and the Passover meal, especially in the Synoptic Gospels. In the Fourth Gospel, however, such a concept is entirely and intentionally foreign. While it is usually assumed that the Synoptics make the connection clear, this assumption finds no direct warrant from Scripture itself. Brown, for example, suggests that Christians read back into the Lord's Supper the Passover imagery, not because it is stated as such (it is not) but because the theological comparisons are implicitly present.[8] Even more, Meier helpfully shows that several historical details in the common understanding of the Synoptics' chronology are difficult to reconcile with commonly known Jewish practices and regulations, specifically that "the supreme Jewish authority in Jerusalem" would arrest, hold a formal trial, reach

5. Contra Keener, *John*, 2:1100.
6. Brown, *Death of the Messiah*, 2:1372.

7. Frederick Dale Bruner, *The Gospel of John: A Commentary* (Grand Rapids: Eerdmans, 2012), 1064.
8. Brown, *Death of the Messiah*, 2:1371.

a decision, and hand the criminal over to gentile authorities for a same-day execution all within a few hours of Passover day. "Yet this is what the Synoptic passion chronology and presentation of the Jewish 'process' basically demanded."[9]

It is really only Mark 14:12 – 16 that allows for the suggestion of a Passover
meal connection, and even in this verse there is no exegetical demand to view
the Lord's Supper as a Passover meal. A few reasons can be provided. First, the
reference to Passover-meal "preparations" in Mark 14:12 is made by the disciples, not Jesus. While Jesus does give them instructions for the preparation of
a meal, he never once refers to the meal as the Passover meal; the disciples assume it is a Passover meal because of the approaching Passover Feast. Certainly
the meals are theologically related, but they are also (and necessarily) distinct.
This might be exactly what the text intends to depict in its implicitness, with
the absence of a Passover lamb (because it was not a Passover meal) making
the point explicit — Jesus was to be *the* Lamb (John 1:29). Even if the disciples
thought it was a Passover-like meal (Mark 14:16), that does not mean that it was
viewed as such by Jesus. For him this meal was instituting (proleptically) the
new covenant in his blood.

Second, there is no reason to suggest that the time of the meal in Mark 14:12
is on Friday, for on the normal Jewish method of reckoning days this meal would
be on the evening *prior* to the sacrifice preparations, since the Jewish day was
normally understood to begin at sunset of the previous day (as Mark's Gospel
makes clear in Mark 15:46). "In other words, he [Mark] was as clearly aware as
John was that Jesus held his Passover meal not on the official day, but deliberately one day earlier."[10] And similar to the Gospel of John, we would argue that
such an adjustment was not merely out of historical necessity but also for very
important theological reasons.

Third, the statement by the narrator in Mark 14:2 that the Jewish authorities were seeking to kill Jesus "but not during the feast" for fear of the people's
reaction, adds further support to the chronology depicted by John. Unless the
Jewish authorities changed their mind (about which the reader was not made
aware by the text), this rules out the possibility that Jesus was arrested on the
evening when everyone else was participating in the official Passover meal.
That is, by Mark's own account, Jesus had to be arrested on the previous evening before the actual day of the Passover.

Fourth, the Barabbas incident (vv. 39 – 40; cf. Mark 15:6 – 14) is best explained
by John's chronology.[11] The obvious premise of the Barabbas release — an

---

9. Meier, *A Marginal Jew*, 1:396.

10. R. T. France, *The Gospel of Mark: A Commentary on the Greek Text*, NIGTC (Grand Rapids: Eerdmans, 2002), 561.

11. This argument is adapted from Meier, *A Marginal Jew*, 1:400.

amnesty or pardon granted to some Jewish prisoner at Passover — is that amnesty was given precisely so that this Jew, upon release, could take part in the Passover meal. The common Synoptic chronology that relates the Lord's Supper to the Passover meal is unable to explain the point of Barabbas's release, for the meal would have already been celebrated! The Barabbas incident only makes sense if the Passover meal had not yet occurred and if the Lord's Supper (as recorded in the Synoptics) is not the Passover meal.

For these reasons, then, the solution to the apparent contradiction between the chronology of the Synoptics and John is just that — only apparent, rooted in the connection between the Lord's Supper and the Passover meal. By making the Passover meal the implicit background of the Lord's Supper (per Mark) or Jesus's final meal with his disciples (per John), the Gospels transfer the theology of Passover and the old covenant (the lamb, the blood, the ceremony) to Jesus and the new covenant. This is why John (and the Synoptics) is so careful to connect the final meal of Jesus to the Passover but not define it as such. For this *final* meal was actually the *first* Lord's Supper and the only one that would look forward and not back, situated between the "Passover" meals of both covenants so as to make Jesus the fulfillment and subject matter of them both. In several places the Gospel has employed the historical reality of the Jewish "Feasts" in order to highlight the cosmological forces at work in the narrative (see comments on 10:22). The use of the Passover in John is no exception.

18:28 Then they led Jesus from Caiaphas to the praetorium. It was early and they did not want to enter themselves into the praetorium in order that they might not be defiled but may eat the Passover (Ἄγουσιν οὖν τὸν Ἰησοῦν ἀπὸ τοῦ Καϊάφα εἰς τὸ πραιτώριον· ἦν δὲ πρωΐ· καὶ αὐτοὶ οὐκ εἰσῆλθον εἰς τὸ πραιτώριον, ἵνα μὴ μιανθῶσιν ἀλλὰ φάγωσιν τὸ πάσχα). The first verse of the pericope provides an introduction to the scene, explaining the transition from the Jewish trial in the court of the high priest (18:15) to the Roman trial in the "praetorium" (τὸ πραιτώριον), a Latin loanword that came to designate the official residence of a governor of a province.[12] The narrator's comment "It was early" (ἦν δὲ πρωΐ) gives the temporal context, but also the cosmological context: "The day of the victory of Jesus over the world is breaking."[13]

The narrator is careful to explain how religiously precise the Jewish authorities acted in transferring Jesus to the Roman governor "in order that they might not be defiled" (ἵνα μὴ μιανθῶσιν) on the morning of the Passover meal. Although the statement does offer insight into the chronology of events (see comments before v. 28), this explanation is hardly evincing a concern for Jewish regulations and purity laws.[14] The narrator focuses the reader's attention entirely on the irony of the scene;

12. BDAG 859.
13. Bultmann, *John*, 561.
14. Cf. Barrett, *John*, 531–33; Keener, *John*, 2:1099–1100.

while taking great care to be ritually pure before their Passover by not entering the praetorium, "the Jews have ironically prepared for the arrival of the true Passover by leading Jesus to the praetorium to be put to death."[15]

18:29 Then Pilate came outside toward them and said, "Who brings an accusation against this man?" (ἐξῆλθεν οὖν ὁ Πιλᾶτος ἔξω πρὸς αὐτοὺς καὶ φησίν, Τίνα κατηγορίαν φέρετε κατὰ τοῦ ἀνθρώπου τούτου;). The second section of the pericope (vv. 29 – 32) takes place outside the praetorium (the front stage; see comments before v. 28) and involves the Jewish authorities and Pilate, the Roman prefect (or more generally, "governor"; see Matt 27:2) of Judea in AD 26 – 36. Only Pilate's name is given, for the "praetorium" provides the necessary context regarding his role and relationship to the Jews and Jesus. In every important respect Pilate *is* Rome; the authority he assumes, the questions he asks, and his interaction with the Jews and Jesus expresses as much to the readers.[16] Pilate's entrance "outside" (ἔξω) signals that the encounter between the Jews and Pilate has begun.

Pilate's question formally initiates the judicial proceedings. The question is directed at the local subordinates, the accusers, upon whom the Roman officials would consult. In essence, Pilate's question is a request for a charge.[17] And by the response of the Jews in v. 30, it is probably to be interpreted as more demand than request. Pilate may be mocking their decision regarding Jesus as a mere accusation.[18] Thus the trial has begun, with Pilate serving as the judge, the Jews serving as the prosecutor, and Jesus, the accused, without defense.

18:30 They answered and said to him, "If this man was not doing evil, we would not have delivered him to you" (ἀπεκρίθησαν καὶ εἶπαν αὐτῷ, Εἰ μὴ ἦν οὗτος κακὸν ποιῶν, οὐκ ἄν σοι παρεδώκαμεν αὐτόν). The response of the Jews is intentionally indirect, as they seek to secure Pilate's authority without offering details of the charge. In fact, their response to Pilate's question is an attempt at leveraging their own position of authority against his, giving them political advantage. With shocking impudence, the Jews attempt to gain a foothold on the proceedings by retorting in a manner that declares Jesus guilty without evidence or qualification — not even a charge. The proof that "this man"[19] is "doing evil" (κακὸν ποιῶν), that is, is a "criminal," is grounded in and established by his very deliverance to Pilate.

While the Jews' reluctance to state the charge directly might be due to the unwarranted appearance of such accusations on Roman ears, the interaction itself suggests that their reluctance is rooted in the social dynamics of the scene. The interaction between the Jews and Pilate is almost certainly in substance functioning like a social challenge (see Introduction). The Jews are trying to use Pilate (just as Pilate will try to use the Jews) to access his authority and obtain their intended political (and religious) victory. The scene depicts two worldly authorities fighting over a claim to power that ultimately belongs to neither.[20]

18:31 Then Pilate said to them, "You take him yourselves and judge him according to your law." Then the Jews said to him, "It is not lawful for us to kill anyone" (εἶπεν οὖν αὐτοῖς ὁ Πιλᾶτος,

---

15. Heil, *Blood and Water*, 46.
16. Cf. Helen K. Bond, *Pontius Pilate in History and Interpretation*, SNTSMS 100 (Cambridge: Cambridge University Press, 1998), especially 163 – 93.
17. Keener, *John*, 2:1104.
18. Brown, *John*, 2:847.
19. Brown is right to suggest that this is "a contemptuous

use" of the demonstrative pronoun (*John*, 2:848). Cf. BDAG 740.
20. According to Helen K. Bond, "The Literary Function of Pontius Pilate in Josephus' Narratives," in *Narrativity in Biblical and Related Texts*, ed. G. J. Brooke and J.-D. Kaestli (Leuven: Leuven University Press, 2000), 213 – 23, this account between Pilate and the Jews matches other encounters.

Λάβετε αὐτὸν ὑμεῖς, καὶ κατὰ τὸν νόμον ὑμῶν κρίνατε αὐτόν. εἶπον [οὖν] αὐτῷ οἱ Ἰουδαῖοι, Ἡμῖν οὐκ ἔξεστιν ἀποκτεῖναι οὐδένα). Pilate's response not only reflects a move to disassociate himself from the (Jewish) legality involving "this man" but also serves to strike back at the Jews (per a social challenge) by leveraging their own laws against them. Pilate's argument is as follows: if your laws can so easily and with little qualification declare his actions as "evil," then they should just as easily be able to declare him guilty. This argument brings to light the real intentions of the Jews and forces them to qualify and explain their need for Pilate (and Rome more generally).

The Jews then explain, "It is not lawful for us to kill anyone" (Ἡμῖν οὐκ ἔξεστιν ἀποκτεῖναι οὐδένα). This statement has not been easily interpreted. There is no need to doubt the historicity of this statement, as if the Gospel is not itself a source into the legalities of a vassal state (Israel) under a foreign power (Rome) or a trustworthy source for understanding such authority in the first century.[21] But the issue may have less to do with Roman authority and more to do with the regulations described by their own law, perhaps especially in light of Passover. This latter sense fits well with the Gospel itself, where the Jews not only freely speak of killing Jesus with no regard for Roman permission (e.g., 5:18; 7:1; 11:53) but are even the ones to whom Pilate hands Jesus over to be crucified (see 19:15–16; cf. Jesus's prediction of this in 8:28). The expression, "It is not lawful," is almost always used in the Gospels to refer to what is either permitted or forbidden to Jews by their own law of Moses, which

makes it difficult to interpret the statement as a reference to Roman law alone.[22] Even the immediate context of the statement is helpful, for it would be odd (historically) to suggest that the Jews needed to remind Pilate of what Roman law did or did not permit; just as it would be odd (chronologically) to suggest that the Jews would defer to Pilate's Roman authority (v. 31b) seconds after he had just ordered them to act on their own authority (v. 31a).[23] Such a statement, then, serves as an ironic word of self-condemnation, a confession that they were not allowed to do the very thing they were about to do.

18:32 [This happened] in order that the word of Jesus might be fulfilled, which he spoke to indicate what kind of death he was about to die (ἵνα ὁ λόγος τοῦ Ἰησοῦ πληρωθῇ ὃν εἶπεν σημαίνων ποίῳ θανάτῳ ἤμελλεν ἀποθνῄσκειν). The narrator intrudes to offer a brief theological commentary on the result of the interaction between the Jewish authorities and Pilate. That which was illegal for the Jews and less than desirable for Pilate would still be accomplished, for as the narrator rightly explains, its authority was established by "the word of Jesus" (ὁ λόγος τοῦ Ἰησοῦ) — neither Jerusalem nor Rome serve as the true source of authority over the sacrificial death of the Son.[24] The use of "fulfillment" language makes clear that this is another example of the narrator equating the words of Jesus to Scripture (see comments on 18:9).

The phrase "what kind of death" (ποίῳ θανάτῳ) focuses the fulfillment upon the mode by which Jesus dies: Roman crucifixion — in place of, for example, the traditionally Jewish mode of death by stoning.[25] The depiction here is slightly strange,

---

21. Cf. Keener, *John*, 2:1104–9.

22. See J. Ramsey Michaels, "John 18.31 and the 'Trial' of Jesus," *NTS* 36 (1990): 474–79 (474–75).

23. Michaels, *John*, 917.

24. Cf. Aquinas: "The words … do not indicate the intention the Jews had, but the arrangement of God's providence" (*John*, 3:218).

25. According to Keener, "Although the severest form of execution Pharisaic law acknowledged on the basis of the Hebrew Bible was stoning (*b. Sanh.* 49b–50a), Jewish rulers had used crucifixion before the Roman period. Under Roman rule, however, all official, public executions belonged to the Romans" (*John*, 2:1104).

since not much has been agreed upon by both the Jews and Rome; the narrative is obviously speaking with foresight into the account it is still providing — three times Pilate will tell them, "I find nothing in him that is a basis for a charge" (v. 38; 19:4, 6), before finally agreeing to their demands (19:16). Yet the narrator's commentary already signals what is coming. Jesus *will* be crucified under Pontius Pilate. In a sense this offers the narrator a brief pause so as to comment on the action as it is occurring.[26] The narrator's commentary and its important insight for the reader serve to conclude the second section of the pericope (vv. 29 – 32).

18:33 Then Pilate entered again into the praetorium and summoned Jesus and said to him, "Are you the king of the Jews?" (Εἰσῆλθεν οὖν πάλιν εἰς τὸ πραιτώριον ὁ Πιλᾶτος καὶ ἐφώνησεν τὸν Ἰησοῦν καὶ εἶπεν αὐτῷ, Σὺ εἶ ὁ βασιλεὺς τῶν Ἰουδαίων;). The third section of the pericope (vv. 33 – 38a) takes place inside the praetorium (the back stage; see comments before v. 28) and involves a private discussion between Jesus and Pilate. Since it took place inside the praetorium, the Jews could not enter if they wanted to avoid defilement before the Passover (see v. 28). Just as Jesus had been interrogated in the court of the high priest (see 18:15), now he is to be interrogated in the court of the Roman prefect. Still arrested and probably still bound, Jesus is "summoned" (ἐφώνησεν) by Pilate and brought before him in what is an ironic reversal of the sovereign and the servant.

Pilate begins his interrogation of Jesus with a potent question, "Are you the king of the Jews?" (Σὺ εἶ ὁ βασιλεὺς τῶν Ἰουδαίων;), with the "you" (Σὺ) placed in an emphatic position. This title "king of the Jews" plays a significant role in the ensuing dialogue and has a controlling importance in the

narrative that follows (chs. 18 – 19).[27] Although the Jews never explicitly stated the charge against Jesus (see v. 30), Pilate's question suggests that this is the issue at stake. It is difficult to know if Pilate's question is incredulous and derisive ("*You* are a king?") or straightforward ("Do you consider yourself to be a king?"). The question may openly intend both realities and therefore functions contemptuously not only toward Jesus but also the Jews.

The clear issue confronting both Jerusalem and Rome, however, is the messianic activities and claims of Jesus. While Jesus rarely spoke in such terms, he did refer to the kingdom of God in his dialogue with Nicodemus (see comments on 3:3; cf. 3:5) and did receive the treatment and attention of a king from both his disciples (see 12:1 – 11) as well as the Jerusalem crowd (see 12:12 – 19). Thus to the Jews and to Pilate, Jesus was a kingly claimant in both word and deed.

18:34 Jesus answered, "Do you speak this of your own accord or did others speak to you about me?" (ἀπεκρίθη Ἰησοῦς, Ἀπὸ σεαυτοῦ σὺ τοῦτο λέγεις ἢ ἄλλοι εἶπόν σοι περὶ ἐμοῦ;). Jesus's response to Pilate makes clear that the opening question was disrespectful. By asking his own counterquestion, Jesus offers his own challenge to Pilate's judgment of his identity. Jesus lists two challenging options: Do you speak this "of your own accord" (Ἀπὸ σεαυτοῦ) or did "others speak to you about me" (ἄλλοι εἶπόν σοι περὶ ἐμοῦ)? The latter question links Pilate to the politically charged social dynamics with the Jewish authorities, suggesting that Pilate was manipulated or controlled by the judgment of the Jews. The former, however, challenges Pilate on his own to make the right judgment regarding Jesus. Similar to the Jewish "trial," Jesus again has reversed roles so that the interrogator receives the

---

26. If there is vagueness in the account, it is intentional, for the narrator wants the entire trial to be seen under the explanation of "fulfillment" (Bruner, *John*, 1066).

27. Barrett, *John*, 536; Carson, *John*, 592. Cf. Martinus C. de Boer, "The Narrative Function of Pilate in John," in *Narrativity in Biblical and Related Texts*, 141 – 58 (147 – 48).

interrogation and the accuser becomes the accused (see comments on 18:13).[28] The very foundation of Pilate's rule is being challenged by the probing counterquestion of Jesus.

18:35 Plate answered, "I am not a Jew, am I?" Your nation and high priests handed you over to me. What did you do?" (ἀπεκρίθη ὁ Πιλᾶτος, Μήτι ἐγὼ Ἰουδαῖός εἰμι; τὸ ἔθνος τὸ σὸν καὶ οἱ ἀρχιερεῖς παρέδωκάν σε ἐμοί· τί ἐποίησας;). Pilate quickly and emphatically disassociates himself from the Jews and counters by reversing the suggested connection — *you* are a Jew and *you* are being charged by the Jews! By asking a question that assumes a negative answer, Pilate attempts to place the issue of Jesus's kingship on his ethnicity, his nation, and his religious leaders. As much as Pilate tries to remove himself from the Jewish nation and issues, this "trial" has already shown that the two sides (Jewish and Roman — the represented world) need each other and are collaboratively at work (cf. v. 30).[29] Pilate reveals his involvement when he says that Jesus has now been "handed over" (παρέδωκάν) to him.[30] Pilate even asks a further question that focuses more directly upon Jesus: "What did you do?" (τί ἐποίησας;). This question seeks the crime Jesus committed such that the Jewish authorities found it necessary to hand him over to Pilate.

18:36 Jesus answered, "My kingdom is not from this world. If my kingdom was from this world, my servants would be fighting in order that I might not be handed over to the Jews. But now my kingdom is not from here" (ἀπεκρίθη Ἰησοῦς,

Ἡ βασιλεία ἡ ἐμὴ οὐκ ἔστιν ἐκ τοῦ κόσμου τούτου· εἰ ἐκ τοῦ κόσμου τούτου ἦν ἡ βασιλεία ἡ ἐμή, οἱ ὑπηρέται οἱ ἐμοὶ ἠγωνίζοντο [ἄν], ἵνα μὴ παραδοθῶ τοῖς Ἰουδαίοις· νῦν δὲ ἡ βασιλεία ἡ ἐμὴ οὐκ ἔστιν ἐντεῦθεν). Pilate may be able to disassociate himself (at least in principle) from the Jews and Judaism, but Jesus offers a response that disassociates him from this world. Jesus declares emphatically, "My kingdom is not from this world" (Ἡ βασιλεία ἡ ἐμὴ οὐκ ἔστιν ἐκ τοῦ κόσμου τούτου). This phrase has been interpreted in three ways:[31] (1) the spiritualistic (spatial) interpretation, which interprets Jesus's kingdom as internal, spiritual, and private and not material; (2) the future-eschatological (temporal) interpretation, which interprets Jesus's kingdom as something that will exist in the world to come, not in this transitory world; and (3) the ethical-religious (political) interpretation, which interprets Jesus's kingdom in the functional sense of "dominion" or "kingship."

The third option is the most viable, for the first two options force too much separation between Jesus's kingdom and its relationship to the world. The prepositional phrase "from this world" (ἐκ τοῦ κόσμου τούτου) primarily depicts the *source* of Jesus's kingdom, not its *space* (territory). Jesus's kingdom is not grounded in this world or established by means of this world. This kingdom has an authority "from above," above and beyond the authority of Jerusalem and Rome. It is a difference in the kind of kingdom and not the degree of kingdom, which stands in sharp contrast to the trifling kingdom challenge between Jerusalem and Rome.

---

28. Cf. Lincoln, *John*, 461. See also Bart D. Ehrman, "Jesus's Trial before Pilate: John 18:28 – 19:16," *BTB* 13 (1983): 124 – 31 (128).

29. See Christopher M. Tuckett, "Pilate in John 18 – 19: A Narrative Critical Approach," in *Narrativity in Biblical and Related Texts*, 131 – 40 (135).

30. The term "handed over" in the Gospel has become a term of betrayal involving both Judas (see 6:71; 12:4; 13:2, 11, 21; 18:2, 5) and the Jews (see 6:64). Cf. Ernst Bammel, "The

Trial before Pilate," in *Jesus and the Politics of His Day*, ed. Ernst Bammel and C. F. D. Moule (Cambridge: Cambridge University Press, 1984), 415 – 51 (415 – 16).

31. The following is adapted from Reimund Bieringer, " 'My Kingship Is Not of This World' (John 18,36): The Kingship of Jesus and Politics," in *The Myriad Christ: Plurality and the Quest for Unity in Contemporary Christology*, ed. T. Merrigan and J. Haers; BETL 152 (Leuven: Leuven University Press, 2000), 159 – 75 (161 – 65).

In short, "the world" and all its kingdoms are a subset of Jesus's kingdom.

It is common for scholars to interpret the term "kingdom" (βασιλεία) as "kingship" to emphasize that Jesus's rule is not defined by a *place* but by a *power*—the sovereign reign of God.[32] There is no need to make a sharp distinction between the two, however, as if the "kingship" of Jesus did not also involve and include a "kingdom." The use of the term "kingdom of God" in 3:3, for example, also demands that both senses (rule and territory) are likely in view (see comments on 3:3). The prologue is helpful here, for only by understanding the two-stranded plot of the Gospel (i.e., the historical and the cosmological) can the true nature of Jesus's kingdom and kingship be grasped. Jesus's kingdom may not find its source "from" this world, but its power and authority are clearly at work *in* this world.[33] That is, we must be careful to note what Jesus does *not* say: "He does not say that this world is not the sphere of his authority, but that his authority is not of human origin."[34] And Jesus does make a territorial claim in this Gospel when he refers to himself as the one who comes "from above," which he connects directly to the kingdom of God (3:3). For this reason we will use the translation "kingdom," not with the intention to deny Jesus his "kingship" or to posit "realm" over against "reign" but to suggest that the reign of Jesus is not elsewhere but everywhere — even when he is bound and arrested and standing trial in the ruling courts of both the Jews and the Romans in Jerusalem. As if the Creator does not have a territorial claim over his creation? The kingdom and kingship

of Christ have an *in-but-not-of* relationship to the world (participation without accommodation) that is similar to how the disciples' identity in Christ makes them participants *in* but not *of* the world (see comments on 17:14 – 16).

Jesus offers evidence that his kingdom is different in kind. If his kingdom was established by this world, "my servants would be fighting" (οἱ ὑπηρέται οἱ ἐμοὶ ἠγωνίζοντο [ἄν]) against the other kingdoms. The word "servants" (ὑπηρέται) is identical to the term used earlier to depict the "assistants" of the Jewish authorities who arrested Jesus (see 18:3). The fact that Jesus's servants have not been called upon suggests that Jesus's kingdom is so beyond the powers of this world that nothing is happening that is beyond his sovereign control. In a sense, the powers of this world (the Jewish and Roman authorities) have been functioning all along as Jesus's "servants," subordinates doing his will for his purposes.[35] And at this point his newly appointed "servants" to the world, the disciples (see 17:18), still need him to serve them.

18:37 Then Pilate said to him, "So you are a king!" Jesus answered, "You say that I am a king. For this reason I was born and for this reason I came into the world, in order that I might testify to the truth. Everyone who hears my voice is from the truth" (εἶπεν οὖν αὐτῷ ὁ Πιλᾶτος, Οὐκοῦν βασιλεὺς εἶ σύ; ἀπεκρίθη ὁ Ἰησοῦς, Σὺ λέγεις ὅτι βασιλεύς εἰμι. ἐγὼ εἰς τοῦτο γεγέννημαι καὶ εἰς τοῦτο ἐλήλυθα εἰς τὸν κόσμον, ἵνα μαρτυρήσω τῇ ἀληθείᾳ· πᾶς ὁ ὢν ἐκ τῆς ἀληθείας ἀκούει μου τῆς φωνῆς). Pilate responds with a question that functions like an emphatic statement, denoted by the

32. See Beasey-Murray, *John*, 330. Cf. Michaels, *John*, 922.
33. Schnackenburg, *John*, 3:249.
34. Hoskyns, *Fourth Gospel*, 520. Cf. Bultmann, *John*, 654.
35. For a helpful discussion (and warning) of the political issues involving this verse, see Ridderbos, *John*, 594 – 95. For example, according to Martin Hengel, "Reich Christi, Reich Gottes und Weltreich im Johannesevangelium," in *König-sherrschaft und in der hellenistischen Welt*, ed. Martin Hengel and Anna Maria Schwemer; WUNT 55 (Tübingen: Mohr Siebeck, 1991), 163 – 84 (182): "The Gospel of John is the end of all political theology" ("*Das Johannesevangelium bedeutet das Ende aller politischen Theologie*"). For others, like Calvin, this is simply the start of a very different kind of "politics" (*John 11 – 21*, 166 – 67).

term translated as "so" (Οὐκοῦν).[36] This explains how Jesus can interpret Pilate's words as some sort of witness to his identity. Jesus's response "*you* say that I am a king" (Σὺ λέγεις ὅτι βασιλεύς εἰμι) could be interpreted as either an affirmation or denial of Pilate's inference. The emphatic "you" is intended to be contrasted with the emphatic "I" (ἐγὼ) that begins the next clause, so that Jesus can describe the real reason for his presence in the world. That is, Jesus neither affirms nor denies Pilate's statement simply because the nature of his work, his mission, and his kingship is so other and of such a different order from the categories of Pilate and "this world" that he can only denote the contrast.

Jesus offers an important response to the "king" inference of Pilate. Since this world's category of "king" is too small to contain the fullness of King Jesus, he describes his kingship (and the nature of his rule) by explaining his mission's purpose (truth telling) and result (truth hearing). Jesus offers here a significant summary of the goal of his ministry to the world, and his explanation uses language that echoes the message of the prologue, for he speaks as if he had not always been "in" the world. Almost certainly Pilate did not grasp what Jesus was saying, but the reader is able to make sense of this explanation by means of the cumulative message of the Gospel. Two aspects briefly need to be explained.

First, Jesus explains the purpose of his mission: "In order that I might testify to the truth" (ἵνα μαρτυρήσω τῇ ἀληθείᾳ). The otherworldliness of his "coming" is contrasted by the language of his birth — in the "flesh" (1:14). The personal nature of Jesus's arrival and presence in the world must set the context for the nature of his work of truth telling. That is, the truth about which Jesus witnesses is overtly personal. His purpose was to speak truth or, better, to make manifest what is true. The personal nature of this truth is important here, for Jesus is "the truth," which means that he is the *reality* through which participation in God and even (human) existence is confirmed and finds its meaning (see comments on 14:6). This explains why Jesus alone must define his kingship, for he is the king of truth, and his testimony to the truth is the enactment of his sovereign reign.[37]

Second, Jesus gives the results of his mission: "Everyone who hears my voice is from the truth" (πᾶς ὁ ὢν ἐκ τῆς ἀληθείας ἀκούει μου τῆς φωνῆς). The result of his mission is the creation of those who can hear his voice, that is, those who respond to the truth. This explains why Jesus's "servants" (ὑπηρέται) are not "fighting" his arrest (v. 36), for the battle is more cosmic than human kingdoms; the battle is between falsehood and the truth, between darkness and the light (1:5). For the real fight is not merely external, the "flesh and blood," but the "powers of this dark world" that enslave — a personal power that rules over people (Eph 6:12). For this reason Jesus, the king of truth, was born and came, so that those who come to know the truth can be set free from the enslavement of sin (see comments on 8:32) and that freedom may be given to the true "sons and daughters" in the "house" of God (8:35–36). Jesus refers here to those who "hear" and know the voice of the Good Shepherd, whose reign is displayed by a self-sacrifice that provides the "sheep" with life "in abundance" (see comments on 10:10–11). With this concluding statement Jesus puts the judge on trial in regard to the truth or, more graciously, invites him to participate in it.[38]

18:38a Pilate said to him, "What is truth?" (λέγει αὐτῷ ὁ Πιλᾶτος, Τί ἐστιν ἀλήθεια;). The brief response of Pilate in the form of a question is almost

---

36. BDAG 736.

37. Hoskyns, *Fourth Gospel*, 520–21.

38. Cf. Lincoln, *John*, 463; Culpepper, *Anatomy of the Fourth Gospel*, 143.

certainly a rebuking rejoinder to Jesus; it is a potentially violent and abrupt statement that concludes the interrogation.[39] It is difficult to know the exact intention of Pilate, and in this situation it is almost unnecessary, for in this interrogation the meanings of Pilate's statements have been explained by being contrasted to Jesus and his statements. Pilate's question is itself his answer to the issue surrounding the person and work of Jesus. But Pilate asks the wrong question, for truth is not a "what" (Τί) but a "who" — the *person* of Jesus Christ.[40] Pilate addressed this question to the very one who was the answer. By concluding the interrogation in this abrupt manner, the narrator wants the question to do more than offer insight into the person of Pilate; it is intended to echo in the mind of the readers. In this way the third section of the pericope (vv. 33 – 38a) comes to a conclusion.

18:38b And after he said this, he went out again to the Jews and said to them, "I find nothing in him that is a basis for a charge" (Καὶ τοῦτο εἰπὼν πάλιν ἐξῆλθεν πρὸς τοὺς Ἰουδαίους, καὶ λέγει αὐτοῖς, Ἐγὼ οὐδεμίαν εὑρίσκω ἐν αὐτῷ αἰτίαν). The fourth and final section of the pericope (vv. 38b – 40) takes place outside the praetorium (the front stage; see comments before v. 28) and involves a final interaction between Pilate and "the Jews," a designation which suggests that alongside the Jewish authorities a larger crowd may have also assembled. Almost as if there was no need to record the response of Jesus to Pilate's concluding question, the narrator keeps the focus on Pilate and describes him leaving the back stage with Jesus and moving "out again" to where the Jews had earlier assembled. After the first interaction between Jerusalem and Rome regarding Jesus (vv. 29 – 32), the

assumption is that the negotiations and political gerrymandering would continue.

In what appears to be a more formal announcement, suggesting he was addressing a crowd, Pilate declares that he finds no "basis for a charge" (αἰτίαν), that is, no "basis for legal action."[41] From Pilate's perspective, there was nothing Jesus claimed about himself that warranted legal or disciplinary action according to Roman law. The serious "truth" question behind Pilate's concluding statement to Jesus may suggest that he heard Jesus say nothing that would contradict the truth that he knows or the truth that Rome oversees. It is fitting that neither Jerusalem nor Rome can fully claim to oversee the truth of Jesus (cf. v. 31).

18:39 "But it is a custom for you to release one person to you on the Passover. Do you want me to release to you, then, the king of the Jews?" (ἔστιν δὲ συνήθεια ὑμῖν ἵνα ἕνα ἀπολύσω ὑμῖν ἐν τῷ πάσχα· βούλεσθε οὖν ἀπολύσω ὑμῖν τὸν βασιλέα τῶν Ἰουδαίων;). Since the Jews had no problem responding quickly to Pilate's statements in their first interaction, it is likely that immediately after declaring Jesus innocent that Pilate offered a possible solution. Although we can only estimate, by connecting his decision regarding Jesus to Jewish customs, it appears that in the opinion of Pilate Jesus was only a legal problem for his own people, the Jews. For this reason then he decides to use one of their own rules, a Passover "custom" (συνήθεια), to handle Jesus so that he is ultimately judged (or released) by Jewish legal practices.

While there is no evidence for this "Passover amnesty custom" outside of the four Gospels, there is also no warrant for rejecting it.[42] The "custom" may not have been an annually practiced custom,

---

39. Cf. Andreas J. Köstenberger, "'What is Truth?' Pilate's Question in Its Johannine and Larger Biblical Context," *JETS* 48 (2005): 33 – 62 (60).

40. Cf. Haenchen, *John*, 2:180.

41. BDAG 31.

42. Cf. Brown, *Death of the Messiah*, 1793 – 95; Keener, *John*, 2:1115 – 17.

but possibly was a legal allowance for which there was already a precedent. Certainly the Jews do not challenge the existence of their own "custom" or appear unfamiliar with it. Rather, they not only understand Pilate's suggestion but without any intramural discussion offer an apparently unanimous answer in reply (v. 40). If the Passover custom was not intended to publicly mock the Jews, it is almost certain that it was the intention behind Pilate's title for Jesus, "the king of the Jews" (τὸν βασιλέα τῶν Ἰουδαίων). By forcing the Jews to respond positively to his offer, Pilate implicitly forces them to acknowledge the title — something the Jews clearly do not want ascribed to Jesus.[43]

18:40 Then they shouted again saying, "Not this man but Barabbas." And Barabbas was a robber (ἐκραύγασαν οὖν πάλιν λέγοντες, Μὴ τοῦτον ἀλλὰ τὸν Βαραββᾶν. ἦν δὲ ὁ Βαραββᾶς λῃστής). The strategy of Pilate forced the Jews to be confronted with Jesus as "their king" befittingly at the Passover which commemorated the deliverance of the Jews from the wrong "king" — the Pharaoh of Egypt.[44] Ironically, the very king that had freed them from the wrong ruler in Egypt — God himself — was here being personally rejected by them; they would soon declare a foreign ruler to be their king — the Caesar of Rome (see 19:15). The careful reader should take care to note that this is no throwaway verse. The description of the actions of the Jews, and even more the name and identity of Barabbas, are extremely important to the narrative, serving as a climactic ending to the pericope.

The narrator explains the response to Pilate's offer to release Jesus with careful detail. Their answer was a resounding no to "this man" (τοῦτον) — they will not even speak his name. In his place they

choose a specific person they call by name: Barabbas. Little is known about "Barabbas" (Βαραββᾶς), who is only known from the Gospels.[45] The title given to him, "robber" (λῃστής), suggests that he was one of those violent, lawless men, often bandits, whom Josephus describes in Palestine in the first century (e.g., *J.W.* 2.13.2 – 3; 2.17.9).[46] The title is significant, however, which we will explain below.

The fact that the narrator provides his name is significant. The Gospel has clearly used both anonymity (e.g., mother of Jesus, lame man, blind man, and "Beloved Disciple") and specific names (e.g., Nicodemus) with narrative intentionality. Barabbas is likely another example of the latter. "Barabbas" is a patronymic, that is, a father's name used to make a distinction between men who bear the same personal (first) names. For example, when two men have the same personal name in one village, they would often be designated by means of their father. "Not infrequently only the patronymic is used in a description,"[47] even though it was more common for a personal name to be combined with a patronymic: Simon Barjona (Matt 16:17); Joseph Barnabas (Acts 4:36); John and James, sons of Zebedee (Mark 1:19). Thus, the name Barabbas means "Bar-Abba," that is, "son of [a person named] Abba" or "son of the father." Since the author was well aware of the meaning of the name Barabbas, by stating it twice and calling Jesus simply "this man," the narrator implicitly directs the reader to a potent realization: the Jews have exchanged the Son of the Father for a son of a father.

The pericope concludes with a description of this other "son of the father," Barabbas, describing him as a "robber" (λῃστής). The title is of only

43. Carson, *John*, 595.
44. Ridderbos, *John*, 598.
45. See Helen K. Bond, "Barabbas Remembered," in *Jesus and Paul: Global Perspectives in Honor of James D. G. Dunn*, ed.

B. J. Oropeza, C. K. Robertson, and Douglas C. Mohrmann; LNTS 414 (London: T&T Clark, 2009), 59 – 71.
46. Cf. Brown, *Death of the Messiah*, 1:686 – 88.
47. Brown, *Death of the Messiah*, 1:798.

general significance outside of John, as discussed above, but its use earlier in the Gospel magnifies its meaning here. This is one of the key titles contrasted with the Good Shepherd (10:1, 8). In contrast to the Good Shepherd, Jesus described the way of the thief and "robber" (λῃστής), who "does not come except to steal and kill and destroy" (10:10).

The antithesis is Jesus, who comes to give life — by laying down "his life for the sheep" (10:11). In the larger context of the Gospel, the contrast is sharp. The reader is aware that the Jews have chosen the exact opposite of what they really need — they have chosen the "robber" instead of the "Good Shepherd" and the wrong "Son of the Father."

Theology in Application

This pericope guides the reader to see more clearly how the impending death of Jesus is the sacrifice of God for the world. Like the previous pericopae (18:1 – 12; 18:13 – 27), even while being arrested, bound, and questioned Jesus is in complete control, dictating the terms and guiding his own interrogation. The reader is exhorted to see Jesus as the true King and the answer to Pilate's question, "What is truth?" Through this pericope the reader is coming to understand the true meaning of Passover and how Jesus fulfills the roles of both the King of kings and the Lamb of God.

The Passover Lamb and the Lord's Supper

The Passover context of this pericope serves as the backdrop against which it must be read and interpreted. The great concern with which the Jews showed to avoid defilement by not entering the praetorium — the very place they sent Jesus — creates by means of irony a clear portrait of the theological significance of the Feast. The cumulative effect of the Gospel has been to depict the person and work of Jesus by means of the Passover — Jesus *is* the Lamb of God, *the* sacrificial Passover Lamb. This is why the date of the crucifixion is so important to John and why Jesus's death is described as occurring at the same time the other lambs were being slaughtered in preparation for Passover (see 19:14). The meaning of Passover was forever changed as the sun arose in the early morning of that day "when the great God through his slaughtered Son will [make] the final and all-fulfilling Passover sacrifice for the sin of the whole world."[48]

For this reason the church honors the fulfillment of the Passover meal by replacing it with the Lord's Supper, which has traditionally and simply been called "Thanksgiving" (the Eucharist). It is the meal of the new covenant that declares the gospel, the redemptive sacrifice of the Son of God. At this "supper" no lamb is needed, and the symbolic elements are now limited to two, for the prepared lamb is the flesh of Christ (1:14), and the symbolic elements include the bread and the cup

---

48. Bruner, *John*, 1064.

representing his body and his blood. The Lord's Supper therefore is the Feast of the second exodus, commemorating the defeat of sin, death, and the "Pharaoh" (ruler) of this world (12:31).

The Trial of the King

If the previous pericope (18:13 – 27) used irony to depict the Jewish "trial" of Jesus as the trial of Judaism, the Roman "trial" of Jesus depicts the trial of both the Romans and the Jews; it is the trial of "the world." In this scene the narrative carefully reveals how the authority of the world was no match for the authority of King Jesus. No accusation could be brought against Jesus (v. 29), nor did either Jerusalem or Rome have the legal right to judge him (v. 31). This was no accident, for the entire interrogation and trial served the greater (cosmological) purpose of declaring Jesus innocent and the world — both Jew and gentile — guilty. Yet as the narrator revealed in v. 32, all of this "fulfilled" the purposes of God. That is, the reality of the love of God was most clearly expressed in this hate-filled scene, for Jesus was arrested and bound not by the powers of Jerusalem and Rome but by his own kingly power and authority. He gave the world permission to bind him and ultimately to crucify him so that they — again both Jews and gentiles — could be released from their bondage of sin and death. While the world was busy hating the Son of God, God in the person of Jesus was fully expressing his love for the world (3:16).

"What is Truth?"

Pilate's rebuking question to Jesus guides the reader to one of the primary messages of the Gospel: Jesus *is* truth. Pilate actually words the question incorrectly, for truth is not a "what" but a "who," the *person* of Jesus Christ. Ironically, Pilate addressed this question to the very person who *was* the answer. Jesus is "the truth" in that he is the *reality* through which Christian existence and participation in God are confirmed and find their meaning (cf. 14:6). Jesus is the embodiment of the supreme revelation of God and the standard for what is real in this world and true about God, for he is the one who reveals God and is the authority regarding the meaning and purpose of God (1:18). Jesus, the Son of God, says and does exclusively what the Father has given him to say and to do (5:19; 8:29). He is the perfect expression of God (1:14). For this reason Jesus is the plumb line for all things — seen and unseen, the lens through which the world is interpreted and by which it must be judged. He is the gracious extension of light (actuality) into a world confined by darkness (distortion). It is because Jesus is *the* truth that his mission to the world was called the "good news" by the church, for it was recognized as the foundational account of all truth, even life itself.

The Great Substitution

The powerful conclusion to this pericope involves the long-standing custom of the Jews (v. 39) to release one prisoner, a person already convicted and declared guilty — and sentenced to death. The custom of release probably intended to display "in the flesh" the redemptive power of the ancient exodus event. Little did either Pilate or the Jews know that God himself had a long-standing custom he was about to start on that very day involving the release of all prisoners already convicted and declared guilty — and sentenced to death — in order to display "in his flesh" the redemptive power of his love for the world. Although the Jews thought they were deciding between a "son of man" (Barabbas) and *the* "Son of Man," it was really God who was initiating his eternal "custom" with the world, the new covenant. The lamb, the blood-covered wood, the firstborn son, the slavery — these things are intended to "impress" upon the reader how God "passed over" us and applied his wrath upon his own Son, who was the lamb, the source of blood on the wooden cross, and the King-become-slave. Jesus is the great substitute, whose person and work has become for us the atoning work of God. He is the Son of Man exchanged for the sons of men. O church, we were Barabbas, sons of mankind, but now we are the children of God (1:12) and true sons of the Father.

John 19:1 – 16

Literary Context

This pericope continues to depict the events surrounding the sacrificial death of the Son of God. Jesus has already been arrested and interrogated by the Jewish and Roman authorities. In this pericope both Pilate and the Jewish authorities (i.e., "the world") finalize their collaboration and announce the verdict regarding the person and work of Jesus. Themes that began earlier in this section of the Gospel continue in this pericope, especially those related to the tension between Jerusalem and Rome, the Passover sacrifice, the reluctance of Pilate, and the issue of Jesus's kingship. The narrative continues to contrast Christ with the significant characters in the narrative primarily by means of irony. The reader is guided to see even more clearly how the authority of Jesus is "from above" and to interpret the conclusion of the trial proceedings before Jerusalem and Rome in light of his kingship, including the verdict that announces his crucifixion.

VIII. The Crucifixion (18:1 – 19:42)
    A. The Arrest of Jesus (18:1 – 12)
    B. The Jewish Trial and Its Witnesses (18:13 – 27)
    C. The Roman Trial before Pilate (18:28 – 40)
→   **D. The Verdict: "Crucify Him!" (19:1 – 16)**
    E. The Crucifixion of Jesus (19:17 – 27)
    F. The Death and Burial of Jesus (19:28 – 42)

Main Idea

Jesus took on humanity's condition of death (the second Adam) and became the sacrifice for humanity's sins (the Passover Lamb). For this reason God made him the King of kings so that one day all people will kneel and confess that Jesus is Lord.

Translation

John 19:1–16

1a	Rapid Sequence of Action	Then **Pilate took Jesus**
b		and **flogged him.**
2a	Satirical Parody (2–3)	And **the soldiers wove a crown of thorns**
b	Sequence of events (2a–3d)	and **placed it on his head,**
c		and **they clothed him in a purple robe.**
3a		Then **they went up to him and said,**
b	Mocking Praise	*"Hail,*
c	Mocking, Ironic Title	*king of the Jews,"*
d		and **they gave him slaps in the face.**
4a	Progression of Action	Then **Pilate again came outside**
b		and **said to them,**
c	Exclamation	*"Behold,*
d	Announcement	*I am bringing him outside to you*
e	Intended Result	*so that you may know*
f	Content: Innocence	*that I find nothing in him that is a basis for a charge."*
5a	Progression of Action	Then **Jesus came outside**
b	Manner	wearing the crown of thorns and
c		the purple robe.
d		And **Pilate said to them,**
e	Emphasis	*"Behold,*
f	Presentation/Title	*the man!"*
6a	Circumstance	When the high priests and servants saw him
b	Result	**they cried out,**
c	Demand: Judgment	*"Crucify,*
d	Emphasis	*crucify!"*
e	Response	**Pilate said to them,**
f	Rejection of Request	*"You take him*
g		*and crucify him yourselves.*
h	Basis	*For I myself do not find in him a basis for a charge."*
7a	Response	**The Jews responded to him,**
b	Basis of e	*"We have a law,*
c		*and*
d	Standard: "Law"	*according to the law*
e	Judgment	*he is required to die,*
f	Basis (Indictment)	*because he made himself out to be*
g	Ironic Contrast to 5f	*the Son of God."*
8a		When Pilate heard this statement,
b	Reaction	**he was very afraid.**
9a	Progression of Action	And **he entered into the praetorium again**
b		and **said to Jesus,**
c	Question	*"Where are you from?"*
d	Silent Rebuke	But **Jesus did not give him an answer.**

Continued on next page.

Continued from previous page.

10a	Response	So **Pilate said to him,**
b	Interrogative Counterrebuke	*"You do not speak to me?*
c		*Do you not know*
d	Ironic "Authority"	*that I have authority to release you and*
e	Ironic "Authority"	*I have the authority to crucify you?"*
11a	Response	**Jesus responded to him,**
b	Rebuke	*"You have no authority over me*
c	Exception	*except that which was given to you*
d	Source	*from above.*
e	Basis (11a–d) of f, g	↓ *For this reason*
f	Description/Condition	*the one who handed me over to you …* ↓
g	Result/Indictment	*… has the greater sin."*
12a	Narrator's Aside	*From then on*
b	Character's Thoughts	**Pilate wanted to release him,**
c	Contrast	but **the Jews were shouting,**
d	Condition	*"If you release this man,*
e	Inferential Judgment	*you are not a friend of Caesar.*
f	Description/Condition	*Anyone who makes himself out to be a king …*
g	Result/Inference	*… opposes Caesar."*
13a		*After Pilate heard these words,*
b	Reaction	**he brought out Jesus**
c		and **sat upon the judgment seat,**
d		*in the place*
e	Identification	*called the Stone Pavement, but*
f	Translation	*in Aramaic,*
g		*Gabbatha.*
14a	Context	Now **it was the day of preparation for the Passover;**
b	Time	**it was about the sixth hour.**
c	Progression of Action	And **he said to the Jews,**
d	Emphasis	*"Behold,*
e	Presentation/Title	*your King!"*
15a	Reaction	Then **they shouted,**
b	Demand	*"Away with him!*
c	Emphasis	*Away with him!*
d	Demand	*Crucify him!"*
e	Response	**Pilate said to them,**
f	Question	*"Shall I crucify your king?"*
g	Response	**The high priests answered,**
h	Answer	*"We have no king but Caesar."*
16a	Reaction	So **then he handed him over to them**
b	Purpose	*in order that he might be crucified.*
c	Reaction	Then **they received Jesus.**

Structure and Literary Form

The structure of this pericope is different than the basic story form (see Introduction). The structure is guided by the trial motif that defines the pericopae leading up to the crucifixion: the Jewish trial (18:13 – 27), the Roman trial (18:28 – 40), and the verdict (19:1 – 16). This pericope's narrative structure continues the geographic back-and-forth movement of the previous pericope (inside-outside-inside-outside). With a kind of dramatic technique, the narrator "employs the device of two stages upon which the action is exhibited, a front and back stage," with the reader receiving access into the events of both stages (see comments before 18:28).[1] The "trial" before Pilate (Rome) has been completed except for the announcement of the verdict. Before the verdict is declared under the authority of Pilate, Jesus is taken inside and given a preliminary punishment that bears the markings of the trial's ironic point of contention concerning Jesus's kingship (vv. 1 – 3); the scene then moves to the outside where Pilate presents Jesus to the Jewish authorities and the public (vv. 4 – 7); the scene again moves inside where Pilate questions Jesus one more time regarding his identity (vv. 8 – 11); finally the scene moves outside where the verdict regarding Jesus is finalized by Pilate and the Jewish authorities (vv. 12–16).

Exegetical Outline

➡ **D. The Verdict: "Crucify Him!" (19:1 – 16)**
   1. Treatment for a King (vv. 1 – 3)
   2. "Behold, the Man!" (vv. 4 – 7)
   3. Authority "from Above" (vv. 8 – 11)
   4. The Judgment Seat (vv. 12 – 16)

Explanation of the Text

19:1 Then Pilate took Jesus and flogged him (Τότε οὖν ἔλαβεν ὁ Πιλᾶτος τὸν Ἰησοῦν καὶ ἐμαστίγωσεν). The first section of the pericope (vv. 1 – 3) continues the outside-inside movement that began in the previous pericope (18:28 – 40). After the public negotiation concerning Jesus (18:38b – 40), Pilate has Jesus taken inside and has him punished, probably inside the praetorium. Although the verbs imply that Pilate was the subject, certainly his soldiers performed the actual task. In this way, however, the narrator explicitly links Pilate to the treatment and condemnation of Jesus, in spite of Pilate's own attempt to remove himself from the conviction of Jesus (vv. 4, 6; cf. 18:38). Some attempt to interpret the intentions of Pilate here (probably via Luke 23:16, 21) and suggest that he is trying to meet the Jews' demand that Jesus be punished.[2] Keener notes that the flogging "is not at all incompatible

---

1. Dodd, *Historical Tradition*, 96.

2. See Beasley-Murray, *John*, 334; Carson, *John*, 596. Cf. Morris, *John*, 699.

with Pilate's belief that Jesus was innocent"; other Roman officials were known for brutally flogging innocent men simply because they disrupted public order (see Josephus, *J. W.* 6.304).[3] At this point, however, the reader can only note the direct connection the narrator is careful to make between Pilate and the flogging of Jesus.

The term "flogged" (ἐμαστίγωσεν) is the normal term for punishment by "whipping" or "scourging."[4] It was a common form of punishment that was used in both Jewish and Roman legal systems. Although the narrator does not explain the details of the flogging, the first-century reader would have certainly been familiar with the general procedure. The actually flogging would have been extremely violent.[5] It is likely that Jesus was stripped, tied to a post or thrown to the ground, and beaten with *flagella* — leather whips to which were attached pieces of iron, bone, or spikes, which would shred the skin, often leaving it hanging from the victim's back in strips. Unlike the thirty-nine maximum lashes prescribed by Jewish law (Deut 25:3), the Romans did not limit the number of lashes, thus leaving the victim helpless to the cruelty of the supervising soldiers. The flogging would have been a public event, which added shame and familial humiliation to the physical pain. Even before the announcement of the verdict, the punishment of Jesus has been officially initiated.

19:2 And the soldiers wove a crown of thorns and placed it on his head, and they clothed him in a purple robe (καὶ οἱ στρατιῶται πλέξαντες στέφανον ἐξ ἀκανθῶν ἐπέθηκαν αὐτοῦ τῇ κεφαλῇ, καὶ ἱμάτιον πορφυροῦν περιέβαλον αὐτόν). Although the narrator spends little time on the physi-

cal suffering of Jesus, the shame applied to him is described in detail. It is not enough to abuse his body; the Roman "soldiers" (οἱ στρατιῶται) abuse his reputation also by enacting the title "king of the Jews" given to him in the politically charged interactions between Pilate and the Jews and use it to make a mockery of him (see 18:39). By now the assumed accusation against Jesus is that he claimed to be king, a political threat to the Romans and more of a religious threat to the Jews (see v. 7). The kingly authority of Jesus becomes a primary theme of this pericope.

After stripping him for the flogging, the soldiers decide to cover his shameful nakedness by dressing him as a king so as to add even further shame. The kingly garb is intended as a caricature, not as a further instrument of torture, even though it would have been also been painful.[6] The scene depicted by vv. 2 – 3 is a theatricalized parody and satirical imitation of the royal coronation of a king, with the crown and royal-colored robe serving as the marks of investiture.[7] The term "crown" (στέφανον) is normally used to denote a wreath of victory rather than a "royal crown" (διάδημα).[8] In this context both senses are implied. In this way they "honor" him as a victorious king so as to highlight what in their minds is clearly the opposite of this man before them, who is a defeated and dying criminal.

19:3 Then they went up to him and said, "Hail, king of the Jews," and they gave him slaps in the face (καὶ ἤρχοντο πρὸς αὐτὸν καὶ ἔλεγον, Χαῖρε, ὁ βασιλεὺς τῶν Ἰουδαίων· καὶ ἐδίδοσαν αὐτῷ ῥαπίσματα). The theatrical parody of the soldiers comes to a climax when they come toward him, almost certainly one at a time, offering him mock

---

3. Keener, *John*, 2:1118.

4. Barrett, *John*, 539.

5. The following is adapted from Keener, *John*, 2:1118 – 19, and Brown, *Death of the Messiah*, 1:851 – 53. Cf. Paul W. Walaskay, "The Trial and Death of Jesus in the Gospel of Luke," *JBL* 94 (1975): 91 – 93 (90).

6. Beasley-Murray, *John*, 336.

7. Heil, *Blood and Water*, 61.

8. BDAG 943 – 45.

homage as king, likely by kneeling before him, after which they would strike him in the face. Their statement of adoration, "Hail, king of the Jews" (Χαῖρε, ὁ βασιλεὺς τῶν Ἰουδαίων), emulates the kind of worship given to Caesar, before whom worshippers would kneel and cry, "Hail, Caesar!" But rather than offering him a kiss of loyalty, they struck him in the face, either with their hands or with rods (cf. Matt 27:30). Almost certainly proud of their theatrical wit, the soldiers make Jesus a plaything, treating him as if he were a clown-king. But these anonymous soldiers were unaware that one day they would perform this very act, kneeling before him and confessing with their tongues that he is Lord (Phil 2:10 – 11).

19:4 Then Pilate again came outside and said to them, "Behold, I am bringing him outside to you so that you may know that I find nothing in him that is a basis for a charge" (Καὶ ἐξῆλθεν πάλιν ἔξω ὁ Πιλᾶτος καὶ λέγει αὐτοῖς, Ἴδε ἄγω ὑμῖν αὐτὸν ἔξω, ἵνα γνῶτε ὅτι οὐδεμίαν αἰτίαν εὑρίσκω ἐν αὐτῷ). The second section of the pericope (vv. 4 – 7) begins as Pilate moves outside again and addresses the crowd. Pilate announces that he is also about to have Jesus brought outside to him and before the crowd, to which he adds again the qualification he made earlier that he finds no "basis for a charge" (αἰτίαν) in him, that is, no legitimate basis for legal action (see comments on 18:38). Pilate prefaces his announcement with the particle of exclamation, "Behold" (Ἴδε), which is used in Greek to draw attention to what follows. When used before a verb it serves as a "prompter of attention," setting the tone regarding the importance to be placed on the person being introduced (see comments on 1:29).[9] This preparatory introduction of Jesus with the explanation of presumed innocence makes sense if Pilate is trying to remove himself from the verdict of Jesus. At the same time it serves as a potent "prompter of attention" to Pilate's significant description of Jesus to follow.

19:5 Then Jesus came outside wearing the crown of thorns and the purple robe. And Pilate said to them, "Behold, the man!" (ἐξῆλθεν οὖν ὁ Ἰησοῦς ἔξω, φορῶν τὸν ἀκάνθινον στέφανον καὶ τὸ πορφυροῦν ἱμάτιον. καὶ λέγει αὐτοῖς, Ἰδοὺ ὁ ἄνθρωπος). Probably at the command of Pilate, Jesus comes out dressed in what the soldiers had intended to be a kingly costume, barely covering what was certainly a beaten and bloodied body that had just received a flogging. Although the narrative is silent on the physical details, one can imagine that to the crowd "he had no beauty or majesty to attract us to him," but appeared to them as "a man of suffering, and familiar with pain" and "like one from whom people hide their faces" (Isa 53:2 – 3). The focus on the narrative is on his kingly attire, setting the context (even if unintentionally) for the title Pilate was about to use regarding him.

Pilate introduces Jesus to the crowd with the exclamation, "Behold, the man!" (Ἰδοὺ ὁ ἄνθρωπος). Although the particle of exclamation, "Behold" (Ἰδοὺ), serves as a "prompter of attention" before a verb, when it is used before a noun, as in this case, it serves as a "marker of strong emphasis."[10] The Fourth Gospel uses it in the latter sense when there is a challenge to perceive with the mind a truth not outwardly evident to human eyes, as when the Baptist declared, "Behold, the Lamb of God" (1:29; cf. v. 14). For Pilate the "king of the Jews" is nothing more than "a pathetic and harmless figure" — nothing at all like a king.[11] But to the reader the exact opposite is the truth. In fact, just as the reader has been taught to see in Jesus more than the historical

---

9. BDAG 468.
10. BDAG 468.

11. de Boer, "The Narrative Function of Pilate in John," 153.

persons around him were able to see, so also must we see in this title of introduction something even more profound in the context of the Gospel.

The narrative's focus on this title, denoted by its preparatory introduction and its application in this significant moment before the announcement of the verdict, strongly suggests that the narrator intends to make a statement of his own by means of Pilate's words in a manner similar to how the narrator used the words of Caiaphas as his own commentary (see 11:49 – 52). The exact meaning of the title, however, is difficult to determine. There are two types of options that have commonly been offered.[12] Some suggest the title is an abbreviated form of another, more common title: 1) an abbreviation for the title, "the Son of Man," befitting the larger context of the Gospel;[13] or 2) a messianic title common in Hellenistic Judaism, befitting the royal context of the scene.[14] Others suggest the title is functioning as a biblical allusion or echo, with three common suggestions: 1) "the man" of sorrows of Isaiah 53:3;[15] 2) the Lord's word to Samuel in regard to king Saul, "Behold, the man," in 1 Samuel 9:7,[16] which nicely matches the royal context of the scene; or 3) "man" as in the first man, Adam, in Genesis 3:22.

Several of the options are untenable. For example, it is unlikely that the title is intended to evoke by means of abbreviation another title. In this context the title of "king" is entirely in view, and there is little to suggest that the title is ever used as an abbreviation. Rather, it is more likely that the title is intentionally echoing within the larger context of OT Scripture. And as much as the context of the sufferings of Christ find comparisons with Isaiah 53 and the royal context finds comparisons with 1 Samuel 9, neither have an innate connection to the Gospel as a whole that would give them preference. But in light of the Genesis-laden context of the Gospel of John and the Genesis lens applied to its interpretive telling of the person and work of Jesus, the connection to Adam is hardly a stretch. And the "royal" context is also implicit to Adam.[17]

As we have discussed before with similar statements (see comments on 1:29), our interpretation is not limited to the meaning intended by Pilate. The narrator may well have used Pilate's own words in a manner that far exceeds Pilate's grasp — but not the reader's. The irony communicated by the Gospel is expressed not only by the contextually extended meaning of *actions* (e.g., the crown and robe) but also by the contextually extended meaning of *words*. We are also to be reminded how words in the ancient world were "expected to evoke in hearer's minds shared impressions of people and events and things, and shared ideas, generalities, abstract concepts."[18] These "mental impressions" had a creative and flexible freedom within the bounds of appropriate meaning (see Introduction).

Whatever the political (or simply cruel) intentions of Pilate regarding his introduction of Jesus, in the cosmological context of the Fourth Gospel this title provides for the reader rich insight into the person and work of Jesus Christ. A brief explanation of the use of the title in Genesis 3:22 is necessary in order to make the connection to its use

12. The following is adapted from M. David Litwa, "Behold Adam: A Reading of John 19:5," *HBT* 32 (2010): 129 – 43.

13. This is the most popular option. See Michaels, *John*, 930.

14. See Wayne A. Meeks, *The Prophet-King: Moses Traditions and the Johannine Christology* (Leiden: Brill, 1967), 69 – 72. Cf. Brown, *John*, 2:876.

15. See A. T. Hanson, *The Prophetic Gospel* (Edinburgh: T&T Clark, 1991), 205.

16. The similarity in wording makes this allusion quite popular. See Dieter Böhler, "«ECCE HOMO!» (Joh 19,5) — ein Zitat aus dem Alten Testament," *BZ* 39 (1995): 104 – 8. Cf. Lincoln, *John*, 466.

17. See Alan Richardson, *The Gospel according to St. John* (London: SPCK, 1959), 197.

18. Downing, "Ambiguity, Ancient Semantics, and Faith," 146.

here. Although the LXX uses a different noun for "the man" (Ἀδαμ) than the Gospel (ἄνθρωπος), the noun not only means "man/humanity," but the Hebrew term can be translated as "the man," which is how most English translations render it (cf. NRSV, NIV, ESV, NKJV, NASB, NJB, NEB). Even the article "the" in "the man" (ὁ ἄνθρωπος) is significant in the title, suggesting that the allusion is in reference to a particular man, Adam.[19] The title is spoken by God in Genesis 3:22 in the context of God's announcement of the guilty verdict to be placed upon all creation (Adam, Eve, and the serpent). In Genesis 3, then, the title declares the mortality of Adam and assumes an ironic reality, for "Behold, the man" announces Adam's alienation from God and his existence in a state of death. The title announces to the first human life that it now exists in a state of depravity and impending death.[20]

In the Gospel of John, however, a reversal of this state of death has begun with the coming of Jesus. Jesus is the life (1:4; 14:6) who has entered into the depraved condition of the world, into the depraved flesh condition of "man" (1:14), in order to recreate. This is why the Genesis motif is so central to the Gospel. What started "in the beginning" in the first "week" of creation (ch. 1) will be finalized by a renewal of "Adam" in a "garden" (chs. 18 – 20). The "exaltation" of Jesus and his "glory" has continually been directed at the cross, the place of death and humiliation that most clearly expresses the nature of his kingship. By this declaration Pilate's words make the point explicit to the reader. Rather than garnering sympathy for Jesus, as is often assumed, Pilate is extending *publicly* the application of shame to Jesus performed by the soldiers inside the praetorium, serving to expose before the same public his own prideful ignorance. But to the reader Pilate is an "unconscious witness to Christian truth."[21]

19:6 When the high priests and servants saw him they cried out, "Crucify, crucify!" Pilate said to them, "You take him and crucify him yourselves. For I myself do not find in him a basis for a charge" (ὅτε οὖν εἶδον αὐτὸν οἱ ἀρχιερεῖς καὶ οἱ ὑπηρέται ἐκραύγασαν λέγοντες, Σταύρωσον σταύρωσον. λέγει αὐτοῖς ὁ Πιλᾶτος, Λάβετε αὐτὸν ὑμεῖς καὶ σταυρώσατε, ἐγὼ γὰρ οὐχ εὑρίσκω ἐν αὐτῷ αἰτίαν). The Jewish response to Jesus was unanimous and bold; they demanded that he be crucified. If Pilate wanted to earn pity for him, he failed, but if he wanted to fuel the hate of the Jews, he succeeded. This is the first occurrence of the term "crucify" (σταύρωσον) in the Gospel, and it is significant that the narrative only lists two primary speakers among the crowd: "the high priests" (οἱ ἀρχιερεῖς) and their "servants" (οἱ ὑπηρέται).

Pilate responds for a third time with the claim that he finds no "basis for a charge" (αἰτίαν) against him (cf. 18:38; v. 4). Pilate creates an emphatic contrast between "you" and "I" to make this "man" their issue and to try to remove himself from the case. The entire Roman "trial" has been based on the shared legal authority between Jerusalem and Rome and the innate political tension expressed in the interaction between the Jewish authorities and Rome (see comments on 18:31). Pilate again raises this issue and puts pressure on the Jews. While Pilate's intentions may be political and therefore taken as a sarcastic taunt, if we take his threefold denial of a "charge" against Jesus at its face value, he may have also doubted the judgments made against Jesus. Either way, the repeated one-word command from the Jews, "crucify, crucify," may have sounded more like a demand than a request (the verbs are imperative).

19:7 The Jews responded to him, "We have a law, and according to the law he is required to die,

---

19. Litwa, "Behold Adam," 135.
20. Ibid., 136, 139.

21. Hoskyns, *Fourth Gospel*, 523.

because he made himself out to be the Son of God" (ἀπεκρίθησαν αὐτῷ οἱ Ἰουδαῖοι, Ἡμεῖς νόμον ἔχομεν, καὶ κατὰ τὸν νόμον ὀφείλει ἀποθανεῖν, ὅτι υἱὸν θεοῦ ἑαυτὸν ἐποίησεν). Up to this point in the Roman trial, the Jews were unwilling to explain themselves to Pilate (see comments on 18:30). But now the Jews are forced to explain to Pilate that according to their law this man "is required to die" (ὀφείλει ἀποθανεῖν) for blasphemy (see Lev 24:16). That is, "he made himself out to be the Son of God" (υἱὸν θεοῦ ἑαυτὸν ἐποίησεν), which the Gospel already explained was the judgment of the Jews during his public ministry (see 5:18). This legal charge is certainly not a surprise to Pilate, who first broached the subject with Jesus directly when he asked if he was "the king of the Jews" (18:33). But by giving warrant based upon "their law," the case is not only political but also religious. That is, the Jews are forcing Pilate's hand by demanding that he use his (Roman) political authority to support and facilitate their (Jewish) religious authority. As much as the Jews were to become like the Romans (see vv. 12, 15), here this Roman was forced to become like a Jew, supporting the local laws and customs of the Jews over which he had been placed by the Romans. The Gospel again describes how the whole world formed a unified front against God in the person of Jesus Christ. In these last two verses the truth of the Gospel is unconsciously spoken by both opponents of Jesus: "Pilate proclaims the sinlessness of Jesus, and the Jews declare His death to be the fulfillment of the Law."[22]

19:8 When Pilate heard this statement, he was very afraid (Ὅτε οὖν ἤκουσεν ὁ Πιλᾶτος τοῦτον τὸν λόγον, μᾶλλον ἐφοβήθη). The third section of the pericope (vv. 8–11) moves from the outside back to the inside; though before it moves inside the praetorium the narrator begins from the *in-side* of Pilate. The narrator explains that Pilate was "afraid" (ἐφοβήθη), with the addition of an adverb making the fear even greater: "He was very afraid" (μᾶλλον ἐφοβήθη).[23] This may be Pilate's first response in regard to Jesus that was religiously (or at least superstitiously) motivated, denoted by the questions he is about to present to Jesus. It is possible that a polytheistic Roman was more open to claims of divine sonship than a monotheist, which facilitates further the irony of the Gospel, for a Roman outsider proves more ready to believe something divine about the Son of God than his own people (see 1:11).[24]

19:9 And he entered into the praetorium again and said to Jesus, "Where are you from?" But Jesus did not give him an answer (καὶ εἰσῆλθεν εἰς τὸ πραιτώριον πάλιν καὶ λέγει τῷ Ἰησοῦ, Πόθεν εἶ σύ; ὁ δὲ Ἰησοῦς ἀπόκρισιν οὐκ ἔδωκεν αὐτῷ). The narrative's focus is so intently placed on Pilate that no mention is made of how Jesus was brought into the praetorium. Pilate asks Jesus a question that places emphasis on the "you": "Where are *you* from?" (Πόθεν εἶ σύ;). In this context the emphatic pronoun might suggest incredulity. Bultmann is probably right to suggest that Pilate's question is asking if Jesus is a man or a god.[25] For the reader of the Gospel thus far, however, the answer to Pilate's question is also quite clear. Jesus is "the one who comes from above" (see 3:31).

Pilate asks Jesus the question of questions, and Jesus remains silent. The silence of Jesus is almost certainly a rebuke of Pilate. He is neither worthy to judge such matters (they are above his paygrade), nor is he able to handle such truth. Jesus has already revealed to Pilate, even if only by contrast, the nature of his work, his mission, and his kingship (see 18:36–37). But Pilate cannot (or will not) understand the fullness of Jesus Christ, the Son of

---

22. Ibid.
23. BDAG 613.
24. Keener, *John*, 2:1125.
25. Bultmann, *John*, 661.

God, and the depths of his person and work. This understanding is rooted in faith (see 20:31).[26]

19:10 So Pilate said to him, "You do not speak to me? Do you not know that I have authority to release you and I have the authority to crucify you?" (λέγει οὖν αὐτῷ ὁ Πιλᾶτος, Ἐμοὶ οὐ λαλεῖς; οὐκ οἶδας ὅτι ἐξουσίαν ἔχω ἀπολῦσαί σε καὶ ἐξουσίαν ἔχω σταυρῶσαί σε;). Pilate then attempts to force Jesus to speak, probably irritated or offended at the silence of Jesus. Pilate's first question, with the emphatic pronoun "to me" (Ἐμοὶ) is probably to be understood as an expression of astonishment: "You do not speak *to me*?" The implicit rebuke is this: "A bound, beaten, bloodied, and soon-to-be-crucified prisoner will not speak to me, the Roman prefect!" By this Pilate establishes the ground for his next question, which he bases on his authority either to release or to crucify Jesus, with the twice-stated "I have authority" (ἐξουσίαν ἔχω) making a strong claim to the power he has over Jesus.

19:11 Jesus responded to him, "You have no authority over me except that which was given to you from above. For this reason the one who handed me over to you has the greater sin" (ἀπεκρίθη αὐτῷ ὁ Ἰησοῦς, Οὐκ εἶχες ἐξουσίαν κατ᾽ ἐμοῦ οὐδεμίαν εἰ μὴ ἦν δεδομένον σοι ἄνωθεν· διὰ τοῦτο ὁ παραδούς μέ σοι μείζονα ἁμαρτίαν ἔχει). Jesus ends his silence with these final words, serving to close this section of the pericope (vv. 8 – 11). Jesus makes clear that any authority Pilate has was given to him "from above" (ἄνωθεν). By this statement Jesus declares all authority to have its source in the authority of God, that is, in his own authority. Jesus is not absolving Pilate, for although he is not his own source of authority he does bear responsibility for the authority given to him "from

above." For "greater sin" (μείζονα ἁμαρτίαν) clearly implies that Pilate too has sinned. Yet Jesus explains that a greater sin has been committed by "the one who handed me over to you" (ὁ παραδούς μέ σοι). The singular "the one" probably suggests that Jesus is referring to the high priest, since the context of his interaction with Pilate has centered upon competing "authority," even though the sense intended here is almost certainly collective or representative, referring to the powers of Jerusalem (cf. 1:11; 11:52).[27]

19:12 From then on Pilate wanted to release him, but the Jews were shouting, "If you release this man, you are not a friend of Caesar. Anyone who makes himself out to be a king opposes Caesar" (ἐκ τούτου ὁ Πιλᾶτος ἐζήτει ἀπολῦσαι αὐτόν· οἱ δὲ Ἰουδαῖοι ἐκραύγαζον λέγοντες, Ἐὰν τοῦτον ἀπολύσῃς, οὐκ εἶ φίλος τοῦ Καίσαρος· πᾶς ὁ βασιλέα ἑαυτὸν ποιῶν ἀντιλέγει τῷ Καίσαρι). The fourth section of the pericope (vv. 12 – 16) returns for a final time to the outside, making this the seventh and final scene involving movement between front and back stage (see comments before 19:1). Before the official announcement is made, the narrator reveals that Pilate "wanted" (ἐζήτει) to release Jesus; the imperfect tense of the verb suggests a series of "attempts" or "strivings." The phrase translated temporally, "from then on" (ἐκ τούτου), could also be interpreted causally, "for this reason." Either way the phrase suggests that the backstage conversation with Jesus had facilitated this desire, though no specific reason is provided. It certainly was not because Jesus excused Pilate from sin or guilt (cf. v. 11). If anything can be deduced from the previous interaction, it is that Pilate saw something in this "Son of God" that threatened him (cf. v. 8). But "the Jews" (cf. v. 6) are said to offer a quick

---

26. Cf. Beasley-Murray, *John*, 339.

27. Other suggestions for "the one" include Judas or, more cosmologically, the devil, with the latter referring to the great betrayal of Genesis 3, befitting the second-Adam theme.

response to the hesitant judgment of Pilate. The narrative does not explain how the Jews knew of Pilate's desire to release Jesus, but the reader has clearly seen how the political gerrymandering between these two authorities is slowly combining into the unified opposition of "the world" against Jesus.

The Jews forcefully present Pilate with an argument that eventually persuades him not to release Jesus and to carry on with the guilty verdict. In a symbolic maneuver, the Jews contrast Jesus to Caesar and demand that Pilate choose between them. Without knowing it, the Jewish authorities here invoke the very authority Jesus informed Pilate was "from above" (v. 11) as a veiled threat against him.[28] The thrust of the argument is based on the phrase "friend of Caesar" (φίλος τοῦ Καίσαρος), which although it may have a more simple meaning is more likely referring to a recognizable title of honor (amicus Caesari) for those in close partnership with the ruler, something in which Pilate may have actually been enrolled in as a trusted associate of Caesar (cf. Tacitus, Ann. 6.8).[29] Whether or not Pilate was officially a member of this illustrious fellowship is beside the point. Even the suggestion that an extension of mercy to Jesus is a treasonable behavior toward Caesar is enough of a threat to dissuade Pilate, especially when made publicly. The threat of denunciation as unfaithful to Caesar forces Pilate's hand. This was hardly an impotent threat, for the writings of Josephus suggest that later in his career Pilate so agitated the Jewish people that he eventually helped create an open revolt,[30] leading to his humiliation by Caesar.[31] Like for the leader of Jerusalem, Caiaphas (11:49–52), the solution became clear for Pilate. Rather than

becoming a sacrifice himself (social-politically or even physically), political prudence made it necessary for Pilate to make Christ the sacrifice.

By forcing Pilate to choose Caesar over Jesus, the Jews have ironically forced themselves into the same corner and have chosen Caesar the Roman over a fellow Jew, Jesus. The Jewish authorities have now secured the upper hand in the political gerrymandering between Jerusalem and Rome, but at a very great cost. They have become one with Rome. The Gospel's use of irony is overtly clear when the Jews suggest that an alliance with Jesus "opposes Caesar," for the reverse is also true. In this moment (and even more clearly in v. 15), the Jews have become Roman, rejecting their God-given right to be God's people and their God-given King for a pagan existence under a pagan ruler. Blinzler explains the irony: "The highest Roman official in Judea has to endure being accused of lack of loyalty to the emperor by the representatives of a nation more passionately seething with hatred for the Roman yoke than almost any other in the empire"[32] — and all of these at Passover, the celebration of the God-given liberation! As the reader fully understands, this decision was only political at the surface; deep down this was a spiritual issue, symptomatic of the sin of "the world" (both Jew and gentile) that had been separated from God (1:5).

19:13 After Pilate heard these words, he brought out Jesus and sat upon the judgment seat, in the place called the Stone Pavement, but in Aramaic, Gabbatha (Ὁ οὖν Πιλᾶτος ἀκούσας τῶν λόγων τούτων ἤγαγεν ἔξω τὸν Ἰησοῦν, καὶ ἐκάθισεν ἐπὶ βήματος εἰς τόπον λεγόμενον Λιθόστρωτον, Ἑβραϊστὶ δὲ Γαββαθα). Pilate's decision was almost

28. Michaels, John, 938.
29. See Keener, John, 2:1128.
30. Bond, "The Literary Function of Pontius Pilate in Josephus' Narratives," 221.
31. Keener, John, 2:1128. See also Brian S. Messner, "'No Friend of Caesar': Jesus, Pilate, Sejanus, and Tiberius," SCJ 11 (2008): 47–57.
32. Josef Blinzler, Der Prozess Jesu, 4th ed. (Regensburg: Verlag Pustet, 1969), 337. Cf. Beasley-Murray, John, 340.

made for him by the shouting Jews, for the narrator explains that he brought Jesus out before the crowd "after" he heard "these words" (τῶν λόγων τούτων), that is, the political threat made against him. But as the reader has come to understand, this coming announcement was not rooted in the authority of either Jerusalem or Rome — not even Caesar, but by the will of God. The fact of Jesus as the ultimate authority in this scene is depicted by the narrative itself in the description of Jesus being brought out by Pilate. The narrative explains that "he [Pilate] brought Jesus out and sat upon the judgment seat" (ἤγαγεν ἔξω τὸν Ἰησοῦν, καὶ ἐκάθισεν ἐπὶ βήματος). The statement is odd because it is not entirely clear who exactly "sat" upon the judgment seat: Pilate or Jesus. It all depends upon whether the verb "sat" (ἐκάθισεν) is interpreted as an intransitive verb (i.e., a verb with no object to receive the action) or as a transitive verb (i.e., a verb that has an object to receive the action). If it is the former, then it is Pilate himself who sat on the judgment seat, but if it is the latter, then Pilate "caused Jesus to sit upon the judgment seat."

Both options are grammatically possible, and several arguments have been offered for both.[33] We must remember that we are not interpreting the historical event itself but the account recorded in a text (on method, see Introduction). This is not to deny or even minimize the reality of the event but to suggest that the inspired account may intend to communicate truths beyond what was seen by those present (e.g., Jesus the man is also "the Lamb," 1:29). In fact, the narrative's nondescript account may be entirely the point. That is, the narrative wanted to present two coexisting (and competing) realities simultaneously, namely, the "authority" of both Pilate and Jesus, which vv. 10 – 11 made clear was the central issue between

them. From the narrative's perspective, both were sitting on the judgment seat. The historical strand of the Gospel's plot would suggest Pilate was the one seated, for the seat did belong to his Roman office; yet the cosmological strand of the Gospel's plot just as strongly suggests that Jesus was the one seated, for the seat also belonged to his divine office. In order to communicate this, the narrative intentionally makes the sitting of the "judge" explicitly *implicit* so that the scene is presented in the fullness of its historical *and* cosmological contexts. If Pilate placed Jesus on the judgment seat, then he was certainly making a mockery of the Jews, as he would do again when Jesus was placed upon the cross (see 19:19 – 22). But if Pilate himself was sitting on the judgment seat, then the joke was on him, for the place where he sat was given to him by a much higher authority, the very man he was (supposedly) about to judge.

As much as the characters involved in the verdict are emphasized by the narrative, so is the important location of the verdict. The place of "the sitting" is "the judgment seat" (βήματος), the "judicial bench" for the ruling magistrate.[34] The term in the NT is also used to refer to the judgment seat of God or Christ (Rom 14:10; 2 Cor 5:10), which helps explain the narrator's intentional play regarding the one who "sat" upon it.[35] The narrator also explains that the judgment seat is "in the place called the Stone Pavement" (εἰς τόπον λεγόμενον Λιθόστρωτον), for which he also provides the Aramaic name "Gabbatha" (Γαββαθα; see comments on 5:2). Although a "stone pavement" is a generic term referring to stone or mosaic pavements, this one in particular is known as "*the* Stone Pavement" probably because it was a public landmark where crowds could assemble for public meetings. While it is difficult to define the exact place, the reference

---

33. For a summary, see Barrett, *John*, 544.
34. BDAG 175.

35. Barrett, *John*, 544.

to "the Stone Pavement" and the Jewish equivalent, "Gabbatha," the root of which means "height" or "hill,"[36] probably depicts a large, elevated platform connected to the praetorium and Pilate's palace complex that featured a large open area accessible to the public where the ruler could hold public court while seated above on "the judgment seat."[37]

19:14 Now it was the day of preparation for the Passover; it was about the sixth hour. And he said to the Jews, "Behold, your King!" (ἦν δὲ παρασκευὴ τοῦ πάσχα, ὥρα ἦν ὡς ἕκτη. καὶ λέγει τοῖς Ἰουδαίοις, Ἴδε ὁ βασιλεὺς ὑμῶν). The same symbolic force with which the narrator depicts the place of the verdict of Jesus is also applied to the time of the verdict. The narrator notes that "it was the day of the preparation for the Passover" (ἦν δὲ παρασκευὴ τοῦ πάσχα), which suggests that it was about noon, since the counting of hours would begin with the rising of the sun (about six in the morning; on the Jewish time system, see comments on 1:39). Thus, Jesus was about to be crucified at the very time the great feast was beginning to be prepared all across Jerusalem, with thousands of lambs being slaughtered and hearts being prepared for the climactic moment of the Passover (on chronology, see comments before 18:28).

The allusion to the slaughtering of the lambs is intended to declare that Jesus is the true Passover Lamb first announced by the Baptist (1:29, cf. 1:36). The motif of Jesus as "the Lamb of God" is one of the primary theological statements the Gospel is making, through which all of Jesus's authority as Judge (5:22 – 27) and King (vv. 2 – 5; cf. 12:1 – 19) must be understood. Jesus has continually been depicted by the Gospel of John as the fulfillment of the Jewish feasts (see comments on 10:22; 15:1)

and here is depicted as the fulfillment the Passover. The image created by this pericope's connection between Jesus the King (vv. 2 – 5) and Jesus the Lamb is nicely displayed by the portrait provided in the Revelation of John: "I saw a Lamb, looking as if it had been slain, standing at the center of the throne" (5:6), about whom it is said, "Worthy is the Lamb, who was slain" (5:12).

Pilate presents Jesus to the Jews and the crowd one final time with the title, "Behold, your King!" (Ἴδε ὁ βασιλεὺς ὑμῶν). Similar to the first introduction of Jesus, the particle of exclamation, "behold" (Ἴδε), serves to draw all attention to Jesus (cf. v. 5). It is possible and commonly assumed that Pilate offers a final mockery of Jesus with this title — he had lost ground in the political gerrymandering with the Jews (v. 12) but still has the power to humiliate them politically by means of Jesus. ("What your people call a king [cf. 12:12 – 19] we declare a criminal!") Surely this is partly the case here. Yet something regarding Jesus, if nothing more than the possibility that he is "a/the Son of God," caused Pilate to be "very afraid" (v. 8). By mounting the elevated platform, Pilate has already made his judgment, but with this last title Pilate may be speaking more straightforwardly than often assumed. The reader is aware, however, that no matter what Pilate intended to say by his words, the title given to Jesus was perfect in every way.

19:15 Then they shouted, "Away with him! Away with him! Crucify him!" Pilate said to them, "Shall I crucify your king?" The high priests answered, "We have no king but Caesar" (ἐκραύγασαν οὖν ἐκεῖνοι, Ἆρον ἆρον, σταύρωσον αὐτόν. λέγει αὐτοῖς ὁ Πιλᾶτος, Τὸν βασιλέα ὑμῶν σταυρώσω; ἀπεκρίθησαν οἱ ἀρχιερεῖς, Οὐκ ἔχομεν

---

36. Cf. John J. O'Rourke, "Two Notes on St. John's Gospel (Jn 19,13: *eis ton topon*)," *CBQ* 25 (1963): 124 – 28 (126).

37. John F. Wilson, "Archeology and the Origins of the Fourth Gospel: Gabbatha," in *Johannine Studies: Essays in Honor of Frank Pack*, ed. James E. Priest (Malibu, CA: Pepperdine University Press, 1989), 221 – 31 (228).

βασιλέα εἰ μὴ Καίσαρα). If the intentions of Pilate were more subtle at this second presentation of Jesus, the response of the Jews was crystal clear. They were spewing verbal hate at the very expression of God's love for them. They had already cornered Pilate with political threats (see v. 12); now they aim their demands at Jesus and clamor for his crucifixion, denoted by three imperatives that are probably stronger than imperatives of request (entreaty or polite command), which is normally used to speak to a superior.[38]

Befitting a dialogue technique, Pilate asks if the Jews really want their own king crucified, with "king" in the emphatic position. The response of the Jews is telling and consistent with their earlier political maneuver (cf. v. 12): "We have no king but Caesar" (Οὐκ ἔχομεν βασιλέα εἰ μὴ Καίσαρα). By choosing Caesar over Jesus, the Jews declare themselves to be Roman or, as the Gospel introduced those who oppose and deny God, to be members of "the world" (1:11). In the midst of this irony, however, stands real truth, for just as Pilate spoke more truthfully (we argued) in regard to Jesus, so did the Jews. That is, no longer were they living a lie filled with Sabbaths, feasts, and sacrifices, things they mocked by their pretensions. For the first time they were speaking the truth about themselves and their true loyalties. God was not king to them, and here they finally gave testimony to that about themselves. In a real sense, they were as much "friends of Caesar" as Pilate (v. 12).[39] And

these self-condemning words become their last, for the Jews do not appear again in the Gospel.

19:16 So then he handed him over to them in order that he might be crucified. Then they received Jesus (τότε οὖν παρέδωκεν αὐτὸν αὐτοῖς ἵνα σταυρωθῇ. Παρέλαβον οὖν τὸν Ἰησοῦν). The pericope concludes with the brief and seemingly undramatic handing over of Jesus to be crucified. The narrator explains that the order was given and that Jesus was "received" (Παρέλαβον), but quite remarkably none of the characters are named except Jesus. While Pilate is certainly the subject of "handing over," who is the referent of "to them" (αὐτοῖς), and why does the narrator not say this plainly? At the historical level it was certainly the Roman soldiers who received Jesus and performed the actual crucifixion (see 19:23). But as v. 11 explained, the "greater sin" here was committed by the Jewish authorities, who also become the natural referent. The narrator is intentionally directing the reader to see here the dual referent in the pronoun at the cosmological level of the Gospel (cf. v. 13). The intimate connection between Jerusalem and Rome creates a powerful image in light of this anonymity. Just as the whole world had just condemned Jesus to death, it would be the whole world that would take him to the cross. This verdict had always involved the whole of humanity, from the first Adam to the second Adam. This is the context out of which the crucifixion of Jesus must be understood.

Theology in Application

This pericope functions almost like a prologue to Jesus's crucifixion (19:17 – 27) and death and burial (19:28 – 42). Like the previous three pericopae (18:1 – 12, 13 – 27, 28 – 40), even while being arrested, bound, and bloodied, Jesus is in complete control. But the control Jesus exhibits in this pericope is not depicted merely with

---

38. Cf. Wallace, *Greek Grammar*, 487 – 88.   39. Cf. Heil, *Blood and Water*, 83.

words but with the fuller meaning of every cruel act directed at him. The narrative guides the reader to see how the evil-intended treatment and titles given to Jesus by his opponents rightly declare him to be the good-intended fulfillment of God's promises in the OT. Through this pericope the reader is confronted with the condition of the world that is enslaved to sin and the gracious response of the Passover Lamb whose sacrifice provides for the world a second exodus.

Jesus, the True King

The scene begins (vv. 2 – 3) with an almost unbearable description of the graphic mocking of Jesus as Roman soldiers dress him as a clown-king and pay him homage by slapping him in the face. Could there be a more vile moment in the world's treatment of its true King? Yet the reader is keenly aware that as much as the soldiers did everything they could to demean the royal status of Jesus, everything they did declared to perfection the kind of king he truly is. It is in the midst of the parody and cruelty of this scene that the reader comes to understand the deep message of the gospel. God's love of the world and the life that he offers is expressed specifically through the suffering and death of Jesus Christ. This *is* Jesus's kingship, and befitting his mission to the world a crown of thorns is the perfect adornment for the King who is also the Suffering Servant. For as the prophet Isaiah explained long ago: "The punishment that brought us peace was on him, and by his wounds we are healed" (Isa 53:5). The true King brings peace without the sword, and no fighting is needed to guarantee his eternal reign. For his power was expressed through weakness, and the humility of his suffering became his victory. The very actions that were intended to shame him were what Scripture would later explain to be the source of his exaltation by the Father, from whom he received after his crucifixion the name above all other names: Jesus *the* Lord (Phil 2:9). One day these soldiers will perform this very act, though with an entirely different intention and understanding, when they kneel before him and confess with their tongues that he is Lord, the true King (Phil 2:10 – 11).

Jesus, the Second Adam

The title applied to Jesus in v. 5, "Behold, the man," is not easily interpreted. We argued that an allusion to Adam is in view, which not only fits the kingly context of Adam as the king of creation (Ps 8) but also befits the Genesis-laden context of the Gospel as a whole. In Genesis 3 the same title was spoken by God as he announced the guilty verdict to be placed upon all creation. In Genesis the title declares the mortality of Adam and his alienation from God, and announces to the first human life that it now exists in a state of depravity and impending death. But its occurrence in the Gospel of John is the announcement of the reversal of this state of death in the person of Jesus, who receives in his person the condition of depravity and death originally applied to the first Adam, but now applied — and fulfilled! — in the person and work of the second Adam. On the surface Jesus was presented to "the world" as a broken individual, weakened and unable to avoid his impending death. But in reality Jesus was standing before God as the representative of the world, broken by the world's sinful condition that he embraced willingly and without sinning himself so as to take in his body their impending death.

Jesus, the Passover Lamb

This pericope takes great care to depict the events leading up to the crucifixion as parallel to the preparation for the Passover taking place at the exact same time. This Passover was in the eyes of God the last Passover, for the perfect and eternal Passover Lamb was prepared that year, Jesus Christ, the Son of God. On that Friday, which was the day of the great feast of Jewish liberation, Jesus himself became the great liberator, releasing the bondage of his enslaved people not merely from the wrong king (Pharaoh) but from the ruling bondage of depravity and death. For this reason the church refers to this Friday as Good Friday. And this celebration no longer involves the preparation of lambs, for such lambs have now been made obsolete. Jesus has become *the* Lamb of God, the one who takes away the sin of the entire world (1:29). For this reason Passover is now fulfilled, just as all the OT feasts have been fulfilled in Jesus, for the eternal Passover Lamb has been sacrificed for our liberation, and we have experienced true freedom (8:36).

The church celebrates the Lamb of God alone because his sacrifice is not merely national but international, offering freedom not merely from physical enslavement but also from spiritual enslavement. The primary Christian holidays have become personalized and focused entirely upon Jesus Christ, with celebrations of *his* birth (Christmas), *his* death (Good Friday), and *his* resurrection (Easter). For in Jesus death has been defeated and life has been recreated. And this is what Jesus offers to the world still in need of redemption and what the church proclaims by means of its "ministry of reconciliation" (2 Cor 5:11 – 21).

41

John 19:17 – 27

Literary Context

This pericope continues to depict the events surrounding the sacrificial death of the Son of God. The Jewish and Roman "trials" have concluded and the verdict has been declared. The "hour" of Jesus has now arrived (see 2:4). The narrator's depiction of the crucifixion of Jesus is not merely focused upon the physical suffering of Christ — the historical details of the event — but also on the theological significance of the cross of Christ and the nature of the person hanging upon it — the cosmological details of the event. The reader is guided to see in the death of Jesus the fuller meaning of his person and work. It is specifically the crucified Jesus who has now fulfilled the perfect plan of God as the King, Priest, and Son of God.

VIII. The Crucifixion (18:1 – 19:42)

    A. The Arrest of Jesus (18:1 – 12)

    B. The Jewish Trial and Its Witnesses (18:13 – 27)

    C. The Roman Trial before Pilate (18:28 – 40)

    D. The Verdict: "Crucify Him!" (19:1 – 16)

➡   **E. The Crucifixion of Jesus (19:17 – 27)**

    F. The Death and Burial of Jesus (19:28 – 42)

Main Idea

The crucifixion of Jesus is the "hour" when God declares that death has given birth to life and that the crucified Christ is the true King (ruler of the world), the true Priest (mediator for the world), and the true Son (creator of the world).

Translation

John 19:17–27

	Scene 1 (17–18)	
17a	Description	Carrying his own cross
b	Action	**he went out**
c	Destination	to what is called the Place of the Skull,
d	Translation	which in Aramaic is called Golgotha,
18a	Crucifixion	where they crucified him, and
b	Characters Entrance	with him two others—
c	Description of Setting	one on each side, and
d		Jesus in the middle.
	Scene 2 (19–22)	
19a	Character Reentrance	**Pilate also wrote a title**
b	Description of "Cross"	and **placed it on the cross,**
c		which had written upon it:
d	Name	*"Jesus*
e	Description	*the Nazarene,*
f	Ironic Title	*the King of the Jews."*
20a	Description of Scene	**Many of the Jews read this title,**
b	Basis #1: Location	because ↑ the place
c	Description	where Jesus was crucified was near ↺ the city, and
d	Basis #2: Trilingual	it was written in Aramaic,
e		Latin, and
f		Greek.
21a	Character Reentrance	Then **the high priests of the Jews said to Pilate,**
b	Demand	*"Do not write,*
c		*'the King of the Jews,'*
d	Correction	*but that he said,*
e		*'I am King of the Jews.'"*
22a	Response	**Pilate answered,**
b	Rejection of Demand	*"What I have written …*
c	Emphasis	*… I have written."*
	Scene 3 (23–24)	
23a	Character Reentrance	Then **the soldiers …**
b	Timing of Action	when they crucified Jesus,
c	Action	**… took his clothes**
d		and **divided them into four parts,**
e	Description	a part for each soldier,
f	Exception	↑ except for the tunic.
g	Allusion: Lev 21:10	**The tunic was seamless,**
h	Description	woven throughout from the top.

Continued on next page.

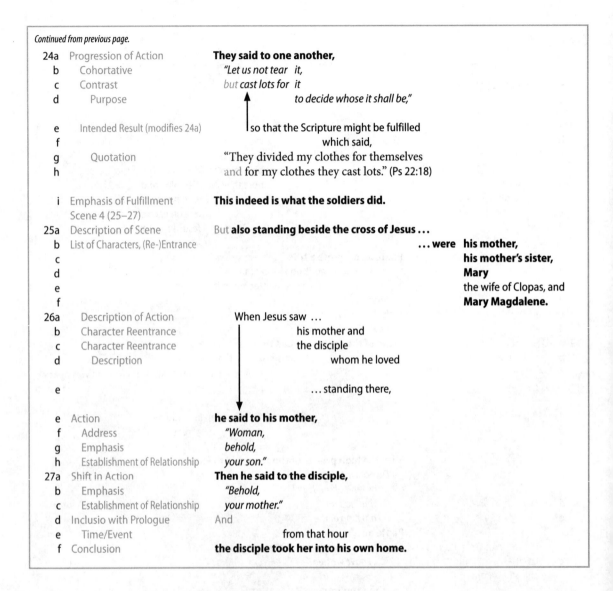

Structure and Literary Form

The structure of this pericope is different than the basic story form (see Introduction). Unlike the previous three pericopae that were guided by the trial motif (18:13–27; 18:28–40; 19:1–16), the next two pericopae (19:17–27 and 19:28–42) are guided by the details of a Roman crucifixion, with the account of the death of Jesus falling naturally into seven scenes between both pericopae.

This pericope is broken into four brief scenes that detail one significant aspect of such a death. The first scene succinctly describes the place and procedure of the crucifixion of Jesus (vv. 17–18). The next three scenes, similar to the trial scenes, are guided by a geographic perspective: the title *above* the crucified Christ, the tunic *below* the crucified Christ, and the family *in front of* the crucified Christ. Thus, after the brief first scene summarizing the crucifixion, the second scene describes the title Pilate had placed above the cross to depict Jesus as the *King* (vv. 19 – 22); the third scene describes and explains the soldiers' apprehension of the seamless tunic of Jesus to depict Jesus as the *Priest* (vv. 23 – 24); and the fourth scene describes the final moments between Jesus and his family in order to depict Jesus as the *Son* (vv. 25 – 27).

Exegetical Outline

➡   **E. The Crucifixion of Jesus (19:17 – 27)**

1. "Place of the Skull" (vv. 17 – 18)
2. The Title of the King (vv. 19 – 22)
3. The Tunic of the Priest (vv. 23 – 24)
4. The Family of the Son (vv. 25 – 27)

Explanation of the Text

19:17 Carrying his own cross he went out to what is called the Place of the Skull, which in Aramaic is called Golgotha (καὶ βαστάζων αὐτῷ τὸν σταυρὸν ἐξῆλθεν εἰς τὸν λεγόμενον Κρανίου Τόπον, ὃ λέγεται Ἑβραϊστὶ Γολγοθᾶ). The first scene of the pericope (vv. 17 – 18) depicts the place and procedure of the crucifixion of Jesus. The explanation is intentionally sparse in vv. 17 – 18; the crucifixion has been so central to the developing message of the Gospel that it only needs to be stated as historical fact. Only the place and the people crucified with Jesus are mentioned, and then only briefly. The narrator does explain that Jesus was "carrying his own cross" (βαστάζων αὐτῷ τὸν σταυρὸν), which was a common practice in Roman crucifixion. The condemned criminal would normally be forced to carry the transverse beam or crossbeam of the cross (the *patibulum*) to the site of the ex-

ecution where soldiers would attach it to the (permanent) upright stake that was regularly used for executions.[1]

The narrator depicts a movement outside the city, implied by the adverbial prefix of the verb "he went out" (ἐξῆλθεν) and stated explicitly in v. 20, to a place called "the Place of the Skull" (Κρανίου Τόπον).[2] The narrator explains that its "Hebrew" name, which almost certainly means "Aramaic" (Ἑβραϊστὶ) since that was the common language in the first century (see comments on 5:2), was "Golgotha" (Γολγοθᾶ). It is common for contemporary Christians to use the Latin translation, "Calvary" (*Calvaria*), which also means "skull," when referring to the place of Christ's death. By giving both the Greco-Roman and Jewish names, the narrator emphasizes the particular location of Christ's death, the Place of the Skull.[3]

---

1. Keener, *John*, 2:1134. Cf. Chrysostom, *John*, 85.1.317.

2. It is unclear why the place was called "Skull." See Brown, *John*, 2:899 – 900.

3. The location has long been debated. See Brown, *Death of the Messiah*, 2:937 – 40.

19:18 Where they crucified him, and with him two others — one on each side, and Jesus in the middle (ὅπου αὐτὸν ἐσταύρωσαν, καὶ μετ᾽ αὐτοῦ ἄλλους δύο ἐντεῦθεν καὶ ἐντεῦθεν, μέσον δὲ τὸν Ἰησοῦν). Jesus was not alone, as the narrator notes, for two other criminals were also crucified, one on each side of him (cf. Isa 53:12). John (unlike the Synoptics) is silent on the transgressions committed by these criminals; the point is simply to contrast the sinners with the sacrifice. It is fitting that the narrator is careful to mention the placement of Jesus among the three crosses; he was "in the middle" (μέσον), a seemingly insignificant detail.[4] But the center was the place of greatest honor (or in this case, shame), possibly making Jesus the most visible to the massive crowd that had gathered for the Passover Feast.

Roman crucifixion was familiar to the ancient world, which partly explains the brevity of the Gospel's account. While there were some standard procedures for the crucifixion, similar to the flogging (cf. 19:1), the executioners could perform their duties in a variety of manners, "limited only by the extent of their sadistic creativity."[5] Crucifixion for all people — Jews, Romans, and barbarians — was "an utterly offensive affair, 'obscene' in the original sense of the word."[6] The whole point was the utmost indignity of the individual.

The general procedure would look something like the following. The criminal would be flogged and then forced to carry his own crossbeam to the place of the execution, often scourged on the way, both of which were intended to torture the criminal before the crucifixion itself.[7] If not already fully stripped, the criminal would have his cloth-

ing removed and confiscated, thus stripped of both possessions and honor.[8] Then the criminal would normally be fastened to the cross with either ropes or nails through the wrist (see 20:25); in Roman crucifixion the feet of the victim were often fastened to the cross as well.[9] The nails were typically five to seven inches in length, long enough to penetrate both the flesh and bone and the wood of the cross to secure the body to it.[10] The upright stake would have been no more than ten feet high, which had in the middle a small wooden "seat" and near the top a groove to receive the crossbeam, thus leaving the criminal hanging just above the ground. Once placed on the cross, the body of the criminal was fully accessible to external conditions, with scores of flies attracted to the bodily wounds or animals assaulting the feet of the victim. The suffering also would cause severe bodily distortions, including the loss of bodily control (waste) and enlarged, swelling body parts. The prisoner, attached to the crossbeam, would hang in this agonizing position until released by death, which usually came about through difficulty in breathing and stoppage of circulation, not so much through blood loss. The body of the victim was attached to the cross in a manner that facilitated prolonged suffering. If the criminal could lift himself up to get breath, he would survive longer than if the unsupported body was deadweight; yet to lift oneself was designed to cause severe pain. If death was slow in coming, the end was often hastened by means of clubbing, stabbing, or poison.[11] The normal Roman practice was to leave the body on the cross until it rotted, but Jewish law demanded that the body of a hanging man had to be buried on the day of execution to

---

4. Cf. Bruner, *John*, 1099.

5. Keener, *John*, 2:1135.

6. Martin Hengel, *Crucifixion*, trans. John Bowden (Philadelphia: Fortress, 1977), 22.

7. Ibid., 22–32.

8. Malina and Rohrbaugh, *John*, 264.

9. Hengel, *Crucifixion*, 31. Cf. Nicu Haas, "Anthropological Observations on the Skeletal Remains from Giv'at ha-Mivtar," *IEJ* 20 (1970): 38–59.

10. See Brown, *Death of the Messiah*, 2:949–50.

11. Bo Reicke, *The New Testament Era*, trans. David E. Green (Philadelphia: Fortress, 1968), 186–87.

prevent the land from being defiled (Deut 21:23). The execution served as a crude form of public entertainment, with the crowds often ridiculing and mocking the victims.[12]

19:19 Pilate also wrote a title and placed it on the cross, which had written upon it: "Jesus the Nazarene, the King of the Jews" (ἔγραψεν δὲ καὶ τίτλον ὁ Πιλᾶτος καὶ ἔθηκεν ἐπὶ τοῦ σταυροῦ· ἦν δὲ γεγραμμένον, Ἰησοῦς ὁ Ναζωραῖος ὁ βασιλεὺς τῶν Ἰουδαίων). The second scene of the pericope (vv. 19 – 22) directs the reader to look above the crucified Christ to the title placed at the top of the cross. It was common for the criminal to be forced to carry in his hands or hanging around his neck a plaque (*tabula*) on his way to the place of execution, making public the "charge" (αἰτία) against him.[13] In some cases, however, the criminal had "the notice of the complaint" attached to the top of the cross.[14] The "charge" was not a mandatory part of the crucifixion; it would often be used as a public warning or as a continuation of the mockery of the criminal. The narrator refers to the notice above the cross as "a title" (τίτλον), which is different from the Synoptics which refer to it as "an inscription" (Mark 15:26; Luke 23:38) or more simply, "a charge" (Matt 27:37). The term "title" has a more majestic or "royal" emphasis, suggesting that the message is intended for the general public and probably reflects the continuation of the political gerrymandering between Pilate and the Jews (see comments before 18:28).[15] This might explain why the narrator explains that Pilate "wrote" (ἔγραψεν) the title, in order to connect it to the authority by which it was created and to the context in which it must be understood.

The "title" posted above the cross read as follows: "Jesus the Nazarene, the King of the Jews" (Ἰησοῦς ὁ Ναζωραῖος ὁ βασιλεὺς τῶν Ἰουδαίων). The title includes both Jesus's personal name and professional "title." The crowd of authorities and soldiers that came to arrest him in the garden were looking for "Jesus the Nazarene" (cf. 18:5, 7), but the title "the King of the Jews" has been the primary title applied to Jesus throughout the trial scenes in order to mock not only him but also the Jews (cf. 18:39). Thus, the "title" above the cross brings closure to the whole narrative of chapters 18 – 19.[16]

19:20 Many of the Jews read this title, because the place where Jesus was crucified was near the city, and it was written in Aramaic, Latin, and Greek (τοῦτον οὖν τὸν τίτλον πολλοὶ ἀνέγνωσαν τῶν Ἰουδαίων, ὅτι ἐγγὺς ἦν ὁ τόπος τῆς πόλεως ὅπου ἐσταυρώθη ὁ Ἰησοῦς· καὶ ἦν γεγραμμένον Ἑβραϊστί, Ῥωμαϊστί, Ἑλληνιστί). The importance of the title is magnified by its trilingual presentation to the gathering Passover crowd. The narrator takes care to describe how the title was written in the three major languages of the Mediterranean world so that it could be read by all: "Aramaic" (Ἑβραϊστί), the language of the Jews and the vernacular of the region (cf. 5:2), "Latin" (Ῥωμαϊστί), the language of the Romans and the vernacular of the government, and "Greek" (Ἑλληνιστί), the language of the rest of the cultured world and the vernacular of trade and commerce.[17] Beyond the intentions of Pilate, the trilingual title announces to the world the judgment and victory of God in the person and work of Jesus Christ. "The Cross is international the moment Jesus mounts it."[18] Ignorantly Pilate, like Caiaphas before him (11:51), served as an OT prophet (cf. Ps 96:10). The trilingual title

---

12. Malina and Rohrbaugh, *John*, 264.

13. Ernst Bammel and Moule, "The *titulus*," in Bammel and Moule, *Jesus and the Politics of His Day*, 353 – 64 (353).

14. Reicke, *New Testament Era*, 187.

15. Brown, *Death of the Messiah*, 2:962 – 63.

16. Cf. Michaels, *John*, 949.

17. Schnackenburg, *John*, 3:271.

18. Bruner, *John*, 1101.

announces "the universal condemnation of those who condemned Jesus, and the universal offer of salvation to the universally condemned."[19]

19:21 Then the high priests of the Jews said to Pilate, "Do not write, 'the King of the Jews,' but that he said, 'I am King of the Jews'" (ἔλεγον οὖν τῷ Πιλάτῳ οἱ ἀρχιερεῖς τῶν Ἰουδαίων, Μὴ γράφε, Ὁ βασιλεὺς τῶν Ἰουδαίων, ἀλλ᾽ ὅτι ἐκεῖνος εἶπεν, Βασιλεύς εἰμι τῶν Ἰουδαίων). The reader is hardly surprised to see the Jews reject the title and respond to the climactic political statement of Pilate with disapproval. The present-tense imperative, "Do not write" (Μὴ γράφε) is surprising and is probably to be understood to be demanding that the sign be changed: "Alter what you have written!"[20] The command is given by those described almost tautologically by the narrator as "the high priests *of the Jews*" (οἱ ἀρχιερεῖς τῶν Ἰουδαίων), with the genitive qualifier serving emphatically to establish them as the representative voice of the whole of Judaism. Implicitly these high priests (correctly) interpret the charge in reference to them and want the charge redirected to the person beneath the plaque, Jesus the Nazarene, about whom they want explained that this was *his own* claim (see comments on 19:7). But Jesus was specific that his kingdom was "not from this world" (see comments on 18:36). The otherworldliness of his kingship was itself being declared as he hung on the cross, the place of his exaltation.

19:22 Pilate answered, "What I have written, I have written" (ἀπεκρίθη ὁ Πιλᾶτος, Ὃ γέγραφα, γέγραφα). The response of Pilate to the Jews is majestic in its own right, silencing all further discussion and allowing the trilingual title of Jesus on the cross to stand. Pilate declares twice in two perfect-tense verbs, "I have written" (γέγραφα),

which echoes the sacred scriptural preface "it is written" (γεγραμμένον) used elsewhere in the Gospel (2:17; 6:31, 45; 8:17; 10:34; 12:14; 15:25; cf. 7:38 and 20:31). The first perfect functions more like an aorist and may have been normally stated as such, which suggests that the use of two perfects increases the strength of finality.[21] While Pilate's formal statement was only intended to silence the challenge of the high priests and to serve as a final rebuke, it simultaneously serves a Scripture-like function declaring that the true authority had always belonged to the King on the cross. This entire section of the Gospel (18:1–19:42) has detailed how in every moment Jesus was in control, dictating the terms to both Jerusalem and Rome. The authoritative declaration of Pilate to the Jews cements this fact, so that even from the cross Jesus was exacting *his* rule over all creation.

19:23 Then the soldiers, when they crucified Jesus, took his clothes and divided them into four parts, a part for each soldier, except for the tunic. The tunic was seamless, woven throughout from the top (Οἱ οὖν στρατιῶται ὅτε ἐσταύρωσαν τὸν Ἰησοῦν ἔλαβον τὰ ἱμάτια αὐτοῦ καὶ ἐποίησαν τέσσαρα μέρη, ἑκάστῳ στρατιώτῃ μέρος, καὶ τὸν χιτῶνα. ἦν δὲ ὁ χιτὼν ἄραφος, ἐκ τῶν ἄνωθεν ὑφαντὸς δι᾽ ὅλου). The third scene of the pericope (vv. 23–24) directs the reader to look below the crucified Christ to the garments of Jesus lying on the ground beneath him. This is a surprising aspect of the crucifixion for the narrator to focus the reader's attention upon. It is not the soldiers' behavior that is surprising, for the confiscation of the criminal's possessions was a common penalty attending executions or other sentences of judgment. Roman crucifixions were performed with the victim naked, which heaped greater public shame on the criminal.[22] The specificity given to the garment

---

19. Barrett, *John*, 549.
20. Moulton, *Grammar*, 3:76. Cf. Moule, *Idiom*, 21.
21. BDF § 342.4.
22. Keener, *John*, 2:1138.

by the narrator suggests that this aspect of the crucifixion is important.

It appears that four soldiers, half of a normal Roman military unit that was likely dispatched for this work detail,[23] took the freedom they had as executioners to claim Jesus's clothes, both outer and inner garments. The outer garment(s), represented by the word "clothes" (τὰ ἱμάτια), was probably a traditional rectangular-shaped cloth (a "cloak") draped around the body, but it might also have included a belt, sandals, and even a head covering. The inner garment, represented by the word "tunic" (ὁ χιτών), was normally "worn next to the skin and was essentially a long, tight-fitting shirt made of two pieces of cloth sewn together," often sleeveless, and made of "wool, linen, or leather."[24] It was the outer garment(s) that the soldiers divided amongst themselves, either by separating the cloak into four parts at the seams or by giving one of the likely four items (cloak, belt, sandals, and head covering) to each of the soldiers. The seamless tunic, however, according to v. 24, was viewed as too worthy for division, so the soldiers decided to cast lots to decide to whom it would belong.

While it might be suggested that there is no symbolic significance in the tunic, the textual details suggest otherwise for a couple of reasons. First, the Greek syntax in this verse related to the tunic "is rather labored."[25] The narrator not only mentions that the tunic is seamless but gives details about its weave and construction that practically demands that something significant belongs to the depiction of the tunic itself. Second, the Gospel has already portrayed clothing in a manner that endows it with symbolic significance, as in the symbolically untied grave clothes of Lazarus (11:44; cf. 20:6 – 7), the symbolic taking up of a slave's towel by Jesus before washing his disciples' feet (13:4), or the symbol-laden royal garments mockingly placed on Jesus at his Roman trial (19:2, 5).[26] The Gospel's use of symbolism and double meaning has not decreased but increased as it moves toward its conclusion. It is exceedingly difficult to deny symbolism to this scene when the scenes surrounding it are also drenched with such narrative-directed symbolic significance.

What, therefore, is the symbolic significance of the seamless tunic? There are three options that have commonly been offered.[27] The most common suggestion in church history is that the tunic represents the unity of believers. This symbolic interpretation finds support in the Gospel as a whole regarding the ingathering of "other sheep" into one flock (cf. 10:16; 11:52; 17:20 – 23). Yet there is nothing specific to vv. 23 – 24 that make such symbolism explicit.[28] Moreover, the robe is no longer in the possession of or attached to Jesus. If unity is in view, why is the tunic depicted in isolation from Jesus?

The second option holds that because of the discarded tunic, the tunic highlights the self-giving of the Son. Seeing a parallel with 13:1 – 20 where Jesus laid aside his garments and became a

---

23. Ibid., 2:1139.

24. James S. Jeffers, *The Greco-Roman World of the New Testament Era: Exploring the Background of Early Christianity* (Downers Grove, IL: InterVarsity Press, 1999), 43.

25. Helen K. Bond, "Discarding the Seamless Robe: The High Priesthood of Jesus in John's Gospel" in *Israel's God and Rebecca's Children: Christology and Community in Early Judaism and Christianity*, ed. David B. Capes, April D. DeConick, Helen K. Bond, and Troy A. Miller (Waco, TX: Baylor University Press, 2007), 183 – 94 (184).

26. The Gospel also symbolically describes other physical objects, like the "night" in order to depict conflict with the light (3:2; 13:30), the jar left by the Samaritan woman (4:28), the loaves used to feed the large crowd (6:9), the charcoal fire (18:18; 21:9), and the great catch of fish without tearing the net (21:11). Cf. R. Alan Culpepper, "The Theology of the Johannine Passion Narrative: John 19:16b – 30," *Neot* 31 (1997): 21 – 37 (27).

27. The following is adapted from Bond, "Discarding the Seamless Robe," 185 – 89.

28. See Schnackenburg, *John*, 3:274.

humble servant, in this scene Jesus fulfills the ultimate act of service he promised in chapter 13, not by removing his own clothes (cf. 13:4) but by having them forcefully removed as he served and cleansed his disciples by the cross.[29] Yet like the first option, the parallel can only be claimed at the general level. The seamless nature of the tunic and the nature of its weave are entirely incidental to this interpretation of the symbolism. And unlike the foot washing scene in which a servant's towel was used (13:4), the use of the term "tunic" (χιτὼν) does not innately give the impression of debasement and humility; in fact, its seamlessness suggests quite the opposite.

Finally, some have suggested that the tunic is intended to evoke the symbolism of the high priest. In the first century this kind of clothing would have at least been recognized as ceremonial, and even more so in the context of the Jewish temple. The priestly garments are given careful depiction and emphasis in the Old Testament, reflecting the glory and honor of both the priesthood and the God it represents (cf. Exod 28:2). But this symbolic allusion is not primarily to be based upon vestment awareness in the first century but upon the specifics of the narrative itself.

Even beyond the narrator's depiction of the "seamless" tunic is his explanation that it was "woven throughout from the top" (ἐκ τῶν ἄνωθεν ὑφαντὸς δι' ὅλου).[30] Several things are worthy of note here. First, the adjective "woven" (ὑφαντὸς) only occurs in the LXX when referring to priestly garments (Exod 28:6, 32; 35:35; 36:10, 12, 15, 29, 34; 37:3, 5, 21) and in Josephus when he refers to

priestly garments and the drapes in the sanctuary. In fact, Josephus' depiction of the tunic of the priest is a strong parallel (Ant. 3.161). Second, the fact that the tunic was "seamless" (ἄραφος) adds to its priestly nature, since the priestly garments were created and preserved with great care.[31] Finally, the concern not to tear the tunic (v. 24) may echo the injunction of Leviticus 21:10 against tearing the high priestly robes.

The larger context of this section of the Gospel gives credence to this symbolic interpretation, for the narrative has taken great care to present Jesus as the true Priest (see comments on 18:10, 13). Even more, this entire section has given a dual portrait of Jesus as the priestly king, with the depictions of Jesus as *king* and *authority* (18:28–19:16) being surrounded or framed by the depictions of Jesus as *priest* and *sacrifice* (18:1–27 and 19:17–42). Thus, if vv. 19–22 are declaring Jesus to be the true King, then these verses (vv. 23–24) are declaring Jesus to be the true Priest—the Priest of the Most High God (cf. Heb 7). It is fitting that the tunic is no longer being worn by Jesus, for "it is Jesus, and no longer an earthly Jewish high priest, who takes away the sins of the world. God's people are about to be reconstituted around the person of Jesus, and the role and functions once reserved for the high priest—intercession, sacrifice, reconciliation, cleansing, and forgiveness from sin—are now fulfilled and superseded by Jesus himself."[32]

19:24 They said to one another, "Let us not tear it, but cast lots for it to decide whose it shall be," so that the Scripture might be fulfilled which said, "They divided my clothes for

---

29. See Carson, *John*, 614–15.

30. Elizabeth G. Pemberton, "The Seamless Garment: A Note on John 19:23–24," *ABR* 54 (2006): 50–55 (53).

31. See Heil, *Blood and Water*, 90–92.

32. Bond, "Discarding the Seamless Robe," 189. Cf. John Paul Heil, "Jesus as the Unique High Priest in the Gospel of John," *CBQ* 57 (1995): 729–45 (742). While the third option is

to be preferred as the primary symbol intended by the seamless tunic, there is no reason to suggest that the other options are not also (secondarily) in view. Certainly the second option (the self-giving of the Son) is part and parcel of the nature of Jesus's priesthood. But the first option (the unity of believers) is even more innately represented by the symbolism of the high priest.

themselves and for my clothes they cast lots." This indeed is what the soldiers did (εἶπαν οὖν πρὸς ἀλλήλους, Μὴ σχίσωμεν αὐτόν, ἀλλὰ λάχωμεν περὶ αὐτοῦ τίνος ἔσται· ἵνα ἡ γραφὴ πληρωθῇ ἡ λέγουσα, Διεμερίσαντο τὰ ἱμάτιά μου ἑαυτοῖς καὶ ἐπὶ τὸν ἱματισμόν μου ἔβαλον κλῆρον. Οἱ μὲν οὖν στρατιῶται ταῦτα ἐποίησαν). The soldiers voice their reason for not tearing the seamless tunic of Jesus, but the narrator explains that God had a much bigger reason. The action of the soldiers (i.e., the dividing of the garments and the casting of lots) according to the narrator fulfills what Psalm 22:18 had declared long before. Psalm 22 is quoted or alluded to fourteen times in the Gospels, twice in John (here and 19:30), and is an "altogether fitting ... expression of what he was experiencing on the cross and why he was there."[33] The majority of the OT passages quoted in relation to the crucifixion of Jesus come from the Psalms, most of which are "royal lament psalms" used "to portray Jesus as the King who was maltreated, pursued, or deserted by his contemporaries."[34] The movement of the psalms from suffering to triumph "is correlated hermeneutically with the story of Jesus's death and resurrection."[35]

Even the closing statement of this scene, "This indeed is what the soldiers did" (Οἱ μὲν οὖν στρατιῶται ταῦτα ἐποίησαν), with the phrase translated "indeed" (μὲν οὖν) serving as an emphatic expression (i.e., "certainly" or "to be sure"),[36] underscores the importance of the scriptural fulfillment performed unknowingly by the soldiers.[37] By using Psalm 22 the narrator presents Christ "not as a desperate King seeking protection from his enemies, and rescue by a seemingly absent God, but as a righteous King vindicated by God against those who falsely accuse and pursue him."[38] Even as Christ is nailed to the cross, the soldiers below him, gambling on the garments previously belonging to him, do nothing outside the will and control of God. They are doing, quite simply, what God said long ago they would do.

19:25 But also standing beside the cross of Jesus were his mother, his mother's sister, Mary the wife of Clopas, and Mary Magdalene (εἱστήκεισαν δὲ παρὰ τῷ σταυρῷ τοῦ Ἰησοῦ ἡ μήτηρ αὐτοῦ καὶ ἡ ἀδελφὴ τῆς μητρὸς αὐτοῦ, Μαρία ἡ τοῦ Κλωπᾶ καὶ Μαρία ἡ Μαγδαληνή). The fourth scene of the pericope (vv. 25–27) directs the reader to look in front of the crucified Christ to the family members standing before him. The narrator turns from the objects near Jesus to the people "standing" (εἱστήκεισαν) beside him. The public nature of crucifixion would have involved the family and friends as well, who by their relation to the criminal would have shared in his shame. While the soldiers would have normally disallowed people from approaching the cross directly, there is evidence that mourners, especially women, were allowed to be within hearing range of the criminal.[39] The narrator introduces or names each of the four women standing beside the cross of Jesus. The first two women are only introduced by their relation to Jesus, whereas the second two women are named. The Greek syntax offers a comparison between the four (male) soldiers and the four women also standing nearby, with the

---

33. Richard D. Patterson, "Psalm 22: From Trial to Triumph," *JETS* 47 (2004): 213–33 (228).

34. Marianne Meye Thompson, "'They Bear Witness to Me': The Psalms in the Passion Narrative of the Gospel of John," in *The Word Leaps the Gap: Essays on Scripture and Theology in Honor of Richard B. Hays*, ed. J. Ross Wagner, C. Kavin Rowe, and A. Katherine Grieb (Grand Rapids: Eerdmans, 2008), 267–83 (269).

35. Richard B. Hays, "Christ Prays the Psalms: Israel's Psalter as Matrix of Early Christianity," in *The Conversion of the Imagination: Paul as Interpreter of Israel's Scriptures* (Grand Rapids: Eerdmans, 2005), 101–18 (111).

36. BDAG 737.

37. Ridderbos, *John*, 610.

38. Thompson, "They Bear Witness to Me," 279.

39. Keener, *John*, 2:1141; Barrett, *John*, 551.

"but" (δὲ) functioning contrastively: "This indeed (Οἱ μὲν) is what the [four] soldiers did, but (δὲ) also standing beside the cross" were four women.[40]

The first woman mentioned is "his mother" (ἡ μήτηρ αὐτοῦ), whose only other appearance was at the wedding in Cana (see 2:1). The name of Jesus's mother (Mary) is never given in the Gospel, which we argued earlier was intended to facilitate the contrast between the mother of Jesus and his Father (see comments on 2:3–4). A similar contrast is likely in place here, since Jesus will again distance himself from *his mother* (v. 26).

The second woman mentioned is "his mother's sister" (ἡ ἀδελφὴ τῆς μητρὸς αὐτοῦ). The identity of this woman is directly related to her potential relation to Mary the wife of Clopas, for it has been suggested that this phrase is intended to be read in apposition to the one that follows, thus making "Mary the wife of Clopas" the sister of Mary the mother of Jesus. But as we will see below, this is almost certainly not the case, since it is unlikely that there would be two sisters both named "Mary." Thus, this unnamed woman is simply designated as the sister of Mary, the mother of Jesus, and therefore is *Jesus's aunt on his mother's side.*

The third woman mentioned is "Mary the wife of Clopas" (Μαρία ἡ τοῦ Κλωπᾶ). The Greek construction with the genitive is used here and elsewhere (e.g., Matt 1:6) to suffice for the meaning "the wife of."[41] Clopas, then, is the husband of this "Mary." But who is Clopas? According to Christian tradition he was the brother of Joseph, the husband of Mary, the mother of Jesus. According to the second-century writer Hegesippus, we know that the

successor to James the Lord's brother as head of the Jerusalem church was Simon (or Symeon), the son of Clopas (Eusebius, *Hist. eccl.* 3.11; 3.32.6; 4.22.4). Clopas's son's succession to James "is part of the pattern of dominance of relatives of Jesus in the leadership of Palestine Jewish Christianity down to the early second century at least."[42] Thus, "Mary the wife of Clopas" was Jesus's mother's husband's brother's wife. Since her son Simon "was the most important Christian leader in Palestine for half a century," she could have easily been identified by her relation to him.[43] But by relating her to her husband, Clopas, the narrator also then relates her more directly to Jesus, who is the son of Clopas's brother, Joseph, and therefore is *Jesus's aunt on his father's side.*[44]

The fourth woman mentioned is "Mary Magdalene" (Μαρία ἡ Μαγδαληνή). This is the first appearance of this "Mary" in the Gospel, though she plays a prominent role in the resurrection scenes (see 20:1–2, 11–18). Although she is the only woman at the cross not related to Jesus, she is the best known woman disciple of Jesus in the early church, appearing in every grouping in every Gospel.[45] Even though this "Mary" is just as briefly introduced as the other women at the cross, early sectarian groups often focused on her, and recently popular books (and films) have given her an inordinate amount of attention and mystique.[46] But there is no mystery behind Mary Magdalene or repression of her role by the church. Rather, it is her intimate connection to the death and resurrection of Jesus that explains the emphasis given to her by the Gospel of John and the other Gospels.[47] She

---

40. Cf. Carson, *John*, 615.

41. Richard Bauckham, "Mary of Clopas (John 19:25)," in *Women in the Gospel Tradition*, ed. George J. Brooke; SWR 31 (Lewiston, NY: Edwin Mellen, 1992), 231–55 (235).

42. Ibid., 237. See also Bauckham, *Jude and the Relatives of Jesus*, 45–133.

43. Ibid., 238.

44. Ibid., 242.

45. Bauckham, *Jude and the Relatives of Jesus*, 11.

46. See Dan Brown, *The Da Vinci Code* (New York: Doubleday, 2003).

47. Richard Bauckham, "Salome the Sister of Jesus, Salome the Disciple of Jesus, and the Secret Gospel of Mark," *NovT* 33 (1991): 245–75 (257).

serves as "an apostle to the apostles" (cf. 20:1 – 2, 18) in the events immediately following the crucifixion, becoming *the first witness of the resurrected Christ*.[48]

19:26 When Jesus saw his mother and the disciple whom he loved standing there, he said to his mother, "Woman, behold, your son" (Ἰησοῦς οὖν ἰδὼν τὴν μητέρα καὶ τὸν μαθητὴν παρεστῶτα ὃν ἠγάπα, λέγει τῇ μητρί, Γύναι, ἴδε ὁ υἱός σου). The narrative shifts from the crowd's observation of Jesus to Jesus's observation of his family, specifically Jesus's mother and one of his disciples, whom Jesus notices from the cross and briefly addresses. While some might suggest the statement of Jesus is simply an act of familial faithfulness, ensuring that his mother is cared for after his death, for two reasons this scene demands to be interpreted primarily with a symbolic significance, making familial (historical) concerns the secondary concern of the narrative message. First, since every other statement of Jesus during his crucifixion is focused upon and is to be understood by his divine (i.e., cosmological) mission, "it would be truly astounding if these words to his mother constituted a solitary exception."[49] Second, if vv. 26 – 27 is primarily an act of care for his mother, why is the disciple entrusted to Mary and not *vice versa*?[50] If the care of his mother was his primary concern, he should have directed the disciple (the new "son") toward his mother so as to make him the active agent who is to receive her as his own mother. Thus, however we explain the symbolic significance of Jesus's statement, what is clear is that he is making the *sonship* of this anonymous disciple a primary concern.

The symbolism is given direction by the statement of Jesus itself: "Woman, behold, your son"

(Γύναι, ἴδε ὁ υἱός σου). The meaning of this statement is strongly dependent on a related statement Jesus made to his mother at her first appearance in the Gospel at the wedding at Cana (cf. 2:3 – 5). The two prefatory aspects of the statement need to be explained. First, the use of "woman" (Γύναι) to address his mother must be viewed as parallel to its use in 2:4 where it was functioning at least minimally as a distancing mechanism, even if it is enveloped within a healthy and loving relationship between mother and son. This choice of word must be drawing attention away from Mary's blood relationship with Jesus. This need not be a distancing that denies the mother her son but locates it in the larger context of a much greater and more foundational relationship between the unique Son and the Father (see comments on 2:4).

Second, the use of the particle of exclamation "behold" (ἴδε) has become common in the Gospel, serving as a "prompter of attention" before a verb; yet when it is used before a noun, it serves as a "marker of strong emphasis."[51] The Fourth Gospel uses it in the latter sense when there is a challenge to perceive with the mind a truth not outwardly evident to human eyes (cf. 1:29; 19:5, 14). Thus, the concept of "sonship" Jesus is about to introduce is clearly to be viewed as different in kind from the traditional, familial concepts of sonship. As much as this is certain, however, it is difficult to know exactly how this grander category of "sonship" is to be interpreted, especially in relation to the mother of Jesus. We will discuss this more fully below (see v. 27).

It is important to note that the context the narrator establishes for Jesus's symbolic statement includes not only his mother but also the "son" about whom he speaks, who is depicted as "standing

48. F. S. Spencer, "Women," in *Dictionary of Jesus and the Gospels*, 2nd ed. (Downers Grove, IL: InterVarsity Press, 2013), 1004 – 13 (1013).

49. John McHugh, *The Mother of Jesus in the New Testament* (Garden City, NY: Doubleday, 1975), 376.

50. Ibid.

51. BDAG 468.

there" (παρεστῶτα) with Jesus's mother at the cross. Implicit in the narrator's description is that standing beside the four women was an anonymous disciple, whom he describes as "the disciple whom he loved" (τὸν μαθητὴν ὃν ἠγάπα). This is another occurrence in the Gospel of the "Beloved Disciple," who was officially introduced in the farewell discourse and appears throughout the end of the Gospel (for an overview of the "Beloved Disciple," see comments on 13:23). In this scene two things are important to note regarding the developing identity and role of the Beloved Disciple. First, while not mentioned at first (v. 25), in this verse he is clearly included among the four women as a personal witness of the final words and the death of Jesus. Second, according to Jesus's own instruction, the statement of Jesus makes the "son" intimately connected to the mother of Jesus and therefore to the family of Jesus.

The more obvious significance of this verse is that the "son," who is also the Beloved Disciple, is positioned by Jesus in this verse to be the object of the maternal focus of Jesus's mother. As much as the son's parental focus will also be directed toward his (nonbiological) mother in v. 27, it is certainly striking that the mother is addressed first, especially when in the historical context the traditional priority would be the care of the mother by the son. Since the symbolism of this scene in the pericope is rooted neither in the son nor the mother alone but in the relationship between them, we must include an analysis of v. 27 to determine its meaning.

But one thing has already been established by this verse: *Jesus's statement is intended to establish the true nature of sonship.* By focusing on the son before the mother and by distancing himself from his mother with the use of "woman," Jesus's statement from the cross expresses the complex nature of sonship that has been developing throughout the

Gospel. The prologue explained the comparison and contrast between the "children of God" (1:12) and the "unique Son" (1:14). While it is the cross that most clearly distinguishes the sons from the Son, it is also the cross alone that unifies them in the same Father. This is why Jesus addresses the needs of the son before the needs of his mother as he hangs on the cross, for in the context of his mission from the Father, the mother of Jesus is no less in need of this "sonship" than the Beloved Disciple, for by this act she too becomes a child of the Father. Jesus is addressing the cosmological identity of his family from the cross, not their historical identity (1:13).

19:27 Then he said to the disciple, "Behold, your mother." And from that hour the disciple took her into his own home (εἶτα λέγει τῷ μαθητῇ, Ἴδε ἡ μήτηρ σου. καὶ ἀπ᾽ ἐκείνης τῆς ὥρας ἔλαβεν αὐτὴν ὁ μαθητὴς εἰς τὰ ἴδια). In light of v. 26 we have determined that the first part of Jesus's statement from the cross was intended to establish the vertical nature of sonship. Jesus is the unique Son, and his disciples and even his own kin are the children of God by means of his person and work. But what is the meaning of the second part of Jesus's statement to his family, which he addresses to the Beloved Disciple: "Behold, your mother" (Ἴδε ἡ μήτηρ σου)? Like v. 26, the particle of exclamation is to be noted, guiding us to perceive with the mind a truth not outwardly evident to human eyes. And with v. 26, this second part of the statement is clearly to be understood in relation to the first part of the statement.

A host of interpretations has been offered to explain their relation, falling somewhere under one of three primary approaches to the symbolism.[52]

(1) *The son's (physical) care of the mother.* Protestants historically have restricted the significance of the statement to Jesus's personal care for his mother,

---

52. See also Schnackenburg, *John*, 3:279–81.

probably in response to the exaggerated symbolic significance applied to the mother of Jesus. But as we discussed above, the first part of the statement is so emphatically focused on the issue of sonship that it is difficult to see the care of the mother as the primary intention. In light of the first part of the statement, the care of the mother cannot be viewed as distinct from the nature of the "son."

(2) *The mother's (spiritual) care of the son.* Catholics in contrast have at least since the twelfth century found support in this statement for the understanding of Mary as the spiritual mother of the church.[53] In fact, since the papal citations of the passage constitute an authoritative doctrine, the spiritual motherhood can arguably be declared Roman Catholic Marian doctrine.[54] But the emphasis on sonship in the first part of the statement makes it difficult to see this interpretation as the primary meaning. Certainly the role of the mother of Jesus cannot be viewed in isolation from the role of the Beloved Disciple. This interpretation also has the added difficulty of requiring the mother of Jesus to be treated as an individual (Mary) while the Beloved Disciple is treated as a general symbol for every Christian (the church).[55]

(3) *The symbolism of mother and son.* Finally, a variety of interpretations has been offered that interpret the two figures (mother and son) as two equal figures. For example, Bultmann suggests that each figure represents and serves to unify the Jewish and gentile sides of Christianity.[56] But the text does nothing to suggest a symbolic ethnic distinction between the two figures. Others have suggested that the mother of Jesus represents Eve, the "woman" of Genesis 2–4, so that Mary becomes the new (second) Eve and the mother of the disciples of Jesus, represented by the "ideal" disciple, the replacement son promised to Eve by God (Gen 4:25; cf. Rev 12). The danger of these symbolic approaches is that they emphasize the individuality of the figures. The text, however, does not show concern with the figures in their individuality but in their *mutuality*.[57] When Jesus addresses the one, he is speaking about the other.

The symbolic significance of Jesus's two-part statement therefore lies not in the individual symbols but precisely in the new relationship that can now be understood to exist between them. If the first part of Jesus's statement emphasizes the *vertical* nature of sonship, that he is the unique Son, the second part of his statement expresses the *horizontal* nature of this same sonship, that his disciples, including his own kin, have been declared by him to be a newly created family (cf. 2 Cor. 5:17). Jesus does not relegate his family relations before he dies but announces by his death the formation of a new family with new family relations, represented by the two people with whom he was likely the closest (cf. Matt 12:46–50).[58] The primary symbolism of Jesus's (anonymous) mother and the (anonymous) Beloved Disciple then is their relationship, with both representing the unique nature of this new community. Mary, by being distanced from her role as the mother of Jesus, from now on will represent the *maternal* nature of the children of God and their corporate life together.[59] And the Beloved

53. See Christian Paul Ceroke, "Mary's Maternal Role in John 19, 25–27," *MarStud* 11 (1960): 123–51.

54. Brown, *John*, 2:925.

55. Raymond E. Brown, Karl P. Donfried, Joseph A. Fitzmyer, and John Reumann, *Mary in the New Testament: A Collaborative Assessment by Protestant and Roman Catholic Scholars* (Philadelphia: Fortress, 1978), 217.

56. Bultmann, *John*, 673.

57. Cf. Heinz Schürmann, *Jesu ureigener Tod* (Freiburg: Herder, 1975), 20.

58. Barrett suggests that the statement "behold, your mother" recalls legal adoption language (*John*, 552). Culpepper suggests the language is "performative language" and is like a marriage declaration ("Theology of the Johannine Passion Narrative," 30).

59. Cf. the "hospitality" motif employed elsewhere in the Gospel.

Disciple, by being distanced from his role as the biological son of another, from now on will represent the *adopted* nature of the children of God and their continued work together.

It is in this light that the final statement of the pericope "and from that hour the disciple took her into his own home" (καὶ ἀπ᾽ ἐκείνης τῆς ὥρας ἔλαβεν αὐτὴν ὁ μαθητὴς εἰς τὰ ἴδια) can be understood to speak beyond the mother's new resi-

dence. The terms in this pithy statement — "hour" (cf. 2:4), "receive" (1:12), and "his own home" (τὰ ἴδια; 1:11) — are each rooted in the Gospel's macrothemes. Rather than depicting the place to which the mother of Jesus was going, this closing statement by the narrator speaks more about the place to which Jesus is going. For as Jesus explained in the farewell discourse, his departure is less an ending and more a new beginning (14:18 – 20).

Theology in Application

The climax of the Gospel — and the ministry of Jesus — has long been described as "the hour" (cf. 2:4), and in this pericope the hour has arrived. The cross is the place where the person and work of Christ is explained and proclaimed, and it is at the cross that the narrator takes the reader on a tour to explain the threefold message it declares about Christ as the fulfillment of God's work in the world: that he is the King, the Priest, and the Son. The narrative guides the reader from the perspective of the cross to see how the historical realities surrounding the death of Jesus — his title, his tunic, and his family — declare the cosmological realities of God. Through this pericope the reader is presented with the "grace and truth" that comes through the person of Jesus Christ (1:17) and is exhorted to embrace him as the King, the Priest, and the Son of God.

The Place of Death and Life

Although few details of the crucifixion of Jesus are given, the narrator goes into surprising detail regarding the place of the crucifixion, which as he explains is called "the Place of the Skull" (v. 17). The symbolism of the place of the death of Jesus are clear: the *place* of the Skull has been overtaken by the *presence* of the Savior! The reader is well aware at this point in the Gospel that Jesus is not hanging on the cross as a victim but voluntarily and by his own authority. For in that "hour," the place of death was transformed into the place of life. For this reason Christians claim the death of Christ as the source of their life and the cross as their symbol. For when Jesus's life ended that day, eternal life was born. And the Place of the Skull, or Calvary, would forever be known not by the thousands of people's lives it claimed but by the millions of lives it produced through the vicarious death of one person, Jesus Christ.

The Cross Declares the Kingship of Jesus

It is fitting that just inches above the head of Jesus, as if it were a crown, rested a sign — intentionally called "a title" (v. 19) by the narrator — which declared in every necessary language the day that Jesus was the King. The ironic reality of the title above the cross is clear. The political gerrymandering and rhetorical wrangling between the authorities of Jerusalem and Rome ended with a climactic, Scripture-like declaration that was so true that only the reader could comprehend its fullness: the crucifixion of Jesus *is* his exaltation (cf. 3:14). This declaration of the kingship of Jesus was the simultaneous announcement of the judgment of the world and the victory of God. The cross announces that "the LORD reigns" and "will judge the peoples with equity" (Ps 96:10). For this reason Christians speak of Jesus as both Savior and Lord, for the cross is both the source of redemption and the scepter of his rule, through which he "hands over the kingdom to God the Father after he has destroyed all dominion, authority and power" (1 Cor 15:24). One day people from every nation and government, both slave and sovereign, will bow their knees and confess with their tongues that Jesus Christ is Lord — not in spite of the cross but because of it (Phil 2:10 – 11).

The Cross Declares the Priesthood of Jesus

It is fitting that resting on the ground beneath the broken and bloodied body were the garments of Jesus that the narrator intentionally describes with imagery reflecting the robes of the high priest (vv. 23 – 24). The symbolism of the seamless tunic below the cross is clear: the crucified Christ is "the Lamb of God" (cf. 1:29) who as the high priest of God (Heb 7) offers a one-time sacrifice for the sin of the world. By his own authority (as King), Jesus makes himself the propitiation for the sins of the world, taking the wrath of God upon himself and reconciling the world to God. The sacrificial overtones have been developing throughout the Gospel so that the symbol-laden priestly tunic of Jesus lying unworn beneath the cross proclaims that the crucified Jesus has fulfilled and superseded the role of both the Passover lamb and the high priest. The garment need no longer be worn, for like the temple it has been replaced by the body of Jesus (cf. 2:12 – 15). The reader is guided to see that everything once expected from the high priest — intercession, sacrifice, reconciliation, cleansing, and forgiveness from sin — is now accomplished completely through Jesus on the cross. For this reason Christians come to Jesus as the royal High Priest "who sat down at the right hand of the throne of the Majesty in heaven, and who serves in the sanctuary, the true tabernacle set up by the Lord, not by a mere human being" (Heb 8:1 – 2). The crucified Christ *is* the sacrificed Priest, who by his own blood is the mediator of eternal redemption and a new covenant (Heb 9:12, 15).

The Cross Declares the Sonship of Jesus

It is fitting that standing just feet in front of the cross of Christ was the family of Jesus: his mother, two aunts, and two intimate disciples (a woman and a man), to whom Jesus speaks with words that describe them all in familial terms (vv. 25 – 27). The symbolism of the family of Jesus before the cross is clear: the cross declares Jesus as the unique Son from the Father and reestablishes the disciples through his own blood as a newly created family, the "children of God" (1:12). The familial language is intended to establish the true nature of Jesus's sonship, through which the sons and daughters of God are born (ch. 3). Paradoxically, then, while it is the cross that most clearly distinguishes the sons from the Son, it is also the cross alone that unifies them in the same Father. This is why the Gospel exhorts the reader to believe that Jesus the Christ is *the Son* of God (20:31), for it is through the Son of God that the children of God are given life, complete access to the Father, and full participation in the family of God, the church. For this reason Christians call one another "brothers and sisters" and are commanded to live together as a family. The source of life for the Christian has never been grounded in the blood, desire, or will of humanity, "but from God" (1:13) alone, whom we now may address as "our Father" (Matt 6:9 – 13).

John 19:28 – 42

Literary Context

The pericope concludes the events surrounding the sacrificial death of the Son of God. Just as the Gospel was careful to detail the symbol-laden meaning of the crucifixion of Christ, so also will it depict his death and burial with sensitivity to both the details of the event and their intentional significance. The reader is guided to see how the end of Jesus's life is also the completion of the promises foretold by Scripture long before. The death and burial of Jesus is the completion of the first half of the biblical story, but it is also the beginning of the rest of the story the Bible tells — and it all centers around "a garden" (see comments on 18:1). For just as the first part of the biblical story began in a garden (Gen 2), so also will the second part end in a garden (Rev 21 – 22), and at the center of this story is this garden in John 18 – 20, the place of the death (19:41) and resurrection (see 20:15) of Jesus Christ, whose death gives life to the world, fulfilling in his person the entire biblical story.

VIII. The Crucifixion (18:1 – 19:42)
    A. The Arrest of Jesus (18:1 – 12)
    B. The Jewish Trial and Its Witnesses (18:13 – 27)
    C. The Roman Trial before Pilate (18:28 – 40)
    D. The Verdict: "Crucify Him!" (19:1 – 16)
    E. The Crucifixion of Jesus (19:17 – 27)
➡   **F. The Death and Burial of Jesus (19:28 – 42)**

Main Idea

Jesus is the perfect sacrifice of God, completing in full the Passover requirements God established long before in Scripture. Beginning and ending in "a garden," the death and burial of Jesus fulfills the entire biblical story.

Translation

John 19:28–42

28a	Scene 1	After this,
b	Character Reentrance	**Jesus ...**
c	Character's Thoughts	knowing that all things ...
d	"Complete" #1	... had already been completed,
e	Result	so that the Scripture ...
f	"Complete" #2	... might be completed,
g		**... said,**
h	Assertion/Allusion: OT & NT	*"I am thirsty."*
29a	Setting	**A jar ...**
b	Allusion: Ps 69:21	full of sour wine
c		**... was standing there,**
d		
	Sequence of Action (#1)	so putting a sponge
e	Allusion: Ps 69:21	full of the sour wine
f	Allusion: "Passover"	on a hyssop,
g	Character Entrance (#2)	**they brought it to his mouth**
30a	Progression of Action	When Jesus had received the sour wine,
b		**he said,**
c	Announcement/"Complete" #3	*"It is completed,"*
d	Sequence of Departure #1	and **he bowed his head**
e	Sequence of Departure #2	and **gave over his spirit.**
31a	Scene 2	Then
b	Characters Reentrance	**the Jews asked Pilate**
c	Purposed Sequence #1	to break their legs and
d	Purposed Sequence #2	have them taken away,
e	Basis of 31f	since it was the day of preparation,
f	Intended Result	so that the bodies would not stay
g	Ironical Juxtaposition:	on the cross
h	"Cross"/"Sabbath"	on the Sabbath,
i	Explanation	for **that Sabbath was a great day.**
32a	Result of 31	So **the soldiers came**
b		and **broke the legs**
c	Progression of Action	of the first man and
d		the other man
e	Description	who had been crucified with him.
33a	Contrast to 32	But
b		when they came to Jesus
c	Action	**they saw that he had already died,**
d	Result	so they did not break his legs.

34a	Continued Contrast to 32	Instead
b	Character Entrance	**one of the soldiers ...**
c	Sequence of Action #1	**... pierced his side with a spear,**
d	Sequence of Action #2	and
e		immediately
f	Allusion: "Sacrifice"	**blood** and
g	Allusion: "Spirit"	**water came out.**

35a	Narrator's Intrusion	**The one who has seen it ...**
b	Assertion	**... has given witness,**
c	Assertion	and **his testimony is true.**
d	Character's Thoughts	**He knows that he speaks the truth,**
e	Purpose	in order that you also may believe.

36a	Explanation	For **these things happened**
b	Prophetic Fulfillment #1	so that Scripture might be fulfilled:
c	"Passover Lamb" & "Father"	*"His bones will not be broken."*
37a	Prophetic Fulfillment #2	In addition **another Scripture says,**
b	"Sacrifice" & "Solution"	*"They will look at the one they have pierced."*
38a	Scene 3	And
b	Scene Shift	after these things
c	Character Entrance	**Joseph of Arimathea ...**
d	Identification	a disciple of Jesus, but
e	Description	a secret one
f	Basis	for fear of the Jews,
g	Request	**... asked Pilate**
h	Purpose	to take away the body of Jesus.

i	Reaction	And **Pilate granted him permission,**
j	Progression of Action	so **he came**
k		and **took away his body.**
39a	Character Re–Entrance	And **Nicodemus came also,**
b	Description	the one who came to him first at night,
c	Simultaneous Action	bringing a mixture
d	Burial Items	of myrrh and aloe,
e	Quantity	about a hundred pounds.
40a	Restatement of 38k	So **they took the body of Jesus**
b	Burial of "Jesus"	and **wrapped it in linen cloth with spices,**
c	Historical Description	as is the burial custom of the Jews.

41a	Historical Location of Burial	**In the place where Jesus was crucified ...**
b	Allusion: OT & NT	**... was a garden,**
c	Description	and **in the garden a new tomb,**
d	Emphatic Description	in which no one had ever been laid.

42a	Basis #1 for 42c	On account of the Jewish day of preparation and
b	Basis #2	because the tomb was close,
c	Conclusion	**they placed Jesus in that place.**

Structure and Literary Form

The structure of this pericope is different than the basic story form (see Introduction). Combined with the previous pericope (19:17 – 27), these two pericopae are guided by the details of a Roman crucifixion, with the account of the death of Jesus falling naturally into seven scenes between both pericopae. This pericope is broken into three scenes that detail one significant aspect of his death and burial. The intentional symbolism prominent throughout the Gospel and magnified in the previous pericope is also on display here, with carefully chosen language and descriptions that serve to display in each scene important aspects of the significance of Jesus's death. The first scene depicts the final words of "the Word," his declaration that his death is the completion of his mission from the Father (vv. 28 – 30). The second scene involves the narrator's commentary on the death of Jesus as the perfect sacrifice, fulfilling what was promised in the OT (vv. 31 – 37). The third scene describes how two lesser-known disciples of Jesus gave the body of Jesus a fitting burial (vv. 38 – 42). In what could be described as the final act of the public ministry of Jesus, the reader is a witness to the full biblical significance of the death and burial of the Son of God.

Exegetical Outline

→ **F. The Death and Burial of Jesus (19:28 – 42)**
    1. "It Is Completed" (vv. 28 – 30)
    2. Testimony to the Perfect Sacrifice (vv. 31 – 37)
    3. Buried in a Garden and a New Tomb (vv. 38 – 42)

Explanation of the Text

19:28 After this, Jesus, knowing that all things had already been completed, so that the Scripture might be completed, said, "I am thirsty" (Μετὰ τοῦτο εἰδὼς ὁ Ἰησοῦς ὅτι ἤδη πάντα τετέλεσται, ἵνα τελειωθῇ ἡ γραφή, λέγει, Διψῶ). The first section of the pericope (vv. 28 – 30) records the final words and actions of Jesus and the moments leading up to his death. The opening phrase "after this" (Μετὰ τοῦτο) signals the start of a new pericope (see comments on 2:12), but it also serves to focus the reader's attention from the details surrounding the cross to the person hanging upon it. The Gospel here is giving insight into the meaning of

the death and burial of Jesus as it is occurring in narrative time.

According to the narrator, Jesus knew "that all things had already been completed" (ὅτι ἤδη πάντα τετέλεσται). The narrator gives us insight into Jesus's perspective of his own death even while he is hanging on the cross. Like the trial scene, Jesus is depicted in complete control (see 18:4); but more is likely intended by this statement. The use of the term "completed" or "fulfilled" (τετέλεσται) suggests that Jesus had accomplished all the work given to him by the Father (17:4; cf. 4:34; 5:36; 17:4). Since he will shortly declare it completed with one Greek word (v. 30), here the narrator offers the reader insight into what that one-word statement is referring to. The crucified Jesus has now accomplished "all things" (πάντα) assigned to him by the Father.

The next phrase, "so that the Scripture might be completed" (ἵνα τελειωθῇ ἡ γραφή), is more difficult to explain. While it might seem like one of several fulfillment formulas, there is a potentially significant difference. In every other occurrence of such a formula in the Gospel, the verb "fulfilled" (πληρωθῇ) is used, both before (12:38; 13:18; 15:25; 17:12; 18:9, 32; 19:24) and after (19:36) this particular fulfillment formula. But in this unique occurrence, the Greek word equally translatable as "fulfilled" is different, which is why we used a different, even if overlapping, translation of "completed" (τελειωθῇ). While a case should not be made that there is a serious distinction in meaning, for the terms are overlapping enough to be generally synonymous, the change in words is certainly intentional and facilitates meaning — a stylistic variation not uncommon to the Gospel (see 21:15 – 17). The word change is almost certainly related to the occurrence of two identical words in the immediate context which also come from the same Greek word group (τελ-): "completed" (τετέλεσται) in v. 28a and "it is completed" (Τετέλεσται) in v. 30. Thus, by using nearly identical terms three times in such close proximity, the narrative offers an emphatic threefold declaration that the work assigned to Jesus by the Father is *completed* on the cross. And in the context of a fulfillment formula, the work of Jesus not only "completes" the work assigned from the Father but also "completes" Scripture.

It is difficult to know, however, if the fulfillment formula is referring to what preceded it, the "completed" work, or to what comes after it, Jesus's statement, "I am thirsty" (Διψῶ). There are two grammatical possibilities: (1) the fulfillment formula concludes the preceding clause and refers to Scripture as a whole, or (2) the fulfillment formula prefaces the clause that comes after it and refers to one particular Scripture: "I am thirsty." In support of option (1), normally a final clause introduced with "so that/in order that" (ἵνα) is related to a governing verb that precedes it.[1] And it is undeniable that the clearly interconnected terminology with the preceding statement is intended to create some sort of functional connection. In support of option (2), however, normally the fulfillment formula modifies the statement that comes after it, as it does in every other occurrence in the Gospel. And while it is not impossible that the formula offers a concluding statement, it is much more likely that the fulfillment formula is prefacing what follows.[2]

Thus, we have an interpretive conundrum. This fulfillment formula is grammatically (and arguably equally) connected both to what it concludes *and* what it prefaces. Rather than choosing between the two, the text seems to be suggesting by its very construction that we let this fulfillment formula function simultaneously in both directions. And this might be precisely the point! By concluding the preceding clause (option 1), the formula declares at the general level that the crucified Christ brings the Scripture to its completion. The crucified Jesus *is* the completion of Scripture.[3] It is the fulfillment of everything that was promised in Scripture and the foundation of everything still to come. At the same time, however, by prefacing the clause that follows (option 2), the formula also declares that Christ's thirst is itself a specific fulfillment of Scripture. To the smallest detail the death of Christ is the fulfillment of what Scripture foretold long before.

---

1. Brown, *John*, 2:908.
2. Cf. Barrett, *John*, 553.

3. Hoskyns, *Fourth Gospel*, 531.

Jesus's one Greek word, translated into English as "I am thirsty" (Διψῶ), is rightly taken by most scholars as a fulfillment of Psalm 69:21. Not only has Psalm 69 been quoted twice before in the Gospel (2:17; 15:25), but the response of the soldiers to Jesus's thirst makes the connection clear (see v. 29). But by not providing a specific quotation that is fulfilled, the narrator allows Jesus's word itself to stand as that which is fulfilled. That is, while the thing imaged through the connection to Psalm 69 is certainly the deep reality of the suffering of Christ depicted by the thirst and drink language, the lack of a specific referent suggests that the image intended is not fully confined to Psalm 69 alone but also includes comparable allusions in the Gospel.[4] For example, the last time Jesus asked for a drink was in 4:7 when he spoke to the Samaritan woman while sitting by Jacob's well. In 7:38 – 39 Jesus refers to another obscure OT passage when he speaks of a thirst that only he can quench. The connection between this "drink" and the Spirit has many parallels with this pericope (see v. 30). Finally, when Peter tried to prevent his arrest, Jesus responded in 18:11, "The cup which the Father has given to me, shall I not drink it?"

Thus, when Jesus speaks of his thirst and takes a drink (v. 29), his drinking symbolizes not only "the cup" from the Father, but how by his own thirst he fulfills in his person the thirst-quenching promise he declared long before. Just as the allusion to Psalm 69 is not about thirst and drink per se but is intended to depict the depth of Jesus's suffering, so also is Jesus's single word here intended to depict how his thirst is a *representative* thirst.[5] The cross of Christ is the source of living water. This makes all the more sense in the context of this particu-

lar fulfillment formula, which also speaks generally about the completion of Jesus's work from the Father. Jesus really was thirsty as he hung on the cross, and the narrator describes it in a manner that allows the reader to understand the full depth of Christ's thirst and the full solution to all thirst.

19:29 A jar full of sour wine was standing there, so putting a sponge full of the sour wine on a hyssop, they brought it to his mouth (σκεῦος ἔκειτο ὄξους μεστόν· σπόγγον οὖν μεστὸν τοῦ ὄξους ὑσσώπῳ περιθέντες προσήνεγκαν αὐτοῦ τῷ στόματι). Although the reader knows that Jesus's one-word statement was inclusive of a much greater "cup," the soldiers, who we may presume are the ones offering the drink to Jesus, respond to Jesus by offering him an actual substance to drink. The narrator explains that standing near the cross was a jar full of "sour wine" (ὄξους). This sour wine is often described as "the usual refreshing drink of laborers and soldiers," and therefore was intended for the soldiers to drink.[6] Thus, it is possible that the gesture was sympathetic, although in the context of a crucifixion where abuse and mockery have run rampant this would be somewhat surprising. Some have suggested, in contrast, that the drink was intended "to revive Jesus lest he die too soon."[7] Some have even argued (based primarily on Mark 15) that the wine was a form of torture, based upon the corroding mixture of wine and vinegar/myrrh.[8] While this cannot be verified from the text alone, the probable allusion to Psalm 69:21 strengthens the possibility, where the drink given to the victim is an act of hostility to increase suffering. What is clear is that the response of the soldiers is the fulfillment of Scripture and highlights the cup of suffering Jesus must drink.

---

4. Culpepper, "Theology of the Johannine Passion Narrative," 32.

5. Ibid., 33 – 34.

6. Keener, *John*, 2:1147.

7. Brown, *Death of the Messiah*, 2:1064.

8. See Erkki Koskenniemi, Kirsi Nisula, and Jorma Toppari, "Wine Mixed with Myrrh (Mark 15.23) and Crurifragium (John 19.31 – 32): Two Details of the Passion Narratives," *JSNT* 27 (2005): 379 – 91 (especially 379 – 86).

The narrator explains how the soldiers (again, presumably) filled a sponge with the wine and put it to Jesus's mouth for him to drink; this was the only means by which liquid could be given to a person on a cross. While the mode of drinking is quite normal, the oddity in the scene is the mention of a "hyssop" (ὑσσώπῳ) upon which the sponge was placed. The hyssop lacked a substantial stalk needed to place a wine-filled sponge and hold its weight; it is a small, bushy plant with leaves and flowers that are highly absorptive and thus suitable for sprinkling (Lev 14:4 – 7; Num 19:18).[9] For this reason it was famously connected to the sprinkling of the blood of the Passover lamb on the doorposts as recorded in Exodus 12:22. The very implausibility of the description of this plant serving this task at the crucifixion reinforces the probability that its use here is intended to reinforce for the Gospel the Passover imagery (see comments on 1:29 and 19:14).[10] There is no need to suggest that the narrator is fabricating the account for theological purposes. In the providence of God the Roman soldiers, entirely unfamiliar with the theology of plant parts used to provide a drink, used a particular plant that communicated perfectly the nature of the drink received by Jesus. The cup given to Jesus by the Father was perfectly displayed by the symbol-laden hyssop given to him by the soldiers.

19:30 When Jesus had received the sour wine, he said, "It is completed," and he bowed his head and gave over his spirit (ὅτε οὖν ἔλαβεν τὸ ὄξος [ὁ] Ἰησοῦς εἶπεν, Τετέλεσται· καὶ κλίνας τὴν κεφαλὴν παρέδωκεν τὸ πνεῦμα). The narrator then describes the last moment of Jesus's life. After drinking the wine from the hyssop branch, the narrator explains that Jesus did two further things. First, Jesus again

speaks a one-word statement: "It is completed" (Τετέλεσται). This is the third occurrence of nearly identical words used in the immediate context (see v. 28) that emphasize the completion of the work assigned to Jesus by the Father. The fulfillment theme in this section of the pericope reaches its climax here. The cross of Christ is the completion of the work of the Father through the Son, fulfilling the whole of Scripture to the smallest detail (see comments on v. 28). And the nature of the completed action is magnified by the verb's perfect tense, which describes a past action with continuingly present-tense force.[11]

This one Greek word is the final statement of God, declaring that everything he wanted to accomplish has been completed to perfection in the person and work of his Son, Jesus Christ. This is no cry of defeat or mere announcement of imminent death; it is an announcement of victory![12] Even more, it is the announcement of "the victory of the victim."[13] In this moment of suffering and despair, God in the person of Jesus Christ declares victory over the forces of sin and death — a victory secured not in spite of but by means of the cross. With this word the Word speaks forth a new creation (1:3), and the light shines forth in the darkness (1:5). For this one word summarizes the "good news" of the gospel and reveals the constant foundation of the Christian faith.

Second, the narrator explains that Jesus "bowed his head and gave over his spirit" (κλίνας τὴν κεφαλὴν παρέδωκεν τὸ πνεῦμα). It is significant that the narrator continues to describe Jesus as the subject of the verb; death itself has no authority over him, for he lays down his life by his own authority (10:18). The statement is almost certainly intended to depict the moment Jesus released his

---

9. Brown, *Death of the Messiah*, 2:1075.

10. See F. G. Beetham and P. A. Beetham, "A Note on John 19:29," *JTS* 44 (1993): 163 – 69.

11. See BDF § 340: "The perfect combines in itself, so to

speak, the present and aorist in that it denotes the *continuance of completed action*."

12. Cf. Carson, *John*, 621.

13. Hoskyns, *Fourth Gospel*, 531.

life and thus the moment when it was *truly* completed. It has been commonly noted, however, that the final phrase is also intended to be interpreted symbolically, since the Greek does not use a personal pronoun ("his") and could be translated as "he gave over *the* spirit" (παρέδωκεν τὸ πνεῦμα). If the verb is translated as "gave over" (παρέδωκεν), the sense expressed is in reference to the surrendering of life; but the verb could also be translated as "handed over," thus communicating that the object, "his/the spirit," is given to someone, with the options being the disciples (see comments on 20:22) or God the Father.[14]

As before in the Gospel, this is another example where the narrative does not intend for us to choose between the two options. The awkwardly phrased language does not only depict the physical death of Jesus, but with symbol-laden words the Gospel also depicts the immediate connection between the death of Christ and the Spirit, of which the Gospel has already spoken (see comments on 7:39).[15] Our argument is that the Gospel is using language in a manner that reflects in calculated simultaneity both the historical and cosmological strands of its plot (see comments before 1:1). What is being communicated is that the "spirit" of Jesus is directly related to "the Spirit of Jesus" (2 Cor 3:17; Gal 4:6; Phil 1:19), so much so that it is Jesus who sends the Spirit (see 16:7) precisely by his departure, which begins with his death. When Jesus "gave over" *his* spirit, he also "handed over" *the* Spirit. While our translation of this "very strange language"[16] can only reflect the surface-level meaning, our interpretation must work hard to grasp the fullness of its theological symbolism.

19:31 Then the Jews asked Pilate to break their legs and have them taken away, since it was the day of preparation, so that the bodies would not stay on the cross on the Sabbath, for that Sabbath was a great day (Οἱ οὖν Ἰουδαῖοι, ἐπεὶ παρασκευὴ ἦν, ἵνα μὴ μείνῃ ἐπὶ τοῦ σταυροῦ τὰ σώματα ἐν τῷ σαββάτῳ, ἦν γὰρ μεγάλη ἡ ἡμέρα ἐκείνου τοῦ σαββάτου, ἠρώτησαν τὸν Πιλᾶτον ἵνα κατεαγῶσιν αὐτῶν τὰ σκέλη καὶ ἀρθῶσιν). The second section of the pericope (vv. 31 – 37) records the treatment of Jesus's body and the confirmations regarding his death. For the first time in the Gospel, Jesus is not an active agent; in this scene of the periocpe we are dealing with his lifeless body. The narrator explains that for reasons of ritual purity the Jews wanted Pilate to confirm the death of the criminals and have their bodies removed from the cross. The Jews had important purity regulations regarding dead bodies, and the narrator has already described how adept the Jews were at avoiding defilement (see 18:28). The irony is clear. The Jews think the corpse of the Son of God is the source of their defilement at Passover, when in reality his "flesh" is the true Passover Lamb and the only source of true purification.

The day of preparation was on Friday, the day of the great feast of liberation (see comments on 19:14). According to the narrator, this particular Sabbath was important to the Jews: "That Sabbath was a great day" (μεγάλη ἡ ἡμέρα ἐκείνου τοῦ σαββάτου). While the adjective "great" (μεγάλη) might also be translated as "high" in the historical context of Passover, that is, the great or high Sabbath of Passover, the irony of the situation forces

---

14. See David Crump, "Who Gets What? God or Disciples, Human Spirit or Holy Spirit in John 19:30," *NovT* 51 (2009): 78 – 89 (79 – 82). While Crump is correct to suggest that the Father is likely the primary indirect object of the handing over of the Spirit (e.g., 3:34; 14:16 – 17, 26; 15:26), the silence of the narrative allows for the indirect object to be inclusive of the church as well — though in the proper sequence (83 – 84).

15. See Robert Kysar, " 'He Gave Up the Spirit': A Reader's Reflection on John 19:30b," in *Transcending Boundaries: Contemporary Readings of the New Testament: Essays in Honor of Francis J. Moloney*, ed. Rekha M. Chennattu and Mary L. Coloe, BSR 187 (Rome: Libreria Ateneo Salesiano, 2005), 161 – 72.

16. Hoskyns, *Fourth Gospel*, 532.

our translation.[17] For while the religious leaders of the Jews were preparing to perform their Passover duties on behalf of God for the people, God himself had personally already "completed" the task. This truly was the great day — perhaps Christians should refer to this Friday not as Good Friday but as Great Friday.

The concern of the Jews to remove the bodies before Sabbath (Saturday) suggests that it was later in the day. Since the verdict of Jesus took place around the sixth hour, that is, at about noon, it is likely that the crucifixion process took several hours, making it late in the afternoon on Friday. Since in Judaism the calculations of days were based upon the light of the sun, the Sabbath (Saturday) would begin at the setting of the sun. This explains why the Jews would be pressuring the Romans to complete the crucifixion and remove the corpses, for the darkness of the evening was likely approaching. The breaking of the legs (*crurifragium*) was a common form of Roman punishment in its own right, often used to create a horrible deterrent effect.[18] It may also have been used to impose a final act of bodily mutilation and suffering.[19] The severe addition of this punishment, however, often turns into a merciful deed since it would hasten the end of the suffering.[20]

19:32 So the soldiers came and broke the legs of the first man and the other man who had been crucified with him (ἦλθον οὖν οἱ στρατιῶται, καὶ τοῦ μὲν πρώτου κατέαξαν τὰ σκέλη καὶ τοῦ ἄλλου τοῦ συσταυρωθέντος αὐτῷ). Apparently Pilate gave his approval, for the narrator describes how the soldiers broke the legs of the two men on each side of Jesus. Nothing more is stated; the implication is

that shortly thereafter the crucifixion of those two men would be completed. For by this act the death of these anonymous criminals was hastened.

19:33 But when they came to Jesus they saw that he had already died, so they did not break his legs (ἐπὶ δὲ τὸν Ἰησοῦν ἐλθόντες, ὡς εἶδον ἤδη αὐτὸν τεθνηκότα, οὐ κατέαξαν αὐτοῦ τὰ σκέλη). But the narrator is careful to note that the legs of Jesus were not broken because there was no need to do so, for "he had already died" (ἤδη αὐτὸν τεθνηκότα). The importance of the fact that Jesus's legs were not broken will be given significance from Scripture in v. 36. This detail does not only intend to confirm Jesus's death but may also highlight the manner in which he died. Befitting the Gospel thus far, especially in the trial and crucifixion scenes, the implication might simply be that Jesus was the acting authority over his life until its very end (cf. 10:18), choosing to die once "all things" had been "completed" (v. 30).

19:34 Instead one of the soldiers pierced his side with a spear, and immediately blood and water came out (ἀλλ᾽ εἷς τῶν στρατιωτῶν λόγχῃ αὐτοῦ τὴν πλευρὰν ἔνυξεν, καὶ ἐξῆλθεν εὐθὺς αἷμα καὶ ὕδωρ). Although the narrator already declared the death of Jesus, the soldier took his "spear" (λόγχῃ), a lance about three and one-half feet long with an iron point on a long stem joined to a shaft of wood,[21] and pierced the side of Jesus. This action was commonly used to give final verification that the criminal was dead, but it could also have been one final act of cruelty by the soldiers. Even if the latter is intended, the former is provided conclusive proof. Jesus is dead.

Yet the narrator had already explained that Jesus

---

17. Michaels also suggests "special Sabbath" (*John*, 966).

18. See Joseph A. Fitzmyer, "Crucifixion in Ancient Palestine, Qumran Literature, and the New Testament," *CBQ* 40 (1978): 493 – 513.

19. Brown, *Death of the Messiah*, 2:1076.

20. Koskenniemi, Nisula, and Toppari, "Wine and Crurifragium," 387 – 89.

21. Everett Ferguson, *Backgrounds of Early Christianity*, 2nd ed. (Grand Rapids: Eerdmans, 1992), 49.

was dead and that he had been horribly abused throughout the trial and crucifixion. So why does he include this particular detail? In a Gospel (and section of the Gospel) so symbol laden, the reason must be found in the final part of the verse: "And immediately blood and water came out" (καὶ ἐξῆλθεν εὐθὺς αἷμα καὶ ὕδωρ). This statement has long been debated regarding the possibility of its symbolism. In the modern era interpreters have been hesitant to interpret the symbolism as anything more than physical proof that Jesus was dead, and usually this is taken as the obvious or most natural interpretation. Yet it is not quite obvious that a merely physical description of the hanging corpse of Jesus is the statement's clear communicative intention. The often assumed more objective resources of medical science are hardly the source for a clear interpretation: Has the heart been pierced, possibly the pericardial sac?[22] Or did the brutal flogging he received earlier that day produce a hemorrhage in the pleural cavity between the ribs and the lungs?[23] Not only do these more *historical* suggestions, which commonly criticize the uncontrolled (allegorical?) interpretations of more *theological* suggestions, offer a variety of uncontrolled (reconstructed?) interpretations themselves, but on their own they fail to offer an interpretation of the intentions of the Gospel by the inclusion of this statement.[24] None of this is to deny that the narrator is describing at the historical level of the Gospel's plot that Jesus was officially dead; what is being argued for here is that at the same time at the cosmological level of the plot, the Gospel is also speaking in a theologically symbolic manner about Jesus's person and work.

Thus, since the narrator has already declared Jesus to be dead, we must assume (and have rea-

son to do so in this Gospel!) that the narrator is explaining the death of Jesus to the reader. By placing our interpretation within the confines of the Gospel itself, the (theological) intentions behind the reference to "blood" and "water" can be more accurately deduced. Our argument will be that the terms "blood" (αἷμα) and "water" (ὕδωρ) create textually guided "impressions" (see Introduction) derived from the cumulative theology of the Gospel (cf. 1 John 5:6 – 8).

The reference to "blood" is almost certainly intended to evoke the image of sacrifice, and in light of the immediate context of the Gospel — "unless one is canonically tone-deaf" — this imagery is being directly connected to the Passover sacrifice.[25] The image of blood, then, serves to declare Jesus as the Passover Lamb *par excellence* and therefore the fulfillment of Passover. This is one of the primary messages of the Gospel as a whole, and it is certainly befitting the Gospel's bent to use a potentially insignificant and unnecessary detail to express that which the developing narrative has been pointing.

The reference to "water" is almost certainly intended to evoke the image of the Spirit, who the narrator already explained — on a "great day" of a feast and in a manner replete with OT allusions (see comments on 7:37 – 38) — was directly connected to the death of Christ *and* the image of water. After Jesus spoke of the flowing of streams of "living water" in 7:38, the narrator intrudes in 7:39 to explain that Jesus was referring to the Spirit, though none of this would happen until Jesus was "glorified," that is, until Jesus makes this possible from the cross (see comments on 7:39). Like "blood," then, the symbol-laden term "water" does not express biology but theology. The death

---

22. W. D. Edwards, W. J. Gabel, and F. E. Hosmer, "On the Physical Death of Jesus Christ," *JAMA* 255 (1986): 1455 – 63.

23. A. F. Sava, "The Wound in the Side of Christ," *CBQ* 19 (1957): 343 – 46.

24. See Kevin J. Vanhoozer, "Body-Piercing, the Natural Sense, and the Task of Theological Interpretation: A Hermeneutical Homily on John 19:34," *ExAud* 16 (2000): 1 – 29.

25. Ibid., 21.

of Jesus has now made possible the Spirit, fulfilling not only what OT Scripture foretold but also what Jesus himself foretold.

The point, however, is not the meaning of the terms in isolation, but their functional relationship.[26] It is significant that both blood *and* water flowed from the side of Jesus. The mixture of blood and water forcefully unites the purification of the blood with the power of the Spirit, creating a universal and eternal atonement for the sins of the world.[27] The narrator is not primarily giving proof here of the death of Jesus, but proof of the life his death now offers to the world.[28] The death of Jesus is the source of life so that it "immediately" (εὐθὺς) flowed from his side, that is, from within him, for "in the Word was life" (1:4). Augustine may be forcing an "impression" when he suggests that the narrator's reference to "the side" (τὴν πλευρὰν) of Jesus finds its explanation in the creation account. He writes that just as the first woman, "the mother of all living," was "formed from the side of the man when asleep," so also "this second Adam bowed His head and fell asleep on the cross, that a spouse might be formed for Him from that which flowed from the sleeper's side."[29] Yet Augustine rightly grasps the theological subject matter of this symbol-laden depiction of the crucified Christ. There is no need to choose between a historical or theological significance to this verse, for both are intended. In fact, the paradox of that moment is precisely the point. When the Roman soldier thrust his spear into the side of Jesus to confirm his death, he was unwittingly declaring to the whole world that true life had just begun.[30]

19:35 The one who has seen it has given witness, and his testimony is true. He knows that he speaks the truth, in order that you also may believe (καὶ ὁ ἑωρακὼς μεμαρτύρηκεν, καὶ ἀληθινὴ αὐτοῦ ἐστιν ἡ μαρτυρία, καὶ ἐκεῖνος οἶδεν ὅτι ἀληθῆ λέγει, ἵνα καὶ ὑμεῖς πιστεύσητε). After a remarkable collection of symbol-laden depictions of the death of Jesus Christ, the narrator intrudes into the story to offer an explanation of its significance. The importance of v. 34 is emphasized by the inclusion of this verse.[31] The narrator has intruded into the narrative before to offer insight and interpretation (see comments on 3:16). In this case, however, the narrator includes a claim about himself. He is "the one who has seen it" (ὁ ἑωρακὼς). In this remarkable moment, the narrator is revealed to be a character in the story, the anonymous "Beloved Disciple," who was the only disciple mentioned by the narrative to be at the scene of the cross (vv. 26 – 27).[32] We have summarized the Gospel's depiction of the Beloved Disciple and have no need to rehearse it here (see comments on 13:23 and 21:24). This disciple is presented by the Gospel as an intimate associate of Jesus and therefore an "ideal disciple" and an "ideal author." In this way, then, his insight into the things he has "seen" becomes the foundational witness of the Gospel itself (on the authorship of the Gospel, see Introduction).

The narrator declares emphatically that he has given "witness" or testimony to what he has seen and that "his testimony is true" (ἀληθινὴ αὐτοῦ ἐστιν ἡ μαρτυρία) and "he knows that he speaks the truth" (ἐκεῖνος οἶδεν ὅτι ἀληθῆ λέγει). The language here is the statement of an eyewitness,[33] with

---

26. Cf. Schnackenburg, *John*, 3:294.
27. Cf. Heil, *Blood and Water*, 106.
28. Cf. Westcott, *John*, 284 – 86.
29. Augustine, *John*, 120.2.434 – 35.
30. Brown, *John*, 2:950.
31. Carson, *John*, 625.

32. This does not guarantee that the narrator is the Beloved Disciple, but it is logically implicit from the narrative presentation. The similarity between this statement and the narrator's statement in 21:24 also supports the link with the beloved disciple. Cf. Bauckham, "The Beloved Disciple as Ideal Author," 73 – 91.
33. See Bauckham, *Jesus and the Eyewitnesses*, 358 – 411.

the second "he" (ἐκεῖνος) serving as an emphatic declaration about himself. It is important to note that the thing about which the narrator/Beloved Disciple gives testimony is the fact and meaning of the death of Jesus Christ. Since there is good reason to support the identification of the Beloved Disciple with John the apostle (see Introduction), then the Gospel's potent literary structure is made manifest, initiated by the somewhat odd introduction of the Baptist simply as "John" in 1:6: "The two great Johns bear solemn witness to the effective sacrifice of the Lamb of God, the one at the beginning of the narrative, the other at its conclusion."[34] The first John declares Jesus the Lamb of God who takes away the world's sin (1:29), and the second John sees the concrete fulfillment of the prophecy and testifies to its truth.

The purpose for which the narrator speaks the truth and declares his testimony (ultimately in the form of this Gospel) is "in order that you also may believe" (ἵνα καὶ ὑμεῖς πιστεύσητε). The statement nearly parallels the purpose statement of the Gospel in 20:30 – 31, containing even the same textual variant, and should be understood in the same way (see comments on 20:30 – 31). The Christian message rests on the eyewitness account of the disciples, who were called and sent out for this purpose (cf. 15:27; 17:21).[35] It is important to note the witness's desire is that "you *also* (καὶ) may believe," which suggests two things. First, it suggests that the narrator already has an a priori belief in that to which he witnesses. His witness is grounded in a truth he already believes and trusts in its veracity. Second, it suggests that the witness is not only correct but competent. He has seen firsthand what needs to be

seen — the whole truth — so that when he "speaks the truth" he does so in regard to both the record *and* interpretation of the events at hand.[36]

19:36 For these things happened so that Scripture might be fulfilled: "His bones will not be broken" (ἐγένετο γὰρ ταῦτα ἵνα ἡ γραφὴ πληρωθῇ, Ὀστοῦν οὐ συντριβήσεται αὐτοῦ). After intruding briefly into the narrative to highlight the significance of the death of Jesus, the narrator uses a fulfillment formula common to the Gospel (cf. v. 28) to give two further Scripture references to explain even more precisely the meaning of Jesus's death. The first one is negative and highlights the fact that the soldier did not break a single bone of Jesus. There is no perfectly matching Scripture from the OT, though three are closely parallel: two in regard to the bone of the Passover lamb (Exod 12:46 and Num 9:12) and one in regard to God's care for the righteous man (Ps 34:20).[37] While the latter fits the use of "royal lament psalms" of one protected by God the Father (see comments on 19:24), in light of the overt Passover imagery the former is almost certainly in view. The fact that no bones were broken testifies to the fact that Jesus, "according to the law of Passover" (Num 9:12), was the perfect Passover sacrifice. It is quite possible that the Gospel has both simultaneously in view — Christ fulfills the role of the Passover Lamb but not without the constant care and protection of the Father.[38] The point of significance, however, must be the negative assertion that no bone was broken on the Lamb of God.

19:37 In addition another Scripture says, "They will look at the one they have pierced" (καὶ πάλιν

34. Hoskyns, *Fourth Gospel*, 534.
35. Cf. Ridderbos, *John*, 622.
36. Bauckham, "The Beloved Disciple as Ideal Author," 88. On the relationship between this verse, the purpose statement (20:30 – 31), and the seventh sign, see comments before 20:1.
37. See Brown, *Death of the Messiah*, 2:1184 – 86.
38. Cf. Lindars, *John*, 590; Beasley-Murray, *John*, 355; Maarten J. J. Menken, "The Old Testament Quotation in John 19,36: Sources, Redaction, Backgrounds," in *The Four Gospels 1992: Festschrift Frans Neirynck*, ed. F. van Segbroeck, C. M. Tuckett, G. van Belle, and J. Verheyden, 3 vols., BETL 100 (Leuven: Leuven University Press, 1992), 3:2101 – 18 (2117 – 18).

ἑτέρα γραφὴ λέγει, Ὄψονται εἰς ὃν ἐξεκέντησαν). Unlike v. 36, while the OT text being alluded to is quite clear here (Zech 12:10), its relationship to this particular context is less clear. The introductory formula "in addition another Scripture says" (καὶ πάλιν ἑτέρα γραφὴ λέγει) suggests that the two Scriptures are to be understood together. Zechariah 12:10 says immediately after this statement that the people "will mourn for him," suggesting repentance and despair. But the Fourth Gospel focuses on the piercing, which forces Michaels to suggest that the "they" refers to the Roman soldiers who physically "pierced" Jesus on the cross (v. 34). But the textual evidence suggests that the "piercing" cannot be fully explained by a soldier's spear. In the larger context of Zechariah 12, especially the section immediately after the quoted text, a reversal is declared by God: "On that day a fountain will be opened … to cleanse them from sin and impurity" (Zech 13:1). We argued earlier that the language of Zechariah 13 has been implied in several places in the Gospel, such as in Jesus's message about "living water" to the Samaritan woman (see comments on 4:10, 17 – 18) and in the more related message Jesus publicly gave to the religious authorities at the Feast of Tabernacles in 7:37 – 39. By referencing this text the narrator declares to the reader that the death of Jesus is not only the *perfect sacrifice* (v. 36) but also the *perfect solution* to the plight of the world (cf. Rev 1:7). The very one they "pierced" is the one to whom they must look for the sake of their salvation.[39] In this way the second section of the pericope (vv. 31 – 37) is concluded.

19:38 And after these things Joseph of Arimathea, a disciple of Jesus, but a secret one for fear of the Jews, asked Pilate to take away the body of Jesus. And Pilate granted him permission, so he came and took away his body (Μετὰ δὲ ταῦτα ἠρώτησεν τὸν Πιλᾶτον Ἰωσὴφ ὁ ἀπὸ Ἁριμαθαίας, ὢν μαθητὴς τοῦ Ἰησοῦ κεκρυμμένος δὲ διὰ τὸν φόβον τῶν Ἰουδαίων, ἵνα ἄρῃ τὸ σῶμα τοῦ Ἰησοῦ· καὶ ἐπέτρεψεν ὁ Πιλᾶτος. ἦλθεν οὖν καὶ ἦρεν τὸ σῶμα αὐτοῦ). The third section of the pericope (vv. 38 – 42) records the burial of Jesus. The opening phrase "and after these things" (Μετὰ δὲ ταῦτα) signals the start of a new section (cf. v. 28; 2:12). The narrator explains that a man named Joseph of Arimathea secured permission from Pilate to provide for Jesus a proper burial, an important practice in Judaism. Even though the bodies of criminals were often mistreated after a crucifixion (often left for the vultures), the Jews were pleased to have it removed (cf. v. 31), and the narrative does not reveal any further maneuvers by Pilate.

Little is known of this Joseph. The fact that all four Gospels attest to his role in the burial of Jesus (cf. Matt 27:57; Mark 15:43; Luke 23:51) suggests that his identity in relation to Jesus's burial is significant, probably because he became a permanent fixture in the early Christian tradition. Joseph may have been an influential man, suggested by the fact that Pilate did give him permission to take the body of Jesus. The presence of this Joseph in Jerusalem suggests that although he had an estate near a town called "Arimathea" (Ἁριμαθαίας), he lived mostly in Jerusalem or visited frequently, and the tomb to which he took Jesus almost certainly belonged to him (cf. Matt 27:60).[40]

The narrator does reveal an important part of his identity. He was "a disciple of Jesus, but a secret one for fear of the Jews" (ὢν μαθητὴς τοῦ Ἰησοῦ κεκρυμμένος δὲ διὰ τὸν φόβον τῶν Ἰουδαίων). It has been commonly suggested that this Joseph (and Nicodemus) is depicted here as a representative of those mentioned in 12:42 – 43: "Many of the rulers believed in him, but because of the Pharisees they were not confessing … for they loved the glory of

39. Cf. Ridderbos, *John*, 624.

40. Bauckham, *Jesus and the Eyewitnesses*, 81 – 82.

humanity rather than the glory of God." But the narrative almost certainly intends to portray Joseph's treatment of Jesus in a positive light. By this action Joseph of Arimathea is depicted as reversing what was known of him, for his actions before Pilate and with the highly politicized criminal's body was anything but cowardly. Possibly motivated by a growing understanding of the nature of Jesus's death, Joseph makes quite a statement with this action.[41]

19:39 And Nicodemus came also, the one who came to him first at night, bringing a mixture of myrrh and aloe, about a hundred pounds (ἦλθεν δὲ καὶ Νικόδημος, ὁ ἐλθὼν πρὸς αὐτὸν νυκτὸς τὸ πρῶτον, φέρων μίγμα σμύρνης καὶ ἀλόης ὡς λίτρας ἑκατόν). Joseph was not alone, for the narrator explains that another man joined him, Nicodemus. The narrator reminds the reader that Nicodemus was "the one who came to him first at night" (ὁ ἐλθὼν πρὸς αὐτὸν νυκτὸς τὸ πρῶτον), which is almost certainly intended to be an equally negative depiction of Nicodemus that parallels the previously fearful status of Joseph. This suggests two things. First, it offers confirmation that the "first" encounter between Nicodemus and Jesus "at night" was negative (see comments on 3:1–2). Second, similar to Joseph of Arimathea, it likely suggests that Nicodemus's actions here are also to be taken positively.[42] In some way the death of Jesus caused Joseph and Nicodemus to respond to Jesus differently than they had before.

The narrator explains that Nicodemus brought with him "a mixture of myrrh and aloe" (μίγμα σμύρνης καὶ ἀλόης). Myrrh was commonly used for embalming the dead. It was used in Jewish burial to offset the unpleasant odor. Aloe was a powdered perfume that created a pleasant fragrance. A customary honorable burial would have involved washing the body, anointing it with oil, and/or placing spices (i.e., myrrh and aloe) within the wrappings placed around the body (cf. v. 40). When mixed together, the two spices would have created a pleasant fragrance with which to honor the body of Jesus.[43]

What is surprising is that Nicodemus brought with him "about a hundred pounds" (ὡς λίτρας ἑκατόν) of spices. The reader should remember that when Mary anointed the feet of Jesus with perfume in 12:3, she brought only one "pound" (λίτραν), which means one Roman pound (cf. 12:3). While the perfume Mary used was of a very high quality and we are not told of the quality of these spices, the comparison is stark: if one pound of perfume was a ridiculously lavish amount of fine perfume to be used all at once, how much more lavish was a hundred pounds? If Mary anointed Jesus with about one-year's wages of perfume, did Nicodemus bring over a lifetime of wages (about a hundred-year's wages!) to anoint his crucified body? If so, this is further proof that Nicodemus was a man of great status and wealth (see comments on 3:1). Even though the term "anoint" is not used like it was in 12:3, there can be little doubt that the lavish amount of perfume to be placed on Jesus's body is to be interpreted as a highly honorific act, with this act paralleling the royal symbolism used by Mary to denote the perfume that is applied to a king.[44] In this case, however, it is applied to Jesus at the exact time he requested in 12:7: "For the day of my preparation for burial" (see comments on 12:3). The royal-burial motif of

---

41. Cf. Ridderbos, *John*, 625–26.

42. For a survey of interpretations regarding Nicodemus, see Raimo Hakola, "The Burden of Ambiguity: Nicodemus and the Social Identity of the Johannine Christians," *NTS* 55 (2009): 438–55 (439–45).

43. Brown, *Death of the Messiah*, 2:1261–64.

44. See Brown, *John*, 2:960.

this scene is not only grounded in the extravagant application of perfume but also in the mention of a "garden" in v. 41 (on which, see below).

This is the third appearance in the Gospel of Nicodemus, the only character outside of the disciples who is progressively developed throughout the narrative. Interpreters are often hesitant to make judgments regarding Nicodemus's faith response, suggesting instead that the narrative "leaves his status unresolved."[45] But this is likely rooted in a misreading of Nicodemus's first appearance, his dialogue with Jesus (3:1 – 15), which we argued was negative. His second appearance (7:48 – 52), however, was clearly different. In this brief encounter among the Jewish authorities, Nicodemus was displayed as the outsider, challenging those with whom he was more closely associated on behalf of Jesus. Finally, in his third appearance, with no words at all, Nicodemus stands beside a (once secret) "disciple of Jesus" with his own, extravagant offering for the crucified Jesus. Once the first encounter is less than ambivalent, as we tried to show by means of the challenge dialogue, the developing portrait of Nicodemus's response to Jesus can be seen to be progressively positive (see comments on 7:52).[46] The Gospel's concern is not with the conversion of Nicodemus per se, however, but with the message Jesus offered through his encounter with Nicodemus (3:14 – 15). He comes this time as "night" approaches with an entirely different agenda, knowing full well that Jesus, not he, is the true "conqueror" (cf. 3:1), made manifest and possible by his death.

19:40 So they took the body of Jesus and wrapped it in linen clothes with spices, as is the burial custom of the Jews (ἔλαβον οὖν τὸ σῶμα τοῦ Ἰησοῦ καὶ ἔδησαν αὐτὸ ὀθονίοις μετὰ τῶν ἀρωμάτων,

καθὼς ἔθος ἐστὶν τοῖς Ἰουδαίοις ἐνταφιάζειν). Befitting the Jewish customs, Joseph of Arimathea and Nicodemus take the body of Jesus and wrap it in linen clothes with spices. A corpse would be wrapped tightly with shrouds of cloth from head to toe, including the tight wrap around the head and face to keep the mouth closed (cf. 11:44; 20:7).[47] The spices (myrrh and aloe) were probably mixed together and applied to the body under and around the linen. The Gospel's concern here is less the Jewish customs and more the fact of Christ's burial, reflected in the church's later creeds: he "was crucified for us under Pontius Pilate; He suffered *and was buried*" (Nicaea/Constantinople).

19:41 In the place where Jesus was crucified was a garden, and in the garden a new tomb, in which no one had ever been laid (ἦν δὲ ἐν τῷ τόπῳ ὅπου ἐσταυρώθη κῆπος, καὶ ἐν τῷ κήπῳ μνημεῖον καινὸν ἐν ᾧ οὐδέπω οὐδεὶς ἦν τεθειμένος). The narrator is not only concerned with the *fact* of Jesus's burial but also with *the place*. The narrator gives two important qualifications about "the place" (τῷ τόπῳ). First, the narrator explains that "in the place where Jesus was crucified was a garden" (ἦν δὲ ἐν τῷ τόπῳ ὅπου ἐσταυρώθη κῆπος). This statement not only situates the tomb in which Jesus was laid in the vicinity of the crucifixion, but it also connects the crucifixion to "a garden."[48] Jesus was arrested in a garden (cf. 18:1), and now he is crucified and buried in a garden. He will also rise from the dead in a garden (cf. 20:15). As we argued earlier, the Gospel has so clearly applied a Genesis lens to the story that the reader is expected to see the connection between this "garden" and the first garden in Genesis 2:8 – 16 (see comments on 18:1).

Second, the narrator explains that in this garden was "a new tomb, in which no one had ever

---

45. R. Alan Culpepper, "Nicodemus: The Travail of New Birth," in *Character Studies in the Fourth Gospel*, 249 – 59 (59).

46. See Farelly, "An Unexpected Ally."

47. Keener, *John*, 2:850.

48. See Gabriel Barkay, "The Garden Tomb: Was Jesus Buried Here?" *BAR* 12 (1986): 40 – 57.

been laid" (μνημεῖον καινὸν ἐν ᾧ οὐδέπω οὐδεὶς ἦν τεθειμένος). The place of Jesus's burial not only "impresses" (see Introduction) upon the reader the importance of his death but also the importance of his person. Schaper has shown that in the OT and other ancient literature there is an explicit connection between gardens and kings. The careful and intentional reference to a garden as the place of the burial of Jesus "was intended to make an extremely important symbolic point: the tomb of Jesus, like that of David and other Davidic rulers, is located in a garden."[49] And along with the lavish amount of spices (v. 39), the "implicit statement is that Jesus is the legitimate heir of David and the Messiah of Israel."[50] This "royal garden" motif, which began at the arrest and betrayal of Jesus (18:1 – 2), is made even clearer in the context of the resurrection scene (see 20:15). This is no traditional king, however, for reserved for him was an unused tomb, declaring the uniqueness of the person intended to occupy it.[51] But the presence of Jesus in this "new tomb" was doubly unique. For not only was it the tomb for God himself, but it was also the first tomb in human history that was needed for only three days! Jesus was the first person to walk out of a tomb on his own power. The uniqueness of this tomb, then, was that it became the womb of life, "the place" where the dead body of Jesus took on a resurrected life.

19:42 On account of the Jewish day of preparation and because the tomb was close, they placed Jesus in that place (ἐκεῖ οὖν διὰ τὴν παρασκευὴν τῶν Ἰουδαίων, ὅτι ἐγγὺς ἦν τὸ μνημεῖον, ἔθηκαν τὸν Ἰησοῦν). The narrator concludes the pericope by describing the relation between Jesus's burial and the Jewish practices of the "day of preparation" (Friday), on the eve of the great Sabbath (see v. 31). In the mind of Joseph and Nicodemus and possibly the servants assisting them, it was entirely practical to place Jesus in a nearby tomb before Sabbath began. The Jewish authorities may have been pleased that the burial of Jesus avoided ceremonial defilement and possibly satisfied that Jesus was buried alone and not in a family tomb, befitting the treatment of a criminal. The narrator, however, was likely thinking other thoughts. "That place" would shortly provide for an unmistakable witness to the victory of life over death.[52]

Theology in Application

The climactic "hour" (cf. 2:4) of world history took place on the eve of the great Sabbath Day of Passover when the Son of God was crucified by the combined authorities of Jerusalem and Rome. But the seemingly common crucifixion performed that day was a *novum*. For one of the three men crucified was not a victim (criminal) but a victor (the Christ!), who received death by his own authority so that by that same authority (cf. 1:12) the world could have life. Death exchanged for life, God's life for eternal life, a perfect sacrifice for the perfect solution to the plight of the world. In this pericope the narrative guides the reader to the true meaning of the death and burial of Jesus Christ, declaring the full reality of the work of God accomplished through Jesus Christ.

---

49. Schaper, "The Messiah in the Garden," 25.
50. Ibid.
51. Cf. Aquinas, *John*, 3:251.
52. Beasley-Murray, *John*, 360.

"It Is Completed"

With one word (in Greek), his final word, Jesus declares the completion of the work assigned to him by the Father. Done! Finished! Jesus completed it all. His "thirst" is what gives us complete satisfaction (vv. 28 – 29). By giving up his spirit, we have received the Spirit (v. 30). The person and work of Jesus has fulfilled the OT Scriptures. To the smallest detail it is completed — all things for all people for all time. This *is* the gospel. With one word all sin is paid in full. With one word the ruler of this world is defeated. With one word creation regains its hope. With one word death is defeated. With one word life is redefined. With one word the love of God is made manifest. Everything makes sense because of this one word. At the moment the Word of God spoke this single word, a new creation "happened," just as it did at the original creation. When the author of this Gospel first wrote the words "in the beginning was the Word" (1:1), he was certainly thinking of a person (the Word), but not far behind was this other beautiful "word" that signifies the work this person has now completed.

The Perfect Sacrifice of God

The second section of the pericope (vv. 31 – 37) is a testimony to the perfection of the sacrifice God offered on behalf of the sins of the world. Jesus is the *perfect* "Lamb of God" (1:29), fulfilling to perfection the Passover requirements God himself established long before. Everything the OT expected for the removal of sin God himself met and applied to his Son, Jesus Christ. The crucifixion of Jesus is not merely the climax of the ministry of Jesus; it is the climax of the entire biblical story. The crucifixion of Jesus is the context from which every biblical verse and passage must be read. It is also the context from which every biblical Christian must live. For his perfection was intended to counter our imperfection. Every detail this Gospel explains of the perfect life and mission of the Son of God is a rebuke of the entirely imperfect life and obedience of the children of God. Yet in Christ there is now no condemnation. "For what the law was powerless to do because it was weakened by the flesh, *God did* by sending his son in the likeness of sinful flesh to be a sin offering. And so he condemned sin *in the flesh*" (Rom 8:3; emphasis added). Yes, "God did … in the flesh." It is a beautiful truth declared by means of a horrific Roman crucifixion. This is why we are no longer condemned, for God has placed all such condemnation on his Son — the Lamb of God. His condemnation is our victory!

What Is Jesus Worth?

If the elements Nicodemus brought to anoint the body of Jesus can be compared to Mary's anointing (12:3), then Nicodemus brought over a lifetime's worth of an average person's wages to anoint Jesus's corpse. Is Jesus worth that much to us? Are we willing to give the value of our working lives as our gift to our Lord? Nicodemus's actions are arguably more than a depiction of a sentimental gift; they are prescriptive of the kind of giving expected of all Christians. Christ gave his life for us; will we give our life back to him?

The Garden Tomb

The "garden" motif frames the passion narrative (chs. 18 – 20) and is used again here to develop further the full-orbed contrast between the first and second garden, related to the first and second Adam. But is it not strange to link a tomb (a place of death) to a garden (a place of life)? Not for the Gospel of John. For the death of Jesus is declared by this Gospel to be the means of life for the world. The uniqueness of this tomb was not merely its newness, but that it was "the place" where life itself was renewed, where the corpse of Jesus took on a resurrected life as the "first fruits" of eternal life (1 Cor 15:23). The "tree of life" in this garden is the wooden cross, which the church has since transformed into the symbol for new life. The paradox of the "garden tomb" is the foundation of the Christian faith: death is the source of life. Not any death but the particular death of Jesus. As Jesus himself explained, "Unless the seed ... falls to the ground to die, it remains alone. But if it dies, it produces much fruit" (12:24). Jesus is the "gardener" of his garden and the seed that dies to produce much fruit — the church!

John 20:1 – 10

Literary Context

This pericope is the first of four sections of the final section of the narrative proper, "The Resurrection" (20:1 – 31), which brings climactic resolution to the Gospel story. Jesus has been crucified and buried just as he foretold, and the narrative was careful to depict the full significance of his death. But the death of Jesus is not the end of his person or work, for as Jesus also foretold the Jewish authorities, using a metaphor for his body, "Destroy this temple and in three days I will raise it" (2:19). As the Gospel will now make clear, the third day has now arrived. In this pericope the reader is exhorted to believe that Jesus has been raised from the dead and is guided to see how the resurrection of Jesus is the completion and restoration of the person and work of Jesus and the inauguration of the restoration of all things.

➡ **IX. The Resurrection (20:1 – 31)**
    A. The Empty Tomb (20:1 – 10)
    B. The Appearance to Mary Magdalene (20:11 – 18)
    C. The Appearance to the Disciples (20:19 – 23)
    D. The Appearance to Thomas and the Purpose of the Gospel (20:24 – 31)

Main Idea

The empty tomb declares that Jesus has risen from the dead. He is no corpse; he is Christ the Lord, whose resurrection is the defeat of sin and death and the declaration that the renewal of creation has begun.

Translation

(See next page.)

John 20:1–10

	Introduction & Setting (1–2)	
1a	Time of Week	On the first day of the week,
b	Character Reentrance	**Mary Magdalene came to the tomb**
c	Time of Day	early,
d	Description	while it was still dark,
e	Action	and **saw the stone had been taken away from the tomb.**
2a	Reaction	So **she ran**
b	Character Reentrance	and **came to Simon Peter and**
c	Character Reentrance	**to the other disciple**
d	Identification	whom Jesus loved,
e		and **she said to them,**
f	Announcement	*"They have taken the Lord from the tomb*
g	Inference	*and we do not know where they have placed him."*
3a	Reaction	Then **Peter departed,**
b		and **the other disciple,**
c		and **they set off for the tomb.**
4a	Description of Action	**The two were running together,**
b		and **the other disciple ran ahead more quickly than Peter**
c	Arrival	and **came first to the tomb.**
5a	Description of Action	Kneeling to look,
b	Action	**he saw the linen clothes**
c		lying there,
d		but **he did not enter.**
6a		**Then Simon Peter …**
b	Description	who was behind him
c	Arrival	**… also came**
d	Contrasting Action to 5d	and **he went into the tomb;**
e	Progression of Action	**he also saw the linen clothes**
f		lying there, and
7a	Allusion: Exod 34:33–35	**the face cloth,**
b	Description	which was placed upon his head;
c	Location	**it was not lying with the linen clothes**
d	Contrast	but **was folded in one place by itself.**
8a	Action	So then **the other disciple …**
b	Description	who had come first to the tomb,
c		**… entered also;**
d		and **he saw**
e	Reaction	and **began to believe.**
9a	Narrator's Explanation	For **they did not yet know**
b	OT & NT	the Scripture
c	Teaching of "Scripture"	that it was necessary for him to be raised from the dead.
10a	Conclusion	Then **the disciples went again to their homes.**

Structure and Literary Form

This pericope corresponds to the basic story form (see Introduction). The *intro-duction/setting* is established in vv. 1 – 2, explaining the location and people around whom the plot's conflict will focus. In vv. 3 – 7 the *conflict* of the pericope is dramatically displayed by the race between Peter and the Beloved Disciple, which depicts their different approaches and responses to the empty tomb. The *resolution* of the plot is explained in vv. 8 – 9, with the narrator offering further insight into the full nature of the conflict. Finally, a brief but significant *conclusion/interpretation* closes the pericope in v. 10.

Exegetical Outline

➡ **A. The Empty Tomb (20:1 – 10)**

  1. The Location of Jesus (vv. 1 – 2)

  2. Run to the Tomb (vv. 3 – 7)

  3. Belief in the Resurrection (vv. 8 – 9)

  4. The Location of the Disciples (v. 10)

Explanation of the Text

IN-DEPTH: The Seventh Sign

We have already explained the six "signs" that are identified as such by the Gospel (see comments on 2:11). After working through the entire narrative proper of the Gospel, we may now make a more conclusive judgment regarding the identity of the seventh sign: *the death and resurrection of Jesus is the seventh sign*. Our developing analysis of the Gospel has yielded three arguments for this conclusion.

First, we noted that it is likely significant that the first of the six stated "signs" occurs in the same pericope as the last of the six stated "days" (2:1 – 11). Similar to John's use of the six "days," the six "signs" are intended to be viewed as a corporate unit, unfolding throughout the remainder of the Gospel. It is not surprising then that on the sixth "day," when the image of God is made known to his creation, that the "signs" have their "beginning" (see comments before 2:1). We should expect the implicit seventh sign not to be hidden in the middle of John somewhere but to be fully manifested only at the end, at the transition point between work and rest alongside the implicit seventh day. Thus, the Gospel's symbolic use of the creation week is directly related to the identity of the seventh sign (see comments on 20:1).

Second, we argued that Jesus announced a "sign" to the Jews and the disciples in 2:19, which he described as both the "destruction of this temple" and "its resurrection in three days." The death and resurrection of Jesus Christ is the seventh sign, the final and conclusive proof that Jesus is the Christ and the Son of God (see comments on 2:18 – 22). Here Jesus unites his death and resurrection, which the rest of the Gospel explains cannot be separated, for they are to be understood as one unified event — his "glorification" (cf. 1:14; 2:11; 7:39; 12:23).[1] Thus, while the other six signs are described as such by the narrator, it is likely that the Gospel intentionally allows Jesus himself to announce the seventh and climactic sign. This prophetic announcement of Jesus occurring in 2:19 is quite important, for the rest of the developing narrative is needed to prepare the reader for the *sign*-ificance of the seventh sign, Jesus's death and resurrection.

Third, the narrator's more personal intrusion right after the death (19:35) and resurrection (20:30 – 31) of Jesus, unlike the intrusions at the end of other pericopae (3:16 – 21 or 3:31 – 36), strongly supports the developing significance of this two-part event. Just as Jesus predicted (2:19), the seventh sign involves not only his destruction but also his rebuilding, and the narrative uses the final three chapters of the Gospel proper (chs. 18 – 20) to articulate and express this seventh sign. Even more, since the narrator's comments at 19:35 and 20:30 – 31 are the only two places in the Gospel where the reader is explicitly invited to "believe" and since both occur after each of the two aspects of the seventh sign — Jesus's death (ch. 19) and resurrection (ch. 20) — it is likely that the narrator's statements here are to direct the reader to see and understand not only the seventh sign but also the purpose of the Gospel as a whole.

Helpful here is Köstenberger, who has provided three criteria that can be used to determine the seventh sign: (1) Is the sign performed by Jesus as part of his public ministry? (2) Is an event explicitly identified as a "sign" in the Fourth Gospel? (3) Does the event symbolically point to God's glory displayed in Jesus, thus revealing Jesus as God's true representative?[2] This is not only a helpful overview of the purpose of the "signs" but a guide to determining the actual seventh sign. Based upon these criteria, Köstenberger is correct to say that only the cleansing of the temple pericope (2:12 – 25) specifically uses the term. How-

---

1. See Udo Schnelle, "Cross and Resurrection in the Gospel of John," in *The Resurrection of Jesus in the Gospel of John*, ed. Craig R. Koester and Reimund Bieringer, WUNT 222 (Tübingen: Mohr Siebeck, 2008), 127 – 51.

2. Andreas J. Köstenberger, "The Seventh Johannine Sign: A Study in John's Christology," *BBR* 5 (1995): 87 – 103 (92 – 95). How-

ever, he is incorrect when he demands that the cleansing itself is that which is signified by the use of "sign" (2:18). The sign Jesus announces is his crucifixion and resurrection three days later (2:19). The Jewish authorities do not ask if his preceding action was the sign; rather, they demand him to perform a sign (in the future!). And when Jesus answers their demand, he does not look back to his preceding action and declare it the sign but looks forward to an action still to come. As much as Köstenberger was correct when he identified this text as foundational to the announcement of the seventh sign, he applied the "sign" terminology to the wrong event.[3] The words of Jesus themselves (2:19) and the narrator's comments that immediately follow (2:21 – 22) make clear that the subject matter of this "sign" is to be found specifically in his death (the destruction of "this temple") and his bodily resurrection ("in three days").

In this way the narrative carefully (not cryptically) announces the seventh and climactic sign of Jesus that publicly declares his glorification and that he is the complete and final representative of God. The death and resurrection of Jesus has continually been depicted by the Gospel as the glorification of Jesus, and the portrayal of Jesus as the true fulfillment of humanity/Adam (see comments on 19:5) and the required sacrifice of God/Passover (see comments on 19:14) finds its culmination in his death and resurrection, through which the new covenant is grounded and inaugurated. Befitting the theological chronology of the Gospel, the seventh sign is on the "seventh" day of the week, completing the first week of the old creation (see comments before 2:1), with the resurrection occurring "on the first day of the week" (20:1), the first week of the new creation.

---

3. Köstenberger ("The Seventh Johannine Sign," 97 – 100), makes several unnecessary judgments regarding the connection between the seventh sign and the death/resurrection of Jesus. First, he inappropriately disassociates the crucifixion from the public ministry of Jesus, relying too strongly on source-critical theories that label chapters 1 – 12 of the Gospel as the Book of Signs (see Introduction). Second, he assumes the signs point to the crucifixion/resurrection and therefore cannot be included among them. But the signs point not to any single work of Christ but to that which is also accomplished by his person. Third, he defines the signs as "preliminary in nature" and having only a "temporary function" (98). But nothing in the Gospel demands such a definition. In fact, the signs are not best defined temporally but qualitatively, that is, as symbolic anticipations of a greater reality of which each sign is already a part (see comments on 2:11). Fourth, he minimizes the implicit connection between the seventh sign and the purpose statement (20:30 – 31), the narrator's personal commentary (see above), even though he clearly assumes the statement works in tandem with the death and resurrection of Jesus. Finally, he suggests that the seventh sign as the death and resurrection would have "appeared inappropriate (if not blasphemous)" to Jesus's disciples, who would have seen the crucifixion and resurrection as different in kind in their understanding of its salvation-historical and personal uniqueness. While certainly the death and resurrection is the climactic sign and does more than the work of any other "sign," this does not imply it is not also a visible sign that can and should be understood in light of Jesus's entire ministry. It not only accomplished what God intended but serves to instruct the disciples thereafter that everything that had been *done* to him had also been *told* by him and Scripture long before (see 12:16; cf. 20:9).

20:1 On the first day of the week, Mary Magdalene came to the tomb early, while it was still dark, and saw the stone had been taken away from the tomb (Τῇ δὲ μιᾷ τῶν σαββάτων Μαρία ἡ Μαγδαληνὴ ἔρχεται πρωῒ σκοτίας ἔτι οὔσης εἰς τὸ μνημεῖον, καὶ βλέπει τὸν λίθον ἠρμένον ἐκ τοῦ μνημείου). The first section of the pericope (vv. 1 – 2) introduces the characters of the story (Mary, Peter, and the Beloved Disciple) and the issue the conflict centers upon: the body of Jesus. The Gospel moves quickly from the death of Jesus on Friday to the resurrection of Jesus three days later on Sunday. No time is spent depicting the reaction of the family of Jesus as they left the site of the crucifixion or the disciples as they are confronted with what just occurred. Perhaps even more significant, the great day of the Passover is not even mentioned; what took place on the day of preparation consumed all the attention.[4] For the Gospel it is almost as if the sun itself was controlled by the body of Christ, descending below the horizon just after Jesus gave his life and waiting until Jesus had risen from the dead before rising (in narrative time) above the horizon. Thus, "early" (πρωῒ) in the morning, with the "dark" (σκοτίας) still present but fading, Mary Magdalene arrives at the tomb of Jesus. The pervasively negative use of "darkness/night" in the Gospel (see 1:5; 13:30) makes its use in this context potent. The darkness that had for so long "overcome" (cf. 1:5) the world and had tried to do the same to the Son of Man was here taking its last breath before the Son — the light of the world — arose to claim his victory on the third day!

The narrative explains that Mary Magdalene was the person who arrived early at the tomb. Although only she is mentioned, the first-person plural verb in v. 2 "we do not know" (οἴδαμεν) sug-gests she came with others (cf. the Synoptics: Matt 28:1; Mark 16:1; Luke 24:10). But the narrative fo-cuses all its attention upon Mary. Mary Magdalene first appeared in the Gospel as the only woman not related to Jesus standing the before the cross (see comments on 19:25). Her appearance at the cross and the resurrection of Jesus makes her a pri-mary witness of these foundational set of events. Upon her arrival at the tomb, she discovers it in an unusual condition — the stone covering the front of Jesus's tomb had been removed. She infers (or looks inside to see) that the body of Jesus had been removed (see v. 2), since the removal of such stones was neither easy nor expected.[5]

The Gospel has so clearly applied a Genesis lens to the story it tells that it is difficult not to see the opening phrase "on the first day of the week" (Τῇ δὲ μιᾷ τῶν σαββάτων) in light of the Gospel's cre-ation motif.[6] The anonymous "garden" (see com-ments on 18:1) and the second Adam theme (see comments on 19:5) direct the reader to hear with these words the announcement of the first week of the new creation. The entire Gospel has been crafted within a "creation week" structure (see comments before 2:1 and on 12:1; cf. comments before 1:19). The creation of man was literally re-newed at the incarnation (1:14). The focus of the majority of John was on the sixth day, the creation of the God-man, awaiting the seventh day, the day of rest, to arrive. But the seventh day has now come and gone! Jesus, "the man" (19:5), has completed his work (see 19:30), ceasing from all his activities. The biblical irony is stark: the Son of God rested from his creative work in a new tomb located in a garden (19:41). In this one statement the entire biblical story is summarized, for all of creation has been reborn. From this garden tomb life (eternal)

---

4. Cf. Hoskyns, *Fourth Gospel*, 539.
5. Keener, *John*, 2:1179.

6. See Jeannine K. Brown, "Creation's Renewal in the Gos-pel of John," *CBQ* 72 (2010): 275 – 90.

was recreated. Thus, as the sun rose on this new "day," so did the unique Son, for whom this day would henceforth be named "the Lord's Day."[7]

20:2 So she ran and came to Simon Peter and to the other disciple whom Jesus loved, and she said to them, "They have taken the Lord from the tomb and we do not know where they have placed him" (τρέχει οὖν καὶ ἔρχεται πρὸς Σίμωνα Πέτρον καὶ πρὸς τὸν ἄλλον μαθητὴν ὃν ἐφίλει ὁ Ἰησοῦς, καὶ λέγει αὐτοῖς, Ἦραν τὸν κύριον ἐκ τοῦ μνημείου, καὶ οὐκ οἴδαμεν ποῦ ἔθηκαν αὐτόν). The narrator does not spend much time depicting what Mary saw at the tomb; it is her reaction to the tomb that is stressed. It is notable that the narrator explains that Mary "ran" (τρέχει) to the disciples, specifically to Peter and the "Beloved Disciple" (see v. 3), to share the state in which she found Jesus's tomb, for the narrator will describe how they also will "run" as they go to the tomb (see v. 4). Nothing is revealed regarding Mary's observation inside the tomb. The reader is expected to assume what Mary likely inferred, that an opened tomb suggested foul play of some sort.[8] Her message to the disciples suggests as much.

Mary's announcement to the disciples — though only two are mentioned — describes what she understood (assumed?) from her observation of the tomb of Jesus. Two aspects of her statement need to be addressed. First, Mary explains, "They have taken the Lord from the tomb" (Ἦραν τὸν κύριον ἐκ τοῦ μνημείου). But who does Mary believe "they" are? While grave robbers were not unknown, they were quite rare and the text does not give even a hint in this direction.[9] The only contextual evidence in John, though not overt, points in another direction: "the Jews."[10] The evidence in-

cludes the following: the Jews had been complainants at the trial (19:7), the Jews wanted proof of his death by the breaking of his legs (19:31), Joseph of Arimathea had already acted in fear of the Jews (19:38), and the disciples would later act according to a similar fear (20:19; cf. 20:26). While Mary's assumed antecedent for "they" cannot be determined from the text, her stated concern notably places emphasis on the *body* of Jesus (see comments on 20:17).

Second, Mary adds, "And we do not know where they have placed him" (καὶ οὐκ οἴδαμεν ποῦ ἔθηκαν αὐτόν). Again the antecedent of another pronoun is often noted as significant: Who does Mary include with her when she says "we?" There is no need to assume Mary came alone simply because the narrator mentions only her, just as there is no need to assume Mary's announcement regarding the Lord's tomb was only spoken to Peter and the Beloved Disciple.[11] The Gospel has often focused scenes on individual characters (e.g., 3:1 – 9; 4:7 – 26; 5:1 – 9; 9:1 – 7; 11:20 – 37), for all accounts are interpretive in their selectivity and emphasis.

The issue that should not be missed, however, is Mary's concern regarding the *location* of Jesus's body. The implied antecedents of "they" and "we" are eclipsed by the clear antecedent of "him," that is "the Lord" (τὸν κύριον), an important christological title (see 20:18, 28) that occurs with the definite article here for the first time in the Gospel (the anarthrous "Lord/sir" has occurred several times). The connection between "the Lord" and his location is important in the Gospel as a whole. Moreover, Mary's question reflects the topic raised several times by the Gospel regarding the location of Jesus. The entire Gospel message is supported

---

7. See Augustine, *John*, 110.6.435. Cf. Did. 14:1; Ign. *Magn.* 9:1; Barn. 15:8 – 9.

8. See Keener, *John*, 2:1180 – 81.

9. See Barrett, *John*, 562 – 63.

10. Paul S. Minear, " 'We don't know where …' John 20:2," *Int* 30 (1976): 125 – 39 (126).

11. It is unlikely that a woman in a first-century context would travel alone at such an hour and to such a place.

by Christ's identity as the one who came ("from above") and the one who goes (to the Father).[12] Not only has Jesus rebuked his accusers with this premise (8:14; cf. 6:62; 7:32 – 36), but the Gospel has continually made Jesus's location a point of emphasis, often at the expense of the crowd, the Jews, and even the disciples (e.g., 7:11; 12:35 – 36; 13:1 – 3, 33 – 38; 14:28; 16:5, 16, 18, 28). Although this theme will come to a climax in the next pericope — again involving Mary Magdalene (see 20:17), its importance is here introduced.

20:3 Then Peter departed, and the other disciple, and they set off for the tomb (Ἐξῆλθεν οὖν ὁ Πέτρος καὶ ὁ ἄλλος μαθητής, καὶ ἤρχοντο εἰς τὸ μνημεῖον). The second section of the pericope (vv. 3 – 7) introduces the conflict of the pericope. The narrative turns now to the two disciples who received Mary's announcement. According to the narrator, Peter and the Beloved Disciple begin making their way to the tomb where Jesus had been buried. This is the third pericope that mentions the Beloved Disciple (for an overview of the "Beloved Disciple," see comments on 13:23), but it is the first time that the "Beloved Disciple" is directly connected with the less common but significant occurrences of the anonymous "other/ another disciple" (for an overview of the "other" disciple, see comments on 1:40). This anonymous disciple has not only become an "ideal author" as one who has been with Jesus from the beginning of his ministry and an "ideal disciple" as one who has special access and intimate relationship with Jesus (see 13:25), but he also serves as an "ideal witness" as one who will see the empty tomb with his own eyes and come to understand its true significance (see v. 8).

20:4 The two were running together, and the other disciple ran ahead more quickly than Peter and came first to the tomb (ἔτρεχον δὲ οἱ δύο ὁμοῦ· καὶ ὁ ἄλλος μαθητὴς προέδραμεν τάχιον τοῦ Πέτρου καὶ ἦλθεν πρῶτος εἰς τὸ μνημεῖον). Just as Mary "ran" to tell the disciples about the tomb (v. 2), so the two disciples ran to the tomb, though the Beloved Disciple ran faster than Peter. It is difficult to know what the narrator intends to communicate by comparing the pace of the two disciples. The narrator certainly does not intend to communicate that "the faster running of the Beloved Disciple shows ... his greater degree of love and ... keener predisposition to faith."[13] The ancient explanation might still be best: the Beloved Disciple was simply a younger man than Peter. This is not to deny, however, that some level of conflict or dissonance is in view (see 21:15 – 25).

This is the second of four comparison-like depictions of Peter and the Beloved Disciple (13:22 – 25; 20:3 – 9; 21:7; 21:20 – 23). The first occurrence, however, depicts not competition but unity (cf. 13:24), and the last is raised by Peter (not the narrator) and sharply rebuked by Jesus (cf. 21:21 – 22). Even here the narrator carefully describes them as running "together" (ὁμοῦ). And although the Beloved Disciple arrives at the tomb first, it is Peter who first enters the tomb — again carefully described by the narrator (v. 6). In fact, the so-called race might be intended merely to set the context for another comparison: the order of their entrance into the tomb.[14] Comparison was a standard rhetorical technique, employing comparison of characters in ways useful to the point of the narrative.[15] For this reason the point of comparison must involve not only the running but also the entrance into the tomb. And since the narrator in

12. Minear, "We don't know where," 130.
13. Contra Brendan Byrne, "The Faith of the Beloved Disciple and the Community in John 20," *JSNT* 23 (1985): 83 – 97 (86). Cf. Moloney, *John*, 519; Bultmann, *John*, 685.
14. Michaels, *John*, 989.
15. Keener, *John*, 2:1183.

v. 9 compares the response of both disciples to the message of Scripture, it is likely that neither disciple is intended to serve as the paradigm.

20:5 Kneeling to look, he saw the linen clothes lying there, but he did not enter (καὶ παρακύψας βλέπει κείμενα τὰ ὀθόνια, οὐ μέντοι εἰσῆλθεν). Although the Beloved Disciple arrived at the tomb first, the narrator is careful to note that he was not quick to enter. He did, however, look into the tomb. The participle translated as "kneeling to look" (παρακύψας) can be used to depict more metaphorical "looking" or intellectually trying to figure something out, but here probably only suggests that the Beloved Disciple looked into the tomb with curiosity or great interest.[16] The Beloved Disciple knelt because the tomb like most ancient tombs "had a low entrance and a step down into the central, rectangular pit, with shelves cut into the rock around the pit" (cf. 11:38).[17] The fact that "he saw the linen clothes lying there" (βλέπει κείμενα τὰ ὀθόνια) is given importance, since Peter will also be described as seeing the exact same thing.

20:6 Then Simon Peter who was behind him also came and he went into the tomb; he also saw the linen clothes lying there (ἔρχεται οὖν καὶ Σίμων Πέτρος ἀκολουθῶν αὐτῷ, καὶ εἰσῆλθεν εἰς τὸ μνημεῖον· καὶ θεωρεῖ τὰ ὀθόνια κείμενα). Although second to the tomb, Peter was the first to enter it, apparently moving right past the Beloved Disciple, who remained at the entrance. If the Beloved Disciple was the first *to* the tomb, Peter was the first *in* the tomb. Our analysis above in v. 4 is important here. What is the point of such details? Why does the narrator make such comparison-like depictions of the disciples? Our goal is to discover the narra-

tive's rhetorical point expressed by the comparison technique. Several points need to be made.

First, clearly the comparison is not simply concerned with foot speed. The narrative is more concerned with what is inside the tomb than with its exterior. Thus, for the Gospel this could not have been a "race" to the tomb.[18] Even more, there are several aspects of the narrative that place the so-called competitors in an equivalent position. In the greater context of chapter 20, Mary, Peter, and the Beloved Disciple all have some privileged position in relation to the tomb's exterior, interior, and belief that separates them from the other two, yet not one of them can be clearly distinguished as more significant than the others. Even further, each of them is rebuked for their understanding or belief either by the narrator (20:9) or Jesus himself (20:17) in a manner that recontextualizes their particular positions of privilege. That is, the Gospel interprets their interpretations. Their privileged places are not enough; more sight and belief are needed.

Second, the narrative gives emphasis to "seeing and believing" in this pericope (20:8) and the one to follow (20:18) These two acts are best taken as a unified whole, first introduced by the words of the Beloved Disciple and presented to all the disciples by Jesus's own initiative. The Gospel proper will end with this emphasis, with Thomas serving for the reader less as "the doubter" and more as the final disciple to come to an understanding of the relationship between sight and belief in Jesus (see 20:24 – 29).[19]

For these reasons, the relation of all three disciples to the tomb or the body of Jesus is intended to create a greater (cumulative) comparison. The rhetorical technique of comparison intends to point the reader away from a tomb or a corpse and

---

16. BDAG 767.
17. Rodney A. Whitacre, *John*, IVPNTC 4 (Downers Grove, IL: InterVarsity Press, 1999), 473.
18. Cf. Calvin, *John 11 – 21*, 193.

19. Cf. Larry Darnell George, *Reading the Tapestry: A Literary-Rhetorical Analysis of the Johannine Resurrection Narrative (John 20 – 21)*, StBibLit 14 (New York: Peter Lang, 2000), 57 – 64.

direct it to the resurrected Lord himself. The point of the narrative then was not between the disciples at all — no race (v. 4), no superior belief (v. 8) — but between the "flesh" the disciples had known and the Word they were from this point on to know by faith and through the Spirit. Jesus had spoken to the disciples about this in the farewell discourse, but the reality of the resurrection and shortly thereafter the gift of the Spirit would have to drive it home. It is ultimately the resurrection of Jesus that becomes the hinge that unites the cosmological and historical strands of the plot of John — the full understanding of the person and work of Jesus (see comments on 2:22). The depth of this transition, however, would need to be explained over several pericopae; the whole of chapter 20 will be needed to convey this new reality of the immediate access of the children of God to God the Father by means of the risen Lord and in the Spirit.[20]

20:7 And the face cloth, which was placed upon his head; it was not lying with the linen clothes but was folded in one place by itself (καὶ τὸ σουδάριον, ὃ ἦν ἐπὶ τῆς κεφαλῆς αὐτοῦ, οὐ μετὰ τῶν ὀθονίων κείμενον ἀλλὰ χωρὶς ἐντετυλιγμένον εἰς ἕνα τόπον). The narrator now goes into great detail describing all that Peter "saw." Between vv. 6 – 7, two items are mentioned as having been seen by Peter. The first item (v. 6) is "the linen clothes" (τὰ ὀθόνια). Befitting Jewish customs, a corpse would be wrapped tightly with shrouds of cloth from head to toe, including the tight wrap around the head and face to keep the mouth closed (cf. 11:44; 19:40).[21] The second item is "the face cloth" (τὸ σουδάριον), separate from the linen clothes; it is a term borrowed from Latin which can refer to "a napkin," or "a cloth for

wiping off perspiration."[22] The face cloth was tied around the head of the corpse in order to keep the mouth closed, usually placed on the outside of the linen clothes and therefore detached from them. "The napkin (a square) was so folded so as to make a triangle putting an angle upon the opposite angle of the napkin. Then the large side of the triangle was rolled [folded] around the head ... and finally its two opposite angles tied together."[23]

The narrative's description of the face cloth is difficult to interpret, but clearly the specific focus gives it emphasis. Much of the meaning is based upon the Greek phrase that explains that the face cloth was "folded in one place by itself" (χωρὶς ἐντετυλιγμένον εἰς ἕνα τόπον). In the context the phrase explains that the face cloth was located in a different location, "by itself" (χωρὶς), and not in the "same place" as the linen clothes. By explaining that the face cloth was folded and placed to the side away from the rest of the shrouds of linen, the narrative implies that after rising from the dead, Jesus removed the cloth from his face and folded it nicely to the side of the stone slab upon which he had just been lying.

The imagery created by the depiction of the grave clothes is stark. A couple observations are warranted. First, the neatness and placement of the grave clothes is evidence that grave robbers had not stolen the body of Jesus. In fact, if the body had been taken at all, why would someone remove such elaborate shrouds of linen (covered with a hundred pounds of perfume and spices; cf. 19:39) and neatly fold a face cloth and place it to the side? This evidence was famously described by Chrysostom as a proof or "a sign of the resurrection."[24]

Second, the imagery of Jesus's grave clothes is intended to serve as a stark contrast to the grave clothes

20. Reimund Bieringer, "'They Have Taken Away my Lord:' Text-Immanent Repetitions and Variations in John 20,1 – 18," in *Repetitions and Variations in the Fourth Gospel: Style, Text, Interpretation*, ed. G. van Belle, M. Labahn, and P. Maritz, BETL 223 (Leuven: Peeters, 2009), 609 – 30 (630).

21. Keener, *John*, 2:850.
22. Barrett, *John*, 403.
23. Fausto Salvoni, "The So-Called Jesus Resurrection Proof (John 20:7)," *ResQ* 22 (1979): 72 – 76 (74).
24. Chrysostom, *John*, 85.4.320.

of Lazarus, who was depicted as coming out of the tomb with both the linen clothes and face cloth still tightly wound about him, needing to be freed from the chains of the grave. Even more, the folded face cloth serves as a sign of his triumph over death.

Third, the term "face cloth" (τὸ σουδάριον) is semantically related to the Greek translation of the Hebrew word for the veil covering the face of Moses in Exodus 34:33 – 35. Although this Greek term is close in meaning to the term for the veil used to cover the face of Moses, this Latin-based word speaks more specifically to a "covering for the face" (cf. 11:44).[25] In light of the OT context, this term would have recalled the face veil of Moses. The fact that Jesus did not merely drop the face cloth or veil but carefully removed, folded, and placed it to the side is telling. "Like Moses, who put aside the veil when he ascended to meet God in glory, Jesus, the New Moses, has put aside the veil of his flesh as he ascends into the presence of God to receive from him the glory which he had with the Father before the world was made" (cf. 17:5).[26]

The second section of the pericope (vv. 3 – 7) concludes with a powerful presentation of the pericope's conflict. The conflict has nothing to do with a race to the tomb, the courage needed to enter it, or grave robbers, or even the Jewish authorities. The conflict of this pericope, rather, is the understanding of the disciples regarding the location and body of Jesus, that is, the meaning of the completion of his work and the nature of their new relationship with him. As much as this conflict will require all of chapter 20 to come to a full resolution, it begins in the very next verse.

20:8 So then the other disciple, who had come first to the tomb, entered also; and he saw and began to believe (τότε οὖν εἰσῆλθεν καὶ ὁ ἄλλος μαθητὴς ὁ ἐλθὼν πρῶτος εἰς τὸ μνημεῖον, καὶ εἶδεν καὶ ἐπίστευσεν). In the third section of the pericope (vv. 8 – 9), the resolution of the pericope's plot is presented through a cryptic statement regarding the Beloved Disciple, followed by an important explanation by the narrator. The narrator emphasizes the temporal connection between the entrance of Peter into the tomb and the delayed entrance by the Beloved Disciple with the emphatic connective "so then" (τότε οὖν), which presents a "fuller sense" of "now" (in contrast to the preceding time).[27] Although the Beloved Disciple initially only looked into the tomb from the outside, he now enters it for himself.

The narrator gives a two-verb commentary on the reaction of the Beloved Disciple that is climactic and yet difficult to interpret in the immediate context: "And he saw and began to believe" (καὶ εἶδεν καὶ ἐπίστευσεν). The importance of "seeing and believing" has a unified and thematic importance in this pericope (see v. 6) and the one to follow (20:18) — and in the Gospel as a whole (cf. 20:30 – 31) — so that its occurrence here is significant and foundational. It is important to note that the two verbs do not have an object. The first verb is the third occurrence of three synonymous verbs used to depict the fact that the disciples "saw" (εἶδεν), making emphatic this particular "seeing" (see v. 6). The object of sight may be absent, but the narrative could not have been clearer about the object in view. The immense detail about the seemingly unimportant articles of grave clothes, both their folding and location, makes clear that these are the objects the Beloved Disciple "saw."[28]

But what is the object of the Beloved Disciple's

25. Sandra M. Schneiders, "The Face Veil: A Johannine Sign (John 20:1 – 10)," *BTB* 13 (1983): 94 – 97 (96).

26. Ibid.

27. BDF § 459.2; cf. BDAG 1012.

28. Steven A. Hunt, "Nicodemus, Lazarus, and the Fear of 'the Jews' in the Fourth Gospel," in Van Belle, *Repetitions and Variations in the Fourth Gospel*, 199 – 212 (208).

belief? This is the more difficult question to answer, for it must assume something about the nature of the Beloved Disciple's belief — his understanding of the person and work of Jesus. What also makes the nature of the Beloved Disciple's belief difficult to interpret is v. 9, which explains that the disciples were lacking in understanding about the resurrection. It has long been argued that the object of belief was the announcement of the empty tomb made to them by Mary (v. 2).[29] The warrant for this interpretation, however, is strongly challenged by the force of "believe" in the Gospel as a whole. When used absolutely, as it may be intended by the narrator here, the term refers to genuine faith (e.g., 5:44; 6:47; 19:35; 20:29).[30] The more likely object of belief is the resurrection itself. The preceding context certainly favors this, with such a dramatic buildup of detailed, tangible evidence. And Mary's announcement seems to have served more to raise their concerns and direct them to the tomb than to serve as a statement worthy of belief.

It is important to note, however, that while the preceding context seems to demand that the object in view is the resurrection, the subsequent context explains that the object believed was not fully grasped and that there was still some misunderstanding, similar to the earlier presentation of Mary (v. 2). There is warrant to suggest therefore that the aorist-tense verb often translated more generically as "believed" functions as an ingressive aorist, which stresses the beginning of an action or the entrance into a state: "He *began* to believe."[31] Rather than assuming the verb is, for example, a constative aorist, which views the action as a whole, in the developing context of chapter 20 the object-less verb is intended to make a counterannounce-

ment to Mary's that a real and greater clarity was being perceived by the Beloved Disciple. "It was like a new certainty that took hold of this disciple while understanding was still lacking."[32] The irony of this pericope is that the resolution of its conflict is provided more for the reader than the disciples themselves, as the next verse will make clear.[33]

20:9 For they did not yet know the Scripture that it was necessary for him to be raised from the dead (οὐδέπω γὰρ ᾔδεισαν τὴν γραφὴν ὅτι δεῖ αὐτὸν ἐκ νεκρῶν ἀναστῆναι). The resolution of the conflict (vv. 8 – 9) is so significant (and complex) that the narrator interjects the necessary explanation (cf. 2:21). Comments by the narrator that provide necessary insight are common in John; in every instance they serve to add insight to the scene at hand, even to the historical details. This is precisely how this comment by the narrator functions. The narrator explains the nature of the object believed by the Beloved Disciple — and Peter, for the verb is plural. The plural verb guarantees that the Gospel has no intentions of pitting one disciple against the other.

It is surprising that the narrator begins his explanation with "for" (γὰρ) and not "but" (δὲ), a contrastive conjunction, although "for" can function as a "marker of clarification" for the purpose of explanation, even in a manner that parallels "but" (δὲ).[34] The narrator makes an important clarification that "they did not yet know the Scripture" (οὐδέπω γὰρ ᾔδεισαν τὴν γραφὴν). While the verb "know" (ᾔδεισαν) might be better translated as "understand," in the context the important word is the negated adverb translated as "not yet" (οὐδέπω), which is used for "the negation of extending time up to and beyond an expected

29. Augustine, *John*, 120.9.436; Luther, *John*, 69:297 – 98. See Minear, "We don't know where," 127 – 28.

30. Beasley-Murray, *John*, 373.

31. Wallace, *Greek Grammar*, 558.

32. Ridderbos, *John*, 633.

33. Kelli S. O'Brien, "Written That You May Believe: John 20 and Narrative Rhetoric," *CBQ* 67 (2005): 284 – 302.

34. BDAG 189. Cf. Bultmann, *John*, 685.

point."[35] Without v. 8, the statement here would suggest that (without the Scripture) the disciples did not know at all about the resurrection, but v. 8 demands that they did know or understand something, just not everything. Thus, the narrator offers insight regarding the disciples, that they were limited in their understanding, but also regarding "the Scripture" (τὴν γραφὴν), that it serves as a fuller, even explanatory, testimony to the fact and meaning of the resurrection of Jesus. The Scripture would reveal that the resurrection was "necessary" (δεῖ), divinely ordained and willed by God.

This statement conjoins two important aspects of belief for the Gospel of John: the resurrection and Scripture. As Jesus explained to the Jewish authorities in 2:22, the resurrection explains the Scripture (what is read), and the Scripture explains the resurrection (what is seen and experienced) in a manner similar to how bifocals serve as correctives for both nearsightedness and farsightedness. While any number of particular Scriptures might fit the subject matter, the singular "the Scripture," which the Gospel has used before (cf. 2:22; 10:35), suggests the whole is in view.[36] This passage even implies that belief in the resurrection came *before* it was interpreted as being foretold in the OT. This is not to suggest that the first Christians manufactured a resurrection in their interpretation of OT prophecy; rather, the fact of the resurrection facilitated a fuller meaning in their reading of the same OT.[37] The resolution this pericope provides is grounded not only in what the disciples have already seen in the tomb but what they are still to see in the word of God — and even shortly from the

Word of God himself. The ultimate resolution of this pericope and all chapter 20, then, is true belief (20:30 – 31).

20:10 Then the disciples went again to their homes (ἀπῆλθον οὖν πάλιν πρὸς αὐτοὺς οἱ μαθηταί). After such dramatic detail of running to and from the tomb and the various ways the disciples entered into it, the conclusion is quite unremarkable. The narrator briefly explains that the disciples left the tomb and returned to where they had been before. The verse serves as a transition, bringing this pericope (vv. 1 – 10) to a conclusion and setting up the context for the next pericope (20:11 – 18), in which Mary is alone at the tomb.

The phrase we translated as "to their homes" (πρὸς αὐτοὺς) is likely an abbreviated form of the phrase used earlier, "to their own homes" (εἰς τὰ ἴδια), in two significant passages: 1:11 and 16:32. It could be argued that the earlier phrase (used in 1:11; 16:32) is a prophetic statement that is fulfilled by this statement: "You will be scattered, each to his own home." The incomplete understanding of the disciples is likely revealed by this verse, so unlike the response to come (20:18, 25; 21:7). For this reason, Jesus will be the one to pursue them. Just as he came to the world (to "his own"; cf. 1:11), so also will he come to his disciples, even "to their homes" to which they returned; not even closed doors can hinder his mission to them (see 20:19, 26). At this point the disciples have not fully understood the meaning of his death or the power of his life, let alone the truth that their life finds its meaning in him (14:19).

---

35. BDAG 735.

36. The Gospel can use the singular, however, to refer to one particular passage (see 19:37). Some of the suggested ref-

erences include Psalm 16:10, Hosea 6:2, Jonah 1:17, and Isaiah 53:10 – 12 (cf. 1 Cor 15:4).

37. Morris, *John*, 737. Cf. Hoskyns, *Fourth Gospel*, 540.

Theology in Application

The Jews with the help of the Romans destroyed the temple — the body of Jesus — fulfilling in their own actions the first part of Jesus's prophecy in 2:19. Here Jesus completes the prophecy by raising it — himself — on the third day. This pericope begins on the third day since his crucifixion, and it serves to announce to the reader the fact and reality of the resurrection of *the* Lord. This pericope begins a chapter-long explanation of the meaning of the resurrection. The narrative testifies to the reader that Jesus has been raised from the dead and guides the reader to understand how the resurrection of Jesus is the inauguration of the restoration of all things.

The Fact of the Empty Tomb

This pericope goes to great lengths to testify to the fact of the empty tomb. In these ten verses, the Gospel of John proclaims to the reader that Jesus has risen from the dead. The detail with which the narrative explains the empty and forsaken grave clothes is intended to serve as a witness for the reader (vv. 5–6), explaining that such garments had never been in command of this body but were simply used like a garment for sleep, soon to be folded and prepared for a person who would actually use it (v. 7).

The message of this passage is clear: "Christ is risen!" The church has used this Easter greeting for centuries. It serves as a declaration that the work of Jesus has been accomplished and fulfilled and serves as a promise that the restoration of all things has now been guaranteed.[38] The resurrection is the foundation of the Christian faith, as the apostle Paul also makes clear (see 1 Cor 15:14). And as Paul explains, the fact of the empty tomb declares that all people who believe in him shall be resurrected to life eternal.

The Location of the Lord

None of the followers of Jesus — Mary, Peter, or the Beloved Disciple — grasped the full reality of the empty tomb. Mary's concerned statement regarding the location of "the Lord" was especially revealing. Yet when she speaks of the Lord she attempts to define him by the location of his body. It has been the primary thrust of the entire Gospel from the start that the Lord *was* before he "became flesh" (1:14), for he was in the beginning with God (1:1–2). How then could his body be misplaced or taken? How could the Lord be defined or confined by his body? Moreover, when we think of the location of the Lord, the only place that defines him is God himself — the Trini-

---

38. See N. T. Wright, *The Resurrection of the Son of God*, Christian Origins and the Question of God 3 (Minneapolis: Fortress, 2003), 685.

tarian God — for the entire Gospel message defines his location by his movement. Jesus is the one who came ("from above") and the one who goes (to the Father).

The disciples, evidenced by Mary, misunderstood that this (mis)location was actually a "sign" that he was closer than he had ever been. For he had now destroyed all things separating himself from them — even death itself — and was fully able to do what he promised them in his farewell discourse: "I will not leave you as orphans; I am coming to you ... the world will no longer see me but you will see me, because I live you also will live. On that day you will know that I am in the Father and you are in me and I am in you" (14:18 – 20). That day has come. It is resurrection Sunday, known henceforth as "the Lord's Day."

The Testimony of Scripture

The primary importance given to historical evidence regarding the resurrection of Jesus does not in any way minimize the primary importance also given in v. 9 to Scripture as a witness to the resurrection of Jesus. Without in any way denying the absolute historical fact of the resurrection, a fact supported by verifiable historical evidence seen and recounted by the disciples and many others (see 1 Cor 15:3 – 8), the narrator's commentary on the nature of the disciples' belief makes clear that the testimony of Scripture is itself an essential and irreplaceable piece of evidence for the resurrection. In fact, the narrative suggests that without the testimony of Scripture, the disciples would have been unable to believe that Christ had risen from the dead. The Christian must ensure that the greatest testimony to God and his work — even his historical works — is the Bible.[39] While there is a place for apologetics that relies on historical and philosophical proofs, one must be careful not to avoid or deny the primacy of Scripture for securing belief and its certainties.

Death, Life, and Creation Renewed

This pericope brings together several Genesis-creation motifs that have been central in the progressive unfolding of the Gospel narrative. It is no surprise that the "seventh sign" of the second Adam (cf. 19:5) takes place in a garden (cf. 18:1) on "the first day of the week" (v. 1). In light of the rest of the Gospel, this pericope offers a climactic summary of the whole biblical story. The reader is directed to understand that Jesus Christ has completed his mission from the Father and has inaugurated the new creation, with the empty tomb declaring that death itself has been defeated and all creation has been offered new life. The apostle Paul makes a similar declaration, "For as in Adam all die, so in Christ all will be made alive" (1 Cor 15:22). It is because "he is risen!" that death itself has been defeated. This is more than just a fact of this life, for it is also what gives this life its meaning and purpose. He is risen indeed!

---

39. Luther calls the testimony of Scripture "the external Word" of Christ (*John*, 69:297).

44

John 20:11 – 18

Literary Context

This pericope is the second of four sections of the final section of the narrative proper, which brings climactic resolution to the Gospel story. The previous pericope (20:1 – 10) emphasized the fact of the empty tomb and the location of Jesus; in this pericope Jesus makes his first postresurrection appearance, which serves to explain further the reality of his resurrection and the nature of his relationship to his disciples. In this pericope the reader learns how the resurrection conquered the grief of Mary Magdalene and is guided to participate in her growing understanding of new-covenant life in the family of God.

IX. The Resurrection (20:1 – 31)

   A. The Empty Tomb (20:1 – 10)

➡   **B. The Appearance to Mary Magdalene (20:11 – 18)**

   C. The Appearance to the Disciples (20:19 – 23)

   D. The Appearance to Thomas and the Purpose of the Gospel (20:24 – 31)

Main Idea

The resurrected Jesus makes the tomb a place of grace not grief, declaring that he has fulfilled the old covenant and established the saving power and presence of the Lord through his death, resurrection, and ascension. The Gardener has returned to reclaim his Garden.

Translation

John 20:11–18

Introduction & Setting (11–12)

11a	Contrasting Action of "Disciples"	But **Mary was standing at the tomb**
b	Description	weeping outside.
c		As she was weeping
d	Progression of Action	**she knelt to look into the tomb,**
12a		and **she saw two angels**
b	Description	in white seated,
c	Location	one at the head and
d		one at the feet,
e	Location	where the body of Jesus had been lying.
13a		And **they said to her,**
b	Address	*"Woman,*
c	Question	*why are you weeping?"*
d	Response	**She said to them,**
e	Assertion	*"They have taken away my Lord,*
f	Inference	*and I do not know where they have placed him."*
14a		After she said these things,
b	Escalating Progression of Action	**she turned around**
c		and **saw**
d	Character Reentrance!	Jesus standing there,
e	Reaction	and **she did not know that he was Jesus.**
15a	Action	**Jesus said to her,**
b	Address	*"Woman,*
c	Question #1	*why are you weeping?*
d	Question #2	*Whom are you seeking?"*
e	Character's Thoughts	Thinking that he is the gardener,
f	Response	**she said to him,**
g	Address	*"Sir,*
h	Condition	*if you removed him,*
i	Request	*tell me where you have laid him,*
j	Purpose	*and I will take him away."*
16a	Response	**Jesus said to her,**
b	Address	*"Mary."*
c		After turning
d	Response	**she said to him**
e	Language	in Aramaic,
f	Recognition of "Jesus"	*"Rabboni"*
g	Translation	(which means, Teacher).

Continued on next page.

Continued from previous page.

17a	Response	**Jesus said to her,**
b	Prohibition	*"Do not touch me,*
c	Basis	*for I have not yet ascended to the Father.*
d	Contrast to 17b	*But* go
e	New Status: "Family"	to my brothers
f	Message (g–k):	*and* say to them,
g	Ascension	*'I am ascending*
h	Destination: "Father"	to my Father and
i	Mutual "Father"	your Father, and
j	God's Identity: "Father"	to my God and
k		your God.'"
18a	Reaction/Conclusion	**Mary Magdalene went to the disciples**
b		announcing,
c	Announcement	*"I have seen the Lord,"*
d	Delivery of Message (17g–k)	and **that he had said these things to her.**

Structure and Literary Form

This pericope corresponds to the basic story form (see Introduction). The *introduction/setting* is established in vv. 11 – 12, explaining the location and people around whom the plot's conflict will focus. In vv. 13 – 15 the *conflict* of the pericope is presented, directed by the twice-asked question to Mary, "Why are you weeping?" (vv. 13, 15). The *resolution* of the plot is explained in vv. 16 – 17, with Jesus addressing Mary and giving insight into the full nature of his relationship to the children of God. Finally, in v. 18 the pericope is given a brief but significant *conclusion/interpretation*.

Exegetical Outline

➡ **B. The Appearance to Mary Magdalene (20:11 – 18)**

    1. The Throne of Grace (vv. 11 – 12)

    2. "Why Are You Weeping?" (vv. 13 – 15)

    3. The Ascension (vv. 16 – 17)

    4. "I Have Seen the Lord" (v. 18)

Explanation of the Text

20:11 But Mary was standing at the tomb weeping outside. As she was weeping she knelt to look into the tomb (Μαρία δὲ εἱστήκει πρὸς τῷ μνημείῳ ἔξω κλαίουσα. ὡς οὖν ἔκλαιεν παρέκυψεν εἰς τὸ μνημεῖον). The pericope begins directly in front of the tomb, with the "but" (δὲ) contrasting the departure of Peter and the Beloved Disciple with Mary, who remained "at the tomb" (πρὸς τῷ μνημείῳ).[1] Like the Beloved Disciple, Mary did not go into the tomb but simply "knelt to look" (παρέκυψεν) inside (see comments on 20:5). The narrator explains that she was standing "outside" (ἔξω) the tomb "weeping." The twofold depiction of her "weeping" (κλαίουσα; ἔκλαιεν) highlights her state of grief. This is the introduction of Mary's grief, which both the angels (v. 13) and Jesus (v. 15) will address as they initiate conversation with her. There is no warrant for interpreting the reason she remained outside the tomb or what she observed in the tomb. The narrative is not reconstructing the fullness of the event but directing the reader with interpretive intentionality to aspects of meaning and significance.

20:12 And she saw two angels in white seated, one at the head and one at the feet, where the body of Jesus had been lying (καὶ θεωρεῖ δύο ἀγγέλους ἐν λευκοῖς καθεζομένους, ἕνα πρὸς τῇ κεφαλῇ καὶ ἕνα πρὸς τοῖς ποσίν, ὅπου ἔκειτο τὸ σῶμα τοῦ Ἰησοῦ). Upon kneeling to look into the tomb, the narrator explains that Mary saw two angels dressed in white sitting at the head and foot of the place where Jesus had been lying. This is not the first mention of angels in John (cf. 1:51; 12:29), but it is the only pericope in which angels participate as characters.[2] The narrator adds that the angels were dressed "in white" (ἐν λευκοῖς), the common color of attire for angelic beings (cf. Ezek 9:2; Dan 10:5; Acts 1:10; Rev 3:3 – 4; 4:5) and priests in the Mediterranean religions, including Judaism (cf. Josephus, *J.W.* 5.229).[3] The presence of the angels makes clear that this place, and the body previously lying upon it, is hardly a place left in disarray by grave robbers. In the least the narrator uses the presence of the angels to highlight the sacredness of the site, for their presence where the corpse previously lay implies that God had something to do with it.[4]

The detailed focus of this verse, however, is not merely on the presence of the angels or the angels' attire or even the response of Mary, but on the places where the angels were seated. No specifics are provided about the inside of the tomb; like many first-century tombs there would have been space on a carved stone bench or ledge for the angels to be visibly seated, probably running along the inside wall.[5] The narrator does not focus on the kind of bench upon which the angels were seated but on their specific locations on the bench at the "head" (κεφαλῇ) and "feet" (ποσίν) of the place "where the body of Jesus had been lying." Why does the narrator focus on this particular detail? The majority of interpreters make no mention of the unique location of the angels, or they suggest that the point is simply the fact of the empty tomb.[6] However, not only did the previous pericope (20:1 – 10) already make that declaration, but the miraculous presence of two angels hardly brings focus to the absence of Jesus; indeed, it might even

---

1. Cf. BDAG 874.
2. See Jan Van der Watt, "Angels in the Gospel according to John," *JECH* 1 (2011): 185 – 204.
3. Keener, *John*, 2:1188.
4. Cf. Beasley-Murray, *John*, 374.
5. Cf. Carson, *John*, 640.
6. Ridderbos suggests their location is "to mark the emptiness of that space" (*John*, 636). Morris suggests that "the angels do not play a major part; their one function is to ask Mary why she is crying" (*John*, 739).

eclipse it if their presence was not serving a different function. A few interpreters suggest that the details provided by the narrator serve a more symbolic function. Augustine, for example, suggests that their position "signified that the gospel of Christ was to be preached from head to foot, from the beginning to the end."[7] Aquinas suggests that two further things are also signified by the two angels: the two testaments and the two natures in Christ.[8] But none of these options finds direct support from the narrative's details.

There is another option that finds sufficient warrant from the narrative. The location of the angels at each end of the place where Jesus had been lying intends to signify the angels at the two ends of the mercy seat on the ark of the covenant. The narrative's emphatic particularity of the location of the angels in relationship to the place where Jesus had been lying is remarkable in its resemblance to the instructions given to Moses regarding the ark: "Make two cherubim out of hammered gold at the ends of the cover. Make one cherub on one end and the second cherub on the other; make the cherubim of one piece with the cover, at the two ends" (Exod 25:18 – 19; cf. Exod 37:1 – 9). The place between the two angels was "the place of propitiation" or "the mercy seat" (ἱλαστήριον in the LXX), the cover of the ark that was associated with the sin offering on the Day of Atonement. It is the place where God authoritatively atones for sins. For this reason Luther's translation of the term in Exodus 25 is a most fitting description of this place: "The throne of grace" (*der Gnadenthron*).[9] It is important to state that our interpretation is driven by the emphatic particularity of the narrative itself, which like elsewhere in the Gospel creates for the reader an "impression" that qualifies as such by being rooted in the deep

structure of the narrative. Such impressions find their impulse from macrothemes in the OT and surface as a demonstrable theme in the Gospel as a whole (see comments on 4:18; see Introduction).

There are numerous verbal and conceptual links that support this interpretation.[10] First, there is a spatial relationship between the location of the ark and the body of Jesus. The ark was in the innermost chamber of the tabernacle and separated by a veil (Exod 40:3, 21); Jesus's body was placed in a burial chamber and separated by a rock and a veil-like "face cloth" (20:7). Second, the occurrence of shared terms like "take/carry" and "put/place/lay" serve to create a conceptual relationship, with the latter having a significant role in the plot of both John 20 (vv. 2, 13, 15; cf. 19:41 – 42) and Exodus 40 (vv. 2 – 3, 5 – 6, 22, 24, 26, 29). Third, both locations/objects involve the use of spices as an act of anointing or consecration: the ark (Exod 30:26) and the body of Jesus (12:3; 19:39). Fourth, just as the Jews with respect to the sanctuary were forbidden to "go in to look at the holy things, even for a minute, or they will die" (Num 4:20), both the Beloved Disciple and Mary Magdalene are hesitant to enter the tomb. In a related manner, just as there is the prohibition not to "touch the holy things or they will die (Num 4:15), so Mary Magdalene will shortly be commanded not to touch Jesus (v. 17). Fifth, there is a conceptual relationship between the ark and the resurrected Christ in that both express the idea of glory. Just as the glory of the Lord filled the tabernacle (Exod 40:34 – 35) and appeared to Moses between the cherubim on the ark (Exod 25:22, 29:43),[11] so also is the resurrection one aspect of Christ's "glorification." This is most clearly explained by the narrator in 12:16: "At first the disciples did not understand these things, but

7. Augustine, *John*, 121.1.437.

8. Aquinas, *John*, 3:260 – 61.

9. *Die Bibel nach der Übersetzung Martin Luthers* (Stuttgart: Deutsche Bibelgesellschaft, 1999).

10. The following is adapted from Nicholas P. Lunn, "Jesus, the Ark, and the Day of Atonement: Intertextual Echoes in John 19:38 – 20:18," *JETS* 52 (2009): 731 – 46.

11. Cf. Westcott, *John*, 291.

when Jesus was glorified then they remembered," which nicely parallels 2:22, which explicitly refers to the resurrection (see comments on 12:16).

The cumulative weight of these links strongly suggests that the narrative is fashioning a "deliberate allusion, linking the events described in the Gospel to certain passages of the OT."[12] Just as the Gospel declared Jesus to be the fulfillment of the Jewish feasts (see comments on 10:22), the Passover lamb (see 1:29; 19:31 – 37) and the manna (see 6:32 – 35), so here he is declared to be the fulfilling manifestation of *the saving power and presence of the Lord.* For with this symbolism Jesus is depicted as both the *atoning sacrifice* of God in the holy of holies and the one who "*sits enthroned* between the cherubim" (Ps 99:1, emphasis added; cf. 1 Sam 4:4; 2 Sam 6:2; 2 Kgs 19:15; Ps 80:1). The Gospel of John has articulated a full replacement of the temple and its predecessors (Bethel and the Tabernacle) in the person (his body) and work (his death and resurrection) of Jesus. Jesus is not merely analogous to the temple; he is its full replacement (see comments on 2:23). This includes the entire sacrificial system. Jesus is *the atonement* for the people of God — the world; it is his blood that covers our sins.[13] All Christian worship is founded upon his sacrificed "flesh" and empowered by the Spirit (4:23). All of this was being symbolized by the narrative's emphatic focus on the location of the angels, "building a picture of Jesus in terms of Mosaic categories" in order to depict this place and the person who had occupied it as the saving power and presence of God, with the empty tomb serving as the ark of the *new* covenant.[14]

20:13 And they said to her, "Woman, why are you weeping?" She said to them, "They have taken away my Lord, and I do not know where they have placed him" (καὶ λέγουσιν αὐτῇ ἐκεῖνοι, Γύναι, τί κλαίεις; λέγει αὐτοῖς ὅτι Ἦραν τὸν κύριόν μου, καὶ οὐκ οἶδα ποῦ ἔθηκαν αὐτόν). The second section of the pericope (vv. 13 – 15) presents the conflict of the pericope, uniquely provided by the angel who speaks — only this once in the Gospel — by addressing Mary with a question. No attention is given to what Mary actually understood regarding the presence of the angels, let alone their location. Instead the narrator focuses on the emotional response of Mary to the tomb. The conflict is clear: the throne of *grace* presented in vv. 11 – 12 is nothing more to Mary than a cause for *grief.* The narrative's threefold depiction of her weeping (vv. 11, 13, 15) and the same twice-asked question of Mary by the angels and Jesus makes clear that Mary's grief in the context of the throne of grace is the point of contention.

The angels are the first to speak. The third-person plural verb "they said" (λέγουσιν) suggests that they both were speaking, though the narrator may simply be viewing them as a unit, befitting the symbolic "impression" depicted just before. The angels address Mary as "woman" (Γύναι), a term used to address three other women in the Gospel: the mother of Jesus (2:4; 19:26), the Samaritan woman (4:21), and the woman accused of adultery (8:10). Jesus will also address Mary as "woman" (v. 15). The normal use of the term demands that it be seen to function at least minimally as a distancing mechanism, even when a relationship is presumed or respect is maintained (see comments on 2:4). Mary's grief before the "throne of grace" contextualizes the distancing mechanism of the term. It also puts the angels' question into context: "Why are you weeping?" (τί κλαίεις;). Grief is distant

---

12. Lunn, "Jesus, the Ark, and the Day of Atonement," 734.

13. See George Carey, "The Lamb of God and Atonement Theories," *TynBul* 32 (1981): 97 – 122.

14. Lunn, "Jesus, the Ark, and the Day of Atonement," 736.

Lunn makes an important qualification: "The significance of such an image, though implicit, is unmistakable — of Jesus, not as the typological, but as the actual means whereby atonement is attained."

from grace; it is not a befitting response. The question suggests that Mary does not understand what she has just seen.

Mary answers the question of the angels, repeating almost verbatim what she first announced to the disciples (20:2). Mary's response makes clear that she is still concerned with the location of Jesus's body, which as we argued earlier was misguided in its focus on the nature of Jesus's presence and the meaning of the empty tomb (see comments on 20:2). Quite simply, even with the angels in the cherubim positions on the "throne of grace," Mary only understands grief. She cannot see how this tomb now symbolizes life not death.

20:14 After she said these things, she turned around and saw Jesus standing there, and she did not know that he was Jesus (ταῦτα εἰποῦσα ἐστράφη εἰς τὰ ὀπίσω, καὶ θεωρεῖ τὸν Ἰησοῦν ἑστῶτα, καὶ οὐκ ᾔδει ὅτι Ἰησοῦς ἐστιν). Without any further comment the brief dialogue between Mary Magdalene and the two angels in the tomb of Jesus is concluded by the narrator; not another mention is made of it, for the point has been made. Rather, and in dramatic fashion, the narrator focuses on Mary as she "turned around" (ἐστράφη εἰς τὰ ὀπίσω) from the tomb, though what caused the turn is left unexplained (see vv. 15–16).[15] The drama climaxes, however, when after turning the narrator describes how Mary "saw Jesus" (θεωρεῖ τὸν Ἰησοῦν). Although translated as a historic present ("saw"), the verbal tense perhaps describes the up close encounter and could be translated as "she is seeing Jesus." This is the first encounter with the risen Jesus, and yet she "did not know" (οὐκ ᾔδει)

that he was Jesus. The irony is stark. The answer to her concern had been before her the whole time, both the throne of grace in the tomb and now the resurrected Lord himself, and yet she cannot "see" him (cf. 20:8).[16] At this point the conflict of the pericope reaches its climax.

20:15 Jesus said to her, "Woman, why are you weeping? Whom are you seeking?" Thinking that he is the gardener, she said to him, "Sir, if you removed him, tell me where you have laid him, and I will take him away" (λέγει αὐτῇ Ἰησοῦς, Γύναι, τί κλαίεις; τίνα ζητεῖς; ἐκείνη δοκοῦσα ὅτι ὁ κηπουρός ἐστιν λέγει αὐτῷ, Κύριε, εἰ σὺ ἐβάστασας αὐτόν, εἰπέ μοι ποῦ ἔθηκας αὐτόν, κἀγὼ αὐτὸν ἀρῶ). Jesus addresses Mary Magdalene just as the angels did, not only by using the same distancing term, "woman," but also by asking the same question regarding her weeping (v. 13). It is best to assume that Jesus's question is probing the same issue of grief in the context of grace.

Yet Jesus asks a further question: "Whom do you seek?" (τίνα ζητεῖς;). Jesus asked this exact question to the Jewish and Roman authorities coming to arrest him in the garden (see 18:4). This "garden" question, however, is spoken not in the context of betrayal but in the context of the empty tomb. The questions of Jesus in the Gospel are rarely straightforward, for usually they probe more deeply into the true reality of the scene or person (see 5:6). Jesus had asked his disciples almost the same question before (see 1:38), probing their intentions, that is, what they truly desire.[17]

The narrator provides an important explanation of Mary's mistaken assumption regarding the iden-

---

15. Chrysostom offers an imaginative suggestion that "while she was speaking, Christ suddenly appearing behind her, struck the Angels with awe ... and this drew the woman's attention" (*John*, 86.1.323).

16. Cf. Marianne Meye Thompson, "Jesus: 'The One Who Sees God,'" in Capes, *Israel's God and Rebecca's Children*, 215–26.

17. Alison Jasper, "Interpretive Approaches to John 20:1–18: Mary at the Tomb of Jesus," *ST* 47 (1993): 107–18 (111). There are several parallels with 1:38 (e.g., "turning" and "Rabbi").

tity of Jesus. Mary was "thinking that he was the gardener" (ἐκείνη δοκοῦσα ὅτι ὁ κηπουρός ἐστιν). Mary's assumption is further expressed when she questions him to see if he is responsible for the missing body of Jesus. Although Mary's statement to Jesus would have been enough to show that she did not recognize him, certainly the narrator intended to state the assumption for the readers, guiding them to see the beautiful portrait of *this* Gardener in *his* Garden. The narrator again shows how another character in the Gospel is speaking so beautifully beyond themselves in spite of their ignorance (cf. 11:49–52). Like the term "garden" (see comments on 18:1), the term "the gardener" (ὁ κηπουρός) makes an intentional "impression" on the reader (see Introduction). The Gospel has so clearly applied a Genesis lens to the story it tells that the reader sees again the "garden" theme developed throughout chapters 18–20 (cf. Gen 2:8–16).[18]

20:16 Jesus said to her, "Mary." After turning she said to him in Aramaic, "Rabboni" (which means, Teacher) (λέγει αὐτῇ Ἰησοῦς, Μαρία. στραφεῖσα ἐκείνη λέγει αὐτῷ Ἑβραϊστί, Ραββουνι [ὃ λέγεται Διδάσκαλε]). The resolution to this grief-filled, dramatic encounter between Mary and Jesus takes place when Jesus simply speaks her name. Although it is impossible to know the tone of his voice, the theology of the Gospel as a whole suggests that this voice was both warm and inviting. Immediately Mary responds to his voice, fulfilling what Jesus had promised earlier: "The sheep hear his voice, and he calls his own sheep by name" (10:3; cf. 10:4, 16, 27; 18:37). Mary responds to him

using a term in Aramaic, "Rabboni" (Ραββουνι), which the narrator explains means "Teacher" (Διδάσκαλε) in Greek (cf. 1:38). By mentioning the Aramaic, the narrator may simply intend to describe the scene as it really occurred in its original language and not to suggest that this particular Aramaic term bears a different meaning than the seven other occurrences of the related term.[19] At this point Mary recognizes the resurrected Jesus. The reader is given no deep insight into the exact nature of her understanding, though both of their responses to come yield some insight.

It may be significant that according to the narrator, Mary is again described as "turning" (στραφεῖσα). If Mary had already turned away from the angels and toward Jesus in v. 14 (denoted by the same verb), why would the narrator explain that she had to turn back toward Jesus when he spoke to her? Had she not just been in conversation with him, supposing him to be the gardener (v. 15)? Did she look back again to the tomb, to the angels? The long history of explanations suggests that the statement is at least awkward, if not out of place.[20] While it might be safest to make nothing of this detail, the emphasis on "turning" in the Gospel and this pericope is suggestive (see comments on 1:38).

This would not be the first time the Gospel has spoken through the apparently normal circumstances to something other (e.g., the "baptism" of Jesus in 3:22; "this feast" in 7:10). The double turning perhaps depicts how Mary was turning between the angels in the tomb and the Lord and misunderstanding them both. Ironically, her

18. This interpretation of this allusion is given little credence by the majority of interpreters, who prefer a more strictly historical interpretation. A few older commentators suggest that the theological connection is intentional (Lightfoot, *John*, 322; Hoskyns, *Fourth Gospel*, 542). See also Adele Reinhartz, "To Love the Lord: An Intertextual Reading of John 20," in *The Labour of Reading: Desire, Alienation, and Biblical Interpreta-*

tion, ed. Fiona C. Black, Roland Boer, and Erin Runions, SBLSS 36 (Atlanta: Society of Biblical Literature, 1999), 53–69 (63).

19. Contra Brown, *John*, 2:991; Hoskyns, *Fourth Gospel*, 543.

20. Cf. Karl Kastner, "Noli me tangere," *BZ* 13 (1915): 244–53; Bultmann, *John*, 686–87; Michaels, *John*, 999.

misunderstanding was blinding her to see what she "saw" as she stood at the tomb that Sunday morning.[21] For at that moment, as she turned back and forth, she was speaking with two unique conversation partners, both of whom represented the presence of God: the ark of the new covenant and the resurrected Lord.

The portrait painted by the narrative's repeated reference to "turning" can be explained this way. On one side of Mary the physical position of the angels declared in Mosaic categories that Jesus's body was offered as a sacrifice for others, and the tomb in which the angels were sitting likewise announced that God is accessed *through* this death. On the other side of Mary, the physical presence of Jesus declared that the resurrection proves that he was not taken by the authority of others but was given for others by his own authority (10:18). And unlike the angels, it is important that Jesus stands *outside* the tomb because his intercession on behalf of his sheep is not accomplished by his death alone but also by his newness of life. While the "lifting up" or "exaltation" of Jesus certainly includes the irony of the cross, it is not entirely defined by humiliation but also by his "glorification," the "hour" when the Son of Man enacts and receives all the authority assigned to him by the Father (cf. Acts 2:33, 36). *It was this that Mary stood between at the tomb: the declaration of the resurrected Lord outside the tomb and the declaration of the sacrificial Christ in the tomb.* In that moment Mary could declare like David: "Before a word is on my tongue you, LORD, know it completely. You hem me in behind and before.... Where can I go from your Spirit?" (Ps 139:4–7).

20:17 Jesus said to her, "Do not touch me, for I have not yet ascended to the Father. But go to my brothers and say to them, 'I am ascending to my Father and your Father, and to my God and your God'" (λέγει αὐτῇ Ἰησοῦς, Μή μου ἅπτου, οὔπω γὰρ ἀναβέβηκα πρὸς τὸν πατέρα· πορεύου δὲ πρὸς τοὺς ἀδελφούς μου καὶ εἰπὲ αὐτοῖς, Ἀναβαίνω πρὸς τὸν πατέρα μου καὶ πατέρα ὑμῶν καὶ θεόν μου καὶ θεὸν ὑμῶν). It is not an exaggeration to claim that this verse "belongs to a handful of the most difficult passages in the New Testament."[22] There are several issues that compound the difficulty that must be addressed in turn. Since the pericope thus far has been concerned with the physical location/presence of Jesus, we should assume that Jesus's statement here is intended to address that issue.

Although the narrator does not give much detail about the actual encounter between Mary and Jesus, his command to her "do not touch me" (Μή μου ἅπτου) causes some to suggest that Mary had grabbed or reached for him in some manner. However, while the negated present imperative can function as a progressive and serve to stop an action already in progress ("Stop touching me"), it can also function as a customary and have the force of a general precept ("Do not touch me").[23] Since the "action may or may not have already begun," it is ultimately context and not verbal tense that determines the force of the present imperative.[24] Interpreters debate whether Mary is grasping Jesus and therefore told to stop doing so (progressive) or Jesus is simply giving a general prohibition that addesses Mary's preoccupation with the physical body of Jesus (customary). The former (the progressive interpretation) has been the preferred view of the twentieth century in the translations and commentaries. This interpretation finds support by the fact that in just a few verses Jesus will command Thomas to touch him (20:27). It is also

21. See O'Brien, "Written That You May Believe," 296, who argues that the narrative intends for the reader to identify with the misunderstanding of the characters.

22. Carson, *John*, 641–42.
23. Wallace, *Greek Grammar*, 724.
24. Ibid., 721, 725.

supported by the Gospel of Matthew where the women at the tomb (including Mary Magdalene) upon meeting the resurrected Lord "grasped him by the feet and worshipped him" (Matt 28:9; cf. Luke 24:5).[25] For this reason, it is argued, Jesus's command must be specific to Mary and her theologically inappropriate grasping at Jesus. Yet such an interpretation requires the interpreter to infer that Mary was at that moment touching him, perhaps grasping at his feet. And the narrative's silence should at least caution us about reconstructing the actions of Mary, especially when those actions will be used to determine or explain the force of the prohibition. If Mary was grasping Jesus, why would the narrative not have described her action in that way, like the other Mary in 11:2?

When the narrative wants the reader to infer something only implied by the context, it usually leaves a statement that rests somewhat awkwardly in the immediate context (see 3:22; 7:10; cf. "turning in v. 16). But this is not awkward in this kind of way. It is quite reasonable to assume that Mary would have wanted to hold on to Jesus, and there would be nothing shocking if Jesus asked her to let go so as to send her to announce his presence to the rest of the disciples. No, the awkwardness only exists if she was *not* touching him at that time and grasping him uncontrollably. The awkwardness occurs when the statement is isolated from Mary's actions and speaking in a general way. For by such a statement Jesus would be addressing not primarily her action but his — not her physicality but his.[26] "The command does indeed warn Mary off from the embrace that might accompany a greeting, but its strangeness should be underlined rather than modified."[27]

There is good reason therefore to assume that the customary force of the prohibition is intended in the command of Jesus. In fact, a general prohibition would fit nicely with this pericope's focus (and all of ch. 20) on the physical location and nature of Jesus. It is also important to note that in this statement the prohibition of Jesus "is strictly preliminary to the main thing Jesus wants to say" to Mary and to the rest of his disciples.[28] The issue then is not whether he can or should be touched; Jesus is simply not concerned with Mary's approach toward him at this moment. Rather, Jesus is concerned that Mary — and every other disciple — comes to understood how he is to be approached from this moment onward. The function of the command is to call attention to the unique state that now exists between Mary and the resurrected Lord.[29]

The resurrection appearance to Mary has been guiding the reader to ask the more appropriate question regarding the location of Jesus: *Where is the Lord encountered?* That is, in what way is Jesus (i.e., his person and presence) now to be accessed differently? For this reason Jesus's opening command does not prohibit Mary from touching him at that moment but guides her to see that her intense search for the location of his physical body had been misguided. *What needs to stop is not a particular act of touching but a misplaced reliance on the physical presence of Jesus.* The body of Jesus and his location need to be redefined in light of his death, resurrection, and ascension as well as the coming of the Spirit/Paraclete. This is why the touching of Jesus by Thomas is not in contradiction at all with this prohibition, for the narrative is also interested in addressing a further question: *How is the Lord encountered?* That is, the Gospel

---

25. David C. Fowler, "The Meaning of 'Touch Me Not' in John 20:17," *EvQ* 47 (1975): 16 – 25. Cf. Schnackenburg, *John*, 3:317 – 18; Brown, *John*, 2:992 – 93.

26. Cf. Origen, *John*, 6.37.378.

27. Mary Rose D'Angelo, "A Critical Note: John 20:17 and Apocalypse of Moses 31," *JTS* 41 (1990): 529 – 36 (531 – 32).

28. Michaels, *John*, 1001.

29. D'Angelo, "A Critical Note: John 20:17," 532.

is intent on serving as a witness to the reader of the reality of the resurrection of Jesus from the dead.[30] The Christian faith is faith in the *living Lord*, who returned to the Father after his earthly ministry (per the Thomas account), and who is now encountered *in and by the Spirit* (per the Mary account). It is no wonder that the narrative places between Jesus's appearances to Mary (20:11 – 18) and Thomas (20:24 – 31) the giving of the Holy Spirit (20:19 – 23).[31]

Ultimately, the Gospel of John answers the "where" of Jesus not primarily by referring to his spatial or geographic location but by describing his mission from the Father. Jesus was in the bosom of the Father (1:18), and he was sent into the world to create the children of God for the Father (1:12 – 13). He will then depart to resume again the glory that properly belongs to him in the presence of God (17:5), thus facilitating for his disciples, the children of God, the full manifestation of his presence through the Spirit, the second Paraclete.[32] So where, then, is Jesus present? Jesus is present in the church! For the church is "God's temple," and "God's Spirit dwells in your midst" (1 Cor 3:16).[33]

Jesus follows his prohibition with an important and related statement: "For I have not yet ascended to the Father" (οὔπω γὰρ ἀναβέβηκα πρὸς τὸν πατέρα). The conjunction "for" (γὰρ) is functioning causally, expressing the basis of ground for the prohibition. The ground or reason why Jesus creates a separation between his physical presence and Mary is because he has not yet "ascended" (ἀναβέβηκα) to the Father. The "hour" about which Jesus spoke (see 2:4) does not merely refer to his

death and resurrection but also to his "ascension" and the sending and permanent "dwelling" of the Spirit (14:16). For Jesus to be fully "present" with his disciples, he must depart from them and return to "the Father." Jesus's statement here is anticipated in his farewell discourse (see 13:1, 3; 14:12, 28; 16:5, 7, 10, 17, 27 – 28; 17:11, 13, 21 – 26; cf. 6:62). By these words Jesus explains that his relationship to his disciples is intended to extend well beyond his physical bodily presence. For by his ascent to the Father, Jesus will eliminate entirely spatial and temporal separation, opening the way for the reciprocal indwelling in and by the Spirit.

Since the ascension (and the subsequent giving of the indwelling Spirit) completes Jesus's work, he now turns to Mary and gives her a work to do. Jesus commands Mary to go and share this announcement with the other disciples. Interestingly, Jesus refers to the disciples as "my brothers" (τοὺς ἀδελφούς μου), with the masculine plural noun serving to denote inclusively both male and female disciples ("my brothers and sisters").[34] This is the first time in the Gospel that "brothers (and sisters)" is used for the disciples (cf. 21:23); the term had previously been used only for biological kin. Its occurrence here, therefore, is telling. Something has changed. For as Jesus explains, Mary is to announce to them that "I am ascending to my Father and your Father, and to my God and your God." While maintaining a distinction between the Father's relationship to the unique Son and the Father's relationship to his other sons and daughters, this statement brings the children of God in proper relation to God the Father through God the Son.

---

30. See Sandra M. Schneiders, "Touching the Risen Jesus: Mary Magdalene and Thomas the Twin in John 20," in Koester, *The Resurrection of Jesus in the Gospel of John*, 153 – 76.

31. Our interpretation of the two angels in the tomb of Jesus in v. 12 is also relevant here.

32. Sandra M. Schneiders, "John 20:11 – 18: The Encounter of the Easter Jesus with Mary Magdalene — A Transformative

Feminist Reading," in *"What is John?" Readers and Readings of the Fourth Gospel*, ed. Fernando F. Segovia, SBLSymS 3 (Atlanta: Scholars Press, 1996): 155 – 68 (157 – 58).

33. Cf. Minear, "We don't know where," 134.

34. Contextually, as long as the group was mixed gender, the masculine plural would extend to both genders.

Jesus's words here are the fulfillment of 1:12 – 13. The ascension not only finalizes and substantiates Jesus's role as the unique Son but fully enables the disciples to receive in their persons the promised sonship (14:1 – 4, 12, 20 – 28; 16:5 – 23, 28). Mary is not merely announcing the resurrection of Jesus but also his impending ascension, which means she is declaring the fulfillment of all the things Jesus taught. It is the inauguration and reality of the gospel of Jesus Christ![35]

20:18 Mary Magdalene went to the disciples announcing, "I have seen the Lord," and that he had said these things to her (ἔρχεται Μαρία ἡ Μαγδαληνὴ ἀγγέλλουσα τοῖς μαθηταῖς ὅτι Ἑώρακα τὸν κύριον, καὶ ταῦτα εἶπεν αὐτῇ). The pericope concludes with Mary's obedient response to Jesus's command. She left the resurrected Lord and went to the disciples to announce what she saw and what Jesus said to her. Mary has had a remarkable role in "the hour" of Jesus: she was near the cross at his death (19:25), she was the first to discover the empty tomb (20:1), and she was the first to see and talk with the resurrected Jesus (vv. 14 – 17). Here she is given the commission to make this important announcement to the disciples. Several interpreters have suggested that Mary's unique position and role has her serving as "an apostle to the apostles."[36] For this reason it is argued that Mary's testimony "deserves to be called apostolic."[37] If anything, however, Mary should be viewed no differently than John the Baptist, both of whom were sent by God and therefore function as part of his self-witness (see comments on 3:29 – 30, 32). Just as the Baptist preceded the start of Jesus's public ministry and heralded his arrival in the flesh (cf. 1:6 – 8), so also Mary preceded the conclusion of Jesus's public ministry and heralded his arrival in and by the Spirit (cf. 14:16).

Theology in Application

The tomb is empty, but where is the Lord? In this pericope the reader follows Mary Magdalene's journey from a place of grief to the "throne of grace" as she encounters Jesus. Standing between the angelic tomb-throne and the resurrected Lord, Mary becomes a witness to the new reality of God's presence and the necessity of the ascension. In this pericope the narrative guides the readers to understand their new relationship to God through Christ (and in the Spirit) and exhorts them to embrace the Father in the fullness of his presence.

Grief versus Grace

This pericope offers a beautiful contrast between Mary's grief outside the tomb and the grace declared inside it. The narrative's threefold depiction of her "weeping" (vv. 11, 13, 15) and the same twice-asked question of Mary by both the angels and

---

35. The Gospel's account is in conformity with the account of the ascension given elsewhere in the NT (Luke 24:51; Acts 1:9 – 11). Cf. Reimund Bieringer, " 'I am ascending to my Father and your Father, to my God and your God' (John 20:17): Resurrection and Ascension in the Gospel of John," in Koester, *The Resurrection of Jesus in the Gospel of John*, 209 – 35.

36. Spencer, "Women," 1013. Cf. Schneiders, "John 20:11 – 18," 168: "Mary Magdalene, contrary to what generations of condescending male commentators would have us believe, is by all accounts an official apostolic witness of the resurrection."

37. Lincoln, *John*, 495.

Jesus make clear that Mary's grief in the context of the "throne of grace" is an issue of misunderstanding. To Mary, the empty tomb was cause for grief; the reader, however, was guided to see that it was the exact opposite. The tomb is a symbolic declaration of the victory of God over the power of sin and death. The Gospel shows how Jesus overturns grief with grace, established and declared specifically by his death and resurrection.

The Ark of the New Covenant

The narrative offers a powerful counter to Mary's grief at the tomb with the symbolic "impression" of the ark of the covenant from the OT (Exod 25:18 – 19) created by the specific placement of the angels at the head and feet of the place where the body of Jesus had been lying. Without even speaking, the angels' carefully described positions declare that Jesus is the fulfillment and replacement of Judaism. Even more, their presence declares that Jesus is the full manifestation of the saving power and presence of the Lord. The irony of ironies is that this tomb has become the new holy of holies, for with this symbolism Jesus is depicted as both the *atoning sacrifice* of God and the one who "*sits enthroned* between the cherubim" (Ps 99:1; emphasis added). Rather than being empty, the tomb serves as the ark of the *new covenant*, "the throne of grace." Golden angels were not capable of adorning this holy of holies; this place of atonement required angels not made by human hands (cf. Acts 17:24 – 25). The words of the prologue regarding Christ have now been made even more concrete: Jesus is "grace in place of grace" (1:16).

The Ascension

The Gospel of John makes a significant contribution to the church's understanding of the ascension. It was Irenaeus who suggested that the ascension marks the completion of the divine act of creating humanity in the image of God. Through his own U-shaped history (descent from above and incarnation, baptism, death, resurrection, and ascension), Jesus recapitulates the entire experience of fallen humanity and restores the gift of the Spirit (Irenaeus, *Haer*. 3.24.1).[38] The Heidelberg Catechism (Question 49) suggests three benefits that we receive from the ascension that are worthy to note. First, it declares that the resurrected Lord is also our advocate in heaven in the presence of the Father. Second, it declares that we have our own flesh (i.e., proof of a physical, bodily resurrection) in heaven as a sure pledge that Christ our head will also take us, his members, up to himself. Third, it declares that he sends his Spirit to us on earth as a corresponding pledge, a promise and guarantee of our inheritance. This pericope and the pericope to follow (20:19 – 23) fully support this

---

38. Cf. Douglas Farrow, "Ascension," *Dictionary for Theological Interpretation of the Bible*, 65 – 68.

list of benefits, declaring the impending finality of Christ's work and preparing for the arrival of the Spirit.

The Gardener in his Garden

The pericope develops further the Gospel's symbolic depiction of this garden as "the garden," most notably this time with the presence of "the gardener" (see v. 15) in the garden. The garden is the place where the world betrayed God, making a garden a fitting place for his final betrayal and also a fitting place for it to be overturned. The narrator reveals Mary's mistaken assumption primarily to reveal what *God* — not Mary — had in mind. "The cross to be in Paradise, as the tree of life from which the first man had been raised from the dust as the primordial King, now the second Man, also raised from the dust in resurrection, took up his rightful place in the garden … tilling the soil and caring for Eden from which the first Man had been banished."[39] For Jesus had fulfilled in his person the demands of God and therefore had become the second Adam, the Gardner assigned by God (see Gen 2:15), here standing in his "garden" on the first day of the "week" (cf. 20:1). In the second Garden, the Gardener himself came to tend his (new) creation (Gen 2:15; Rev 21 – 22).

The Woman in the Garden

It is common for interpreters to highlight the significance of Mary, a woman, serving as the first witness of the resurrected Lord and thereafter the first messenger of the fact of the resurrection (v. 18). Without limiting the significance of the Gospel's intention to highlight the role of women in the earliest moments of Christianity, it is also important to note another likely comparison between the characters in the first and second gardens. In the first garden a woman was asked a question that would soon reveal that the questioner intended to become the source of grief (Gen 3:1), but in the second garden a woman is asked a question that would soon reveal that the questioner had already become the source of grace. The serpent promised that the first woman would be *like* God, whereas Jesus announces that the second woman would be *with* God. The difference is stark, for the actions in the second garden return the creation to the intended state of the first garden.[40] The concern of early Christianity (cf. Matt 28:1 – 8; Mark 16:9 – 11; Luke 24:1 – 10) to connect the *garden of Easter* with a woman may have less to do with gender in the first century and more to do with gender in the first garden, the *garden of Eden*. In this way Jesus fulfills and repairs the fall of his creation in every way. Even the serpent has been

---

39. Wyatt, "Supposing Him to Be the Gardener," 38. Cf. Schaper, "The Messiah in the Garden," 25.

40. The first woman tells the serpent that God had commanded that the tree not be touched (Gen 3:3), paralleling the command not to touch in v. 17.

silenced and his grief-inducing question has been replaced with a grace-filled response of the true Gardener!

Children of the Father

The Gospel began with the promise that God the Son would unite the children of God to God the Father in a manner that would be entirely "from God" (1:12 – 13). In this pericope, that promise is fulfilled. For the first time the fatherhood of God is applied to the disciples and kinship language is required between the disciples. Just as the disciples now relate to God more fully in the Spirit, so they also relate now more fully to one another as "brothers and sisters" in the church. This pericope explains that the true Judge and King (5:22 – 29) has declared the church to be "adopted children by grace," the newly created family of God.[41]

41. Aquinas, *John*, 3:267.

John 20:19 – 23

Literary Context

This pericope is the third of four sections of the final section of the narrative proper, which brings climactic resolution to the Gospel story. The previous pericopae explained the fact of the empty tomb (20:1 – 10) and the reality of Jesus's resurrection and impending ascension and the nature of his relationship to his disciples (20:11 – 18). The Gospel has taken care to establish that the saving power and presence of God has been made manifest through the person and work of Jesus. In this pericope the reader is guided to see how this power and presence is also bestowed upon the disciples — the church — and is exhorted to participate in the mission of God.

IX. The Resurrection (20:1 – 31)
    A. The Empty Tomb (20:1 – 10)
    B. The Appearance to Mary Magdalene (20:11 – 18)
➡   **C. The Appearance to the Disciples (20:19 – 23)**
    D. The Appearance to Thomas and the Purpose of the Gospel (20:24 – 31)

Main Idea

On the first Lord's Day, Jesus transformed the founding church by replacing their fear with his forgiveness, the true peace of God, and commanded them to participate in the continuation of the work of God by obediently responding to the mission of God in the Spirit of God.

Translation

John 20:19–23

19a	Introduction & Setting	When it was evening on that day,
b	Time	the first day of the week, and
c	Setting	with the doors closed
d	Location	where the disciples were
e	Basis	for fear of the Jews,
f	Sequence of Action #1	**Jesus came**
g	Sequence of Action #2	and **stood in their midst**
h	Sequence of Action #3	and **said to them,**
i	Declaration	*"Peace to you."*
20a		And
b		after he said this,
c	Progression of Action	**he showed his hands and**
d		**side to them.**
e	Reaction	Then **the disciples rejoiced**
f	Circumstance	when they saw the Lord.
21a		Then **he said to them again,**
b	Redeclaration of 19i	*"Peace be with you.*
c	Comparison	*Just as the Father has sent me,*
d	Assertion	*I also send you."*
22a		And
b		after he said this
c	Progression of Action	**he blew**
d		and **said to them,**
e	Command	*"Receive the Holy Spirit.*
23a	Condition	*If you forgive the sins of anyone,*
b	Inference	*they have been forgiven them.*
c	Condition	*If you retain theirs,*
d	Inference	*they have been retained."*

Structure and Literary Form

The structure of this pericope is different than a basic story form (see Introduction). In this first postresurrection appearance of Jesus to his disciples, the pericope is facilitated by means of four statements by the Lord that climactically summarize the theology of the Gospel and ultimately the new covenant and the mission of the church. The first statement, set in the context of Jesus's supernatural appearance to the disciples, involves a symbol-laden greeting that serves to declare the peace of God (vv. 19 – 20). The second statement is the announcement by Jesus that the mission of God now includes the sending of the disciples (v. 21). The third statement of Jesus is the bestowal of the Spirit of God (v. 22). Finally, in the fourth statement Jesus declares that the disciples share in the ministerial authority of God (v. 23). This pericope and the statements of Jesus derive their meaning not merely from this section of the Gospel (ch. 20), but from the entire Gospel narrative.

Exegetical Outline

➡ **C. The Appearance to the Disciples (20:19 – 23)**
> 1. The Peace of God (vv. 19 – 20)
> 2. The Mission of God (v. 21)
> 3. The Spirit of God (v. 22)
> 4. The Ministerial Authority of God (v. 23)

Explanation of the Text

This short five-verse pericope abounds with the theological force of the entire Gospel. Yet its theological freight is often easily eclipsed by the notorious interpretive crux in Johannine scholarship regarding Jesus's breathing/blowing and giving the Spirit to his disciples in v. 22.

IN-DEPTH: The Johannine Pentecost

The Gospel's portrayal of the Spirit-Paraclete comes to a climactic conclusion in v. 22, where the narrator describes how Jesus "blew" and said to his disciples, "Receive the Holy Spirit." The narrative appears to be describing a giving of the Spirit, often called a "Johannine Pentecost" that in some manner rivals the giving of the Spirit and Pentecost described in Luke-Acts, specifically Acts 2. Interpreters wrestle with two primary aspects of this verse: What did the "breathing/blowing" of Jesus actually do to or for the disciples, and how does this giving of the Spirit relate to the coming of the Spirit in Acts 2? The variety of responses to these questions can be combined into seven major interpretations:[1] (1) the symbolic interpretation, a symbolic (future) promise of the gift of the Spirit at Pentecost; (2) the apostolic ministry interpretation, a gift for empowerment,

---

1. The following is adapted from Cornelis Bennema, "The Giving of the Spirit in John's Gospel — A New Proposal?" *EvQ* 74 (2002): 195 – 213. See also idem, "The Giving of the Spirit in John 19 – 20: Another Round," in *The Spirit and Christ in the New Testament and Christian Theology: Essays in Honor of Max Turner*, ed. I. Howard Marshall, Volker Rabens, and Cornelis Bennema (Grand Rapids, Eerdmans, 2012), 86 – 104.

equipping, or qualification for apostolic ministry exclusively for the apostles; (3) the proclamation interpretation, a gift of the power of proclamation and teaching that leads to eternal life; (4) the "Johannine Pentecost" interpretation, the definitive gift of the Spirit that is the Gospel's version of Acts 2; (5) the embryonic Paraclete interpretation, a partial (or inaugurated) gift of the Spirit who will become the Paraclete later; (6) the salvation interpretation, an act that signifies the moment when the disciples become regenerated and are promised the coming Paraclete; and (7) the progressive glorification interpretation, the gift of the Spirit is a three-stage process related to Jesus's glorification — symbolically at the cross 19:30, the Spirit of salvation in 20:22, and the Paraclete at Pentecost in Acts 2.

While each of these proposals interprets significant aspects or emphases of this verse, there are some further interpretive issues that also need to be addressed. First, because of the natural comparison between this pericope and Acts 2, interpreters are too easily drawn into a historical-apologetic approach to this verse rather than a textual-interpretive approach. The goal of interpretation, however, is not primarily to reconstruct an event but to read a text (on method, see Introduction), and this text in particular is concerned with much more than the metaphysical or material realities, especially when the text intends to image a reality that extends beyond that which can be perceived with the senses.

Second, the historical comparisons between the giving of the Spirit in John and Acts are often done in a manner that pits Scripture against itself. In some manner, each of the interpretive options above succumbs to this mistake. While it is common for interpreters to address this issue by treating the two texts and their authors as working independently of one another, such an approach fails to treat adequately both John and Acts as unitary Scripture. A Christian doctrine of Scripture demands that the two texts be read speaking ultimately to the same subject matter, the nature and coming of the Holy Spirit (see Inroduction).

Third, and related to the previous point, one of the most dangerous mistakes made in the interpretation of this pericope is to treat the Holy Spirit as a commodity, merely something to be used. We explained earlier that the meaning of "God" is rooted not in "what God is," but in "who God is" (see comments on 1:1). Since "Holy Spirit" (πνεῦμα ἅγιον) is a "God" word, it "ought to lead to the question how then one understands the identity of Jesus and, in turn, how one understands the very identity and character of God."[2] It is here where most (all?) of the interpretations above fall short, for by interpreting the Spirit by means of

2. Thompson, *God of the Gospel of John*, 187.

the disciples' reaction or behavior or even apostolic calling, the Spirit is defined relationally to those *particular* men and not to the *particularity* of God.[3] If that results in a more undefined and less historically explainable interpretation of the account, then so be it! Because "Spirit" is "a distinct way of envisioning God's activity and presence in the world, the functions that are exercised necessarily imply the very activity and presence of God"—definable only in the relational unity of the Trinitarian God.[4]

There can be no doubt that the actions and words of Jesus in v. 22 are difficult to interpret, and the interpretive issues we raised above are not intended to alleviate this interpretive crux. While we will explain the details of the verse more fully below, two further and preparatory comments are necessary. First, sensitivity to the textual (and not just historical) context reveals that this entire pericope, not just v. 22, functions as a climactic summary of the Gospel's theology and purpose. The depictions and statements, therefore, should be expected to employ and make sense of the developing theology of the Gospel.

Second, the theological freight placed upon this verse at the end of the Gospel demands that the interpretation of its meaning must include not only a historical depiction of "breath/blow," "receive," and "Spirit" but also a theological depiction.[5] That is, as much as this statement speaks about what is seen, it simultaneously speaks about "the unseen" (see comments before 1:1) and witnesses to its fuller subject matter. If the first Paraclete (the Son) has been defined by both the historical and cosmological strands of the Gospel's plot, certainly the Second Paraclete (the Spirit) must also be defined in that way. As the Gospel has already explained, God had always intended a multifaceted sending of himself, the first *and* second Paraclete(s), inaugurated and established by the work of the Son and appropriated and maintained by the work of the Spirit (see comments on 14:16). And it is in this pericope that the full presence of God with his people comes to fruition, the presence of the "God" whose identity must be defined as from the Father, through the Son, and in and by the Holy Spirit.

Following the declaration of the empty tomb in the first pericope in chapter 20 (20:1 – 10), the next three pericopae involving the appearances of Jesus each play a different role. While this pericope can be said to depict the first meeting of the church, with Jesus founding and declaring its identity in the person and (continuing) work of God, the appearances of Jesus to individuals surrounding this pericope each depict a different aspect of relating to Jesus. The appearance to Mary (20:11 – 18)

---

3. Cf. Reginald H. Fuller, "John 20:19 – 23," *Int* 32 (1978): 180 – 84 (183).
4. Ibid.

5. Cf. Augustine, *Teaching Christianity*, 2.14.135: "Signs, for their part, can be either proper or metaphorical."

functions for the Gospel as an explanation of how Jesus is to be related to *physically*, and the appearance to Thomas (20:24–31) functions for the Gospel as an explanation of how Jesus is to be related to *textually*, especially by concluding with the Gospel's purpose statement (20:30–31).[6] This pericope, however, speaks more directly to the church and its relation to the fullness of God's person and work, guiding the reader to see how the church is now participating in the mission of God through Christ and in and by the Spirit.

20:19 When it was evening on that day, the first day of the week, and with the doors closed where the disciples were for fear of the Jews, Jesus came and stood in their midst and said to them, "Peace to you" (Οὔσης οὖν ὀψίας τῇ ἡμέρᾳ ἐκείνῃ τῇ μιᾷ σαββάτων, καὶ τῶν θυρῶν κεκλεισμένων ὅπου ἦσαν οἱ μαθηταὶ διὰ τὸν φόβον τῶν Ἰουδαίων, ἦλθεν ὁ Ἰησοῦς καὶ ἔστη εἰς τὸ μέσον καὶ λέγει αὐτοῖς, Εἰρήνη ὑμῖν). The pericope begins with a temporal designation that explains that the events to follow are taking place on the same day as the previous events in chapter 20, though now in the evening. As we discussed before, the phrase "the first day of the week" (τῇ μιᾷ σαββάτων) makes this more than a chronological marker, for it simultaneously echoes again the Gospel's creation motif (see comments on 20:1). It is no wonder that the earliest Christians were convinced that this day, Sunday, the first day of the week, was the most appropriate day for the gathering of the church. Not only was it the day of the resurrected Lord, the day creation itself was reclaimed by God, but according to this pericope it was also the day the "church" met for the first time.[7] While such a designation is a theological deduction, it is interesting that the gathered disciples also qualified as a congregational quorum or minyan of ten men (no Judas or Thomas) according to Jewish regulations (cf. Num 14:27; Ps 82).

This first meeting of the church started as anything but glorious, for these soon-to-be-appointed apostles of the resurrected Lord were not gathered for worship on this first Lord's Day but were hiding from the Jewish authorities behind "closed" (κεκλεισμένων) doors, a verb which can also be translated "locked," which is certainly implied in this context.[8] No specific reason is given; the reader of the Gospel can only assume that the political power the Jews wielded during the trial of Jesus and the link between the now-crucified Jesus and his disciples made them hide in fear. The irony is stark: on the greatest day in the history of the world, a day when God defeated death itself and inaugurated the restoration of his creation, his closest followers were not celebrating but cowering in fear.

Yet the narrator may have mentioned the locked doors more to explain the appearance of Jesus than the presence of the disciples, for even with the doors closed the narrator explains that "Jesus came and stood in their midst" (ἦλθεν ὁ Ἰησοῦς καὶ ἔστη εἰς τὸ μέσον). This cryptic description of Jesus's entrance is often used to interpret the nature of Jesus's resurrected body (see vv. 20, 26; cf. 1 Cor 15:44). While a miraculous entrance might be implied, the text only refers explicitly to his appearance among them, not to the mode of his entrance.[9] In light of the rest of the Gospel, this appearance serves as a final and climactic "coming" of the Lord to his people (see 1:9); Jesus had said, "I am coming to you" (14:18; cf. 14:28), and this coming is guaranteed.

---

6. Sandra Schneiders, "The Raising of the New Temple: John 20.19–23 and Johannine Ecclesiology," *NTS* 52 (2006): 337–55 (339–41).

7. Cf. John P. Meier, "John 20:19–23," *Mid-Stream* 35 (1996): 395–98 (395).

8. BDAG 546–47.

9. Cf. Morris, *John*, 745; Augustine, *John*, 121.4.438.

What Jesus said to the disciples is even more important to the narrative than his miraculous entrance: "Peace to you" (Εἰρήνη ὑμῖν). This traditional Jewish salutation typically meant nothing more than "peace be with you" or "may all be well with you."[10] But in light of the OT's use of the term (*shalom*) and its importance in the NT and early Christianity, certainly more is intended, especially in this context.[11] "All that the prophets had poured into shalom as the epitome of the blessings of the kingdom of God had essentially been realized in the redemptive deeds of the incarnate Son of God."[12] On the evening of Easter, Christ's use of the term "peace" is less a greeting and more a pronouncement of blessing, a declaration that the peace of God — the eschatological peace promised in the OT — has now been made accessible through Jesus Christ. This symbol-laden greeting is the equivalent of "it is completed" (19:30), though now in its postresurrection translation.[13] It is no surprise that every epistolary greeting of Paul in the NT includes "peace" along with "grace," for "the throne of grace" (20:12) is the place of peace. Jesus had spoken of this peace in the farewell discourse (14:18, 27; 16:33), and he will speak this same pronouncement greeting two further times to the disciples (v. 21; 20:24).

20:20 And after he said this, he showed his hands and side to them. Then the disciples rejoiced when the saw the Lord (καὶ τοῦτο εἰπὼν ἔδειξεν τὰς χεῖρας καὶ τὴν πλευρὰν αὐτοῖς. ἐχάρησαν οὖν οἱ μαθηταὶ ἰδόντες τὸν κύριον). The potency of Jesus's statement of greeting to his disciples is based not only on the words he spoke but also on his actions: "He showed his hands and side to them" (ἔδειξεν

τὰς χεῖρας καὶ τὴν πλευρὰν αὐτοῖς). Just as Jesus's greeting in this context was symbol laden, so is his display of wounds from the cross.[14] But "there must be more here than a reductionist reading of the narrative logic might demand."[15] The display of wounds is not simply an act of identification, a proof to the disciples that the man standing in their midst is Jesus. Rather, they explain the source of his peace. The peace of God was entirely dependent on these specific wounds — the *scars* from the crucifixion declare *shalom* for the world. Isaiah was speaking about this very encounter when he announced that "the punishment that *brought us peace* was on him, and *by his wounds* we are healed" (Isa 53:5; emphasis added).

The narrative continues by saying that "then the disciples rejoiced when they saw the Lord" (ἐχάρησαν οὖν οἱ μαθηταὶ ἰδόντες τὸν κύριον). In light of the context as well as the use of the title "the Lord," we must assume that the response of the disciples is not merely in regard to his *presence* but also his *person*; he is the resurrected "Lord." His scar-filled presence declares the defeat of both sin and death, and as the narrative stated earlier the disciples were now beginning to understand the fullness of his person and work (see comments on 12:16). Jesus had promised to turn their "grief" (like the "weeping" of Mary Magdalene; see 20:11, 13, 15) into "rejoicing" (16:20–24; cf. 15:11; 17:13). And that transformation occurred in the presence of his transformed person on the evening of the first Lord's Day. The narrative's details craft for the reader an image of heavenly worship, with believers standing around Jesus and worshipping the slain Lamb of God (Rev 5:11–12).

---

10. Barrett, *John*, 568.

11. Gerhard von Rad, "εἰρήνη," *TDNT* 2:402.

12. Beasley-Murray, *John*, 378.

13. Johannes Beutler, "Resurrection and Forgiveness of Sin. John 20:23 against Its Traditional Background," in Koester, *The*

Resurrection of Jesus in the Gospel of John, 237–51.

14. For a description of the nature of his wounds caused by Roman crucifixion, see comments on 19:18.

15. Stephen R. Holmes, "Trinitarian Missiology: Towards a Theology of God as Missionary," *IJST* 8 (2006): 72–90 (75).

20:21 Then he said to them again, "Peace be with you. Just as the Father has sent me, I also send you" (εἶπεν οὖν αὐτοῖς πάλιν, Εἰρήνη ὑμῖν· καθὼς ἀπέσταλκέν με ὁ πατήρ, κἀγὼ πέμπω ὑμᾶς). The repetition of the symbol-laden peace greeting further clarifies that this is no simple greeting. Acting as a preface to the statement that follows, it suggests here that peace is to accompany the disciples in their forthcoming mission.[16] Moreover, "just as" the mission of the Son of God involved peace, so also will the mission of the children of God involve peace, the proclamation of the eschatological *shalom* of the OT and that Christ's victory over the powers of evil has been accomplished.[17]

Jesus announces to the disciples what earlier he had only prayed to the Father (cf. 17:21): "Just as the Father has sent me, I also send you" (καθὼς ἀπέσταλκέν με ὁ πατήρ, κἀγὼ πέμπω ὑμᾶς). With this statement Jesus declares that the disciples — and the church as a whole — are called to participate in the mission of God in a manner similar to the Son. As we mentioned earlier, there is an important difference in senders (the Father sends the Son; the Son sends the disciples), which means the roles of the sent ones are also different (see comments on 17:18). Jesus's specific choice of words also reveals a distinction, for he uses two different synonyms for "sent/send" (ἀπέσταλκέν/πέμπω). While the Fourth Gospel frequently uses related or overlapping words synonymously across the narrative (e.g., 13:10; 21:15 – 17), when they are used in close proximity (especially in the same verse) there is usually a carefully nuanced distinction or comparison intended between them. In this case the distinction is provided by the senders. The Son was participating in the work of the Father, and was doing what *only* the Son can do. In a similar way, then, the disciples are participating in what is ultimately the work of the Son, a work made possible through the Son alone (see comments on 17:19). Although the church is sent "just as" (καθὼς) the Son was sent, the mission of the church is defined by the Son who sent them, from whom the nature and direction of its mission are derived.

The derivation of the mission of the church needs to be more carefully defined. It is common for interpreters to connect the missions of the Son and the church to "structural similarities" and historically based parallels[18] or to use Jesus's mission as a "model."[19] But this approach is not complex enough to grasp both the continuity and discontinuity between the missions of the Son and the church. More precise theological categories are needed for grasping the unique yet participatory nature of the mission of God in and through the church. While theologians may simply refer to the account of the divine economy and the indivisibility of the divine works as a reflection of the *nature of God's mission*, some theologians suggest even further that this account is also reflective of *the very nature of God*. That is, the works of God have their origin in the very nature of God, the pattern of relationship between the Father, Son, and Spirit.[20] While the Father's sending of the Son might merely be an expression of the economic Trinity (functional), it can also be grounded in the immanent Trinity (ontological), "reflecting on the eternal inner-triune relationships of love which Father, Son, and Spirit share, and in which the church is called to participate."[21]

---

16. Raymond E. Brown, "The Resurrection in John 20 — A Series of Diverse Reactions," *Wor* 64 (1990): 194 – 206 (202).

17. Cf. Fuller, "John 20:19 – 23," 183.

18. See Eckhard J. Schnabel, "'As the Father Has Sent Me, So I Send You' (John 20:21): The Mission of Jesus and the Mission of the Church," *Missionalia* 33 (2005): 263 – 86 (263).

19. See Craig S. Keener, "Sent Like Jesus: Johannine Missiology (John 20:21 – 22)," *AJPS* 12 (2009): 21 – 45 (45).

20. Cf. Augustine, *The Trinity*, trans. Edmund Hill (New York: New City Press, 1991), 2.9.103.

21. Holmes, "Trinitarian Missiology," 82.

While both economic and immanent readings are possible in this verse, it is worth reflecting on the implications to be drawn from an understanding of the immanent Trinity. Several can be described. First, the apostolic mission given to the church is in direct relation to the eternal life of God. The sending of the Son and the Spirit — the gospel story — is neither foreign to God nor an afterthought (an act intending to repair unforeseen damage). Rather, "God's own life is gospel shaped ... what happens on Calvary is a repetition of the pattern of God's eternal life."[22]

Second, the church does not merely imitate the sending of the Son but participates directly in the very same mission of God. "The reason why mission is of the very being of the church is that mission is not just *imitating* the sending forth of Jesus. It is a *participation* in the Father's own sending of the Son ... mission is rooted in the very being of the triune God."[23] The sacrifice of Christ then was always intended to occur as such and is part of God's self-determination of his own life — "it is part of who God is, not just what God has done."[24]

Third, the logical conclusion is that the church's participation in the mission of God is a response to the nature of God. Just as God is love or is holy, so also is he *missionary*. And the church's worship of God must match the full nature of God. "Just as the church is called to love in ways that mirror the eternal relationships of love that Father, Son, and Spirit have shared from all eternity, so the missionary nature of the church derives ultimately from the missionary nature of God's own life."[25] Ultimately, then, if God is to be properly described as "missionary," then appropriate Christian worship of God can only be done by a missionary church.

And since God is missionary in his eternal identity, the mission of God in which the church now participates can never come to an end.

It is important that the reader see the developing and logical progression of this pericope. The apostolic mission[26] declared by Jesus here is rightly situated between the peace-creating crucifixion wounds of Jesus (v. 20) and the Spirit-received command of Jesus (v. 22). And in light of this verse, then, the giving of the Spirit that follows is not merely empowerment for the mission of God but a divine manifestation for participation in it.[27] That is, the church participates in the missionary life of God by *remaining* in Christ (15:4) and *receiving* the Spirit (v. 22).

20:22 And after he said this he blew and said to them, "Receive the Holy Spirit" (καὶ τοῦτο εἰπὼν ἐνεφύσησεν καὶ λέγει αὐτοῖς, Λάβετε πνεῦμα ἅγιον). In light of the previous verse, the transition from the mission of God to the Spirit of God is both logical and warranted. Even more, it is in light of this larger context that the giving of the Spirit is to be understood. This verse is not doing something distinct from the mission just announced. The Spirit, as God, is the key component of this mission, for this mission is ultimately the mission *of God*, who is the ground and goal of Christian mission. The narrative makes the connection clear by including the temporal connection "and after he said this" (καὶ τοῦτο εἰπὼν). The words of Jesus function as commentary on the forthcoming action of Jesus.

The narrator explains the action of Jesus with one word: "He blew" (ἐνεφύσησεν). This term only occurs here in the NT, though it occurs ten times in the LXX. While nearly every translation expresses

22. Ibid., 83.
23. Paul Fiddes, "Mission and Liberty: A Baptist Connection," in *Tracks and Traces: Baptist Identity in Church and Theology* (Carlisle: Paternoster, 2003): 249 – 73 (251).
24. Holmes, "Trinitarian Missiology," 85.
25. Ibid., 86.
26. Cf. Hoskyns, *Fourth Gospel*, 544; Calvin, *John 11 – 21*, 203.
27. Cf. Thomas R. Hatina, "John 20,22 in Its Eschatological Context: Promise of Fulfillment?" *Bib* 74 (1993): 196 – 219 (218).

the verb as "breathed," there are other, more common NT words that are normally used for breathing: "breathe" or "breathe out" (ἐκπνέω) in Mark 15:37, 39 and Luke 23:46; "breathe" or even "blow (softly)" (πνέω) in Matthew 7:25, 27, Luke 12:55, Acts 27:40, Revelation 7:1, and twice in the Gospel at 3:8 and 6:18. In John 3:8 (see comments on 3:8) it is clearly being used playfully with its cognate noun "wind/breath/spirit" (πνεῦμα). Why did the author not use the cognate form of Spirit here, especially when involving the giving of the Spirit? The cognate verb for Spirit is more commonly used for "breathing" or "soft blowing" (πνέω), but context is needed to determine its sense.[28] The verb in this pericope likewise needs further context. When compared to other uses in the LXX, its sense is much stronger than "breathe," for it is used in Job 4:21 of a hot wind and in Sirach 43:4 of igniting coals of a blazing furnace.[29] Thus, this particular verb is more commonly used to describe a stronger or more powerful breathing, best translated as a kind of "blowing."[30] Derrett is correct when he suggests that "the desire to read 'breathed' may derive from an attempt to explain this strange behavior."[31]

Striking in its absence is the lack of a direct object. While the disciples are clearly the implicit recipients of Jesus's blowing, the lack of a direct object distances the act from this specific situation and emphasizes the symbolic nature of the gesture. In light of the fact that the verb "he blew" (ἐνεφύσησεν) is more common in the OT (LXX) than the NT and in light of the Genesis-laden context of the Gospel of John and the Genesis lens applied to its interpretive telling of the person and work of Jesus (see comments on 18:1), it is difficult not to see a connection to Genesis 2:7, where the exact same verb is used: "Then the Lord God formed the man from the dust of the ground and *blew* [ἐνεφύσησεν] into his nostrils the breath of life, and the man became a living person." Given this rare use of this verb, the use of it here is clearly intended to echo the first story of human enlivenment. The Gospel guides the reader to see here an act of creation.[32] This connection is strengthened even further by the use of the same verb in Ezekiel 37:9 (LXX), which envisions the breath/wind/Spirit of the Lord recreating the temple and the people of God: "*Blow* into these slain that they may come to life."[33]

At this climactic moment at the end of the Gospel, the narrative signals again the creation theme with which the narrative began. In the context of Genesis 1–2 and Ezekiel 37, the "blowing" of the Spirit by Jesus is the re-creation of the temple of God and the people of God. At this moment this quorum of ten fearful men were being established as a new creation, the church — a "new humanity" (Eph 2:15) and even a "new Israel" or priestly class in light of the connection to Ezekiel 37:9. That is, Jesus is establishing by the Spirit his body as a ministering agent in the world, and by the same Spirit Jesus is empowering this new humanity to do what Adam and others had failed to do: to be God's representatives and ministers in the world.[34] This final Genesis allusion creates a bookend for the theme of creation that functions as a frame for the entire story of Jesus told by the Gospel. "The climax of the Fourth Gospel presents Jesus as ['blowing'] upon the apostles after the pattern of the creating God who [blew] upon the Edenic couple; now

28. BDAG 837–38.

29. Cf. LSJ 551.

30. E. Stauffer, "ἐμφυσάω," *TDNT* 2:536–37.

31. J. Duncan M. Derrett, "Why Did Jesus Blow on the Disciples? (John 20,22)," *BeO* 40 (1998): 235–46 (236).

32. Brown, "Creation's Renewal in the Gospel of John," 282.

Cf. du Rand, "Creation Motif in the Fourth Gospel."

33. Jon D. Levenson, "The Temple and the World," *JR* 64 (1984): 275–98 (286–87).

34. Cf. G. K. Beale, *A New Testament Biblical Theology: The Unfolding of the Old Testament in the New* (Grand Rapids: Baker, 2011), 569–72.

they receive the Spirit, and not simply the gift of life."[35] And this creation motif extends to the end of chapter 20, when the narrator explains the purpose of the Gospel that the reader may have "life" re-created in Jesus Christ (20:31).

In light of our discussion above, the meaning of Jesus's command, "receive the Holy Spirit" (Λάβετε πνεῦμα ἅγιον), must be understood with its two-part preface of participation in the mission of God (v. 21) and this symbol-laden act of "blowing." Jesus does not give the Spirit as if some sort of transaction were taking place from one party to another, but invites the disciples to participate in the Spirit — in his Spirit — and therefore also in the Son. Jesus had prayed for the disciples (the church) to experience "in-one-ness" with God (and one another) that was directly connected to the mission of God: "I in them and you in me, so that they may be brought to completion as one, in order that the world may know that you sent me" (17:23). This kind of "in-one-ness" cannot be obtained by a human process but can only be an act "from above," a unity that is divine from start to "completion." It is a unity in and by the Spirit, not by an organization (see comments on 17:23). In this first meeting of the church on the Lord's Day, on the first day of the (new creation) week (see v. 19), Jesus declares in word *and* deed that the church is one with God and therefore is now to work according to his nature and for his purposes in full participation with him.

This new-creation work of God can be defined further in three ways. First, as we discussed above (before v. 19 and on v. 21), this new-creation work is a work involving the fullness of the Trinitarian God. The fact that the Spirit is involved merely signifies that all three persons of the Trinity are now fully involved economically (functionally). Second, the Gospel as a whole "focuses specifically on the Spirit as the agent through whom God imparts life to others."[36] Just as in Jesus "was life" (1:4), the Spirit gives life (3:3, 5). The giving of the Spirit, therefore, is the inauguration of *eternal* life (20:31). Third, although God is still doing the work, with the Spirit the church is now truly able to be participants in the work of God. It is not God's work without God; for this reason the presence of God means that for the first time in redemptive history the church is now fully included in the mission of God. In this remarkable moment, the church becomes both a *recipient* and a *minister* of the renewing work of God. For this two-sided response to the gospel is ultimately one unified work.

But what actually happened? That is the question this verse has seemed to raise the most. As much as we want to interpret a text and not an event (see Introduction), our interpretation in no way denies that Jesus said these words and performed this gesture. While the narrative demands we be only minimally reconstructive, several aspects of what happened can be explained before we give a more definitive answer.

First, as much as there is a temptation to determine if the Spirit was given here or in Acts, a judgment regarding the economic Trinity (the what), the issue is at least partially resolved by balancing it with an understanding of the immanent Trinity (the who). Since the Spirit can never be defined or located in isolation from the Son, depicted as a commodity or something for use, then the manner in which we speak of the Spirit cannot be isolated from the Son. In this instance, then, the doctrine of the Trinity helps our interpretation to maintain the unity of the persons of God, so that

35. Edith M. Humphrey, "New Creation," *Dictionary for Theological Interpretation of the Bible*, 536 – 37 (536).

36. Marianne Meye Thompson, "The Breath of Life: John 20:22 – 23 Once More," in *The Holy Spirit and Christian Origins:* *Essays in Honor of James D. G. Dunn*, ed. Graham N. Stanton, Bruce W. Longenecker, and Stephen C. Barton (Grand Rapids: Eerdmans, 2004), 69 – 78 (77).

the particular manifestations of God are not self-destructive to the identity of God. Since the Gospel here describes the Spirit and his "coming" in such personal/relational categories, no chronological designations can be precise, at least not without underemphasizing an aspect of God's identity.[37] So, did disciples receive the Spirit at this moment? Yes. But is this John's version (replacement) of the Pentecost in Acts? No. Relying again on theological criteria, it would be wrong to press for a chronological foundation as a starting point. When has the Spirit *not* been at work and present? This is not to deny a newness of the Spirit here but to suggest that the Spirit is hardly new to the biblical narrative (including the OT). If anything, the giving of the Spirit serves to mark a different *kind* of chronology.[38] There is no need to interpret the disciples' actions to see if it worked or to account for the absence of Thomas,[39] for the Spirit's work is not limited by its newly participating coworkers. The Spirit has been actively working independently long before the church (see comments on 15:26), even before the creation of the world (Gen 1:2).

Second, the Gospel's account of the giving of the Spirit should be interpreted as relating thematically to "the hour," the technical term established by the Gospel that is intimately and directly connected to the death of Jesus. Yet it also connects to Jesus in a much broader sense, not only at the point of the cross but also in his going to the Father and his glorification. That is, the death of Jesus is only the beginning of "the hour." The "hour" never came to its conclusion during the life of Jesus, for its true completion is rooted in the life of Jesus beyond this world — the life of Jesus rooted in the cosmological plot of the Gospel's narrative depiction (see comments on 2:4). Just as "the hour" is not a literal sixty minutes, so also is the giving of the Spirit a complex chronology.[40] And just as "the hour" was inclusive of several, interrelated events, so also did the Gospel carefully describe the elements necessary for the giving of the Spirit (cf. 7:37 – 39). This is not to say that the giving of the Spirit is a process, as Bennema suggests,[41] for this not only distorts the identity of God but also inappropriately suggests that the cross and the resurrection were performed independently of one another and only vaguely shared ties to "the hour." No, "the hour" is the single, even if multifaceted, concluding work of the Son, involving his death, resurrection, insufflation (of the Spirit), and ascension.[42] And the giving of the Spirit is part of "the hour," which at this moment was occurring both cosmologically and historically, with neither part overtaking (or eclipsing) the other.

For this reason, then, the time-bound giving of the Spirit is best defined by relating the two givings of the Spirit (John 20 and Acts 2) to the two final events of "the hour" to which they are most connected — the resurrection and the ascension. With Westcott this would be a "relation of quickening to endowing"; John depicts the power of the resurrection and Acts depicts the power of the ascension — "the one to victory and the other to sovereignty."[43] But only when interpreted symphonically as Scripture is the reader presented with the full manifestation of the identity of God in the person of the Spirit. Befitting this pericope, which abounds with the theological force of the entire Gospel, this one verse speaks out of the context of the whole biblical story, with the "last Adam" as the "life-giving spirit" (1 Cor 15:45 – 49) at the beginning of the new creation.[44]

---

37. Cf. Beasley-Murray, *John*, 382.

38. Tobias Hägerlund, "The Power of Prophecy: A Septuagintal Echo in John 20:19 – 23," *CBQ* 71 (2009): 84 – 103 (95).

39. Contra Carson, *John*, 653.

40. Cf. Moloney, *John*, 532.

41. Bennema, "The Giving of the Spirit in John 19 – 20," 87.

42. See Newbigin, *The Light Has Come*, 270.

43. Westcott, *John*, 295.

44. Newbigin, *The Light Has Come*, 268.

The modern reader, overly sensitive to the historical particulars of this event, is directed to see more imminent than economic Trinity in this text. Yet a problem remains. For if this text depicts the start of the new creation, the beginning of the in-one-ness of Jesus with his disciples, and the inauguration of the church's participation in mission of God, how can these things be described in tangible, physical terms and categories? Said another way, if the giving of the Spirit in this text is the inauguration of eternal life, how can our commentary explain it in words of everyday life? Just as there are four Gospels and yet only one gospel, so also are there are two givings of the Spirit (John 20 and Acts 2) and yet only one giving. Do not misunderstand: words were spoken and air was blown. But even if we had been standing there, we would have understood more by faith than by sight. And it would have only been after the event and in light of its continuing manifestation (in Acts 2) that the disciples would have understood more clearly not only what God had done (the "hour") but what he had done to them (cf. 2:22). To assume we can explain the imminent Trinity in economic terms is to confuse categories. The full reality of this event cannot be historically reconstructed in a manner that adequately explains or shows what truly happened. If God is comfortable to leave the modern reader less than satisfied with the account of the original creation (Gen 1 – 2), certainly he can do the same with the account of new creation.

20:23 "If you forgive the sins of anyone, they have been forgiven them. If you retain theirs, they have been retained" (ἄν τινων ἀφῆτε τὰς ἁμαρτίας ἀφέωνται αὐτοῖς, ἄν τινων κρατῆτε

κεκράτηνται). The pericope concludes with a final, theologically loaded explanation by Jesus. Jesus addresses here the ministerial authority of the disciples. Like Jesus's other statements in this pericope, this statement is brief but potent and is often compared to two similar statements in Matthew 16:19 and 18:18. Although he addresses the disciples standing around him, the generic nature of the subject matter about which he speaks serves to address the newly created church established upon these apostles (Eph 2:20). For this reason it would be wrong to suggest that the authority given to the (ten) apostles is specific to them, contra Brown, who argues that "the power to absolve and to hold men's sins is explicitly given to (ten of) the Twelve in 20:23."[45] This is Jesus's authority, and it belongs to *his* person and work — and *his* Spirit — and therefore to all *his* people. By this statement, then, Jesus shares his authority (5:22 – 29) with his disciples; or better, Jesus joins his disciples to his already established and already operating authority with which their functional (not ontological) authority finds its source and purpose.

Jesus declares that the disciples have an authoritative role in the forgiveness of sins, which he explains both positively and negatively. In both the positive and negative statements, conditional relative clauses (ἄν plus a subjunctive) are followed by main clauses with verbs in the perfect tense,[46] signaling that something definite has already been accomplished.[47] The function of the perfect tense here has been variously interpreted, especially in reference to time. But it is verbal aspect theory that should explain this use of the perfect tense.[48] And since the verbs are perfect passives, it is clear that the primary actor is God, not the disciples. The sense communicated here then is that a state

---

45. Raymond E. Brown, "The Kerygma of the Gospel according to John: The Johannine View of Jesus in Modern Studies," *Int* 21 (1967): 387 – 400 (391).

46. On the text-critical issues involving this verse, see Metzger, *Textual Commentary*, 219.

47. Michaels, *John*, 1013 – 14.

48. See Porter, *Verbal Aspect*, 471 – 74.

of forgiveness is in effect, without any allusion to the time of its inception or termination.[49] Positively, therefore, a person's sins "stand forgiven" or "are in a state of forgiveness," and negatively their sins are not in such a state.[50] The verb "retain" (κεκράτηνται) must be understood in direct relation to "forgive," so that they are caused to stay in a condition or state of being unforgiven.[51]

The meaning and significance of the state of forgiveness (or lack thereof) must be defined by the preceding context, which includes the "peace" declared by the crucifixion wounds (vv. 19–20), the mission of the disciples (v. 21), and the giving of the Spirit (v. 22). As we have discussed above, this pericope has made clear that the mission of the church is wrongly viewed if it is not understood to be participation in the missionary life of God. For this reason, it is not surprising that the Gospel connects the mission of the church specifically to the forgiveness of sins. The total mission of the church could be summarized by the forgiving and retaining of sins. For "everything the church does is a prolongation in time and space of the victory of the Lamb over the world's sin by making it a victory over our sins."[52] This explains *why* Jesus had

to show his scars from the crucifixion (v. 20), and this explains *how* peace has been established and can now be declared. The *message* of the church is the forgiveness of sins through Christ, and the *mission* of the church is to liberate the world from the power of sin.[53] And this commissioning cannot be narrowed to a single task but is prescriptive of the very life of the church.[54]

This final statement, therefore, is not an add-on or supplement to the already declared mission of the church and the work of the Spirit; it is the final result. It is the ministry of the new covenant.[55] The old covenant itself looked forward to this day, as in Jeremiah 31, where a day was described in which God would be fully known by his people and sin would be removed. The words God began to speak through the prophets among Israel are concluded as his Son speaks here among the "new Israel." For there, *in the midst* of his disciples encircled around him, was the Lamb standing as if he had been slain (Rev 5:6) on the evening of this historical (Easter) and eschatological or cosmological (new-creation) day, summoning his people to his very person (the body of Christ) that they may both experience and extol this slain lamb before the world.

Theology in Application

On the first Lord's Day, Jesus stood in the midst of his fear-filled disciples and replaced that fear with the Holy Spirit, declaring that they are now participants in his mission, the mission of God. The disciples never say a word; in this moment *the Word* needed to do all the talking. In this pericope, the narrative guides the reader to understand what the sacrificial death accomplished for the people of God — peace and forgiveness of sins — and how such an understanding is prescriptive for both the life of the church and its mission in the world.

---

49. Ibid., 473.
50. Cf. Carson, *John*, 655.
51. BDAG 564–65.
52. Meier, "John 20:19–23," 397.

53. Fuller, "John 20:19–23," 184.
54. Holmes, "Trinitarian Missiology," 85.
55. Cf. Schneiders, "The Raising of the New Temple," 338.

His Wounds Brought Us Peace

When Jesus stood in the midst of his disciples and showed them his wounds from the crucifixion, he was declaring with his body what the prophet Isaiah declared with words centuries earlier, that the Suffering Servant "brought us peace … by his wounds" (Isa 53:5). It was Christ's death on the cross that provided for us the eschatological peace (*shalom*) promised in the OT. Christ did not merely give us this peace; he became our peace, the Prince of Peace (Isa 9:6), by removing the distance between us and God by this work. His wounds are the source of our peace, for his wounds gave healing to our own — the forgiveness of sins. Our brokenness was applied to his body, and his life was given for ours.

The Mission of the Missionary God

As much as this pericope can be called John's equivalent to the Great Commission (Matt 28:18 – 20), it is so much more. For according to this pericope, it is not the church but God who is the primary actor. Before the world even knew of its condition or could recognize its Creator, God "sent" himself to the world. God is the first and foundational missionary. The fact that God "sent" is itself a declaration regarding the true nature of God. The actions of God are a reflection of the very life of God — that "God's own life is gospel shaped."[56] Just as God is rightly described as loving or sovereign, so also is he rightly described as missionary.

The church's participation in the mission of God is ultimately participation in the life of God. And the response of the church to the mission of God is a response to the nature of God and, more specifically, to the missionary God. The church's worship of God must match the full nature of God. Just as the holiness of God prescribes to the church the goal and manner of its holiness (see 1 Pet 1:16: "Be holy, because I am holy"), so also the missionary nature of God prescribes to the church the goal and manner of its mission. Ultimately then, if God is to be properly described as missionary, then appropriate Christian worship of God can only be done by a missionary church. The lack of missions in so many of our churches is not to be explained by poor strategies or programs but by poor worship. By "worship" we do not mean music and singing but the alignment of the church to the nature of God and the linking of our ecclesial life to the eternal life of the Trinitarian God. The more we participate in God and according to God, the more missional our churches will become. Quite simply, the more we look like God in the person of Jesus Christ — cruciform and self-sacrificing — the more we will act like him and live "sent."

---

56. Holmes, "Trinitarian Missiology," 83.

The Holy Spirit

Throughout Scripture the Holy Spirit is the climax of God's personal and powerful expression in the world. At the beginning of both creation (Gen 1 – 2) and the new creation (20:22), the Spirit of God was directing the actions of God in the world. According to this pericope it is the Spirit who unites the church to God, allowing them to participate in the very life of God. The Gospel as a whole depicts the Spirit as the agent of life, the one through whom God imparts life to others. Just as in Jesus "was life" (1:4), so the Spirit gives life (3:3, 5). The giving of the Spirit therefore is the inauguration of *eternal* life (20:31).

In this pericope, which abounds with the theological force of the entire Gospel, v. 22 speaks out of the context of the whole biblical story, with the "last Adam" as the "life-giving spirit" at the beginning of the new creation (1 Cor 15:45 – 49). And what is this new creation? It is the church, the descendants of the second Adam! Here Jesus Christ has established his disciples as the founding representatives of the newly created people of God, a new humanity and Israel, who by the Spirit become God's temple, founded on the death of Christ (v. 20) and commissioned to declare the peace of God (vv. 19, 21) for the forgiveness of sins (v. 23). Like the first creation, in this moment Jesus spoke into creation the "holy temple in the Lord ... a dwelling in which God lives by his Spirit" (Eph 2:21 – 22).

Unfortunately, it is common for the Holy Spirit to be misapplied in our churches today. To some the Spirit has been inappropriately relegated to a commodity, like an electrical outlet for spiritual power. To others the Spirit has been inappropriately elevated, placed in a position that moves beyond the biblically defined identity of God. Christ's command, "Receive the Holy Spirit," is a command to receive God in his Trinitarian fullness. The Spirit is not an additional gift from God but a continuation and magnification of the gift of the Son from the Father. In short, the Spirit is the final and climactic statement of God's love for the world (3:16).

The Church of God

In this pericope the second Adam gives the life-giving Spirit at the beginning of the new creation to the church, whose people become descendants of the second Adam. In this way Jesus Christ has established his disciples as the founding representatives of the newly created people of God, a "new humanity" (Eph 2:15) and "new Israel" or new priestly class (Ezek 37:9), who by the Spirit become God's temple, founded on the death of Christ (v. 20) and commissioned to declare the peace of God (vv. 19, 21) for the forgiveness of sins (v. 23). The creation of the church establishes the "holy temple in the Lord ... a dwelling in which God lives by his Spirit" (Eph 2:21 – 22). The church has become "God with us" in a manner that carries on the presence of Christ by the Spirit. According to this pericope, the Trinitarian work of God is now joined to the church in such a way that it functionally represents the work of God in the world. As much as the gospel finds its origin in the life of God, the gospel is tangibly expressed by the ministry of the church. As the apostle Paul explains, "We are therefore Christ's ambassadors, as though God were making his appeal through us" (2 Cor 5:20).

The Authority to Forgive Sins

In the first three centuries, the church often related v. 23 to the confession of sins as admission to baptism. After the Reformation, however, while the Protestants limited the verse to the proclamation of the gospel (i.e., the power of preaching God's forgiveness of sins in Christ and the admission of sinners to baptism), Catholics responded at the Council of Trent by affirming that it should be applied to the power of ordained priests to forgive sins, proving that Jesus Christ himself instituted the sacrament of penance for dealing specifically with postbaptismal sins.[57]

What this text must be explaining is that the Trinitarian work of God is now *joined to the church* in such a way that it functionally represents the work of God in the world *without being confined to the church*. For just as the mission of the Son is different than the mission of the church (see v. 21), there is also a difference between their ministries of forgiveness. For the church is not only a herald of God's forgiveness (a witness to the world) but also a recipient (an example of its work), the "bearer of that effective action" in the flesh.[58] For this reason it is not merely the church's words that declare the gospel but its very existence; the life of the church witnesses to the nature of forgiveness that has been embraced both within the church and extended outside the church. The resurrected presence of the Lord by the Spirit is now with his people in such a way that the church's ministry is ultimately his ministry (see 13:20: "the one who receives the one I send receives me"), with the church serving as the God-established "embassy of salvation and eternal life" in the world.[59]

57. Dennis C. Duling, "Binding and Loosing: Matthew 16:19; Matthew 18:18; John 20:23," *Forum* 3 (1987): 3 – 31 (26). Cf. Beasley-Murray, *John*, 384.

58. Newbigin, *The Light Has Come*, 269.
59. Calvin, *John 11 – 21*, 208.

46

John 20:24 – 31

Literary Context

This pericope is the fourth of four sections of the final section of the narrative proper, which brings climactic resolution to the story told by the Gospel proper. This chapter has announced that Jesus has been raised from the dead (20:1 – 10), that the "garden" tomb has been changed from a place of grief to a place of grace (20:11 – 18), and that the fear of the disciples has been transformed into the mission of the church (20:19 – 23). The resurrected Lord has initiated his new-creational reign in the world, beginning with the disciples themselves. What about the future disciples of Jesus, those to whom the apostles will be sent? In this pericope the reader is exhorted to grasp the manner in which a disciple relates to Jesus and is guided to understand how the Gospel's purpose has been to testify to and to present Jesus to the reader.

IX. The Resurrection (20:1 – 31)

    A. The Empty Tomb (20:1 – 10)

    B. The Appearance to Mary Magdalene (20:11 – 18)

    C. The Appearance to the Disciples (20:19 – 23)

➡   **D. The Appearance to Thomas and the Purpose of the Gospel (20:24 – 31)**

Main Idea

The Gospel of John is an apostolic testimony of *the* gospel, entrusted to the disciples of Jesus who are eyewitnesses of his person and work and the approved witnesses for the church. The Gospel was written to serve as a textually mediated encounter with the Lord Jesus Christ, so that the reader may come to believe in Jesus and participate in the life of God.

Translation

John 20:24–31

24a	Introduction & Setting	Now
b	Character Entrance	**Thomas . . .**
c	Description	one of the Twelve,
d	Identification	the one called Didymus,
e	Predication	**. . . was not with them**
f	Circumstance	when Jesus came.
25a	Conflict	Now **the other disciples were saying to him,**
b	Exclamation	*"We have seen the Lord."*
c	Response	But **he said to them,**
d	Emphatic Conditions/Series	*"Unless I see the mark of the nails in his hands and*
e		*I put my finger in the place of the nails and*
f		*I put my hand in his side,*
g	Negative Inference	*I will not believe."*
26a	Resolution (26–27)	After eight days
b	Setting	**the disciples were again inside**
c		and **Thomas was with them.**
d	Setting	Although the doors were shut,
e	Sequence of Action #1	**Jesus came to them**
f	Sequence of Action #2	and **stood in their midst**
g	Sequence of Action #3	and **said,**
h	Declaration	*"Peace to you."*
27a	Reaction to 25c–g	**Then he said to Thomas,**
b	Series of Commands #1	*"Reach your finger here;*
c	Series of Commands #2	*see my hands.*
d	Series of Commands #3	*Reach out your hand*
e	Series of Commands #4	*and put it in my side.*
f	Series of Commands #5	*Do not be unbelieving but*
g	Series of Commands #6	*believing."*
28a	Conclusion (28–29)	**Thomas answered**
b	Reaction	and **said to him,**
c	Declaration	*"My Lord*
d		*and my God."*
29a		**Jesus said to him,**
b	Circumstance	*"Because you have seen me*
c	Result (Rebuke)	*you have believed.*
d	Pronouncement	*Blessed are those*
e	Contrasting Circumstance	*who have not seen and*
f	Contrasting Result	*have believed."*

Continued on next page.

Continued from previous page.

30a	Narrator's Interpretation (30–31)	So **Jesus also performed many other signs in the presence of his disciples,**
b	Description	which are not written in this book.
31a	Explanation	For **these things have been written**
b	Purpose #1	in order that you may believe
c	Content:	that Jesus …
d	Title	… is the Christ,
e	Identification	the Son of God, and
f	Purpose #2	that …
g	Means	by believing
h		… you may have life
i	Source/Sphere	in his name.

Structure and Literary Form

This pericope corresponds to the basic story form (see Introduction). The *introduction/setting* is established in v. 24, explaining the location and people around whom the plot's conflict will focus. In v. 25 the *conflict* of the pericope is presented, directed by Thomas's rejection of the witness of the other disciples. The *resolution* of the plot is explained in vv. 26 – 27, with Jesus addressing Thomas and giving insight into the manner in which he is to be encountered by his disciples. Finally, the pericope concludes with a two-part interpretive *conclusion/interpretation*. The first is in vv. 28 – 29, ending the pericope proper, where Thomas's reaction to Jesus provides for a significant exhortation by Jesus to future disciples regarding belief not based upon physical sight. The second is in vv. 30 – 31, ending the Gospel proper, where in collaboration with the message of the pericope the narrator provides the first of a two-part conclusion to the Gospel as a whole (20:30 – 31; 21:24 – 25), explaining the purpose for which the Gospel was written.

Exegetical Outline

➡ **D. The Appearance to Thomas and the Purpose of the Gospel (20:24 – 31)**

1. The "Absent Thomas" (v. 24)
2. The Witness of the Disciples (v. 25)
3. Not Unbelieving but Believing (vv. 26 – 27)
4. Belief in Testimony (vv. 28 – 29)
5. The Purpose of the Gospel (vv. 30 – 31)

Explanation of the Text

The last two verses of this pericope, vv. 30 – 31, are considered by a majority of scholars to be the original ending of the Gospel. It is commonly argued that chapter 21 is an appendix added later, so that the original Gospel consisted of merely chapters 1 – 20. We will argue, however, that chapter 21 is original to the Gospel as a formal epilogue, performing a balancing function with the prologue (1:1 – 18). Its relation to 20:30 – 31 demands that we explain the literary conclusion of the Gospel, with a full discussion of the epilogue to be addressed in the next pericope (see comments before 21:1).

IN-DEPTH: The Literary Conclusion of the Gospel of John

The structure of the concluding parts of the Gospel is coherent.[1] The Gospel ends with a narrative epilogue (21:1 – 23) framed by a conclusion divided into two carefully designed stages, with 20:30 – 31 functioning as the first stage and 21:24 – 25 functioning as the second stage.[2] The two-stage conclusion serves to fence off the narrative in chapter 21 from the main narrative of the Gospel (chs. 1 – 20), thus indicating its status as an epilogue.[3] This suggests (among other things) that the epilogue, framed with its two-stage conclusion, was intended to be part of the original design of the Gospel narrative. One obvious narrative reason is to provide structural and thematic balance with the prologue. "The Prologue sketches the prehistory to the Gospel's story, while the Epilogue foresees its posthistory. Just as the Prologue goes back in time to creation, so the Epilogue previews the future mission of the disciples."[4]

It is important to understand the role of the first stage of the conclusion (vv. 30 – 31) and its relation to the second stage (21:24 – 25). Several aspects are important to discuss. First, the two-stage conclusion forms a progressive development that is parallel but not repetitive. At every point where the two stages of the conclusion are parallel, the second stage of the conclusion takes the matter a step further: from "many other signs" (20:30) to "many other things" or deeds in general (21:25). In this way then "the first stage of the conclusion accurately and appropriately indicates the end of the Gospel's narrative specifically of 'signs' and with it the completion of the Gospel's main aim of enabling

1. The following is adapted from Bauckham, *Jesus and the Eyewitnesses*, 364 – 69.

2. Cf. Fernando F. Segovia, "The Final Farewell of Jesus: A Reading of John 20:30 – 21:25," *Semeia* 53 (1991): 167 – 90 (174 – 75).

3. Armin D. Baum, "The Original Epilogue (John 20:30 – 31), the Secondary Appendix (21:1 – 23), and the Editorial Epilogues (21:24 – 25) of John's Gospel: Observations against the Background of Ancient Literary Conventions," in *Earliest Christian History: History, Literature, and Theology: Essays from the Tyndale Fellowship in Honor of Martin Hengel*, ed. Michael F. Bird and Jason Maston, WUNT 2.320 (Tübingen: Mohr Siebeck, 2012), 227 – 70.

4. Bauckham, *Jesus and the Eyewitnesses*, 364.

Christological faith, while the second stage equally accurately and appropriately marks the end of the whole Gospel."[5]

Second, the two-stage conclusion progresses in regard to the witnesses upon which the Gospel is based. The first stage speaks generally of Jesus's disciples as a whole (e.g., 20:30: "In the presence of his disciples"), whereas the second stage speaks specifically of one disciple, the Beloved Disciple. That is, whereas the first stage focused on the general witness of the disciples, as Jesus commanded them to do (15:27: "You also will testify, because from the beginning you have been with me"), the second stage focuses on the testimony of the Beloved Disciple as the particular witness. The reason is that while the Gospel is based upon the corporate experience and witness of the disciples (and even some beyond the Twelve), the narrative form and contents of the Gospel were authored by the Beloved Disciple (21:24: "The one who wrote these things"). In this way, the two-stage conclusion balances and forms an *inclusio* with the prologue, which not only spoke of the Baptist as a witness, matching the second stage of the Gospel (1:15), but also as one who "came as a witness ... so that all may believe through him" (1:7), matching the first stage of the conclusion.

Third, the two-stage conclusion progresses in regard to the context of the Gospel narrative to which it relates. The first stage clearly relates to what has come before, with an initial connection to the immediate pericope — Jesus's appearance to Thomas — which is connected by means of Jesus's own exhortation to future believers, inclusive of the readers of this Gospel (see comments on vv. 28 – 29).[6] But the first stage also initiates a conclusion to the entire narrative of the Gospel proper, all of which mediates between those who have seen, the disciples (witnesses), and those who have not seen. The epilogue that follows (21:1 – 23) then previews symbolically the church's mission, which is how the disciples' witness will enable many to believe in the person and work of Jesus. In fact, the emphasis on "signs" in the first-stage conclusion (v. 30) gives further warrant to our interpretation of the death and resurrection of Jesus as the seventh sign (see comments before 20:1). For example, because it is commonly suggested that the "signs" conclude in chapter 12 (see Introduction), Van Belle considers it "a curious fact" that the term is used in the conclusion to the Gospel proper, since in his view such a term does not fit the whole Gospel. His solution is to suggest that the evangelist moved the original conclusion of the signs source (chs. 1 – 12) and used it to conclude the Gospel as a whole (chs. 1 – 20).[7]

5. Ibid., 366.

6. Cf. J. Smit Sibinga, "Towards Understanding the Composition of John 20," in Van Segbroeck et al., *The Four Gospels*, 3:2139 – 52.

7. Gilbert van Belle, "The Meaning of σημεῖα in Jn 20,30 – 31," *ETL* 74 (1998): 300 – 325 (301).

But if chapters 19–20 serve as the detailed depiction of the climactic seventh sign, then the reference to "signs" at the conclusion of chapter 20 is perfectly placed to provide a climactic conclusion not only for the final sign but also for the entire Gospel — all twenty chapters — declaring in brief the apostolic message of the early church.[8]

For these reasons, then, it is appropriate to speak of vv. 30–31 as the *purpose statement* of the Gospel, as long as the reader is aware that this statement is also the first of a two-stage conclusion that frames the Gospel's epilogue. While the second stage of the conclusion will speak about the author and his identity, in this first stage the reader and his identity are addressed. Such statements were intended to guide the reader to properly read the content of the narrative and to appropriate properly the message of the narrative. While this kind of a more technical purpose statement was commonly located at the end of the narrative,[9] it is clear that the prologue was also intended to guide the reading of the Gospel and declare in a robustly theological manner the purpose of the Gospel (see comments before 1:1). In this way, while vv. 30–31 serve as the first stage of the Gospel's conclusion, it serves almost equally (though not technically) as the second stage of the Gospel's purposeful introduction. At both ends of the Gospel proper, the reader has been guided to read and appropriate the message and ultimate subject matter of the narrative.

20:24 Now Thomas, one of the Twelve, the one called Didymus, was not with them when Jesus came (Θωμᾶς δὲ εἷς ἐκ τῶν δώδεκα, ὁ λεγόμενος Δίδυμος, οὐκ ἦν μετ' αὐτῶν ὅτε ἦλθεν Ἰησοῦς). The pericope is introduced by identifying the main character, Thomas, but also by explaining what becomes important for the pericope's plot, namely, that he "was not with them" (οὐκ ἦν μετ' αὐτῶν) when Jesus first appeared to the disciples (20:19–23). The designation "one of the Twelve" (εἷς ἐκ τῶν δώδεκα) is important because it highlights Thomas's role as a member of the (apostolic) Twelve. The reason for Thomas's absence is not provided to the reader, though in the circumstances to follow it serves an obvious and significant purpose.

For many contemporary readers, the focus of this pericope is eclipsed by the long-established popularity of the "Thomas" character, commonly known as "doubting Thomas."[10] In fact, in two established dictionaries a "doubting Thomas" is "a person who refuses to believe something without

8. See Dominik Markl, "Spielen Joh 1,1; 20,30f; 21,24f auf den Rahmen des Pentateuch an?" in *Führe mein Volk heraus. Zur innerbiblischen Rezeption der Exodusthematik*, ed. Simone Paganini, Claudia Paganini, and Dominik Markl (Frankfurt: Peter Lang, 2004), 107–19 (110–13).

9. Carl Wendel, *Die griechisch-römische Buchbeschreibung verglichen mit der des Vorderen Orients*, HM 3 (Halle: Niemeyer, 1949), 28–29.

10. Stan Harstine, "Un-Doubting Thomas: Recognition Scenes in the Ancient World," *PRSt* 33 (2006): 435–47 (436–39), argues that for the Greek fathers, Thomas's reputation for doubting was of secondary concern.

proof"[11] and a person "who is habitually doubt-ful."[12] Since Thomas is given the most personal focus in this pericope, it is this pericope alone that is used to define him as this kind of character. All four Gospels and Acts mention Thomas, but only in lists of the Twelve (cf. Matt 10:3; Mark 3:18; Luke 6:15; John 21:2; Acts 1:13), except in the Gospel of John, where Thomas plays a much more promi-nent role. In 11:16, for example, Thomas exhorts his disciples to follow Jesus even unto death; in 14:5, Thomas's question to the cryptic teaching of Jesus provides the opportunity for Jesus's sixth "I am" statement in the Gospel. This pericope is the only place in the NT where Thomas the disciple is given any explanation.

There are two ways in which this focus on Thomas is misguided. First, a focus on Thomas often moves inappropriately beyond the narra-tive to the historically reconstructed event behind it. Beyond the methodological concerns of such an approach (see Introduction), it is often done in distinction from the portrait of Thomas pro-vided earlier in the Gospel, especially the much more positive response of Thomas in 11:16. Sec-ond, a focus on Thomas can eclipse the pericope's intentional focus beyond his person to the per-sons he represents: the readers who also have not seen or touched Jesus. If the appearance to Mary (20:11 – 18) functions for the Gospel as an explana-tion of how Jesus is to be related to *physically*, that is, *where* the Lord is encountered (see comments on 20:17, 19), then the appearance to Thomas (20:24 – 31), as we will argue below, functions for the Gospel as an explanation of how Jesus is to be related to *textually*, that is, *how* the Lord is encoun-tered. This is made especially clear by occurring just before and in collaboration with the Gospel's purpose statement (vv. 30 – 31).

20:25 Now the other disciples were saying to him, "We have seen the Lord." But he said to them, "Unless I see the mark of the nails in his hands and I put my finger in the place of the nails and I put my hand in his side, I will not believe" (ἔλεγον οὖν αὐτῷ οἱ ἄλλοι μαθηταί, Ἑωράκαμεν τὸν κύριον. ὁ δὲ εἶπεν αὐτοῖς, Ἐὰν μὴ ἴδω ἐν ταῖς χερσὶν αὐτοῦ τὸν τύπον τῶν ἥλων καὶ βάλω τὸν δάκτυλόν μου εἰς τὸν τύπον τῶν ἥλων καὶ βάλω μου τὴν χεῖρα εἰς τὴν πλευρὰν αὐτοῦ, οὐ μὴ πιστεύσω.). The conflict of the pericope stems from the absence of Thomas, who was not present when the risen Jesus first appeared to the disciples. Although the dis-ciples provide a unified and emphatic witness to what they have seen, denoted by the first-person plural and perfect tense verb "we have seen (the Lord)" (Ἑωράκαμεν [τὸν κύριον]), Thomas claims he will not believe without physical evidence that is particularly concrete. He needs to see and touch the wounds from the crucifixion. While Thomas's request might seem absurd for its detail, it also serves to declare the eyewitness account of the dis-ciples as absurd. The very disciples who had just been sent with the Spirit-empowered authority of the Lord to announce his person and work to the world (20:21 – 23) were immediately rejected by one of their own — indeed, by one who had already exhibited belief in Jesus. The conflict pre-sented here, therefore, is not primarily about *what* Thomas believes but about the *warrant* Thomas requires to believe. The question the Gospel now poses to the reader is *how* is the Lord encountered in his physical absence?

20:26 After eight days the disciples were again inside and Thomas was with them. Although the doors were shut, Jesus came to them and stood in their midst and said, "Peace to you" (Καὶ μεθ' ἡμέρας ὀκτὼ πάλιν ἦσαν ἔσω οἱ μαθηταὶ αὐτοῦ καὶ

---

11. *The Oxford English Dictionary*, 2nd ed. (Oxford: Clar-endon Press, 1989).

12. *The American Heritage Dictionary of the English Lan-guage*, 4th ed. (Boston: Houghton Mifflin, 2000).

Θωμᾶς μετ᾽ αὐτῶν. ἔρχεται ὁ Ἰησοῦς τῶν θυρῶν κεκλεισμένων, καὶ ἔστη εἰς τὸ μέσον καὶ εἶπεν, Εἰρήνη ὑμῖν). The resolution of the pericope begins the moment Jesus arrives in a manner identical to his first postresurrection appearance to his disciples (see comments on 20:19). There is something else that is identical: the day of this appearance is also the Lord's Day, just one week later. For, according to the Jewish mode of reckoning time, with both the first and last day being counted, this appearance was exactly seven days after the first appearance to the disciples, which occurred on "the first day of the week" (20:19).

The silence of the narrator on so many other issues (e.g., Why were the doors locked again, even after the first appearance? Why did Jesus appear and greet in exactly the same manner?) emphasizes the mentioning of the specific day of the appearance. It is as if the narrator magnifies the importance of this day, the Lord's Day, imaging in his account what all Christians receive when they gather on Sunday, the presence of the Lord with his people, the church. Although this is impossible to know, it is almost as if the disciples had decided to meet again on the next Lord's Day, one week later, starting what would become the customary day of gathering for the church. In any case, Jesus appeared a second time to them (cf. Rev 1:10).[13]

20:27 Then he said to Thomas, "Reach your finger here; see my hands. Reach out your hand and put it in my side. Do not be unbelieving but believing" (εἶτα λέγει τῷ Θωμᾷ, Φέρε τὸν δάκτυλόν σου ὧδε καὶ ἴδε τὰς χεῖράς μου, καὶ φέρε τὴν χεῖρά σου καὶ βάλε εἰς τὴν πλευράν μου, καὶ μὴ γίνου ἄπιστος ἀλλὰ πιστός). Following the same order of events as his earlier appearance to the disciples,

after his symbol-laden greeting Jesus displays his crucifixion wounds. But this time he shows them specifically to Thomas, whom he commands to "reach" (Φέρε) and touch the physical markings on his body derived from the cross. It is as if Jesus had heard Thomas's comment in v. 25, for Jesus commands Thomas to do exactly what he had demanded when presented with the witness of the disciples. The narrative does not reveal if he does touch Jesus's wounds, and that may be precisely the point.[14] Based upon what the text reveals, the issue is less the physical experience of Jesus and more the nature of a legitimate witness to him. For while Thomas may not have touched Jesus, he certainly did see him, just like the rest of the disciples had the Sunday before and declared afterward to Thomas (v. 25). Part of the resolution of this pericope, then, is not merely the "touching," which can only be implied from the text, but the "seeing," which the text makes explicit. And this is confirmed in v. 29 when Jesus says that Thomas's belief stems from seeing him; touching is not mentioned.

But Jesus gives a further command to Thomas: "Do not be unbelieving but believing" (μὴ γίνου ἄπιστος ἀλλὰ πιστός). This is an awkward expression that could be rendered in several ways.[15] The terms "unbelieving" (ἄπιστος) and "believing" (πιστός) are the same Greek work except for the former having the negating prefix; thus they are antitheses. Although our translation understands the words to be functioning adjectively, they could also be functioning substantively ("Do not be an unbeliever but a believer"), which is how they more commonly function in the NT (cf. 1 Cor 6:6; 7:12). But nothing in the Gospel suggests that Thomas is less than a believer (cf. 11:16). That is, the actions of Thomas suggest that he is acting in an unbelieving

---

13. See Richard Bauckham, "The Lord's Day," in *From Sabbath to Lord's Day: A Biblical, Historical and Theological Investigation*, ed. D. A. Carson (Grand Rapids: Zondervan, 1982), 221 – 50.

14. Cf. Beasley-Murray, *John*, 385.
15. See Brown, *John*, 2:1026.

manner, not that he is an unbeliever. He is willing (and able) to believe, as he himself confessed (v. 25), but only on his own terms. Thomas wants to return to his preresurrection faith relationship with Jesus, the Jesus in the flesh. "He is demanding that Jesus be for him as he had been prior to the glorification."[16] This is not doubt, as it is often interpreted; this is rebellion, a refusal to relate to God on his own terms.[17] It is no less prideful than what the Jewish authorities displayed, who would not relate to God through Jesus but demanded the former mode of mediation — their temple and their laws. Thomas likewise pits life with Jesus against life in the Spirit and chooses only to relate to the former. He was not rejecting the disciples when he denied their witness, he was rejecting God.

Ridderbos is almost certainly right when he suggests that Jesus's first command, his offer for Thomas to touch his wounds, was intended to shame him.[18] Just as he did with Nicodemus (3:1–15), Jesus took on Thomas's challenge in every way — literally to the smallest detail — and presented his crucified form as his forceful rebuke. This helps explain the certain force and tone of Thomas's words to follow (v. 28). Thomas is not in need of a conversion (from unbeliever to believer) but a transition from the old to the new covenant now mediated by the crucified Lord and his Spirit.[19]

20:28 Thomas answered and said to him, "My Lord and my God" (ἀπεκρίθη Θωμᾶς καὶ εἶπεν αὐτῷ, Ὁ κύριός μου καὶ ὁ θεός μου). The conclusion of the pericope brings closure to the encounter between Thomas and Jesus (vv. 28–29) but also — as discussed above (see comments before v. 24) — between the reader and the author of the Gospel (vv. 30–31). Thomas does not extend himself toward Jesus with his touch but with his words, for God in the person and work of Jesus can only be grasped fully by faith, by the words of a prayer or confession, and by statements of adoration. The last pericope of chapter 20, the resurrection chapter, guides the reader to understand and appropriate the fullness of the incarnate presence of God-with-us by means of the death and resurrection of Jesus. And it is this climactic confession by Thomas that serves as "a narrative bridge between Easter Sunday and the life of the believing community."[20] It is fitting that the last word of the Gospel proper by a character other than Jesus is a confession of his identity as Lord.

Thomas declares, "My Lord and my God" (Ὁ κύριός μου καὶ ὁ θεός μου). While the titles could be functioning as true nominatives and thus be translated more as a statement of recognition — "It is my Lord and my God" — the context also suggests that the titles are in the form of an address, with the nominatives functioning as vocatives. The latter sense, though more likely here, is also more unusual and therefore emphatic. But that is because Thomas speaks not to Jesus but about him in the manner of a true confession: "*You are* my Lord and my God."[21] As much as Jesus is *the* Lord and God, he is at the same time fittingly described by Thomas as "*my* Lord and *my* God." In this way, Thomas not only acknowledges the identity of Jesus but also his personal relationship to him.

Thomas's ascription of these two titles to Jesus are a fitting conclusion to the Gospel. A character in the narrative comes to complete agreement with the opening declaration of the narrator that "the Word was God" (1:1), forming an *inclusio* between the beginning and end of the Gospel proper.

---

16. Schneiders, "Touching the Risen Jesus," 168.

17. See Harstine, "Un-Doubting Thomas," 443–44.

18. Ridderbos, *John*, 647.

19. Cf. Schneiders, "Touching the Risen Jesus," 170.

20. Dorothy A. Lee, "Partnership in Easter Faith: The Role of Mary Magdalene and Thomas in John 20," *JSNT* 58 (1995): 37–49 (48).

21. Bultmann, *John*, 695.

Thomas's statement speaks beyond the confirmation of the resurrection and addresses the meaning of the resurrection. The resurrection reveals who Jesus truly is! Yet it is not an abstract theological definition concerning the person of Christ, for at the same time Thomas speaks of the Lord as "my Lord" and of God as "my God."[22] By this the uniqueness of the Christian faith is made clear. The God of creation can be claimed by the believer as "my God" and even "my Father." The Gospel is the declaration that all the cosmological purposes of God and his grand love for the world through the person and work of Jesus Christ are ultimately applied to specific individuals. The good news is not only universal but also particular; it is for Thomas and therefore also for the individual reader.

20:29 Jesus said to him, "Because you have seen me you have believed. Blessed are those who have not seen and have believed" (λέγει αὐτῷ ὁ Ἰησοῦς, Ὅτι ἑώρακάς με πεπίστευκας; μακάριοι οἱ μὴ ἰδόντες καὶ πιστεύσαντες). Jesus offers the final word when he responds to the confession of Thomas. Jesus makes two statements. The first is concluded with a question mark by NA[28], but because early manuscripts rarely have punctuation, the context suggests this sentence makes more sense as a statement.[23] Even if Jesus is asking a question, it is certainly rhetorical and therefore functions as an emphatic statement. But is the statement a rebuke of Thomas, continuing the rebuke that began in v. 27? If it is a rebuke, it is certainly a gentle one.[24] But it appears to be a rebuke nonetheless.

Because Jesus's first statement is directly related to his second statement, with the two statements serving to form some sort of comparison between

Thomas and future believers, we must be clear regarding the meaning of the first statement. The first statement provides the cause for Thomas's belief, denoted by "because" (Ὅτι). The comparison is not between seeing and touching (cf. v. 27) but between seeing and believing. Or more specifically, the comparison is between the fact that Thomas was able to see Jesus but later believers will not be given such an opportunity. It is common for interpreters to suggest that all sight is inappropriate and unrelated to faith, but this is to misunderstand the Gospel, which used seven signs (with six being explicit) to *sign*ify something beyond the mere miracle.[25] Even if the statement is a rebuke, which we suggest it is, it cannot be a rebuke of Thomas's demand for physical proof. The Gospel as a whole prohibits such an interpretation. The rebuke would have to stem from the fact that Thomas did not believe the signs already presented or the witness of the disciples.

In this way then, besides the historical location of Thomas in relation to the occurrence of the signs (which includes the resurrection of Jesus), there is less difference between the experience of Thomas and future believers than normally assumed. If we can refer to the disciples and the signs as *two kinds of witnesses*, then Jesus's rebuke of Thomas was in reference only to the former. He failed to trust those to whom the mission of God had been entrusted (20:21). But Jesus does not rebuke Thomas for the latter, for he had not yet seen for himself the full seventh sign, the resurrection. In fact, Jesus's appearance here to Thomas provides him with nothing beyond what the other disciples received earlier; the exactness in appearance and presentation supports this observation (cf. v. 26). Carson suggests the rebuke (or the accusation of

---

22. Beasley-Murray, *John*, 385.

23. See Schnackenburg, *John*, 3:334.

24. Some take it as a statement of approval; cf. Morris, *John*, 753.

25. Cf. D. A. Carson, "Is Faith in Christ without Evidence Superior Faith? A Re-examination of John 20:29," in Marshall, *The Spirit and Christ in the New Testament and Christian Theology*, 105 – 18 (108).

"doubt") is unfair since Thomas was not present with the disciples at the first appearance.[26] But that only excuses him from being accountable to the second witness (the final and climactic sign); it does not excuse him from disbelieving the witness of his fellow disciples. Our interpretation must account for this pericope's emphatic presentation of Thomas's rejection of the disciples' declaration, "We have seen the Lord" (v. 25). Jesus's rebuke of Thomas is not for what he had yet to see but for what he had already seen (and yet failed to believe) through them (cf. 4:48).[27] And in this way the reader is given a comparable analogy for their own belief and reception of the apostolic witness.

The second statement of Jesus uses the disbelieving rebellion of Thomas (cf. v. 27) as a platform from which to exhort future believers — the readers. Jesus's second statement is the last word from its main character in the Gospel proper: "Blessed are those who have not seen and have believed" (μακάριοι οἱ μὴ ἰδόντες καὶ πιστεύσαντες). This statement is a beatitude, the only true beatitude in the Gospel, and is related in form (and therefore function) to the well-known beatitudes in Matthew 5:3 – 12, which also each begin with "blessed" (μακάριοι). A beatitude is essentially "an expression of praise of congratulations."[28] Rooted in its use in both testaments, the term "blessed" means more than good fortune (i.e., happiness) or even good fortune in the future, but something very present — "that an eschatological state has been made possible" (cf. 13:17).[29] The kind of blessedness Jesus is declaring is "a divine gift,"[30] and in the immediate context this "eschatological state" is available to those who follow Thomas in belief. This beatitude

serves as a perfect conclusion to the Gospel proper and transition to the Gospel's purpose statement.

Jesus's appearance to Thomas, therefore, is to confirm the original testimony of the disciples. In the providence of God, Thomas's absence allowed him to function as an example of a future believer, who had to rely on the testimony of the disciples — one of whom wrote this Gospel! — as eyewitnesses to the person and work of Jesus Christ. Although the physical appearance to Thomas confirmed his own role as an apostle and personal eyewitness, the repetition of the appearance with all the disciples was intended to rebuke Thomas for disbelieving the witness and to confirm for the disciples that their testimony is both valid and authoritative. By his dismissal of the disciples' testimony, Thomas undercut his own role as an apostolic witness.[31] For this reason Jesus reestablishes it, giving freight to the apostolic mission in the previous pericope (20:19 – 23) and making clear that the apostolic ministry is a necessary ground upon which the mission of God will continue. The body of Christ is to declare the resurrection of the body of Christ and therefore both his lordship and participation in the divine identity of God. In a similar but not identical manner, just as Jesus is *the* representative of God (1:18), the disciples (as the apostles) are the representatives of Jesus, and the church, having been "built on the foundation of the apostles and prophets" (Eph 2:20), continues this representation to the world.

What, then, is the significance of "sight?" In light of the importance of "seeing" in the Gospel, Jesus certainly does not deny its place. "Seeing" in the Gospel can refer to physical observation or

---

26. Ibid., 110 – 11.

27. Contra Bultmann, *John*, 695 – 96. See Newbigin, *The Light Has Come*, 272.

28. Raymond F. Collins, "'Blessed are Those Who Have not Seen': John 20:29," in Chennattu and Coloe, *Transcending Boundaries*, 173 – 90.

29. Brown, *John*, 2:553.

30. Stevick, *Jesus and His Own*, 36.

31. Cf. Peter J. Judge, "A Note on JN 20,29," in Van Segbroeck et al., *The Four Gospels*, 2183 – 92 (2188).

perception, but it can also be used metaphorically. "Seeing" can refer "to the insight to perceive or understand the significance or truth about a person or thing."[32] Only this explains what the disciples can claim to have seen in the prologue: "We saw his glory" (1:14). Therefore, just as Jesus mediates the presence of the Father and is the one through whom the Father is "revealed," in a similar manner the disciples mediate the presence of the Lord, made possible by the Spirit, who as we argued earlier is the source of the disciples' sight, a cosmological vision (see comments on 16:16). "Seeing" in the Gospel therefore is both "sight" and "insight," and the belief exhorted by this Gospel requires them both.[33]

20:30 So Jesus also performed many other signs in the presence of his disciples, which are not written in this book (Πολλὰ μὲν οὖν καὶ ἄλλα σημεῖα ἐποίησεν ὁ Ἰησοῦς ἐνώπιον τῶν μαθητῶν [αὐτοῦ], ἃ οὐκ ἔστιν γεγραμμένα ἐν τῷ βιβλίῳ τούτῳ). Although vv. 28 – 29 could independently function as the fourth scene of the pericope, offering its own conclusion and interpretation, vv. 30 – 31 clearly function in an intentional partnership with it. It is common for vv. 30 – 31 to be interpreted as an independent conclusion, especially when chapter 21 is deemed a later addition and therefore not the original conclusion to the Gospel. If chapter 21 is considered unoriginal, then the weight of the Gospel's closing statement is forcefully placed upon these final two verses, forcing them to serve the entire Gospel and not merely vv. 24 – 29.

These two verses, however, are connected to the preceding scene in that they are an explanatory intrusion by the narrator, not uncommon in John (cf. 3:16), in which the reader is given key information for interpreting the previous encounter. Nothing in the grammar separates v. 29 from v. 30. Even the particles, which are often left untranslated, which we translated as "so ... also" (μὲν οὖν καὶ),[34] serve not to redirect the reader to a new topic or section but to connect vv. 30 – 31 logically with what precedes.[35] This is especially clear when one of the particles in v. 30 (μὲν) is seen to be connected to another particle in v. 31 (δὲ), creating an often untranslated construction that implies, "on the one hand ... on the other."[36] In this way then Jesus's appearance to Thomas serves as "an illustration of the reception of testimony."[37] While vv. 24 – 29 could function as their own complete pericope, they are developed by the inclusion and placement of vv. 30 – 31.

This is not to deny, however, that these two verses have an "air of finality" to them, in that they look right past Thomas to address a new character to whom Jesus is now also appearing: the reader.[38] These verses not only provide the purpose of the Gospel but speak of its selective character, almost as if the narrative is speaking about itself in the third person (i.e., "this book"). Its selectivity was always directed toward the reader, for whom it (or he, the author) had been making a presentation — a witness, beginning from the first verse. By these verses the narrator makes clear that the ministry of Jesus was intended from its very "beginning" to be inclusive of the (most contemporary) reader of the Gospel. This Gospel is an extension of Jesus's ministry, declared by "those approved by God to be entrusted with the gospel" (1 Thess 2:4). The

---

32. Thompson, "Jesus: 'The One Who Sees God,'" 218.

33. Ibid., 226. Augustine calls sight "a kind of general sense," which speaks of every sense (*John*, 121.5.438).

34. According to BDAG 736, the particle we translated as "so" (οὖν) is "inferential, denoting that what it introduces is the result of or an inference from what precedes."

35. See Brian D. Johnson, "Thomas and *marturia*: John 20:24 – 31," *ProcGLM* 25 (2005): 169 – 78 (173 – 75).

36. Carson, *John*, 660 – 61.

37. Johnson, "Thomas and *marturia*," 169.

38. Brown, *John*, 2:1057.

reader should hardly be surprised at the intentionality with which the Gospel is now to conclude. Just as the content of the entire Gospel is *described* by the prologue, the purpose of the entire Gospel is *prescribed* by the epilogue, including this first stage of a two-part conclusion.

The narrator provides the first stage of the Gospel's conclusion by explaining its locution and illocution — its content and force (v. 30) — and then its perlocution — its purpose (v. 31). The narrator reveals that the form of the Gospel was selective in content and that the (seven) signs it presented to the reader were appropriate for the task. There were other signs which could have been included in the Gospel that were also performed by Jesus and were "witnessed" by the disciples, who function as eyewitnesses and apostolic representatives (cf. 20:21 – 23). In the least this suggests that the signs chosen were done so with interpretive intention, giving credence to the expectation of seven signs (see comments before 20:1).

20:31 For these things have been written in order that you may believe that Jesus is the Christ, the Son of God, and that by believing you may have life in his name (ταῦτα δὲ γέγραπται ἵνα πιστεύσητε ὅτι Ἰησοῦς ἐστιν ὁ Χριστὸς ὁ υἱὸς τοῦ θεοῦ, καὶ ἵνα πιστεύοντες ζωὴν ἔχητε ἐν τῷ ὀνόματι αὐτοῦ). The narrator concludes the purpose statement by explaining the Gospel's intended response from the readers (its perlocution). The narrator plainly states the twofold purpose for which the Gospel was written. Both aspects emphasize that the expected response is "belief," the single word that can alone express the purpose of the entire Gospel, used nearly a hundred times. The twofold

purpose of the Gospel involves belief in the Gospel's twofold subject matter: the person (v. 31a) and work (v. 31b) of Jesus Christ.

The first of the two-part purpose statement is "that you may believe that Jesus is the Christ, the Son of God" (ἵνα πιστεύσητε ὅτι Ἰησοῦς ἐστιν ὁ Χριστὸς ὁ υἱὸς τοῦ θεοῦ). The statement is clouded by the text-critical uncertainty regarding the verb "believe," which occurs in two different tense forms in the manuscript tradition: (1) a *present* subjunctive, which may emphasize the continuous aspect of belief — "in order that you continue to believe" (πιστεύητε); and (2) an *aorist* subjunctive, which may emphasize the initiation of belief — "in order that you may come to believe" (πιστεύσητε). While the former might suggest that the Gospel was written for Christians and therefore was written to direct and encourage their already existing faith, the latter might suggest that the Gospel was written to bring unbelievers to faith.[39]

While there is a text-critical issue that warrants resolution (i.e., there is an original reading), for two reasons a resolution is not essential for understanding the purpose of the Gospel. First, the evidence from textual criticism is unable to resolve the issue.[40] While the present subjunctive, option (1), can be taken as having a greater claim to being the original reading with a reasonably high probability, there is still nothing close to certainty. Thus, the form of the verb (present or aorist) cannot be clearly determined. Second, it is just as difficult to determine the difference in function between the options. Even if one knew the present subjunctive was the original reading, Fee is correct when he admits a reluctance "to press for that much intent in the use of tense alone."[41] Here Carson agrees:

---

39. For a helpful exchange between these two options, see D. A. Carson, "The Purpose of the Fourth Gospel: John 20:31 Reconsidered," *JBL* 106 (1987): 639–51; idem, "Syntactical and Text-Critical Observations on John 20:30 – 31: One More Round on the Purpose of the Fourth Gospel," *JBL* 124 (2005):

693 – 714; and Gordon D. Fee, "On the Text and Meaning of John 20,30 – 31," in Van Segbroeck et al., *The Four Gospels*, 2193 – 2205.

40. See Metzger, *Textual Commentary*, 219 – 20.

41. Fee, "On the Text and Meaning of John 20,30 – 31," 2204.

"This is not because no legitimate distinction can be made between the semantics of the aorist and the semantics of the present, but because the present tense forms, in this ἵνα construction, can be clearly applied to believers and unbelievers alike."[42] The multiform and complex sense of "believe" in the Gospel must be held in tension, which engages all readers with the identity of God in the person and work of Jesus Christ. This certainly matches the use of the Gospel in Christian history.

The object of belief, not just the act of belief, is also in question. Is "Jesus" the subject of the predicate nominative, which would seek to answer the question, "Who is Jesus?" Or is "Christ" the subject, which would seek to answer the question, "Who is the Christ/Messiah?" Related to the previous issue, Carson suggests that Christians would not be interested in the latter question, because they already knew the answer.[43] While grammatical arguments have been made to suggest that the subject of the predicate nominative usually has the article ("the Christ"), this rule is made complex by the use of a proper name ("Jesus"), which at times also functions as the subject, especially (in both John and the whole NT) when functioning in ἵνα-clauses and ὅτι-clauses.[44] Even more, the directional force of the entire Gospel has made Jesus the subject of its message and purpose (see 1:17). If anything, it is Jesus who is needed not only to explain Judaism but also to complete it. What is clear is that Jesus is the appropriate content of belief.

The purpose of the Gospel was to explain Jesus to the reader. Who is Jesus? He is "the Christ, the Son of God" (ὁ Χριστὸς ὁ υἱὸς τοῦ θεοῦ), two apposite titles that in relation to Jesus become func-

tionally similar.[45] As much as these titles might be helpfully defined by the first-century (and Jewish) context of the Gospel, that is, the Gospel's historical plot, the reader has now been advantaged to see through the cosmological plot of the Gospel the fuller significance of the terms in relation to the purposes and plans of God. The first title, "the Christ," speaks of the Messiah or the Anointed One of God. "Jesus is the Messiah of Israel, but in a way that can no longer be expressed in the traditional messianic categories and far exceeds them in content."[46] The Baptist declared that he was not the Christ at the very beginning of the Gospel proper, and the narrator applies it to Jesus at its very end (see comments on 1:20). Serving like a frame, then, the entire Gospel has been explaining how Jesus alone fulfills the role of the Christ, the one sent by God to do his work and to make him known. *As the Christ, Jesus is intimately related to everything that God does.* All the plans of God — past, present, and future — are made manifest in the work of Christ.

The second title, "the Son of God," speaks of the intimate and lofty relationship between Jesus and God, that is, between God the Father and God the Son. In this Gospel it is the most exalted Christological expression, matching the prologue's section of Jesus as "the unique Son" (see comments on 1:14) and as the one who is in intimate union with the Father (see comments on 1:18).[47] Again, like a frame around the Gospel, the actions of Jesus throughout the Gospel are best viewed as depicting the very presence and purpose of God through Jesus. *As the Son of God, Jesus is intimately related to everything that God is.* By making Jesus the subject matter of the Gospel and the object of faith,

42. Carson, "Syntactical and Text-Critical Observations on John 20:30 – 31," 707.

43. Carson, *John*, 662.

44. Cf. Harald Riesenfeld, "Zu den johanneische ἵνα-Sätzen," *ST* 19 (1965): 213 – 20; Lane C. McGaughy, *Toward a Descriptive Analysis of EINAI as a Linking Verb in New Testa-*

ment Greek, SBLDS 6 (Missoula, MT: Society of Biblical Literature, 1972); and James V. Brownson, "John 20:31 and the Purpose of the Fourth Gospel," *RefR* 48 (1995): 212 – 16.

45. Cf. Morris, *John*, 756.

46. Ridderbos, *John*, 653.

47. Schnackenburg, *John*, 3:339.

the Gospel of John has confronted the reader with God himself through the *person* and *work* of Jesus Christ. This God can only be accessed and understood *through* Jesus and *by* faith. In short, as the "Christ" Jesus is the *powerful expression of God*, the king and judge of the saving sovereignty of God, who has enacted the new creation; as "the Son of God" Jesus is the *personal expression of God*, who makes God known and accessible to humanity.[48] God has established his rule and relationship to the world through Jesus Christ.

The second of the two-part purpose statement is "that by believing you may have life in his name" (ἵνα πιστεύοντες ζωὴν ἔχητε ἐν τῷ ὀνόματι αὐτοῦ). Again the purpose statement is using language that has been given in-depth definition throughout the Gospel.[49] The "life" (ζωὴν) Jesus offers the reader

is eternal life, an eschatological life in which the reader is invited to participate in the cosmological plot to which the Gospel has been pointing. This life is both provided by Jesus and grounded in him (1:4; 14:6). What Jesus offers therefore is all-embracing, extending beyond what any person can grasp about physical and spiritual life (even the afterlife). The "life" is rooted "in his name," that is, in the character of his person — his power, authority, and love (see comments on 1:12). This Gospel was never "merely a recollection of things past but a proclamation addressing the present."[50] The author of the Gospel has witnessed to this reality and, like Thomas did ultimately, the reader is exhorted to believe his testimony. The message of the Gospel has become part of "the gift of God" to the reader (4:10).

Theology in Application

Beginning a pattern that continues to this day, the disciples met on the second Lord's Day only to have Jesus appear again in their midst, declaring again the completion of his work and the continuation of his mission through them. This time, however, the focus was on one disciple, Thomas, who became representative of all future disciples who are to believe in the apostolic witness of Jesus's disciples. In this pericope the narrative instructs the reader how the Lord is encountered through the mediated witness of the apostles in general, and specifically this Gospel's author, the Beloved Disciple, exhorts the reader to "see" and "believe" and receive "life" through Jesus Christ.

The Apostolic Witness of Thomas to the Reader

Jesus's rebuke of Thomas not only directs the reader to see what Thomas failed to do but also to see what he has been reinstated to become. In the Gospel's opening chapter, John the Baptist was positioned in redemptive history to be the voice of both an OT prophet and an apostle, for he transitioned from looking *for* him to looking *at* him (see comments on 1:15). In the final chapter of the Gospel proper, Thomas

---

48. Beasley-Murray, *John*, 388.

49. Cf. Gilbert van Belle, "Christology and Soteriology in the Fourth Gospel: The Conclusion to the Gospel of John Re-

visited," in Van Belle, *Theology and Christology in the Fourth Gospel*, 435 – 61.

50. Moloney, *John*, 542.

was also positioned by God in redemptive history to be the voice of both a disciple and an apostle, for he transitioned from being a witness *of* him to a witness *for* him. This Gospel is established upon this witness. To read this Gospel is to see both the historical and cosmological realities of God, for it serves as an apostolic testimony of Jesus, who himself was sent to make God known. In this way the concluding statement of Jesus places the readers within the historical and cosmological strands of the Gospel's plot, making them participants in its authoritative and living witness. "From this moment the company no longer consists solely of eleven disciples gathered at that particular time and place; every reader of the Gospel who has faith, to the end of time, is included in Christ's final beatitude."[51]

Signs … Written in This Book

The story a narrative (or a Gospel) tells is an illocution, something which makes assertions, yet it is also something more, for "a narrative displays an interpreted world."[52] Even more, a narrative not only displays a world but communicates a way of viewing it. Its "basic illocutionary activity is ideological instruction; its basic plea: hear my word, believe and understand."[53] The Gospel's "signs," therefore, were never intended to be an illustration, but are "a symbolical anticipation or showing forth of a greater reality of which [the sign] is nevertheless itself a part."[54] In light of the biblical sense of the term, the "signs" about which the narrator speaks are innately eschatological (cf. 2:11), for they declare to the historically located world the cosmological reality now made manifest, expressing what the prologue and introduction foretold: "We beheld his glory" (1:14) and "you will see heaven open … upon the Son of Man" (1:51). These signs, then, are the aftershock of "God with us." Their purpose is fulfilled in the disciples, who believed not in the signs themselves but in the one to whom they pointed (see 2:11). The "signs" ultimately declare the cosmological narrative of God and his work in the world, a world defined entirely by the person and work of Jesus Christ, whose actions make God redemptively present in word and deed. And the reader is presented with this same "sign"-declared reality by means of this Gospel.

The Purpose of the Gospel

The Gospel of John has one goal — that the reader would believe in Jesus Christ. Everything written in the Gospel has this as its goal. Any other use of the Gospel (e.g., as a historical source for the life of Jesus or as guidelines for moral living) would be secondary at best. Its stated purpose is to invite the reader to participate in God,

---

51. Dodd, *Interpretation*, 443.
52. Vanhoozer, *Is There a Meaning in This Text?* 341.
53. Susan Snaider Lanser, *The Narrative Act: Point of View* in *Prose Fiction* (Princeton: Princeton University Press, 1981), 293.
54. Barrett, *John*, 76.

now made possible through Jesus Christ, by becoming members of his family and participants in his ongoing mission to the world (20:21 – 23). The Gospel's intention is ultimately to invite and instruct the reader to live in, with, and for God in all things. In every way, then, this Gospel speaks about Jesus (and God) in a manner inclusive of the reader. This was never a story of something past; it has always been a story about the present — and even the future. To read the Gospel in any other way is a misinterpretation. And not to respond to the Gospel is a form of rebellion, a rejection of the living voice of God.

Jesus is the Christ, the Son of God

This "biography" of Jesus (see Introduction) is clear regarding his person and work: "Jesus is the Christ, the Son of God" (v. 31). By this statement the Gospel declares that Jesus is the perfect agent of God and representative of God. There is nothing that God does or is that is not made manifest and accessible through Jesus Christ. To be "in Christ," to use the favorite expression of the apostle Paul, is to have received by faith the person and work of God in Jesus Christ. Jesus Christ has become for the world everything God *does* and *is*. A "Christian" is a recipient of Christ and therefore a child of God. To speak of God without Christ is not to speak of God at all. If denying Christ is denying God, believing in Christ is to receive the fullness of God. The Gospel of John was written to explain that Jesus is the powerful and personal expression of God and to invite the reader to share in God's love for the world through Jesus Christ. This Gospel is therefore a witness to *the* gospel.

47

John 21:1 – 14

Literary Context

The Gospel proper concludes with the proclamation that Jesus Christ has risen from the dead, followed by the corresponding exhortation to the reader to believe and participate in the resurrection life. The story the Gospel tells, however, is not yet finished, for just as this story started "in the beginning" (1:1) so also does it continue, as Jesus explains, "until I return" (21:23). This story does not conclude with the Son of God but begins with him, for its conclusion must also be inclusive of the children of God (1:12), the majority of whom will meet Jesus through the testimony of the Gospel (cf. 10:16). In this pericope, the first of two in the epilogue of the Gospel, the content of the narrative transitions from the life of Jesus to the life of his disciples and from the particular mission of Jesus to the mission of his disciples and the church.

→ **X. Epilogue (21:1 – 25)**
   A. The Mission of the Church: Jesus and the Fishermen (21:1 – 14)
   B. The Ministers of the Church: Peter's Reinstatement and the Beloved Disciple's Testimony (21:15 – 25)

Main Idea

The life and ministry of Jesus is present in and empowering the life and ministry of the church, whose mission is to participate in the ongoing mission of God to the world, for it is in the church where the presence and purposes of God are made manifest.

Translation

John 21:1–14

1a	Introduction & Setting (1–3)	After these things
b	Character Reentrance/Action	**Jesus appeared again to the disciples**
c	Place	at the Sea of Tiberias.
d		**He appeared in this way.**
2a	List of Characters/Reentrance	**Simon Peter,**
b		**Thomas,**
c	Identification	the one called Didymus,
d		**Nathanael**
e	Place of Origin	from Cana in Galilee,
f		**the sons of Zebedee,** and
g		**two others of his disciples were together.**
3a	Action	**Simon Peter said to them,**
b	Assertion	*"I am going to fish."*
c	Response	**They said to him,**
d	Agreement	*"We will go also with you."*
e	Sequence of Action	**So they went out**
f		and **got into the boat,**
g	Contrast to Intentions	yet
h	Time/Context	that night
i	Result	**they caught nothing.**
4a	Conflict (4–6)	But
b	Time/Context	as it was becoming morning,
c	Action	**Jesus stood on the shore,**
d	Reaction	though **the disciples did not recognize that it was Jesus.**
5a	Action	**Jesus said to them,**
b	Address	*"Children,*
c	Assertion	*you do not have any fish,*
d	Rhetorical Question	*do you?"*
e	Response	**They answered him,**
f		*"No."*
6a	Progression of Action	Then **Jesus said to them,**
b	Command	*"Throw the net on the right side of the boat,*
c	Predicted Result	*and you will find some."*
d	Reaction	**They threw it,**
e		and **they were no longer able to lift it**
f	Basis	because of the large number of fish.
7a	Resolution (7–8)	Then
b	Character Reentrance	**that disciple …**
c	Description	whom Jesus loved
d	Progression of Action	**… said to Peter,**
e	Exclamation	*"It is the Lord!"*
f		After Simon Peter heard that it is the Lord,
g	Sequence of Reaction #1	**he wrapped the outer garment,**
h	Aside	for **he had taken it off,**
i	Sequence of Reaction #2	and **threw himself into the sea.**

8a	Reaction	**The other disciples came in the boat,**
b	Manner	dragging the net of fish,
c	Explanation	for **they were not far away**
d	Distance	from the land but
e		about two hundred cubits.
9a	Conclusion (9–14)	Then
b	Arrival	when they arrived at the land
c	Action	**they saw**
d	Setting d–g	**a charcoal fire**
e		already prepared,
f		**a fish lying on it,** and
g		**bread.**
10a	Reaction to "Arrival"	**Jesus said to them,**
b	Invitation	*"Bring some of the fish that you caught just now."*
11a	Reaction	Then **Simon Peter went up**
b		and **dragged the net onto the land.**
c	Description of "net"	**It was full of large fish,**
d	Quantity	153,
e	Concession	but even with so many
f	Further Description of "net"	**the net was not torn.**
12a	Progression of Action	**Jesus said to them,**
b	Reinvitation	*"Come and eat a meal."*
c	Characters' Thoughts	**Not one of the disciples dared to question him,**
d		*"Who are you?"*
e	Basis	**They knew it was the Lord.**
13a	Sequence of Action	**Then Jesus came**
b		and **took the bread**
c		and **gave it to them,** and also
d		**the fish.**
14a	Concluding Assertion	**This is now the third time Jesus appeared to his disciples**
b	Postresurrection	after he was raised from the dead.

Structure and Literary Form

This pericope corresponds to the basic story form (see Introduction). The *introduction/setting* is established in vv. 1 – 3, explaining the location and people around whom the plot's conflict will focus. In vv. 4 – 6 the dual *conflict* of the pericope is presented: secondarily the absence of fish and primarily the absence of Jesus. The *resolution* of the plot is explained in vv. 7 – 8, with the recognition of Jesus by the Beloved Disciple and the bold move toward him by Peter. Finally, in vv. 9 – 14 the pericope is given a lengthy and symbol-laden *conclusion/interpretation*, with v. 14's announcement that this is the third appearance of Jesus to the disciples serving as a fitting summary of the pericope, forming an *inclusio* with the "appearance" language in v. 1.

Exegetical Outline

➡ **A. The Mission of the Church: Jesus and the Fishermen (21:1 – 14)**
  1. Fishermen without Fish (vv. 1 – 3)
  2. Disciples without Jesus (vv. 4 – 6)
  3. "It Is the Lord!" (vv. 7 – 8)
  4. Jesus's Third Appearance to the Disciples (vv. 9 – 14)

Explanation of the Text

The epilogue of John provides the authoritative conclusion for the entire Gospel and serves as the lens through which the message of the Gospel must be applied to the reader. While the epilogue functions to offer a conclusion to the narrative's account of the Gospel (of John), it simultaneously offers an introduction to the continuing participation of the church in the proclamation of *the* gospel (of God). It is of great importance that the magnificent imagery of the epilogue not detract the reader from grasping its functional significance for directing the application of the Gospel.[1]

IN-DEPTH: The Epilogue

The majority of scholarship on the Gospel of John considers the entirety of chapter 21 to be a later addition to the Gospel. The primary basis of this assumption is the manner in which the purpose statement of 20:30 – 31 functions as a fitting conclusion to the Gospel (see comments before 20:24).[2] The argument for this can only be based on internal evidence, however, for there is not a shred of evidence from the manuscript tradition that suggests the Gospel ever existed without chapter 21. No existing copy of the Gospel ever ends at 20:31, nor are either pericopae in chapter 21 ever found elsewhere in the Gospel. This is significant evidence and makes certain that the burden of proof is placed upon those who argue that chapter 21 is not original to the Gospel.[3]

Even without external support, however, the majority of scholarship continues to argue that chapter 21 is a later addition. Several reasons have been given. First, in the past it was commonly argued that chapter 21 is stylistically and/or grammatically divergent from the rest of the Gospel. This position has been shown to be untenable, even by those who still claim that chapter 21 is a later addition, like Bultmann, who claims that "language and style afford no sure proof."[4] Smith offers an insightful explanation regarding the reasoning

---

1. See Hooker, "Beginnings and Endings," 201 – 02.
2. Brown writes, "The clear termination ... seems to preclude any further narrative" (*John*, 2:1078).

3. Cf. Paul S. Minear, "The Original Functions of John 21," *JBL* 102 (1983): 85 – 98 (86).
4. Bultmann, *John*, 700.

of Bultmann (and certainly others): "The redactional material of the Gospel is identified primarily by theological analysis, with contextual considerations playing a secondary role."[5] As we will see below, the internal argument against the originality of chapter 21 now stems from similar theological presuppositions.[6]

Second, if not divergent in style, then it is argued that chapter 21 is divergent in substance; the contents of chapter 21 are so loosely related to the rest of the Gospel that it can only be considered independent and secondary.[7] The reasons for this difference in content are variously presented and undeniably subjective, an interpretation themselves. There are at least two important connections in content between chapter 21 and the rest of the Gospel. First, chapter 21 provides a necessary end to the story of the two disciples, Peter and the Beloved Disciple, who from chapter 13 on have played very conspicuous roles in the Gospel. It is in chapter 21 where these two characters and their developing roles in the narrative are given an important conclusion.[8] Second, chapter 21 provides a necessary conclusion to the character spoken to directly by the narrator: the reader. A major function of chapter 21 is that it expresses a strong and continuing interest in the disciples of the second generation and even all future readers. Jesus prayed for all future believers in chapter 17, and in chapter 21 the Gospel also extends itself to the future believers, the readers to whom it was created to minister. If chapter 1 attempted to connect the story of Jesus to the people of God pre-Christ, chapter 21 is attempting to connect the same story to the people of God post-Christ. Ultimately, however, it is a slight readjustment in subject matter — in this case a shift toward future disciples — that makes an epilogue an epilogue, a related yet distinct conclusion.[9]

Third, and related to the former, it is argued that the divergence in substance suggests that the purpose statement of 20:30–31 is the intended conclusion of the entire document, so that chapter 21 must be an afterthought of some sort, an appendix or a postscript. This is by far the most common interpretation of the Gospel's conclusion. The charge that chapter 21 is anticlimactic is itself an interpretation and assumes that the Gospel's purpose statement at the end of chapter 20 fulfilled the progressive intention of the narrative. However, there are several examples of literary works that have a conclusion to the main body of a work and yet still include a substantial epilogue. There are several kinds

5. D. Moody Smith, *The Composition and Order of the Fourth Gospel* (New Haven: Yale University Press, 1965), 227.

6. According to an extensive linguistic comparison, B. de Solages, *Jean et les Synoptiques* (Leiden: Brill, 1979), 191–235 (234) even suggests that chapter 21 is actually in a closer linguistic relationship than chapter 20 to chapters 1–19.

7. See Alan Shaw, "Image and Symbol in John 21," *ExpTim* 86 (1975): 311.

8. See Edmund Little, "Peter and the Beloved Disciple: Unfinished Business in John 21," *Stim* 18 (2010): 36–43.

9. Richard Bauckham, "The 153 Fish and the Unity of the Fourth Gospel," in *Testimony of the Beloved Disciple*, 271–84 (274).

of ancient literary forms which have appendices as a normative feature. This was especially common in legal documents, for which "to label this ... an 'appendix' or a 'supplement' is consequently misleading; it was not a mere postscript, dispensable as such, but rather the crucial means by which the business at hand was made legally binding upon its principals."[10] Chapter 21 bears many resemblances to such legal documents, especially 21:24, which assumed the disposition of eyewitness testimony. This makes the subscription a requirement for the witness to be official, certifying the veracity of its report (see comments before 21:15). Thus, chapter 21 must be viewed as a necessary conclusion to the Gospel that provides for the reader a final explanation of the story told by the narrative and a necessary legal statement that certifies the trustworthiness of its eyewitness testimony and, therefore, its author.

All this fits perfectly well with the proposed structure of the concluding parts of the Gospel (see comments before 20:24). The Gospel ends with a narrative epilogue (21:1 – 23) framed by a conclusion divided into two carefully designed stages, with 20:30 – 31 functioning as the first stage and 21:24 – 25 functioning as the second stage. The two-stage conclusion serves to fence off the narrative in chapter 21 from the main narrative of the Gospel (chs. 1 – 20), thus indicating its status as an epilogue. This structure suggests that the epilogue, framed by its two-stage conclusion, was always intended as part of the final Gospel, for some of the reasons suggested above (i.e., narrative conclusion and legal statement). The epilogue has a literary (genre) relationship to the prologue. If the literary function of the prologue was to introduce the important characters in the narrative, situate them within the story, and give some understanding of their importance, the epilogue functioned to conclude the importance and story of those same characters. The validity and narrative importance of the epilogue should be viewed as coterminous with the validity and narrative importance of the prologue (see comments before 1:1).[11]

Therefore, in a manner entirely consistent with and corresponding to the prologue with which the Gospel begins, the Gospel concludes with a formal epilogue, the narrative conclusion to a (dramatic) text that is intended to bring completion to the story, offer a legal statement by the author, and provide applications for the reader.[12] Epilogues were common in both Greco-Roman and

---

10. Howard M. Jackson, "Ancient Self-referential Conventions and their Implications for the Authorship and Integrity of the Gospel of John," *JTS* 50 (1999): 1 – 34 (4).

11. For a fascinating argument regarding the interconnection between the prologue and epilogue based upon intentional numerical compositon (496 syllables and words — a triangular number), see Bauckham, *Jesus and the Eyewitnesses*, 364. A similarly intentional numerical correspondence exists between the two-stage conclusion (20:30 – 31 and 21:24 – 25), both of which consist of exactly forty-three words.

12. Baum, "The Original Epilogue," 231.

Jewish literature.[13] And in the ancient world both prologues and epilogues "were written as a rule by the authors of the books themselves and not by someone else."[14] But they were intended for the reader. In fact, the entire Gospel has displayed sensitivity to the reader, guiding the reading of the narrative at both ends of the Gospel. Just as the Gospel began with a double beginning consisting of the prologue (1:1 – 18) and an introduction to the narrative proper (1:19 – 51), so the Gospel has a double ending consisting of a two-staged conclusion (20:30 – 31; 21:24 – 25) that frames the epilogue (21:1 – 23). In collaboration with the two-stage conclusion, chapter 21 serves as a technical epilogue and "carries forward" the theme and message of the entire Gospel, not only by bridging the gap between the reader and the content of the narrative but also by bridging the gap between the reader and the authoritative witness and identity of the author.[15]

Just as the Gospel's prologue serves to *lift* the reader so that he may grasp the full cosmological significance of the person and work of Jesus Christ, so the Gospel's epilogue serves to *land* the reader so that he may be guided in the newly established relation with God and mission of God. Similar to the prologue, then, the epilogue of the Gospel casts a vision for the reader, providing the spectacles needed for seeing the cosmological story of the Gospel in the real world, that is, in the reader's world. For this reason the reader can expect the epilogue to be more symbolic in presentation. The prologue's generic, symbol-laden language and depictions that speak of things beyond what the eye could see (e.g., life, light, darkness, children, flesh, Son, grace, truth) are matched by the epilogue's equally symbolic depiction of the final appearance of Jesus with his disciples that speaks beyond the things it addresses.[16] In the epilogue, the narrator has in mind not merely the story he has been telling but also the reader to whom he has been speaking. We should expect, then, for the narrative to depict even more explicitly the coalescence of the historical and cosmological strands of the Gospel's plot into the world of the reader. For in the same way the prologue directs the reader from their (historical) world and to its narrative (cosmological) world, the epilogue directs the reader from its narrative (cosmological) world and back to their (historical) world.

Between these two symbol-laden (dramatic) genres of prologue and epilogue, the Gospel frames its message and invitation to the reader. The Gospel

---

13. See Markl, "Spielen Joh 1,1; 20,30f; 21,24f auf den Rahmen des Pentateuch an?," 107 – 19.

14. Baum, "The Original Epilogue," 233.

15. See John Breck, "John 21: Appendix, Epilogue, or Conclusion," *SVTQ* 36 (1992), 27 – 49.

16. On the nature of symbolism, see Sandra M. Schneiders, "John 21:1 – 14," *Int* 43 (1989): 70 – 75, who explains how symbols "mediate transcendent reality" (71).

begins with the exhortation to "follow" Jesus (1:37 – 43) and ends with a nearly identical exhortation (21:19 – 22), though now with full access to the Father, through the Son, and in and by the Spirit. Befitting the purpose of the entire Gospel, Segovia helpfully speaks of the epilogue's rhetorical intentions and strategic functions.[17] Primarily the epilogue performs a didactic and exhortative service, but not without admonitory and consolatory aspects: the need for mission in and to the world, the message that nothing is possible without Jesus, the explanation that love for Jesus and "following" Jesus is discipleship and the nature of "shepherding," that the loss of life is a real possibility, and the significant role of the disciples. Ultimately then, the Gospel ends where it started, with the mission of God to the world. At the end of the Gospel, however, it is no longer merely the mission of the Son who was sent by the Father but now also the mission of the church who is sent by the Son (20:21).[18]

21:1 After these things Jesus appeared again to the disciples at the Sea of Tiberias. He appeared in this way (Μετὰ ταῦτα ἐφανέρωσεν ἑαυτὸν πάλιν ὁ Ἰησοῦς τοῖς μαθηταῖς ἐπὶ τῆς θαλάσσης τῆς Τιβεριάδος· ἐφανέρωσεν δὲ οὕτως). The introduction and setting of the pericope (vv. 1 – 3) begins with a generic connective phrase, "after these things" (Μετὰ ταῦτα), which occurs frequently in the Gospel (see comments on 2:12), directing the reader to read this pericope as a continuation of what precedes it. Combined with the adverb "again" (πάλιν), this opening statement serves to "bind" the following story to those of 20:19 – 23 and 20:24 – 29. If the reader thought 20:30 – 31 was the Gospel's conclusion and not simply its purpose statement, this verse "must make him change his mind."[19]

This verse introduces for the reader another "appearance" of the resurrected Jesus to his disciples. This third appearance (see v. 14) occurs not in a locked room like the first two, but on the shore of the Sea of Tiberias. If it was fitting for Jesus's first two appearances to take place at the gathering of the earliest church (cf. 20:26), it is appropriate that Jesus's final appearance was out in the world, even beyond the confines of Jerusalem (see comments on 6:1). In all three appearances, Jesus met his disciples where they were, for Jesus has always been and remains "the coming one" (see 12:13).

By using the verb "appeared" (ἐφανέρωσεν) twice in the opening verse and once in the final verse (v. 14), the pericope creates an *inclusio* that establishes the appearance or "revelation" of Jesus as "the announcement of a theme"[20] and "the key doctrine of the passage."[21] This appearance is not to establish the fact of his presence, for that was already accomplished — and emphatically with Thomas. Rather, this appearance establishes the *continuation* of his presence, how the risen Lord will reveal himself to and be present with his disciples in all future times. The revelation of the Son of God — and God himself (1:18) — is a major theme

---

17. The following is adapted from Segovia, "The Final Farewell of Jesus," 184 – 85.

18. Cf. Schlatter, *Der Evangelist Johannes*, 363.

19. Lars Hartman, "An Attempt at a Text-Centered Exegesis of John 21," *ST* 38 (1984): 29 – 45 (30).

20. Schnackenburg, *John*, 3:352.

21. Bruner, *John*, 1204.

in the Gospel (e.g., 1:31; 2:11; 3:21; 7:4; 9:3; 17:6). The revelation of Jesus was intended for Israel (1:31) and for the purpose of revealing his "glory" (2:11), which the prologue connected directly to Jesus's dwelling presence, his "tabernacling" (1:14). In this pericope, filled with numerous symbol-laden details, Jesus will explain further the continuing nature of his presence with his disciples, the church.

21:2 Simon Peter, Thomas, the one called Didymus, Nathanael from Cana in Galilee, the sons of Zebedee, and two others of his disciples were together (ἦσαν ὁμοῦ Σίμων Πέτρος καὶ Θωμᾶς ὁ λεγόμενος Δίδυμος καὶ Ναθαναὴλ ὁ ἀπὸ Κανὰ τῆς Γαλιλαίας καὶ οἱ τοῦ Ζεβεδαίου καὶ ἄλλοι ἐκ τῶν μαθητῶν αὐτοῦ δύο). The narrator introduces the characters to whom Jesus would reveal himself. The seven characters are described as his "disciples" both here and in v. 1, even though Nathanael was not one of "the Twelve" (see 1:45). Clearly the term is being used more expansively here, and rightly so in light of the Gospel's shift from present to future disciples (20:29 – 31). The presence of seven disciples may be intended to symbolize a perfect or complete number, and not merely a truncated twelve. The number is clearly symbolic in biblical literature, even Johannine literature (Rev 1:20), and the obvious symbolism used later in the pericope makes it difficult to avoid the implicit "impression" (see Introduction) crafted by the narrative.[22] It could even be argued that the Gospel has made "seven" a thematic number (e.g., seven "signs"; seven days of the week). The narrator could have expressed his symbolic intentions more clearly, however, if he had stated the number explicitly and not required the reader to do the counting.[23]

Since v. 7 mentions the presence of the Beloved Disciple, he is certainly to be included among the seven disciples and is almost certainly one of the two unnamed disciples who are the sons of Zebedee, mentioned only here in the Gospel (John and James; see Mark 1:19). This finds strong agreement with the traditional identification of the Beloved Disciple as John, son of Zebedee (on authorship, see Introduction). Befitting the epilogue and conclusion of the Gospel (20:30 – 21:25), the author reveals more insights into his identity, though the continued anonymity facilitates further his significant connection to the testimony of the Gospel (see comments on 21:24).

21:3 Simon Peter said to them, "I am going to fish." They said to him, "We will go also with you." So they went out and got into the boat, yet that night they caught nothing (λέγει αὐτοῖς Σίμων Πέτρος, Ὑπάγω ἁλιεύειν. λέγουσιν αὐτῷ, Ἐρχόμεθα καὶ ἡμεῖς σὺν σοί. ἐξῆλθον καὶ ἐνέβησαν εἰς τὸ πλοῖον, καὶ ἐν ἐκείνῃ τῇ νυκτὶ ἐπίασαν οὐδέν). Simon Peter, the leader and spokesperson for the disciples (cf. 1:40, 42), announces that he is going fishing, and the rest of the disciples decide to join him. There is nothing in the text to suggest that Peter's announcement is an abandonment of the apostolic mission. Numerous commentators relate this particular activity to the disciples' former occupation and therefore interpret this more extremely as "complete apostasy,"[24] or less extremely as an "aimless activity undertaken in desperation."[25] The text alone, however, does not demand such interpretations. Rather, the scene detailed by the narrator intends to depict a real-life circumstance into which the newly assigned apostolic mission can now be contextualized.[26] The narrative does not show any interest in *why* Peter (and the others) went fishing; it is more concerned to describe *how* their fishing

---

22. See Aquinas, *John*, 3:283.
23. However, this would not be the first place where the reader is benefited by counting (see comments on 1:17).

24. Hoskyns, *Fourth Gospel*, 552.
25. Brown, *John*, 2:1096.
26. Cf. Morris, *John*, 760.

went. Moreover, it is not Peter who should be interpreted symbolically but the act of fishing, which Scripture uses as a metaphor for the apostolic mission of "catching people" (see Luke 5:10).[27] And it is not their decision to fish but their inability to fish that Jesus will address (vv. 5 – 6).

The disciples went fishing but "caught nothing" (ἐπίασαν οὐδέν) that night. The narrator explains their lack of success because it is directly related to the plot of the Gospel. The lack of fish, however, is not the true conflict in this pericope. The Gospel has already used a miracle story to depict a far greater conflict, even if the miracle was employed to depict it (see 2:1 – 4). The occurrence of the term "night" (νυκτὶ), in light of its use in the rest of the Gospel, strongly colors the context of the scene. Since the term always has negative connotations in the Gospel and often in regard to the cosmological strand of the Gospel's plot (see comments on 3:2), it is likely used in a similar way here. There is evidence that fishing was commonly done at night (e.g., Luke 5:5),[28] but with their lack of success the term creates the "impression" that there is more going on here than fishermen's luck. The disciples of Jesus are still grasping at the reality of the resurrection and their participation in the life of God through Christ. Something (or someone) is still missing. Jesus had said to the disciples, "You will be scattered, each to his own home, and to leave me alone" (16:32), and their actions here likely fulfill his prophecy. With this verse then, the reader has been given the introduction and setting for the narrative to follow.

21:4 But as it was becoming morning, Jesus stood on the shore, though the disciples did not rec-
ognize that it was Jesus (πρωΐας δὲ ἤδη γενομένης ἔστη Ἰησοῦς εἰς τὸν αἰγιαλόν· οὐ μέντοι ᾔδεισαν οἱ μαθηταὶ ὅτι Ἰησοῦς ἐστιν). The conflict of the pericope (vv. 4 – 6) is introduced by the narrator's robustly theological description of the appearance of Jesus. In every appearance to his disciples, Jesus is described with the verb "stood" (ἔστη), as if he just appeared before them (see 20:14, 19, 26). While the narrator shares with the reader the deliberation of the disciples, their departure from that place, and even their entrance into the boat (v. 3), Jesus's appearance on the shore is given minimal detail. This cryptic maneuver is almost certainly intentional (see comments on 20:19).

Although the disciples went out to fish at "night" (v. 3), Jesus appears before them on the shore "as it was becoming morning" (πρωΐας δὲ ἤδη γενομένης). The term "morning" (πρωΐας) refers to the "early part of the daylight period."[29] The night "impression" created in v. 3 is facilitated further by the contrastive sense here. As the sun appears over the horizon, Jesus appears on the shore. The statement "but as it was becoming morning" serves to explain not the chronological order of events but the cosmological reality in which the disciples now exist.[30]

The contrastive context has been introduced (e.g., disciples and Jesus; night and light), but what is the pericope's conflict? It is introduced formally at the end of the verse: "Though the disciples did not recognize that it was Jesus" (οὐ μέντοι ᾔδεισαν οἱ μαθηταὶ ὅτι Ἰησοῦς ἐστιν).[31] There is no need to speculate regarding the reason for their inability to see Jesus, natural or supernatural,[32] for the Gospel has used before the inability to see or recognize Jesus in order to highlight the true nature

---

27. Both testaments use the catching of fish to symbolize the catching and ingathering of people (for the OT, see Jer 16:14 – 16; Hab 1:14 – 15). Cf. Heil, *Blood and Water*, 153 – 54.

28. See Keener, *John*, 2:1226 – 27.

29. BDAG 892.

30. But the narrative is even more intentional. For the theological significance of the verbal root of "becoming" (γενομένης), see comments on 1:17.

31. BDAG 630.

32. Contra Bultmann, *John*, 707; Brown, *John*, 2:1070.

of his presence (see comments on 20:14). While the absence of fish will be quickly remedied in this pericope, it is the absence of Jesus that becomes the intended focus of the narrative details. The narrative is already guiding the reader to see that the inability or inadequacy of the disciples to catch fish reveals that something deeper is missing.

21:5 Jesus said to them, "Children, you do not have any fish, do you?" They answered him, "No" (λέγει οὖν αὐτοῖς [ὁ] Ἰησοῦς, Παιδία, μή τι προσφάγιον ἔχετε; ἀπεκρίθησαν αὐτῷ, Οὔ). Like the previous appearances to the disciples, it is Jesus who speaks first. Jesus calls out to his disciples by using the title "children" (Παιδία), which should be interpreted as synonymous with the significant term in the prologue that also is translated as "children" (τέκνα).[33] The Fourth Gospel frequently uses related or overlapping words synonymously across the narrative; it is only when they are used in close proximity (especially in the same verse) that there is usually a carefully nuanced distinction or comparison intended between them (e.g., 13:10; 21:15 – 17). This is further supported by the interchangeable use of these two terms in a letter of John (e.g., 1 John 2:14, 18 and 2:1, 12, 28; 3:7, 18; 4:4; 5:21). Fittingly then, Jesus reaches out to his disciples with a title that can only now be bestowed upon them after his death and resurrection. It is only because of the authoritative name of the Son of God that they can receive the name "children" of God (1:12).

Jesus addresses not only their new identity ("children") but also their condition, their lack of fish. He asks them a simple question that expects a negative answer, and they give an even simpler negative response. The narrator is establishing that both sides are aware of the situation at hand, though Jesus's knowledge of their lack of fish highlights how much else he "recognizes" that they do not. Jesus uses a far less common term for "fish" (προσφάγιον) that generally is used to refer to fish to eat.[34] The term facilitates a further contrast between Jesus and his disciples: while they were unable to provide a meal for themselves, Jesus himself will provide the fish to eat (v. 9).[35] This is not the first time the reader of the Gospel has seen Jesus ask a question for which he already knew the answer (see 5:6).

21:6 Then Jesus said to them, "Throw the net on the right side of the boat, and you will find some." They threw it, and they were no longer able to lift it because of the large number of fish (ὁ δὲ εἶπεν αὐτοῖς, Βάλετε εἰς τὰ δεξιὰ μέρη τοῦ πλοίου τὸ δίκτυον, καὶ εὑρήσετε. ἔβαλον οὖν, καὶ οὐκέτι αὐτὸ ἑλκύσαι ἴσχυον ἀπὸ τοῦ πλήθους τῶν ἰχθύων). Still standing on the shore, Jesus commands the disciples to throw their net on the right side of the boat, where he promises fish will be present. Without any verbal response, they obey his command and receive in their nets a bountiful catch of fish; it is so large that the disciples were not physically able to lift the overcrowded net into the boat. The miraculous solution to the lack of fish "is described with the greatest reserve."[36] The quick resolution further supports the argument that the pericope's conflict is the absence of Jesus, not fish.

The narrative gives no indication that the commands of Jesus are unique or somehow the point. There is no historical evidence that the right side of the boat had any such significance for fishing. To

---

33. The NIV's translation "friends" obscures the likely intentional connection to "children" in 1:12. In the historical context of the Gospel, however, the term could function as an affectionate colloquialism. Cf. Michaels, *John*, 1031.

34. BDAG 886. The term only occurs here in the NT and does not occur in the LXX; it is even rare in Greek literature. It is the first of three different terms for "fish" in this pericope. Cf. Moloney, *John*, 552.

35. Cf. Barrett, *John*, 580.

36. Morris, *John*, 761.

suggest that the right side was the side of fortune, as some commentators suggest, is to read pagan practices into Scripture.[37] The extravagant catch of fish strongly suggests that something beyond the plain sense of catching fish is in view. Some suggest that a moral lesson is intended — that obedience to the master is a significant aspect of discipleship.[38] But it is more commonly suggested that some kind of symbolic representation is intended. Even the absence of fish as the direct object of "you will find *some*" (εὑρήσετε) strongly implies that the object about which Jesus speaks is less fish and more people.[39]

The magnitude of fish is not intended for a meal (see v. 9) but to symbolize "the effective authorization and promise of the Risen One to fulfill the missionary mandate that he has given to his disciples."[40] This might also explain the willingness of the disciples to obey a stranger's command from the shore. In this moment the disciples were more shepherds than fishermen (1 Pet 5:2 – 4), for they heard and responded to the "voice" of the Good Shepherd (10:16). The lack of an explicit seventh sign has led some to suggest that this miracle is the seventh sign.[41] If this were some sort of sign, however — and it is not! (see comments before 20:1) — then it would be a symbolic anticipation of the apostolic mission and not the mission of the Son.[42] If the Gospel proper describes the Son's role in the mission of God, then the Gospel's epilogue prescribes the church's role in the mission of God.

21:7 Then that disciple whom Jesus loved said to Peter, "It is the Lord!" After Simon Peter heard that it is the Lord, he wrapped the outer garment, for he had taken it off, and threw himself into the sea" (λέγει οὖν ὁ μαθητὴς ἐκεῖνος ὃν ἠγάπα ὁ Ἰησοῦς τῷ Πέτρῳ, Ὁ κύριός ἐστιν. Σίμων οὖν Πέτρος, ἀκούσας ὅτι ὁ κύριός ἐστιν, τὸν ἐπενδύτην διεζώσατο, ἦν γὰρ γυμνός, καὶ ἔβαλεν ἑαυτὸν εἰς τὴν θάλασσαν). The resolution of the pericope (vv. 7 – 8) begins with a recognition scene similar to the scenes in chapter 20 and with an exchange between the two primary disciples in the Gospel, Peter and the Beloved Disciple.[43] Though at first unrecognized, the Beloved Disciple sees and announces to his fellow disciples that the man giving instructions from the shore is Jesus, which he announces almost certainly in the form of an emphatic witness: "It is the Lord!" (ὁ κύριός ἐστιν). The Beloved Disciple has had a significant role in the Gospel (see comments on 13:23), and it is in the epilogue where the nature of his identity is more clearly revealed (see 21:2, 24). By recognizing Jesus and declaring him before the other disciples, the Beloved Disciple is again functioning as an ideal witness to the person and work of Jesus Christ.

This is the third of four comparison-like depictions of Peter and the Beloved Disciple (13:22 – 25; 20:3 – 9; 21:7; 21:20 – 23). In contrast to the implied race between them in the previous comparison (see comments on 20:4), this encounter is similar to the first (13:22 – 25) where collaboration is depicted. Although the Beloved Disciples is the first to recognize Jesus, it is Peter who is the first to respond — and in a radical manner. Comparison was a standard rhetorical technique, employing comparison of characters in ways useful to the point of the narrative.[44] For this reason the point of comparison must involve not only the recognition of Jesus but also the intensity of the movement toward Jesus.[45]

37. See Barrett, *John*, 580.
38. Keener, *John*, 2:1228.
39. Heil, *Blood and Water*, 155.
40. Ridderbos, *John*, 660.
41. See Stephen S. Smalley, "The Signs in John XXI," *NTS* 20 (1964): 275 – 88.
42. Cf. Aquinas, *John*, 3:286; Augustine, *John*, 122.7.442.
43. With the modifying demonstrative, "that" (ἐκεῖνος) Beloved Disciple, the character is given a more technical introduction (cf. 13:25; 19:35).
44. Keener, *John*, 2:1183.
45. Similar to the second comparison, the Beloved Disciple

If the Beloved Disciple exhibits an awareness of Jesus (he recognized the voice of his Shepherd), Peter exhibits a desire for his presence, underscored by the fact that he "wrapped" (cf. 13:4 – 5) his garments around him (which the labor of fishing had required him to remove) and leaped into the sea, apparently in order to swim to Jesus, leaving the other disciples to tend to the fish. The fact that the narrator does not describe Peter's arrival to the beach suggests that his initial response is the fact of importance. It is almost as if Peter were bringing his belongings with him so as to follow Jesus.[46] In the least, this displays for the reader the kind of response one should have to the Lord.

21:8 The other disciples came in the boat, dragging the net of fish, for they were not far away from the land but about two hundred cubits (οἱ δὲ ἄλλοι μαθηταὶ τῷ πλοιαρίῳ ἦλθον, οὐ γὰρ ἦσαν μακρὰν ἀπὸ τῆς γῆς ἀλλὰ ὡς ἀπὸ πηχῶν διακοσίων, σύροντες τὸ δίκτυον τῶν ἰχθύων). This verse serves to explain further the radical departure of Peter. Not only did Peter leave the other disciples with a net crammed full of fish that was too heavy to lift into the boat (v. 6), so that the disciples were "dragging" (σύροντες) the net alongside the boat until they could reach the shore, but Peter also jumped into the water so that he had to swim a good distance to the shore. The narrator explains that when Peter jumped into the sea, the boat was about two hundred "cubits" (πηχῶν) from land. Since one cubit is an average man's forearm (the distance from the elbow to the end of the middle finger), which is about 45 – 52 centimeters or 19 – 20 inches, two hundred cubits would be about 330 feet or 110 yards (100 meters).[47] Peter's dramatic movement toward Jesus is only slightly more extravagant than the disciples, who are similarly exerting themselves to get the fish Jesus procured for them from the overflowing net being pulled behind their boat to the shore. En route to Jesus, the conflict of the pericope is given resolution. The missing element in their previous activities now stands before them, ready and waiting.

21:9 Then when they arrived at the land they saw a charcoal fire already prepared, a fish lying on it, and bread (ὡς οὖν ἀπέβησαν εἰς τὴν γῆν βλέπουσιν ἀνθρακιὰν κειμένην καὶ ὀψάριον ἐπικείμενον καὶ ἄρτον). The conclusion and interpretation of the pericope (vv. 9 – 14) is a lengthy selection of symbol-laden details that direct the reader to grasp the ministerial presence of Christ and the nature of the apostolic mission. It seems that when the disciples had been busy in their inadequacy, Jesus had prepared on the shore for them a charcoal fire with fish already being grilled upon it and some bread. Jesus did not merely catch fish, he prepared a meal.

The second occurrence of the term "charcoal fire" (ἀνθρακιὰν) creates a potent contrast. At its first appearance Peter was warming himself at the fire prepared by the enemies of his Lord (18:18). Now, however, he is warming himself at a fire prepared by his Lord. "What is happening around this charcoal fire is the work of the resurrected Lord."[48] An unsuccessful night's work draws to its end, and the disciples are only beginning to realize the reality of Jesus's words "apart from me you can do nothing" (15:5).[49] It is important to note that this redemptive charcoal fire is the context in which the Gospel will end (21:15 – 25).

---

is the first to see (20:5), but Peter is the first to take action (20:6). The connection between this pericope and 20:1 – 10 gives further credence to the originality of the epilogue. Cf. Beasley-Murray, *John*, 400.

46. Especially since swimming with a wrapped tunic would be cumbersome. Cf. Keener, *John*, 2:1229 – 30.

47. BDAG 812.

48. Angus Paddison, "Exegetical Notes: John 21:1 – 19," *ExpTim* 118 (2007): 292 – 93 (293).

49. Newbigin, *The Light Has Come*, 277.

21:10 Jesus said to them, "Bring some of the fish that you caught just now" (λέγει αὐτοῖς ὁ Ἰησοῦς, Ἐνέγκατε ἀπὸ τῶν ὀψαρίων ὧν ἐπιάσατε νῦν). Jesus never intended to prepare this meal on his own, for he commands his disciples to bring some of the caught fish to him, that is, to this meal. For a fishing story, this is a strange request. The singular "fish" in v. 9 provides an interesting contrast with the plural "fish" here, suggesting that this meal had always required a shared responsibility. It is when the disciples bring the fish they too have caught that the meal receives its full significance. It is surprising that Jesus credits the disciples with the catch of fish, for certainly he was the one primarily responsible.[50] It seems clear that the catching of the fish and the preparation of the meal is intended to portray the nature of the disciples' involvement and participation in the mission of God. At this moment the resurrected Lord is teaching his disciples how to "share in his resurrection power" and "continue his work on earth."[51]

The ministry of Jesus is framed in this Gospel by meals he prepared: in 2:1 – 11 Jesus produces the wine for a wedding feast, and here Jesus provides the fish and bread for his disciples.[52] While the first meal set the context for the work he would do for his disciples, the last meal (the true last supper!) would set the context for the work his disciples would do through him for others (cf. Jesus's forthcoming command to Peter in 21:15, 17: "Feed my lambs/sheep").[53]

21:11 Then Simon Peter went up and dragged the net onto the land. It was full of large fish, 153, but even with so many the net was not torn (ἀνέβη οὖν Σίμων Πέτρος καὶ εἵλκυσεν τὸ δίκτυον εἰς τὴν γῆν μεστὸν ἰχθύων μεγάλων ἑκατὸν πεντήκοντα τριῶν· καὶ τοσούτων ὄντων οὐκ ἐσχίσθη τὸ δίκτυον). Peter, again the first to respond to Jesus, "went up" (ἀνέβη) into the boat, that is, he "climbed aboard," and he "dragged the net" (εἵλκυσεν τὸ δίκτυον) onto the shore, apparently on his own. The text is not suggesting that Peter displayed some sort of miraculous strength by dragging the net by his own power. The emphasis is on the inclusion of the disciples' fish, not on their delivery. The strength of delivery that is emphasized is in regard to the net, which the narrator notes was full of so many large fish. The symbolic nature of the epilogue suggests that "something more" is being told to the readers here. The intended symbolism might be of the net's physical power so as to depict how Christ is never overstrained, or of the net's unifying power so as to depict how through Christ "the church remains one, in spite of the number and variety of its members."[54] It might be best, however, to let the symbolic "impressions" created by the scene be reflected in several directions, since both of these options (even if there are more) are clearly true of Christ.[55] The provisions and powers of Jesus are true for both fish and followers.

The most debated symbolism, however, is the number of fish in the net: "153" (ἑκατὸν πεντήκοντα τριῶν). No analysis of this number in the history of the church has brought anything close to an agreeable resolution. The more specific the solution the more it feels fabricated or forced, yet to ignore the fact that the narrator did not give a round number is equally unsettling. There are five primary options offered to explain the depiction of the 153 fish.[56]

---

50. See Aquinas, *John*, 3:289 – 90.

51. Ridderbos, *John*, 662.

52. Regarding allusions to this meal as an allusion to the Lord's Supper or Eucharist, see comments before 6:22.

53. Keener, *John*, 2:1231.

54. Barrett, *John*, 582.

55. See Heil, *Blood and Water*, 157.

56. For a more comprehensive survey and bibliography, see R. Alan Culpepper, "Designs for the Church in the Imagery of John 21:1 – 14," in *Imagery in the Gospel of John: Terms, Forms, Themes, and Theology of Johannine Figurative Language*, ed. Jörg Frey, Jan G. Van der Watt, and Ruben Zimmer-

IN-DEPTH: **The 153 Fish**

1. *Historical Description*. This interpretation denies that the number has any symbolic intentions. Its purpose, rather, is much more mundane: to provide the exact count of fish from the catch.[57] The specificity does affect the reader's understanding of the scene, but only in a manner that helps "fulfill their natural purpose" by providing "a vivid account of human experience"[58] or by offering a detail that is representative of its eyewitness testimony.[59] While this minimalist interpretation is attractive, in light of the Gospel's use of symbolism — especially with numbers — it is difficult to believe that this is the only intention.

2. *Natural Symbolism*. This interpretation maintains a historical basis for the number but suggests that it is also directing the reader to a symbolic message. Jerome, in his commentary on Ezekiel 47:6 – 12, argues with the assistance of Greek zoologists that there are 153 different kinds of fish, which by implication declares the fullness of the catch, representative of the church.[60] Unfortunately, not only has Jerome's appropriation of zoological information been proven inaccurate,[61] but such a suggestion is also inaccurate according to contemporary standards of natural science.

3. *Biblical Symbolism*. This interpretation moves from the natural world to the textually mediated world of the Bible and argues that the number employs an already established symbolic number from Scripture. Guilding suggests that the number is an allusion to the 153,300 workers assigned to building Solomon's temple recorded in 1 Kings 5:15 – 16.[62] While the image fits nicely with the building of the church, the suggestion is not clear from 1 Kings 5, for the reader would have to do their own calculation. A more thematic connection is suggested by Brooke who uses the Dead Sea Scrolls, which calculates that the flood in Genesis occurred for a total of 153 days (from its start to the grounding on the mountain).[63] Again, while this allows for Brooke to suggest that the Gospel employs Jewish exegetical traditions to connect the pericope to the Noah narrative and even further to the baptism typology in the Petrine tradition (1 Pet 3:20 – 21), one wonders if his solution has become more complicated than the original problem.

mann, WUNT 200 (Tübingen: Mohr Siebeck, 2006), 369 – 402 (383 – 94).

57. Bernard, *John*, 2:699 – 700.

58. Timothy J. Wiarda, "John 21.1 – 23: Narrative Unity and Its Implications," *JSNT* 46 (1992): 53 – 71 (60, 67).

59. See Brown, *John*, 2:1076.

60. See J.-P. Migne, ed., *Patrologia Latina*, 25:474c.

61. See Robert M. Grant, " 'One Hundred Fifty-Three Large Fish' (John 21:11)," *HTR* 42 (1949): 273 – 75.

62. Aileen Guilding, *The Fourth Gospel and Jewish Worship* (Oxford: Clarendon, 1960), 226 – 27.

63. George J. Brooke, "4Q252 and the 153 Fish of John 21:11," in *Antikes Judentum und Frühes Christentum: Festschrift für Hartmut Stegemann zum 65. Geburtstag*, ed. Bernd Kollmann, Wolfgand Reinbold, and Annette Steudel, BZNW 97 (Berlin: de Gruyter, 1999), 253 – 65.

4. *Mathematical Symbolism.* This interpretation suggests the solution is to be found in a mathematical approach that depicts or displays a theological truth. Origen is said to have been the first to suggest that the number represents the Trinity, for it can be divided into three parts of which to themselves are "three:" $153 = (50 \times 3) + 3$.[64] Augustine seems to do something similar and adds a further dimension that 153 is the sum of the natural numbers from 1 to 17 (a triangular number), which he saw as symbolizing the Ten Commandments plus the seven gifts of the Holy Spirit.[65] While Origen helpfully shows the agency of the Trinitarian God by the number, and Augustine shows how all "who are sharers in such grace are symbolized by this number."[66] What they do not show is the necessity of such calculations from the specifics of the narrative context.

5. *Gematria.* This interpretation is the most technical option and suggests that the solution is to be found in the numerical values assigned to letters in Greek (and sometimes Hebrew). If every letter represents a number, then the value of a word's constituent letters added together equals a determinable number. This is hardly unique in Scripture (e.g., the number 666 in Rev 13:18). Because of the variety of possible options, an equally wide range of interpretations has been offered. One of the most recent and carefully defined is by Bauckham, who relies on what he thinks is the neglected work of Menken[67] to reintroduce the use of numerical composition in biblical and related literature.[68] Bauckham makes a number of arguments using gematria that make fascinating connections within John, to the rest of Scripture, and even between chapters 20 and 21. For example, Bauckham explains how the key words of 20:30 – 31 are "sign," "believe," "Christ," and "life," with each occurring for the last time in those verses. If the occurrences of each of the words are counted, the result is as follows: "sign" (17x), "believe" (98x), "Christ" (19x), and "life" (36x). It is not a coincidence, according to Bauckham, that the sum of the last three of these numbers is 153, and that 17, the number of the first (sign), is its triangular number and therefore declaring in the opening of the Gospel's epilogue a numerical statement that projects the "word statistics" of the theological message of the entire Gospel.[69] While the vast majority of contemporary readers of the Gospel will perceive none of the instances of numerical composition, the story is still fully intelligible. For Bauckham, the numerical literary techniques simply "add dimensions of meaning to the text

64. J. M. Ross, "One Hundred and Fifty-Three Fishes," *ExpTim* 100 (1989): 375.

65. Augustine, *John*, 122.6 – 9.441 – 43.

66. Ibid., 122.8.443.

67. M. J. J. Menken, *Numerical Literary Techniques in John: The Fourth Evangelist's Use of Numbers of Words and Syllables*, NovTSup 55 (Leiden: Brill, 1985).

68. Richard Bauckham, "The 153 Fish and the Unity of the Fourth Gospel," 283 – 84.

69. Ibid., 280 – 81.

for those who discern them, but they are not required for understanding the message of the Gospel and they do not impede 'ordinary' readers who are not likely to discern them."[70] While nothing regarding gematria feels ordinary to the modern reader, its use in the ancient world and the functionality of word statistics is worth noting.

The symbolism of the 153 fish is "as elusive as it is evident."[71] The lack of a qualification, unlike the one supplied in v. 8 ("about" [ὡς]), strongly suggests an intentional specificity, if only "on the principle that where there is smoke there is fire."[72] Yet our interpretation must be directed by an equally important principle: any intended symbolism must match the subject matter of the context. The complexity of interpretive possibilities suggested for this number forces this interpreter to remain cautious regarding its specific intention. The symbolic (genre) conventions of the epilogue, along with the other symbols and images more clearly established in the pericope, provide an interpretive freedom, bounded by the context, for the application of one or more exegetically derived "impressions" regarding the number's meaning. In the least the number symbolizes further what the pericope as a whole is intending to express: the magnitude of the Christian church and the comprehensive nature of its mission and the detailed and particular power and authority of God that facilitates the church's mission.[73] While this interpreter is comfortable to allow the Gospel to speak with a higher or more complex level of numerical-theological intentionality (on method and its relation to the doctrine of Scripture, see Introduction), not all interpreters

will function under the same doctrinal-exegetical freedom.

21:12 Jesus said to them, "Come and eat a meal." Not one of the disciples dared to question him, "Who are you?" They knew it was the Lord (λέγει αὐτοῖς ὁ Ἰησοῦς, Δεῦτε ἀριστήσατε. οὐδεὶς δὲ ἐτόλμα τῶν μαθητῶν ἐξετάσαι αὐτόν, Σὺ τίς εἶ; εἰδότες ὅτι ὁ κύριός ἐστιν). The fish that Peter "dragged" onto the shore are never mentioned again. Jesus has always been the provider of the food, even if the disciples (the church) have a role to play. Jesus invites his disciples to the meal that he prepared for them. Jesus's invitation to his disciples to "come and eat," which are apparently the last words Jesus speaks to the disciples as a group in the Gospel, match perfectly the first words spoken by Jesus as an invitation to the disciples, "Come and see" (1:39).[74] As the narrator explains, however, the disciples say nothing as they take it all in. The entire focus of the scene is the mysterious and overwhelming nature of Christ's presence and the disciples together with him.[75]

The narrator offers a fascinating and interpretive insight into the disciples. Although Jesus was recognized by the disciples in v. 7, the narrator explains here that the disciples wanted but were unwilling to ask about his identity — they knew his

---

70. Ibid., 283 – 84.

71. Culpepper, "Designs for the Church in the Imagery of John 21:1 – 14," 401.

72. Brown, *John*, 2:1075.

73. According to Aquinas, part of the number's meaning is its mystery (*John*, 3:291).

74. Cf. Raymond E. Brown, "The Resurrection in John 21 — Missionary and Pastoral Directives for the Church," *Wor* 64 (1990): 433 – 45.

75. Ridderbos, *John*, 664.

identity, that he was the Lord. The verb translated as "to question" (ἐξετάσαι) is often used of a persons who "try to find out by use of careful methods … personal scrutiny."[76] They wanted to do more than ask a surface-level question; they wanted to cross-examine Jesus and ask about "the deep things of God" (1 Cor 2:10). But they remained silent (cf. comment on 16:23: "In that day you will not ask me anything"). The only reason given by the narrator is that in spite of their legitimate question, they already "knew" (εἰδότες) the answer, for they already knew "the Lord" (an important title in this Gospel; cf. 20:2, 28) and that his person was the subject matter of all their questions.

Why did they not speak their questions? The force of the verb, which refers to a cross-examination, is stark in its similarity to the kind of examination Thomas wanted to perform on Jesus in 20:25.[77] Is it possible that the disciples learned from Thomas and now respond rightly to their Lord? The narrative suggests that they have gained a knowledge that "although it might want further assurance, inspires so much awe that it does not dare require that confirmation."[78] Even though they have not seen, they believe and therefore decide to receive in themselves the blessing promised by Christ (20:29). No further "signs" were needed, just the continuous belief to "see." Their confession, unlike Thomas's ("the Lord"; cf. 20:28), is silent — in the form of a prayer only the Lord could hear.

21:13 Then Jesus came and took the bread and gave it to them, and also the fish (ἔρχεται Ἰησοῦς καὶ λαμβάνει τὸν ἄρτον καὶ δίδωσιν αὐτοῖς, καὶ τὸ ὀψάριον ὁμοίως). The pericope ends with a meal. The ministry of Jesus begins (2:1–11) and ends with a celebratory meal. This meal is "Jesus's cli-

mactic means of self-revelation in this life."[79] The Gospel has made certain that the true meal Jesus provides is his body and blood, but this has been proclaimed in this Gospel by real food and drink — a real meal. Just as Jesus more fully declared his person and work in the context of such a meal (cf. 6:22–71), so here the disciples are again confronted by Jesus in the context of a meal. The reader cannot avoid interpreting this meal in relation to the feeding of the large crowd and the bread of life dialogue in chapter 6 and therefore as a depiction of the Lord's Supper or Eucharist (see comments before 6:22). The symbolic nature of the epilogue suggests that "something more" is again being told to the readers.

This meal with the resurrected Lord therefore is the meal set apart by the Lord for his disciples and thereafter for the church. Just as the disciples share in the presence of Christ at this meal, so also does the church participate together in Christ at their "Supper of the Lord." It is important to note that Jesus is not described as eating at this meal but serving. This is *his* meal, but it is *from* him and not *for* him.[80] The epilogue helps the reader grasp the cosmological reality now made accessible through Christ and in and by the Spirit. When the church gathers together, the Lord is present with them (see 14:18–20), serving them by his very own person and work.

21:14 This is now the third time Jesus appeared to his disciples after he was raised from the dead (τοῦτο ἤδη τρίτον ἐφανερώθη Ἰησοῦς τοῖς μαθηταῖς ἐγερθεὶς ἐκ νεκρῶν). The pericope concludes the way it started (see v. 1), forming an *inclusio* with what is now the third use of the verb "appeared" (ἐφανερώθη), matching what is the third physical

---

76. BDAG 349.
77. Hartman, "Text-Centered Exegesis of John 21," 41.
78. Ibid.
79. Bruner, *John*, 1215.

80. Bultmann, *John*, 710. This pericope works with the motif of "hospitality" that has already been established in the Gospel (see comments before 4:1).

appearance to his disciples. The numerical indication "the third time" (τοῦτο ἤδη τρίτον) suggests "that there is full certainty as to the fact of the resurrection."[81] But as this pericope has made clear, this appearance primarily intends to establish the continuation of Jesus's presence and how the Lord is revealed and present with his disciples, the church. The era of the new creation has been inaugurated, beginning the moment Jesus "was raised from the dead."

Theology in Application

The story of the life and ministry of Jesus, which the Gospel proper explained (chs. 1 – 20), transitions in the epilogue to the life and ministry of the church (ch. 21). Just as the epilogue serves to conclude the story told by the Gospel proper, it also introduces the continuation of the same story lived by the disciples. Serving as a parallel to the introduction provided by the prologue, the epilogue guides the reader in their newly established relationship with God and his mission. In this pericope, the narrative explains to the reader the nature of the continuation of the presence of Jesus with his disciples and guides them to understand and to be faithful to their identity and calling in the ongoing mission of God.

The Ministry of an Epilogue (and a Gospel)

By concluding with an epilogue, the Gospel expresses further its interest in the reader. As much as the Gospel of John is about the good news established in the life and ministry of Jesus Christ, it is also intent on establishing the reader into the life of Jesus by means of his ministry. The generic conventions of an epilogue make clear that the subject matter of the Gospel is not merely the past but also the present. The readers are also part of the Gospel's message, for by participating by faith in its witness, they substantiate its very purpose and existence. This story of things past is intended to communicate with things present. As much as the Gospel of John is not the book of Acts, its presentation is so inclusive and sensitive to the reader, especially by means of the epilogue, that it shares many similarities. The Gospel reflects the gospel not only with its words but also with its actions (perlocutionary intentions). In a manner similar to Jesus's incarnational ministry to the world, the narrative of the Gospel enters into the world of the reader, giving the spectacles needed to grasp not only the sin-filled reality of the human condition but also the grace-filled extension of God through the person and work of Christ to that same humanity. The message of the Fourth Gospel therefore is as relevant and contemporary as the person who reads it, because its subject matter is "the living Father" (6:57) and his Son, Jesus Christ — who is the same yesterday, today, and forever (Heb 13:8).

---

81. G. Delling, "τρεῖς, τρίς, τρίτος," *TDNT* 8:222.

The Life and Ministry of the Church

The theme of this pericope is the continuation of the presence of Jesus and the mission of God in the life and ministry of the disciples and thereafter the church. Jesus had already commissioned the disciples by word and Spirit to continue by participation in the mission of God (20:19 – 23); in this pericope, the nature of that participation is explicated. Several things are explained. First, the mission of the church can be depicted by the metaphor of fishing, the "catching of people" (see v. 3). The church is the ministerial extension of God in the world, seeking people to "come and see" Christ. In a real sense, by the Spirit the church is called to "tabernacle" as the body of Christ in the world. Second, the church's work is ultimately a work of God. It cannot (and will not) succeed without his direction, empowerment, and presence. The mission of the church is a subset of the mission of God. Third, the life of the church is participation in the presence of Christ, which the pericope places symbolically in the gathering of the disciples and their sacred meal with Christ, that is, by means of the divinely instituted manifestation of God in the church. The Gospel has made clear that the arrival of Jesus means that God is truly "dwelling" among his people, first by the incarnation of the Son and now by the incarnational presence of the Spirit. Just as God has intimately made himself manifest to and in his church, the church is called to make God manifest through its corporate life and ministry.

The True Fisherman

In this pericope the true catcher of fish was Jesus, not the disciples; the narrative makes this very clear. Yet Jesus makes an important statement when he commands the disciples to bring to him "the fish that you caught just now" (v. 10). Certainly the disciples cannot claim much responsibility for this catch of fish, for Jesus was the one primarily responsible. Even more, Jesus had no apparent need for them, for he already had a fish of his own cooking on the fire (v. 9). The narrative does not intend to present a contradiction but the paradoxical reality of life in God and by his Spirit. Through the narrative, the reader is instructed regarding the life lived by the knowledge of Christ and the ministry done by "the power of his resurrection" and even "participation" in the fullness of his person and work (Phil 3:10).

In this way, the lesson of the narrative is clear. While the church is to be faithful in its participation in the mission and work of God, it also knows full well that its success is entirely dependent upon God. Calvin offers the correct theological explanation to this paradox: "Thus we call it our bread, and yet, by asking that it may be given to us, we confess that it comes from God's blessing."[82] If our life in him finds its source and success in God, so also must our life for him, the church's ministry: "For

82. Calvin, *John 11 – 21*, 217.

from him and through him and for him are all things. To him be the glory forever!" (Rom 11:36).

Believing without Seeing: The Role of Doubt and Faith

This pericope offers a final portrait of the disciples that brings together several major themes in the Gospel's message. Although the disciples recognize Jesus in v. 7, the narrator reveals that they wanted to know more; they wanted to cross-examine him and have him answer the plethora of questions and concerns they still had. Yet they said nothing! The narrator simply says they already "knew" who he was, and in some way that was enough. The disciples were able to rest securely in the person and work of Jesus even though there were other things they still did not know. This is not to minimize their fears and doubts but to make them subservient to their faith — even more, to the object of their faith, Jesus Christ. As we said above (v. 12), the disciples decided to receive in themselves the blessing promised by Christ through the beatitude he shared with Thomas (20:29). They were willing to believe without fully "seeing," for seeing Christ was more than satisfactory.

The combination of doubt and faith presented by this verse is intended to be both prescriptive and encouraging. The contemporary Christian is no different than the disciples. Living the Christian life is to live in a constant combination of belief and doubt, of worshipping and wondering. This combination will only be finally overcome when the Lord appears to us at his return, when all questions and doubts are fully removed by the fullness of his presence.[83] Until then, however, our faith is sustained by the trustworthiness of its object, Jesus Christ, whom we cannot fully know or see, yet in whom we believe. The testimony of the Gospel serves to facilitate this faith, as does what the Reformers called the internal testimony of the Spirit (*testimonium internum Spiritus Sancti*). By this we see and know, even if not yet fully. It is ultimately the objectivity of Christ that silences the subjectivity of everything else.

---

83. Bruner, *John*, 1215.

48

John 21:15 – 25

Literary Context

The Gospel concludes with an epilogue that serves to explain the incorporation of the children of God into the mission of God and their specific participation in the life and ministry of Jesus. The epilogue begins with the mission of the church (21:1 – 14) and concludes in this pericope with the ministers of the church and, more specifically, the personal nature of their ministries with a particular focus on Peter and the Beloved Disciple. By focusing on these two specific disciples and the particularity of their callings, the Gospel explains how the message communicated by the narrative is manifested in an overtly personal manner, with the ministry of the Beloved Disciple being directly related to the production of the Gospel itself. In this pericope, the second of two in the epilogue, the reader is presented with the conclusion to the developing testimonies of two disciples of Jesus, Peter and the Beloved Disciple, in order to facilitate their understanding and application of believing and living the message of the Gospel.

X. Epilogue (21:1 – 25)
   A. The Mission of the Church: Jesus and the Fishermen (21:1 – 14)
➡   **B. The Ministers of the Church: Peter's Reinstatement and the Beloved Disciple's Testimony (21:15 – 25)**

Main Idea

The Christian life is directed by a love for Christ and displayed by an obedient following of Christ. A true disciple of Jesus Christ believes in his person and work, participates in his life, and strives for his glory.

Translation

John 21:15–25

15a	Progression of Action	Then
b	Setting	when they had finished eating,
c	1st Interlocution	**Jesus said to Simon Peter,**
d	Address	*"Simon,*
e	Identification	*son of John,*
f	Question #1	*do you love me*
g	Comparison	*more than these?"*
h	Response	**He said to him,**
i	Affirmation	*"Yes,*
j	Address	*Lord,*
k	Emphasis	*you know that I love you."*
l	Response	**[Jesus] said to him,**
m	Command	*"Feed my lambs."*
16a	2nd Interlocution	**He said to him again**
b		a second time,
c		*"Simon,*
d		*son of John,*
e	Question #2	*do you love me?"*
f	Repeated Response	**He said to him,**
g		*"Yes,*
h		*Lord,*
i		*you know that I love you."*
j	Response	**[Jesus] said to him,**
k	Repeated Command	*"Shepherd my sheep."*
17a	3rd Interlocution	**He said to him**
b		a third time,
c		*"Simon,*
d		*son of John,*
e	Question #3	*do you love me?"*
f	Reaction	**Peter became sorrowful**
g	Basis	because he said [this] to him a third time,
h		*"Do you love me?"*
i	Emphatic, Repeated Response	**He said to him,**
j		*"Lord,*
k		*you know all things;*
l		*you know that I love you."*
m	Response	**[Jesus] said to him,**
n	Repeated Command	*"Feed my sheep.*

Continued on next page.

Continued from previous page.

18a	Amen Formula	*Truly, truly I say to you,*
	(Prophetic Illustration)	
b	Circumstance	*when you were younger*
c	Sequence of Action #1	*you dressed yourself and*
d	Sequence of Action #2	*walked where you wanted; but*
	(Contrast)	
e	Circumstance	*when you grow old*
f	Sequence of Action #1	*you will stretch out your hands and*
g	Sequence of Action #2	*others will dress you and*
h	Sequence of Action #3	*lead you*
i	Destination	*where you do not want to go."*
19a		**He said this**
b	Purpose	in order to indicate what kind of death he would glorify God.
c		And
d	Progression of Action	after he said this
e		**he said to him,**
f	Command	*"Follow me!"*
20a	Progression of Action	After turning
b	Character Reentrance	**Peter saw the disciple**
c	Series of Descriptors	whom Jesus loved
d		following them
e		(the one who also reclined on his chest at the dinner and he said,
f		*"Lord,*
g		*who is the one who betrays you?")*
21a		After Peter saw him
b	Action	**he said to Jesus,**
c	Address	*"Lord,*
d	Question	*what about him?"*
22a	Response	**Jesus said to him,**
b	Condition	*"If I want him to remain*
c	Duration	*until I come,*
d	Interrogative Rebuke	*what is that to you?*
e	Repeated Command	*You follow me!"*
23a	Result	**This saying went out among the brothers and sisters**
b	Description of "saying"	that that disciple would not die.
c	Contrast	But **Jesus did not say to him that he would not die;**
d	Contrary Statement	rather,
e		*"If I want him to remain*
f		*until I come,*
g		*what is that to you?"*
24a	Character Identification	**This is the disciple**
b	Description	who testifies concerning these things and
c	Description	who wrote these things,
d	Assertion of Certainty	and **we know that his testimony is true.**

25a	Conclusion of Gospel	And **there are also many other things**
b	Description	which Jesus did,
c	Description:	which …
d	Condition	if each one were written down,
e	Inference	… I suppose not even the world itself ↵ could contain the books
f	Description	that would be written.

Structure and Literary Form

The structure of this pericope is different than the basic story form (see Introduction). This pericope is a combination of a basic story form and a dialogue, which the Gospel commonly combines in its narrative (see comments before 13:1). The narrative sets the context for the entire epilogue in the first pericope (21:1 – 14), with the disciples gathered for a sacred meal (cf. 21:13) around a charcoal fire (21:9; cf. 18:18) that creates a scene that facilitates reconciliation both within the group (for Peter especially) as well as to the world outside. Thus, this story-dialogue is carefully integrated with the context and movement of the previous pericope. In this sense then, the interaction of this pericope is a continuation of what precedes it; the epilogue functions as a unit.

Although this dialogue involves three people, Jesus, Peter, and the Beloved Disciple, the third person is only involved by the others near the end, though when he finally speaks it is neither to Jesus nor to Peter but to the reader. This dialogue is unique in that it is a symbol-laden dialogue with few words, befitting the symbolic nature of an epilogue (see comments before 21:1). In vv. 15 – 19, Jesus initiates a symbol-laden and pithy dialogue with Peter that brings resolution to his denial of Jesus in chapter 18. In vv. 20 – 23, Peter's question provides Jesus with an opportunity to bring resolution to the implicit tension between Peter and the Beloved Disciple. Finally, in vv. 24 – 25 the Beloved Disciple reveals that he is the author of the Gospel and provides information regarding the Gospel's origin.

Exegetical Outline

➡ **B. The Ministers of the Church: Peter's Reinstatement and the Beloved Disciple's Testimony (21:15 – 25)**

    1. The Love and Sheep of Jesus (vv. 15 – 19)

    2. "You Follow Me!" (vv. 20 – 23)

    3. The Origin of the Gospel (vv. 24 – 25)

Explanation of the Text

The argument of this commentary is that chapter 21 is the intended and original conclusion to the Gospel and a significant part of its coherent structure and purpose (see comments before 21:1). While this pericope is the second of a two-part epilogue, its final two verses (vv. 24 – 25) are also the second of a two-stage conclusion (see comments before 20:24). Just as the first stage of the conclusion (20:30 – 31) raised several issues regarding the *purpose* of the Gospel, the second stage of the conclusion (vv. 24 – 25) raises several issues regarding the *origin* of the Gospel, primarily in relation to the identity of the Beloved Disciple (for a summary, see comments on 13:23) who reveals himself to be personally involved in the origin of the Gospel and, by extension and invitation, the belief of the reader.

21:15 Then when they had finished eating, Jesus said to Simon Peter, "Simon, son of John, do you love me more than these?" He said to him, "Yes, Lord, you know that I love you." [Jesus] said to him, "Feed my lambs" (Ὅτε οὖν ἠρίστησαν λέγει τῷ Σίμωνι Πέτρῳ ὁ Ἰησοῦς, Σίμων Ἰωάννου, ἀγαπᾷς με πλέον τούτων; λέγει αὐτῷ, Ναί, κύριε, σὺ οἶδας ὅτι φιλῶ σε. λέγει αὐτῷ, Βόσκε τὰ ἀρνία μου). The scene of this periocope has not changed from the previous one (21:1 – 14). On the shore of the Sea of Tiberias, Jesus had prepared a symbol-laden meal for his disciples with fish, bread, and a charcoal fire. When the meal ended, Jesus addressed Peter with a question about the object of his love. In light of v. 20, where Peter "turns" and sees the Beloved Disciple "following," it is not a stretch to suggest that "we are probably to think of Peter walking down the beach with Jesus," with the Beloved Dis-

ciple following not far behind and the rest of the disciples present implicitly.[1]

The last time Peter was asked a question about Jesus in the presence of a charcoal fire, he denied Jesus three times (see 18:18). Thus it is fitting that around this charcoal fire Peter is again asked a question about Jesus three times. This time, however, the questions are in an entirely different context and therefore have an entirely different agenda. For this time the questions come not from accusers but from the one who was himself the foremost accused, and this time the questions come not before but after the death and resurrection of Jesus. That is, the questions Jesus asks do not seek to take life but to restore it, for the person asking the question has already paid the price with his own life.

Even if this was a private moment between Jesus and Peter, Jesus's formal address includes Peter's father's (family) name, "Simon, son of John" (Σίμων Ἰωάννου), matching Jesus's first address of Peter at the beginning of the narrative (see comments on 1:42). It gives this conversation "an air of solemnity."[2] It might even signal that in what follows the nature of their relationship needs to be reestablished.[3] This engagement between Jesus and Peter has traditionally (and rightly) been understood to be the reinstatement of Peter.[4] The reader is being guided to understand that the discipleship and ministry of Peter — and the church thereafter — is facilitated not ultimately by courage (ch. 18) or competence (ch. 21), but by Christ.

This section of the pericope is directed by the significant question Jesus asks Peter: "Do you love me more than these?" (ἀγαπᾷς με πλέον τούτων;). Love is a — if not *the* — major motif in the Gos-

---

1. Carson, *John*, 675.
2. Morris, *John*, 767.
3. Lincoln, *John*, 517. Cf. Brown, *John*, 2:1102.

4. This is clearly the dominant interpretation in the history of the church. Cf. Bruner, *John*, 1224 – 26. For a discussion of other suggestions, see Beasley-Murray, *John*, 404 – 5.

pel. The love of God for the world (3:16) finds reception in the new commandment given to the church for mutual love (e.g., 13:34 – 35), which has as its source the mutual love between the Trinitarian God, most visible between the Father and the Son (e.g., 3:35; 14:31).[5] Thus, the question brings the message of love presented by the Gospel full circle: Will the love of God that was first given to the world be appropriately returned to him? And just as the love of God for the world was most clearly expressed by the death of Jesus on the cross, will the love of a disciple for God be similarly expressed?

Jesus focuses the question by narrowing the comparison: "Do you love me *more than these*?" But what or who is the exact referent? The two most common options are the fishing (a way of life) or the disciples. The latter makes the most sense, but it is still not exactly clear. Does it mean "more than these disciples love me" or "more than you love these disciples"? Again the latter makes more sense, since the point of the comparison is the object of Peter's love. The former option is quite possible and preferred by several interpreters, especially because the disciples are repeatedly urged to love one another (13:34 – 35; 15:12, 17).[6] But just as Christ made the care for the poor secondary to or a subset of devotion (i.e., love) to him (see comments on 12:7), so here Jesus makes love for others, even for brothers and sisters in Christ, a subset of a love for Christ. In this way, then, just as the threefold denial of Peter revealed whom he loved (or feared) more, so befitting the reinstatement Jesus asks Peter again to compare his love for Jesus with his love for others. Even still, the ambiguous nature of the comparison serves to establish the ambiguous comparison between the synonymous words to follow (i.e., "love" and "sheep").

Peter answers Jesus's question with a strong and emphatic affirmation: "Yes, Lord, you know that I love you" (Ναί, κύριε, σὺ οἶδας ὅτι φιλῶ σε). Peter's answer appeals to Jesus's knowledge of him. Such an answer does not intend to rebuke Jesus (i.e., "Why ask me? You don't know me, do you?") but to make an appeal grounded upon Jesus and not himself.[7] If his own actions speak with hesitation at best, the Good Shepherd's knowledge of his sheep becomes not only the most secure foundation but also ultimately the (theologically) correct answer (2:24 – 25; cf. Job 16:19). Peter may not be answering the question in regard to its comparison, but he rightly grasps that the point of the question was in regard to his love of Jesus.

The most difficult issue presented by this verse and one of the most well-known in the Gospel is the use of different verbal forms for "love." The Greek word for "love" (ἀγαπᾷς from ἀγαπάω) used by Jesus — *agapaō* — is different than the word for "love" (φιλῶ from φιλέω) used by Peter — *phileō*. In the first two questions Jesus uses *agapaō* and Peter uses *phileō* (vv. 15 – 16), but in the third question Jesus and Peter both use *phileō* (v. 17). Interpreters have long wrestled with the question of whether the alternation of verbs is narratively significant. Contemporary scholarship has almost unanimously concluded that there is no intended difference in meaning by the verbal alternation; it is simply a stylistic preference for using different but synonymous words (rather than repeating the same word).[8] The reason for this is clear: "Attempts to draw a dependable semantic distinction between *agapaō* and *phileō* are doomed to failure whether in

---

5. See Jörg Frey, "Love-Relationships in the Fourth Gospel: Establishing a Semantic Network," in Van Belle, *Repetitions and Variations in the Fourth Gospel*, 171 – 98.

6. See Michaels, *John*, 1042 – 43; Barrett, *John*, 584; Carson, *John*, 676.

7. Ridderbos, *John*, 665.

8. See Moulton, *Grammar*, 3:76 – 77, in a section entitled "Pointless Variety in Style."

Greek literature generally, the Septuagint, the NT, or John's Gospel itself."[9] The strongest example of this is the fact that both verbs are used for the Father's love for the Son (e.g., *agapaō* in 3:35 but *phileō* in 5:20), and certainly God's love is eternal and unchanging.

Yet as the Gospel narrative has revealed in five separate instances, while the Fourth Gospel frequently uses related or overlapping words synonymously across the narrative, when they are used in close proximity (especially in the same verse) there is usually a carefully nuanced distinction or comparison intended between them (see 13:10; 16:16, 23; 20:6, 21).[10] Although this would suggest that a carefully nuanced distinction is intended, the options are not best determined from a reconstruction of the historical event, as in the common suggestion that since *agapaō* denotes a higher (or more divine) kind of love and *phileō* denotes a lower (or more human) kind of love, Peter is unable to claim the higher form of love, (graciously) forcing Jesus to accommodate to Peter. But neither are they to be determined from a purely narrative-critical analysis, as in the more recent suggestion that the use of *agapaō* by Jesus is an intentional allusion to 13:31–38, intending to continue the last conversation between Jesus and Peter.[11]

In each of the previous five instances, however, the meaning is derived directly from the narrative pressures innate to the specific pericope. But can the carefully nuanced distinction or comparison intended between them be determined in this peri-

cope? It was not until the nineteenth century that interpreters pressed the distinction; even the Greek commentators (e.g., John Chrysostom and Cyril of Alexandria) with the rest of the early church were unwilling to press a real distinction between the terms.[12] In the least we can agree with McKay, who argues that although the variation in forms is not pointless, its contextual distinction "is not blatant, but gently significant."[13] Even interpreters who cannot see a distinction in meaning see clearly the distinction in terms, so that all readers can agree that the alternation is a "signal" of sorts to the reader.[14] And this may be precisely the "gently significant" point.

Here at the end of the Gospel, with the message of the love of God in full view, the different terms for love used by Jesus and Peter need not mean anything at all for Jesus and Peter; in fact they might just be stylistic and rhetorically emphatic.[15] For the reader, however, the difference might still be real and meaningful.[16] The fact that Peter uses a different word than Jesus imposes itself upon the reader in a manner that cannot be (psychologically) reconstructed from Jesus or Peter. Without denying that the words are often used as functionally synonymous, the apparent comparative interaction between them in such close quarters stands out to the reader. Whatever the intentions of Peter, who remained consistent with his use of *phileō* in all three answers (vv. 15–17), the fact that Jesus changed from *agapaō* to *phileō* to match Peter in his third question (v. 17) suggests that the disso-

9. David Shepherd, "'Do You Love Me?' A Narrative-Critical reappraisal of ἀγαπάω and φιλέω in John 21:15–17," *JBL* 129 (2010): 777–92 (777–78).

10. See Leon Morris, *Studies in the Fourth Gospel* (Grand Rapids: Eerdmans, 1969), 293–319, in a chapter entitled, "Variation—A Feature of the Johannine Style"; see also Francis T. Gignac, "The Use of Verbal Variety in the Fourth Gospel," in Chennattu and Coloe, *Transcending Boundaries*, 191–200.

11. See Shepherd, "Do You Love Me?"

12. Keener, *John*, 2:1236.

13. K. L. McKay, "Style and Significance in the Language of John 21:15–17," *NovT* 27 (1985): 319–33 (333).

14. Cf. Caleb O. Oladipo, "John 21:15–17," *Int* 51 (1997): 65–66 (66). See also James Barr, "Words for Love in Biblical Greek," in *The Glory of Christ in the New Testament: Studies in Christology in Memory of George Bradford Caird*, ed. L. D. Hurst and N. T. Wright (Oxford: Clarendon Press, 1987), 3–18 (15).

15. See Keener, *John*, 2:1236.

16. Cf. Heil, *Blood and Water*, 161.

nance caused by the first two exchanges is resolved (in some manner) in the third. And befitting the message of the Gospel, it was God (not Peter) who bridged the gap. Even if the reader cannot draw any real meaning from this alternation in words based upon the words themselves, the narrative pressures the reader to desire a resolution to the dissonance caused by the different words and even between Jesus and Peter. The reader is directed by the scene to desire the love that matches the question of Christ.[17] And befitting the purpose of an epilogue (see comments before 21:1), the dissonance is resolved neither by Peter nor Jesus but by the reader, the one for whom the written account of this threefold questioning is ultimately intended. The "interpretive" issue presented to the reader in the final pericope of the Gospel is not truly lexical; it is personal.

Jesus follows Peter's answer to his first question with a command: "Feed my sheep" (Βόσκε τὰ ἀρνία μου). Jesus's response to Peter's answer is not in the form of a correction but a commission. As we discussed above, just as love is not merely descriptive but also prescriptive, so also a love for Christ should be expressed in a fitting manner. Jesus commissions Peter to serve as a shepherd in his absence in view of his imminent departure.[18] If the first pericope in the epilogue (21:1 – 14) concerned the work of God outside the church and in the world, this pericope is concerned with the work of God within the church. The qualification "*my sheep*" (τὰ ἀρνία μου) makes clear that this is the command of the Good Shepherd to an undershepherd, for just as there is "one flock," there is also only "one Shepherd" (10:16).

Interestingly, in a manner similar to how the word "love" alternates in form in vv. 15 – 17, so do the following two other terms: "*Feed my lambs*" (Βόσκε τὰ ἀρνία μου; v. 15);[19] "*shepherd my sheep*" (Ποίμαινε τὰ πρόβατά μου; v. 16); "*feed my sheep*" (Βόσκε τὰ πρόβατά μουν; v. 17). As before, even though the terms are generally synonymous, when they are used in close proximity there is usually a carefully nuanced distinction or comparison intended between them. In the context of this commission, the alternation reflects the variety of sheep and the range of shepherding required. The distinction in meaning is more obvious in the verbs but reflects the same intention. As the undershepherd, Peter is to care for the Shepherd's sheep as the Lord cares for them, feeding them and performing all the duties of a shepherd in a manner entirely distinct from the "hired worker" in 10:12 – 13. This command of Jesus is ultimately the fulfillment not only of the expectation that Peter love him (vv. 15 – 17) but also of the new commandment given to the church for mutual love (13:34 – 35), which fittingly occurred earlier in the Gospel just before Jesus announced the betrayal of Peter (13:38).

21:16 He said to him again a second time, "Simon, son of John, do you love me?" He said to him, "Yes, Lord, you know that I love you." [Jesus] said to him, "Shepherd my sheep" (λέγει αὐτῷ πάλιν δεύτερον, Σίμων Ἰωάννου, ἀγαπᾷς με; λέγει αὐτῷ, Ναί, κύριε, σὺ οἶδας ὅτι φιλῶ σε. λέγει αὐτῷ, Ποίμαινε τὰ πρόβατά μου). Without waiting for Peter to respond to the commission, Jesus repeats "again a second time" (πάλιν δεύτερον) the question with which he began. The second exchange between Jesus and Peter almost directly

---

17. Hoskyns gets near the point: "The author varies his terms in order to express the perfection of the knowledge of Christ and of the Love and devotion which He demands" (*Fourth Gospel*, 558).

18. Michaels, *John*, 1044.

19. We translated the word τὰ ἀρνία as "lambs" and not "sheep" in v. 15 to show the occurrence of a different Greek word, but no substantial difference can be determined by its use, for according to BDAG, the word can refer to "a sheep of any age" (133).

parallels the first, with the continuation of the word variations discussed above. The comparison of the first question ("more than these") is not repeated; the focus is now entirely on love for Jesus in both its descriptive (i.e., "Do you love me?") and prescriptive (i.e., "Shepherd my sheep") forms. By numbering this next question of Jesus as "second" (δεύτερον), as well as the "third" one to follow (v. 17), the narrator highlights the unitary purpose of vv. 15–17 and their parallel to the previous threefold denial by Peter. The repetition thus becomes a cumulative statement of its own; loving Jesus and pastoring the church are interrelated.

21:17 He said to him a third time, "Simon, son of John, do you love me?" Peter became sorrowful because he said [this] to him a third time, "Do you love me?" He said to him, "Lord, you know all things; you know that I love you." [Jesus] said to him, "Feed my sheep" (λέγει αὐτῷ τὸ τρίτον, Σίμων Ἰωάννου, φιλεῖς με; ἐλυπήθη ὁ Πέτρος ὅτι εἶπεν αὐτῷ τὸ τρίτον, Φιλεῖς με; καὶ λέγει αὐτῷ, Κύριε, πάντα σὺ οἶδας, σὺ γινώσκεις ὅτι φιλῶ σε. λέγει αὐτῷ, Βόσκε τὰ πρόβατά μου). The "third" (τὸ τρίτον) question and commission concludes the threefold exchange in a manner that again nearly parallels the first two. There are a couple noticeable differences. First, the absence of "yes" (Ναί), which was present in both v. 15 and v. 16, makes Peter's answer more forceful.[20] Second, the narrator actually provides Peter's internal response to this final question of Jesus. Peter "became sorrowful" (ἐλυπήθη), a verb likely functioning as an ingressive aorist, which stresses "the beginning of an action or the entrance into a state."[21] The word can denote emotional distress, offence, irritation, insult, or — as we have translated it here — sadness, sorrow, and grief (cf. 16:20).[22] The narrator's com-

ment suggests that Peter did not understand the intentions of Christ. Even without fully understanding Jesus's purposes, Peter understood his person so that what Peter said to Christ during his public ministry at a moment of confusion he similarly speaks now: "Lord, to whom shall we go? You have the words of eternal life" (6:68).

21:18 "Truly, truly I say to you, when you were younger you dressed yourself and walked where you wanted; but when you grow old you will stretch out your hands and others will dress you and lead you where you do not want to go" (ἀμὴν ἀμὴν λέγω σοι, ὅτε ἦς νεώτερος, ἐζώννυες σεαυτὸν καὶ περιεπάτεις ὅπου ἤθελες· ὅταν δὲ γηράσῃς, ἐκτενεῖς τὰς χεῖράς σου, καὶ ἄλλος σε ζώσει καὶ οἴσει ὅπου οὐ θέλεις). After the threefold exchange, Jesus offers an explanatory statement that begins with an authoritative preface, formalizing the remarks to follow (see comments on 1:51). Jesus presents Peter with a prophecy in the form of a comparative "illustration" (i.e., a symbolic saying), not uncommon in the Gospel (see comments on 10:6), in which a "younger" (νεώτερος)[23] Peter has the freedom to move and live freely but an "old" (γηράσῃς) Peter will lose his ability to move and live freely. More specifically, Jesus explains to Peter, "You will stretch out your hands" (ἐκτενεῖς τὰς χεῖράς σου), which was understood in the ancient world to refer to crucifixion.[24] The given order of the events need not be chronological, for the saying is an "illustration" and the manner of death is likely thrown forward for emphasis.

21:19 He said this in order to indicate what kind of death he would glorify God. And after he said this he said to him, "Follow me!" (τοῦτο δὲ εἶπεν σημαίνων ποίῳ θανάτῳ δοξάσει τὸν θεόν. καὶ τοῦτο

20. See Michaels, *John*, 1046.
21. Wallace, *Greek Grammar*, 558.
22. BDAG 604.
23. This form need have no comparative force and could simply be translated as "young."
24. Haenchen, *John*, 2:226–27.

εἰπὼν λέγει αὐτῷ, Ἀκολούθει μοι). Jesus explains *what* will happen to Peter, the narrator explains *why* to the reader. The narrator confirms that Jesus was speaking prophetically about Peter. Evidence from the tradition of the early church agrees, reporting that Peter died by crucifixion (Tertullian, *Scorp.* 15) and probably upside down (Eusebius, *Hist. eccl.* 3.1). The narrator also explains that by his martyrdom Peter "would glorify God" (δοξάσει τὸν θεόν). Although this is a prophecy for Peter alone, certainly the glorification of God is required of all disciples.

Jesus concludes this illustration in the same manner as he did the exchanges in vv. 15 – 17, with a command: "Follow me!" (Ἀκολούθει μοι). In this way, Jesus ends his ministry with the same command with which it began (1:43). Coming at the end of the Gospel and directly after the prophecy of Peter's violent end, this command is made more potent and necessary. Moreover, similar to the command "feed/shepherd my sheep" in vv. 15 – 17, this command becomes a second commission. Just as Peter's ministry is to look similar to the ministry of Christ, Peter's life is also expected to look like the life of Christ, a life that ended with a sacrificial death. While Peter's ministry is not a replacement for the life and ministry of Jesus, it is a subset of his life and ministry. The link to the denial of Jesus is now made clear. Peter denied Jesus three times in chapter 18, but this comes after the exchange in 13:36 – 38, where Jesus not only predicted Peter's denial but also hinted at the similarity of their deaths. As Jesus prophesies again here, Peter will follow Jesus in a similarly sacrificial manner.[25] Jesus's prophecy is only partially about "the end of Peter's life" and primarily about the nature of his life in Christ. In this way the first section of the pericope concludes (vv. 15 – 19), with a final exhor-

tation by Jesus to Peter that extends directly to the reader as well.

21:20   After turning Peter saw the disciple whom Jesus loved following them (the one who also reclined on his chest at the dinner and he said, "Lord, who is the one who betrays you?") (Ἐπιστραφεὶς ὁ Πέτρος βλέπει τὸν μαθητὴν ὃν ἠγάπα ὁ Ἰησοῦς ἀκολουθοῦντα, ὃς καὶ ἀνέπεσεν ἐν τῷ δείπνῳ ἐπὶ τὸ στῆθος αὐτοῦ καὶ εἶπεν, Κύριε, τίς ἐστιν ὁ παραδιδούς σε;). The second section of the pericope (vv. 20 – 23) is connected to what comes before, though the focus on Peter and the participle of motion, "after turning" (Ἐπιστραφεὶς), signals to the reader that a new section is beginning. The language of "turning" has played a significant role in the Gospel both at the beginning and end of Jesus's ministry (see comments on 1:38 and 20:14 – 16). In both of those occurrences, the motion was theologically significant. While this occurrence is less clear, the oddity of the statement suggests that a similar importance is in play. In short, the "turning" of Peter serves to depict for a final time in the Gospel Peter's misunderstanding regarding his calling and the Christian life. Peter had just been commanded, even commissioned, to *follow* Jesus. Why, then, is he not focused solely on him?

The narrative reveals quickly that the issue confronting Peter is that he is comparing himself with another disciple — but not just any disciple. When Peter turned, he saw the Beloved Disciple, whom the narrator explains in great detail to be the one who was reclining intimately on the chest of Jesus at the meal at which he gave the farewell discourse (see comments on 13:23). The scene that the narrator briefly recounts (see 13:24 – 25) brings to the surface again the Gospel's depiction of an implicit competition or tension between Peter and the Beloved Disciple. This is the fourth

---

25. Cf. Augustine, *John*, 123.4.445.

of four comparison-like depictions of Peter and the Beloved Disciple (13:22 – 25; 20:3 – 9; 21:7; 21:20 – 23). In this final comparison, the implicit competition is made explicit and is rebuked by Jesus, giving the reader insight appropriate for an epilogue regarding the faithfulness expected of each disciple of Christ.[26]

21:21 After Peter saw him he said to Jesus, "Lord, what about him?" (τοῦτον οὖν ἰδὼν ὁ Πέτρος λέγει τῷ Ἰησοῦ, Κύριε, οὗτος δὲ τί;). Peter "sees" the Beloved Disciple and brings him up to Jesus, raising a question that implicitly asks about the assignment of the Beloved Disciple. Since Peter just heard prophetically from the Lord about the life he has been called to give back to God, he now wonders what is to become of his fellow disciple. What kind of life-stretching assignment has the Lord assigned to him?[27]

21:22 Jesus said to him, "If I want him to remain until I come, what is that to you? You follow me!" (λέγει αὐτῷ ὁ Ἰησοῦς, Ἐὰν αὐτὸν θέλω μένειν ἕως ἔρχομαι, τί πρὸς σέ; σύ μοι ἀκολούθει). Jesus responds to Peter with a counterquestion that serves as a rebuke. The question is rhetorical and hypothetical, as the narrator explains in v. 23, and functions to make a separation between what Jesus "wants" (θέλω) for Peter and what he wants for the Beloved Disciple. The emphasis here is on Jesus's authority, power, and will.[28] And in his statement Jesus speaks as if he had already departed.[29] Jesus offers a rebuke that challenges Peter's assumption that his life and calling can be compared to that of the Beloved Disciple. Quite simply, Peter is told that the life assigned to the Beloved Disciple is none

of his business (cf. Job 38 – 41).[30] Jesus restates his "follow me" commission with the significant addition of an emphatic pronoun: "*You* follow me!" (σύ μοι ἀκολούθει), which denies Peter the ability to change the subject of "follow."[31] The "you" changes everything, for it demands that discipleship be viewed as "a single-minded following of Jesus."[32]

These are the last words of Jesus in the Gospel of John, and they echo his very first: "What do you seek?" (1:38), "Come and see" (1:39), and "Follow me" (1:43). From start to finish, and forming something akin to an *inclusio*, the Gospel has invited the reader to *follow* Jesus Christ by believing in his person and work and receiving life in his name (cf. 20:30 – 31). Befitting an epilogue, the Gospel concludes by explaining that "following" Jesus is not one-size-fits-all. Using Peter and the Beloved Disciple as "representative characters,"[33] the Gospel declares that the various *lives* assigned to the disciples of Jesus Christ are equally grounded in the one called *the Life* (1:4). As the apostle Paul explains, at the same time "to each one of us grace has been given as Christ apportioned it" there is still "*one*" body, Spirit, faith, Lord, and baptism, and "one God and Father of all who is over all and through all and in all" (Eph 4:4 – 7).

21:23 This saying went out among the brothers and sisters that that disciple would not die. But Jesus did not say to him that he would not die; rather, "If I want him to remain until I come, what is that to you?" (ἐξῆλθεν οὖν οὗτος ὁ λόγος εἰς τοὺς ἀδελφοὺς ὅτι ὁ μαθητὴς ἐκεῖνος οὐκ ἀποθνῄσκει. οὐκ εἶπεν δὲ αὐτῷ ὁ Ἰησοῦς ὅτι οὐκ ἀποθνῄσκει, ἀλλ᾽, Ἐὰν αὐτὸν θέλω μένειν ἕως

---

26. For the first time Peter (not the Beloved Disciple) is the first to see, but this time Jesus (not Peter) is the first to take action.

27. Interestingly, ancient commentators interpret Peter's intentions positively. See Chrysostom, *John*, 88.2.332; Aquinas, *John*, 3:304.

28. Ridderbos, *John*, 668.

29. Michaels, *John*, 1051.

30. Carson, *John*, 681.

31. Michaels, *John*, 1051.

32. Newbigin, *The Light Has Come*, 280.

33. Augustine, *John*, 124.7.451.

ἔρχομαι[, τί πρὸς σέ];). Although v. 22 brings conclusion to the issue Jesus had with Peter, in this verse the narrator himself notes that Jesus's statement to Peter also stirred other disciples in the earliest church to make assumptions about the life of the Beloved Disciple. In one sense, this offers a fitting conclusion to the second section of the pericope (vv. 20 – 23), showing that all disciples must learn to commit themselves to a single-minded following of Jesus. In another sense, however, it transitions the narrative to the Beloved Disciple, who will reveal in v. 24 the assignment given to him by the Lord.

By providing such a detailed summary of Jesus's statement to Peter in v. 22, the narrator, who is about to reveal himself as the Beloved Disciple, wants to make explicit what Jesus was not saying so that he could explain in his own words what Jesus was saying in regard to his ministry. This verse suggests that if Peter's calling involves the ending of life, the Beloved Disciple's calling involves the continuation of life, with each serving a different purpose.[34]

21:24 This is the disciple who testifies concerning these things and who wrote these things, and we know that his testimony is true (Οὗτός ἐστιν ὁ μαθητὴς ὁ μαρτυρῶν περὶ τούτων καὶ γράψας ταῦτα, καὶ οἴδαμεν ὅτι ἀληθὴς αὐτοῦ ἡ μαρτυρία ἐστίν). The third section of the pericope (vv. 24 – 25) concludes not only the epilogue but the Gospel as a whole. As we argued earlier, vv. 24 – 25 are the second of a two-stage conclusion that frames the epilogue; 20:30 – 31 provide the *purpose* of the Gospel and vv. 24 – 25 explain the *origin* of the Gospel (see comments before 20:24). In a manner similar to 20:30 – 31, which were connected with the verses that preceded (20:24 – 29), vv. 24 – 25 are also directly connected to the preceding verses, serving as the answer to Peter's question regarding the Beloved Disciple in v. 21 ("Lord, what about him?"). It is not Jesus, however, but the narrator himself who answers this question and who reveals that he is the one about whom Peter spoke. The narrator *is* the Beloved Disciple. In these verses, the person and the ministry of the Beloved Disciple are now explained, both of which are directly related to the production of the Gospel itself. This verse provides three insights into the identity and function of the Beloved Disciple.

First, *the Beloved Disciple is established as the authoritative witness of the Gospel*: "This is the disciple who testifies concerning these things" (Οὗτός ἐστιν ὁ μαθητὴς ὁ μαρτυρῶν περὶ τούτων). The Beloved Disciple declares himself to be an eyewitness of the things written in this book and therefore to be personally connected to the people and events themselves.[35] Although the character called the "Beloved Disciple" did not explicitly appear until chapter 13, he was almost certainly implicitly (i.e., anonymously) present in 1:40 with Andrew, Peter's brother, as one of the two first disciples of Jesus. The placement of the Beloved Disciple as a witness at both the very beginning and very end of the Gospel creates a technical literary device common in the ancient world called the *inclusio* of eyewitness testimony. This technique not only makes clear that this disciple fulfilled the requirements of apostolic testimony ("from the beginning you have been with me" [15:27]), but it also serves to solidify the witness as participating in the reliable practices of historiography.[36]

---

34. Cf. Bultmann, *John*, 716; Lincoln, *John*, 521.

35. See Vanhoozer, "The Hermeneutics of I-Witness Testimony."

36. Bauckham, *Jesus and the Eyewitnesses*, 127 – 29, 390 – 93.

IN-DEPTH: Peter and the Beloved Disciple

At the end of the Gospel of John, the relationship between Peter and the Beloved Disciple finds resolution. The resolution is grounded in the literary-historiographic practices of eyewitness testimony. For example, the *inclusio* of eyewitness testimony with reference to the Beloved Disciple frames the witness of Peter in order to privilege the witness of the Beloved Disciple, which this Gospel embodies. Just as the Gospel of Mark in a similar manner creates an *inclusio* of eyewitness testimony with reference to Peter to employ a literary device that indicates "precisely this qualification on the part of their eyewitness sources,"[37] so John employs the same device to ground its testimony in the Beloved Disciple, who is depicted through the Gospel as the "ideal witness" and the authority of the Gospel's content[38] and the most important source of the Gospel's historical narrative. This suggests that the "comparison" in this Gospel between Peter and the Beloved Disciple exists even between Gospels. The comparison, however, is not intended to create a competition but to establish a distinction in the roles and functions of these disciples.[39] Implicitly from 1:40 and explicitly beginning in chapter 13, the story this Gospel records of Peter and the Beloved Disciple shows how each became qualified for different kinds of discipleship — Peter for *active service as an undershepherd* and John as *perceptive and authoritative witness and disciple.*

Peter is portrayed as the disciple most eager to follow and serve Jesus (13:6 – 9, 36 – 37; 18:10 – 11, 15). Although Peter misunderstands the nature of following Jesus on numerous occasions before the resurrection, after the resurrection and in this specific pericope Jesus allows Peter to become the first disciple to grasp the full meaning of following him. Peter is ultimately assigned the office of the undershepherd of Jesus's sheep and is called to follow Jesus by giving his own life for the sheep. The Gospel does not portray Peter's misunderstanding or misapplied self-will to denigrate him but to present him typologically as the disciple who through failure and grace is restored to become a pastor of the church. The self-will of Peter is now enabled to be applied to the will of God.

The Beloved Disciple is portrayed as superior to Peter only in that which qualifies him for his particular role as the perceptive witness to Jesus. This role is signified in four key ways throughout the Gospel. (1) He enjoys a special intimacy with Jesus, beginning in 1:35 – 40 with his early acquaintance with Jesus.

---

37. Bauckham, *Jesus and the Eyewitnesses*, 124.

38. See John A. T. Robinson, "'His Witness is True': A Test of the Johannine Claim," in Bammel, *Jesus and the Politics of His Day*, 453 – 76 (454).

39. The following is adapted from Bauckham, *Jesus and the Eyewitnesses*, 395 – 402.

It is formally displayed in 13:23–26 where the intimate title (or epithet), "the one whom Jesus loved," is first used and is climactically established at the cross in 19:26–27 when Jesus entrusts his mother to him.[40] (2) He is present at key points in the story of Jesus, formally at 19:35 as a witness of Christ's death and implicitly in several other significant moments in the Gospel narrative (e.g., 1:35; 18:15–16; 19:31–37; 20:3–10). (3) His appearances in the narrative are marked by observational detail, which suggest that the Beloved Disciple is qualified to give eyewitness reports of the events at which he was present. His observations are not merely unique in their description of the event's details but also interpretively significant for grasping the true meaning of the event. (4) Related to the previous point, he is portrayed as a perceptive witness, as one having spiritual insight into the fuller meaning of the events and their (cosmological) significance (see 20:8). In this way then, the Gospel portrays the Beloved Disciple as qualified to be the ideal witness to Jesus, the account of his life and ministry, and the meaning of his person and work.

Second, *the Beloved Disciple is established as the author of the Gospel*: "This is the disciple ... who wrote these things" (Οὗτός ἐστιν ὁ μαθητὴς γράψας ταῦτα). Although Johannine scholars have often treated authorship as a historical issue, it is more properly a hermeneutical issue. Interpretation of this Gospel has taken the form of a quest for the historical author. "The result: conservative and liberal commentators alike have treated authorship as a matter of apologetics rather than interpretation."[41] But if the origin of the Gospel is grounded in an eyewitness, then it is a testimony that demands that the author be taken seriously. A "witness" demands to be attended to and respected. "Of all literary forms, testimony most vigorously resists an interpreter's reading something into it."[42] It is a generic form that innately requires the reader to "believe." This does not guarantee the testimony is true; it might be a false witness. But the reader can only determine its truthfulness from the inside as one who receives the witness.[43]

Several aspects of the Gospel's "witness" discussed in the first point are also directly related to the Gospel's "author." For example, an "insider" position is assumed by the author, for whom this Gospel is part of his eyewitness testimony, an ancient, historiographic practice (on eyewitness testimony, see Introduction). Other examples include the use of anonymity, the literary device of the *inclusio* of eyewitness testimony, and the representation of the Beloved Disciple as an ideal and authoritative witness. Just as a faithful witness is an author (of a testimony), so a faithful author (of a testimony) is also a witness. Only in this way does the "author" of the Gospel of John become as much a hermeneutical and theological issue as he is a historical one (on the identification of the historical author, see Introduction). To treat the authorship of the Fourth

40. See Hengel, *The Johannine Question*, 78.
41. Vanhoozer, "The Hermeneutics of I-Witness Testimony," 367.
42. Ibid., 376.
43. Ibid., 380.

Gospel as an isolated debate is to compartmentalize inappropriately the message from its messenger.[44] The role of eyewitness testimony in ancient historiography therefore is not primarily based on a relationship to a text (in this case, the Gospel) but to an author, one whose (interpretive) witness explains the text's origin. The Gospel is ultimately the Beloved Disciple's synthesis "of history and story, of the oral history of an eyewitness and the interpretive and narrativizing procedures of an author."[45]

IN-DEPTH: The Anonymity of the Beloved Disciple

The anonymity of the Beloved Disciple is a classic example of a common procedure of the best of ancient historiography. There is some evidence that anonymity was used as a stylistic device in the ancient world by authors of historical books for depicting themselves as "comparatively insignificant mediators of a subject matter that deserved the full attention."[46] While this generic convention has some merit, its actual function is only implicit in the data. It has also been suggested that the device was appropriate for historiography by "bestowing an air of disinterested objectivity and impartiality on a narrative that might otherwise be mistaken for polemic."[47] But this too quickly separates the witness from the interpretation of his witness, which as we will discuss below cannot (and should not) be separated. As we have discussed before, anonymity is a narrative tool which requires the reader to "interact with, analyze, or construct the unnamed characters on a basis other than the proper name," namely, "to focus the readers' attention on the role designations that flood into the gap that anonymity denotes."[48] For this reason Bauckham is correct when he argues that the Gospel employs the literary device of anonymity "to mark out the Beloved Disciple, who is the author, from the other disciples in the narrative in which he appears with them. His anonymity makes him not just one named disciple among others or even the closest to Jesus but, so to speak, different in kind. It gives the reader/hearer the sense that this disciple is in a different category from the others."[49] This explains the use of the third-person for the author, a well-established historiographic practice, which served in the first century "to distinguish [the] reporting self from the self who lived then ... by placing a nominal and pronominal distance between the two 'selfs.'"[50] In short, anonymity allows the Beloved Disciple to function as both a character within the narrative and an "agent" over it — a witness in the fullest sense.

44. See Vanhoozer, "The Hermeneutics of I-Witness Testimony," 368.

45. Byrskog, *Story as History — History as Story*, 304–5.

46. Armin D. Baum, "The Anonymity of the New Testament Historical Books: A Stylistic Device in the Context of Greco-Roman and Ancient Near Eastern Literature," *NovT* 50 (2008): 120–42 (142).

47. Jackson, "Ancient Self-referential Conventions," 25, 27.

48. Reinhartz, *"Why Ask My Name?,"* 188.

49. Bauckham, "The Beloved Disciple as Ideal Author," 91.

50. Derek Tovey, *Narrative Art and Act in the Fourth Gospel*, JSNTSup 151 (Sheffield: Sheffield Academic Press, 1997), 145.

Third, *the Beloved Disciple is established as the model disciple of the Gospel*: "And we know that his testimony is true" (καὶ οἴδαμεν ὅτι ἀληθὴς αὐτοῦ ἡ μαρτυρία ἐστίν). This is not the first time the narrator has described his witness as true (see comments on 19:35). By "model" disciple we are not suggesting that the Beloved Disciple functions as a more virtuous or more "Christian" disciple, but that he functions for the reader as an ideal reader, for he prefigures the ideal reader who receives, believes, and is affected by the testimony of the Gospel. "The Beloved Disciple is a model reader who not only follows testimony in the sense of understanding it, but follows out its implications to the point where his or her own life becomes a life of testimony. The aim of the author is to make the reader a disciple."[51]

The reader models the Beloved Disciple by receiving his testimony, "by accepting the role of the narrate,"[52] and by responding according to the rhetorical strategy of the narrative's witness. As the first stage of the conclusion explained, the Gospel desires the reader to believe and have life in Jesus Christ (20:30–31). Just as the Beloved Disciple "saw and began to believe" (20:8), the reader of the Gospel "reads and believes." By using the "we" of authoritative testimony (see comments on 1:14), the Beloved Disciple gives "added force to the self-reference," for "the plural intensifies the authority expressed."[53] Its use in the epilogue forms an *inclusio* with the authoritative "we" in the prologue (1:14). The entire Gospel therefore has become the confession of a personal eyewitness of the person and work of Jesus Christ. The Gospel invites the reader to participate not only in the Beloved Disciple's authoritative testimony but also in his personal confession of faith.[54]

21:25 And there are also many other things which Jesus did, which if each one were written down, I suppose not even the world itself could contain the books that would be written (Ἔστιν δὲ καὶ ἄλλα πολλὰ ἃ ἐποίησεν ὁ Ἰησοῦς, ἅτινα ἐὰν γράφηται καθ᾽ ἕν, οὐδ᾽ αὐτὸν οἶμαι τὸν κόσμον χωρῆσαι τὰ γραφόμενα βιβλία). If v. 24 is in reference to the author (the Beloved Disciple), then v. 25 is in reference to the text (the Gospel of John). The Beloved Disciple, speaking for the first time in the first person, concludes with a "hyperbolic praise" of his Gospel's subject matter, a common literary convention, although the robust Christology of the Gospel and the truth of its subject matter reduce the hyperbole to reality.[55] By referring to what could be written but was not, the author magnifies Jesus as worthy of endless description and gives greater emphasis to what was written.[56] Since v. 24 alludes to the prologue, it is likely that this verse is as well. The Jesus to whom he bears witness is the incarnate Word, the one through whom "the world" (τὸν κόσμον) was made; there is not enough space in the world to contain the "words" needed to make known the fullness of *the* Word.[57] While the use of this canonical Gospel should not be minimized, it is fair to say that even this part of God's special revelation is unable to say all that could be said about God.[58]

---

51. Vanhoozer, "The Hermeneutics of I-Witness Testimony," 381.

52. Davies, *Rhetoric and Reference in the Fourth Gospel*, 368.

53. Bauckham, *Jesus and the Eyewitnesses*, 372.

54. This explains further the Gospel's concern to depict Peter and the Beloved Disciple comparatively. If Peter is called to shepherd the church at large, the Beloved Disciple is called to shepherd the reader. Cf. Brown, "The Resurrection in John 21," 445.

55. See Keener, *John*, 2:1241–42, who provides several related examples.

56. This verse implies that the contents of the Gospel were selected by the author for his precise interpretive purposes (20:30–31). Cf. Moloney, *John*, 562.

57. Cf. Carson, *John*, 686; Beasley-Murray, *John*, 416.

58. Cf. Aquinas, *John*, 307–8.

This final verse makes clear that this Gospel was never intended to say it all, something the church clearly recognized with its appropriate reception of four authored Gospels. Yet as this Gospel has made clear, there is only one gospel of Jesus Christ, and this Fourth Gospel, the Gospel according to John, has intended to make it known. Let the reader believe its message and the church receive its life.

Theology in Application

The Gospel concludes in a personal way, depicting the ministerial callings of the two primary disciples in the Gospel, Peter and the Beloved Disciple, in order to orient the reader to the life and ministry of a disciple of Jesus Christ. This final pericope in the narrative serves as a conclusion to the Gospel and an introduction to its author, who is revealed to be the Beloved Disciple, for whom this Gospel was his personal ministry to its readers, the church. In this pericope the epilogue brings conclusion to the narrative of the Gospel by facilitating the readers' understanding and application of believing and living the message of the Gospel.

The Christian Life: To Love and Follow Christ

According to this pericope, the Christian life is given direction by a *love* of Christ and is displayed by an obedience to *follow* Christ. The two-part nature of the Christian life was first expressed by the alternation of words for "love" between Jesus and Peter, which caused a resolution-requiring dissonance that encourages a proper love for Christ. Just as God's innate love explains his intentions and purposeful response to the sinful world, so also does the Christian's love of Christ explain and give guidance to their purposeful life in God. The foundational love is not our love for God but God's love for us, for it was not we who loved first (as if his love were contingent upon ours) but God who first loved us (1 John 4:10). Christian love of God is not merely a result of his love; it is also a response to his love. And in this Gospel the logical expression of Christian love is action, just as God's expression of his love for us is displayed in the person and work of Jesus Christ. That is why Jesus, after grounding Peter's discipleship in a love for him, immediately commands for its expression to be in the form of an obedient and sacrificial following of him. To follow Christ is to make one's own life a subset of the life of Christ. Just as the love of God was expressed by the cross, so the Christian's life is to be a cruciform expression of their love of God.

Life, Death, and the Glory of God

The kind of discipleship Jesus commanded of Peter was a "life of outstretched hands." But God's intention was not ultimately the end of his life (death) but its fullest expression, that he "would glorify God" (v. 19). The church has long believed that the glory of God is "the chief end of man" (*Westminster Shorter Catechism* 1), and according to this pericope Peter's end would do just that. The death and resurrection of Jesus Christ serves as an invitation for the disciples of Jesus, who are invited to participate in their fullness — his death and the new life he provides — and therefore to participate in the fullness of life in God through Christ and by the Spirit. Ultimately, just as Christ gave his life as a gift to his children, so the Christian gives their life as a gift to their God. In this way all Christians are called to martyrdom, becoming a living sacrifice for God for the glory of God (Rom 12:1; 1 Cor. 10:31).

Shepherding the Sheep of the Good Shepherd

The exchange between Jesus and Peter reveals several aspects of the ministry Peter represents. First, the reinstatement of Peter is representative of every minister of Christ, who is equally in need of the grace and forgiveness Jesus provides. The gracious work of Christ in the life of the minister reminds them of both their place and purpose in relation to Christ and forces them "not to examine themselves facilely but to scrutinize [themselves] thoroughly."[59] Peter's reinstatement required an understanding of the entire Gospel's message regarding the love of God that not only is founded upon Christ's person and work but properly ends with him (see v. 15).

Second, the commission of Peter, because it has been variously interpreted, needs to be properly applied. Beasley-Murray suggests that this is "the one issue in the entire Gospel where members of different Christian confessions not only divide, but find difficulty in understanding the answers of others."[60] Although Roman Catholics have used this pericope to establish the primacy of Peter as the first pontiff (often in connection with Matt 16:13 – 20), there is nothing in this narrative that explicitly supports such an interpretation.[61] The narrative does, however, establish the primacy of Jesus as the chief pontiff, not only by giving the commission to Peter but also by calling the sheep his own ("my sheep"). There is nothing explicit in vv. 15 – 17 that suggests a unique role (as the "highest" undershepherd) or a distinct authority for Peter in relation to the other disciples. In this pericope Peter is restored to his intended apostolic role, not as the replacement for Christ's role. Peter represents all ministers in the church who receive the role and authority to shepherd the sheep of Christ assigned to them. And their love for Christ is directly reflected by the manner in which they feed and shepherd Christ's flock.

Receiving the Testimony of the Beloved Disciple

In this pericope the Beloved Disciple becomes for the reader the conduit or access point. The personal nature of the Beloved Disciple's witness gives direction to the kind of reception required of the reader by displaying how the testimony of the Gospel is to affect the reader. That is, as both the author of the Gospel and a character

---

59. Calvin, *John 11 – 21*, 221.
60. Beasley-Murray, *John*, 406.

61. Cf. Bultmann, *John*, 713. Contra Schnackenburg, *John*, 2:365 – 66; Brown, *John*, 2:1114 – 17.

in the Gospel, the Beloved Disciple is able to fasten himself to the reader (and their reading experience) in such a way that he guides the interpretation of the very book he authored. The appropriate reader follows the lead of the Beloved Disciple by "accepting the role of the narratees, by understanding Jesus from the perspective of belief."[62] The Beloved Disciple therefore is not merely the author; he is also a maker of disciples and fellow followers of Jesus: "It is his hope that each reader will be so drawn by the Gospel to believe in Jesus and to follow him, that he will discover himself in the true discipleship of the Beloved Disciple."[63] In this way the origin of the Gospel (21:24 – 25) perfectly matches its purpose (20:30 – 31).

The Origin of the Gospel

Scholarship on the Gospel of John has been fascinated with the Gospel's origin, its author(s), source(s), and its historical location. Yet when the Gospel addresses its own origin, it places it in the true witness of a believing testimony (v. 24). Even more, the Gospel primarily locates its origin in its subject matter, Jesus Christ, about whom books filling the world would be too few (v. 25). While scholars have called the mystery of John's origin "the Johannine Problem," that is, an unanswerable question, it might best be viewed as its own kind of answer. Helpful here is Hoskyns's description of the author's concern with his Gospel's origin: "At the end of our inquiry he remains no more than a voice bearing witness to the glory of God.... The author of the book has effaced himself, or, rather, has been decreased and sacrificed, in order that the Truth may be made known and in order that the Eternal Life which is in God may be declared."[64]

This Gospel is God's Word, and its content directs us to its true subject matter, God himself. At the end of the Gospel, both author and reader alike are beckoned to believe and find life in the one who was "in the beginning" (1:1). For this Gospel declares the gospel of Jesus Christ. This is not a problem; it is the answer to the question of (eternal) life itself.

---

62. Davies, *Rhetoric and Reference in the Fourth Gospel*, 368.   64. Hoskyns, *Fourth Gospel*, 19.
63. Lindars, *John*, 640.

Theology of John

The Gospel of John has long been recognized for its theological depth, often paired with Romans as one of the most robust doctrinal books in Scripture. Some of the earliest commentators in the church recognized the significant theology presented by the Fourth Gospel, giving it the title, "the Spiritual Gospel."[1] The commentary proper has tried to assist the reader of the Gospel in an examination of the narrative in a manner that was attentive to the theological intentions and categories it applied to the person and work of Jesus Christ. And in the "Theology in Application" section at the end of each pericope, we examined the theological issues driven and being developed by the specific section of the narrative. It is fitting that we conclude the commentary with a macrolevel overview of the theology of John, using the larger categories of biblical and systematic theology along with sensitivity to the historical doctrines and practices of the church.

God

The Gospel could not be clearer: God *is* the beginning (1:1) and the end, that is, the goal or purpose of human existence — what the Gospel simply calls "life" (1:18; 20:31). In this Gospel God is emphatically described as the one through whom all things were made (1:3), in order to make clear to the reader that nothing that has been, is, or will be is outside the authority and plan of God. In the Fourth Gospel, God is the main character — not just generally but specifically in every pericope. Every part of the Gospel describes what God is doing, with other characters — the disciples, "the Jews," or the Roman authorities — serving as minor characters that reflect by their lives the purposes and identity of God. In this way, the characters in the Gospel's narrative are no different from humanity in general, whose primary task is "to glorify God and to enjoy him forever" (*Westminster Shorter Catechism* 1).

Reflective of the early Christian concern to take belief in "God" seriously, the Gospel depicts God not by his nature, based upon Greek philosophy, but by his identity, rooted in the already-established biblical depictions of his person and work in

---

1. Clement of Alexandria (in Eusebius, *Hist. eccl.* 6.14.7). Cf. Augustine, *John*, 36.1.208.

the Old Testament — the God of Israel (see comments on 1:1). In the Gospel, "God" is defined not by ontological categories but by relational or personal categories. While God can easily be spoken of as having attributes befitting his "divinity," such as eternal existence (8:58), the power to create (1:3), and omniscience (2:24 – 25), the Gospel directs the reader to understand such attributes as belonging more properly to the identity of God, not to some vague category of "divinity."

When the Gospel of John speaks or refers to God in any way, it depicts the divine identity of God as Father, Son, and Spirit. In short, from beginning to end the Gospel is Trinitarian, presenting as its *theo*logical subject matter what the church would recognize as present throughout all Scripture. Thus, to speak of "God" is to speak about his three-person identity. As the church has long understood and explained, while the Father (or the Son or the Spirit) is fully God, God is not fully the Father. The Gospel reflects God as Trinitarian in nature in every pericope. When God is mentioned in any way, all three persons of God are relationally and functionally involved. The question often asked of this Gospel as to whether it is christocentric or theocentric (i.e, patricentric) is entirely misguided.[2] The Fourth Gospel would never make such a distinction, for not only could the Father and Son not be divided in such a manner, but both — not to mention the Holy Spirit — are essential to the identity of God. To be christocentric is to be theocentric. The Son honors himself when he defers to the Father (5:19). And the Son's presence is magnified at his departure and the arrival of the gift of the Spirit (14:16; 16:7). To make such a choice is to pit God against himself. Since the Gospel demands that God be understood in his Trinitarian form, it is necessary for us to summarize the Gospel's teaching on each person of the Trinity.

God the Father is listed first elsewhere in Scipture (cf. Matt 28:19) and is presented similarly in the Gospel of John. The order is not one of rank or importance but economy, for it is the Father who sends the Son. Quite simply, the work of God is directed by the Father and done for the Father (17:4). In the Gospel of John, everything God is doing is directed from and for the Father (5:19 – 27). The Fourth Gospel describes God the Father as the source and starting point of all God's activity. The Father sends the Son (3:16; 20:21), and the Son does the will of the Father (4:34). The Father expresses his love for the world by giving his own Son (3:16) so that he might receive through him more children (1:12 – 13). In short, the Father is depicted throughout the Gospel as the giving and receiving one, the sending agent who directs and structures the divine activity so that the work of God can properly be described as beginning and ending with the Father, that is, "to the glory of God the Father" (cf. Phil 2:11). This depiction of the Father, of course, is simply to speak in a manner that depicts or emphasizes the economic Trinity, for certainly the Son, as part of the divine identity of God, is just as involved in the sending as he is in being sent.[3] While the Father's sending of the Son might merely be an expression of the economic Trinity (function), it should also be grounded in the immanent Trinity (ontology).

---

2. See Barrett, "Christocentric or Theocentric?"   3. Augustine, *The Trinity*, 2.9.103.

God the Son, though a distinct person in the identity of God, must also be defined by his functional (economic) relationship to the Father. The Son is listed second elsewhere in Scipture (cf. Matt 28:19) and is presented similarly in the Gospel of John, not because of rank or importance but economy, for the Son is the "one sent" from the Father (e.g., 4:34; 5:24, 37; 6:44; 7:29; 8:29; 20:21). The Gospel of John is a biography of the Son and his coming to the world and becoming "flesh" as Jesus Christ. The reason for this is clear; God the Son is the expression of the love of God for the world. If the Father is the sending agent, the Son is the sent agent, the one who does what the Father wills. The Son is the doing of God (5:19), the one who comes, who joins, who completes, and who fulfills. Jesus is the Son of God, the Son of Man, the unique Son; each of these titles reflect divine status and purpose and are given definition and expression throughout the Gospel narrative. But Jesus does more than complete the will and pupose of God — he does the same for humanity. Jesus takes on "flesh" (1:14) so that he can become and perform everything humanity needed to do and to be. Three areas can be briefly summarized.

First, *Jesus Christ is the fulfillment of all human persons*. The Gospel frames its entire narrative with symbols and allusions to Genesis and the creation story in order to depict Jesus as the second Adam (19:5) and therefore as the fulfillment of human life. Jesus is the faithful man who lived under and fulfilled the old covenant expectations of God — a sinless life that gave full glory to God, making possible the perfect, sacrifical offering for a new covenant. In this way then, *Jesus fulfills the role of prophet* (4:44; 6:14; cf. 1:21), since he lived in such a way that his life spoke and directed others toward God and true (eternal) life.

Second, *Jesus Christ is the fulfullment of all human religion*. The Gospel drenches its pages with OT practices, symbols, allusions, and even direct quotations to declare emphatically that Jesus's person and work is the completion of Judaism, and therefore everything God required of human religion. Jesus, specifically his crucified and resurrected body, is the true temple of God (2:19–22), for he is "the tabernacling one" (1:14). Jesus is also uniquely both the sacrifice, the Lamb of God (1:29), and the High Priest (18:12–27; 19:30), the one who offers the sacrifice. For this reason Jesus completes in himself the cycle of sacrifice and sacrificer, allowing it to come to its completion in his person and work and making obselete any human religion which tries to mediate between God and humanity. It is not enough to say that Jesus replaces human religion, or even Judaism, and perhaps fulfillment language only reflects the economic (Trinity) reality of what Jesus has performed. For Jesus is the perfect and long-awaited means (e.g., 5:46: Moses wrote about him) by which God would redeem humanity from sin and death and declare himself the way, the truth, and the life (14:6). In this way then, *Jesus fulfills the role of priest*, since he offered perfect and eternal mediation for all humanity on behalf of God and for God and on behalf of humanity.

Third, *Jesus Christ is the fulfillment of all human kingdoms*. The narrative works hard to declare that Jesus speaks about and with the authority of another kingdom — the kingdom of God (3:3, 5). Jesus has received "from above" all power and authority and is the judge over both the living and the dead (5:22 – 29). Jesus has also defeated all enemies, even "the ruler of this world" (12:31; 14:30; 16:11), and has received again the glory properly belonging to him (17:5) even before "the beginning" (1:1). In this way then, *Jesus fulfills the role of king*, since he defeated all opposing powers and claimed the exalted throne of authority and judgment that has always belonged to him.

The church has long spoken of Jesus as fulfilling the roles of prophet, priest, and king. These are categories for God's person and work that are projected by the OT Scriptures and find fulfillment in the careful depiction of Jesus's person and work in the Gospel of John. In this Gospel, Jesus establishes the creation of a new humanity (children "born new"), a new religious people (the church), and a new kingdom (the kingdom of God). Yet he is only the first Paraclete — the foundation of the work God had inaugurated in the new covenant. The second Paraclete (14:16) was only able to come after God the Son had completed his role.

God the Spirit, though a distinct person in the identity of God, must also be defined by his functional (economic) relationship to the Father and the Son. The Holy Spirit is listed third elsewhere in Scipture (cf. Matt 28:19) and is presented similarly in the Gospel of John, not because of rank or importance but economy, for the Spirit's coming and work — the Spirit's sending — is dependent upon and rooted in the Father's sending of the Son and the Son's person and work (14:16 – 20). The Gospel of John provides Scripture's introduction and teaching about the Spirit as the Paraclete, who is a witness to God and a spokesperson for God as well as a counselor, teacher, and helper for God's people. The Spirit is "another Paraclete" (14:16), the functional presence of Jesus for his disciples (14:18 – 21). The Spirit/Paraclete has a special relationship to the disciples — he is the indwelling presence of God with the people of God. The Spirit/Paraclete also has a unique role in the world to convict the world of sin, righteousness, and judgment (16:8). The Spirit/Paraclete is the "Spirit of truth" (14:17), the functional presence of God in the church and for the world. The disciple of Christ lives in and by the Holy Spirit. According to the Fourth Gospel, the Christian life is to be lived in Christ, by the Spirit, and for the glory of God.

The World

The term "the world" becomes foundational in the Gospel of John, appearing seventy-eight times in the Gospel, over five times more frequently than in the Synoptics (fourteen times). Although the term can refer to the physical, created universe (17:5; 21:25), it is used in the Gospel in a more personal and relational manner. The Gospel narrative depicts the world in the fullness of its relationship to its Creator, not merely as the "good" object that he made (Gen 1) but also as an evil entity that is best defined as "darkness" (1:5), that is, as something opposed to God, who is the light (1:4 – 5). In this way then, "the world" refers primarily not to the earth but to its people, a particular class of people who by their darkened nature are in conflict with God. In this Gospel the world is both the place where and the people with whom God works.

In the Gospel of John, "the world" is a character in the narrative. In a very important way the world is the primary opponent of God, made up of fallen creation and humanity, the latter of which includes both Jews and gentiles. Even the disciples, those with whom Jesus most intimately works, are shown to be "worldly" in their inability to understand or obey the instructions of Jesus. The world is ultimately depicted, in line with the rest of Scripture, as defiled and dominated by the darkness (1:5). It distorts reality and is enslaved to sin (8:31 – 36) and therefore is in need of the light (8:12; 9:39), the truth (14:6), and the freedom (8:36) that only Jesus can provide.

The story the Gospel tells of God and the world is one of conflict, reflected in each interaction Jesus has with opponents, whether they be the Jewish authorities, the Roman authorities, the various people with whom he ministers or speaks, and even his own disciples, who are only just beginning to see the light standing in the darkness before them (1:5). While many people are just seekers or onlookers, they are still by definition opponents, challengers of God by their unfaithful existence to their Creator and Lord. It is likely for this reason that the Gospel provides seven dialogues (see Introduction) that depict in theologically substantive words the issues God has with humanity and the means by which he plans to defeat his challengers — to offer himself as the defeated one. God did not defeat the world as he could have with the magnitude of his holiness and justice, but with grace and truth (1:17). That is, God defeated the world — every single opponent — with love. For in the Fourth Gospel the world may be the opponent of God, but it is also the object of God's love. This is why this Gospel (along with the other three) was entitled by the church as "the gospel," for it declares the "good news" for the whole world.

Sin and Death

The world was in darkness because it was plagued, stained, and enslaved to sin. Early in the Gospel the narrator explains that the work of Jesus was intended to take away "the sin of the world" (1:29). The world was so darkened by sin that it did not recognize (1:5), know (1:10), or receive (1:11) God in the person of Jesus. The Gospel of John speaks about sin in a manner that matches its discussion throughout Scripture. Sin is a condition or state of all people, and it can only be cleansed or remedied by God. Jesus enters into the sinful state of the world, best exemplified by the prologue's depiction of Jesus becoming "flesh" (1:14), a term which presents the incarnate body of Jesus like both a corpse and a sacrifice. The Gospel does not spend much time defining sin, because it assumes that the rest of the biblical story has made it clear. The clear connection to Genesis is prerequisite for this Gospel. The failure of humanity (Gen 3) requires repair, for sin is now innate to human existence (8:7).

The Gospel also makes clear that sin has its consequences (5:14). As much as the Gospel invites every person to understand how God has provided redemption and forgiveness from sin through Jesus Christ, it also exhorts those who have already been redeemed to live a life free from the influence and stain of sin. Said another way, the Gospel does not merely invite the readers to become "children of God" (1:12 – 13), but demands that the already "born new" (3:3 – 8) children live as sons and daughters in the household of God and not as slaves to sin (8:35 – 36). The conflict in the Fourth Gospel is not presented in statements alone but also in situations. The narrative depicts the consequences of sin, often detailing a person's condition, such as the blind man (9:1 – 41), the lame man (5:1 – 15), and the Samaritan woman (4:1 – 42), with the last suggestive of religious illness. The Gospel makes clear that sin is everywhere and that Jesus is the Savior who not only redeems a person from sin but instructs them to embrace a life that is Spirit filled not sin filled.

The ultimate consequence and result of sin is death (8:24). Jesus, however, is the provision that allows the person who believes in his person and work — in the gospel — to pass from death to life (5:24). Death in the Gospel is the fullest manifestation of sin, and yet it also becomes the means by which sin and all its consequences are defeated, including death itself. In this Gospel death is countered by the Life (1:4), who offers "eternal life" (3:16; 20:31), which can only be defined by the source and substance of life itself — Jesus Christ (1:1 – 3). Eternal life is participation in God through Christ in and by the Spirit. To view life as something outside of or even beside God is to speak not of life but death. God is the source of life and the meaning of life, and everything not (re)sourced or defined by God is death.

The Historical and Cosmological Plot

The Gospel of John narrates a story that conceptualizes by its emplotment the two realities simultaneously at work in the story. These two realities are best defined as two narrative strands that run parallel and interpenetrate one another throughout the Gospel. The historical strand of the Gospel's plot is the visible persons and events that happened in time-and-space history in the life and ministry of Jesus. The cosmological strand of the Gospel's plot is the invisible God — his forces, workings, and purposes. Neither strand of the plot is complete on its own; in fact, each strand is supported by and intertwined with the other. This is vital information that the prologue (1:1 – 18) reveals to the reader and provides as hermeneutical (i.e., reading) instructions in order that the Gospel's message can be fully understood and rightly applied.

The two-stranded plot of the Gospel is what makes it the "spiritual Gospel" or, better, a historical narrative that is robustly theological. In every pericope the reader starts in first-century Palestine (the historical strand) and without ever leaving sees in the visible historical persons and events the invisible realities of God and his purposes (the cosmological strand). The historical persons and events are not minimized or declared untrue — not at all! Rather, they are given interpretation and meaning in light of the cosmological context into which the narrative places them. Said another way, the cosmological strand is the background and foreground out of which the historical strand of the narrative must be interpreted. Without the cosmological insights, the historical details would be incomplete. In this way, the story of the Gospel is not merely about the Jesus of history or as he could be understood by means of historical investigation alone, but it is about Jesus the Word, who must be understood in the fullness of Scripture and its (theological) subject matter. Again, this is not to deny in the least the historical referents of the Gospel but to show what (or who) the true and ultimate referent really is. Jesus really did become flesh, but the flesh is not for the purpose of demotion but promotion — his exaltation (3:14; 12:32).

The reason for the Gospel's use of a two-stranded emplotment is its subject matter: the person and work of God. In order to grasp the fullness of who God is and what God is doing, the narrative needed to be able to be flexible and complex enough to contain and express the nature and workings of God. By placing the historical strand of the narrative into the cosmological strand, "The two- to three-year time span of Jesus's earthly mission ... are placed in the continuum of the Word's preexistence with God and the eventual return of the Word and his disciples to God's realm, that is, the 'story time' of the cosmological [story]."[4] And it is God who connects and interconnects the two strands within the narrative itself. While the cosmological strand narrates the arrival of the Son, the historical strand narrates the events of his arrival into the world, with both reaching their climax in the crucifixion and resurrection of Jesus. This is where the events of history (Jesus the man, the disciples, the world) meet the intentions of God (Jesus the one sent from above, God, the coming Paraclete) in a unified way. Thus John is able to speak simultaneously about real space-time history and God's activity in one story. The cosmological strand serves as the metastory, allowing the narrative to present a cosmic drama that serves as the overarching temporal, geographical, theological, and narrative framework for the entire Gospel.[5] The cosmological aspects are employed by the narrative by the use of biblical symbols and allusions (e.g., the signs, the "I am" statements), irony, paradox, and at times even apparent narrative contradictions (e.g., 3:22 and 4:1 – 2; 7:8 – 10), all of which assist the reader to see the invisible in the visible.

It would not be a stretch to suggest that each of the two strands of the Gospel's plot expresses one of the two aspects of the divine identity of God: the historical strand portrays the economic Trinity (function), and the cosmological strand portrays the immanent Trinity (ontology). While this is not fully accurate, it gives further warrant for our reading of the Gospel, for it assumes that God's activities in even the most

---

4. Reinhartz, *Word in the World*, 4 – 5.   5. See Klink, "Light of the World."

basic historical aspects of the world are unable to be grasped without a multidimensional and theological lens. To limit God to what can be seen or analyzed by historical investigation (what he does in the flesh) is to deny that God is unique (the unique Son!), the Creator (not creation), and free from the constraints of time and space. When the prologue provides for the reader the two strands of the narrative's plot, it was not simply giving methodological definition to the Gospel. Rather, it was giving theological definition to the nature of God and his intentions for the world.

The church was not wrong to suggest that the Gospel of John was the "spiritual" Gospel, but it was incomplete when it explained, as Augustine suggested, that John "disdained to walk on the earth" and wrote instead as he "soared … above the earth."[6] Such a depiction emphasizes the cosmological and minimizes the historical. No, John was standing firmly on the ground as he wrote and yet saw every historical detail "from above." John cannot speak of a "historical Jesus" (per the scholarly construction) if that disallows the Word who was "in the beginning with God" (1:1). Jesus was real "flesh" (1:14) at the same time as he was the second person of the Trinity. This apparent paradox is the message of the Gospel, and the entire narrative is written with this paradoxical ink.

Scripture

It would not be accurate simply to examine the Gospel's use or application of OT quotations, allusions, or symbolisms when describing the relationship between the Gospel of John and the rest of Scripture. This would be too thin of a description of the canonical relationship between John and the OT, let alone John and the rest of the NT. Our exegesis of the Gospel revealed that at the most foundational level, the Gospel is so tied to the rest of the biblical story and canon that its own ("Johannine") meaning is rooted in not merely its historical context but also its biblical-canonical context. Two aspects need to be briefly discussed.

First, the Fourth Gospel participates in the biblical story told by the OT. The Gospel is telling its story in dependence on, in participation with, and with the perspective of the past in what is a *backward reading*. The story it tells requires the story already told about Adam (19:5), Abraham (8:31 – 58), Moses (1:45; 5:45 – 47), David (7:42), and all Israel (15:1 – 8). To read the Gospel as if it is the beginning of the story or a self-contained story is to misread it. This is the continuation of a story already underway and already told, even if only in part. In this way the Gospel not only continues the OT story but retells it, showing how Jesus fulfills, replaces, exposes, rebukes, and even is and does what the OT promised God would be and do. It might not be enough, then, to describe the Gospel as the continuation of the OT story, for it also is commentary on the OT; even more, it is a second telling. The Gospel of John

---

6. Augustine, *John*, 36.1.208.

does not merely use the OT or add one more chapter to the same volume. Without ever replacing it, the Gospel rewrites the OT. Said another way, the subject matter of the OT and the Fourth Gospel are so intertwined that they can only be rightly understood when read symphonically (on method related to canon, see Introduction). The Gospel makes clear that the OT was looking to the same object: the life and ministry (especially the death and resurrection) of Jesus Christ. The OT, then, is not mere background but the shared foreground of the Gospel's content and message.

Second, the Fourth Gospel also participates in the biblical story told by the rest of the NT. The Gospel tells its story in dependence on, in participation with, and with the perspective of the present and future in what is a *forward reading*. Throughout our exegesis in the commentary proper, it became clear that the Gospel was speaking about topics or a subject matter that not only resonated with the message of the rest of the NT (in part or in whole) but also necessitated expression from other NT books and authors. At times we even used language or discussion from other NT books and authors to help express or elucidate what John was also intending to communicate (see comments on 13:23 – 25). Our interpretation was not merely based upon conceptual links but an alignment or overlap of sorts in subject matter that made the description, analysis, or categories of the NT essential to grasping the actual meaning of the Gospel of John. Such collaboration does not intend to stir together individual sections of Scripture so as to make them unrecognizable but to let them speak in concert or symphonically in regard to their related and shared subject matter.

The Gospel of John instructs its reader to read all Scripture, for the subject matter it addresses — Jesus Christ, the Son of God, and life in his name (20:31) — is the message of the whole Bible and needs the whole Bible for its expression. According to John, Jesus explained to the Jews that he is (and had always been) the subject matter of Moses's writings: "For he wrote about me" (5:46). Such a statement not only provides hermeneutical instruction for reading Scripture in light of its shared subject matter but also shows how the Jesus that John portrays in this Gospel has always been a sixty-six-book Jesus, so that the primary context for understanding the Gospel of John is the canon in which it has been rightly placed and published by the church.

The Gospel of Jesus Christ

It is not an oversimplification to state that the basic message of the Gospel of John is the gospel of Jesus Christ. That is, the Gospel tells *the* gospel. This is not to say that John is the gospel, but as a Gospel it participates in the fourfold telling of the gospel. Since all four Gospels have the same title prefacing four different authors, the title makes a striking claim: there is *one* gospel written or expressed in *four* different accounts — "according to" Matthew, Mark, Luke, and John. Thus, there is one gospel and four Gospels, with each Gospel offering a necessary perspective, witness, and interpretation of the one and only gospel. (On the title and function of "Gospel," see Introduction.) As the *Fourth* Gospel, John (the author and text) is one of the evangelists, declaring and defining the gospel. As the fourth, John is neither the climactic statement of the gospel (though the canonical order is certainly significant), nor is John only able to address one-quarter of the gospel. In the providence of God, each of the four Gospels tells the full gospel without ever being the authorized account of the gospel, for the authorized gospel requires four Gospels. Our discussion here is not to confuse the reader but to guide him or her to read the Gospel of John for its subject matter, the gospel of Jesus Christ.

What is *the* gospel, according to the Gospel of John? In short, the gospel is the person and work of Jesus Christ and all that it means. Clearly John does not describe the gospel in a merely past-tense manner, something that happened back then; yet neither does he describe it in a merely present-tense manner, something only for the present day. According to this Gospel, the gospel is both descriptive and prescriptive in that it is based upon facts about God and drives toward faith in God. Even more simply, the gospel is both believed and lived (20:30–31). Both these aspects need to be briefly defined.

First, according to John *the gospel is a description of fact*. The gospel that John announces centers upon the meaning and significance of the death and resurrection of Jesus Christ. The entire Gospel aims at the cross, and the time spent on the last week of Jesus's life and ministry is by far the longest section of the narrative. For John the gospel is the fact that Jesus died and rose again, and the meaning of that fact: that Jesus has now accomplished the full purposes of God. The Gospel presents Jesus as the fulfillment of all human persons (the Second Adam), religions (fulfillment of Judaism and the true High Priest), and kingdoms (the true King) with numerous maneuvers in the narrative that help express their fuller meaning and subject matter, as in the "exaltation/lifting up" theme (3:14; 12:32), which helps express not only the nature of the King but also his relation to the necessity of sacrifice.

Second, according to John *the gospel is a prescription of faith*. While the factualness of the gospel is strongly rooted in what God accomplished through Jesus Christ in the past event of the cross, such a foundation necessarily invites the world to "believe" — a central term in the Gospel. And belief, though inclusive of propositions, is ultimately a manner of life. The word is used a total of ninety-eight times, which is more than any other NT author, nearly doubling the use of the term by the apostle Paul (fifty-four times). Belief in John is about both alignment and allegiance. Upon believing the gospel, the believer is properly aligned to God. He or she becomes a new creation (recall the Genesis theme) by being "born new" (3:3). Such are received as "children of God" (1:12) who enjoy the full rights of sonship in the house of God (8:35) and friendship with God (15:15). This is the passive effect of the gospel. But there is also an active effect of the gospel. Upon believing, the believer is exhorted to be aligned to God. He or she accepts God as the Father, Jesus as the mediating unique Son, and the Spirit as the source and guide of this new life. The believer submits and entrusts himself to God, remains in him (15:1 – 8), follows his guidance and instruction (16:5 – 15), and participates in his continuing mission to the world (17:18; 20:21).

According to the Gospel of John, therefore, the gospel of Jesus Christ is both the fact of God and faith in God. It is Jesus Christ as the High Priest and the Lamb of God. But it is also Jesus Christ as brother, friend, and King. Stated more simply, as much as the gospel is Jesus Christ "the truth," it is also "the way" and "the life" (14:6). The Gospel of John calls the reader to grasp both doctrine and discipleship, and it denies that any dichotomy or wedge can be placed between them. The gospel is the word of the Word, which like the Greek term "w/Word" (ὁ λόγος) refers to both a message (word) and the person of Jesus Christ (Word). Jesus is the Word who speaks a word, and their intersection is the gospel. It might be for this very reason that the author of the Gospel decided to use this broadly defined term "w/Word," allowing the reader to see at the end of the narrative how the multifaceted meaning of the term with which the Gospel began explains how Jesus's life and ministry *is* his subject matter and therefore the "good news."

Eschatology

Scholarship on the Gospel of John has often emphasized its "realized eschatology" and minimized its "futuristic eschatology." As instructive as such language is for interpreters, both phrases have a tendency to speak right past the other. The present reality of the "eternal life" that Jesus gives need not deny its future implications or reality. For example, the healed man in 5:14 could be warned quite strongly about something worse happening to him in the future only because he had already experienced something bad in the present. Likewise, Jesus can speak of the gift of life in the present without thwarting in any way the glorious aspects of the life to come (see 14:1 – 4). Another example is when Jesus qualifies the aspects of "life" in 5:24 by claiming that the believer "does not come into judgment" and "has passed from death to life." Both of these aspects speak right through the present to the future. It seems that modern interpreters have been so captured by the cosmological strand of John's emplotment (without designating it as such) that they have imputed to the Gospel an overly realized eschatology that according to their reading either denies or strongly mutes the futuristic eschatology of the Gospel. But such an imbalance is altogether missing from the Gospel. In fact, for John the promise of a future eschatology is the best argument for the reality of a present eschatology. The fact that Jesus will be the life and the Judge in the future is proof that he is serving as the life and the Judge in the present (5:28 – 29).

This balance is important because according to this Gospel, Jesus, the Word-become-flesh (1:14), unites the past, present, and future in his person (cf. Heb 13:8).

While John may provide for the biblical-canonical witness a more nuanced and even emphatic presentation concerning the manifest presence of God and his kingdom in the present, this in no way allows for a reading of the Gospel that denies futurist elements. The Gospel of John fits within Scripture's overall presentation of an "already-not yet" eschatology. Such a position allows eschatology to be defined not merely by its linear development, especially as an "end times" reality, but also as a subset of God's in-breaking into human history. Thus, as the NT authors recognized, even the coming of Jesus was eschatological in the sense that God had become "the tabernacling one" (1:14) and was now working in a way that inaugurated the eschatological reality that the OT had promised long before. The Fourth Gospel's portrait of the person (the incarnation) and work (the cross, the resurrection, the Spirit) of Jesus portrays "eschatology" in a theocentric manner, so that eschatology is not merely a period of time or a particular event but is everything that God does.

The emplotment of the narrative we discussed above is significant for the Gospel's presentation of eschatology. For the Gospel of John, the first-century events of Jesus's life and ministry need to be placed in their cosmological context. That is, the Gospel is careful to show how human history is a subset of something more; it is a created thing that is not a self-contained and closed entity but is formed and ruled by a Creator. Thus, when God enters into his creation, his presence and work can rightly be defined as eschatological (i.e., cosmological). For example, the "Word became flesh" (1:14) was an eschatological event, just as the resurrection was eschatological in that it was the sign and seal of the new creation (20:1, 19). This is why the rest of the NT commonly refers to the time since Jesus as "the last days" (e.g., Acts 2:17; 1 Tim 3:1), for Jesus's presence and ministry inaugurated the final work of God in the world.

The fullest expression of Scripture's presentation of inaugurated eschatology is the Spirit, who is the most permanent and intimate manifestation of God's presence. The Spirit is the ultimate sign of God's presence and grace, the seal of his power and the deposit of his promise (Eph 1:13 – 14; cf. Rom 8:23; 1 Cor 1:18 – 22; Gal 3:14). The Spirit is a manifestation of the fact that the believer is now sharing and participating in God's life, that is, "eternal life." Even though sin and death have not yet been vanquished, their defeat has been guaranteed. The Christian, then, is exhorted to live in light of their newly bestowed eschatological status as children of the light not darkness (1 Thess 5:4 – 8; 1 John 1:5 – 10; 2:8), and as heirs of the kingdom of God and not as slaves of sin and death (John 8:34 – 36). In this sense, therefore, the Christian life is eschatological.

The Church

The Gospel of John states as its opening concern to reach the world (1:1 – 18) for the purpose of establishing a new people, the "children of God" (1:12), who are to live and serve as a family under God the Father. Biblical theologians over the last century, primarily in America, have debated the relationship between Israel and the church. Dispensational theologians have pressed for various levels of distinction, claiming that the people Jesus establishes are not a replacement of the people of Israel. Covenant theologians, on the other hand, press for continuity, claiming that the people Jesus establishes are the fullest and cumulative expression of the people of God, inclusive of all people for all time, Jews (Israel) and gentiles. Although the discussion is rooted in an analysis of the whole of Scripture, the Fourth Gospel offers something to the conversation.

The Gospel shows precise connections between what Jesus accomplishes by his person and work and the Jews and Judaism. There is nothing in the Gospel to suggest that Jesus is creating a people who are primarily gentile or non-Jew, that is, who are different from the people God established in the OT. Rather, the Gospel intentionally shows how Jesus repairs and restores Israel through his person and work. There is also nothing in the Gospel to suggest that the Jewish people are firmly established in God's covenant without Jesus and that only others are in need of him. From the perspective of the Gospel, it is Jesus who finally establishes or becomes the temple, the High Priest, the presence of God, the Lamb of God, the final sacrifice for sins, and the final and eternal (new) covenant (Heb 13:20). There is no evidence in the Fourth Gospel, therefore, to suggest that Israel has some ministerial role that is outside of what Jesus has already done or that is distinct from the church. While this author is well aware that a discontinuity approach is rooted in much larger biblical-theological and hermeneutical issues,[7] the Gospel strongly presents continuity between the two testaments, between the two covenants, as they are centered upon and established by Jesus Christ.

The people established by Jesus can be described as the recreated people of God, who through Jesus have fulfilled the old covenant and are now in the new covenant relationship with God the Father through God the Son and living in and by God the Spirit. That is, the people of God in the Fourth Gospel, inclusive of both Jews and gentiles (the world!), is the church. The church is the Spirit-indwelt and Spirit-empowered people of God, who have been created to reflect God in two ways.

First, *the church is to participate in God's love* by obeying and fulfilling the love commandment (13:34–35). Jesus commands his disciples to display God's love for them to one another. And this love manifests itself in sacrificial service, best exemplified by Jesus's action at the start of the farewell discourse where he washed the disciples' feet (13:1–17). According to the Gospel, this act of service is to be expressed not only as a ceremony but as a lifestyle. The church is to live as the family of God, with all members (brothers and sisters) functioning as servants of one another and

7. See Klink and Lockett, *Understanding Biblical Theology,* especially 59–75.

ultimately, therefore, of God. In this way the love of God manifests its presence in and through the people of God.

Second, *the church is to participate in God's mission* by being sent by the Son and therefore also the Father to the world in the power and truth of the Spirit. Just as the Father sent the Son, the Son sends his church (20:21), bestowing upon them his Spirit and authority (20:22 – 23) to do the work assigned to them by the Father. The foot washing (13:1 – 17) and the prayer of consecration or dedication (17:1 – 26) is the preparation for service, the initiation of Christian discipleship. The foot washing is done not only to one another but also as part of the mission of God to the world, heralding the new covenant and the gospel of Jesus Christ. And since Christ was superior in every way to those whose feet he washed, no Christian may ever claim to be so superior that he or she is above washing the feet of another. This means that, according to the "example" of Christ, "the last will be first, and the first will be last" (Matt 20:16). The significance of the church for the mission of God is surpassed, however, by God himself, who by the Spirit will be the primary ministering agent at work in the world (16:8).

The Reader of the Gospel

The Gospel of John is written for the reader and stated clearly as such (20:30 – 31; cf. 21:24 – 25). But the reader is not embraced by the Gospel and its intentions by a purpose statement, for he or she is quickly grasped by the beauty and majesty of the Gospel's subject matter, the person and work of Jesus Christ, and is graciously invited to "follow." Like the earliest disciples, the reader of the Gospel is confronted by Jesus and asked, "What do you seek?" (1:38). Through the Fourth Gospel, Jesus questions the reader and invites him or her to believe in him and to have life in his name (20:31), that is, to become his disciple.

Every reader of this Gospel, no matter their relationship to God or stage of their Christian walk, is beckoned to "come and see" (1:39, 46). In this Gospel, the Beloved Disciple comes alongside the reader and shares his testimony and life with the reader. Just as the Gospel begins with a disciple of Jesus (Andrew) seeking his brother (Peter) and leading him to Jesus (1:41), so the Gospel ends with a disciple of Jesus (the Beloved Disciple) leading a brother or sister (the reader) to Jesus. Ultimately, the mysterious identity of the Beloved Disciple is eclipsed in importance by his ministerial role as author of the Gospel, and it is the reader who becomes the referent of this mystery as he or she receives the Gospel's message, believes its subject matter, and lives as a disciple of Jesus Christ. And since all disciples are sent by Jesus, even the Beloved Disciple's text-based ministry is an extension of the love of God to the reader, an ongoing invitation to believe in Jesus Christ and receive life in his name. Amen.

Scripture Index

Genesis

1 . . . . .93, 930
12 . . . . 862, 865, 868
1:1 86
1:1 – 5 .93, 95, 161
1:2 . . . . 96, 198, 312, 864
1:3 . . . . .93, 94, 95, 96
1:5 . . . . .93, 94
1:6 94
1:8 . . . . .93, 94
1:9 . . . . .93, 94
1:11 . . . . .93, 94
1:13 . . . . .93, 94
1:14 94
1:15 . . . . .93, 94
1:19 . . . . .93, 94
1:20 . . . . .93, 94
1:23 . . . . .93, 94
1:24 . . . . .93, 94
1:30 . . . . .93, 94
1:31 94
2 . . . . 733, 739, 805
2 – 4 801
2:2 – 3 276
2:7 . . . . 289, 439, 862
2:8 – 16 . . . . 733, 819, 845
2:15 851
2:19 – 20 460
3 . . . . 779, 781, 786, 932
3:1 851
3:1 – 5 733
3:3 851
3:4 420
3:5 609
3:9 . . . . .701, 735
3:22 . . . . .778 – 79

3:24 739
4:25 801
9:4 339
12:1 – 3 657
12:2 – 3 244
12:3 . . . . .235, 244
13:6 – 10 357
17:19 425
21:6 425
22 . . . . .139, 303
22:8 . . . . .133, 139
22:9 738
22:13 113
24:1 – 27 236
28 . . . . .154, 157
28:12 154
28:17 462
29:1 – 12 236
32:28 148
37:19 353
47:29 – 49:33 571
49:10 150
49:11 172
49:33 572
50:20 . . . . .355, 519

Exodus

2:15 – 21 236
3 . . . . .246, 309, 312, 313,
                              314, 411, 425, 715
3:6 . . . . 252, 312, 332
3:10 – 15 97
3:14 . . . . .264, 332
4:22 – 23 152
9:14 429
12 179

12:22 811
12:46 816
13:21 – 22 406
14 314
14:19 – 25 406
15:25 303
16 341
16:2 . . . . .334, 339
16:4 303
16:7 335
16:7 – 8 335
17:1 – 7 240
17:2 339
19:5 103
20:2 332
20:5 436
23:22 103
24:9 – 11 117
24:16 – 17 109
25 842
25:9 122
25:18 – 19 . . . . .842, 850
25:22 842
28:2 796
28:6 796
28:32 796
28:38 133
28:41 525
29:43 842
30:26 842
31:18 394
32:15 395
33 – 34 . . . . .116, 117
33:11 448
33:18 . . . . 109, 111, 116, 619
33:18 – 22 116

33:19 111
33:20 117
33:22 109
34 116
34:6 . . . . .111, 116
34:7 133
34:8 116
34:33 – 35 833
35:35 796
36:10 796
36:12 796
36:15 796
36:29 796
36:34 796
37:1 – 9 842
37:3 796
37:5 796
37:21 796
40:2 – 3 842
40:3 842
40:5 – 6 842
40:21 842
40:22 842
40:24 842
40:26 842
40:29 842
40:34 – 35 842

Leviticus

10:17 133
11:33 166
14 133
14:4 – 7 811
14:25 133
17:11 339
17:14 339
19:18 605
20:10 393
21:10 796
24:16 . . . . .479, 780

Numbers

4:15 842
4:20 842
6:26 641
9:6 – 12 516
11:12 118
14:22 109

9:12 816
14:27 858
19:18 811
20:2 – 13 240
20:11 . . . . .240, 376
21 203
21:4 203
21:4 – 9 203
21:5 203
21:7 203
21:8 203
24:6 – 9 376
24:17 150
27 461

Deuteronomy

1:31 152
2:14 270
4:12 117
5:24 109
6:4 295
7:6 103
8:2 303
8:3 248
8:16 303
9:10 394
10:17 90
11:29 242
12:23 339
13 426
13:1 – 5 442
13:6 118
13:9 391
14:2 103
15:11 . . . . .529, 531
17:6 407
17:7 391
18 . . . . 195, 197, 328, 563
18:11 129
18:15 . . . . 150, 242, 306
18:15 – 19 . . . . 129, 195, 240
18:18 245
18:18 – 19 . . . . .150, 563
18:36 129
19:5 407
19:15 291
21:23 793
22:22 . . . . .392, 393

22:23 – 24 393
25:3 776
26:18 103
27:4 242
27:4 – 7 242
27:12 242
28:25 373
28:33 249
30:4 373
30:19 520
30:20 289
31:10 – 11 376
32 706
32:6 . . . . .152, 418
32:39 286
33 706

Joshua

1:8 – 9 293
7:19 446
22 – 24 571
22:24 164

Judges

3:1 – 4 303
6:3 249

1 Samuel

2:6 286
4:4 843
8:11 – 13 525
9 778
9:7 778
10:1 – 13 525
10:24 543
15:1 195
15:25 133
16:1 195
16:12 – 13 525
25:28 133

2 Samuel

6:2 843
7:14 . . . . .152, 418
16:10 164

1 Kings

3:20 118

4:25 151
5 900
5:15 – 16 901
17:18 164

2 Kings
1:8 129
3:13 164
5:7 286
8:31 151
14:25 380
17:24 – 41 235
19:15 843
23:34 148
24:17 148

1 Chronicles
28 – 29 571

2 Chronicles
20:7 657
30:17 – 18 516

Nehemiah
8 – 9 376
9:15 329
9:20 376

Job
4:19 439
4:21 862
9:8 . . . . .312, 313
10:9 439
10:12 289
16:19 913
33:4 289
38 – 41 918

Psalms
2:7 . . . . .152, 481
8 786
11:6 738
16:10 835
16:11 289
19:7 644
20:1 105
22 797
22:18 797

23 . . . . .463, 468 – 69
23:2 469
25:5 . . . . .682, 685
27:1 406
28:11 641
32 156
32:9 586
34:20 816
35:19 667
36:9 . . . . .238, 289
41 719
41:9 . . . . .586, 719
46 314
46:6 314
46:10 314
46:11 314
60:3 738
66:16 – 20 449
69 . . . . .183, 187
69:5 667
69:7 187
69:9 . . . . .181, 187
69:21 810
78:24 329
80:1 843
80:4 145
80:5 145
80:7 – 15 651
80:8 145
80:8 – 16 650
80:9 145
80:19 145
80:20 145
82 . . . . .480, 481, 482, 858
82:3 – 4 481
82:5 481
82:6 . . . . .480, 481
82:6 – 7 481
82:8 . . . . .482 – 83, 485
85:6 145
85:7 145
89 377
89:27 418
89:32 436
90:13 . . . . .145, 155
96:10 . . . . .793, 803
97:2 117
99:1 . . . . .843, 850

103:8 170
105:40 329
106:36 – 37 421
107:23 – 32 313
107:30 313
109:7 449
118 . . . . .475, 536 – 38, 540, 541
118:25 – 26 536
118:25 – 27 537
118:26 . . . . .536, 537
118:27 536
119 644
119:11 293
119:105 . . . . .406, 427
119:105 116
139:4 – 7 846
147:2 373

Proverbs
4:23 376
5:15 376
6:23 406
15:29 449
26:12 452

Song of Solomon
1:2 526

Isaiah
3:8 559
3:9 559
5:1 – 2 650
5:18 559
5:19 559
6 . . . . .559, 561
6:1 560
6:3 560
6:5 . . . . .138, 561
6:8 . . . . .97, 195
6:9 – 13 559
6:10 559
7:14 684
9:6 867
11 . . . . .135, 638
11:1 150
11:1 – 9 136
11:2 135
12:3 . . . . .240, 376

25 308
25:6 172
25:9 172
27:2 – 6 650
29:9 – 10 738
30:6 537
35:6 272
36:16 151
40 – 55 . . . . .411, 425
40 558
40:3 130
40:9 539
40:10 558
41:4 . . . . .411, 425
41:8 657
42:1 136
42:1 – 9 558
43:10 411
43:13 . . . . .411, 425
43:21 103
43:25 411
44:3 376
44:6 152
46:4 411
48:12 411
48:14 558
49:1 – 6 558
49:6 . . . . .373, 406
49:10 376
50:4 – 9 558
51:5 558
51:17 738
51:21 – 23 738
52 – 53 559
52:10 558
52:13 558
52:15 558
53 . . . . 139, 559, 778
53:1 . . . . .558, 559
53:2 – 3 777
53:3 778
53:5 . . . . 429, 786, 859, 867
53:7 133
53:8 429
53:10 429
53:10 – 12 835
53:11 515
53:11 – 12 133

53:12 792
54:13 . . . . 335, 336, 641
55:1 – 3 331
55:1 – 5 240
55:6 – 7 331
55:10 331
56:7 180
57:19 641
60:19 – 22 406
61:1 137
62:5 219
63:6 738
63:16 418
64:6 680
64:8 418
66:18 109

Jeremiah
1:4 – 7 97
1:7 195
2:13 238
2:21 650
3:4 418
3:19 418
16:14 – 16 896
17:13 238
22:10 691
23:5 – 6 150
25:15 – 29 738
30:3 238
30:31 – 34 238
31 866
31:9 152
31:31 – 34 198
31:33 – 34 694
31:34 102
34:17 373

Lamentations
4:21 738

Ezekiel
1:4 406
1:13 406
1:26 – 28 406
3:16 – 21 409
9:2 841
9:6 395

10:4 109
10:18 – 19 109
11:16 – 20 198
13:18 – 23 103
15:2 – 6 650
17:5 – 10 650
19:10 – 14 650
23:31 – 33 738
34 . . . . .461, 466
34:15 – 16 464
34:22 467
34:23 464
36:24 – 28 198
36:25 – 26 137
36:25 – 27 .238, 376
37 . . . . 198, 200, 862
37:9 . . . . .862, 868
37:36 641
40 – 48 198
47:1 – 12 . . . . .239, 376
47:6 – 12 901

Daniel
3:26 90
7 . . . . 154, 290, 638
7:13 289
7:13 – 14 . . . . 154, 290, 450
9:18 680
10:5 841
12:1 – 2 290

Hosea
2:16 – 23 219
6:2 835
11:1 152
13:14 704

Joel
2:28 – 29 239
3:18 . . . . .239, 376

Amos
9:11 – 15 376
9:13 249
9:13 – 14 172

Jonah
1:17 835

Micah

4:4 151
5:2 377
6:8 449
6:15 249
7:18 133

Habakkuk

1:14 – 15 896
3:3 – 4 406
3:3 – 15 638

Zephaniah

1 37
3:15 152
3:16 539

Zechariah

1:3 145
3:8 150
3:10 151
9 . . . . 538 – 40, 638
9:4 – 7 538
9:8 538
9:9 . . . . 538, 539
9:10 538
9:11 . . . . 538, 539
9:15 538
9:16 538
12 817
12:10 817
13 817
13:1 . . . . 239, 241, 242, 376, 817
14:8 . . . . 239, 376
14:21 180

Malachi

2:10 418
3:1 – 4 129
3:7 145
3:17 103
3:23 – 24 129
4:5 – 6 129

Matthew

1:6 798
1:23 684

3:4 129
3:11 131
4:13 178
4:18 – 22 144
5:3 – 12 880
5:13 – 16 566
5:14 122
5:34 580
6:9 – 13 804
7:13 – 14 462
7:25 862
7:27 862
8:29 164
9:1 178
9:9 144
9:22 145
10:3 . . . . 149, 876
11:14 129
12:45 275
12:46 – 50 801
13:55 – 56 178
13:57 259
14:1 – 12 . . . . 216, 220
14:5 242
15:28 163
16:13 – 20 . . . . 148, 925
16:14 129
16:17 . . . . 148, 768
16:18 149
16:19 865
16:22 345
16:23 145
16:24 . . . . 683, 740
17:12 129
18:18 865
20:16 . . . . 588, 940
21:1 – 11 534
21:9 536
21:12 – 13 175
22:1 – 14 172
22:34 – 40 656
25:1 – 13 218
25:31 – 46 470
26:6 – 13 . . . . 495, 496, 523
26:13 526
26:57 – 68 458
26:73 418
27:2 761

27:30 777
27:37 793
27:57 817
27:60 817
28:1 828
28:1 – 8 851
28:9 847
28:19 . . . . 215, 928, 929, 930
28:18 – 20 . . . 225, 278, 622, 643, 659, 867

Mark

1:1 720
1:6 129
1:7 – 8 131
1:14 216
1:16 – 20 144
1:19 . . . . 768, 895
1:24 . . . . 164, 345
2:13 – 14 144
2:19 – 20 . . . . 168, 218
2:28 275
3:5 508
3:16 148
3:18 . . . . 149, 876
5:7 164
6:3 178
6:11 586
6:14 260
6:14 – 29 216
6:15 129
7:1 – 13 . . . . 131. 193
7:3 – 4 166
9:13 129
10:18 357
10:45 542
11:1 – 11 534
11:10 536
11:15 – 17 175
11:17 180
11:18 178
11:32 242
12:18 – 27 504
12:28 – 31 606
12:28 – 34 656
14:2 759
14:3 – 9 . . . . 495, 496, 523
14:9 . . . . 496, 526
14:12 . . . . 757, 759

14:12 – 16 759
14:16 759
14:53 . . . . .744, 817
14:53 – 65 458
14:64 744
15 810
15:6 – 14 759
15:26 793
15:32 328
15:37 862
15:39 862
15:46 759
16:1 828
16:9 – 11 851

Luke

1:17 129
1:41 – 42 112
3:2 . . . . .514, 746
3:16 131
3:19 – 20 216
3:23 425
4:18 – 19 396
4:24 259
4:31 178
4:34 . . . . .164, 345
5:1 – 11 144
5:5 896
5:10 896
5:24 396
5:27 – 28 144
6:14 149
6:15 876
7:9 145
7:12 117
7:16 242
7:36 – 50 . . . . .495, 523
7:44 145
8:28 164
8:42 117
9:19 129
9:23 . . . . .383, 740
9:38 117
10:23 145
10:25 177
10:25 – 27 605
10:25 – 28 656
10:38 – 42 . . . . .495, 496

12:55 862
14:25 145
15:2 596
16:11 184
18:19 357
19:29 – 38 534
19:45 – 46 175
21:37 391
21:38 387
22:50 737
22:57 163
22:61 145
22:66 – 71 458
23:16 775
23:21 775
23:38 793
23:43 462
23:46 862
23:51 817
24:1 – 10 851
24:5 847
24:10 828
24:51 849

John

1 . . . . 125, 155, 162, 259, 779, 891
1 – 12 . . . . .65, 827, 874
1 – 19 891
1 – 20 . . . . 873, 874, 892, 905
1:1 . . . . .22, 27, 38, 86, 90, 91, 93,
106, 107, 111, 118, 139, 202,
215, 221, 244, 259, 277, 285,
287, 289, 296, 316, 334,
343, 370, 411, 419, 425,
438, 451, 474, 479, 497, 511,
562, 615, 616, 620, 641, 643,
703, 713, 715, 717, 812, 821,
856, 857, 875, 878, 887, 892,
926, 927, 928, 930, 934
1:1 – 2 . . . . .335, 836
1:1 – 3 . . . . 95, 408, 411, 932
1:1 – 4 95
1:1 – 5 . . . .97, 99, 111, 112, 161, 214, 427
1:1 – 18 . . . . . . .65, 116, 141, 143, 158,
873, 893, 932, 938
1:1 – 51 160
1:2 . . . . . .97, 101, 251, 342, 413, 423, 448
1:3 . . . . .87, 94, 95, 96, 104, 114 – 115,
171, 264, 276, 290, 425,

449, 500, 505, 587, 618,
669, 724, 811, 927, 928
1:3 – 4 105
1:3 – 5 . . . . .101, 270
1:4 . . . . .94, 121, 200, 209, 264, 288,
289, 330, 406, 419, 439, 467,
476, 500, 504, 618, 779, 815,
863, 868, 884, 918, 932
1:4 – 5 . . . . 98, 207, 499, 931
1:5 . . . . . 57, 102, 121, 207, 209, 210, 218,
248, 288, 294, 332, 350, 352,
358, 365, 377, 405, 406, 410,
428, 445, 451, 467, 469, 473,
481, 559, 561, 599, 702, 735,
739, 766, 782, 811, 828, 931
1:6 . . . . .94, 98, 103, 111, 112, 115,
121, 125, 136, 155, 215, 218,
220, 291, 292, 293, 816
1:6 – 7 96
1:6 – 8 . . . . 98, 111, 484, 849
1:7 . . . . .99, 121, 126, 135, 250,
291, 667, 874
1:8 . . . . .96, 121
1:9 . . . . 98, 107, 412, 858
1:9 – 10 418
1:9 – 14 . . . . 99, 110, 111, 112
1:10 . . . 94, 103, 106, 115, 121, 199, 205,
221, 424, 636, 664, 691, 749, 931
1:10 – 11 . . . . 99, 104, 201, 559
1:10 – 12 221
1:11 . . . . . . 121, 155, 184, 221, 251, 275,
277, 344, 460, 576, 598, 667,
733, 780, 781, 785, 802, 835, 931
1:12 . . . . 94, 111, 115 166, 184, 186,
207, 244, 260, 328, 344, 347,
380, 416, 418, 420, 428, 446,
450, 466, 469, 529, 552,
562, 576, 587, 605, 619,
623, 636, 657, 665, 722, 727,
749, 771, 800, 802, 804, 820,
884, 887, 897, 936, 938
1:12 – 13 . . . . .91, 106, 199, 200, 356, 557,
848, 849, 852, 928, 932
1:12 – 14 718
1:13 . . . . .167, 198, 209, 344, 347,
420, 715, 753, 800, 804
1:14 . . . . .88, 93, 94, 99, 100, 102, 113,
115, 117, 118, 135, 137, 146,
155, 161, 169, 180, 182, 201,
203, 204, 215, 277, 295,
324, 335, 338, 357, 359, 376,
411, 414, 419, 451, 463, 475,
497, 499, 508, 553, 560, 562,

598, 618, 619, 620, 633, 635,
645, 653, 678, 682, 713,
717, 722, 724, 749, 758, 766,
769, 770, 779, 800, 826, 828,
836, 881, 883, 885, 895, 923,
929, 931, 934, 937, 938
1:15 . . . . 94, 113, 115, 134, 206, 217, 220,
370, 484, 506, 537, 559, 562,
874, 884 . . . .
1:15 – 18 111
1:16 . . . . 192, 356, 850
1:16 – 17 359
1:16 – 18 113 . . . .
1:17 . . . . .39, 94, 97, 99, 101, 104, 107,
110, 112, 128, 161, 186,
235, 245, 271, 356, 414,
538, 588, 679, 682, 722, 750,
802, 883, 895, 896, 931
1:18 . . . . . . 89, 91, 94, 110, 115, 139, 154,
157, 161, 180, 186, 197, 202,
204, 220, 221, 243, 244, 250,
251, 263, 275, 277, 285, 296,
314, 328, 335, 336, 340, 371,
373, 408, 423, 448, 451, 477,
479, 483, 485, 561, 562, 587,
594, 618, 619, 620, 641, 652,
666, 682, 689, 699, 703, 714,
715, 716, 718, 724, 725, 770,
848, 880, 883, 894, 927
1:19 . . . . .83, 130, 132, 134, 181, 196,
234, 259, 272, 334, 353, 366,
409, 441, 443, 467, 475, 502,
512, 529, 534, 700, 828
1:19 – 28 . . . . 125, 160, 292
1:19 – 34 . . . . 125, 141, 143, 484
1:19 – 51 . . . . 141, 143, 158, 893
1:19 – 2:11 161
1:19 – 10:42 486
1:19 – 12:50 65
1:20 . . . . 148, 217, 218, 377, 476, 883
1:20 – 21 . . . . 139, 306, 748
1:21 . . . . .377, 929
1:22 – 23 132
1:23 . . . . .292, 558
1:24 . . . . 193, 234, 372, 391, 441, 512
1:25 123
1:27 . . . . .135, 139, 220, 506,
525, 537, 559, 578
1:28 495
1:29 . . . . 128, 135, 136, 139, 144, 157,
251, 274, 465, 475, 484, 679,
735, 752, 758, 759, 777, 778,

783, 784, 787, 799, 803, 811,
816, 820, 843, 929, 931
1:29 – 34 .125, 160
1:30 . . . . 112, 215, 506, 537
1:31 . . . . 132, 139, 895
1:31 – 32 292
1:32 139
1:32 – 33 . . . . 340, 414
1:32 – 34 221
1:33 . . . . .112, 131, 138, 139,
198, 215, 676, 718
1:33 – 34 327
1:34 91
1:35 . . . . .162, 921
1:35 – 40 920
1:35 – 42 . . . . .98, 143, 160
1:35 – 51 125
1:36 . . . . 148, 157, 758, 784
1:37 . . . . .149, 894
1:37 – 39 250
1:38 . . . . .146, 149, 152, 155, 195,
326, 392, 498, 585, 735,
844, 845, 917, 918, 940
1:39 . . . . .150, 153, 247, 261, 262,
315, 450, 508, 550, 637,
784, 903, 918, 940
1:40 . . . . .149, 304, 593, 719, 746,
830, 895, 919, 920
1:40 – 41 377
1:41 . . . .145, 146, 150, 326, 345, 484, 940
1:42 . . . . 145, 146, 304, 895, 912
1:43 . . . . 145, 274, 917, 918
1:43 – 46 620
1:43 – 51 . . . . 143, 148, 160
1:44 . . . . 195, 303, 550
1:45 . . . .195, 197, 326, 345, 735, 895, 934
1:46 . . . .152, 247, 249, 315, 460, 637, 940
1:47 156
1:47 – 48 . . . . 342, 735
1:48 484
1:49 . . . . . .91, 134, 137, 326, 345, 526, 537
1:50 622
1:51 . . . . .157, 161, 162, 169, 170, 196,
197, 201, 202, 243, 272, 285,
289, 329, 337, 339, 342, 412,
415, 422, 425, 450, 459, 461,
464, 551, 555, 585, 587, 593,
603, 604, 841. 885, 916
2 . . . . .187, 256, 607, 621, 650,
678, 680, 690, 692

2 – 12 544
2:1 . . . . .125, 132, 141, 144, 149,
217, 259, 442, 524, 733,
798, 825, 827, 828
2:1 – 2 163
2:1 – 3 158
2:1 – 4 896
2:1 – 11 . . . . 160, 164, 169, 173, 214, 218,
226, 233, 260, 307, 825, 900
2:1 – 3:21 210
2:3 162
2:3 – 4 798
2:3 – 5 799
2:4 . . . . 158, 170, 171, 235, 243, 354,
355, 371, 395, 409, 439, 516,
539, 551, 576, 596, 643, 675,
713, 729, 732, 739, 788, 799,
802, 820, 843, 848, 864
2:5 164
2:5 – 8 160
2:6 172
2:7 181
2:8 219
2:8 – 10 172
2:9 – 10 172
2:9 – 11 .160, 167
2:10 . . . .167, 171, 746 . . . .
2:11 . . . . . . 160, 170, 173, 182, 183, 204,
259, 263, 302, 306, 326, 375,
412, 442, 473, 497, 558, 560,
621, 666, 825, 826, 827, 885, 895
2:12 . . . . .164, 196, 215, 269, 302,
352, 353, 808, 817, 894
2:12 – 15 803
2:12 – 17 175
2:12 – 25 214, 226, 329, 338, 475, 540, 826
2:13 . . . . 303, 353, 516
2:13 – 23 179
2:13 – 25 260
2:14 . . . . .180, 234
2:15 – 17 175
2:16 . . . . 133, 276, 614
2:17 . . . . 150 185, 186, 205, 540, 794, 810
2:18 . . . . .177, 827
2:18 – 19 204
2:18 – 20 175
2:18 – 22 826
2:19 . . . . 179, 823, 826, 827, 836
2:19 – 22 929
2:20 179

2:21 . . . . 179, 243, 758, 834
2:21 – 22 175, 181, 205, 329, 376, 540, 827
2:22 . . . . . . 150, 180, 182, 185, 186, 540,
737, 832, 835, 843, 865
2:23 . . . . .179, 196, 215, 269,
303, 512, 516, 843
2:23 – 25 . . . . 175, 413, 561
2:24 413
2:24 – 25 306, 327, 342, 343, 735, 913, 928
2:25 . . . . 192, 193, 210, 242, 292, 701
3 . . . . .56, 105, 154, 256, 260, 382,
554, 680, 691, 727, 804
3:1 . . . . .196, 372, 379, 380,
512, 746, 818, 819
3:1 – 2 . . . . .131, 818
3:1 – 9 829
3:1 – 11 . . . . 104, 184, 410, 665
3:1 – 13 559
3:1 – 15 . . . . 205, 377, 379, 819, 878
3:1 – 21 . . . . .56, 214, 473
3:2 . . . . 197, 199, 201, 330, 392, 475,
506, 537, 597, 748, 795, 896
3:3 . . . . .198, 202, 380, 383, 407,
414, 428, 448, 763, 765,
863, 868, 930, 936
3:3 – 5 416
3:3 – 8 932
3:5 . . . . .197, 200, 380, 414, 428,
448, 763, 863, 868, 930
3:6 343
3:7 . . . . .220, 235
3:8 862
3:9 116
3:10 . . . . 131, 134, 194
3:11 . . . . .221, 438
3:11 – 12 343
3:12 204
3:13 . . . . 201, 204, 220
3:13 – 15 204
3:14 . . . . 39, 109, 220, 235, 342, 357, 412,
526, 555, 702, 722, 803, 933, 936
3:14 – 15 . . . . .468, 819
3:15 . . . . .240, 330
3:16 . . . . . . 103, 117, 164, 185, 203, 207,
220, 244, 249, 286, 294, 303,
307, 338, 355, 408, 412, 418,
420, 422, 425, 428, 450, 465,
467, 483, 496, 498, 514, 518,
519, 551, 562, 595, 599, 603,
608, 634, 640, 651, 655, 660,

669, 685, 699, 703, 722, 723,
770, 815, 868, 913, 928, 932
3:16 – 17 .298, 451
3:16 – 18 91
3:16 – 19 562
3:16 – 21 . . . . 204 – 205, 220, 223,
470, 666, 826
3:17 . . . . 97, 294, 355, 426, 463
3:17 – 18 .287, 562
3:17 – 19 554
3:17 – 21 483
3:18 . . . . 117, 209, 555, 565, 679
3:18 – 20 666
3:19 . . . . 288, 294, 298
3:19 – 20 96
3:19 – 21 207
3:20 678
3:20 – 21 221
3:21 . . . . 204, 366, 451, 682, 895
3:22 . . . . 178, 226, 234, 845, 847, 933
3:22 – 24 214
3:22 – 36 .226, 484
3:24 495
3:25 – 26 214
3:26 . . . . .234, 483
3:27 292
3:27 – 30 .214, 218
3:29 . . . .168, 172, 224, 225, 233, 656, 720
3:29 – 30 849
3:30 . . . . .235, 367
3:31 . . . . 224, 448, 559, 780
3:31 – 32 224
3:31 – 36 . . . . 205, 210, 214, 826
3:32 . . . . 220, 224, 849
3:32 – 35 682
3:33 224
3:34 . . . . 221, 413, 812
3:35 . . . . 224, 683, 913, 914
3:36 . . . . .91, 206, 224, 452, 679, 738
4 . . . . . . .56, 185, 233, 256, 268, 650, 680
4:1 . . . . 131, 305, 578, 904
4:1 – 2 . . . . .215, 933
4:1 – 3 234
4:1 – 42 . . . . 56, 260, 307, 932
4:2 . . . . .215 – 216
4:3 – 4 234
4:3 259
4:4 . . . . .234, 237

4:6 249
4:7 . . . . 167, 243, 810
4:7 – 26 829
4:8 . . . . .205, 246
4:9 127
4:10 . . . . 245, 817, 884
4:10 – 11 376
4:10 – 14 . . . . .198, 375
4:11 242
4:12 423
4:14 . . . . . 116, 242, 245, 247, 326, 331
4:15 . . . . 167, 239, 242
4:16 – 18 237
4:16 – 19 151
4:17 – 18 817
4:18 . . . . 342, 735, 842
4:19 . . . . 239, 242, 251
4:20 615
4:21 . . . . .165, 843
4:21 – 24 245
4:22 . . . . 246, 252, 371
4:23 . . . . 165, 233, 246, 256,
288, 305, 421, 843
4:23 – 24 .91, 682
4:25 . . . . 145, 148, 242, 251, 506, 537
4:25 – 26 476
4:26 312
4:27 247
4:27 – 28 247
4:28 . . . . .234, 795
4:29 . . . . .242, 250
4:34 . . . . 641, 676, 808, 928, 929
4:35 . . . . 250, 254, 260, 303, 307, 510
4:38 – 39 259
4:40 . . . . 233, 260, 305
4:41 250
4:42 . . . . .236, 330, 355, 406,
407, 413, 465, 541
4:43 – 45 .162, 259
4:43 – 46 258
4:43 – 54 .169, 353
4:44 . . . . .263, 929
4:45 259
4:46 259
4:47 . . . . .258, 439
4:47 – 48 270
4:48 . . . . .153, 880
4:48 – 51 258

4:52 – 54 258
4:53 . . . . .259, 614
4:54 . . . . 162, 258, 259, 260, 306
5 . . . . 268, 352, 554, 650, 680
5:1 . . . . 178, 302, 474
5:1 – 5 268
5:1 – 9 . . . . .272, 829
5:1 – 15 932
5:1 – 18 . . . . 169, 287, 292, 294, 297, 306,
            313, 368, 371, 374, 441, 442
5:1 – 8:11 . . . . 309, 311, 384, 386, 399, 486
5:2 . . . . 783, 791, 793
5:2 – 3 274
5:3 271
5:3 – 5 269
5:6 . . . . .116, 274, 275, 286, 701,
            735, 784, 844, 897
5:6 – 10 .268, 272
5:7 270
5:8 . . . . .270, 273
5:9 . . . . .116, 442
5:9 – 18 272
5:11 – 12 357
5:11 – 15 268
5:12 784
5:13 . . . . 270, 426, 557
5:14 . . . .178, 277, 286, 437, 749, 932, 937
5:16 . . . . 127, 392, 406
5:16 – 18 . . . . 268, 513, 641
5:17 . . . . 277, 285, 479
5:17 – 18 273
5:18 . . . . .91, 369, 371, 392, 406, 423,
            446, 479, 480, 762, 780
5:19 . . . . .206, 286, 370, 513,
            618, 770, 928, 929
5:19 – 20 201
5:19 – 23 . . . . 287, 366, 480
5:19 – 24 . . . . .284, 289
5:19 – 27 928
5:19 – 29 152
5:19 – 30 641
5:19 – 47 .58, 571
5:20 . . . . .622, 914
5:20 – 22 .286, 287
5:21 . . . . 287, 289, 297, 343, 486
5:21 – 22 284
5:21 – 29 .504, 505
5:21 – 30 340

5:22 . . . . . . 289, 290, 295, 297, 343, 393,
            396, 455, 471, 680, 722
5:22 – 27 . . . . . . .405, 407, 422, 478, 622,
            750, 751, 752, 784
5:22 – 29 . . . . 500, 511, 852, 865, 930
5:22 – 30 . . . . 206, 554, 563
5:23 . . . . .297, 422
5:24 . . . .340, 419, 676, 680, 929, 932, 937
5:25 . . . . 91, 165, 290, 504, 511
5:25 – 29 .284, 289
5:26 . . . . 119, 121, 297, 419, 476, 618
5:26 – 27 . . . . 284, 291, 396, 722
5:27 . . . . 297, 450, 454, 503, 623
5:28 . . . . .165, 297
5:28 – 29 . . . . 288, 290, 328, 333, 937
5:29 297
5:30 . . . . 291, 413, 676, 714
5:30 – 47 750
5:31 . . . . .294, 407
5:32 . . . . .293, 294
5:33 – 35 291
5:34 297
5:36 . . . . 168, 291, 305, 621, 666, 808
5:37 . . . . .414, 929
5:37 – 38 .668, 670
5:38 . . . . .414, 653
5:37 – 38 .291, 332
5:38 343
5:39 . . . . 150, 183, 298, 482
5:39 – 40 291
5:39 – 47 557
5:41 561
5:41 – 47 294
5:42 298
5:42 – 44 91
5:43 . . . . 104, 195, 260, 633
5:44 . . . . .91, 104, 834
5:45 563
5:45 – 46 448
5:45 – 47 . . . . 116, 377, 424, 934
5:46 . . . . 298, 325, 929, 935
6 . . . . . . 56, 154, 268, 302, 303, 306, 311,
            316, 324, 338, 609, 650, 904
6:1 . . . . 178, 324, 894
6:1 – 4 301
6:1 – 15 . . . . 169, 309, 316, 326, 340
6:2 . . . . .265, 306
6:4 . . . . 179, 269, 302, 352, 516

6:5 510
6:5 – 9 301
6:6 . . . . .375, 444
6:7 149
6:8 – 9 148
6:9 795
6:10 – 13 301
6:11 324
6:12 333
6:14 . . . . .129, 220, 326, 336, 377,
            506, 537, 559, 929
6:14 – 15 . . . . 301, 307, 325, 513, 539
6:15 . . . . 303, 311, 325, 326, 526
6:16 – 17 310
6:16 – 21 .316, 325
6:18 862
6:18 – 19 310
6:19 116
6:20 . . . . .310, 314
6:21 310
6:22 . . . . .900, 904
6:22 – 24 335
6:22 – 71 . . . . .56, 309, 904
6:23 302
6:24 341
6:25 116
6:25 – 71 302
6:26 . . . . 332, 334, 335
6:26 – 27 336
6:27 . . . . 91, 331, 339, 340
6:27 – 29 91
6:28 – 29 .290, 437
6:29 . . . . .290, 366
6:30 . . . . 302, 331, 337
6:30 – 33 328
6:31 794
6:31 – 33 303
6:32 – 33 91
6:32 – 35 843
6:33 . . . . 329, 331, 342, 355
6:34 – 40 330
6:35 . . . . 198, 248, 312, 337, 338, 406,
            408, 411, 461, 463, 473, 504,
            587, 616, 617, 650, 735
6:36 343
6:37 . . . . 338, 460, 713, 715
6:37 – 39 343
6:37 – 40 335

6:38 . . . . 260, 342, 413, 676
6:38 – 39 334
6:39 . . . . 305, 339, 586, 676
6:40 . . . . 206, 334, 339
6:41 . . . . 339, 342, 348, 357, 372
6:41 – 42 . . . . 337, 342, 406
6:41 – 51 334
6:42 341
6:43 . . . . 342, 370, 690
6:44 . . . . . . 106, 328, 336, 338, 339, 343,
556, 586, 713, 716, 929
6:45 794
6:45 – 46 91
6:47 . . . . 338, 834
6:48 – 51 337
6:49 . . . . 317, 338
6:49 – 51 337
6:50 – 51 342
6:51 . . . . 339, 340, 341, 343, 355,
464, 515, 657, 722
6:51 – 56 . . . . 108, 758
6:51 – 58 167
6:52 . . . . 334, 337, 341, 406
6:52 – 59 . . . . 324, 338
6:53 . . . . 345, 347, 439
6:53 – 58 330
6:54 586
6:56 . . . . 414, 653
6:57 . . . . 637, 905
6:58 342
6:59 . . . . 132, 749
6:60 . . . . 344, 345, 350
6:60 – 61 343
6:60 – 71 343
6:61 . . . . 357, 370, 372, 675
6:62 . . . . 830, 848
6:63 198
6:63 – 65 344
6:64 . . . . 182, 205, 346, 444, 593, 733, 764
6:65 347
6:66 345
6:67 . . . . 162, 306, 341, 529
6:68 916
6:68 – 69 753
6:69 . . . . 347, 506, 718
6:70 . . . . 436, 576, 586, 593
6:70 – 71 527
6:71 . . . . 182, 345, 375, 444, 593, 733, 764

7 . . . . 56, 268, 382, 386, 405, 458
7:1 . . . 103, 178, 357, 446, 498, 541, 762
7:1 – 2 352
7:2 . . . . 269, 374, 474
7:3 355
7:3 – 5 . . . . 178, 352
7:4 . . . . 178, 355, 749, 895
7:5 . . . . 182, 205, 353
7:6 409
7:6 – 9 352
7:7 . . . . 103, 358
7:8 . . . . 357, 365, 374, 515
7:8 – 10 933
7:10 . . . . 357, 365, 368, 845, 847
7:10 – 13 352
7:11 . . . . 406, 830
7:12 . . . . 358, 359, 372, 378
7:13 . . . . 354, 359, 445, 513
7:13 – 14 551
7:14 . . . . 374, 391, 415, 474, 749
7:14 – 19 369
7:14 – 52 . . . . 56, 365, 409, 415, 458
7:15 . . . . 373, 406
7:15 – 19 366
7:16 . . . . 381, 676
7:16 – 17 365
7:16 – 18 682
7:18 676
7:19 . . . . 369, 408, 446
7:20 467
7:20 – 24 369
7:23 . . . . 271, 481
7:24 . . . . 382, 680
7:25 . . . . 373, 445, 446
7:25 – 27 . . . . 440, 442
7:25 – 29 . . . . 369, 372
7:25 – 36 369
7:26 . . . . 357, 373, 476, 749
7:27 373
7:28 . . . . 112, 195, 372, 374,
407, 561, 676, 749
7:28 – 29 665
7:29 929
7:30 . . . . 165, 354, 372, 378, 392,
406, 409, 483, 513, 539
7:31 . . . . 265, 372, 373
7:32 . . . . 131, 178, 193, 357,
378, 392, 406, 512

7:32 – 36 830
7:33 . . . . 557, 676
7:34 . . . . 409, 605
7:35 606
7:35 – 36 406
7:36 387
7:37 . . . . 370, 381, 474, 561
7:37 – 38 . . . . 198, 376, 381, 814
7:37 – 39 . . . . 150, 240, 365, 374, 817, 864
7:38 . . . . 374, 794, 814
7:38 – 39 810
7:39 . . . . 182, 198, 375, 540, 812, 814, 826
7:40 . . . . 129, 377
7:42 . . . . 195, 934
7:43 . . . . 442, 467
7:44 . . . . 387, 392
7:45 . . . . 193, 357
7:45 – 46 . . . . 372, 701
7:45 – 49 406
7:45 – 52 513
7:47 – 48 357
7:47 – 49 131
7:47 – 52 131
7:48 357
7:48 – 52 819
7:50 – 52 . . . . 178, 378
7:51 383
7:52 . . . . 387, 390, 819
7:53 – 8:2 386
7:53 – 811 . . . . 386 – 90, 405, 455, 471
8 . . . . 56, 405, 458, 471, 557
8 – 9 458
8:1 – 2 390
8:2 . . . . 393, 395
8:3 . . . . 394, 441
8:3 – 6 386
8:5 394
8:6 . . . . 391, 392, 395
8:6 – 8 386
8:7 . . . . 395, 396, 932
8:8 391
8:9 – 11 386
8:10 843
8:11 . . . . 396, 397, 405
8:12 . . . . 96, 145, 331, 405, 407, 427, 429,
438, 451, 458, 485, 557, 562, 931
8:12 – 30 . . . . 412, 413
8:12 – 59 . . . . 56, 430

8:12 – 10:42 . . . . 399, 426,
      452, 455, 468, 471, 481, 483, 486
8:13 131
8:14 . . . . 291, 428, 830
8:14 – 16 408
8:14 – 18 407
8:15 408
8:16 . . . . .428, 676
8:15 – 16 . . . . .206, 422
8:17 .480, 794
8:17 – 18 408
8:18 . . . . 411, 413, 676
8:19 665
8:20 . . . . .132, 165, 341, 354,
      413, 426, 539, 749
8:21 . . . . 410, 428, 429, 605
8:21 – 30 . . . . .413, 417
8:23 . . . . 103, 260, 421, 428
8:24 . . . . 275, 420, 428, 429, 932
8:26 . . . . 221, 222, 419, 676
8:26 – 29 682
8:27 444
8:28 . . . . .109, 422, 555, 702, 722, 762
8:29 . . . .417, 605, 618, 641, 676, 770, 929
8:31 . . . . .127, 416, 419, 422, 424,
      427, 428, 429, 631, 653
8:31 – 32 . . . . .340, 415
8:31 – 36 931
8:31 – 38 396
8:31 – 58 934
8:31 – 59 413
8:32 . . . . 420, 424, 429, 682, 766
8:32 – 36 . . . . .451, 718
8:33 421
8:34 . . . . 414, 429, 451
8:34 – 35 505
8:34 – 36 938
8:35 . . . . 429, 614, 615, 936
8:35 – 36 . . . . 657, 766, 932
8:36 . . . . 206, 414, 505, 619, 787, 931
8:37 . . . . 414, 417, 418, 427, 446
8:38 . . . . 419, 420, 467
8:39 418
8:40 . . . . 418, 419, 446, 682
8:41 423
8:41 – 42 . . . . .91, 426
8:42 . . . . .91, 195, 631
8:42 – 43 682

8:43 . . . . 411, 414, 427
8:44 . . . . .418, 420
8:44 – 46 682
8:46 679
8:47 421
8:48 418
8:50 423
8:51 . . . . 414, 427, 505
8:52 . . . . .414, 467
8:54 . . . . .91, 603
8:54 – 55 480
8:55 414
8:56 . . . . .427, 560
8:58 . . . . .87, 93, 116, 246, 312, 332,
      504, 560, 650, 928
8:59 . . . . 436, 479, 557
9 . . . . 56, 459, 462, 471, 481
9:1 438
9:1 – 3 500
9:1 – 7 .452, 829
9:1 – 41 . . . . 56, 169, 468, 570, 932
9:2 . . . . 442, 443, 449, 452, 454
9:3 . . . . 168, 438, 453, 496, 666, 895
9:3 – 5 . . . . .437, 449
9:4 . . . . 194, 235, 440, 498, 676
9:4 – 5 557
9:4 – 6 454
9:5 . . . . .96, 406
9:6 . . . . .438, 441
9:6 – 7 438
9:7 . . . . 145, 150, 198, 450
9:8 – 12 . . . . .440, 441
9:8 – 34 452
9:9 442
9:11 . . . . .442, 446
9:12 . . . . .446, 448
9:13 . . . . 442, 446, 512
9:13 – 17 . . . . .441, 443
9:14 . . . . 439, 442, 454
9:15 . . . . .442, 447
9:16 . . . . 131, 377, 447, 467
9:17 . . . . .242, 447
9:18 – 23 . . . . .443, 444
9:21 . . . . 439, 446, 448
9:22 . . . . .127, 358, 436, 449, 450,
      512, 513, 561, 675
9:24 . . . . .448, 453
9:24 – 34 446

9:25 448
9:27 . . . . .116, 448
9:28 450
9:28 – 29 131
9:30 – 33 448
9:31 . . . . 366, 447, 450, 453
9:32 436
9:34 . . . . .450, 460
9:35 . . . . 274, 440, 454, 701
9:35 – 38 . . . . 441, 443, 450
9:35 – 41 . . . . .450, 452
9:36 452
9:38 450
9:39 . . . .103, 116, 206, 407, 454, 639, 931
9:39 – 41 . . . . 449, 451, 453, 666
9:40 – 41 131
10 . . . . 56, 458, 486, 519, 616
10:1 769
10:1 – 5 . . . . 458, 461, 463, 468, 698
10:1 – 9 461
10:1 – 21 . . . . .58, 455, 468, 469, 471,
      476, 481, 571
10:3 . . . . 466, 468, 845
10:3 – 5 . . . . 120, 470, 477
10:4 . . . . .468, 845
10:5 468
10:6 . . . . .416, 458, 461, 498, 500,
      551, 650, 691, 698, 916
10:7 . . . . 331, 463, 469, 476
10:7 – 10 461
10:7 – 18 458
10:8 . . . . .463, 769
10:9 . . . . .331, 459
10:10 .95, 769
10:10 – 11 .766
10:10 – 16 .461
10:11 . . .332, 466, 475, 476, 515, 650, 758
10:11 – 16 .463
10:12 – 13 .915
10:13 478
10:14 . . . . 332, 475, 515
10:15 .466, 469
10:16 . . . . .235, 469, 515, 597, 795,
      845, 887, 898, 915
10:17 . . . . 222, 465, 469
10:17 – 18 . . . . .577, 582
10:18 . . . . . .133, 469, 478, 515, 516, 517,
      596, 605, 670, 735, 811, 813, 846
10:19 377

10:20 367
10:21 . . . . 458, 467
10:22 . . . . 269, 458, 475, 535,
                          748, 760, 784, 843
10:22 – 23 474
10:22 – 42 . . . . .56, 455, 471
10:23 . . . . .466, 749
10:24 . . . . 479, 698, 749
10:24 – 30 480
10:25 . . . . .483, 621
10:25 – 30 . . . . .476, 479
10:26 . . . . .478, 483
10:27 . . . . .475, 845
10:28 . . . . .479, 719
10:29 – 30 719
10:30 . . . . 467, 476, 480, 485, 641
10:31 483
10:32 . . . . .168, 666
10:34 794
10:34 – 36 482
10:35 . . . . .721, 835
10:35 – 36 91
10:36 . . . . .91, 475, 485
10:37 . . . . .168, 666
10:38 . . . . .621, 718
10:40 – 42 . . . . .483, 495
10:42 486
11 . . . . .483, 524
11:1 . . . . 132, 195, 483, 496
11:1 – 2 496
11:1 – 4 378
11:1 – 16 494
11:1 – 57 . . . . 169, 521, 523
11:1 – 12:50 . . . . . 486, 521, 530, 532, 544
11:2 . . . . .524, 847
11:3 . . . . 483, 497, 499
11:4 . . . . 91, 499, 517, 603, 713
11:4 – 6 501
11:5 . . . . 483, 498, 499, 500, 517, 595
11:6 518
11:7 178
11:8 . . . . .501, 502
11:8 – 10 502
11:9 . . . . .416, 557
11:10 . . . . 194, 518, 597, 748
11:11 178
11:11 – 13 . . . . .511, 512
11:11 – 14 . . . . .501, 504

11:13 182
11:14 . . . . 501, 504, 749
11:15 510
11:16 . . . . 145, 606, 876, 877
11:17 – 37 . . . . .494, 502
11:18 495
11:19 . . . . .501, 507
11:20 506
11:20 – 37 829
11:21 . . . . 505, 507, 509
11:21 – 22 510
11:22 507
11:23 – 26 511
11:24 503
11:25 . . . . . . 332, 518, 520, 521, 530, 618
11:25 – 26 510
11:26 . . . . .518, 520
11:27 . . . . 91, 220, 537, 559
11:28 392
11:29 – 31 503
11:30 502
11:31 614
11:32 509
11:33 . . . . 509, 519, 593
11:35 519
11:36 595
11:38 . . . . .519, 831
11:38 – 44 494
11:39 . . . . 133, 501, 503
11:40 . . . . .154, 713
11:40 – 41 91
11:41 712
11:44 . . . . 369, 510, 795, 819, 832
11:45 127
11:45 – 46 . . . . .502, 512
11:45 – 57 494
11:46 131
11:47 . . . . .193, 486
11:48 . . . . 133, 615, 744
11:49 . . . . 514, 516, 746
11:49 – 52 519,
           541, 700, 722, 736, 778, 782, 845
11:50 . . . . .515, 678
11:50 – 52 746
11:51 . . . . 375, 514, 516, 793
11:51 – 52 . . . . .182, 758
11:52 . . . . .91, 781, 795
11:53 . . . . 517, 523, 529, 541, 746, 762

11:54 . . . . 132, 354, 523, 749
11:55 . . . . .179, 303
11:55 – 56 . . . . 269, 529, 535
11:57 . . . . .193, 512
12 . . . . 65, 130, 558, 874
12:1 . . . . . . 516, 526, 535, 550, 575, 828
12:1 – 3 523
12:1 – 11 . . . . 521, 532, 534, 763
12:1 – 19 784
12:2 . . . . .251, 523
12:3 . . . . 527, 528, 614, 818, 821, 842
12:4 . . . . 593, 733, 758, 764
12:4 – 6 523
12:6 . . . . 182, 375, 529, 597
12:7 . . . . 526, 818, 913
12:7 – 8 523
12:8 557
12:9 . . . . 531, 534, 541
12:9 – 11 . . . . 513, 523, 535
12:11 127
12:12 – 13 534
12:12 – 19 . . . . 521, 526, 763, 784
12:13 . . . . .134, 152, 220, 506,
                          537, 540, 559, 894
12:13 – 15 526
12:14 . . . . .534, 794
12:14 – 15 . . . . .534, 536
12:15 – 16 150
12:16 . . . . .180, 532, 534, 540,
                          827, 842, 843, 859
12:17 – 18 529
12:17 – 19 . . . . .512, 534
12:19 . . . . 131, 535, 550
12:20 – 22 556
12:20 – 36 549
12:20 – 50 . . . . .58, 521, 549 – 50, 571
12:21 195
12:21 – 22 149
12:22 148
12:23 . . . . . . 165, 182, 553, 554, 556, 560,
                     561, 576, 603, 713, 826
12:23 – 26 550
12:24 . . . . . . 555, 556, 564, 691, 698, 822
12:24 – 26 551
12:25 553
12:26 . . . . .145, 617
12:27 . . . . 165, 181, 554, 593
12:27 – 28 . . . . .554, 682

12:27 – 36 552
12:28 . . . . 564, 603, 713
12:29 . . . . 549, 570, 841
12:31 . . . . .96, 206, 642, 681, 702,
721, 722, 727, 930
12:31 – 32 554
12:32 . . . . 109, 526, 933, 936
12:32 – 33 181
12:33 . . . . .182, 375
12:34 . . . . . . 109, 204, 235, 549, 570, 702
12:35 . . . . .96, 558
12:35 – 36 830
12:36 . . . . 560, 561, 653, 694
12:36 – 43 259
12:37 541
12:37 – 42 670
12:37 – 43 . . . . 549, 558, 565
12:37 – 50 549
12:38 809
12:38 – 40 451
12:38 – 41 130
12:40 . . . . 561, 565, 716
12:41 116
12:42 . . . . 131, 445, 558, 566
12:42 – 43 817
12:43 . . . . .559, 566
12:44 . . . . 112, 370, 563, 676
12:44 – 50 . . . . 549, 550, 561
12:45 . . . . .620, 676
12:46 195
12:46 – 48 562
12:47 463
12:47 – 48 206
12:47 – 50 682
12:48 633
12:48 – 49 641
12:49 676
12:49 – 50 563, 605
13 . . . . 65, 796, 891, 919, 920
13 – 16 729
13 – 17 . . . . .571, 578
13:1 . . . . .48, 165, 354, 524, 577, 587,
593, 595, 597, 603, 604, 610,
613, 627, 631, 638, 639,
643, 644, 646, 650, 661, 664,
671, 674, 686, 689, 698,
706, 712, 732, 848, 911
13:1 – 3 . . . . 575, 576, 577, 830
13:1 – 5 . . . . 570, 575, 578

13:1 – 17 . . . . 307, 939, 940
13:1 – 20 . . . . 590, 592, 598, 795
13:1 – 29 603
13:1 – 30 . . . . 573, 574, 600, 705
13:1 – 17:26 . . . . 571, 573, 706
13:1 – 18:1 572
13:1 – 20:31 65
13:2 . . . . 524, 584, 593, 735, 764
13:3 . . . . 91, 195, 222, 683, 848
13:4 . . . . 524, 795, 796
13:4 – 5 . . . . .575, 899
13:5 . . . . 198, 581, 584
13:6 – 9 920
13:6 – 11 . . . . 570, 579, 584
13:7 584
13:8 587
13:10 . . . . .584, 586, 588, 595, 652,
689, 758, 860, 897, 914
13:11 . . . . 205, 593, 764
13:12 . . . . 581, 585, 586
13:12 – 17 586
13:12 – 20 . . . . . . 570, 582, 583, 584, 587
13:13 . . . . .392, 582
13:14 . . . . .392, 581
13:14 – 15 605
13:15 582
13:16 . . . . .665, 676
13:17 880
13:18 . . . . 593, 719, 809
13:18 – 20 586
13:19 . . . . .104, 642
13:20 . . . . . . 104, 620, 666, 676, 676, 869
13:21 764
13:21 – 22 592
13:21 – 30 719
13:22 598
13:22 – 25 . . . . 594, 830, 898, 918
13:23 . . . . .45, 118, 147, 746, 747, 800,
815, 830, 898, 912, 917
13:23 – 25 935
13:23 – 26 . . . . 592, 593, 921
13:24 . . . . 594, 598, 606, 747, 830
13:24 – 25 917
13:25 . . . . 599, 830, 898
13:26 598
13:27 . . . . 572, 597, 598, 599, 642
13:27 – 30 . . . . .592, 596
13:28 598

13:30 . . . . . . 194, 475, 572, 576, 598, 603,
605, 638, 748, 795, 828
13:30 – 31 644
13:31 . . .574, 574, 598, 602, 615, 663, 697
13:31 – 32 .604, 608
13:31 – 38 574,
602, 603, 607, 610, 622, 627,
646, 661, 671, 686, 695, 697, 914
13:31 – 14:31 573
13:31 – 16:33 . . . . .58, 573
13:33 . . .557, 604, 606, 622, 676, 678, 717
13:33 – 38 830
13:34 . . . . .608, 728
13:34 – 35 . . . . 656, 725, 913, 915, 939
13:36 . . . . .677, 678
13:36 – 37 920
13:36 – 38 . . . . 606, 752, 917
13:38 . . . . 574, 602, 697, 738, 915
14 . . . . 636, 654, 689
14:1 . . . .610, 616, 617, 619, 624, 641, 642
14:1 – 2 . . . . .91, 617
14:1 – 4 . . . . 613, 849, 937
14:1 – 6 . . . . .691, 720
14:1 – 7 185
14:1 – 14 . . . . 574, 605, 606
14:1 – 31 . . . . .613, 630
14:1 – 15:7 667
14:1 – 16:24 695
14:2 . . . . 260, 605, 639, 657, 659
14:2 – 3 . 307, 610, 614, 635, 637, 639, 724
14:2 – 6 678
14:3 636
14:3 – 6 575
14:4 . . . . .605, 618
14:5 876
14:5 – 7 .616, 617
14:6 . . . . . . 172, 202, 222, 263, 292, 332,
381, 411, 419, 424, 463, 605,
625, 633, 634, 635, 643, 681,
682, 683, 684, 694, 699, 717,
725, 766, 770, 779, 848, 849,
857, 884, 929, 931, 937
14:7 . . . . .633, 676
14:8 – 9 149
14:8 – 14 619
14:9 . . . . 154, 451, 633
14:9 – 11 .619, 621
14:10 . . . . .168, 340, 414, 622,
625, 653, 666, 723

14:10 – 11 . . . . .637, 723
14:11 153
14:12 . . . . .438, 453, 575, 623, 626,
634, 658, 848, 849
14:12 – 13 438
14:12 – 14 . . . . 619, 621, 668, 699
14:12 – 15 610
14:13 . . . . 206, 623, 654
14:13 – 14 . . . .
575, 623, 626, 631, 654, 658, 692
14:14 613
14:15 . . . . .630, 638, 639, 641, 642,
643, 644, 655, 657
14:15 – 18 113
14:15 – 21 . . . . .631, 638
14:15 – 31 574
14:16 . . . . . . 573, 631, 636, 637, 640, 667,
677, 692, 721, 725, 928, 930
14:16 – 17 . . . . 633, 636, 637, 640, 812
14:16 – 20 930
14:17 . . . . .245, 340, 633, 634,
653, 667, 681, 930
14:18 . . . . 575, 634, 701, 858, 859
14:18 – 19 528
14:18 – 20 . . . . 802, 837, 904
14:18 – 21 . . . . .573, 930
14:19 . . . . 557, 605, 636, 689, 835
14:19 – 20 . . . . .678, 692
14:19 – 24 689
14:20 . . . . . . 340, 633, 636, 653, 718, 723
14:20 – 28 849
14:21 . . . . .552, 630, 639, 641, 642,
644, 655, 657, 699
14:22 – 24 638
14:23 . . . . .552, 575, 605, 614, 630,
633, 636, 637, 641, 642,
644, 655, 657, 699
14:24 676
14:25 . . . . 653, 674, 698
14:25 – 31 639
14:26 . . . . .579, 631, 632, 633,
667, 681, 718, 812
14:27 . . . . 575, 677, 693, 702, 859
14:27 – 29 . . . . .613, 630
14:28 . . . . 830, 848, 858
14:28 – 29 677
14:30 . . . . 555, 681, 727, 930
14:30 – 31 . . . . .702, 721
14:31 . . . . . . 572, 573, 605, 630, 631, 644,
649, 654, 655, 657, 732, 913

15 . . . . .609, 614
15:1 . . . . 332, 649, 652, 658, 784
15:1 – 3 . . . . .653, 654
15:1 – 8 . . . . 650, 654, 698, 934, 937
15:1 – 10 307
15:1 – 11 575
15:1 – 16 573
15:1 – 17 574
15:1 – 16:33 573
15:2 . . . . .133, 654
15:3 654
15:4 . . . . 340, 414, 654, 655, 861
15:4 – 5 . . . . 633, 654, 668
15:4 – 7 . . . . 651, 653, 654
15:4 – 10 340
15:5 . . . . 332, 452, 654, 899
15:6 . . . . .654, 655
15:7 . . . . .655, 658
15:7 – 8 699
15:8 . . . . .654, 682
15:9 222
15:9 – 10 660
15:9 – 11 . . . . .654, 656
15:9 – 16 700
15:10 . . . . .605, 693
15:11 . . . . 658, 692, 720, 859
15:12 . . . . 649, 658, 728, 913
15:12 – 17 . . . . 656, 658, 663, 725
15:13 721
15:15 936
15:16 . . . . .664, 699
15:17 . . . . 649, 663, 913
15:18 . . . . 649, 663, 668, 677
15:18 – 19 . . . . .103, 667
15:18 – 21 . . . . 575, 665, 718
15:18 – 25 . . . . .702, 720
15:18 – 27 574
15:18 – 16:4 573
15:18 – 16:24 .667
15:19 . . . . 595, 609, 669, 720
15:20 . . . . .103, 669
15:21 . . . . .676, 720
15:22 – 25 . . . . 665, 666, 667
15:23 676
15:24 275
15:25 . . . . . . 103, 669, 676, 794, 809, 810
15:26 . . . . . . 245, 631, 633, 635, 640, 667,
670, 681, 721, 812, 864

15:26 – 27 667
15:27 . . . . 676, 816, 874, 919
16 689
16:1 . . . . 663, 676, 698
16:1 – 3 103
16:1 – 4 .674, 676
16:1 – 15 . . . . 574, 668, 688
16:2 . . . . 165, 445, 676, 683, 691, 702
16:2 – 3 91
16:4 . . . . 165, 663, 675, 683, 691
16:4 – 6 . . . . 674, 676, 677
16:4 – 7 . . . . .680, 700
16:5 . . . . .830, 848
16:5 – 15 937
16:5 – 23 849
16:6 674
16:7 . . . . .575, 631, 633, 667, 674,
689, 690, 812, 848, 928
16:7 – 15 . . . . 674, 677, 683
16:8 . . . . 633, 685, 930, 940
16:8 – 11 . . . . 674, 678, 702, 721, 725
16:8 – 15 678
16:9 275
16:9 – 11 . . . . .678, 679
16:10 848
16:11 . . . . 206, 555, 642, 727, 930
16:12 682
16:12 – 15 . . . . 635, 674, 678, 681
16:13 . . . . . . 245, 540, 579, 623, 633, 635,
640, 684, 698, 703, 721, 725
16:13 – 14 . . . . .640, 698
16:13 – 15 668
16:14 633
16:16 . . . . .154, 605, 688, 691,
692, 830, 881, 914
16:16 – 18 . . . . .688, 689
16:16 – 19 557
16:16 – 24 . . . . .557, 574
16:17 . . . . .154, 848
16:18 830
16:19 154
16:19 – 24 . . . . .688, 690
16:19 – 31 495
16:20 916
16:20 – 24 859
16:21 . . . . .165, 698
16:23 . . . . 623, 699, 904, 914
16:23 – 24 575

16:24 . . . . 552, 656, 694, 720
16:25 . . . . .165, 461, 551, 650,
691, 700, 702, 749
16:25 – 28 . . . . .698, 700
16:25 – 33 . . 574, 602, 610, 627, 646, 661,
671, 686, 697 . . . .
16:27 91
16:27 – 28 848
16:28 . . .195, 574, 602, 697, 701, 830, 849
16:29 . . . . .461, 749
16:29 – 31 703
16:30 . . . . .195, 701
16:31 – 33 701
16:32 . . . . . . 165, 574, 602, 697, 835, 896
16:33 . . . . 574, 575, 663, 717, 859
17 . . . . 510, 701, 702, 729, 740, 891
17:1 . . . . .165, 206, 354, 510, 682,
712, 713, 717, 723, 726
17:1 – 2 .713, 714
17:1 – 5 . . . . 706, 712, 724
17:1 – 8 712
17:1 – 26 . . . . 573, 574, 940
17:2 . . . . .712, 713
17:3 . . . . 91, 116, 715, 716, 725
17:3 – 5 91
17:4 . . . . 248, 808, 928
17:4 – 5 715
17:5 . . . . .89, 101, 682, 712, 713,
723, 726, 930
17:6 . . . . .104, 184, 712, 718,
719, 721, 725, 895
17:6 – 8 . . . . 716, 720, 725
17:6 – 19 706
17:8 . . . . .721, 722
17:9 712
17:9 – 19 . . . . .716, 722
17:10 . . . . 683, 712, 718, 726
17:11 . . . . .664, 712, 713, 719, 720,
721, 725, 727, 848
17:11 – 12 . . . . .720, 721
17:12 . . . . 717, 727, 737, 809
17:13 . . . . 656, 727, 848, 859
17:14 . . . . 712, 718, 721, 722, 725, 727
17:14 – 16 765
17:15 . . . . 718, 727, 833, 848
17:16 . . . . 104, 184, 720, 727
17:17 682
17:17 – 19 718
17:18 . . . . 721, 765, 860, 937

17:19 . . . . 721, 728, 736, 758, 860
17:20 712
17:20 – 23 795
17:20 – 26 . . . . .706, 722
17:21 . . . . . . 712, 713, 724, 727, 728, 860
17:21 – 23 340
17:21 – 26 848
17:22 . . . . 712, 724, 726, 728
17:22 – 23 552
17:22 – 24 . . . . .682, 713
17:23 . . . . 633, 728, 863
17:23 – 26 222
17:24 . . . . 712, 713, 724, 725, 726
17:25 . . . . .713, 725
17:26 . . . . .633, 712
18 . . . . 911, 912, 917
18 – 19 . . . . 152, 763, 793
18 – 20 . . .61, 739, 779, 805, 822, 826, 845
18:1 . . . . 572, 573, 603, 644, 734, 805,
819, 828, 837, 845, 862
18:1 – 2 820
18:1 – 3 . . . . 731, 733, 734
18:1 – 12 . . . . 752, 769, 785
18:1 – 27 796
18:1 – 19:42 . . . . .739, 794
18:2 . . . . .735, 764
18:3 . . . . 193, 735, 738, 748, 750, 765
18:4 . . . . 145, 245, 735, 808, 844
18:4 – 9 . . . . 731, 735, 737
18:5 . . . . .764, 793
18:6 739
18:7 . . . . .145, 793
18:9 . . . . .762, 809
18:10 . . . . 607, 735, 751, 796
18:10 – 11 . . . . 731, 748, 920
18:11 . . . . .729, 810
18:12 . . . . .731, 734
18:12 – 27 929
18:13 . . . . .514, 746, 748, 749, 750,
751, 752, 757, 764, 796
18:13 – 14 . . . . .743, 744
18:13 – 27 731,
743, 756, 769, 770, 775, 785, 790
18:14 . . . . .678, 745
18:15 . . . . 147, 593, 760, 763, 920
18:15 – 16 921
18:15 – 18 . . . . 607, 746, 748, 751
18:17 751

18:18 . . . . 795, 899, 911, 912
18:19 . . . . 744, 745, 751
18:19 – 20 341
18:19 – 24 . . . . .746, 750
18:20 . . . . .354, 476
18:21 753
18:22 751
18:24 . . . . .745, 748
18:25 – 27 607
18:28 . . . . . 134, 524, 575, 576, 756, 757,
760, 763, 767, 775, 784, 793, 812
18:28 – 40 . . . . . . 743, 756, 775, 785, 790
18:28 – 19:16 796
18:28 – 19:27 41
18:29 770
18:29 – 32 . . . . 756, 761, 763, 767
18:30 . . . . 763, 764, 780
18:31 . . . . 767, 770, 779
18:31 – 32 59
18:32 . . . . .770, 809
18:33 . . . . .537, 780
18:33 – 19:3 526
18:33 – 38 . . . . 756, 763, 767
18:36 . . . . 152, 197, 766, 794
18:36 – 37 780
18:37 . . . . 195, 776, 845
18:37 – 38 682
18:38 . . . . 763, 775, 777, 779
18:38 – 40 . . . . 756, 767, 775
18:39 . . . . 537, 771, 793
18:39 – 40 759
18:40 511
19 . . . . 383, 526, 826
19 – 20 875
19:1 . . . . .781, 792
19:1 – 3 775
19:1 – 16 . . . . 743, 756, 775, 790
19:2 795
19:2 – 3 . . . . 162, 307, 526, 786
19:2 – 5 784
19:3 537
19:4 . . . . 763, 775, 779
19:4 – 7 .775, 777
19:5 . . . . .162, 733, 784, 786, 795,
799, 827, 828, 837, 934
19:6 . . . . 511, 763, 775, 781
19:7 . . . . 776, 794, 829
19:8 . . . . .781, 784

19:8 – 11 775, 780, 781 . . . .
19:10 – 11 783
19:11 . . . . .782, 785
19:12 . . . . 511, 780, 784, 785
19:12 – 16 . . . . .775, 781
19:13 785
19:13 – 22 526
19:14 . . . . . . 133, 179, 303, 524, 575, 757,
        758, 769, 777, 799, 811, 812, 827
19:14 – 16 127
19:15 . . .133, 367, 511, 768, 780, 782, 929
19:15 – 16 762
19:16 763
19:17 . . . . .145, 802
19:17 – 18 . . . . .790, 791
19:17 – 27 . . . . 785, 790, 808
19:17 – 42 796
19:18 859
19:19 . . . . 526, 537, 803
19:19 – 22 . . . . 783, 791, 793, 796
19:20 791
19:21 537
19:23 785
19:23 – 24 . . . . . . 791, 794, 795, 796, 803
19:24 . . . . 795, 809, 816
19:25 . . . . 800, 828, 849
19:25 – 27 . . . .
        178, 593, 594, 746, 791, 797, 804
19:26 . . . . . . 147, 164, 395, 758, 798, 843
19:26 – 27 . . . . 799, 815, 921
19:27 799
19:28 . . . . 178, 811, 816, 817
19:28 – 29 821
19:28 – 30 808
19:28 – 42 . . . . .785, 790
19:30 . . . . .543, 797, 809, 810, 813,
        821, 828, 856, 859, 929
19:31 . . . . 133, 524, 817, 820, 829
19:31 – 37 . . .808, 812, 817, 821, 843, 921
19:33 – 36 758
19:34 817
19:35 . . . . .97, 593, 746, 826, 834,
        898, 921, 923
19:36 . . . . 116, 134, 813, 817
19:37 835
19:38 . . . . 133, 178, 195, 358, 829
19:38 – 40 380
19:38 – 42 . . . . .808, 817
19:39 . . . . . . 194, 525, 530, 820, 832, 842

19:40 . . . . .818, 832
19:41 . . . . 61, 733, 734, 805, 828
19:41 – 42 842
19:42 524
20 . . . . .826, 831, 832, 833, 834,
        835, 847, 857, 858, 864 – 65,
        875, 878, 891, 898, 902
20:1 . . . . 169, 495, 733, 827, 837, 849,
        851, 858, 874, 882, 898, 938
20:1 – 2 . . . . 798, 799, 825, 828
20:1 – 10 . . . . .41, 593, 746, 835, 838,
        841, 853, 857, 870, 899
20:1 – 31 823
20:2 . . . . .133, 147, 585, 828,
        834, 842, 844, 904
20:2 – 5 147
20:2 – 8 747
20:3 829
20:3 – 7 . . . . 825, 830, 833
20:3 – 9 . . . . 594, 830, 898, 918
20:3 – 10 921
20:4 . . . . 183, 832, 898
20:5 . . . . .841, 899
20:5 – 6 836
20:6 . . . . 830, 833, 899, 914
20:6 – 7 795
20:7 . . . . 819, 836, 842
20:8 . . . . .147, 830, 831, 832,
        835, 844, 921, 923
20:8 – 9 . . . . .825, 833
20:9 . . .150, 182, 205, 235, 827, 831, 837
20:10 825
20:11 . . . . 843, 849, 859
20:11 – 12 . . . . .840, 843
20:11 – 18 . . . .
        798, 835, 848, 853, 857, 870, 876
20:12 . . . . .848, 859
20:13 . . . . . . 133, 840, 841, 842, 849, 859
20:13 – 15 . . . . .840, 843
20:14 . . . . 845, 896, 897
20:14 – 16 917
20:14 – 17 849
20:15 . . . . .133, 145, 733, 734, 805,
        819, 820, 840, 841, 842,
        843, 849, 851, 859
20:15 – 16 844
20:16 . . . . 145, 392, 847
20:16 – 17 840
20:17 . . . . .91, 342, 829, 830, 831,
        842, 851, 876

20:18 . . . . .585, 799, 829, 831,
        833, 835, 840, 851
20:19 . . . . .358, 642, 829, 835, 863,
        868, 876, 877, 896, 938
20:19 – 20 . . . . .855, 866
20:19 – 23 585,
        848, 850, 870, 875, 880, 894, 906
20:20 . . . . 585, 858, 861, 866, 868
20:21 . . .485, 643, 659, 676, 721, 855 – 56,
        859, 863, 866, 868, 869, 879,
        894, 914, 928, 929, 937, 940
20:21 – 22 . . . . .38, 634
20:21 – 23 . . . . 876, 882, 886
20:22 . . . . 136, 718, 812, 855 – 57,
        861, 866, 868
20:22 – 23 940
20:23 . . . . 855, 865, 868, 869
20:24 . . . . .145, 501, 859, 872,
        878, 890, 892, 919
20:24 – 29 . . . . 501, 831, 881, 894, 919
20:24 – 31 . . . . 848, 858, 876
20:25 . . . . .585, 792, 835, 872,
        877, 878, 880, 904
20:26 . . . . 829, 835, 858, 879, 894, 896
20:26 – 27 872
20:27 . . . . 846, 879, 880
20:28 . . . . 585, 641, 829, 904
20:28 – 29 . . . . 872, 874, 878, 881
20:29 . . . . .148, 149, 285, 451,
        834, 877, 904, 907
20:29 – 31 895
20:30 . . . . .873, 874
20:30 – 21:25 895
20:31 . . . . . 50, 54, 66, 105, 116, 137, 206,
        261, 264, 268, 286, 287, 289,
        295, 348, 369, 371, 411, 416,
        469, 470, 484, 497, 498, 506,
        625, 635, 678, 679, 719, 781,
        794, 804, 863, 868, 873, 881,
        886, 890, 927, 932, 935, 940
20:30 – 31 . . . . .28, 170, 183, 214,
        245, 278, 562, 639, 816, 826,
        827, 833, 835, 858, 872, 875,
        876, 878, 881, 890 – 94, 902,
        912, 918, 919, 923, 926, 936, 940
21 . . . . . 873, 881, 890 – 94, 902, 905, 912
21:1 . . . . 873, 889, 904, 911, 912, 915
21:1 – 3 .889, 894
21:1 – 7 .593, 746
21:1 – 14 . . . . 908, 911, 912, 915
21:1 – 23 . . . . 873, 874, 892, 893

21:1 – 25 65
21:2 . . . . .47, 145, 150, 162, 195, 876, 898
21:3 . . . . 194, 597, 748, 906
21:4 – 6 .889, 896
21:5 – 6 896
21:7 . . . . .147, 594, 830, 835, 895,
898, 903, 907, 918
21:7 – 8 .889, 898
21:8 903
21:9 . . . .748, 795, 897, 898, 900, 906, 911
21:9 – 14 .889, 899
21:10 906
21:11 795
21:12 907
21:13 911
21:14 . . . . .889, 894
21:15 . . . . 892, 900, 916, 925
21:15 – 16 913
21:15 – 17 . . . . .581, 689, 809,
860, 897, 914, 915, 916, 917, 925
21:15 – 19 . . . . .911, 917
21:15 – 23 752
21:15 – 25 . . . . .830, 899
21:17 . . . . 900, 913, 914, 915
21:19 . . . . 59, 145, 375, 924
21:19 – 22 894
21:20 . . . . 145, 147, 524, 912
21:20 – 22 595
21:20 – 23 . . . .
594, 830, 898, 911, 917, 918, 919
21:20 – 24 . . . . .593, 746
21:21 919
21:21 – 22 830
21:22 . . . . .145, 919
21:23 . . . . .848, 887
21:23 – 24 .45, 47
21:24 . . . . . . 45, 85, 98, 109, 147, 594, 815,
874, 892, 895, 898, 912, 926
21:24 – 25 . . . . 872, 873,
892, 893, 911, 912, 919, 926, 940
21:25 . . . . . . .101, 183, 387, 873, 926, 930

Acts

1:8 668
1:9 – 11 849
1:10 841
1:13 . . . . .149, 876
1:21 – 22 .97, 144
2 . . . . .855 – 56, 864 – 65

2:17 938
2:22 151
2:23 516
2:24 467
2:33 . . . . 203, 412, 556, 702, 846
2:36 846
2:38 238
3:8 240
3:12 151
3:22 129
4:12 . . . . 314, 411, 469
4:36 768
5:5 – 6 502
5:10 502
5:17 372
5:35 151
7:37 129
7:53 116
8:17 – 20 238
9:4 665
10:37 . . . . .97, 144
10:38 136
10:39 144
10:45 238
10:48 215
11:17 238
13:16 151
13:24 144
13:24 – 25 97
13:26 144
17:24 – 25 850
21:28 151
23:8 504
24:5 150
27:40 862

Romans

1:1 – 2 43
1:1 – 5 713
1:4 467
3:2 184
3:19 428
3:20 . . . . .416, 428
5:8 655
5:13 666
6 429
6:15 – 23 397
6:17 – 18 186

6:18 – 19 656
7:12 – 16 116
7:24 – 25 298
8 104
8:3 821
8:11 633
8:14 633
8:23 938
8:26 – 27 694
8:28 . . . . .453, 519
8:34 699
8:38 – 39 . . . . 501, 509, 635
9:4 151
9:27 112
10:13 680
11:1 151
11:36 . . . . 298, 624, 907
12:1 925
14:10 783
14:17 . . . . .656, 720

1 Corinthians

1:18 – 22 938
1:23 . . . . .140, 599
2:1 – 5 469
2:10 904
2:11 633
2:14 698
2:16 186
3:5 723
3:16 . . . . .122, 848
4:7 381
6:6 877
7:12 877
9:17 184
9:21 . . . . 368, 656, 660
10:31 925
12:3 . . . . .633, 637
12:27 . . . . .122, 749
13 470
13:12 263
15:3 – 8 837
15:3 – 70 639
15:4 835
15:14 836
15:22 837
15:23 822
15:24 803

15:44 858
15:45 – 49 . . . . .864, 868
15:54 – 55 704
15:55 . . . . 518, 565, 645
15:57 645

2 Corinthians

1:20 359
2:15 531
3:6 342
3:7 – 18 462
3:17 .633, 812
4:4 . . . . 420, 428, 555, 599, 727
4:5 – 6 428
4:7 171
5:10 783
5:11 – 21 787
5:17 . . . . .427, 801
5:19 723
5:20 869
11:22 151

Galatians

1:6 – 7 634
2:7 184
2:20 340
3 – 4 104
3:7 657
3:14 938
3:16 416
3:26 – 29 466
4:6 . . . . .633, 812
5:22 .656, 720
6:2 . . . . 368, 396, 428, 656, 660
6:16 .157, 515

Ephesians

1:4 – 5 509
1:13 – 14 938
2:2 555
2:8 – 9 659
2:10 . . . . 564, 656, 659
2:14 – 18 238
2:15 . . . . .862, 868
2:20 . . . . .47, 865, 880
2:21 – 22 868
2:8 – 9 453
4:4 – 7 918

4:7 222
6:10 – 17 . . . . .642, 645
6:11 – 12 735
6:12 766
6:13 599
6:19 466

Philippians

1:19 .633, 812
2:6 – 8 582
2:8 – 9 530
2:9 . . . . 542, 588, 786
2:9 – 10 295
2:9 – 11 543
2:10 – 11 . . . . 530, 739, 777, 786, 803
2:11 .542, 928
3:10 .703, 906

Colossians

1:6 564
1:15 – 20 699
1:18 185
1:24 .665, 683
2:18 277
3:1 – 4 685

1 Thessalonians

2:4 . . . . 184, 668, 881
5:4 – 8 938
5:17 626

2 Thessalonians

2:3 719

1 Timothy

1:11 184
3:1 938

Titus

1:3 184
3:6 633

Hebrews

1:1 – 2 .497, 703
2:10 713
4:14 .737, 741
4:15 .397, 519
4:16 .157, 397

6:4 238
7 . . . . .796, 803
7:22 514
7:24 514
7:25 511
8:1 – 2 .514, 803
9:12 803
9:15 803
11:10 416
11:16 416
11:17 117
12:2 . . . . 187, 542, 604, 608
13:8 . . . . 120, 398, 684, 905
13:20 939

James

2:23 657

1 Peter

1:4 727
1:5 599
1:15 – 16 718
1:16 .656, 867
2:11 .669, 727
3:20 – 21 900
4:13 683
4:14 187
5:2 – 4 898

2 Peter

2:22 461

1 John

1:1 . . . . .87, 109
1:1 – 2 668
1:3 714
1:5 – 10 938
1:6 – 7 492
1:7 – 9 581
1:8 660
1:9 . . . . .582, 725
2:1 . . . . 631, 634, 667, 897
2:1 – 2 582
2:7 599
2:8 938
2:12 897
2:14 897
2:18 897

2:20 694
2:23 665
2:28 897
3:7 897
3:13 664
3:18 897
4:4 897
4:7 – 5:3 703
4:8 588
4:9 . . . . .117, 204
4:10 . . . . 644, 699, 924
4:19 . . . . 40, 253, 588, 608
5:6 – 8 814
5:10 222
5:18 – 20 721
5:21 897

Revelation

1:5 581
1:7 817
1:10 877
3:3 – 4 841
4:5 841
4:8 718
5 140
5:6 . . . . 133, 530, 543, 866
5:9 581
5:11 – 12 589
6:10 718
7:1 862
7:9 536
7:9 – 10 157

7:16 – 17 239
12 801
12:7 – 9 555
12:12 108
13:18 902
14:1 – 4 133
14:10 738
16:19 738
17:14 133
19:7 – 9 .168, 172
19:13 . . . . .87, 581
21 – 22 . . . . 734, 805, 851
21:6 . . . . .239, 376
22:1 133
22:3 . . . . .133, 185
22:13 27

Other Ancient Literature Index

Apocrypha

2 Esdras

7:21 100

1 Maccabees

1:59 535
4:36 – 59 474
4:46 129
13:51 535
14:41 129

2 Maccabees

1:29 513
5:19 513
10:7 535

Sirach

26:15 113
33:24 537
43:4 862

Tobit

2:2 597
7:9 581

Wisdom of Solomon

19:3 507

Pseudepigrapha

1 Enoch

72 – 75 462

2 Baruch

29:8 329

4 Ezra

2:18 129

Jubilees

2:20 418
19:28 – 29 421
19:29 418

Odes of Solomon

17:6 – 11 462
42:15 – 17 462

Psalms of Solomon

17:42 152

Testament of Levi

9:11 581

Josephus

Jewish Antiquities

3.161 796
4.310 105
6.151 128
8.100 353
11.341 239
12.316 – 25 474
12.320 – 21 535
13.171 131
13.297 . . . . .131, 193
14.172 – 73 749
14.366 737
18.26 – 35 745
18.28 149
18.35 514
18.36 302
18.95 513

20.118 235
20.198 745
20.199 372
20.201 – 2 193

Jewish War

1.21 182
1.229 516
1.648 131
2.13.2 – 3 768
2.17.9 768
2.162 .131, 193
2.163 504
2.168 149
2.232 235
3.375 410
5.229 841
6.290 516
6.304 776
6.427 550

Life

86.207 162
269 235

Philo

On the Special Laws

3.57 304

On the Posterity of Cain

145 113

Rabbinic Literature

m. 'Abot

1:5 246

m. Niddah

4:1 237

m. Shabbat

7:2 . . . . .273, 442

24:3 442

m. Sukkah

5:1 353

b. Sanhedrin

49 – 50. 762

b. Shabbat

55 436

108 441

b. Sukkah

27 380

Early Christian Literature and Ancient Church

Barnabas

15:8 – 9 829

Didache

10:6 536

11:4 – 5 251

14:1 829

16:5 675

Eusebius — *Historia ecclesiastica*

3.1 917

3.1.1 60

3.1.2 60

3.11 798

3.32.6 798

3.39.4 46

4.22.4 798

Ignatius — *To the Magnesians*

9:1 829

Irenaeus — *Adversus haereses*

1.9.1 – 3. 46

2.22.5 46

3.1.2 45

3.3.4 46

3.24.1 850

Tertullian — *Scorpiace*

15 917

Classical Writers

Diogenes Laertius — *Lives of Eminent Philosophers*

6.2.44 132

Polybius — *The Histories*

26.1.12 – 14 526

Tacitus — *Annales*

6.8 782

Confessional Documents

Heidelberg Catechism

49 850

Westminster Confession of Faith

2.3 119

Westminster Shorter Catechism

1 . . . . .924, 927

Subject Index

abiding. *See* remaining

Abraham, 139, 223, 236, 242, 244, 252, 286, 303, 414–18, 422–25, 427, 429, 560, 657, 934

Adam, 107, 460, 485, 701, 733, 739, 777–79, 781, 785, 786–87, 815, 822, 827, 828, 837, 851, 862, 864, 868, 929, 934, 936

angel(s), 90, 97, 129, 153–55, 202, 269, 480, 553–55, 841–46, 848, 849–50

anonymity, 42–47, 58, 60, 147–48, 162, 172, 217, 269–70, 373, 437, 440, 442, 495, 593–94, 719, 732–33, 739, 746–47, 750–51, 768, 777, 785, 799–801, 813, 815, 828, 830, 895, 919, 921, 922

ark of the covenant, 841–43, 846, 850

ascension, 342, 556, 574–76, 577, 604–6, 608, 615–18, 634, 641–42, 676–78, 685, 689–92, 700, 717–18, 846–49, 850–51, 864

authority, 22–23, 30, 104, 109, 127, 131, 148, 157, 180–82, 193, 195–96, 202, 221, 289–90, 295, 327, 342, 366, 377, 388–90, 395–96, 397, 405, 408, 417, 438, 460, 466–67, 478–82, 504–6, 538, 543, 559, 577, 596, 623, 639, 654, 666, 682, 713, 735–36, 738, 761–62, 764, 770, 776, 780–81, 796, 811, 846, 865, 869, 918, 920, 925, 930

baptism, 131–32, 135–36, 139, 215–16, 220–21, 234, 327, 483, 578, 581, 583, 869

belief, 105, 204, 206, 261, 262, 287, 293, 295, 327–28, 331, 332, 336–37, 354, 371, 410, 413–14, 419, 450–51, 476–77, 483, 500–501, 505–6, 510, 511–12, 519–20, 557–63, 587, 613–14, 699–701, 703, 722–23, 815–16, 833–34, 876, 877–78, 879–84, 907

Beloved Disciple, 45–47, 147, 496, 593–96, 598–99, 746–47, 800–801, 815–16, 829–34, 874, 895, 898–99, 912, 917–18, 919–24, 925–26, 940

birth (new), 104–6, 154, 184, 196–200, 202–3, 380, 410, 691

blindness, 184, 220, 273, 294, 327, 371, 412, 436–37, 451–53, 559–61, 565–66, 679

blood, 105, 339–40, 348, 813–15, 843

body, 106–7, 122, 181–83, 199, 245, 254, 340, 342, 606, 665, 668, 792, 817–19, 828–29, 831–33, 836, 844, 929

bread. *See* food

burial, 509, 526, 528, 817–20, 842

"came/made/became," 93–94, 96, 101, 104, 107, 112, 114–16, 271

children (of God), 104, 105–6, 110–111, 121–22, 416, 515, 557, 604, 852, 897, 918–19

church, 22, 29–31, 36, 40, 50, 61, 109, 120, 122, 157, 158, 172, 185, 215, 219, 223–24, 254, 465–66, 469, 470, 598, 605–6, 728, 753, 868–69, 906, 938–40

cross, 57, 165, 203, 244, 338, 348, 376–77, 409, 412–13, 466–67, 515, 530, 551, 554–55, 556, 565, 576, 580–81, 582, 603, 608, 691–93, 702, 791–92, 802–4, 809, 812–13, 846, 936, 938

crucifixion, 340, 412, 524, 556, 565, 670, 691, 739, 757–60, 762–63, 784–85, 792–93, 794–99, 812–20, 821, 827, 859, 876, 916–17, 933

darkness, 57, 95–96, 101, 107–8, 121, 194, 206, 207–10, 288, 294,

311, 332, 405–6, 427–28, 451, 557, 562, 599, 605, 666, 702, 735, 828–29, 930–31. *See also* night

date of the crucifixion, 757–60

David, 128–29, 136, 152, 377, 464, 466, 571, 820, 846, 934

death, 496–97, 499–500, 501, 503, 551–52, 556, 931–32

demon, 164, 345, 367, 420–23, 467–68, 576

departure. *See* ascension

Devil. *See* Satan

dialogue, 52–54

  legal challenge, 55, 236, 404–5, 421, 425–26, 435

  rhetorical challenge, 55, 227, 233, 236, 237–39, 243–44, 250

  social challenge, 55, 177, 192–201, 204, 206, 208, 317, 330, 334, 341, 353, 361, 369, 372, 379, 417, 435, 473, 479, 761–62

discipleship, 147, 156–57, 186, 207, 223–25, 263, 298, 314–15, 328, 344, 346, 382, 413–14, 429, 468–69, 518, 530–31, 589, 599, 608–9, 654, 659, 659, 660, 669, 683, 693–94, 703–4, 727–28, 740, 752–53, 821–22, 916–17, 918, 924–25

donkey, 537–40

drinking, 337–41, 348, 375–76, 737–38, 740, 808–11

dwelling/tabernacling, 108, 122, 356–57, 359, 639

eating, 337–41, 348, 912

election, 335–36, 343–44, 345–46, 347, 555–56, 558–63, 586, 658

emotion, 507–8, 509, 519, 552, 593

epilogue, 697, 873–75, 890–94, 905

eschatology, 288, 333–35, 337–41,

503 – 5, 554 – 55, 563, 614 – 17,
624 – 25, 639, 641 – 42, 837, 937 – 38
eternal generation of the Son, 119
eternal life. *See* life
Eucharist, 305, 307, 324 – 25, 338, 343,
578, 583, 650, 769, 900, 904
exit device, 573 – 74, 642 – 44
exodus (theme), 303, 429, 516, 770, 786
expulsion from the synagogue,
444 – 46, 561, 675

faith, 624, 907
family, 358, 797 – 802, 846 – 49, 918 – 19
farewell discourse, 571 – 75
Father (God), 110 – 11, 118, 180, 222,
248, 275 – 76, 284 – 87, 292 – 93,
326 – 30, 332, 340, 343, 381, 408 – 9,
412, 417 – 18, 421 – 25, 465 – 66,
476 – 79, 483, 510, 552 – 53, 563,
575 – 76, 614 – 15, 617 – 23, 638,
650 – 51, 654 – 55, 657 – 58, 683,
692, 698 – 700, 703, 712 – 13,
717 – 18, 723 – 25, 737 – 38,
846 – 49, 852, 860 – 61, 928 – 29
father of lies. *See* Satan
feasts/festivals (Jewish),
268 – 69, 355 – 57, 374
Dedication/Hanukkah, 458,
474 – 75, 484 – 85
Passover, 134, 178 – 79, 185, 260,
303, 356, 516, 523 – 24, 534 – 35,
550, 575, 597, 760 – 61, 767 – 68,
769 – 70, 784, 787, 812 – 13, 820
Tabernacles, 353, 355 – 56,
365, 374, 375, 405 – 6
finger, 393 – 95
fire (charcoal), 748, 751
fish, 897 – 903, 904, 906
flesh, 106 – 8, 199, 338 – 40,
342 – 43, 348, 407
food, 248, 303 – 6, 328 – 31, 337 – 38,
348, 595 – 97, 899 – 900, 904
foot washing, 577 – 84, 588 – 89
forgiveness, 578, 865 – 67, 869, 925, 932
freedom, 286, 347, 396, 414 – 16,
427, 429, 451, 559, 619,
660, 766, 787, 931
friend, 218 – 19, 225, 464, 499,
595, 599, 656 – 58, 660,
781 – 82, 785, 897, 936 – 37
"from above," 196, 198, 202 – 3,
220 – 21, 292, 329 – 30, 410,
414, 448, 559, 665, 781, 930

fruit, 551 – 53, 564, 650 – 54, 656, 658,
659, 682, 720, 822. *See also* seed

garden (theme), 732 – 34, 739,
751, 777 – 79, 819 – 20,
822, 844 – 45, 851 – 52
gematria, 902 – 3
Genesis (theme), 86 – 87, 93, 94, 95,
96, 161 – 62, 176, 312, 732 – 34,
777 – 79, 786 – 87, 819 – 20, 828 – 29,
844 – 45, 851 – 52, 858, 862 – 63
gentile, 88, 128, 179, 234, 244, 254,
260, 373, 421, 465 – 66, 515,
550, 734, 801, 931, 939
gift, 238, 252, 381, 715 – 18
glory, 65, 108 – 11, 116, 154 – 55,
168 – 69, 259, 366 – 67, 376,
422 – 23, 446, 496 – 97, 510,
540 – 41, 542 – 43, 550 – 51, 553,
554 – 55, 560, 564 – 65, 566, 603 – 4,
608, 622 – 23, 654, 682, 712 – 13,
714, 717, 723, 726, 916 – 17
God (title), 89 – 91, 366, 480 – 82,
846 – 49, 927 – 30
Gospel of John
audience, 61 – 65
authorship, 42 – 47
basic story form, 50 – 52
date, 59 – 60
genre, 47 – 50
identity of "John," 45 – 47
"Johannine community," 61 – 65
"Johannine problem," 41 – 42
literary forms, 52 – 58. *See also*
dialogue and monologue
outline, 67 – 74
provenance, 60 – 61
structure, 65 – 67
title, 42 – 45
gospel, the, 935 – 37
grace, 27, 28, 97, 108, 11 – 14, 116 – 17,
122, 137, 239, 297, 376, 483 560,
579, 583, 586, 644, 679, 716, 750,
842 – 44, 849 – 50, 859, 938
Greeks, 167, 550 – 51, 556, 564

hate, 207, 209, 355, 418, 470, 552 – 53,
664 – 67, 668 – 69, 675 – 77, 720, 785
Holy Spirit, 640, 855 – 57,
861 – 65, 868, 930
Paraclete, 631 – 35, 636 – 38, 640,
644 – 45, 667 – 68, 677 – 81, 684

Spirit, the, 135 – 37, 198 – 200,
222, 245, 342 – 43, 375 – 76,
381 – 82, 684 – 85
Spirit of truth, 635 – 36,
667 – 68, 681 – 82
hospitality, 233 – 34, 236, 251 – 52, 253,
260, 305 – 6, 307 – 8, 578, 581, 586
hour, 165, 170 – 71, 243 – 44, 288,
354 – 55, 371, 409, 550 – 51,
552 – 53, 575 – 76, 675 – 76,
683, 698 – 99, 701, 712 – 13

I AM, 246, 312, 331 – 32, 405 – 6,
408, 410 – 11, 425, 427 – 28,
438, 451, 461 – 62, 463 – 65,
504, 587, 616 – 19, 635,
650 – 51, 735 – 36, 876, 933
illustration (literary function),
459 – 68, 498, 551 – 52, 579, 581,
582, 584, 587, 650 – 54, 691,
698, 700, 881, 885, 916 – 17

Jesus
fulfillment of OT/religion, 26,
108, 112 – 17, 137 – 38, 150,
166 – 67, 171 – 72, 181, 185,
198, 214, 271 – 72, 275, 277,
307, 658 – 59, 821, 929 – 30
eternal generation, 119
Christ/Messiah, 128 – 29, 147 – 48,
245 – 46, 253 – 54, 345, 370,
371, 377, 475 – 76, 505 – 6,
556 – 57, 882 – 84, 886
Door, the, 461 – 63
gardener, 844 – 45
God, 878 – 79
Good Shepherd, 463 – 65, 925
Holy One of God, 345
king, 152, 524 – 26, 528, 530,
538 – 40, 542 – 43, 765 – 66, 770,
776 – 79, 784 – 85, 786, 803
king of the Jews, 763, 767 – 68,
793. *See also* king
King of Israel, 535. *See also* king
lamb of God, 133 – 34, 139,
144, 180, 769 – 70, 787
Lord, 451, 496, 584 – 85, 829 – 30,
878 – 79, 898 – 99, 903 – 4,
912 – 16, 917 – 18
Nazarene, the, 735 – 36, 793
rabbi, 145, 151 – 52, 195, 217,
326, 498. *See also* teacher
Son of Man, 154 – 55, 202 – 3, 204,

289 – 90, 297, 326, 339, 342, 412, 450, 550 – 51, 556 – 57, 602

Son/Son of God, 104, 137, 139, 152, 206, 222, 284 – 87, 289, 297, 332 – 33, 482 – 83, 496 – 97, 505 – 6, 712 – 13, 779 – 80, 804, 882 – 84, 886, 929 – 30

teacher, 392, 506, 584 – 85, 845. *See also* rabbi

"unique Son," 110 – 11, 117 – 18, 120, 134, 204, 206

Jews, the, 127 – 28, 134, 192, 234, 242 – 43, 259, 275, 334, 352, 357 – 58, 365 – 66, 373, 467, 506 – 7, 529, 779 – 80, 793, 812 – 13, 819, 858

high priest(s), 513 – 15, 516 – 517, 529, 734, 737, 744 – 52, 752, 779, 784 – 85, 794, 803

Israel, 134 – 35, 934

Levites, 125

people of Jerusalem/ Jerusalemites, 369 – 70

Pharisees, 130 – 31, 193 – 94, 234, 372, 378, 391 – 92, 441 – 42, 512, 734

Priests, 125 – 26

ruling officials, 193 – 94, 378 – 80

Sanhedrin/meeting of the council, 512 – 13

scribes, 391 – 92

servant(s) of the high priest(s), 734, 737, 738, 779

Johannine Pentecost, 855 – 57, 861 – 65

John the Baptist, 97 – 99, 111 – 12, 121, 125 – 37, 144 – 47, 214 – 23, 234, 483 – 84

joy, 218 – 19, 424 – 25, 501, 604, 656, 658, 660, 677, 690 – 93, 720, 727 – 28, 859

judgment, 206 – 7, 286 – 91, 396 – 97, 405, 411, 422, 426 – 27, 451, 485, 554 – 55, 559 – 63, 565, 639, 678 – 81, 782 – 84

kingdom, 130, 152, 155, 172, 196 – 99, 202, 290, 380, 420, 538, 565, 586, 626, 637, 682, 763 – 65, 794, 803, 859, 929 – 30, 936, 938

law, 114, 379, 392 – 93, 397, 408, 480 – 81, 556 – 57, 667, 761 – 62, 779 – 80

lambs. *See* sheep

life, 94 – 95, 206, 224, 239, 248, 262,

264, 286, 287 – 88, 293 – 94, 330, 337 – 41, 342 – 43, 345, 348 – 49, 419, 463 – 64, 475 – 76, 477 – 48, 504 – 5, 518, 552, 553, 563, 606 – 7, 617 – 19, 637, 643, 645, 713 – 14, 726 – 27, 882 – 84, 902, 927, 937

"lifted up," 203, 220, 412 – 13, 526, 555 – 57, 564 – 65

light, 95 – 96, 99 – 100, 204, 207, 405 – 6, 427, 438 – 39, 498 – 99, 557

literary conclusion, 873 – 75

living water, 238 – 241, 245, 248 – 49, 307, 374 – 76, 381, 810, 814, 817

love, 205 – 6, 208, 298, 466, 496, 497, 517 – 18, 575 – 76, 605 – 6, 631, 638, 639, 644, 656 – 57, 660, 664 – 65, 685, 699 – 700, 703, 723 – 25, 912 – 16

love commandment, 605 – 6, 608, 658, 660, 939

mercy seat. *See* ark of the covenant

method, 22 – 24, 31 – 41, 134

biblical reader, 39 – 41

canonical "impressions," 37 – 39, 118, 194, 233, 292, 303, 305 – 6, 324, 369, 375, 394, 411, 414, 439 – 40, 508, 578, 675, 732 – 34, 739, 748, 814 – 15, 842 – 43, 845, 850, 895 – 96, 900 – 903

critical vs. confessional, 23 – 24

historical-critical/grammatical exegesis, 22 – 23, 31 – 33

historical reconstruction, 302, 926

symbolism, 166, 650, 900 – 903

text versus event, 34 – 36

theological exegesis, 31 – 33, 41, 298

mission, 33, 50, 97 – 98, 110 – 11, 115, 128 – 29, 134 – 35, 156, 164, 170, 206, 227, 235 – 36, 249, 251 – 52, 254, 287, 328, 333, 366, 370, 371, 407 – 8, 413, 482 – 83, 561 – 63, 577, 585, 587, 685, 699 – 700, 714, 723 – 24, 728, 860 – 61, 867

monologue, 57 – 58, 284, 457 – 58, 549, 567, 570, 571

Moses, 97, 109, 111, 114, 116, 129, 135, 150, 195, 197, 202 – 203, 223, 236, 238, 240, 242, 246, 295 – 96, 302 – 3, 305, 312, 314, 328 – 31, 334 – 40, 346, 348, 356, 367 – 69, 392 – 95, 407 – 8, 424, 447 – 48,

462, 563, 571, 619, 650, 666, 706, 762, 833, 842, 929, 934 – 35

name, 39, 90, 105, 207, 294 – 95, 459 – 60, 622 – 23, 665, 692, 694, 699, 715, 725, 882 – 84

narrator, 85, 168, 204 – 6, 220, 325, 343, 354

night, 194 – 95, 437 – 38, 475, 498, 576, 597, 599, 605, 795, 818 – 19, 828 – 29, 895 – 96. *See also* darkness

numbers. *See* gematria

Palm Sunday, 534 – 41, 543

peace, 538 – 39, 575, 640 – 41, 645, 677, 693, 701 – 2, 786, 855, 858 – 61, 866, 867, 868, 876 – 77

plot, 84 – 86, 932 – 34

cosmological, 85 – 85, 99, 100, 206, 285, 353, 356 – 57, 370, 475, 505, 812, 896, 932 – 34

historical, 85 – 86, 99, 353, 370, 812, 932 – 34

poor, the, 527 – 29, 531, 597

prayer, 510 – 11, 552 – 53, 623 – 24, 626, 694, 712 – 25

prologue, 83, 84 – 86, 116, 204, 873 – 75, 890 – 94

prophet, the, 98, 128 – 36, 240, 251, 306, 308, 326, 328 – 29, 374, 377, 380, 443, 563

purification, 126, 157, 166 – 67, 171, 198, 214, 217, 219, 516, 583, 812, 815

purpose statement, 170, 816, 827, 858, 873 – 75, 882 – 84, 885 – 86, 890 – 91, 894, 940

reader, 39 – 41, 884 – 85, 870, 880 – 84, 940

remaining, 135 – 36, 146, 223, 340, 414, 422, 424, 452, 562, 614, 620 – 21, 636, 653 – 56, 659 – 60, 664, 861, 937

remembering, 180 – 81, 183, 540 – 41, 640, 665, 669, 675 – 76, 843

resurrection, 466 – 67, 504 – 5, 828 – 35, 836, 904 – 5

revelation, 22, 25, 26 – 27, 29, 34, 100, 116, 117, 118, 122, 134 – 35, 154, 157, 201, 243, 246 – 47, 287, 293, 332, 336, 345, 424, 450, 559, 579, 587, 618 – 19, 638, 682, 714 – 15, 719, 721, 770, 894 – 95, 904, 923

righteousness, 633, 678 – 80,
685, 724 – 25, 930

Romans, 146, 367, 498, 513 – 14,
734, 760 – 70, 776, 780,
792, 793, 813, 836

ruler of this world. *See* Satan

Sabbath, 272 – 73, 275 – 76,
368 – 69, 441 – 42, 812 – 13

sacrament. *See* Eucharist

salvation, 50, 95, 96, 102, 238, 241,
243 – 44, 248, 335, 344, 347, 414,
463, 467, 515, 555, 556, 565, 653,
656, 660, 700, 719, 856, 869

Samaritans, 233, 235 – 36, 242 – 43,
250 – 51, 420 – 22

Satan, 345 – 46, 416, 419 – 22, 463, 527,
554 – 55, 565, 576 – 77, 593, 596,
599, 642, 719 – 21, 739, 781

Scripture, 21 – 41, 365, 540 – 41, 586,
718 – 19, 736 – 37, 762 – 63,
796 – 97, 808 – 10, 816 – 17,
834 – 35, 837, 934 – 35

doctrine of, 22 – 23, 24 – 31, 398

historical nature (creation), 25 – 27

literary nature (canon), 27 – 29

theological nature (creed), 29 – 31

security (in God), 477 – 79

seed, 377, 414 – 17, 551 – 53,
555 – 56, 564, 822

sheep. *See* shepherd

shepherd (theme), 459 – 65,
468 – 70, 477, 912 – 16, 925

sight, 117 – 18, 135 – 36, 150 – 51,
153 – 54, 156, 157, 197, 221,
260 – 61, 270, 285, 303, 326 – 27,
336, 439, 447, 451 – 52, 452 – 53,
510, 559 – 63, 565 – 66, 619 – 20,
689 – 90, 831 – 32, 833 – 34, 849,
859, 876, 877 – 78, 894 – 95, 904 – 5

sign, 168 – 69, 181 – 84, 204, 264, 302,
306, 307, 326, 328, 371, 442, 446,
541, 558, 825 – 27, 881 – 82, 885

sin, 121, 133, 209, 241 – 42, 274 – 75,
277, 396, 397, 409, 410,
415 – 16, 428 – 29, 442, 448 – 49,
452, 666 – 67, 678 – 79, 781,
865 – 66, 869, 931 – 32

soldiers (Roman), 734, 738,
776 – 77, 794 – 97, 813 – 15

son(s) and daughters(s). *See* children.

Spirit. *See* Holy Spirit

Synoptic Gospels, 53, 57, 97, 100,
125, 127, 129, 130 – 31, 136, 144,
149, 153, 169, 175 – 78, 180, 197,
216, 220, 242, 259, 275, 302,
307, 324, 327, 345, 377, 391,
458, 461, 494 – 96, 523 – 24, 526,
534, 555, 576, 732, 733, 744,
757 – 60, 792 – 93, 828, 930

temple, 108, 122, 179, 181 – 83, 185, 274,
338. *See also* body and dwelling

temple cleansing(s), 176 – 78

testimony. *See* witness

text-critical problem of
7:53 – 8:11, 386 – 90

time. *See* hour

trial, 399, 404, 454, 458, 744 – 52,
760 – 69, 770, 775 – 85

Trinity, the, 26, 29, 30, 38, 51, 119,
139, 198, 221 – 22, 238 – 39, 244,
254, 287, 291, 296, 328, 340, 376,
407, 465, 476, 485, 497, 508, 510,
519, 562 – 63, 578, 608, 618, 620,
625, 634 – 35, 637, 639, 640, 641,
644 – 45, 656, 658, 678, 682 – 83,
692, 694, 713, 714, 718, 720, 725,
857, 860 – 61, 863, 865, 868, 869,
902, 913, 928 – 29, 933 – 34

true vine, 332, 574, 650 – 54

"truly, truly" (authoritative preface),
153, 196, 198, 201, 285, 287, 288,
329, 337, 339, 415, 422, 425,

459, 461, 551, 585, 587, 593,
607, 621, 677, 690, 692, 916

truth, 111, 114, 116, 209, 221 – 22,
224, 244, 249, 251, 292, 366 – 67,
370 – 71, 406 – 8, 411, 414, 419, 429,
617 – 19, 677 – 78, 681 – 82, 721 – 22,
765 – 67, 770, 815 – 16, 919 – 23

voice, 459 – 62, 465 – 66, 477, 553 – 54

water, 131, 134 – 35, 154, 166 – 67,
171 – 72, 198 – 203, 233,
237, 238, 813 – 15

way, the, 617 – 19

"we" (literary function), 109,
196, 199, 201, 438, 923

wedding (theme), 162, 165, 167 – 68,
171 – 72, 218 – 19, 223, 225, 233

week, 125, 141, 143, 160 – 63, 523 – 24,
733, 779, 826 – 27, 828 – 29,
837, 858, 863, 877, 895, 936

will, 248, 250, 366

winter. *See* night

witness, 98, 121, 125 – 26, 133, 138 – 39,
144 – 45, 184, 218, 291 – 96,
297 – 98, 406 – 8, 453 – 54, 476, 541,
668, 670, 750, 753, 815 – 16, 849,
881 – 84, 884 – 85, 919 – 24, 925 – 26

Word/word, 87 – 89, 106, 120, 250 – 51,
264, 413 – 14, 416 – 18, 422, 424,
620 – 21, 639, 652, 665, 703,
715 – 16, 720 – 23, 736 – 37, 762 – 63

work, 248, 250, 276, 278, 285 – 86, 290,
326 – 28, 355, 417 – 18, 437 – 38,
453, 476 – 77, 479 – 80, 483,
620 – 22, 625 – 26, 666 – 67, 714 – 16

world, 100 – 101, 103, 204, 251, 353 – 54,
355, 438 – 39, 541, 554 – 55,
562 – 63, 638 – 39, 642, 664 – 65,
668, 669, 701 – 2, 714 – 18, 720 – 25,
726 – 27, 739 – 40, 923 – 24, 930 – 31

worship, 243 – 45, 253, 254, 550

Author Index

Adam, A. K. M., 36

Alexander, Loveday, 48

Allen, R. Michael, 24, 32

Allison Jr., Dale C., 238

Aloisi, John, 679

Alter, Robert, 233

Anderson, Paul N., 302, 324, 445

Aquinas, Thomas, 97, 215, 306, 452,
    515, 524, 526, 541, 558, 603,
    613, 725, 733, 762, 820, 842, 852,
    895, 898, 900, 903, 918, 923

Arterbury, Andrew E., 233, 246

Ashton, John, 62, 101, 572, 575

Attridge, Harold W., 54, 706

Augustine, 27, 108, 215, 220, 221,
    222, 285, 304, 307, 308, 313, 325,
    328, 331, 336, 357, 366, 382, 395,
    438, 441, 464, 478, 482, 500, 511,
    528, 531, 543, 552, 564, 566, 576,
    577, 579, 606, 609, 617, 619, 620,
    623, 633, 637, 639, 641, 656, 668,
    684, 700, 715, 718, 815, 829, 834,
    842, 857, 858, 860, 881, 898,
    902, 917, 918, 927, 928, 934

Auld, A. Graeme, 45

Aune, David E., 271

Aycock, Don M., 724

Bammel, Ernst, 764, 793

Barkey, Gabriel, 819

Barr, James, 354, 914

Barrett, C. K., 84, 87, 88, 89, 102, 104,
    116, 117, 127, 130, 131, 134, 146,
    153, 167, 169, 180, 192, 193,
    207, 219, 237, 242, 245, 250, 269,
    273, 276, 290, 292, 294, 297,
    302, 305, 311, 313, 328, 329,
    332, 340, 343, 345, 346, 353,
    367, 369, 372, 373, 406, 407, 409,
    410, 414, 424, 436, 440, 442, 444,
    459, 462, 464, 465, 466, 467, 476,
    478, 480, 496, 497, 500, 507, 509,
    511, 529, 549, 554, 556, 563, 606,
    614, 617, 622, 631, 635, 638, 650,
    658, 665, 668, 677, 679, 681, 682,
    692, 700, 719, 720, 723, 725, 732,
    734, 745, 747, 760, 763, 776, 783,
    794, 797, 801, 809, 829, 832, 859,
    885, 897, 898, 900, 913, 928

Barth, Karl, 27, 32, 89, 91, 94,
    97, 101, 106, 107, 112, 113,
    144, 146, 153, 156

Bartlett, David L., 599

Barton, John, 23

Barton, Stephen, 48, 863

Bauckham, Richard, 42, 43, 44, 46, 64,
    90, 109, 148, 150, 178, 194, 201,
    429, 438, 495, 501, 583, 594, 798,
    815, 816, 817, 873, 877, 891, 892,
    902 – 903, 919 – 20, 922, 923

Baum, Armin D., 873, 892, 893, 922

Beale, G. K., 111, 862

Beasley – Murray, George R., 41, 57,
    406, 458, 459, 508, 549, 554, 555,
    556, 563, 604, 606, 616, 622, 682,
    706, 732, 765, 775, 776, 781, 782,
    816, 820, 834, 841, 859, 864, 869,
    877, 879, 884, 899, 912, 923, 925

Beetham, F. G., 811

Beetham, P. A., 811

Bennema, Cornelis, 136, 446, 855, 864

Berding, Kenneth, 645

Berger, Klaus, 153

Bernard, J. H., 153, 268, 312,
    339, 367, 459, 650, 901

Beutler, Johannes, 859

Betz, Otto, 536

Beutler, Johannes, 302, 311

Bevan, H. B. H., 643

Bieringer, Reimund, 127,
    764, 826, 832, 849

Billings, J. Todd, 26, 27

Bird, Michael F., 873

Black, C. Clifton, 572

Black, David Alan, 712

Black, Fiona C., 845

Blinzler, Josef, 782

Block, Daniel I., 409

Blomberg, Craig L., 32, 176

Bock, Darrell L., 176

Bockmuehl, Markus, 84, 733

Boer, Roland, 845

Boers, Hendrikus, 252

Böhler, Dieter, 778

Boice, James Montgomery, 291

Bond, Helen K., 761, 768, 782, 795, 796

Bondi, Richard A., 420

Borchert, Gerald L., 48, 50, 109

Borgen, Peder, 277, 329, 337

Botha, J. Eugene, 235

Bowald, Mark Alan, 34

Bowden, John, 42, 792

Boyle, John L., 574, 602, 656, 697

Brant, Jo – Ann A., 54 – 56, 195,
    197, 198, 200, 201, 326,
    339, 367, 408, 499, 524

Breck, John, 893

Bridges, Carl B., 387, 388

Brock, Brian, 733

Brodie, Thomas L., 41, 89, 549

Bromiley, Geoffrey W., 27, 91

Brooke, George J., 761, 798, 901

Brown, Dan, 798

Brown, Jeannine K., 27, 828, 862

Brown, Raymond E., 63 – 64, 89, 113,
    126, 128, 164, 235, 245, 249,
    273, 302, 312, 343, 346, 375,
    396, 407, 410, 415, 436, 437, 440,
    446, 474, 475, 476, 482, 508,
    509, 513, 516, 525, 526, 563, 572,

586, 615, 632, 635, 650, 676, 712, 715, 724, 732, 733, 734, 737, 751, 757, 758, 761, 767, 768, 776, 778, 791, 792, 793, 801, 809, 810, 811, 813, 815, 816, 818, 845, 847, 860, 865, 877, 880, 881, 890, 895, 896, 901, 903, 912, 923, 925

Brown, Tricia Gates, 632

Brownson, James V., 883

Bruce, F. F., 86, 423

Bruner, Frederick Dale, 758, 763, 769, 792, 793, 894, 904, 907, 912

Bruns, J. Edgar, 526

Brunson, Andrew C., 506, 535, 536, 538, 539

Bryne, Brendan, 494, 830

Bryan, Steven M., 270, 271, 275, 276, 614

Büchsel, F., 110

Bultmann, Rudolf, 57, 66, 92, 93, 98, 101, 105, 112, 126, 147, 166, 168, 198, 217, 223, 240, 247, 251, 268, 285, 305, 312, 332, 342, 366, 374, 378, 410, 413, 414, 419, 424, 440, 449, 450, 451, 462, 477, 496, 499, 503, 504, 507, 512, 514, 515, 537, 541, 549, 551, 555, 560, 562, 585, 593, 603, 605, 606, 615, 617, 621, 623, 631, 635, 636, 639, 658, 676, 682, 694, 700, 701, 704, 717, 718, 721, 724, 725, 748, 749, 760, 765, 780, 801, 830, 834, 845, 878, 880, 890, 896, 904, 919, 925

Burge, Gary M., 135, 388, 632, 651

Burkholder, Benjamin J., 117

Burnett, Richard E., 22 – 23

Burridge, Richard A., 48

Busse, Ulrich, 59

Byrskog, Samuel, 44, 922

Caird, G. B., 461

Calvin, John, 97, 110, 128, 132, 133, 135, 156, 186, 220, 222, 236, 239, 241, 244, 252, 270, 278, 296, 306, 325, 327, 328, 347, 366, 382, 397, 407, 410, 412, 420, 423, 425, 437, 465, 477, 497, 518, 529, 560, 565, 582, 589, 618, 621, 634, 643, 670, 680, 682, 689, 712, 716, 719, 720, 723, 725, 748, 765, 861, 869, 906, 925

Capes, David B., 795

Carey, George, 843

Carse, James P., 45

Carson, D. A., 32, 66, 87, 88, 89, 95, 100, 111, 112, 126, 132, 137, 149,

161, 162, 176, 196, 198, 200, 202, 218, 219, 223, 269, 303, 305, 324, 327, 331, 332, 341, 345, 376, 391, 425, 439, 452, 474, 486, 503, 508, 510, 537, 552, 556, 576, 577, 582, 604, 615, 638, 642, 654, 657, 663, 665, 667, 677, 678, 679, 692, 700, 713, 718, 719, 721, 723, 745, 763, 768, 775, 796, 798, 811, 815, 831, 841, 846, 864, 866, 877, 879 – 80, 881, 882 – 83, 912, 913, 918, 923

Ceroke, Christian Paul, 164, 801

Chennattu, Rekha M., 575, 812

Childs, Brevard S., 469

Chrysostom, John, 94, 215, 791, 832, 844, 918

Cirafesi, Wally V., 65

Coakley, J. F., 525, 536, 538

Collins, Adela Yarbro, 49

Collins, Raymond F., 880

Coloe, Mary L., 108, 575, 578, 812

Coppens, J., 297

Cosgrove, Charles H., 526

Cotterell, F. P., 195

Crump, David, 812

Culpepper, R. Alan, 302, 572, 594, 766, 795, 801, 810, 819, 900, 903

Cyril of Alexandria, 94

Dahms, John V., 119

Daly – Denton, Margaret, 536

D'Angelo, Mary Rose, 847

Daube, David, 238, 737

Davies, Margaret, 101, 923, 926

Davies, W. D., 572

de Boer, Esther A., 45

de Boer, Martinus C., 763, 777

DeConick, April D., 795

de Jonge, Marinus, 285

de La Potterie, Ignace, 617

Delling, G., 905

Denniston, John D., 106

Derrett, J. Duncan M., 451, 689, 862

deSilva, David A., 176, 177

de Solages, B., 891

Dewey, Kim E., 461

Dietzfelbinger, Christian, 622

Dodd, C. H., 53, 57, 66, 109, 132, 214, 259, 399, 430, 435, 494, 497, 549, 604, 616, 643, 651, 715, 723, 757, 775, 885

Donfried, Karl P., 801

Downing, F. Gerald, 39, 578, 778

Draycott, Andy, 733

Duke, Paul D., 442, 757

Duling, Dennis C., 869

Dunn, J. D. G., 330

du Rand, Jan A., 94, 862

Dwight, Timothy, 108

Easterling, P. E., 54, 572

Edgington, Allen, 583

Edwards, Mark, 196

Edwards, Ruth B., 113, 116, 581

Edwards, W. D., 814

Ehrman, Bart D., 764

Elliott, J. K., 523

Ensor, Peter W., 285, 603, 604

Evans, Craig A., 559, 586

Farelly, Nicolas, 380, 819

Farmer, William R., 536

Farrow, Douglas, 850

Fee, Gordon D., 374, 621, 882

Ferguson, Everett, 813

Fewell, Danna Nolan, 233

Fiddes, Paul, 861

Fitzmyer, Joseph A., 536, 801, 813

Förster, Hans, 499

Fortna, Robert T., 62, 66

Fowl, Stephen, 32, 36, 326

Fowler, David C., 847

Fowler, Robert M., 744

France, R. T., 759

Frei, Hans W., 30, 35

Frey, Jörg, 900, 913

Freytag, Gustav, 50

Fuller, Reginald H., 857, 860, 866

Funk, Robert W., 59

Fürst, Walter, 91

Gabel, W. J., 814

Garland, David E., 736, 737

Gaventa, B. R., 62

Gentry, Peter J., 37, 38

George, Larry Darnell, 831

Germond, Philippe, 537

Giblin, Charles Homer, 734

Gibson, David, 575, 578

Gignac, Francis T., 914

Godet, Frederic L., 108, 420

Goldingay, John, 181, 475, 481, 536

Grant, Robert M., 901

Grassi, Joseph A., 45

Grayston, Kenneth, 632

Green, David E., 792

Green, Joel B., 581

Grieb, A. Katherine, 797

Grigsby, Bruce, 440

Guilding, Aileen, 901

Gundry, Robert H., 205, 615

Haas, Nicu, 792

Haenchen, Ernst, 59, 270, 312, 767, 916

Haers, J., 764

Hägerlund, Tobias, 864

Hagner, Donald A., 84

Hakola, Raimo, 818

Halliwell, Stephen, 50

Hamilton Jr., James M., 633

Hanson, A. T., 778

Harris, J. S. Randolph, 508

Harris, Murray J., 90, 91, 110, 117, 118

Harstine, Stan, 875, 878

Hartley, Donald E., 558, 560

Hartman, Lars, 894, 904

Hasse, Wolfgang, 271

Hatina, Thomas R., 861

Hauck, F., 461

Hauerwas, Stanley, 578

Hawthorne, Gerald F., 536

Hays, Richard B., 797

Head, A. H., 260

Heath, Jane, 357

Heil, John Paul, 748, 761, 776, 785, 796, 815, 896, 898, 900, 914

Heinz, Donald, 664

Hengel, Martin, 42, 46, 765, 792, 921

Hill, Charles E., 47, 59

Hill, Edmund, 27, 860

Hoare, R. W. N., 57

Hofius, Otfried, 509

Holloway, Paul A., 573

Holmes, Stephen R., 859, 860, 861, 866, 867

Homcy, Stephen L., 482

Hooker, Morna D., 84, 204 – 205, 220, 890

Horbury, William, 665

Hoskins, Paul M., 108

Hoskyns, Edwyn Clement, 32, 60, 87, 94, 104, 106, 108, 117, 136, 145, 199, 207, 220, 248, 296, 303, 329, 334, 342, 348, 357, 368, 373, 397, 409, 410, 411, 416, 461, 498, 500,

504, 514, 526, 552, 555, 557, 559, 562, 576, 586, 595, 603, 604, 605, 606, 617, 618, 619, 620, 622, 638, 640, 641, 655, 656, 658, 664, 666, 667, 677, 682, 691, 700, 706, 714, 724, 747, 749, 765, 766, 779, 809, 811, 812, 816, 828, 834, 845, 861, 895, 915, 926

Hosmer, F. E., 814

Howard, W. F., 135

Howell, Russell W., 205

Hultgren, Arland J., 578

Humphrey, Edith M., 863

Hunn, Debbie, 415

Hunt, Steven A., 167, 833

Hurst, L. D., 914

Jackson, Howard M., 892, 922

Janzen, J. Gerald, 406, 722

Jasper, Allison, 844

Jeffers, James S., 795

Jeremias, J., 116

Jeske, Richard L., 550

Johnson, Brian D., 881

Johnson, Keith E., 119

Judge, Peter J., 880

Just, Felix, 445

Kaestli, J. – D., 761

Kastner, Karl, 845

Keener, Craig S., 48, 57, 83, 95, 101, 117, 129, 131, 132, 133, 135, 151, 162 – 63, 167, 216, 219, 246, 269, 273, 276, 287, 312, 374, 380, 406, 424, 439, 443, 446, 462, 463, 464, 475, 502, 503, 507, 509, 512, 513, 514, 515, 516, 525, 526, 527, 536, 594, 605, 632, 641, 650, 656, 657, 720, 732, 734, 737, 744, 745, 747, 749, 758, 760, 761, 762, 767, 776, 780, 782, 791, 792, 794 – 95, 797, 810, 819, 828, 829, 830, 832, 841, 860, 896, 898, 899, 900, 914, 923

Keith, Chris, 387, 391, 393, 394, 395

Kelley, Nicole, 437

Kellum, L. Scott, 573

Kinman, Brent, 537

Klink III, Edward W., 26, 28, 61, 64 – 65, 96, 100, 148, 164, 167, 172, 179, 445, 933, 939

Koester, Craig R., 108, 251, 619, 826

Kollmann, Bernd, 901

Koskenniemi, Erkki, 810, 813

Köstenberger, Andreas J., 46, 47, 59, 65, 111, 169, 176, 329, 388, 466, 482, 538, 621, 634, 667, 767, 826 – 27

Kovacs, Judith L., 555

Kurek – Chomycz, Dominika A., 526

Kysar, Robert, 812

Labahn, M., 832

Lacomara, Aelred, 571

Ladd, George Eldon, 153

Laney, J. Carl, 652

Lanser, Susan Snaider, 885

Larcher, Fabian, 97

Larsen, Kasper Bro, 233, 435

Lee, Dorothy A., 634, 878

Leithart, Peter L., 39, 435, 441, 444, 451

Leung, Mavis M., 466, 536

Levenson, Jon D., 862

Levine, Amy – Jill, 495

Lierman, John, 193

Lieu, Judith M., 451

Lightfoot, R. H., 260, 293, 845

Lincoln, Andrew T., 98, 126, 292, 399, 405, 410, 421, 430, 458, 526, 529, 539, 561, 632, 633, 679, 717, 719, 764, 766, 778, 849, 912, 919

Lindars, Barnabas, 110, 665, 816, 926

Little, Edmund, 891

Litwa, M. David, 778, 779

Livet, Jacques, 537

Lockett, Darian R., 26, 939

Longenecker, Bruce W., 863

Lundin, Roger, 40

Lunn, Nicholas P., 842, 843

Luther, Martin, 95, 106, 176, 186, 328, 331, 343, 347, 381, 396, 406, 618, 636, 680, 834, 837, 842

Lyons, John, 604

Macchia, Frank D., 583

Macintosh, Fiona, 643

Malina, Bruce J., 163, 177, 179, 436, 524, 792, 793

Manning Jr., Gary, 372, 461

Manns, Frédéric, 733

Markl, Dominik, 875, 893

Martyr, Justin, 421

Maritz, P., 94, 714, 832

Marrow, Stanley B., 101

Marshall, I. Howard, 855

Martyn, J. Louis, 62 – 64, 436, 445

Maston, Jason, 873

Maxwell, Elisabeth, 415

McCaffrey, James, 615

McDonagh, Francis, 270

McDonough, Sean M., 96

McGaughy, Lane C., 883

McGlasson, Paul C., 35

McHugh, John F., 88, 97, 98, 99, 100, 102, 104, 107, 109, 110, 117, 118, 126, 128–29, 133, 134, 135, 137, 145, 148, 150, 152, 154, 163, 168, 180, 195, 219, 234, 238, 240, 244, 245, 249, 261, 330, 799

McKay, K. L., 914

McKeague, Ian, 312

McNeil, Brian, 665

Meeks, Wayne A., 64, 778

Meier, John P., 757, 758, 858, 866

Menken, Maarten J. J., 536, 816, 902

Merrigan, T., 764

Messner, Brian S., 782

Metzger, Bruce M., 94, 137, 269, 295, 387, 411, 438, 478, 580, 615, 619, 682, 865, 882

Michaels, J. Ramsey, 83, 84, 134, 144, 150, 154, 168, 175, 180, 199, 202, 214, 220, 234, 247, 259, 261, 268, 269, 271, 273, 274, 276, 289, 305, 311, 312, 328, 338, 340, 342, 343, 370, 380, 392, 395, 405, 406, 412, 416, 420, 421, 424, 443, 447, 448, 449, 450, 451, 462, 465, 476, 478, 479, 480, 482, 483, 500, 509, 510, 514, 515, 524, 527, 539, 555, 556, 557, 558, 561, 576, 577, 579, 581, 586, 587, 593, 594, 596, 614, 617, 653, 676, 690, 700, 706, 716, 733, 736, 745, 747, 748, 762, 765, 778, 782, 793, 813, 830, 845, 847, 865, 897, 913, 915, 916, 918

Migne, J. – P., 901

Mihalios, Stefanos, 290

Miller, Susan, 525

Miller, Troy A., 795

Milligan, G., 525

Minear, Paul S., 715, 724, 829, 830, 834, 848, 890

Mlakuzhyil, George, 570

Moberly, R. W. L., 24

Moffatt, James, 62

Mohrmann, Douglas C., 768

Moloney, Francis J., 93, 233, 249, 450,

494, 526, 528, 575, 576, 603, 674, 712, 756, 830, 864, 884, 897, 923

Morris, Leon, 84, 88, 96, 98, 104, 105, 133, 149, 160, 169, 176, 199, 202, 234, 247, 260, 289, 331, 333, 335, 366, 369, 370, 373, 391, 393, 405, 409, 411, 420, 425, 440, 442, 444, 448, 452, 460, 462, 465, 468, 475, 476, 477, 481, 494, 498, 499, 500, 501, 503, 513, 514, 515, 537, 552, 559, 584, 586, 603, 607, 621, 623, 633, 637, 657, 664, 682, 700, 734, 747, 750, 757, 775, 835, 841, 858, 879, 883, 895, 897, 912, 914

Motyer, Stephen, 55, 413, 418

Moule, C. F. D., 518, 524, 764, 794

Moulton, J. H., 135, 180, 261, 345, 438, 525, 535, 794, 913

Moyise, Steve, 536

Nation, Mark Thiessen, 578

Neale, D., 446

Neill, Stephen C., 45

Newbigin, Lesslie, 252, 616, 652, 676, 680, 684, 713, 864, 869, 880, 899, 918

Neyrey, Jerome H., 55, 103, 330, 354, 366, 410, 413, 481, 525, 585

Nicol, Willem, 107

Nicholson, Godfrey C., 556

Nisula, Kirsi, 810, 813

Nof, Doron, 312

O'Brien, Kelli S., 834, 846

O'Day, Gail R., 305, 308, 312, 392, 620, 702, 717

Okure, Teresa, 233, 235, 237, 238, 241, 242

Oladipo, Caleb O., 914

Origen, 96, 133, 847

Oropeza, B. J., 768

O'Rourke, John J., 784

Oswalt, John N., 558, 559

Paddison, Angus, 640, 899

Paganini, Claudia, 875

Paganini, Simone, 875

Painter, John, 436, 449

Paldor, Nathan, 312

Pancaro, Severino, 368, 369

Parker, T. H. L., 97

Parks, Ward, 195

Parsenios, George L., 53, 54, 435, 458, 571, 572, 596, 603, 643, 718, 732

Patterson, Richard D., 797

Pemberton, Elizabeth G., 796

Pennington, Jonathan T., 43, 49, 50, 96, 197

Phallis, Alexander, 476

Phillips, Gary A., 233

Pink, Arthur W., 652

Pollefeyt, Didier, 127

Porter, James I., 527

Porter, Stanley E., 32, 87, 100, 483, 604, 615, 865

Potter, David S., 527

Powell, Mark Allan, 49

Poythress, Vern S., 24, 37, 83, 387

Priest, James E., 784

Pryor, John W., 102, 103, 259

Rabens, Volker, 855

Rae, Murray A., 26–27, 35

Reicke, Bo, 792, 793

Reifenberg, Abraham A., 536

Reinbold, Wolfgang, 901

Reinhartz, Adele, 85, 127, 147, 415, 421, 426, 461, 495, 514, 525, 594, 746, 845, 922, 933

Rengstorf, Karl H., 97

Rensberger, David, 101, 437

Renz, Gabi, 193

Resseguie, James L., 744

Reumann, John, 801

Richards, E. Randolph, 176–78, 181, 183

Richardson, Alan, 778

Ridderbos, Herman N., 93, 95, 105, 107, 116, 127, 132, 146, 154, 165, 168, 241, 272, 285, 296, 303, 305, 329, 330, 337, 338, 342, 353, 354, 394, 396, 417, 418, 425, 437, 452, 460, 462, 477, 478, 482, 503, 505, 515, 541, 552, 554, 560, 577, 582, 585, 593, 605, 607, 634, 638, 651, 655, 658, 666, 689, 690, 692, 699, 713, 724, 735, 765, 768, 797, 816, 817, 818, 834, 841, 878, 883, 898, 900, 903, 913, 918

Richards, Kent Harold, 38

Riches, John K., 57, 270

Richter, Georg, 581

Riesenfeld, Harald, 883

Roberts, R., 118

Robertson, A. T., 371

Robertson, C. K., 768

Robinson, John A. T., 269, 584, 920

Rohrbaugh, Richard L., 163, 179, 436, 524, 792, 793

Romanowsky, John W., 556

Ross, J. M., 902

Rotelle, John E., 27

Roth, John K., 415

Rowe, C. Kavin, 38, 797

Rowe, Jonathan, 733

Runions, Erin, 845

Ryken, Leland, 51

Ryle, John Charles, 284

Sadananda, Daniel Rathnakara, 635, 706

Sailhamer, John H., 34, 35

Salier, Bill, 535

Salier, Willis Hedley, 558, 559

Salvoni, Fausto, 832

Samra, Jim, 254

Sanders, E. P., 126, 131

Sanders, Fred,   119

Sava, A. F., 814

Schaper, Joachim, 733, 820, 851

Schlatter, Adolf, 93, 107, 110, 112, 134, 146, 219, 344, 439, 658, 699, 715, 894

Schnabel, Eckhard J., 32, 860

Schnackenburg, Rudolf, 59, 100, 102, 128, 151, 154, 164, 196, 202, 207, 245, 249, 268, 333, 339, 356, 357, 370, 415, 418, 425, 436, 438, 458, 464, 468, 480, 495, 503, 509, 513, 554, 555, 559, 603, 605, 606, 618, 619, 640, 678, 679, 718, 722, 736, 765, 793, 795, 800, 815, 847, 879, 883, 894, 925

Schneiders, Sandra M., 193, 833, 848, 849, 858, 866, 878, 893

Schnelle, Udo, 826

Schrage, Wolfgang, 554

Schürmann, Heinz, 801

Schwemer, Anna Maria, 765

Scouteris, Constantine, 724

Segovia, Fernando F., 572, 575, 604, 653, 663, 848, 873, 894

Seitz, Christopher R., 38

Shaw, Alan, 891

Shepherd, David, 914

Shillington, V. George, 634

Sibinga, Joost Smit, 260, 874

Sloyan, Gerard S., 235

Smalley, Stephen S., 898

Smith, Barry D., 757

Smith, D. Moody, 28, 47, 59, 62, 549, 677, 891

Smyth, Kevin, 59

Snodgrass, Klyne, 461

Soulen, R. Kendall, 427

Spencer, F. S., 799, 849

Sproston North, Wendy E., 494

Stagg, Frank, 596

Staley, Jeffrey L., 270, 435, 436, 444, 745

Stanton, Graham N., 43, 863

Staton, John E., 723

Stauffer, E., 862

Strachan, R. H., 374

Stegner, W. Richard, 586

Stenger, Werner, 680

Sternberg, Meir, 36

Steudel, Annette, 901

Stevick, Daniel B., 575, 584, 586, 603, 608, 880

Stibbe, Mark. W. G., 245, 254, 494, 507, 511

Stibbs, Alan M., 339

Stout, Stephen O., 47

Stovell, Beth M., 32

Stroumsa, Guy G., 733

Swain, Scott R., 23, 634

Tabb, Brian J., 559

Temple, William, 88

Thatcher, Tom, 272, 442, 445

Theissen, Gerd, 270

Thomas, John Christopher, 576, 578, 580, 581, 582

Thompson, Marianne Meye, 90, 289, 797, 844, 856, 863, 881

Tolmie, D. Francois, 167

Toppari, Jorma, 810, 813

Torrance, Alan J., 494

Torrance, David W., 97

Torrance, Thomas F., 27, 97

Tovey, Derek,   922

Tozer, A. W., 277

Treier, Daniel J., 32

Trites, A. A., 679

Truemann, Carl R., 30

Tsuchido, Kiyoshi, 549

Tuckett, Christopher M., 764, 816

Turner, Max, 581, 678

Turner, N., 135

Vandecasteele – Vanneuville, Frederique, 127

Van, Harvey A., 23 – 24

Vanhoozer, Kevin J., 22, 27 – 28, 32, 36, 40, 45, 814, 885, 919, 921 – 23

van Belle, Gilbert, 94, 816, 832, 874, 884

Van der Watt, J. G., 94, 458, 650, 841, 900

van Segbroeck, F., 816

van Tilborg, Sjef, 60

van Unnik, W. C., 584

Verheyden, J., 816

Via Jr., Dan Otto, 461

von Rad, Gerhard, 859

Voorwinde, Stephen, 500

Vriend, John, 93

Wagner, J. Ross, 797

Walaskay, Paul W., 776

Wallace, Daniel B., 89, 92, 95, 104, 118, 126, 135, 180, 181, 202, 205, 218, 237, 244, 261, 274, 304, 311, 327, 333, 342, 353, 369, 393, 394, 410, 423, 448, 478, 496, 502, 503, 509, 516, 553, 579, 605, 613, 616, 635, 636, 653, 785, 834, 846, 916

Walters, Geoff, 508

Warfield, Benjamin B., 34

Watson, Francis, 25, 36, 714

Way, Kenneth C., 537 – 38, 539

Webster, John, 25 – 26, 28, 29, 31, 33, 40, 65, 389

Weisheipl, James A., 97

Wells, Samuel, 578

Wellum, Stephen J., 37, 38

Wendel, Carl, 875

Westcott, B. F., 87. 98, 111, 204, 286, 357, 614, 706, 815, 842, 864

Whitacre, Rodney A., 831

White, L. Michael, 585

Wiarda, Timothy, 738, 901

Wink, Walter, 128

Willemse, Johannes, 161

Williams, P. J., 83

Williams, Ritva H., 163

Williford, Don, 193

Wilson, John F., 784

Witherington III, Ben, 45, 88, 176

Witkamp, L. Th., 271

Wright, N. T. (Tom), 45, 90, 836, 914

Wright IV, William M., 440, 441, 442, 451, 596, 734
Wuellner, Wilhelm, 494
Wyatt, Nicolas, 733, 851

Yarbrough, O. Larry, 585
Yeago, David S., 30, 560
Yocum, John, 31
Young, R. A., 503

Zahn, Theodor, 104
Zimmermann, M., 219
Zimmermann, Ruben, 167, 219, 900
Zola, Nicholas J., 596